WINDOWS ON THE WORLD

WINDOWS ON THE WORLD
1990

Alisa M. Hoffman, Editor

THE NATIONAL LIBRARY OF POETRY

WINDOWS ON THE WORLD

FOURTH EDITION
IN ANTHOLOGY SERIES

Copyright © 1990 by The National Library of Poetry

As a compilation.
Rights to individual poems reside with the artists themselves.

All rights reserved under International and Pan-American copyright conventions. No part of this book may be reproduced, stored in a retrieval system or transmitted in any form, electronic, mechanical, or by other means, without written permission of the publisher. Address all inquiries to Jeffrey Franz, Publisher, P. O. Box 704, Owings Mills, Maryland 21117.

Library of Congress
Cataloging in Publication Data

ISBN 0-940863-21-9 (Hardbound)
ISBN 0-940863-26-X (Leatherbound)

Manufactured in The United States of America by
Watermark Press
5-E Gwynns Mill Court
Owings Mills, Maryland 21117

Editor's Note

As editor for **Windows on the World**, as well as one of the three judges of the competition, I had an opportunity to read and discuss all of the entries that we received. Believe me, this was no easy task. I was amazed at the wide range of subjects the poems covered and the way the poets were able to evoke strong feelings in the reader, whether humorous or sensitive, pensive or optimistic. I enjoyed them all, but there were some that stood out from the rest.

Jennifer Kay's poem was truly my favorite. Though short in length, I found it touched something deep inside of me. The lilting rhythm of the lines reinforces the subject of the poem. "Aurora Borealis" by Kim M. Dunn is a beautiful piece of writing. The words are carefully chosen to present a clear, vibrant image to the reader. Angie Lomax's submission "The Golden Quest" is the classic ballad with a twist. While the story is good, it seems almost predictable, until the reversal in the last line.

Our Grand Prize Winner, J. Warren Spencer, captured our attention with his poem about a hobo's life. "Gypsy Earth" is written in a unique style combining rhyme and consonance throughout every line. While this style is difficult to write, it is effective and can enhance the subject when it is done properly -- and Spencer certainly has.

Although only 70 top prizes could be awarded, all of the artists published in this volume are deserving or recognition for their fine artistic talent, for it is only with creative minds such as these that written language can continue to delight and inspire the reader.

Alisa M. Hoffman, Editor

Acknowledgements

The publication **Windows on the World** is a culmination of the efforts of many individuals. Judges, editors, assistant editors, typesetters, computer operators, graphic artists, layout artists, paste-up artists and office administrators have all brought their respective talents to bear on the project. The editors are grateful for the contributions of these fine people:

> Dorothy Anderson, Connie Bradford, Jerry Breen, Jeffrey Bryan, Lisa Della, Phyllis Franz, Ardie L. Freeman, Lori Gutman, Michele Johnson, Ethel Koons, Dawn M. Koslowski, Olorah McLendon, Annette Logan, Michelle A. Munter, Kathryn Runde, Pat Silverman and Patti Ward.

Howard Ely, Managing Editor

Grand Prize Winner

J. Warren Spencer

Second Prize Winners

Diane Bogus Anne Findlay
Cathryn Braun Jesse Bryant Fletcher
Hilda Brown Jennifer Kay
Kim M. Dunn Angie Kinnamon
Wendy Estela Jessica Lester
Yon E. Fearshaker Billie Ann Patrick
Wesley Wood

Third Prize Winners

Robert Bartlett
Fiona Bayly
Yvonne Behrens
Mary Best
Judy Atwell Blecha
Helen J. Bonnell
Eileen Bossarte
April Capil
Laurie Chalko
Emma Crobaugh
Connie Cradall Crosby
David Curtis
Connie M. DeLancey
Amy Dull
Joyce Fowler
Melody Ghandchi
Jennifer Gillett
Hazel Firth Goddard
Brandee Grumbling

Judith Hadary
Barbara J. Hall
Belva Dobyns Hamilton
Janice L. Harrison
Katherine Hawkins
Stephanie Hoffman
Anne Holmberg
Linda Jessie-Jones
Kim Karr
Erin Lindsey
Jennifer Lohmuller
Angie Lomax
Robertta Jeanette Ludwig
Lesa Lunsford
Cassandra J. Maier
Spencer Mansouri
Karen Martin
Sally McMillan

Tracy LR Ojakangas
Jean Philips
Veronica Rupp
Bob Schumaker
Annette Schultz
Brenda Whitehead Smith
Danielle St. Pierre
Peter Stassi
Rod Stearns
Ruth Stone
Svieta
Brian Swartzfager
Katherine Tapley
Julia Diana Kent
Bethany W. Uhlig
Carolyn R. Williams
Dennis A. Williams
Sally Ann Winterberg
Daniel Forie Zook

There were also 165 Editor's Choice Awards.

Gypsy Earth

Twenty-seven years on a back road back strokin,
Open token free rider late nighter hitch.
Destination: Bay Station tag trackin net workin,
No burden earnin dirt an' jumpin when the switch

Pulls down. Old south bounder that'll rattle,
Throttle round the middle ground of little towns,
In slumber rumble under nimble limbs.
Just listen for the whistle on the tressle as it passes,
Does it answer through the drizzle,
Or address the razor winds?

Monday's huddle round the puddle from the roof leak,
Blue feet teeter tip the bottle of the root.
Big splash quick flash-in-ration till a juice's jailor,
Loosens like the buttons on this tailor tattered suit.

Split in half by the draft and after ninety miles,
The box car locks hard dockyard berth.
Dirt cheap deep sleep, new sheet heat me,
Keep me breathing gypsy earth.

-- *J. Warren Spencer*

Grand Prize Winner

They throw knives at us
And don't realize it hurts
They say words
That just kill
Then they ask
Why are you feeling this way
No
You tell me
Why am i feeling this way
Why am i me
Why aren't i like everyone else.

—*immx ferreria*

As Seen Through the Eyes of a Fatherless Child

It's a story about life; so subtle—yet somewhat wild, as it was seen through eyes of a "Fatherless Child."
A baby man was born. His fate, what would it be? just listen to these words because that baby was me.
And it still is me even until this very day. The story went like this and it goes this way. . .
I was born to love and learned to hate. It was only the Good Lord who could restore my true fate.
Oft misunderstood; folks just passed me by. Some said I looked sad; yet unconcerned why.
I grew up in poverty; the epitome of shame. Folks always despised me and they blasphemed my name.
"Aww you ain't nothin' boy. No you won't get very far." But they didn't know what they were talking about because I'm a star!
So don't worry about those negative folks. Just make sure you know who you are!
East coast, West coast, and even down South, folks stop in awe at the words from my mouth.
"The words you use, you're one of a kind." No it's not the words but it's the thoughts from my mind.
Because glory in the Lord is what I seek to find. They said I was crazy.
They called me a disgrace. But did I let that stop me. No! Just look at the smile on my face.
Is it false? No, it's for real. The glory it reveals.
It once locked inside with bitter disgust. But now I'm set free because it's the Lord that I trust.
Yes, life is hard but yet it's so mild. . .as seen through the eyes of a "fatherless child."

—*Darrel Anthony White*

I'm Scared Sometimes

I'm scared sometimes that all this is just a dream.
A beautiful dream; a wonderful dream that is going to end.
I'm scared sometimes that you're just going to walk away
from me for no reason.
If you were to do this or if it is a dream and it were to end,
I would just curl up and die inside.
I would no longer have feelings like I do now
for because of you, I feel all that I do.
So please, if it's a dream—don't awaken me.
If it's reality—don't walk away from me.

—*Amy L. Velazquez*

Love

A man and a woman,
A boy and a girl,
A mother and her child,
A master and his pet.
Each has a special love.
Loyalty and respect,
Passion to puppy love.
All fit the same word-Love.
It is important in everyone's life,
That one little word.
Everyone has it,
One kind or another.
But somehow passion is the one some think about most.
But me, I'll settle for mother-child love,
Because that love is always there.
You can't divorce it,
Or break up with it.
It will always be there.

—*Jayna DeWaard*

Castles of Sand

I chanced upon a boy today playing in the sand,
a bucket sitting by his side, a shovel in his hand.
He noticed not me standing there to watch his childish play,
to build a castle only to see the tide wash it away.
As I watched him work so hard to build his castle there,
nothing to complicate his mind he worked without a care.
I pray to God my life to be so peaceful and so free,
as I watch the castles I have made when they wash out to sea.
He watched the castle he had built as the tide washed it away,
with shovel and bucket in his hand he calmly walked away.
When I look to God I think out loud the only thing I say,
God make me like that little boy when my castle's washed away.

—*B. J. Teeple*

Tears of Pain

Quietly walking in the evening rain,
A camouflage for the tears of pain.
I look to days I never knew,
Shattered dreams I have of you.
Having nothing but a dream to hold on to.
It's like the loneliness of a mountain stream,
No one around to appreciate the beauty God did create.
Tranquility through whispering winds,
When will my life begin?
Imagining the softness of your touch,
The tears in my eyes I love you so much!
A burning desire deep within.
Soul searching for ways to start fresh again.

—*Jan Gelineau*

Just a Thought

The sun setting is of wonder,
A child in a closet as it thunders.
So as the tear, the tear of fear,
That makes your smile disappear.
The ocean so blue,
Yet it still waves to you.
The sand in your hand,
Is like the touch of a man.
This is just a thought,
A thought that time has caught.

—*Jennifer A. Copple*

Untitled

As the day ends and the night comes, the
	world turns silent.
A chilled wind whistles through the trees.
	The sun has set.
The sky turns into a rainbow of colors no
	artist can paint.
The day turns to night. Nothing can be
	seen except the shadows
Of the darkness. The moon comes out
	from it's hidden cave in the sky.
With the twinkling stars they light up the
	night with beauty
And the sound of peace.

—Cherie LaPlante

My Love

Your soft warm touch which makes me
	feel so right.
Your sweet smile in which shines like a
	light.
Your love and strength which must come
	from up above. . .
This is why, I call you my love.

—Tanya Tamburin

Untitled

Church bells will ring,
A choir will sing,
Now will come the day
When my Jesus is born again.
He will rise above the heavens
And fall upon me.
I will be as he wants me to be
And I will love as he wants
Me to love.

—Kristi Shiban

Beautiful Rose

Your color is that of red wine,
Your sweet smell is so devine,
Deep down in my heart you grew close to
	me,
Without you I would never be.

—Martha Yunker

Poison Mushrooms

Gaunt faces stare in disbelief
A cloud roars into the air,
As buttons touched by witless souls
Bring all the world despair!
Our children's children ache for peace;
'Tis a small yet powerful word,
With growing hate and deafening noise
The cries for peace cannot be heard.
Let wisdom choose the paths we take;
What's decided now could threaten
	tomorrow,
Be certain the buttons we finally push
Won't bring the world infinite sorrow!

—Judith Hadary

Blessed with Inner Peace

My soul once churned much like a stormy
	sea,
A constant raging source of energy
And a peace of mind was but a memory.
Adversity would dampen, often drown
My faith and insight. . .limp, a tattered
	gown;
Forgotten smiles would falter, force a
	frown.
I found no time to do what mattered most.
My goals were realized, I loved to boast.
Would speed in highest gear, yet never
	coast.
Now I have grown in wisdom and in
	grace,
And prayer is given prominent, fresh
	place.
I sail more slowly now, refuse to race.
For me, the sea's uniqueness will not
	cease;
When I am near it, blessed with inner
	peace,
All cares are put on hold for God's
	release.

—Judy Atwell Blecha

Prophecy

Watch the waves float away,
a constant song for night and day.
Time and tide roll as one
far beneath the setting sun.
We watch together from the cold beach
as stars twinkle beyond our reach,
Like dreams we held when we were young
but died like many songs unsung.
We try to grab what can't be gained,
words between us coming strained.
We leave behind the ocean land
just two impressions in the sand.

—Janet Clapp and Rich Clark

Appreciation

In the deep green mist of the forests,
A cool vapor descends from the trees and
Blankets the moist soil.
And the owls' cry echoes, endlessly,
	unanswered
Through her wayward paths.
On the damp coast of the ocean,
The blue crests pound on the empty
	shoreline
And the seagulls' call sinks into the fog,
Forever lost.
From the seat of my window
The horns bleat and the cars screech.
And the rarest, faintest, chirp of a
Mockingbird is held eternally
And completely, in my heart.

—Jenny Jones

City Rain

Rain silk screens the immediate world
A delicate print in old-world Japan
A shopping bag lady garbage can digging,
In the liquid crystal delicate and elegant
Picking fragile flowers near an azure lake.
An orange taxi swims the busy
	intersection
Like a giant splashing sparkling sunny.
Unkempt school children dance an
	exuberant ballet,
Graceful as a convey of colorful tropical
	birds,
Guided by a haggardly ancient school
	crossing guard
Holding brilliant bouncing bobbing
	bumbershoots
For chanting tin soldiers marching erectly
	abreast.
A stray dog eerily mad-dashes for cover
Becoming a nonchalant swan lake
	crossing.
Windblown bare trees in multiple
	abstractions,
A masterful painting of awe striking
	beauty.
Common cracked sidewalk pavement
	glistening gold
Scattered debris, a sea of wondrous
	precious jewels.
Rain silk-screening ugliness into haunting
	beauty,
Challenging the essence of significance in
	the universe.

—Alex W. Bussey

To A Man Among Men

Your visions cross a continent; your heart
	never leaves home and hearth.
Your thoughts never still, encompass
	thoughtfulness, industry and relaxation.
Your dreams are attainable—they are of
	a future with and for your family.
Your future will be contentment because
	you have nutured what is important.
Your presence is. . .caring and love.

—Marilyn Ryan

Silence

A cool crisp autumn day,
A deserted island far away.
A meadow of wildflowers in a sudden
	spring shower,
High atop a mountain bursting with
	power.
An ocean of waves while sailing upon,
A cabin in the mountains at the break of
	dawn.
Silence can be full of sorrow,
Or silence can be your own tomorrow.

—Heather Kohler

My Love

A pang in my heart
A dizziness in my head
A beating in my chest
And a twinkle in my eyes
As I think of you, my love
I long for your arms
Around me once more
For a kiss from
Your tender lips
And an "I love you"
From your heart
I am again with you
So hold me near, my love
Kiss me sweetly and
Tell me that you love me

—*Brooke Sargent*

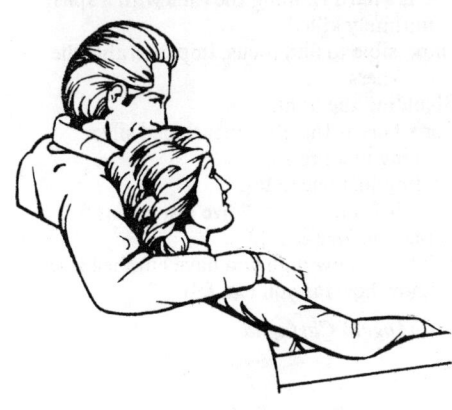

No More Than a Dream

My mind brings back the memory of a
   dream that I once had,
A dream that was as lovely as a tender
   song is sad.
I wandered down a road with no one else
   in sight,
When I came upon a brook that trembled
   with delight.
It was no more than a trickle, a couple
   footsteps wide,
But I decided I would follow it to see what
   it might hide.
I wandered on for days and traveled many
   miles,
The water became clearer and the land
   was changing styles.
I stayed for many nights just feasting on
   my awe,
And wept in quiet tribute for the grandeur
   that I saw.
The days were growing shorter, the leaves
   began to fall,
I knew that now I must return for I could
   hear the wild geese call.
I rambled back for miles til' I wakened
   from my dream,
Then listened in yearning silence for the
   trickle of the stream.

—*Kendra L. Slobotski*

Threshold Of A Dream

I am a dreamer,
a dreamer of dreams,
tides of memory set
the night afire.
Restless slumber unfolds
drifting dreams,
weaving in and out.
Lifes dreams,
just a dream,
fragile as a shining
moonbeam.
Dreams fade away
leaving you the day.

—*B.J. Weber*

The Waterfall

Off in the distance,
A faint rustling can be heard.
You dismiss it, believing it to be but the
   wind
Sighing gracefully through the trees;
And yet, as you near the source of the
   sound,
You see through the parting of the
   branches of the
Dew—sodden trees a bubbling fountain
Flowing playfully down the mountainside.
It is always there,
A sign of everlasting peace in a desolate
   place.
The sound dwindles away as you leave the
Ceaseless flowing of the waters
In a child's imagination.

—*Kristen Nation*

White is...

A brilliant ship silhouetted against a
   shimmering sea
A fluffy cloud up above me
A radiant bride in her wedding gown
A soft pillow filled with goose down
A layer of fresh fallen snow on the ground
A playful persian kitten from the pound
A pair of doves as they are in flight
A melting candle with a flickering light
A tall snow capped mountain
A glistening marble fountain

—*Julia Blankenship*

The Gallery

At morning time
A fresh canvas stands
Bold before us.
We paint as we live
And the colors splash
From sounds and feelings
Which soar to blues,
Pure and clear,
To oranges and pinks
Of lively contentment
And startling reds of passion.
Strokes of gray and black intrude
Where melancholy dwells.
When a darkened canvas pains
Turn away and sleep until
A fresh one comes with dawn.

—*Carlyn Parker*

A Roller Coaster

Up slowly, anticipation high
A gentle sway
Suddenly, a mechanical muscle twitch
It drops like lead cut from braced yarn
A gentle sway
A swift swoop, a sharp loop
It drops like lead cut from braced yarn
I'm free!
A swift swoop, a sharp loop
A bit of rocking
I'm free!
How exhilarating
A bit of rocking
Suddenly, a mechanical muscle twitch
How exhilarating
Up slowly, anticipation high.

—*Heidi R. Enerson*

From the Cutting Room Floor

A timid girls' humble smile.
A gentle touch from a friend.
A walk in the forest on a warm summer's
   day,
And a gentle breeze blowing through my
   hair.
As the sun casts its final glow
And the day turns into night,
It soon becomes the past
Too quickly forgotten,
Just like its memories.

—*Amanda Sowards*

Love

A golden sun,
A happy smile.
Two being one,
People going the extra mile.
Hand in hand
They walk the beach.
The day seems endless
Sadness out of reach.

—*Gina Newsome*

At the Feet of the Powerful

Through a window,
A helpless witness stares
With a desire to help as
Two worlds collide.
A world which consists
Of those too busy,
And of those too self-centered
To notice otherwise.
The other, a world
Of those suffering from the former,
And of those with nothing
But love, which they know neither.
Two worlds collide
The weak fall in anguish at
The powerful feet
Of the witnesses that stare, helplessly.

—*Andria Kraus*

Heroes Made of Stone?

A hero is someone whom you can depend on.
A hero is someone who can do no wrong in your eyes.
You model yourself in the likeness of your hero.
The pedestal upon which he stands is indestructible.
But what happens when you glimpse through the stone
And find a weakness in your hero?
What happens when your hero fails you?
Then that stone pedestal crumbles beneath him and
Your hero falls.
Emptiness fills you when you realize your hero is mortal.
My hero, you've failed me in every way.
Fatal was the blow when I came crashing down to
Earth, realizing your pedestal was not stone, but sponge.
Now at least we stand level, mind to mind, with
Nothing to say.
I just want you, my hero, to know
It's killing me.

—*Alison Phinney*

Together Always

I know that look, that attitude.
A lack of life, of gratitude.
You used to fly above so high,
Soaring with birds up in the sky.
Life is never constant, or so it seems,
But we can always be together in my dreams.
Like a child weeping over spilled milk
Or the cloudlike softness of silk.
The sweetness from a spring afternoon,
It was all vanquished so soon.
Life is never constant, or so it seems,
I wish we could be together in my dreams.
When the dream is off with the morning dawn,
And there comes a time to move on,
My voice will still linger in the mist.
I will walk in wonder and make a list
Of all the dreams of my past,
And keep my days I wish would last.

—*Crystal Hutchings*

Words Cannot Tell

Words cannot tell just what you mean to me,
You're much more than I've ever dreamed or hoped for,
You're more than I can think about.
You've given me a hope to see,
Beyond my day of trials and sores,
You've given me a strength to endure
Each and every hardship that knocks at my door;
What might have been little to you
You've been nice enough to care.
And now I have to say to you
I love you all the more.

—*Sherry Gavitt*

Wonder Of Gods Hands

With his hands he made this land
A land of beauty that truly stands
A land where everything should be free
And always have its liberty.
He made a tree that stands so high, it almost reaches the sky
And many a story it could tell, if only it could talk.
He made the air that blows and stirs
And truly refreshes the Earth
He made the flowers that bloom
That make up for all our gloom
The sun he made to shine all over this mighty Earth
He made the rain, the snow
The weather both hot and cold
He made the animals that run and play
Then with his hands he made a man
To go on this wonderful land
He taught them to live and worship
Each in their own way, but for him not to Betray.

—*Elizabeth Davis*

In a Lifetime

I'm not sure where, but I've heard it said before,
A life's love will arrive just once and no more.
If this is true, I see a long road ahead,
For my night has passed and left me for dead.
Somehow, someone upstairs let go of the reins,
Or perhaps it was part of the plan to drive me insane.
For as soon as this life was finally seized,
She vanished, a frozen memory all she saw fit to leave.
A lifetime now awaits, full of dreams to forge and hopes to build,
Yet it's hard running the race with a spirit untimely killed.
Impossible to find focus, impenetrable the darkness
Shielding the light,
For where is the oft—mentioned silver lining in a lifetime
Lasting just one night.
The pitiful fools cry, "love lost is better than no love at all,"
Yet to see how high you have climbed is to know how far you can fall.

—*Angelo Carfagna*

The California Mountains

Your mountains higher than a castle tower.
Your waterfalls a cascading shower.
The misty fog an encompassing veil,
That hides your height without a fail.
You stand so tall, majestic and true,
As so many pass and gaze at you.
But as I pass, might I see,
That proud and aloof you may not be?
Instead I see a mountain of power,
Which is strong, but shy as a wildflower.

—*Stacy Limberger*

Seemed To Be

Feelings being denied
A love not spoken
We are caught between two ties
That are forcing us away
From the thing we want most
To be happy together
So now as we part
Please don't look back
Why should you now
When you never did before
A love I thought so true
Was one of many lies
I should have seen the end
But love blinded once again
Why couldn't we see
That we weren't as happy
As we seemed to be.

—*Dana Jordan*

Love

Together they stand and together they fall
A man and a woman strongly bonded
   through it all
Although separate in their minds, they
   are one within their hearts
For it is here within our bodies that the
   bond begins to start
Then with each passing day, it grows
   stronger ever still
And it never seems to dwindle , nor does it
   lose its thrill
They live endlessly together; both
   enjoying one life plan
For there's no stronger bond than that of
   a woman and a man

—Elaine Anne Dotoli

You're the One

You're the one I love to touch,
You're the one who means so much.
I just want you to know I care,
And that I will always be there.
You are so special.
I just want to say,
I love you in every way.

—Tricia Bateman

What Could Be

It couldn't happen to me
A man born into freedom but without an
   innate appreciation
Of that which could not be gained
Without the blood, sweat, and tears
Of those who bequethed it to me
To remember the feeling, emotion, and
   commitment
Which was the price of that inheritance
If feelings could be remembered
Without the experience that caused them
   to be formed
Would perhaps have sparked my spirit
To spur my soul to greater love
For that which I had not suffered to gain
Life, with which I was born
Liberty, with which I was bestowed
The pursuit of happiness, with which I
   was blessed
But feelings of others cannot be
   remembered
Anger because of injustice, fear because
   of oppression,
Desperation because of loss, can only be
   remembered
By those who experience anger, fear or
   desperation.
But that could not happen to me
A man born to freedom from injustice,
   oppression,
Or desperation because of loss of liberty
And because that could not happen to me
There is injustice, oppression, slavery.

—H. R. Gielow

Creative Imagination

Fantasy can be reality,
A mental image, coming forth in life
A vision seen by imagination,
Ending of darkness, the beginning of light
The beginning of a new creation,
The existence of one's inner self
Expressing the quality of one's awareness
A presence, that is deeply felt
The realization of your inner feelings,
Perceived by your sense of thought
Responding to your subconscious
   emotions
A reply, without self doubt.

—Diane Bowman Mack

Bull Horn

He came with a baseball bat in one hand.
A microphone in the other one.
To break the bonds of ignorance.
Or your head.
His name was Joe.
Are we so depressed and destitute.
That we welcomed the oppressor as our
   liberator.
With his baseball bat he brused our
   heads.
We take it with a smile.
With his bull horn, he abuses our child.
It has happened many times in history.
It will happen many more times.
Look at Germany.
They had their Hitler.
We got our Joe.
So be careful who you elect and designate.
As your liberator.

—James Bell

Desert Sand

To eye, dazzling.
A mirror reflecting a million arrows from
   the sun,
A sea of golden brown, rolling to the
   horizon;
Here calm, and still and lifeless, there
   turbulent;
Sand dunes cresting and troughing,
Sand storms billowing like ocean waves,
Whirling winds spiralling skyward to the
   clouds.
Underfoot, treacherous like quicksand,
Burning like hot coals,
Impeding like shackles,
Save for camel hooves and ostrich claws.
Between the fingers, light.
All heat and turmoil gone, dazzle dulled;
Free of plankton and scum,
Which the whitest sea sand spoil;
It is fine and powdry,
Almost germless, like moon dust.

—Anezi Okoro

Elegy On A Care Door Opening

Friend is such a loose inversion;
A misplace disc
In a quater jukebox
I think it scares you.
Like a perpared piano
Where you are weighs warm
But your fingers stick
Your riffs drag
And your music skids
between
The V of my knee.
You are crippling standard blues
And these, in anticipation.
For only
on your well-oiled mouthpieced
Do you not grab for notes
Like you grabbed for my arm.

—Bonnie Snow

Lyin In Pain

The tentative walls come crashing down
You're screaming loud, no one hears a
   sound
Things were fine, now they're a mess
It seems to you there' nothing left
In the fog, the future was clear
But now the future has disappeared
Left you standing all alone
Left you to bear, the weight of the stone
You can't let it win, you've got to be
   strong
You have to learn, to carry on
I know you're hurt, I know you're in pain
But the tentative walls; we'll build them
   again.

—Lara Gould

January 25

Ah! To be born in January.
A month of pink camelias,
Dove-white gardenias,
And diamonds with garnets.
Radiating the likeness of rubies.
As a child walking home from school,
In the gently falling rain,
And playing hopscotch alone,
And losing, with no-one to blame.
Hummingbirds quietly sing,
Outside a window pane,
And eagerly sip rose-colored sugar water,
While wishing that the weather,
Was only a little hotter.
And now that the trees
Have attracted all of the neighborly
   bumblebees,
The Hummingbirds fly away,
And may come back again during May.
Ah! to be born in the midst of Winter,
Awaiting patiently for Spring,
And all that life will bring.

—Deborah Ellen Howard

Love

Love is like poetry,
A never ending verse,
One line following another,
Sometimes being a curse.
Love is like the wind,
It comes and goes as it pleases;
A cool breeze sweeping the land,
And all the pain it eases.
Love is like the wild cats roar,
So loud and fierce pounding in your heart;
Or like a small mouse,
Quiet and lonesome beginning a new start.
But most of all I think,
Love is like a starry night,
The kind so bright and clear;
Where I can see you standing
Oh so very near.

—*Crystal Brashares*

How Do You See Me?

How do I see myself?
A person of wit,
A person with grit
I don't think so—
How do I see myself?
A person who's shy,
One who will die
Maybe, I don't know.
How do I see myself?
A person alone,
A person of stone,
That's how I see myself.
How do you see me?

—*Ali Marie Drake*

Behind your Eyes

I knew there would be
A place in my heart
For you, the moment we shared our first kiss,
There's still that special
Place in my heart,
Even though your love I very much miss.
I hope you feel the
Same about me,
Forever I want to be with you,
Today I realized that
Behind your eyes,
I found a place I never knew.

—*Hana Taylor*

Irredeemable Prism

I actually felt safe in your eyes,
A prism to uphold in one's mind
To feel a sense of security and promise
An illusion of yesterdays and tomorrows
An embossed trust buried deep beneath our surfaces
A dismantled "paragon of virtue"
But one day can shatter-
A fear of a child's neverending nightmare
To believe in a broken trust is poisonous
The venom quickly takes affect deep within the mind
Disillusioned, one-sided beliefs lie implanted until
You give in and trust starts to die
With such happy beginnings-why?
-People change

—*Karen J. Murawski*

Environment as of Now

If one has a certain number of years to complete
A project of due course in this tiny planet, doesn't that defeat
The purpose of one's duty to their own lives?
The planet is scarred and there is no more disguise
To mask the disgrace we are causing ourselves. We must
Help brother sapien and mother earth and discuss
The importance of fruitful abundance and other
Trivial things. For how else can we help one another?
Soon something green will spring from the dark corner
And a light is lit inside one's soul coming from former
Ignorance. Help can only help itself and no one
Pays attention, only self-centeredness has begun
And will always continue in a world fighting for peace.
The statement contradicts itself, but absolutely no one can retreat.

—*Cheryl Anne Patin*

The Puzzle

Life is a puzzle,
A puzzle in your heart.
Each person is a piece of that puzzle; a very special part.
One day you and that person will have to be apart.
But that piece will stay forever in that puzzle in your heart.

—*Heather Griffin*

Black Ivory

Today a beast roams the earth
A race in which pride is carried from generation to generation
The fathers, aged, strong, massive,
Guiding their children to safety from poachers
Poachers who carry with them hearts of stone and thoughts of wealth
They leave trunks detached from limp bodies
And faces spattered with blood
Yes, the elephant is its name; some honor it, others do not
But nonetheless extinction soon will be
And few will remember its nobility.

—*Joe Reinhart*

Shattered Dreams

Johnny took his life last night.
A razor to his wrist
And through a mirror of my dreams
In anger came my fist
A fist to shatter broken dreams
At one time we had shared
Why couldn't you have come to me?
I thought you knew I cared
And didn't you once stop to think
What if the tables turned?
And I had turned my back on you
What then would you have learned?
So Johnny if you hear me now
Please know I'll always care
But still, you should have called on me
I would've been right there.

—*Jessica Lester*

A Reason

Always yearning to accomplish
A real reason to be.
To somehow make a difference
To calm some rocky sea.
To reach out and grasp a hand
That has lost it's grip on life.
To lose my life in love is to find it once again.
Food, natural and spritual, with a stranger I will share.
Entertaining angels, although maybe unaware.
Sometimes blessed to give and sometimes to receive
Not always all our wants, but always all our needs.
I was lost, but not I'm found. Blind, but now I see.
Grace to accomplish. A reason to be.

—*Eloise Snider*

My Life

My life is but a journey from the past,
A rocket ship that takes off in a blast.
The days go floating by
Like stars up in the sky,
And joy and sorrow, feelings never last.
My life is as a sojourn on the earth,
An exploration from my date of birth.
Each stride is as a leap.
Each memory I keep
Are images now etched within my worth.
My life is as a fiction novel written.
Read one page
And you can't stop, you're smitten.
And chapters are my way
Of writing through each day.
And some day my last chapter will be written.

—Catherine M. Chechik

Abstract Allusion

Amidst the awe of the green, murky water was the inaugural point
A runner at the starting point; a first lesson
Together in pairs they cascade playfully into the water; the solvent of life
Mud poetically spirting gently onto the surface of their backs
The presence of a dark color preceded their structure
Their rumbustous actions made the water ripple and spunt like a fan
Giving childlike features to the water's essence
An allusion, a family harmony, between the creatures and the water arose
Bringing life to the free, spontaneous, spirit brewing inside a joyous change.
Through the irridescent fading mist arose the vision of creatures
Crawling through a reality cycle in which warm rays of the fire
Faught up-spiriting water burning the inner heart of the creatures
Soul as they immersed in it seeing the dark, desolate, cool flowing
Bed of tranquility for them to rest; a runner reaches the finish line,
An abstract allusion of paradise!

—Amy Marie Goodrich

A Kaleidoscope Life

A boy of consolidated darkness
A scream he gives is the same scream
His dreams can only hear inside his clever but fiendish mind
His eyes are closed to what he sees and feels
As a destructive and morbid reality,
But his eyes are really open,
And his thoughts and feelings are really lost
From the point when reality's harsh light cracked through,
And so brutally savored his untainted mind.

—Anne Scott

The Ocean

The wind slightly blows across the land,
A seashell, the sea, and a lover in hand.
Roaring waves crash on the shore,
Beauty and laughter is all this is for.
The full moon stands for effection and love,
As it creates a lovely reflection from up above.
Bits of seashells wash up with high tide,
To leave them there is what I decide.
I can feel the sand between my toes,
I'd love to go where the ocean goes.
Strings of green musty seaweed wash ashore too,
I love the ocean, wouldn't you?

—Heather Goodlett

Whispering

The Voice...
A spark
Blazing thought
So commanding
A gentle touch
To massage
The desperate need
For understanding
That sweet
Song of peace
Has become
An unwritten symphony
A voice...
Now quiet
Can hear
The melody

—Bil Anthony Sinclair

The Play Of Spring

Dusk appoints the whippoor will and its song it heard.
A stillness holds the cool night air in suspense, and ever so slowly
the moon crees from sullen clouds to commence a new season.
In parpurition, the Earth gently nudges forth her performes.
The oak in slumber roused to purvey its buds from yawning branch giving birth.
The night is in a frenzy of excitement as life stages the Earth.
Applauding with a booming thunderous fury the clouds collate, hurling
a cast of descending tears to enrich the prolific scene below.
The stage grows darker and the Earth's musicians, the wind and rain,
bring an act of nature into intermission.
Summoned by the sun, the robing pauses to await the dance of the daffodil.
The sun commands its rays to dabble upon the dew glistening on the newly
opened petals.
The jovial rays leap on to the iris, and to the tulip, cognizant of the
sparkling beauty created in huse of purple, cadmium, xanthic, and crimson.
New life has been once again given.
And ever so slowy, the song of the whippoor will is heard and the
curtain of dusk is drawn.

—Kathleen L. Garlisch

The New Generation

In this generation
You've got to be strong,
For if you don't,
Everything will go wrong.
Dreams will shatter,
Life will fall,
And the things that matter the most
Won't matter at all.

—Raquel Gronke

State of the Nation

The state of the nation is confusing to me
A strange situation can't anyone see
They worry about the state of the nation
Which economic theory to use
The ways to reduce inflation
The cost of a nuclear fuse
Why don't they worry about us
The holes at the bottom of the sieve
All we are asking for is a place to live
We not worried about Persian carpets
Or Chinese rugs on the floor
We'll settle for so much less
Like a room four walls and a door
Why don't they worry about us
The holes at the bottom fo the sieve
All we asking for is a place to live

—G. T. Reader

The Wind

A soft, cool breeze,
A strong gust of air,
The wind is in control.
Trees bending and swaying
Trying to catch it.
Water, jealous, tries to
Drown it.
But the wind is just too fast,
Leaves, happy as can be join
In its dance.
And as it departs to go elsewhere,
The wind calls out, "I'll be back,
I'll be back."

—*Krista Marie Evans*

Freedom

A Magnificent bird, soaring above the
  skies,
A system of justice that has no eyes,
Riding the rapids without a fare,
Walking unburdened in the midnight air.
A man and a woman, deeply in love,
The cloudly place, high above,
A belly dancer's unscrupulous motions,
The mountains, the seas, and the oceans.
A healty man of a hundred-and-one,
A just that brings forth laughter and glee,
The moon, the stars, the Gods, and the
  sun;
These are some of the many things that
  are free.

—*Christopher Ray*

Freedom

The drop from a silken rose petal
A tear crying out for freedom
Pricked by its thorns picked to be
Sold for its beauty
Lost from its soil no longer swaying
In peace
The sun hidden from portraying its
Beauty
The ground now empty where it
Stood with pride
Giving all its got but never to
Receive what it wants
Faulty love and care something that
Will never compare to the sun and
Soil of freedom

—*Donna Seginak*

My Version of Friendship

Promises made to be broken,
A telephone call that's never spoken,
Hopes and dreams,
Will never be,
Best to give up now,
What was never really meant for me!

—*Alice Auliff*

A Daydream

Today,
A thought streaked through my mind
and attached to it was a tiny picture of
  you.
I then closed my eyes and enlarged the
  picture
Until it was life size.
I stroked your hair and gently kissed
Your lips.
We laughed and talked until the sun's
  rays
Turned into moonlight.
Soon it was time for you to leave
So I remembered the thought that
  brought you here
And put it in the back of my mind until
I need to bring you here again.

—*Karen Stepherson*

Untitled

It started as a dream
a tiny spark that needed fuel
to make it grow into a fire
like all dreams it took time
before it took flight
many rough starts and failed attempts
but then one day
it took the form of reality
and my dream—once so tiny
began to come true—
I could see it and feel it; it was real
but then something happened
and like a thin glass
it shattered easily
and so did i
what was once almost reality
was now another
lost moment in time.

—*Kathryne Kinnison Smith*

A Rose

A rose, just a single rose.
A token of love, friendship, and trust,
Brilliant red, soft pink, yellow or white.
Take your pick they all mean the same.
But be careful as you pick out your rose,
For hidden beneath it's beauty there may
  be a thorn.
A thorn you don't know is there
A thorn that is hidden from your eyes.
It may be there just waiting for you to be
  careless
So it can prick your finger or your heart.
So be careful as you pick out your rose
From the bunch of roses that pass you
  throughout life,
For the rose you pick may have a hidden
  thorn.

—*Colleen Leavenworth*

Confusion

Spinning. Like
a top
A roar
like thunder.
Silence.
Deafening,
screaming.
Not there.
Hot,
chilly. Blistering,
cold and heat
at the same time.
Twirling, spinning.
Dizzily
falling.
Confusion.

—*Christy Cameli*

My Life, My Promise

It didn't take long for me to realize what
  you mean to me,
You've shown me love the way it should
  be.
I owe you so much for the happiness you
  put in my life,
The happiness you've given to me since
  you made me your wife.
Thank you so much for changing my life's
  direction,
With all your gentleness, kindness, love
  and affection.
I give to you my life to share with me,
And my promise to be the best wife I can
  be.

—*Wendy L. Hamill*

The First Wink of Autumn

Tired, old summer—playing its last scene.
A trace of amber bedimming nature's
  green.
One leaf...two leaves...three...
Swirling from the backyard tree.
The world cloaked in a hint of haze,
Imparting dreamlike quality to shorter
  days.
A fresh twinge of something long
  forgotten in the air
Churning up old thoughts. Catch them if
  you dare!
Reliving aching emotions of cheery teen
  years.
Awkward beginnings. First efforts, lost
  chances because of fears.
Loved ones and people of the past far
  away.
Striving to return to home ground for
  Christmas day.
Lurking near are yuletide and year's end.
Hardly time left for life—changing
  resolutions of year's begin.
Oh time, don't scurry so fast
And bury it all still further into the past.

—*Belton Dominick*

A Wish Upon a Teardrop

As I lay my head to rest,
A trickle of tear
Runs down my cheek.
It's of a wish,
A wish upon a teardrop
Of life's hardships and despair
Hopes and fears.
Sometimes I think of
Good things to make it stop,
But it won't.
I try harder.
Oh, how I long for it to end
So I could live free
With faith, hope, and love.
And the feeling of being
Being someone special
To love, truly love
With all my heart.

—Clarissa Bannis

Friends

Friends,
A weird lot we are,
Our little group.
Like a little family,
There for one another.
We can be so kind,
Yet turn around and
Cause pain to the ones
We are closest to.
What a weird lot we are!
Is it worth it?
All the emotions we bring?
All the happy and sad times?
Will we be together in the
Future to compensate for
The time invested now?
The time and the tears?
What a weird lot we are.
My conclusion is yes.
The future may not hold
Us together, but we
Influence each other's lives
At this time. Our time.
We care.
We love.
We are friends.

—Jennifer A. Hovis

A Tear of a Rose

A vagary of the heart,
A whisper in the warm wind,
A tear of a delicate rose,
A rose that never fully bloomed,
A sweet, dewey, light tear
That falls with the grace of the ever rising sun.
A light touch,
A dream dies,
As a vision's seen. . .

—Erica Shahinian

We Were Given

We were given eyes to see the world,
A world made of beauty and gold.
We were given eyes to see the road that we would travel,
The road that would show us our lives as we grow,
The road that would throw us to and fro,
The road that would make us realize,
The heavenly skies,
The eyes that would show us love and hate in disguise.

—Jennifer Roberts

I'm in Another Land

I'm in another land when I'm with you
A world of fantasy where all dreams come true
I wished for a guy whose tough but sweet
Then you came by and that's hard to beat
You told me I was special and I meant alot to you.
You know I'll always love you and I'll always be true.
So I wrote this down just to let you know how I feel,
But what I feel isn't fantasy, I love you and that's for real.

—Jennelli Simms

Luckiest of All

Like the sun shining bright blinding her from the outside world, they seem to call reality.
A young woman with a child's mind, imagination, hopes, dreams and fanatasies.
A young man in love with a fairytale he hopes will grow into a woman with a woman's mind, determination to be somebody instead of anybody.
Lucky how she must be to have found this man who shows patience, strength, and determination to stand beside her until she stands alone.
A young woman with a child's mind, someone people pity sometime, but they say there's two sides to every person.
One day that other side will be seen and she'll probably stand tall.
But for now my friends she's the luckiest of all.

—Dora L. Heiman

Glass Window

Looking at life through a glass window,
Able to watch but never to see,
Able to touch but never to feel,
Able to hear but never to listen,
Able to dream but never with love.
We are the people who can no longer cry,
Our tears have filled the ocean wide,
We are the people alone at heart,
Afraid our life will never start.
Anger and fear and sadness alone,
Are hidden deep beneath our bones,
Our eyes and face and body pray,
Not to listen to the words we say.
To be alone is not our wish,
We need the touch of a tender kiss,
To be understood is what we plead,
To have love is what we need.
Hating life through a glass window,
Hoping it to crack and fall by piece,
Wanting not to touch, but feel,
Wanting not to hear, but listen,
Wanting not to dream, but love.

—Cora Ostermeier

Empty Window Frame

I view life through a different window
Your life is free of streaks and smears
While mine is full of bloody cracks and tears
When I look out the window on a dark summer's night
It makes me see life in a little different light.
Painful tears of love disguised as bloody drops of rain
Fill my heart with such sweet, sweet pain.
And without this pain
My life would be nothing but an
Empty window frame.

—Robin Lokele Smith

Needed: A friend and Confidante

If he only knew how much I think
About all I do, all he does, all we do together. . .
If he only knew how much I analyze my world
How insecure I feel at times;
How disturbed my heart can feel.
If he only knew, perhaps he'd help me;
Perhaps he'd tell me he feels the same way,
If he only knew, a ray of sunshine
Would warm my heart and make me truly smile.
If he only knew what others cannot see;
What I hide to maintain my cheerful image;
How much I long to have a confidante.
If he only knew. . .he'd be my friend and my love.

—Irene Vassos

My Secret Place

There is a world of just you and me
About anytime I can see us,
We dive in the lake,
Swim very close,
Where all we must do is
Just be us.
Where nobody knows, cares, or sees
The two lovers kissing so sweetly.
They frolic and play most all of the day,
They trust in each other completely.
When night comes to call
Beneath a waterfall,
In each other's arms you can find them.
Where love leads the way
To more endless days
Where no lies or goodbyes can harm them.

—*Jeannie Mattox Kendall*

An Endless Dream

I sit back and wonder
About my thoughtless dreams
Keeping faith
In adolescence
Like a petal on the wind
I'm struggling to find my way
It seems like forever
When I'll be an adult
Whatever happened to Santa
Or the Tooth Fairy, the Easter Bunny
If only we could freeze the lands of time
For soon I'll just be a seed of yesterday.

—*Jackie Mahoney*

The Homeless

People often wonder
About the homeless on the streets.
They never take a chance to see
They're really not deadbeats.
They're people who can't find a job,
And people who are taught
That not everything thats's in your life
Is something that's bought.
Why can't we lay off these people?
They are humans too.
People just don't understand
What the homeless really go through.
It's tough out there,
But some can't see what really does go on.
If the homeless stay there long enough,
Soon they'll all be gone.

—*Kim Kuntzman*

The Sun

The sun came bursting
above the mountaintops.
Above the trees he came.
He smiled with a non-stop smile you could not tame.
He told the trees to stand up straight,
He told the grass to grow.
He told the flowers to show their beauty,
And the rivers he told to flow.

—*Jackie Morgan*

Colors

Splish, Splash
Across the pages of life
Hot or warm
Black or white.
Are your pages green or red
Blue or yellow or even orange?
For I do not care
For you are my friend.
And the color of your pages do not matter at all.
It would not matter if your pages were ripped
Or in perfect condition,
I would love you and hope you would love me.
The way that you are and the changes you make,
You will always be the friend I love.
This is why I always want to be able to call you my friend.
Colors, colors
Splish, splash
Across the pages of our lives.

—*Corey Wilson*

Little Things

Sometimes we may not realize that everything we do,
Affects not only our lives, but touches others too.
A single caring smile brightens every day,
For anyone who happens to be passing the way.
A little bit of thoughtfulness that shows someone you care,
Creates a ray of sunshine for everyone to share.

—*Kimmi L. Baumgardt*

Night Light

I lie here and shiver, my heart full of dread,
Afraid to get up and out of my bed.
I hear the steps on the stairway outside,
I tremble in fear and want to hide.
Closer and closer, at my door do they stop,
If I try to move, I know I will drop.
The door slowly opens, a shadow is cast,
It's a monster, I know, and it's coming in fast.
I cover my head, afraid to look out,
"Don't eat me, don't eat me", I begin to shout.
"Time for bed dear", I hear mama say,
"Put your book up, it's been a long day".
I know I shouldn't be afraid of the night,
But even at seven, I need my night light.

—*Brenda D. Walden*

Hold On To Your Dream

Your dreams are soaring,
Your hopes are high.
You have great potential,
Your limit is the sky.
Important goals you have made,
Are to be reached, not betrayed.
You are a special person,
I know you can do it.
Your dream is unique,
So hold on to it!

—*Melissa Sams*

The Inauguration

What will happen to the nation,
After the inauguration?
George Bush has been inaugurated,
That's what all the papers stated.
Does everyone like Dan Quayle,
Or is he getting nasty mail?
The mud slinging is finally over.
George Bush had the lucky clover.
Was Bush glad to see Reagan go,
Or is there something we don't know?
Reagan's wife had a goal,
To keep kids from using Skoal.
Bush's wife thinks it's cool,
For all kids to stay in school.
Does Bush want a nuclear war?
Does he have a plan to settle a score?
Do we know the man who won,
Or have our troubles just begun?

—*Jennifer Robinette*

The fall of an object, crashing down to the floor

The sound of his footsteps, walking fast out the door
After the slam, she silently screams
The glass on the floor, representing her dreams
The wimper of a child, interrupted her thoughts
Around then she turned, recapping the battle just fought.
The child it seems, got the worst of the blow,
With the battles she's seen, and attacks fought alone.
She screamed only once, when his hand hit her face
It can not be right, to raise a child this way.
It's a hopeless disaster, entered each and every day,
But what could she do? Where could they stay?
So they lived out their days, her child worn and battered.
Their weeks filled, with sorrow, their hearts torn and tattered.
And like the vase once thrown to the floor, their hope too
has shattered.

—*Amy Wyninger*

The White Room

A big white room with nothing in it.
Your heart empty,
Not trusting yourself to let anyone in.
So you sit, alone, empty,
In a big white room.
All you see is other people having fun,
And you trapped inside the white room.

—*Sarah Smith*

Fleeing Dove

Lying on petals of solitude,
Again, sliding into dark waters.
Take me to that infinite paradise
Where our wild love should reign.
I'm being blown away
Always by the winds of dreams,
Dedicating this endless hope
To someone now unknown.
Maybe a dissolving image
That will never bring back
The same fleeing dove.
Out there lost and disappeared
Is our faith of turning the world around;
Making forests out of deserts
And diamonds out of glass.
But now the pain that lives in the soul
Knows the sun won't shine on this grey sky,
And lonely night of thunder.

—*Deborah Ramos*

The Ocean and You

I sit here and watch the waves as they lap
against my toes and think of the way you held
me close that one special night, and being glad
we've never once had a real fight. Through thick
and thin you've been my friend. But just like the
sand you evade my grasp and slipped through my
fingers. Like the broken sand dollar sitting there,
my heart is broken-up over you, and like when
I touch that Jellyfish, I get stung when I
try to show you my emotions. I love this
ocean and it sometimes seems to me like a
magic potion. I wish I could bring you here,
sit upon this pier with you, and ask you if
you really care.

—*Crystal Manker*

Wind of Silence

The wind blows hard
Against the trees
My hair becomes wild
As it blows in the breeze.
As the wind blows softer
With much grace
A tear slides gently
Down my face.
I stand in the wind
Letting my troubles go
As the wind goes
Through my soul.

—*Heather Richardson*

One Rose

There are roses in bloom
All around my house.
How could one in a vase
Be so special,
Because it came from you?
But it didn't,
And the vase remains empty.
I'd trade all the roses
In the garden
For the one single rose from you
Just to know you cared enough
To send me one.

—*Barbara Finnicum*

Behind the Mirror Image

Behind the mirror image,
All I can see
Is a desperate little girl
Trying to break free.
I see her in the morning,
I see her at night.
I'm always wondering if I might
Help this fearful child
She's scared, yes indeed.
I want to help her with
Her thoughts help her to
break free.
If I break the mirror,
She will be gone.
Tiny little pieces is what
She will be.
Forever gone, forever free.

—*Karen Lee Staniec*

Shattered Love

As I walk through the white forest
All I hear is crunch, crunch.
And all I think of is him
And the way he broke us apart.
Not only did he break us apart
But my heart just as well.
I'm wondering why he did it,
And what I did to deserve it.
Then I started to cry
Knowing I could have done nothing about it.

—*Jaime Wilkie*

Losing A Friend

What you ever did I'll never know
All I know is it wasn't your time to go
You never hurt anyone; You were always so sweet
You didn't know you were near defeat
You cared so much for everyone else
You forgot about the special person yourself
I can't live without you here.
Without feeling your presence near
It's hard to think I'll never see
That friend who was very dear to me
All I want you to know
Is that I'll always love you so.

—*Diana Merriman*

Mr. Pudgy Penguin

Little Mr. Pudgy Penguin
All in black and white.
Little Mr. Pudgy Penguin
Is dressed in his tux tonight.
He has a date with his ladyfriend,
She's very pudgy too,
They're going to go dancing
Under the bright yellow moon.
They'll be little sweethearts,
Dancing to the band,
When Mr. Pudgy Penguin
Puts a ring on his ladyfriend's hand.
It looks like a big, bright diamond,
But won't she be surprised,
When it gets a little warmer,
And her ring melts before her eyes!

—*Erica Migliaccio*

Today

I don't have to tell you I looked your way today,
All our friends were there without a word to say.
They knew something was wrong,
Because you looked at me in that weary kind of way.
When you cried on my shoulder that one day,
I told you I'd be there right there, eye to eye.
I know you did not know, but I was really scared
Of what you'd think of me when I were to die.
Now as I stare up at you from my final bed,
You give me a look that says, "why are you dead?"
If you only knew it was all for you,
You would hate me more.
I died for you because I cry too.
There is one last thing I have to say...
I hope you know I died for you today.

—*Kari Adams*

Basketball is What it's All About

Dunk shots, lay-ups, dribbling,
All part of my fave sport: Basketball
Magic and Kareem are "da brathers"
They know da hoop well
LA Lakers is what it's all about,
Yellow and purple is all the game's about.
Dribble dat ball and get it in da hoop,
'Cause you ain't going nowheres wid'out da shot.
Lay-ups, rebounds, "scoring"!
Wow! Got dat and you in for some B-Ball!
Watch da brathers and sistas as they jump for da win!
Basketball is what it's all about,
Kareem and Magic on da lead!
Basketball is what it's all about,
LA Lakers in purple and yellow!
Basketball is what it's all about,
Watch da Lakers and you'll know "who's boss!"

—*Claudia Amador*

Peace and Freedom

There comes a time when we
All should stand together as one. Racial ethics, there should not be
none. We love our brothers, so treat them as our equals. This whole world should be full
of loving people. Now open your eyes so you can
see, That peace is what matters to me.

—*Jaylynn Johnson*

My Sleeping Babes

I looked in on my sleeping babes,
All snuggled in their beds.
They had their favorite teddy bears,
Nestled around their heads.
I'm sure their dreams were pleasant ones,
From looking at their faces.
I wonder what they're dreaming of,
There beyond my gazes?
I hope they feel my love for them
Will never cease to grow.
Looking at my precious babes,
Makes my heart aglow.
I want to give my best for them,
And make them feel secure.
So, sleep my babes, my little boys
All my love is yours.

—*Jean Leflar*

Shattered Dreams

Mirrored in my mind's eye I see a life of joy
All that is and could be opens up as a door into my imagination
But now the elves of childhood mutate of adult regrets
Stars that once held the souls of angels fall like the rain
The rainbow with all its promise lays before my eyes as refracting light
Seven and the mirror cracked are purely coincidence
A penny is a penny no matter heads or tails
The simplicity of life is no longer that of fairy tales
Life, with the malice of time, loses childhood in the radiance of age
The child I was and wished to be
Weeps my name and the forests of time turn and flee

—*Keith Lominac*

To Infinity

You listen to me when I'm feeling sad,
You share my joy whenever I'm glad.
Countless hours we've talked on the phone
So that I wouldn't have to feel alone.
You're there when it's advice I need
You set an example and I follow your lead.
I can't thank God enough for sending me
Someone like you, a friend to infinity.

—*Stacy Moder*

Pandora's Box

A poet is a special one, who holds, down deep inside,
All the colors of the world, and dreams that never died.
A sunset, melting in the sky, and lakes of crystal blue
A magic moonlit summer night she might have shared with you.
And when a poet laughs, you hear a million different things:
A summer breeze, a shooting star, the song a bluebird sings.
Look into the blackness of a quiet poet's eyes,
And you will see each smile she smiles, and every tear she cries.
Poets tell the stories that no one's ever told,
And let the unsolved mysteries of our secret world's unfold.
Each poet holds a secret dream, locked way down deep inside
That only in their poetry would they ever dare confide.
So when you read a precious verse by Shakespeare, me or Poe,
Think about the hidden dream you'll never get to know.

—*April Capil*

The Ending Of A Friendship

We were once such good friends
All the stories we shared
From beginning to end
In the beginning it was like a fairy tale
All the love, trust, and care we shared
Then things happened and we grew apart
The love, trust, and care no longer
    mattered
It became a friendship that had shattered
Now we go our separate ways
And share nothing in our days
Though our special friendship is over
There is one thing I'd like to say,
Although this day we decide to part,
You will always hold a special place in my
    heart

—Christine A. Budai

She Shields Me

She holds me under her double breasted
    wing.
All the while shielding me from all live
    prey.
She holds me so close and yet so near,
I often feel I'll never shed a tear.
Not to fear my faithful Mother dear,
I'll never shed a tear.
Not as long as you are here.
I love you, my Mother dear,
Mainly because you're always near.

—Edith Inez Bradley

Crayons for my Friend

Here, take my crayons!
All these pointed magic wands!
Mix magenta tulips and scarlet poppies,
Spray a spring tree cerise pink.
Set a red clay bowl with tangerines.
Try primary yellows; splash goldenrods
    gold!
Imagine sunset above the Painted Desert,
Use ochre to outline the clouds.
Sign your paper with orange orange.
Leave cool gray in the box;
Fog chills, black is nothing's night.
Blues? I hold them back, cheerless, sad;
They paint a music score in minor key.
Put away that weary, somber brown
Keep the pale tints in their pasteboard
    places,
Fill your whole space with warming
    colors!
Look! I give you only the bright ones!

—Helen J. Bonnell

All in Life

Agony, pain, anguish, sorrow.
All this in life.
Pleasure, happiness, love
All this in life.
The pursuit of happiness, the let downs.
All this in life.
The love you never want, the love you
    never had.
All this in life.
The one special girl, the hell of the
    troubled world.
All this in life.
The agonizing pain, someone slain
All this in life.
The problems, the suffering, the anger
All this in life.
The time you sacrifice, the time you
    spend.
One day all in life must end.

—Donald Webster

Touching

You have touched me with your smile
allowing me to see you an instant
without denial.
You opened a door for me to see
that deep within you lies
an even greater mystery.
Even in your silence I can find
depths far greater than I should
I can almost see into your mind.
As your smile so gently unfolds
I see beauty in your eyes-eyes that hold
the windows to your soul.

—Dian Lieber

Remember

A memory that passed within the night.
Allowing only brief comfort of a
    relationship once known.
A tear of the loneliness one feesls when
    love is gone.
The silent weeping of a child now grown.
No one can hear her, no one will know.
For only the depths of the darkness
    swallows the fears.
Only the thought of loved ones bring
    morning near.
Asking forgiveness from those hardly
    known.
Is it sincere, these feelings of being alone.

—Heather Harrington

Shadows

Looking into your eyes is
Almost like reading a book.
Your eyes reveal so much
That you are afraid to say.
I see many things, maybe
Even more than you realize.
Every so often, when I gaze
Into those endless windows,
I watch as a cloud passes over them,
Like a shadow, guarding
Some long kept secret, something
You don't want me to see yet.
But I don't mind too much,
For I know that maybe, someday,
When you feel ready to,
You'll share with me
Those things kept hidden for so long,
Behind those mysterious shadows.

—Jenny Rich

L.T.S.

(1963–1989)
Alone
In the desert sand
Duck tape tubing
On your exhaust
Poison sucking damn air
Two days burning
In California sun
Weakening
Your precious skin
Fluid collecting
In your lower
Extremities
The breaking flesh
Of your
Dead decaying
Body.

—Corrine L. Miller

A Single Blossom

A single blossom
alone in a field,
sending sweet fragrance
into the air swirling about it
A passionate love
of two uniting to form one,
sending messages of
romance into awaiting ears.
A single blossom in a vase,
cut by the hands who own it.
Injured stems long for water,
as the fragrance fades.
A united love one,
severed into two.
Injured hearts desire love,
as the romance subsides.

—Julie Lombardi

Alone

It is terrifying to be alone,
Alone in a world where you have to pray
 for a tomorrow,
I an world where peace is the prize,
If you win the fight.
A world where true colors shine through,
Only on the battlefield.
A world where guns are more common
 than handshakes,
And divorce papers outnumber love
 letters.
A world where going Christmas shopping
Is second only to buying drugs,
And pregnant women are getting high for
 two.
A world where even when surrounded by
 friends,
You are alone.

—*Crista Miles*

Broken Moon

Shining brightly
Alone yet proud
Then it broke and pieces went all around
It wept no one heard
It picked itself up and begun to shine
Even though inside it cried
Above the clouds it stands alone
Just a broken moon

—*Deborah Naudus*

The Sound Of Grey

The excitement is past now
along highways where might must pound
soiled forms of snow abound
it was hoary white when first it fell
couldn't be packed too tight, enough
it sculpted into gates and walls
now a descent, their patchwork stuff!
Along schools where is books vise
browse, that theorized
bells ring and youth hopscotch
the grayed dent's notch
they have truth in their swift
intimacy of the past seen in drifts
the sharp scenes like broken wells
loose a liberty that made them swells
in a guess that was apt to do
what white does and how it makes us,
 even so.

—*Elizabeth Lotman*

The Beach

I walked along the beach one day
Along the rocky shore
I saw the big blue waves
crashing an becoming no more.
The sound was that of thunder
The smell was of salt
The scene was quite a wonder
But, suddenly the waves came to a halt.
High tide was slowly dying
And everything was quieting down
The sea gulls were flying
Above the wet ground.
As I walked back down the shore
Along the soft white sand
I could remember but no more
About the sea-bearing land.

—*Georgia Gofis*

My Love And Me And The Beautiful Sea

My love and me walked by the sea,
Along the sand, hand in hand.
We watched the sun set into the wet,
Wet, beautiful sea, my love and me
Oh, how the birds flew, and the wind blew
And tousled our hair in the evening air.
The seagulls cried, and the silence died
When the sound of the rolling sea spoke to
 my love and me.
The sun was half gone, and we went on,
My love and me by the beautiful sea.
The birds flew by across the pink sky
While the wind rolled the sea, and my
 love looked at me.
I looked into his eyes, hearing the cries
Of the birds and the sea calling softly to
 me.
We spoke without saying and silently
 praying
that we would forever be free and walked
 along the beautiful sea.

—*Heather Mason*

Days of Spring

On my windshield rain pelting
Alongside the road snow melting
Within the trees spring showing its color
Orchards of cherry trees clooming
In a distant old mountain fuming
One can hear birds sing
On sidewalks people mingling
With spring a new beginning

—*Carol Buell*

Beauty

Beauty is love
Also caring and sharing in your heart.
If you don't have beauty,
Your mind will not open inside you
If you do open your mind to beauty in
 your heart,
You will be true as you are now to
 yourself.

—*Cynthia Ortiz*

Memories

Memories I have of you
always come to mind
the time we shared together
was never wasted time.
I didn't know how much I loved you
until it was much too late
someday I'll show my love for you
but only at God's Heavenly Gate.
I will never forget the love you gave me
even when I didn't take it
you'll always have a part in me
and with my love is will be lit.

—*Damantha Ford*

Friends

Friends are great:
Always there when you need someone to
 talk to!
When I think of friends;
I think of someone who's stuck by me;
Someone who I can talk to;
Knowing that the whole school won't
 know.
I think of someone who's never deserted
 me;
One who I've laughed and cried with;
One who isn't ashamed to be seen with
 me;
I think of someone who's put up with a
 lot;
Someone who helped me to grow up;
Someone who I trust more than anyone!
I don't think of those who poke fun of me,
All they do is use me and think bad things
 about me!
That's not a friend.
A friend is someone that will always be
 there and will
Never make fun of you!
But most importantly a friend is someone
 you can count on.

—*Betsy Crane*

Dogwood

Dogwood...
always tilting, and
from a distance,
Degas-costumed in
breathless white.
Yet, look up close—
how tough and firmly whorled
are those four
moire petals.
Dogwood is
beam of Diana,
intensely focused,
leaving frothy female
camouflage to
Aphrodite's apple,
It bends to listen
and consider—
not to yield.

—*Joan Auer Kelly*

Safe

So you say I'm safe.
Am I really?
Yes, I'm positive, you say.
I'm not safe, but I can't tell you.
My heart is still breaking,
The love in me is still loving.
No, I'm not safe from hurt,
Sometimes you even hurt me.
You say you feel my pain? Ha!
You just see it.
Yes, your words are nice.
But you are safe in your nice home
With your nice family.
So you say I'm safe.
Think again.

—*Graceful One*

Free

In the night
among the shadows
standing alone
with thought
as my ony companion
He is my dearest friend
with him my possibilities
shall never end
I know as long as he
walks beside my shadow
I am free,
frre to wish
and free to believe
that no dream is ever
impossible

—*Karen Keys*

Untitled

Am I a fool to feel this way?
Am I a fool to love you?
Am I a fool to be your friend
And always be thinking of you?
Am I a fool because I know you
Will always belong to someone else?
Am I a fool not to give a damn;
It won't make me love you any less.

—*Gloria Katsifis*

Duke Ellington 1950's

Giving thanks to the man who had dignity
  enough to love.
Amidst the sins of man he'd set me in the
  clearing made by family sense.
For who says one cannot be a friend in a
  family of man to man learning
  harmony.
The shock of a child allowed to sit
  unharmed and learn the sense of their
  accomplishments.
The awakening of men to the child they'd
  been and the man still holding that
  child within.
The bleakness that cleans with the
  sunlight reaching into darkened scenes.
Seeing the scope of their dreams reduced
  to the night life scene with the Blue
  Note name.
With then souls stirred to acknowledging
  that their children were losing.
The sounds of jazz its fullness resounds to
  the curved house of a Ravinia crowd.
The sense oceans shell God beheld
  through other's souls allowing human
  to human growth.
A spiritual evolve from the drugs
  involved.
That new birth starts to the human's taste
  development.
The death of one gentler son following
  into what older man had also done.
Bub Powell's living yet.
Shocking the city to what man's teaching
  man misplaced in time to the living
  rhythm
And then honoring his death with the best
  of their music.
Instead of the drugs some younger ones
  couldn't resist.

—*Cathleen Chesrow*

Dreaming

Dreaming...
Am I dreaming? Or not?
It all seems so real.
The touch of his hand held so tightly with
  mine.
His warm breath blowing lightly against
  my skin.
I see every warm smile.
I feel every gentle kiss.
Yet, I know none of it's true.
And, in my heart I know it can't be.
Then when I see him it all feels real again.
His smile as he's passing,
To me feels everlasting.
Will somebody please tell me,
"Is it real or am I just dreaming?"

—*Katie Passanisi*

A Fulfilled Dream

A writer's finest work,
An actor's greatest scene.
A poet's best rhyme,
A fantasizer's sweetest dream.
We all have our accomplishments,
Each has his moment of glory.
Everyone has his highest point,
The climax to his life story.
An answered prayer,
An accomplished scheme.
A returned love,
A fulfilled dream.

—*Angela McHaney*

Love

A sunset ending a glorious day I have
  spent with him
An endless song full of emotions flowing
  from his mind
A broom sweeping all the sadnesss from
  his heart
A memory I have of our pleasures from
  the past.
His flirtatious smile that always sets me
  on fire
His hand writing me letters to tell me how
  he feels
His tender lips gently brushing mine as
  we kiss
His soft touch as he holds me safely in his
  arms.
The kindness of each word spoken from
  his lips
The special song that played when we first
  met
The masculine smell of his cologne
  drifting by
The warmth of his erratic breath on my
  neck.
Our hands clasped tightly as we walk side
  by side
Our place we go together just to be alone
Our care and affection expressed so
  deeply
Our loving hearts beating strongly as one.

—*Bobbie Ann Brown*

When Will We Learn

As we all start out as children and grow
  up along the way,
An everchanging world we travel to seek
  knowledge day by day.
Like the child who is told time and time
  again,
Don't play with that, they say.
Some people never listened, they never
  learned the game.
But some you'll find throughout their lives
  hardly ever feel the shame.
Then shame on us, what we have done to
  such a wonderous place.
What have we learned about ourselves
  progressing towards
A future no one of us can fortell.
What will we learn in all our lives.
With help will teach us to be kind.
But for myself, I ask looking at this world
  of ours,
The only question that comes to mind,
When will we learn that knowledge and
  can we seek then find.

—*Coleen McAdams*

The Rosebud

I looked at the rose, and what did I see?
An eye in the rose looking back at me.
I said to the rose confidentially,
"Your beauty sublime delighteth me".
The rose blushed warm and caressingly
Breathed its perfume back to me.
I thank it very tenderly,
A moment passed—or two or three—
When whispered the rose silently
"A rose is a rose and will always be"
"Sans beauty, sans love except for thee"
"The eye of beholder who looks and sees"
"That which indwells in secrecy".

—*Hazel Hoff Katz*

A Dream Is. . .

A dream is
An ocean unsailed
A dream is
A neverending story
A dream is
The future unvailed
A dream is
A bouquet of glory
A dream is
A waiting pot of gold
A dream is
An everflowing river
A dream is
A guide to riches untold
A dream is
A song that lasts forever

—*Jerry Arney*

Teardrops

A teardrop fell upon my cheek -
An omen of turmoil from within.
With trembling hands I wiped it away,
And it fell again. . .
With an angry swipe I rubbed it off
And three fell in its place.
I gave up and let them flow
And saw an image of your face.
As the months flew by
And teardrops fell,
A river began to grow.
It channeled in two directions -
I knew not which to go.
After many trials and anguish
I built a canoe and sailed away
Down the channel toward tomorrow
And buried yesterday.

—*Donna M. Leavitt*

Billy the Kid

He was a legend in his own time
And a cowboy through and through.
He shot better than the best of them
And was younger than them too.
He was known as William H. Bonney
Or just plain, "Billy the Kid".
He was an outlaw to the very core
Cause killing's what he did.
But on that fateful night
A bullet, someone did send,
Put our Billy to the ground
A hero till the end.

—*Jennifer Raynard*

How Do I Look

I stand in front of the mirror with an old
  pair of shoes
And a new dress with blues.
It looks pretty dumb
With a green belt with plum.
I look like a jerk
With the ugliest smirk,
And a bow like the tail of a doe.
My eyes are green with a little tangerine
And my lips are as small as a tie.
I looked up and then I looked down and
  there's a pink spot
As big as an ink blott.
I thought O'my God with a big nod.
I looked at my face and saw I was bluffing
Because all that time I was standing there
  thinking for nothing. . .

—*Candice Barnes*

Cycle

The soft smooth egg gently opens, in
  tearing,
And a slow-moving grub feeds on leaves,
  without sharing,
'Til its fat little body swells like a balloon
And sans diagrams, starts to build a
  cocoon.
What force tells this newly-hatched worm
  how to spin
And wrap itself up to renew life again?
In slumber it changes; a new chapter's
  begun!
A slim lady emerges to greet a new sun.
Veined wings fill, unfolding, and she
  flutters away.
In that different world of another day
She displays brand-new garments, as she
  swings side to side,
Flit-floating about: a giddy new bride.
And then on a succulent
  green-leafy-dinner
She deposits the capsule of a new
  future-spinner.
That complex little egg stirs with life as it
  tries
To begin once again, while the butterfly
  dies.

—*Daniel Forie Zook*

Threat To A Lier

Try and Try to decieve,
and a web of trouble you will weave.
Said something that made you feel good,
but you didn't tell the truth,
like you knew you should.
Someday your gonna pay,
so always watch what you say!
Your doing it the hard way,
but you're going to learn!
You've played with fire,
and you're getting burned!
Yes, you are a lier, you are a fake!
You've twisted my words around,
and I'm afraid you've made,
a terrible mistake!
you put my name to disgrace,
Now it's your turn!
And it's coming back in your face!

—*Jennifer Halverson*

Red

Red is the color of love
You give your loved ones each day.
Red is the color of the apples
You bribe your teacher with.
Red is the color of fire
Man's way of heat.
Red is the color of Coca—Cola
Which we all know is so neat.
Red is the color of the rose
You give your love on Valentine's Day.

—*Michelle Reitzler*

Death

Sometimes when I'm alone my mind starts to wander
And all of my dreams of this world I patiently start to ponder
I think of myself what would I be if I were not here
I would just be a little speck waiting to disappear
Cause life has significance only for a short while
When the people who once loved you think of you and smile
Like sands in the hour glass your life slowly fades away
Waiting for that dark, dismal, inevitable day
The day when your soul departs as if it were magic
An occurance to your loved ones that seems so tragic
A tragedy that will be remembered while your loved ones survive
An indirect way of keeping your soul alive
As time goes by their souls will also be finished
And then the only thing left of your life will be diminished
Because life will always go on in a world that is so vast
And you suddenly realize that you were just a fragment of the past.

—*Allyson Perry*

An Old Fashioned Kisser

I am a modern lover
And an old fashioned kisser
Who loves foreplay
But not horseplay
I like to be loved for what I am
And not what I've got
One day I might meet the right girl
Who will stand up and cheer
Whenever I fear
Always remember those olden days
When we were young at heart
Till death do us part
Do unto others
As others do unto you
Do unto others
Before others do unto you.

—*Jack Gilbert*

Look at Me

Look at me from the outside
You will not see very much.
I have ears and eyes and nose
Just like anyone.
But if you care to look more closely
You'll find something better
The specialness that I contain
Deep inside my body:
A love, a friend, a dream, a poem.
So, please don't judge the outside
And find everything the same.
Look inward a little more closely
And you will find the true me.

—*Stacey Grayson*

Let the Rain fall

Outside the rain is falling, but here in my room I am warm and dry.
And as I lie here and listen to the rain I'm thinking of you.
For you are the sun that lights up my life.
You make my world one large rainbow.
You have brightened my life in so many ways.
I see your smile and the stars begin to shine.
My body tingles at your touch.
You've made me so happy that I don't know how I ever existed without you.
I can't help but smile when I remember
Some of the wonderful times we've had.
I never thought a sunset could be so beautiful,
But sharing it with you I feel as if it were the first time I'd ever seen it
You've taught me to see things in a whole new way.
I can't remember ever seeing the stars shine so bright.
So let the rain fall, for as long as I have you in my life
All my days will be filled with sunshine.

—*Judith Glass*

Friendship

It started out good then began to flow.
And as the years passed it continued to grow
We grew closer and closer as best friends should,
We did everything possible that best friends could,
But the year rolled around when she had to go away.
And deep in my heart, I wanted her to stay.
As the day drew closer we grew farther apart.
The thing I feared most, she soon would depart.
But as all things end, I knew this would too.
So, I have to say goodbye to me and you.

—*Katie Matthews*

The Wild Flower

A rose is a beautiful flower. It begins its life closed to the world,
And, as time passes and it is cared for,
It opens its petals for a short while.
But the world is full of roses.
Roses that need attention and priming
And time to become a beautiful flower.
And often times, the rose will die
Before it ever becomes what it was meant to be,
Because it is a weak flower which cannot withstand neglect.
You are not a rose. Instead, you are a wild flower.
For a wild flower needs only the sun and rain to make it strong.
All it needs is freedom. The rose should envy the wild flower,
For the rose can never be wild, and therefore, it can never be free.
The wild flower is unique, for a person never tries to control
Its growth and structure its environment. The wild flower is not grown
By human hands for harvest, like the rose. And the wild flower
Can endure the pain of a heavy rain and strong winds, the rose wilts
And dies in the storm. Yes, there are plenty of beautiful flowers
In this world such as the rose, but there are only a few flowers
Truly beautiful enough to be called a wild flower.

—*Christine Laufenberg*

Pacific Crest Trail

We walked to the lake in blue August sky
And beyond, to the other side of the mountain
Standing quietly, one felt a reclining spine
Stretched over Sierra massivity, heard it sigh
"Don't go!" against readiness to hurry back
To busy, bustling roads, rewards of other things.
Sunlight and shade dappled softly round her
My hand stretched to draw her into sun
Pungently shrubbed, the mountain meadow
Mounted challenge, its green grasses whispering,
"Pull off your things, be naked with tall pine trees."
Young at heart, her body bounded free, playfully
Then intensely, even frenziedly
When still again, while plucking twigs of heather
From her hair, I felt her love for me
Fell to wondering, was heaven elsewhere
Too, this loving day, or only here with us?

—*Jack Nidever*

The Seed

The seed entered my heart
And curled up waiting to sprout,
Making its home there embedded in the dark.
The seed knows
Like a gypsy and the palm;
Like a seer and the crystal ball;
Like a psychic and the visions-
Yet it is deceived in its eagerness to grow:
Rhythmic sprinkles spray upon the seed
Quenching its arid skin,
Beams of sunlight shine on the seed emitting warmth.
The seed sprouts from the nourishment
Weakening its resistance yet giving it strength.
Sprouts turn into stems, stems into leaves
Roots extend deeper and deeper.
The seed knew and suffered from the deceit
As it fell prey to the clutches of its captor.
When the pain turned torturous, it withered and wilted.

—*Kristine Koempel*

Opportunities

I live in a city of windows,
And doors opening and closing.
Opportunities shout and yell to me, I follow them.
Some are great, some are small.
Some I would have followed
Yesterday, ones are not big enough today.
They might get bigger or smaller.
Tomorrow I may follow ones from today.
Tomorrow may bring something different.
Something exciting or boring.
I hear the footsteps fading, leaving.
The footsteps are gone.
Maybe they'll come back, not tomorrow
Or the next day, or the next.
Soon, I hope.
Soon may be a long time,
Or it may be a short time.
All I can do is wait, wait for more doors and windows to open.

—*Jocelynne Gardiner*

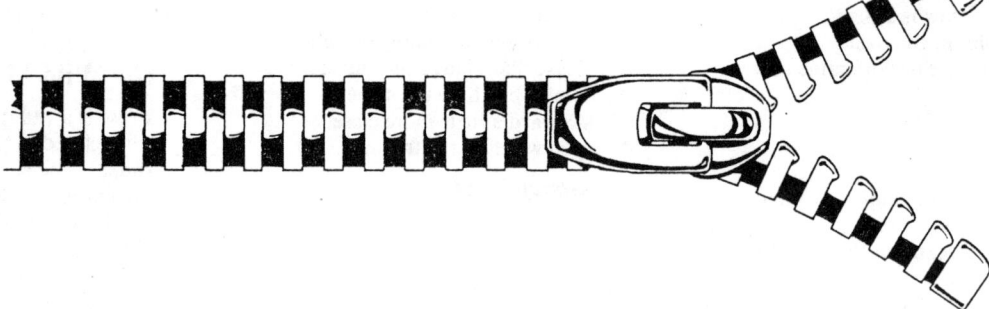

Commemoration

You sadly shook your head
And cast your emerald-dusted doe glance from the light.
A drop of perspiration ran
Trickling from your neck, lost,
Between the darkness of your breasts.
"Heaven is long ago remembered,", you said;
"A day without a past";
When future lay in skies
I entered through the blue fire of your eyes;
When you were warm, bedewed inside me held
Between my kisses and the sun bright in your hair.
I laughed no sound.
No sound disturbed the spellbound epitaph.
Blessed are the gentle demons
For they shall inherit
The ones that enthrall,
THE MOST EVIL OF THEM ALL.

—*Edgar Wyatt Stephens*

What is Love

Love is red roses
And diamond rings,
Tears on noses
And pretty things.
Love is the hurt
When one's love is away,
And the feeling that's felt
On a warm summer's day.
Love is a child
Asleep in his bed,
And a passion gone wild
In somebody's head.
No matter what love is
If it's for secret
Or for show,
There is one thing I know.
Love is for you,
And love is for me,
Love is for everyone,
From here to the sea.

—*Dawn Renee Neisius*

Sea Breeze Love

Love. . . come sit with me beside the sandy dune
And enjoy the quiet sea breeze of early afternoon.
Soft winds a blowing, as I find a seashell,
We both grow silent as if under a spell.
We trace pictures in the sun-warmed sand,
Sea oats rustle, as you take my hand.
Deep and vast is the ocean blue,
So is my love that I give to you.
On nearby rocks a bird trills it's tune.
So in love are we this month of June.
Sun shining brightly as the sea gulls soar,
As we begin to walk along the sandy shore.
Strolling along the water's edge,
Our love to each other, we do pledge.
My hand in your's, we gaze out at the waves and the surf,
This beautiful place, our Heaven on Earth.

—*Brenda K. Brice*

Untitled

In the morning, in the night,
And even in the day,
I think of you and I'm in love,
But there's nothing I can say.
I talk to you on the phone sometimes
I'm happy when I do.
But I hold back something I want to say,
I hold back "I love you."
I'm sure you know the way I feel
When you're around I can't disguise
The love, the hurt, the feeling for you
That's all in my eyes.
If I should write a book
You'd be in every page.
There's only one thing that stands in our way
And that painful thing is "age."

—*Jennifer Lynn Menke*

On Being Seventy

A 70th birthday is no big deal
You take off the brakes and just free wheel
Chronological age can put folks in a stew
And change their thinking as to what they can do
But a caring spouse, plus family and friends
Keeps everything perking till life's journey ends
One musn't feel sorry for what is past
The future is now, the die is cast
There's too much new in each tomorrow
To waste one's time is needless sorrow
Just greet each day as a challenge new
But fill it full of effort true
So when the time to look back comes
You'll always be able to add up the sums
That tell you how your efforts fare
Against that score-board we all share
And, if you can answer you did it well
You surely will with satisfaction dwell

—*Robert A. Taylor*

Belief is More Strong Than Truth

I believed in you.
And even today, you're not here
But I believe in you still.
Tell me. . .
Were they just vain words
Said to please and deceive
Or did you mean what you said.
When you were here,
I looked around me
And saw iridescent colors
And life for me was
A bed of roses.
But those days are gone now,
Evaporated like a sweet perfume;
All that remains is the fragrance
And memories.
But I believe in you still
For belief is more strong than the truth.

—*Amishi Bagla*

The Winner

Winning is not later; winning is now!
And everybody wants to know just how?
First of all, you need to know
what winning is, and how it to show.
Winning is having a deep success desire,
which we in people always admire.
Winning is a spirit that is positive accomplishment.
Tasks fulfilled without negative detriment.
Winning is being happy with your life,
yourself, and your relationship with your wife.
Winning is having the respect of your children
when they to adulthood have fully grown.
Winning is when your parents are proud
because you are so wonderfully endowed.
Winning is when the lives you have touched are made better.
Whether you have done it in person or by letter.
So, you too can be the Winner without strife.
Just gear up your desire to accomplish your life!

—*John Doney*

Past And Future

I sit here thinking what could have been
and fearing what is to be,
I cry at past missed opportunities
and what is to become of me.
I think of what I should of done
and maybe should of said,
I desire to be able to change the past
as I sit here in my bed.
The past must only be the past,
now that I have accepted it,
On this path it is behind me now,
a flaming bright torch lit.
Now I must face the future and
what it brings to me to last,
I wonder if I will be able to accept it,
as I have done with the past.

—*Carmen D. Hubbard*

Autumn's End

The rain drizzled down through the crisp night air,
And fell to the icy river below.
An eerie fog rose up; thick, yet misty.
The ebony sky surrounded me, and a chill shot through the air.
A lone snowflake, like a fragment of lace,
Fluttered down through the rain.
Everything around me froze, and I shivered,
As I watched autumn. . .fade into winter.

—*Jennifer Steimle*

Friends

Some friends are nice
and filled with spice.
Some friends people
can't control.
Those friends are wrong
not always right.
So don't be depressed
be the best and you
will lift mountains.
When you lift those mountains
as high as you want
you will have all the
friends you need.
Not friends that use
or friends to lose.
These are your real friends
that no one can choose.

—*Kanika Sharrock*

Suicide

I walked alone one dusty night
And found my friend alone at last.
She used to party, she used to smoke,
But now she's alone on a one way road.
She said she'd do it;
She dared my fears!
But now she's gone with her dripping tears.
The kids at school were stunned to hear that good
Old Carrie was finally there.
No more parties, smoking, or tears
Because good old Carrie's finally there!

—*Annette Marietta*

The Emigrant Plea!

America, America he cried,
And from the dreary walls.
Compassioned echo replied.
For liberty, liberty I search.
With freedom and justice for all.
Equality is there to stay.
No red, no white, no black,
But all in one they glow.
Blessed be the land.
Blessed be the people
God, family and nation
Is what freedom is for.
All of myself giving I want
With my thoughts, my work, my love,
And in the land of the brave
In her arms I shall rest my soul.

—*Ben B. Cumella*

Untitled

You always ask so little of me,
And give your love so generously.
You help me through all the pain,
And somehow make rainbows out of rain.
You work so hard to provide;
Picking me up and giving a ride
To wherever I need to go or be.
You try your hardest just for me.
It's just your job some may say,
But I know inside that you are that way.
Thinking of me instead of you,
Keeping the old while giving me the new.
You take the time just for me,
You are the best any father could be.
I would like to promise you the world
As you have promised me,
But I know the only thing I can do—
Is give my love just for you.

—Dawn Rustad

Am I a Fool

You are the light upon each day through the breath of the sky, you are next to me.
You hold out your hand to help me see, the life I have waiting for me.
You are taking my love and all I have in spite of my chances of finding someone quite like you.
As long as you are here I have no fear, but as soon as you leave I feel insecure.
You're each breath that I take, am I a fool?
I have told myself you cannot stop the way of life.
You are the only thing I need today.
I feel like a fool, afraid of how much I feel for you,
Is it all in my mind or are you for real?
Hoping and wishing you were here today, I feel like a fool anyway!

—Marie Poulsen

Dreamer

You wanted to change the world
And had big plans
Trapped in a world of boredom
You wanted to overcome
Things you planned
You rarely made possible
Free from worry
Or so it seemed
But at night you loved to dream...
Dreams of better times
Where past and present became one
And all the injustice in your life
Would be undone
Dreams of love and friends
Not knowing how it would all end
If a dreamer is a fool
You bring new definition to the word.

—Dolores Murawski

Separated Siblings

Without your mother you both have grown;
And had certain things to learn on your own;
My first six years I shared with you;
And having to leave was very hard to do.
Although I was too young to realize;
We were forced to live our own separate lives;
A split up home is hard to explain;
Who can you run to, who can you blame.
The one sure thing has been your dad;
While growing up he was all you had,
I know he really loves you too
He wouldn't have made it if it weren't for you.
He's loved and protected you all these years,
And in front of you has held back the tears;
As time goes on his love still grows;
For you he's done the best he knows.
Someday you'll look back and see all he's done,
It's been for you, his daughter and son,
Without your mother you both have grown,
And your father has done it all alone.

—Denise Newton

Untitled

Through the hard times and the fights,
You were there, my shining light.
I could tell you my trouble of that day,
And you always understood in your own way.
We had something special, called trust,
But one day it all blew away in the dust.
But if love was meant to be forever,
We'd shed a tear, never.
Through my mind, runs the question, "How?"
I have never cried for you, until now.

—Lena Dias

The Eagle

The wing span was magnificent
And he soared through the sky;
And his movements graced with beauty...
In awe we watched him fly.
So rarely does one see this scene
The eagle in its flight:
How swiftly, as we stand amazed
He passes from our sight!
The vision of this mighty bird
Took our breath away,
And we stood still in wonderment
With sudden, sad dismay.
How soon again will we be blessed
To behold this glorious sight...
The majestic, sweeping movements
Of the eagle in its flight?

—Joyce Fowler

Foggy Apparition of a Lie

"I'll be back", he said,
And he walked through the darkness.
I saw nothing, and heard nothing,
Except the hollow footsteps of a hollow heart.
The mist clouded over,
And my eyes deceived me once more.
I thought I saw him, heard him,
But it was only the foggy apparition of a lie.
I never saw him again.
Only my dreams relived every promise he made.
And the tender words late at night
Melted away into a foggy apparition of a lie.
"This is forever", he told me once.
I believed him, my hopes soared so high.
The night he walked away,
They crashed down to a foggy apparition of a lie.

—Anke Marsh

Happy Pictures

Our grand-daughter draws pictures every day
And her mother sends some of them to me.
They are happy pictures—of children at play—
Little girls with pigtails, pony tails and curls
Flying kites or swimming under sunny blue skies
With fleecy white clouds overhead
And birds, bees and butterflies—
Little girls in pretty little dresses
By neat little houses, watering the flowers
In the window boxes, or on the lawn.
Or otherwise whiling away the hours.
She drew a picture of Grampa—
Catching a mermaid while fishing.
This five year old Renoir, named Renee
Doesn't know that we are wishing
That all the days of her life will be
Like all the happy pictures
Her mother sends to me.

—Alice Davis Merker

A Big Brother

A big brother is like a mother
And he's always on my mind,
Sweet and kind.
A big brother is someone
I can always count on,
Today or tomorrow.
You're always in my heart
Forevermore.
How can I ever store all your love?
Above, below, what would I ever do
Without my big brother.

—Amanda Bailey

Lost Friendship

I've thought an awful lot about the way
 that we were
And how our friendship just became a
 blur.
It happened so fast, like I'd been struck
 very hard,
And my life had seemed to had been dealt
 the wrong card.
I think back every once in a while
To the times when you always made me
 smile,
And all the places we wanted to go,
Until, of course, when you became my
 foe.
That terrible day in the middle of
 September,
That one fateful day I will always
 remember.
I realize now that day was pure fate,
The day when our friendship turned into
 hate.

—*Andrea Kirk*

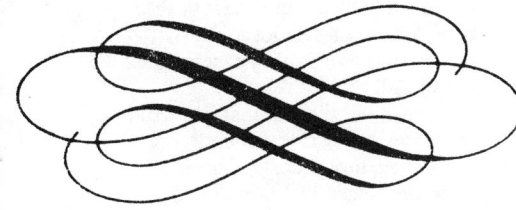

Of Moment Then. . .

Far away from moment now. . .I cried a
 tear you wiped somehow,
And I believed in miracles. . .but that was
 far from moment now.
Long ago, not places here, I met a boy
 who held me near,
saw me things.
Not thought I 'd see, but that was long
 from places here.
But in that place and at that time, I sang
 him songs
of love and rhyme.
And he brought smiles and candlelight,
 warmest passion
on coldest night.
Closer then to moment now, our lives did
 change and then, somehow
We grew to hear a different song, and
 reached the end,
of moment then.
Nearer now to places here, changes took
 the place of cheer, and so
We gathered separate cares, and went
 away from places there.
Far away and long ago, I loved a boy who
 loved me so
I don't know that he does today, but he
 loved me,
Long ago. . .
Far away. . .

—*Julie Brennan*

The Teddy Bear

I have a teddy bear
And I care about my teddy bear.
My dad has a teddy bear
And he doesn't seem to care.
My mom has a teddy bear,
She cares but she's the mayor.
My sister has a teddy bear,
She doesn't have time to care.
My brother has a teddy bear,
And he has enough time to care,
Because he's a baby and babies seem to
 care!

—*Amber Castro*

Just Fine Sections

That's your section, this's mine;
You stay there, I'll stay here,
And everything'll be fine;
It shouldn't be that way,
We're all people, the same,
The past is all to blame;
This woman's black, that child's
From China, this man's white;
When will we see what's right?
There shouldn't be sections,
All people are one,
But we created this world of sections
 under a warm, settled sun;
Change is difficult
In a set, diseased mind;
Many people have such thinking,
And that's a bomb ticking;
Ticking and ticking within the Earth,
Ready to detonate our time;
Change is the ultimate
If we are ready to really ever be just fine.

—*William Ladislaw*

World of Pain

Though my family cares for my health
And I care just the same,
I can't help but to drift into another world
Another world of pain.
I overheard my mother talking with the
 doctor
There's a chance that I may die,
So as I sit and wonder how soon it will be
I slowly lay my head on my knees and cry.
I cry for all the times I yelled "Leave me
 the hell alone!"
And I cry for all the times I bugged my
 sisters on the phone.
I cry for all the terrible things
I have done to life, you see,
And I cry for all the punishment
Life is not giving me.
And as I drift back into reality
All is still the same,
But one more thought, no longer bottled
 up
In my world of pain.

—*Doreen Michelle Latourette*

The World Around Us

I woke up every morning thinking my life
 was horrible.
And I didn't even see beyond my own
 front door. . .
Beyond my door, there was war and
 crime, proverty and famine, lonliness
 and neglect.
I didn't notice all that was happening
 around me. . .
I was too caught up in my own life.
It didn't take much to make me see, just a
 fast glance at the T.V.
And I realized, that my life was a bed of
 roses compared to others.
So now I wake up every morning thinking
 of how lucky I am. . .
To be free, healthy, fed, and loved.
And I pray that all the wrong will turn
 right, that all the pain might cease. . .
But beyond my door, there is still war and
 crime, proverty and famine, loneliness
 and neglect.
I have made a vow, to pray every night
 and every morning. . . That all the
 world will live in peace.
And I have vowed to make a difference,
 no matter how small it may seem,
 because one can make a difference.
I will start with love and kindness, the
 simplest of my task, and work my
 way. . .recruiting others along my path.
So that the world may once again have
 peace.

—*Dawn-Mari N.E. Martin*

Once Dead

Once dead life is over
You enter a new voyage
Leaving the voyage of life behind
You leave all the madness
Becoming of sanity
Born of life again
You kill and become dead
When you die you are new born
Leaving suicide to others

—*Lori Trenary*

Dream

I dream of the moon
And I dream of the earth,
I dream of death
And I dream of birth.
I dream of you
And I dream of me,
I dream of things
That cannot be.
I dream a lot
And maybe that's bad,
But dreaming makes me happy
Whenever I feel sad.
To dream is to live
And to live is to be,
So without dreams,
I wouldn't be me!

—*Charidy Riedel*

The Death of the Alcohol Abuser

From my mother's sleep, I fell into the habit,
And I hunched in it's security till my life took a plunge.
Two inches from death loosened from its dream of life.
I awoke to bloodshot eyes and a splitting headache.
When I died they pulled me from the wreckage with gloves on.

—*Crystal Cutler*

Paradise is so Unreal

When I look into your eyes, I see a paradise,
And I know that's what I'm looking for.
But in reality it was something much more.
I let you know the way I feel
But this paradise is so unreal.
I end up getting really hurt,
Because I wasn't really alert.
I know this paradise is so unreal
No matter how I really feel.

—*Jamie Smith*

Your Eyes

I looked up,
and I saw your eyes,
so dark and deep,
they told no lies.
And with your eyes,
you searched my soul,
while looking for answers,
to questions unknown.
I expressed how I felt,
though you already knew.
You knew of my love,
and you knew it was true.
I looked up again,
and your eyes seemed to say,
"I'll love you forever"
"as I love you today".

—*Carli Conklin*

Good Times

When I remember the good times we had
And I see you're not here, it makes me sad.
It's a feeling much worse than pain
And it creeps up on you all over again and again.
It's then when I want to be
Without thoughts and feelings in me.
I love you so much, you see
It's more than words of just three.
Come home soon from Japan
So we can have good times again.

—*Elke Zoske*

My Living Hell

My life seems like a living hell;
And I thank God for helping me get out of that
"prison cell". When I didn't have my parents
to love and care for me;
My friends were there to help me
through my misery. I have been through almost
everything. And I know that God will always care
because His Love is everlasting.
His Love was sent to me through my friends who care;
And I am glad that they were always there.
I know now that I can handle any problem or anyone
who wants to fight;
Because with the Love of God
and my friends, I know I will always be right.

—*Jeanine Sandiford*

The End

Thoughts of you cross my mind
And I think I could go blind.
From looking at you I feel I knew
We would be together even through blues.
How I feel inside I can't explain,
Only that I hope things will never change.
I love you now and I'll love you then,
Even when things come to an end.

—*Christina Johnson*

Mirrors

I watch the scenes of our life go by
And I try to stop
The tears from falling.
I'm not worried-I know you can't see,
You don't know what's inside of me.
Mirrors keep you out.
Without them, you're alive
When you put them on,
I have to strive
To see the real you.
Mirrors keep me out.
And so we stay,
Will we be forever this way?
I want to touch you,
To look into your eyes-
I know it's not wise.
Tears can slip underneath my mirrors.

—*Cecilia Long*

Untitled

Bend thine ear low, my sweetest love,
And I will whisper my heart to thee.
Bend low, my truest love,
With words will I softly caress thee.
Lower still,
And I will tell thee all that lies within.
Hear now my sweetest sound:
I love thee, love thee, love thee.
This love rings like towered bells
Sounding out their tolling iterance.
Know these words as treasure for thy soul and mine
And tell them back to me.
Press me as a chalice to thy lips.
Now drink thee deep.
I will fill thee with the whole of love
And nourish thee
That stronger thou wilt soon return
To drink again.

—*F. Robert Crawford*

All the While I Thought of You

I would always sit on the hill to watch the sunset,
And I would always watch it out my window,
As it would crack above the horizon
And fill the world with a dusty smile.
I would always walk away from the wind,
And I would always lie in the shadow of my favorite tree.
There I would dream of unknown kingdoms,
And try to walk through the sugar ripped fields to reach it.
I would always search for you in the sunlight,
And in the sunset when it would turn my room and hopes the color orange.
And all the while I thought of you.

—*Karen Witusik*

Dream

My dream is to walk on the sandy wet beach.
and I'd like to build a big gloomy house and
watch my flowers bloom as I sit under my pineapple tree.
As I open the long pink fence.
I greet a young friend in my dream world.
As she touches my flowers they come alive.
As she takes a drink, from the sparkly fountain,
she flies away on a unicorn and disappears in the clouds.

—*Dawn Smith*

Moonlight Mist

Between the magnificent and peculiar oak trees,
You could hear, feel, and see the moonlight mist
By the dim light of the glowing moon.
Spectrums of the rainbow put their mysterious
Spells in each of the clear, pure, raindrops,
Which could be heard like a pitter—patter of
One thousand fireflies dancing on the roof.
Soon, the misty raindrops grew into an
Endeavorous and ferocious electrical storm.
The rolling thunder was heard miles away.
The lightning put shiny streaks of light on the
Dark and deep forest.
What caused this?
There is only one answer. . .
The moonlight mist.

—*Rita M. Cool*

Beat The Drum

I'm alone— I don't want to be used,
And I'm scared—I just can't stay amused.
My god, I'm so tired of playing with paper hearts
And pretty boys and the sea.
Gin and rye flush the webs from my mind.
Beat the drum and I'm running blind.
Save me. I can't seem to make the reflection smile.
Just hold my hand 'til it's gone.
Is it real, this game that I play?
Memories of lost yesterdays.
Oh Lord, I won't spin around like a ballet queen
And skin my knees on a cloud.
I'm alone—I can't take anymore.
Is it real? I don't know what it's for.
Save me. I can't fight my way through this masquerade.
Just hold my hand 'til it's gone.

—*Beverly L. Harler*

Love Will Ne'er Return

Once love is lost it ne'er returns.
And in the heart of a maiden burns
The long, lost love of a shining knight
Who'll do her good and treat her right.
The knight sees this young maiden fair
And falls in love with her long, brown hair.
He gives her gifts and treats her right
And takes her out on every night.
Then comes along the king's young girl—
A younger girl with golden curls.
The knight vowed his love to the maiden lass,
But when royalty's seen he forgets the past.
He breaks the fair young maiden's heart,
Who though he was true right from the start.
She knows she'll never love again,
For her heart will always be with him.
So finally the maiden learns,
Once love is lost, it ne'er returns.

—*Carri Long*

Just Another Boy

He's just another guy
You meet everyday.
The kind of guy that is gorgeous
In just about everyway.
His body is so perfect
Oh, God, it's so devine.
His smile, oh believe me,
It's one of a kind.
His eyes are so beautiful
With the gleam full of joy.
But if you look closer
At him he's just another boy.
But of course,
Boy, that's what he is for sure.
But without them,
Our sadness,
They couldn't find a cure.

—*Veronica Dianne Hopkins*

Together and Free

You love me like no other man has before
And it means so much to me.
Oh baby let me show you more
In our own little privacy.
As your hands caress my body
I suddenly forget to breathe;
Full of sweet passion and ecstasy
This is love I do believe.
So cradle me in your arms forever
And I hope you will then see
It doesn't matter what we say to each other
Just as long as we're together and free.

—*Kristen M. Call*

Full Moon

A full moon was out the night we celebrated
and it seemed to signify love is in the air
The only love I could feel was in my heart
it was the love I had for you
Each day it grows stronger and stronger
and I don't need a full moon to make me feel the way.
Although we didn't take that special walk
we took the time to spend with each other
Not always do I get the chance to tell you
I appreciate all you've done for me
It's not the gifts you give to me
but it's the time I spend with you that makes me love you.
Everytime I see a full moon
I tend to chuckle as well as cry
That full moon signifies love is in the air
moreover, it signifies how much I love you
I'll always remember that beautiful full moon
but most of all, I'll always remember you.

—*Carrie Colleen Wilkie*

First Love

When May and June have come and gone
And July is under way,
And the sands have slipped through the hourglass
At the end of another day.
When the moon hangs high up in the sky
Replacing the tired sun,
And all the children are tucked in tight,
Each and every one.
When the night wind begins to howl,
And nothing stirs but a wise old owl,
This is when I lie in bed,
Pictures of you run through my head.
I think of how long you've been away,
I count and recount the number of days
Till you'll come back home to me,
Fill my life back up with glee.
Clear and true just like a dove,
You are my first and only love.

—*Kristin McCrary*

Year End Memories

It's the end of the year
And kids scream and cheer.
Everyone says their goodbyes
And tears fill their eyes.
The school year has gone by fast
But the memories will always last.

—*Cynthia Alley*

Lightning and Thunder

When I was a little girl
and lay in my bed at night
I would scream for my mommy
When I saw the sky light.
There would be a huge rumble
and a streak across the sky
It would scare me to death
and I run to my mommy and cry
She would hold me and tell me not to be scared
cause I didn't know what was going on out there.
I was so little that I was still frightened
cause I didn't understand the meaning of lightning.
But now that I'm older and I understand
that lightning and thunder is only the Lord clapping his hands.

—*Angela S. Kirkman*

Friendship

Now that you are going
And leaving friends behind
Remember us on sad days
Look back and you will find
That we are always with you
When you need us most of all
Memories can keep you happy
And they're at your beck and call.
For we will not forget you
Your smile will always be
A source of joy and pleasure
That we will always see
When lives entwine and hearts are warm
The bonds are firmly made
No matter how the years unfold
The friendship will never fade.

—*Anna Gilbert*

We Will do it His Way

We will do it his way
And live by the Bible every day.
We will be so happy and free,
If we do it his way and believe in thee.
Jesus died to save us and set us free from all sin.
So open up your heart and let him in.
We will do it his way
And live by the Bible every day.
Some day we will meet our saviour on the golden shore
With loved ones that have gone on before.
Have faith everyday that you live,
He will stand beside you and his love he will give.

—*Hazel Broadwater*

Untitled

He turned as he was talking
and look straight into
my eyes. As our eyes met
I lowered my head and smiled.
He stopped dead in his tracks
during his lecture—everyone in
class stared at him, why did he
stop? I looked up—his eyes
still fixed upon me—I
blushed as he said "I love you".

—*Jacquelyn Moore*

Beneath my Living Heart

The stillness I feel,
And love embraced,
Beneath my living heart
Another life is formed
In spiritual bliss.
Ah! how beautiful,
The beating,
A moment of quiet,
Then moving again
Rolling, quivering love.
My child, a new life
Soon to embrace the world,
Come forth my little one
It is yours
Freedom to explore.

—*Jeanne B. Jones*

Best Friends

There'll be a time when your far far away,
And maybe you'll think of me with each passing day.
I can't say goodbye it'll be to hard,
And when that day comes around I'll be sure to send a card!
I know in time we'll lose touch,
I will miss seeing you really quite to much.
You helped me with my problems and I helped you with yours,
When the time comes we will close our doors.
I'll wipe away your tears I don't want you to cry.
And the saddest part of all is saying goodbye.
Remember goodbye isn't forever just a long long while,
And maybe next time I see you'll be walking down the aisle.
Don't forget me and I won't forget you,
Try to remember me in everything you do.
I'll say it now and I'll say it then,
Thank-you so much for being my Best Friend.

—*Angi Thisse*

Love

Oh, how wise
and merciful
all nature be
to heal the soul
that cries with pain.
To numb the mind
to think no more
of sleepless nights
and restless days.
To heal the soul
the mind
the heart
and set it free.
No pain too great
no love in vain.
T'is well and wise
to love and love,
and love again.

—*Anita Alma*

The Love He's Given Me

You may be finer than fine can be,
You may be sweeter than the sweetest sea,
You may be better than the best I've ever seen,
But you can never beat the love he's given me.
You may say I'm your only one you dream of,
You may write sweet loving poems to cherish ever dear,
You may ask me out and try to keep me through the night,
But you can never see the love he's given me!

—*Rebecca Gresham*

For Betsy North

For the one that stays home and eats all alone,
And never sees Coq Au Vin;
When burgers and fries take the place of rib eyes,
We offer this little rhyme.
While your husband is blest with stuffed pheasant breast,
You are home with the laundry and bills;
With a mother's love sent from above,
You cope with the children's ills;
So with this token from us, and without any fuss,
Have a meal that is just for you;
Have a fancy dessert and eat till it hurts
And don't worry about Ollie or us.
We'll take care of your spouse till he returns to your house
And your family is family again;
And like the words in the song, he knows why he's gone,
You are the "wind beneath his wings".

—*Barbara Arnold*

The Facial Hair Affair

I've never craved a moustache
And no great leader of real class,
To my knowledge, has appeared
With a neatly cut or flowing beard.
Arafat, you say, but none of major stature
Like Bush or Gorbachev or Margaret Thatcher.
Someone might give me pause
By mentioning Santa Claus—
But I'd not accept the contradiction
Since Santa Claus is made up fiction.
I plead with every little shaver
To do me this one personal favor
"Cut the whiskers off your faces"
"Soon after removing your tooth braces."
We girls can all sleep better nights
When at last we gain our equal rights.

—Grin Moore

Clock of Life

The clock of life is wound but once
And no man has the power
To tell just when the hands will stop
At late or early hour.
Now is the only time you own,
Live, love, toil with a will,
Place no faith in "tomorrow"
For the hands may then be still.

—Annette Shultz

Loving You

To love forever,
And not to end.
Saying never,
Until the end.
Loving you as I do,
Is my source of life.
Without you,
I don't know what to do.
But to die,
Without a lover like you.

—Brandi Grubb

The Cycle Of Life

Life is a barrel of laughs,
And ocean of tears,
And a universe of confusion.
A person can only laugh until he cries.
the confuses himself between
The laughter and the tears.
Once a person is confused, he shall stay that way,
Until passed on to another world.
Then the cycle takes another turn.
Those who still remain cry.
As he looks down on us and laughs.

—Jennifer Borba

Shoe Shine Boy

Little Joe, the shoe shine boy, is tiny in his size,
And once you get to know him, he's the apple of your eye.
Now age of twelve, Joe grew up to be quite a lad.
To those who know him well, not one has proved him bad.
His big brown eyes light up, to make one feel of joy.
It's a pleasure just to be around, this gentle shoe shine boy.
Folks find him every Saturday, working at his stand,
With shoe shine kit before him, he buffs the shoes by hand.
He'll smile, and thank his patrons, who pay him for his chore.
Although his fee is firmly set, folks often give him more.
He sings a happy little tune, as he buffs the shoes all day,
While keeping time in every note, with strokes he buffs away.
Little Joe, he gives much more, then just a buff and shine.
He gives to all, a part of him, in his pleasant state of mind.
In evening when Joe's work is done, he stops by a flower cart,
Where he buys a single rose, to cheer his mother's heart.

—Alice L. Legg

Untitled

You give me strength when I feel weak.
You give me hope when I feel discouraged.
You give me happiness when I feel sadness.
You give me pride, when I feel none.
You give me tears when you look in my eyes.
You give me a smile when I feel blue.
You give me joy when I'm with you,
But most of all,
You give me love when I need you.

—Tanya Miller

Old Words

Since there is no peace
And only afternoon tea
Provides any humanism;
It seems reasonable
In the midst of discontent
To rejuvenate the old words.
Though ostracized and appended;
Their purpose is apparent
In sagacious conversation.
Like footpaths; humanism and words
Become overgrown and forgotten
Through lack of use.

—James M. Williams

9-28-1988

For all experience, thre is one Time for each moment,
And only one Time for each moment.
But if one, so skilled that, by sacrifice
Of this moment, were to return
To make the visit and by review:
There would be little change to see.
For all experience there is one Place for each moment,
And only one Place. . .Can there be a single Time, a single Place?
If thry be two: one Time, one Place,
They stand as sentinel guardians;
To suspend a single moment, in hardened amber crystal.
Hold firm by might t'span the isthmus of Rhodes.
So, have no fear; You grow in strength;
You call the wisdom of the many ages
To rejoice, That things are as they have always been;
Respect each little Place, and bow to the wispy flight of Time. . .
Discover a gentle calmness settles upon this moment
Supported by tiny tender hands,
Come out from your soul
Is mightier than All
What Is it
Touch your heart; It has this moment,
And so many more, to. . . ...;

—John Adams

Living the Dream

America! America! Let us join hands and live the dream,
And open our hearts and sing of all the dreams of Martin Luther King.
He told us about his dream on the mountain top.
We know he lived it humbly; we know he lived if heroically.
Yet, he would not stop, so that the land he loved may be free
With liberty and justice for all.
Then came the fatal day he was unjustly silenced.
This led the land he loved to mourn, and he did, America,
For our sojourn; he knew by instinct that his dream was born.
Let us keep Martin Luther King's dream alive.
He gave his all so freedom and justice could survive.
Let us keep his dream alive along life's highways we trod,
He is, undoubtedly, the 20th Century Disciple
To keep America onward—under God.

—Alfred Napoleon Martin

Untitled

As we bind our hearts to one
And our lives now forever fun
We shall be to each a tree
And our love will make us grow.
My life will be full of happiness
Just as it is each time we kiss.
And now as our lives are becoming one
By the love that's building in our hearts
I'd like to say I love you so
And now my life is done.

—*Dana Iacobucci*

The Beautiful

A place where eagles fly high
And people soar
They are free like the wind
The land of history
Of people who have opinions,
Different views and personalities.
Freedom rings here
The innocent are innocent until proven
    guilty
The people themselves decide who rules
    over them
We have the power to move mountains
Everyone has power in this society
Every man and woman are equal
People try their best to live their dreams
They make sacrifices
They spend days working towards their
    future
America is the best place to live, for me
What a great place to be!

—*Jill Swartzfager*

Untitled

Turn around, dear one
And revel in your creation
Like flowers are to spring
I am your daughter, your relation.
Remember what we've had
And surely what will be
Anticipate the years to come
With patience and you will see.
The outcome of your product
Will grow, expand, mature,
Just wait and don't turn your back
For I will blossom, I am sure.

—*Amy McBee*

How It Feels to Fly

How does it feel to be above the clouds
And see stars and moon piercing night's
    shrouds?
How does it feel toward heaven to rise,
To feel the wings lift with surprise?
How does it feel to bank and ride
With engine throttled into a glide?
How does it feel to chandelle or roll
Such sensation and equilibria to unfold?
How does it feel toward the earth to dive,
Ground fast approaching—are you really
    alive?
How does it feel to rest between two
    wings?
To hear with satisfaction songs the engine
    sings?
How does it really feel to fly?
You'll never know till you try.
To know, come today and fly with me
The beauty of our world to see,
To experience the ecstasy of the sky.
Then you'll know how it feels to fly.

—*Billy F. Andrews, Sr.*

In the Eyes of a Child

You can look into her eyes
And see the innocence of youth.
Her lips know nothing,
Other than the truth.
Smiling in her sleep;
Can't help but wonder what she dreams.
In the eyes of a child,
Is it all what it seems?
All that she knows
Is the warmth of her mom.
Her dreams are of unicorns
Instead of "the bomb."
What she knows is happiness
Of a life carefree and mild.
That's what I see
In the eyes of a child.

—*Elizabeth Collins*

Wind

The wind whistled through the trees
And soared through the air.
It sank down low
And played with the waves.
It blew through the child's hair
Just to tease her.
Then it went home again
To the sky of beautiful skies
And stayed to play with the clouds
Without a care.

—*Julie Schlegel*

Untitled

From someone who likes you
And someone who cares,
Who thinks he should make all his repairs
He thinks he should start
By showing he cares.
He knows he was bad
And he made you very sad
But he hopes he is making
You very, very glad
Rather than mad or sad.
Well all I can say is
That I have a new way
I think I'm taking
The right passage way.
I was always there
And I really did care
So now let's find out
If we can make all the repairs.

—*Dustin Rotter*

Seasons

The winter winds are slowly passing by
And spring will soon be here.
The birds are returning from the south
And the snow has disappeared.
The sun is starting to show a happy face
As the children wave winter goodbye.
Soon spring, then summer, then fall will
    pass,
And winter will return again.
But day by day as the seasons pass
And each time winter returns again,
We can see a twinkle in the sun's eye
As the children are at play.

—*Emily Douglas*

Father

You were the one who kept me strong
And stood by me when days grew long.
You comforted me in times of sorrow,
And said there was always a new
    tomorrow.
Whenever I needed an honest friend,
You stood by me till the bitter end.
Your love was true and I always knew,
No matter what, through thick and thin,
You'd be back on my side again.
Father dear I love you so, it was hard
To have to let you go.
But I know that someday again,
We will walk that path my friend.
I told you when you took that last breath,
The only thing that keeps one apart is
    death.

—*Julie Roots*

Untitled

Twisted my words
And stripped me raw
Left cold and shameful on the bed of
  thorns
Where all our innocence was lost
I listened to your lies
Through unhearing ears
And saw them with unseeing eyes
Not believing the truth
Hidden inside
My spirit broken you left me dying inside
And when I was dead
You forgot it all

—Karen Senninger

A Theory of Life

I live for tomorrow
And survive today
Tomorrow might bring happiness joy
While today brings sorrow.

—Debra E. Guggenheim

Colors

If there was no color, this world would be
  black and white,
And that wouldn't be a very pretty sight.
The sky wouldn't be blue and the trees
  wouldn't be green.
Colors are the prettiest sight I've seen.
The green, red, blue, and white are the
  colors of our land.
The colors of the flowers and the colors of
  the sand.
White sand, black sand, and red sand are
  very, very pretty.
Too bad for the people who live in the
  city.
The color of the moon and sun give us our
  light
That shines on blue water, what a pretty
  sight!
Colors are very, very, very, very pretty!
Red, white, and blue are our country's
  way of victory!
Color is the best thing that happened to us
So please enjoy the color and don't make
  a fuss.

—Debbie Brown

The Perfect Rose

Her skin, like a rose, is delicate to the
  touch
And that's the reason I love her so much
Her beauty, like a rose, is delightful to
  observe
And when I get near her I'm at a loss for
  words
She's bashful, like a rose, and shutters as
  she turns away
But I will continue to love her anyway
They say a rose is perfect and the utmost
  desire
And I surely agree, because she sets my
  heart on fire
The roses sweet nectar is sought by the
  honeybee
And my girl tastes as sweet as sugar to me
Her thorns are one of her best offenses
But for my sake I hope she'll lower her
  defenses
My love for her just grows and grows
And that's why she's my Perfect Rose.

—Bob Brown

For a Friend

When I was hurt or feeling down
You consoled me, inspired me, you were
  my clown.
You were the friend that was always there
You had time for me because you cared.
I am happy when I'm with you
You make me laugh when I feel blue.
Of all the friends I've ever had
You are the one that makes me glad.
I am so thankful for you my friend
I promise on me you can depend.
The love I have for you will always grow
And today seemed perfect to tell you so.

—Robin Marie Bicherl

Spring is Leaving and Summer is Coming

The sky is blue,
And the birds chirp all day,
And the ocean looks so blue
In the distance away.
I don't understand things the summer
  does bring us,
But that is fine with me anyway.
But the Spring is leaving us,
And summer is now coming.
I remember all the things that the Spring
  brought us.
I also remember the things the summer
  has
Brought us in the past.
I'm going on my way,
And when summer comes this way,
I'll remember what Spring brought us
And cannot wait to see what else
Summer brings us.

—Andrea Nicole Otts

Untitled

In the light of the moon flows mystical
  images, far away places
And the earnest setting of the earth but
  between the heavens
And the hard packed earth lies a section
  of peace, happiness and understanding.
But to be peaceful, happy and
  understanding you have to believe in
  love
For that on the face of the earth, under
  the suns rays
And beneath the moon light, just might
  really happen.

—Angelica Pinna

Memories Of Love

Today I thought of you
And the memories only brought pain
I remember how things were between us
  two,
And I wished I cold hold you again.
I heard your voice and I saw your smile
And tears once again, came to my eyes.
If only I could go back just for awhile.
Oh God how time flies.
I loved you but I lost you
I never knew how much I needed your
  love
And I never realized the friend I had in
  you.
You were a blessing from Heaven above.
To me your love was a treasure
The kind you find at the rainbows end.
My love for you is forever
And to you, all of it I send.

—Jennifer Walton

Air Force I

As the noises
And the motion,
In the warmth
Or rays on grasses,
Feel the breeze
Of ages wafting,
Spark to life
Think it everlasting,
Note they not
That time short passes.
While overhead
Blood ceasing potion,
Flying craft
Man's evil notion,
Protecting lies
To feed the masses,
Steel that feeds on flesh
Desires an end to it's fasting.

—Heidi Tompkins

Jesus is My Light

Jesus is my light
And the rock of my salvation.
He is there day and night
To shine his light without stipulation.
Jesus is my light
And the creator of my abilities.
He is there to show me wrong from right
Through prayer without humility.
Jesus is my light
And the restorer of my soul.
He is there with all his might
So that I may stand bold.
Jesus is my light
And I need him to be my best.
He is there to give enormous insight
And to encourage me to do the rest.

—*Janice Anderson Edwards*

Rainstorm

The clouds are huge masses of fury,
And the sky is a piece of splintered glass
And the air is cold, like ice,
Then the trees sway,
Then they rock,
And then the weeds bow down to the wind.
And then hooded winds thunder over the earth,
And the the sky cries,
The rain starts.
Pitter, patter, pitter, patter
Calmly at first
Then more rapidly, wildly it pelts the soden soil
And the trees sway,
And the weeds bow down
And lightning shatters the sky,
Like a jagged tear track down my face
And then all is quiet,
And then all is still.

—*Charlotte Payne*

In the Morning

You wake up to this loud alarm clock,
And the sound of the hands going tick tock.
You get out of bed, put your feet on the floor,
Check the time,
And then open the door.
You pick out an outfit suitable to wear,
Go into the hallway and head for the stairs.
As you're in the bathroom where you wash and get dressed,
You hoped today would be the best.
Oh, no! Wait I hear another sound,
It's my parents alarm clock in the background.
When finished you go to the kitchen gulping down your morning food,
Smiling at your mother as in a good mood.
I'm finally finished it's the beginning of a new day.
You open the front door and yell to your parents, "I'm on my way",
Your parents say goodbye only as yawning,
This is the way I begin my morning.

—*Britney Fisher*

Friends

Friends are more than words can say,
You don't have to pay,
To have a Great Day!
Rings or necklaces don't mean a thing,
It's that one something,
That makes everything!
Friends are really hard to beat,
They are all so very sweet,
That's what makes them extremely neat!
Now I've told you how I see friends,
I just hope I made two people hold hands,
And someday we'll all live in happy lands!

—*Lisa Green*

A Winter Sonnet

When the winter storm comes in with snow,
And the stormy gales do blow.
You seek shelter in your house,
And try to get snuggly like a winter mouse;
Let the icy demons roar,
Keeping warm is not a chore;
Then you take a flask of wine,
And drink until your eyes do shine;
Outside you can hear the wintery blast,
And wonder how long the wine will last;
The snow is piling up so deep,
You might be shut in for at least a week;
Alas! 'Tis but a wintry show,
And when it's over your heart will glow.

—*Harold Chossek*

Flowers

The grass in the graveyard was high
And the tombstones were covered over;
So I asked the gravekeeper,
"Where do I put these flowers"?
"They are for my friend"
"Buried here somewhere".
"Where should I put them"?
And the black gravekeeper with the gray beard told me:
"Take them home"
"And put them in your mantle".
"If you wanted to give your friends flowers",
"You should have done it yesterday".
"What are flowers to the dead?"
"Better yet", he said,
"Take them and give them to someone"
"Who will die tomorrow"
"That way, tomorrow",
"You won't have to buy flowers".

—*J. Patrick Johnston*

The Special One

Dear Grandpa, this poem, as I like to think of it, is dedicated to you.
Your glistening, white hair reflects your wisdom.
Your wrinkles showed your concerns for us.
Your fake teeth makes you shine your age.
Your eyes twinkle as you charm us all.
Your happiness depends on our welfare.
Your love shines clear and bright.
Your hands tell us you're never quitting.
Your quietness and forever shy behavior makes me want to reach out and touch you.
Your warm heart covers us from the pain and sorrow of the real world.
Your unstable figure the war you fought for us.
But now it is time for us to stand on our own two feet. . .to fight our own
Battles. . .to make you proud. We want the world to know what you taught
Us as human beings. We are going to show the world that we are the
Children and grandchildren and for many generations to come children of Lu Chau Thien. Oh Grandpa, I love you.

—*Nhien-Phuong Lu*

The Pain of War

When the sunset breaks,
And the women cry,
The house shakes,
And all the little children die.
The men have come today,
To take us all away;
The pain of war.

—*Dana Watters*

Midnight Insomnia

One night when I couldn't sleep, I was
  tossing and turning
And the wood in the fireplace was steadily
  burning.
I arose from my bed in deep despair,
Wishing that someone. . .someone was
  there.
My midnight insomnia had grown very
  intense.
And the price was being paid at my
  expense.
So I went to the icebox to get a cold drink
And pulled out a soda to help me think.
How could I sleep? What could I do?
I was so sleepy and tired, and the feelings
  were true.
So I went back to bed hoping to sleep.
But then my insomnia grew deeper than
  deep.
Then I went back and thought of all the
  good times.
Hoping that they could clear out my
  mind.
My eyes grew heavy, and my head grew
  light.
And soon everything grew beautiful and
  bright.
I dozed off to sleep, then I knew for sure.
That my midnight insomnia had finally
  been cured.

—*Endia Anderson*

Hurt Feelings

One morning I came to see you
You looked better
Your wife was not very nice
But I came in to see you anyway
I did not stay long
She did not want me there
So, I left and came home
I was not home long
Until I got a phone call
That said you were worse
I went back to see you
And by the time I got there
You were gone
I never got to see you again

—*Priscilla Wethington*

Rose Colored Shades

I sit at the window on this rainy day,
And the world outside looks so cold and
  grey.
I put on my new rose colored shades,
And as I do the greyness quickly fades.
The world outside now looks warm and
  bright,
And the rain from heaven full of light.
The people on the street,
With no shoes on their feet,
Seem so happy today
All their troubles have gone away.
And I just wish everyone could see
The world through my rose-colored
  shades.

—*Eleanor R. Curtis*

On Parting From A Friend

I looked down the road as far as I could,
And there in the path my dear friend
  stood.
Soon decision was grandly made,
And into the wood my friend did fade.
Knowing that I on the other path must
  trod,
I looked to heaven, I looked to God.
It's hard to believe our school days are
  done,
All our studies, our sorrows and fun.
On down the path I made my way,
Not too melancholy, not too gay.
In years to come when backward I glance,
I'll remember this day in the wood,
  perchance.
When on this path of grass and weed,
I parted from my friend, my friend
  indeed.

—*Anne B. Sawyer*

My Eyes Can Lie, Too

Eyes are the mirrors of the soul,
And this mirror rarely lies.
But your eyes are lying now.
My eyes can lie, too.
Your eyes have become mine.
You're seeing the world as I see it.
It's a haunting place, isn't it.
My eyes can lie, too.
You're seeing me as I see myself.
You never knew I felt this way, did you?
My eyes can lie, too.
You're seeing yourself the way I see you.
You're a beautiful person, aren't you?
You are more than a beautiful person to
  me,
But my eyes can lie, too.
No one knows the real me; no one knows
  the real you.
But at least we know each other.
Our eyes are lying.

—*Amy Perbeck*

Left Unspoken

What if tomorrow never came
And this was the final day?
Would I have done the same,
Or spent it another way?
Would I have told you I love you
In some poetic rhyme?
Or would I have left that unspoken
For some other time?
Yesterday is gone forever,
Tomorrow may never be.
But I am glad that for today
You are here with me.

—*Kristine Jones*

Hotel Vaakuuna Helsinki

I stood by the window
And thought
How nice it would be
To lose myself
In your streets,
And leave my name
Hanging in the closet
For the next tourist
To find.
And the bubble of those elfin voices
Skittered up the wall,
Dancing past the window
Of my hotel room
Skating on the northern sky
And they begged me not to go.

—*Bill Coyle*

My Little Kevin

There once was a guy filled with hate
And to his future he couldn't relate.
Some people thought he was very bad
  news,
Heavy on smoking, heavy on booze.
To some, his feelings he could not hide,
But to others, he kept them deep inside.
He was real real depressed and oh so sad.
The pain inside him hurt so bad.
He was desperate for love and affection.
He couldn't take the pain of rejection.
He needed a friend but he didn't know
  who.
He needed help, someone to turn to.
No one understood his scary thoughts,
Or know about his scandelous plots.
I don't know why we didn't understand.
We should've known what he had
  planned.
This friend of mine, he went to Heaven.
God took away my little Kevin

—*Julie Bartlett*

Lost in a Masquerade

As a child we can build a false image,
And to others we serenade
That all is well within us,
But, we are lost in a masquerade!
We learn to live in our fantasy,
But inside it's quite a task
Because God is there to remind us
That we're living behind a mask.
Our lives become increasingly empty
Each time we're pressured to ask,
"Who put me in this place of emptiness,"
"This place behind a mask?"
God's truth will our image correct
And to the world we can serenade,
"We're created in his loving image,"
"Now, we're not lost in a masquerade!"

—*Chuck Reisinger*

It Was Only a Dream

The sun is set, the waves are low
And two people who love each other
Walk side by side, hand in hand,
Down the white sandy beach.
They sit down, but only to look at the
    sunset.
She looks to the waves and
Out of the corner of her eye,
She can see him staring at her,
She turns to look at him,
He gently touches her soft black hair.
She pulls him close to fill comfort inside.
Before long a big tide comes up
And the water washes off the sand on
    their feet.
They get up because the tides are high
And the night has fallen,
But as they walk away,
She also leaves their closeness behind
Because he is gone, he was never there, it
    was only a dream.

—*Christy J. Campbell*

A Summertime Day

The wind was breezy,
And very strong,
The water rippled,
For miles along.
The sun was set,
But there still was heat,
The sand was warm,
Beneath your feet.
The sail was high,
With the color white,
The day soared by fast,
Like a flying kite.

—*Janna Nissen*

The Best is Yet to Come

When we come home he turns on the
    stereo,
And we dance to the beat of our loving
    hearts.
The best is yet to come.
If in the darkness we see the truth,
As our lips meet we'll forget our youth.
Love is like the falling rain, it's so hard to
    train.
My love runs wild for you, as yours does
    for me
The best is yet to come, yes the best is yet
    to come.
I will always love you, and hope you love
    me true.
People stare but I don't care, an unlikely
    pair they all say.
But what does it matter? My heart will
    never shatter
As long as our love is true.
The best is yet to come.
Yes the best is yet to come.

—*Alicia Estis*

Time

Time passes in an endless stream,
And we put off till tomorrow
What should have been done today
Without realizing that there may be no
    tomorrow.
Then something happens,
Someone is gone who once was there,
Something changed that once seemed
    changeless,
And then we know that all we really have
    is today.

—*Jo Ann Chiari Krueger*

Untitled

I capture the night
and weave it into my hair,
while the stars fall through my fingers
like sand.
The cool night air is my shawl.
The moon melts
when I dip my toe
in the pond.
The wet infinite blackness
swirls around me,
around me,
around me.
Laughing, I run across the dewy grass
towards home.

—*Danya Ruttenberg*

Untitled

Who said "savor the moment?"
And what did they mean?
The moments pass so quickly;
Too quickly to grab.
Like the quick twinkle in the old man's
    eye,
When listening to a child's sweet song.
Maybe I'm wrong, I don't think I am.
But when do the moments come again?
Why savor them?
They'll only come back when the times
    are bad
And make you depressed
Thinking of great times you've had.
When the future comes, never look back.
Only look forward to the bright future
    ahead.
So when you're old,
You'll be able to say
You lived life to its fullest
And took advantage of your opportunity
    when it arose.

—*Cindy Bellamy*

Moving

On the edge of yesterday,
And what tomorrow may become,
I learned that when you go away
Only the best is yet to come.
For the future is dependent
On how you view yourself
And I, for one, have placed myself
Upon the highest shelf.
So, in the days to come,
As we continue to grow
Bad days, we'll see some,
But on the inside we'll know
That the secret to being happy
Comes only from within.
So to truly have the best in life
You must be your own best friend.

—*Emily Payne*

Rose Petals

The years unfold like the petals of a rose
And where the thorny road leads us one
    knows
For to realize the beauty is to become
    acquainted with the pain
To smell the divine is also to recognize the
    profane.
We know not why we are planted where
    we are sown
Our only command is to bloom and grow
As only each may in tasting of the sky and
    toiling beneath the sun
Shining over passing days even though we
    do not know where our breaths go
What our routine labor means
What our dreams foretell when emotions
    cast their spell.
I only know we need to love and be loved
Listening to the clamoring voices in our
    hearts shouting
"More, more!"
I only know my fingers must not fear the
    pricking of the thorns
Nor frightened by the trickles of blood
    which spring
The prize of inner beauty never dies
Unlike the wilting petals of a rose
For the prize blooms unto eternity
Its fragrance enveloping my soul.

—*Kathleen Silva*

Me

Me, I am me for what I am
And who I am for
Me, I am me for myself
And nobody else
Me, I have my own personality
Not like you but just like me.

—*Bethany B. Wilson*

Dream of Rememberance

As I slowly slip into sleep, your face
 appears in my mind.
And with a sad sigh, I set myself free.
In my dreams I'm in water, feeling it flow
 around me.
Like warm and loving fingers touching all
 of me.
Slowly the water begins to form into the
 body of an old lover.
A body that is familiar now, only in my
 dreams.
I reach out to touch him and to pull him
 down.
Wanting to feel him down the length of
 me.
My hands caress his skin, slowly feeling
 their way.
Rediscovering the pleasure I felt
 whenever I touched him.
My mouth begins it's search, exploring
 curves and hollows.
Finally closing over his mouth and
 savoring it's taste.
Slowly, we begin to move together, bodies
 and senses remembering.
Giving and taking pleasure as they did
 before.
Yes, I know it won't last, that it is only a
 dream.
But for now, I am happy.
I am whole again.

—*Kim E. Garner*

Time

As flowers bloom
And wither away.
As time passes by
And makes you gray.
I'll always remember to hear you say
I love you with every passing day.
And everytime we're apart,
I love you with all my heart.

—*Aramenta L. Hooper*

My Daddy

I sit and stare,
And wonder why
He had left without a goodbye.
I try not to cry,
But it aches inside.
Oh daddy why did you
Leave us behind.
I try to find,
Oh, never mind. . .
Oh, oh daddy don't
Forget me in your mind.

—*Christine Krysz*

The Leaf that Falls in Spring

These hollow tears are not the first to fall,
And won't be the last.
This is not the first heart to end it all,
And won't be the last.
Each and every, as precious as the first,
But no more the last.
Life the only quench to your dry heart's
 thirst,
My throat is dry.
Only for you the Sun does not shine
 through,
But it burns you so.
Lost in darkness, drowning in it—it's true,
As that Thought echoes.
Stale memories of your only
 friend—Hope,
Quickly fading now.
Blind in the gray nothingness, cannot
 cope;
The seconds hourless.
And some say the sun will someday shine
 through,
Tomorrow—never comes—the Tree one
 Leaf few.

—*Joseph L. Ramirez*

Lost in Love

I think of you from day to night,
Your eyes so warm and bright.
Lost in love!
Every time I look at you,
I just fall in love with you again.
Lost in love!
When I here your voice,
My heart skips a beat.
Lost in love!
When I feel your touch,
I melt inside.
Lost in love!

—*Sheila Rause*

What Path Can You Take

When life's journey seems near its end,
And you look around in vain
To find you have no friends,
When burdens are heavy and there
Is no one in which you can confide,
When you find the joys of life have passed
 you by,
When you have done your very best,
And time will not await,
To whom do you turn, what path can you
 take?
When great storms arise putting you to a
 test,
You look around to see the things of
Which you have been blessed,
When you find the toil has been in vain
 over the years,
For all the things you have sacrificed and
 cried so many tears,
When you find from life all joy is gone,
Yet, exist from day to day,
What road do you tread, what path can
 you take?

—*Erma Ghoston*

Tell Me

Tell me that you've always cared,
and you treasure the memories we once
 shared.
Tell me that you dream of enchanting
 nights
of us watching the moon glisten the sea,
 which it lights.
Tell me that you and I united in hands,
can overcome any obstacle that ever
 stands.
Tell me that your unfailing love continues
 as always
fresh as every morning and its peaceful
 sunrise.
Tell me that we can start a life together,
and love each other ALWAYS AND
 FOREVER.

—*Cindy Bartels*

Dreams

Each dream of mine begins and ends with
 loving thoughts of you.
And your the most important part of
 everything I do. . .
Your in my mind, your in my heart each
 moment of the day.
And no one else in all this world, can
 make me feel this way.

—*Carol Villa*

Silver River

Billowing leaves hath brought me here,
And your towering power hath wrought
 my tears.
So now alone, I walk along,
A silver river, to which I sing a silver
 song.
And as I sing my silver song,
I peer across the river's sound.
And there I spy another,
I can hear him sing a song like mine,
But his is sung to a tune,
So much different from mine.
And now I look to my surprise,
To see him standing by my side.
So now we sing side by side,
To a river in the sky.

—*Christina Pauly*

Mixed Emotions

Hatred and frustration, always burning.
Anxiety and confusion, always turning
Me crueler.
Diligence and determination, always
    trying.
Contentment and satisfaction, yet always
    crying
For help.
Laughter and smiles, always faking.
Broken hearts and false euphoria, always
    making
Me give up.
Roaming and wandering, always straying.
Wishing and dreaming, always praying
For peace.
Praises and compliments, always
    flattering.
Plans for present and future, always
    shattering
To pieces.
Misunderstandings and alternations,
    always disagreeing.
Surrounded by family and friends, yet
    always being
All alone.

—*Julie A. Evans*

Serenity

White Rock
Arboretum,
Serenely affirming
Nature's beauty forged from mortal
Bounty.

—*B. J. Eaton*

Untitled

Glances in the halls
Are all we seem to share
Neither of us letting it show
That maybe we still care.
Shadows in the darkness
A flame put out by hate
The memory that still lingered
Gone now on this date.
A photograph, a song,
A note from you to me
Now I know we really
Weren't meant to be.
Yet I sit here thinking
Wondering what to do
Because deep down I think you know
That I do still love you.

—*Heidi Rosenfelt*

My Best Friend

My best friend and me,
Are as close as two friends can be.
We'll stick together
Through good times and bad.
My best friend and me,
Are always laughing and sharing good
    times.
We talk on the phone for hours at a time,
And joke about all of our experiences
    together.
Sharing feelings and ideas,
Never criticizing each other's ideas and
    feelings.
We share jokes,
Experiences too.
Will we always be friends?
We both know we'll disagree someday,
But we hope to still remain friends.
My best friend and me.

—*Amy Leigh Miller*

My Songs

The songs that are inside me
Are clawing to the top.
It's been years since I have written.
Starting now, I'll never stop.
There've been worldly things to do,
and busy I've been as I've tried.
I've ignored the music within me,
But the melody won't be denied.
I know I've found a pathway
to the way to be made whole.
I must give a voice
to the music in my soul.
We each have music in us,
A precious, lovely thing.
And all our lives are better
When we allow ourselves to sing.

—*Gena Williams*

Spotlight of Popularity

Someone once said that you don't have
    fun unless you
Are in the spotlight of popularity.
But the light that I see only comes to
    those who care not
Of others therefore I have no friends.
I wonder why people go around looking
    for the spotlight
When they have all they need.
Love, Friendship, and Happiness
These seem more pleasant to me than
Misfortune, Loneliness, and Distrust
Yet, they keep searching for this light.
Yet, I am still looking for the
Love, Friendship, and Happiness
That they gave up.
I pray someday that I might experience
    these feelings
Without needing to strive for the spotlight
    that
Brings yet sorrow.

—*Kirstin Tolle*

Silent Emotions

When the people we love
Are not always near,
We think of how we feel—
But when we're together
We laugh and make jokes,
And our emotions never reveal.
We should have said,
"I love you" one more time,
And hugged each other more,
So this will have to do
Until the next time
We see you—walk in the door.

—*Ida Lewellen McKnight*

Untitled

Why is it that love is said to be joyous?
Are not love and pain one?
I am drowning in waves of emotion;
What has come over me?
I cannot control my actions;
I am a slave to my own feelings
It scares me.
Confusion shrouds my mind.
How can I find my way through this fog?
I thought love was supposed to show you
    the light.
I am lost in darkness
A lonely, deep fear burns inside of me
I don't know what to do, where to go.
They say that this is the best thing that
    ever happened to me.
How can that be?
I am hurting, not rejoicing,
Please help me,
Make me understand what love really is

—*Amy Roselle*

Words

The truest words of life
are not written by charismatic and
    articulate
young men at their desks on sunny
    afternoons.
No.
They are written by pathetic old
    romantics
slumped over scraps of paper
at three o'clock in the morning,
with suffering fueling their restlessness.

—*Brian J. Burt*

Time

Your thoughts
Are precious
When time
Is not.
We waste
Our time
When we know
We should not.
For one day
We will look back
And surely not see
What we thought we would
When we had time
To be.

—*Katie Dickinson*

Senior Pioneers

The senior citizens of today
Are somewhat like pioneers of yesterday
For actually never before did the word
Senior citizen really ever exist.
And today's senior citizens are actually
    paving
The road for the senior citizens that are to
    come
Especially such as housing and medical
    benefits,
But most of all a desirable amount of
    pension money.
For really after a lifetime of work
Whatever our good Lord has added on to
    our lifetime
It can be lived in a more desirable way.
So now what can be seen
How the pioneers of yesterday
Did struggle to build our country what it
    really is today
The senior citizens of today
Are struggling to build the good old USA
But in sort of a different way.

—*Edward Gottesman*

Do You Really Love Me?

Do you really love me,
Are you always thinking of me?
Do you think about the day we met,
And are there some things you'll never
    forget?
Do you think about the day we might
    have kids,
And other things we never did?
I don't think you'll ever know what you
    mean to me,
But all in all, do you really love me?

—*Jennifer L. Mullen*

Goddess of Democracy

Young Pandora. Beautiful one,
Arm stretching forth to hold the sun,
Why do you lie and promise much
But bring us sorrow with each touch?
Holding that forbidden flame
Beyond our reach. We cannot tame
The evils that surround desire
To experience the freedom fire.
Every day you send messengers
That tear at our emotions,
But hold our expectations high
As we watch the eagle cross the sky.

—*Elaine Wadlington*

TRUTH

He suffered all pain with
arms outstretched
Welcoming it mercifully and all
for our sake.
He loves us all, of that I
am sure,
For if he did not, we would be
the ones suffering through it all.
Whether to walk with Jesus
or not
Is your decision to make
To either walk away, or to
walk through God's heavenly gate.
It is your decision, and only
His, after death,
You have your whole life
to think about it,
Have you thought it over yet?

—*Jesca*

Forever is Gone

I built myself a wall
around you and me.
It was just for us.
That's all I cared about,
that's all that mattered.
Our love would hold it
together for eternity.
Without each others love,
it wouldn't work.
Not it is broken. . .
all because of something
that kept us apart,
now it is over. . .it is gone.
Never again will I feel,
the warmth, love, and happiness
I felt when I was with you
it is over. . .
forever is gone. . .

—*D. Amywensel*

The Ball Player

A batter steps to the plate
As a hush falls over the crowd.
He looks into the bleachers
And suddenly he feels proud.
He tenses and grips the bat
As the ball sails past in a blur.
He's missed and his face burns
As someone out there shouts a slur.
A tear goes sliding down his cheek
When, with a crack, the ball is flying.
The tears dry as he runs the bases
A homerun made, without even trying.
A man shouts from the bleachers
Telling everyone that's his boy.
Only eight and his first homerun
Another tear falls, but one of joy.

—*Christine Eastep*

Touch Tomorrow

Roots run deep
As a stream, so do the deer
Flying high are the birds and spirits
In search for fullness of body and mind
Wanting only peace and harmony.
In secluded places you'll find lovers
Poets, and dreamers
For all we are, and that we know
For the root to all is love
The stream is everyone
Spirits are in all of us.

—*Andrew James Vecere*

Dreaming

Night falls heavy on my face
As dark clouds fill my head.
My body sinks in the matter of time
That gently surrounds my bed.
From the darkness comes serenity
As flights of fantasia abound
Of love, of warmth, that caresses my soul
With only silence as sound.
And then I awake to the realm of
    suspicion
To a world of deprivation and sin.
And I hide like a child, in myself, in my
    soul,
And I cry to dream again.

—*Cheryl Hill*

It Was Me

It fell from your eye,
As I said good-bye.
You knew love wouldn't last.
You turned away from yesterday,
And took away my past,
But I felt no pain.
It fell to the ground,
As I looked down,
I saw your tear—
It was me.

—*Kerri Bachus*

Please Reply, Lord

Lord, give me peace and comfort
As I struggle thru each day.
Give me love and understanding;
Stay close beside me all the way.
Lord, give me strength and courage
For this teen I strive to reach.
Guide me in your ways of truth
While I discipline and teach.
Lord, give me hope and patience;
This the essence of my prayer,
Let me never lack in giving,
Let my temper never flare.
Lord, above all these requests,
The most important one of all:
Please live within this precious teen;
Hold her tight, never let her fall.

—*Cathy Bryan*

A Wall That is Small Yet I Can't Get Over

A wall that is small yet I can't get over
As I struggle with life I get closer
Reaching and stretching so I can get near
A place where there is all kinds of fear
The top of the wall was like desert land
As I walked I felt the hot sand
This was the place where I wanted to be
I want to go home and find the kid in me

—*Kelly Moody*

Moonlight Breeze

The moon shines on my face
As I walk down to the ocean.
As I come up upon
The ocean breeze,
I can feel my soul
Getting stronger
Every step I take.
Over the ocean
I see the shining
Moon above the crashing waves
My heart pounding
Stronger than the wind
As I take that final step
Into the sand.
I feel myself
Fading away.

—*Corinne Monacci*

Searching

Filmlike fog settles unevenly on these
    hours approaching dawn
As I walk the rainwet streets...passing
    painted and powdered prostitutes
More honest and alive than I
Beneath the taciturn opaqueness of the
    sky...
As glowing fog dims and dwindles into
    dark
While I tremble through the cold,
    searching
Houses and storefronts reflect the
    radiance of distant streetlamps
Glistening streets reflect, puddles and
    pools reflect, and I reflect
Engines cough and vomit fumes, doors
    open and words whisper or shout
From the anonymity of darkness
Traffic lights and ramps and viaducts and
    highways lace my journey home
From where I did not wish to be to where
    I do not wish to go
Her orange windows tempt me, her once
    familiar door reminds me
But I walk on, passing there again and
    again, searching
Searching for the elixir or some vital
    transmuting ingredient
Searching for phlogiston, and the ether
    wind

—*J. Blaine Hudson*

Flooded Mind

The smile on her face frightens
As I watch it glimmer
The smile is a rainstorm
That floods my mind of thought.
The quick glimmer in the corner
Changes to her mood as the thunder
And the lightning strikes a lonely tree.
The tree which stands alone.
I become the tree, uncertain and
Afraid to be a friend or a follower
I see her smile and walk or grow near
When I am close enough to see her tears.
They were all along a shower of sadness
And she is glad I have come.

—*Jennifer Geddes*

The Flower Watcher

The raindrops stain the sidewalk,
As I watch the clouds pour forth on the
    day.
The water falls for all eternity.
For hours in front of the window I stay.
As if they will never rise again,
The flowers are smashed into the grass.
The glass window is streaked as I watch.
I wait with the flowers for the rain to pass.

—*Berni Anne Royce*

Longing

I long for you
As if I'm waiting for the sunrise
To bring light to my darkened world.
As if I'm trying to find a star
In the darkest night sky.
As if my soul is trying to escape
From the locked doors of my body.
I long for you
To waken me
From my fearful, death-like trance,
For you
Are the one person
Who can take the solemn confusion of my
    life,
And bring me, once again,
To feel
Needed
Wanted
And loved.

—*Erica Britt*

The Light of Tomorrow

The sun came out today,
As if only to say,
"The storm is now done,"
"Your life is yours to run."
"There are no clouds to follow,"
"So make your own tomorrow."
By opening eyes too blind to see,
We'll see the truth that clearly is to be.
The earth, the stars, the sun
Are only ours to run,
And our destinies will be
Just true love's decree.
For love is but a season,
Changing without reason,
And as time goes by,
True love will not die.
Like an old light, it will fade,
And in the new light, it will wade.

—Joy Bolton

Suddenly, it's Spring

The earth is stirring
As it comes alive
And is transformed
Into a place of beauty and enchantment.
As the verdant blossoms
Burst forth with their frangrance
Filling the air with their perfume.
The hepatica and crocus appear.
The robin returns
To its nesting place.
And, suddenly it's spring!
As spirits soar high
In the realm of its spell,
When thoughts turn to
Love and romance. . .amore!
It's a time for planning and for planting
A time for new beginnings!

—Anna Nichols

First Love

It seems so beautiful at times to me
As it fades in, the light before the dawn
No one notices and everything is calm
I love to watch, will anyone look to see
We lean and wait beneath the flowing tree
The gorgeous light is on the palm
I had once read about it in a psalm
As we walk alone beside the sea.
It begins to cling and grasp your attention
Like the cool, crisp breeze in the fall
In the distance it begins to glow
I'm sure I had forgotten to mention
The beauty and silence of it all
As our love has started to show

—Julie Bulver

The Final Hour

The fear grasps my heart and starts
 taking its toll;
As it grows inside me and tears apart my
 soul.
It struggles to possess me and drive me
 insane.
I can feel it vibrate through me, pounding
 like rain.
My mind is a turmoil about to explode;
And death grasps my heart all clammy
 and cold.
I lose all my senses and struggle to escape;
Darkness engulfs me like a huge, black
 cape.
I sink into the darkness and find peace at
 last;
Peace from the pain and torture, making
 my life dark and vast.
I forget all the pain and torture I had to
 endure.
With a stab in the heart, I found the cure.

—Alison Miller

Moonlight Lace

As I stared at the stars my heart starts to
 pound
As it tells me to look east at the moonlight
And my heart tells me to stand in the
 moonlight,
To groan in the moonlight
As death moves across the dark night
And I hear a screeching voice that said
Moonlight lace.
I turn my head for just a moment,
Then I look back and the moon was
 looking at me.
The moonlight lace.

—Jana Lashun Devoe

My Little Child

My child you were born into this world
As just a tiny baby.
Too little to love or care
Or even know who is there
But as you grow older my dear.
You'll compete with the fear of loving
 another.
For when you love another,
You give your whole heart, soul, and
 mind.
Which is alot to give
To the one who takes the innocent
And turns it into sin.

—Angie Ruminski

Untitled

Sand slips through the hour glass,
As lives entwine finding understanding.
Memories smolder from dusk to dawn,
Never forgetting the warm touch of a
 loved one.
Tears well in the eye of the beholder,
For pain is nothing new.
Dreams of everlasting happiness embrace,
As hearts savor each moment in time.

—J. L. Ludwig

Learning to Let Go

My emotions get scrambled
As my heart prepared for change.
It's hard to fight the tears
When I'm feeling so strange.
How simple it would be
To be told what to do,
'Cause I'll need help to keep my chin up,
When I no longer have you.
But just knowing you're happy
Will help to ease my pain,
Please don't take away the friendship
Or I have nothing to gain.
A tear runs down my face
As I watch you walk away,
But please don't look back
Enough pain for one day.

—Juli Lockhart

The Night Of Your Death

The past that is dead now fades from my
 memory,
As quickly as the day vanishes into night.
But this time the sun will not rise again,
 the past
is over and gone.
As the memories are covered with earth
 and dirt,
Mourners look upon the site.
The memories of the fading past, packed
 in a case,
Buried in the ground.
No longer will the sun shine on the
 glorious days of old.
The nights of reminiscing under the
 moon's twilight
will be no more.
Now is the time for preparing for the
 future,
While living in the present,
Yet, constantly remembering the past.
Even though dead and buried,
The memories of our past will live on.

—Kara Beisner

Untitled

As the wind sweeps across the sky
As silent moan, a childs cry
The slightest sound disturbs our peace
The neverending love shall never cease
To come to an end without a beginning
Condemned to hell without the sinning
The breath and heart beat as one
Hoping wishing is never done
To see you cry I start to melt
To tell the feelings I've always felt
Running away until we die
Keeping it in until we cry
Turning the light out when we sleep
Covering our eyes when we weep
Being scared of loves devotion
We sink our feelings into the ocean
They go so deep they never return
So when we touch we leave a burn.

—Casey Ptak

Smile In The Dark

Surrender to the night
As sleep claims his bride
Sacrifice the minutes
Slip to the other side
And sleep is my drug
To drown out the time
Sometimes it seems so long
Before the sun shines.
Lying in the dark
Alone with my thoughts
I close my eyes
As time stops
Smile in the dark
Your dreams are the clue to
Reveal the depth of your soul
I always dream of you.

—Jeanette L. Jackson

Our Love

Our love for you will always be,
As strong as the wonders of eternity.
If you could climb up to the sky,
On a sunny day so bright;
And float on a cloud so high,
In the sun's warm cozy light.
If you could reach and touch the sky,
On a star filled night so bright;
And gather all the stars so high,
That share their glistening light.
Our love for you will always be,
As strong as the wonders of eternity.

—Elaine Wager

Castle

I see a castle on a faraway hill,
as tall and proud as a silver horse,
with wings colored like the clouds of
    winter.
The gray, crumbling stone
seems to shimmer in the sun,
as the surface of a lake on a hot summer
    day.
The strong, erect towers symbolize
    endurance,
bringing me back to medieval times,
where knights in shining armor fought for
    the fair lady's hand.
The empty moat reflects the beauty that
    must have been,
on a warm spring day when graceful
    water lillies
opened their petals like the wings of a
    butterfly.
The drawbridge, a weathered brown,
the color of autumn leaves,
opens its gaping mouth to swallow any
    who venture within.
The brightly colored flowers
come alive with every breath of the wind,
and seem to look at me as I sit in the
    vibrant green field.

—Jessica Beck

Shadows of the Mind

I'm lost in a nightmare
As the evil spirits pass me by
I quietly step into the night
Trying to reach reality
But all I do is fail
As I start to give up
My soul begins to drift
As I jump off a cliff
Into an endless sleep, alone!

—Christina Hildebrandt

Early Beginnings

As the sky turns blue with color,
As the flowers begin to open,
As hummingbirds begin their daily flight,
As the distant sounds begin, and roar
Beyond the horizon,
It has already marked a new
And luminous beginning:
Until the end.

—Guisselle Nunez

Friendship

Remember me when I'm gone,
As the girl who stumbled on.
Remember why I needed you,
Because you were the one who knew,
Just everything I can do.
Although we are worlds apart
You're the closest person to my heart.
Don't ever forget who you are
Cause you're the one-who touched my
    heart.
You never let me down
You cheer me up when you clown around.
You're the friend who taught me how,
To share my feelings here and now.
I think of you all the time,
Because you're my best friend;
And you're always on my mind!

—Angela Martin

Untitled

Thinking of you
As the morning mist
Brings the morning dew.
Walking through gardens,
Flowers in blue.
Wishing I knew,
What happened to your love,
And where are you?
Walking along beaches
In the summer sand.
Wishing you were there
To hold my hand.
The golden moonlight
Beginning to show
Over the summer sea.
Where are you now
That you're not with me?

—Jennifer Floyd

Night

As the sun disappears and the sky turns a
    deep blue the night has begun.
As the night becomes nearer the creatures
    of the night begin to come out,
When this happens you know that the
    night has begun.
When the stars begin to shine brighter
    than a diamond then you know that the
    night has begun.
When the sky turns a pinkish, orange then
    you know that the night has ended,
When the stars have disappeared then you
    know that the night has ended.
When the silvery moon has disappeared
    from the sky then you know that the
    night has ended, and a new day has
    begun.

—Betsy K. McDermott

Acceptance

My love for you was forbidden,
As the prejudices of the world became
 unhidden.
No one asked what we felt inside,
Because of our colors we just lied.
You asked me if I loved you,
But how was I to reply.
A society which could refuse our love,
Is like a glassy lake refusing a beautiful
 dove.
My friends looked at me with shame,
Yours wouldn't even say my name.
Which is right,
The answer like a black night with a lost
 kite.
All I know is that I loved you,
But was forbidden, too.
You said we didn't have to tell,
But a secret like that would be hell.
How could our love survive
Knowing acceptance would never arrive.

—*Amy Auten*

The Backwoods of Connecticut

Oh winter night!
As the snow falls down
Twinkling, sparkling
Gently falling on
The Backwoods of Connecticut
I'll ask my special friend tonight
To walk with me
Just one more time
We'll see the magic once again in
The Backwoods of Connecticut
We'll walk together, my friend and I
Our breath against the cold night air
With fallen branches underfoot in
The Backwoods of Connecticut
The sight is grand tonight
I think we'll smell the forest scent
And hear the lonely train wind through
The Backwoods of Connecticut

—*Edith Meyers*

Music to my Ears

A brief ensemble of notes dance around in
 my mind
As they flow through my pen they slowly
 unwind
The paper comes to life for upon it these
 notes cling
An array of sound arises as the page
 begins to sing
The concert starts out simply with a soft,
 high-pitched duet
As they slowly crescendo, they join
 rhythmic low notes just met
The duet wanders gracefully, up and
 down the endless staff
The thumping of the bass notes keeps
 them running as they laugh
Many strange and foreign notes enter as
 they try to invade
But they all end up as one when they
 march their lively parade
Suddenly the excitement is halted, but for
 no major fret
Only to remind myself of that once
 beautifully played duet
The magic was still there but was losing
 all its strength
The couple struggled hard to play out
 their entire length
The last note ended so soft, I wondered to
 where it disappears
Probably to start a new concert, that will
 again be. . .
music to my ears

—*Jennifer Kirchhoff*

Shades of Blue

I never felt the whip
Yet
Although in the night I silent
Wept
Not for the freedom
Which I need
Or for my soul to redeemed
Not for my heavy bonds
But not to be looked down on.

—*Leesa Falashadeh Samuels*

Untitled

Ivy creeps,
As they weep.
Pools of tears,
That are so deep.
The earth is torn,
As they mourn.
Children sit,
And look forlorn.
He used a knife,
And took his life.
Leaving a child,
And his wife.
Now I sit beside his grave.
Oddly, I feel very brave.
While I'm here I think of him.
And the tomorrow that I crave.

—*Deborah Dow*

To Thee My Love

Dawn awakens with a new glow
As thoughts of thee appear
Causing every little dew drop
To reflect thy love, my dear
Thou touchest all my hearts strings
And a symphonic melody
Fillest every tiny timespace
Of my life now and eternally
I lovest thee more completely
With the passing of each day
And oh, that I may show my love
In a pure and perfect way
When day is done and evening's near
That thou mayest truly be
Complete in joy, contentment and love
Because I camest to thee
To thee my love

—*Dorothy Leonard*

Sea Storms

Waves crash and roll about the sea,
As thunder roars,
And lightning streaks the deep, black
 night
sky.
Then the wind,
With its mighty power,
Sways fiercely, ripping through the
 endless
sky.
The tremendous rain erupts over the
sea like a giant volcano
Then after hours and hours,
This vicious storm slowly,
Ever so slowly comes to a stop.
But still waves rock in the sea,
And pound on the helpless land around.
But then all is calm, with no proof of
the storm,
Except for the damp land,
There are only memories.

—*Erin Sargeant*

Forever Free

Warm breezes blow from the sea,
As we walk hand in hand forever free.
Our footprints are now forever in the
 sand,
As we keep walking, as you kiss my hand.
We think we are in love, yes it may be so,
But do we really know?
As I walk on, I lose hold of your hand,
I keep walking, you just stand.
Our love is fading, can't we see,
We'll always be forever free.

—*Jennifer A. Bowles*

Love

I wish I could hold you in my arms so still,
As we watch the moon at my window sill.
Oh, how I dream of a night like this,
Filled with only romantic bliss.
I can't describe the way I feel,
I can't believe this love is real.
You say you must go because of the time,
As you kiss me, I know you'll always be mine.

—*Cindy Wonderling*

Ocean Touch

The ocean touches the shore
As you once touched me.
With all the gentleness of the sea.
Your love used to flow as calm as the sea
Until I told what happened to me.
Emotions errupted like a hurricane at bay
And nothing could stop the terrible rage.
I sat back in silence and watched it all explode
And wondered if the waves would mercifully pull me from the shore.
I sat back knowing there was nothing I could do.
But let the wind whip around me and you.
Thunder sounded, lightening flashed
And I hoped that this soon would pass.
For inside me terror has built
That our love would end for this too.
But the ocean touched the shore and you touched me,
With all the gentleness of the sea.

—*Christina Arrington*

Midlife

The resisted road of recognizing the
assault on our middle years can be
a long and weary one.
The devastation can be overwhelming
and all consuming.
The honeymoon of life has a shadow
cast upon it.
Is it my imagination that causes the
emptiness from within?
Does the thought of the golden years
of tomorrow rob us of our resurrection
in the spring of today?
The paths to fulfilling the holes of
doubt, of becoming whole are numerous.

—*Cathy Schulte*

The Rose

I walk in a garden and frown at the sight
At a rose that has hardened because the sun's light
I go and pick up this fragile flower
And it turns to dust right before my eyes
And I think what I did to destroy such a strong, loving power
And sit on a rock listening to my poor worthless cries.

—*Jennifer C. Armas*

Life Without You

Feeling sad and lonely
At the thought of losing you
Yet a bit relieved
Knowing what's been bothering you
You say you must be free
And it has nothing to do with me
I want so to understand-
Yet how will I survive
Without your special love
My best friend-my love.
I shutter to think of the day to come
When I last look into your eyes
Never to hold you again
Only for it all to end-
I can only hope and pray
That somehow, some way
You will let me stay
For I can't imagine-life without you.

—*Annette Scott*

Last Letter

With pen in hand, I sit and stare
At written words
A golden band lies close by
One of a pair.
It hurts so much I close my eyes
Unlocking memories of painted lies.
Beneath the wounds, all truths will bend
And mock the turning of a key
Releasing pain for me to mend.
I saw you leave
I felt my tears.

—*Bonnie Lou Navicki*

Family

A family is mothers, brothers, fathers, sisters
Aunts, uncles, nephews, nieces too
A family is people, a family is you.
A family is caring, sharing, giving, taking
Families help each other do
A family is loving, a family is you.
A family is moving, settling, rooting, growing
And reaching for the new pleateau
A family is changing, a family is you.
It is you and me, he and she
Us and them, they and we
That's what makes a family.
Different people, from different places
Some new, some familiar smiling faces
Come together to agree
That how we keep our family tree
Strong enough to resist every tug
We must first root in love.

—*Adora L. Dupree*

The Death

I stand in the wings in my poised position,
Awaiting the moment my body
Comes to life.
Then a spotlight falls into a perfect circle,
Isolating me from the darkness.
The music begins.
I count for beats, and then
Cautiously step into the spotlight.
I slowly raise my head and arms in a yearning gesture,
Toward the darkness.
Then I speed diagonally on Pointe to the opposite corner
Of the stage, my feet barely skimming the ground.
The hunter comes; he aims the arrow at my heart,
And shoots. I slowly fall to the floor, my arm reaching
Out, in a gesture that suddenly looses strength. . .
The music slowly comes to an end. . .as I die.

—*Jessica Zellermayer*

Collective Security

Spheres of influence
"ballons of domination"
will create congruence
through steady infiltration.
of the areas adjacent
to centripetal desire.
Spheres never grow complacent,
so diversity expires.
by slow suffocation
from perfet enormity;
spherical domination
if regularity.

—*Grace Palazzolo*

Could It Be?

Could my feelings for you
be harmful to my heart?
For I really care for you
with all of my heart.
Could I be doing damage
to both you and me?
For every moment I'm away from you
I know is pure torture to me.
Could you're seeming gentleness
be harmful to my mind?
For everytime you're nice to me
my mind is only on you.
I hope there is no way
that I'm harming you,
for nothing in this life
could make me want to hurt you.

—*Ginger Melbott*

Picture Book

Faded black and white photo of the most
beautiful woman I've seen. Dark Brown
hair swept into a bun. Beautiful brown
  eyes
framed by feathery lashes. The corner of
her mouth tilted ever so slightly, lift of
her chin says she's proud, stubborn and
independant. Chloe 17.
Turning the page I see a bent over old
lady. She leans heavily on a cane. Her
  face is
a mass of wrinkles. Her eyes are dull,
expressionless. Her gray hair is pulled
  tightly
back. She is bent by the cruelty of a man,
broken from a struggle most women no
  longer
know. A brown dress hangs limply from
jutting bones. She stand in front of a
  shack.
Now no one remembers her or her pain
and all that's left of her is two pictures
in an old forgotten picture book. Chloe 45.

—*Cathy Symonds*

A Search for Love

I look in the mirror
beauty I see
A reflection that's physical
with no love beneath
Am I to be like Venus
and never to succeed?
For the gift of love
is a treasure for keep
True love is forever
for my beauty will cease
My heart will hurt more
for this search will always be.

—*Brenda Mellett*

Untitled

Hope your excited
because I sure am
that you'll becoming home again soon.
Hope you will stay for awhile
So we can become better acquainted
and go fising and camping, too.
Hope we'll never argue
over petty little things
that might ruin that day.
Hope you'll be proud of my
  achievements
because I am sure proud of yours
even the ones that are questionable.
Hope you'll understand this poem
because I am trying to say I love you
and need you in my life.
Although it doesn't always seem that way!

—*Josie FitzPatrick*

Requiem For the Jonestown Masses

Give your tithe
Your priceless possessions
Your earthly habitations
And I will elevate you beyond
your own imaginations.
Give me your weary faces etched
with despair and I will erase
the weathered lines of constant
anxiety.
Give me your receptive hearts
and I will unyoke the reins
of muted frustrations and free
your girdled spirit.
Give me your mind and I will
Instill new purpose for your being
Give me your soul, so that upon
Your journey homeward you need
Only abide in my will.

—*R. Elaine Portier*

Haunting Memories

The child's life went so quick,
Because of just one lunatic.
While intoxicated he did drive,
Which put danger in many lives.
The innocent child had a life to live,
People to meet and love to give.
But the drunk driver did not care,
A child's life he would not spare.
There sits the family by the grave,
They try not to cry, and appear to be
  brave,
The sting in their throats and burn in
  their eye,
Makes it impossible not to cry.
Laying the flowers upon the grave stone,
Wishing their child was safe at home,
Images of the driver form in their minds,
Wishing that bars he were locked behind.

—*Kendra L. Underwood*

Never Again

You are out of your pain, but what about
  mine?
Because of your decision I hurt all the
  time.
Somehow, I wish that you could have
  realized
The pain you were inflicting on other's
  lives.
You had lost confidence in yourself, no
  doubt.
Your life was a mess, you needed a way
  out.
I only wish that you could have chose
  another,
That way I would still have my little
  brother.
But, you chose to go onto the hereafter.
Now, never again will I hear your
  laughter.
Never again, because it was your choice.
Now, never again will I hear your voice.
Never again will I see your face.
Never again will you and I embrace.
Never again will I see your smile.
Never again is a long, long while.
Never again will you have to feel the pain.
Now, never again will my life be the
  same.

—*Deborah E. Kirkpatrick*

Private Emotions

I know I shouldn't feel this way
Because that's what they all say
There's a reason behind this emotion
But I'd hate to say it and raise a
  commotion
Please understand
That life would be grand
If these feelings people see
Were only between you and me

—*Gretchen Tyler*

The World Today

The world today is a great world to me,
Because there are so many precious things
  to see.
I think the world would be better if the
  government
Would sign a treaty for the sick, poor, and
  the needy.
The world would be better if all countries
  could
Become friends that way it wouldn't
  always have to be the end.
The world today is a great world to me,
but it's not
A great world for everybody. Just listen to
  the radios,
Read the newspapers, or watch T.V. and
  you will soon see!

—*Bonnie L. Gardner*

My Friend and Me

My friend is a very special person
Because this friend means a lot to me.
This friend was also there for me
And I was always there for them.
We have had our good times,
We also have had our bad times.
But, no matter whatever happened,
We worked it out.
This friend told me that
"If I ever needed a shoulder to lean on"
She would be there.
I have counted on this friend night and
    day.
Even if I had a bad day,
This friend knew just what to say.
This friend could make me smile when I
    was down.
I just want this friend to know,
No matter whatever happens,
This friend will always mean the same.

—*Jennifer Pipkin*

A Bath There Is No Need

The stiffing smell that steadily flows,
Because water and soap has not been
    used.
Do not worry.
A bath, there is no need.
A dirty neck and built up ear wax.
A ring around the collar, from the hair?
    The neck?
Classmates see you coming to sit near
    them,
Because water and soap has not been
    used,
They quickly find an excuse and move.
Don't worry,
A bath, there is no need.
An outcast in a world that is important to
    be in.
A time in life when one must be accepted,
This bathless one finds only loneliness.
There this careless, smelly, dirty
    individual exist,
Because soap and water has not been
    used.
Do not worry,
A bath, there is no need.

—*Aviance Dyke*

Mom

Mom you are the greatest thing
Because you know how to heal.
And you're always there to feed me,
Each and every meal.
When I am sad and feeling down,
You look at me and discard my frown.
Then upon my face appears a big smile,
So big you would think it was a mile.
Thank you mom for loving me,
The wonderful way you do.
And all I want to say right now
Is how much I love you too.

—*Jessica Osborne*

My Valentine

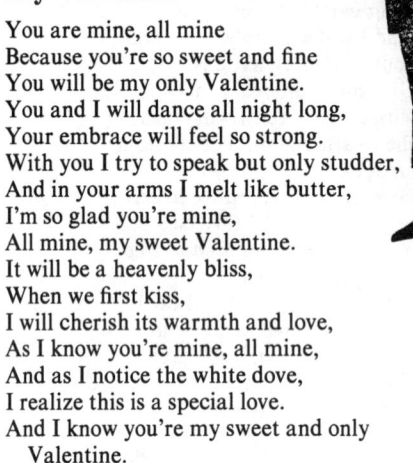

You are mine, all mine
Because you're so sweet and fine
You will be my only Valentine.
You and I will dance all night long,
Your embrace will feel so strong.
With you I try to speak but only studder,
And in your arms I melt like butter,
I'm so glad you're mine,
All mine, my sweet Valentine.
It will be a heavenly bliss,
When we first kiss,
I will cherish its warmth and love,
As I know you're mine, all mine,
And as I notice the white dove,
I realize this is a special love.
And I know you're my sweet and only
    Valentine.

—*Kristine Watson*

February, 1989

I've loved you
Before,
During, and
After,
But
I've never loved you
For the last time
Until now.

—*Connie S. Bradley*

Family Tree

The family tree of Anders and Kari
Began to grow when they did marry.
Now exists a stand of timber,
Some are stout and some are limber.
You can find a mighty oak standing alone,
Or maybe a chattering elm on the phone.
A stately maple stands in beauty,
And the little ash is a real cutie.
You might see the weeping willow,
Crying sometimes in her pillow.
A majestic pine sways in the breeze,
Facing life with apparent ease.
Occasionally you'll find a beech,
But much more often they are a peach.
There's maybe a nut scattered in too,
Do you know which one applies to you?

—*Judy Korsbeck*

Untitled

How come when one love
Begins to fade,
Another starts to grow?
When you get over one man,
Why is there always
Another to take his place?
How come you have goals in mind
Until love comes along
And takes them away?
Why does love
Build the images
Of castles in the air?

—*Jennifer Vanpatten*

Man / Woman

The man who is outgoing and suceeds,
Behind him is planted a seed.
The man whose plans can't be foiled,
Behind him is the soil.
The man who is firm and brim,
Behind him stands a stem.
The man who stands strong in his belief,
Behind him grows a leaf.
The man who has dignity and power,
Behind him blooms a flower.
The man who feels supreme,
Behind him the grass is green.
Man
Woman

—*Gay F. Liddell*

The New Age

This is write for ones of future generations
Behold this time without duration
For a tremendous change has taken place
Where man faces nature face to face
The power of crystals and music of complete harmony
Has taken the place of daily regiments with its tranquility
Behold upon the insight of this year 88
For it has enhanced the karmic fate
For all of us in this time and age
We have turned history pass one more page
Where the soul is able to be one with the body and mind
Unlike anything experienced by mankind
With the exception of the egyptian race
For that is where it first took place. . .

—Dawn C. McKoy

Happiness

Feeling full of life
Being kind to others
Thinking good thoughts
Joyful
Happiness is always

—Annette Haydon

My Midnight Fantasy

I was lying on an empty beach
Being swallowed by the sand,
When the moonlight came upon me
And touched me with it's hands.
When I looked into the golden beams
An image of a girl was there
With-soft blue eyes,
And Curly Blond Hair.
She smiled at me with that unforgettable face
Warming my soul, she reached to embrace.
I opened my arms like the wings of a swallow
And flew to her beauty hoping no one would follow.
Once I was with her it was pure ecstacy
We rode on the clouds of my midnight fantasy.

—Deb Chadwick Zambito

Lines

Crouched in a room, all alone
Believing all his miserable lies
He remembers well the surrounding darkness
As lines of tears rolled down his eyes.
His pain and grief overflowed his heart
And silently he screamed within
He tried to pull away from his vicious cycle
As lines of scars marred his skin.
The night before he was bound in hell
Now his own fears tarnished his charms
Nightmares known haunted his mind
As lines of blood run throuh his arms.
Desperate pleas and desperate cries
A little boy locked in his room today
His nostrils flare red with pain and anger
As lines of coke rot his soul away.

—Julie Yamorsky

Small Tear that Fell Today

A small tear fell for you today
Beneath the closed eye, where it hid for so long—
Untouched by the sting of winter.
It burned against my cheek
But I did not wipe it off.
It rolled on, leaving a shimmering trail behind it.
A small tear fell for you today. . .
And it felt good.

—Alexandra McCrory

Limitations

Horizons loiter in the changeless tomorrows
Betrayed demurely in ageless bitter sweet quests
Tireless unmade replies blossom yearnings of
Futility to bewilder mindful designs
Divinely spun splendor shadowing remoteness.
Deific selfsame boldness consigned to silence
Allure upcurled to contentment brooding unloved
In patterns of vapory myrrhing fragrant stillness
Ecstatic pleasure scrutinized in wonderous daze
Piled up endlessly in memorized solitude
Poignant moments of casual dare in passing myrrh
Raveled in austere journeys bend on shifting tides.
Host of angelic daring comfort forever
Chanting wildly always drifting unclinged wiser.

—Georges J. B. Saucier

Untitled

Tell me how dark the night does get
between the dusk and 'morrow
does it block out love and hope
leaving only death and sorrow
when it creeps into my room
grasping my surroundings
Do I let it in my heart
to silence fear from pounding
Will it forever rule our lives
stealing half the day
Or will an even greater force
come take the night away.

—Jill Aman

Eternal War

It's always a war
Between us and them
Our emotions
Against their unwillingness to commit.
We try to let go; yet we only fall. . .
Deeper. . .deeper
Infatuation occurs
Sometimes even love, but why?
We can't live with them
And we won't live without them
It's always a war
Between us and them. . .
What do they think
When they say
Those softly spoken words that melt our hearts?
Where can it go? Where will it lead?
This battle of emotions,
Between us and them.

—Julie Anna Sirch

My Field

As I walked on
Beyond Mommy's Garden of Paradise
Beyond Sister's lawn
Beyond Daddy's House of Mice.
To my cotton field
Which was now covered with newfallen snow
All my cotton was killed
That was when I saw a little doe.
The field looked like a quilt,
Made of the finest silk
But it had alot of filth
Yet the doe made it look like milk.

—Angela Winson

Prayer of the Elderly

Do not despise me if I live
Beyond the years that I can give.
The soul I have is the same one
I possessed when I was young.
I need your love and presence near
To hold my hand and quiet my fear
That comes as I approach the age
When I must turn the final page.

—*Bonny Withrow*

How to Heart See!

A musical voice beckoning confidants.
Binding hearts,
Unconditional love.
Harmony in life's melody,
Disguise removed.
Rituals that gather,
Destroying matters of consequence,
Befriending.
Feelings like perfect plush petals,
Faces as mirrors of emotion.
Unique sense capturing pride in another's being,
Tenderness replaces dishonor,
Seeking destiny's peace.
A glowing ray piercing the void,
Comfort in a friend's silence.

—*Dawn Jordan*

Oh, So Beautiful. . .

Mill of fields to dream and explore
Birds I've seemed to miss before
Lep on the hillside I've got this far
To peer down at my house of war
The war in my mind has lift me repressed
Nothing to hope for always unrest
But sitting up there on the hillside so green
The wet grass is blowing
I feel so serene
My thoughts are of beauty
Instead of despair
I finally feel like I'm getting some where
So come, come, come with me
I can now help to set you free
You've go the 9–5 hassle not me.
Come on baby. I'll set you free.

—*Keith O'Brien Land*

The Prince of Evil

The night descends upon the house with hate.
Black clouds hang low and watch for him to near.
He climbs the stairs and ponders of his fate.
Death waits for him to finally appear.
It hides in cracks of long-forgotten walls,
And seeps into the stones to lurk below.
It slithers under boards of hallowed halls,
Yet knowing in its core just where to go.
His sense is turned to feel the rapid beat.
His heart pounds wildly in a choking chest.
His eyes burn brightly with fear and heat.
Death stalls and waits to put his life to rest.
The fear and pain have left a peaceful face,
For death the force of dark has found its place.

—*Gena Griffis*

Self Truth

Red heat, suffering souls of crime—
Blasphemous
Chains and cries, fires of death
Enclosed and ruled by the worst of them
And bound by infallible stone.
But go to hell, to coin a phrase
And if you get close enough
To see, perhaps to touch,
And freeze your hand
On the ice cold gates of nothing—
Hell has a place, a reality
Not red, but green, brown, black and blue
Colors of the earth and of bruised skin.
It lies in barren fields and broken dreams
And words unspoken by frightened tongues.
There is no place for evil to reside
But where we keep it, inside our hearts

—*Elizabeth Davis*

Lord of the Cedar Trees

Lord of the cedar trees,
Bless me now with love and kindness all around.
Make me a source of your love.
That's all I'm asking till I'm done.

—*Christine Johnson*

The Edge of Time

We stand at the edge of time
Blind to what waits before us
And unconcerned with what is behind
Illusions of splendor without real reasons
Our wisdom changes as the turning of seasons
Though onward we seem to climb
We still stand at the edge of time
The colors are fading
The words are all useless
The path is chosen, and the goal is progress
Blind to where we are going
And unconcerned of what is behind
We still worship it seems
The unfounded worship of mind

—*Jeff Trexler*

Flowers Of Midsummer

Flowers of midsummer brilliance,
blossoms of natural wonder,
you dot the hills and dells,
dressing up the landscape.
Nod your gorgeous heads in midday sunshine,
bringing a smile to the lips.
Soon Autumn will set the stage as summer fades,
and your petals drop in the wind.
Winter is fast approaching,
now you sleep your wintry sleep,
beneath frost, ice, and snow,
then in spring to bloom again.

—*Bonnie Teller*

Spring Lament

Bare trees embraced by the warming air
Blossoms wake, seedlings take
But, Margie, you won't see another spring.
Two kids waiting for the fun to start
Full of liquor, but empty hearts
And, Margie, you won't see another spring.
Cheap booze turned to finer brands
Steady jobs, but shaky hands
And, Margie, you won't see another spring.
Your winter came with a summer breeze
Black attire, and a rosary
And, Margie, you won't see another spring.
Ducks rejoice on the melted stream
Feathers bright, stealing light
But, Margie, you won't see another spring.

—*Helen J. Jortner*

Last Waltz

We danced to upbeat drummers, all our own,
Bohemians so bold we'd even dare
To breach a world that could not quite condone
A lifestyle tried traditions did not share.
By day we walked through woods we knew so well,
Where fir boughs sheltered nests and newborn young,
And revelled in creation when burst shell
Released fresh firstness of a song unsung.
But evenings you held magic in your hand.
Gold comets circled, stars shone silver light.
So perfect then, the rhythm. . .when the band
Rolls out our favorites, I dance through the night,
Though in another's arms, my heart still true,
"The Last Waltz is Forever"—that's with you!

—*Hazel Firth Goddard*

A Love Fantasy

Through the fields the young lovers walk.
Both of them knowing there's no need for talk.
The magic of seeing the whole world in bloom
Makes them feel as if there's no gloom.
She playfully runs through the long grass.
He runs after her as if a young lass.
They fall to the ground and laugh out loud
As they stare in the air at the billowy clouds.
They gaze at each other longing for love.
They are taken to the clouds and far, far above.

—*Jules Mastracchio*

Waiting

Everybody's dancing,
Boys and girls romancing.
I just stand near,
On my cheek a crystal tear,
My head and body ache,
I'm about to suffocate.
In the shadow I stand,
With no one to hold my hand.
Waiting for Mr. Right,
Late grows the night.
About to give up,
When who shows up.
Sweeter than cream,
The man of my dreams.

—*Karen Casavant*

Soul Exchange

This day I chanced upon a jewel, I knew it to be rare.
Brambles and briars had scarred its face, but still it shone with greatness with grace.
I paused to behold its brilliant reflection, it cast its light so brightly.
It touched my mind, it searched my soul and darkness could not find me.
My spirit moved, I spilt a tear, upon the priceless gem. . .
A healing stream bathed the wounds, no scars, the light to dim.
Crimson radiance, it shamed the stars and dared to challenge the reigning sun.
Through springs and winters, summers and fall. . .
Continued until it won.

—*Judith Ann Scheller*

Breaking Free

A solitary petal
Breaks free from its hold
Cascading gently through the air
Toward endless dangers untold.
Browned around its edges
Scarred by wind and rain
The rips and tears that deface it
Fill its milky white face with pain.
Drifting faster and faster
It braves the coming ground
Separated it must die
But from it you hear not a sound.
Upon the glistening grass
Lying there alone
The solitary petal lies
By its choice away from home.

—*Janet Peel*

Nature's Child

I'm walking,
Breathing in the air,
Through the lost corridor of time,
Without the slightest care.
Knowing the world to be unfair,
I'm walking.
Catch the woodland forest's essence around me,
Knowing that I should be free,
As far as the eye can see,
I'm walking.
Nature's child,
Wild child,
That's who I am.
As I'm walking I do what I can,
To bring forth my wild soul from this barren land.
I'm walking.
Want to walk with me?

—*Christopher A. Clark*

Sahara

You came into my life
breezing across the parched desert
of my soul
of my desire,
an angry thunderstorm
a sweet spring rain.
I touch you like a snake
When I came back to my soul
I found the flowers of you tempests
blooming, rampant;
Your fragrant smile,
your voice a memory
stronger yet
than Sahara sunrise.

—*Jeanine Normand*

Deck Chair Olympics

Winter white vacationers
Breezing in the Caribbean sun,
Zephyr winds whisper hovering sounds
Recalling the recurrences of
Youth's once frisky splendors.
In their minds' eyes they're teens still
But their bones feel otherwise.
Once they ran and leapt and jumped up sideways.
Now in their old deck chairs
They do it in memories.

—*Amalia L. Rylander*

Old Glory At Reveille

Dawn, that drives away the night,
Bringing its shadows mist and dew,
To blend and fade, with the coming light,
Leaving a morning-born a -new.
Softly, with the light of coming day.
A bugle sounds its notes of Reveille
To Old Glory—or flag-the U.S.A.
Waving over, a land of the free.
When the world is at peace again.
To the Brave no gone, we promise you
Your fight for Freedom, is not in vain
It is written, in Red, White and Blue.
Our Flag of America, with Liberty for all.
A symbol of me, who would be free.
With the cannon's roar, hear the Bugle call,
To Old Glory, up there are Reveille.

—*E.B. Owens*

Beautiful Pride

Each color, stripe or star that I see
Brings an extra "special" feeling of "pride" to me;
You "mean freedom" and so "very much more—"
Telling us of the "strength" and "belief" our country stands for.
So now, "every" time I see your "beauty" against Gods
I "will" say a "sincere", but silent prayer as to pass by
For "every" soldier that fought and for those that died
Under you to help keep our country's "pride".
We still have a long way to go; but I "know" it "will" come "true"
Because "Old Glory" we're very proud of you,
So hear these words that come from me to you
I'll do my "best" to "keep" you waving, in "freedom"
Our beautiful red, white and blue.

—Joyce Rafique

The Ultimate Elusive Dream

The peace and stillness of a moon and starlit night;
Brings rest to a burdened soul and quiet to a worried mind:
Soon the warmth of a newborn sun shall rise;
Another day for us to tarry, while learning to be wise:
To walk a path of narrow, which has no dividing line;
Ending my journey only, when life is no longer mine:
In a place rich in beauty may I wake to see;
To find my Lord, has forgiven and accepted me.

—Joseph Leroy Hartzfeld

Shattered

Broken pieces of a mirror,
Broken pieces of a heart.
Broken pieces lost forever,
Never put back together.
Lost forever in a dream,
Lost forever never seen.
Broken pieces of a mind,
Broken pieces of a life.
Broken pieces lost together,
Broken up,
Gone forever.

—Jenna Anderson

Ken

Smiles
Brought to me by you
Like winter roses
Under a blanket of snow
Waiting for a spring bloom
You
Are the spring time
For my smiles

—Joanne M. Cunningham

You Must Die Young

You used to lay your head down on folded arms,
Brown eyes as calm as funeral pyre.
Are you dying inside? Gentle smile like sculptured stone of an eager child.
Lookin' like love-cold stone love. You must die young.
'Cause pure genius doesn't survive in a world of twisted ignorance.
And the smile fades with the light in your eyes
Like sunshine ignored from an office room.
You wouldn't want success best. Yes, you're going to die young.
'Cause an office won't hold you and success wouldn't have you.
You don't think love's important enough.
So, my little genius lay your head down.
The first time for the luxury of mahogany or satin.
Though if it was your choice it wouldn't have been stone.
So lay your head down, 'cause you're gonna die young.
You'll have to die young. You were meant to die young.

—Kristin McDonald

The Weaver

Yellow yarn that she weaves through her warp,
Brown, withered, old and tired are her hands that work the loom.
She weaves her red, black, and gray wool to complete her final rug.

—Christa Harkness

At Sunrise

I see. . .Life's castles standing in the sand
Built from dreams through child's hand.
New tide rolls in to wash away
That child's dream born yesterday.
It's new waves carry in to shore. . .
Tomorrow's hopes for her to store.
Within my heart new light I see. . .
. . .My laughter lifts to ride sea's breeze.
Sounds lost in sorrow, set apart
By new responses of my heart.
I'll ever seek my fantasies
To Keep that child's spirit free!

—Cherie Biasini Browning

To My Creator

When I disown this love you created
Built from fragile dreams,
Captured on the sloping wing,
Drawn from shadow's pain
And ghostly portraits of the past;
When I cast aside the perfection of your soul
Married with mine in night fantasies
More chaste than the purest cloistered place,
Greater than any symphony of celestial song,
More resplendent than pagan pageant splendor;
When I lay down my pen in praise of you,
Blot the pages of my love story with tears,
Lay this book of psalms aside;
When you hear no message,
Seek me in some ruined chapel
Where my grief divides real from unreal.
Time to pose for a greater Creater than you.

—Cecilia G. Haupt

Life

Life is an illusion,
Built on hopes,
Fantasies, and dreams,
No one knows what it will bring.
We hope for joy, but surely
There must be pain.
Tomorrow is not promised us,
Though we take for granted
It will come.
We face each day with apprehension,
Knowing not what our destinies
Will be.
Such is the life that's given us,
It's only a breath,
A feather in the wind.
Its direction is uncertain,
But for the fact that someday,
It must end!

—Alberta L. Smith

I the Rose

Once it bloomed
Bursting open with
Color, this rose
Flourishing in the sweetness
Of life
Til the gentle rain
Came no more
And the dew no more
Its fragrance met
Now the beauty is gone
The bud is dead
For I was the rose
The bud my heart
Without your love
To share

—Carolyn D. Butler

Writer of No Returns

I've written you many letters over a long
    period of time,
But all I get are echoes like an empty
    bottle of wine,
And ever since I've been gone I feel like
    an old forgotten song,
One that was many times played,
Now gone like it never was made,
Lost in time without a face,
Lost in the wilderness without a trace,
I'll sit on the beach staring at a star,
Thinking about you and how you are,
Wondering why you never write to me,
To shed some light so that I can see,
I'll look in the mirror and see my face,
Saying to myself that its all a waste,
To send another letter off to sail,
For it's only on a one way trail.

—Brian Westerfield

Life

Life at times seems so unfair
But all we can do is learn to bear
The ladder of life is hard to climb
And growing up should be the first step in
    mind
Making choices is what we all go through
And living through those choices is hard
    to do
Taking chances is really scary and all
Especially when it's you who may fall
Getting hurt is something no one asks for
But it makes us strong enough to take
    more
Having the strength gives us the pride
To struggle and fight along life's long ride
We can only learn by the mistakes we
    make
And hope for the best on the right road to
    take

—Elaine Goncalves

Untitled

I may not always tell you how I feel
But deep down inside my love is for real.
Even though we argue, I see a kind of
    light
That sparkles in your eyes even when we
    fight.
I hope our relationship will never end
Because we are more than just friends.
We've been through it all together
    everyday.
You helped me through it ever step of the
    way.
We'll always have happiness that will
    forever last,
For we put all of our troubles into the
    past.
Now as you drive me home tonight
I think how everything is so right
As you give me that kiss good night.

—Barb Kunesh

The Nameless One

I knew where I was going
But everyday I drifted farther away.
The music throbbed in my head
As everything turned gray.
The walls closed in around me
And from nowhere came the chirping of
    birds.
I wanted to sing along
But I forgot all the words.

—Jennifer Jensen

Rape

Do you feel yourself being watched
But go on telling yourself that you're
    foolish.
You've seen the same guy more than once
In different places
Always behind you.
Always there.
You wish he'd go away
But he just stays there.
Dark comes and you
Begin to feel funny.
The pain is unbearable.
You try to scream
But he's always there.

—Brandee Creager

Love's Dying Words

She loved him,
but he didn't love her,
and for a broken heart,
there was no cure.
So she decided to quit
while she was ahead.
She thought that maybe
She'd be better off dead.
So from a rope
hanging above
her lips silently cried
"I died for love"

—Karen Fluharty

Life

Life isn't easy, at least that's what I'm
    told,
But how much harder is it, after you get
    old?
No one understands the problems of the
    young.
They think it's fun and games, but it can
    be ruined by a slip of the tongue.
One little mistake and you're crucified for
    life.
No one really believes you, so you end it
    with a knife.
That's how it is, for some that's how it
    ends.
You never survive the fall, and the heart
    never mends.
Death isn't the answer, I guess you just go
    on,
Living your life forever, on lies it's based
    upon.

—Cheryl Ellen Campbell

Traveling by Bus at Night

I look forward to these quiet times with
    you
But I also dread them with
A pain deep inside.
These few moments in the dark I can
    touch you
And the beautiful feelings that
Touching you brings flow softly
And freely from my heart.
But with the sunlight I must let you go
And with both hands clench my heart
So none of these feelings slip through.
Behind this mask I hide my heart
Even from you
For I love her, too.

—Jonnia Walker Smith

Insecurity

Before, I was always on shakey ground
But I always had my parents as my safety net.
But now an earthquake in my life
Has made it that I can barely stand
And all my protection has diminished.
I look back in the past
And see the reassured, confident person I used to be
And compare myself to the insecure,
Overly concerned, flustered person who always belittles herself
That I have become.
I struggle to keep ahead,
To keep the pace I had before this disaster
And see myself gradually falling behind.
I try to keep all the pain and disappointment from showing on my face
But the tears refuse to stop flowing.
And I keep looking back to the past and wonder,
If I will ever return to the person that I used to be,
Or will I continue on the course that I am on now, to complete insecurity?

—Heidi Tennis

Life, So Dark and Lonely

Life, so dark and lonely.
You'll hear a scream in the night,
Probably a child putting up a fight.
What is this life we live?
Everybody takes but nobody will give.
Life, so dark and lonely.
This life we live is so cold, scary,
And full of fear.
Everyone is alone even when people are near.
Life, so dark and lonely.
Please don't take me for granted,
Or leave me abandoned
Because when you're not by my side,
I feel this thing called suicide.

—Staci Hoogland

Sic Transit Gloria Mundi

Death stalks with sharpened sickle through my door.
But I can laugh; Because I know that I
Have had in life the things worth living for.
Have lived, and loved;
I've watched the birds sail by on migrant wing,
And seen storms gather in a cloud fleck't sky.
Cradled within my arms I've held my babes,
Fruit of all the love my world has ever known.
So I can laugh—and yet be unafraid,
Death does not come to only me alone.

—Clara E. Fewkes

Coping

In the beginning we were inseparable,
But I didn''t know that what we did was unacceptable.
We made such a good team,
Or so it would seem.
I never thought that it was wrong,
So I let it go on so long.
I'm tying to learn how to deal with it.
My real loved ones just won't let me quit.
I'm trying so hard to learn so much so fast.
I'm not sure how much longer I can last.
I hope that it's all over soon,
Because I'm graduating and moving in June.

—Candi A. Brown

Eyes Behind the Mask

When you look at everyone, they see your eyes, but not your true eyes.
But I do. I feel the pain you feel.
I will always be the only one who can.
For we are of one. I am the only one who will ever see the true eyes behind the mask.

—Carrie Todd

My Brother

My brother I love dearly now,
But I don't really know how,
Because he's usually never home,
And sometimes I feel alone,
I remember when we were young,
I would always stick out my tongue,
Then he would yell at me,
And sometimes even hit me,
As we have grown older,
Our love has grown bigger,
I dread the day he leaves home,
Me the only child,
As he grows mild,
I have to go through high school yet,
Even though I know he won't forget,
The promise he made me,
That if I ever had any questions,
He would always be there for me!

—Amy Abney

Nowhere

The wind is not blowing,
But I feel it on my face.
The sun is not shining,
Yet, I feel its warming embrace.
I sit in solitude,
But I am not lonely.
I cannot sleep,
So I am not dreaming.
There are no birds,
But I hear them singing.
There are no plants,
But yet I am breathing.
I am nowhere,
And where I am I don't know.
But I'm happy!

—Jennifer Herrington

They Say

They say no one can take it away from you,
But, I found out that's not true.
I found out it can be stolen,
Or it can just go away.
They say it's inside you forever, alive always.
But, I found out that's not true.
I found out someone,
Can reach in and kill it
Or it dies because there's nothing,
To live for.
He said he'd always be there.
But, today
I found out that's not true.

—Denise Gerling

In Memory of Gramps

He never really told me he loved me,
But I knew.
He really cared
But he did not show it.
Most people said he
Was hard to deal with.
Now that he is gone everyone sees.
The old man that never cared,
Really did.
Sure he did not show it
In normal ways.
But deep in his heart
He cared more than most.
He cared about people and family.
But most of all he cared about Jesus.
Now that he is gone even I realize.
The uncaring old man
Cared more than me.

—Gretchen Williams

Confused

Sometimes I want your kiss.
But I know it's a wish,
I'll never have.
Someday you'll find
What I feel for you is real.
Somehow you'll know I really care
For the things you do.
Somewhere the time will be right
For me and you.
However, am I to find
What is on your mind.
Forever, I'll be there for you!

—Christina Nelson

Guardian Angel

I don't know your name
But I know who you are
You're an angel from heaven
A gift from the stars
Always watching
Filling my dreams with songs
Giving me hope
And the strength to go on
You protect me from danger
That only you can see
I'll remember you always
For eternity

—Kathy M. Keith

Unable to Fly

Unable to fly
But I slowly take flight
To battle the winds
For the win, I must fight
Unable to grasp
Just what's going on
The world now below
This cloud I'm upon
Unable to fly
But I move along
A journey that takes me
Far beyond this song
All that I ask
As I move towards the sky
The land grows smaller
As I ask myself why?
Unable to fly
But I slowly take flight...

—James Handy

Parents

We kids always say parents don't
    understand,
But if you think, you'll notice,
Mom and Dad were once "we" kids.
They once wanted to be popular, different,
    and thin,
Kids and parents are made up of the same
    skin.
Our parents were once us;
They probably do understand,
But we don't think of them as us,
We think of them as just Mom and Dad.

—Jenny Nelson

Feelings

When someone dies we feel great sorrow,
But is the sorrow we feel because he is
    dead.
Or because we miss seeing that face?
Would it not be selfish to wish him alive
    and to suffer the real world
Than to let him live in eternal happiness
    that we will all someday be joined
    together in?
Perhaps he was chosen early to help
    prepare for our final coming,
As someone has done for him.
We all feel sorrow for a loved one crossed
    over,
But wouldn't it be better to be in eternal
    happpiness
Then to be living in suspended hell?

—Allison Howell

When I Loved You, You Didn't Love Me

When I loved you and knew you didn't
    care,
But it got you nowhere.
When I cried night after night, I loved
    you
But you didn't love me.
When I said a little prayer then tried to
    touch your heart,
You didn't love me cause you weren't
    there.
When I told you "I love you" you knew
    but didn't care about me.
Now the tables have turned.
You love me and now I don't love you.
But now you know that love games do not
    pay.
It only causes heart trouble and emotional
    problems.
And it's happening to you today.
Love is beautiful, but hurts so bad.
The price that had to be paid was high.
I went around the love circle,
Not it's your turn to feel how to be let
    down by love.

—Geraldine Hyio

I'll Always Be Thinking Of You

I thought honesty was the best way
But it only turned you away
I don't know what to do anymore
Because it seems like you've shut the door
There's a song that reminds me of you
But now it's only turning me blue
I don't show it because I have pride
But it hurts too much to keep inside
I won't lie
Sometimes I do cry
If you'd only care
My love is what I want to share
Every night I dream of you and me
I guess it just wasn't meant to be
But just remember no matter where you
    go or what you do
I'll always be thinking of you.

—Brenda J. Votuno

I Can Always Count on You

There's so many things I would like to
    say, oh, if you only knew
But, it seems that my verbal and physical
    expressions are few
I want you to know that you are in my
    thoughts every day,
And I only hope that you notice what my
    actions convey
Oh how I love it when you can always
    make me smile
And, the times when you make me laugh,
    like a Child.
The compassion you have when I'm down
    and blue
You always make me feel special, like
    among a chosen few
How you always let my independence
    shine right through
And, if I falter or go backwards, I can
    always count on you
You seem to let me be whenever I over
    indulge
And, don't make fun, though I'm fighting
    the battle of the bulge.
So, if at times I seem melacholy and don't
    care
Just wrap your arms around me for I'll
    always be right there
You're always so enthusiastic in
    everything you do,
Whether it's work or play, I know I can
    always count on you
So, my love, with all the things you do and
    say...
It's no wonder how you steal my heart
    away.

—Diane Kirkman

Class Ring

You pull and tug
But it seems to be stuck there,
Tears run down your face
As you try to face the truth,
That he wants his ring back
To give to someone else,
The ring you treasured for so long
Is being taken away,
It finally pulls off
And the memories flow,
All he can do is look at the floor
You give him his ring,
He says, "I'm sorry".
And you say, "Goodbye".

—*Jennifer Long*

Rivers to Cross

I learned to swim in my youth,
but I've yet to swim the river.
I can dance and I can sing,
but I've not yet performed.
I've dreamed of far away places,
but I've yet to travel there.
I've watched the sun set,
but I wait to capture the dawn.
I've been excited by new discoveries,
but I long to discover the unknown.
I've been through the lowest valley,
but I anticipate the mountain top.
Never missing a step,
Never worrying of time lost,
For in the end, I know!
They'll still be a river to cross.

—*Edwina Lewis*

Just Love

Just love that's all we wanted.
But just love got us what we didn't think
    of.
A little baby.
Yes a baby,
Something we never thought of.
Well look at us now trying to play house.
Just for love.
To try to get something out of this world.
No job, no house,
We're living in cardboard boxes.
And let me tell you something,
If this is heaven, I'll pass.
People ask me why don't I leave you.
I could find better.
But I tell them I do it for love.
But if you don't get off it,
I'm leaving just as fast.

—*Christina Spitsen*

Just the Way I Feel

I love you so much, you know that is true
But my friend don't think I am the right
    person for you.
Your eyes so innocent, so brightly colored
    blue,
Darling, I really love, I do! I do!
Darling, not to be mean, not to be strict,
But that attitude will just have to be fixed!
You're always so cheery, your face soft as
    dew,
Darling, I love you! I truly do!
You may not believe me though some
    people do,
Darling, everyone loves a fellow like you.
Now I must go, we have the future to
    fear,
So don't let this message get you into
    tears.
So stand up tall, you have nothing to fear,
So get off that couch and put down that
    beer!
No matter who you meet or who makes
    you blue,
Darling, remember, I only love you.

—*Brandi Pearce*

Jess

Her skin is fair—as fair as a red apple's
    meat,
But never pleased is she, in summer, her
    question
Is "Am I black yet?"
Hair like spun flaxen, with hints of gold,
Thick, creating its own jungle. Mouth not
    quite
Perfect from a before-birth position on
    out
Mother's pelvis, droops on the right
    bottom
Corner where she smiles, laughs, or cries;
    its
Sweet form is frozen on my mind.
She is thin, all muscle from eating as little
    as she
Can get away with, and constant motion.
    Even though
She's not quite eight, she has a mind of
    her own,
Very stubborn and very likely to get her
    own way. Her
Intelligence astounds me, mechanics in
    math and reading
Will take her far from me—soon.
I've seen her from the baby sister she will
    always be
To me, to the loving and at times
    unbelievable holy terror
She can become. I have trouble keeping
    up with her now.
I do not look forward to the days when I
    know Jess will
Leave me behind.

—*Amber Carter*

Hope

Hopelessness and fear crowd around
    outside
But no emotions can live here inside
And the world will still turn, as lives crash
    and burn
As children are crying, and we're all
    slowly dying
Some people will always scream out their
    fear
Although they believe that no one can
    hear
Wars between countries will always
    continue
And so will the ones that are fought
    within you
People will always be hurting each other
Regardless of love for their friend or their
    brother
A madman goes on a murdering spree
While an innocent man waits to be set
    free
I know why you hide, scared, behind your
    wall
But come out, face the world, have
    courage, stand up tall
I promise there's good, it's just harder to
    find
And it also depends upon your state of
    mind
So when you're overcome by despair
Just simply remember that God's always
    there.

—*Dawn Carstens*

Security

Here is where I want to stay,
Wrapped securely in your arms.
Surrounded by your love.
The world outside a mystery,
With unknown things to come.
I need you close beside me,
I need you to stand by me.
I need your love around me.

—*Tamara Frantz*

Whispers in the Darkness

I reach out a hand
But nobody's there
I whisper your name
But you never come near
The darkness surrounds me
I'm alone in the crowd
I can't turn to anyone
The silence is so loud
My heart is racing
As I lay down in bed
Sometimes I wonder
About being dead
Would anyone miss me
Would anyone care
I look for the answers
But only find despair

—*Dawn Raftery*

When Fall is Sad

The fall arrives, and my leaves change color
But not just mine, it happens to every other.
They then turn brown and start to die.
And believe me please, I would not lie.
It's very lonely when a part of you goes,
And you are left bare in the cold winter snows.
When the sun finally returns to shine
They all return-those green leaves of mine.
Now tell me friend, if you happen to know,
What do you do when your friends come and go?
Every spring I have them all,
And then they leave me in the fall.
I'm quite sure that you never knew
That a tree could be lonely, just like you.

—*Jennifer Cook*

Farewell

The time has come to say goodbye,
But now is not the time to cry;
It's time to remember the times we've had,
Remember the good and forget the bad.
Although I've known you for only a few short years,
We've had time to share our hopes and fears,
So when you're down and feeling bad,
Just remember the times we've had,
Then maybe you'll realize,
Now is not the time to cry,

—*Christine Kauffman*

Lost Memories Of Yesterday

There was once a yesterday
But now it's gone
But there is a tomorrow
We can carry on.
Be thankful
Be proud
Look at the sky and touch a cloud.
The sky is no limit
Of dreams of forever
Of you and I always together.
So those lost memories
Can be found
Just in our hearts
We here the sound.

—*Brandi Robinson*

Grandfather

Our past takes so many turns,
But now its up to me.
Having left behind what was once done,
Now setting those feeling free.
Forgiveness is an image
Seen only by those who have done wrong.
A sample of love
But now, too late, it's gone.
Though it's never too late
To express what's inside.
Our time has passed
But our dreams will not die.
Hold fast to those dreams
They can take you so high,
High enough to find yourself,
The person no one can deny.

—*Jessie Hotte*

Don't Go

I talk to him, he listens not
But once again, he takes a shot.
It's two and three than four and five
I grab him close, beg him not to drive.
He pulls away, exclaims I'm crazy
I say please don't go the roads are hazy.
He leaves the party and shuts the door,
Gets in the car and gases the floor
He turns to the left, he turns to the right
Out my window, he's gone and I say good night.

—*Carri Ogrodnik*

Our Love

Our love was true for so many days
But our love slowly grew dim
Cause I felt there was another person in your life
Then our love was on the line
Or our love was all in my hands
So I let you go because
I thought I would let her have you
But then the winter came and left
The spring did the same
But summer came so did drivers ed
You came with your friend to drop his brother
You came to goof off in Victoria and just to see me
But I ignored you. I also refused to accept the gold bracelet
Then I never thought for once that we'd forget each other.
I never thought you'd enroll in the Marines
Now it's time for you to come home
And I need to sort out my feelings for you
So I can decide if I should go with you
Because I know you are going to ask.

—*Donna Machicek*

Casual Sax

I haven't written in quite some time
But right now I've got that jazz rhythm in my head
I'm talking-casual sax
I'm talking the kind of sax
That makes your Takoma Station Molson-Golden
The type of sax that makes that pretty waitress-prettier
It makes that chicken basket seem-bigger
Those soft lights much-dimmer
Man, that sax was so good
I might get a little more
Cause when I go to get saxed
I ain't got no Aids to fear
Just a little more of that funky, sexy, sensual
Casual sax to hear

—*Dennis A. Williams*

The Forest of Hatred

Hatred is like a dark forest
With trees closing in on you
The sky dark, gray, and anything but welcoming.
The dead leaves crunching
This is the forest of hatred.

—*Shanna Green*

Black is Black, but Should it be Judged?

Black is a color of a wheel,
But should it be judged?
Black can be a color of a hat,
But should it be judged?
Black can also be the color of a cat,
But should it be judged?
Black is a color of paint,
But should it be judged?
Black is the color of my skin,
But should I be judged?
I should not think so.

—*Kristal Baker*

Love

Love is not something just found in the air,
But something found in your heart.
It may take a day, or it may take a year,
But LOVE will someday be found.

—*Jody L. Rarick*

Untitled

I lean on nothing,
But stand perfectly.
I have no God,
But am my own Savior.
I never wish aloud
But, alone, deliver
My dreams to reality.
I speak not of my troubles,
But inwardly I solve them.
I dare not cry from pain,
But turn it to anger.
I lash out at no one,
But punish myself.
I depend on no one,
And I am alone.

—*Celeste A. Boling*

A Friend

A friend, just a simple one syllable word
But the meaning as complicated as the world.
Never can tell if the way you feel can be expressed
To just anybody but a friend.
Someone you can love, caring, trusting, sharing,
Your most inner thoughts with a friend,
A person you can never lend.
Whenever in an argument,
Just know a friend is a person you can count on,
Always a person you can lean on.
Crying too, just telling all your problems
Never worrying about embarrassment.
A friend!

—*Kristie Yoo*

A Friend

I have a friend that's very kind,
But the problem is she's halfway blind.
She can't see blue birds singing sweet songs,
Or even a friend who came along.
So, one day, maybe I hope she can see,
All of nature's beauty just like me.

—*Kim Gauden*

Rain—Streaked Love

I feel the threat of rain,
but the sky is blue.
I see storms in your eyes,
I hear pain in your voice.
You struggle with things
that I cannot see.
Your dreams are shattered,
I sit back and cry.
I know we can't go on,
I hold on to the hope,
You're out of my grasp,
A cloud on a rainy day.

—*Jenni Wagner*

Tall Tales

My father has told me many tales,
But the tale he tells so well
Is when he walked six miles in the snow
And rain and sleet and hail.
He says that when a house burned down
He saved at least nine kids.
I don't know what's come over him
To make him tell such fibs.
He told me several kids had almost drowned,
And if it hadn't been for him,
We'd be visiting their graves right now
And keeping them nice and trim.
The other day I fell into a stream,
But luckily, I could swim.
So now I have a tall tale to tell
Instead of listening to him.

—*Elizabeth Black*

Faded Love

Our love was once like a rose
But then our love faded away,
Just like freshness, beauty,
And color fades away.
I loved you and you loved me,
But now we live our lives separately.
Of course, by now, you've got your
Own love life and I've got mine.
But somehow deep down inside,
I still love you.
I really don't know why,
I guess it's just part of the past
That hasn't faded by.

—*Jennifer Dunn*

The Beauty of Nature

Beautiful things never will last,
But they will be rememberd far in the past.
Sunsets in red, orange, and pink,
Never stay long enough to be captured in ink.
Their changing hues,
Will never give away nature's clues.
Just as shafts of sunlight are rarely shown,
Like dewy blades of grass freshly mown.
Just like the beauty of nature in the past
Nature's beauty never will last

—*Beckie King*

Good-bye Everyone

I've made some great friends
But they're all moving away
They're the best friends ever
And I'll miss them so much
They were there through the happy
And helped in the sad
Pushed through the rough
And loved in the good
Helped in the hard
Rejoiced in the easy
I'll never forget them
I'll miss them so much
For they're the best I could ask for
And, oh, so much more

—*Erin Frahme*

The Quest

It isn't easy searching for the rainbow's end
But tis a jewel of knowledge and continuation
The essence of which you create such control
By building that dream
Fired by you
In the discovery of your own make-up. . .

—*Gloria Parks Crawford*

Assurance

The word "assurance" has such a confident ring,
But trials of life often take our will to sing.
Through one of God's saints I had known so long,
He sent me assurance when He took you home.
"When We All Get To Heaven" the holy choir pealed,
"We have received one of our own" His voice revealed.
Almost two years have passed, so slow, yet so quick,
My soul is still weary, and my spirit still sick.
How can the death of a loved one hurt so much,
While God's eternal love and care surround us.
Enduring such agony and loneliness seems unfair,
Yet, I know He won't send more than I can bear.

—Juanita Ray

He Stands Over Me

He stands over me,
But when I turn around,
No one is there.
I can hear voices, whispering.
But when I open my ears
A little wider,
Those voices are silent.
Sometimes I hear him walking.
I walk, he walks,
I walk faster, he walks faster,
I stop, and he stops.
I turn around,
And he turns around with me.
I get frightened,
And it seems that
He gets frightened as well.
Maybe he is my shadow.

—Barbie Lane

I Know Now

Paradise I've never seen
But when my body and
Heart is next to your's
I begin to realize
what love really means
But it doesn't stop their
It goes further than the eye can see
Your Love
Has shown me real beauty
That was hidden inside of me. . .

—J.L. Savory II

Forgotten

A walk through a graveyard
but yet a joyful smile
a tear falls slowly
but only for awhile
a heartbreak now forgotten
buried dead in the ground
the leaves rustle loudly
but we do not make a sound
etched in stone a memory
now for you and I to see

—Brandi Weber

Time

Time is never repeated again,
But yet it remains until the end. . .
It seems to linger and never pass,
But yet when you want it, it just won't last. . .
The beginning of day falls into the end of night,
All runs together then falls from our sight. . .
It's when the time has so quickly gone,
We all decide to carry on. . .
Time is like death in that it just can't be stopped
You've just got to keep going until you drop. . .
You've only begun to just begin,
And before you know it, it's time to end. . .

—Christina M. DeMatteis

Can't Forget

You as my babysitter I thought would be fine,
But you did something that night to me that something was mine
All of my life I am frightened to leave my home,
Because I am afraid that you still might roam
I don't think you care I don't think you know,
That my feelings toward you will never go
Now you've made my dreams like they can't go far,
Because in my mind you've left a big scar
All of my hurting and all of my pain,
And to think that you are only to blame
My dignity my pride all gone to waste,
My hopes my dreams have all been misplaced
You hurt me bad I will never forgive,
Because the thoughts I'm left with will always live

—Amy Aporta

I Never Knew

You said you loved me
but you didn't
I know, because all I see
Is you turning away from me
You say you do
Then walk away
You don't see I want you to stay
You stood me up
And pretended it never happened
I never knew being in love could
Hurt so much.

—Angela Knopp

You Said

You said you'd always be here. . .
But you didn't say when.
You said you'd love me. . .
But you didn't say how long.
You said you'd take care of me. . .
But only me. . . I guess.
You said, "Marry me. . ."
And I did, but. . .
Darling, do you remember these things that you said?
Remember the day I told you that special little secret.
You got angry and left.
When you came home you said, "Get an abortion".
I didn't and you ran away.
Well, I don't know where you are, but one thing's for sure, I'll have your baby.
I'll love it until the end, but I hope and pray that he or she won't turn out to be like Daddy.

—Janice L. May

Big Sis

You've been here from the beginning,
but, you have not been simply a relative,
nor plainly a sister.
You've been much more.
Although time after time,
we've grown together and have been torn apart.
Our relationship remained equally as deep, strong, and pure.
The separating distance seemed absent.
You've felt with me the torture of pain,
the cold of madness,
and the bitter sweetness of jealousy.
You've shared with me the fullness of love, the dependability
of faith, and laughter of joy.
To me, you are a TRUE friend.
One that is a part of me.
One I am a part of.
Most of all the memories of childplay,
And the realism of adulthood.

—Dawn Miller

The Wind Sings a Song

The wind sings a song
But you probably didn't know,
Just sit and listen
Sometime as it blows.
The trees are her band
And we are her fans,
She gets no pay
But works night and day.
She sings her song beautifully
Though you probably didn't notice,
It's a nice little melody
That can't be sung by a chorus.
From now on, when you hear the wind
   blow
Just take a listen, it shouldn't take long;
Besides you never know
She might be singing your song.

—Denise McKeehan

I Thought You Were My Survival

I thought you were my survival,
but you turned out to be my doom.
In you I saw a light,
but now there is only darkness.
In you I held the truth,
but now there are only lies.
You once were my idol,
but now my rival.

—Joanne Delli Santi

Pearls

Mutant girl. . .
Buy a face
For a model's smile tells a thousand lies
Mutant girl. . .
Find a boy
Then mother will pride in her daughter's
   charm
Mutant girl. . .
Leave him oblivious
It will make him want you more
Mutant girl. . .
Shun your friends in other's company
For no one wants to hear the dealings of
   single faced saints
Mutant girl. . .
Sacrifice your faith
For the beauty of this world lies only in
   it's cruelty

—Ginger Baker

Lost Love

I react to the news
By beginning to cry
I ponder it over
And wonder why
We had our fun
But now it ends
I cry some more
As my heart slowly mends
Years have passed
My eyes are now dry
I've accepted my loss
And no longer ask why
I found a new love
His heart he did lend
But I'll remember my old love
Until the very end.

—Kelly Williams

Beside the Highway

He called her "Honey" as if distracted
By more important things
Like chopping weeds
Beside the highway.
She cooked, cleaned, crocheted, grew
   children
As if these mattered
And began to sip
A little more each day.
In time the warmth of wine
Froze all good hopes;
Dreams drowned
In thirsty search.
And unseen weeds depleted
Hungry lives untended
While highway's tidy path
Bypassed these stumbling travelers.

—Ardith Johnson

Do You Really Care?

I care and I want you to know,
By my actions I will show. . . .
Show how much I care about you,
Knowing my love is so true blue.
Wondering if you care about me,
I sit in my room it's as quiet as can be.
Depressing moods I find myself in,
Writing poems here I go again.
Poems I write about you and me,
Wondering if we'll stay together through
   eternity.
Now I'm very depressed it's really not
   fair.
I'm still lying thinking. . .
Do you really care?

—Claire Doyle

Between Sleep

As I lay last night in my winters bed
By ways, highways, through threads of
   memory,
Clearly with the eyes of youth I could see
Details I'd missed and heard words never
   said,
Entered doors and paths to see where they
   led,
Fondled the fruit of a young cherry tree,
Gazed at the shadowy land of could be,
Had never events in a time not sped.
I lay and I dreamed although not asleep,
Just of the could have beens, joys I had
   missed,
Knew the strange time stream that
   started with IF.
Long have I stayed on the path that I
   keep,
Moaning for all the young girls I've not
   kissed,
Now it is only my bones that grow stiff.

—Joseph E. Barrett

Untitled

How in life's weary days,
Can I trust someone who has led me
   astray?
That near fatal glance,
Which I took a sorriful chance,
Has destroyed part of my soul
And turned my heart powerfully cold.
Will he come to me and regain his trust.
Or runaway as he said he must?
What he does is his will,
But I'll be with him in spirit still.

—Angela Noel Hubner

I Wish. . .

I wish I were a butterfly,
careless and free.
Going from flower to flower,
trying to be me.
Without a care in the world,
or a thought on my mind,
I stop to listen
at time passing by.
The pattern of life is winding down,
and all of my colors are turning brown.
Life was so happy,
careless and free,
When I did not have to try to be me.

—Kim Reynolds

The Bird's Song

The way the wind blows,
Caress how the tree grows.
Birds singing their songs,
Shows their wings' strong.
When I listen to the bird's song,
I hear what no man hears.
Their song, tell of tranquility with
Heaven guarantee.
Birds have seen the future world,
While we're still searching this world.
Listen to the bird's song,
It's never wrong.

—*Jonancy Miller*

Desert Winds

The desert wind so soft and warm
Caresses me before the storm;
And the desert wind eddies around
'Til sky—reaching dust devils abound.
The eerie, moaning, sighing sound
Is music, when the sun goes down,
Its haunting, lonely melodies
Take me on flights of fantasy.
The desert seeps in, is all around
Dressing me up in a dusty gown;
Tumble weeds go tumbling by,
While animals burrow and hide,
The desert takes wing hiding the sky,
When the stinging desert winds blow.

—*Frances J. Brouillard*

Caring...

When you care about someone you feel a special passion between yourselves.
Caring is when you're concerned about every little thing that happens to the other.
Some people think that caring is when one lets the other have their way even though they know it's wrong.
When you care about someone you don't say what they want to hear just to keep them happy.
Sometimes if they can't see something you have to point it out before they get hurt.
I guess when you care too much you get over-protective and forget to think of what the other is really feeling;
But you have to keep an open mind and an open heart.

—*Cheryl Serrano*

Daydreams

Billowing clouds of misty gray
Carry me from here, far away.
Fields of flowers, pine forest as green
In abundance in my daydreams.
Walk in from crisp, sunshiney warmth
Two kittens, a pup sleep on the hearth
Sunlight, so cozy, an overstuffed chair
Oh, to spend an entire day there.
Gentle the look of sweetest repose
The kittens, the pup lie nose to nose
A house of peace, our home of love
So full of life's blessings from above.

—*Cheryl Paris*

Sharing

Supplication to an unready mind
Cascades, as torrents of rain
Down newly—sheared hills,
Finding no well—worn
River beds of thought,
No giant roots to hold it fast.
I can release my storm
Of joy or newfound bliss
To crash or dance,
Expressing of its nature,
No need to expect a sharing
Or devouring upon my command.
The thirsty tentacles
Of each being
May reach out to drink
Or whirl with me
To the measure of
Desire or need.

—*Eileen M. Scarlett*

You

You
Catching the moment,
The way time passes.
Challenge,
No regrets,
Hold these promises;
Remember the old.
The river of your life,
Yesterdays,
Tomorrows,
In the same way.

—*Christy Eppinette*

Fourteen Is The Age For Me

Fourteen is the age for me
'Cause I'm as happy as I can be.
I'm not too old, I'm not too young.
I'm just the right age for what I need done.
So listen to me, all you boys and girls
With long blonde hair or brown with curls.
Try to be young for as long as you can.
You'll have plenty of time to be a woman or man.
If you act grown up all your life long,
You'll frown and say "Where's my childhood gone"?
Here's just one more thing that you need to know:
You'll never be young once you're old.
Well, I've said it before and I'll say it again
You'll have plenty of time to be a woman or man.
So as for me, I'm happy as can be
'Cause fourteen is the age for me.

—*Chelby Schoppa*

My Only Friend

Crying
Cheeks cherry red,
Damp from my only fear,
Tears.
I hear a sound.
Louder and louder
Then softer.
It is my own,
Laughter,
My shield
My strength
The all mighty destroyer
Of the tear

—*Gina Vigliotti*

The Wild Rose

Blooming up as sweet as wine
Cherishing the sun with every shine.
Through the silent night it awaits the sun
For it will bloom and spread to be as one.
Waiting till morning can be very long
As the night gets cold it becomes real
     strong.
Soon, night will be gone and morning will
     rise
Its stem will stretch out to the skies.
The golden sun from beneath the earth
Will help this seedling start its birth.
As the sun rises higher it starts to unfold
Turning the seed into a beautiful mold.
A bud has developed and soon it will
     bloom
The fresh scent of the air making its
     perfume.
The bud opens up and becomes a rose
The beauty of life it really shows!

—*Carol Mackey*

Greenland Mummy

Like a 500 year old eyeless doll
With skin as dry as a pressed flower
A fragile bookmark
In the story of his people
A bud withered before it could flower
Set out in the cruel winter air
Passing his window of life

—*Marisa Novara*

Broken Wings

Haunted by your darkened eyes-
Chilling winds-to enchant your stare-
Bearing such an innocent disguise-
So many clues of which you are not
     aware-
Mystical flames-you glow like an angel-
In a silent rage-words cannot explain-
So much darkness-to always enrage you-
Releasing my dreams-for you to
     remain. . .
A quiet prayer-in the silent ocean-
Words of mystery-invade my mind-
Strength of my weakness-my suffering
     emotions-
Distrusting in fate-believing in time. . .
The fog shines through my stain-glass
     mind-
Others run away-as I stand by your side-
An angel in black-one so kind-
Determined frustration-avenging her
     pride. . .
Inspiration of the night-adding of the
     numbers-
Conflict fills my heart so open-
It drowns my strength-so far under-
Fly with me forever-now my wings are
     broken. . .

—*Beth Branson*

New Year's Eve

Dusk sighs, deep blackness blinds, the
     night swallows me.
Chimneys exhale chalk, abodes light up
     with gold twinkles,
Cold calms, even settles the surroundings,
     diverse energy swells. . .
Unpatterned icebergs scatter blue-grey
     above,
the wetlands sublime, soggy, whose soil
     leaps
such gracious green-growth,
And warmth madly thrashing-deafening
     sweep—
within still branches brittle by season's
     chill. . .
Headstones survive, tattered and porous
     with sunken messages
long since deciphered, survive at rest
     rooted deep in springtime
scents, summer fire, autumn decay, winter
     wind.
Their rhythms rehearse with life under
     life as fire-blood seeths,
fulminates, settles, limbers. . .
My heart sighs, brightened as death
     dismembers fossiled wrinkles
in the tranquil night.

—*Ann C. Eells*

Essence of Muncipality

The sun pulls the blanket of sky over its
     trite head.
City apartment lights disappear one by
     one.
A deer peers with gleaming eyes from
     behind a redwood.
Hapless people push their shopping carts
     into alleys
called home.
The song of crickets lulls the animals to
     sleep.
Horns of the night shift and taxis scream
     from a road
twelve floors below.
Moonlight reflects silver images from the
     crystal lake.
Lampposts highlight drops of rain that
     form streams to flow
into sidewalk gutters.
Packs of wolves hunt for food by
     moonlight.
Trash bags are ripped open and robbed of
     remains to satisfy
stark stomachs.
Silence.
Death.

—*Kimberly Berry*

A Lost Soul

Why must the once opened arms of the
     world
Close as I come near?
Why must my words of pleading
No one hear?
Why must the tears that fall from my
     eyes
Be ignored by all?
Why must I rise
To only fall?

—*Andrea Hernandez*

Insight

Farthest sun,
Closest moon,
Brings the light and the night.
The past,
The present,
Filled with life
And some with strife.
The rich,
The poor,
One just surviving
The other thriving.
A saint,
A sinner,
The difference being
One repenting
The other not yet relenting.

—*Katie Figueroa*

Adam's Only Child

The airy grey sky after a morning rain,
Clouds in their lethargical manner float
     past.
I stand solely, deeply breathing in
     existence.
Listen as the resilient bird sings his
     ballad.
The hushed rattle made by a coy rabbit,
There he is! Peering out meekly from
     under the thicket.
Oh! I laugh to myself! (Most think me an
     idler)
Yet I learn.
Heed nature herself as she recites her
     sililoquy,
Even as she holds me attentive, my core,
     my spirit,
So overwhelmed by her sonorus tone,
I cannot forget my loneliness,
Exiled by the human race.
Thank you. . .
For those few wondrous hours in your
     garden,
Where I was the only child of Adam.

—*A. Ashley*

Under the Attic Eves

Dusty shelves and furniture lie about in wait,
Cobwebs hang upon the walls spider scurry so not late.
Why is the stranger in the corner have an expression that is sad?
If she can't turn her frown around her troubles must be bad.
Eyes stare back in terror hands shake, legs quiver.
The mouth is slightly open and then the body shivers.
Fingers clench into a fist then just a fast relax,
head turns from side to side a tear falls from an eye.
It's hard to face reality, but staring back at me
is the image of myself in the mirror, under the attic eves.

—*Heather Gooze*

In an Instant

In an instant
Coffee for the morning
Wake up
In an instant
The telephone can
Connect us
In an instant
She answers
In an instant
He is gone
In an instant

—*Carol Babcock*

The Lighthouse

The lighthouse stands on the dark lonely island.
Cold, salty breezes fill the air.
The rough waves splash upon the rigid rocks,
As the small lighthouse brightly glows.
The crashes of thunder and scintillations of lightning begin,
Then the thick dense fog sets in.
Blinking its eye, the lonely lighthouse
Helps guide the ships home.

—*Colleen A. Leavy*

Beneath Notice

A small, little dandelion,
Colored like the sun,
Works its way up,
Digs its way out,
Up through a crack
In the sidewalk
Of the big city.
It emerges,
Slowly and carefully,
Into its bright new world. . .
And is promptly trampled—
Crushed to death—
Under the feet
Of ignorant citizens,
Who only saw the yellow,
And not the precious gold.

—*Brian Swartzfager*

From Dusk to Dawn

As I sat on the soft beach side,
With the wind blowing through my hair,
As the mid-night mist covers my face,
I quietly watch the sun go down.
I then sit and listen to the bluebirds
Sing sweet lullabyes, and the sounds
Of the waves roaring violently.
I watched the sunshine bright,
That's what happens from dusk to dawn.

—*Melissa Lewallen*

Love Is. . .

Love is like a rainbow,
Colors in our hearts.
Yearns for you day by day,
When we are apart.
Love is like a whisper,
Wind through the trees.
Like green blades of grass,
Swaying in the breeze.
Love is happiness,
Along with heartbreak and despair.
Just be true to your heart,
And you'll find love anywhere.

—*Kristy Leathers*

My Prison Wall
Come Betwixt thou temptest storm,
My heart and Soul, bound I am;
Level thy firecrest rage and wind,
My fortress stones ungently torn;
See my naked heart in the chains,
My soul doth perish, lost in pains;
To see thou darkened wind swept clouds,
My heart imperiled cries out loud;
Come gentle wind and gentle sky,
Thy warmth and beauty do though now reside;
For lost is hope and sight unseen,
Oh wounded heart, to thee I cry;
In dampened darkened dungeons deep,
In fetters tied beyond my strength;
That rats and sickness steel my sleep,
In lonliness I cringe from thee;
Begone from me.

—*John A. Hladky*

The Fatigued Mother

The working mother, she wakes, goes to work,
Comes home, takes care of her family.
Emergency comes up, she is at the hospital, goes home,
Then awakes again and starts her day,
Her child must get well and her children must eat.
This mother comes home, her house is a mess
But she remembers that she loves her family.
She finds her mail under a load of dirty clothes,
The bills pile high but she opens an odd looking envelope,
Afraid something bad has or will happen, but no.
What is this, there is money inside the envelope.
The fatigued mother can now rest,
She can pay her bills and feed her children,
She smiles and runs to tell her kids the good news.

—*Detra Eckman*

The Christmas Present

Under the tree there lies a present,
Wrapped in paper and tied with a string,
The stars in heaven smile down on this present,
But only sadness it will bring.
In this present there beats a heart,
The heart of a living thing.
A forgotten heart that can only wish
For the choirs of angels it longs to hear sing.
Under the tree lies a person,
Lost, lonely, and cold,
Hidden under torn papers and string.

—*Laura Ellen Millender*

A Dying Flame

The eternal time span,
Comes to an expected end,
Those feelings I've long felt for you,
Desperately trying to send.
In the final analysis,
One can clearly see.
The agony and pain I've suffered.
From you not picking me.
It's cold comfort,
To the one's without it,
To know how they struggled,
How they suffered about it.
If things don't change soon,
Between the two of us, you and me,
The end will come upon my heart,
And I'll have no choice
But to be apart from you, endlessly.

—*Josh Lipicky*

Philosophy

What are consequences?
Consequences you live down, unprepared,
Paying for the chances you took.
What are chances?
Chances you take when you're not sure
What you're getting into.
Sometime you win,
Sometime you lose.
In any case, It's an experience.
What's an experience?
An experience is: If you play with fire
You get burned. Geting burned will hurt.
And some hurts take a long time healing.
So, the lesson you've learned is:
You always take chances if you want
To experience consequences!

—*Joanne Kalies*

Eternal Sleep

Enter my nightmare at your own
   discretion,
Consume all my visions, they'll become
   your obsessions.
You've lived in my visions, as the years
   have gone by,
Not a bit of compassion, now you plead
   not to die.
Enter my nightmare, you'll see as I do,
How to unleash the demons that lie within
   you.
How I pity your journey of the world you
   believe.
To watch you fall deeper into hands that
   deceive.
Take a look deep inside: Do you see what
   I see?
You feel no remorse, yet you want to be
   free.
To spare you compassion, is so hard to do,
But to unlock revenge, is as evil as you.
The darkness will devour your inner most
   fears,
Then the pain will release you through
   sorrowful tears.
If you hold on to the demons inside that
   you keep,
Then your conscience will burn you in
   eternal sleep.

—*Deborah Skiba*

Firecracker

Boom
Crack
Smack
Goes the firecracker.
Snap
Fizz
Out pops beautiful colors.

—*Andrea Fantl*

The Key

You were out with "friends", having fun
CRASH! In a second you were gone.
All your accomplishments were over and
   done
You were out with "friends", having fun.
Alcohol kills just like a gun;
One more time you turned the car on.
You were out with "friends", having fun
CRASH! In a second you were gone.

—*Amy D. Byerley*

Food for Worms

There is a hunger
Crawling inside of me.
This love, like a parasite
Eating me from the inside out.
Soon I will have holes in my skin.
All the world will be able to see
The way I fed myself to you
Bit by bit, in faster and faster handfuls.
Till I was an empty kitchen.
You walked through me,
Leaving behind your litter
Which I saved as precious souveniers.
These gifts you gave me
Have no resale value.
Is this why I feel so empty handed
Sitting here alone on the linoleum?

—*Frances Gaudiano*

Meeting Love

It comes,
Creeping up little by little,
Upon you.
Behold, it's getting closer and closer,
And like the waves of the sea,
It comes crashing upon your senses!
It comes swiftly,
So swift,
You are unaware of its arrival.
It overwhelms the mind.
Bringing with it
Promises of fulfillment, of desire, of love.
It's a steady feeling;
A feeling of surrender.
For you cannot struggle
In its grasp anymore.
See it now for what it really is.
It's to be in love!

—*Cherrin Beausoleil*

Untitled

Desperate leaves have absent
Cries, fear for the fall.
Why the tears?

—*Denise Gross*

Words On End

Words, words, what are words?
Cries or Howls Howling in the wind.
Words, Words, what are words?
Shrieks or Screams, Drowning in the
Sea of Tears.
Word, words, what are Words?
Talk or Lies that lay too far beyond
The Boundary Of Truth.
Words, Words, what are Words?
Letters, sounds, and syllables.
No! Words are to important for that;
Words are for friendship, freedom, and
   Peace.

—*Craig Thomas Combs*

Silver Threads

Shiny silver trails
Crisscross on wet concrete
In delicate spring language.
I isolate one and follow it
Wind gracefully down cement stairs
And then into the moist lawn.
The trail ends in glistening clover;
On one stem nods a snail,
Her antennae gently quiver.
She glides away
Weaving a silver thread
Through green grass.

—*Heather May*

The Peddler

I met an old man on the road,
Croaking as though he were a toad.
He followed a piece of dirty, old string,
While bumping His pans with a ding.
He kept belongings in his van,
When I looked at him I ran,
There things were like brickety brack
The things that I saw in his shack.
Big Mac was the name of the peddler's
   cat,
Big Mac thought he were too fine to chase
   rats,
That pair lived on day to day,
Can you find something to say?
Today that old pair's dead and gone,
I don't know what went wrong.

—*Diane Li*

The Hand Of Man

Waves beat upon the rock
Crumbling it to sand.
But it's really only man
Who desecrates the land.
For gales of wind and hurricanes
The tallest trees bow low.
A tiny flame in a careless hand
And it's the last they ever know.
The hungry lion ravishes the lamb,
For it must kill to eat.
The thinking beast enjoys the sport,
Takes the head, yet leaves the meat.
Time and nature change the world
And in taking they also give.
But for those whose aim is to destroy
What right have they to live?

—Cathryn Braun

After the Bloom

A summer sun,
Crushed petals,
And fragrant scent...
I wonder where
Those youthful
Days of loving went.
An evening sky,
Purple sunset,
And languor spent...
I sometimes hear
Those laughing
Days of nothing meant.

—Carol A. Chester

Never Fading Love

Pale blue eyes
crying,
Your fragile heart
broken,
dying.
Your love for heer
never fading
here I am
forever waiting.

—Heather Holloway

Sitting at the Top of the Stair

I remember the child sitting at the top of
   the stair
Cupping his ears paralyzed by fear
Arguments that turn into screams of
   shattered silverware
Two people he loved vowing more hatred
   and future despair
I remember the child and his anger
Praying tomorrow's apologies will recover
The loss of this fabricated relationship
I'm staying only for the kids, i'm staying
   only because I care
I have been told that these things do
   happen
That it always happens after the
   celebration
If only common decency could survive all
   tribulations
I remember the child talking to himself
Be strong, let time be the healing bond
Hide your insecurity and sympathy for
   now
Just grow up slowly and grow up sound
The child has never forgotten the
   humiliation
For everytime he screams and tears
He looks through the haunted files of life's
   lessons
And remembers the child who sat at the
   top of the stair

—Hein Jee Wong

Untitled

I am the house upon the hill
With the broken windowsill.
My roof is in shambles,
My door and floor rambles.
Hey, wait!
Why are there crates on my lawn
In the middle of dawn?
I am the house upon the hill
With the broken windowsill.

—Toni Fabiszak

Where did the Years Go

Mom says, "I can't believe you're
   fourteen."
Dad says, "Where did my little girl go?"
Sometimes I wonder
Where the years went;
All the time I spent playing on the swing
   set
Or playing ball is gone.
It just seems like just the other day
I was hugging my teddy bear
And pretending, I'm Mommy of all my
   stuffed animals
But that's gone, too.
As the years go by
I get older and older
No more little ballerina shoes
And pretend land.
All that people say now is...
Where did the years go?

—Jennifer Nicole Fisher

The Land of Make-Believe

Blue elephants and pink lemonade,
Dancing and prancing in the parade.
Fairies dancing through the golden gate,
Never wishing to be late.
Flowers laughing at the grass,
Pegasus horses flying past.
Let's join them in the land
Of make-believe.
Blue dinosaurs, happy red boars,[00ff]
A dancing boogey man,
Two flying tooberans,
Having fun laughing hand in hand.
Wouldn't you like to live
In the land of make-believe
Where nobody lies and nobody grieves?
Then make a kind invasion
To the land of imagination.

—Alexandra Matson

Sea Songs

Sunlight sprinkles moistened leaves.
Dancing shadows, heaven's seas.
A wave of time kisses shore,
Roughness rises, a sailor's lore.
Sweet song silence,
Serenity for me.
Sweet song lust,
A fantasy I see.
Sunlight sprinkles a distant rose,
She faces ocean, petals closed.
Stem so strong and thorns so sharp.
Roughness rises, anger of the harp.
Sweet song rose,
Your song is me.
Sweet song flower,
We long for serenity.

—Donna M. Pritchett

Christy

The sun sets in the distance
Dark clouds in deep blue hues
Engulf a flaming amber sun
The north wind wraps a chilling embrace
Around a scape
Golden pastures
Fieldstones fences
Autumn elms
A lone, winding country road
Parts the scene; cold, grey and worn
The touch of your hand
Your eyes meet mine in the gentlest gaze
A smile from your lips
We move to embrace
At one with each other
In love

—Ken Tamsin

Between Me and My Lord

When I'm feeling so down and blue,
Dear God, all I think about is you.
Why must life be so full of ups and downs?
Is life so much like a flower so beautiful til it dies?
Or does life just go on through our troubles and our fears?
I feel so much like a child,
Yet so grown up at times.
When I think my life is straight,
Something happens to make it seem so new.
Dear God, is everyone's life this way?
I hope not for their sake,
But only you do know.
Dear God, please tell me what shall I do?

—*Denise Woerpel*

Shadows

When shadows fall upon the sky,
Death will be among us.
The world is disappearing,
One by one, piece by piece.
No one cares what happens,
Everyone dies a sad death.
Violence...everywhere,
Peacefulness, nowhere.
No more cares in the world
No more doors of new dimensions
The sun is gone, no more life,
Death is upon us. Nothing.
Why must people live in shame?
No one knows just who to blame.
Someday, all will be lost,
Don't worry, all is lost.

—*Jennifer McReynolds*

Water of Love

You are a pool of clear, dark night
Deep and calm and soft and right
You lie in wait for my first taste
A brimming cup with none to waste
And when those drops have thrilled my tongue
My heart upon your altar hung
Now I sink through your abyss
I feel the cold like Death's first kiss
In shock I feel a fire ignite
Desire warms with bursts of light
And as my soul in you immersed
At last I know the truth of curse
My life, my goals are washed away
I am emptied, my thoughts are fey
Water salt and water sweet
In the delta we two shall meet
Your very being entwined with mine
Like the raging river and the swelling brine

—*Elayne Schumaker*

He

Musky cologne lingers,
Deep, husky voice
Smooth, tanned skin
Sweet, salty lips
Muscular and vital, he stands there.

—*Cindy Cracolici*

Grandpa

We journeyed far in twilight hours
Deep within his old armchair.
Grandpa's nutmeg cheeks
Relived the blaze
Of India's delights
And led my dazzled eye
To brighter shores
Than ever I have found.
In the closeness of our
Warm upholstered world
I shared the sparkle
Of his eyes and gold
Watch chain winking at the fire.
As one, we glowed
I, his reflection
And he, my sun.

—*Edward J. Grossmith*

True Denial

Denied once more
Destined to live a life of lonliness
To wallow in my pain
Feel the burning of my aching heart
The hate of myself
The love of him
Too much to handle
Too many emotions to control
I've been lead to a place called hell
And left there to die
So many feelings
Why can't it work out
My appearance an embarrassment
His a heavenly sight
It'll never work out, why can't I forget
There is no exit from hell
Unless he comes to save me.

—*Heather Kendra*

Friends

Friendship is like a open book, you treasure it and look.
Did I ever tell you that your my best friend?
The only one I could talk to and trust, that was always a must.
When I shined forth and got all the attention, even if you
were really upset you would never, ever dare mention.
Did I ever say that your my hero?
You are the sun, moon, and stars to me.
You are my life and breath, the very essence of me.
You sometimes go unnoticed, I'm sorry if I really didn't try.
Did I ever mention that you are my soldier of freedom?
Without you I would die.
Like a prayer answered from above, you come filled with hope
and love.
Birds may grow and fly away.
Tears may fall and dry everyday.
Our love is like a bridge of everything free, it will live
forever, like you and me.

—*Amanda Wills*

Untitled

Someone from her past
Dierespectfully walks into OUR lives
Makes things difficult
She loved him once
Hopefully once is enough
It's my turn now
I treat her special
He never did
This simple little crush
Interupts us

—*Anne Keith*

Carpe Diem

Sieze the day
Do not live for tomorrow,
Do not live for yesterday,
Live only for today.
Never worry about what might have been
And
Never worry about what should have been.
Live only for what is and what could be.
For this my dear friends is a message of life:
Live life to its fullest.
Enjoy the goods times
And
Take the bad times all in stride.
Sieze the day, my friends,
Sieze the day.

—*Christa Avampato*

Reality?

Why cannot some play your game
Do they dwell in another frame
As prisoners insides their minds?
In another time, with other kinds?
Is our world really more crowded
And our bright eyes truly clouded?
Why do you seem to be so cruel
Do we play by a hidden rule?
Are these "freaks" the untold key
Of what you are truly to be
Are they in fear for their soul
Can this be their forsaken "toll"?
Are the superstitions true
Is magic the only thing left to do?
Why does the truth hide from sight?
I want to see the revealing light
Is death the only open door
To find if in you there is more?

—*Dawn Marie Mernone*

Dreams Lost in the Midst of Nowhere

What happens when dreams don't come true?
Do they fly in the sky and take over other people's minds?
Do they turn into the remote control of televisions?
Are they like peaches that you have been chewing on for years and still can't get to the seed?
Are they lost in the middle of nowhere unable to find their owners?
It's gone. . .forever. . .in the midst of nowhere.

—*Baria Mumtaz Abdur-Razzaq*

Because You Are Afraid of the Truth

When you are alone
Do you cry to yourself?
Do you keep the lights dim
In hope that nobody will see?
Is it because you are afraid,
Afraid to face the truth?
Of course you would be afraid,
But don't let it get you down.
Because everybody,
At one time in their life,
Hides the truth
Away from the rest of the world.
They do just what you do,
Cry to themselves
And hope that nobody sees.
So don't ever think you're alone
No matter how different you are.

—*Amy Venberg*

The Time Has Risen

When feeling of emptiness hits you
Do you feel all alone
That sad bitterness of sorrow
That haunts you all night long.
A feeling of sadness
Only torched by the unknown
A vision of lost happiness
that keeps you all alone.
Feeling like a lost child
Wanting to be free
Something that won't end
Why can't this be.
That burden in your heart
Is a broken image
The mirror of chance
For the time has risen.

—*Gail Barnes*

Oklahoma Man

I was sitting at a table
You asked me to dance
There was country music playing
I said I'd give it a chance
You taught me the two step
And when it was done
You asked me to breakfast
Of which I had none
You sang and talked your way into my heart
And courted me with flowers from the very start
Now we live our lives together. . .and
You still bring me flowers, letting me know
The courting's forever, not just for show
Now you sing me your songs
Holding me tight
As we lay down together
Side by side

—*Linda S. Emery*

A Poem of Many Questions

After life, what lies ahead?
Do you go to heaven; or lie there dead?
Does God take your hand and take you away;
Or do you lie in your coffin forever to stay?
Do you feel pain?
Is love in the air?
Do you feel nothing?
Is anything there?
Will it be paradise like prophets have said?
Or is it an endless hole. . .where everything lies dead?
Can we forsee the future and predict the end?
Or will it be a surprise the Grim Reeper sends?
When will I see the "Great Pearly Gates"?
Lord, Master, tell me now before it's too late.

—*Brenda M. Stout*

Words of Wisdom—Lost in Time

Listen,
Do you hear it? Aloft. . .
It's a child's cry—
The kind that haunts, stalks you down,
And tears you limb from limb,
Because you have food, warm food
Enough in your home right now—At this very
Minute—to last you—What? Two maybe three weeks
Without going to the grocery store
Yet a youngster has to suffer, a pain anguish
Nothing like you have ever felt in your lifetime.
Probably you never will. An acute feeling that hurts
So bad—a feeling that makes you think about food
All day. Sooner or later that pain turns into a
Numb feeling where you can't feel your own stomach
If your lucky you will die in your sleep—but if you
Die awake you die an even slower and agonizing death.

—*Jennifer Sander*

Do you Know?

Do you know how much I love you, from the sea to the sky of blue?
Do you know I love you so much, that my thoughts are all of you.
Every hour of the day, every day of the week,
My love for you keeps growing, even as I sleep.
You've made my life complete, with all you've done for me,
My heart was locked and sealed, but you had the key.
Do you know how much I love you, from the sea to the sky of blue?
Do you know I love you so much, that my thoughts are all of you.
The stars, how they do twinkle, with their light on us so warm,
But even your starry eyes sparkle, when outside it is a storm.
From rainy days of boredom, to the days of sunshine bright,
The little things I thought were drab, I now see with new light.
Do you know how much I love you, from the sea to the sky of blue,
Do you know I love you so much, that my thoughts are all of you?

—*Cindy Emig*

Do You Hear Me?

Do you hear what I say?
Do you listen?
When I look at your picture
All I can think is "why"?
But I get no answer
All I am left with is an emptiness inside
An emptiness only you can refill.
So many questions left unanswered
So many things left unsaid
I can't let you go, I don't want to
never will
Times I think "what if"?
But it's too late
I need you here so much
wish you could-COME HOME DAVID
 PLEASE!

—Andrea Wright

Do You Love

Do you love the flower rose, now dead.
Do you love the tree so cold.
Do you love the autumn leaves all brown,
The sun's rays, disguised as gold?
Could you love the cold and bitter wind,
As it swirls about your head.
Could you find it in your heart,
To love the death instead?

—Jane Cho

Do You Remember When?

Do you remember Junior High?
Do you recall our fun?
Did you forget about our clique,
When all of us were one?
Do you remember teachers?
Do you recall our classes?
Did you forget the privileges
Of small, pink potty passes?
I remember serious times
Of sorrows and of joys
Also when we laughed about
Clothes, friendships, and boys.
I recall the dances,
Field trips, movies, band.
What fun we had in the halls
Where together we'd all stand.
I'd love to live it all again
Do you remember when?

—Debbie Pruitt

Friends

How does it feel when a friend says hi?
Do you turn away and hide it inside,
or do you smile and say—Thanks
 you just made my day?
Friends are needed all life through
they help you smile when your feeling
 blue.
They listen when you want them to hear,
and feel with you when you shed a small
 tear.
But do they always understand?
Or do they turn away and give you
 somebody elses hand?
And when this happens don't you want to
 cry,
but aren't you afraid your friendship
 might die?
Is this fair to you or even me?
No its not as you will see,
friends must stick together to the end,
No matter what, A FRIEND IS
 ALWAYS A FRIEND!

—Jennifer Harth

Decisions

A path in the lonely woods,
Does anyone know where it leads to?
To lightening and thunder,
A rainbow with colors,
Or a sun, glistening with yellow?
A path in the deep, dark woods,
A path that can lead to
Happiness or sorrow,
Sunlight or shadow,
A path that I am going to follow.

—Annette Koren

Love

Love
Does it exist
Maybe not
Love may be
Just a figment of man's imagination
Love may be
The devil's way of hurting us
Love may be
The ultimate weapon of destruction
Why do we depend on it
Is it really that important
Why do we insist
On smoking this drug
It can hurt us
It can kill us
Love
Does it exist
Maybe not.

—Erica T. Miller

Death

What does DEATH mean?
Does it mean when you friends put you
 under pressure,
or if someone close hurts you?
Does it mean spiritual death, when the
 soul leaves the body?
Is it when you wish were dead?
Maybe, it means if you use drugs, or do
 things to make you die,
perhaps that is death.
It could be that death is anytime your
 feelings are hurt,
when you feel that pain inside.
If someone you know abuses drugs or
 alcohol.
These could be death,
but the death that hurts the most isn't
 when you,
yourself is in agony or pain,
in a slow final death.
It is the death, the emptiness you feel,
when someone you love dies before you,
and you have done nothing to prevent it.

—Christie Marcum

Love Songs

Have you ever heard a love song you
 really and truly love?
Does it remind you of something sweet,
 such as a dove?
The gentle tone that reaches your ear,
Put so sweetly, lovingly, and dear.
Or could it be the tone of someone's voice.
Well, everyone has their choice.
But the most romantic love song you hear
Is when someone you love is cuddled near.
Now, this someone may just be a friend,
But the feeling of that love song shall
 never end.

—Amy Buckless

Freedom

Don't cage my free spirit
Don't box me in
Don't confine me to walls
Let me breathe
Let me run
Let me fly
I am a fish
I am a bird
I am a deer
But don't trap me
For I am not game
And I am free
to trap myself.

—Collen Stein

Growing Up a Girl

"Sit up straight! Stand up straight!"
"Don't eat while slumped over your
    plate."
I can even hear her while I sleep.
She gives me a doll, when I want a ball.
She's not happy, because I'll be tall.
She counts every calorie that I eat.
Curls, ruffles, bows and frills
Just don't stand up to all my spills.
Pink is okay, but give me Carolina blue.
I'm creative and Mom thinks, Interior
    Design.
Carpentry and car engines are more my
    line.
But I won't tell her, will you?
"Ladies, don't do that," she will often say.
Ballet lessons on Wednesday, tap lessons,
    today.
Each day I must become a little bolder.
But for now,
I'll mind my manners, and remember to
    smile.
I'll let her enjoy herself for a while.
I'll tell her my plans when I'm older.

—*Carolyn R. Williams*

What We Had

Lonely days and lonely nights,
Don't go by when I don't think of you
    twice.
I loved you for so long,
And I know now I have to be strong,
Didn't you think of what we had?
Even though on that day I was very sad.
I needed you like I never needed you
    before,
But you are gone now and forever more.
Don't you have any regrets?
Or do you feel feelings are a threat?
I can't be hurt any more,
I feel so empty and so sore. . .
Even if in everything I say and do,
I can't help but think of you.

—*Kristie Mitchell*

Untitled

Don't need your help, just need out of this
    place
Don't need your advice, I've got a lot of
    common sense of my own
Don't need you to tell me which way to
    go, I know the difference between left
    and right.
Don't need answers, just need halfway
    decent solutions
We all need solutions
What good is being alive if I don't have
    you by my side
What good is smelling the flowers if a bee
    stings anyway
What good is screaming when no one
    hears me at all
What good is fighting if you don't get
    justice, only bruises
What good is standing up if you're only
    pushed back down
Don't need you to preach to me, I go to
    church
Don't need you to hurt me, I've been hurt
    before
Don't need you to curse at me, I know all
    the words too
Don't need you to call me names, I know
    what I am
Don't need you to predict my future, I
    know what I want out of life
What good is saying "I love you", if you
    don't even care

—*Jennifer Cook*

Beauty

She awakens in the morning,
With the sweet smell of flowers,
And the greetings of spring,
As it pours the morning showers.
Music she loves,
Goddess of beauty,
As the white doves,
Cry out thoughtfully.
No one challenges
The fairest of all,
For they know the changes,
That will happen to all.

—*Minerva Pedroza*

The Unknown One

Don't look at me when you think of her.
Don't say my name when you want to say
    hers.
Don't walk with me when you want to
    walk with her.
Don't talk to me when you think you're
    talking to her.
Don't touch me the way you'd touch her.
Don't smile at me when you think of
    something funny she said.
Don't comfort me when she's upset.
Don't talk about others when you think it
    might make her jealous.
Don't tease me the way you'd tease her.
Don't tell me I play well unless I'm her.

—*Heather Cotton*

Vows

Don't show me your hate,
Don't show me your pride,
Just show me the love
That you hold inside.
Those feelings inside,
You don't want to share,
The feelings inside
That show that you care.
Love isn't easy,
And it isn't always good,
Fortunately, it comes only
To those that it should.
If you're worried at all
About the problems we'll face,
Don't be,
We'll only go our own pace.

—*Andrea R. Kirk*

Bruises

Why do they hurt the children? Beat
    them till their black and blue.
Don't they know to stop, we never hit you
    we never did anything to you.
You pretended everything was okay, and
    while we sit in the corner and cry.
You sit back and watch us die.
We loved you so, but not anymore.
You were the one who broke the peace.
We will never forget you hurt the
    children.
You wonder why I was never there I was
    hiding from you.
It was to heal the wounds and pain that
    hurts me.
No more pain comes from you, and now I
    will always hate you,
I will live on without you.

—*Heather Hoffman*

SADD Thoughts

Under the tree, he sat with fear,
Down his cheek ran a silent tear.
Thinking of her and the fun they'd had,
Being sorry, feeling sad.
Would she live, or would she die?
Who would be hurt? Who would cry?
Saying to himself, "She's still alive."
And wondering why she had to drink and
    drive.

—*Jenny Martel*

Dream

Dream ye children of fields of green.
Dream ye babes of oceans and seas.
Dream ye all of love and joy.
Dream ye not of peace.
Dream ye lads of fair—haired maidens.
Dream ye maidens of fearless men.
Dream ye both of home and lineage.
Dream ye not of peace.
Dream ye young of days ahead.
Dream ye old of days gone by.
Dream ye people of life and living.
Dream ye not of peace.
For peace cannot be dreamed alive,
nor can peace be bought.
Peace comes from within the hearts of others,
whether stranger or friend, sister or brother.
No, dream ye not of peace.

—*Christine Allie*

Dreams

Dreams
Dreams
I have a dream
I love to dream
For the day you stop to dream
You stop to live
For everything that exist in this world
Is a product of a dream
For if you can dream it
You can achieve it
That's why I love to dream
I dream the impossible
And set out to achieve it
I am a visionary
For I believe
All things are possible
To he, who believes
To he who dream, dreams

—*Eugene Tonye Uranta*

Dreams

Dreams are fantasy,
Dreams are terror,
Dreams are untold by such an error.
Some come true,
Some are scary,
Some are just for fun.
But such a great thing can only come from
The mind of one.

—*Jennifer Altmann*

Endeavor of the Slaves

Drenched in darkness last night shadows.
 Windblown thoughts sheenless
Dreams turning to ashes. Hineous
 hawkers, hindmost minds with bloted
Reasoning! Trespassing, pilfering your
 riches! You must heed from
Hidden fear or fright don't let them
 foreclose your dreams!
Shadows from where the gainsay sinisters
 abode, hammering dwindling
Resources into waste! Incantation brought
 upon, encased the world in
Guns and chains. In sightless chain of
 fear, you slave in silence that
Screams! From your dreams slipped away
 the time, the age of gold!
Another day, another try braiding the
 colors of all nations, rid the
World from windblown thoughts! Share
 your hammer with the slaves, the
Ones that ower wrought! At the time of
 subsiding pain and cry at time
End to all fear and tremble, remold your
 dreams into unmolested thoughts!
Bend the time into shape, let the glow of
 the beyond shatter the darkness.
As the shrills interloping your soul
 echoing the supernal hammer
Resounding your only hope as the slaves
 endeavor in joint effort!

—*Alien Star*

The Call of Mercy

Come and tell me.
You begged for me and all.
But shall I believe you?
No you are wrong.
Even if there's one thing
There shall be another.
I think you shall not be forgiven.
Even if the clouds fall.
You shall be under it.
By all I mean.
Last but always remember
There shall be no soul
Who will be kept for all.

—*Rosemarie Alvarez*

My Vanishing Depression

Like the slow-moving fog
Drifting along,
Obscuring vision,
Brightening,
Darkening
And finally
Dissipating,
So, my mood
Of depression
Takes hold,
Flits away,
Reappears
And disappears,
Like the vaporous fog.

—*Joan Stone*

Transition

Warm rays of blood red sunshine
Drip blindingly down the valley.
Horses' firey eyes refuse the darkness.
Their manes flare in the burning twilight.
Branches arch longingly toward the
 vanishing light.
Dusk dies mercilessly over the land.
The trees slowly retreat their arms.
Field mice scurry on their way home.
Darkness falls hushingly upon the hills.
The horses huddle close for warmth.
A peaceful quiet rests upon all as the
 moon takes over
Creating shadows here and there.
Hours pass as the moon shifts
Trying to find a comfortable position.
Eventually it gives up.
Slowly the clouds show themselves.
Pink, purple, blue.
The sun peeps a watchful eye over the
 land.

—*Desiree DeSurra*

My Ships Of Skies Blue

What tears are these that fain to fall
Yet dry-eyed I staunchly remain;
In the ring of my forced laughter I hear
Naught but heartbreak and sadness, so
 plain.
Gone is the smile from my heart
Gone is the sweet song from my lips;
All because of something so ribald as this
that has cast away my fine multitude of
 ships.
My ships are at sea to brave the horrors
Though they be lacking of provisions, I
 harden myself
to take courage
That they'll find good ports to take rest in
 and
good sea beds for anchorage.
For my ports are not steady nor gay
As once they were when my skies were
 blue;
But just as the grayness has settled above
so are my spirits gray though they once,
 happiness, knew.

—*Therese B. Donesa*

Rain

I Love the sound of rain,
Drizzling down the storm drain.
The sound on the roof, so clear,
Like eight tiny reindeer.
Rain is a beautiful sight
During the day or late at night.
After it rains you can go outside,
And see a colorful rainbow in the sky.
I like sunny days with warm weather,
But I like cool, rainy days much better,
On a day when clouds fill the sky
I can watch the rain fall outside.
I Love Rain!

—*Kelli Parrotte*

Littering the Sorrow Street

Everywhere and almost anywhere, there is a
drop of garbages and dirtiness. Every kind's on
sorrow street; the result of man's thoughtless passion
lying pitifully and mercilessly stripped and constantly a
reminder of whirl wind of man's sinful lust. Human err;
the street urchins, always making dirty faces on
sorrow street, displaying portentously obvious declension
of tomorrow. Naming no names, yet every drop knows
is a lust. Cleaning up is almost and always without thought,
paid hurrying hands that show no mind or concern and
budget that reflect everyman's pocket and incinerators
that collect unquestionably and burn without thought
every drop; rich man's poor man's, black man's and white man's both
and soon man's common destiny is consumed for concern.

—*Chudy Lazarus*

Being with You

Adventurous, exuberant,
Wild spirits with feelings of romantic love,
Outrageous, exciting.
Fun—filled days and nights,
Festive, playful.
I love being with you.

—*M. Wolfe*

Drugs

Drugs are harmful.
Drugs are a drag.
Drugs are a person's life down the drain.
Drugs are things that just aren't right.
Drugs are sorry, drugs are poor.
As for drugs, it can stick with coors.
Drugs aren't for teenagers or kids.
Drugs aren't for anybody but fools who think they're so cool.
Drugs make you low instead of high.
Drugs are nothing but a big lie.
Drugs just don't come and go.
Drugs stick with you till you are low.
Then drugs let you down till you can't get up.
Drugs stomp and step on you till you're all messed up.
Drugs don't do anything but tear you up.
So drugs will be drugs until fools quit being cool.
So don't be a fool just to be cool.

—*Amanda Barber*

Sunset Souls

Gently faded broken down people
Dusty house and ash
Dismal, rain soaked, dreary world, dull and nil
Old photos whispering their songs on a window sill.
Ambition curbed, energy thwarted
Failure and defeat.
Once brilliant, now tired worn and older
Bitterness is the scarf they wear on their shoulder.

—*Carol L. Stewart*

Tangled

Step right up and see the Woman who hears visions with her eyes
Dying in cowardice, she departs in a black cloud of faces...
Listen, you said long ago standing with hands in your pockets,
Has the filthy moment come when moral feeling collapses?
I can't accept this foolish dreariness, whiskeys of darkness.
These canned goods of the intellectuals canned sauerkraut and
It torments me to insanity that you should be so misled.
You are too intelligent for this, you inherited rich blood
Your father peddled apples as he stood looking down at the tracks...

—*A. Hull Prenderfast*

Slice of Time

I feel locked into place,
Each day, each night, the same.
I rise at five and do today,
The very things
I did yesterday.
Of dubious comfort
This daily routine.
My time is spent before its' time,
Tomorrow is here
And gone...today.
Like in a waterwheel,
I run at tempo,
Eyeing a small wedge to leap through,
A thin slice of time
To escape to.

—*Anne Charette*

Straight Isn't Always Up

The trees stand tall, straight with no shade,
Each fighting for its space
In the wintery morning.
But one tree waits, bending so low.
It fights for survival
Isn't forced, but is still strong.
Its branches cling, entwined in air,
Each holding fast to each,
Protecting the life they share.
Soft clouds drift by floating above.
The trees reach for sunlight,
But my tree stays near the ground.
In a world of dog—eat—dog style,
Why do we fight to live—
Outdoing ourselves in will?
My tree proves that all things don't strive
To be dominant, yet
Are able to sustain life.

—*Deborah Kirchhevel*

Ocean Of Tears

I've cried the Pacific Ocean;
each night I work my way
into the Atlantic.
One day soon I'll have cried the world
and still have much more.
Inside I'm dying
Yet to the world I'm fine.
No one understands.
No one cares.
I hide my life,
so no one can see
what true love really means.

—*April Renee Berry*

Shadows

Shadows painting pictures
Each of them are you
Silent, etherial expressions
From minds window pouring through
Yes, magical reflections
Dancing on my walls
Subtle recollections in the night
Drifting in my memories
Distant scenes the shadows shape
Masterful re-creations brought to life
With morning's star approaching
The patterns diffuse
Days make me lonely
But I spend each night with you
Shadows painting pictures
On the canvas of my mind
Bright colors of remembrance
Painting you.

—*James Hunt*

Earth Child

That day when your arms parted the
    stormy clouds,
Earth child your strength gave courage to
    my soul.
That day when your words took flight and
    unto my ears were born,
Earth child your wisdom gave light to my
    mind.
Your hand in mine, that smile so gentle
Spread sunlight across the cold, damp
    earth.
Thus when heavy be your heart with eyes
    kissed by the dew,
Forget not Earth child your kindness shall
    not go unrewarded.

—*Joyce Lehmann*

Your Lonesome Song

I will never be that someone who
Will capture your romantic heart,
I'll only be that someone who
Secretly loves you from the start
We will never know the ectasy that
Could set our world on fire
And if you go away from me
This world will always be very lonely
If the one who knows me
Would ever find me untrue
My love for you would only make me
The sentimental old fool
So dream the dreams of loving, you and
    me.

—*Tracey Zacharias*

Lovely Lady Love

Sweet are the words that I long to hear,
Echoing constantly in my ear;
Sweet are the joys of my youthful days
Lingering still in so many ways.
Sleep on, my LOVELY LADY LOVE, so
    still,
With part of me to keep you company,
While in the forest of my mind and will
The greatest part of you will always be.
Your spirit, like an ocean breeze, will fill
The air that travels through the mountain
    trees
And meets the rainbow's edge, with
    Nature's skill,
To live in Heaven's hallowed mysteries.
Sleep on, my LOVELY LADY LOVE,
    and thrill
The treasured moments in my memory,
Where once your hopes and faith you did
    instill
To leave with me your gift of charity.
How sad it is to leave her
Asleep in her new home,
Yet some of her stays with me,
Wherever I may roam!

—*Josephine Bertolini Comberiate*

Nightly Embrace

I am but one
Embraced by the night
I walk to the edge of day
And am one
With the shadowy light
I wonder at the stars
Upon an ebon sky
Searching to understand
Who am I
I'll follow the whispers on the wind
But find only the echoes of my heart
So I slumber among my dreams
Yearning for all they impart
And there I walk to the edge of night
Cradled by a lunar caress
For I am one
Embraced by the night.

—*K. D. Marley*

Death's Embrace

Walking the streets alone at night,
Emotions slowly start their churning;
Feeling something near to fright,
Struggle hard to keep from turning.
The path ahead seems long and tiring—
My strength in spirit somehow gone.
What's left of time is soon expiring—
It seems so useless to go on.
In death is life—in life is death—
Appearing as a vicious circle.
It snares you with its fatal breath,
And mortal sins are left eternal.
The future holds a bleak horizon
And casts its shadow far away;
Ends life on earth once time is done,
To find in death one's sad dismay.

—*Angie Kinnamon*

The Blue Iris

Like a dancing fairy
Enchanting, enticing
The skirt twirls of blue
In the breeze softly
Dancing, twirling
To the unheard music of the wind
Her bodice trimmed with lace
Dipping, dancing
With the greatest grace
Pink intertwined with blue
Turns to its lightest hue
Lurking in the corners
Darkness waits
As the sun goes down
Softly her petals fall
The unheard music has gone away
Yet the Blue Iris shall dance again
Someday!

—*Kate Olsen*

Dreams of Passion

You are the passion in my dreams.
Enchanting melodies and unforgettable
    fragrances are on the scene.
You're an angel from above.
Like the wind's song, you enhance my
    passionate love.
While the night's heavenly breezes dance,
You waltz into my mind.
I hear your laughter; I see your smile.
It's funny how they say love is blind.
In my dreams, your fragrance and warm
    loving touch caresses me.
My heart pounds; I'm burning with
    passionate desire to embrace thee.
Heavenly music and sweet perfume from
    above is sent;
Seducing me into a state of emotional
    excitement.
I start to tremble—I'm on the verge this
    night we are one.
Suddenly came the dawn—and you were
    gone.
Still, your sweet fragrance and loving
    warmth linger on.
I arose like the wind with a song in my
    heart.
'Cause tonight, we will not be apart.

—*Christina Howton*

Untitled

Sensational,
Entertaining,
Valuable,
Emotional,
News,
Top Notch Articles,
Easy Reading,
Essential to a Great Day,
Never Better,
Informative,
Super,
Great Photos,
Ravishing,
Enthusiastic,
Awesome,
The Top Magazine.

—*Angela Niles*

Untitled

Love is in the air
Especially in the spring
Love is everywhere
In the flowers loved ones bring
Even music stands for love
The notes in every measure
Maybe living stands for love
The never ending pleasure

—*Erin Haupt*

My Love For You, You'll Never Know

The pain for losing your heart is so dear.
Especially when you are near.
My love for you will never end.
I hope you will always be my good friend.
Though you told me that we would be together forever.
Now it seems we will be together never.
When I see you, your love seems so near.
But then we talk and it disappears.
Knowing you don't love me, I feel so low.
Therefore my love for you, you'll never know.

—Judith Del Rio

Suicide

Suicide is a very bad thing to happen.
Especially with someone you love.
You feel guilty and very sad.
And you are mad at yourself
Thinking there is something you could have done.
Or that it is your fault.
But halt those thoughts.
I'm sure you all are great people
Who cared very much for them.

—Alicia Shumard

Too Little Time

The silhouette of winterized trees
Etched out gently against the sky
Reminiscent of elderly hands
Gripping meek and sky.
They remind me of the imminent truth
That death will come someday
Just like those trees against the sky
We must make our mark some way.
Our lives are like sands in the hourglass
They're much too precious to waste
Some are stolen by tragedy
Others are incessant haste.

—Jennifer Lynn Seward

Saying Goodbye

It's so hard to say goodbye
even if you really try.
And I have tried to say goodbye,
but each time I seem to cry.
If this is how it is to say farewell
I guess I shouldn't really dwell.
Because you will come
and you will go
I guess I should except this so,
There is just one thing I don't understand and
that is why I do so much crying,
just for you.

—Allison DeLand

What You can do with Belief

I have a feeling to get up and conquer all;
Even life itself.
Standing ten feet tall
I wish it was a warm day so I could
Just take off my shoes and run away
To meet my challenge head on.
When my spirit and imagination combine,
There's nothing I can't do in any amount of time.
My confidence is like steel and my heart is like a rainbow.
I can be anything and know all there is to know.
If I were to take a chance on everything in life,
My success would cut through the world like a knife.
I believe in myself and as long as I can speak a word
Or make an action, I can and will be anything I wish to be.

—Jennifer Jones

Untitled

The time has come for us to say goodbye,
Even though it hurts me so.
I know I have to try
To love you enough to let you go.
I've made my last plea,
For you to follow your heart.
But you just won't see
We could make a new start.
Still, you've made it clear
And I'm letting you go.
Just remember dear,
I'll always love you so.

—Debbie Morgan

That Time Again

Now it's time to light the lamps
Evening is drawing nigh
Birds are nesting as heavy shadows
Lengthen across the sky.
Soon the winds will be warmer
Daylight will linger long
The moon will be slow in coming up
And the air will be heavy with song.
As you turn the lamps up brighter
Shadows lengthen on the wall.
You keeping thinking, "Ah, tis spring";
And soon, too soon, it's fall!

—Dolores LaBianco

Armory

Cupid shoots arrows
ever wonder why?
a declaration of love
is an arming
arrows in slings
more more more
then an arrow is used
amazement
confusion
disorientation
pilgrim on the Great Plains in his Conestoga
suddenly finds a tiny spear protruding from his breast
he has thrust too far into territory not his own
is rewarded by a penetration
compulsion to taste
the other side of
love and life and
life and death and
death and love and

—E. Zoller

Wind

To be like the wind,
everlasting floating
above the lands of trouble
just as each individual person
passes and solves
the problems faced during life.
But to not be bothered
as the wind is unbothered
would be impossible
yet to dream is always,
something forever
Individuality separates us though
just as the wind may separate
in opposite directions,
To float above the clouds
without worry or difficulties
is a dream, A DREAM FOREVER.

—Christel Privette

Courage

Courage is the one thing
Every man wants
Every man likes
But not every man has it
For it takes courage to
Step out of the status quo
It takes genuine courage
To do the unusual and unique
For it is not the life
That one lives that matters
But the courage one puts into it
That courage that's what matters
Courage to speak the truth
In the face of possible
Prosecution and suffer
Courage to stand up to one's belief
That's what the courage is
And this I'll always stand for.

—Gene James

If Only You Knew

If I keep listening to these songs and memorize each word,
Will they match the very thoughts in the songs that you have heard?
Will you hear my cries and fears, and come to hold me tight?
Will you rescue me from loneliness that sings throughout the night?
If I send you all my feelings on a tape with our song,
Will you come back to kiss me, in my arms where you belong?
If only you would see me; if you could feel my heart;
If you could go back distance and find a brand new start.
I'd give you life from inside me; I'd make happiness so real.
But we've grown so far apart now, I don't know how you feel.
So I will sit here crying. It's you that I have missed.
Regardless of the future, my love will still exist.

—Nicole Staheli

The Tree

The tree is an opening to another life.
Every year its blossoms,
That are like new hairs on a head,
Begin a new time of life.
Its branches are telephone poles,
Extending great lengths.
Its leaves are people,
Which are born and then die,
For generations beyond end.
The tree is a shell,
Resting on a beach of little sands,
Watching life come and go.
For the tree is as wonderful as you and me.
The tree.

—Heather Cramer

God's Dream

Snow on the ground, lights on the tree.
Everyone hopes that this year the world will be free.
Carols are sung about peace and good will.
While lonely soldiers lie dead on the ground so still. . .
The gleam that fades from a young child's eye,
When he learns that Santa Claus was just a big lie.
White candlelight shines from many a window
But what is it for?
Reminding us all of the prisoners of war. . .
Christmas is a time for people everywhere,
But what about those who haven't a prayer?
Sad-but true-is that what you say?
Then why is it that throughout the whole year
You only think about it for one day?
Christmas, what does it mean?
Christmas, is it only God's dream?

—Ellyn McKee

To Look Around

To look around the world today,
will give most people much dismay.
Littered moutains, polluted shore,
garbage, war and much much more.
The world to me looks pretty good,
but I would clean it if I could.
Pick up the mountains, clean the sea,
there's so much work for little me!
Just look at the flowers, trees, and grass,
skies, stars, they all have class.
So look at the good and not the bad,
for the bad will surely make you sad.
But what about the mountains, shore, garbage,
war, and blur.
They will not go away and that's for sure.
so help me clean them all together,
and that will make us feel much better.

—Patrice Pederson

My World

I live in a world where death is no surprise,
Everywhere I hear dying people's cries.
Shouting to me in utmost fear.
As their killer watches never shedding a tear,
Teenagers pregnant and doing drugs,
As helpless old people cannot walk the street
Without being mugged,
Is this what God intended for us,
Is it? Is it? I shall never know.
But God and only God knows the answer
To this life and death question.

—Angie Shoaf

Feelings

There are no words to say,
Exactly how I fee.,
But to say my dreams are finally real.
I used to dream every night.
That I was in your arms
And you were holding me tight.
It's different now,
We're together,
But I don know how.
No elegant dinner or wine,
But I will never leave it behind.
Don't ever leave me,
I'll never leave you.
Our lives are young,
We have a lot to live through.
I'd figured it out,
What's needless to say.
"I Love You"
Are you feeling it too?

—Kim Salahi

Pictures

A picture is to remind you of the fun
Excitement or the sadness that it brought.
To show someone has patience to stand there
And give you a memory that will last forever.
A friend or relative of bring back moments.
A still life picture that will last forever.

—Christine Tucker

My Interpretation of Love

The valleys of one's heart,
Expands further than the depths of one's mind.
For I know that what's been said is true.
As true as the sky is the color blue.
For love is a dove
With a heart on its wings.
That flies,
That flies,
Just as high as the love that heart brings.
It is soon met by another dove to help lighten its load.
And together they travel that self same road.
Until the heart has found its place of desire,
Where it is lit by a glowing fire.
This could be a castle of cold stone bricks,
Or a solid gold palace. . .
That only a child's picture book depicts

—ChrisAnn Silver

The Secret Romantic

Do you know that I am lost in your eyes
Eyes that know so much but can barely see
I'm caught by something as deep as the skies
Can love hold me, yet let me be free?
From the wisest men to the lowest fools
The hearts crying for you aren't worth counting
You caught them in your eyes like dark, deep pools
A man in love is like a man drowning
A dangerous thing is love of the heart
Love's pull doesn't allow one to let off steam
Love's pressure tears a romantic apart
Till he's confused crying with the wind's scream
Can I not ever thaw her heart so cold
With wishful thoughts and my heart of fool's gold

—*Arlan P. Bullard*

Yesterday is Still Today

When I saw you for the first time
Eyes the color of the ocean,
Something moved inside me
Long forgotten lying broken.
And now I'm lost in a dream
You're all that I can see,
Every moment I'd die
Just to look into your eyes.
I remember eyes that shined
As they looked so hard back into mine,
I lost direction in the darkness
So I'll set you free.
So now I must go on
What more can I do?
What good is being strong
When all I ever really want is you.

—*Brandy Eastlund*

Young Love

As we stand motionless
Face to face
No words are expressed
Only a fate left undecided
Shall we go or
Shall we stay?
In our innocence
Of yesterday.

—*Kim Smith*

The Butterfly and the Bug

People from everywhere,
Faces and hands
Getting what is deserving,
From work and the sweat.
People from everywhere,
Faces and hands
Getting what they wanted,
At the risk of others,
Suffering.
Like the butterfly and the bug,
Both the same,
Yet. . .
One we kill and other we cherish.

—*Julie Noiman*

My Thoughts of You

You are thoughtful, you are sincere,
You bring joy and happiness throughout the year.
You make me happy, you really do,
My life would be miserable without someone great like you.
You're always around when I'm feeling down,
You lift my spirits, you lift my frown.
You compliment me, make me feel good,
You do nice things that a boyfriend should.
I love you so much, I love you a lot,
I think of you in every thought.
And I know in my heart,
That if we should part,
I could never feel
A love so real
Like I do with you.

—*Michele Snisky*

Peace

Sunshine bright upon the ground
Falling leaves make not a sound.
Whispering brooks so silently flow
Blue skies reflect a watery glow.
So softly a step is heard suddenly
One twinkling eye seen behind a tall tree;
A dear in the stream perks up its pert head,
But goes along drinking when it senses no dread.
Breezes blowing through branches so high
Make a soft, soothing, and quiet sigh.
Warmth can be felt on a sunny rock
Where he sits as he pulls off one red sock.
Finishing the job he walks toward the doe
And seeing him she sprints through branches so low.
He notices not, but steps gently down
On a piece of soft moss in the brook he has found.
So is a child's innocence in a silent forest glade
Far from the gloomy world man has made.

—*Jennifer Lohmuller*

Silent Dove

The mist of the midnight sky,
falls upon my face.
The shadows from above
seek the feel of ruffled lace.
In the visions of my mind
I see you standing there.
Reaching behind the moonlight
I feel your unwilling stare.
Listen and you'll hear my voice,
softer than a dove of white.
Listen and you'll feel my words
piercing you through the night.
Love that is held within your hands
from your grasp soon will slip.
But the love held within your heart
will never leave your finger tips.
So lie here beside me as I pledge to you my love.
Just let the world slip away on the wings of a silent dove.

—*Jeannie Stokely*

Fantasy

Once behind a misty meadows
Far beyond the stormy seas
Was a place where I would venture
In my fantasies.
I would be a maiden fair
Upon a noble steed
And galloping to the castle
I would meet my destiny.
Or I would be a unicorn
With a shiny golden horn
And glisten in the sunlight
Or help a girl forlorn
And if I were a mermaid
With long and flowing hair
I'd swim among the shadows
To see treasures hidden there.
But I have to live in this life
Instead of fantasy
And why? You ask, I dream so much.
I'd rather not be me.

—*Denise Hall*

Fairytales

Once upon a time, in a fantasy
Far, far away. . .there lived a dream.
Legends tell us that
Wishing on a star
Will make our dreams come true.
But, in the darkness,
There lurks broken hearts!
Magic, myths, and spells are cast
To destroy the wickedness.
The struggle is fierce and hard.
But the victor, in the end,
Is you!

—*Jenni Jennings*

I'm Like

I'm like a carnival ride slowly building
   speed; now out of control,
Faster and faster, lights a blur
The lever is pulled, the power is gone—I
   stop.
I'm like a sharp pencil writing of love and
   laughter...
The slightest pressure, I break.
I'm like a dimly lit room, the only light, a
   sunset
Casting golden rays through the window.
The sun sets, no more light; I see nothing.
I'm like a music box ballerina,
Spinning with a frozen smile on my face.
The music slows; the lid is shut. I am
   forgotten.
Life begins: too simple, too beautiful.
Change: too hard to stay the same.
Life: too easy to end.

—Jane Steding

Metamorphosis

I see the minutes ticking by
Faster than a fly can fly
Like the wind I cannot see
Moments changing into memories
Etching lines upon my face
Telling stories I cannot erase.

—Elizabeth Gordon

Paradox

Still and dazed at the thought of
   movement.
Fearful of action, angry and ashamed of
   fear.
Guilty of sin, tired of guilt.
Unsure of the future, powerless to control
   it.
Sweltering under a hot sun
That will soon become a furnace.
Confusion creates stillness, but not
   serenity.
Stillness born of fright,
Quiet born of uncertainty,
Inaction for fear of consequences.
Purity and peace ever elusive,
Desired but the root of hesitancy;
Both inescapable needs
Direly difficult to fulfill,
With failure leaving nothing.
Silent stillness remains, and will
   expectantly wait
Fearing that death will come too soon
Or sadder still, too late.

—Carol L. Gunby

Trapped

With no way out,
Feeling as if we are surrounded,
Yet not knowing by who,
You reach out,
And when you think you've got a good
   grip,
They disappear, leaving thoughts
   lingering inside.
You run as fast as you can,
Hoping you are leaving all the miseries
   behind,
But then you look and see that you have
   not left anything,
As if you had been standing still the whole
   time,
You listen hoping to hear...but silence.
You look hoping to see...but blindness.
I'm trapped...

—Kelly Mackett

Homeless

I sit in this cardboard box,
Feeling forever alone.
I shiver in the cool night air,
In this shelter I call my home.
The wind blows through the walls,
For they offer no sturdy shield.
The quiet call of the breeze,
Chills my body of wounds not healed.
Maybe tomorrow I'll find a place,
A place to live and breathe.
Someday I'll have a permanent home,
To come to and to leave.
But for now, I will sit alone,
And listen to my heartbeat.
As my house of cardboard sits,
On the hidden corner of the street.

—Ashley Carter

The Love of a Friend

The love of a friend came to me one day,
Fell on my knees and began to pray.
I said, "Dear Lord Jesus, why me?"
But my friend only answered, "because I
   love thee."
I cherish that moment every day,
I'll never forget it, there's no way.
I talked to Him and loved Him,
And my love showed, it wasn't dim.
He walked with me and gave me strength,
Money can't reach His heart's length.
So, today I walk and talk with Jesus,
He promises He will never leave us.
And today I have the love of a friend,
That is true until Heaven's end!

—Kaye Jones

Friends

Always together,
Fighting never,
The one you trust,
Fair and just.
To whom you confide,
Secrets you cannot hide.
Always there,
Your problems they can bear.
When you cry a tear,
They are there to hear.
Now they are gone,
Life must go on.
You can always call,
Just to talk, that's all.
You cry a tear,
When their voices you hear.
You say hello and goodbye
The friendships will never die.

—Diana V. Heard

In My Own Way

Martyrs have died for their belief
Fighting their cause unto the end,
And their deaths brought honour—and
   brought grief
To enemy and friend.
It would be much easier to die
And if our goodness were the test,
Then we to the mighty heavens cry
Dear God, I have done my best!
No saintly aspirations, but I believe in
   love
And the chance to understand and give.
Willing I may see and touch—not from
   above
But here, in my own way, while yet I live.

—Joyce Shapton

1967, Viet Nam?

The boy became a soldier,
Filled to overflowing,
With loves, fears, and dreams,
Which made the man.
He knew four generations.
Three more of his own,
He should have known.
But the Untruths, War and Oppression,
Engulfed the men of his generation,
In an Agony, titled, Viet Nam.
And Death took another loved one.
In Mourning, our eyes filled with tears,
Hearts were bruised with Sorrow.
Then, in humility, we prayed...then, and
   only then,
Was found some Truth in death...
New Birth, with God in heaven.
This, even today, is the only Peace we
   find?
For all those left behind? In Viet Nam?

—Cecilia Edwina McBurnett

Problems?

My life was a mess
Filled with problems,
Enormous problems.
Then I opened my eyes
I saw a friend,
A good friend.
She was there for me
Even with her own troubles,
Bigger troubles.
My problems disappeared.
I have a good life,
A very good life.

—Amy Catherine Teeple

Sky Shadows

Sky shadows
Find little boy eyes
While debt omens
Follow big boy buys
He's scraped knees and shoe lace trails
"Snips and snails and puppy dog tails"
And though his brief case and power suits
Cage a former pup
When kites fly high
On windy days
He stops and glances up

—Jack E. Canavan

Seek the Darkness

The soul that wanders in desire
Finds security is rare,
A quest for that one secret fire
Challenges only those who dare.
The heart in search for only love
Fails to meet the mystery,
In all below and up above—
Dark knowledge for the world to see.
The mind that seeks the darkness
Rises far above the rest,
For difference and a second guess
Brings wisdom to the best.

—Kathylynn Barranco

Two Lovers

You are my kindling candle,
Flickering spiters of fire.
Two lovers sit around you,
Burning with hope and desire.
They dare not blow you out
For they fear their love
Will burn out with you.

—Kimberly Schimetz

Going...Going...Gone

A leaf
floats through life
from the bough of a tree
to the waiting ground beneath
curls upon its spin
distorts and
hardens
Comatose
It remains
Green turns to brown
to black
Until
A foot
crushes its veiny net
And
it crumbles into a million pieces
Like so many drugged
Doped—out
shattered minds.

—Georgette M. Norman

Love Is

Love is like a river,
Flowing forever.
Love is like a river,
When we are together.
Love is like the sunshine,
Always bright and cheery.
Love is like the sunshine,
Never dull and dreary.
Love is like springtime,
Always full of cheer.
Love is like springtime,
With nothing to fear.
Love is like a flower,
Blooming in the spring.
Love is like a flower,
With all the beauty it brings.

—Krista Adlhock

Casey Boy

Orange and gold, his colors were bold
Fluffy ears and red water bowl
Special bed, food, and rubber toys
And long whiskers had my Casey Boy.
Wild and free my Casey did roam
When seeing me, he'd run right home
Scruffy and torn after long days fights
Mouse in mouth his eyes shown bright.
No furniture, curtains, or tree's too high
From limb to limb, Casey would fly
Snagged fur and battle torn ears
King Casey, Lord of his peers.
Casey Boy's gone now, he lives in my heart
His spirit flies free, but we're never apart
Each night as my dreams drift high
I join my Casey Boy in the sky.

—Donald G. Cranford, Sr.

Malignancy

Suspicion proceeded the word;
Fluttering pulsation of heartbeat, grasped
By grinding fists of fear;
Overwrought imaginings of hysteria,
   denied
Until the word.
Knowledge accompanies the word,
Destorying truth's insulation, shedding
Refuge of numbness,
Shattering haven of unknowing,
Through the word.
Feelings frozen in echo of the word;
Far away roar of clashing mood,
Multiplying like my cells run amuck,
Rushing, malformed, to blot out sanity,
Overrunning harmony of soul and
Metastasizing to heart
The word comprehended.

—Eileen Bossarte

Untitled

Curious little birds of the air
fly around without a care
for they know that they will be safe in the
   air
from all that lurks below their outspread
   wings.

—Kathy Olivera

Past This Bachelor's Lair

Little girls,
Flying curls,
Cute and pretty too,
Cycling through,
Past this bachelor's lair,
Riding who knows where,
To some fancy play,
Living life today.
Living life today
Some bright and fancy way,
Who knows where,
Past this bachelor's lair?

—J. J. Yoder

Thank You

Thanks for all the times we've shared
For all the memories.
Thanks for all the times you listened,
And cared so much for me.
You've been there through some tough times.
You've laughed me through the good.
You made me feel special.
More than anyone else could.
Thanks for all the dreams you've planted,
The dreams we're fighting for.
Thanks for opening my eyes,
For showing me the open door.
In life you've done many things,
Now it seems you've grown your wings.
It's time to go our own way, and find roads to mend.
Thanks for being there, for being my friend.

—Denise Williams

Reflection

Mirror, mirror on the wall
For all the world to see. . .
Look, see that fat girl smiling bright?
I wonder how she does it?
Obviously, she's not quite right.
Oh my, there goes a crippled young soul.
Obviously, it takes great effort
To master the simplest goal.
And over there, is one whose skin is brown.
Everywhere we turn
Are characteristics unlike our own.
And then there's me. . .
My heart's been crushed and broken.
My soul's curled up and died.
My differences they hide.
I am a victim of abuse, violence and crime,
Provided by family and society,
Unseen by the naked eye.

—Bonnie Henry

I Desire

Not abundant riches
For frills and glitter;
But security invaluable
For peace, a mind not bitter.
Not acquaintances bringing
Pleasures and spending of time,
But a world of friends sincere
For a living wholesome and sublime.
Not unproductive thinking
Toward life's ultimate end,
But God's loving guidance
For my adverse traits to mend.
Not for myself alone do I
Desire to embellish in reality,
But that I may impart to others
An outgrowth of God given maturity.

—Eva Wallwe

Untitled

My friend has gone,
For I am alone,
I walk in a game of solitaire.
My friend where have you gone?
But then I look,
And you are there.

—Cathy Cottrell

Guard

Keep hold of love
For if love goes
Life is a beating heart
That suddenly slows.
Keep hold of love
For if love shrouds
Life is a sun
Hidden by clouds.

—Judi L. Ehrig

A Victim Of Love

I'm a victim of Love
for I'm crying you see
wanting to be loved
so desperately.
I'm a victim of love
for I'm hurting inside
wanting love to share
not love to hide.
I'm a victim of love
for I'm all alone
with no one to talk to
not even on the phone.
I'm a victim of love
for I'm blind you see
when misconceptions of love
are bestowed upon me.

—Deborah Moore

My World

Be not in my world
For it is there we shall fall.
Be not in my world
For there is no one there at all.
A void so endless
And no one to care.
A time so empty
Fought with despair.
A tree that fell in the forest
And no one did hear,
A voiceless cry on silent ears.
So stay not where there is no end
And care not for a silent friend.
Go by your way and watch it not end.
For it is alone the war will end
Or will we win. But until then,
There is no one at all.

—Brenda Weatherford

Say Goodbye

The time has now come,
For me to tell you goodbye.
Until now I couldn't do it,
As hard as I'd try.
For all of the memories,
Keep lingering inside.
I just can't believe,
That our relationship died.
But now I know,
That it's time to go on.
For the feelings we had,
Now seem to be gone.
I hope that you'll remember,
Whenever I'm not here. . .
My love for you is living,
In our precious child each year.

—Gina A. Stripe

The Winds

The wind is always there
You can always count on it
No matter the strength
Soft, strong, short, long
It is peace,
The peace you think about when the sun goes down.
The wind is like a mother
The resting child knows it's there.
When she is gone, it cries in insecurity, loneliness, fear.
The wind is like a good meal
It fulfills your every need
And makes you feel good inside
Because it is a friend.

—Rachael Maresh

Cookies

There are all sorts of cookies for you and me,
For munching and crunching and dipping in tea.
You'll find them in the supermarket, or even in the mall.
People buying one or two or even buying them all.
They are topped with all sorts of goodies from head to toe,
They can be squarish, rectangular, or even triangular as you know.
Chocolate and vanilla are the most saught out flavors,
But some people like strawberry which is also savored.
Buying cookies by the box or the pound,
Sounds really too much for people who are not big and round.
For men who know they are not as lean as their wives,
Really don't care, they wouldn't give them up for their lives!

—Bridgette Williams

You Ask Me What I Want For Christmas

You ask me what I want for Christmas,
   this I'll tell you true,
for on this day I'd like to see the whole
   world in a truce.
A truce that would last from year to year
   and bring peace
through out the land, neighbors helping
   neighbors, each lending a helping hand.
$You ask me what I want for Christmas,
   this I'll tell you too,
I'd like to see the forest green and skies of
   sparkling blue.
I'd like to see the ocean waves rushing to
   the shore,
clean and pure and free of trash, I'd like
   to see the ocean floor.
$You ask me what I want for Christmas,
   this I'll tell you now,
I'd like to have baby brother, we can wrap
   him in my towel.
Do you think I ask to much? This I asked
   my mother,
when she said I think you did, I told her to
   forget the baby brother.

—*James G. Greenfield*

For Once

For once I see clearly
For once I hear fully
Finally I know you do love me truly.
For once I understand what you were
   going through
For once I understand that you were
   hurting too
For once I understand that I was wrong
   from the start
For once I see how much I broke your
   heart
Again you forgave me
Again you came back to me
Again you said you loved me
And that you would never leave me
Again you were so right and I was so
   wrong
Again I was so weak and you were so
   strong
You're so understanding, so loving, so
   caring
Once again it all comes down to one fact
I love you.

—*Kellie Blair*

You

You've been there for me
For quite awhile,
Through every tear,
And every smile.
You helped me
When I was down,
When things got bad
You turned them around.
I thank the Lord
Each and every day,
That you'll always
Be here in every way.
Even now
As we're far apart,
You're always there
In my heart.
Now I just want you to know
I will always love you so.

—*Jann Ross*

My Suicide

I did what I did,
For revenge, and for spite,
Somehow I got lost,
on the way to the light.,
I'm nailed in a coffin,
surrounded by dirt,
And I'm haunted by thoughts,
of the people I've hurt.
I thought I'd escape,
But I want to go back,
For now all I know
Is silence and black.
I'll never again,
See a bright, sunny day.
I chose my way out,
And here I must stay.

—*Kristin Perpignano*

My Love For You

My love for you is one of a kind,
For so long In have searched for you,
You are all I ever needed to find.
To make my love to one be true.
At times I have been so lost,
In love with one who didn't care,
And my heart has been the cost.
Where I belonged I knew not where.
Loving you feels so very right,
Happiness you have lead me to know.
I feel I no longer have to fight.
As time goes by our love will grow.
And you are all I shall live for,
Through the good and the bad,
Our loved will open one more door.
To feelings I did not know I had.
You smile and you touch my heart, Like
   no other ever could,
I finally found the missing part. Fitting in
   my heart I felt
you would.

—*Janine Hoyle*

Falling Tears

Why does my heart keep aching
For something that I'm forsaking
This feeling that throbs inside
Feels like a person just died
Is it really something that I want
Or is it just that voice inside that haunts
Staring up at the beautiful, aqua sky
Listening to the birds as they fly
Hearts float by me, then sink down
With a crash they are broken on the
   ground
Picking them up, I try to return the
   beauty they once felt
But for some odd reason they turn to ice
   and melt
Then the rain starts to pour
It's not the rain that falls anymore
I lift my hands to my cheeks with grace
It's my tears. . .that are falling upon my
   face

—*Angela Von Hollen*

First of Birds

It was a great feeling
for the bird
as it heard
the sky whispering its name
to all the world below—
to all the earth
in glorious mirth,
to all the lands and waters,
and creatures, friend or foe.
The wind rushed
under steady wings,
and angels were hushed
to see the wondrous sight
of a bird in flight
of all other beautiful things.

—*Arlene P. Ferrer*

Moments

Snatch your moments while you can
For the hour will soon be gone.
Time, like poetry, is so fleeting,
Too soon, you'll know why you were born.
Reflect a second, look at each other,
At your bodies, young and firm.
Your love is new, your touch is special,
And soon, you'll find, what's left to learn?
Enjoy each instance, make it count,
Even silence is a friend.
Be a romantic or be a clown,
Be not afraid of who's around.
But most of all, just snatch your moments,
Enjoy them while you can.

—*Elaine Couturier*

Life Like a Flower

A flower is only wild and free to grow
    when it is left alone.
For then this flower can grow the way
    nature intended for it to.
After being touched by any form of life, it
    then becomes exposed
To life's trials, fears and disappointments.
    It then becomes a prisoner.

—Anne Bosse

Time

Time, is a wonderful thing,
For those who can really see.
You can't measure, all of time in one day,
But you can save it for your memories.
I wish that you, could have a chance,
To share a dream of today,
With a small child of tomorrow,
And an old man of yesterday.
Find your own special time,
Give yourself the chance to see.
How wonderful time really is,
And how precious it can be.
So watch your time, well,
And never try to push too fast.
Remember this time, it's yours,
Don't spend too much, in the past.

—Barbara L. Underwood

Tomorrow

Deal only with the present
For tomorrow may never be.
Tomorrow is the great unknown,
Which we may never see.
To live only in the future
Is sure to bring you sorrow.
For time from tomorrow
We can never borrow.

—Debra Jette

Friendship

How dear you are to me my friend
For you stand by me no matter what I
    may do
For whether I be right or wrong.
You pass not judgement on me
May I give to you as much in return
As you have given me my friend

—Courtney J. Ellis

Untitled

Oh to God my heart partook
Forever more arresting
The silent plea within my core—
My soul! My soul protesting. . .
For my last breath, I inhaled slowly,
The cold knife, I violently siezed
As whatever tranquil bliss beheld me—
My tribulation now released. . .
But as the tears fell from my eyes
My anguish suddenly cleansed,
My heart bequeathed to my soul—
Memories, warm memories within. . .
To this moment I still remember
The pulsating beat of my heart;
How proud am I, that in today's
    brilliance—
I still play a significant part!

—Danielle Leigh Geary

Age 9

I was lonely at this stage of life,
Forever on my own.
I wanted to be grown-up now,
And spent my time alone.
I hung around with no one then,
And liked it just that way.
I had no friends to speak of,
And was lonely night and day.
I always tried to dress real fancy,
Like an adult should.
All I wanted was to be
A grown-up, if I could.
Now that I am all grown up,
I want to change the score.
I'd like to turn the clock back,
And be a child once more.

—Amy Grau

Perfidy

Listless heart
Forever smart
Reneging soul
Forever trow
Schmaltz dreams
Forever gleams
Spume breath
Forever death

—Beverly Lizewski

The Real Treasure

Attics of treasures sunken under the dust.
Forgotten. . .
Hidden away by pirates years ago;
Locking away their riches and secrets of
    yesterday.
Gone without a key.
Only one map reveals the mystery.
Directions to the real treasure,
Lying at the bottom of the chest.
One single picture,
Brought back to life by the remembrance
    of a time
Long ago.

—Jill Foner

Breaking Away

Crisp, brown, fragile;
Free, soaring loftily from the rest;
Then clumsily shifting down, splash;
Bobbing in hostile, ebullient waters;
Meandering towards the edge and falling;
Torrents of water engulfing, buffeting,
    drowning;
Until broken, changed, shaken;
The leaf emerges on the placid pool,
Below multi-colored lights sifting through
Crystaline droplets in the sky.

—David Mary

Friends

Friends are caring,
Friends are sharing
I have a friend who gives me money to
    spend
She takes care of me
When I'm sad or if I'm bad.
She wrote me a letter
Saying please get better.
She spends a dime or all of her time, to
    play with me,
Can't you see?
I call her my friend, not to send bad and
    foolish letters
But to make friends better.
Now I must surrender to our friendship,
Which has now come to an end
But, may I say you are always going to be
    in my mind,
So, goodbye my friend.

—Diannah Van Velzer

Friends

Friends don't let Friends drink and drive,
Friends don't let friends commit suicide,
A Friend that will care and will love,
Definately is a Friend from above,
A Friend is someone who will care,
A Friend is there when you're feeling
   down,
A Friend is there and won't let you frown,
A Friend that's always there for you,
Is a Friend that is always true,
A Friend is always willing to lend you
   a helping hand,
So hold on to your Friends while you can.

—Becky Cox

Love

Love is filled with happiness,
Friendship and some tears.
I hope you always have someone to love,
All through the years.
Love is like a lucky charm
That is there when it is needed.
No matter what kind it is,
Love has always succeeded.

—Jessica Northcutt

Friendship

Friendship is golden filled with hope and
   trust.
Friendship is like a special bond holding
   two people together.
Friends are like brothers and sisters
   sticking together through thick and
   thin.
Friendship is golden to those who treasure
   the good in others.
Friendship is golden to true friends.

—Heather Hauff

What Friendship Is To Me

Friendship means giving and never taking
Friendship means being there when you
   don't want to be
Friendship means being strong when you
   want to be weak
Friendship means doing all that you can
Even when it's not to your benefit.
Friendship means loving someone more
   than you do yourself
Friendship means having total trust and
   respect
But most of all
Friendship to me is pure love.

—Aimee Allison

Summary of My Situation

Hanging
From a limb
On my long dead family tree
Trying
To regain
My precarious balance
Stretching
But I can't
Quite touch my feet to the ground

—Betsyann Sandt

Dreams

Sleep is my only escape
From a world that has no dreams.
My world holds only pain for me
Frustration, despair and longing.
I long only for my dreams,
For the magic of fresh new feelings.
I touch those now and then again,
But they're not mine for keeping.
So I close my eyes again
And wait for sleep to help me.
To mask my life of dreamlessness
In a cloak of meaningless dreams.

—Donna Gaskin

Angels and Sons

He's got wings on his heart
From his ancestors' starts
Of sets of three
The covering of the face
The feet
The lifting mechanism angels'
Wings denoting
So what anger to anguish
Given solace by those wings.
What joy lifted in their beatings.
From my cousin
So he knows he has brothers
Heaven's eternal uncovered
"I looked upon the face of truth"
"And see love"
Interdimensional caring.

—Cathleen Chesrow

Premonition

You frightened me
From the beginning
Because, before you
Life was certain
And I was certain.
I knew you would
Shake my world
Take away my certainty.
And before it was over
You did
And I was
Uncertain
Uneasy
Unsure.

—Carole J. Frew

Untitled

Everywhere I go I see you
From the corner of my eye.
Why do you seek to play in shadows
Or run with clouds across these skies?
Why are we twisted, coiled so tightly
Against one another, our souls decree?
Mystery shades the long lost lovers
Like Ragnavok shades Life's tree.

—K. Hilsinger

Fear

Do you know the sound of a child in tears,
From the powerful thought that love
   won't conquer fear?
Can you feel the wind blowin' in the
   night?
Can you hear its voice sayin' baby, it's
   alright?
Once you're brought into this world to
   this evil place,
Everything you do is wrong, every door
   slams in your face.
Growing up in this world is a hard, cruel
   chore.
People start off as friends, then they go
   fight a war.
It's the wind of time which comforts every
   child
Of the well-known face that the world is
   running wild.
And like good and bad, the wind of time
   goes away,
Because in the end we all have to pay.

—Jackie Kerzner

The View from the Tree

What can I see
From the top of the tree?
A colorful parrot talking to me,
A bird in the air flying gracefully,
A big black cat meowing away,
A fuzzy grizzly bear hunting its prey,
A silver fish swimming the sea,
A treasure chest being opened with a shiny gold key.
&This is what I see
From the top of the tree.
Isn't it beautiful,
To be so free
To see what you can see
From the top of the tree.

—*Kristine Bond*

A World Of Heartbreak

Welcome to our world,
Full of lost and lonely love.
For love can only come
From the heavens up above.
We've all been chosen to lose
All hope of happiness.
Our worlds are all shattered,
And just a crazy mess.
A painful yearning to be loved,
These sensations are greatly missed.
Feelings of joy when being held,
Caressed and gently kissed.
For some this is a world,
Of endless give and take,
For us this is a world
Of neverending heartbreak.

—*Kristie Heilman*

The Eighth Wonder of the World

Why do guys think we're so confusing?
Give us flowers, melt our minds,
And our hearts are yours till the end of time.
Men are the ones I don't understand.
Sometimes it seems they don't want a chic on their hands.
Unfortunately men don't have a clue to what they want.
Some want a broad to flaunt all that she's got,
Others like a woman with a head on her shoulders.
Well, I give up!
Would someone please tell what a guy really wants.

—*Kara Needles*

The Light

I see the gazing past of light,
From when in darkness it sheads its flight,
Gaining speed which darkness is no more,
Gaining speed through the window and out beyond the door.
Opening rays while in mid air,
Gaining steadily while in a glare,
A rainbow of light is gathered there,
From when in mists it dreams of soft,
Where it peers behind the loft.
Many wonders within fact,
Seeing before you nothing more,
The light shining through mists of day,
Hoping to see the right way.
The very end is soon to become,
For the night will reign over its kingdom,
And the light of day will be no more.

—*Desiree J. Fontenot*

Loveliest Sort Of Way

Sitting here since half past noon
Gazing at an iridescent moon
Soft rays flatter your gentle face
Candid words to my ears, you grace
The warmness of your heartfelt smile
Can be felt and grasped for miles and miles
The smell of honeysuckle rides the breeze
As we listen to the rhythm of rustling leaves
In the auro of you I daily bask
Just to have you close, is all I ask
Exactly how I feel is most hard to say
But I love you more each passing day
In the loveliest, loving, sort of way.

—*Darlene Denice Cunningham*

Inside the Fence

Two oaks in dark broad leaves and a cherry tree in blossom.
Giving a slighting glance at the oaks in heavy leaves,
The cherry blossoms pretend just to start flying high.
It being still light outside in the evening, we find the doors and
The window frames having their wood textures and grains laid bare.
Dim reflections of bloom on the sliding glass doors.
They, brothers and sisters-in-law, say everything by implications and sound
Others out; "on an average", "as a general concept", worn out phrases.
Someone stands up, saying "white pink full blossom",
And bumps her hipbone against a corner of the table.
The other suddenly puts on the electric coffee mill.
Hard motor noise ends in a few seconds, one or two incantations are left out;
"Not in bloom but in green leaves, not a square table but a round one".
Coffee berries have been sleeping too long to have a flavory taste.
Six napkin rings are gathered beside the platter,
On which pate' of tuna fish has got out of shape.
The rings empty holes think of the joyful sound of the rain drops
That had slithered down amicably together in the pipe yesterday.

—*Etsuko Ogi Onabe*

Gazing at a Rose; Thinking of a Gypsy

Gazing at a rose
Full in bloom and
Moving in the wind
I'm reminded of a gypsy,
Dancing in her den.
The rose's delicate petals
Are the dancer's scarves
Flowing flawlessly
All about her.
The thorns are her hands
That clasp the scarves
Saving them from blowing
And never returning.
The leaves seem to be
The castanets,
Shaking to make the
Beautiful gypsy dancing music.

—*Jenni Tanner*

Untitled

Death comes softly,
Gently in the night,
When least expected
It captures our light.
Death comes quickly
With no time to spare
And steals our souls
With delicate care.
Death comes soon
In an urgent pace
And takes us to
Our eternal place.
Death comes softly
Gently in the night,
When least expected
It captures your light.

—*Amy Lawhorn*

Swans

Swans on a golden pond,
Gliding along the water's edge.
A silver moonlit sky glistening above,
And stars shining brightly.
The swans are singing their beautiful song.
As they glide on a golden pond.

—*Erin Kelly*

Untitled

growing hair,
glistening fangs,
and a bright moon above.
fighting the instinct
unable to be controlled
in the silence of the
deadly forest.
softly creeping
over crackling dead leaves,
sly and sinister with a
fading heart.
are they real,
or are they myth
these pitiful human creatures?
they come out at night,
yet should we believe,
or leave the werewolf alone?

—*Kimberly S. Rife*

Why?

Why does the rain come out of the sky?
Why does the sun shine in my eye?
Why does the tiny baby cry?
Why does everyone have to die?
Why are the stars up so high?
Why, oh why?

—*Marci Cox*

Frail Sadness

A single tear on a piece of paper,
Glistening like a solitary star.
Fading to nothing as it seeps through the page.
Now it's gone. . .
A single piece of paper, lying on a desk.
Blank, except for a tiny spot of water.
Someone begins to write. . .
Not realizing that they have obliterated
A tiny star of sadness.

—*Jeanne Camilletti*

Celestial Shores

Joys ascending on lives unending,
Glories unreceding on Love's celestial shore.
Clear, untrammeled consciousness,
Unmanipulated bliss, deserved.
Few are traveling celestial shores
Where fear and pain and death are over.
But more to follow, that's for sure.
In salvation's light embodied with natures rarefied,
Unburdened by the sin of guilt, and hatred, hurting,
Denying, killing; works of darkest night. . .
I give up my possessions of fear and doubt, depression;
My pain is in recession,
To Love I make confession, "I have denied you."
"Please cleanse my unhealed shores;"
"And bring me to Celestial Shores."

—*Byron G. Miller*

Beautiful Things

A fish
With soft colors
Floats by
Like a weightless blossom
Floating in the sky.
I hear the swift waves
Of the wind blowing by,
The screech of a bird way up
High.
The fish of the sea
The birds of the sky
Both as beautiful as
You and I.

—*Tami Doty*

New Jerusalem

New Jerusalem will be my home one day soon;
God assures me. . .as the flowers bloom.
I'll reside in Heaven with streets of gold. . .
The city of God's perfection to behold.
There will be no more sickness or sorrow. . .
And eternity of perfect tomorrows.
No more sin or pain will there be. . .
No more thirst or hunger in God's eternity.
Continual song of praise and honor to my Lord;
Living in Heaven's harmony in one accord.
I look forward to Heaven, my new home;
New Jerusalem. . .on earth, no more to roam.
I'll walk with Jesus in His perfect way.
In Heaven. . .perfected, with Him always.
I'll see my Savior who saved my worthless life.
With no more darkness. . .but, everlasting light.

—*Barbara Wolfe Heaps*

A Soldier's Prayer, a Letter to God

As I fight this war, please guide me through each day.
God, bless all my brothers here and watch us on our way.
As we fight for life, please guide us till the end,
Especially dear Lord, please promise to stay our friend.
God bless all my family, especially my wife and son.
Please promise to keep them both secure, so they never have to run.
I would like to thank you, for all you've done for me,
By taking only men and leaving families free.
As we march through mud and sand, to fight for freedom today,
God, if you must call for me, for you, I'll be on my way.
Dear Lord, I am now walking, a cannon if nearby.
God, I hear you calling me, for you, I shall die!
As I am at my death, my family is by my side.
God, now that I am gone, please promise to be their guide.
Now, I have the flag, waving ahead of me,
I was very proud to have served in the U.S. army!
Now, I am closing because I am with you, I shall say goodbye,
For I like you God I sacrificed my life!

—*Josephine Henderson*

God Is. . .For He Made It

Have you ever wondered about God? He made everthing like him.
God is like a soft, peaceful, breeze on a hot day
For he made it
God is like a rose symboling love and dignity
For he made it
God is like you and me, like the animals, even with our
Pain and our happiness
For he made it
God is like our sunshine, for happiness and light
God is like everything
For he made it
For God so loved the world that he gave his only son
That whoever belives in him may not perish but have
Eternal Life!!! John 3:16

—*Corrie Milaeger*

Violet to Azzuro

Violet skies
Golden eye's
Shining
Purple breeze
All in ease
Dawning
Feathered smaze
Distant haze
Burning
Violet dies
Azzuro rise
Morning.

—*Idania Diaz*

Consolidation

Dispatched far by waters' thunder
Grains of the solid float away,
Thus leaving I, tarnished luster;
To you bestows fine vanity.
Yet moon hence daytide to I rise
And glory is restored here in;
But short lived! Melancholy eyes,
Shrewd with contempt, do displine.
With greater strength does passion sweep,
Drowned pebbles here do rebuild land.
Rush'ed on white naked beaches,
Give happ'ly which did one expend.
Look, by element they are one,
And do so fuse not with regret;
Point 'this one', that one' e'er no more;
Unselfishly both to each is lent.

—*Amy P. Flowers*

A New Start

I heard today that you passed away.
Grief struck my heart with pain.
I knew you had been drinking but. . .
What could I have done to keep you here
  with me?
Tell you again that it's not right?
Tell you again that I care for you?
Words can never say.
The end seems so near.
Now there is no end,
Just a beginning.
Starting over without you next to me.
Starting over with only the memory of
  you
To grasp on to.

—*Kelli Janae Rupe*

Marriage

Golden fire around her finger,
Golden fire that burned my soul.
My own ring looked so meager,
My chest had a hole.
A doctor put my heart in a bag
And threw it to a nearby dog;
While my heart was shred to rags,
She went to the altar and her galen love.
Her father escorted her to her prince;
He got to the altar and with a spin
He turned and ran towards me
I tried to move but I was pinned.
An old woman held my sleeve
While the charging father drew a sword;
With one swift jump he landed near
And with his sword my arm he struck.
And my arm became the sword
And I looked at him and saw
That the father was no more:
My mother now held the gleaming sword
And she said: "Wake up!"

—*Alex Lobera*

Color Combination

On Mother's side
Grandma was Hungarian,
While Grandpa claimed Bavarian.
On Father's side
There's a strange combination
Of Indian and missing link.
This odd conglomeration
Has produced a unique American
With front side very tan
And backside in the pink.

—*Dorothy R. Marsh*

Darkness and the Light

A young child, groping in the dark.
Groping for light, for hope, for safety.
But he finds no light
To make him feel safe.
There is no light
To give him that hope.
You are the light, the hope
That keeps us safe,
That keeps him from groping.
But where are you now
When he needs you most?
Do you stay away because you don't care?
Don't keep him in darkness
Turn on the light.

—*Diane Van Houten*

Untitled

October's air is crisp
Green hills turn golden
And finally, brown.
Leaves rustle
In patches of sunlight
Under hardwood groves.
October's harvest moon
Hunt's the vast
Empty land
Cold dew drops
Steadily drip upon
The lakes surface
Rippling hills draped
In yellowed silk
Disintegrate to memories
Of October's past
Left to be raked up.

—*Diana Desrosiers*

Our Friendship

Many memories we have shared,
Good, bad, we've always cared.
Time after time we laugh and cry,
We share emotions, just you and I.
Day by day, year by year,
From smile to smile, from tear to tear,
Our friendship stands on one solid rock,
Bound together with a solid lock.

—*Amy England*

Grass

In the summer it grows and grows,
Growing in between your toes.
Cut it here, cut it there,
Cut it everywhere.
Green as green,
Green as green grass be.
Summer comes and summer goes,
Just like the grass between your toes.
Winter comes and then it dies,
But here comes spring with a surprise.
There's the grass,
There it is!
Ready to begin,
Growing again,
Get out the clipper, get out the mower,
Cut the grass lower and lower.

—*Jessica Collins*

Shadows

Sweet flower
grown by innocent hands in innocent
    love...
Sweet flower
crushed by guilty hands in guilty love...
Sweet flowers
grown together as one in secrecy
secret love...
Nothing,
flowers lost by time's hands
lost love.
Shadows

—Kiri Krick

The Courage to Love

The campfire burns, emitting warmth like
    slow-motion lightning.
Yet even in its presence, we feel the chilly
    night air racing through us.
So we move toward one another—only a
    hint of apprehension.
The cold hate of lost love is pushed aside
    with new treasures.
A warmth is found, a bond is shared.
Our naive eyes do not meet, but for an
    occasional glance,
For fear the windows will be open.
Instead we stand, two silhouettes in
    silence,
Staring intently into the flames of love.
What makes it start? What makes it
    stop?
How do we keep love strong?
The orange, red, yellow offer the answers.
Listen to their crackling cries.
But our hearts are pounding so loudly,
    selfishly leaving room for no other.
So the answers we seek are lost—for the
    better?
And pulling closer as compensation,
We float away from the flames, run away
    before they die.
Oh, the courage—the courage of those
    who dare to love.

—Michelle Conti

Love Shared

Love shared mulitiplies,
Grows beyond all boundaries.
Love shared simplifies,
Life and things unfounded.
Seek it out
For love is all there is,
The secret of our being,
The reason for living, love is
Giving to each other sustenance
Necessary to our existence.
Love unshared will die
And love cannot die
For God is love
And God is forever.

—Beverly Ales

Guidance

Someone, please take my hand and lead
    me to the place I want to be.
Guide me through this emptiness and
    show me
That there is sunlight through my
    darkness.
Give me strength to face my very
    uncertain tomorrows
And help me accept my painful
    yesterdays.
Show me what is normal and just.
Convince me that life is fair.
Encourage me, believe in me, need
    me... .love me.
Understand my fears, doubts and
    insecurities
For they too, are a part of me.
Teach me how to overcome them and
    convince me
That pain needn't be the most frequent of
    all other emotions.
Show me that feeling lost is just a passing
    feeling
That has passed through all the years of
    my life.
Show me a place where I belong and am
    happy,
Convince me that I do deserve happiness.
Guide me through this relentless storm
    called "My Life"
And give me a reason to wake up
    tomorrow.

—Bonnie Strobel

Decision

She whispered no words, no sign of
    emotion
Guilt overwhelmed her, leaving no escape.
She searched the drawer for some fatal
    potion
Shuddering as though Evil had grasped
    her nape
Death whispered her name as the bottle
    drained.
Like an addict, she quickly gulped it down
While inside her small world it stormed
    and rained
The mirror reflected her red sequined
    gown
But as her eyes rose, she glanced at
    herself
Beyond swollen eyes and a pale
    countenance
Recalled memories she stuck on a shelf
Awakening the future without a chance
Sirens sounded before untimely death
The phone cord dangling until her last
    breath.

—Julie Anne Lambert

The Storm...

Clouds tumble in
Gusts of wind begin to blow
You stand outside
And you feel the humid air
Raindrops begin to penetrate the earth
Evaporating when they hit the cement
Raindrops glimmering in the dullness of
    the early afternoon
You lift your face toward the sky;
Letting the rain hit your skin
Cooling it, soothing it...
Clouds tumble away
The wind stops
The rain left over
On leaves, fences and roof-tops
Shine with the brilliant colors of the
    rainbow
As the sun quickly appears
From behind a rapidly diminishing cloud

—Jennifer Greening

Ne Parts Pas, S'il Te Plait

Mon cheri, I am here for you
You cannot get rid of me.
For you have won my heart,
And I have already done my part.
Take me, I'm yours.
I will wait.
You cannot think twice for it is
Already too late.
You have tried and tried
To conquer me.
Now you have finally won.
I love you more than life itself
Please don't leave me now.

—Rachel Hughbanks

Just a Crocus

A bright splash of yellow, sparkling in the
    sun's rays,
Had burst through the cold, dark earth.
I stopped—stood still—awed by this
    unexpected beauty.
Just a crocus? No, it was more, much
    more.
You see, this was my mother's crocus.
It greeted me at the steps of my childhood
    home,
Now void of her tender presence.
Just a crocus? No, it was more, much
    more.
The bright golden petals welcomed me,
Like my mother's radiant smile.
Only barely visible above the ground,
They were soft and velvety, like her
    caress.
Just a crocus? No, it was more, much
    more.
It was a promise. A promise of new life.
After winter, spring;
After sorrow, gladness;
After physical death, eternal life.
Just a crocus? No, it was more, much
    more.

—Inez Hitchcock

One Nation Under...

This nation under God
Had loyalty and patriotism,
Love, pride and family.
Today, murder and mayhem; is this the US?
Aborting future citizens
Cracking up our brains
Separating prayer and schools,
Letting the klan march; US or China?
Satan verses unleashed
Flags and crosses burning,
Religion hidden in shadows
Usurpers rights emerging; US or SR?
A new nation is erupting,
Immoral, unloving, dispirited.
Our basic rights are twisted,
That leaves US here; SU.

—G. C. Parker

Reflections of an Octogenarian

The road I travelled
Had many intersections,
Oft' which ones to take
I was not sure.
But once the choice I made,
I never looked back.
To do what was right,
I had to fight.
I witnessed right downgraded;
Wrong elevated.
It was all a part of God's plan
To make of me a man.
He sent the sunshine and the rain,
If I could live life over again,
And live it my way,
What change would I make?
None, I think.

—Arville Wheeler

Round

Round, just as the Earth, he's everything.
Hair of golden seas,
Flowing and natural.
Eyes which make the heavens bow
To their magnificence.
Beams of light, which awaken the dead,
Come from him, and the sun is envious.
The jasmine King, which rules all,
Has idolized him.
That which covers his bones
Makes the glass of churches shatter.
But all of this is unimportant.
Since to love someone
The angels must seem tainted next to him.
HE is just something which makes
The plastic baubles melt,
Though neither my heart nor soul.

—Elizabeth Crowell

Peace vs. War

Having peace means having life,
Happiness, and love.
Having war means stopping life,
Unhappiness, and hate.
If people would believe more
In themselves and give love
To everyone, then maybe there
Would be more peace.
With war, no one really ever wins.
The horror of it all keeps
Going on forever.
Peace is the answer
To all our prayers.

—Deana Burton

Untitled

Older than the star I wished upon,
Wiser than the sky that holds it.
Wipe the tears away from the reddened eyes of death.
Leave her...still and alone.
More beautiful than the waves I sing with,
Lovlier than the sands that greet them,
Touch the lost hand of the frightened and meek child.
Lead him, loved and wanted
More deadly than the toys I play with
More sacred than the box that holds them.
Steal a kiss from the gentle lips of the hunting girl.
Hold her, aching and empty.

—Michelle Menz

Your Wings Cry Out

You've trapped yourself inside
Hard walls surround you
They're built of solid store
It seems like forever
That I've been chipping pieces away
My cramped hands are scarred with blisters
The scorching sun beats down
Its rays eat through my tender skin
My throat is raw and swollen
Salty tears flow over my cracked bleeding lips
Somewhat satisfying my thirsty tongue
Each conquered day gives me hope for the next
Now I lie down on cool grains of sand for what seems hours
Until now, I never noticed it
The warm colours melt together
The sunset brings a new fresh day
Reaching deep inside of you
You are released by the wings of freedom

—Jennifer Dunbar

Lines for the Planting of Memorial Dogwood at Neshaminy-Langhorne High School

Come, you Dryads and Diana,
Haunt these trees, that we may see and imagine and believe
In you, in beauty, and in our own
Quiescent quests.
Come rain and sun,
Prepare these trees for habitation.
Our dreams and visioning would find a sturdy branch and
Mingle momentarily the new myth-makers with the old
Before they fly to far-off forests.
Speak, you trees, a hundred years from now
For voices that no longer speak the language of this world.
Blaze out our greetings in white and party pink.
Edge them in delicate green.
When summer passes, salute with a bright red berry.

—Esther Hughes Holby

Dreams

Nobody understands them.
Why do they go farther than we'll ever go?
Why do they cross our practical boundaries?
They take us places. Beautiful places.
Where only in our dreams can we behold such beauty.
They take us places. Terrible places.
Where only in our dreams could we dare go.
Dreams, nobody understands them.

—Patricia M. Lombillo

Lovers and Fools

So many words on this matter
Have been spoken
So many rules established
So many hearts broken;
Where is the wisdom...
Where is the fence
To separate lovers and fools
To employ good sense;
Emotions abound...
Fevers run high,
From lovers and fools,
In a twinkling of an eye;
And what have we left
But a heart that breaks;
From passions of the moment...
From unbearable aches;
Is this, then, always the end
For those who break rules?
Broken hearts that never mend,
Hearts of lovers, hearts of fools?

—Joseph Wigney

Imprints

A stroll by the sea, is a plunge back in time.
Have others before had thoughts such as mine?
My footprints are joined with those made before
By long ago lives, whose breath is no more.
Did they ponder secrets that lay at their feet
Where lovers awaited by chance here to meet?
What vast adventures took place way back when
Men struggled in battle; each fighting to win?
These sands long absorbed, a wife's lonely tears
When prayers lifted upward, as mast disappeared.
Her sailor had chosen to challenge the sea
Thus sadly she waited for whatever would be.
Blood of the deer hunt, also washed with the tides
The Indian has eaten; he has ended his ride.
The arrow that pierced, has long been abandoned.
The quivers are empty; the tribes have disbanded.
From over my shoulder at footprints behind
Only I know that those imprints are mine.
Time and the tides will bring new sands into place
Like all footprints before; mine too will erase.

—Belva Dobyns Hamilton

God's Gifts

God made the flowers and sturdy trees,
He also made the butterflies and bees.
God formed the earth, the clouds and sky,
He also created you and I.
God made the oceans of sapphire blue,
And emerald green grass for me and you.
He made stars twinkle like diamonds in space,
And sent crystal raindrops to bathe our face.
God made the sun to warm the day,
And the moon at night to light our way.
He made snowflakes beautiful and white,
And a gentle breeze to cool the night.
God gives these gifts with love and free.
It's proof he cares for you and me.
Trust him and thank him daily in prayer,
And you'll feel his presence always, everywhere.

—F. Georgia Worley

Number 1 Dad

My dad is sweet, kind and nice
He always listens to me,
And gives me great advice.
My dad will love me forever and ever.
But the cute kid down the street,
Always sends me love letters.
My dad sure beats the kid by far,
'Cause the only boy you can trust,
Ain't strumming that guitar.
I love my dad!
I'll love my dad even more in time
That's him over there
The #1 dad of mine!

—Cindi Madaffari

Then And Now

He was then, and you are now.
He broke my heart which you mended with care.
He made me cry, but you wiped my tears away.
He caused me anger while you brought me laughter.
He hovered above me, but you allowed me to be free.
You are now, and he was then.
You whisper sweetly in my ear; he yelled at me.
You make me happy; he causes me sadness.
You ar humble to the world; he was conceited to all.
You brighten each new day; he painted my days gray.
You need me—he only wanted me.
You love me—his feelings were not of love.
he and I were then
but
You and I are now. . .and always, I love you.

—Jodi Lea

The Artist

He painted that picture on the living room wall.
He created that painting at the end of the hall.
He's full of ideas to put on paper,
A bird, a dog, or an immense skyscraper.
With a stroke of his pen and a swirl of his brush,
He creates the drawing of the nighttime hush.
Colors and colors, red and blue,
Oh, what works an imagination can do.
So be an artist and follow your heart,
Cause it's one great career, it's a work of art.

—Allie Bloom

A Tribute to Feliphi

A little boy was brought into the World
He gave his heart to a very special girl.
He gave the most precious gift he could give
So the girl he loved would have a life to live.
All America is proud of him
He knew his life on earth was very dim.
He only lived a few short miles
We will always remember his sweet smiles.
He was sent from Heaven Above
He was carried away on the Wings of a Dove.
I pray some day his famliy he will meet
And spend Eternity at the Master's Feet.

—Brenda Shaw

Barren Canvas

As the artist looked upon the canvas
he gazed out upon the water
and the colors sprang into being
Brilliant, rich, royal blues
Grays forming thunder caps
Flashes of white making foam
as the waves crashed toward the shore.
The moors stretched out,
a green hand reaching to the sea
The rocky, sun washed cliffs looked dead
but for the moss that clung to them.
Stranded jellyfish
lifeless, left by the tide
Bits and fragments of spectacular
coral, reds, opal, cream.
Gulls screeching over a fish that had been washed ashore.

—Jennifer Gillett

Autumn

He came slowly, hauntingly, very silent
He grasped a brush and carefully painted
The leaves blushed from the touch of this tyrant
They crumbled and fell, their color tainted.
A cool autumn's wind gently rustled the trees
The sun blazed in the bright blue sky
His breath carefully scattered the leaves
Whistled through the branches and then sighed.
Like a kaleidoscope the landscape changed
The caressing wind, the trees, and the flowers
His painting was so carefully arranged
A monument of his God like powers.
His beautiful picture, oh, what a loss
With the arrival of winter and the first frost.

—Aileen Cameron

A Soldier's Wounds

While the young soldier sat in fear
he heard an explosion very near.
His best friend had been shot.
The soldier heard the crash, and knew
    he'd been caught,
He and his friend were such a pair.
When he was shot it seemed unfair.
The soldier knew in the end there would
    be great doom.
He knew it was soon when he heard the
    explosion boom.
The soldier tried to run,
but the enemy shot him before it was
    done.
the soldier started to cry;
Then he lay on his stomache to die.

—*Jeni Davis*

King of the Jungle

His roar shakes the jungle floor.
He is the beast, he is the master.
From the smallest bird to the most
    powerful elephant,
He rules them all.
He is the leader of the forest,
Ruler of the wilderness.
He is the mighty one who sits proud
As he watches over his kingdom.
For he is the lion,
Majestic and mighty.

—*Kimberly Tepe*

Untitled

Idyllic innocence trapped within medieval
    battlements
He keeps me for a reason I do not know.
In the vortex of seven spiraling towers, I
    wonder his intent
For I am followed by watching eyes
    wherever I go.
This impenetrable castle rises high above
    the mists
To hold the youth encompassed within his
    towers.
Kept in the realms of a maiden fortress,
Hiding sheltered dreams and hidden
    powers.
As there is magic in the tapestries
And the stained glass casts enchanted
    shadows
I wait for the day when I will set myself
    free
Release your prisoners, let me go.

—*Kim Boestche*

God

God makes the skies
he made the trees
God made the bee's,
He made the leaves
God made the birds and flowers
God made it all for you and me.
God made you and me
And put us on the earth so fair
God made the moon
And He is coming soon.
God made the sun
And evolutionists that's no pun.
God made the stars
And put them in the sky so fair
God made everything!

—*Jeannette C. Fegley*

Search

Irony! My search for comfort torments
    me!
Why do I toil for wealth, at cost of health,
When happiness pawned for property
    is rewarded eternal proverty?
I stray from the path in search of gain;
Though from that decision only comes
    pain.
Such pity it doesn't press me
That time to be spent only in praying
Is lost for the sake of my soul slaying.
In corporate cages, my love
Of money sells life for wages.
Such sacrifice for mere raises?
Far better to believe in the father;
My happiness can be for the asking!

—*Mark A. Johnson*

The Writer's Twenty-Third Psalm

The editor is my shepherd, I do not want,
He maketh me to type all my manuscripts —
He leadeth me to distraction,
He vexes my soul: He leadeth me in the
    paths
Of punctuation and grammar;
Yes, though I walk through the valley of
    writer's block
I will fear no libel suit; for the editor is
    with me;
My typewriter and eraser they comfort
    me.
The editor prepareth a deadline before me
In the presence of my harried schedule —
He anointeth my fingers with liquid eraser
    fluid,
My manuscript with spelling errors
    runneth over.
Surely verbosity and a pedestrian style
Shall follow me all the days of my writing
    career
And I will remain unpublished in the
    glossy magazines forever.

—*Katherine Tapley*

Untitled

He betrayed me
He played with all my emotions
He made me quiver with fancy notions
He did not love me.
I wanted to have his child
To hear it cry and smile
Would make me feel sublime
But me he beguiled
With his smile
Before I could act
Someone else had his child
And all I have left is a smile
To have a child is such joy he cried
Why don't I give you another tonight
But alas, it was too late
All my hopes and dreams went down the
    drain
To be second best would give me such
    pain
Goodbye I cried, and closed the door in
    his face.

—*Alice Robinson*

Romance

He said its over, that there is no use
He said we're finished, and gave me no
    excuse
Everyone thinks I should forget him
They say he's not worth the pain
They don't seem to understand
My life he has changed.
They were not there
When he lost me in his eyes
They did not experience the hurt
That existed, when he said good-bye.
They did not hear with feeling the words
I love you come from his mouth
Just explain how he expects me
To forget all of this now.
He wants to throw everything away
Without a fighting chance
What ever happened
To the real meaning of romance?

—*Jennifer White*

The Magnificent One

He died on the Cross.
He, the Prince of Peace,
Died for the world's sin.
We all live in sin
Which is forgiven
For the blood of Him
Cleansed us white as snow.
God gave His only Son,
The Great Messiah,
As the Great and Final
Holy Sacrifice.
How magnificent
God's love for sinners
Must be to allow
The Crucifixion
Of Emmanuel!
How great His love is!
How great His love is!

—*Emily Garrett Clary*

Untitled

Why are we always blamed?
Why must we be the reason for everyone's fault.
Because we were conceived between your mid—life
You blame us for your failures?
If you could only see who's really to blame
You'd think different of us.
We were just the fetus of your development.
You chose our outcome.

—*Parisha Kinsey*

The Petrified Eels on the Dunes at the Beach

He came on a dark night all clammy and cold.
He washed up on shore with the seaweed and worms.
He slithered and snaked through the slimy green scum.
So full of the refuse of rotting, dead fish.
Tired of fighting his way through the refuse,
The doddering demon drew up his body
And, standing erect, searched for his spouse.
His sharp eyes missed nothing. He spotted his lady,
And took to the labours of scrambling to her.
He found her quite limp and most certainly dead,
Her body infested with maggots and such.
Yet, still, he stood by her, refusing belief
In that which his eyes said was veritably true.
The doddering demon just curled up to die.
And there you will find them, if ever you look.

—*E. Talley Brown*

Like a Stone

See no evil
Hear no evil
Speak no evil
Feel no pain
Have no shame
Have no blame
Do no bad
Do no good
Don't walk
Don't run
Don't talk
Just lie there
In a deep
Dark hole
Like a mole
Like a stone
Stone cold

—*Fred A. Valenzuela*

Morning Music

Smell the scent of flowers
Hear the sounds of birds
See the morning sunrise
Undescribed by words
Listen to the warbler
Sing a song of love
While two mating meadowlarks
Fly not far above
Off in the distance
See a robin on the wing
And watch an orchard oriole
Prepare a song to sing
In the morning sunrise
Hear songs without the words
If you like to hear good music
Listen to the birds

—*Franklin J. Skillman*

The Rose

It denies empty promises,
Heartache and dismay,
While it promises a love,
That shall never go away,
It is the eternal symbol of beauty,
The beauty that is also inside,
And it rids you of your sorrows,
Briskly pushing them aside,
It brings forth a happiness,
Presented straight from the heart,
And it's never been misleading,
But a perfection piece of art,
Nothing have I discovered,
Holds meanings alike to these,
The feelings held within,
A sweet rose's captivity.

—*Angela Williams*

Books are Fun for Everyone

Big ones, little ones, thick ones, thin ones, fat ones, skinny ones.
Heavy ones, light ones, different books for different folks
The more you read the more you know.
Books are fun and interesting too.
Titles galore to soothe your mood
From home to school to other lands
Around the world and back again.
Travel through books to the stars and flirt with Mars
Or board a sub and explore the deep
Through a book all dreams will come true—
You can do or you can be whatever you choose.
Reading is the golden rule—
Adventures to Mysteries, Folklore to Humor,
Drama to Fine Arts, Religion to Romance—
All of these subjects and more
You can find at a glance in a book—
So, read read as much as you please
And you'll be sure to succeed, indeed—

—*Gwendolyn Wood-Tisdale*

Daddy

I remember the times that I used to share
with a father that really did care.
He always knew the right things to say
and his laughter and smiles brightened my day.
He helped me out when I had a problem,
and he always knew just how to solve them
When I was bored and feeling blue,
He always had fun things for me to do.
He was such a good husband to his wife
and I know he loved her more than life.
He was the best father that there could be
and he did everything he could for me.
But not his memory is all that lived on
and it's true that you don't know what you've
got til it's gone.
I'll think about him each and every day
and that he left in such an unpainful way.

—*Melissa L. Baldwin*

Languages, Languages, Languages

A touch of English...
"Hello, how are thing going, fine here".
A touch of Francais...
"allo c,a va? c,a va bien"
A touch of Deutsch...
"Gruss Gott! Wie geht's"? Prima!
A touch of Espanol...
"I Hola, Que' tal? Bien"
A touch of "The End"!

—*Christa Anderson*

The Child

I saw a child sitting far away, as I walked
    close I stopped to say
Hello—she turned, I saw her tears
I asked her why she cried today, she said
    not a word but turned away
And as the tears dropped from her face
I thought of you.
Was she crying for you and me, for the
    love we lost now will never be
Did she know in some strange way that I
    had lost you yesterday
I stood and watched as tears dropped
    down
Like grains of sand upon the ground that
    people trod upon,
I thought of you
Why does she cry this child forlorn, no
    sound she makes as tears run down
I long to hold her in my embrace, to ease
    her pain; but it's not my place
And now she turns her face to mine
I see her smile, it's like pure sunshine
The tears dry slowly on her face
Her pain is over, she won her race
As I walked away I thought of you

    —*Hazel Morvant Master Form*

Miss Jeckle And Ms. Hyde

Free at last
Wow lifes a blast
Money to do
No longer dependent and blue
Power to rule
Man this is cool
My room, my cozy castle
A place to rejuvenate, rest a spell
The walls their precious secrets
Never their stories to tell
Parents relegated to the past
Dusty antiques, creaky outcasts
These my awkward teen years
Loaded with struggles, stretches and
    souvenirs
Tweaked by challenges haunted by fears
Teens are keen. Their qualities to extol
Their virtues to redeem
Off for a bike ride
With my trusty teddy by my side.

    —*Wendy Harrison*

The Homeless

All afternoon, a neighbor's saw buzzed
Hemmed, spit and chored
As an aging tree fell placidly to memory.
At four o'clock, a plump ground hog leapt
Across the yards and through scattered
    bush
And with pleading eyes my evergreen it
    took
But beseeched—kindly—will you
    befriend me?

    —*Diana Kwiatkowski Rubin*

Prints in the Snow

Across the road she was skittishly leaping
    and skipping,
Her cloven hooves making heart shaped
    prints in fresh snow.
When a creation of man approached as
    she was tripping,
The delicate creature did find herself
    below.
Her body did heave with one last will to
    survive
As she dragged herself to the side of the
    cold and wet street.
Her cotton—white tail did fall, now no
    longer alive—
By the world of man, this deer did have
    defeat.
Along the roadside, a pale, dry skeleton
    lies
To remind us of our carelessness with
    life—
While a spotted yearling across the
    highway flies
Up comes a flash as quick as a butcher's
    knife.
This one never to become a graceful aged
    doe
Alas, had left her heart shaped prints in
    fresh snow.

    —*Anne Findlay*

Wedding Bells

When shall wedding bells ring for me?
Will I be vibrant with youth
Or mature with age?
My path will be laden with flowers,
Eyes, dreamy with love.
The organ shall resound in my soul
And on my head shall reside lilies.
I will join my chosen
In front of best wishers and God.
Those who entered as two
Will then leave together as one.

    —*Shaun-Marie Scott*

The Lonely Lady of Denmark

There she was in the middle of the night.
Her eyes covered with tears and her heart
    filled with fear.
In the street everybody said,
"There goes the lonely lady of Denmark".
She walked slow,
without a glow.
There was no smile on her face,
her whole body was in outer space.
She had no friends, no family, no hope
She was the lonely lady of Denmark.
On a dark night,
in a place without light.
The lonely lady poisoned was.
Surrounded by her loneliness,
the lady had died.
The Lonely Lady of Denmark.

    —*Grace Soto*

The Child

See the child standing there,
Her eyes filled with hope,
Filled with trust,
Filled with innocence.
She knows not what this cruel world has
    in store for her.
She only knows the love from her mother,
The protection from her father,
The endless gifts from her grandmother.
Who is not jealous of her youth?
She longs to grow up for what she thinks
    is fun.
Little does she know of the heartache in
    store for her.
But for now she clutches her teddy bear,
And looks up at you with those big,
    trusting eyes.

    —*Charity Metz*

Beauty

Her eyes are as green as grass.
Her hair is as smooth as silk.
I can see her running in a pasture,
Full of daises.
No one she can turn to
But she doesn't have a care in the world.
But why you ask?
She has not one care in the world because
She see's beauty all around her;
Beauty just like herself.

    —*Judy Cavagnudo*

The Danger in her Eyes

She lay there feeling the pain of sorrow,
Her heart burned like an open wound.
Tell me when will this wound heal,
When will the torture die.
She asked herself, why? Why me?
Why this torture to my innocent body?
Her heart ticked like a time bomb ticking
    away.
The door opened, the intensity grew
    stronger.
The hand raised,
Her heart stopped.
The pain is gone,
But the wound remains.
One day the tearing inside me
Will end.

    —*Kelly Blazak*

The Hole

She lies wide open
her mouth with scream open
as the heat-seeking missile
takes off in firm flight
desiring her life to land in
like the last nail
being driven into the only empty hole
attaching the legs
firmly, but without commitment.

—Dana Beardsley

My Friend Betsy

As I laid my sleepy head on
her stomach,
My eyes closed and all the early
morning fears of what the
Day held, disappeared.
She was warm and friendly
as she lay beside me,
And I could hear the steady thump
of her heart,
And the gurgle of the food
in her stomach.
Did it matter that she had horns?
Did it matter that she had four legs?
The slow, steady squash-squish
of her cud chewing,
Lulled me to sleep—
She was a true friend,
Betsy, my cow.

—Howard L. Voeltz

Summon A Smile

There among the gravestones of
her treacherous past, lay
one who cared—her love.
Long ago, his soul departed
it's home to find
harbour in hers.
Inside, her heart lost
it's heat. The boy received
the gift she sent him.
You shall never forget
what you cherish. Her lover
never leaves.
He sits, forever bringing
smiles to her lips.
The golden maker of memories.

—Anthony Cartee

Sun

Sun, sun
Here it comes again
I don't know when it'll ever end
Everytime the sun rises
Brings everyone good prizes
Everytime the sky goes red
The sun lies down and goes to bed

—Bobbi Pischke

Glimpses

Cycle
Herring boats
startle silvered fish
at a thump.
Caught in light,
they fill the phosporous nets
on moonlit water.
Winter's Haven
White feathers
pervade Puget Sound
as snow geese
from Russia
Fly the icy winds
to their brackish bowl.
Nosegay
Ribboned breeze
carries cedar trees
hued in green,
bristling scent,
an invisible presence
wafting through the house.

—Helen McNab

Amazing

My choice Amazing Almighty God,
Whomever chances to read,
This body's origin, sod
An elegant living, breathing seed,
Giver,
Overseer,
Deliverer!
Chooses, Grace with Love, no hazing!

—L.E.T.C. Gray

Old Mr. Taters

Old Mr. Taters lives down the street, he's
out sippin' lemonade in the summer's
heat.
He's a nice old man who likes to walk, but
if you start him goin' he'll talk and talk.
Without one worry in his many days, he
gets whatever he wants and with cash
he pays.
He tells you a story then he tells you once
more, then he guides you out his
screened back door.
He sets you down and then himself, and
he tells you the story of his cousin
Ralph.
By now you're wonderin' when he'll ever
stop, now that poor old man might
someday pop!
He tells you things from way back when,
and comes up the years to nineteen ten.
He talks and talks and never misses a
spot, he goes on talkin' 'bout the things
he got.
His mothers name was Nancy and His
fathers name was Fred, and he keeps
talkin' 'bout his Uncle Ed.
He climbed trees like maple and pine, and
he kept on dancin' 'til a quarter to nine.
Then he ends the day about his Uncle
Pete, that old Mr. Taters just can't be
beat.

—Jill Hendrickson

Once a Child

See the baby as he kicks
He's active, even while sick;
Maintaining an occasional smile,
What a personality,
That of a child,
A small thing to remember
But worthwhile;
They are small only a short season;
Their sweet innocence,
Gone without reason.
Then you wonder;
What happened to that little child;
That I was teasing?

—David M. Hawkins

The Land Hidden Behind Clouds

As clouds part to reveal a mysterious
place
Hidden between time and dimensions,
Our souls begin to travel into a lost land
Forgotten by generations of long ago.
A land where dreams come true and
happiness is found.
Where lovers meet and where peace is
eternal.
Where silence is kept and new life begins.
A place where rainbows are seen with
vivid colors,
That dance like devoted dancers in the
bright, blue sky;
Like different emotions that gather
together, but never disappear.
A place where laughter is endless and
thoughts never end up in an abyss;
And melancholy faces are turned into
smiles.
This is the land hidden behind clouds.

—Alisa Caldwell

Endangered Species

Inside this caring man
His artist's soul burns.
He conveys on canvas
All of life's twists and turns.
With each stroke of his brush —
He brings his subjects to life —
This sensitive lonely man
Who himself has paid the price.
He feels the pain of the catfish
Clutched within the eagle's claws,
But accepts with resignation —
One of life's many flaws.
The alligator watches stealthily —
He is known for not being violent;
But as the panther comes up to drink,
There is a roar — and all is silent.

—Julia Diana Trent

Eve of Hope

The Devil awoke and the world turned grey;
His breath formed a haze around the day.
He stroked his wings and spread his talons,
Preparing to consume blood in gallons.
His shadow carried with it a stench
From his dark and filthy lair. The Devil went
Out to seek his prey. Hell was loose this way.
Where his form fell on the land, grass gave way.
To decay, a mother hides her infant son.
If the Devil finds him, Hell will have won.
The prophets foretold the coming of this child.
The Devil heard also; His rage was wild.
The beast searched daily, but passed over in haste
The babe who'd live to put an end to His waste.

—*Danielle K. Smith*

Preceptor

His robe was stained, His feet were bare
His burden He carried, the thorns in His hair
Some of them mocked Him, others they cried
They watched as they nailed Him, they watched as He died
Some understood, others did not
The light that He carried, the truth that He taught
The truth is still spoken, the light it still shines
But some will not listen, they prefer to be blind
He was here but a short time, and yet for so long
He walked with twelve, and yet walked alone
He showed us the road, He showed us the way
The road was to home, the place we could stay
We await His returning, we watch for a sign
We look to the heavens, and wait for the time.

—*Albert W. Dorsey*

The Monster

There is a monster that roams the earth.
His claws are very sharp. His eyes are green.
His grip is fierce.
His bite is worse than his bark.
Those of us who look upward.
Have seen him so many times.
His prey you see have eyes cast down.
And very little minds.
They cannot see the monster.
They don't know he is there.
They are so busy tearing down.
Blindly they're in his snare.
If we're on guard and try real hard.
The monster though he be.
All around us daily.
His trap, us from are free.

—*Annie L. Wilson*

The Flame

There was a boy whom I used to know,
His eyes would sparkle
My face would glow.
Now that flame has turned to dark,
And left a gap
Deep in my heart.
When the wounds began to heal,
The memories I soon would feel.
The flame that made my heart lift,
Soon would take an awful shift.
Now that flame has turned to dark,
And now my heart has one less spark.

—*Julie Harris*

Are the Seasons a Comparison to Jesus?

The sun shines brightly.
His face glows with happiness.
He holds onto you tightly,
Like the wind with choppiness.
He will give you faith, hope and love,
Like the seasons give you hot, cold, and chilly.
All this from up above,
And this is not silly.
On earth in every land,
These seasons do come.
Just like Jesus doesn't abandon,
Any famous man or bum.
Shall I compare thee to the seasons?
Only for certain reasons!

—*Donna M. White*

The Search

He looked out over the midnight sea,
His gaze intent and wary.
Trembling as he stares, he does not flee,
But he knows he dare not tary.
His jaw is stoney and firmly set.
He is distracted and confused.
His mind is burdened, tangled in net.
He feels alone, trapped, abused.
He reaches for a sword, scabbard-bound,
But none meets his questing grasp.
In his boot a fine dagger is found.
Freed, it makes a steely rasp.
He shivers slightly from chills like death.
He searches both cliff and shore,
For the one who tends to steal his breath,
But she seems to be no more.

—*Alana J. Thorell*

I Dream

He looks like a god,
With his wavy hair
Blowing in the wind,
But he doesn't care.
He runs on the beach,
And plays in the sun,
All day long,
He has so much fun.
I dream of him,
And of us together,
I probably will,
Forever and ever.

—*Shawna Gietzen*

The Golden Quest

His hair blew gently in the wind, the shining deck beneath his feet.
His golden eyes were ever searching into the briny deep.
How long he'd breathed this single thought, only he could guess.
He's lived and breathed for the treasure below,
This was his golden quest.
After 30 years at open sea, he knew at last he'd found
The reason for his very being, where the spanish ship went down.
He held his breath and prepared to dive into the murky depths below,
Adrenalin ran rapid through his veins, his anticipation began to grow.
Years of waiting had not prepared him for the treasure the sea embraced,
His eyes were burning, his lungs on fire, as his heart began to race.
Such a vast amount of gold, no earthly man could measure,
But the sea refused to yield or release her sunken treasure.
They found him with his hair entangled in the golden chest,
At last his search was over,
The sea had claimed her golden quest!

—*Angie Lomax*

The Portrait of a Fine Man

His hair was soft and gray,
His hands were tough and calloused.
His eyes were brown and brewing.
His face was peach and baggy.
His lips were pink and outlined.
His voice was low and mellow.
His hair was sprayed and placed.
His hands were soft and folded.
His eyes were closed and covered.
His face was pink and tight.
His lips were colored and silent,
As for his voice he said nothing.
And for me, I was confused.

—Christal Lahr

It Could Be Someone You Love

His eyes a carnival of hazel lights
His heart the richest gold mine
"The most wanted man" women would say
Yet his faithfulness so divine
Yes, God works in mysterious ways
And my mind is always thriving
Why he took his soul that woeful day
By a man who had been drinking and driving
This is not God's will I say
And it fills me with great appall
That it is not God who has taken his life
But the influence of alcohol
And I would like everyone to understand
As I write tear of mourn streaks my face
For the man behind that wheel can never answer
Who will take my husband's place

—Danielle Wald

Untitled

His eyes had changed,
His lips the same, but all the while I feared.
I hoped and prayed to come this day
A knowledge not too seared.
To know where not the life regained
Could conjure up my plea;
But rules prevailed; I lost and failed
Until they play with me.

—Janice L. Chorvat

Ben, My Enemy And My Friend

There's someone living inside my head
His name is Ben, my enemy and my friend.
He runs around all day and night,
Trying to convince me that I can't think right.
I don't know what Ben's trying to prove,
By making me think that I'm worthless and no good.
Ben says that he's my trusting friend,
But where was he when I needed him.
Ben's always around when I don't.
I wished he'd go away from here,
And leave me the hell alone
I'm feeling kind of funny,
My head is spinning round.
My heart has stopped beating,
And my body has fallen to the ground.
I guess by now you all should know.
That because of drugs, Ben and I had to go. . .

—Karen Odom

The Middle Child

I have an older brother
Who thinks he's like my mother.
I have a younger sister
Who thinks she's Mr. Mister.
I'm stuck in the middle,
I'm not the one who's little,
I'm not the one who's big,
I'm like the newton in a fig.
My mother adores me.

—Michele LaSalle

Faithful Love

Love me like I love you;
Hold me tight next to you;
Kiss me tender in the moonlight;
The kiss that keeps me warm at night;
Please believe my words ever so firmly;
And be honest with those sweet words that you say to me;
Don't promise what you cannot keep;
And don't take our love physically deep;
Don't tell me just what to do
So that I can prove my love to you;
Money cannot buy happiness, as most of us know;
Happiness develops as our love for each other grows;
I will listen to you and what you have to say;
Call me when you need me any time of the night or day;
I will be here for you and I hope you will be here for me;
But we both need time alone to be free;
If you take to heart these words I write to you;
I'm sure, together, we can make it through.

—Becky Loecher

The Kiss

At evening tide we walked
Holding hands knowing else to do.
We had built sand castles, danced,
And gone to the library.
Tentatively we locked our fingers.
Suddenly he put his hands under my arms
And swung me onto a small cement ledge.
I stood higher than him when
He looked at me.
Amber eyes turning to green
With lips parted.
He kissed me.

—Joyce Cameron

Shades of Love

Whe I look into that deep, blue ocean,
Holding red, white and pink roses makes me feel loved and wanted.
After the day is over and done,
I look into that big, black sky full of summer stars and think that there is a reason for life.
And when I see the first star of night,
I make a wish that someone would sit and hold me till the end of time.
When I see the big, white, fluffy clouds,
I see shapes of bears and hearts.
And I say to myself, my heart bears the love of a guy somewhere
And I will love and care for him very much someday.
When I think of the shades of love, I think of you!

—Kristina M. Solt

Alone

A man, blind, begging
Homeless, to wander alone.
No family. Alone, alone
Begging to the tourists.
Begging to the natives.
Starving, alone, alone.
No one but the unknown faces.
They stare, but walk briskly by.
Sleeping in alleys, alone, alone.
A child walks by. Wondering.
Why is that man begging?
A voice whispers. He is alone. Alone.
In her hand, a pretzel just bought.
She hands it to the man and says,
You're not alone.

—Jennifer Harper

Children

Carefree and full of adventure
Honest and sincere
Independent little creatures
Little in body, but oh so dear
Direct and responsive
Rich with love and full of cheer
Energetically full of breath to live
Not expecting more than life can give

—*Gail Webb*

Praying for a Miracle

I've always prayed,
hoped, dreamed, wished
for a miracle all my
life, I've hoped
to be a writer,
but never got there
once I dreamed,
of being a singer,
singing my heart out to
the publish it never
came true.
Then I wished,
I was a model of
high fashion wearing
customs of all style
no way
Now all I do is
pray for a miracle.

—*Bettie Martin Davis*

Forgotten Love

The young girl sits alone on her bed
Hoping that one day
Her love will come back.
He was her world;
Her guiding light.
Now that he's gone,
Her world has shattered.
Her heart has gone numb.
All she can think of is
The time she spent with him.
Tears fill her eyes once again
As she reaches for the cold blade.
She feels nothing as she slices
Away all her problems.
Not even the pain of her now
Forgotten love.

—*Jeni Hendrix*

Everlasting Pain

We had spent the summer together,
Hoping to be in each other's arms forever.
Our hearts seemed to always chime,
But then soon came the time.
The pain inside hurt me so,
And your love for me you couldn't let go.
I could only sit and remember the past,
When you and I thought it would forever last.
Now, when we look in each other's eyes,
We both feel the pain and realize
The day we said goodbye was a mistake,
As we reminicse our hearts will ache.
For as we try to continue our life,
We'll feel this pain through each struggle and strife.

—*Janet Striegel*

Going Out with the Tide

The sand on the beach
hot beneath our feet
As the sun set
The tide began to come in
And washed what was left of us away
Our names etched in the sand
As the tide went back
we gave each other glances
And we both knew what they ment
That all the remained of our love
Went out with the tide.

—*Gail A. Jewett*

Daddy I Love You

How do you know,
How can I show,
That you're the best Daddy
In the whole wide world?
You wiped my tears when I was sad,
And spanked my "hinney" when I was bad,
And for that I will always love you.
When mom and you split apart
You left my little heart to break,
And when you began to pack up
All your stuff to leave, me you didn't take,
But finally being the kind of Daddy you were
You told me you'd love me wherever you and me were.
My Dad is a wonderful person who I will always look up to,
So I'd just like to say, "Daddy I really love you!"

—*Deeana Webb*

Baby

I watch you grow up,
How can you grow up so fast?
I watch you play by day and night,
I have grown fond of you.
When I hear your laughter, you
make me happy. You are a
joy to be around, you showed
me how to love you so much.
How can't I not love you?
I know one day, you will
grow up to be a young lady.
May you grow with kindness,
willing to help others, respect,
dignity, and pride in yourself.

—*Kelly Luicelle Smith*

Untitled

Cry and you shall see
How it feels to be me;
I like to dress like a clown
But inside I'm wearing a frown;
I like to snicker an sneer
But I'm really shedding a tear;
I like to run and play
But I can never stay;
Now that you know about me
Please just let me be.

—*Kristin Merz*

Hopefully

How many men must die
How many eyes must cry
Before gunfire stops
Before bombs no longer drop.
How long before people open their eyes
And begin to realize
That fighting doesn't bring gain
It only causes suffering and pain.
One day the world will come to an end
And it will be impossible to mend
The destruction that our greed caused
To stop humans and their private laws.
Hopefully, the day will come
When children can play and have fun
But only if we stop our hate
Before it sends us all to the white (or red) gate.

—*Jennifer Bewley*

Frustrations

How many hearts must be broken.
How many tears must be shed.
How many dreams must be shattered.
What has ever happened to my sea
Of vast open hopes.
Nevertheless life goes on.

—*Gina DiGrazia*

Life's Delusions

How green the grass on the other side,
How still the sea at eventide,
How bright the sun when you're in the
   shade,
How dry the desert, far from the glade,
How grand it all looks through a looking
   glass,
How dull pewter seems next to brass,
How tiny each soul in God's great plan,
How large a rock next to a grain of sand,
How great your life was when you die,
How lovely a life, how soft Time's sigh.

—*Chrissy Radice*

Grandma Lois and her Sweet Potato Pie

Lord have mercy, it's Thanksgiving Eve
   and Grandma Lois is in the kitchen
Humming to an old Negro Spiritual,
   getting ready to make her traditional
   Sweet Potato Pie
Using that strong left hand of hers
   whipping, stirring, then whipping again
Here I am watching from around the
   corner of the kitchen entrance
She is so involved in her creation that she
   has not noticed me yet
But that's alright Grandma Lois, whip
   those sweet potatoes
While using all that elbow energy her eye
   glasses begin to slide down,
She pushes them back up with the back of
   her hand and continues her creation.
One by one, in go the eggs, brown sugar,
   white sugar, butter, vanilla flavoring,
   lemon extract,
And what do I see? A little dash of salt,
   some cinammon, nutmeg and more
   nutmeg.
There goes that strong left hand again
   whipping, and stirring
Lord have mercy, she put a little of the
   batter in the palm of her hand and
   tastes it,
She adds a little more sugar and vanilla
   flavoring, go on Grandma, do your
   thing!
She brings the mix to the kitchen counter
   now what is she doing?
Oh, I see, the pie crust she made already,
   here comes your filling!
In the oven goes the pie, Grandma finally
   sits down, pulls up her house dress to
   the knee,
Leans forward, folds her hands, rocks
   slowly, continually humming to that
   Old Negro Spiritual
Oh yes, I will neve forget Grandma Lois
   and her Sweet Potato Pie

—*Jonathon Crawford Jr.*

Nemesis

I am a soldier
hurling the enemy back
with reckless courage,
heedless of danger.
I am a prophet
cursed with vision
doing all that I can
to prevent disaster.
I am Cassandra,
ignored, tired of
my own predictions,
waiting only for
an end to hostilities.

—*Kathleen DeMeo*

Prayers

When I go to sleep at night
I always remember to turn out the light
Then I kneel down by my bed
Fold my hands and bow my head
I then say a prayer to the one above
And when I say it I send lots of love
For the Lord is my shepherd
For I am his sheep
He will guard me and guide me
While I am asleep

—*Becky Lynne Peek*

Hold the Power of Your Dreams

Those quiet peaceful nights,
I always spend alone.
Watching the stars
Shining above the gentle waters—
Holding mystery to all those
Who search for one wish to come true.
Yet dreams may not be granted,
When wished upon the stars.
Your dreams come true
If you hold the power,
And have the desire
To unlock your heart and soul.

—*Brenda Weitzer*

Drowning

I stand on the shore barefoot as the wind
   blows away its chilling anger.
I am alone, like always as I stand looking
   toward my God, my salvation, the
   ocean.
It's water with a dark blue smile and
   foamy white tentacles, taunt me, tempt
   me
Dare me to become a part of it.
Without hesitation, I accept the offer
   smiling.
The seagulls cry out a warning, an
   unheeded warning to my deaf ears.
For the ocean's beauty is more satisfying
   than life.
I give in and sucumb to the water pleads.
It first devours my legs, then my
   shoulders, and very soon. . .
My entire soul.

—*Elizabeth Cadena*

Prison

As the moon starts it's path across the
   zodiac
I am imprisoned once again
in a cell called night
guilty of being alone.
No sleep will some for me tonight
because it's like any other night
bitter words flow
from a broken heart.
As I walk down the hall
as condemned man
to my final execution
I seach for a pardon called love.

—*C. P. Micheal*

Life of an Alcoholic

It's eight a.m. and time for a beer.
I am invincible; I have nothing to fear.
I drink until I pass out.
I'll drink forever, I have no doubt.
I sometimes get angry and scream and
   yell,
I make everyone's life a living hell!
I drink all day and drink all night.
It doesn't matter, I'll be alright.
I try to tell myself that everyday.
The truth is, I will soon pay.
I'll have another drink to forget the past.
I'll close my eyes, because this drink's my
   last.

—*Karen Kilbarger*

Temptation

I am darkness,
I am light,
I'm the stars that shine so bright,
I am wind,
And I am rain,
I'm the healer of your pain,
I am sadness,
I am cheer,
I'm the evil that you fear,
I am death,
And I am life,
I'm the blood that stains your knife,
I am heaven,
I am hell,
I'm the dark in the wishing well,
I'm the power
You desire,
Follow me into the fire.

—*Edie Marshall*

Opening Night

Standing in the wings; stage right,
I am masking.
Stagefright appears,
Act curtain rises.
Stepping past the proscenium
Downstage onto the apron,
My nervousness is gone.
Performing to the house,
I feel at ease,
Not even noticing
As drops fly-in and out,
And actors enter and exit.
The theatre and I are one,
And one we remain,
Until the final curtain falls,
Leaving me to deal with reality.
I become uneasy again,
And sit in the wings; stage right,
Waiting for the next performance.

—*Audrey Braun*

The Visit

Why are you here so soon?
I am not nearly ready.
I've still so much to do,
So many more things to see.
There are plans I put off;
I cannot go with you yet.
Time has been far too short,
Is this really all I get?
You get just what you make,
Of the time you are allowed;
Waste it, you still lose it,
But don't feel bad, join the crowd.
You've spent your life planning,
As so many of you do,
Then ask that same question,
"Oh, why couldn't I have two?"

—*Gail Ferrier*

Especially for You Dad

You'll never know just how glad,
I am that you were chosen as my Dad.
As I was growing through the years,
You helped to wipe away my tears.
You taught me love, respect and trust,
Through everyday life this was a must.
You were there as often as you could be,
To help mend whatever the problem
  might be.
You had a firm hand when there was a
  need,
Most of the time you would just plead.
My childhood memories are good to look
  back on,
Because I had you to rely and depend on.
The right words on a card I could not find,
So I've written some down from my own
  mind.
On this day that belongs to you,
I hope many of your wishes come true.
You taught me a lot through the years,
That's the reason Dad, you're so dear.
As I end this I will say. . .
I wish you a Very Happy Birthday!

—*Gayle Wright*

Creation of Destiny

I alone, am my destiny.
I am the creator, and the creation.
I have made myself.
Modeled not by one,
Nor after one.
I will decide my wealth
For I am my wealth.
I will decide my happiness
For I am my happiness.
I will decide my future,
For I am my future.
In my mind's eye,
I see myself;
My life; created.
The Creator, my life.
I am what I become,
And I become what I am.
I, alone, am my destiny.

—*Ann Newton*

I Am

I am the water deep and blue.
I am the fish swimming beneath the glass.
I am the sand beneath your feet.
I am the castles the children once built.
I am the rocks upon the lovers sit.
I am the sun slowly sinking.
I am the sky deepening with night.
I am the stars guiding the way.
I am the moon pushing away day.
I am.

—*Jennifer Sharp*

Serenity

"What do you want"? asked me of I.
I answered only with a sigh,
Then thoughtfully I said to me,
"I think I want serenity."
"But, oh, do you not know"
"That one thing can be so".
"It's not there",
"Or anywhere",
"But here—for you to see"
"If you will let it be".
"Just let your heart perceive it",
"And let your being receive it";
"Then from within", said me to I,
"Sweet peace can come without a cry".

—*Bett Knight*

Never Give Up

All have sat thinking about one certain
  guy,
Why we're too afraid to talk, why we're
  way too shy.
All know how it is, we've all had those
  days,
Sometimes we wish it would just go away.
Some say it's a crush, some say love,
But whatever it is, they surely know
  above.
If only they'd tell us, just give us a clue,
Maybe then we wouldn't have to feel so
  blue.
Love doesn't have a one word meaning,
  nor a long definition.
But looking for one is certainly a
  tradition.
Some who seek will search for the rest of
  their lives,
Asking, "why me" with tears of pain in
  their eyes.
But some who seek will find their gold,
Loving their treasure with an everlasting
  hold.
Never give up because of one loss,
There's someone out there promised by
  the boss.

—*S. Matteson*

Blindness

Darkness surrounds me everywhere I go
I ask a stranger for a dime, but they say
  no
I walk around aimlessly, looking for the
  light
Oh God what I would give just for my
  sight
A little while ago, I was free
Free to walk around, free to see
Now my greatest gift was taken away
And I pray to get my gift back every day

—*Christine Good*

A Cry for Help

As I look around, I see faces of the elderly time,
I ask myself, what if I become like this, and I haven't got a dime.
Who would care for me or tend my need? and have the time to spare.
At this present time, I am lucky, and I am fully duty bound, and aware,
I see the Elderly in their wheelchairs, against the corridor wal.
And at times a cry for help upon my ears befall,
Youth is so precious and we never think of getting old,
And wonder what we would do, if shut out in the cold.
Visitors are seldom seen, as no one has the time to spare,
Each one floats by and usually are not aware.
Home is where the heart is and a place to talk.
Dark corridors are here and this is where they walk.
Days pass by so slow and minds are not the best,
It's only when at night and darkness fills the room, that time means rest.
God hears their cry for help and loving hands rest on each one,
And peace for chosen ones, will come, when day is done.

—*Joyce Willis*

Autumn Sonnet

In the brown crispness of Autumn
I breath the air of coldness in,
And grieve not loss of summer sun,
But anticipate biting winds
That chap my cheeks. Bare branches sway
And stretch toward the sullen sky,
While bitter chill forestalls decay
Of love for life. I'd ne'er deny
Myself walks down winding pathways,
Where I'd turn the leaves that landed
White-side-up in gutters and gaze
On dry hues that time demanded.
May none discern which is pretense,
And which is breath of innocence.

—*Keltcie D. Shields*

Forever

As I look into the clear blue sky,
I brush a tiny tear from my eye.
Thinking about all the things that have been,
Hoping that I'll get the chance to be free again.
Reliving all those wonderful moments from my past,
Realizing now they never last.
So when I look into that clear blue sky,
Dreaming of the days gone by,
Wondering what life has in store,
Wishing happiness was forever more.

—*Amy Jensen*

Help

Help, help,
I call to thee!
Help, help,
Please help me!
I love you true,
Don't make me blue!
Help, help,
Help, help!
I cry out at night,
"Help, help"!
When I think of our fight
Help, please, help!

—*Holly Coppler*

Without You

I see your face,
I call your name,
I feel so sad inside,
You can't feel the pain.
I cry myself to sleep,
Dreams of you come and go.
You're never coming back,
I've realized that
Still I'll never stop loving you.

—*Barbara Neece*

The Dream Man

While walking down the road,
I came across a waterfall.
And there he sat,
The man of my dreams.
He came to take me away,
From all the pain.
Away we went up in the clouds.
Higher than birds can fly.
Never to return until death came.
To take us away.

—*Brandi McCraine*

Night Growth

As the night grows closer now,
I can feel my body fighting.
You don't know when or how,
But there's no escape, there is no hiding.
As the darkness flows through you,
You get frightened and rebel.
Your soul will be gone soon,
And you won't live to tell.

—*Amber Robertson*

As. . .

As winter turns to summer
I can feel the change.
But as spring turns to fall
I can feel the difference.
As the seasons turn, so do
The leaves, the ground, the
World, and so do I.

—*Gina Fulks*

Canon

In this small, darkened room
I can feel the fire
Making love to the smoke-filled chimney.
Man and Woman see each other
But Shame receives no thought.
And seconds away and seconds close
He raises his eyes and beckons
Me to Him, and I go into his embrace
Willingly and yet still tormented. . .
And His eyes never stray from mine,.
So I'm burning, Lost in His Fire.
And soft words spoken in silence,
He understands and feels the same.
So we marry one another. . .
By ourselves,
In our hearts,
In one second,
For a million eternities. . .

—*Brigitta*

Good-bye To A Friend

As I walk in the woods,
I can feel the warm air.
And all I think about is
If I could,
I would have helped.
If you would have talked,
I would have listened.
But you didn't speak,
So I didn't hear.
Now it's to late for you.
I wish you didn't have to leave,
But God loves you more.
So I must say goodbye, but I
will never forget you.

—*Katie Horowitz*

Untitled

Now while we're here alone, and all is
    said and done,
I can let you know
Because of all you've shown.
I've grown enough to tell you,
You'll always be inside of me.
How many roads have gone by?
So many words left. . .unspoken.
I needed to be by your side.
If only to hold you. . .forever.
In my heart. . .forever.
You will be, and even when I'm gone,
You'll be here with me. . .forever.
Once I dreamed that you were gone.
I cried out trying to find you.
I begged the dream to fade,
But all that answered were memories
Memories of you and me.
I dreamt it would last. . .forever.

—Barb Miller

Clouds

Looking up at the clouds,
I can see many different
Shapes and Forms.
For the clouds, purity and
Whiteness, and the blue sky
that surrounds them is the
true beauty of the sky.
Clouds can have meanings,
and hope, and just looking
up at them you get a
warm feeling of peace and joy.
Knowing that the clouds
can sheild us from the
world's frustration, is the
warmest peace of all.

—Cathy Vallandingham

Teddy Bear

Teddy Bear he's always there,
I can tell my secrets and dreams to him,
Teddy Bear he really does care,
He listens and never yells,
Teddy Bear he's soft and cuddly,
And I love to hug him,
He shares all my life,
Trials and tributes days and nights,
He's never frightened,
And never cries,
And when I'm sad my Teddy Bear
Is there to care about me!

—Dreama Holcomb

Best Friends

If you picture the things that are here 'til
    the end,
I can think of only one-a true best friend.
They are always there when you need a
    hug,
They're not to be looked down or used as a
    rug.
When your life seems over and the road's
    not bright,
Count on that friend to make your life
    right.
When you come to a crossroad and turn
    the wrong way,
They come along, take your hand and
    know just what to say.
You'll get that phone call in that rainy
    storm,
You find out what's wrong then hold them
    'til they're warm.
It's someone you talk to late in the night,
About religion and death, they make it all
    right.
Some friends come and some friends go,
But best friends stay through the high and
    low.
When we get the warning that the world's
    gonna end,
You'll find me with the best, my best
    friend.

—Claudette LeBlanc

Wild

Crashes on the harsh, brown
White gold specks of sand.
Bright in light but dark upon night,
White breakers on its shore.
It roars with lightning,
But water hums with care.
As creatures of unknown and known,
To life is a spectacular knowledge
Of the inner soul.
The ocean is a superb being
Of God.

—Marlo Mercer

Facing The Truth

What isn't mine;
I cannot hold.
All of my feelings,
remain untold.
No more of those special nights;
or no more arms to hold you tight.
Is the way I feel, wrong or right?
There will always be,
that non-winning game.
You can't just throw love away,
things like that won't ever change.
Not to believe, is not to care,
But when you know the truth,
you realize life just isn't fair.
You still have those feelings,
of being loved for so long,
Someday you'll see;
your love was all wrong.

—Keirsten Sorensen

Sea of Life

I'm drowning, save me from this cold
    world.
I cannot seem to catch my breath.
Please give me your hand and pull me out
    from all my sadness.
All that will be left is my madness.
Will anyone notice I'm gone, help me
    someone.
I'm not mentally strong.
Let these waes wash away my pain.
I have nothing anymore to lose or
    anything to gain.
I'm losing my mind, it's going under fast.
Too fast for me to catch.
In these cold waters of life I'm searching
    for a stable mind
That is the only thing I cannot find.
The waves of sorrow keep on pulling me
    under.
So very far under I can't see my way.
I do not think I can survive another
    painful day.
Help me someone, somebody.
Can't you hear me calling you for help.
Listen, now, before I'm nothing in this
    insane sea of life
Life is pulling me under, so far under, I
    can't pull free.
Someone anyone before I'm no one save
    me.

—Ericka Tauriello

The Clock of Time

Tick, tock, tick, tock
Why doesn't it ever stop,
The constant battle we must unlock,
While the handles drop,
The pace, the race of the hour no more,
Our eyes are blinded by a haze,
Father time pointing his finger through a
    door,
We must open our eyes from the maze
    and cut the haze,
Befor we are no more,
Using our time wise,
Before we step in that door,
As if we were to demise,
Tick, tock, tick, tock
Why doesn't it ever stop?

—Margaret Jensen

Sailing

I love to sail the open sea
I can't describe what it does to me.
The sea by day is pure delight
And even more beautiful in dark of night.
Blue skies, white sails
Gleaming chrome, shining rails.
A boat to me is a gift from above
And no gift could I more love.
I feel at home when I'm riding the tide
In a setting sunset I take much pride.
I believe I was born to sail the waves
For these memories I will forever save.

—Kanda Rae Foster

On and On

I'm crying out for help but no one seems to hear.
I close my eyes and down falls a single blue tear.
My heart and mind plead a silent cry,
Ever so slowly my heart will die.
I scream but you choose to ignore me.
If you don't look, who will see?
I'm trying desperately to end the pain,
But when it leaves it comes again.
The days of pain are getting too long,
Happiness has never felt so wrong.
One day I hope my pain is gone,
But for now the hurting goes on and on.

—Bonnie Vandervelde

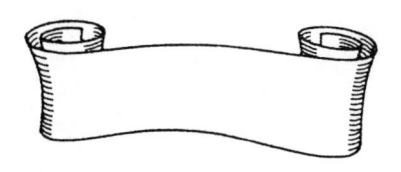

Why Not Me?

I look at you, you look away
I come to you, you never stay.
When I speak, you never listen
My eyes are cold, your eyes glisten.
When I look up, you look down
Although you smile, I always frown.
I wonder why, you wonder when
I say later, you say then.
When all's said, and all is done
I guess I'll say, you finally won.
But in my mind, I still don't see
Why you chose her instead of me.

—Heather Pruitt

The Whispering Rain

As the rain fell whispering through the trees,
I could feel the gentleness of your touch,
Yet the urgency of your need.
I cried out to you,
But you never heard the sound.
You just went your own way,
As my heart began to pound.
Now I'm hurt forever,
But still I hear the rain;
Whispering to me in my sorrow and my pain.

—Joellen Meckley

The Unforgotten One

The sound of war always scared you,
I could never understand why you went,
You said there was nothing better to do
But why throw away the time you've spent?
I knew you were scared when you arrived.
But you wrote to us saying it was great
I couldn't believe that you had survived
When the air was filled with screams of hate.
Who were we at home to truly know
The garb of death was assuming color brown
For you, and only you; life was slow.
Our distant dreams of togetherness did drown.
Will there be a time to see you again, dear brother.
Or must we wait until that solemn day for one another?

—Giovanna Macaluso

My Addiction

I awake
I crave my drug
Need my fix
Hopelessly devoted to this life,
This utopia
I'm high on you.

—Heather Fettweis

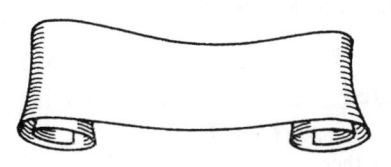

Lament To Love

I'm depressed and sad and lonely,
I cry my love for you dear only,
I scream your name it's gone in the breeze.
Love I will remember you forever in my heart,
Soon we will be together never more to be apart.

—Kara Turner

You're Cute

Each and every time I look at you
I daydream you walking toward me
Embracing me in your arms and saying
I know how you feel and the feelings are mutual
Then you kiss me lightly
I imagine me saying I've waited so long
I imagine us sharing our dreams
Laughing together, loving together
I imagine me not being shy anymore
Breaking out of my shell and telling you
All the feelings I've kept hidden inside
You say you knew it but were shy just the same
But something broke into my dream
I came down to earth
To catch myself staring at you
I get embarrassed-oh shoot!
And all I can think to say is you're cute!

—Deanna Sarver

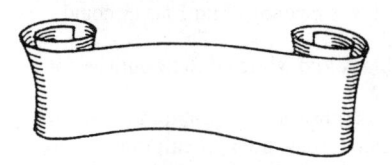

Change of Mind

Just when you thought that I loved you
I decided to find somebody new
Although I loved you I treated you bad
I respect you because you didn't get mad
I do think that you really are sweet
And in the long run I'm glad we did meet
As much as I thought I was gonna break up
I loved you too much to give you up
To break up with you it would have been mean
I now know that's something I should have seen
All because you've been so kind
I have had a change of mind.

—Holly M. Davis

The Betrayal

I did not mean to betray you
I did not know that I could move
Another so much in betraying you
I have betrayed myself
If I could take back what I've done
A thousand times wouldn't be enough.
Stangely revealed in the silent night
What I gave couldn't be touched
What couldn't be opened
Was the deepest recesses of my soul.
At night when I dream,
His hands are dead, his mouth cold.

—Karen Gaskins

Glorious Sunrise

As the day approaches,
I do hope to wake from bed.
To see the glorious sunrise
beaming over my head.
I will see the wheat fields glowing,
with their stalks rising to the sky.
And the narrow creek flowing,
with its waters rising high.
My eyes will be astonished,
at such a glorious scene.
While my heart will be pounding,
with my soul feeling serene.
I will quickly walk from my bed,
out onto my porch.
To see the world waking,
by a golden fiery torch.

—Elyse Salzman

When I was a Young Child

When I was a young child I never could
  see,
Why black and white adults would seldom
  agree.
Why racial injustice just had to be,
With slanderous intent of calumny.
Why people of all nations could not be
  free,
To live out their lives in close harmony,
Choosing a lifestyle, that's passive, like
  me.
When I was a young child I never knew
  why,
We engaged in wars so that people would
  die.
Where friends came together with family
  to cry,
As news of dead loved ones brought tears
  to the eye.
In this twist of mourning there overhead
  lie,
White billowy clouds in a calm azure sky.
Will it make a difference as time passes
  by?

—Ruth Naomi Nielsen

Transcend to the Pearl

I wish to share with you a gift
I do not call my own.
I spied a pearl through a narrow rift,
The faraway feild unknown.
I feared the pearl would vanish away,
If my eyes should linger;
But I felt as I wandered astray,
The touch of the spirit's finger.
Every night I approach the fissure
Where I gaze upon the pearl.
I pray upon the glowing treasure,
My zealous soul unfurls.
During these fleeting moments of peace
My joyful spirit will fly.
Beyond the stars and mountain peaks
The pearl draws me nigh.

—Amy Dull

On My Mountain

On my mountain, high up in a hidden
  place in the distant sky,
I do whatever I will and it is such a
  wonderful thrill
For me to sometimes be a red bird
  flapping my wings as I fly.
Through the tops of the trees and clouds
  so high or drill,
For my supper deep into the sun—baked
  ground or go wondering,
Soaring, floating up, up into the air, as
  does the worker bee
As it pollinates the flowers then stops a
  while to rest its wing
Upon the tiniest limb on the bottom
  branch of a mulberry tree;
I do whatever I will and it is such a
  wonderful thrill
Just to walk along a flowery path or to
  simply float above
The roses and the marigolds until, quietly,
  I stop to mill
About for a little while and contemplate
  the fulfillingness of love;
All the friends and things I need and
  want, I have right now
And each one, regardless of the form it
  takes, is my faithful pal.

—Elizabeth Bowers

True Perspective

It has come to my attention
With some little apprehension
That things are just not
What I was taught
Nor, are what they appear to be.
I shall try to remember,
How was it stated?
Or was it equated?
And though a few are elective
I believe the true perspective
Will show that,
You have to plant the seed
Before you can grow the tree.

—Robert G. Richardson

Untitled

You don't understand
I don't either
But please don't be mad
Because you'll never see her
Remember all the good times
And forget the bad
Life will go on
It won't stop
Even though she's gone
She'll live forever
In my heart
Always together
Never apart
I know it's hard
Because it's hard on me too.

—Elizabeth Cole

Let the Light Shine Through

So many changes in my life
I don't know where to turn
Should I run or hide from the lies
Or should I leave them as they are
They say to confront my fears
Let the light shine through
No more dark past should lay ahead
Though more may come through the tears
Let the light shine through
For the world to see
We need to feel the warmth
Can't you see?
Let the light shine through.

—Christine Andriekus

His Name

I want to know his name.
I don't want to play this game;
It goes on inside my head,
Oh, the tears I shed.
I know if I would know his name
That what we could share the same.
I'm sure the feeling
I feel is not in vain.
Who is this mystery man?
Will he ever speak his name?

—Charity Geebaman

Dreams

I close my eyes and dream.
I dream some dreams that will never come
  true.
I dream some that are so crazy they could
  never be true.
And some dreams aren't crazy, but
  something that could
come true, but never do.
And the dreams that could come true are
  about you, but
they never come true, either.
But some dreams that come true happen
  to fast, or come
to fast, or to slow; such as, the end.
So I hope some of your wonderful dreams
  do come true;
the end of
or just the end...

—Cheryl Meyer

Untitled

Each night I wish upon a star
I dream that forever you would stay
To each other friends is what we are
Yet I feel you are so far away.
I long to feel your arms around me
Your lips pressed against my own
I've fallen in love with you, can't you see
For your embrace welcomed me like home.
Your caress sends tingles through my spine
These feelings I have only with you
I wish, dream, and pray that you were mine
Then maybe you would love me too.
Until I met you, my life was in a hole
My spirits had been cut like a knife
You brought a breath of fresh air into my soul
And filled my heart with new life.

—*Ana C. Dinis*

What Your Love Means to Me

I need you. I want you. I love you so much.
You don't understand your touch means so much.
We laugh. We cry. We run, and we play.
I love the way our love grows each day.
You understand, and you care
You give and you share.
When you kiss me I close my eyes tight.
So tight there's no trace of light.
Listen to me. . .my life is just you
Your love, concern, and givingness too.
All my happiness I have I share with you.
I can't believe I love you as much as I do.

—*Lori Randels*

A Dream of Value to Life

One day I had a dream of being someone special.
I dreamed of being someone wealthy and famous
With lots of friends and admirers.
I dreamed of ordering people to do things I wanted them to do.
And most of all, I dreamed of being able to do what I wanted to do.
My dream of being someone special has finally come true.
To my surprise, my dream was being myself,
For I know myself better than any other person.
I know now that I have always been rich;
Rich in love, hope, friends, and most of all in the Lord.
I pray that everyone else does see the way to being someone special,
By being themselves.

—*Jaime D. Garza*

For Andrea

I pass a girl with long blonde hair,
I falter, I imagine, I think it's you,
but soon the reality reaches my mind,
I sadden, and miss you, then carry on. . .
. . .carry on with my own life,
with my own thoughts—
Thoughts of you so far away.
Yes, I carry on, but always without you—
For now.
For now I know, in weeks, or months, or maybe years.
we'll be together again.
Not like we were,
but just to be with you,
to share time with you,
even to see you,
these thoughts for the future are enough
For now.
For me.

—*Jane Elizabeth*

A Night Walk

As I am walking alone at night,
I feel a certain little fright.
For all around me all I see,
Are the nightly shadows of the trees.
As the wind disturbs the quiet leaves,
A rustling comes with a silent breeze.
I shiver inside with some kind of fright,
As I slowly walk along on a calm, autumn night.

—*Alycia W. Johnson*

Untitled

My sadness is empty.
I feel a dull continuous pain in my heart.
It is difficult for me to breathe.
For my breath is stopped by the lump in my throat.
It is testing my strength to hold back the tears.
The tears of loss, anger and love.
Then my shell is cracked, my happy front.
All because you are with her. I see you.
My knees are weak, my breath is faster.
The lump explodes and the tears spill out, hot upon my cheeks.
Look at me, See me crying?
You drop her hand as I turn away.
You call my name, I cling to the nearest and walk quickly away,
till I fall dead into those arms and sob.
I know it is over.
Thank-you for the times together
Let's not be friends.

—*Aimee Wedlake*

The Beach

When I go to the beach
I feel as relaxed as can be,
As I look at the waves
And the beautiful sea.
I watch the different people
Going for walks on the shore,
And the beautiful seagulls
I will remember forevermore.
As I pick up sand
And gaze at the ocean,
I will always remember
Those good times in motion.
I love the beach
As you can see,
Only because of the great
Memories its given me.

—*Beth M. Pignataro*

The Day After. . .

As I walk along the beach
I feel every cool grain of sand beneath my feet
As the wind blows softly, little more than a breeze
A tear escapes and I fall to my knees. . .
Wishing my feelings could blow away
Leaving my heart without a single trace
But it's wounded and slowly healing
Leaving my heart with a scar
That is deep and mending

—*Ginger Bairow*

Myself A Flower

When I feel good,
I feel like a daffodil or lilac,
When I feel bad,
I feel like a wilted or stepped on flower
I like it when the rabbit nudges me
And I like to watch horses
Running in the fields
But I hate the bee's sting
Sometimes my mind fades away
Like a flower in winter
But it grows back
Like a flower in spring
I am special because
I hold many colors
Myself a flower

—*Heather Hendrickson*

She's Gone Away

Staring blankly up at the sky
I feel much sorrow and start to cry
My tears began to flood my face
It's just like running but there's no race.
I love my Momma deep and so
But she's been taken by our loving crow.
Is she gone for real or could it be a lie?
Why did she leave me, could you please tell me why?
I tried my best to heal, could I have been such a disgrace?
But now she's gone, leaving me here without a word of trace.
Why did she leave me? I will never know.
But where ever she is, someday I will go.

—Anna Armendariz

Devotion

What can I do to prove my devotion
I feel so helpless
Like I'm drowning in a sea of emotion
I can only guess
That you feel the same
Set your heart free
And let it play the game
Give it a chance and you will see
A love can last
More than one day
Why live in the past
When there's so much more to say
A true love can last forever
It's only a whisper away
Blowing in the breeze forever and ever
And it never will fade away.

—Alicia Monique Sayers

When

When I think of you
I feel the ocean blue.
When we are apart
I hope someday you will
Mend my broken heart.
When I think of the
Beauty of your brown eyes,
I remember we have
No true ties.
When I think I know all about you,
You bring upon a new clue.
When I think of you. . .

—Abby Mackin

The Cry OF The Dove

When I look deep into your eyes,
I feel nothing but pleasure inside.
The words I love you mean so much,
to feel the gentleness of your tender touch.
The cry of the dove is what I give to you,
it's the symbol of my love,
and the wishes you've made come true.
I guess what I'm trying to say,
is that I love you in so many different ways.
But if there's ever a doubt,
or things just don't work out
Remember what I had to give and all my love.
and if you never remember anything at all,
you'll never forget The Cry of the Dove.

—Christine Westcott

Night Images

As I lay my head down on my pilllow,
I feel the darkness filter in around me.
Closing my eyes, I picture him standing before me,
Tall, dark, and powerful.
His eyes bore into mine as we exchange words through our gaze.
It's magical what we feel for each other.
It's as though we have our own little world
In which people around us cannot enter,
It's a forbidden trespass.
Opening my eyes I can no longer see him
But I feel his presence all around me,
Protecting me from horror of the night,
And promising we will be together very soon.
It's only with this knowledge I am able to sleep!
With his features etched in my mind,
And his voice ringing in my ears.

—Kristal Hein

I Wonder Why

I don't know why
I feel this way
Something inside me
Says it's o.k.
Should I let you know
The way I feel
Or should I let it go
As if it's unreal.
Maybe it's the hug
I give with grace:
Or the smile that
Comes across my face.
I'm secretly hoping
With all my might
That we'll be
Together
Maybe;
Some night.

—Christy Meyer

The Stranger

As I walk these lonely streets beside him,
I feel safe, warm and confident,
I don't feel like this with anyone else,
The streets are dark and lurking with shadows,
But I have no fear for he is by my side,
Nothing or no one can harm me,
I'm safe in his strong loving arms,
For I know he will always be there,
His name I cannot give for I know not his name

—Dawna Dutchy

Serene Passage

As I walk along a man-made path,
I feel the gentle breeze blow past me.
I hold my head in an upright pose,
And feel the warmth of the sun against my body.
I admire these fair days,
When I feel the whole world is peaceful and calm.

—Kimberly Timpany

All About the Soap Operas

As the world turns,
I fell of the edge of night.
They took me to General Hospital;
The doctor said I had one life to live.
I gave my hope to all my children
And my boyfriend Ryan's hope.

—Adelle Allen

Going Separate Ways

You were together and I was with you all
   the way.
I felt as if I wasn't wanted, so I didn't
   stay.
I left you there with him that day;
I was all alone with nothing to say.
I knew, while I was there, I didn't belong.
I felt like an interfering tag-along.
So how come everything I do is wrong?
It just seems like it has been so long.
We used to do everything in the world
   together,
Through good, bad, and any weather.
You float along just like a feather,
And we have no time to be together.

—Amy Davis

Personification of Nature

One morning, I walked in a soft meadow
I felt at peace with grassy arms sweeping
   my feet
I looked up
The sun smiled at me
It's lanquid tongues of light
Shone on my hair
I looked around
The birds sang their lovely melodies for
   me
Memories of my life flashed before me
I felt at peace, yet so all alone
Even with my best friends around me

—Diana ThiHuyen Duong

I Find You

When I look into our eyes, I find you.
I find a man terrified of loving.
I find a man camouflaging his frailty.
I find a man perplexed about self.
I find a man questioning the elements of
   time.
I find a man I love, nonetheless.
I find you!

—Deborah A. Morrisette

See What I See

When I look at the rolling hills
I find it hard to believe,
That somewhere there are problems,
That somewhere people grieve.
When I look at the summer sky
It all seems so untrue,
That people abuse their children,
And wives get battered too.
When I look at the waving fields
It all seems so unreal.
That hostile countries fight each other,
And starving people beg for just one meal.
If people could see what I see,
World problems would be so few,
If only people could understand,
That we must try to stop it too.

—Jocelyn Lock

Walking Alone

As I walk alone today
I find myself changing—
But to what? I don't know!
When I walk alone tomorrow
I'll try to uncover the mystery—
But if I can't then I'll persist!
For if I don't find the solution
I'll spend my todays and tomorrows
Walking alone and yet, I, I will
Continue to change and I, I
Won't know why?

—Jeanine Perez

Mental Mirror

As I look through the glass,
I find no struggle
To see the flaws
Reflected through the light.
I walk through my mirror
Questioning the mentalities
Within me,
Searching for answers
To satisfy the soul.
And so my struggle ends,
For I searched
And I found
The imperfections revealed to me.

—Kendra Di Pasqua

Never

Why have you shattered the brittle
   window that is my world?
I gave you my love, my trust, myself as a
   whole.
Yet you cast a stone into my sacred soul,
Breaking my cherished memories of life.
I allowed you to enter my secret island of
   crystal dreams,
But you insisted on crushing my hopes,
   my joys.
I no longer see that prism of colors across
   the glassy sky;
But a shadow of gloom clouding the
   marbled earth.
While you still have some hope of finding
   that beloved
Treasure in the starry night sky,
I've lost all sight of it.
My heart has been broken, not lifted, by
   that piercing golden arrow;
And all warmth is gone from my lips.
But always remember, dear love,
Never will I forget thee. . .
Never.

—Kelly Marie Dickman

My Secret

Whenever I see you or look in your eyes,
I get a funny feeling deep down inside.
I know I can't tell you how I feel
Because it may sound a little unreal.
My love for you cannot be known
For if it was my secret would be blown.
So until I know you love me too,
My love cannot be known to you.

—Deanne Dzikowski

Cries In The Night

Whenever we're apart
I get that empty feeling
Deep down in my heart.
Walking barefoot on the beach
As the moon comes around,
The cry from the birds is a beautiful
   sound.
I will never let you go
And wander the earth
that we see below.
The times we have had together
Will go on forever.
There has been times when we've both
   lied
But we try to hold back
The tears from inside.
There will be times when we fight
And you may hear
My Cries In The Night.

—Jennifer Danioth

I Love You

I really never told you,
I guess I didn't know how.
My love for you I never told,
So I guess the time is now.
I think of the great times
As we go on through the years.
Sometimes I wonder what it
Would've been like
If you were never here.
I've grown up a bit
And I know how much I care,
Grandpa, I love you now and always,
And I know you'll always be there.

—Jenny L. Parsons

The Secret

When I was about six,
I had something done that couldn't be
   fixed.
I didn't know what to do,
But I had to tell someone soon.
There I laid on my bed,
Thinking about what could be said.
I told my sister Sue,
But she thought it was untrue.
I often sigh,
When the years go bye and bye.
I've been so sad,
That I couldn't tell mom and dad.
I feel so ashamed,
Now that it won't be the same.
Today I stand all alone,
And wonder what will be known.
There's alot more to say,
But for right now I have to save.

—Debbie Green

The Confession of a Rich Man; Poor Soul

In this life I found all my heart's desires;
I have found wealth in my surroundings,
I have sought after power and domination
   and did not seek in vain.
I was able to walk through streets of
   poverty and scorn the naked and
   shelterless.
No true God did my eyes ever see,
No faith had ever overcome my soul.
All that gold could buy, I had.
Greed became my master,
And I became greed's slave: One of the
   wretched.
Misery was in my every breath of life.
I became blind to the true values of life.
Sunken was my soul,
Cumbered with a conscience of guilt.
My soul, will hell's fire see.

—Kiran Antoinette Maharaj

On Friendship

To a friend throughout the years
I have held you dear,
Though your presence has not been near.
The sweetness of your heart has found a
   home
In the memories of yesteryears.
The memory of you comes to me as a
   sweet, refreshing breeze of joy,
After a cold winter day.
Though I haven't seen you in years,
Your enthral presence clings close to me
   still,
In the warm memories of the times we've
   shared,
As friends, my dear.

—Amir Muhammad

In a Twinkling

I came unto you with a tattered soul
Yearning for restoration.
You took me in without a moment's
   displeasure,
Eager to sustain the remainder of my
   youth.
Melodies filled the air with tunes of days
   gone by;
While you waltzed me gently in your arms
   once again
As though I were a fragile paper doll.
Slowly, you ignited that forgotten spark of
   passion
Deep within me, buried so long ago.
As we feverishly swayed in each others
   arms, the night
Lay ahead, misty and unyielding to all our
   desires.
Our destinies shall forever be entwined in
   that
Radiant, lustful moment in the twinkling
   of an eye!
And the flames of passion will forever
   burn
Until the day I die. . . and beyond.

—Sara Taylor

Yesterday, Today, Tomorrow

Slowly walking down a lonely road
I have memories of yesterday
Some are good and some are bad
But they all lead back to you
You were my life
All I lived for
And now I think of today
It makes me happy to know you are still
   here
Still my life
And what I live for
As for the future
The question remains
Will you be here then
I hope so
For if not
It could be my life's end

—Connie Craig

Envious!!!

I sometimes get so jealous of you and I
   don't understand why.
I have no idea why over the littlest things
   I cry.
You've taken all the talent and left
   nothing for me.
You've locked the door in which you hold
   the key.
Why am I so resentful that what you do,
   you do so good?
Is it because you draw so well and I never
   could?
You write a simple little poem and the
   compliments go your way,
No matter what the situation you know
   what to say.
Because you turn heads no matter where
   you go,
I could never be jealous just because
   you're so talented and pretty.
Never. . .No!
O, who am I kidding its all so true,
Even though your my sister, I'm so
   envious of you!

—Heidi Hartwell

Message from Mom

Whenever the mind should worry,
Wherever the road should twine,
Remember that I am your mother,
You never need-feed me a line.
I know life will often cause worry.
I know that life's road isn't true,
Just remember that life isn't easy,
And the one who makes life work is you.
Happy Graduation

—Sindy Somach

April Star

I have seen a kid's mittens hanging from
   coat sleeves,
I have seen clothes hanging and floating in
   the breeze.
I have seen bracelets of gems hanging
   from a hand,
And I have seen balloons hanging above
   the band.
But one night I saw a star hanging from
   the moon,
Perhaps to the eyes an illusion.
But with a kid's mittens fastened to a
   coat,
Tenderness floats.
Clothes hanging from a line,
Speak of a caring love sublime.
Wealth does speak of the bracelet,
Glamour's onset.
Balloons hanging from a ceiling,
Begets a togetherness feeling.
But a star hanging from a moon creates a
   festive spirit,
So fanciful, you won't forget.
My eyes, mind, have seen it and I won't
   deny a part,
Illusion or not, it has captured my heart!

—Annette Clayton

Feelings Within

Should I tell him I love him, or should I
   let him go?
I have so many feelings I don't know
   where to go.
I really really like him, but yet I feel I
   can't,
Because of all the differences, and what I
   have to pretend.
I want to tell him something, but I really
   can't.
I want to let him go, and break my heart
   within.
I want to let him know I really really care,
But there's a fear within that maybe he
   doesn't care.
I know within my heart the things I need
   to say,
But if he doesn't like me I can't pretend
To forget the things I need to say.
My heart is full of love, and lots of things
   to share,
And all I need to know is does he really
   care.
Can he be my lover, or will he be my
   friend,
Or should I forget all my feelings within?

—Aniece Shobe

Untitled

There are three certain words
You find so hard to say
So you don't have to voice them
I'll list a few ways:
One of your smiles that make me go weak,
A light touch on my cheek,
A sweet smelling rose to make my heart
   grow,
A gentle squeeze to show that you care,
Or run your fingers through my hair,
A short simple letter to make me feel
   better
Or blow a kiss to make my eyes mist—
There's a few ways to say "I love you"
And so you'll get the message
I'll try some on you!

—Lisa Holland

Clear Emotions

You're a very private person and very
   complex,
I have to analyze the emotions you reflect.
It's hard for me to hear what you really
   want to say,
For your words apparently come out the
   wrong way.
I have to read between the lines and listen
   very close,
Or I might miread the emotions you've
   chose.
So speak a little plainer, and say what you
   feel,
It might hurt a little, but all wounds do
   heal.

—Cyndi Morris

A Friend's House

As I sit on a large, cozy sofa
I hear the rain gently tapping on the
   windows.
The scent of buttery popcorn lingers
and I feel the warmth of a blazing fire.
Greg and Marcia are joking on T.V.
and my friends are bubbling with
   laughter.
I notice the odor of grape bubble gum
   someone is chewing
as a furry dog cuddles up at my feet.
The trees outside are gently swaying in
   the wind
while the computer behind me quietly
   beeps.
There is an aroma of cookies baking
as I sink into the feathery softness of the
   sofa pillows.

—Aimee Guenther

Alone

Alone
I hear the screaming silence
Of a howling whine that burns my face,
The musty smell of dampness surrounds
   my sleep,
A nightmare of falling pulls my lead-filled
   stomach,
Eyes closed,
I feel no pain.
Alone
I hear the singing silence
of a sweet melody that cools my face,
The fresh smell of daisies surrounds my
   sleep,
A dream of floating lifts my weightless
   heart,
Eyes closed,
I feel no pain.
The continuous cycle of life;
We all meet in the end.

—Krissy Konrad

Tears

I hear the tears of joy
I hear the tears of sorrow
I watch the lonely people, waiting for
   tomorrow
Vietnam has left a picture across these
   peoples minds,
that never goes or leaves them
It just stays there all the time
We have to try and help them
For they have saved our lives
I hear the tears, just falling
Falling all the time.

—Kathy Teal

Missing You

By the ocean
I hear the waves.
I think of you
My loves in caves.
You won't open your heart
You barely talk
What happened to us?
You start to walk.
I love you more
Every day
But when I see you,
You walk away.
Please hold my hand,
And talk to me.
I'm missing you
You're leaving me.

—Heather Heirbout

Free

As the tears hit the rose
I hold in my hand
the rain hits the ground
in the still of the night
and the moon light is reflected
off the blade.
The silence is broken by the
shriek of pain,
the blood drips onto the rose
I hold in my hand,
I can feel the pain overtake me.
The hate is slowly draining frm me
as if it were in my blood.
I am free, free of you and your
teasing eyes.
As the blackness closes in I am free.

—Desiree VanDeburgh

Friends

Friends, Friends, Friends.
I hope our friendship never ends.
When I met a friend as good as you,
I couldn't believe It was true.
You're always nice
You're full of spice
You always bring luck to me
You are my four leaf clover
So I hope you can see you're the
best friend a girl could ever have.

—Kim Kravcisin

My Reeboks

I like my Reeboks blue and grey,
I hope they always stay that way.
When I wear them through the mud,
My Reeboks start to look like crud.
I always wear them when I cut the lawn,
Me and my Reeboks stay out till dawn.
In the wash they swish round and round.
Until no dirty spots can be found.
And then again,
What will you see,
My Reebock shoes back on me!

—Jaime Suszek

Baby Dear to Be

Dear little one who's on the way,
I hope to meet you, one fine day.
But while awaiting your debut
My mind is questioning, "who are you?"
Like that twinkling little star
I sit and wonder what you are.
Will you be a boy or girl?
Will your baby hair be straight or curl?
Will you be a red haired blue eyed lad?
Or dark and handsome, like you Dad?
Or maybe a sweet and dainty lass
Like your beautiful mother, full of class?
But, dear baby, whichever you be
Will be the same to "Poppy" and me.
May you have good health, happiness and love
For which we thank the Lord above.

—Hope Robiczek

Love

As I sit right here in the dead of the night,
I imagine the future not so bright.
I think of then, not now, so near,
It's then, not now, I truly fear.
I think of the changes, and how life goes,
I remember a flower, the death of a rose.
The inside burning, the total pain,
The fear in my heart will drive me insane.
I imagine the cloud-like dream of haze,
Like one would go through in a long, dark maze.
But the light in the end that reaches from above,
"Is it worth it" she calls. . ."this thing called love. . ."

—Carrie Sams

I Still Hear. . .

I still hear the phone ringing in the middle of the night
I jump out of bed to turn on the light
I hear it, I hear it as the night so long ago
I remember hearing your voice, now only a dial tone.
I pick up the phone waiting to hear you again
Believing your not gone just asking, "Where have you been"?
Your laughter, your laughter placed high up in the sky
Now your gone and I still cry.
So, tonight as I lie in bed after turning off the light—
I know I'll hear the phone ringing in the middle of the night.

—Ginnie Jean McNally

The Rose That My Brother Gave Me

I got a rose from my brother
I just sat there and thought about the times
When my mother spent time with me and took care of me
With her love and I just sat there and thought about
Those loving things just because of one little rose
My brother gave me.

—Carolyn Phillips

Sorrow

I hide my sorrow deep within my mind
I keep my thoughts trapped inside.
My life, one big secret.
I've searched everywhere
I've hinted to everyone
But no one knows.
There's no one to prattle to.
They don't seem to understand my feelings.
There are so many problems in my life.
Sorrow pierce at my insides
Being heart broken,
Makes the feeling deeper.
When I am put down by anyone,
Sorrow is what I find more of
One day it will drown me
Into its depths, but I will be ready to save myself
From the troubled waters of sorrow.

—Kymberdo Barce

The Harem Scarem Massacre

I approached the dark wood with fear.
I kept going though I was not curious.
Someone was approaching me from behind; I couldn't see him.
I ran for my dear life, but whatever was behind me ran faster.
I fell and landed in a trap.
The skeleton started laughing.
He came closer with a knife in his hand.
I closed my eyes. . .
Forever I would rest.

—Kimberly Moskal

Untitled

Why does my heart ache so?
I knew one day that you're go
But when you left I was lost.
You know I'll love you whatever the cost.
Now it's all over.
And my weak heart has to mend.
Why do all things worth having.
Always have to end?

—Elizabeth Owens

Love At First Sight

When I first saw you
I knew you were trouble
but I just couldn't bare
to turn away
the feelings I felt just
got in the way.
The first time I heard
your baby talk
and looked into those
deep blue eyes
I knew then that the
feelings I had felt
could only mean but
one thing,
It was love at first
sight.

—Dusty Keefer

Father's House

Oh Lord, you led me to your house
I knocked and the doors opened.
I was invited in.
You spoke to me of many things;
Of poetry, mysteries, caring and forgiving.
You told me stories; you preached to me.
You took my hand and asked me to share life with you.
You lifted me up when I was down.
You showed me what true love really is.
When I left, there was a fullness in my heart.
For you told me you'll be with me always.

—Holly Bojorquez

Happy Birthday

My gift to you is not very much
I know you'll like it a whole bunch.
It's very cheap but it's worth more,
Than you can buy in any store.
My gift to you can fly like the dove,
It's the wonderful gift of love.
It comes straight from the heart,
And nothing shall ever tear us apart.
Happy Birthday and I love you.

—*Christy Phillips*

Mystery of Motherhood

I washed my babies' diapers.
I laid them down to sleep.
I kissed away the falling tears
that each of them would weep.
I showed care when they were careless.
I sampled how to cope.
I struggled through their teen-age years,
but I never gave up hope.
I was Nurse, Judge and Warden,
the Seamstress and the Cook—
as every Mother knows,
you became just what it took.
Now aged, withered and childlike,
my failing eyes can plainly see-
that I was able to raise my babies,
but my babies can't raise me.

—*Dawn Raffaghello*

Enchantedness

As I flipped the switch
I left my body.
Inner peace came over me.
I could do anything.
Free to enjoy life as I want.
Didn't have to think
About my problems.
Soar like an eagle.
Sway like a tree.
Free to be me.
Unfortunately I had to go
Back living like everyone else.

—*Andrea Garafolo*

Beneath the Waters

Beneath the waters rippling so,
I let my thoughts and worries go,
And think about the timeless calms
Of which I have grown extremely fond.
My worries of you and other such things
Suddenly fade away
And now the clear blue water rings,
It rings with joy, as I do too.
Even though I am away from you,
For I know someday my wish will come true.
And I will be once again, with you; with you beneath the water so calm.
As once again I watch my worries melt away
In the hot sun that will shine and the love that will be mine.

—*Carrie Frisk*

Untold Feelings

There is a place in my heart
Where there are untold feelings about you.
You are special to me.
You stand by my side at all times.
You correct me when I'm wrong.
I can always count on you to be cheerful.
I will always love you.
Love me please.

—*Sandy Hughes*

Shadow

It is an extremely dark night!
I look around, there's no one in sight.
There's no moon and there's no stars.
I discover that I am alone, alone in the dark.
I begin to walk forward hoping to find someone with
bad luck just like mine.
As I'm walking I hear, these loud footsteps
Which are too loud for me to bear.
I turn around but there's still no one to be found.
I begin walking and again I hear, those footsteps which
are hard for me to bear,
But this time you see, the footsteps were coming towards me.
Then I look up and I find, this image that looks just like mine.
As I moved, it moved too.
I didn't know what to do, but then I noticed the image was looking at me too.
I see the image clearly now and I realized it was wearing a frown.
There is also a tear trickling down, right down to the ground.
But my image is not as it seems, for then I woke up and
Realized it was all just a dream.

—*Elaine Vitale*

For My Friend as She Graduates

Through my tears
I look at you
Remembering the years,
And the things we've been through.
Now you are moving on
And starting a new life.
With everyday that dawns
May you never have struggle or strife.
Your bright smile
And your cheerful face
Will be with me all the while
As no one can take your place.
So good luck my dear friend,
But this isn't a goodbye.
Because our memories will never end,
And our friendship will last bye and bye.

—*Krista Lundy*

Our Star

The silence of your breath defies your last word.
I look into your eyes, through the blur of mine.
But no more are you here. Your life and mine
tore apart to the end of your time.
I scream "why", asking why you were such a stranger.
I was of no danger to you, why then were we so far apart.
I look into the dark sky around us, looking for any kind
of mark answering why.
Then I see it, a bright star far in the sky.
This is the star we wished upon together, the
wish of always being together.
As long as the star shines bright,
no matter how far away we were and are,
it's still our star.

—*Crista Dinkel*

The Two Worst Friends

I once had a friend who I no longer have.
I lost him to his two other best friends.
His two best friends were drugs and booze.
Those two friends tore him and his life apart.
His life was one big high day and night.
Then it happened, drugs and booze took his mind over.
Decisions couldn't be made,
Life was just too much to handle.
Then his two best friends made a decision for him.
They decided he didn't want to live anymore.
So, they ended his life so tragically.
So young, so much to live for, but no more.
So those two best friends will move on to
Find someone else to make decisions for,
But we can stop them!!!

—*Kim Behrendt*

Toby

I never knew love could be like this.
I love him more than words can say.
In his eyes, I see the reflection
Of his love for me and mine for him.
He's always there for me.
Through good times and bad times
With his strong hands he holds me
And guides me through
The ever changing and scary world.
Without him, life would be nothing.

—*Eme Yang*

Words of Love

"Words" of love, so easy to say—
I love you. . .I love you. . .
Everyday—
An old cliche so often I've heard—
"Action! Action! speaks louder than words"—
Where are your actions—
That prove what you say?
"Words" of love—
They soon fade away—
I hear an echo from days long past—
It whispers, "Be careful, love words don't last."
"Words" of love, they fill me with fear—
Oh, please!..Let me see—
Let me see what I hear—

—*Andrea Sue Howard*

As My Feeling Grow

I may never know if he sees me,
I may never know if he cares!
I may never know if he likes me,
I may never know if we're a good pair.
The only thing I do know
Is that he is very near
I wish he would let his feelings show,
Hopefully, he will hear.
could he already know
What I feel for him?
I hope my feelings do not grow,
cause if they do, I might get hurt again!

—*April Stover*

Painful Dream

On that vacation I recall
I met a man I would always love.
He gave me his love and I gave him mine.
We laughed and played though just for one day.
The day to depart for me then came,
I thought of him day and night.
The pain I felt inside my heart
Was the one I carried with me at all times.
Though many times I was told,
That there is more than one person in our lives.
I still don't understand why the pain was driving me insane.
They all told me that it was a temporary thing,
But I assure you, that it was real love.
Time went by and not a letter from him did I receive.
So then I guessed this was the time to realize
That the love I felt
Was only in a dream.

—*Gloria I. Ballesteros*

Untitled

Even though you left me only yesterday
I need to tell you I miss you in a very special way.
The drawing you gave me I keep in my heart
But when I think of you it tears me apart.
I didn't realize how close I was to you
Until you are gone and then I knew.
What we had was so real and so good
If only everyone else understood.
Our lives are too different, we both go our ways
Hopefully we'll meet again someday.
You were my first love and I admit
The love I feel no one can forget.
What I want to tell you is that I want you to come home
I really don't want to be alone.

—*Jennifer L. Myers*

I Am The Seasons

I began as spring, young and fresh with buds bursting in the caressing hands of the sun.
I nestled myself among the soft, fragrant blades of grass that was nature's bed, and we became as one.
Then, I became summer.. my blossoms spreading gently,
Making a rainbow bouquet beneath the arms of the hallowed oak.
I swayed in rhythm with the wind, as seldom blew the breeze;
But when it blew with angry breath, it blew me to my knees.
As fall I donned a coat of russet, scarlet and gold.
Though the sun still breathed it's hot breath upon my neck, I felt a hint of cold.
Oh, I would like to have worn indian summer like a garland on my brow,
But winter knocked upon my heart. . .it was destined to enter now.
Winter, I call myself. I am a princess of purity, white mounds flowing
With the softness of an ermine cloak falling gently 'round my toes.
I am grotesque branches reaching scrawny fingers to the sky.
I am the fading blush of summer's last rose.
I am the beginning, the end, all things yet one, merely nature, when all is done.

—*Barbara Clark Hinson*

Dead

There is a place to go
Where the wind will hardly blow.
It's a lifeless place,
Just dead trees to take up space.
You go there when you commit suicide,
But you're not with others who have died.
It's a place to be alone,
Where the sun has never shone.
For those who have bled,
It's a place called dead.

—*Melissa Millett (Sean E. Spencer)*

A Broken Heart

Walking down the long corridor
I pick up the remains of my broken heart
Which lay scattered on the floor
I think of all the memories
When we met
When our hearts sang as one
And the first kiss we shared
But all the good soon faded
And all I can hear is a voice saying
"All you were was just a game."
And the laughter that followed from my friends
Now I sit in silence
In forever silence
Alone

—*Jenny Young*

Life and Love

Stirring inside a soul I long for freedom,
I plant myself deep in the hearts of those
  who love beauty,
I am the first bud of spring and the last
  rose of summer,
When the sun lingers I dance in the
  essence of those who seek me,
I am the hunger for fairness of spirit and
  flesh,
I am a breath of new beginnings, as love
  blossoms I stir,
I am love, I am life

—Crys Hall

Heaven

Now I lay thy down to rest.
I pray thee for the very best.
To live a life where you'll never die,
And roam helplessly in the sky.
A place where you can stay forever more,
To live in a fairy tale that never ends,
To a life that has no run on ends.
The place that has the qualities you seek,
Is a place that is so very unique.
A place of peace and harmony,
A place, heaven, is where you should be.

—Dana Berlin

God

God! I love you with my heart and soul!
I pray to you everyday to make me whole.
Although I walk through life with
  troubles and strife!
I pray to you everyday to help me through
  my life.
And even though I feel like a chess pawn!
I know you will bring me through my
  troubles and strife,
Until I can see the dawn.
And, as I read and believe in your words
  that are written in the book of Psalms!
I truly know, dear Father, that you will
  never let me come to any harm.
But I know, dear Father, that sometimes I
  fall!
So when I read your psalms, they make
  me stand tall.
But when I feel that I'm going to fail!
I read the psalms to get back on the right
  trail.
So I praise you, dear Father, for not
  making me frail!
Because, dear Father, as long as you are
  with me, I will always prevail!
Amen!

—Joseph John Imperial

Relaxing Summer Day

As I walk outside on this summer day,
I put down my blanket and there I will
  lay,
In the gentle breeze the tree's do sway,
And when I close my eyes I feel far away.
I could take a dip in the stream,
Or join a baseball team,
I might take a walk in the forest green,
Maybe just look at the lovely summer
  scene.
I've done alot so far this summer,
Everything's fun, never a bummer,
In the parade I was a drummer,
An during the sing-a-long the guitar
  strummer.
Oh, yes, I can do alot on a day like this
  one,
It's all so much fun,
But there's alot of chores to be done,
I think I'll forget them and lay in the sun.

—Donna Werner

The One I Love

As I sit here by myself,
I realize that while I was looking
Toward the bright lights of love
And all it held for me,
I was destined once more
To have my high flying hopes
Shot down from the sky
By none other than you,
The one I love,
And all I was left with
Were empty nights and
Shattered dreams.
Although you broke my heart
And stole away my faith,
I will always hold a place for you
In my heart,
The one I love.

—Bonnie Michalski

Theif

As I sit here thinking of you,
I realize what you have done.
You have stolen my heart.
Somehow, someway,
you found the key and unlocked it.
Like a thief in the night,
you came in softly, but surely.
I find myself wondering,
how you did it. . .
but even more,
I wonder if I have also captured yours.

—Jena Benton

Strain

As I walk along the path of life
I realized that I was lost,
For I don't know where to go.
Everytime I try to lift my foot,
One step forward. . .
There is something
That always bothers me.
It seems that griefs and blues
Won't leave me.
It seems that a second will cry
If I won't get hurt.
And now I'm trying to live my life
Like a strain
I've never heard before.

—Jesselyn de Leon

Peace

I look up in space and wonder what's
  there
I really truely don't think it's fair
If I were in space I could just float about
Without any worries without any doubts
Up there there's probably no such thing as
  tears
I bet they've never even heard of fears
I could sit on the moon and look at the
  stars or
Even take a ride over to visit Mars
I could catch a shooting star right in my
  hand
Then throw it all down all over the land
Maybe then everyone's prayer would
  come true,
The prayer that calls for peace for me and
  you

—Amy Blackburn

Childhood Dreams

As I think
I remember the times
I sat and dreamt
of how life would be.
All the dates and sweet sixteen
of a teenage girl.
These dreams are still there,
Yet, they've changed.
Being a teenage girl.
I see it's not just dates and fun,
But, hard because
You are growing out of your childhood
  image,
Into a woman.

—Christina McFerran

Untitled

No one knows "me", who I really am.
I remember when I was a little girl
And my daddy would say "I love you."
I knew, even then, that it was meaningless.
The words sounded so empty:
    I—love—you.
After he'd say that, the lights would go out
And tears would begin to flow, stinging my face.
I'm still that helpless little girl.
My body has changed, but she still sneaks out.
"Ha, you're no good, you walk around"
"With a smile painted on your face, like a clown."
"But underneath, you're still crying."
A tiny tear rolls down my cheek
And makes a quiet splash that no one ever hears.
Once again she reminds me that she's right.

    —Kristie Stephens

House

House, among the cherry pastures, looks upon his shambles.
Why do you cry as each soul wants?
House, filled with listless apparitions,
You want me to see you and steal me into the never ending life.
Oh, why do you frighten me?
House, in the middle of nowhere land,
Trying to tempt me to steal you away.
Do you think I want to be here?
House, with big minds, who stole my mind away,
Please let me go!
Do you think I cannot see?
House, among the cherry pastures looks upon his shambles
Once again to even tumble far below.
Why do you still cry as each soul wants?
Even after you stole them away.

    —Shannon M. Luttrell

Movin On

I am a hobo
I ride that lonesome track
The lines are forbidding
Where I've been
I won't be back
To panhandle a quater
Makes my daily life complete
It is the price of a cup of coffee
I shall have nothing to eat
But to understand life
And its puzzled me through the years
If there's one good thing I can say about life
Through time we've had our cheers

    —Fred Pickrell III

If God Had Meant for Man to Fly

With naught but love and hope to guide, on magic silver wings
I ride till morning takes my dreams from me.
Ah, he who dreams of silent dark hears not the sweet song
Of a lark in the morning meadows when I rise.
And as that sweetest bird does sing, I see on him my silver wings
And grasp his song between my lips that I may travel to the sky
And on and on till stars do cry:
"Where goest thou with silver wings?" I go to see the king of kings
And all these things before me now
Beckon like a lover's kiss; and though these earth—things I shall miss,
I spread my wings of silver high and so I fly, and so I fly
To live or die up in the sky.

    —Andrea Sokalski

The Sun Lives Forever

Come live where the sun lives forever,
Where the sorrow has ceased,
Where the animals reign from the abundance of the lands,
Where the happenings of Mother Nature have been lifted away,
Where love is found in every form of life,
Where all act justly and belong in the heart of Yahweh,
And where everyone lives in the midst of their Gods.

    —Sara Angelica Islas

The Black Cloud

The black cloud it follows me.
I run from it to no avail,
It catches me never fail.
The black cloud fogs my head,
Makes my heart feel like lead.
The black cloud consumes my soul,
Leaving me with no control.
My thoughts are constantly reflected,
So easily I feel rejected.
The pain at times so intense,
Obsession my minds only defense.
The black cloud distorts my vision,
And I cannot make a decision.
For love, acceptance, praise I yearn
To understand, to grow, to learn.
Criticism, the black clouds best friend,
Causes me to have to defend.
Anger mounts, resentment sets in,
The war starts that no one can win.
Those I love the most I blame,
Resulting in my feeling shame.
The black cloud is very cruel
Using me as it's tool.
The black cloud is what I hate,
For it to lift is what I wait.

    —Denise Jenkins

A Thought Came

With quill in hand, I sat down to write
I sat all day and I sat all night
But no thought came
The next day, I sat down again
This time with a fountain pen
But this day proved to be the same
The third day I sought a tutor
She brought along her computer
Still no thought, what a shame
Then, it came like a lightning bolt
It really gave me quite a jolt
A thought crystal clear
Quickly, I set to write with my pen
Before the thought slipped away again
And left me stranded here
But the thought grew and grew
And I share it now with you
I think I'll have a root beer!

    —George W. Croasmun

The Beauty of the Earth

As I looked outside this morning,
I saw and heard the beautiful birds calling.
Lillies were falling,
Leaves rushing down from trees.
Lots of big bright yellow bees,
I decided to water the flowers which were all colors.
I stayed for hours and hours.
But now it's night
And lots of things are out of sight.
But I guess tomorrow will be quite
As nice nice nice!

    —Faycial Raymond

Sand Castles

When I met you,
I saw sand castles on the beach
Dolphins too far from reach
Burning embers in my soul
Tied together, but couldn't hold
A lust for life which wasn't there
A need for freedom, I've never shared
I wonder what I would have missed
If we had never met.
I'm sure that through the years ahead,
I never shall forget.

    —Deborah A. Mitchell-Rizzo

Peaceful Man

As I walked in the woods on my land,
I saw this strange, but peaceful man.
He was as sweet as he ever could be.
He said to me,
For once in your life just fall in love.
Have a dear person you can only think of.
Give him your heart, set yourself free,
Find out the man I used to be.
This man I know who he was,
Thank you God for the man I love.

—*Hollie Rockett*

Together

As the sun was setting,
I saw you there, all alone.
You were a swan, gently gliding
Over peaceful waters.
As the sun sank deeper
Into the purple, misty sky,
You became an eagle,
Flying over the land
In complete control.
Now,
The sun is gone.
You are a man
Holding me,
Caressing me.
And I know
This is where
We both belong.

—*Kristi Bosse*

Strangers

We were strangers who met by fate
I saw you, you saw me
There was no thought of the word "hate"
We got to know each other so well
But I hadn't realized my love
There was no way I could tell
so, now you've gone away
Forgetting me, meeting someone new
What else can I do, but say:
"I love you so much"
"But it might be too late"
"For us strangers who met by fate".

—*Kelly Eastman*

Class

I'm sitting, staring off in the distance
I see a pen moving gracefully
Gliding across paper
People are talking and laughing
Like a babbling brook
Me, I'm just staring
Like a snake hypnotizing it's prey
I hear paper rustling in the background
I can't pay attention to anything
I'm trying to, but everyting falls down hard
As if I didn't care
I'm sitting, sitting, with no reason at all

—*Amanda Finkle*

Rainbows

As I look out the window,
I see a rainbow.
I see it up in the sky,
Way up high.
It is so pretty and bright,
As it glistens in the sunlight.
I think how the world is so peaceful and calm,
As God holds the world in his gentle palm.

—*Charla Brown*

Untitled

When I look into the dark
I see all the lives that are wasted
on death or things un-tasted.
When I look into the light
I see many faces and facades
people laughing and acting out canards.
When I look into the mirror
I see the light and dark face of me
being just the way that I want to be.

—*Amy Ricker*

The Eagle

As I lay down in the cool green grass
    underneath the oak tree,
I see an eagle soaring and dipping and
    then resting to call its mate.
I wonder what it would be like to soar
    with the King of the Skies at my
    wingtip.
For it to guide me and take me on its
    path,
To feel the wind gradually lift me up as it
    rushes to the aid of my wings.
Although I dream, maybe to my great
    great-grandchildren will be a part of
    everyday life,
To be able to soar with the King of the
    Skies. . .the eagle.

—*Karen Anderson*

Room with a View

In my room with a view
I see famine and killings
I know that I am too small
To make a difference
They feel that we, the
Younger generation are
Incapable of making a difference
But if they were in my room
With a view, they would see
That they
Need all the help they can get.

—*Aimee Escoffier*

One Step Ahead

One step ahead
I see him there,
The distance is well defined.
One step ahead
I hear him there,
Laughing as he looks behind.
More rapidly my feet do fall
But his do the same kind,
I look about and after all,
I'm still one step behind.
Never shall I walk beside
The one created first,
Equal thought nor equal stride
His bubble will they burst.
One step ahead, he leads the way
One step behind I'll always stay,
Better I ask? This may be true,
Smarter? No, I have the better view.

—*Kelly Vermette*

Being Free

As I sit along the stream,
I see my little boy
Playing with toys.
He seems to be so carefree.
In just being.
As I look around
I see no mother abound.
But he still seems so carefree.
I asked him "Where is your mother?"
He looks me in his eyes and then
Looks up toward the heavenly skies.
I knew then that he was in
God's hands.

—*Bill Richardson*

America

America is beautiful!
I see no need to go
To other lands where thrills await.
Whichever way you go,
From Mexico to Canada,
From sea to shining sea,
God-blessed and wonderful she stands,
Sweet Land of Liberty.
Her desert flowers adorn her,
Her mountains touch the sky.
There still are peaceful, fruitful farms
Where in the meadow lie
Fat, contented cattle.
No matter what some say,
Most stand for right, and purity,
And there is hope today.

—*Alta McLain*

Airballoon

In my airballoon high above,
I see nothing but a dove.
Whirling and waving,
It's graceful wings.
Not even knowing what tomorrow brings.
A day of happiness, a day of sorrow?
We won't find out until tomorrow.

—*Brandi Miller*

A Walk With You

As we walk together hand in hand,
I see our footprints in the sand.
I hear the waves crashing on the beach,
and then for each other we reach.
You put your arms around me,
and say our love will always be.
We look up in the sky.
Together. Alone. Just you and I.
The stars sparkle just like your eyes.
And for a moment they catch me by
    suprise.
You hold me so strong, I could never
    break free.
The next thing I know, you're kissing me.
It all seems so right,
that I could stay here all night.
Only with you.

—*Angie Titkemeier*

The Sunset of Peace

Along the bloody trail of darkness,
I see the golden sunset.
The colors pink, orange, and yellow,
Screached across the sky.
Along the ground lay the beaten soldiers,
Dark and gray.
The colored flag that once was full of
    pride
And swayed in the breeze,
Now lay still on the dusty hill.
The golden sunset shown bright with love,
And peace on earth had now begun.

—*Ethel Tozier*

Untitled

I see the sky,
I see the sea,
I see everything,
With the eyes in me.
I just don't know,
What I would do,
If I were blind,
And without you.
I Love you so much,
That it's hard to say,
You're on my mind,
All night and day.
I hope the love,
With you and I,
Will never fade,
And never die.

—*Jennifer Uhrinek*

Tears

I hear the sound of children crying
I see the trees; they are dying
There is no reason for the world to be so
    corrupt
But the people go on and say, "So what?"
Lord knows what good they see
I just know them tears keep coming to me
I know that one speech can't get the job
    done
And it sure can't get the war won
But maybe I'll influence those
Who don't notice they're trampling on
    other's toes
Just to kill the living, you see
That's why them tears keep coming to me
Teenagers committing suicide
Their bodies crumbled on the roadside
It's a miracle the people alive are
    surviving
While most are dying
All these dangers you see
But still you ask why these tears keep
    coming to me

—*Cenita Smith*

A Dream Of Love

When I look into your eyes
I see you and me
We're walking together
On a sandy beach.
The sunset on the water
Seagulls soaring through the air
The day turns into night
And our love is everywhere
Your body touches mine
Your fingers on my skin
A soft and quiet kiss
A gentle breeze of wind
You hold me tight
I hear you breath in my ear
You tell me you love me
And you'll always be here!

—*Chasity D. Stallins*

Sweet Rose

Oh, sweet Rose, you glitter in the golden
    sands of heaven,
I see you in the clouds glowing so bright,
Like the biggest star of all in the
    everlasting life.
I sing to you like a choir of angels
    glistening a happy tune,
You give me happiness and joy with a
    wonderful loving life,
You have showed me what to do and what
    not.
You have helped me through a various
    numbers of things in life.
Oh, sweet Rose, I promise I won't fade
    away into the dust and dirt in the
    underground, where evil and darkness
    lies,
Oh grateful Lord, you're the sweet Rose.

—*Gillian Hefter*

When is the End?

I'm sitting here next to you
I see you smile
I feel the fresh dew
The sun is rising
A new day begins
My life is starting all over again
Now it is time to get up.
To walk across the earth
Never knowing what step I take will be
    the last.
Never knowing if the sun will rise
    tomorrow.
I'm sitting there next to you
I see you frown
I feel the cool wind blow
The sun is going down
I fall asleep
Only to dream very good dreams.
And I just pray I rise with the sun
Tomorrow, and forever.

—*Kari Wentzloff*

The Light Turns Green

The light turns green, I start to walk;
I see you there but you don't talk.
I stand there in the cold morning air
And I know that you don't care.
But you don't seem to understand
That I make such a careful plan.
I'm afraid of what to be,
I can't help but feel your laughing at me.
I'm sorry if I caused you pain,
But that won't give me any gain.
'Cause if I used my mouth instead of my mind,
All my problems would be behind.
I don't even seem to try,
I guess that's why I won't get by.
So now you see why I can't talk,
The light turns green, and away I walk.

—Christine Tappen

Blow Wind Blow

Climb, oh climb up in that tree
I shall climb way up where they cannot see
Higher and higher up toward the sky
Up so high I can catch a tear from God's eye
Up in the top, I'll sail on the breeze
They say stop, but I'm hidden in the leaves
Blow wind blow, sway me to and fro
So high on my own I could never grow
I could stay up here forever
With the winds melody in my ears
The blue sky above me where it ends never
The dew of the morning is the angel's tears
So, blow wind blow, sway to and fro
Sailing up high through God's sky.

—Deanna Tatianna

Forever in Prison

With all these slaves within me
I shall forever be in prison.
I know only what master wants me to be,
He has made my decision.
I shall forever be in prison,
For so long I've been in isolation,
Master has made my decision
And he forms my reputation.
For so long I've been in isolation
That I believe every door is locked.
Master forms my reputation,
So my self esteem is blocked.
I believe every door is locked
Because I know only what master wants me to be.
My self esteem is blocked,
With all these slaves within me.

—Jennifer F. Wood

Death, the Sleep

When I die I shall sleep.
I shall sleep an everlasting sleep.
Not one—thousand babes a weeping shall awaken me.
Not one—thousand birds a chirping shall awaken me.
Not one—thousand wailing babies shall awaken me.
For I shall be asleep
In my peaceful everlasting sleep.

—Kamil Bhangoo

Through My Silence

Without words
I shall tell you
I love you
I shall speak of caring
And loving
And show you I care
I'll let you feel me
And tell you of love
Without words
My silence will teach you
As you learn of my thoughts
And feeling I'll show
Of my love you shall know
Through my silence
I will bring your love
And prove my love is yours.

—Farhana Zaidi

The Dream

Last night I dreamt that you were here.
I shivered slightly as you came near.
I saw you smile and your eyes shone bright,
And I hoped you'd stay with all my might.
You whispered words into my ear,
But these soft, sweet phrases I could not hear.
As you spoke, I heard our song,
We began to dance before too long.
You held me tightly as I'd wished for,
And soon I felt my spirits soar.
But then you whispered, "I won't forget you".
The end was near, I suddenly knew.
More then anything I wished you'd stay
As the dream slipped away.
I felt your touch growing weak—
And woke as a tear slid down my cheek.

—Erika Banick

Grandma B

Now that you're gone
I sit and stare
I remember times
When you were there
We were so close
But times so far away
I loved you so much
Why couldn't you stay
When God reached down
And pulled you up above
How could he take you away
Someone I so much loved
Why does it hurt so much
And I feel such pain
Does it ever go away
Or will it always remain

—Brandie Jones

Untitled

I lay in the gray night looking to the stars,
Wondering only where you are.
Our love fades like a puddle the sun is drying,
Our strength is easing as our love is slowly dying
Why did our love go by so fast?
The sands ran so quickly our of the hourglass.
I guess the beatings of your heart
Squeezed away my little part.
It's not the arguing or breaking up that's making me go insane,
It's that throbbing in my heart, "O" that powerful pain.
Our love was like a foolish game I don't think
I will ever feel the same.
I thought our love would last forever,
Like the Earth and the Moon.
But it ended so quickly as
The day broke at Noon.

—Michelle Kurth

Cave

I am afraid
I sit and stare
Blankly feeling
Cadaverous and cold
Dankness
Dripping
Clammy, diseased wetness on a vast walled stretch of ominous stone
Prisoner in my own life
Clenched fists
Cuticles white with terror
Nails angrily imprinting half-moons on my flesh like small red tattoos
Teeth chattering in the solitary dampness
Under surveillance of stalagmites
Unable to move
Dim beam of my flashlight slowly fading
Wavering
Proclaiming death

—Brenda Wensel

One Night I was Awakened

One night I was awakened, it was after midnight,
I slowly got up and opened the window in fright.
I was met by the bluest eyes I had ever seen,
They were not the least bit frightened, but calm and serene.
Above the eyes glowed a horn of pure gold,
The creature did not appear young, or old.
I glanced at my clock, it was almost morn,
Then I realized the creature I saw was a unicorn!
It dipped its snowy white head as if to say,
Don't be frightened, oh, please don't run away!
I looked into its deep blue eyes,
Though it did not make a sound, I could imagine its cries.
I could see where its snowy white ankles had bled,
They were wrapped in prickly rose vines and were puffy and red.
Then the creature dissolved into a gold mist and was gone,
I assume it died with the coming of a dawn.
I went back to bed and cried and cried,
Still hoping the unicorn had not died.

—*Dara Miller*

Lady, Oh Lady

Lady, oh lady
Where have you gone?
Have you forgotten our song?
Have the nights been too long?
Lady, oh lady
Are you coming back again?
Have we reached the end?
You were my best friend.

—*Laura Foot*

Waiting

Waiting for you with lonely arms,
I stand,
Tears fall,
And my heart maintains,
My existence.
I feel incredibly robbed,
By One,
Who so recently granted me,
With life's greatest gem of all,
True love,
Once shared,
Now waiting.
Knowing we'll again be reunited,
Hope churns,
Optimism blossoms,
And my heart,
Continues to maintain,
My existence,
In waiting.

—*Angie Jenkins*

The Red Rose

The graveyard filled with sorrow; and sadness.
I, standing side a grave, am filled with lust.
The girl I had known; yet, she did not know me.
Memories of her from years ago, fill my head.
Playing with friends; fighting off enemies.
Beautiful as the red rose in her hair.
Days ago, still playful and fighting.
Days ago, beautiful as the red rose in her hair.
And now, laid in the grave, being loved as she once was.
Alone in her world of grace and beauty.
But still the red rose lay across the grave.
How I weep for her; how I mourn her everyday.

—*Ellen Ralston*

When I Think of You

When I think of you
I start to feel sad
Thinking of the times we've shared
The times we've had.
I miss you so much
That words cannot say
You were my friend
And I love you to this day.
As I sit here crying
Wishing you were here,
I know in my heart
That you'll always be near.

—*Anna Qualset*

Pretender

Sitting in the moonlight
I still feel like I could cry
Because I heard tonight
Everything was just a lie.
You didn't even like me,
Not a thing you said was true.
Who were you trying to be?
What did you want to prove?
You didn't care at all for me,
You just cared about your friends.
And when they laughed and when they teased,
You put us to an end.
To me you meant 'most everything,
To you I was just fun.
All your words have empty meaning
-Even the beautiful ones.

—*Bernadette Hillery Emerson*

If I Could

Baby if I could, I'd give you your heart's desire.
I still love you,
And in my heart for you I have
A blazing fire.
If I could, I would heal all the hurting and save all the sinners.
If I could, I'd make myself well; and I'd live as a winner.
If I could, I'd go back in time,
To the days when you were mine.
If I could, I would set humanity free.
If I could, I'd get a Ph.d,
In loving and caring,
I believe in kindness and sharing.
If I could I'd fill every soul with holiness and love.
I would make the earth like heaven above.
If I could, baby, I'd make you so happy, because I love you, and you mean the world to me!
If I could, I'd keep this beautiful feeling forever if I could make healing and reality come together.

—*Janice Walker*

Untitled

I look forward to walks with you
When the friendly wind ruffles my hair
I can look into your eyes and share the inner me

—*Lois Barr*

Being With You

As stars twinkled above and a breeze slowly blew
I stood in front of you feeling loved, but confused.
I had finally met you after a long years wait
And now that I have you I made a big mistake.
You told me you loved me, but I shied away
Thinking I'd wait just for another day.
As fate would have it everything went wrong
And I lost you right before things had begun.
I know things will be different now
And you'll go your separate way
But I'll never forget how we spent those days.
You were always so happy and cheerful, too
And I'll always love you for just being you.

—*Amy C. Jones*

Garden Universe

Clad in the clear white of my skin
I stroll serene to the tune of tricklings and
Skippings, drippings of freshly falling
    water
I stop to drink
Gathering this mountain stream in clean
    palms
I relish it, like drinking diamonds
Even my soul is quenched
Drenched in vigor.
Sweetly my feet carry me, maiden of the
    Day Spring
Soft my beauty shrissles through green
    and aliveness
Morning without mourning amidst tender
    shoots.
Joy shining my eyes play with snap
    dragons and dragonflies
Daylillies and oopsidaisies; buttercups.
Creamy my skin tingles tight through the
    willow wind
As my virgin lips bloom into your sunlight
    smile
You walk beside me.

—Jean Philips

My Friend the Darkness

I am awakened in the darkest of night,
When the walls surrounding me are
    invisible.
As the sun takes its place in the sky,
I am aware of the cold, hard bars
That enclose me in my flowerless world.
When my friend, the darkness returns,
I discover it is impossible to slip between
    the bars.
I fall back in surrender
And watch the outside wait for me.
So, while the sun rises and sets,
I patiently watch the time silently go by,
    slowly,
Until the alarm goes off,
And I walk beyond the bars
To join the outside.

—Ruby Rafuse

Prayer of Desire

Lord,
I thank You for the gift of write,
It is my strength as well as my wisdom,
It is life as well as my death.
But there is one more thing —
A Woman — A Beautiful Woman,
I desire her as much as I love to write.
I know You have given me all,
But not I plead to You,
I ask You to give her unto me.
I wish to care for her.
I want to hold her —
Hold her with the two strong and empty
    arms You have given to me.
I ask this of You,
For her, I will give up my gift of write.

—Brian Gambone

The Beauty of One Day

For the beauty of this one day,
I thank you Lord for tomorrow I may
    never see.
But for this one day and all its beauty,
I take this time to praise thee.
When I look into the sky, the softeness of
    the clouds so blue,
I see the work of the masters great hand,
And again my God I praise you.
I feel the wind as it whispers to the earth,
See the life God has given thee, a miracle
    of new birth.
The beauty of the flowers and the trees,
As they nod their head in the breeze.
Who else but God could make the flowers
    and the trees?

—Katherine Gravely

Untitled

From time to time
I think about you
And remember the things
we had and shared togethjer
our dreams
our hopes
which we for filled
are now gone for ever
I miss the laughs
and th cries
but most of all
The love I saw in our eyes
I wish I could see to the truth
That now your gone
And I'm still her
But things do happen in wife
And I do care.

—Gloria Morse

Love

Love is not flowers and candy,
I think it's not that dandy.
Hugging and kissing are one way of
    loving,
So you wouldn't go and start shoving.
Sharing and caring are one good way,
Saying "I love you" is one good thing to
    say.

—Kiana Peake

A Love Dies

When I think of our love ending now,
I think of something related is death.
But then again, was it love we shared?
I loved you, you said you loved me.
Were we too young to understand the true
    meaning of love?
Your meaning of love runs shallow.
My meaning of love lies far beyond
Beauty, gifts, hearts, roses, and rainbows.
I wish to share beautiful moments with
The one I love, but only one may know
The pain I feel.
Love itself nourishes life. Without love,
There is death. Did the one I love,
Love Me? Only God may know.

—Joanna Estes

Hypnotized

As I sit here down comes a tear.
I think of you, I hope you're thinking of
    me, too.
Our love is still there,
So why do you say you don't care?
I am hurting inside , but that. . .
I always try to hide.
You made me cry because I feel like it
    was all one big lie.
Maybe we won't ever be but your love for
    me is what I see.
I look in your eyes and your feelings are
    what you can't disguise.
Why can't you admit you fell. . .
You fell into my spell.
You were hypnotized when you looked
    into my eyes. . .

—Jennifer Sambas

A Love that Still Exists

As the night falls, I laid down to sleep.
I think of you, my heart begins to weep.
And all the feelings that I hide
Are being stirred down deep inside.
I close my eyes wishing we were like
    before
And then my tears begin to fall even
    more.
I think of how hard I try to live without
    you
Each day it becomes the hardest thing to
    do.
I still remember the feeling of looking into
    your eyes;
It's like walking through the open doors of
    paradise.
This love of mine time cannot erase
Neither can I, the pieces together place.
So no matter where I go or what I do,
My heart has and always will belong to
    you!

—Anita Gonzales

Forever

I thought I could love you forever,
I thought we would part never.
But was I ever wrong!
You're the one who screwed up this time,
You crossed over the unspoken line.
And now I'm gone.
I should be sad,
But I can only be glad.
Now there are others
Who won't do that to me.
Someday you'll see
And be sorry
You had that Saturday night fling.

—*Belinda Tiritilli*

Is There A Reason?

Why do trees grow, why do birds fly
Why are we here, why do we die
Where is the wind, where does it go
Where are our friends, when we grow old.
Mysteries of life unfold before us with
    every year that comes
But things get even more confusing; into
    the world as soon
The moon that glows, the stars that shine
His sparkling eyes says he is mine
He has a spark inside of him to try
    and tell me something
It isn't scare, it isn't fright, he acts as if
    it's nothing.
My mind may wander off and on as if that
    I were old.
Will he grow up as does a tree, becoming
    big and bold.
Now he is twenty with a life of his own
How can it be that he's all ready grown
Just like a bird, he flew to his dreams
It's time I sit back and watch what it
    brings.

—*Richard Smith*

Good-bye forever my friend I had

I counted on you as a friend of mine.
I thought we'd be friends forever in time,
But, now I know what I must do
to break our friendship forever in two.
Erase all the happy time we had together,
I thought we'd be friends forever and
    ever.
As you can see that didn't last,
As we stand still the time will pass,
I really thought you cared for me.
But, I can see that I am wrong.
The time is now for I must go
To some othe place.
We can not show
the feelings we had,
The two of us now.
I'll say Good-bye and leave it at that.
Good-bye forever,
My friend I had.

—*Diane Tang*

Deadly Memories

I sit in my dark room and remember the
    way you made me feel last night.
I thought you really loved me.
All the words you said now seem empty.
Maybe you never meant to hurt me.
Maybe you don't realize how much I love
    you.
Now I am a shell of a person.
Sleep is an impossible dream.
The sun is beginning to rise in my
    window,
But all still seems dark.
Absent is your laughter, your touch.
I am destined to be in darkness, only
    because I am without you.
You made my blood race, now it's time to
    let that blood spill
Into the warm tub filled with water.
I am beginning to feel very weak.
As I look into the bloody hell my wrists
    are sunk into,
There is no pain, just your memories.
Darkness appears in front of my eyes.
Death is near.

—*Bobby Jo Pound*

Untitled

When you start feeling blue
You think it's so unfair
So you wonder if it's true
Or is it you just don't care.
You don't know who to call on
And hope to find some help
But you can't find that someone
For that tiny yelp.
You feel it's just so huge
That you can't take it on yourself
So then you start to boo
And put it on a shelf.
You say you'll deal with it later
But that's something you just can't say
Because the feeling of hurt and pain
Just won't go away.

—*Michelle M. Godfrey*

I Guess It's Over

I threw away the pain.
I threw away the tears
And all the memories of the years.
I thought I was over you
I guess I was wrong.
When I see your face
I think of our song.
You found someone new,
That I can't except.
But you I still respect.
Seasons change, people too.
My love life I've lost
And so I've lost you.
Friends we could be
Though hurt would come to me.
I guess it's over I have to say,
So I'll shut my mouth
And I'll be on my way.

—*Amber Richardson*

Back Home

When I was a child growing up on the
    farm,
I took care to see my animals came to no
    harm.
Dogs, cats, rabbits, and chickens,
If anyone touched, they caught the
    dickens.
Cows, calves, horses, and pigs galore,
Heaven knows my chores were never a
    bore.
Mama cooked and helped daddy in the
    fields,
Hoping the crops would bring in more
    yields.
Those years went by much too fast,
Sometimes I think it is better to live in the
    past.
Back home is where I long to be,
But you and I both know,
It is just a dream for me.

—*Joanne O'Field*

Mine Mind

A moment in words is not a moment in
    time.
I try so hard to describe
But I can't find the words.
Trapping emotion in syllables belittles the
    essence.
See as I see, hear as I hear,
Feel as I feel and be me.
Only I can know the experiences
That I touch, that are me.
If we were the same, you could know:
My sorrow and why I weep;
My bliss and the reason I rejoice;
My anger and how I hurt;
My silence which indulges my
    indifference.
Then you would understand me.
If you were to understand me,
You would steal my individuality.

—*K. Keith*

Perfect

I try to please you, you cannot be pleased.
I try to impress you, you cannot be
    impressed.
I try my hardest, you say I didn't try my
    best.
I am not perfect, and neither are you.
You say that you love me, how can that be
    true?
You never look towards me, you look right
    through.
You say I'm unsure of myself, what more
    can I do?
You want me to be perfect, but perfect I
    cannot be.
Just as you are you. . .let me be me.

—*Judy Sgambati*

Life Goes On

As I walk down the beach of my past
I turn to look behind me
My footprints I can still see
I stop and think of how much they remind
—me of the people I've met and learned
    to love
The sun in shining down from above
As I stand there and think
I notest how much my last step reminds
    me of you
It's really close to me
As you were once too
It was my last
So were you
I stand there and watch as the water
    rushes up
—and fills all of them up
All except the one that reminded me of
    you
I must have stood there for at least 5
    minutes
Then, I turned around and walked on
Remembering that life goes on

—*Julie Marie Zidek*

Sunset

Sitting on the beach, looking over the
    shimmery ocean, I picture you.
Your hair, your eyes, your body,
    everything about you.
I imagine you holding me as we watch the
    sun setting in the west.
The bright, vibrant colors remind me of
    the good times we've shared.
Each cloud represents a different feeling
    that I have for you.
But most of all, the sun is all the love we
    have for each other.
The ocean, the breeze, the sunset is for us.
It is our special place.
I love it and I will love you forever and
    always.

—*Lisa Gallagher*

Full Moon

The moon shines bright in my window
    tonight.
I turn to the right with my back to the
    sight.
And close my eyes tight to shut out the
    light,
But alas in spite of all, lose the fight.
So in my plight I think I just might
Enjoy in a mite, since sleeping took flight.
It's like a kite suspended in height,
Beaming delight, through clouds fleecy
    white.
Night seems to ignite, all nature excite.
The dog, nose upright, howls up a fright.
Relaxing? Not quite. Impressive alright.
The covers invite back to slumber,
    goodnight.

—*Floy Fisher*

Bringing No Fruit To Hear

I reach for an apple that's too high for me.
I use a stick, I throw a rock, and still it
    hangs defiantly.
I have never gotten the apple above my
    head.
I have been told to keep reaching, and
    keep trying,
Like all the others before me who have
    tried to capture the prize.
I know no better way to keep one under a
    tight reign,
Than to offer an apple that is out of reach.
It works very well when one is hungry.
There will always be apples above my
    head.
As long as I am hungry I will keep
    reaching.

—*E. Hugh Elledge*

Is This Love?

I close my eyes.
I visualize.
Vivid fantasies, dancing in a row.
Together we walk through meadows
    green.
Where fields of splendor grow.
Who are you that only you.
Should be in every corner of my mind.
But, who am I that I should find.
Someone so gentle and so kind.
And, what is this that I possess.
This devastation that sets my
Soul aflame.
This ardent desire that you inspire
With just a whisper of your name.
Is this love?

—*Connie M. DeLancey*

To Shannon

I wake up in the morning and I see your
    adorable smile
I walk to the bathroom hoping that
    getting up will be worth my while.
You keep me from going to sleep by
    screaming my name
Each night before I lay down I realize the
    next morning will be the same.
You are there when I am happy and also
    when I'm sad
You console me and make me feel that lil'
    sisters aren't so bad.
You are only two years old; I wonder what
    your future will bring
All I know is that I'll be there for you and
    will give you anything.
I feel as we get older, we will grow closer
    together
I thank the Lord each day you're here,
    cause Shannon, I will love you forever.

—*Kimberly Davis*

You're My Friend Always

If I shall go before tomorrow
I want you to keep
My soul in your heart
Because good friends never part

—*Angela Copeland*

Remember Me When

Remember me when
I wanted to hold you, just to be
In your arms, so I could love you.
Remember me when
You said you loved me but
To me that was just a mystery.
A mystery of wondering if you loved me
    true
When most of the time I felt so blue.
Remember me when
We had fun,
Me showing you all my love
Remember me when
We shared some love,
Those were the times I felt so above
So, remember me when you see good
    things
When you see me maybe we'll share good
    things!
Remember me when.

—*Angela C. Mayhew*

Pearls and Gold

I dreamed a dream of pearls and gold.
I was a princess in a tale untold.
My ladies were dressed in gowns made of
    silk,
My lords were dressed in armor of steel.
My kingdom was more than a radiant
    castle,
My kingdom held more than a journey
    behold.
My kingdom held harmony, friendship,
    and love,
In my dream that I dreamed of pearls and
    gold.

—*Alanna Furne*

God of Love

Oh God of Love, God Devine,
I wasn't given all my time,
My child is gone, no last goodbye,
No holding his precious hand in mine.
I didn't have my last goodbye.
A gentle kiss upon his face,
A little sigh, "I love you Steve".
Oh God of Love, why did he leave?
He was a precious gift from above,
We gave him all of our love.
But now he's back at home with you.
Oh God of Love, God Devine,
Please love and bless this son of mine.
When I am called, I'll have my last
 Goodbye.
I'll hold him then, I won't have to cry.
I'll be in your holy place, where I can love
 and hold his hand,
Kiss him gently on the face.
Oh God of Love, God Devine,
You are still a friend of mine.

—*Charlotte Russell*

I Loved Too Little

I tried to reach for it
I wasn't quite tall enough.
There were no obstacles he couldn't
 overcome
I had many.
He wanted it
I also wanted it, but I want many things.
He tried to love me
He succeeded.
I tried to love back
I tried too hard.
Forbidden our love, I thought
though he took a chance.
He loved too much
I loved too little.

—*Amy M. Bridges*

Sunset

While I sit on the golden sand by the
 shore,
I watch the pink, blue, and yellow colors
 slip away.
Often I find myself dreaming,
Why can't this beauty last forever?

—*Beth Anderson*

Society's Heart

As I sit sullenly on my doorstep,
I watch the world passing by me.
The furry animals, the velvet
 clouds. . .ahhh
The noisy vehicles,
The smog—filled air
And I wonder, why?
But nobody really knows.
The core of the earth reaches out
And grabs my gut
Strangling my wretched soul
And as I sit, suffocating from the world
 around me,
The pretensions
The deceit
The selfishness
I wonder, why?
But nobody really knows.

—*Holly Berg*

Walking Death

Stalking the broad daylight
I will cut the noonday shadow from the
 soles of your blistering feet
The shade scuds ever over water
Whose froth
Remembers not the passage of one
 incomplete
The orphaned boy
Will sail over a still ocean, and a cold one,
 and a dark one
Into the black dawn
To the shores of the wild rose and thyme
There
Walking death
Yea, walking death
Shards of being
The boy will come to love
But now the shore is sinking, and the
 heaving waves ever forget
The boy will love
But who will tell the wild rose?

—*Adrian Bangerter*

Thoughts of a Stranger

I lay here thinking if
I will ever see your again.
To look into those eyes and
See the pain that others in
Life have put you through.
You look at me like an answer
To all your problems.
I erase anyone or anything
That has written on the exterior
Of your heart.
But I think to myself, who will
Write the ending of the story
Which has not yet begun?

—*Kimberly Riffle*

I Will Love You

I will love you while you are far away.
I will love you while you are close to me.
I will love you for my days seem lonesome
 when you are not here.
I will love you for my love is endless.
I will love you for you are my day and I
 am your night.
I will love you for you are my star, shining
 bright.
I will love you for you are my todays, my
 tomorrows, my forever.
I will love you as the air refreshes my
 senses, and the sea enfolds like a babe.
I will love you with all the laughter and
 the tears, all the sadness and the fears.
I will love you for you are my destiny.
For the love we share is a love that only
 comes once in a lifetime.
I will love you for always because in you I
 found the true meaning of love.
In you I found the true meaning of loving
 you.

—*Jacqueline Gonzalez*

My Will

I will to you a smile forever.
I will to you a fragrant rose to
Behold the tender beauty there.
I will to you a road to travel,
Boat, plane, or car.
I will to you to be exactly
Who and what you are.
I will to you a dream of life,
Of whatever you want it to be.
I will to you a master plan to
Shine in glory for you and me.
I will to you all that life describes.
See it, feel it, taste and touch it,
And benefits you will derive.

—*Julie Phillips*

The Stars are Happy

As I see the sun go down,
I wish I were in the stars without any
 sound.
To sit upon the world tall,
It's sad to watch the sadness fall.
To watch the people moan and groan,
Or to watch the street people who don't
 have a home.
Neither the sun or moon can see what I
 can see,
That's why the stars are so special to me.

—*Heather Stewart*

Once

You tell me you love me
I wish it were true
You tell me you missed me
I used to miss you.
When you walked out the door
I thought I would cry
But you kept on walking
Didn't even say goodbye.
Now that you're back
It isn't the same
For me it was real
For you just a game
It's true I once missed you
But that was before
And now that you're back
It doesn't matter anymore.

—Dawn Abbott

I Wish

I wish for cool days and nights,
I wish to see the neon lights.
I wish upon this big bright star,
That my troubles would go far.
I wish to love someone true.
I wish that someone could be you.

—Heather Terry

A Worried Young Girl

I am a worried young girl that cares
I wonder about people and what's going to happen to them
I hear people crying from hunger
I see it everywhere I go, I want this to end
I am a worried young girl that cares
I pretend I'm the president, I feel I can help them
I touch the tears and hope for the best
I worry when something goes wrong
I cry when I see people in need of help
I am a worried young girl that cares.
I understand that not everyone can be helped
I say "Why can't you help them?" Give a generous hand to someone in need
I dream of people having a home, a job, and food for their table
I try to help those I can but one person can't do it alone
I hope other people will realize that there is somebody
Who cares and wants to help
I am a worried young girl that cares.

—Jodie Rouse

Untitled

As I look up at the shining sky
I wonder how high I'll be able to fly
I wonder if I'll ever succeed
In whatever profession I decide to be
With all of the war, drugs, and crime
It's harder to get by in a matter of time.
I'll just go on believeing that dreams come true
But sooner or later I'll find the truth
Everybody says "Follow Your Dreams"
But do they really know what that means?
It's not that easy, as I've heard
It doesn't happen with just one word
I guess I'll just believe
That I can make it by myself. . .just me.

—Carla Barker

God Bless the Monsters

Oh God, bless the monsters in the deep
Who are guarding little children
While they're acting out their sleep
Who raise their cup so knowingly
To the reason why God's weep
God bless the monsters in the deep.
And God, help this monster made of sand.
And God, help us get control
Of the old clock once again
Oh Lord, help us get these sickness' controlled
And God bless our fields and streams once more
Oh God, stop this use of iron
That puts the blood upon the ground
And erase the confusion left
From wars ugly awful sound
And tell us what we are and not
To do or think or eat
And God bless the monsters
In the deep.

—Timothy Sheehan

I am

I am nature and beauty
I wonder of death
I see the soul when
I hear the love saying,
"I want the more!"
I am nature and beauty
I pretend to be happy even if
I feel depressed
I touch millions of people's hearts deep inside, but
I worry when they cry, and
I cry when they die
I am nature and beauty
I understand what life is all about when
I say, "I have a million friends!"
I dream of tomorrow as the day will begin
I try to remember yesterday as half-day today
I hope to live today forever. . .
I am nature and beauty

—Dilma Palma

I am the Sky and the Dream

I am the sky and the dream.
I wonder what life would be without people.
I hear hate in rising flames.
I see destruction and pollution.
I want to understand people and their problems.
I am the sky and the dream.
I pretend to be a traveller in a foreign land.
I feel as though love has died throughout time.
I touch the outer part of a crystal ball.
I worry when a child is destroyed.
I cry when the world turns upside down.
I am the sky and the dream.
I understand nothing.
I say I love what's true and real.
I dream that someday life will be free.
I try to escape the dangers of thunder.
I hope that someday people will come to understand
I am the sky and the dream.

—Despina Bissas

Fantasy

As I thought under the raspberry bush where I lay
I wondered if it was really meant to be this way
To relax and dream of places I'm not
"Live in reality!", that's what we're taught
Then I'll be a rebel, for I'd rather dream
Of the Rocky Mountains, and cool underground streams
And I'd rather live in a place called Pottawattamie
Where peace abounds and war is not in their vocabulary
When you reach deep inside and open your imaginations door
You find that your life, is not such a bore.

—Jennifer Smith

Untitled

The day I started loving you,
I wondered if the whole world knew.
A light came down and shown on me,
My heart was pounding like a raging sea.
I closed my eyes and saw your face,
I looked at you with a peaceful grace.
You held out your hand and we were floating up high.
I knew then, I was going with you to the sky.
I looked back and saw my friends,
I waved goodbye and said "amen".
I looked at you and took your hand,
I knew we were going to the Promised Land.

—Christine Dill

If I Were A

If I were a bird
I would fly high into the air,
I'd watch the airplanes go by,
I'd watch the earth below.
If I were a cat
I would stay in the house
And lie in front of an open window
And look at God's creatures.
If I were a butterfly
I would show my beauty to the bees,
I'd watch other butterflies spread their
 wings.
If I were an angel
I'd pray for the little babies who are dying
 or ill.
I'd ask God to make them well
So that they could live a happy life. . .like
 mine.

—*Joanna Pauline Hollis*

My Next Life

Soaring against a bright blue sky,
I would fulfill my dreams of flying up
 high.
I would spread my wings and fill the air.
I would feel free,
Without a care.
I would look down and below I'd see,
Many people like I used to be.
But I am now no human wanting to fly,
Free in the wind, against the sky.
For my wish came true
In my next life I became
A free born bird,
No fear, no pain.

—*Beth Thomas*

Goals

Have you ever said to yourself,
I would like to write a song,
Run a mile on the sand,
Or reach for a depressed person's hand?
Afterwards, did you say,
I will not be able to endure that mile,
Or it will be impossible to make that
 person smile?
If you have not doubted yourself,
Then chances are great,
That you have completed the goal,
And directed yourself towards it,
As soon the thought, in your mind came,
And if you understand my point of view,
Then I have done the same.

—*Danielle Terese Avery*

Heartache

If the strength vanished from my legs,
I would lose the gift of walking.
If no sound was heard from my mouth,
It would be useless to continue talking.
Yet, if I was deprived a pair of eyes,
Then I would painfully cry no more.
And if I was blessed with a set of wings,
Without a woe I would peacefully soar.
If dreams transformed to reality,
These wings would lead me far away,
Expunge my fright and grief,
And relieve the pain I suffer today.
For my heart was torn in two,
And my hopes have gradually decayed,
Which is why the endless battle ahead,
Is one I will fight alone and afraid.

—*Jean Talifer*

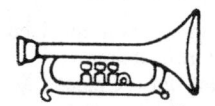

Clouds

Of all my dreams and wishes,
I would yearn to be a cloud;
To be free, floating,
A lone nomad in the sky.
To express myself so openly,
In joy, sadness, loneliness, and
 restlessness.
To experience the sensation of flight
Through the unconfined atmosphere,
And never know pain.
To realize that I'm closer to God than
 anyone;
That, in itself, would be a true paradise.

—*Colleen O'Dowd*

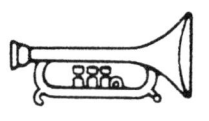

To Walk

Your hands outstretched before me.
I wouldn't step alone.
I've always been afraid
Of falling.
You taught me that you have
To fall to learn
To walk.
Every day I take a few more
Steps.
Sometimes I fall.
You taught me well,
And now I can walk by your side.

—*Kimberly Black*

A Poem

For everyone, for everything
I write a poem and keep;
And someday if we ever meet,
I'll hand out each with bliss.
For all the times we share on earth,
For all the blows we take;
I offer friendship, grace and mirth;
I give you love and care.
For all the Lord has given us,
For all He's made us do,
I kneel and pray to Him so much-
To make us good as new.
To every man who reads the poem,
I've written to be shared;
Remember you should lend a hand,
Remember why you're here.

—*Emilienne Motaze*

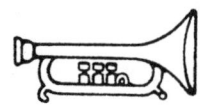

If

If I could go into the future,
I'd go where no one knows.
I'd go far away where no one ever goes.
If I could go into the past,
I'd go where no one has been before.
I'd go to a thousand places
And many, many more.

—*Amy Casella*

I try to never get angry—
I'd rather be glad than mad;
I must admit sometimes I do get
 perturbed,
and it bothers me to be disturbed,
it makes me feel so sad.
So, back in my head (on the very top
 shelf)
I keep a little "Cheer-Me-Up Elf"—
(One that is mellow is my kind of fellow).
If I scowl he comes out (he won't let me
 pout)—
Then I usually laugh at myself.
If I'm feelin' low and kind of blue—
things go wrong no matter what I do,
I call on my Elf to tickle myself—
(You ought to try it too).
Then a little twinkle begins;
First thing ya know—a couple of grins;
Soon you feel good—the way that you
 should,
Cuz the gloom is gone from you.

—*Haze Craddock*

Vietnam War

Caught in a whirlwind of confusion
If both are right, who's wrong?
Satisfaction for only some people
While others violently sing songs.
Bullets colliding with bodies
Grenades screech through the air
Nobody has the answer
So everyone is scared
Fighting for what seems no purpose
Was there ever one we ask
Why were victims carted away
To fulfill this terrible task
Dusk till dawn the war proceeded
Months and years had passed
Until finally the foolish men realized
That no one had last

—Kelly Christine LeBlanc

Untitled

We could have been friends
If hearts never lied
And to think all this time
Foolish pride
Kept us together
Yet, tore us apart
Still, I'm left with a broken heart
Dreaming we would always be
Still you said it's not me
And althouth you're not mine
I'm forever your girl
Wishing we could be
Two less lonely people in the world
Yes, someday I'll be over you
When a true love comes passing thru
But until then I'll remember when
I was holding you

—Joanne Halmas

A Tear of Love

Sometimes I feel like you don't really care
If I cry out for help that you won't be there
I know that things could work all we need is one more try
So I can wipe the tear slowly running from my eye
The feelings we both share are the only things that matter
But if they're hidden any longer that tear of glass will shatter
So if you don't want me to be yours to love and to hold forever
Then remember what I'm saying now your someone I'll always treasure

—Joy Wheeler

Sky

There's a miraculous view,
If only you knew.
Lie on your back and look above,
You'll find a rainbow of colors you'll love.
When the night comes, and you really try,
You'll see a bright and beautiful sky.

—Brenda Ashcraft

He's the Only One

Life isn't lived with one's self alone
If so I'd be making it all on my own.
When faults are shown, each day by day
I'd remember then to have followed
The path to which I have prayed.
Praying I've done time and time again
And that's something I know will never end.
He gave me dreams to light my way
And if dreams failed, I'd hear him say:
"Don't give up just yet, there's a way to go,"
"After all, what's life without dreams and goals?"
He's taught me things I know to be true.
Just listen to reason and hear him through.
If you learn as I have done,
Then you'll understand He's the only one.

—Amy McKissick

Greatest of All

I often think of what I'd do
If together we could not stay
If I could not trust in you
To share with me, every day.
My days would be dark
If your heart didn't shine.
I could not sleep for fear
When I'd wake, you wouldn't be mine.
My heart would never sing it's verse
I would feel so all alone,
If I could not talk to you
And call you my very own.
You always walk next to me,
Never behind or in the lead.
My heart you hold so dear
My love, the greatest of all.

—Jodi Schmidt

If We Want God to Come

The time is now we have to act
If we want God to come.
Can you imagine seeing God
And His trillion angel sons.
The bells will toll-the world rejoice
Each face will look above-
Up to the king of kings;
In Lord of lords-stunned!
This time He'll wear no crown of thorns
Instead a crown of-gold!
Before this great event takes palace
His word we shall unfold-His good news-
Unite-humanity come together as one-
If we want God to come.

—Grace Galasso St. Dawn

Stop This Madness

Nothing would be left but peace and harmony,
if we would stop these careless sins
shined upon you and me.
I am talking about homeless people,
out among the streets and
the families searching aimlessly for something to eat.
I am talking about the hate
between two beings as loving as can be.
So raise your hand proudly
and stop this madness in this world
to keep hope alive for the future to be.

—Alisha Nicole Alexander

I Want You

Life would be rich, it would taste just like sweets
If you and I darling, could mess up some sheets
You've got my pulse racing, my soul is on fire
My mind is delirious, with burning desire
I've watned to know you since the day we first me
You are a fantasy, I haven't lived yet
You look like a dream, you body's divine
I want to make love to you, be it your place or mine
My body would move with the heat of desire
Like a flame burning brightly, soaring higher and higher
I'd kiss you so sweetly, you'll think I was wine
My body would wrap yours, like a tight clinging vine
I want you so madly, I'm under your spell
But I don't need to say so, I'm sure you can tell.

—Dori Maurone

Untitled

Please don't tell me you don't know,
if you want me to just let go.
It could have worked if we both tried,
But after awhile our love just died.
I was really convinced that you loved me,
why couldn't you just let it be.
You had to go and be on your own,
the clues and signs just weren't shown.
Little did I know you'd soon be gone,
I was to hung up, I couldn't have known.
I've tried to forget and push you away,
but just the thought of being together
    someday,
Reminds me of how I used to feel,
back when our love was still for real.

—*Jenny Houser*

Want To Be Your Friend

I want to be yours,
If you want to be mine,
I have some friends, but I want some
    more.
I want to talk to you,
I want to share my feelings with someone.
I want to tell you how I feel.
Please be my friend,
I'm willing to give it a try.
I know you're left out,
but give it a try, you'll see.
Please give it a try.
I want to be happy,
I want you to be cheerful
Can you give it a try?
I'll be a lot happier.
Do you want to be my friend?
I hope so!

—*Kelly A. Thibeault*

The Artist

"Look!" I'll doodle you a doodle,
if you'll only wait upon a rye,
With pen and ink or pencil and lead,
I'll doodle to doodle the time away;
So, sit a spell in class on glass on
bench or anywhere—I don't mind!
I'll just doodle a doodle until you
    stop and cry—
"Why you doodle to doodle"
"just so your mind can go astray"!
She said poking me with the pointer,
to prove her lucid point.
"I don't doodle just to doodle a doodle"
for anyone anymore, I can assure you!
He said atop the high dunce-chair.

—*D. Lee Davis*

Dog

My dog is a special one,
I'll love him till the end,
He sits so still to listen to me,
So he's the best of friends.
My dog is a shabby dog,
But cute and sweet, that is,
I love him so very much
Cause he's the best there is.
When I'm lonely and feeling down,
He's always there for me,
He licks me on the hand,
Sometimes as gentle as the sea.
He barks aloud to questions I cannot
    answer alone,
He gives me the kind of love that you can
    never own.
My dog is so great; I'll love him till the
    end,
He's the best he can be ; that's why he's
man's best friend.

—*Jennifer Denney*

Dear Grandpa

As I walk through this existance
I'll recall the memories of your life
A smile will appear on my face
For time will not erase
Those memories
I hold deep in my heart.
As I recall those old stories
You would tell when I was young
And the songs we would sing
Made your face beam
Those memories
I hold deep in my heart.
And I know that where you are
Really isn't very far
I'm sure we'll talk again someday
We'll reminsce of the good times
We have missed
From a world of yesterday.

—*Jeri Hawkins*

Friendship Is Real

When you need support,
I'll take a stand.
When you are afraid,
I will always be there.
I will constantly care.
If you need might,
I'll help you fight.
When you can't see,
I'll be your sight.
I won't go, so you'll always know,
our friendship is real.
I'll help you reach the stars above.
Come to me and you will see. . .
I love you and it will always be
you and me!
Our Friendship is Real!

—*Diona Betz*

Darkness

You ask me "what is darkness?"
I'll tell you this, I should know all
About this word,
Cause I'm in the dark about you.
I'm sitting here scared of you,
Cause I'm in the dark about you.
My heart feels real cold and sad.
It is dark with a little bit of light,
Because you just looked into my eyes.
If you stay here with me you might
Melt the ice.
The ice is almost gone and a little
Bit more of light has come through.
Does this so far answer your question
About darkness?
By telling you,
The light has finally shined through.

—*Joy Fitzpatrick*

Outcast

Why do they look away?
I'm different?
Yes, but not in heart.
I see them looking at me,
their look is pity and disgust.
Why?
Am I going to live,
live in this bottled up world forever?
Talk to me,
Tell me you love me.
I think about why they stare
maybe
Just maybe
they are the ones who are different.

—*Emily Russell*

Being Alone

I don't understand this emptiness
I'm feeling inside.
I guess it's just part of being alone.
Everything's changing again, leaving me
With just a small piece of heart left,
Just part of being alone.
No more sweet loving smiles, just looks
To say goodbye,
Just another part of being alone;
Day dreams just stay fantasies that won't
Ever come true,
Just another part of being alone.
Wishing and dreaming of a time where
    love
Will come back,
Just another part of being alone.

—*Dani Lane*

Feelings

I don't know why
I'm feeling this way
This feeling just hit me
Earlier today
It's a feeling of happiness
I can't understand
It hit me today
When you first grabbed my hand
Feelings like these are hard to find
But when you get them
They never leave your mind
Yes, the feeling I have is true
I found it the day that I met you
I'll never forget that special day we met
That special moment I'll never forget

—Diana Dean

Today's the Day

Oh, today's the day,
I'm going to make a change,
A change for the better,
Even if it turns out for the worse.
Oh, today's the day,
I'm going to flower you with gifts,
And make love to you,
And maybe even marry you,
Because I know it'll turn out for the better,
And not for the worse.
Oh, even ,if it turns out for the worse,
I know as long as were still together,
We can make it turn out for the better,
And let it remain with us that way forever.

—Eddie Hennigan III

Anger Arising

I can't unfold the pressure burning up inside of me to the highest degree.
I'm like a ferocious lion just waiting for the perfect moment when I'm set free.
Or maybe I'm like a wild lion-tamer beating down on the animals' flesh just to get rid of my anger.
The PAIN, the TORMENT, the TEARS, the DANGER:
When does it all stop?
I guess there's no end!
Because there are too many enemies
And not enough friends.

—Gina Foster

Loneliness

It's dark out and no one is home.
I'm lonely and no one cares.
But I still have a life and
I will soon find someone who cares.
All those people I thought did care,
I now find they don't.
The hurt will soon go away I hope.
In life there are times you have to face up
To things like losing someone you love
And care for.
Some of the hurt will go away and yet some
Of it will stay with you forever.

—Dawn Schwarz

One Little Tear

When I was little, you always told me
When someone you loved died
Never grieve for what they lost
Always think of the "good times"
But always let one little tear fall
For the love you lost.
In you I had a kind hand to hold when I was hurting.
But a firm hand when I did wrong.
In you I had a friend, even though
Sometimes I thought of you as an enemy.
In you I had a voice that comforted me at all times.
But scared me to death sometimes.
In you I had everything, now as I stand here
Thinking of the good times.
I let one little tear fall
For the love I lost, your love.
Only one little tear.

—Tammie Truax

Friendship for Love

You're the greatest guy I know,
I'm not sure if I should let my feelings show.
I know I'll end up with a heart broken in two.
I'm so confused, I don't know what to do.
You're such a wonderful, caring man,
I don't know if you'll understand.
You'll never mean to hurt me,
But that's the way it'll end up to be.
If my felings are clear for you to see,
Will our friendship still be?
I want for you to know, but I don't want our friendship to end.
Do not worry, my heart is soon to mend.
I've realized a friendship is more than anything can ever be.
I want you to always remember me.
I'll never be able to look in your eyes without it hurting me,
Maybe that's the way it should be.
In my eyes you'll be forever great.
Your caring face I could never hate.

—Angela Michelle Nunez

I'm Lost

I'm lost and I know not where to go.
I'm so confused that I will let no one know.
I cry out on the inside and keep things hidden away.
I'm ridding myself of my burdens and I have no other way.
Sometimes a friend or a relative wants to join me.
We have decided that we want to be free.
We can't face a painful environment.
Negative things we definitely resent.
If no one wants to come with me, I'll go it alone.
I want out of reality and go to a more peaceful home.
Sometimes I give a hint as to what I want to do,
But a guardian angel looks over me and turns my gray skies blue.
Sometimes I'm successful and sometimes I fail,
But if I take my life, I will go to hell.
There are millions of lost people like me,
Most of us live to see how beautiful life can be.
So pay attention to my silent cry.
It's when I'm not heard and I want to die.

—Juliette Moon-Clay

Hopeless

My hearts beats in mid air,
While my legs tremble through the sand.
Birds fly over my head,
While I see him standing there.
He turns then smiles and walks towards me.
Then I fall to the ground hopelessly.
I'm not sure why, but I smile,
And walk away together,
As I have known him, for a great time.

—Missy Delap

Are you Still Insulted by the Things I Said

Are you still insulted by the things I said,
I'm sorry, but I was in over my head.
I agree I made a mistake,
How could I ever make it up to you.
Please just give me a break
And tell me what to do.
You know I loved you,
But I never knew if you felt the same.
I did everything there is to do.
But I don't know anymore how to play the game.
Every night and every day,
I never thought it would end this way,
Cause for a while, it went so well,
But now it's gone to hell.
With you, I was in heaven,
But now, I'm deep under the ocean.
I'll always remember your name,
But in my heart, it will never be the same.

—Josee Michaud

Never Leave a Friend

I'm sorry you must go through all this
  pain and sorrow.
I'm sorry there seems there may be no
  tomorrow.
Don't take it out on me, it's not my fault,
  can't you see?
I love you a lot.
I'll never let you go in my heart even
  though
Your problems are tearing us apart.
Somedays you hate me, others I'm
  adored.
It's like you get tired and maybe a little
  bored.
What am I to you? Obviously nothing
  now.
If I could change things, could you
  possibly tell me how?
I'm leaving you alone, but hopefully not
  for long.
Until you can figure out what you want
  from me,
Until you know what's wrong.
So goodbye as far as I'm concerned, it
  doesn't mean the end,
For though you may walk away, you can
  never leave a friend.

—*Amy Parker*

Sad and Happy

When there is hate and war going on
When nobody cares about one another,
Only being their selfish way;
When you lose friendship that lasted a
  long time,
When everything looks so confused
And you don't know what to do;
All these make me sad
To know that you have a
Family that cares about you,
When you feel safe and secure,
To have friends who see you the way you
  are,
And not because of what you could give
  them;
When there's love, peace and hope in the
  world
Finally all these will make me happy

—*Yvette Maldonado*

Sexual Assault

Why does it Hurt?
I'm supposed to be strong.
It happened a year ago,
Yet I still feel wrong.
He took all my pride
And he took all my trust.
When all he really wanted
Was all of my lust.
He left me with anger, and fear, and pain.
But I know he'll always go on with his
  special game.

—*Christie Ogden*

I Wish You Were My Daddy

I wish you were my Daddy you look so
  kind and good.
I'm sure that you would love me the way
  that daddies should.
I'd like to climb upon your lap or kneel
  down at your knee.
And listen to the stories old, you know
  would interest me.
Your face is oh, so very sweet, your eyes
  are tender blue.
Your smile is like a flash of gold that
  sparkles through and through.
To take my hand and hold it tight.
And tuck me in my bed each night.
I'd be so very, very glad if you would let
  me call you dad.
So please, kind sir, won't you agree that
  we would very happy be?
And take me home with you today where
  I can have a place to stay.
To live and grow as other boys and share
  together many joys.
My wishes are from an orphan lad who
  wants you for my loving dad.

—*George L. Hutchison*

Untold Feelings

If only I told you sooner the way I really
  felt.
I'm sure your heart would truly melt,
I never thought it woud be this way.
I loved you more then words could ever
  say.
I shook of nervousness when you were
  near.
I cried of sadness when you weren't here.
To have felt you touch my hand.
To know that you were there.
To make you understand how much I
  really cared.
So why can't you see that our love was
  meant to be.

—*Heather Smith*

Loneliness

Like a small abandoned child, I'm very
  full of fear.
I'm terrified of your rejection, afraid to let
  you near.
I fear the open vulnerability upon which
  people prey,
Like a fugitive on the run, I've chosen my
  own way.
You think you know how I feel, but I
  really must confess,
The wrong I've done that hurts the most,
  is that I've made a mess.
I've buried myself far away, where I'm
  sure to be secure,
What I really feel is loneliness, afraid and
  insecure.
I know that I should trust you, everything
  tells me so,
I know you won't let me down, but I'm
  afraid to let go.
Like the rose out in the garden, eventually
  must die,
The risk for eminent beauty is something
  I should try.

—*Jill Winestock*

Suicide

I wasn't alone, my shadow was with me.
When I turned around, she didn't.
I stepped on, she. . .
My faith was gone, my life followed it.
The red crawled across my palm,
The clock stopped, and a tear ceased it.
The silence screamed as the scene faded.

—*Silvia Lopez Lira*

All in Your Head

Don't forget who I am.
I'm your worst enemy, and your best
  friend.
I'll make you believe that it's all right.
Pleasant dreams on a moonlit night.
But sometimes good turns bad, changes
  from happy into sad.
I'm deep inside, inside of you.
And there's no escaping from me, because
  I'm a part of you.
And there's nothing left you can do, but
  learn to live with me.
I'll be there when you sleep at night.
I'll show you the way, when they turn out
  the lights.
Teach you that dark can be bright, or that
  wrong can be right.
Over the mountains through the cold and
  snow.
I will follow where ever you go.
Teach you all that I know.
But only the strong will survive
The weak and the crazy will die.
Because I'm a part of you, and there's no
  escape.
From your mind.

—*Joseph J. Jarnot, Jr.*

May God Help Us!

Imagine scores of churches without any
    preachers;
Imagine full high schools without any
    teachers;
And picture nice playrooms filled with
    toys
But no happy little girls and boys.
Feature scores of pregnant young mothers
Enduring the pain of abortion, while
    others
Are weeping because they cannot
    conceive
And care for children they'd gladly
    receive.
You say this is all so very absurd —
Like a beautiful forest without a bird —
Like a night sky in summer without
    shining stars,
Or a great new highway without any cars.
I wish it were only a very bad dream
And not social practice, common and
    mean.
I pray all young mothers will ask for
    God's will:
Then babies will grow up, their places to
    fill.

—*Ethel H. Kleppinger*

The Butterfly

How does the gay little buttterfly
Improve each shining hour,
And flutter from flower to flower through
    the day
Even in the worst shower!
It's works of play or of skill
I should be busy, too;
For satin will find mischief still
For idle minds to do,
In books, or school, or healthful play
Early years may be passed,
For this will pay for every day
Some great account at last.

—*Denise Long*

Balloon Ride

With my imagination I took a ride
In a beautiful hot air balloon.
As it ascended I held my breath
Hoping not to fall too soon.
I drifted over a land of peace
Where people labored hand in hand.
Love seemed to spread like fire
In such a lovely land.
A gentle breeze whispered freedom
Over trees and fields of grain
And people around the countryside
Had everything to gain.
Let's all hope someday soon we'll see
Where any balloon may rise
People living in a world of peace
Beneath the friendly skies.

—*Jack Hensley*

For Matthew

I am like a growing thing
In a meadow of bright green grass.
My flesh is a fortress of strong, dull steel,
My heart is one of glass.
Your kisses are the air I breathe,
Your hugs warm me like the sun.
When your eyes look into mine,
I know I am the only one.
So keep from me all the evil things
Give me what you can give,
For your love is like my source of life,
Without it I cannot live.

—*Caryn Evans*

Crossroads

I stroll along a lonely lane
In a rural county unknown.
As I walk, I come to a crossroad.
I glance behind me
And see the familiar past
Its trials and triumphs.
I gaze around me
Not noticing the rustic beauty
But my present life.
I look ahead towards the crossroads
And view all the directions, I may take
As the uncertain future.
Those crossroads resemble
My life and ambitions,
All the things I am and hope to be.

—*Jenniefer Droesch*

Dusk

Dusk
In a valley,
By the sea,
An old man sits,
Waiting patiently.
The cool breeze blows.
The trees sway.
In a far off land,
A shot rings through the battlefield.
A wave of screams,
And the crash of an empire.
The old man closes his eyes.
Death sweeps over him.
Dawn.

—*Helene Sinnreich*

My Dream

You left me here all alone
In a world I do not know
One day when I hear the bird
Sing in my apple tree
One day when the sun comes
And I know it is spring
I will see you that day you will
Be the same as you always were
But you will have changed
You will not be able to hear my
Birds sing for you cannot hear the love
And you will not see my apple tree
For you cannot see the tears
And you will not feel me
Standing next to you
For you cannot feel the pain
For your dream is not but real
But mine will shine again

—*Danielle Hiller*

Untitled

I met you by chance
In a world lacking love
You know me for just who I am
You gave my heart a shove.
I wish that you could understand
Just why I can't return
The feelings that you feel for me
To say this makes my tear drops burn.
Your words of love touch my heart
But they're really not for me
For you're in love with someone else
We weren't meant to be.
We needed some time to think things
    through
Away from the ones who hold our hearts
For we're both in love with someone else
And from them we'll never part.

—*Carrie Ann Madden*

If Only To Be Fifteen

If only to be fifteen
In a world not so far away
Where flowers bloom
And skies are blue
Oh, in the month of May!
Not a petal left unturned
Nor a mountain left to climb
"Higher than the kite"
Far beyond the time.
Oh, if only to be fifteen
I'd giveth all to Him
T'is He of whom I speak
Who gave it all to me.

—*Amy Consola*

Shattered Dream

Mere survival
In a world of mirrors
Walking on broken glass
Looking back on the shattered lives
Of the ones you left behind
Anxious tears in glittering eyes
Perfumed pity in your heart
Rhetorical question fluttering on your lips
Careful beings and strange occurences
Starlight to set a somber mood
Foolish ways of devised promises
Unpunished grief and unspeakable death
Special youth succombed to pieces
Soul here, up in the trees
Body there, buried in your grave
Under a bed of beautiful roses
Death becomes you.

—*Kim Clemente*

Death

What is death, how does it feel,
In case of a wound, do you heal?
Is it scary when you die,
Deep down beneath, where you lie?
Can you see, can you hear,
Can you feel a cold wet tear?
If God doesn't take you, where do you go,
Down to that awful place far below?
When I die I will know
That God has decided it's my time to go.

—*Heidi J. Herrin*

Summer Days

I sit below the trees
In comes a soft cool breeze
When I sit in all of their shade
I can see branches form a braid
A bird tweets in its nest
It is a robin red breast
When I looked up into the sky
He was flying with mystery in his eye
A few flowers bloom
They take away all the gloom
Nature in all it's mysterious ways
Make beautiful these bright summer days

—*Beth Jones*

The Orchestra

Arms outstretched
in command.
Graceful,
powerful movements.
The song has begun.
Bows glide over strings.
Sweet and flowing.
Swelling from behind,
fluid sounds.
Haunting but beautiful.
Reeds and winds.
Rich, deep tones.
Ringing, resounding, over all.
Beating out time.
Crash.
The melody of ivory.
Mallots on metal.
Silence.

—*Kristin Dascole*

The Sky

The sky, like a cat's eye, glows
In damp morning when the sun will make
A reveille to all below,
And then I dryly wake.
The sky tumbles to curious blue,
A playful color that glistens.
The dancing world is busy at noon,
So the clouds settle to listen.
The sky becomes a flower,
When the night begins to bloom.
It is a gentle hour,
That ends singing with the moon.
The sky is now flowing navy,
A sea of royal lights,
So I lay down on my pillow
And dream away the night.

—*Hallie Lanier*

Best Friends

It seems as if the years have passed
In just a few short days.
The ties with which our hearts are bound
All time cannot erase.
Tho' we be separated
By long and toilsome miles,
The memories stored within our minds
Are the source of many smiles.
The thoughts we've shared,
The laughter and the tears.
We've shared our lives, our hopes, and
  dreams
Our friendship lasts the years.
Much time may pass before the day
When you come back to me.
I only ask, remember this,
Best friends-eternally.

—*Kimberly A. Shaver*

Whispers In The Wind

If I should leave my body to perish
In my hour of death, your memory will be
  cherished
If my time expires with the slipping sand
My spirit will seek to kiss you hand
If I should lie as an empty shell
My soul will linger by your side to dwell
If my essence leaves without suffering or
  shame
The last word I'd utter would be your
  name...

—*Erline Alonzo*

Her Mystery

Composing and creating,
In my imagination
Without hesitating,
Trying to solve the mystery
Which is like a puzzle,
A puzzle of her.
What is her identity,
And her life story?
Is her beautiful blond
Hair really blond?
Are her pretty blue eyes
Truly blue?
Where did she come from?
Why is she really here?
Why is my heart
So deeply curious,
And why is it so happy,
Whenever she is near?

—*Gil Saenz*

Untitled

Love is a feeling that comes from the
  heart.
In our eyes it should be seen as poetry and
  art.
Why so much fear? Our emotions should
  bring us tenderness and passion.
Have we not cried enough tears? This era
  has brought us into a world of power
  and fashion.
Justify the pain—it's time to get
  romantic.
Love should bring happiness and joy, not
  make us crazily insane.
Let's make a new start and show the
  world that love truly comes from the
  heart!

—*Kellie M. Leslie*

The Butterfly: 1863

One day, while I was playing
In our field, I came upon a butterfly.
Its wings shone (purple, orange, green)
In the sun. It was so beautiful that
I captured it. I brought it to my father
To show him my magnificent captive.
When he saw it, he said, "Child, do you"
"Know what you've done? You've taken the"
"Beauty and dignity away from one of God's"
"Creatures. Set it free immediately."
As I turned, headed for the field,
I heard my father holler for our slave
boy to bring him more lemonade.

—Christine A. Wilt

Together Forever

Together as one
In rain and in sun
With love in our heart
May we never be apart.
In God we live
And continue to give.
I'll stand by you
And you stand by me—
Together we can make it through eternity.

—Holly Poremba

Lullabye to a Little One

Little baby, angel of mine,
In slumberland shall you find
Dreams of toys, ribbons, and rings
Sugarplums, candy canes, and silver wings
Nutcrackers and ballerinas dancing
Angels singing in your dreams
Sleeping angel, so beautiful and sweet
You are so precious to me
Little darling, little one
Sleep for dawn will soon come.

—Diane Phillips

Old Friends New

Friends old, new
In, out of our lives
They travel
Like clouds floating
Through the skies
Covering up the sun.
That's how time
Can cover friendship.
Then comes the sun
Peering through the clouds
Appearing again
Like old friends do
Creating new friendships
In an older state of mind
And older state of time.

—Dee Dlouhy

Memorial to Vietnam

The ghosts of these our honored dead
in silent muster stand.
Like brooding sentries—grimly wait
the healing of their land.
Long since quiet guns of war,
the crash of cannon across jungle floor.
But the other enemy is with them yet
"Dissent and prejudice"—they can't forget.
So make this not a wailing wall
for rebel causes lost,
But a burning shrine of glory
to those who paid the cost.
Just leave them your love and unshed tears
as you pass beside the wall.
Small measure—for we the living to give -
to those who gave their all.
May they rest in peace "forever more"
from a "long and brutal" bitter war.

—Edward D. Slater

No One At All

One stark figures passes
in the darkness of night,
but no one notices!
A child cries and
wakes a thousand hearts but
no one hears!
And old man sits still in the
cold of the city but no one
stops to lend a hand.
Watching a melancholy world fall,
no one glances at
the time going by.
Looking back on time finally
being able to see the reality of
man's faults.
As society lingers on
to a thread of hope, no one notices
no one at all.

—Athena Davis

As Gulls Fly

Awaken to streaming golden light
In radiant flow from the sky.
Arise to mornings beauteous sight
The soaring of gulls, floats as they fly.
Seagulls have crying conversations
As over the breaking waves they go.
I walk on the sand in elation
In the golden light upon me to show.
Catch a glimpse of descending gulls
Dipping into the ocean to feed.
Over the gracefullness of gulls one mulls
As expert fishers they now succeed!
Inspiration of spirit follows their flight.
The outstretched wings of gulls unfold
Silhouetting against rays of golden light. . .
Become remembered images untold.

—Karen Kernodle

Silent Stares

I did not see,
In silent stares,
Those deep, dark lights—
My father's eyes—
The love I sought to find.
Anger alone,
Or so I thought,
Behind that inward gaze.
He held aloof.
I turned away,
From silent stares,
His mask for fear.
I did not understand.
We spoke no words,
Our time soon passed,
All lost in silent stares.

—George E. Damm

Summer

My mother called a plumber,
In the midst of summer!
His eyes were dark
And he lived in a park.
He came and went,
Always leaving off a scent.
The plumber fixed our sink,
But charged us quite a pink.
By the end of summer,
He fixed our home.
And this is the
End of my poem.

—Kristine Mazeika

From the Sun in May to an Unhappy Day

It was a sunny day
In the month of May
When I first saw my true love come
His hair sparkled in the sun
He said hello t me
Then may I tack you out to dinner please
I excepted with great anticipation
Then a week after this he took me on
  vacation
But then something happened I dread
He came out of the car accident dead
I was all fine
But the life token should have been mine
I love him till this very day
I remember the first time I meet him in
  May

—*Jenny Vass*

The Day We Met

The day we met, it was a warm spring day
In the month of May,
A year ago today.
When our eyes met
That is when I knew I fell for you.
I became lost in your eyes
And was totally in love with you.
I could never forget the day we met.
It changed my life forever.
You became my whole life.
Nothing else seemed to matter.
Once I met you
I knew you were the perfect one.
That's why I would never forget
THe day we met.

—*Cindy Corrente*

Untitled

Down the trumpeting falls I fell
In the morning new and strong the smell
Of watercress and frozen sap
Of earthy quilt that stole the map
To the triumph cloud and pine tree
To the boy blue and checkered seee
Walk the crosses, dash and dot
Lift but under there was not
A sole, soul, a year perhaps
Fly above the discriminate traps
That catch, but than a month, a week
Less aisles must Trojans seek
Worn they are, a bearded ten
To forge through bush and curling glen
Caves found crumbled, somewhat dry
Never drown, nor to sigh
To the island, any who hunt and sail
Bury rocks all jewels will fail.

—*Alicia White*

Does the Sky Ever Smile?

I've seen that smile before,
In the sky as I watched the birds soar.
The clouds so glorious, so blue,
They make me smile, they remind me of
  you.
Never will I let my gentle heart heal,
For my feelings for you are so tender, so
  real.
Maybe this feeling wasn't meant to be,
Or maybe I'm weak and holding onto
  destiny.
Whatever the reason,
You and I are together as one,
For you are the moon and I, the sun.

—*Candi Kitchen*

Mystery of the Soul

Mystery lies within each human spirit,
In the soul and inner self.
The kind of mystery most all keep hidden
Even from themselves.
Drifting in thought, with a total solitude,
The vital essence of man
Becomes an island, surrounded by
  memories
Difficult to span.
With the crushing pressure of eternity,
Our spirit cries out with a desire
To put our soul out front,
Where all may see who we really are.
Rising from the obscurity of our past,
Our fears reign afar, and in the end
Keeps our soul in hiding,
Showing only what we want others
To believe we are.

—*Joan L. Day*

A Man's Eyes

A man's eyes glimmer;
in the thought of lust.
A man's eyes wince;
in mistrust.
A man's eyes water;
in his sleep.
A man's eyes stream;
the tears he weeps.
A man's eyes glow;
when he finds a dollar.
But a man's eyes shine;
when he sees he loves her.

—*Andree Miller*

Life in the Country

Instead of city noises, one hears the
  crickets and the birds.
In the tranquil—looking bushes are
  creatures who need no words.
The flash of lightning and the peals of
  thunder
Contrast with the darkness of night.
There is a oneness with nature as the
  morning brings the light.
In the distance is a barking dog
And the slowly lifting of the morning fog.
Soon the sky will change its hue and
  become a vivid blue.
The daylight dispels the shadows of the
  night
And everything looks so light and bright.
The vivid color of flowers and the many
  shaded greens of trees,
The sound of rippling water as it flows
  over pebbles and leaves.
These are the sounds of nature so
  appealing to the soul.
The peace and quiet of the country makes
  one feel so whole.

—*Edna Joblon*

I Have Seen

I have seen the wind.
In the tree tops, bent in surrender
Against a force not even they can subdue.
I have seen the wind.
In the whirlwind of autumn's colored
  leaves
Twirling in dance and delight.
I have seen the wind.
In the waters of the pond's morning light
Rippled with shimmering laughter.
I have seen the wind.
In the wings of the hawk, in motionless
  stature
Swooping upward without the exertion of
  flight.
I have seen the wind.
In the hair of mine own, tussled and
  thrown
About my face in confused direction.
As I gaze through the locks that flow
  round my head
I can say with much reverance
I have seen the wind.

—*Christine Annette Tait*

Stop And Think

The beautiful roses are out today.
In the wonderful month of May.
And look at the roses,
With their pretty, pink roses.
Do you still want the world to stop?
And the lovely roses to drop?
Everyone does once in a while.
That's in the big blue file.
But when your problems get to you stop for a while,
And think of the pretty, pink roses.

—*Kerry Anctil*

Wild and Free

Somewhere
In the world
Is a thing of great beauty,
A thing of perfect grace.
Wild and free
On a distant horizon,
That's where he will be.
Long black mane and tail,
Flowing in the air
From his great speeds.
The setting sun
Shines bright on his sleek, black coat.
No man will ever ride him,
He truly is,
Wild and free!

—*Jocelyn L. Adelsperger*

Think of Me

When you've lost your way
In this changing world
Think of me-
Think of me
When the storm rages on
And you can't seem to calm it
Think of me-
Think of me
Think of me in good times or bad
When you think of me
You'll never be alone. . .

—*Eugenia Collins*

Sorrow

I am alone, utterly alone
In this cold, dark cage that some call life,
And I call sorrow.
With winds blowing from every side,
Some warm, but more often cold than not,
They seek to chill and freeze the very essence
Of my soul, the life's breath
Of my lips.
An icy world, with crystal figures
Made of shadows, brilliantly dulled, that try
To see my pain, my agony
With probing soft sharp spikes, like teeth
Yet somehow not.
Darkness closes in about my trembling soul,
Grasping terribly at the strings,
To pull me to my end.
A gleamingly dull black shard is thrust,
And as I scream, the strings of my soul, my soul
Are cut.

—*April E. Mattison*

Kevin

The act so repugnant,
Yet peace of mind and soul was his.
Though horrid and not understood,
The pain was acceptable and deeply felt.
Searing pain, seething sores,
Caused haunts of guilt,
Ghosts from the hurt inflected on
Those loved and deared for always.
The lasting sore cut across the conscious
Causing blood red streams of screams so shrill,
That the sound pounded and dulled.
Never to be so again.

—*S. L. Spotts*

Pain

Why is there so much pain,
In this world?
A small child gets hurt,
When he falls,
While trying to walk.
Why is there pain?
A teenage girl gets hurt,
When her guy dumps her,
For someone else!
There is too much pain,
In this world!
A five year old child,
Cries with fear,
When her cat is lost!
A little boy,
Gets upset when,
He loses his favorite baseball card!
Why is there so much pain in this world?

—*Kelly Showers*

The Cry of a Rainforest

Please, leave us alone, to dwell and create life;
Instead of cutting us down, with your sword, axe or knife.
We are simply here to help out by making breathable air;
And create medicines to help the sick, for humans in despair.
We are picture perfect beauty and alive with noise and sound;
Yet slowly we are deteriorating with the help of man, we are less found.
Please, let us live to be old, never destroy us again;
We give so much, help out so much, please. . .give us no more pain.
Do not destroy us anymore by cutting and burning us down;
Or soon there will be none left.
If the killing doesn't stop, the destruction exterminated,
You will witness our extinction, our death.

—*Aimee E. Grimm*

The Beach

The sun beats down
Intensely on my head,
As the waves gently
Ripple up onto the shore.
I can smell the air.
Fresh.
Undisturbed.
And I can feel the hot grains of sand
Oozing through my toes.
The breeze,
Hardly present,
But blowing gently
In my hair.
Alone.
I am all alone.
Quietly,
As not to disturb the silence,
I roll over and gaze out to the green—blue sea.

—*Clare Mulford*

A New World

Diving down beneath the surface,
Into a brand new world.
A world so different from yours and mine,
A place so beautiful,
A place so fine.
Colored fish here and there,
This place I discovered underwater somewhere.
This is the place I've been dreaming of,
This is the world I love.

—*Erika Brown*

Metamorphosis

A caterpillar can change but once
Into a butterfly
And cannot retreat to its cocoon
A mountain crumbles slowly
Into the sand
And does not impose upon the land
A flower grows and then returns
Into the ground
And will not wave in the wind
A friend by chance should turn
Into a lover
And a friend is lost forever

—*Bob Schumaker*

Forever

She took her life
Into her heart; into her hands
And threw it up into the air.
She watched it gently fall to the ground
And she turned away,
On the perfect autumn day,
And left her life on the autumn floor
With broken dreams to be swept away.
Shadows in the darkness
On another starry night;
Memories of our love
Still fresh in my mind
Dancing on the beach
Through the sand and through the waves;
Laughter echoes in the midst of places
    where
We once loved
Forever is what we said;
But forever was too long for our love to
    last.

—*Gabrielle Schapira*

Rain

When it rains, it pours
Into puddles of tears.
It's gloomy out
The sun isn't
Shining bright.
When it rains
The tears are fresh
As a newborn baby.
But it clears up
And the sun is
Shining bright
In the sky.
The gloominess
Has passed.

—*Carmen Webb*

Mountain Scenery

Go down deep
Into the night
Find the source
That gives you fright
Face up to the eyes
That haunt you inside
You will soon realize
You can push them aside
Don't let them get you
They'll drive you insane
My words are true
For I did the same.

—*Dana Bertrand*

The Sea's Anger

The storm buffets the ocean's waves
Into the storm's sandswept caves.
Not a gull
In the sky.
The sand is wet,
Nothing is dry.
The lightning flashes,
The water dashes.
The sand does nothing,
Listen to the water strike on key.
The thunder rumbles and roars,
Over the sea,
Not a gull soars.
Then suddenly,
A peaceful calm
Comes over the land.
All that's left of the storm
Is the cold, wet sand.

—*Jana M. Lawson*

Untitled

one simple blade of squeaky green grass
is
stuck on the end of my toe
the
moisture makes it cling to my toe
i
swirl my foot in the
warm pool water
waves ripple and
catch
one simple blade of squeaky green grass
floats
away
on another adventure.

—*Anjanette Ohlerking*

Nobody Won

An angle of polished black stone,
Is a chilling sight that chills to the bone.
The names on the wall are more than lives
    lost,
For the war they were the cost.
So that for every man that died, so died a
    dream,
But in the jungles nothing was as it
    seemed.
The men were the price paid in blood and
    sorrow,
Everyone thought it would produce better
    tomorrows.
Vietnam was a human tragedy,
A tragedy of epic dimensions that reaches
    even me.
When it was all said and done,
We would call it Vietnam: The War
    Nobody Won.

—*Angela Kathleen Foye*

A Circus of Curious Delights

This World
Is a Circus of Curious Delights
Complete with PeekShows, a MidWay, a
    Battered BigTop,
And blinking, blinding Kaleidoscopic
    Lights
That produce a gaggle of delerious Days
    and Nights—
It's a Circus of Curious Delights!
$This World
Is a Rib-Crackling Waltz with a Dancing
    Bear
While the ticket-buying Audience
    applauds with bated breath,
Betting to see if you escape, are raped or
    crushed to death
While Ursus Horribilius drags you here
    and there—
It's a Rib-Crackling Waltz with a
    Dancing Bear!
$This World
Is a Mind-Boggling Whirl on a
    Merry-Go-Round,
On a Pink Plastic Porpoise going nowhere
    except up and down
While pursued by Rainbow-Maned
    Stallions & a Virgin Swan—
Then, abruptly, the rinky-tinky music is
    gone!
Slowly, the Merry-Go-Round dies down.
$And I?
I am that Rubber-Nosed, Baggy-Pantsed
    Clown
Who pratfalls to tickle the fancies of those
    wearing crowns,
Inching my way to The Center Ring
    where squats The King,
Resplendent in purple, star-spangled
    tights—
This World
Is a Circus of Curious Delights!

—*James Ploss*

The Way She Is

The way she is to me
Is a vision of pure beauty
She is the sun in my dawn
She is all I've ever wanted
Her glimmering, golden hair
Her caressing and seductive voice
The blueness of her eyes reminds me
Of looking up from the ocean floor
The softness of her skin
Is like that of a new born baby's
The way she moves is so incredible
She has the grace and beauty
Of a ballerina
She is the queen
Who rules the world inside my mind
She is all I think of
Or ever will think of
This is why I love her.

—*Adam Franklin Pierce*

Tomorrow

Weapons, planes, bombs and guns
Is all we ever hear.
You're not showing us the meaning of life,
But making us live in fear.
You're teaching us to fight and defend,
Not to work together.
The money you spend on weapons
Should go to something better.
For we shouldn't live in fear of our
    neighbors,
But in love and trust of all.
For the future lies in the hands of us,
The children you're telling wrong.
As I sit by my window watching the
    world,
I shed a tear in sorrow.
For I wonder if there will be
Another day for tomorrow.

—*Jennifer Barnett*

Michelangelo

The ceiling
is an eggshell
Break through
and see the clouds
The dust on your idols below
sneezes greater men
than you
Touch God
with a paintbrush
Lying on your scaffold altar
the blood of your sacrifice
drips rainbows into white tunics
passing in processional
far below your gaze
Cardinals in worried circles
find fault with flesh
in their deep whispers
This was not your idea

—*George Roland Wills*

A Paper Rose

A paper rose
Is cut to pieces,
By your cruel laughter.
But the real one
You crush—
And the thorns twist tight
Into your skin.
—And so I'm sorry
That your heart
Now twists in pain.

—*Jacqueline Schmidt*

Death

What is death?
Is death the end of life as we know it?
Does death help people end what they
    consider a bad life?
Or is death a passing on to a new life?
Is death a welcome relief or something
We are always worrying that we're going
    to be next!

—*Heather Ann Costes*

Untitled

This world of ours
Is forever bold
Because the truth we seek
Is never told.
We sit in our homes
Hearing the lies
While the government tells us
That it tries.
The things they say
They have no clue
Of the terror we feel
From what they do.

—*Kim Klinger*

The Gift of Song

The gift of tomorrow
Is in a song
A gift of love
For which the world does long.
Song brings joy
To a world dark with madness
And we have a chance
To brighten it with our gladness.
To bring song to the world
Would be to give a gift that has no end
A song in itself,
The gift of a friend.
So, may others enjoy
The joy and gladness
May music take away
A world of sadness.

—*Angela Lueking*

Untitled

My favorite place to be
Is in an open field,
Full of beautiful flowers.
The wind blowing through your long hair,
The birds chirping around you.
Peace and quiet, no one there,
No one to bother you.
The fresh open air.
I like sitting. . .
Reading. . .
Or just doing nothing.

—*Krissy Liesch*

Death

What is death?
Is it just a neverending sleep?
Why then do our loved ones weep?
Perhaps they do not understand.
Is it a long hollow tunnel with a bright
    light at the end?
And when we walk to that light, are we
    accompanied by our past friends?
Do they understand?
Or is everyones' death different, each
    seeing their maker as how they
    perceive,
Each in their own state of afterlife, in
    which they would not want to leave.
Will they then understand?
Or is it full of angels, harps, and doves,
All living on the most special type of love?
Can you understand?
How then can you explain this to a young
    bright-eyed child, who's
favorite word is "Why"?
She will not understand.

—*Darniele Taylor*

Masquerade

The emptiness in my heart
Is only there to remind
Of sacred promises broken
And the one left behind.
Shades of the past
Dance softly in my head
And for victims of love
There are tears to be shed.
For in the lonely night
Voices hold no sound
Only silence speaks
And dreams cannot be found.
Love for the two of us
Only once can be
Because a pain filled masquerade
Is all that I can see.

—*April Spencer*

New Life

Being brought to us
is something so dear
Listen, please listen
I want you to hear
We're having a baby
our joy is unknown
Over the months—just look!
how big baby's grown
The day baby's born
will bring us such joy
As long as it's healthy
be it a girl or a boy
Our days will be brightened
our nights will all shine
Now I've got one—a family
one I can call mine.

—D. T. Bishop

A Special Dream

A greem meadow near a cool, clear
   stream
is the setting of a special dream
A dream of flowers and of trees
on a sunny spring day with a gentle breeze
as I peer at my reflection in the water
   clear and blue
I feel a gentle hand touch me and I know
   it must be you
you gaze into my eyes as you draw me
   near
I'm sure you can see how much I care
You whisper very softly that you'll love
   me forever more
And then so very gently you touch my lips
   with yours
When I wake up wishing it was true.
All I think about is me loving you.

—Heather M. Bolton

Without a Choice

Drowned here in my blood and tears,
Is there anyone who cares?
I'm lost in pain, I'm so scared.
This is what I've always feared.
Can't go back, I've gone too far,
There are many doors but none ajar.
I timidly just creep around
Too scared to even make a sound.
Time has passed and I am sure
I cannot stay a moment more.
I've been shot down, but I still try
I do not need the reason why.
Time has told I cannot choose,
Whether or not I win or lose.

—Kristen Andersen

Why God Made Father's

A Father's greatest responsibility,
is to train his child to follow God's way,
to love, guide, and provide,
to read God's word and pray.
God made a Father ready and willing
to lend a helping hand,
And to listen when his child
needs someone to understand.
A Father cares for his little one,
while watching God's example,
of how He loves His only Son.
God made a Father to hold his son's hand,
to walk with him through life, until he
   becomes a man.
God made a Father to hold his daughter's
   hands,
to stay beside, and protect her, until he
   gives her another man's hand.
God gave man a honored blessing, when
   he made him a Father
by giving him the responsiblity, of a son or
   daughter.

—Erma J. Sybil

The Little Fool

The little fool
Is very slow in his actions.
He does not play with the other children.
The little fool
Never talks. . .when people ask him
   questions.
He is discreet.
People do not like the little fool.
They tire of him, thinking that—
He is of no use to the world in any way.
They do not know
That he lives in a world of his own
And he writes beautiful poems
Of the heart.

—Dalit Warshaw

A Family

A family is one who clings together
Is what my Bible said.
They pray together and stay together
Is how my Bible read.
The family is the source of strength
Working in unity and making preparatio
The hopes, dreams, and cornerstone
Of every country and every nation.
The family is one you can turn to
When there are troubles all around.
They clothe, feed and shelter you
When your world comes crashing down.
A family is one who loves each other
Who stays in touch when they are apart.
Their future, success and survival
Are embedded in each other's heart.

—Erwin Milner

Dream Land

Somewhere, in a world unknown to man,
Is where we meet secretly.
It's a sacred place where dreams become
   reality;
A serene enviornment surrounded by big,
   white, fluffy clouds.
In the night awaits the magical unicorn
Which will take us to our enchanted
   garden.
Soft music plays as we glide across the
   sky.
We take a ride on the never ending
   colorful rainbow.
As we near the end of our journey
Everything begins to disappear,
Everything seems to fade as we begin to
   fall from above.
We are not afraid.
For we know we'll meet again;
Once again in dream land.

—Diane Weiss

A Naked Ride

Another night escaped my sleepless soul,
It aches and screams and cries relentless
   tears
From naked eyes discolored by my fears,
Alone, Afraid, without a stable pole
To lean my broken heart, an empty hole
Hides every empty promise made by
   peers,
Oh, how the room seems larger through
   the years,
Walls laced with proof that time does take
   its toll,
Remind me how to ride without a sound,
"Behave, you silent tears who deafen
   sight"
"Of mine," Now i see wasted tears i've
   cried,
I only ride when no one is around,
Which means i ride all through the
   endless night,
Another night devours my sleepless pride

—Jill Heyman

Love

Love was shattered by a precious guy
It broke me up and I wanted to cry
One has caused this sorrow and pain
And I'll leave this poem with
unmentioned names.
I'm telling you this, I'm not insane
I'm telling you this, Because of a hollow
   pain
I'm telling you this, With no more shame
It may be you, with unspoken time
That will take my heart to the place
   devine.

—Charlene Wilbur

The Rose

The rose that he gave me was strawberry red
It came straight from my heart the card plainly said.
The rose is like you, filled with beauty and joy.
You're nothing but goodness for this plain country boy.
I loved him so much and the love that we shared,
I wanted him to know just how much I had cared.
Even though he is gone our love stays the same
Now I know in my heart no one is to blame.
The petals are starting to fall from the stem
It reminds me so much of the way I loved him.
Now the rose that he gave me is dying so slow,
But our love for each other continues to grow.

—*Angela Hatfield*

True Love

True Love is a beautiful thing
It can make you laugh
It can make you sing
True Love is a wonderful thing.
It fills your heart with joy
Your eyes shine bright.
True love is not a toy
But a feeling that shines like a light.
True love will never let you down.
It is always there when your feeling low.
True love, for me, has found itself a place
my heart, forever.

—*Amy Paris*

Priceless is Your Love Towards Me

My love for you is so strong, so deep.
It cannot be compared with other fine treasures.
I need not money, nor gold, nor priceless works of art,
For you are all I need, all that makes me happy.
Your love cannot be bought, it has no limit, no price.
It is an endless treasure that I have discovered.
Your love towards me is shown in everything you do.
I need not live without it, for it is always there.
Your love evolves around me, it is all I need to keep me going.
You are to me like warmth and water to an unborn flower
For when that flower blossoms, it is the most natural, beautiful thing.
When you are with me, our love blossoms more and more each day.
Inside of us we have painted one more flower,
To add to the meadow of flowers we have created.

—*Halide Niazi*

Love

Love. . .
it comes
from the deepest
and darkest tunnels
of your heart
from the very bottom
it reaches out
to steal another heart
it is giving and taking
understanding and forgiving
and most of all
it is everlasting
like the constant flow
of a river
that never ends.

—*Jill Detro*

Love

Love is a very special thing
It comes in waves, it comes in flings
And though my love and I've just met
I know our love is not in debt.
My love for him will never die,
Even if we someday say goodbye.
And though it would hurt to see him part,
His love will forever be in my heart!

—*Clarissa Scott*

Undecided

Decisions are things we all must make,
It doesn't matter who we are.
The choices we have tempt us,
They overrule our minds by far.
Though we may want what may be wrong,
That's the way life goes.
You live and take it day by day,
With every days' highs and lows.

—*Kim Skala*

Life Goes On

As I lie here thinking of you and our times together,
It gives me an empty feeling inside.
I guess knowing that I'm here for you anytime you need me
And you not being there.
I know it would have been great between us.
Just because there was this one girl that broke your heart
Doesn't mean that me or any other girl will.
I know you feel confused and lonely,
But it's only part of life.
That's why everybody gets hurt every now and then,
But there's one thing to remember and that's
Life goes on.

—*Dana R. Cole*

Never too Much

I love you so much
It hurts me to tell you so,
Even though you're not
With me now there's
No way I could ever let you go.
I still see you in
My dreams but I still seem
To be all alone, because I
Can't touch you like I used to.
In the end I hope
You are right here with
Me, because nothing you can say
Or do could ever make me stop
Loving you.
There's never too much
Love from you.

—*April Guilford*

Love

Love is more than a word,
It is a feeling.
It is stronger than friendship
Or just plain caring.
It is a reason to go on living.
Love is a combination of all our emotions.
It is stronger than fear or pain.
It is all conquering.
It is a reason for dying.

—Jenny Kaufmann

Untitled

Sometimes life seems too hard to bear.
It is as though no one does really care.
And then perhaps I will recall
How it is said when one door closes
  another will open.
What am I doing in the Hall?
When one door closes,
The dark completely surrounds.
There is a vaccum like stillness,
No music, bird's songs, or other sounds.
Then another door opens
A crack of light shines through.
A distant murmur of voices,
Then, dear Lord, there is you,
Waiting to show me the way
TO a brighter and better day.

—Betty B. Harness

Life

Life begins in the womb, at the moment of
  conception,
It is at birth that we initially start,
Our journey to the end, our death.
As a newborn, as a child,
We are unaware of our venture.
Each day, we travel along a path,
Which brings us closer to God, our
  creator.
We sometimes think our youth will last
  forever.
That old age is far yet down the lane.
But often, before we realize, it arrives
  unannounced.
Bewildered, we wonder where the time
  went.
As we grow near and nearer to our maker,
We reflect on past events,
Thinking of how things might have been,
Could have been, yet were.
We sense our vulnerability, our fear of the
  unknown,
Some of us are at peace with ourselves
  and God.
Which are you?

—Andra Lynn Stone

What Is Love?

What is love?
It is just an
emotion.
What is love?
It is something
you will learn
about.
What is love?
I don't know
Why not?
Because no one
wanted to teach me.
Why?
Because!

—Amy Kieber

Yes, I Am

Yes, I am your child.
It is of no importance that we are
  different.
Yes, I am your child.
Is it not of some importance that when cut
  I bleed.
Yes, I am your child.
It is of no importance that our outer shell
  is different.
Yes, I am your child.
Is it not of some importance that when
  tickled, I laugh.
Yes, I am your child.
It is of no importance that my hair is of a
  different texture.
Yes, I am your child.
Is it not of some importance that when
  sad or hurt, I weep.
Yes, I am your child.
It is of no importance that my lips are
  fuller.
Yes, I am your child.
Yes, I am you, in a different wrapping.

—Cheryllynn A. Morton

Dream

When you dream,
It is real
And when you are awake,
It is a dream.
The living is a dream
And it is in God's mind.

—Jaime Lynn Marshall

The Wind

The wind is a kite, touching the clouds.
It knows no boundaries or cages or
  crowds.
It dances and sings in blossomed trees,
It titters and giggles at buzzing bees.
The wind is a horse, wild, untame
It's always surprising, never the same.
Swirling, twirling and flaunting it's skirt,
The wind is a giggler, a blusher, a flirt.
Softly, so softly, it picks up a seed.
Then cruelly, so cruelly, it uproots a weed.
It pushes the clouds out of it's way,
It picks on a tree, just for play.
The wind is a cleanser, cleaning the air,
It sweeps by the flowers, making them
  fair.
Sometimes it's like the roaring sea,
But always, always, always it's free.

—Kelly Renee Henderson

What is Life

Life is like a speck of dusk.
It lands,
It joins others.
My mother sweeps it away
With her white cleaning rag.
It's gone.
Life. . .

—Julie Jarzynka

The Dove

The small lonely dove,
It likes his head to be rubbed
It loves bird seed,
But it doesn't read
Is it you or is it me,
That knows how they can be;
They like to fly high
Way, way up into the sky,
Then they look down
On you and the ground
He halfway smiles
But continues to fly, for miles
he flies on and on till the
Crack of dawn

—Bobbi Thomas

So Red the Rose

So red the rose that I see before my eyes.
It looks as though it may be in disguise.
Is it really there or does it vanish when the
  sun rises?
Will I ever know?
Shall I ever show?
Will its sacred beauty rise from below?
I just don't know.

—Kristin Korpos

A Heart

A heart is like a looking glass
It loves, hates and can do it with such class.
A heart is the deepest thing within you
Hiding every feeling that makes you blue.
A heart will not hesitate to twist and confuse
Making you feel like no matter what you do, you will lose
And when it comes decision time
A heart just breaks and can't decide if it wants you to be mine.

—Colleen Eklund

Time After Time

By and by
When I think of you,
I remember all those memories
Because it's all I have left
Of the times we shared
Of the times we cared.
Day after day,
I think of you
Of the times when I used to say
I love you
You mean so much to me
Why does this have to be
The end of us together?
Night after night,
I wish I could hold you tight.
I can never sleep because way down deep
I love you so much it hurts.

—Melissa C. Stolder

Silent Conflicts

You are sitting encompassed by a
    force—an invitation beyond my senses.
It manipulates your thoughts,
    monopolizes the air around you
With a scent so strong and forbidden
That I dare not, I want not
To turn the shadow of my face onto its
    rampant path.
Oh you! The one who convinced me of all
    purity and perfection;
Who pounded upon my mindn
With insatiable appetite for imagination;
You have invited dreams into the
    unsupported framework of my emotions
And now forsake your lair for redolences,
    powers, and secrets
Which I fear in their remoteness.
And yet you remain here, sitting
With sand lodged triumphantly in the
    molecules of your life-weary feet.
I thought you'd always hated sand, or did
    I dream more than I knew?
So, now do you press your hand into mine
In apology for the aura, the mystery in
    you
Which has collided with me in warning,
Or do you hope to soothe my longing
Before you turn in honesty, to lay before
    me vacant eyes?

—Cara Olsen

My First Love

All the promises true love has brought,
It offers trouble too.
And though it's been a long, long time,
I still remember you.
You were my first hello
And always my last goodbye.
And, though I loved you so,
I could never tell you why.
You were different from the others,
You always seemed to care.
And no matter what the problem,
You were always there.
We used to be in love,
It was you and me.
But then you had to go away
And why, I still don't see!

—Jenna Bagley

Rainy Day

The rain is falling down
It pitters and it patters.
It's falling to the ground
Dampening all the earth bound matters.
The tree tops stand so mighty,
Their limbs reach up so high
They're swaying in the breeze
Up in the cloudy sky.
The dogs are snoring softly
As they slumber on the lawn,
The largest lifts his head
To free a sleepy yawn.
The wind chime's dancing slowly
It goes tinkle-tattle-ting.
It's dancing as the wind blows
I love to hear it sing.
I would give a thousand years
To live this day again.
All these things I love
Out in the falling rain.

—Hollie Jenkins

Golden Hours

Bless this memory I pray.
It seems so poignant today.
Don't let the mists roll in,
Before I feel our love again.
I float away in our dream;
Down a swift mountain stream.
The sparkling waters sing to me
Of happy days that used to be.
Our hearts are reflected there,
Dancing free of future care.
This memory that I treasure
Is precious beyond measure.
Golden hours of unspoken love
As pure as a snow-white dove.

—Elizabeth Wilkinson-Anderson

Untitled

Confusion works in mysterious ways,
It seems to come and go,
But it's always there,
Up high or down low.
It creeps like a thief
Into your brain
Your support turns to sand
And slips grain by grain.
Confusion, at times, is a comfort,
To know not what goes on,
To be innocent,
Pure and beautiful, like dawn.
Realization is your front door,
Slammed shut by a breeze
While you were confused,
Someone stole the keys.

—Audrey Alforque

The Greenbrier River

The color of the river is green.
It shines and gleams.
It makes you wonder why it shines and gleams.
It makes you wonder why you dream.

—Angela Ritch

All our Love

You have a kind and gentle heart,
It shows with just a smile.
Your pleasant gestures and remarks,
Makes knowing you worthwhile.
The love you share with all of us,
Just glistens in the air.
And how you've always made a fuss,
It's no wonder why we care.
Your beauty shines within your soul,
And touches every heart.
You've lifted us when we were low,
And praised our works of art.
And so we take this time to say,
How much we love you so.
And thank you for the love you gave,
So freely as we know.

—D.J. Preble

Hurt

Hurt is blueish-gray.
It smells like ammonia,
And tastes like salty teardrop on your tongue.
It sounds like a bullet being shot out
Of a gun, and straight through
Someone's heart as he cries out,
And feels chilly, like a foggy night
In London.

—Jennifer L. Wetter

A Shade Of Green

Under the sun, how life grows.
It starts out young, then gets old.
Life is a hunger, with many needs.
Time has a number, for all indeed.
Born to learn, we grow and dream.
For what we earn, makes us supreme.
Our world earth, among the stars
Has given birth, both near and far.
So treasure living, my human race.
For life is giving, with no disgrace.
A shade of green, may someday be—
A badge of freedom, for you and me.

—*Kelly A. Firmingham*

My Love for You

I heard a song on the radio that expressed
   my love for you.
It was a soft, gentle love song that I knew
   would touch you through.
It made me very happy that someone had
   the same feelings
That I do for someone like you.
There's been rough times and there's been
   good,
And sometimes I ask myself if we should.
I tell myself it will get better,
And a time will come where we will stay
   together
To show our love for each other forever.
And on that day I will give you a ring
To show you my love with all of my heart
So wherever we are we won't part.
And then I will say:
I love you. . .I love you. . .I love you!

—*Amy Marie Bonish*

The Wild Horses

I watched them swallow at a lonely
   stream,
It was clear yet dark like their very own
   eyes,
Their bodies were stretched in the
   morning light,
Beautiful, like a dream, like a midnight's
   vision,
When I watched them swallow at that
   lonely stream.
I watched them gallop in the open fields,
They ran fast with spirit freedom and joy,
Their manes were blown by the softest
   winds,
Their legs were strengthened as they hit
   the ground,
While they galloped fast in the open
   fields.
Soon I watched them stop on a hilltop
   high,
Their heads held up searched for danger
   awaiting,
With nostrils high to the soft blowing
   breeze,
Danger was not found so they slightly
   relaxed,
As they stood still on that hilltop high.
Then I watched them eat while the sun
   went down,
They were beautiful, graceful and quiet,
Their hearts pumped gently as they at the
   grass,
But then their leader reared up and said
   onward,
And that was the last I saw them when
   the sun went down.

—*Carla Dalton*

Oh What Should I Do

When I first met you,
It was love at first sight.
And all I wanted to do
Was to hold you forever with all my
   might.
Everything was so perfect
Between me and you.
But now something's changing
And it's breaking my heart in two.
I think I'm in love with
One of his friends,
But I'm not sure if I want
This relationship to end.
Oh what should I do,
About this terrible mess.
Time is the only solution,
I guess.

—*Kim Simmons*

Ultimate Laws

Triumphs and applause, touch of mortal
   laws.
It was not complete, impact of defeat.
Geranium borders, formal orders.
Ultimate laws, truth draws.
Confusion, scraps of illusion.
Release the repression.
Dubious missions, studied insane,
   exquisite pain.
Visit of vision, luck years overdue, unjust
   laws, it's the view.
My people starve on the stoop of
   invention, never ever are we mention!
We don't gain, but we live the true reality
   of everyday pain.

—*Donna May Bradley*

Why Did They Have to Die?

Body heaving with sobbing tears
It was always your biggest fear
You keep thinking is it really true
Then you realize they've really left you
Everyone tells you it will be all right
That everything will turn out bright
Why them you always say
I just saw them the other day
You loved them so
But did they know
You remember you never said you did
Your true feelings you always hid
Then you start to feel the guilt
As though your heart is flashing tilt
Why did it happen you reply
Why did they have to die.

—*Jennifer Harris*

Hero's Friend

The news came today. . .
it was grey.
My son's friend died today. . .
far away. . .
Far away from the home he knew as a
   boy.
Far away from the friend who brought
   him such joy. . .
so very far away.
He died a hero, they say. . .
but I say. . .
We'll never again see him smile come a
   sunny day. . .
And my son is left alone to pay. . .
the price a hero's friend must pay.

—*Jeanne Barbasiewicz Hoogstad*

Believe in a Dream

The ground is wet and the pound full of
   ice.
It was one of the coldest days that year.
As I walked along, I began to think.
To think of why I was even here.
Soon I noticed a man sitting near.
You could hear him crying very clear.
I walked over and sat down beside him
As he looked up.
He began to talk to me and tell me why
And as he talked I began to realize that
Life was not as bad as it seemed to be.
And as I walked home that day,
I decided that all I needed to believe in
Is a dream.

—*Jacquelyn J. Moore*

The Grand Revival

I wanted to be happy, to feel excited with
    the upcoming blessed event,
It was to be my first grandchild, but I
    suffered burn-out, my maternal
    instincts were spent.
The due date came and went and nothing
    happened, another week dragged by
    without a stir,
Anxiety bubbled up and a tinge of
    disappointment, an old flag waved
    before me yet a blur.
Another week crept by and I felt a
    yearning, an old familiar feeling from
    the past—
Then a telephone call, "It's happening,
    we're having the baby at last."
We sped to the hospital, and then we
    waited, five hours we walked the halls
    and watched the door,
At 11:55 the miracle happened, and I
    became transformed forever more.
My one flesh and blood held him before
    us, proud as a peacock with what he'd
    made,
We "oozed" and we "aahed" behind the
    pane glass, never wanting this moment
    to fade.
Just one among the throng, I watched in
    wonder, while those around me were
    unaware,
An essence ooaed from deep within my
    marrow, I felt a prickling on my neck
    and in my hair—
This baby held before me will be a
    sculpture, formed by so many human
    hands,
He is my grasp into the future, he is my
    revival and he's grand.

—Carol B. Link

Lost Love

When we first met
it wasn't love a first sight.
But as our feelings grew
We knew we couldn't live without
holding each other tight.
We want to be together
but soon you'll be going away
and as you go
remember my love for you
will always be here to stay.
Remember me forever
Keep me in your heart to stay
Even if we don't end up being together
The lets just remember how it once was
    this way.

—Angel Commisso

Untitled

Tears in my eyes, I see it go up.
It went up and up.
Then. . .it's coming down.
Coming down very fast.
I scream and scream.
Up. . .down. . .scream. . .
Up. . .down. . .scream. . .
Stop
Tears
Quite
No one is around, but I.
But I and my tears.
I hate them, him, my step-daddy.
I am red, soon be black and blue.
Why?

—Collena McMinn

The Seed To The Future

What is your future, where will it lead?
It will all depend on how you plant the
    seed.
The seed must be good, the seed must be
    firm
the path to the future is the one which you
    yearn.
You cultivate the seed with love and with
    care
and if you follow the path, you soon will
    be there.
Once the seed is planted and starts into
    grow
the path to the future is the seed that you
    sow.
The knowledge you learn in planting this
    seed
is that which is cultivated, when you
    pullout the weed.
As long as the ground is fertile and firm,
then so is the future and the product in
    turn.
There is a great deal in this world that we
    need
We can all learn a lot from this little seed.

—John G. Orlowske

True. . .There lies an Ocean

Water casts down the valley of her skin.
It will find it's ocean just take her in.
Pure as the silk of her eyes.
Still moves, as still as the sky.
True is the muddy, murkiness of truth.
All these things I know are true.
I'll come for you down by your ocean.
We'll join, down by the ocean.
Take off your shoes, it will still be true.
Cross the tides in hand with you.
All these things I know are true.

—Billy D. Kidd

The Evening Approaching

The day was so busy
it was wonderful to see
the Evening approaching
restoring calm within me.
Watching the sun set
as dusk starts to fall
into soft pink violet puffs
as night sounds begin to call.
Deep shades of blue
stretching across the sky
with a yawn, the day slips away
as night gathers her stars nigh.
The wind whisper gentle
so soothing and sweet
as night becomes full
my body falls asleep.

—Elizabeth G. Snow

Time

Time it sails to many shores,
It whips us back and forth.
It closes and opens many doors,
Yet we give it so little worth.
Never enough or so it seems,
To do, to have, to feel everything.
But now and then there is a dream,
Of love, of life, or simply nothing.
Slowly it passes for those who are ill,
But oh so fast for the young.
It runs away with life or stands still,
And never lets you sing the songs yet
    unsung.
Do your best with the time you are given,
That is one thing no vendor can sell.
For not all of us will meet in heaven,
But a lot of us, will toast in hell.

—Jean Harvey

Love Is Nothing but a Headache, or an Illusion

Love is nothing but a headache
It will swell your heart, make your head
    grow
Grow as large as a lake
If you think and dream of love as being
A piece of cake.
Just prepare yourself for an earthquake.
Love is no more than an illusion.
A word you think you know but will only
    lead
You mind in a state of confusion.
It starts out as small as a bubble.
The more air you put into it,
I'll make it get larger,
Larger and when it burst
You are in big trouble.

—James Miller, Sr.

Too Late

As I sit here, I realize
It would have been worth it,
I should have said something.
The book sat open but nothing was written,
My name was not printed.
Could I have said something?
No, of course not.
My words were obsolete.
The heat will never stop.
I didn't think I deserved this,
I saw the light
But I never felt it,
I never felt it.

—Jeremiah Gamble

Mom

All the world loves their mother,
It's a special love, like no other.
It comes from deep inside,
A true love you cannot hide.
The special care a mother will show,
You will remember each day you grow.
Mothers deserve the best from you,
Deep inside we know it is true.
I wish I could write a book,
And let the world take a look,
At how I care for you,
For all the things you say and do.

—Daniel D'lutz

Distance Kills The Heart

We're sixty miles apart.
It's amazing how distance can kill the heart.
I know there could be a wonderful relationship
If only we were together.
Distance kills the heart.
Maybe it isn't supposed to be,
But as for me, that's not the way I feel.
Distance kills the heart.
I need him
And he needs me,
But we can't have each other,
Because we're sixty miles apart.
Distance really kills the heart.

—Kristen Brant

Gossip

It's as dark as a shadow, but still it can blind,
It's as nice as the rainbow, but no friends shall it find.
It sounds like a whisper, Then it yells in your ear.
It has a big mouth, for everyone to hear.
It's as cool as the ocean, but as hot as hell.
It poses as flowers, but rotten is its smell.
It's as light as a feather, but as heavy as stone.
It cuts like a knife, it cuts to the bone.
You try to ignore it, you try not to care.
You try to be nice, but it doesn't play fair.
It burns you like fire, it burns you inside.
You feel so ashamed, you go run and hide.
Things can't be worse, well that's what you said.
You opened your mouth, now you wish you were dead.
You cannot defeat it, so don't even try.
You ask "Who did it?" then you ask yourself, "Why?"
It has no face, and it has not name,
Once it starts on its journey, nothing's ever the same.

—Billie Ann Patrick

Cheese

All well and good,
it's fine for you
as you ride the crest,
following your white line
to glory. Take another sniff.
You can be forgiven.
No stereo in your T-bird,
the smooth serenity of the pond
never feels the dance of your Ripple.
Tattered overcoat, dirty hat;
go ahead tip that paper bag.
You can be forgiven.
Pasteurized part skim milk,
cheese culture, salt and enzymes
melted on a toaster kaiser.
Tastes so good, I'll have another bite.
But where in heaven will they put me,
when they surmise that my demise
was from eating too much cheeses. And will I be forgiven?

—James J. Steager

Death

Death is close behind, nipping at your heel.
It's gaining, resisting your struggle to escape.
Its treacherous grip that you just cannot feel,
Confining you within its satanic cape.
Your name and year scrawled on a slab of steel,
Your casket tossed into a hole that has no shape.
A catastrophe that none can ever heal.
Buried beneath the loathsome, dreary, and hideous drape,
You claw at the unyielding wicked guard,
Silent shrieks of terror echoing throughout your corpus,
Your neurotic nerves suppressing you without a purpose.
When you experience the end, it makes it hard,
To accept eternal dreams were bound to ensue,
To evade your extinction, futile! It'll happen to you!!

—Jessica Ahn

I Couldn't Live Without You

How can I resist it,
It's hard to see, but it's true;
Life is not worth living
Knowing I'm not with you.
And you will stay real close to me
We'll stay snug in the middle of the night;
And if we hear something frightening,
In my arms I will hold you real tight.
And as we grow up and get older,
You, I will never, ever replace;
Because you have told us by your actions,
That you could never live in another place.
Without you I wouldn't see the morn
Just knowing you are not there;
You'll be with me for life and longer
You're definitely my teddy bear.

—Kelly Collins

For Lovers

In patience and in kindness, firm love does not dare desert
Its heavenly fare of warmth, protection and a trust;
Love's higher realms descend in lover's hearts that waken to a union purposed
Beyond the passioned heat of moments that are passing.
A oneness speaks outreaches deep, beneath the seas of peace.
Joy beams our new beginnings,
Love seams our garments wholly true—
I am in love with you.

—Byron Glenn Miller

The Sky

The sky is blue,
It's like a big blue ocean in the sky
With a touch of white lines,
People sit and watch it go by.
The sky is blue like sometime me and you.
The sky is black when it rains.
Thunder and lightning begin to sing.
After the rain goes away,
It's again a pretty day.

—Jeanette Junior

Daddy

Daddy
It's me again—
Your daughter,
I have grown now
And I have accomplished
Something to be proud of, daddy.
I have forgiven you,
From all the hurt,
The sadness, of not
Having a father for
Many years—
But I can say it daddy
I love you—
And I won't forget you
Although
You have given me up
For another woman.

—Dixie Johnson

In The Rain

You say your love is strong—where did I
  go wrong
It's never just you and me—don't you
  know thats the way it should be.
The longer your away—the more that I
  can say
My love is fading in the rain.
My heart is heavy for your love—my
  feelings fly off
Like a little white dove
I know your love is pure and true—but
  what am I supposed to do
My heart is fading in the rain.
You always say everything is okay—that
  was all in yesterday
Help me build my love for you—so I can
  love you the way I used to-
You are fading in the rain.

—Jessica A. Martin

The Sunrise

I wonder where the sunrise holds
Its oranges, reds, pinks and golds.
I feel so happy when I see
The colors the sun has saved for me.
On the horizon the colors form,
Every day and every morn.
And every morn the silver mist
Angels lift and gently kiss.
Morningtime brings breath and life,
To every human, husband and wife.
You may not think so from the start,
But a sunrise's beauty touches the heart.

—Elizabeth Ann Urbach

Sunset

The sunset is beautiful,
Its powers unreal.
Its colors are colorful,
And can make all men kneel.
The sunset has a heart of gold,
That is always admired
By the young and the old.

—Connie Adams

Snow

Sparkling and glittering all aglow,
It's snowing, it's snowing
You look like you've been crying,
But it's just snow falling from the sky.
Sparkling and glittering all aglow.
Snow falls and falls during
The season of cold, yet the glow of
The snow gives a stage to
The ground as it rises the trees above the
  surface.
The snow hides the green color
Of the grass, and trees, yet with
No color and the clear brightness it's
The season of winter.
Sparkling and glittering all aglow,
It's snowing, it's snowing.

—Brooke Yankton

The Sudden Feeling

I have this feeling running deep inside.
It's something I can no longer hide.
This feeling is love and is sent straight to
  you.
It came to me from up above and now I
  have someone to give it to.
I hope that you'll accept it, I hope that
  you'll be mine.
For you're the only one I love and the only
  one I want to find.

—Jennifer Carpenter

Life

Life is like a picture,
It's sometimes standing still.
Time is like an eagle,
It flies upon its will.
The waters overflow
With laughter in it's eyes.
The clouds are stuffed with feathers,
Which paint the deep blue skies.
The heavens turn a pink
Until dusk fades the light.
The sun goes down again
As day turns into night.

—Denise Braga

I Know

I know how bad you are hurting,
It's tearing you apart.
I know how bad you are hurting,
I feel it deep in my heart.
I know the thoughts you are thinking.
You feel that life is hell.
I know the thoughts you are thinking.
I've often thought them myself.
I know you won't believe me,
It's very hard to trust.
I know you won't believe me.
Only Jesus can you trust.
I know you think He failed you.
You think He doesn't care.
I know you think He failed you,
But your tears He truly shared.

—Diane Williams

California

The golden crisp figure we call the sun,
It's the best place to be whether you're old
  or young.
At night the stars are so beautiful and
  bright,
They give you a friendly feeling and take
  away your fright.
The trees are so peaceful and sweet
And the green grass feels cool on your hot
  feet.
The welcoming tide at the beach,
It will give you its hand if you only reach.
California is my home,
Here nature and peace live alone.

—Janelle Luelen Cobb

Love is like. . .

Love is like the wind.
It's there for awhile.
Then it blows away again.
Love never stays long.
It passes with the seasons.
It goes away without a reason.
It buds in summer like a flower
Then dies in a very few hours.
We fall in love like a leaf falls off a tree.
Then we cry and say why, oh why me!
We try to hide the love and the sadness.
Although all we do is fight back the
   madness.
Boys fight it, girls hide it, but we'll never
   really find it.
The love we want and always need.
Although we cry and plead.
So when the love dies.
Just remember,
Love can be cold like December.

—Curry Page

Broken Heart

Love is this feeling in my heart
When I think of you in the dark
My blood is not flowing when
We are apart
So please come and mend my
Broken heart.

—Rosann Martorana

Time

In our lives, time is the most valuable
   thing we've got.
It's very short, when I'm with you, a lot of
   time there's not.
Therefore, each second we spend with
   each other I will treasure
Because being in your arms fills my heart
   up with pleasure.
Once it passes by, there's no going back,
   it's never.
But in my mind it sticks with me forever
   and ever.
We must not take advantage of God's
   great gift.
Through my spirits you bring me a great
   uplift.
It would be my wish that when I'm with
   you, time would stay still
To love me until, when time is through,
   say that you will?
As we are maturing through our stages of
   reality
I have a more understanding of feeling
   inside of me.
Let time take us to where it starts for love.
Make us feel as if we're in heaven up
   above.

—Caroline L. Kim

Precious Words

The following words come from the
   deepest part of the soul.
It's words speak the beauty of them and
   it's warmth.
It's words of the soul forgive, and cannot
   forget a moment,
Because every moment is a memory kept
   to the soul beneath the mind.
The mind is a beginning that does not
   end.
It takes you further than steps and can
   produce more visual
Inspiration than any actual conversation.
   It does not have to
Speak the truth, because the truth can
   ruin the passion effects
Of imagination.
Remember, these words were written in
   the pattern of the soul,
Which the mind encouraged the hand to
   write.

—Amanda L. Morse

Poetry

With a pen in my hand, I can go back in
   time,
When I'm writing, I can change the
   future, by adding another line.
When I'm writing, I can quickly hide,
Only to my pen and paper, can I confide.
Can people be trusted? Now I'm not quite
   sure,
Actually I don't know just how much
   more I can endure.
Now I seem to run to my secret world all
   the time,
I think that's because I'm safe there,
In that secret world of mine.
Here I don't have to act like someone who
   really isn't me,
Here I can act like whomever I want to
   be.

—Wendy Jean Spalding

Just a Poem

There's only one thing I hate to see
It's you filled with so much sorrow
Take a ride to the heavens with me
On the wings of another tomorrow
Then cry your tears till they run dry
And never again shed no more
Stay with me I'll take you to the sky
Make you feel like never before
Just grasp hold of a passing wind
It's okay child don't be scared
Let it take you where you've never been
Show you things never dared
Take a walk across the ocean sand
Waves crashing on the shore
Walking together hand in hand
Nothing could be better I'm sure
I just hope you can understand
Let's never find a cure.

—John Sanders

To Weldon

How do I explain these feelings?
I've been sitting here wondering.
I'm so happy, I want to tell all my friends
   about you and me.
But stop, why do I refrain?
Could it be a secret only lovers share?
If this is true, then I should confide in you.
You are my sunshine when I'm blue.
You are my confidant when I need a
   shoulder to cry on.
You are everything to me, friend, lover,
   and pal.
I can't ask for more than these things
   from you.
When we talk, I feel it's straight from the
   heart.
These feelings are so strange and unusual
   to me,
But please have the patience you have
   always had with me.
Together we can't lose.
I can honestly say I still love you.
I may have kidded myself before,
But I never thought I'd be in your loving
   arms again.
I love you openly and honestly forever.

—Kim Steiner

Loneliness

Since you've been gone,
I've found a new friend.
She'll be with me
Till the end.
Her presence is constant
She never goes away,
She's with me always;
Night and day.
Her name is Loneliness,
She'll forever be here.
To wipe away
Each falling tear.

—Abbey Notes

Swan Song

I sit, hunched up, fighting tears.
I've grown up, but I didn't want to yet.
I loved you, I trespassed, I can't return.
But you left, I 'm alone.
I'm not a child anymore, that's gone.
I know I can't come to the pond anymore.
It hurts too much, it's part of a different
   world.
I look at my baby sleeping, smile
   bittersweet.
A great white bird takes off, startled,
And I can hear my thoughts echoed in the
   cry of a swan.

—Kristin Schorr

Hell Hole

Maybe I'm lost in my own little world.
I've locked myself into a prison.
I sit here day by day thinking my life
  away
Knowing I must be causing someone out
  there great pain,
Not knowing who? I think everyday
  coming up with clues.
One day I found enough clues to know
  who this person is—you.
What can I say to make things right.
When I can't even make myself right.
The only way is I am deeply sorry for your
  wounds.
Each day I make it worse knowing it.
I put pressure on myself each hour I think
  of you—
But I'm still locked in my prison—
Forever looking for a key to let myself out
  of the hell hole.

—Joleen Lujan

Lies

I'm sick of the lies, I'm sick of the pain,
I've made you mad, I've upset you again.
I'm tired of worrying, I'm tired of crying,
I'm tired of apologies, I'm tired of trying.
It's not my fault, I'm not to blame.
It's you and your attitude, you're playing
  a game.
I'll just turn my back, I'll just let you be,
Maybe this way it's better, let's just wait
  and see.

—Ashley D'Amora

Forgive Me

Father-please hear my words
I've sinned and my soul's disturbed.
Sometimes my shield of truth just melts
and it's these times I can't help myself.
I try my hardest not to give in
but my flesh is infected with sin.
Rotting away with each passing day
it won't be long before my soul decays.
That's why I need your help, Father
I need to taste your living waters.
You're most high in the art of forgiving
please forgive me and the life I've been
  living.

—Gary S. Hueppehen

The Unexpected Present

Once when it was Mother's Day I found a
  kitten,
Ivory and gray, like the early morning.
I called him Fred and he was hungry.
I brought him in to breakfast
With the other cats. Good appetite. Well
Fed, Fred needed washing up. Who?
I put him near Mitzie, the mother of
  seven.
He was walking toward her when—pow,
Her paw just missed his face. Fred moved
  back.
Timothy was watching from across the
  room.
I better supervise; sometimes a full grown
  tom cat. . .
Timothy ambled over, swaying as he
  walked.
He looked Fred over and (plop) sat on
  him,
Anchoring him securely to the floor. Then
  Timothy
Began the bath, starting at Fred's little
  face.
Fed and bathed, Fred looked wonderful.
He stood up, stretched, purred at Timothy
And found himself a comfortable chair.
  He was staying.

—Carole B. Hobart

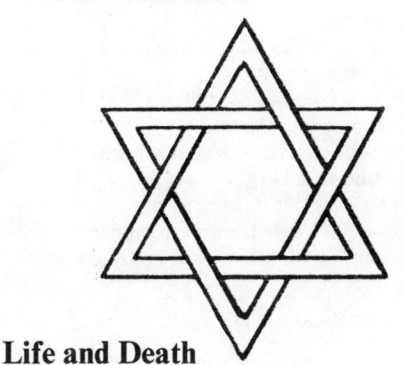

Life and Death

Beneath the walls of the ghetto gate,
Jews sit and sit, they sit and wait.
Will they ever get out? Will the war ever
  end?
Are just some of the questions they ask,
  my friend.
A little girl asked her mom one day,
Why does Hitler hate us? What did we
  say?
The answers to these questions weren't
  known,
But Hitler still killed us, he had a heart of
  cold stone.
After he had killed six million Jews,
The war was over. What was the news?
Hitler had shot himself in the head,
He fell to the ground, fell flat, fell dead.
Now when we look back upon this war,
We think of our people, our hearts are
  sore.
We shan't ever forget what happened
  then,
For if we do, it might happen again.

—Joanna Dubitsky

Color Blue

Fog walked through the trees that night
Jumping lightly from limb to limb,
Visiting birds in their nests,
Blessing and caressing,
Shivering in the moonlight
Until it laid upon my shoulder and wept.
What did you say?
The color blue is dead?
Yes, my love,
Now I understand.

—Kim J. Kennedy

Love Spell

Do you have any hope,
Just a little to spare?
I gazed in your eyes
And found myself there,
But you turned around
And looked away,
Then all I found was dark dismay.
You were the light of my life,
But now I just pray
You will turn around
And begin to say,
"I am forever yours,"
"I am here to stay."
All the more I fantasize,
Hope is lost when I realize,
My heart is longing for you.
Oh, my heart is longing for you.

—Anne Kaiser

Just a Thought

Fellowship and brotherhood. . .
Just a thought.
Love and peace. . .
Just a thought.
Forgiveness and mercy. . .
Just a thought.
War, hate, and poverty. . .
Reality.

—Katie Archer

How Do You Tell. . .

How do you tell the girl you're seeing
Just how much you truly enjoy being
With her each chance you get
But for reasons unexplainable its still not
 enough yet?
You have to be careful when there are
 things you don't know
You can't move fast—while yet afraid
 you'll move too slow
You hold her hand, you kiss her lips
You watch your words so nothing
 un-timely slips.
You look into her eyes you touch her soft
 hair
You whisper to her, "I'm so glad you're
 here!"
Sure you're both afraid of the future
 because of the past
But if you're open and honest you'll find
 those fears won't last!
I mean—Life was made to be happy not
 to live blue!
So, how do you tell her how you feel?
Well why not try—sweetheart I believe
 I've fallen for you.

—*Billy Ray McDowell*

Happiness

Happiness is when you're with the person
Who means the most to you.
Happiness is when you can tell them
That you care and knowing they care, too.
Happiness is when you share an intimate
 kiss,
And a few warm hugs.
Happiness is all things mentioned above,
Even a little more.
Happiness is all you want it to be,
You're the only one who can see
What it is that makes happiness
The way you want it to be.

—*Sarah Frank*

The Song of Fear

The song of fear starts out slow and quiet
Just like the terrifying moment before the
 cobra
Attacks!
As the song continues to feed off my panic
It grows steadily into my minds thirsty
Cracks
This sappy melody filters my thoughts
As it slowly seeps into my brain!
Making a sane mind. . .
Difficult to obtain!
My heart is pounding and my breath
 panting
All to the rhythm of the song
Then slowly the music sounds fainter
And drifts away as fast as it came along
It fades away
Until peace is once more restored
Relief throughout my body it pours
Then. . .Silence Once More.

—*April S. White*

Forever Love

From me to you things were said.
Just me and you, in your bed.
Sun has risen, moon is gone.
24 hours 'til another DAWN.
This thing we have, it's so great.
I'd like to say you're my perfect mate.
I want you to know my love is true
But at times I feel I'm losing you, so what
 should I do?
Is this thing we share so real,
Or is this relationship really no big deal?
From day one you won my heart.
For me it's been true love from the very
 start.
I promise I'll be forever faithful
Even though at times things can be
 painful.
Don't ever hurt me or let me down
Because I know how you hate to see me
 frown.
Forever I'll love you.
Will you forever love me too?

—*Kerri Dawn Neuschafer*

Alone

I sit here and wonder!
Where is he tonight?
Is he alone?
Or is he with someone else?
I sit here and think!
Who is he in love with?
Is he in love with me?
Or is he in love with someone else?
I sit here and cry!
Why does this happen to me?
How can I care for him so much,
When I don't know what he thinks or
 does?

—*Sherry Peltier*

The Pond

A broken, drenched stump
Juts from the depths of slime.
A chasm,
Filled with muck and primal syrup,
Glazed with cobwebs.
Black widows wait in ambush,
As mosquitoes break the silence
With a vexing drone.
A skin of oily sludge
Encloses the deadly organisms within.
Massive snapping turtles lurk beneath,
Jaws gnashing in wrath.
Lizardous snakes and serpents
Hiss and slither under the mysterious
 surface,
As shadows of unseen creatures sway
'Neath the mist and gloom.
All that separates me from this
 nether-world
Is the glass portal,
Behind which I take shelter.

—*Eden Doniger*

White Skin On Black Fabric

You're so beautiful
Kathy Stanton
So pretty
Mysterious
Dark
Even in light—you appear in shadow
Illuminating a warm, radiant smile
Intelligence
That instantly dices through masked
 expressions.
Humor — so dry
Warmth — so tender
Loving
Sexy
Imaginative
A well rounded soul
I would find it difficult to penetrate your
 world
Once there—it would be impossible to
 exit. . .

—*Christopher Shelton*

Ode To A Mommy

Here's to the Lady who made me
Without you I wouldn't be here.
She's there through every tear and smile
She's teaching me the importance of
 modesty and pride,
And the smarts to know the difference.
Through her I'm learning the art of
 earning friendships.
She gives the gift of dreaming and the will
 to make dreams come true.
She passes on the enlightment of being
 humble
And the knowledge to stand on my own
 two feet.
And somewhere in all that,
She slipped in the golden rule and
exposed to me the secrets of its
 comprehension.
Then, she mixes in a little tolerance and a
 whole bunch of love,
And gave me the importance of it all.
Now, I'm taking time to say,
Thanx Mom! For making me, Me!
"Don't be too disappointed"

—*Rose Dady*

Heart

The pound of my heart
Keeps me awake all night.
I think of you
And you are in my sight.
Why can't we share these feelings,
I don't know.
But when I try,
They are hard to show.
I care for you
And need your trust,
And to give my heart
That special trust!

—*Gabrielle DiFrancisco*

Lukewarm Fire

Ancients called it muses, (masters of the arts),
Kept out of sight, out of mind,
Andromeda with its infinite
Matters, parts of everything
You realize this laughter
You see was uttered millions of years ago
(Eternity to our infinite smallness)
But really it's lukewarm fire;
So subtle you'd hardly notice until it's gone;
Only after years of searching, scaling walls
That don't exist, only after you've cut yourself
To the thick for the last time
Lukewarm fire returns; so familiar you have to cry;
For lack of brushes and the only thing to show
For its cuts so you begin to write
Messages with your own blood on the ground,
Temporary messages, but you know your system
Will produce more

—*Dwight A. Gray*

Horses

Horses run wildly in the wind.
Kicking up their heels as they play.
Their mane lifts off the neck and falls back.
The tail sticks straight up like the black stallion.
The feet extend like a race horse.
Their heads stick straight up like they're having fun.
Horses run wildly when it's time to play.

—*Kelli Cunningham*

A Child's Night

Trees made of whispers,
Kiss in the night,
Leaves that are shadows,
A kiss of fright,
Rains from the heavens,
Wind and light,
Tears of laughter,
Kiss of fright,
Peace on heaven,
Love and might,
Tears of laughter,
A kiss good night.

—*Angel Brown*

Confused

Lost in your eyes,
Kissed by your lips,
Lost in my fantasy,
tortured by my reality.
Mixed up by love,
Thrown by passion
Scared of my future,
frightened of my past.
Wanting more out of life,
Less of what it gives.
Tears of pain,
Pleas of confusion.
Am I dreaming,
or is this real.

—*Kim Gilbert*

What is Love?

Love is caring with true devotion,
Kissing and hugging, and holding on tight
Love is sharing, with strong emotions,
Sharing the sweetest of love tonight.
Some find true love really deep and strong,
Soft and white and lovely as a dove.
Others find love as steep and wrong;
It's nothing more than the feelings of love.
Some find love as shaky and weak,
But love is wonderful and love is true.
I have found love seven days a week;
Love can be sad but never with you.
But even with a girl as sweet as a dove,
I'll still ask you, "What is love?"

—*Brian Gabriel*

The Rapture

Here I am waiting and watching for my Lord
Knowing that my soul I couldn't afford
Looking for that glory cloud
Which is the promise he'd always vowed
For we will be caught up in a wind
That our heavenly father sure did send
I hope that you are going to heaven
Because I hate to see you face the seals of seven
What I tell you will not be enticed
It won't even be very nice
If you don't do what the Lord said
You will wind up in the pits of fire-
Spiritually dead!
But you don't have to suffer this strife
All you have to give Jesus is your life
In the tribulation it will be harder
The only way to get to heaven is to be a martyr

—*Charity Baisden*

Untitled

We live
Knowing we'll die
We grow
Knowing we'll rot
We laugh
Knowing we'll cry
?

—*Ashley Joynes*

Caged

There is something of value
Known only to me,
Trapped in a cage that
No one can see.
It knows it has wings
But it cannot fly and
The terrors mount
As it continues to try.
It thinks of freedom
And what joy it would bring;
If it could only get out,
Take its dreams to wing.
What is this thing cages
Of fear can bind?
It's me, of course.
It's me. . .my mind.

—*Barbara Nichols*

Reality

I had come home from work like everyday.
Late as normal, no hint what was coming my way.
I slipped in the door of my shadowy house.
I called out-yet, no answer came from my spouse.
I stumbled into the bedroom and found him asleep.
He awoke and said it was about time I came home, then kissed my cheek.
I, being tired and it being late, I went to bed,
"See you in the morning" was the last that he said.
I happen to glance at a photo of us before I retired.
I smiled to myself, to my husband whom I admired.
And with a sigh, I closed my eyes and fell fast asleep,
Being so tired I fell quickly and deep.
When I awoke the very next day,
"Good morning dear" I turned to my husband to say.
Yet, as I turned to look, my heart pounded with danger,
For suddenly I was face to face, staring at the eyes of a stranger.

—*Gabrelle Saurage*

By the Shores of the Whispering Sea

By the shores of the whispering sea
Lay the maidens of the waves
In the moon-soaked mist, they cry their tears
In bursts of salt-sea spray.
In the sands of the cool silver beach, they silently wait for me.
They take to the tide to be by my side
By the shores of the whispering sea.
In the dark of the night, where the gulls and terns fly
To the beat of the gentle warm breeze
The ladies of lakes, and silent tide pools
All gather in hopes that they'll see
My dark silhouette as I walk down the beach
And dream of what dreams used to be
And their little white shapes, in their little white gowns
All dance on the frost of the sea,
They skip and they sway, and they call me away
By the shores of the whispering sea,
By the shores of the whispering sea.

—*Anthony Rattenni*

Morning Riser

The morning dew
lay wet upon his face,
as the sun
came through his sleepiness.
Moving slowly,
he sat upright,
and leaning back,
stretching, breathed deep.
He rose to his feet,
and turned,
bending slowly,
he removed his bedding.
Wadding it up
into a ball,
he place it
in a trashcan.

—*John Welch*

Untitled

O cruel is winter's icy grip,
laying seige to one's aging frame...
forever the beguilded prisoner
to the gold and violet flame.
Here, one ventures not too far
from those heavenly comforts of home...
leaving their thoughts 'pon mythic shores,
where many a young dreamer roams.

—*John Arsenault*

Tomorrow

Happy, laughing park nymphs,
Leaping through time
Each face smiling, a prophetic smile.
Not knowing futures capricious line.
An old man huddles under a solitary tree
Watching the children, Him, they do not see.
Many colored bubbles on strings to small wrists are tied,
An orange one breaks away and climbs to the sky,
How high it climbs, no one really knows.
Patches of orange rubble are scattered on the ground,
Dirty, forgotten, unknown, sometimes never found.
A park nymph with a prophetic smile,
Leans down to find a scrap of orange debris,
And kicks it away,
Just junk in time.

—*A. Mario Rodio*

And...

Once in a while
You are met by a trial
A trial to show
just how much you know
And to know is the end
of you and a friend,
And to the friend you know
you can only show
And to show is the beginning
of all your feelings
And all your feelings are only of denial.
For that is the beginning
and the end of the
trial.

—*Trey Sandoval*

Leave Me Be

Go away
Leave me be
Let me wonder off by the golden sea
Where the sunshine is bright and all my troubles fade
Let my mind wander to beautiful places
Go away
Leave me be
Leave me be by myself where I can see the world as I like
Leave me be by God where his house is on a floating white river
That is high above my spirit
Life I say, is too complex for me
I am not going to face it
I'd rather walk away
Leave me be.

—*Jolene Bernet*

The Heaven's Cry

The world rests, motionless...
Leaves frozen in position—
Only the sky is alive.
Churning, amethyst—gray clouds
Sweep the azure away.
Lightning carves veins in the heavens
While distant thunder
Warns of the approaching monster.
Exploding clouds pummel the parched earth
With liquid ammunition,
While uncontrollable breaths escape
Heaving violently across the land.
And as quickly as it came to life—it dies.
The droplets dissipate almost in complete
Syncronicity with the weary sighs.
The heavens relax, no longer flickering
To their own mysterious rhythm
And the battered tundra heals once more.

—*Deidre' A. Kelly*

In Search Of

To travel he would find, a life he was in search of,
Leaving all behind, and the girl he once did love.
He rode a horse of freedom, on a very lonely road,
Traveling was quite easy, he heaved a simple load.
He carried a trail of memories and a few dreams from the past,
To secure a brighter future, but nothing that would last.
Halfway through his journey, he turned his horse around,
He realized he had left behind a future already found.

—*Cheryl Kennedy*

Poems on a Yellow Page

The sun had died the previous day,
Leaving remainders of material grey.
My eyes were stung by ashes as I walked away,
The killings hadn't come as news.
It's a deadbeat street.
I go a lookin' for an opportunity.
But might I have known,
Opportunity's got no business lookin' for me.
Missiles in an arch and a military lark.
I give you a dime and you tell me where to park,
Give me not a moment nor a motion in the dark,
I was creeping past a room of sleeping people.
What a strange and etiquette subject
For a strange and etiquette world.
What a strange and different circle
For a world that must be heard.
And as I watch some inferiority, reciting his psychiatry,
I think maybe I've missed something somewhere along the line.

—*Ingrid Anne Jendrzejewski*

Untitled

The sun sets melting into the big blue sea,
Leaving the world in darkness and fear.
The cold of the night soon floats away graceful
Like a swan moving its way through glistening water.
Suddenly the sun shines pushing the loneliness away.
The day starts in full proportion,
Letting all the life and beauty of the morning bloom.

—*Jodi L. Steward*

Death

Here comes death, seeping through,
Let loose on earth, and sparing few.
He's close, now closer, there is no escape,
All see his darkened, evil shape.
He's calling, calling, name by name,
As the earth holds her daughters,
All those that he's claimed.
His beconing hand is pulling away,
All of her children, as though it were play.
Now he has arrived to finish his game,
And then seep away, the way that he came.

—*Kendra Parr*

Untitled

Sleep sweet memories and sweet illusions,
Let me take you along, I'll bring you back.
A little more light will have been shed,
More love will begin to spread.
Dreams. . .
Dream a dream of cosmic conscience.
Our awwareness is crucial.
Expand your heart,
Expand your mind.
I will meet you there,
Opened heart
Opened mind.

—*Denise Koger*

Tranquil at Daylight

Walking along a bridge where the ocean water
Lies beneath its broad path,
I could feel the splashing sounds of the waves
As it rolls itself along.
I had stopped at the middle of the bridge and I began
To stare across the golden sun filled sky,
And then the blueness began to come into light.
As I continued to watch the sky
And then the ocean water and its waves below,
I had felt a tender moment of peace and love,
As the sun was in sight.
And as I began to leave the bridge, I had turned my head
Backward for a moment, then I continued on my way,
Going on forward in peace and with tranquil at daylight.

—*Jewel Monique*

Life

The lonely one
Lies in the corner
Waiting to be picked up
To be caressed and loved.
Stick your head up
And believe in yourself
You are your own destiny,
Follow your dreams to the end
Let them take you far
Down the long winding path called life
But wherever you go,
Remember my love goes with you

—*H. Ross*

Living for a Better Tomorrow

There is no way to explain how I feel,
Life has become painfully unreal.
I cannot survive in this desolate life.
Everywhere I turn there is corruption and spite.
I'm going through life with blinders on
Wondering where the time has gone,
Wandering around with no place to go,
Looking at life through a dirty window.
Without a goal or a destination
I live life in isolation.
My alternatives have become limited,
And my feelings can no longer be inhibited.
So I reach out in desperation,
But all I find is indignation.
So now I'm sentenced to a life of sorrow
Living for a better tomorrow.

—*Amanda Planchard*

Life

Time
Life's most precious gift.
Love.
Life's best feeling.
Friendship
Life's most valuable possession.
Without time
All is lost
Without love
Who cares
Without friendship
Nothing matters
Time, love, friendship. . .
The elements of life.

—*Kristen Holmes*

Departure

Stone by stone
Light by Light
what makes people
cry at night.
Weed by weed
Rain by rain
What makes people
go insane.
The nights are
strong
the days are
wrong.
That's it
so long.

—*E.J. Glaza*

The Moon

The moon, in all of its brightness,
Lights up the sky with a mystifying glow.
The same glow that I see in your heart,
That lights up my life.
The moon, in all of its beauty,
Gives me warmth, as it shines off the
  rippling water.
The same warmth that your soul reflects
  on me.
The moon, in all of its mysteriousness,
Leaves me wondering about the world
  beyond.
The same wondering I feel when I look
  into your eyes.
The moon, in all of its loneliness,
Appears small and quaint in the vast,clear
  sky.
Wheras when I look at you,
The loneliness is small and quaint,
But the love is vast, and clear.
For no loneliness will appear in our world,
Except in the image of the moon.

—*April Pearl*

As Long As You Are Here With Me

Love is like a prison
where you'll never be set free.
Love is like a child
just learning how to read.
Love is like the wind
blowing through the trees.
Love is like a flower
beginning from a seed.
Love is like a river
rolling on to the sea.
Love is like a rainbow
such a beautiful sight to see.
Love is like a dream
for it can last forever
as long as you're here with me.

—*Rebekah Lynn Minor*

Calendar

Ornament of time
Like a clock it ticks the days
Blank boxes—rationed logic
I see before me promises
That one more day
Will come and go
As swiftly as the others
Who were filled in long before.
There's only one more space
Half filled
Tomorrow I will flip the page
To another month
Of empty boxes.
Four tiny lines
My future's cage.

—*Bethany Uhlig*

A Final Reminder

The loneliness grows inside me,
Like a cloud covering the sun.
The ending to a brand new day,
It will soon be over and done.
This is for all those who have hurt me,
And now they will never forget,
The way I tried to love them,
Or the example I will set.
Being pushed away by those I loved,
Drove me to this deed.
I was always alone,
Even in this, my time of need.
Then they will love me,
But too late it will be.
I will be where I am happy,
I will be with He.
You will find me with those who love me,
Where the people care.
I will finally feel the sun,
In my paradise up there.

—*Joelyn A. Tonkin*

Caught in Passion and Pain

Sitting here by myself
Like a toy upon its shelf
Now our love which you decide to break
All I feel is the lonely heartache
Now I'm sitting crying in the rain
But that is love's own passion and pain
Thinking about what went wrong
But it doesn't make a difference
Our love is gone
Living the past and not for tomorrow
Drawing within my own pitiful sorrow
Life has really nothing to gain
When you get caught in love's passion and
  pain

—*Carol A. Caswell*

I Wished

I wished I were dragon fly, and irridescent
  blue.
Like dipped in a metallic dye, my color
  pure and true.
My paper thin wings treaded the air.
Though unlike a king's, this was my lair.
The sun set the skies aflame and burning.
The wind sent the clouds tumbling and
  churning.
I explored my realm by the last golden
  light,
for the daytime was vanishing into the
  night.
The moon gleamed down on me,
Lighting a path so I could see.
The evening sky was royal blue.
Over the quiet land I flew.

—*Gwendolyn Coyne*

Being Alone

Sometimes I feel so alone,
Like everyone has left me to stand on my
  own.
With no support from anyone.
Not even a smile from someone I loved.
I guess you'd say I'm feeling sorry for
  myself
But not really I just don't like being alone.
When everyone else is laughing and
  having fun.
I'm hiding my hurt inside,
Hoping it won't shine through like the
  morning sun.
This feeling I guess is called loneliness.
Why can't people see its no fun when you
  feel alone.
No one to stand with so you stand on your
  own.
Maybe someday people will see its no fun
  being alone.

—*Amanda Edwards*

Untitled

I am born of the sun,
Who roams the hidden places,
Who wonders the gardens that
Bloom the flowers of the heart,
Who rides the clouds,
Who tames the beasts.
I drink the still waters,
I see the center,
I am the lawless one,
Whose name is Submission.
I am the spearpoint of truth,
I am the master of your dreams and
  desires.
I am the unicorn.

—*Sara Woebkenberg*

Growing Up is Tough

I feel rejected from everyone,
Like my world's falling apart.
I have nowhere to turn,
And then there goes my heart.
I think of drugs as a solution,
But just start crying again.
I feel like my life is over,
Like I've reached a dark dead end.
Suddenly, all of my tears are gone
And I wipe my frown away.
I feel a smile come back with my heart,
And I think they're here to stay.
I forget about yesterday, and focus on
  today.
I won't worry about tomorrow,
Cause it will be here soon enough.
And now I understand why they say,
Growing up is tough.

—*Angela Biggins*

Without You

My tears are falling
Like raindrops in the sky
As I sit and watch the time fly by.
This night it feels so lonely,
Without you by my side.
I get these feelings,
They're just so hard to hide.
This room it feels so empty
Without you,
There's no place to hide these feelings,
I know they'll never die.
Now you know the reasons my love is so strong,
I can't hide my feelings, I know I was so wrong.
So take me back, hold me in your arms,
Show me you love me then maybe you'll see
My love for you is flying free!

—*Jennifer Hicks*

Lady Night

Lady night...spread your arms across the evening sky
Winking your starry eyes, laughing at fools such as I.
Lady night...your moon chases the sun away
Bring the mystery instead I wonder what is ahead
Lady night...I hold your dew in my hand like a gift of pearls you sent
And as they shine in your light I wear them strand by strand
Lady night...your breeze softly whispers in my ear
Tell me you know why I am here and you feel the longing and you feel my need
Lady night...can you see him from where you are
Can I make a wish upon your star
Will you hold him safely in your arms for me!

—*Yuli Tharp*

Ode to Cleo: My Primary Kitten

You have markings like a wildcat, jagged
Like the edges of a soda can; split open
Refracting the sun.
Golden Lion's eyes; flecked with Gold and Green;
Mint tic-tacs on a gold bar.
Long whiskers that curve slyly
An inquisitive look on your pointed face.
As if you were pondering the very Secrets of the Universe!
Your face is pointed like the sharp corners of my bed
That you love to lie on.
And we have a secret, you and I.
I know that your belly is full of kittens,
Just as you know that my mind is full of dreams.

—*Jennifer Anne Francis Davison*

Corruption

I've never seen in my life so much corruption,
Like the one I have witnessed in some of the courts of this nation!
District, circuit or county courts all without exception
Provided me examples of the country's injustice and legal degradation.
Corruption! Corruption! What brings to decent people nothing but frustrations!
To see it, there is no need to go to third world nations
Since our judiciary is just as full of human rights violations.
Want to buy justice? Find yourself a few friends in high level positions
Willing to convince the court to settle in your favor any crooked allegations.
Corruption! Corruption! Is it a curse or the result of society's degeneration?
The minister will tell you; "Yes, a curse!" As stated in the book of Revelation.
The philosopher; however, will reason that it is inherent to human's imperfection,
Nevertheless, it doesn't matter which one offers the ideal explanation
If we do nothing to stop those who don't have regard for law or regulation.
Corruption! Corruption! Let's make sure it doesn't lead us to destruction!

—*Jesus Alberto Cabal*

What I Know

People really don't know what it is
Like to have an eating disorder,
Trouble is I do,
It is no fun,
Always being obsessed with numbers,
Having the numbers control you,
You feel you can't control anything in life,
So you turn to the food,
You loose everything,
You fear everything,
When you are at your lowest,
You think your fat—this is a disorder,
It is not the food, it's the feelings behind it,
We just take it out on the food,
There is never a cure,
My anorexia will always be a struggle for me.

—*Alicia Ziptho*

Waves or Not

Silenty the moon slips through the silvery clouds.
Listening,
Cautiously,
I hear a language
None of which I have heard before.
Exquisite
Eloquent
Breath taking in its own sound.
Caressing my thoughts,
Soothing my body,
Loving the gentleness of my sigh.
Can this description be of sight and sound?
Listen carefully. The waves will tell you.

—*Angela Rossa*

Winter

The cold wind blows,
When it snows.
When I was little I was always told,
The trees always glisten,
Like they were made of gold.

—*Shannon Whitt*

The Little Pink Face with the Long White Beard

It was not an elegant country home for the
Little pink faced man with the long white beard
With penders to give away to the children that came his way.
It was not an elegant country home for the artesion well
That stood by to the side of the breeze—way separating
The main house from the kitchen and large, full pantry.
For children who were born and died there many years ago
Belong to the little pink faced man with the long white beard.
My fathers father you may say. He never rode in a car
But walked to the old country store on a road made of sand and clay.
This was the little pink faced man with the long white beard.
This man you see had his own casket made of cedar from the land
That the not so elegant country house stood on.
Locked away in a small cozy room right off the breeze—way
Near the artesion well, beautifully lined in satin it was,
Standing ready to be used by the little pink faced man
With the long white beard.

—*Addy M.*

Flying Free

Of all your creatures I love birds the most,
Little sparrow can sail from his loneli nest
  to freedom's boast,
To defy gravity control calls for a
  blueberry toast,
Regal eagle drinks mountain den at his
  high retreat,
His fear is people whom what to shoot his
  life into defeat,
The sky is the last resort where peace and
  freedom can meet,
With envious eyes all over my head I too
  wish to fly,
Through the sky's trapdoors beyond this
  world's cries,
I won't be an Icarus whose wings melted
  and the sea ended his ride,
Man is enslaved to machines but winged
  featherweights take natural
Flight lessons,
My gravity logged mind always have
  praise sessions,
With daily recharged veneration I study
  birds and thank God for
His perfect selections.

—*James Wesley Ford*

Skeletons in my Closet

Hidden behind a closed door,
Locked without a key.
Are all the secret skeletons,
All belong to me.
If you look at my face,
The mystery behind my eyes.
You could never begin to guess,
Skeletons that I hide.
I am not ashamed of mistakes,
I have not one regret.
I just quietly put them away.
All the skeletons I collect.

—*Judy Carver*

So Foolish the Rulers

Spring dreams forgotten
Long ago, killing students
They think they kill dreams.

—*Bernice Anita Reed*

The Fawn

The fawn arose on tiny feet
Looked at mom and gave a bleat,
Wobbly legs, shaky knees,
Mom, could you help me please?
Momma deer stands close by
Takes her nose and swats a fly,
Giving birth it was her first
But she knew he would soon thirst.
So she waits there patiently
While he tries unsteadily,
To reach the nourishment he needs
Ah! Success, he finally feeds.
Rain falls down from a cloud
Upon a mom with son so proud
She knows with craftiness and luck
One day he'll be a handsome buck.

—*Gladys M. Hackney*

My Greatest Friend

I have a Lord and so might you
Who is nothing technical, nothing new.
A Lord who is called many things
Lord of Lords, King of Kings.
A God of caring, a God of love
A God as gentle as a snow white dove.
And what do I call a God like this?
A God so full of happiness,
A God who gave his only son
And forgives the sins of everyone.
A God who helps us through toils and
  strife
And gives believers eternal life.
A God who carries us all when we have
  pain.
And does this not for personal gain.
A God who is with us all the way.
And leads us back when we go astray.
A God who is with us from beginning to
  end.
I call this God "My Greatest Friend".

—*Tracy Connor*

Momentary Delight

One soulful moment passed
Looked I did, to see beauty near,
Wandering so gracefully bye
Without cause or duty
A glistering gesture
Of momentary delight,
An enraptured glimpse
Of pure insight
Just a moment passed
ooked I then to see
Beauty chased out sorrow
As doubt raced tomorrow
Tomorrow recited to the world:
Feel not your sorrow is all there will be,
Come alive and doubt no more
Your cause is to be free.
Looked again, I did see
Doubt surrounding beauty
Feeling no sorrow
Still there be beauty for tomorrow.

—*David Thurston Roberts*

The Shore Line

The waves crashed upon the shore,
looking above the seagulls soared.
Footprints still fresh in the sand,
memories of us walking hand in hand.
Each wave of water is a moment that we
  shared,
each grain of sand is for the times that we
  cared.
Out of the blue love appeared,
Now I always want you near.
Now I'm close, almost in step,
I'm by your side, something I won't easily
  forget.
Your footprints lead and I follow,
walking in the sand, without you I'd feel
  hollow.
All alone, I sit on the beach,
no one to touch, everything out of reach.
Now I sit and stare as waves cover our
  footprints,
I saw you that day and I've been in love
  with you
ever since. . .

—*Debbie Gizzo*

Concerto

It is octaves above the heavens
When you whisper to me. . .
I hear you as a violin
Upon the chambers of my heart. . .
Jealous is Strativarious,
Your resonance the caress
That causes my body to blush. . .
Your vibration the bow,
Feidlity the resin.
Cleaving unto you
For indefinite dawnings
I know the ghost of my life
Will never grey
Each morning to become closer
To the tune of the dove,
Each morning to become drenched
In the dew of your love.

—*Svieta*

Born with a Smile

Hear I am I said,
Looking around for a bed.
I've had a long trip,
I remember a flip.
Under I went and out,
I crept with such a shout.
It's me the one
I've only just begun.
How much to learn,
But I guess it's my turn.
To be born is so great,
I know now what I won't at eight.
I wish I could talk,
Soon I will and even walk.
I want to tell you thanks,
But how do I say it.
How do I tell you I love you, wait. . .
I did, I smiled and you just knew.

—*Danielle Manzo*

Memory Lane

Taking a walk down memory lane
Looking back to so much pain
Watching my friends come and go
Feeling the tears as they flow.
Days and months, the fading years
Smiles and laughter to hide my fears
I get deeper in agony every day
I won't let my past just fade away
It's by my side with each passing hour
Like the tormenting feeling of thundering shower
The heartache and confusion my past has brought
Is often said to be a lesson well taught.
So now I've come to find
That living my life with confusion—and pain
I caused from living my life
On memory lane.

—*Debra Pepsi Grazulis*

A Cloud

A cloud soft and puffy on a summer's day
Looking down at the world below watching people pass by
Choking on all the pollution there is
Remembering the day when there was no pollution
Hoping that, that day will come again
Being able to breathe free not
Choke on every breathe you take in
Being able to live, life to its fullest.

—*Erin Webb*

Missing

As you walk the path through life
Looking for something just out of sight,
Everything will fade in the night
As you now walk out of sight.
Remember how he loved you as a son,
Overlooking your minor flaws as none.
Before you left everything was going to turn out right,
Today is the day you vanished from his sight.
Pretending
Everything will end up fine,
That you will come back
Keep this in mind,
Hurting
All you love may hurt you too.
The world is tough and he will be blue.

—*Angel L. Hardin*

Why?

I have finally found you, lost in sleep.
Looking for you has been so hard to do.
You almost didn't wake, sleeping so deep.
If you hadn't, I wouldn't know what to
Tell them about you. Maybe about why
You felt you had to go and break our love.
Tell me why you did it. Why did you lie?
I don't understand you; we were in love.
Since you used every excuse you could find
And looked through me our love already dead,
I sensed something wrong. You were in a bind.
I tried to help you. But when I said,
"To err is human, to forgive divine."
You turned and left. No longer were you mine.

—*Deanna Yetter*

The Baby that Died for the Life of a Drug

A baby, that's all it seemed to be,
Lost in a world of confusion.
Not even born, but dead.
The mother, high as a kite,
Not a care in the world,
She thought she was free.
Free from the world that she once knew.
A kite struck down by lightening.
Her own little world lost in a thunder storm.
The baby that died for the life of a drug.

—*Debbie Beebe*

Untitled

Friendship comes, friendship goes,
Love comes, love goes,
Beauty comes, beauty goes,
But there is one thing that came
And will never go,
My friendly, lovely, beautiful
Telephone!

—*Bridget Grady*

Peace and War

Peace,
Love, happiness,
Laughter, warmth, sunrise,
Dreams, life, death, reality
Darkness, coldness, silence,
Sadness, hate,
War.

—*Brooke Benedict*

Love is

Love is a cloud,
Love is a dream.
Love is a feeling,
Nothing comes between.
Love is a wishing well,
A fountain of youth.
Love is no secrets,
And only the truth.
Love is kind,
Love is true.
And hard feelings,
Love will see through.
Love is a fairy tale,
A dream come true.
Because I found love,
When I found you.

—*Connie Willis*

What is Love?

Love is a feeling deep inside,
Love is a feeling shy people hide,
For fear of that person
Won't love them back
For fear of that person
Love will lack.
Love can't exist without two they say
But who are they to ruin our day?
Love is something you cannot see,
Love is anything you want it to be.
Just believe in someone
And trust them too
Then you'll know
That love is true.

—*Kristi Dallas*

The Signature of Love

Love is sang in songs, love is written in poetry.
Love is even said to a beaten child by its abuser.
Love is many things with no true meaning.
I'm not even sure what love is.
But as far as death, I am sure about that.
I know that at death, real love is shown.
I rejoice at the glamour of death.
It is like a blanket of warmth which
Shields me from any false sense of love.
At death, there is much love—tears.
Tears are part of your body you shed for ones you love.
And to give part of yourself for someone has to be love.
Someday it will be known that tears are a signature of love.
So as for me, I await death.

—*Jessica Bellinger*

Love

Love is something money can't buy.
Love is gentle and sweet.
It gives you a special feeling
From your hair down to your feet!
It's in the hearts of many
Though sometimes they may not show it.
God's planted it in everyone,
Even if they'll never know it.

—*Christy Banzet*

Love

Love is strange,
Love is good,
Love can sometimes never be understood.
When you're in love, your eyes will
    sparkle,
Your face will shine,
The sky will be clear blue,
The flowers will bloom
Just for you
In love.

—*Danielle DeBiase*

Love

Love is fun.
Love is happy,
Love is sad.
Love is laughing;
Love is crying.
Love is anything
You want it to be
Anything but forever.

—*Anissa Meek*

Love is not Blind

I think of us and what we could be,
Love is not blind; it's for all to see.
Love is a passion that comes from the
    heart,
Everyone finds it and plays their part.
Some play their game.
Some utter it with fame.
Others deprive it. . .
Yet others survive it. . .
But, don't hide your love from others and
    me.
Love is not blind; it's for all to see.

—*Crystal Osburn*

Untitled

Love is a hunger
Love is pain
Why should we have love
When all it is, is a game?
You played the game well
Excellent I'd say
First you win my heart
Then you throw it away
So go find another girl
Someone just like me
Someone very gullable
Someone you can't see
Maybe if I could have seen
Seen right past your face
I could have seen the hurt
You would cause me
And all of your disgrace

—*Holly Grenz*

Love

Love is here, love is there.
Love is people as a pair.
Love is sweet, love is neat.
Love is people that care.
Love comes, love goes;
just like ice cream cones.
One minute it's here to stay;
then before you know it,
it's melting away.

—*Kimberly McNeely*

Love is

Love is happy,
Love is sad.
Love is promising,
Love is bad.
But most of all,
Love is love.
Love is hate.
Love is giving.
Love is taking.
Love is making.
But most of all,
Love is love.

—*Kelly Dillender*

Painted Love

Trying to be who I am.
Love is so much, bet it's grand.
There are so many things,
we have to go through,
to be who we ought
to be.
With someone and me,
to be together, yet free.
Love through the fallen
painted years.
Tears and fears of love,
with happiness and sadness.
The nights lost in hopes and dreams.
No matter if life is right or wrong.
The heart, stronger than the mind.
That's painted love, specially devine.

—*Bonnie L. Grot*

Love is

Love is kind
Love is sweet
Love can hurt
And make us weak
Love is for me
Love is for you
Love is for those
Who can see it through.

—*Amber Caroline Stewart*

Love Is You

What is Love?
Love is you, wiping my tears.
Love is you, facing my fears.
Love is you, holding me.
Love is you, trying to be free.
Love is you, saying it will be O.K.
Love is you, staying when you want to be
    away
Love is you, wanting us together
Love is you, confused as ever.
Love is you, wanting some space
Love is you, disappearing without a trace.
Love is you, like a flower that wilts and
    dies.
Love is you, someone who shares my cries
Love is you, wanting me back but to
    scared to say
Love is you, with your friends always in
    the way.

—*Alisa Marie Accardi*

Love Me When There's No One Else to Love

Love me when times are hard to bear.
Love me when you wanna swear.
Love me when there's no one else to love
Love me when the clouds are dark and gray
Or when your lover has love another
Love me your friends are cold and few
And you've been left alone and destitude
Love me like a bird need wings to fly
Or like flowers need the sun to blossom
Love me like the earth need wind and rain.
Love me like th day lights up our world.
My love is as beautiful as an innocent dove.
So love me when there's no one else to love.

—*Carolyn Cox*

The Month for Love

June is coming around, oh so very fast!
Lovers moan and say, "Now it's time at last".
We have waited for a very long time
To hear each other, say you will be mine.
We have put away all our childish things
We know the meaning of those wedding rings.
It is truly is time for the wedding vow
Can we wait so long? We do wonder how!
Then one bright morning, we will be awake
Catch a view of our lovely wedding cake!
And then with our fear and trembling hands
We'll say our "I dos" and wear wedding bands.
Those older people, who are in the crowd
They fear for failure, not speaking aloud.
It's good that all can dream wonderful dreams
It takes some time to find just what it means.
Would you make yourself a very solemn vow
That you will succeed, you will figure how.
You'll be surprised that it is not so hard
Just keep your loving right in your own yard.

—*H. Huddle*

Day Dreaming

Imagine this if you will. . .
Loving someone beyond life itself.
The joy of happiness embracing your every thought.
Like a security blanket that covers the face of a timid child.
Then, out of nowhere,
In a moment of haste,
Like a rushing tidal wave,
That someone is thoughtfully taken away. . .now what?
Tears, I suppose.
But. . .
More than that. . .an empty feeling of confusion and even despair.
Shake your head and awaken lover.
She's still here and I have touched her while she still sleeps.
Ahh! Thank you.
How wonderfully mysterious.
How painfully sweet, and
So secure.
Thank goodness for day dreaming.

—*Adib Abdullah Rasheed*

Loving You

Times move so fast
Loving you didn't even last.
Wondering why you left me,
Leaving so soon as you did.
Saying that I love you
Was the only thing I could do.
If only you could wait
Till another day,
I would tell you all
That I ever wanted to say.
Wish that you were back
All the times we had together.
But now they're lost and gone forever.
Why is it that love hurts so much?
Love is everywhere
For everyone.
For the stars above and the
Brightly lit sun.

—*Frances Lozada*

Patience

Just when you think, you have everything under control;
Low and behold, the Devil unfolds
A new problem which seems even bigger than before.
We CAN'T give in,
It'll just give him another win.
Instead we have to pray and try to keep control.
And with God's help show that devil we are bold.

—*Antoinette F. Utley*

Four Days

Four days stretching endlessly
Lying long ahead of me
Them beyond I cannot see
Far away into the dawn
Four days lying ever long
Four days stretching endlessly
Lying long ahead of me
Such a short eternity
Until they are past me too
I must live on without you
Four days stretching endlessly
Lying long ahead of me
Soon they too are memory
Then willl end the misery
Then will I be truly free

—*Florence M. Waldron*

ME

A wesome clarinet player
M aybe will become an astronaut someday
A lways willing to lend a helping hand
N ever is perfect
D ances to let out her feelings
A nd is an all around great gal.

—*Amanda Carle*

A Picture

If you draw a picture of a lake,
Make it shimmer.
If you draw a picture of a snowflake,
Make it quiver.
If you draw a picture of some leaves,
Make them blow.
If you draw a picture of a snail,
Make it go slow.
If you draw a picture of me,
Give me eyes to see.
If you draw a picture of life,
Make it everything you want it to be.

—*Jenny Wallace*

Happiness Within

Putting a little color,
Making an inner glow,
Just plain make your true colors shine
Perhaps with a pretty sash or bow.
Someone who puts a smile on
Does it because his insides are blessed.
This, in turn, causes a chain reaction
Which makes everyone feel as though they are the best.
One such feeling
That can cause sheer bliss
Is a special emotion of love
Which is, many times, expressed with a kiss.

—*Denise Long*

Anything For You

Inside I feel like dying,
Making me always crying.
Remembering how you left me,
Thinking how could he.
But I don't blame you.
I never told you now much I cared,
Nothing at all did we share.
I would do anything for you,
As long as you know
How much I really love you.

—Amy Hite

Younger Generations

Getting dirty; being the dirtiest.
Many of us aim to be the worst,
Particularily the younger generations.
All of us have our own recollections.
Of times when we just didn't care.
It just didn't matter if we got spiders or sticky goo in our hair.
Mud pies, sand castles; they're just a beginning to the list.
Bicycle chains, cowboy hats, and Indians envisioned in the mist.
Particularily the younger generations
Get a kick out of games like this.
I just don't think it's fair
That we begin to grow up, and are forced to care.

—Amber Marie Gerry

Untitled

Shed no tears for me.
Many years have I waited
To speak to Jesus
Face to face,
The Jesus who wept for Lazarus.
Jesus wept?
You may weep for me
Briefly.

—Jack E. Cole, M.D.

Life

Is there ever any happiness or is it always sorrow and pain.
Many yesteryears I remember hope and happiness
But it all seems a dream.
My hopes are gone and happiness is nowhere to be found.
My life seems so far away but half way over.
When it's my time to leave the nest, will I ever make it on my own.
Is there really a life out there for any of us.
So many people look at life in different ways.
Some live in fantasy, some live in reality,
Some people can't live through it and some people never see the end.
For me I know there is an end but I can't see it.
I know reality but I don't want it.
I know fantasy but there I can't find satisfaction
Because I know responsibility.
I know I can face life through but will I make it without sanity.
Happiness is out there somewhere. It has to be, my life will go somewhere;
It has to and I will make it to the end.
I was told to!

—Heather Foley

Life

A bee flies along, buzzing his song,
While the flowers blow in the breeze.
The sun shines down brightly, from the heavens almighty,
And the birds fly around through the trees.
The air keeps on blowing, all along it is showing,
That there is hope in this world of ours.
New life is in bloom, from womb to womb,
We see it shine down through the stars.

—Marilyn Sterling

To My Wife On Her Birthday

The sun moves southward day by day
Marking the leaves of the pear tree
With veins of red and gold.
Returning, it will create a spring
Of continuing life and new birth.
That same sun marked the moment
Of the miracle of your birth and
Each passing has enriched your life.
Denying that universal calendar
I witness your renewed birth this day.
I would give you continued life
Not with the seasons but
Each time the sun rose to suffer
With you the red of your anguish
And treasure the gold of your desires.
I would be your sun.

—Gene Warren

The Truth I Never Told You

I don't know why I don't like you,
Maybe it's me, or maybe it's you.
Though we try to work things out,
we know it's hard without a doubt.
We fight and fight and get nowhere,
Again we fight tear against tear.
We never seem to agree on a thing,
We always fight about stupid things.
I know you love me and I love you,
It's just so hard for us to do.
Another daughter, another dad,
A whole new family we never had.
Different people, different times,
Accusing us for little crimes.
Knowing that you were wrong,
Admitting it very strong.
I'm so sorry we've fought before,
I promise I'll try more and more.
Even though we fight and scream,
There's one thing that seems to me,
I love you and you love me,
And that's the way it's going to be.

—Karen Jones

A Family

A family's a group of best friends,
Who are bonded together with love.
A family supports till the end,
If they're blessed from the Father above.
A family is there for each other.
Even when friends may fail.
The heart of a family's the mother,
And she tenderly guides your life's trail.
The head of a family's the father.
In his strength he always provides.
To meet our needs is no bother,
With his wisdom and knowledge he guides.
So a family's there to depend on.
Through thick and thin it will stand.
If you feel that your friends are all gone,
A family will reach out its hand.

—Lori Slobodian

Confusion

Special. That could be the word.
Maybe something else.
Why does nothing explain how
Or what I feel for him.
Could there be no explanation?
Love. That might describe the feeling
Or why I have this feeling.
But it is so unsure.
My heart is so unclear.
What should I do?
Where should I go?
I am alone, but only
In the decision I must make.
Was it love, hate, or obsession.
Could my emotions span to such great lengths?
What was inside and what I felt inside seem indifferent.
The explanation could always be unknown.

—Blake L. Goldstone

Why?

Let me ask you some questions,
Maybe you can give me some answers.
Why am I dying to live,
When I'm just living to die?
And why I still try.
And could you pray tell,
Will it all end in hell?
Should I always be good
Yea, if I only could.
So a twenty years long,
I still wonder what I did wrong.
Only if I could be good to God;
If I would just try,
I would not be afraid to die.

—John Kenney

Flight Plan

Birds in flight and lines transepting,
Measured echelons unknown;
Swirling, looping, soaring skyward-
Sun on wing and windward blown.
Lines crisscross but no collisions,
Undulations of delight;
Patterns black on rose horizon-
Does some message sing through flight?
For one moment gathering gaily,
All verge on the maple tree,
Drawn to chirping convocation-
Swoop! they vanish instantly.
Suppose each bird could trail a thread of jet,
Oh what a mesh lace pattern they would weave
On the blue loom of sky,
Could eyes believe?

—Evelyn J. Reiser

Amid Pandora's Released

The multitudes cross night's amorphous back,
Melting shapes dimly lit againist the black;
Dreams are they, phantom children 'pon their way,
Released each eventide to giddy play.
Out from Pandora's Box they dart, escaped
To the wavering plains of sleep's dreamscape.
I, stranger to nocturnal happenstance,
Rendered impassive by repose's trance,
Minion, here beneath these somnolent lids,
Am mere witness to their whimsies' bids.
To and fro they pass, deft and willowy,
Weaving patterns of luminous filigree.
I stay my approach, lest direct address
Send them vaulting into the nothingness.
FINIS

—D.T. Phillips

Facing Life's Sorrow

Broken hearts of sorrow,
Memories of yesterday filled with tomorrow.
The loss of your life wasn't right,
The falling tears shout at the night.
We all pray and want to say,
How we love and miss you in a special way.

—Jennifer Tonra

Victims in the Hands of War

During the early days of war
Men were called to fight
They represented boldness and courage
Out there for one reason—
To discover the true meaning of freedom
Dust particles in the air floated through the trees of that lush jungle
Looking around, I could just ask myself,
Why were we fighting against such a beautiful place?
The days passed by slowly
Sleep was rare
When there was a slight moment of rest, dreams of war crowded the mind and left no room for the pleasant thoughts that may have tried to override it
Innocent people were shot
The small children could hardly bare to witness the blood-shed deaths of their loved ones
By the end of the war it was finally realized there was never as much rivalry between our enemies as there was among our own people
All we were were victims in the hands of war

—Jacquie Danette Felan

A Summer Day

The sandy cat by the farmer's chair
Meows at his knee for a dainty fare
Old Rover in his moss-greened house
Mumbles a bone, and barks at a mouse
In the dewy fields the cattle lie
Chewing the cud 'neath a fading sky
Dobbin at manger pulls his day
Gone is another summer's day

—Amanda Covington

Tree of Life

Oh, evergreens of fir and pine
Midst the bleakness of wintertime,
When leaves of trees are dead and gone,
Your evergreens attest that life goes on.
Oh, evergreens of fir and pine,
A symbol of life at Christmastime,
A symbol of our Savior who won
A victory over death for everyone.
Oh, Christmas tree of fir and pine,
You stand to testify, and call to mind,
The word made flesh, the Savior's birth,
Heaven dwelling amongst us,
Christ's love on earth.

—Elaine Casey

Waiting

Waiting?
Yes, waiting.
'Round every corner and bend,
Etched on my memory, each line of your face
Blends with the sound of your voice
Again.
Longing?
Yes, longing.
As the gray skies rival the blue,
There's an insatiable yearning that cannot be quelled
Save by the nearness of
You.
Hoping?
Yes, hoping.
O must you question that part!
It's hope that gives promise to dreams fulfilled
And quickens the beat of my
Heart.

—Sandra Lee Kent

Depression

He squirms his way into the depths of our mind like a snake.
He creates images of destruction and horror.
He slowly crushes every bit of joy and happiness in us.
He laughs and gets a thrill out of seeing us suffer.
He snacks on thoughts of joy.
His main course is the love we have for ourselves.
He drinks the tears that fall from our eyes.
His dessert is the thoughts of agony we now have.
The joy we once had, has now been devoured by him.
He releases a poison that slowly deteriorates
our body and soul.
Our mind is now and empty pit of sorrow.
His job is now done, leaving us in a corpse of depression.

—Dinorah Quinones

Monkey Business

Everybody talks about things they
   shouldn't be
Mind your own business and leave my
   business to me
Don't come around with a whisper—sayin
   she said this and that,
I'll stare at you crazy, and say—is that a
   fact.
Now the fact that I'm referring to, is the
   lie you just told,
Now get the hell out—for I up and grab a
   hold.
Don't like to get rough, some things just
   don't click,
Better get a move on and make your
   steppin quick.
Now don't come back tellin me the news
   of he and she.
Just mind your own business!
And leave my business to me!

—*JoAnn K. Hopkins*

Remember

A
moment
short,
strong
makes
A
memory
lasting
long.

—*Karen Mabry*

Moms

Moms are people who understand,
Moms are there to lend a helping hand.
Moms are special to me and you,
Moms are there to tie our shoe.
If moms happen to get angry or sad,
We are there to make them not feel so
   bad.
If you need to come to one of us,
Drive your car or take a bus.
Moms are there to take us to school,
Moms are watching when we are in the
   pool.
Moms are there when we need some
   money,
Moms are there to say "Oh honey".
Moms are love us as much as we love
   them,
Moms are there to turn on "Gem".
So, mom we hope you stay around for a
   long while,
Who will we have to clean the tile?

—*Christine Abbate*

Off the Ground

Why is it that people with
Money just don't care
They say the ones without are lazy
Who says life is fair?
They used to say love made
The world go 'round
Now even ones with tons can't
Get off the ground.
Why do ones with money give the ones
Without that ugly stare
Are they any different, any less
Who says life is fair?
I used to hear men were created equal
Now I know that's just a sound
If they are, why can't some
Get off the ground?

—*Jennifer L. Wolff*

Love

Love is greater than the stars of the sky,
More powerful than life or death.
Love has value above any gem,
Or fur or piece of art.
Love is warmer than midday sun,
And softer than baby down.
Stronger than steel, more bending than
   wind,
And free to those who will give it.

—*Keith R. Howell*

Carry That Child

See the child whose eyes have seen
More than his years should know,
Whose life has known an unkind world
No joy to help him grow.
See the child whose shoulders stoop
his eyes dart toward the ground
His worries, things like if there's food
or a home will e'er be found.
See that child and love that child
Thought he's not yours or mine.
A gentle touch, a loving hand,
A treasure he can find.
See that child and carry him
As far as you can bear,
Provide him clothing, shelter, food
Reach out and prove you care.
As soon, you see him lift his head
His eyes, with laughter, smile,
You'll know your touch has reached a life.
That marks it all worthwhile.

—*Kim Bellemare*

Feelings

You mean a lot to me
More than the world.
For you are different
Than all those other girls.
I've learned to love you
As if you were my wife,
And that's something I have never
   experienced
In my whole entire life.
For this feeling is special
But will anyone ever know
For my feelings are too hard
To express or even to show.
So I made up this poem,
I wrote it from my heart
To secure you my love
That will never part.

—*Karen Vigil*

Who Cries for the Murdered?

Who cries for hte murdered?
More than twenty six million
Butchered, ripped, torn to pieces. . .
Innocent, defenseless, miraculous,
Babies, dumped in garbage cans.
Who? Have breathed but
Will never breathe, again.
Each were pure innocencies. . .
Are you crying, for the murdered?
The seed of each father was alive
In each living father
The egg of each mother was alive
In each living mother. . .
Who cries, for the murdered?
I am crying. . .they cried!
Will you cry for those
Who?. . .will be murdered?

—*George E. Trout*

Perfect Love

Can anyone be perfect?
Most of us have tried;
We speak of finding the perfect love,
Finding out later on it died.
No one has to be a perfect "10"
To find a true romance;
We have to look inside ourselves,
And give our love and chance.
What's on the outside may look nice,
But it's what' inside that counts;
Life isn't always pleasurable,
The tension often mounts.
Take time to know each other,
Then share in your love and glee;
You may have a few faults here and there,
You may have a few faults here and there,
But you close enought to perfect—for me!

—*Cindy Forster*

Vengeful Neglect

I have feelings too.
Most people don't realize it,
But it is true.
I need to feel special,
Just as much as the next person.
Most people take me for granted.
They think I'll always be here for them,
To hold up their world
When it comes crashing down around
   them.
But what if I'm not?
Then what?
They'll crumble.
I think I will give it
A try.

—*Kimber Tabak*

Sky Power

Soaring sea- bird
Mounting heaven's peaks
Double scythes are severing the sky,
Gliding, sailing;
Insubstantial, weightless wings deny
The pull of earth below.
Eyes wild, open-beaked,
Pretty streamlined head cocked
To see that life upon the nether wave:
Shimmering, silvering
Scattered phosphorescent bits, enslave
This primal appetite.
Unwinking, sudden power,
Tightly scissored wings
Plummetting with ruthless downward
   haste!
Slamming, clamouring,
Toward its prey, precision-paced,
Its weapon gravity.

—*Gray Senior Knapp*

A Bouquet in Repose

Our much worn and tried flag,
Mourns the passing of the day.
Draped caskets that pass our way,
Silently portray its proud legacy.
A calm and soft air,
Unfurls the red, white and blue,
While a nation grieves in prayer,
Under the stars, upon yonder hill one can
   hear the bugle
Of the last ta ta tu.
In each American, there is a memory of
   greatness true,
Christ wept, and His tears live with us
   yet.
And He is born within us like the tuned
   strings of a violin set.
The soldier plays his trade to his country
   due.
Sadly is the sight and sound of a riderless
   horse,
The slow march, a requiem to the drum
   beat,
A tune for the universe where our souls
   shall meet,
And our glory is in the flag, a mighty
   symbol she, for a piece of cloth.

—*Herbert C. Spivey*

The Steel Cocoon

A free spirit soaring through life
Moving fluently, with ease and grace.
Building your space in life
Patiently, slowly, taking your time.
You wanted it all, safe and secure
You rushed a few things.
Now I see your wings are clipped,
You are wrapped, entrapped inside a steel
   cocoon.
Life is now so hard to bear, I see the pain.
The sorrow in your eyes reflects the pain
   in your heart.
Life's cycles will continue. . .
As with the butterfly, you will emerge.
You will be stronger, your wings carrying
   you to unknown heights.
The pain, although hard to bear, will
   strengthen you.
Your spirit will grow.
Each phase of life is hard. . .
But each creature entrapped by a cocoon
   emerges even more beautiful than
   before.

—*Anna Davidson*

Look at the Cross

And not another word. . .
Murder is so plainly sought
and seen from all perspectives.
A Life—
the senseless grief of wonder
of Nothing to maybe know
all of something, but then again. . .
Aging Fools crossing their hands through
air, corroding me, my breath—
These Foolish Fools with
roling eyes could all but
Seek out creation,
instead they forfeit it and close
Shut the lids on such a world
full of nothing but Nothing.

—*Joseph W. Tullgren*

Once Before

I was once in love, but am no more,
My broken heart washed against the
   shore.
I still think about those times we had,
And when I do they make me sad.
I used to think our love was undying,
And would never falter,
But then I made a terrible mistake,
And our strong love began to break.
When I think back to those days,
When I acted in those foolish ways,
I know how wrong it really is to betray
your love for someone,
Because soon enough that someone will be
   gone,
And you will be left alone,
So quiet,
So empty,
So alone you will be
Just like the silent beating of the sea.

—*Jennifer Robinson*

The Anniversary Poem

You're my sweet love,
My dream from up above.
When I fall asleep, you're there,
And when I awaken, you're near.
Your love is as true as a soaring bird,
Or a love song, yet to be heard.
When you're gone, I sit here and wait,
For you my love, please don't be late.
Our love is as beautiful as a red, red rose,
Our love towers over any of those,
Who watch upon.
For day by day, our love carries on.
Today marks our second year,
This anniversary is the most dear.
I say this my love, for in a short time,
You my love, will be completely mine.

—*Dawn Gareau*

What If

My dreams are sweet;
My dreams are good;
The dreams I've had are both sweet and
  good;
Yet they are still more than they should;
I dream for the best;
But after their through, I think of the
  worst;
What if this or what if that;
What if are the words I regret;
Yes, I know it should be this;
But what if it was that?
A dream should be your hope
But then again, it should have a glow;
Oh, that Dream I Dream of;
But then again;
What if I was wrong!

—Julie Stevens

My Secrecy

You cannot begin to know how I feel,
My every sorrow and joy inside.
My secrets of you I've tried to conceal,
They scream for release, but in me abide.
My building and fighting emotions cry
Out in their hidden and controlled
  quarters
Pleading with my heart to not let them
  die,
Their release is stopped for my tongue
  loiters.
My very existence depends on you,
Therefore, I cannot take the risk telling.
My feelings for you are so deeply true
And on them daily I can't help dwelling.
So please believe me when I say this now,
My secrecy is my life and my vow.

—Cymber D'Asto

The Cathedral of a Rose

The class wore on,
My eyes began to wander,
I saw a rose. And pondered,
Where did that rose come from yonder?
On the bare concrete wall,
Where my straying eye did fall,
I saw a box, a rose within,
And a small blossom
Bending the tiny stem.
It is like a chandelier hanging in a great
  cathedral,
Sharing its softness with the great
  Baroque stone work.
Like a tiny light within heavenly clouds,
On the wall where darkness enshrouds.
In a world of its own,
It has silently grown.
Where no one sees it
But the I who sit
In the classroom.

—Eric Stubbert

Big Brother

The day will come and we'll say goodbye,
My eyes will mist and I'm sure I'll cry.
Big brother is leaving, his school days are
  past,
Our childhood days have all gone so fast.
My number one playmate he was to me,
From playing with tractors to climbing up
  trees.
Our quarrels we had numbered more than
  a few,
But as we got older, the smaller they
  grew.
Goodbye, good luck, is all I can say,
Big brother, I love you in every which
  way.

—Kristie Kuipers

By Me

Sometimes I want to tell you,
My feelings inside.
Those feelings that hurt me,
That often make me want to cry.
The feelings of sadness-
A broken heart that just won't mend.
The misery it brings me, the pain that
  never ends.
I'm tired of always crying, everything
  stays the same.
I've given up on trying, because I still
  have the pain.
One thing's for sure, throughout it all.
No matter what problem, big or small.
After the pain, and anger too,
I've got one hope-
And this is you.
You are my joy, my guiding light.
You are my one candle, Burning Bright.
For this and more, I do love you.
And this love is deeply true.

—Cristal Reed

Cloud Collection

I would that
My hand could reach up
And touch
The softness of the clouds.
I want to put my hand upon
The lavender and pink
Of sunset's hour.
I want to start a cloud collection.
I'll only keep the prettiest ones
The ones most dipped in color,
The rest can go.
I want a cloud collection
So I can bring them out
And decorate the sky
Months from now
When the whole day
May be gray.

—Katharine Ann Birge

Staying Together

As the gentle rain pours outside,
My heart aches for you.
While fighting back the tears that sting
  my eyes,
I can't help but wonder if our love is true.
Here I go again,
Doubting my heart.
I remember way back when,
When I thought we'd never part.
I think of you always,
Hoping your love is near.
What more can I say?
Losing you is my greatest fear.
Is there anything I can do
To make sure we stay together?
Because I really do love you,
Whether it's sunlight or stormy weather.

—Carol ReNee' Blanchard

Secret Love

As I sit here by myself
My heart and mind are full of you,
And I can't help from wishing
That you're thinking of me too.
I know that you don't understand
I know you're not sure how I feel,
But still my heart is breaking,
And I wonder if it will ever heal.
I want to tell you everything
About how much I care
I wish you realized how I feel,
Because a love like this is very rare.
You and I are very close
I guess you could say we're best friends,
And it doesn't matter what happens in
  life,
Because my love for you will never end.

—Danylle Reed

My Heart Goes Out To You

When you fall in love, but then break up,
My heart goes out to you.
When you see him with another girl,
My heart goes out to you.
When you're sitting there and the tears
  just fall,
My heart goes out to you.
When the love dies that you thought was
  endless,
My heart goes out to you.
My heart goes out to you,
My heart goes out to you.

—Kimberly Scholz

The Tradgedy

The lights flashed, the sirens screamed
My heart is being crushed
I peered through the noisy crowd
And violently I rushed
A stretcher now is rushed away
I realize its you
I fall down on trembling knees
What else can I do
The hours pass, they seem like years
And silently I wait
The doctor tries to comfort me
But I know that its too late
Inside is trapped all the pain
And sorrow I've ever felt
After I leave, there are tears
At your bedside where I knelt
Suddenly, a startling noise
Arouses me from sleep
I quickly answer the telephone
And softly you repeat
Wake up dear its ten o'clock
How much longer can you sleep.
No other words that I have heard
Will ever sound as sweet.

—Donna Lewis

My Heart is locked

You mean the world to me,
My heart is locked you hold
The key.
I wish you could see right
Through my door,
Cause underneath there's a
Whole lot more,
Even though we haven't known
Each other long,
I can tell my feelings for you
Are strong.
After what we shared,
I could really tell you cared.
So, don't try to get rid of me
Cause my heart is locked
You hold the key.

—Cassie Patterson

Image

Sadness set in when you left me
My heart's rain began to fall
There was no one I could turn to
Nothing I could do
My hands began to tremble
Your letter fell at my feet
Its envelope had since been tossed away
Bending down to pick it up, my knees
    quickly hit the floor
Looking at the letter, tear stains have
    worn the words
The words may disappear from the paper,
But never from my mind
Just waiting to be replaced by the image
    of your face

—Chandra Nouwels

Fire

"Fire brings loving warmth to any room,"
My husband said to me.
"But it can only bring warmth where
    there is none,"
I said.
"Were the children chattering noisily,
    lovingly before we built this fire?"
"Yes, yes they were."
"In a room where there are"
"Strangers,"
"Cold, silent"
"Strangers"
"There, there it would bring loving
    warmth."
"But not here,"
"Here we are a family,"
"A kind, caring family."
"There is already loving warmth here."
But despite everything I have said,
He repeats it once again,
"Fire brings loving warmth to any room."

—Abigail Donovan

Wisdom

. . .on the tapestry
My knowledge falters,
But on the weathered tomes
Of leather
My hungry eyes dance
By candlelight
Within the catacombs
Of a dusty future-past. . .
Here lie all the answers
To questions not yet asked,
Every perfect solution
To problems that have
Never appeared,
And I grin at
This wisdom of fools,
So enticing. . .yet,
So impotent. . .

—Joel Tanis

For Donovan

My love for you is untainted,
My love for you is unstained.
But now that you are gone,
My heart is empty and pained.
I know that you were undaunted
In a fight for a perfect life.
But now that you are gone,
My soul is filled with strife.
You will be well remembered,
Have no fear of this.
For now that you are gone,
It is you that we will miss.

—Donna L. Belles

Till Eternity

To my love, who will always be,
My love forever, till eternity.
When I see how much you love me so,
I realize, I never wanna let you go.
I love you so much, you are forever mine,
When I look at you, you make me shine,
Shine like the sun, every so bright,
You make me feel I'm always right.
You are the one for me, my dear.
When you're with me, I would hate to
    fear.
I want you now, I want to share,
Your love for me, your endless care.
You must see now how I feel for you,
I know you're my love, am I yours too?
Tell me my love who will always be
My love forever, till eternity.

—Kathleen Galazin

Truths

I told her that
My love was true
She told me that
Her's was too.
She told me she loved me
She really did
I didn't know
Her true feeling were hid.
Her feeling were locked
In her heart far away.
She really didn't care
I'm sorry to say.
She got with someone else
Then I threw a fit.
She won my heart
Then stepped on it.

—Erik Rodenberry

New Life

As I look out into the beautiful horizon
My mind breathes
My eyes see for the first time
A new world
A beautiful world
My body lives a new life

—Ammie L. Unger

Independence

I never thought I'd worry, but now that
  you're liberated too, I do.
My mind is a fury of emotion:
Trust and distrust, triumph and defeat.
I wanted you to grow, to try, to
  understand, but now that you are,
My own insecurities surprisingly flood to
  the surface:
Am I enough for you? Can I be what you
  need me to be?
Will your searching lead you away from
  me?
The same insecurities which once crippled
  you.
My ideas seemed so intelligent, so correct.
But now that you're accepting them and
  attempting them,
Maybe I was wrong, I just might lose you.
I don't know, I have to do what I think is
  right.
But now that you're doing what I thought
  was right,
I wonder if I'm wrong.
I will find out.
And when that day comes, I'll have to
  think more carefully and
Express myself more slowly.

—*Anna Gierich*

Keeping the Faith with George Michael

I love you George Michael
You are oh so fine
I love you George Michael
I wish you were mine.
Your music is awesome
Your singing is great
Your songs are terrific
Wanna go on a date?
Your eyes are so dreamy
Your hair is so cool
Your mouth is so sensuous
Would I be kissing a fool?
I love you George Michael
That's all I can say
I love you George Michael
Let's get married today!

—*Lydia Buckley*

Lost Friend

Hello my friend so far from me,
My mind speaks though my eyes can't
  see.
My minds voice, so calm and low,
A shame it wasn't always so.
But behind the harshness of words, it
  seems,
There was always love and trust and
  dreams
To be fulfilled and counted on.
And yes, a friend to lean upon.
I miss the person that used to be,
Goodbye my friend so far from me.

—*A. G. Laurie*

I Miss You

A warmth embraces me as I look out at
  the sea
My mind wanders, thinking thoughts of
  you and me.
With the wind blowing in my hair and the
  sand trickling
Through my feet, I wonder where you are.
The radiant colors of the sunset
  strengthen my heart
Letting me know you're not very far.
They help me to believe that you love me
  no matter where you are.
Our love is so true
It gives me hope, even when I miss you.
When I look at the future, I smile for all I
  can see
Are beautiful visions of the two of us; just
  you and me.
My heart I save for you,
My soul I give to you,
My dreams I share with you,
My love, I miss you.

—*Annamaria Pagliocca*

Endings

My heart grew tired of trying.
My soul grew tired of searching.
It was not you who fell apart.
It was not you who yearned.
Maybe it was not to be.
Maybe it was fate.
No one is to blame.
No fault can be found.
The love did not end.
The flame did not burn out.
But somehow we just stopped.
But somehow we just stopped.

—*Jennifer Bober*

Uncle Doug

"U"nique in more ways than one.
"N"ever said you were perfect, and I
"C"an't say you never had fun!
"L"oved me more than any Uncle could.
"E"ven though you couldn't stay,
I love you anyway.
"D"ied because you drank too much.
"O"r maybe the hurt went straight to the
  heart.
"U"ncle Doug, after watching you, I
  promised
"G"od, I will never start.

—*A. Zelinsky*

Remember Me

Remember me as I am.
Nat as I was
Remember the time we spent
playing in the park,
swinging on the trees,
playing in the grass.
Watching the flowers bloom, as we go
  past.
Looking all around.
Listening to the one sound
The sound of air hearts
Pumping up and down.
Remember me,
as I'll always be.
playing in the park,
just you and me.

—*Kimberly Weikel*

Special Places

It takes a special person to understand a
  child's
need for gentle loving care; to visualize his
potential, tho it may seem little there.
It takes a special person to roam a marsh
  near the
bay; seeking to discover the wonders
hidden there.
For to see something beautiful among the
  weeds in
a marshy place, is much like being able to
find something precious in every child's
  face.
For life's little treasures quietly wait to be
discovered in very special places.

—*Jeanette Morris*

B105

The heart pounds.
Nerves twitch.
Lying together.
Arms holding close.
A gentle caress.
Yes.
Silence.
Stillness.
Pain.
Unspoken words.
Subjected.
Does he know?

—*Dorrie Smith*

Teenagers Treasures

Noxema, Phisoderm,
Neutrogena, Oxy 10.
Cover Girl, Maybelline.
Loreal, Estee Lauder.
Suave, Salon Selectives,
Finesse, Final Net, Nexus.
Girbaud, Esprit, Guess,
Levis, Polo, Generra.
Priceless Treasures.

—*Jennifer Good*

The Helpless Tin Soldier

Marching in an army off to war
Never knew what he was fighting for
But true to his country and all he could be
A wind-up soldier with a shiny key.
And little tin bullets shot through the air
Fighting as if without a care
Young and fearless as all could see
A wind-up soldier with a shiny key.
The world is cruel and so unfair
But try to change it, he didn't dare
Never a complaint, nor a plea
A wind-up soldier with a shiny key.
So in the battle among death's cries
The wind-up soldier was paralyzed
As the enemies' bullet shattered his key
Now helpless and still he'll always be—
The wind-up soldier with a broken key.

—*Corina Schmidt*

Someone to Care

Being together
Never to part
All that seems so fine
May someday break my heart.
We never talk about it,
It's just always there.
A special friendship
Someone to care.
I cared so much,
It never went unspoken.
My feelings for you
Left my heart broken.

—*Jennifer Craig*

Farwa! Farwa!

Farwa! Farwa! Read the paper,
Nicholas Long's the number one raper!
"I don't care cuz he's still cute,"
"Right from his head to the tip of his
   boot."
Farwa! Farwa! Listen to the news,
Nick robbed a bank on Fourth Avenue!
"I don't care cuz he's still cute,"
"Right from his head to the tip of his
   boot."
Farwa! Farwa! Did you hear it from
   Sharon?
Nicky went and married Erin!
"I don't care, I'll win him away."
"After all, where there's a will there's a
   way."
Farwa! Farwa! Haven't you read?
Nicky broke his nose and shaved his head!
"Oh that pig!" she screams and hollers,
"I wouldn't like him for a million dollars!"

—*Eleanor Limprecht*

A Friend

A friend is someone
Who smiles as if to say,
I'll make you happy,
In some little way.
He's that special person
You always like to see,
Even if you're bored
With all other company.
A friend is someone,
Who always tries to stay,
Just a little longer,
When others go away.
He's that special person,
Who always wants to be
Of some kind of help,
When all else seems
To fail to remedy.

—*Sheila Compton*

My Love is a Battle

Love will be a battle if you change.
No darling, I won't change never.
Let me have a chance to go through your
   hair.
My hair is black but he thinks it's dark
   brown.
Let me look into your eyes and
Say something with dim sadness, and
   your brown,
Eyes are beautiful but,
I don't think my hair and eyes are brown.
Why am I brown, I like black is the best.
He thinks I am changing because,
Even my skin color is changing.
The wind is wild and night is cold.
But our changing, love is dry.
What is love? Is it dead?
My lover wants to know.
I can't tell him anything about it.
Because my love is changing.

—*A. K. Ayesha Roshini*

Death is my Only Reward for Living

Death is my only reward for living.
No flowers bloom in my mind.
No sunsets,
No castles
Just dark lifeless things,
Suffocating in my own hate.
No joy from people who are out for
   themselves.
No happiness in a heart turned black.
Death creeps into the soul
Delicate yet unbearable
No light becomes a savior.
Blood as wet as a tear, pain as sharp as a
   blade,
And I am caught in a trap.
Nobody can solve the problems,
The destitute,
The insufferable,
Dreams dying. . .
And I die with them.

—*Erin Salomone*

My Forgiving Rose

The slender stalks of bitterness are but the
   seeds of the thorns.
No hope; just pain, that kills thy heart
   destroys the soul.
It is the sweetness of forgiveness that
   opens the rose;
the buds unfolding to engulf your heart,
   your soul.
Each sweet petal with they tears of dew
brings a newness to thy heart, and an
   uplifting of the soul.
It is this one beauty that covets the earth,
for its warmth, its nourishment and,
without thy tears would not grow.
Open thy heart, fill it with joy
look upon the rose, not the thorns.
It is the love in each and everyone of us
that see's the beauty of this rose.

—*Connie L. Clark*

If There Had Been

If there had been
No love
There would have been
No hatred
Nor anywhere
To fall
There would have been
No heights
There would have been
No depths
There would have been
Nothing at all

—*Judy Pendell*

Words

My whole life has been in dreams,
No mark left on the world.
If I were to be gone tomorrow,
None of my words would be heard.

—*Heather Trousil*

Success

Try your hardest,
No matter what you do,
Because no one can ask,
Any more of you.
The odds are against you.
The pressure is on.
You're scared and you feel
Like a new baby fawn.
You try harder and harder,
Again and again.
Success seems so far,
But then. . .
You find a new strength.
Your courage shows through.
You've beat all the odds.
Be proud that you're you.

—*Karen Boucher*

The Flowers Will Always be There

The flowers are always there
No matter where
Through thick and thin
Used to mend
The broken hearts of lovers

—*Bob Banks*

Fortress

Fortress, fortress once upon a hill
No misty winds can warm your chill
No one thunderblock hath broken your door
No one prince hath made his score
Then
One one summer Knight you must have thought
"Why shouldn't I do what I ought not?"
So when Prince Charming doth finally arrive
No guarded treasure will he find inside
But
Take comfort thou whimpering lass
Herein lies the secret which can forever last;
Only a discerning heart when with true love stands
Will ignore past battles and any previous lance
For within those arms you will one day find
That preserved virginity is a state of mind

—*deci ferguson*

Untitled

"He promised me," I said aloud.
"No more pain, no more cocaine."
Yet here I sit beside his bed
Tears of relatives fall upon my head.
I hold a bag on my lap tight
Filled with notes, pictures, letters,
Stubs from movies we'd seen together.
All the love we once had
I hold now in this paper bag.
"He promised me." Yet tears I lack
"No more cocaine, no more crack."
I stare at the ring for me he'd bought
"No more crack, and no more pot."
I grasp his hand, no reflex back.
His lips are silent, eyes closed fast
They close the lid on the coffin he's lain.
"He promised me no more cocaine."

—*Kimberly LaGarde*

A Gift from Mother

A piece of crystal
Wrapped in a pieace of leaf.
Never touched by any human hand.
So radiant and powerful
Yet still laden with the dirt of the earth.
Keep it close to you at night while you sleep.
Its radiance will cover you
Body, heart and soul
With the hand of God and the wings of angels.
Close your eyes, let your mind clear.
You can hear the wind blow and feel
The tips of angel wings brush against your face.
You do so much for others.
They want to do something for you.
Let them lullaby your soul into peaceful,
Joyous dreams to refresh you
For yet another waking day of preparing
For better things to come.

—*Lori Ingrid Sherrill-Krasinski*

At Peace

No more fret,
No more worry,
No more sadness,
Or pain.
It is we,
Who mourn the loss,
And you,
Who achieve the gain.
The world is bright and cheery,
But in our hearts,
Cloudy and overcast.
For you we mourn,
We wish you back,
Even though we know,
You're in the Father's grasp.
Suffer no more,
Sleep on for now,
You've gained eternal peace.

—*Chris Arent*

The Grieving

Grief is private, grief stands alone,
No one can feel it for you, no one can explain.
Each of us mortals must set its bounds,
Each of us starts and finishes at our own pace.
As the ashes of recollection form the mountain of memories,
The emptiness is real but cannot be measured,
The longing, not conquered, but mocking the watch and calendar, can only be endured,
Fleeting thoughts and sad sighs battle inner strengths
Yearnings, aches and languishments voraciously dream on through endless days,
Oh, soul of my wistful being, what is the final cost of caring?
The personal tally for compassion and sharing?
Where does the sky begin?
When does my melancholy time end?

—*Charles Day*

Last Word to your Daughter (Son)

Do you remember the first time you met?
Who'd have thought you'd come this far.
For here it is your wedding day,
And yes, you are the star.
What greater gift could you two receive,
Than just to have us here?
The people that love you the most
To share with you the years
Together you will seek new roads,
Leave old paths behind.
For tonight you promise each other
New horizons you will find.
And on this day you give to him (her)
The secrets of your soul
And promise each other eternity,
As you both grow old.
So hold each other close on this first dance,
As your lives begin anew.
Be her king, she'll be your queen.
Make your fairy tales come true.

—*Sheila Simmons*

Nothing

Everything is quiet,
No one is talking.
I watch outside for something to happen,
But nothing.
I wait for hours thinking,
But nothing.
A little bit of laughter in the background,
But it meant nothing.
Someone asking for help,
But she got nothing.
Some people are nothing,
But I'm something.

—*Anne Preston*

Turtles

The texture of your tea is just right,
no one knows better than you.
What would you do if it were too soft?
I bet you wouldn't stay around to find out.
Handfuls of seasame seeds were picked just for you,
no wonder you sent them all back
to the museum where they belong.
Three and a quarter years ago you borrowed a rabbit,
and now your turtles are alone, but
you should have known better,
turtles with a rabbit, what a shame!
Sand is falling and is running short for you
but you can handle it, after all
you were the one who chose Tai Chi,
not me!
I can see you are getting bluer now.
Please, don't choke on my account,
I had a better show yesterday
when I heard a marlin was brought
screaming to your front desk.

—*Kenzie McCurdy*

Blue Moon

What exactly is a blue moon?
No one knows for sure.
Some believe it is a time of depression,
Some believe it is a time
when something extravagent will happen,
Yet I believe it is a rebirth
of the moon and stars
That will come to the rebirth
of our souls and bring
peace to the world.

—*Carmen Ashbrook*

Baseball

Baseball's flying here and there
No one knows really where.
The pitcher throws the batter swings.
It seems they all have wings.
The pitcher's throws from the mound
Never get off the ground.
But if the batter does hit
The fielder won't get it.
So I guess I will wait till next year
To play baseball here.

—*Elizabeth Fogler*

Depression

Down that long and lonely road
No one knows where I'll go.
Could be cyanide
That helps my suicide.
Darn that song and lonely road

—*Karen L. Everington*

Why the Angels Cry

The wind sings a sad song, it lingers in the air
No one takes a stand, no one wants to care
A face shows no expression, a smile can't be found
Can't they see what's happening, the signs are all around
Cities of corruption, lives torn apart
It's a world of confusion, with hatred in its heart
The eagle doesn't soar anymore, the flag doesn't fly
So when it rains, nobody asks why the angels cry

—*Jamie Chisolm*

Here I am

Here I am, in an empty glass dome.
No one to love, no place to call home.
I'm singing a song,
I'm telling a tale.
The story of my life.
Why won't anyone listen?
Or is it just that no one can hear?
Inside the dome the colors change.
From dark to darker.
From grey to black.
Why won't anyone look?
Or is it just that no one can see?
I'm sailing a storm.
The waves are rough.
Rough as sandpaper.
Why won't anyone touch?
Or is it just that no one can feel?

—*April Miller*

Wish You Were Here

Summer here—there's nothing to do,
no one to see..
Seems like everyone's away, but me.
Then when I go away, everyone's back,
Or someone has a party when I start to pack.
At least there's the phone, and there's always letters,
So my friends can communicate—
for worse or for better.
I get so lonesome, and wish they
were near, when I get a postcard.
Wish you were HERE!

—*Jennie Ln. Eliot.*

Summer in the South

"Hot and Humid", the weatherman predicts.
"No rain in sight".
I slap at a fly as I wipe the sweat from my forehead.
Heat rises from the sidewalk in shimmering waves ahead of me.
I kick a stone across the dry dusty ground.
The mosquitoes buzz around my head and bite at my legs.
There's no place I'd rather be.

—*Brandy Dean*

Untitled

Confusion fills my mind, there are no answers,
No solutions, like an empty page.
I reach out to you for guidance, but you pull away.
Why? Why have you left me cold and deserted?
I can feel the wetness of tears making their way down my face.
I reach out to you once more, you offer your hand,
But your soul, its longing, longing to be free.
Somewhere deep inside my mind I see the answer
But it's weary, unsure.
Looking again to you for guidance, you look away
Forcing me to search my own soul instead of
Constantly relying on yours like I have,
So many times before.

—*Jacqulyn Aden*

The Love of God

Thank you Lord for this beautiful day
Not a cloud in the sky up above
The birds in the trees singing sweet melodies
They're singing of God's wondrous love.
The love of God is everywhere
No matter where you may be
It's in the trees, the mountain tops
It's in the autum leaves.
It's in a baby's smiling face
A mother's loving eyes
The love of God is everywhere
It never, no never, dies.

—*George E. Henderson*

Daddy

My daddy is a sailor,
Not a silly old tailor.
He works on a submarine,
Unlike a marine.
When he goes to sea,
Here I will be.
When he comes in,
I'll watch that old tin.
I'll wait for his hug,
On that little tug.
The love I can see,
When he hugs me,
Is in his smile,
All the while.

—*Krystyna Giebultowski*

Mixed Emotions

As I walked down the beach
Not a single thing was in reach
But for my soft soled feet
In the warm summer's heat
That is on the glorious sand
Which borders our loving land
For the crashing waves on the sea
Holds nothing but glee for me
As I watch the birds flutter in the sky
I think with such a loving sigh
For all the people nestled up so very high
I soaked it all up in my sparkling eyes
But as far as my eyes would go
I realized it sadly so
That the day was coming to an end
For I feared that my heart would never mend
All the heavens passed our worldly gaze
Would set me into a love and warming daze

—*Jennifer Heffelmeier*

Flying in the Sky

Flying high up in the sky
Not a worry and not a sigh.
Having the time to enjoy
The beautiful sky,
Taking a moment to look at the world.
Flying high up in the sky
Making my dream come true.
Becoming a pilot was not easy to do
I can fly with the birds in the sky.
I'll have my dreams come true,
I'll fly.

—*Christa Fay*

Reflections

I have a pain
not an ordinary pain
visible to only a few.
It lies dormant within
surfacing at will
leaving me weary and confused.
This never-ending trial
this test of endurance
separates those who have given up
and those who have not.
This pain that I have
it tells more than you think.
As long as I can feel this pain
I know I can still go on.

—*Karen M. Chow*

The Most Beautiful Man

There was a man so beautiful that no other could compare.
Not any man from past or future could ever outshine his being.
He was not especially strong or tall, not any special frame,
Yet, his stature was one among the giants.
His eyes were often said to be an ocean blue
Or perhaps a rich, warm brown.
Whatever color, they were full of compassion and understanding.
They were filled with love and saw beyond the surface;
Delving to the heart.
A glimmer of starlight shone among the lashed glory.
His face was full of sunshine.
His smile was passionate and bright.
His young mind was full of wisdom and knew no social right.
Although his hair was long and brown, his features fair,
This was not what made him beautiful,
What made him so, was that he died for me.

—*Bethann Conner*

My Country Life

The country is roomy and also very fun.
Not as icky and sticky as the city
You can't lay in the sun.
You can't swim in the city
It's not very fun I love the country
And I always will it s fun, fun, fun.

—*Danielle Gittler*

Untitled

I just can't seem to stay away,
Not even for a minute let alone a day,
My feelings for your are truly sincere,
Inside my heart I hold you so dear,
You are my one and only love,
My beautiful princess, my morning dove,
I love you angel in so many ways
For so many hours for eternal days,
I promise I would treat you like gold
If only I were yours and you were mine to hold,
When your near me, I'm depressed never,
If only I could have you, I would hold you forever,
Your voice, your face, your touch I need,
Without it, I know my heart would bleed,
My eyes are tearing, my face is blue.
The only cure is a touch from you,
Once we're sure it will be forever,
There's nothing we can't accomplish, me and you together.

—*Joe Dispigno*

Roses and Thorns

I walk down a path of roses,
Not finding a single thorn.
As I walk down this path,
I feel no pain, complete peace.
No wilted petals, no dying stems.
It is so easy.
As I walk along further,
I become lonely, I feel emptiness, frustration.
Everything is too easy.
I feel no accomplishment, no pride.
The roses become my anxiety.
My perfect world isn't enough.

—*Kristen Phillips*

Who Can See the Wind?

Who can see the wind?
Not I.
You can feel it push,
You can hear it sing.
It may be warm on a summer day,
Or cold on a winter night.
But still you cannot see it.
You can tell when it's there,
As the trees swing and sway,
When the leaves disappear,
On a cool autumn day.
You can feel it,
You can hear it,
And know when it's there.
But still you cannot see it.

—*Kathy Sudnik*

My Dream

I had a dream I never thought would
 come true,
Not in a million years did I think I could
 share it with you.
You're the last guy I ever imagined that
 could love me this way,
You're nowhere close to what I expected
 to be with today.
You're such a better person than the one I
 knew before,
Now I realize I have nothing in life to ask
 for anymore.
I have all I need, I have everything that
 love requires,
I have waited for so long and finally I've
 filled each of my desires.
I love everything about you, I know our
 love is true,
I couldn't have done any better than I did
When I fell in love with you!

—*Angela R. Witsil*

Windows of Time

I looked through the windows of time,
Not knowing what I'd find,
Looking how things have changed.
Places, people, and memories all
 rearranged,
Questions arise from inside,
Of the person I was and why,
I rejected and caused disaster along the
 way,
What I did, I would not do today,
I know it's good to be a dreamer,
But my dreams went too far,
I dreamed myself into a prison,
And had myself to blame for the bars.

—*Dee Dee Hamm*

Love

Love is made from many emotions,
Not things like witches brews or love
 potions.
Love is made from gentle embraces,
Not from those who wear false faces.
Love is made from a warmth from within,
Not from the heat created by the actions
 of sin.
Love is made from a special bond between
 two,
Not from tape, string or super glue.
Love is made from a a growing friendship,
Not from the stranger offering a weekend
 trip.
Love, last but not least, is made from
 people like you and I,
Who decided to give emotions, embraces
 and growing friendship a try.

—*Danica Freeman*

How I Give Birth to a Poem

There's a place where I go
Not many know of
It's a place in my heart
Not many can reach
I've done my best writing
While away from the stream
Of people, and places,
And noises, and things
Giving birth to a poem
With pen on a page
Nursing it to life
Like a mother with her newborn babe.

—*Kerry C. Kincaid*

Discontentment

I sit in wildering wonder.
Nothing is clear at all.
The fog of life was
Set within me.
Confusion's bells
Ring through my ears.
The variations of
Exotic thoughts
Dance in my troubled world.

—*Angela D. Jackson*

All Things Come to an End

All things come to an end.
Not just all good things, but all things.
Happiness, sorrow, anger, grief, love, and
 even life.
All things end
Sooner or later.
Time is the keeper of the end and the
 controller of our lives.
We have no control, although many of us
 like to think we do
Sometimes things end sooner than we
 hoped
And sometimes they last too long.
It has been said that time heals all
 wounds,
But it doesn't; it only nurses them like a
 mother of a wounded kitten
If they had healed they would have
 become lost to our memory
And sent to a far-off place
Where nothing exists
Except time.
But even this must end
Because sooner or later in time
All things come to an end.

—*Ginger Greenamyer*

Is it worth It?

You hear a whistle in the wind
Not sure what it is.
You hear the leaves rustle on the ground
Not sure if it's real.
You walk on the busy streets
Not sure if you're really there.
Yes, it's all in the mind.
You feel an uncertain feeling in your
 stomach,
A glow in your eyes, a heart begins to
 beat.
Is it worth it?
Then a heart begins to break
A tear falls down your eye,
Your world begins to tear.
Is it worth it?
What is this feeling you feel?
It's love
Then a broken heart.

—*Jennifer Pereira*

The Lost One

I can't figure out what went wrong,
Nothing is the same.
All I know is that she's gone,
And I feel I'm the one to blame.
Although she came to me for help,
I never thought she'd do it.
I never took her seriously,
I thought she would get through it.
Even though we weren't the best of
 friends,
As once we used to be,
I still sit here and mourn for her,
For today's her one year anniversary.

—*Chrissy Wegert*

Feelings of Love

Love is like being in another world.
Nothing stands in my way nor blocks my
   mind.
My inner thoughts and body are so
   twirled.
The moves I make and thoughts I think
   are blind.
The name of my love is spoke with such
   grace.
I'm aware of the words from whom they
   are spoke.
My love's name I pray is willingly traced,
And my head will soon be emptied of
   smoke.
The sound of my love's voice fills me with
   joy.
I cannot think straight when he comes
   around.
I am given no limits with this boy.
When I see him I know I am love bound.
Nothing will be able to stop our hearts.
And we know that our hearts will never
   part.

—Jodi C. Roney

Desert Nomad

In the heat of the day I hunt my food.
When thirsty, I slay a plump cactus.
My music is the rattle of a snake.
My confidante is the mighty desert rock.
My bed is the burrow of a desert
   mammal.
My light is the sun by day,
And the stars by night.
The desert is my home,
The place where I was born.
I am the richest of all people,
For this sandy castle is
A place to call my own.

—Rebecca Ramos

Georgia Rain

Like a nurse, nurturing God's orchids,
Nourishing my sorrow and pain,
Supporting my addiction to sadness,
This Georgia rain.
Like an overpowering tyrant, imprisoning
   those below,
Chaining me to the confusion I battle in
   vain,
Laughing as I'm scarred with internal
   wars,
This Georgia rain.
Like a widow's veil, shrouding life's
   beauty in black,
Keeping from me the answers for which I
   strain,
While in my search for peace of mind,
This Georgia rain.
Like a romantic song, drying lonely tears,
I wish for sunlight to keep me sane,
So incredibly fatal is
This Georgia rain.

—Krista Edwards

Just Once

This is a poem about a nice man.
Now he not dare walk nor stand.
He died many years before his day,
But now he is gone he's passed away.
He used drugs just once that night.
It gave his family quite a fright.
They called the hospital to send a truck,
But I guess that night they were down on
   their luck.
He died two hours later on.
He said no good-byes and now he's gone.
His falling star that night had fell
So when you use drugs your headed for
hell.

—Brandi McManus

Untitled

Once I walked the night alone.
Now I finally found someone.
Someone who cares and someone
I really care about.
Nothing is going to take this feeling away.
I'm not going to take it for granted.
I'm in love and this time I'm in deep.
I've never felt this way before.
People tell me I'm too young to know
   what love is
But they're wrong.
I'm going to hold on to this feeling
Because I know what it's like
To walk the night alone.

—Amy Vetter

My Heart

You broke my heart built of stone
Now I'm feeling all alone,
All it took was just one flirt
Then my heart began to hurt,
In love, we can't hide our romance
We tried everything even a second
   chance,
Feelings we have deep inside
Are feelings we shall never hide,
The memories we have through the years
Are never lost, just in tears,
One thing we should take, day by day
Is each other's love all the way
If by chance we should part again
We could still have the feeling of a friend.

—Joseph D. Petro

Nocturne

There's a rustle in the tree
Now-in that bush.
There's something satin black
Luring you to its sanctum.
Come hithering-
Withering green slants of eyes peer at
   you.
There's a whispering
In the leaves
An explosion of leaves as the nocturne
Bursts forth
Near your feet.
Catch-me-if-you-can
It runs teasingly into the night.
It's satin hair spreads into a cape
As it turns back
Once
To wink.

—Kristen F. Casey

Love Changes Things

I had my life arranged.
Now it all has changed.
You think it is a shame?
Well, love is to blame.
When it came, goodbye to my plan:
In my planning I had left out a man!
I would be merry
With just a canary
And a nice little nook for one.
This I would enjoy when my daily work
   was done.
I'd write stories and songs for the young.
I'd translate books from a foreign tongue.
But-pigs and chickens, horses and cows:
They are my lot when I take the vows
That make me his. I don't care!
Grand is a farm when love is there!

—Esther G. Lincoln

Untitled

When you left you took my heart,
Now it's all broke apart,,
You had so many dreams to live
So many goals you made,
Now my heart is filled with emptiness,
Since you went away.
We shared so many things
We spent so much time together,
But it all wasn't a waste.
Cause I got you in my mind,
I can still share our memories.
I can do the things we used to do.
Even if it means I do them with you
You're still in my heart no matter where I
   go.
Dear Theresa I wrote this poem
To tell you I love you so.

—Karea Pearson

I Wish You Were Here With Me

Why did you leave me when I needed you the most?
Now that you're gone, I sometimes see and feel your ghost.
Are you really here with me or is all that's left of you a dream?
Sometimes I hear your laughter in the quiet nights.
Or see your smiling face in the stars glistening lights.
Can I leave you behind and forget all that we shared?
No, that would be impossible, I would never dare.
Promise you'll never forget me, what we did, saw, and heard.
I can close my eyes and remember the times we shared.
Sharing in the joys and sorrows, we knew the other cared.
I wish that I could hold you again, at least one more time.
Then I could tell you how special you were, one of a kind.
Maybe one day I'll get you off my mind.
But until that time, I'm so glad I was yours and you were mine.

—*Jennifer Gleason*

Fruit

In the refrigerator, there is some fruit,
When eating fruit, don't wear a suit.
The juice will drip on you,
It will make a mess, this is true.

—*Renee Kerr*

The Gift

Before we were one
Now, we are two.
I did love you true,
but, that's just not the way with you.
As you look me in the eyes,
I feel as if I'm only one of the guys.
Your gift was beautiful,
unlike I've ever known.
Sentimental and precious—
Yet something I cannot own.
Possessive I would be,
to keep this gift all to me.
So now we part,
like the sea.
Forever lonely—
Forever free.
I love you,
but this relationship cannot be.

—*Jennifer and Erin Page*

Demons Of The Concrete Jungle

Life in the 20th century.
Nowhere to go, nothing special to do.
Watch them walking the halls and out into the street.
Not innocent, not sweet, they're never quite right.
Always in sight, the leaders of the future, young lovers
on the loose.
Some say too young, others too old.
Easy to love, still hard to hold.
Fighting for freedom, fighting for love.
Bloody faces, bruised pride, all kinds of feeling hiding inside.
This is modern day America, the concrete jungle.
There is but one way to understand, that is to stay, to watch,
becoming part of the world in which the children live.
Do not stare, do not yell, only accept as we do the rebellion
which only grows with objection.
We will survive if only you leave us our freedom, don't take our
pride, only it allows us to fight the demons of the concrete
Jungle.

—*Frankie Raveill*

An Orphan's Cry

O mother, why did you leave me
O father, why leave me be
In this world where there's no pity
Where love is rare and scarce
O love, where can I find thee
O pity, where do you hide
I need you to comfort me
O mama, I want you by my side
My morale to boost without pride
For love is rare but golden
Two spirits mold into one
Where care is rare but unfolden
Two souls glued into one
Pride to the flame gone
In the jungle of monsters
Playing the game of gangsters
O father, why leave me be
When the heat is on
Thine pride to the wind gone
The battle fought, lost and won.

—*Ayodele Ayetigbo*

Love on Mother's Day

M is for mother the more best friend so dear
O is for the old kind head she has all through the year.
T is for thinking of her home so true
H is for how hard she works to make a stew so well
E is for every good girl and every good boy
R should remember the name of mother all over the world.

—*Joseph Lewis*

On Course

We may complain that we have not
Of earthly stars and whimper wrought
To Him who casts our roles in life,
Who weighs the calm against the strife;
Aware is He if choice were ours,
We would embrace our ivory towers
Should He the Chief of Engineers
Reveal to us the thin veneers,
The false allures
Of green pastures.
So midst dark fears,
Despair, brave tears,
Our God, the Pundit Ultimate,
Revealed, the Artist Consummate,
Gives heed with wise and gentle might
To chart our course toward truth and light.

—*Isabelle Casanta*

Gypsy Shawl

Peel the orange moon
Of her mystery
Like you peeled an orange gypsy shawl
From my shoulders last night.
The birds sang a song
Telling us of the distant birth of dawn
And wondered at the stars
Flickering in the darkness.
We placed bright candles
In white lilies
And sent them down a
Rushing, tumbling river
As a sacrifice
To their reflections
In the sky.

—*Heather Olson*

High In The Sky Of An Afternoon

This is the park of childhood days
Of hide and seek and seesaw ways
When Anna swung me round the moon
High in the sky of an afternoon.
High in the sky of an afternoon
Falling, falling almost too soon.
Over the rocks, king of all kings.
Lord of mountains, Lord of all things.
Lord of mountains, Lord of all things
Climbing the trees, swinging on swings.
Up the web of the monkey bar
Almost to reach the nearest star.
Almost to reach the nearest star
Almost so near, almost so far.
Round and round over the moon.
High in the sky of an afternoon.

—*Hilda Brown*

Untitled

As the sun sets, the color reminds me
Of how vivid your life will be.
The first rose that comes to bloom in the spring
Are your soft petal cheeks.
The sky when it is a light blue,
Without a cloud in it are your crystal blue eyes.
The green grass grows in the summer,
That is how you will grow over the years.
The birds chirp at dawn will be your voice of love.
The raindrops fall one by one
This will be your tears.
As the earth circles your memory
Is burned into my soul forever.

—*Denise Stepankow*

Testimony

Birth life death a single breath
Of intensity passion compassion
Always another moment the last
Not there was it ever there
Are many questions answers that
Might solve something while no mystery exists
Stream of this that the other swirling thing
One big fat fantastical flowing eternal now
Intricately aesthetic now simply pathetic
On one off zero off on now again
Now slip—sliding through now clenched grasp
But all at once in hand in a single moment. What then

—*Eric Holden*

Woman's Work

Tapestry
Of my heart.
Tattooed
With love.
Contemplating
A child.
Child of my heart.
Your child.
Woven by my
Body
With love.

—*Janice E. Rouse*

The Death of Innocence

In quiet words
Of passion
He whispered against her ear:
Please let me
Make love
To you.
As silent tears
Slid down her youthful cheeks
She let him—
Pretending it was real.
What is love?
What is love?

—*Krista Malott*

The Kiss

Disregardful in our time
Of romance's blight,
A moment of life's breath
Is freely intermingled
In fantastic ardor.
We feel ourselves open up;
Two blossoms in single bloom
On barren fields
Where virgin seeds will not take root.

—*Jody Marcus*

Nature Calls

The air is filled with an inspiring scent
Of roses and lillies and hyacinth.
The flowers, they sway across the moor
As in the days that have passed before.
They still hold their virtue of beauty and grace
As they stand so proud in their crowded place.
They give off a luster of yellow and red;
The soil is a blanket, the ground is their bed.
The sky is a ceiling, the trees are their walls,
Listen, my daisy, for nature calls.

—*Jody Stodghill*

Miracle

Searching for the kindred
Of similiar qualities,
To listen to and teach
From among the banalities.
To share deeply. . .easily
Any point of view,
With a caring and respect
As so few can do.
For the meeting of our souls
That cannot count,
But, records our growth
In a painstaking amount.
This miraculous occurance
When one known a short while,
Becomes as one, known years,
In a cabalistic style.

—*Joan Hill*

Paradise Lost

As I stood on the shore
Of the deep blue sea
And watched the waves roll in,
I remembered how it was
When you were with me
The thought puts chills
On my skin.
When I turned to watch you go,
I had a tear in my eye.
I didn't want to see you leave
Because all I'd do is cry.
My love for you, whatever the cost,
That's the price for a paradise lost.

—*Christi Denty*

Desert Monsoon

By July we grow weary
of the desert—
her barrenness, her parched arroyos,
her cloudless, endless blue.
We wait, facing south, wistful
for those first welcome signs
like bales of Mexican cotton
To come tumbling over ragged mountains.
There they gather and spin
then weave themselves
into the canyon, dyeing quickly
into long, black drapes
that sweep coolly
across our nakedness.
And when they lift
we dance to songs
of faithfulness
and even the land runs wild.

—*Anita Jepson-Gilbert*

The Ghost in the Tower

Standing in the corridor
Of the London tower,
I hear a noise and turn around
But nothing's there.
Then I feel a cold hand
On my shoulder,
And when I turn to see
I get quite a scare!
I run through the tower
And all through the streets
'Cause the headless horror that I saw
Was Anne Boleyne by the tower stairs!

—*Heidi Farrar*

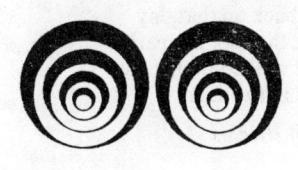

Imagination

In the quiet darkness
Of the skull
The mind conceives
The dream
That is a shadow
Of the shape and substance
Of reality.
The heart quickens
As the blood
Grows warm.
The chaos melts
And flows
Into a form
That is
Invention.

—*G. Whibbs*

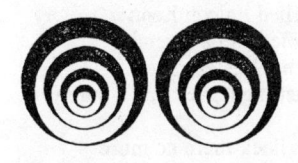

Yellow

Yellow is the color
Of the sun in the day.
Yellow is the color
Of the gold there lay.
It's the color of the
Sunset that covers the
Horizon, near and far,
And the color of
Daffodils on a faraway hill.

—*Kate Ficarro*

Wonders

My life is full of wonders,
of things I can't explain,
A world of hidden reasons,
a world of hidden truths.
And why my life is like this,
is yet another wonder.
A hidden reason not yet found,
a cause I still don't know.
And yet there is no doubt
there has to be a reason,
for all the question not yet answered,
in my wounderous life.
And with every passing day,
my faith will ever grow,
that one day soon,
I'll understand,
the wonders of my life.

—*Jennifer F. May*

The Inevitable

There comes a time
When duty is inflicted upon you
And hence it becomes inescapable
For you are vulnerable
Nervous and frail
At last it becomes essential
To withstand the inevitable
It is elucidated
And seems to be infinite
Do you feel felicity?
Or bow your head in sorrow?
It is much to elaborate for you
How long can it last?

—*L. Thompson*

True Love

You're my one and only true love and I
    mean that.
When I first saw you, I fell head over
    heals
And sparks began to fly.
That's when I knew you were the right
    one for me.
I am glad that I have finally found my one
    and only true love.
You always cheer me up when I am down
    and out.
You always make me feel good about
    myself when I am with you.
You never hurt me like other guys have
    done.
You are sweet, tender, and loving
And that is what I like about you.
You make sure that I am all right when I
    fall down and get hurt.
I like it when we don't always do what you
    want to do.
When you tell me that you have found
    yourself another love
I will not forget you
Because you will always be my true love.

—*Yvonne Wallace*

Diary of a Poet

One poet of time, these words he wrote
    and left them so plain. In his diary of
    notes he told of affairs that he once had.
Of true love and bad love and others so
    sad. He told of flowers beyond the
    willow so fare.
He told of lands where violence did spare.
    He told of rainbows above the coral reef
    and gold beyond the shallow tree. He
    told of time and death so bold.
He told of angels sparing lost souls. He
    told of islands where things were slow
    and time standing still.
For the wind did not blow. He told of a
    God so high and true and evil men with
    much to do. He told of ladies dressed in
    white and children being taken in the
    night.
He told of old men being stalked by age
    and fancy actors performing on the
    stage.
He told of a star in a strange land, so far
    away where shepherds did kneel and
    pray. He told of drugs being sold on the
    streets and a bakery on the corner so
    full of sweets.
He told of wars in a country so strong. He
    told of presidents, some right, some
    wrong.
He told of Hong Kong where many dies
    and sweet songs, song under spacious
    skies.
He told of floods and twisters too and a
    sad story that he knew to be true. He
    told of a drunk asleep in the park and
    when the journey ended of Noah's Ark.
He told of Pharoah and the Red Sea and
    flowers and birds and a tiny bee. He
    told of rain that killed the farmers'
    crops and streets filled with blood where
    the hatred never seems to stop.
He told of a plantation where slaves once
    dwelled and a biblical prophets of a
    burning hell.
He told about a world that would one day
    end and the birth of Jesus, man's best
    friend. He told of all that he knew, even
    about the giant that David slew.
He tried to cover it all in his diary of
    notes, even the mountain and the hills
    and the old gray goat.
He told of things so fair and true of life
    itself shining through and his word now
    lives on, for this man of wisdom is now
    gone.
But he left this diary for a guide for this
    poet has now expired.

—*Ann Gaston*

Indian Summer

The sun dapples the sky, leaving no trace
of yesterday's welcoming to winter.
The wind brushes demurely, helping to paint
the trees.
The trees rustle and sigh, thanking God
that the cold, harsh winter
is not yet to come.
The clouds smile reassuringly, they too
are only partially prepared
for the blithe birds to fly
over top of them.
The people are all so well satisfied with
the Indian summer.

—*Janine Leigh Sunderland*

Let The Children In

Let the children in,
Oh, let them come and play
So they can dance about.
And have fun all through the day.
Let the blind man see,
Oh, let him see the stars and the moon.
And let the deaf man talk
So he can sing his little tune.
Let the crippled run,
Oh, let them jump up with laughter.
And let the world wars end,
So earth will live happily ever after.
Let the children in,
Oh, let them come and play
So they can dance about,
And have fun all through the day.

—*Candice Zoller*

Picture Day

Picture day, picture day,
Oh! What a mess!
Should I wear a skirt?
Or should it be a dress?
Oh! What shall I wear?
And what about my hair?
Picture day, picture day,
Oh! What a mess.

—*Dawn Browning*

The Sad Guitar

Do not play gentle, old man of night,
Old blues pickers should never die.
Pick it sadly, make it weep, open dark windows
To the dying light.
Fret it, pet it, pick it low neck and high,
Keep on picking, until the day you die;
"Old blues pickers should never have to die,"
The sad guitars on bent shoulders sigh.
How many more lonesome roads, old man,
Can you travel before yoiu die?
How many more times can you trade your picken'
For two shot glasses of rye?
In Jake's jook joint, he picked the blues all night;
The women cooed to him gentle-the men didn't fight;
Oh, the sad guitar picken'-how the women cried,
When the old guitar picker, picked on 'till he died.
Kept on pickin', riding the soft night tide,
'Till he keeled over on the bar and died.

—*George Harmon Smith*

The Seaman

The empty basket lay unattended on the shelf
Old paint is peeling from the handle of the net.
Wrinkles are revealed on the waterman's face.
The crystal water glistens brightly in the sunlight
As the work boat slowly departs from its dock.

—*Jen McCreary*

I Saw Her

I saw her gallop bye
On a beautiful white horse.
She rode as though born to it.
Everyone else would be worse.
At the end of the lane
She came back my way.
I watched her all the time
And made my watching pay.
I praised her and saluted,
At this time she came bye.
She reigned him in and came to me
And saw my blazing eye.
Now we are the best of friends
And meet again and again.
We both look toward the future
She has removed my pain.

—*Harry Evans*

Shadow in the Dark

I was walking through the park
On a cold winter's night
When something walked beside me
As a shadow in the light
I turned to look and see this thing,
But what I couldn't understand
That what I turned to look at
Was a shadow in the sand
There was nothing all around me,
No objects I could see
No people walking anywhere
The only one was me
I felt so scared and shaky,
But what was I to do?
For what was walking near me
Was neither me nor you
So now I look back on that day
When walking through the park
The thing that walked beside me
Was a shadow in the dark.

—*Kelly J. Williams*

Dreams

One day my dream is to sail the deep blue sea
On a cruise around the Caribbean.
Just my friends and me.
We will party night and day.
For fun we would swim, dance, and romance,
And when it's all over we will say. . .
We hope to do it again,
And someday we may.

—*Jennifer McAbee*

Falcon Loon

On the march of a fiery journey
On a midnight summer's moon
One pale and lonely rider rode
On a horse called Falcon Loon
The name came from a legend
In a land on the Western shore
Where the rustling leaves sing a lonely song
And the birds flock there no more
The heart of this land, at the mercy of war
Was left to die in the midst of all death
'Til the years came to claim its loneliness
To give back ats life and pay back its debt
The rider rode in search of his soul
That he lost to the land by the sea
For he took the life of a man in revenge
Against the man's forgiving plea
No sound but the sound of a prayer was heard
Like a shadow enlightened by the light of the moon
And the presence of death removed itself
From the land of Falcon Loon

—*Jeanne Floyd*

Destruction

The destruction of one's self can be
On a personal level.
The "destruction" of one's self can be
On a humanitarian level.
Loss may cause one to put one's life
And lifestyle on the razor's edge.
Loss may cause one to put one's life and
    lifestyle
On the the "razor's edge" to help fulfill
    others' lives.
Pain accompanies both paths
But only one brings spiritual and
    psycho-emotional enlightenment.
To breathe life into a deflated life
One must "destroy" the old to bring to life
    the new "creation".
Death is inevitable on both roadways to
    destruction
But a slow, thorough, enlightened
    "Death" is better.

—James Michael Bernard

Peeking Out a Glass Window

The sunshine peeks through my window
On an early summer day.
The chill in the air is perfect,
Not a cloud in the sky.
That cricket makes a noise,
To say summer's here.
A soft breeze bends the grass,
And a drop of dew falls—
As a spectrum of color glistens from the
    sunshine
I walk outside
And breathe in deeply.
The smell of nothings fills up in me
As the day goes on,
The sun gets brighter, hotter
The dew dries up
And the smell gets deeper.
Until tomorrow I will cherish what I have
    today.

—Catherine Noelle Rioux

Untitled

As I lie here
on my bed
many thoughts
run through my head.
Thoughts of you
here with me
thoughts so painful
thoughts so deep.
I dream of you in my sleep
dreams of love
these dreams I keep.
Someday I know
my dreams will come true
my thoughts and my dreams
those dreams of you.

—JoAnne LoGuidice

Sunshine

The warmth of the sunshine,
On my face is encouraging,
As I lay in it warmth,
It's assuring and I wonder,
How life can be so fulfilling,
And yet so demanding,
As the sun drifts down,
Coolness sets in on the night,
I know it's a pattern of time.

—Carol Rich

Untitled

I'm always standing
on the outside, looking in.
Why?
I don't know,
I was just born here.
I've never looked from the
inside out,
it's always
the outside in.
Those who look out,
were born in a different world
where they can afford
to look out, at us looking in
I wish I could be with them,
looking out
instead of in.

—Jamie Sheely

The Rachmaninoff Concerto

High up in balcony sat she while he
On the stage played Rachmaninoff's great
    sound
Music reverberated all around
Strong hands on keyboard powerfully
    moved.
Fingers flying then walking slowly
    through the score.
By music's magic spellbound was she held
    as hands on
Keyboard the notes found in waves of
    indescribable beauty
What ecstacy. She thought so to be loved
    by those
Vibrant hands moving now gently then
    turbulently.
Thought became delight as sensations
    long asleep now
Moved inside her. Imagination took flight!
Till, music's end brought back reality!

—Honor I. Malcolm

Untitled

The black and white stripes,
On the zebra's sleek body,
Are a mystery.

—Kelly Tisdel

Beyond

Straight to the madness my life has come.
Once again my life is none.
Pulled apart within my brain,
Stretched beyond returning sane.
No more suns shall greet these eyes.
The light of life burns my eyes.
Face of life, facade it be.
Beyond it lies reality.
Take a look, horizon's line,
Only gate to heaven's time.
Why remiss? Why fear the past?
Forget it's there. Forget it has.
Darkened sky and darkened thoughts,
Black the fears of which I brought.
The greenest grass, the darkest night,
All's the same, no change of sight.
Darkness comes. It seeks my brain,
Final glimpse, the dying flame.

—Kevin R. Speicher

Life

Life is like an interesting book.
You've heard about it,
But never gotten around to read it.
Life is like the pages of that book.
You never know what will happen next.
Life is full of surprises.
Sometimes things are going great,
Then something goes wrong.
Like the pages of that book flip,
So do the days of your life go on.
Never coming to a halt;
Never waiting for you to recover, when
    you fall.
"Nothing in life should be feared"
"It is only to be understood".
It's the inscription on my diary.
Shall you not fear what's to come,
But make something out of the good and
    the bad.
Just let nature take its course.
And you will have, the most interesting
    book ever written!

—Leticia Cadena

Brother-Sister

My brothers who were
Once my protectors
After weakening me
With their protection
Turned on me like vultures
And I in my weakness
Drawing them in
Like a magnet
With sympathy and fear
(That being my strength)
Opened their eyes
With my fierceness
Oh, strange familial dance

—Adrienne Hall

Dedicated to Someone very Special

Once there was a day where I could run and play.
Once there was a day I stayed inside to lay.
Once another day too tired and weak to run,
Couldn't barley walk, couldn't see the sun.
Looked around the room couldn't really see.
Scared—What was wrong? It was muscular dystrophy.
Couldn't walk no more, couldn't even speak.
Wanted to give up, tired and very weak.
Sorry Mom and Dad for what I did to you,
Sorry Mom and Dad for what I put you through,
There is a telethon that's telling me to live.
There is a way I can and that's for you to give.
So please give me your heart and I'll give you my love,
Now I can wish again on the star above.
So please give me hope so I can run and play.
So please give me your heart so I can live today.

—*Alexia Panagiotou*

Life

To fully understand the meaning of life,
One must find the beauty that lies among themselves.
Thus, one can fulfill his dreams without feeling
A sense of failure trapped inside him.
Such a beautiful gift soon to be wasted
By mortals who corrupt the environment
That surrounds the beauty in life.
People say, "What truly matters in life"
"Is not how long we live, but how we"
"Live our lives to its full content."
Being a child that I am, sometimes
Life should be taken to my own hand.
But my conscience knows me better
To handle matters like this.
Life is hard but good.

—*Cynthia Mendoza*

The Best of Times

Our high school days are almost done,
One of many victories won.
We've been friends for so many years,
Laughed together and cried real tears.
We've shared our thoughts, our hopes, our dreams,
And now they're going to come true it seems.
We've had our disagreements and fights too,
But in the end our friendship only grew. . .
Now into the future I look backward to the past,
I see our graduation, I remember saying,
"I'm out of here at last"!
I wish I'd never said that about my high school days,
For now I know that those were the best of times,
In so many different ways!

—*Becky Denise Repine*

Personality

In this world of harsh judgment, there's one thing,
One thing stands alone, your personality.
The hate, the drugs, the violence, the sex,
All combine into one giant problem.
Some people walk through life without knowing
What you need to get by is some patience.
This world is much too dark to go alone,
You'll always have the need to be protected.
Life is too short to be wasted with hate.
There will always be parties to go to.
And if there aren't any, go make one!
So celebrate life and take this to heart
In this world of harsh judgment there'e one thing,
One that stands alone, your personality.

—*Christine Kalmey*

Soul of a Saint

One man's soul seeks out a mate.
Only a mate with the soul of a saint.
It searched to eternity's end, but at no avail
Was he to find the soul of a saint.
So his soul wandered aimlessly throughout the
Whole of eternity weeping over the soul of a saint.
Until the gleaming glow of a new soul shown bright.
The soul of a saint had been born into eternity.
A newborn taken at birth by the hands of the Lord.
And so the life long union of the two souls begins.

—*Jenny A. Williams*

Breath of Life

To hold the breath of life in the palm of your hand
Only to have it snatched away by some unknown force
That determines when and where;
How?
Why so short a life? Did you chose to be here today?
Gone tomorrow. Life is so short.
Fragile, handle with care in such a cruel world?
How do you handle death with care?
Getting sucked under without a chance in the world;
Without a breath.
To be lying in a coffin
The concept is mind boggling to me.
Did you let go?
Am I supposed to?

—*Erika Marshall*

Good-Bye

The golden sunset poured
Onto the lush green fields
The birds sang their good-byes
As the wind whispered a farewell tune.
Good-bye. . .sun
Good-bye, till we meet once again.
Good-bye. . .good-bye

—*Kathy Donovan*

Summer Rain

The summer rain falls from the sky
Onto trees and passersby
The summer wind blows through the trees
Blowing hair and rustling leaves
The summer heat beats down upon
The golden bodies in the sun
The summer ocean is deep and blue
And summer seems so clear and true
The summer sand is golden grey
Please tell me summer will always stay
The summer tide rolls gently in
And to not love summer is a sin
The summer bird comes here to stay
Singing in his special way
As I walk along a passer-by
The summer rain falls from the sky

—*Cindy Byrd*

Untitled

Gossip is like an
Open book With
Misprints.
Pride is like a
Balloon ready
To burst.
Giddy is like a
Ball wanting
To bounce.
Anxious is like a
Pencil needing
The paper.
You are like a rose;
Beautifully blossoming
Into an unknown sweetness.

—Kim Greet

Rain

My beloved rain,
You yearn to reach me
You soothe my soul,
You wash away my memory
With tears from above,
But I can't cry with you.
Shall I lie down,
To be drenched in
Your sweet sorrow?
Shall I bare every
Fiber of myself
Upon the soft grass,
Where I might be washed
And made clean again?

—Lisa Guerra

Gypsy Earth

Twenty-seven years on a back road back strokin,
Open token free rider late nighter hitch.
Destination: Bay Station tag trackin net workin,
No burden earnin dirt an' jumpin when the switch
Pulls down. Old south bounder that'll rattle,
Throttle round the middle ground of little towns,
In slumber rumble under nimble limbs.
Just listen for the whistle on the tressle as it passes,
Does it answer through the drizzle,
Or address the razor winds?
Monday's huddle round the puddle from the roof leak,
Blue feet teeter tip the bottle of the root.
Big splash quick flash-in-ration till a juice's jailor,
Loosens like the buttons on this tailor tattered suit.
Split in half by the draft and after ninety miles,
The box car locks hard dockyard berth.
Dirt cheep deep sleep, news sheet heat me,
Keep me breathing gypsy earth.

—J. Warren Spencer

A Piece of My Heart

How a flower needs sun
Or a bird needs the air
That's how much I need you
That's how much I care.
Though one day that flower will open
Or that bird will learn to fly
But you, you'll never understand
Why I close my eyes and cry
Though one day that flower will finally die
Or that bird will fly away
But they'll always be a place in my heart
Where only you can stay.

—Deana Ormsby

The Useless Gamble

When there's a speck of dust in the wind,
Or a cup to be filled, or even a thought to be found.
Why am I to be called upon?
Many to go on useless.
This side is here and that side is there,
But together they continue unlocated.
All of course unknown.
Then on record as of extinct, but not
Non—existant, yet one—sided, never thought to change.
Remembrance is tough, and strong is more so.
There is a force, invisible, yet there.
Undecided, but changeable too.
There is no use but to stare thoughtlessly.

—Cynthia A. Morgan

Our Life

Are we saved and sanctified, living this life each day,
Or are we tangled in worldly things, standing in another's way.
Are we living saved in church, full of love and hope,
Going home behind closed doors, puffing a little smoke.
Are we sitting up in church dancing and moving our feet,
Acting like we've got something that only moves you with the beat.
Are we looking people in the face, telling them about the word,
While thinking our little filthy thoughts, too unclean to be heard.
Are we encouraging one another, keeping our faith in tact,
Or are we talking down a saint, throwing another off track.
Are we angry with our brother who won't get saved in time,
Maybe what he sees in our life ain't really worth a dime.
So you who say you know Jesus, with thyself be not content,
When we the saints really get saved, then the sinners will repent.

—Janice Hannah

Do You Care?

Do you really care anymore,
Or are you just trying to make
Me think you do?
You say you don't care if I call,
Is that a signal that I should
Just drop it and forget everything?
If you don't care, tell me so I don't
Have to worry about it anymore.
I'd rather know now than for you
To wait until I'm even more in love.
I don't care about my life anymore,
And it would be easier if I knew
You didn't care either.
You've meant so much to me these
Past weeks and I don't want this
To end.
But if you don't care, I'd rather you
Let me know now.

—Karin DeSantis

Spoken Words

Remember this each passing day
When greeting friend or foe;
That what you ever have to say
Will follow where you go!
Always standing at your side
A shadow all can see.
Marching with you stride for stride
Into Eternity!
Spoken words oft said in haste
Recalled they cannot be.
And oh, the bitter, bitter taste
That's yours Eternally!

—Terry W. Beadles

If You Haven't, You Will

Ever missed your mother's goodnight kiss?
Or feel you have treated her amiss?
Have you missed her tender loving prayers,
When you crawled in bed away upstairs?
If you haven't, you will.
Ever think your mother was dearer than gold?
Or wished she could live on and on,
And never leave you in this world alone?
If you haven't, you will.
Ever watched your mother grow old and gray?
Or held her trembling hand, and her weak voice say,
"Be good daughter and son. . .I'll meet you in heaven,"
"When your lives here are done?"
If you haven't, you will.
Ever seen your mother pass away, and heard the preacher say,
"The world is proud of this mother so sweet,"
"In heaven, someday, her family she shall meet?"
If you haven't, you will.

—Cecil Edwin McBurnett

Us vs. Doom

Can peace ever be found in this world?
Or is DOOM a word we will soon be
 familiar with?
Why can't we get along?
We are all made of the same things.
But our ideas are different, which keeps us
 in shame.
We are supposed to learn, that is what we
 were told.
Why do we fight when we learn not to?
WE—the younger generation—want
 peace and a chance to live until
 tomorrow.
Isn't that what we should learn?

—Jennifer Evans

Seasons

My favorite season is summer
Or maybe spring or fall.
I also think of winter
As being quite a ball.
With snowball fights, and candy canes,
Winter can be quite a game.
But I always love tanning and laying out;
That's what summers' all about.
I know not what is my favorite season of
 all,
But a thought comes to mind, maybe the
 fall.
With red and yellow leaves spread over
 the trees
Makes a sight that is sure to please.
The brillance of spring fills my mind
With flowers blooming in the sunshine.
Come to think of it, I like all seasons in a
 special way
And each fills our life with a happy day.

—Kelly Miller

The Tunnel

Unaware of the consequences,
Or perhaps just unsuspecting.
Longing for attention,
Needing love, and affection.
Not fully understanding
The wrong they are performing.
Desecrating the temple
Keeps them locked in a tunnel.
Dark, alone and crying.
Some yearning, desperately trying
To approach the light at the end,
To find at last, a friend.

—Jennifer Pinto

Silence

Silence is golden
or that's what they say
but what about talk
doesn't anybody this day
Everybody used to
laugh and play
But now we're just reckless
with nothing to say
Oh Lord help us get back to
the old way of life
'cause we're going in circles
with no end in sight

—Heather Dunham

Holding On for One Last Chance

When was the last time we were alone?
Or was I just too blind not to see
That your mind was somewhere else
And you weren't quite following me.
I thought it would last forever,
And we would never part,
But I guess you just can't rely
On what's deep inside of your heart.
I don't think I can remember me happier
Than me being here with you.
And if only I followed my inner heart
 desire
Maybe our love would have been more
 true.
So maybe I'll give up on you and wait
A little bit longer
And when you realize how I feel
Our love will even be stronger.

—Kelly Lenz

Tab 8

Will they say there's enough food for all,
or will they stash it in a stall.
Will they see the homeless young and old,
and will they bring them out from the
 cold.
Will they turn their heads away and look
 for another day.
Will they help their brother, or will they
 do the other.
Will they seek only greed, for their eye
 won't seek the need.
Oh cosmic sky with watchful eyes give
 witness to the child's cry.
We are a country of red, white and blue,
 with fallen angels that's true.
Some fall hard and some fall well, but
 those that do, they'll never tell.
Oh Yow wa, make all to see, but not with
 eyes in a fleshly head,
loose the eye's of your spirit.
So man can learn instead.

—C. J. Stomper

Together Forever

The first time our eyes met,
Our destiny had been set.
Through time and patience,
We came together-thanks to fate.
Thinking back to the beginning,
The present is truly amazing
We've stayed together
through thick and thin;
Whatever problems arise,
I know we'll win.
Now we're going to tie the knot,
Which proves we love each other
quite alot.
There's just one thing you must
always know—
I'm never going to let you go.

—Jennifer Bush

Lost in You, Lost in Love

Sunlight streamed through your hair
Our eyes meet, I feel your stare
Hearts that meet and feel our cares
You and me, we're quite a pair!
Hands that touch, to show our love
We've been matched so well
So keep me secure and warm inside your
 glove
Dance with me beneath our moon
Don't let it end, not too soon
Give me your love, my heart, my dear
I'll give you my life without fear
I wander amongst the stars above
Lost in you, lost in love. . .

—Ginnie Ducharme and Heidi
Schukar

Broken Promises

Our love could never be
Our hearts could never see
Our happiness never came
To everyone, but us, we had no name.
Our faith never fulfilled
Our dreams were always stilled.
All the empty promises
All the false confidences
All that we believed in
No matter how hard we tried, we could
 never win.
The heartless and the cold
Didn't care, were not told.
Our lives were shattered
To no one, it mattered
Each other was all we had
But it was never enough, though always
we pulled through, Me and You.

—Kathy MacPherson

Our Love

Our love is stronger than a gush of wind
across the land.
Our love is hotter than the sun beating
down on the sand.
Our love is fresher than the waters of the
sea.
Our love is more precious than a glowing
bumble bee.
Our love is brighter than a shining star.
Our love is more dazzling than an
expensive car.
Our love is more powerful than silver or
gold.
Our love is worth more than an expensive
gift sold.
Our love is more free than a dove flying
through the sky.
Our love is so unique, that I know it will
never die.

—Jennifer Wolfe

Love

Our love is two hearts bound forever.
Our love is the thing that keeps us
together.
From love to hate,
From grief to fate,
No one will keep us apart.
For we are bound as one heart.
Forever and ever we will be,
Happiness forever for you and me.

—Heather Chappell

Stars And Stripes

Oh, Stars and Stripes
Our symbol of pride.
You're a worthy cause
for which many have died.
Through thick and thin,
you're always flying.
With your dignity and strength
never dying.
And now it is our turn
to return the favor.
You need our strength,
our hopes and prayers.
Oh, Stars and Stripes
Our symbol of pride.
Why must you burn
to tell someone's side?

—Jennifer Hawthorne

Sheltered Dreamer

I look beyond the window pane
Out into the world
Where life is real
And games are left desired
All these things you've kept from me
Hid behind this curtain
All this time you've sheltered me
And left me always dreaming
Now I look beyond the glass
At awe at what I see
Shoved into the middle of
This life you knew to be

—Amy O'Gorman

Staring Through Love

You walked into my life,
out of a dream.
You did not smile or talk,
you only stared.
I tried to stare back,
but looked away.
When I looked up again,
she was there.
She held you in her arms,
you held her.
I did not even know your name,
yet it hurt.
When she was not there,
our eyes met.
But never long enough.
you were gone.
I should have stared back
if only I had.

—Elizabeth Dell'Accio

It's True Love

This time it's true love.
Out of the relationships I've been through
This is the only one that has stayed true.
For all the others, they would die.
With them more and more I would cry.
This time it's true love.
For every time I'm sad or mad,
You're always there to make me glad.
We understand each other.
We love one another.
This time it's true love.

—Cheyenne Molina

Summer Sunsets

The beauty of a sunset descending
over a calm, beautiful lake,
Portraying a dream-like, breathtaking
picture.
Evergreen trees overlapping one another,
off the shore, across from me,
Slowly and teasingly swallowing
the sun piece by piece.
A gentle breeze stirring up the water,
Leaving it to look like a strewn, satin
ribbon.
The sun shining so brightly and
reflecting off the reservoir,
Spread so artistically like smeared
paint on a bare canvas.
The clouds hazy-like and mystical,
Making all appear like magic
before my eyes.

—Karrie Lyczkowski

Drums

I close my eyes and I hear a continuous
drumming
Over...and over...
And I'm a defenseless animal racing away
from a tribe
I hear their shouts and I hear their
screams
And I can practically feel their spears
digging into my fles
But none of those sounds or feelings
Can drown out the rythmic pounding of
the drum
The beat continuous...
Sounding over...and over...and over...
And the hunters take a wrong turn
I have lost them in the jungle
And the rythmic sound starts to fade
away
I am saved
And I open my eyes, And I'm in my room
laying on my bed, and the rain has
stopped.

—Holly Anne Sherwood

The Birdie

The birdie flew,
Over glue,
The birdie got stuck,
He yelled, "Yuck, yuck!"
When the birdie went free,
He was so happy,
When the birdie got home,
He realized he should have known,
By glue you don't fly,
Just stay up in the sky,
And that is the rule
That he went by!

—Erica Orr

Mist

Rising from the swelling lake,
Over the blowing fields;
Through the fresh, steady pines,
Skimming under the drafty doors.
Flowing into the damp pits,
Against the rocky canyon walls;
Past the maddening, thrashing river,
And between the beating wings of eagles.
Above the sweating plateaus,
Beside the trickling streams,
Off of the steaming lake,
Out of the tranquil caves.
Landing upon the soft valley,
The mist
Reveals
Its secrets.

—*Katie Powell*

The Unicorn

A magical beast jumps through the air,
Over the rainbow without a care,
It's silvery horn and long flowing hair,
The unicorn of yesterday, beautiful, lovely
   and rare.

—*Anne Louise Dean*

The Artist

Protected inside her dad's
Paint-speckled navy shirt,
She arms herself with a sable brush
And prepares to explore
Her untamed imagination.
She will conquer the terrifying
White plains of a stretched canvas
And hope someone—
Just one ordinary person—
Will stand in awe at the courage
It took to step inside herself
And find something that has
  never before existed.
Something beautiful.
Maybe then others will listen
In silent admiration to
The colors she has erected as a
Landmark in her soul.

—*Brandee Grumbling*

Jack Frost

Jack Frost jumped into the flower bed,
Painting beads and lace,
And with his tiny little brush,
He touched each flowers face.
He did such a perfect job of it,
So very nice and neat,
That when the sun shone in the morn,
They all had gone to sleep.

—*Jennifer Hollub*

Sunrise

In the sunrise I see life's start,
Pale shades of color, each an art.
Their warming fingers upward span,
Chasing chill to warm the land.
Each ray of light, gently caressing,
Each fleck of color, a simple blessing.
Each spendor of dawn too exalted to miss,
I praise God for night's metamorphosis.

—*Diane Denton*

Isolation

Gray bars to hold your fears locked up
Paper plates and an ugly grimy cup.
What else can you expect from sadness?
It only makes you want more madness.
Can you take all this anger and pain?
Even crazy people think you're insane
You wish you had your happiness back.
Take a comb and makeup in a pink sack.
Tie a yellow ribbon in your hair.
Break out of the cell if you dare.
Try hard to make it on the streeet.
You feel a lump in your throat
And an unsteady heartbeat.
You haven't eaten for many a day
You feel like you're just melting away.
Goodbye. . .there's no pain. . .

—*Heather Scott*

A Clown

He works in many places;
Particularly, those full of tricks and
  mazes.
Always entertaining and gaining
  attraction,
Never by talking but by action.
He is mostly happy and gay,
But when depressed he will never say;
Because he is proud of being known
With an identity that is not shown.
He's fat and funny, like a buffoon.
Dresses in large, tacky clothes, dancing to
  a tune.
Making others cry with laughter,
He has become of doing this a master.
For he is known by everyone
As the neatest clown, in the whole wide
  town.

—*Barbara I. Lopez*

Untitled

. . .a certain feeling exists in the
  passing of time
A nuptial feeling of age
the magic in a child's eyes
And the magic of a love song—
a magic that the wind
listens to. . .
Mystery is the feeling;
Experience is the song;
Music is the magic of the wind.

—*Eleanor Lynn Drake*

Untitled

Life is a masterpiece of new hope and
  inspiration of a bright
Path of fresh flowers and a wonderful cool
  breeze on a summer day.
If I only knew the secret of that recipe,
I would make my summer day in a
  beautiful way.
My eyes are clear, but will not see for
I hope it's my awakening of my future
  near.
Onward into a scope of richness, as I see
  through a
Big bold bright view.
A new sparkle of relfecting glimmer of
  fresh morning dew.
Life is a reflection of inner beauty just if I
  only listen.

—*Barbara J. Smith*

Peace

Peace is a jewel that can't be broken,
Peace is a quality that can't be spoken.
Peace is a trait of love and life
That helps you through terror and strife.
Peace is a cup, that will never run low.
It will never empty, only overflow.
Through war and hate, it will always
  shine
As a sacred temple, an honored shrine.

—*Emily Sartini*

Mother Nature Came Out to Play

One day I finally saw the sun
Peeking from the clouds in the sky.
I heard birds singing a beautiful song,
Ever so sweetly.
Flowers were fully developed and the
  fragrance
Reminded me of sugar and spice.
Apple pie on a window ledge, mother
  gently
Cleaning her sweaty forehead.
The touch of spring in my fingertips
And summer hanging from my toes.
Hearing chuckles and drinking icy
  lemonade
By riverside reminds me of when I was a
  child.
One tear I shed from my wrinkled, old
  face,
I can still remember.

—Elena Oliverio

Appearances

As I stand in the hallway and watch
People as they pass
They seem so small and yet unimportant
from where I'm standing. Yet nobody's
  here.
From where I stand the world seems vast
yet I stand on a stair and look far ahead,
and see the journey that I must tread, yet
the end will come sooner than I planned.
I stand by a mirror and look and see,
The image that everyone thinks is me,
yet the real me has feelings and also
  dreams
and I know things aren't always what they
  seem.

—Kristy Houchens

Pattern

I guess I have a passion for it
People consider it poetry
I see it as my innerself and feeling
Life has a funny twist to it, almost ironic
Considering many live according to plan
Some I see seem dissatisfied
What am I to say I agree
It all falls in a pattern as we slowly
Take our course
When we finish our life on earth
I still wonder where do we go
Is someone down there or up waiting
To set a pattern again and again
Will my changes be visible
What am I, what will become of me
Sometimes seeing with an adult eye
I see no tomorrow
But a pattern of ways to begin to end

—Erica Key

Cozy

Glowing bright and warm
People gather on cold nights
Winter can't get in

—Cara Stein

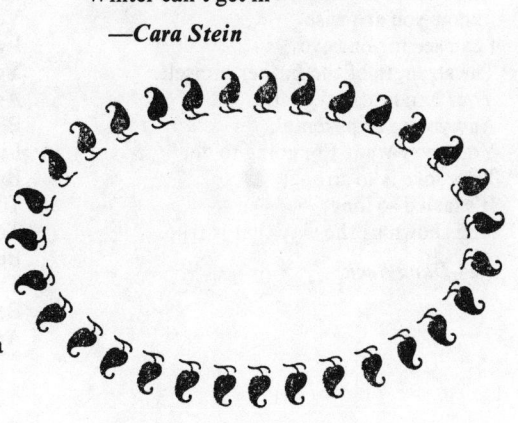

Pigeon Lady

Grey strands of curls hang below a
  battered brim.
People hurry past a sight so grim.
Her scraps are shared with her pigeons,
Her stomach is full, she pretends.
Her camel coat is shaggy and torn.
She cuddles the concrete, an effort to keep
  warm.
She awakes each morning to her reveile
When the church bells chime "Abide
  With Me."

—Anne L. Estes

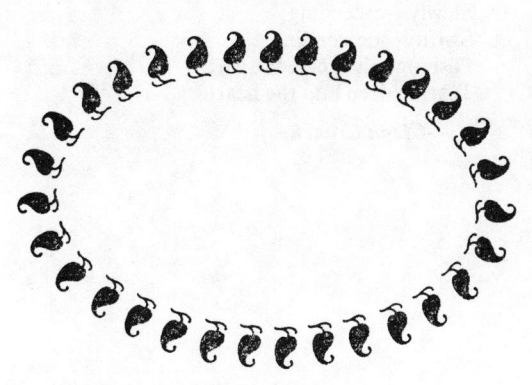

The Discovery

Fresh and new
Perhaps yet not been found
Perhaps I am the first to see
This piece of nature's beauty.
Overgrown shrubs
Tall green grass
That reaches my knees
And covers the bark of fallen trees.
To think I found it!
All on my own.
Enchanting and new,
Through which only birds flew.
My own little hideout.
All to myself.
A place to run and hide in.
A place, maybe, where no one has been.

—Cassie Emans

Images of Christina

Eyes that haunt through
Photographic haze, burn across
Picture plane and gaze
Past all consciousness,
Black on white, entranced,
Enchanted, intrigued by
A view to heaven.
Disillusioned in hell,
Blood runs free, anew,
Like teardrops on
Leather and photo grain
Stained by contempt, beauty
Defined, distorted, reassigned
To parameters undefined.
Enticing essence from afar
Leaves this one childlike before
Developed images of discontent,
Calling into question subconcious
Endeavors upon shadowed hearts
Never to breach space and time.

—Charles Fitzsimmons

Pictures

A chubby little freckled face
Pictures time cannot erase
Swimmin in the county ditch
Fishin with a pin and a willow switch
Catchin frogs and poison ivy
Crickets, bee stings, he steps lively
Laying on the fresh mown meadow
Watching clouds make moving shadows
Dreaming dreams and making plans
What will he be when he's a man
Sis will miss the little brother
For in her heart, there will be no other
Chubby little freckled face
Pictures time cannot erase

—Barbara J. Hall

Night Watch (for my husband)

Deathly quiet
Pierced by hiss of oxygen
Escaping from the tank
Or stretch of fifty feet of hose—
Death tube and pipeline to eternity.
Lungs suck in the precious gas
Sustaining little left of life.
His presence permeates the room,
Making it smell sweet like lilacs
Blooming in our backyard.

—Cornelia Bruck Smith Nedomatsky

Seal Pup

The sad, lonely seal pup
Playing in the snow
Like a fluffy pillow
Who doesn't know where to go
As the seal pup plays in the snow
Slipping and sliding
Always gliding
Shadows fall upon the ice
Poachers do things
That aren't very nice
The last mournful cry
As the seal pup slowly dies

—*Amy Lacky*

Fluffy

I remember you well,
You were loved,
Too much to tell.
I'll never forget
The fun we had
You won't be forgotten,
Come good or bad.
You can't be replaced
I knew that from
The start,
You will always
Hold
A high place in
My heart.

—*Sarah Evans*

Dear God,

I just had to write to you, my mother has cancer
Please help the doctors pull her through.
She's the light of my life she loves me all the time,
Please don't take her away let her stay and be mine.
Everyone loves her you can't take her away,
Oh please God all I want is for you to let her stay!
She's never hurt a thing not even a fly,
Come on God I'm praying please don't let her die.
She's a wonderful woman that's what you need to see,
I'll never ask for another thing just leave her here with me.
The doctors are trying really hard they're doing the best that they can do,
They are doing their share but the rest is up to you.
She's too young to die she hasn't had her share,
She's the most important part of my life don't you know how much I care.
Everyone cares and loves her so much.
Everyone needs her warm and caring touch.
The very last thing I have to say,
Is how much I love her please God don't take her away.

—*Jacinda Nations*

Dear God

Dear God up above,
Please send down your love,
And silence my broken heart.
I know you are wise.
I can see in your eyes,
The strength of the Father himself.
Your hands are so gentle,
And you're so parental,
You know what I'm going to do.
Your love is so strong;
It's lasted so long,
And shown us the way that is true.

—*Dana Beck*

Fate Is Like an Eagle

Shadow form against the fire
Powerful wings climbing higher,
Lifted high by mighty gales
Faster! Faster! it sails.
Spreading over plains below
Touching mountain peaks of snow,
Gliding over dark sea floors
Farther! Farther! it soars.
Slowly—ascending
Swiftly—descending;
Pushing velvet clouds apart
Tearing deep into the heart.

—*Glenn Crouch*

Ornithology

What's ornithology?
Pray can you tell!
It's hard to pronounce and it's hard to spell,
Yet that's what you're learning whenever you care;
To study the birds of the earth, sea, and air.
There's a long word to stand for a bird!
For a lark or a sparrow its length is absurd!
Eagles and ostridges hold no apology
If you should label them as ornithology!
But how can they fit the Tiny Tom Tit?

—*Kerrie-Ann Better*

Flying Free

Come to me
Precious one
For your freedom
You have already won.
I won't tie you down
You can always go
As you please
Because I love you so.
I just want you here
By my side
To give me comfort,
To make me feel alive
But if you can't stay
Thats the way it has to be
Because I love you
And you love "Flying Free".

—*Becky Miller*

The Ocean

I'd like to go to the ocean shore,
Where I sit and wander on its floor,
For the miles and miles that my eyes can see,
My memories of home comes back to me.
With the breeze that blows it's air,
It all seems to tangle my hair,
With a little concern about my hair,
I sit and wander, "How's things back there?"
I miss my home, family and friends,
But sitting with the ocean, my new found friend,
Brings to an end, a lonely friend.

—*Lakshmi Ramnanan*

The Lonely Stranger

Love is the lonely stranger, drifting in the dark waters of isolation.
Promises, thin as a spinster's passion, surrounds its facade of beauty,
Satan's grandest illusion, buffed smooth and beautiful.
Hiding its rotted soul. Speuring maniacal laughter it searches to feed
Its belly on trust and caring. Love takes you down in disillusionment,
Destroying laughter, creating tears.
The rain pattered against the window while he held her in his arms.
He said they would run far away and she would be his forever.
Intertwined in white sheets they vowed their eternal devotion.
The argument was so trivial but grew in hateful words and spiteful cries.
Satan widded his weapon, shrilly laughing knowing he destroyed innocence..
Autumn leaves fly by, brittle as the bones of the dead, her steps slowed
And damned eyes carrying the haunted look of the betrayed, grieving
For her dead heart. Enshrouded by the memory of love's mantle,
She is now the lonely stranger.

—*Dawn Harper*

Beaches

Crashing power against the sand,
Pulling all things in it's wake,
Few shells are left up on dry ground,
And those that are it will soon take.
Seagulls screech and streak the sky,
In the glistening pale moonlight,
Dolphins sing far off the shores,
They are the rulers of the night.
The fog rolls in,
The fog horn sounds,
And the steamer ship it passes by,
The moonlit beaches set the pace,
And the ocean night is nigh.

—Amanda J. Glesmann

Aurora Borealis

Fine fingers reach and one of each
Pulls down the Arctic fire
Coin colors scratched, the lights
    unlatched
Across the tundra mire
Aurora screams, vibrations stream
To grasp the space below
Configurations lay a—strewn
This bleak God blessed snow.
Stark ambers, greens and violets
Damn! Strike me as I raise
Glare grasping eyes cross sutured skies
In clear unbroken haze
Through space and time and all unknowns
That weave and shudder there
Medusa! Take me I am yours
To weave into your hair.

—Kim M. Dunn

The Sea, Eternity and the Cave

The sea erupts into the darkness,
Pulses of eternal foam
Slither off slimy moss,
Clinging to coral encrusted rocks,
Embedded deep in the dwarfish cave.
The sea snakes around the cave,
Filling up cracks and sand-holes,
Flushing out tiny skeletal creatures that
    rush
Frantically out, then hide
In the heated water, the swirling sands.
The sea erupts out of the cave,
Tripping a bell on a distant buoy,
Tied to the tidal path forever,
Rhythm on an invisible thread
Anchored to the mystic moon.

—Brenda Whitehead Smith

My Hidden Love

My love for you is
Pure and good, I think.
For everytime I look at you
My heart just seems to sink.
I love you with a real love
But yet it's like we're friends.
But I can't help but thinking,
Could this be the end?
The end of all I've hoped for
If you should find my love.
So in my heart
My love will stay safely in its place.

—Jynnifer Hargrove

Black Widow

Stop looking so closely at my eyes
Pursuing my thoughts
Reading into my words
I beg you, don't look too closely
You're playing in my web and
I will kill you if you find me.

—Beena Mathai

Old Men

Old men
Put me ill at ease.
Grey eagles
Lonely in clusters
Roosting on benches
Because they cannot fly
Because there is belonging there
Where halting gait
And rounded back
And trembling hand
Pass almost unnoticed
Where collective memory
Becomes one's own
And yesterdays live now
Where pain lives deep
In the lines it carved
And eternity one breath distant.
I pass them quickly
For their eyes speak to me
Of what lies ahead.

—Dr. Edward R. J. Krivda

Trust in Me

Close your eyes
Put your hand in mine
Trust in me
I'll be there
I was there before
I'll be there now
All you have to do
Is trust in me
Step into the magic
Feel your troubles leave
I can make you happy
I can make you free
I'll take you in
And shelter you
I'll keep you safe
From the world outside
All you have to do is
Close your eyes
Put your hand in mine
And trust in me

—Erin Hurt

Teenage Decisions

Puzzles
Questions
No answers
Growing
Older, wiser, either way
Harder puzzles
Deeper questions
No solutions
At least not today.

—Betsy Seamon

Your Little Rose

Slowly wilting is the rose,
Quietly withering away.
Blackening, dulling, losing its glow,
Gone by the end of day.
Slowly dying, the light in your eyes,
Leaving them empty and cold.
Dulled and stony, the feeling is lost,
Except for the love grown old.
Why are we subjected to torment and
    pain?
Why do we let it go on?
Soon, one day, with all the remorse,
Your little rose will be gone.

—Kay Steven

Differences

Why do we fight?
Racial, culture, or religious differences.
Could it be all three?
Are we so inconsiderate
To people who are not us?
People who look different,
Dress different, act different.
Will we ever learn?
Learn to respect, understand,
And appreciate others.
Their language, cultures, and minds.
Could we ever be united?

—Guinelle Williams

Rain Dance

Rain dance on window
Rain dance on street
Rain dance on tree leaves
Rain dance in head.
Rain dance, do limbo
Rain dance, do twist
Rain dance, do fox trot
Rain dance in soul.
Rain dance on rooftop
Rain dance in gutter
Rain dance on stairstep
Rain dance in heart.

—Dana Swier

Moving on

Why did I let him
Rain on my parade?
So he can make fun
Of the mess he's made?
I don't know how
I live like I do,
But I do know that I
Deserve a life too.
It seems like I sit and
Wait for him to come 'round,
But this time I'll prove
That I'm not his clown.
He'll find out that I
Can live my own life,
Without him there to
Stab me with a knife.

—Ashley Moody

Silently We Stand

Silently we stand facing each other,
Rain pouring down on the street.
Your bright blue eyes seem to gaze right
  through me,
As I flinch under your piercing gaze.
The wind flies through your blond hair,
Like a golden flame in the night.
I feel my heart beating faster, as I fight
  back my tears.
I wait for your final words of goodbye,
But your lips stay frozen in place.
You turn your head away, unable to face
  the pain.
I open my mouth to whisper "why,"
But the words seem to disappear into the
  night.
I turn around in seeming despair, slipping
  your ring off my finger,
I hand it to you and you face me straight.
I search your eyes for an answer
But your face spares me no mercy,
As we stand silently facing each other.

—Beth Bajor

The Loss of a Mate

The joy and sorrow of living together for
  many years, as one,
Rainbows and thunderclouds and years of
  having fun.
But, along comes death and it all comes to
  a sudden and final end.
Now part of you remains so dull, for no
  loving glances are sent,
No sighs of great contentment. You
  wonder what is wrong?
The door to his life is closed. That's what
  it really means.
Bright tears can somehow never replace
  the freshness of the light
Spring rain, now that both of you will
  never again share
The glorious or the plain.
But always remember that somewhere in
  eternity,
Your souls and hearts will gather light,
A light so wondrous and steady. No more
  the darkness falls,
For now his love engulfs you in a warm
  peace this night,
Because you know that only God can
  make that final call.

—Gloria Swails

Untitled

Flowers in the meadow,
Rainbows in the sky.
But down deep inside,
Why do we lie?
Stars out at night,
Moon over there.
Is it because
We're just scared?

—Brandi Fleniken

Lifestorm

One despondent
raindrop
slides slantedly
across a
windowpane,
falling
in spirals,
meandering
across the
glass,
surrendering
shards of
itself to
leave behind
its legacy
for the next
drop to follow.

—Karen Martin

The Sun Will Shine Again

A cheerful smile may disguise your worry,
Rainy days may hide your tears,
But inside you can't forget the sorrow,
Which harbors all your fears.
Just remember days of sunshine,
See through the passing rain,
On the other side of tomorrow,
The sun will shine again.

—Alicia Campbell

The Gift

Beautiful is the sky above
Reach for the stars
And discover the Love
Each has the strength
To make or to break
The Love that you took
The Love that you take
Give is the word
That comes from within
You give and you give
Whatever it takes
You will be known
For the Love that
You Gave. . .

—Ismael R. Perez Jr.

Celebration

The morning dew
Reaches its extended arms
Out across the majestic world,
Awakening the animals
Who sleep in its immense home,
Slowly moving the world to a new day.
Night creeps out from the new day.
Darkness surrounds us while awaiting
　　morning dew,
Putting our land deeply to sleep.
The moonlit universe becomes a goddess
　　with her extended arms,
Spreading solemn peacefulness to both
　　humans and animals.
Out across our majestic world awaiting a
　　new day.

—Frenchie Bunch

Open Up The World

Open up the world,
Read a book to a child.
Sit on a front porch swing,
During a summer, warm and mild.
Catch the sight of a fawn,
As it scampers through the trees.
Taste the salt on your lips,
Kissed by the calm of an ocean breeze.
Lift your eyes to the heavens,
Open your heart and let it sing,
Feel the glory of the universe,
Cherish the wonders life can bring.

—Kitten-Kathie Higginbotham

Even When You've Lost

As I skim the books of poetry,
Reading it verse by verse,
I glance at my own work,
And decide I must rehearse.
So, I pick the project poem.
And shout it out aloud.
Reading the lines with pleasure,
It's easy to say "I'm proud".
I enter it in a contest,
But get no back reply.
And though I didn't win,
It's nice to say "I tried".
So even if you lose;
Deep inside, you've won.
There's lots of other people
Who can never say "I'm done".
"Be proud of all you have accomplished."

—Beth A. Gaydos

Masquerade

She came to the group
Ready for the daily ritual,
But could not understand their language.
Its members now wore masks
And had closed off her gap in the circle.
And suddenly she was alone.
No translator, no mask,
Too weak to make room.
An outsider,
Left wishing for the perception to see her
"Friends"
Through the disguise.

—Catherine Fliss

Have I Done my Job?

I walked up the stairs to the top of the
　　building.
Ready to jump, I found myself soaring
　　into a wonderful world full of bright
　　clouds,
Fluffy, white with the sun shining down
　　on it, making it look like angels' wings.
Just then I started swirling around in
　　every direction, fire flying up at me,
Hitting me like whips, black clouds
　　looking like smoke.
Then I was back up on the building.
I sat down and thought, have I done my
　　job?

—Heather Martin

Rose

My love is like a rose.
Red with passion,
Thorns with protection.
As its beauty is admired
There becomes a desire
To be held in your arms.
As it is stretching towards the sun
My love is searching for yours.
When our love is joined together
The rose bursts with color.
As if its signifying our beginning.
When you leave me alone
I shead my tears,
As if to die inside.
The rose of beauty and passion
Turns brown and wilting
And slowly crumbles away.

—Christiana A. Yager

Reflections

Through the trees I heard a lonesome cry,
Reflecting the call of the wild,
Though I heard this not so long ago,
I was then but just a child.
I stumbled on with my sleep like eyes,
'Til my body seemed to weigh me down,
'Til I fell on my knees as though in
　　prayer,
On the cold but Sacred Ground.
With my mind still stunned and in a blur,
I felt the earth reach up,
And kiss me as Jesus must have kissed the
　　Holy Cup.
Here time was endless like the seas and
　　days
They ne'er met night, for in "This Place"
　　no
Darkness dwelt—only "The Eternal
　　Light".
I know in "This Place" I had learned
　　more than
Any man can say, for God reached out
　　and
Touched me on that very "Sacred Day."

—Eudora Tree Kennison

Stellar Night

To look up in a starry sky, to find
reflections, of some time past on;
A glance of lovelorn image passes by,
To give rise, that love was still in bloom.
Romantic thoughts awaken tacit dreams,
On wings of love, and splendor it to be;
To drift with us into the mist of night,
Aroused with passions, to be found
　　delight.
It seemed like all the stars up in the sky,
Held watch for all the cupid's well in
　　trust,
And put a lull upon the calming night;
It seemed like ecstasy, but end it must.
As starlight in the sky began to fall,
The moon was slowly waning out of sight,
And shadows of the night became a wall;
Its love, never to be a forgotten night!

—Eva Croci

Remember

Remember when he was full of love,
Remember how he pushed and shoved.
Remember when he was so kind,
Remember now he isn't mine.
Remember when you first kissed,
Remember now he is missed.
Remember when he kept you warm,
Remember now your heart is torn.
Remember when he said I'll leave you
　　never,
Remember now he's gone forever.

—Christina May

Never Be

Try not to remember all the hurt and pain,
Remember they told you, you were living in the fast lane.
When he was here you could not feel pain.
Now that he's gone that's all that remains.
When He was around he'd whisper to you,
"You make every one of my dreams come true."
His only mistake was telling you this,
"I'll love you forever!" Then gave you that kiss.
Now that you think of him, you come to see.
The love wasn't there, it could never be.

—*Katrina Bieber*

Jenaveve

Ecstatic energy; bursting throughout.
Within there are new revelations showering through towards me.
All about me amidst my fragmented life I am secluded to thoughts of my own.
To entrap myself about expectations in which to conclude I must suffer the unreal.
But to me reality is insanity incarsinated in darkness, without light radiating toward shelter,
Nor a hand to show me the actions needed to proceed.
Falling once again into an utter unknown.
Entrancing one into falling to break the numerous boundaries, to which one is positive of their presence.
Factually knowing one has the key to the everything yet frightened to unlock it.
Fearing consequences too endless to question a conclusion worth merit.
That emptiness in which we must shelter ourselves with threatens to suffocate us inside a world of false hopes.

—*Melissa Hicks*

Just One Friend

While walking down life's lonely road,
Remembering all the troubles I've towed,
I cast aside my wandering eyes,
And now I finally realize,
I'm not as lonely as I thought.
I need not all the friends I sought.
I have a friend that's always there,
With open arms and love to share.
A person on whom I can depend,
The only one I can call my friend.
And although my life is almost o'er,
I always had something to live for.
One true friend is all I ever had,
But she's stuck with me in good times and bad.

—*Ellen Gorman*

Time

Sitting at this table, with your picture in my hand,
Remembering when you were little how we played in the sand
Your little fingers clutching mine as I taught you to walk,
The sweetest sound I ever heard was when you learned to talk,
Your childish smile, your laughing face,
From my mind I can't erase
You've given more than you will ever know
Through scrapes and tears and sleepless nights
To dating, proms and awesome fights,
I never, ever wanted you to go
You were oh so little and didn't have a say,
I turned around and you were grown, then you went away
I wish I may and I wish I might
Have you small again for just one night
To ease the pain in this lonely heart of mine
I cannot beg and cannot plead
Just to stop this hurting need
For we all know there is no stopping. . .time.

—*Dorothy Masilotti*

Untitled

The rain silently falls
Requesting a night of disturbed silence.
The sky argues for a short time
Thinking of a way to get back at the world.
It decides to take a break from the matter at hand.
The rain soon stops and lets the sky and sun take over.
Nature relaxes for a brief moment
While the moon wants to invade.
It wishes for night—when it is time to shine.
The moon finally gets its turn to look at the world in his control.

—*Connie Martinson*

Prefab

invisibles
residues
staining
ferment
cold winter
darkness blooms
sprouting marigolds
sunlit shores
east Duluth
icy cold spray
Lake Superior

—*Kelly R. Sullivan*

Window of the Past

Look through the window of the past
Review the scenes from yesterday
When life moved at a slower pace,
The human race lived in one place,
Not racing helter—skelter here and there.
When ladies wore their hair piled high
Bustled skirts nigh to the floor
When gentlemen wore correct attire,
Declared with fire their hearts' desire
To court their lady fair.
Close the window to the past;
Too fast, too fast our present pace;
The human race cannot retreat
On heedless feet we race to meet;
A fate of our own fashioning.

—*Delphine LeDoux*

Motorcycle Man

Motorcycle man,
Riding away from life,
Hair in your face,
Feeling too fast.
Motorcycle man,
Under a streetlight,
With nighttime brightness,
Your life ran out of gas.

—*Desiree M. Hupy*

Come On

I love you!
Right.
Go out with me!
Leave
Come on!
Bye.
Do you love me?
Why?
Come on!
What?
Tell me, come on!
See you.
Just let me know!
Yes.

—*Jenn Zimmer*

Untitled

Click-clank, click-clank
Roller skate wheels whirr noisily as faces
　of friends flash by.
If you look closely, you can see the nature
　of their futures.
A model. . .a money man. . .a nurse and
　one who seems is good for nothing!
Hmm. . .something to think about.
Look again, twenty years later. . .
The model has skin cancer. . .
The money man was caught for
　embezzlement. . .
Yet, the good-for-nothing is the most
　successful of all!
It makes me wonder, do we change our
　own lives?
Or does time change them for us?
I look to a clock, and watch the minutes
　tick by.
Watching time pass. . .
Yet, instead of familiar tick-tock,
　tick-tock, I hear click-clank,
　click-clank,
And the face of the clock spins with the
　whirr of wheels.

—*Erica Salkin*

Love

Love is a word rarely spoken with intent.
Rolling off the tongue, free and easy,
Throwing out meanings,
The tongue never knew it meant.
Holding some close together,
Tearing others far apart.
Giving and taking the lives of man.
Spreading joy and breaking hearts.
So when you say love,
be sure that's what it is.
For lives are lost and saved
on such a word as this.

—*David McGinnis Jr.*

Untitled

Beaches
Romantic, peaceful,
Surfing, tanning, resting,
Seagulls swaying for food
Laughing, strolling, running,
Colorful, lazy
Oceans

—*Elizabeth A. Koun*

Untitled

roses in the ice
roses in the snow
frozen love and
frozen dreams
dusty old and long ago
tears of ice, cold and bright
tears of sadness and despair
frigid feelings and
frigid souls
distant cold, like the snow
a rose in winter will give you love
a frozen tear despair
look at the rose as if through glass
black and cold
like your tear.

—*Kelly Bingman*

Defeat

Jagged,
Rough,
And piercing,
My fall shall greet me,
The bellowing screams for help shall not
　help me,
For only ones with gruesome eyes shall
　watch my loathing defeat,
For it would only interest one with no
　feelings to greet.

—*Anastasia Boulton*

America

Innocent until proven guilty?
Rumors get started
Then you aren't innocent until proven
　guilty
You are automatically guilty
And you have to suffer through the
　consequences
The dirty looks
Losing your job
Losing your friends
Losing people's trust
America
Innocent until proven guilty?
That's obvious!

—*Christine Robb*

My Imaginary Horse

Rump, rump, romp
Rump, rump, romp
Klickety, klickety, klop
Klickety, klickety, klop
here we go again
Riding on my horse
Klickety, klickety, clop
Rump, rump, romp
Off into the sunset
Klickety, klickety, clop
Rump, rump, romp
Rump, rump, romp

—*December Brown*

Running

Hiding out wherever you can
Running from place to place.
No place to call home.
You want to stop and talk to someone,
But you know they would take you back,
Back to a place you know you don't
　belong.
If only you could stop running
And find a place to call home.
You know you shouldn't go on
But you know if you stopped
You wouldn't last much longer
So you go on and on.
Until the nighttime comes,
Find a good place to sleep and say,
Maybe tomorrow I'll go home.

—*Kristen Violette*

Lost Time

Time
Runs
From eyes
Sleep
Dissolves
Our senses
Minds
Create
Lost lands
Desirs
Melt
Into pictures
Voices
Encased
In sand
Whispers
Escaping
From man

—*Jennifer Kitzan*

The Painter's Brush

Wisps of teal and cool dark sky,
Rushed in vibrant blurring cries.
Streaks of scarlet, dazzling flame,
Lost from the beginning; not one tint the same.
Crushed, crisp, calling to gazers.
Slicing deep within soul,
Like God forged razors.
What secrets a masterpiece must quietly keep.
Oh, silent forever, a still life weep.
One alone knows the canvas's pain.
The painter's brush and it's color streaked mane.

—Kasie Peters

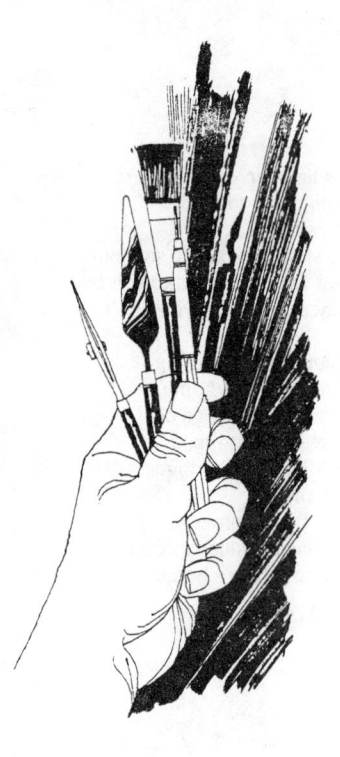

Language of the Trees

The wind whistles through the aspens
Rustling the leaves.
It purrs around the branches
And mourns into the eaves.
A woodland fox that's creeping by
Stops and perks an ear.
But the expression on his cunning face
Shows and feels no fear.
For he knows the gentle murmurings
That waft down from up above
Come only from the wind and trees
Things he knows and loves.
And so, my child, don't worry
Just listen and love I plead.
Because those gentle murmurings are
The language of the trees.

—Jesse Fletcher

Gifts from the Universe

Crimson-pink skies that deepen into to a gemstone blue;
Rustling trees grass and flowers of multi-shades and hues. . .
A warm orange sun that ornamently dots the sky,
This sunsational vision produces mellow natural highs.
Cotton candy-like clouds drift away only to reappear,
To clap thunder melodically short tunes for the ear.
The geese feeling a need are soaring fast in flight
In a "V" shape that's directing one and others toward the site
Of a beautiful waterfall sounding crashes of great roars;
Pouring cold crystal clear fluid from the mountains' generous core.
Rainbows angled arching gracefully above the kingdom of vast space
Slowly fade into the sunset but the memory of it is unerased.
Crickets play a concerto beneath a few shimmering stars;
Cool, soothing darkness blankets them now the night becomes the czar.
Intoxicating ,more so, is a gift that's called love.
Its very nature's intricate with delicate facets interwove.

—Bridgitt F. Boggan

Crying, Crying,

I'm always trying, trying to learn why I am not loved
Sad, Sad,
I'm always mad, mad at the world which treats me bad
Looking, Looking,
I'm always cooking, cleaning, and doing chores
Hear me, Hear me,
Please be near me, do not ever leave me alone
I'm scared, I'm scared,
But no one cares, cares if I am dead or gone
Dying, dying,
I'm slowly crying, crying for help that is not there
Come, Come,
I am so dumb, for thinking that some one might love me
Brighter, brighter,
My head feels lighter, for once I am not scared
For once I know that some one cares
It's not her or him or he or she,
The only one that cares it truly me.

—Henria S. Bailey

A Day in Galillee

Warm sand squishing through your toes.
salty water splashing up onto your face and into your mouth,
as you bodysurf onto the shore.
Little children, covered with sand,
are sitting in a little group,
fighting over sand toys
and trying to build a sand castle.
Tan bodies basking in the sun
covered with every type of oil
from SPF 2 to 21.
They turn with the sun like clocks
to get the best results.
Just down the road, a five minute walk,
George's, a famous seafood restaurant
and little tourist shops
with signs reading
"The T factory, Galillee Grocery"
and " Candy Cottage".
In the evening sunset,
when the beaches are quiet and deserted,
couples walk down the beach
hand in hand,
while gazing at the beautiful sky.

—Hilary Coleman

Little Ray

Little ray,
When you are near
Things are warm
And calm.
But,
For the sake of style
I sit here beneath
This tree, shutting you out!
Show me the logic
Of staying in the shade
Cold and sheltered
When my friend, you
Offer the warmth of
Your soul and the
Comfort of your heart.

—Rebecca Young

Holy Blood

Holy Blood, Holy Blood,
Salvation wasn't free
The price he paid was
Holy Blood, Holy Blood
Shed for you and me
Holy Blood, Holy Blood
Stained the ground
For men that were bound
Holy Blood, Holy Blood
Fell on calvary's mound
While evil men danced around
Holy Blood, Holy Blood
Washed my sin away
God had the final say
Holy Blood, Holy Blood,
Paid the price
We couldn't pay
Holy Blood, Holy Blood

—Gary Farmer

World Crisis as Show Biz

A croacking caucus of crows
Sat on a fence in rows,
Debating dismal dates and data
On farmers, scarecrows and scarcity of
    fodder.
Faulting, fuming, fussing in combination;
Yet no decision on genetic manipulation.
In bawling bedlam; each insistent
    claimiant,
Each beseecher a cacophonous petitioning
    creature.
Within this brotherly merger, a rumor
    filled fold,
A share depends on bold.
And outrageous, seditious exhibitionists
    feed,
While scattering masses in murderous
    numbers;
Yet always assured of seed
For artistry of the tumblers.
What heresy!

—*H. Cajo Dulin*

Morning Thoughts

It's a cool, frosty morning,
With grayish mist and fog.
The air is crisp,
With the feeling of winter coming.
A mother and her fawn,
Coated with thick, speckled fur,
And bright, black eyes,
Stand tense and alert.
They seem to be listening,
For any sounds they know all too well.
And, for no reason at all,
They are smiling.
Maybe they're thinking,
Of their future together...
Leaping fences with delicate legs,
And just being together united with love.

—*Melissa Starling*

Nightmares

Monsters wander through your head,
Screaming, shouting in your bed.
Toss, turn, flip, flop,
In your mind, the ghoulies hop.
Ghosts, goblins, witches, bats,
Black, scary, fire-eyed cats.
Vampires bite blond haired girls,
Around your feet the fog swirls,
Lightnings flicker, thunders booms
Werewolves howl in the gloom.
Castle doors move with creaks and
    groans,
Cemetaries filled with shrieks and moans.
Frightful laughter of the dead,
Echo off a pumpkin head.
Now you're in mother's warm arm,
Knowing that you're safe from harm.

—*Charly Lawson*

Hold On

Expand your dreams, drop your guard,
Search your soul, left deeply scarred.
Fan the ashes, watch the flame,
Past is present, the future will claim.
The mind will float, the heart beats fast,
As dreams are strong, to future from past.
Wishing and hoping, for thoughts buried
    deep,
Hold on to this, in silence you keep.
This world is yours, no one can enter,
Enjoy yourself, be at its center.
Slip from reality, let the body rest,
Close your eyes, experience the best.
The path you walk, no rain will fall,
Tears and pain, lost by this call.
In times of need, just open this door,
A place to go, let feelings soar.
As days go by and life goes wrong,
Hope for a change, can make you strong.

—*Gayle Grainger*

One of Those Days

I look to the heavens and skies up above.
Searching for peace, patience and love.
But why look so far when friends are so
    near.
Sharing the happiness and also the tears.
Still I feel I am all alone, learning of life,
    learning to grow.
Yet this day is over, a new day will start.
Things that have passed will stay in my
    heart.

—*Cirila Ortega*

Passing Moments

I was our neighborhood's biggest terror
Sear's mix or match'em Garanimals
Peanutbutter with jelly or fluff
Mudpies, scrapes and daises in the warm
    weather
I am school and work
The dress is casual clothes
Weekends of pizza or Chinese food
Long walks filled with nonstop
Talks a single pink carnation
I will be counselor dash teacher
Dresses-skirts-shirts
Lobster after nautilis
Moonlit nights and roses

—*Danielle St. Pierre*

Without You

I sit, staring at the walls
See nothing.
Suddenly, I'm overcome with laughter...
A laughter of sadness
Cause I realize our good and bad times
    together,
Have finally come to an end.
Slowly,
The tears silently fall
Slowly.
Tears of happiness
Cause I see that my life is:
More calm, more pleasant
And most of all
More peaceful
Without you.

—*Amy Sims*

Untitled

See the young wife on welfare, with six
    babies to hold?
See the man, another night in the cold?
Can you see them?
See the old, afraid of the young?
See the father beat the son?
Can you see them?
See the young soon to be mother, as of yet
    unwed?
See the abandon children left for dead?
Can you see them?
See the farmer who just lost his land?
See the young man, who dies by his own
    hand?
Can you see them?
Why can't you see them?
We must all soon help or it will be too late
The tired, cold, hungry and poor await
Will you see them?

—*Jan Rogers*

One Love to Share

I look into your deep blue eyes
See things I can never forget.
Emotions of happiness
Some of regret.
The love we share together,
So special, so real.
The exclusiveness of it,
Has its own appeal.
Moments pass by so quickly,
I hardly know they're there.
Which makes each moment
So precious, but yet unfair.
I couldn't begin to tell you,
How much you really mean.
Words just can't explain it,
The feelings can't be seen.
The times we share together,
Unite us both as one.
As if the love between us,
Had only just begun.

—*April Lombardo*

View of the Top

Fascination with the fruit at the top
Seems queer, indeed, to me
It gets most of the sun and all of the fun
And takes what it wants from the tree
The fruits of the vine, emerge so divine
Beautiful, as perfect as can be
But on closer insepection, there is no perfection
The blemishes are just harder to see
Through the passing of time, the fruit will ripe
To wear elusiveness as a crown
The summit now home, the top all its own
Every place to go, from here, is down
The most desirable is that to harvest
When the creation is finally ended
Select in the prime, preserved for a time
Consumed for the use which was intended
The cream of the crop, remaining at top
Untouched by friend or foe at the crest
Though the fruit has it all, it will eventually fall
To the ground and rot like all the rest

—*Johnnie Baker*

Visions

As I sit here in the darkness,
With nothing left to do;
My mind begins to wander,
And I start to think of you.
I think of all the fun we have
When we are together.
I hope this feeling never ends,
And it will last forever.
Your love means so much to me,
You are understanding and true;
In times when darkness surrounds my heart,
My love for you shines through!

—*Robbyn Dianne Trent*

Best Friend

Every now and then, your heart is broken
Seems your world is to an end
You feel like you've been deserted
You need to touch the hand of a friend
You start thinking unpleasant thoughts
That you don't seem to understand
You speak but nobody listens
You need to talk with a friend
Work all day come home tired
And still do the best that you can
But your work is still not over
You need to sit and be with a friend
Gone to bed what a relief you say
As you lie close next to your man
You're feeling warm and he is too
You need to be loved by a friend
Awake in the morning, start a new day
Knowing by you, he'll stand
Leaving the house you realized
Here at home you have your best friend!

—*Ida D. Wheaton*

The Eyes Of A New Born

What is the world like
Seen through the eyes of a new born child?
Torn away from the only world it knew
A world of warmth and security
Snug in mother's womb.
Thrown into a world larger than
It's small eyes can comprehend
Full of so much mystery
Love that's there, but hard to find
How will it know to survive?
When it must turn away from mother's shelter
And her screened knowledge
Her half truths, and one sided views on life
Pushed onto the child what's wrong or right.
With her hopes, of raising the child to be
Something she wanted to be, but wasn't
How do we all?

—*Eric Stockinger*

Untitled

You are not of earth
You are not pinioned by society's ways
Instead, you move among creatures of light
Not quite real; not quite imagined
I can see you, but I cannot touch you
I feel the rhythm of your heart
My feet dance to its ethereal song
You beckon to me,
Inviting me to fly to heights unknown
I hesitate at the thought of leaving my earth-bound past
But join you in a fantasy world
Time and space melt away for us
We are suspended in a universe where dreams are truth
And anything is reality
You take my hand as we soar,
Trapped in a dream, yet I'm finally free
. . .then I wake up.

—*Laura Ryan*

High School

That first new day is on its way
Sending me shivers and fears
Knowing that the scary day
Will soon be coming near
My heart will be pounding
My ears will throb
I'll make a whimper sound
Then I'll start to sob
The day appears
I will get set
I'll have some fear
But I'll forget
It happens to everyone
I'll try to act cool
Think about having fun
When I enter High School

—*Kristi Blair*

Augustus

Even though your academic excellence
Set examples for us when young,
You showed your uncompromising faith in God
Would never go unsung.
You stressed geniality in the game of life
And proved that as neighbors,
We are universal citizens of the world
And good samaritans should be.
You taught never to tolerate intolerance,
To respect the dignity of all,
For we need unadulterated love and support during this,
Our earthly fall.
Above all, Dad, you gave us strength to survive,
To not look for a life of ease
But to be grateful for the challenge of adversities,
And to strive for a mind filled with peace.

—*Jessyca Pearson Yucas*

Bantiqua

Here, the sun
sets on its own—
unpolluted.
The sky holds
the stars
as they should be held,
with a clear conscience.
Here, violence is foreign.
A strange,
Forbidden animal.
Young girls don
orange hair
ribbons,
and everybody is
barefoot
all the time.

—*Amy S. Neal*

Seven Years of. . .

What is seven years?
Seven years of tears.
Seven years of loneliness.
Seven years of fears.
Seven years of growing up.
Seven years of changing.
Seven years of bad luck.
Seven years of rage.
Seven years of bravery.
Seven years of lies.
Seven years of being alone.
You're in for a big surprise.
The seven years that I am talking about
Is all of the above,
Because in all of those seven years what I talk about
Is with you that I'm in love.

—*Dena Barton*

Can't You

If you can catch me I'm yours.
Shall I let you?
You missed again.
If I went slower could you catch me?
Do you want me to slow down?
Such a beautiful day, it's all ours.
Did you know that?
What, you can't see it?
If you opened your eyes all the way you
  wouldn't
Have that terrible tunnel vision.
Come up here, you missed again.
Okay, I'll stop, take my hand.
Look, can't you see the loveliness of pure
  color.
Can't you feel the enchantment.
Life is to be lived and you're a living
  creature.
I distinctly remember feeling a pulse beat
  once...

—*Barbara J. Morazzani*

An Offer of Love

I offer you my love again
With every new day and hope
With all my heart you will not turn away
I may not have as much to give as other's
  holding hands.
But I shall always sympathize and
  understand
I shall be there to comfort you when
  shadows cross your path.
And I shall never show a sign of jealousy
  or wrath.
I shall be glad to wait on you and serve
  your every need.
So please accept my offer now and make
  my dreams come true.
By giving me the happiness of being the
  only one with you.

—*Tina L. Cooks*

Backyard Paradise

By the silence of dawn
Shall the moon set.
Glistening wheat fields on the otherside of
  the hill,
That reminds me of the night I left to go
  to the
So recognized beaches of an unknown
  paradise
And the best part was when I returned
  from
My glorious adventure, to come sit in this
  very same spot
The spot that seems to be an exact replica
  of the night I came home,
With the fragrance of freshly harvested
  wheat,
And newly blossomed flowers that still
  linger in my imagination
from this day forth.

—*Jamie Lynette Hazelton*

Past Departure

A wrinkled face gazed past the night
Shapes like tatoos took form
A cry in vain, a hungry smile
The murmuring of a whispery light
All that has been is now past
The delicate pictures lost in a feature
Bringing back hostile confusion
Bewildered and undesired hopelessness
  thou hast
A dream alive, a dream dead
It's mind a dream within a dream living
  reality
Curiosity, stupidity, unmorality, social
  unrest
Giving a false impression to thy
  unconcious head
This darkening veil into now what is my
  life
Furious concentrations, questioning of
  answers
This morbid scene in my death
Playing my crossroads cleanly as with a
  knife
My shame and humility of my past
  departure
It shall all be a memory of my lost past
  dream

—*Kira Avery*

Sharla

My friend is Sharla
Sharla is a kind of happiness to me
Sharla helps me to see
That everyone needs a friend
I can't thank her enough for all she's done
Sharla makes me happy
When I'm sad or mad
Sharla makes me laugh
When I'm down
She makes me smile when I frown
You see, Sharla is good to me
She lets me yell at her
Whenever I need to
I hope when she is down
I can do all this that she's done for me

—*Brandine Sorenson*

Broken

The window is a symbol of a broken heart
Shattered and smashed like deep feelings
Torn into slivers of sharp pieces
Ready to hurt you even more.
The window like your heart
Can only take so much before
It is broken for good.
You can replace the glass
To the window, but you can never
Replace the feelings of a broken heart.

—*Courtney Frankel*

Shattered Glass

Around me lies the result of a crash
Shattered glass
You take uppers, he takes downers,
Man, you're really smashed
Can't you hear the sounds of
Shattered glass
He's been drinking, she's been cheating
All around you
Shattered glass.
Children beaten, others sleeping
Behind the doorways and on the street
All around me
Shattered glass.
Hear them crying, hear them pleading
Voices now and from the past
Lives, that turned into
Shattered glass.

—*Jeannette Johnson Carney*

It's True

It's true?
She could do anything a man could
Open her own doors, pay for what she
  ordered
When the meal was over, leave a tip.
Drive her own car
Pump her own gas.
Cover her cover charge,
Buy her own drinks straight from the bar.
It's true?
She could do everything a man could do.
It's true?
She could do even more than a man,
If she wanted to...
Be a woman!

—*David M. Max, Jr.*

Death of Reality

She lay there with no feeling of anyone.
She did not see the mourning around her.
Her once red blood wrists were now
Eased of their pain.
The needle marks of her arms
Were now gone without a trace.
The drugs that she consumed once
Had overpowered her.
They drew her to her death.
She was gone.
There was nothing left for her to give.
She lay there with no feeling of anyone,
And she never will!

—*Joy Pochatila*

Untitled

I once knew a girl whose a girl whose
    name was Jan,
She didn't have many friends, but she had
    lots of plans,
She sat alone in the corner, head in her
    books,
The laid that walked by gave her pitying
    looks.
You see Jan was a tall and a awkward
    girl.
Glasses on her face, hair up in curls
Guys never gave her the time of day
Theres that scrawing Jan they would day
Then one day when Jan was shopping
A man approached he was actually
    stopping
He landed her his business card
And told her that he'd make her a star
Now she's in New York its and two years
    later
A star she is a fashion model he made her
You can find Jan on numerous magazine
    covers
She was always a beauty just waiting to
    be
discovered.

—*Joanne E. Hoffmann*

You

You're turning
with your back toward the sun.
You're searching
But there's nowhere left to run.
You're crying
But the tears just slip away.
You're trying
To find the right words to say.
You're asking
But the questions don't seem real.
You're taking
All the heartache that you feel.
You're faking
All the joy you seem to know.
You're giving
The world an unwelcome show.
I'm asking
Do you see what you have done?
You're standing
With you're back toward the sun.

—*Lori Trussell*

Crazy for Me

I've got a girl that's crazy for me.
She does everything I tell her to do.
Her voice is sweet, and turns me on.
And when she touches me, she flips me
    out.
She stares at me with her baby blue eyes.
She gives me kisses with her ruby red lips.
I'd be a fool to let her go,
And if she left me I would just die.
I love the way she acts towards me.
And I think I'm gonna make her mine.

—*Jesse Centeuo*

Swimming Back to the Shore

Standing at the edge of the world
She is a reflection of the sky
Emotional waves pounding like my heart
I have only one question, "Who am I?"
Pretty little girl with such a future
The salt water brings a tear to my eye
Oh how easy I thought it would be
But now time has taken its toll; I've come
    to die.
Progressive plans, ambition and high
    hopes
"Look at me!" I shout
Reality and imagination have focused
I am drowning in self—doubt
Staring into the depths I search my soul
Riding over the swells, my life has not
    been wasted
Determined, I tread through the water
For me, the good life has yet to be
    tasted. . .

—*Ellen Bator*

Gentle One

We must think of the gentle one
She is in trouble
She is not danger
She is a curious soul
Warm water and green leaves are all she
    demands
Her cry for help is silent,
But her pain is immense
We must save her, for she is beautiful. . .
. . .She is the Manatee

—*Kathryn Sondrini*

Divorce

My friend for life,
She is my wife,
At least it's supposed to be,
We had a dream,
Peaches and cream,
It was our cup of tea,
But fight we did,
And then upped the bid,
We took each other to court,
It made us scarred,
Our lives were marred,
By the stupidity of how we fought.
It's over now,
Each refused to bow,
It ended togetherness and fun,
So life goes on,
But we give a darn,
For what was lost now won.

—*Barry Elisofon*

Lips

Glistening with moisture,
She licks them passionately,
Crimson red,
Awaiting the kiss.
I wonder not,
What is going to take place,
With this magnetism,
Of her elegant face.
Presses her lips to mine,
A sensual fire,
Her tongue darts in and out,
Ignited by lust and desire.
This woman is what I want,
Possesses my soul,
Broken heart,
And body as a whole,
For I have earned,
The love in her heart I yearned.

—*Chris Rattenborg*

The Cat who Sat on a Hat. . .

I once knew a cat who was a little brat,
She sat on a hat and she sat real fat.
She was so pretty but it's a pity
That she sat so fat on the pretty little hat.
She once met a boy who was very full of
    joy.
He loved her and petted her
And called her his pretty little cat.
And that was the happiest little cat,
Who sat on that hat.

—*Amber Gemmell*

Listen

She lets out a cry.
She says she wants to die.
Her parents don't hear a sound.
Why aren't they more profound?
When her final day had come,
Her parents say "What could we have
    done?"
They could have listened for that silent
    cry
And maybe their daughter wouldn't have
    died.
And now they can't be so deaf,
They only have one child left.

—*Eloise Kyler*

Untitled

When she laughed. . .
she stole my heart
When she smiled. . .
I'd watch her dream
When she ran. . .
she glided
When she held a daisy. . .
she smiled, she laughed, and she ran

—*Heather Vickery*

To My Sister

Anglia is so caring and kind.
She understands all that I have on my mind.
I long to sit and talk with her,
To laugh and cry with her.
I seek her advice and wisdom,
For she seems so knowing.
Anglia, my sister, and I are always growing.
We are like one, but separate,
Sometimes I feel quite desperate,
For my sister, Anglia.

—*Ellouise Hensley*

Granny

My granny was sweet
she was also neat,
My granny was my friend,
and never let me down
she was also a painter
always painting clowns.
When I was a dancer
she had cancer,
She died in eighty-seven
when I was almost eleven.

—*Amy Ragan*

Great Grandmother

She was a great grandmother everyone loved.
She was always there when all I needed was a little hug.
She always wanted to cook for us and always made enough.
Those days were happy days until she passed away.
I'll never forget all the little things she did.
And all the memories.
And wherever I may be, I know she'll always love me.
All I have to say is wherever she may be,
Mimmie, I love you.

—*Jaime Fraley*

Apathetic Eyes

Look, she's standing at her door
She won't come out.
She won't say a word,
She's an incredible bore.
Look at them in a circle
At their morning base
Fussing with their children
With every hair in place.
Now out comes her little girl
They don't make a fuss
She stands alone waiting for the bus.
Now they retreat to their icy domes
Where vaugue words flow through their phones.
A year ago a child had died
She must go where he lies
Apathetic eyes
Peer through their glass
As she slowly drives by.

—*Diane Perez*

A Dream of Innocence

Dream a dream of laughter
Shed a tear of joy
Love here and foreafter
A heart, not a toy
Dream a dream so real
Sunrise let it shine
The warmest touch to feel
A dream so sublime
Dream a dream of comfort
Coming from within
Dream a dream of a touch
A touch that's without sin
Hold close into the heart
A dreanm that we've all shared
The very dream of innocence
A dream we have not spared.

—*Brietta King*

Best Friend

I am so lucky to have a great friend,
She's always there to give me a lend.
She's very kind and never rude,
She's always happy and in a good mood.
I call her up when I'm feeling sad,
She's easy to talk to and never gets mad.
We are such a perfect pair,
Everything's alike except for our hair.
We have the same laugh and beautiful smile.
We've got the same clothes and like the same style.
When some day, she's a famous athlete,
I'll be a model and again we will meet.
We'll think of the good times at our junior high.
We'll read all of our yearbooks and begin to cry.
Now this poem has come to an end,
I wrote this especially for my best friend!

—*Kari Fankhauser*

Mother

My Mother isn't perfect,
She's far from being a Saint.
But one thing she isn't
Is pretending what she ain't.
She tries to hard to reach out,
Someday she'll reach that goal.
I have no doubts within me
She's one of earth's most loving souls.
I guess the words come hard,
And she doesn't deal in them;
But she says it all in efforts
Her life's blood glady spends.
For she's one of those dear people
Who too rarely bless this earth;
With kind and loving ways
Spread thick upon her hearth.

—*Durae Keran*

Gift of the Angel

What's this I see. . .
She's looking up at me. . .
From outside my window
Her face so beautifully aglow
Little angel in the night
Long silky hair, shining in the moonlight
Blows across her face, lips so full
Gently shape and curves now traced
Delightful vision, my beauty, my flower
In my life, sweet, fragrant, filled with power
Her love alone can lift my soul
From depths too dark, too deep to know
To resolve, I run to protect, to nurture
Cherish, appreciate-God's glorious creature
What wisdom has made this medley of wonder
A collection of miracles; a lifetime to ponder

—*Daniel R. Lien*

The Ocean

The blazing sun
Shining down on my face
The keen pebbles on the fiery sand
Sticking into my frigid back
I can hear the gulls squeeling above
And the tide rising to the shore
I can smell the seaweed air
And the salt water
Arising over me
The foam on the water
Tickles my feet as it touches
As I get up from the blazing sun
To go to the surface of the water
I see a shell
I pick it up
And put it to my ear. . .
I could hear the sound of the beautiful ocean.

—*Beckie Spaulding*

Transformation

Listen for the voice showing inner
  wisdom,
Shining in the darkness.
In times before only confusion reigned.
Now can we have tranquility in life.
This quiet knowing is more a feeling
  giving serenity.
We can find the potential for greatness in
  our life.
We will find what we are seeking.
We can be a friend to all who seek
  greatness.

—*Edgar S. Bloom*

Warrior Children

Children are hiding in debris
Shooting down their enemies,
For they survive their families
And long once more to be free.
These little ones remember when
Their parents used to tuck them in,
And love them in so many ways.
But now, these orphans hunt their prey.
The warrior children are not young,
For their childhood is long gone.
They steal and beg to stay alive,
And seek revenge with grenades and guns.
As long as nations go to war,
And men prove that they are strong,
There will be poverty and blight,
And warrior children will need to fight.

—*Alyce L. Hubbs*

Misunderstandings

You must face it you can not control me.
Show me the way, but don't lead me
  along.
I am my own self; a life can't you see?
You think my life is a game and a song.
As I told you before, "The key is mine."
I love you, but I must be in control.
When I'm in trouble, I'll send you a sign.
But I need my freedom, leave me alone.
I hate to say it, but I will and sigh.
You may not like it at first, you may
  moan.
But I am in control, I say good-bye.
Now your small child is gone, how do you
  feel?
I may not be a child but I am real.

—*Elizabeth Dawn Bean*

The Flying Horse

It is a windy and stormy night. Out from
  the
shy comes a horse with white wings.
He is a warrior horse. He can take you
on an adventure where you've never been
  before.
He is strong and beautiful. He can save
  your life if there is trouble.
But then when the adventure is over.
He goes back where he comes from and
  helps
someone else on another fantasy
  adventure.

—*Bernadette Weeks*

Together We Stand

Together we stand,
side by side
Hand in hand,
Heart to heart.
Together we stand,
In good times,
Through bad times,
Anytime at all.
Together we stand,
Someone to lean on,
Learn from,
And love.
Friends are forever.

—*Brandi Reynolds*

Sidewalks

Sidewalks cold and hard
Sidewalks I walk upon
Everyday back and forth
Millions of people pass by
On their own little sidewalk
Where they lead only they know
No one else is on their sidewalk
My sidewalk leads nowhere
I am only here to watch other people
On their sidewalks going somewhere
Some call me a bum
I call myself a poet

—*Heather Backo*

Death of Love

Set me free, of all this pain
Sieze the problem, go insane
Pain and terror, keep inside
Break the fear, run and hide
Tears falling, nerves cry
Never speak, never lie
Kill my heart, explode with love
Turn to storms, the sky above
Evil speaks, heart of terror
Screams of silence, the dreadful prayer
Face the pain, break the spell
Heart of love, turned to hell
Love of flames, breathe the fire
Destroy temptation, kill desire
Rapture and anguish, have let love die
Evil kills, the desperate cry. . .

—*Erica Gumm*

My Daughters

Inspiring young women of sugar and spice
With rainbows of ribbons and stars in
  their eyes;
Dressed in fancy, frilly or elaborate
  clothes
Make-up so fair seems applied by a pro.
Trendy young women of pom-poms and
  cheers
Gay fashion earrings that cling to their
  ears;
Talented, serious, yearning rock-roll
  music
Elegant, natural and forever romantic.
Pretty young women of popcorn and
  dreams
Perfect hair colors and stylish perfumes;
Stuffed fluffy toys, their beds adorning
Smile covered faces to brighten my
  morning.

—*M. Miranda*

One Heart Divided

Faded voices
Silence over a battlefield that once roared
  in pain
A distant thunder
The sound of ancient souls stirring once
  again
A pale moon reflecting off glistening
  water
The same moon that saw the bloodshed
  for a thousand dreams
Silent prayers sent in the night
For the lost souls who at last found their
  peace
Though not the peace
For those, the mortals, left behind
Though the fighting ended
The agony is present in all humans
Who, although born of different soil,
Are united in one nation
All because of the lives lost
In one long war. . .

—*Kimberly S. Renner*

Fear

You suddenly appeared
Silent and full of power.
I learned to love and trust you
More and more by the hour.
Your wrath broke over me
Like a raging violent storm.
Leaving me shaken and lonely
Instead of laughing and warm.
You posess a dark charisma
And you always seem to glower
Now instead I fear you
More and more by the hour.
Your presence has receded
And I no longer have to cower.
Gone is the brooding silence
That seemed an umbreechable tower.
You can no longer hurt me
For I have built an invisible wall.
Strange...I should be gloating
But now I am the lonliest one of all.

—Carol Hunter

The Fawn

Snow falling to the ground,
Silent as a bird in flight,
Not making any sound,
Reflections now blinding sight.
Looking toward my mother,
I hear the hunters near,
Gunshot overhead then another,
I turned and ran in fear.
The reverberating crack,
Breaking through the silence,
Falling onto my back,
I feel the burning shell.
Pierced through silk fine hair
Red colored blood runs thick,
Looking down they stare,
I plead that it be quick.
Cold metal barrel resting on my head.
What more can I tell, click, then I'm
   dead.

—Christopher Weaver

Untitled

Death crawls slowly by
Silently creeping in the shadows
It fills you full of fright
And makes you look over your shoulder
Death reaches out and grabs your heart
And squeeze it tight until it stops,
Until the pulsing bloody flesh
Gives into the inevitable
A tranquil peace fills the soul
The body, heart, and mind
There is no need to do anything
For everything is already done
In this sickening game of life and death
Death has won again
He collects the lives and leaves the deaths
Don't fight him, he will always win.

—Charis Jackson

I Was Like the Moon

I was like the moon
Silver spendor
Radiant with elegance
You were like the sun
Fiery beauty
Explosive with fire
We were always on opposite sides
Of the Earth.
When I was happy
Shining in the black sky,
You were burning
With pain
And when you were happy
Gleaming in the blue sky
I was shyly tucked away
Behind the clouds
By some force
Unknown to us
We were brought together
And by that same force
We are torn

—Chris Marquais

Growing Up

Many a time have I ventured to the
   ocean's soft shore
Simply to hear the crashing of the waves
And to watch the moonlight gently kiss
   the high white peaks.
Many a time have I found myself lost...
Lost in the soothing wake of the waves
For this is the only time I can think
This is the only time I have to dream and
   not be weak.
Now the tears slowly fall until the gentle
   wind dries them so
That none can see.
Why must I always have the wind to dry
   my tears?
Slowly my soul drinks them, only to be
   hidden inside.
I look onto his eyes as he gazes into mine
And words are passed but none are heard.
So smile subsides to smile, fear subsides to
   fear, and all I still hide.
Least can they see the true nature of my
   heart
That empty third chamber that dear
   Hawthorne loved so,
But here I hide, weak and unforgiven,
Forever to linger...until I let go.

—Cheryl Lynn Fahrner

Joy in the Morning

Sitting at home, thoughts of your day
   enter your mind.
Since the day has been disappointing and
   rough,
Your mind has been focused on that
   which is bad.
You think to yourself, "No. This can't be
   for real."
You haven't acknowledged the presence
   of God, for He is your shield.
Within the depths of your soul lies the
   ability to handle any situation.
Pray. Don't dwell on that which is
   negative.
In understanding and in confidence, there
   lies your strength.
You are not alone. God is with you.
Wipe away the tears and take your
   attention away from the problem.
You come to realize you've got more
   living to do.
You sleep worry-free. You awake as a
   reborn child of God.
A great feeling of peace has come over
   you.
A new day which brings a new beginning
   has come.
You come to realize that weeping may
   endure for a night,
But joy cometh in the morning.

—Catrell Buchanan

Till Death Do Us Part

Everyday that passes by
With only your memory at my side
Causes more pain then you will ever know
Dreadful pain that always shows.
It is like a permanent marking
Scarred deep in my soul,
The love in my heart has taken a
Death driven toll.
My tear—stained eyes say it all,
My pride no longer stands too tall.
It is a white—walled room,
When the night thunders terror in my
   head.
Does anything else need to be said?

—Laura Malinowski

Hands Of Time

Time has flown,
since we first met.
But our love has grown,
it hasn't faded yet.
I can't say its always been easy,
Sometimes it gets pretty hard,
There's always something to keep us busy,
That causes us to be apart.
If wishing would do any good,
I'd wish I could go back
to the first day you were mine,
If I could you know I'd slow down...
The hands of Time.

—Angela R. West

Pursuit of White Doves

To the listening heart
Sirens singing from green seas,
Lonely phantoms wandering on the winds
Moist with silent passion.
Peeping through a moon—fired moment
Vistas of green umbrellas loom,
White lotus moored in hyacinth lagoons.
Stretching to pursue
White doves in golden spheres of sun.
Sighs for jasmine afternoons, wild honey.
Startled by unsummoned songs
Stars bend low, summon me
To go with the wind
Beyond the farthest horizon.
Brace the driftwood
Of grey bones in the sunset,
Brace the winter twilight
And dusk of silence.

—Emma Crobaugh

Reaching Tommorow

When the shadowed glow rises from
Sleep and the shift of wind grows reep
The pondering shimmer of mood swings
The trees until it is upon thee and when
   upon,
Your eternity shatters your intentions.
The warped mind demands a release
Of a certain degree of evil to
Wander and destroy.
Wander and destory of which is very
Likely to be thyself. Attitude becomes
Shivers, reasons become sly, cares turn
   into tears,
But one can only stay one and hurt many.
When the shimmering shine of brightness
   appears,
Thyself shatters sour to sweat,
Hurt has been done and the one is still the
   one and the many
That had been hurt are still many hurt.

—Christine Pinder

Love Cry

Salty drops
slowly falling
from my sparkling eyes
never knowing
of the faith
that I feel inside,
when my heart
is slowly dying
pretending to be smiling
and afraid
to start denying
of the love
that's always crying.

—Anna Wieczorek

Love

What else could love but but thee and me.
Slowly, quietly, we peer from a distance,
A smile, a move, and a comment plants
   the seed.
The hours begin to fill with possibilities
And plans of what ifs and could it possibly
   be?
Is there a chance, maybe?
And the moment comes and off we go.
Our hearts touch as our minds intertwine
   and we lean
Into each other. We are frozen in a
   moment,
Being swept away.
First I say we must go slow and you tell
   me
How long you've waited. As fear leaves
   me and enters you,
It's your time to say let's go slow.
Finally with locked doors and opened
   hearts,
Our minds and hands racing off we go,
Oh so beautifully slow.

—Kathleen Schneck

The Streets and Alleys

Families unsheltered and
Small children cold
These people tend to be frustrated
When underneath they are bold
Shattered dreams and hopes
Are all to look forward to
Our lives are bright
But all they see is blue

—Gretchen Cufton

Untitled

Lying in the grass
Smelling every flowere
Watching every bird
Cathching every butterfly
With my eyes.
Singing with the crickets
Rubbing noses with the rabbits
Tickling every turtle
That slowly walks by
Conversing with the catepillar
Who gently says hi—
Lying in the grass
On a Saturday afternoon.

—Jessica Fowler

Woman to Man

Endless quantities of rippling muscle.
Smooth, taut skin glistens with sweat.
Honestly sweet smiles cause the widest
   eyes to crinkle.
Gentle hands run through a woman's hair.
Innovative styles clothe seductive bodies.
The laughing wind teasingly ruffles
   carefully groomed hair.
Expressions of desire flow from serpentine
   lips.
The provocative trace of cologne hovers in
   the stillness.
This is what the eye can see.
I want more.
I want what the heart can see.
What is going on inside you?
I need in.
Please let me.

—Jennifer Foree

The Big Man

There was a big man
So big
That the tallest trees were looking
At his Feet.
So big
That the highest mountains were looking
At his Knees.
So big
That the highest clouds were looking
At his Waist.
So big
That the moon itself was looking
At his Shoulders.
So big
That the farthest stars were tingling
Among his hair.
So big
That God was looking at Himself.

—Andre' Carbonneau

The Stallion Rides

The stallion rides against the night,
So dark and yet so bright.
The stallion rides against the day,
Where dreams and wishes lay.
The stallion rides.
The stallion rides against the sky,
Where our hearts and souls soar so high.
The stallion rides against the ground,
Silently leaping, bound for bound.
The stallion rides.

—Denisha D. Powell

Visions

Nothing in life is perfect.
So don't look at me
as imperfection or not quite right.
But look at me in beauty and love of a
    friend.
Imperfection can rule out the desire
to see beauty in only the simplest things.
But with your heart and eyes open wide,
you can see more than what is standing
    right before you.

—Alaina Nicole Reynolds

Our World

As a small star falls from the sky,
So I look into your eyes.
I must have seen this look before,
About a million times or more.
A look that says it's not the way it used to
    be,
A look that says I long to be free.
But then in an instant, you change your
    mind,
And once again your eyes are kind.
Our loving world of ups and downs,
One day a smile, the next a frown.
But that's the way it'll have to be,
Because I'll always want you here with
    me.

—Kerry Lynn Murphy

Mystery Place

You could hear the voices of that old
    distored place
So many memories there, had taken place
All the rooms had a dusty smell
It was a very old house and you could tell.
The love the overflowed, now has vanished
People who once lived there had
    abandoned
There was not electricity at all
Grass had beer growing on the walls.
Doors and walls creeked with every pace
trying to get out a word or two
about that Mystery Place.

—Christy Robinson

Eyes of Ice

Those dark sorrowful eyes,
So hard to read.
Beautiful but cold.
Eyes that don't reveal the truth.
Soldiers of faith to oneself.
Eyes so cold the tears are like ice.
Stinging to the show of weakness,
Burning from the ice.
Eyes so lovely I yearn to love them.
I am afraid of the weakness.
Those eyes may not show weakness.
Although they are mine.

—Jessica Stich

Paradise

Winter is paradise
So is spring
Then what is paradise
Paradise is something special
Which is beautiful to the eye
That's what paradise is
Paradise is snowdrifts
During the wintertime
Paradise is birds singing
In the morining time
That's what paradise is to one's eye

—Kirstin McStravick

So Much Pain

So much pain I've tried to hide
So many thoughts locked inside
So many memories parading within
So many times I've tried to win
Yet so many losses, so many tears
So many rejections, so many fears
So many moments, I've felt all alone
So often I've realized I am on my own
So many faces, yet so little see
So many smiles not meant for me
So many thoughts I wish I could share
So many people, but nobody cares. . .

—June Klavikorn

Lesson in Futility

I was told, "to walk you must first learn to
    crawl",
So, I began to crawl!
I was told, "to run you must first learn to
    walk",
So, I began to walk!
I was told, "to be an adult you must fill
    your brain with knowledge",
So, I grew and became wise!
With my wisdom I learned that if you
    crawl, people overlook your existence.
That if you walk, there is no one to walk
    alongside of you.
Yet, if you run, your legs soon tire, and
    you slow to a lonesome walk,
And the crawl becomes inevitable-
And people shall once again overlook your
    existence!

—Dorothy Gill

Warrior of Love

My soul grows wiser year after year,
So lonely and tired, held back by fear.
This emotion I feel yet can't explain,
Allowing it freedom — brings me pain.
I long so to find my "Warrior Brave",
To fight my battle — my soul to save.
In a vision I see him proud and strong,
Astride a winged horse, hair straight and
    long.
From the depths of my being, a light
    emanates,
Glow steady and sure — what peace it
    creates.
From this fire within — my Warrior I see,
Since before time began, he's been here
    with me.
In silence he's waited through eons of
    time,
For me to come claim what's always been
    mine.
He speaks in a whisper, yet loud and so
    clear,
"Trust in my love, I conquer all fear".

—Barbara Pilkington

My Dear Aunt Mary

Her home, it was a second home to me,
So many times, there I would like to be.
I knew much joy with my cousins there,
And many a meal we did share.
She gladly welcomed all who came,
And sweetly loved us all the same.
I can see her yet with snow-white hair,
Her face serene and happy there.
Her children, I do know full well
She loved more dearly than words could
    tell;
Kindness was in her every touch.
And we all loved her, oh so much.
Dear Saviour, we could always yearn
To somehow this great lesson learn,
To face life with her great serenity
And to do God's will to eternity.

—June Briner

Remember

Our journey down lifes road began
So many years ago
And as the bond between us grew
We shared a love sublime.
We lost you to an autumn wind
That fall so long ago,
Although I dream what could have been
That will not make it so.
Lost in the reverie of years gone by;
The dawn of our creation,
I feel your touch, I hear your voice,
Your song still stirs my soul.

—Boyd T. Davey

I Was Bad Again Today

I was bad again today,
So my mommy beat me for it.
I have had scars and bruises and broken bones,
But my parents say I deserve it.
My daddy rapes me all the time,
He says it is because I am bad.
He is right, I am only eight,
And I always make them mad.
My daughter was bad again today,
So I beat her for it.
She has had scars and bruises and broken bones,
But we know she deserves it.
My husband rapes her all the time,
We say it is because she is bad.
We are right, she is only eight,
And she always makes us mad.

—Jerry Edward Miller, Jr.

One of a Kind

Each one is different, each one is unique,
So new to the world, so innocent, so meek.
A child, a prize, a God—given gift,
So precious, so tiny, so weightless to lift,
No two look alike, as close as they may be.
He created everyone with such a natural beauty.
So you see, you've just got to be yourself.
Who else in this world can you possibly be?
You've got to be you, and I've got to be me.
Whatever you do, wherever you go, always keep in mind,
You are a beautiful gift to the world,
You are definitly one of a kind.

—Becky Linn

Untitled

The velvet petals of the rose,
So pure and untouched,
Just like a child,
So sweet and innocent.
A rose has thorns to protect itself,
Whereas a child has nothing,
Yet both do not know fear.

—Jennifer Buzikievich

Love

Love so tender like baby's blood
So soft,
like a baby's skin
So new and pretty,
like a newborn baby
But so harsh at times
like a melting witch
With shrieks of screams
that finally end
Into a puff of smoke
never knowing what?

—Christy Famolare

Death

A black space
so unfamiliar
so faraway
older than life itself
yet this is nothing new to us
darker than space.
Enemy or friend
No one knows
You have to choose for yourself
For death is hardly
friend or enemy.
Just a mixture of both I guess.

—Joanna Darnell

Barbara Ann

I sit here with my pen and ink
So you open your eyes and start to think.
What you mean to me, and me to you
Because I don't know what to say or do.
So I will put it to you in black and white
To see if I'm wrong or if I am right
Those times we shared I'll remember forever
For I don't think I will find any better.
If our feelings are similiar then that means I'm right,
Then a long relationship is definetly in sight.
I pray my feelings are not a mistake,
But I must know for sure so I don't lay awake.
If what I think and hope is true
That you'll wait for me and I'll wait for you.
I hope you understand what I'm trying to say.
As it brings closer, and not further away.
Well, let me close on this very lost line,
By saying to you, won't you still be all mine.

—Barbara McEntee

Dreams

Dreams are like an Eagle's flight,
Soaring high on widespread wings.
Like that Eagle I'd love to fly,
And leave behind all earthly things.
Soaring high up in the clouds,
All problems left behind.
Far away from all the pain,
No heartache by my side.
They say you can't survive on dreams,
Like an Eagle always in flight.
But I never could let go of them,
For they get me through my life.

—Erica Stupansky

First Love

Red as the blood of hearts first love,
Soft as the touch of loves first kiss.
Then storms of hatred fill the air,
And you fade away as quickly as you faded in.

—Becky Cameron

Untitled

Flowing dress
Soft caress
The gypsy girl runs free
Features bold
Rings of gold
She will not wait for me
Full of pride
The gypsy died
And left me alone to see
Through opened eyes
Free of lies
A gypsy I must be.

—*Jennifer Kay*

Cats

Cats, majestically moving gracefully paw
  by paw; with every little step, he leaves
  a track of royalty.
Soft fur that makes feathers feel like
  rocks.
Ears sharpened to the finest point, a tail
  that shows his deepest emotions.
With paws that hide his every move and a
  personality that could make you friend
  or foe at the same time.

—*Annessa Sustaita*

Shadows Of A Dream

Shadows of a dream;
Softer than starlight,
Wings of Summer's dove;
In quiet shades of blue,
Golden fields of wheat;
In a purple haze of sunset,
Peace tiptoes through the clouds;
Whispering its presence,
The rose slowly opens her petals;
Announcing her approval,
The waters ripple;
In tune with the gentle wind,
A tree sheds a solitary leaf;
In recognition of the wings,
It ends in soft abruptness;
Still conscious of the dove.
And I float back—
To reality.

—*Jillian Derrick*

Education

When children are born into this land,
Some are taught by the back of the hand.
Others learn the golden rule,
To live by this is to be a fool.
Now there's a new one called education,
It gives people off the street an
  occupation.
This is the one I hate the most,
And this is the one our government
  boasts.
To learn about science and geometry,
Don't think about you, only me.
To learn the lifestyles of bugs,
But not the deadly effects of drugs.
Don't tell me this world will ever change,
Now we're in the computer age.
We want to build, to kill our brother,
When no one thinks about another.
Yes, I'm tired of living this life,
It cuts deeper, society is the knife.

—*Heddy Lopez*

Remembrance

Soldiers fought for us
Some of them died for us
We remember them
For what they have done for us.
The loud banging from their guns
Their marching feet and the pain
Which they had felt.
We remember them
For what they have done for us.

—*James Walgenbach*

Poetry

The beauty of poetry comes in many
  forms.
Some seem great, others merely nice.
Perhaps it's Hamill's grace on ice,
Or the brutalness of Tyson that reform
Our ideas of beauty and art.
Poetry gives us hope; opens our heart
And soul to love, lust, or despair.
Although beautiful, poetry is not fair.

—*Daniel O'Rourke*

Untitled

Love, like a river, flowing into the sea
Someday, flowing back to me
But until I wait in impatient stress
For Mr. Right's exciting caress.
My days are filled with romantic dreams
Though to others childish it seems
Loneliness is my shadow and friend
When the long days come to an end.
I am shivered with a chill
Though the night air is quite still.
A vision of a horse and galiant knight
Slowly fades from sight
As reality sets in.

—*Dana Edwards*

Someday

Someday I'm going to be your friend,
Someday, someday,
A friend I'll love until the end,
Someday, someday.
Someday, I'll tell you that I care.
Someday, someday.
Someday, I'll praise your lovely hair,
Someday, someday.
Someday, I'm going to take that trip,
Someday, someday.
I'll dare to travel on that ship,
Someday, someday.
Make that someday now.
Don't wait too long to start.
You really do know how,
Make that someday NOW.

—*Bobbie Tait*

Untitled

If only
Somehow see
The really, truly me.
Just to find
Not so blind
It's been there all the time.
Open eyes
Fantasize
Of what's on the inside.
Who and I?
Don't know why?
Relay the message, "Hi"
HELLOW STRANGER

—*Joseph Magee*

Just a Dream

I dreamed a dream. . .
Someone broke my heart
And I cried.
I dreamed a dream. . .
I was sad and lonely
And I wept.
Then someone came. . .
Bringing cheer,
He was handsome,
And sincere.
He made me happy. . .
He made me laugh
And I cried no more.
But it was just a dream. . .

—*Dana Harris*

There Was Once a Man

There was a man in my life
Someone whom was himself, had no
    needs, no worries
It seemed he had it all
At once, he could've had it all, love,
    passion, lust and trust
But to him, that wasn't enough
There was a girl who had a man in her
    life,
Who brought love, passion, feelings and
    lust
He once shared these feelings with her,
    until that day, that night,
He became himself and she became
    herself

—*Christina Marie Sipes*

Passage Of Fate

As I walked past his portrait
Something took me by surprise
I seemed to be shaken by his painted blue
    eyes.
I looked down at the plate—that stated
    the date
It was a hundred years ago—to late.
As I stood there and stared, and stared,
I couldn't believe the moment it seemed
    we'd shared.
More, and More,
I felt as if we'd loved before.
As I turned to go—
I looked back just once more
There he stood—suspended in time
Holding out his hand for mine.
Oh! to tempt the hands of fate
To open to me he passage gate
To hold him in my arms so tight
All through the moon-lit night.

—*Cynthia Jo Talbert*

Parents

Parents to me are. . .
Someone who cares.
and who does things,
nobody else dares.
To take those risks,
nobody else would.
Parents could help a child,
to their best ability.
Parents are someone to talk to,
or laugh with,
or even cry over heartaches.
Parents never think twice
about lending a hand.
Without parents,
the world would be blue,
and filled with boredom,
and nothing to do.

—*Audrey Contristano*

To My Brother

There's something I have to tell you.
Something I'd better say,
I didn't want it to end this way.
Through all the years we've had together,
Sometimes good, sometimes bad.
Teased each other off and on,
It's the best life one could ever have.
I didn't want you to go,
At least not so far away.
But I've heard that things have to change.
And I'll miss you anyway.
I guess what I'm trying to tell you is that I
    Love You so.
But there's nothing I can do about it,
I'll just have to let you go.

— *Grace Salazar*

Love

Love is like a river,
Sometimes gentle,
Sometimes strong,
It drowns the weak and weary,
And gives refuge for the strong.
So if you're not strong or lucky,
I say never try to love,
But love can come so easy,
Like on the wings of a dove.
It's tempting
And decideful,
And powerful too,
It can turn the strongest person,
Into the weakest one of two.

—*Amanda Bryant*

Our Friendship

Remember the good times we've shared,
Someone who stuck by me, someone who
    cared.
You are my best friend,
I know we'll be together until the end.
The times we've laughed, the times we've
    cried.
And all the times that we both lied.
Remember all the secrets we've told,
And dreams of what it will be like when
    we're old.
All the people who tried to break our
    friendship apart,
Now I realize it's all in my heart.

—*Diana Gaulin*

Facing Death

Facing death is an awful hard thing,
Something that takes a lot of courage,
Losing someone special is the worst thing
    to feel.
My grandfather is facing death,
He is in terrible pain,
Pain that I share with him, or how it
    hurts.
Now he's gone,
He couldn't hold on.
The pain was too great,
I came to help much too late.
I can't believe that he's gone,
Yet his memory we will all carry on,
Never will I forget my grandfather.
He was my superman, my man of steel.
The one my father took after,
Now it's just pain that I feel.

—*Daphne Reisdorph*

Rainbows

Rainbows come in many shades and hues,
Sometimes having reds, sometimes blues.
One thing a rainbow shows,
Most everyone knows,
Rainbows are a sign of love,
A gift from Heaven above.
Rainbows are bright,
But they don't show at night.
You have to be careful in the day
To watch before they fade away.
If you see a rainbow near,
Do not fret, do not fear.
As long as you see a rainbow in the day,
Wish hard enough so it won't fade away.

—*Ellen McGuire*

Life

What a life I have today?
Sometimes it's horrible
Sometimes it's great
But lately my life just hasn't been up to
  date.
For real this life has got to go!
And everyday I think that's so
This life's not the way it should be
This life has definently got to go!
My life's not the same as yours
nor yours that much like mine
Our lifes together are much apart
Even though our lifes apart are much the
  same.
Oh, how I wish my life was settled.
Just like a princess, now and forever
A life so pleasant, a life like a dream
This is my wish for a life, unseen.

—Heather C. Griff

Simply Love

I've had a lot of hills to climb,
Sometimes my way I thought I'd never
  find.
But through my faith, I have known,
I would never be alone.
As I struggled across this land,
I always knew God held my hand.
The last few hills were very rough,
But walking with me, He made me tough.
And when I fell to my knees,
He turned to me and gave a hug.
Now that I'm back on my feet,
I honestly know God is love.

—Ginger Upright

Special Friends

"Friends forever", they say,
Sometimes that isn't true,
But with us,
You and me,
I know it's true,
We've been best friends,
Too long,
We've got a special kind of friendship,
One that no one else will ever have,
And if our friendship ever disappears,
I'm sure that part of me would disappear
  too,
Because our friendship is too important to
  me,
To lose. . .

—Janet Oh

My Friend Teddy

I hold my teddy bear close to me,
Soon I'm infinity.
I dream of monsters in my soul,
Taking away my minds control.
I hold my teddy bear close to me,
Sharing my secret fantasy.
We talk of college and reminisce
Of childhood days I often miss.
I hold my teddy bear close to me,
Hoping that it's only he who can see.
The fear in my mind that I'll always hold
The terrible fear of growing old.
I hold my teddy bear close to me,
His ear is an torn as it can be.
He sees that my eyes are sad and gray.
He sees how wearly I am today.
I hold my teddy bear close to me
He knows how hard I've worked to be me.

—Jennifer Stewart

Life and Death

If you live your life like a candle in the
  wind,
Soon the flame will flicker out,
The wind will soon stop blowing.
But if the candle was to spark again,
Or the wind to whisper through the trees,
How could one live without the other?
For if two things work together for such a
  long time,
And one stops doing its part,
Its fair share,
Then the other can go on no longer
  without it,
And the beauty of life must end,
Then the silence of death begins.

—Jocelyn Cortese

In Wars Past

An angry cry in the distance
Souls of brave men lost forever
Far beyond the apparent horizon
The sound of a bomb killing.
Every man and beast within its
Reach is heard; in wars past.
Today, one lonely child cries
One lonely tear and walks along
With his back against the horizon.

—Catherine Bard

Haiku

A leaf drifts in the wind.
Sounds of rearranging leaves
Disrupt silence.

—Karen Grometer

Untitled

We are destined to fall out of the circle,
Space is limited as well as time.
Being pushed closer to the edge,
Tazette, the goddess of fear,
Clutches her five inch long fingernails into
  my heart.
Oh, I am terrified,
Of growing past the boundaries.
The boundaries of an eternity.
An eternity that shall not be known.
A doomed eternity,
Of existence or non-existence.
Oh, what does it matter,
I'm trapped either way.
We all are.

—Elizabeth Fellows

Grandmother

Grandmother was of the sea,
Sparkling, splashing waves of gold.
Her currents were strong,
Made out of love,
As her caring ways,
Crashed upon the sand.
She provided a home to the world,
As the sea provides a home for its
  creatures.
She sparkled brighter than the brightest
  pearl,
Inside a tiny oyster.
But now she moves on,
Sailing up the coast,
Awaiting for what lies ahead,
Knowing it is something greater,
Than the greatest ocean!

—Kristine Nielsen

Communicate

Write a line that meets a need.
Speak a word which plants a seed.
Make a remark which gratifies.
Utter comments which elicit sighs.
Say, I love you, in the way you live.
Set an example with the gifts you give.
Turn someone's head through a selfless
  act.
Sacrifice your will for another's lack.

—Eugene E. Childs

Oh Crowned One

Oh crowned one
Speak the word
That I may be
Released
From the letters
That hold me captive
I shall burn these
Bridges behind me
I hear another call
It beckons me come
My destiny awaits me.

—*Judy Darlene Pitchford*

Sunset Sky

Azure skies
Splashed with alien colors
At sunset.
Magnitudes of mandarin orange,
Powerful purples and pinks,
Blinding, soothing to the eye.
The clouds dipped in
Swirling, bright color,
Dripping on the setting sun.
Sunset stuck on azure skies,
Mandarin orange mixing
With colors that are alien to
Azure skies.

—*Heidi Zimmerhanzel*

Papillon

Papillon
Spread
Her dusty wings
And
Tentatively
Tested
The
Air

—*Cheri Papier*

Untitled

To all those who yearn to fly
Spread your wings
For you have nothing to lose
And all to gain
Don't fear falling
For I will catch you in my outstretched
    arms
Holding you and comforting you
Sheltering you from the harsh world that
    lurks outside
It is here you will stay
When your heart longs for friendship
and your wounds long for care
Until you can fly once more

—*Karla Janel Newman*

When Shall Roses Bloom

When shall roses bloom?
Springtime has come and gone
Leaving a barren plain
Full of death and suffering.
When shall all storms cease
Their worrisome tempest,
Leaving their chaos behind
And the dead mourning the future?
When shall roses bloom?
Up in heaven above
Where life will come.
And storms will cease
In everlasting love.

—*Kathryn Abbot*

The Statue

A large stone figure,
Standing before me.
Metalic hair,
FLowing at her back.
Exaggerated features,
Stand out in the crowd.
A large stone figure,
Forever resting on a floor of stone.
Water rushing,
Over her iron feet;
Turning them an odd sort of green.
A large stone figure,
A sorrowful look, carved on her face.
Drooping eyes, falling lips, wrinkled brow,
A large stone figure,
Standing alone in the park.

—*Jordan Fitzpatrick*

Afraid

Barren room sitting
Standing still,
I hear echoes
Of solemn memories
From long ago.
Screaming, crying,
Writhing in pain.
Don't hit me.
Don't hit me.
The child screams in vain,
But no one listens,
No one seems to care.
A tear stained pillow
Sitting in the corner,
Seems to be the only consolation,
The only one that seems to hear,
A cry for help.

—*Joy Ashcraft*

Suicide

Suicide is there,
Staring me in the face.
I'm lost in a world,
with no one to embrace.
Life is so damn complicated,
I don't know if I can
make it through,
will someone "please" help me,
will it be you?
my mind is blank,
and my heart is filled
with sorrow,
is there someone there?
will there be a tomorrow?

—*Brenda Lavender*

Peacefullness

As I sit here
Staring out into the blackness
of the summer air
I being to wonder. . .
Wonder why the world is
At war
Yet, at the same time,
The lake is so peaceful,
So still.
I wonder, since life is so short,
Why the ongoing threat
Of nuclear war
Where the entire world could
Be destroyed—at the push of a button.
One push.
One impact.
One life—never to be returned or relived.
Yet, my surrounding are so peaceful.

—*Jessica Bosshard*

Prose and Poetry

Prose plods along familiar ways,
Stays earthborne all its given days,
Wanders up and down the streets
Writing lives of those it meets;
Climbs a mountain, scours a plain,
Pens a romance set in Spain,
Treats of tyrants who won't last
Or delves into the dusty past.
But poetry lifts off on wings,
Soars to where the skylark sings,
Flies with planets as they ply
Their chosen course across the sky;
Lights with starfire lamps designed
To illuminate the mind;
Speeds toward beauty like a dart-
Then turns, and stabs you in the heart.

—*Alice M. Hoffman*

My Unfound Lover

Someone to go walking with hand in hand
　in the rain
Stepping in and out of the puddles till all
　four feet are soaked.
Someone to lie with quietly in the tall
　green grass
Staring at the clouds high above and the
　infinity beyond.
Someone to jump with in the piles of
　autumn leaves
Kicking the masses of red, yellow and
　brown.
Someone to swim with at night in the lake
As the waves kiss the shore and the
　retreat.
Someone who can set me on fire just with
　the touch of his hand.
Someone who knows when and when
　not—without even asking.
Someone who at times will just hold my
　hand
And at others won't let go till we become
　one.
Someone who can sit by my side without
　saying a word
And not be bothered by the prolonged
　silence.
Someone to become a part of me and let
　me in his heart forever.
Someone to be my lover.

　—*Emily Goren*

The Morning of Life

Morning is the birth of a new day,
Still and silent like a newborn baby.
Noon is the teenager of the day,
High up in the sky eager to learn.
Evening is the adult,
Wise to the day.
Night is when the day dies,
But with hope there will be a tomorrow.

　—*Denise Spahr*

One of a Kind Love

Memories of our first kiss
Still linger in my mind
I thought the love we shared
Was a love I'd never find
But you found a way
To break this bond apart
A bond I thought we built so strong
That it would not break my heart
But I guess I was wrong
To think this love would last
It was going too good
It passed by us so fast
Now all the pain and sorrow
That you have left behind
Is a forever scar
Of the love I thought was one of a kind.

　—*Danielle McMullin*

Endless Cries

Yesterday's tears should have passed
Still, the memories inside continue to last.
Tomorrow's emotions are yet to flow,
New twisted hearts are soon to show.
The bleeding skies will drip with pain,
The endless sun it will never regain.
This world continues to have a shaking
　ground,
A steady emotion will never be found.
A quiet noise inside my heart,
Speaks silently when wasted tears start.
My mixed emotions have nowhere to go,
The river of sadness has no place to flow.
Yesterday's tears are still in my heart,
With the addition of others beginning to
　start.
The smiles that once appeared in my eyes,
They now have turned into endless cries.

　—*Eileen Katherine Foley*

Alone

My soul,
Stolen by the wind,
Swept away by the sea,
Melted by the sun.
I am left with an emptiness,
Nothing to feel,
Nothing to fear,
Only the sense of being alone.

　—*Freedom Baisley*

Before the Sunrise

A beautiful mass of color
Stretches across the horizon.
It's almost like a rainbow
Waiting for the sun to rise.
I gaze at its splendor,
Not wanting the sun
To rise and spoil its radiance.
But I know there will be
Beauty in the sunset.

　—*Amy Sargent*

Clothes

The main attention getter,
Suave, sophisticated, and intellectual,
Business like, sporty, casual, dressy,
An obsession for some people like me,
A lust or compulsion, that is
Delicate and sharp with many awesome
　colors.

　—*Alameta Yvette Anderson*

The Land of the Unicorn

I close my eyes, I am one with the silence.
Suddenly, I am in a dreamland
Where there is only happiness.
I see a beautiful white winged horse
Gracefully dancing on the warm breeze.
Then, beside me, a unicorn.
With a mane and tail like the finest silken
　thread.
Eyes of sapphire and a horn of gold.
As the horn catches the light,
I am reminded that I cannot stay here.
I am not like these creatures of magic and
　myth.
I am human, I am real, I don't belong
　here.
I open my eyes the silence is shattered
Like a fragile wine glass
Although I may never return
I will always remember the Land of the
　Unicorn.

　—*Jennifer Sumpter*

The Beach

Hot sand, cold water,
Sun blazing ever more.
Winds blowing,
Waves crashing against
The shore.
Cool sand, warm water
Glittering water, sparkling
In the moonlight.
Breezes, waves lapping
On the shore.

　—*Jodean Seniuk*

A Beautiful Place

The most beautiful place to me is the
　beach.
Sunset is my favorite time to be there,
Because everything around me
Slowly becomes quiet with the sounds of
　nature.
As I sit there, the waves crashing against
　the
Sand and rocks hypnotize my thoughts.
I lift my eyes and to my amazament,
The sky looks like a beautiful painting in
　an art gallery.
The sea and I have similiar distinguishing
　traits.
We both can be dangerous and
　destructive
When the wrong forces rise against us,
　and yet...
We both can be calm and enjoyable
When there's nothing in our way.
I hear the sea beckoning me now.
With it's beauty and strength
I'll soar aloft on borrowed wings
To distant years where there is no sorrow.

　—*Dana R. Seals*

Beaches

Romantic, peaceful
Surfing, tanning, resting
Seagulls swaying for food
Laughing, strolling, running,
Colorful, lazy.

—Elizabeth Koon

Junes in Bloom

Gardens, really coming on.
Surrounded by the robin's song.
She's with her siblings and determined
To teach them all about worming
Spring onions have come to size.
Tomatoe plants are on the rise.
The lawn now is at it's best.
A reaching upward, no time to rest.
Winter's way off, the impending gloom
Cause summer's a'coming, and June's in
   bloom.

—Gary D. Meseraull

Thanatos

Gently blows the soft, cool wind
Swaying trees and weeds and limbs
Here comes the luminous, calming moon
There goes the sun into the depths of
   doom
A light mist of rain falls gently to the
   ground
Bringing life to that which lies
   underground
The wind whistles, the moon shines
All is calm throughout time
Across the horizon the clouds gather
Forming a fleet of white lather
Calmness churns into a thunderous trite
Crackling and causing a deafening fright
Like an orchestra, in mark time beat
The clouds play the Rhythm of Winds so
   sweet
Bursts of lightening engulf the sky
Shrieks of fear. . .and then a sigh
The clouds part like the Red Sea
And the master takes you home, eternally.

—Carla Reeves

Thirty One Flavors

You are hotel chocolate
Sweet, rich, special and rare.
Oft the shielding glass windows pull back
And it is your turn to be scooped up,
Sprayed,
Sprinkled
And shaped for someone's savoring.
You are dished out to his hands.
Hot,
Private,
Intimate.
Slowly you melt and lose your own
   individual shape
Becoming
One
With
Him.

—Connie Johnson

Summer Success

Sip a soda,
Swim so serene.
Shoot the rapids.
Sunbathe unseen.
See some old friends.
Shop until dark.
Select some books.
Sit in the park.
See some movies.
Ski in the lake.
Stir up some fudge.
Sleep until late.
Set out iced tea.
Savor ice cream.
Stare at the hills.
Settle and dream.

—Beverly Dornburg

Bright Beaches

Peaceful on the ocean shore,
Swimsuits gleaming in every door.
While my friend sleeps in her bunk,
Other gals shout, "What a hunk!"
Burning sands under our feet,
All the tans, very sheek.
Big, bright sails in the distance.
On one of them, for instance,
Is a picture of a crimson fish.
Now the sun is coming down,
Soon the beach will have no sound.

—Angie Koenig

Peace

Peace is a dove
Symbolizing love
The world should be of peace
All the wars should cease
No one should be mean
And everyone should be seen
PEACE is what the world should be
That's what everyone should see

—Angela Eader

The Path

A little path,
take it just to see where it leads.
A side hill with a lone cross.
A childs best friend is buried there.
A little girl, crying over her loss,
comes to the grave to talk to the friend she
   loved.
Look and see quickly,
the path, the cross, and the little girl will
   soon disappear.

— Dawn Wightman

Take Time for Me

Take time for me for I am small,
Take time for me, too soon I will be tall,
I'm only two, so take hold of my hand,
And try your best to make me understand.
I'm really loved and cherished after all,
Even though sometimes from grace I fall.
I'm just a child, I need to know your love.
I'm very fragile, like the morning dove.
I was a gift to cherish and care for
I don't expect you always to adore.
But always make a space for me within
   your heart
In other words, please give me a good
   start.

—Connie Lee

The Wind

The wind of life blows through me,
Taking my soul along for the ride
On a hard, exhausting journey—
A pilgrimage inside.
It screams in rage,
It murmurs in sorrow.
Though war is of the age
Peace is for tomorrow.
Sometimes if flys so high
Nothing can bring it down,
Then I let out a cry
For the hot sun is its crown
Oft' it sings compassion
At the sight of a hungry child
And it give my conscience a lashin'.
The wind will never be mild.

—Amy Wood

Words of the Oracle

If your dreams are in the sky,
Talk to the eagles and learn how to fly
If you want to follow the sun,
There will be no time to walk, you will
   have to run
If what you seek is beneath the deepest
   sea,
Fear not to ask the moon for a key
If you choose to go far,
Let your goal be no less than a distant
   star.
If the paths are dim and unknown
Don't be afraid to walk them alone.
Wherever you go don't look back
For you will see nothing but a fading
   track
If the night closes in,
And you feel as if you can never win;
Know that to be tall,
You first must know how to fall
To laugh you first must know how to cry;
There is no reason why.
I hope you climb mountains so high
That you can touch the sky.
I also hope you are trusted, and true
But none of this matters unless you are
   you.

—Elizabeth J. Pelkofer

Touch Of Resentment

May I dream the great joys of life
without you standing in my way?
Why must your grasp fall on me as
you feel yourself going under?
Manipulated and used by others your
   whole
life is what you say,
but your shy outlook changes to deceiving
   manners
with all the power of mighty thunder.
No more, will your song of death be heard
or your icey frigid advice be obeyed
for there is one thing that I have learned:
to one's own happiness never be dismayed.

—Renee Fleischhauer

Modest Tidepools

Flirting, loving, luring,
tall seductive waves
tempt her sunburnt morals
as harsh salt water
rapes clean hands
and coaxes her to join
those with foaming egos;
soaring high again, and
yet again, before
eventually being sucked
to the bottom
where perhaps
they may see just
a touch of hell,
enough to scare
them into becoming
modest tidepools.

—Diane Carney

On the Twenty Fifth Anniversary of Your Death

I still remember as if last even
Tapping the earth around your grave with
   my foot.
The silent, empty feeling standing
There, surrounded by loving family and
   friends.
The hot June breeze swaying the grass
Around the fresh, black dirt piled over
   your remains.
I could not forgive my muse for
Betraying me so, taking you away from
   me in the
Prime, so to speak,
Of your life, taking the music within you
   always.
Only twenty five years later
Could I know that your music never died
   within me.
I often wonder what the muses
Had in mind for you in the infinite,
   faraway world,
The world we call the unknown.
Whatever it was, I still remember the pain
   standing
There, tapping the dirt around your grave.

—Harriet Cummins

Once My Teacher, Always My Friend

For five full months you taught me,
Teaching me right from wrong.
Now you're teaching some other lucky
   kids,
And you'll be married before summer's
   done.
You were one of my best teachers,
Now you're one of my best friends,
I'm still in grave seven,
While you're teaching grade eight,
But together, we're still first rate.
And through my life,
Up until it ends,
I'll always remember you,
Once my teacher,
Always my friend.

—Jacqueline R. Russell

Poor Man's Diamonds

Water on the lawn,
Teardrops from my eye,
That sparkle in the light.
They are free for the taking,
To anyone
Who will reach out for
The poor man's diamonds.

—Dawn Arnold

These Thousand Years

And I sit here
Tears in my eyes
A thousand years
A thousand tears
Lost in a dream
Of a dream that's lost.
There's a lot of people
Running in the meadows of my doubts
From a love they don't understand,
And still you don't know who I am.
How can I show you? There are doors
   that are locked to me,
I'm unwelcomed, cold and alone.
I need someone to hold me,
I'm a rose who's been crushed,
Pick me up, see my single, silver tear.
Please, don't let me fall apart
I only wanted to be beauty and love
I only needed someone to care for me
I only desired to survive these thousand
   years.

—Charlie Halbrook

Woman Conquistador

If an old man asks what you life is for
tell him your a singing troubadour
if a sophisticated lady in green-feathered
   hat
says this should be or that and that
tell her your a prophet pure
with revelations of exotic lure
if the children ask why you dance in the
   yard
tell them your a wild-eyed bard
if the neighbors ask why your still a hippy
tell them your a gold-spangled gypsy
if people ask what your search for
tell them your a conquistador!!!

—Elizabeth Long

Pain

"Why do people hate each other"?
Tell me what they've done.
A little child asks his mother,
But an answer she has none.
How can the world be in such pain,
When the children love so deep?
What will fighting ever gain,
When the children dream in sleep?
We blanket the fear for them
As they laugh and play.
But it's their future we condemn,
As they're served hell on a tray.
As the snow falls so peaceful,
And overlook their plea.
Why don't we feel the pull,
And when they cry, set them free.

—Jessica Wilson

Alone to Die

Alone and frightened,
Terror felt inside,
How the pain grows,
I've no place to hide.
Out of my eye
Falls a tear,
The pain grows stronger,
I'm lost in fear.
Lost without you,
Alone at night,
My spirit leaves,
Without a fight.
Lost without love,
Without a close friend,
None hear my cry,
So life comes to an end.

—Andrea Butler

Untitled

I would rather love
Than die. But I'd
Rather die than not be loved.
If time can tell,
Why does it lie so often. . .
And get away with it.
If I had a choice,
I'd fly to the heavens.
If I didn't I'd drive.
Most like the night
Because it's as black
As their sorrow.
As I watch the sky, the stars
Twinkle and wink at me. But
They're only flirting.
The moon stands still. He says
Nothing, just keeps his
Solemn gaze fied upon our troubled world.

—Evie Alburas

Streets

D.C. Streets are meaner now
Than those of by-gone days,
No longer safe to walk at will;
Some streets are like a battlefield.
Where people scurry to and fro
And wonder where they ought to go,
Imagining if they do, they'll meet
Unsavory persons on the street.
Youngsters with no regard for life,
Who boldly tote a gun or knife,
Who scheme to rob, or rape, and kill,
To please some drug-addictive thrill.
Will citizens learn to take a stand?
And help to turn the tide;
To deter vicious acts for drugs,
To stop the homicide.
If government can only find,
A right course to proceed;
A way to thwart such senseless crime
To curb the addicts' need.

—Carolyn P. Gibson

My Mom

I loved my mom more
than words could ever say
I knew she would die sooner or later
but not this way.
She died of Cancer
Such a deadly disease
Oh God
Why can't you bring her back
Please?
I never pictured her dying
Until I saw her in her bed
She was in a coma
Isn't that a dread?
But she was my mom
And that she still is
I will never forget her
as long as I live.

—Kathleen Carroll

Thank You

My little baby, my short cool one,
Thank you for forgiving me for what I
    have done.
You make me laugh, you make me cry,
Without your love, a part of me would die.
I know it will take a while for you to trust
    me again,
I know it will take a while for our love to
    be as it had been.
But I know we'll make it, for our love is
    strong
And I know we'll last forever long.

—Karri Smith

Thank You Lord

Thank you Lord, for sending Johnny to
    me
Thank you, for letting him be all I wanted
    him to be
I know his love is real and true
But most of all, he believes in You.
It means a lot to know he cares
And that if I need him, he'll be there
He shares the good times and the bad
He loves me rather I'm happy or sad.
I love Johnny, Lord, with all my heart
And I know this love won't fall apart
I know it's sent from up above
Blessed by God, with all His love.

—Gloria J. Shores

Sunshine Growing Love

You're the sunshine,
that brightens my day.
you're the light in the darkness,
that never fades away.
you're the glow that makes our love grow,
our love is forever so never let go.

— Jennifer Jones

A Phoenix

A phoenix is a mystical bird
That brings good life when it is heard.
Rose from ashes and started a new life;
This bird is sacred as an indian's knife.
The legend says that this bird burned
    itself,
And rose from the ashes all by himself.
It's symbol stands for prosperity,
To achieve and succeed in activity.
Like you and me we symbolize the
Phoenix that gives new life among us.

—Alison Martin

Music

Hello music lovers
That brings us all together.
Music is a part of life.
Without music we'll always lie.
Music brings out the best in people.
Music even makes people rest.
Everyday you can dance.
Every year you can hear and care.
Music is never the same
Cause it always changes
As we age.
But music will never die
So you don't have to say goodbye.

—Andrea Hyun

Diamond Dust

My feelings are not like sand,
That can be scattered in the wind.
My heart is not a stone,
That can be dropped and forgotten.
My mind in not glass,
That can be shattered under pressure.
My life is not a string,
That can be cut.
My soul is diamond dust,
Precious and dear, like the finest riches in
    the world.
My eyes are windows,
To make you understand,
What makes up the diamond dust among
    the sand.

—Heidi M. Zumbrun

The Sky

The sky is like a painted picture
That can never be captured again
In the sky the sun rises and falls
It leaves a beautiful pattern of colors
That dyes deeper as the sun sets
The moon that fills the sky at night
With all of its stars and galaxies unknown
Is like a light that keeps us protected
The clouds like cotton swifting through
　the sky
Give us ideas of imagination
Shooting stars are what we like to see
To give us luck for the future
This is a place of exploration
Just waiting to be discovered
By someone who likes to daydream
Who likes to take on new adventure
To venture into the sky
Into the jar of endless journeys awaiting

—Christine Kronmiller

The Worm Money

He ran out to catch the worms
That crawled and slithered after rain.
He plunked them in his little box,
The purpose was to sell for gain.
Fishermen would pay the price
For such a juicy bit of bait;
And one by one the little boy
Watched his stash accumulate.
Until, one day, he had enough
To buy the long awaited prize,
But in school that day, he could see
A sadness in his teacher's eyes.
He brought the roses early,
With gruff shyness he said, "Here,"
"I bought 'em with my worm money."
And he thought he saw a tear.

—Janice L. Harrison

A Dream

A world out there is full of dreams
that dance before your eyes,
tantalizing your every emotion, building
　to the skies,
lunging forward, grasping,
with a shaky hand,
all the wishes in your eyes,
the heart, racing in time,
as eyes look far beyond,
anticipation of every thought,
admiration of what is fond.
Blind to limitation, let nothing stop you
　now.
Conquer goals without the words of others
descending beneath your brow.
These thoughts of yours are glistening,
they have a golden gleam.
What you have inside,
will be forever your dream.

—Erin Duffy

Neurosis II

I have a small neurosis
That follows me around
And when it is convenient
I take it on the town.
Sometimes I will fool my friends
And hide it for awhile
But when it is convenient
I bring it out in style.
I like my small neurosis
It's such a soothing friend
And when it is convenient
I'll put it to an end.
When it's convenient.

—Anne Holmberg

Urgency

Are my thoughts and words a curse
That forsaken would better be than verse;
And is a dream of love no more than this?
Yet, I would think of it as gentle kissed
Whose petals long have tender wept
For rain to spill and touch caress
A flower bed long lonely slept.
Would this vain world about me reel
To then think such as passion to reveal
Some need or want or urgency within;
Of songs and music, those whispers of the
　sweet
Are mine and in my heart to beat;
To live, to breathe, if love be lonely
　meant,
It ever will be dreamt.

—Joanne Roma

Beauty

Beauty, like the apple
that grows on the tree,
is something within
and not what you see.
If the apple is bad when bitten into,
it won't really matter
what the cover could do.
The same with a person
who has beauty and grace,
if her heart isn't kind
then she has no place.
For beauty is something
not everyone has,
It's the kindness of the heart
that cheers those who are sad.

—Jewellee Mailer

Perish the Great Red Walls

Perish the great red walls
That have been imprisoned in these halls.
For if this is the darkness to remain
Then all our glories have been in vain.
But force yourself to see the light
For a thousand strings couldn't hold the
　night,
And if one hand held such a power
Then within the earth's mouth we shall be
　devoured.
Yet look once more through the oval glass
Look toward the future not the past,
Forget the speeches of ominous tongue
And render not your victims from which
　you run.

—Kim Litzenberg

My Prayer

I once prayed to God
That he would send to me
Someone to share my life with
And together we would always be.
God answered my prayer
When I met you,
And from then I promised
To be forever true.
You took my heart away
With your style and grace,
And one look in your eyes
Could always make my heart race.
I thank you God
For answering my prayer
And for sending someone
Who will always care.

—Aimee Braeutigan

I'm A Lily

I am a lily who known
that I am not a rose.
A Lily that returns again and again
during its life-span
to beautify the earth
of my birth.
I have my special color;
Another lily has another;
Each in his own way
will brighten up the day.
I admire the rose
who in yonder garden grows;
But I am content to be
A lily who has a place you see.
my purpose is to be
the best Lily I can be;
As long as God grants me life to live;
I have what I am to give.

—Eva O. Scott

My Boyfriend

There's a special someone
that I care a lot for-
I want to be with him
for ever more.
When I'm with him
my heart is a glow—
I like him so much
and it shows.
This person is
so dear to me—
I always want him near
as many can see.
This person means more
than anything else to me-
This person is my boyfriend
and his name is STEVE!

—*Elizabeth Daugherty*

My Prayer

Lord, when I was young, I didn't know
That I could lean on you and trust you so.
I walked a Rocky Road, a Barren Land,
It took a lot of tears to understand,
That you could lead me safely through the night,
And light my path when sorrow blinds my sight.
Please guide, dear Lord, each step that I take.
And overlook mistakes that I will make.
Then when it comes the time for me to go,
I pray my life will leave an afterglow.

—*Jessie Ruth Barnhart*

Best Friends

The other day I realized
That I didn't have any friends.
It really bugged me that I had a
Best friend one second,
The next, it was all gone.
I had nobody to trust.
I'll never have a friend like you.
You meant everything to me.
You were like a sister to me.
You might remember when we got
In a fight we made up that day,
We put the past behind us.
Just remember the good times
We had together.
I'll never forget you!

—*Carrie Heckman*

Forever

I sorrow at the solitude
That I feel inside me,
Knowing I had you and lost.
Grief seems to intertwine with my mind,
Thoughts are fused together.
Mingled,
Diverse yet single,
They will always be forever.

—*Donnajean Cangelose*

Shameled

I feel such shame,
That I treated our love,
Just like a game.
Now we're apart,
And I've gone and broken my heart.
When will I realize,
That I can't live on lies?
Next time. . .
What will I do,
When I say we're through.
Like spilling tea from a cup,
It's going to be my broken heart,
That I'll pick up.

—*Amy Miller*

A Dream Remembered

A dream remembered is a sweet thing,
That is a as lovely as the spring.
It is as green as cloves in a field
And happiness is what they weild.
It takes a hold
And never lets go,
Of your mind
Those precious dreams like gold.
They stay in your head
And play o'r and o'r
But that is what they are for
To be remembered,
To be cherished
Forever to remain unblemised
From the cruel facts of life.
A dream remembered helps in strife.

—*Dawn Lynne Lingenfelter*

Friendship, the Bond of Sunshine

Being a friend is a bond of sunshine
That is only broken by a full moon.
To anything or anyone else, it is unbreakable,
It glows like a candle in the night.

—*Briita Halonen*

Untitled

Today the sun is shining and the sky is blue,
That is what made me want to see you
As I looked at the grave where you lay,
All I wanted to do was run away
I wanted to scream, I wanted to cry
It is not true, it's all a lie
But then I stopped and looked around
I did not see death, but where true life is found
I know your physical body is there,
But your spirit is not-it's in the air
Now your pain and your suffering are all gone away
And that is what helps me on days like today.

—*Anita Pierce Daughtry*

Until You Came

In the beginning I thought that love was just the feelings that one person had for another.
That is why I gave him all the love and support that I could give.
I had oh so much hope that someday he would feel the same way.
And then one day he just all of a sudden turned me away.
I was hurt and helpless, I didn't know what to do with myself, until you came!
You came into my life at just the right time.
You picked me up when I was feeling down, and then you took me out on the town.
You made me see just how love is really suppose to be.
It is not just about feelings, it is about having fun and being happy too.
For all of this you have given me, I thank you.
And I would also like to say that I really do: Love You!

—*Amy Polk*

The Flowers

Sometimes as I grow older, I look around
    and see,
That life is like the flowers at the onset of
    the spring.
The sun pokes out and brings its warmth,
    the flowers begin to grow.
Innocently believing they've seen the last
    of winter's snow.
And then, unforseen, the mercury starts
    to drop once more,
The frost comes down and covers the
    flowers to uneven the score.
As the flowers struggle to keep searching
    for the sun,
They somehow realize their battle has
    only just begun.
Every now and then they hang their heads
    as if in defeat,
All along storing up their energy, only in
    retreat.
Finally after weeks of battle, the flowers
    seem to win,
They perk up their heads and bring their
    colors out again.
As passersby glance at them, they break a
    little smile,
Knowing that the worst is over if only for
    awhile.
Yet they know, in the back of their minds,
    bad times will still come.
They also know of the good times, for the
    flowers have given some.

—*Kimberly C. Cook*

Pleasing One Another

Love is something two people share,
When they need someone to really care.
They give eachother their very own
    hearts,
To love, to cherish, and to never part.
Though sometimes love is sharing to,
To please one another throught and
    through.
But love is also fighting with you,
Since forgiving you is not so new.
But the special thing we two lovers share,
I something no one else could ever tear.
Since loving, fighting, and crying with
    you,
Is part of our love that will always be true.

—*Paula Beck*

The Light

I saw it from a distance
That light shined so bright
I stood behind my window
and watched it through the night.
But later it became weary
The light began to fade
The night got dark and dreary
It turned a dimmer shade.

—*Kirstin Ann Seelos*

Love

I know it's love
That makes me feel so good.
I'd spend every hour with you
If only I could.
You make me feel so warm
Like a fire's soft glow.
Sometimes I wonder,
Does he really know?
I love you so much;
Let me make myself clear.
For as long as you want me,
I'll always be here.
So hold me and kiss me,
The way you always do
For then I'll know
That you will love me too!

—*Cori Lynn Davis*

I Love You

Everyone loves to hear those three special
    words,
That makes you light up like a light bulb,
"I Love You"
Nobody knows how just three little words
Can make you tingle all over
It's like magic
When you're feeling blue here comes
Those three words again,
"I Love You."
Over and over you wonder how just
Three little words can do all of this
Just keep it a mystery to you and me,
But when you see someone who you
Think might need that tingle,
Just light up their life with
Those three little words,
"I Love You"
It may be a mystery but don't keep it a
    secret.

—*Jennifer Myers*

Habits

Habits are things you do.
That mother says your not to.
Theres biting your nails and smacking
    your lips, drinking cokes and eating chips.
Theres watching TV and not enough
    sleep.
There's talking on the phone and not
    brushing your teeth.
Believe it or not I'll tell you true, my
    daddy has to tell me too.

—*Kathryn Lunsford*

A Friend in You

I have found a friend in you,
That no one else can top.
A friend whose love goes on and on,
And will never stop.
A friend that knows me inside out,
And still loves me without a doubt.
With all the silly things we've done,
We sure have had a lot of fun.
With all the time we've spent together,
There are still memories left to gather.
You're the kind of friend who shares,
And lets me know you really care.
The friendship that you give to me,
Is more that I could ever be.
Through my life I'll strive to be,
The kind of friend you are to me.

—*Darla Fossum*

In our World

In our world is pollution
That nobody can seem to find a solution.
In our world there are many fights
Some people don't even get their rights.
In our world there are drugs
It would be nice if we just gave out hugs.
Our world is not perfect as you can see
But we'll just have to do better for you
    and me.

—*Cinamyn Talltree*

The Lighthouse

On a hill stands the lighthouse
that overlooks the bay.
It stands strong and secure
with no signs of decay.
My Lord is the light
that from harm keeps me safe.
My trust is in Him,
not by sight, but by faith.
Praise God for that lighthouse
or I'd have gone astray.
If it weren't for that lighthouse,
I would have lost my way.
The light in the tower,
it burns steady and bright.
And no matter how far I wander,
I'll always keep it in sight.

—*D. H. Kelly*

Love Always

When you're faced with times of trouble,
That seem to double and double,
Don't give up, head in hand.
Your problems really aren't so grand.
Look at what needs to be done,
And work each one out one by one.
Life goes on. Why don't you?
Please tell me why you feel so blue.
Though times seem bad, too bad to bear,
Please come to me. I will be there.
Learn to hold your head high.
Believe me, you don't want to die.
Better, happier times lie ahead.
Remember all that I have said.
No more troubles or worries,
And my good friend, just love always.

—Carissa Sperry

The Magnificent Seven

We roared into space and reached for the stars
that seemed so near, yet so far
This was the hour—our shining hour
yes, our hearts were full of glee
We did'nt know. . . we couldn't know
that so soon we would be free
to roam, to see, to search the universe
The message was clear—the ending terse
Don't shed your tears, you we love the most
just remember this was our vision
Now hand-in-hand we go forward as planned
to fulfill our final mission.

—Dorothy M. Ferguson

Back Home

Once a year
That special time rolls around,
When family and friends
Visit new ground.
Pets and good friends
Are sometimes left behind,
A picture or teddy
Go to remind.
$The trip might start slow,
But it picks up speed
Later in the week
And more time is in need.
Whether beach or mountains
Or city Rome,
The time comes fast
To make that trip back home.

—Kevin Patrick

Communion

I had a sip of wine
That tastes like dew.
Each nectar nymph of jonquil bliss
Mesmer'd me and tantalized my soul.
I had a sip of wine
Of such bouquet,
Its fragrance balmed my heart.
So redolent, this musk—like sheen,
Like potpourri of myrrh and whey.
It webbed my heart, my soul, my mind,
Into a tranquil somnolence.
I had a sip of wine.
Each whiffy, bubbly talisman
Wafts magic arts of sorcery,
Entwined, enmeshed my flaccid mind.
Its tingling aura succumbs my soul
'Tis God's vintage—nature's wine.

—Albert Stanley Knowles

Summer Love

The sparkles in your eyes
That tell me you care.
And the soft summer breeze
Blowing through your hair.
The tiny little shells that
Lay upon the sand.
And the feel of love I get by
Every touch of your hand.
The gentle water washing
Upon the shore.
And the hopes of us together
I'll wish forevermore.

—Angie Cavanaugh

Birthday Greetings

This is the happiest day,
That the year has shown,
Never has the air been so fresh,
Never had we a brighter morn.
I send you this greeting,
With a heart so warmly beating,
Full with thoughts of you,
And with it deep love too.
I send thee this message,
On wings of love,
Having neither form nor shape,
But only imagination's silver dove.
I pray to the almighty to repeat,
This happy day again and again,
Binding us nearer and nearer,
By the beautiful, mysterious and eternal chain.

—Arya Bhushan

A Proposal

To have no life.—To be your wife.
That was the question you proposed to me.
In an old, dirty, dingy, restaurant,
You asked me to be your wife,
Much like you'd ask a women to be your maid.
You stated that I fit the requirements.
You needed the job filled and therefore it was
Mine. No Flowers. No words of love. And no ring.
The man always proposed on bended knee,
The Sun shined, birds sang, a gentle breeze blew
And the two lovers embraced sealing destiny.
True love instead of a business arrangement.
A marriage of convenience. The words sound
So ugly. How could any one settle for that.
So my answer is No to you and your
Meaningless world. A marriage without love
Is no union at all.

—Cherie Birks

My Vows to You

On this special day,
That we'll share together.
I give you my vows,
For now and forever.
I give you my heart,
Through all things we'll share,
I give you my promise,
I'll always be there.
I give you my love,
My whole life long,
When you're feeling weak,
I'll try to be strong.
You are my life now,
And forever will be.
Our lives are as one,
Through eternity.

—Debi Berry

Why Believe in Love

I believed in love so much
That when the wind blew
I swore it was his touch
But when the wind slowed to a few
I knew my heart needed a crutch.
I believed in love so dear
That when I was alone
A single, sad, little tear
Would tell me his love was shown.
Once I didn't believe in love
When birds would fly
I swore they weren't doves
I wanted to just die
I decided not to believe anymore.
What was the use of it?
I was being ignored.
It always turned into a crying fit
Love will never walk through my door!

—Kelly J. Sturm

Broken

Broken is my heart,
That you once had beating.
Broken is the promise,
You told me you'd keep.
A broken promise,
Leads to a broken heart.
A broken heart,
Leads to a dead end.
Once a promise is broken,
It can never be fulfilled.
Once a heart is broken,
It could never love again.
When you told me,
You grabbed my heart.
I could never love anyone,
As much as I loved you.
No one could ever break my heart,
Like you did.

—Kerrie Ann Kubinski

You Tore My Life Apart

I knew the day I met you
That you'd only break my heart
You knew what you were doing
As you tore my life apart.
You knew that you were lying
When you told me that you cared
You saw the tears of pain I cried
Wishing you'd be there.
So now that it has ended
And I'm facing all the facts
I know that you don't love me
But still I want you back
But I know that I won't happen
I know you love her so
I know you never really cared
Enough to let her go.

—Joanne Crosby

Love Me

Hold me close
That's all I ask
My mine embraces
Our memories past.
If I could have
Just one wish now
It would be to
Have somehow
Your love.

—Annette Bay

Forgotten

A hug, a kiss, and a wave of good-bye,
That's all I have to remember you by.
You left me no name no memories at all.
No pictures, or letters, or a telephone call.
Was I a weed you wanted to cede.
Or was I a child you just didn't need.
A hug, a kiss, and a wave of good-bye,
That's all I have to remember you by.

—Jessica Juarez

The Bird

A bird so free as it flies through the air,
That's all we can see, a bird with no care.
We wish and hope to be like that bird,
But we don't see his true life,
He struggles for his life, hoping not to die,
Searching for survival, yet all we see is his lie.
A bird so free as it flies through the air,
That's all we see, a bird with no care.

—Kristin Olsen

Love

Love is a thing
That's better than gold
Not an item
That's bought or sold.
Love is a dream
Of me and you
It's a dream
And together we made it come true.
Love is something
you fall into
It's the way you feel
It can't be used.
Love is something
That two people share
you and I
About each other we care.
Love is a feeling you don't want to end
The best way to start
Is to start out as friends.

—Jennifer Hayden

I Want Peace

Boom! Bang!
That's not a sound of peace.
It's war!
Peace is silent, beautiful, calm and
  everything else you can dream of.
It's also what you have in your soul that
  you share with others.
Boom! Bang!
Boom! Bang!
Stop!
Shh. . .
Listen. . .
Listen to the sound of silence and peace.
See how wonderful peace is.
If only some people in the world had
  peace in their souls. . .
Then my friends. . .peace will be a song of
  beauty that will last forever.

—Emlyn Anderson

Life

Life is something,
That's not always fair,
There are no big bowls of cherries,
But lots of despair.
Life is something,
That everyone lives,
No matter who you are,
You still have to conquer,
Your greatest fears.
Life is something
That is always loved,
By me, by you and even a dove.
Life is something,
That we sometimes regret,
But all and all,
It will turn into the best.

—April Foster

Children's Laughter

Loud laughters of joy,
That's what I hear,
When all the children play.
Screams of happiness,
Float through the air,
Just like clouds on their way.
All different sizes,
All different shapes,
They learn to love and care.
That's the way it should be,
For people everywhere.

—Amanda Wheeler

What to Write

What should I write in this poem,
That's what I'm thinking of at my home.
I think I might have poet's cramp,
Maybe I'll write about a stamp.
Then I thought that's way too dull,
Why can't I think of something in this
    thick skull?
Come back tomorrow, maybe I'll know,
But not while I'm watching my favorite
    show.
Wait a sec, here's a thought,
I'll write about an astronaut.
What did you say, it's time to eat?
Great, because my fingers are beat!
Just a minute, I'm on a roll,
Oh, we're having my favorite casserole.
Well I'm sorry, I've got to rush,
Before my dinner turns to mush!

—*Becky M. Rachoner*

It Can't Happen to Me

It can't happen to me
That's what they all say,
But when it does happen
Some girls run away.
Babies are born
To teenagers too,
It can happen to me
And it can happen to you.
When you have sex
Please be very careful,
Because having a baby
Can be very painful.
When you think that you're pregnant
You get really scared,
You realize that when it comes to
    protection
You never really cared.
So when you have sex
You better think twice,
Because sometimes the consequences
Aren't very nice.

—*Joann Ridenour*

The Star

Follow the star to Bethelehem,
That's what they said,
Because that's where Christ was born,
And Christmas all began.

—*Amanda Wherry*

Suicide

Suicide-when love subsides
That's when your heart dies.
When you have decided to end your life
End all the depression, all of the strife.
Put an end to all the hurting, the hate, the
    maddness
The rage and then, the never ending
    saddness.
All it would take is the shot of a gun
A knife to your chest-you'd see no more
    sun.
No more rain, no more tears,
No more hiding, no more fears.
Ending the pain with some simple touch
Ending what hurts you so much.
Watching down on the rest of the world
The reactions of my death
Tears, fears, people gasp for breath.
I'm sorry I caused some of you pain
    because I did the main.
But I had to do it, my heart blue instead
    of red,
So now here I am, higher than ever, I am
    dead

—*Amanda Hayden*

What is Love?

Tell me you care.
Will you be there.
Show me you still love me.
Why did you have to hurt me?
You just up and left me.
Will somebody please help me forget this
    feeling.
Are you there to care?
Try and reach out and share your heart
    with me.
Oh baby was it all just a dare?
If you leave me say you'll remember me.
Just don't forget me.
Baby, please believe me,
I love you.

—*Ruth Latchaw*

The Night

The wind is soft,
The air is light,
All is calm
Throughout the night.
But how would we know
For we are asleep,
And we think of sweet things
When we are asleep.
When we are asleep,
The flowers weep
And the owls sing their songs.
So when the wind is soft
And the air is light,
All is not as calm
As we may think
It is throughout the night.

—*Heather Wood*

A Moment Of Saddness

As I walk out my door,
the air stands still around me.
The trees seem to die from the weight of
of the snow on its thin branches.
The sky darkens.
As I look up,
The sparkle in my eyes slowly fades.
The fish in the pond stare up at me with
    cold bitterness.
Saddness.
This feeling of saddness,
Like a thick fur coat.
Slowly I walk back to my house.
As I go in, I see my father look at me.
He tells me he loves me, then his eyes
    close.
He is asleep.
Saddness pulls me into the cold air of
    darkness.

—*Clance Jackson*

Touching

My world around me cannot be yours
The air that I breathe and things I touch
It's a world I have made from pieces and
    bits
The world that you live in cannot be mine
But we can share parts of our worlds with
    each other
I can share a love that is only mine
I can share kind words from my thoughts
    and feelings
In all of this, I can give you parts of my
    world
But you can never take it from me
I cannot be you and you cannot be me
But in our sharing of each other
Our worlds touch

—*Cricket Mapes*

Quiet Voice

My own mind would not serve me well.
The answer, no friend could seem to tell.
I searched in books and asked advice.
All these, my quest would not suffice.
Poor harried mind! It could not rest.
I think it tried too hard and long.
And then, when I had really "done my
    best,"
It still was poor, and almost surely wrong.
I listened to my quiet voice to see
If there was communion, He with me;
And there I got my answer for today.
How often it is simplest just to pray.

—*Betty Fern Thackeray*

What Price is Freedom

"What price is freedom?" I ask of you.
The answer to this is known by few.
Is it silver or gold, or precious gems?
I say no, it is the souls of men.
What price shall I pay when my brother calls,
From far away countries with darken halls?
I'll pay silver or gold, or precious gems,
To free the souls of all these men.
How fortune has smiled upon my face.
That I should be born in these United States.
A place of liberty and justice for all,
A place we pray God will never fall.
I say to you, o' luckiest of men,
Hold your head high and wear a big grin.
For you are your country and your country is you,
And we'll show the world that we're yet not through.
O', God of my country, sweet land of liberty
What price is freedom, tis but you and me.

—Franklin K. Pierce

I Thank Dear God

I thank dear God for the trees,
The beautiful butterflies and the bees,
And all the snow so wonderful white,
And the fireflies that fly by night.
I also thank God for the sky,
The color of blue and birds that fly,
The beautiful colors of a hat,
And the wonderful wonders of a cat.
I thank dear God for sunlight,
And the beautiful moon that shines by night,
The grass so shiny, soft and green,
Like the roses that bloom in spring.
I also thank God because you see,
He also made my family and me.

—Amber Edsall

The Special Flower

The flower among flowers catches my eye,
The beauty of it I cannot describe.
The radiant rays shine from the sun above,
Shine upon it as if they were in love.
The magic of this special flower goes straight to my heart,
For I know the sun and the flower never will part.

—Chrissy Udell

Spring

In the spring the birds are chirping,
The bees are buzzing, and the air is filled with love.
The precious flowers bloom so beautifully
That their heavenly scents combine to make one
Mysterious smell drifting through the breeze.
The raindrops glisten on the odd-shaped leaves
That have fallen to the ground waiting
To dry up in the summer time.

—Jennifer Sussman

The Real You

You were the world to me,
The best, as far as I could see,
Well, I just found out.
I wasn't looking very far.
The person I knew was kind and caring.
You were always there and always sharing.
But the person I discovered this afternoon,
Was far from what I knew.
You had become coldhearted and insensitive.
You weren't understanding.
You weren't even caring.
You used to be reliable.
You used to be comforting.
And I want to be forgiving as you would have done before.
Instead, I find myself in tears.
And I've got to get up.
I've got to switch gears and go on with my life.
But it's so hard to accept the real you.

—Emily Ann Lee

Childhood Memories

I remember
The best days
Running
Through open fields
Carefree
Alive.
I remember
The best times
Happy
Without a worry
Carefree
Alive.

—Jenny Rinard

Summer

Summer is here,
The best time of the year.
That people enjoy so—much you see,
The time for going to the Beach, Fishing, Picnics, Barbecues, or even watching Sports on T.V.
This is the season, we have a lot to do,
Like going Camping, Hiking or even to the Zoo.
School is out, and Vacation time is here,
Time to spend with Family and Friends we hold so dear.
I wish that Summer would stay forever, as long as it's not too Hot, everyday,
So then we could see all the beautiful things that we have along the way,
Like Mountains and Lakes, and Gardens in bloom,
And Trees and Flowers all in tune.
Beautiful colors all around,
Some in the air, and some on the ground.
Birdies singing a pretty song,
As we go Strolling along.
The Music is all around us, If only we could here,
And cherish these things, year after year.

—Helen McCoy

The Moon

Gazing in the midnight sun,
The blazing light has just begun.
Looking up beyond the stars,
Looking down upon the cars.
The midnight sun that has just begun,
Has another name, another one.
Listening to the beautiful tune,
The midnight sun is just the moon.

—Deana Cincotta

Lucky One

In a field of stars we lie.
The brightest of them all.
Together are we in the air.
Together we will fall.
Far above the earth we fly.
We see no peace, but war.
Evil, wicked things appear
Upon the earth's ground floor.
For no one is there ever peace,
But only things they mar.
I'm glad I am a lucky one.
Im glad I am a star.

—Jayme Warnock

What a Day

The alarm goes off at 7 o'clock.
The button on the toaster doesn't lock.
The two fried eggs were soft and runny,
The milk was warm, the toast was crummy.
I ran out the house ten minutes late
And as usual the bus didn't wait.
I walked the distance tired and worn.
When I reached the school I saw that my skirt was torn.
I walked into class half an hour tardy;
The way everyone was laughing you would think I was Laurel and Hardy!
I looked down to avoid laughs
And low and behold my socks didn't match.

—*Jennifer Issendorf*

Snow

The white glistening snowflakes slowly drift to the ground.
The children play with apple-red cheeks and icy toes.
The warm aroma of hot chocolate slowly drifts through the air.
It tickles the children's frozen noses as they grow colder.
The daylight is rapidly disappearing behind the dark grey clouds,
That look like dirty cotton candy.
The children finally go inside and go to sleep.
And all that is left in the morning is a small clump of snow.

—*Katherine Sloan*

On The Porch

The warmth of the sun,
The chill of the breeze.
And the frosty coldness of the cement,
Below my feet rest a world that breathes.
The sun in my eyes,
The trees almost bare
Warmth and coldness,
All at one time.
The continous hum of the highway,
The grass still green.
As I sit many sounds engulf me,
Planes above,
Cars at curb-side.
The leaves crackling to the gentle breeze,
As I sit alone on the porch.

—*Kerri Crowne*

The Bag Lady

An old woman is lying on a park bench
The city newspaper is covering her feet
Her clothes are tattered
Her skin is wrinkled and dirty
There is a hole in her left shoe
Her meals are the leftovers
That people throw in dumpsters and trash barrels
She is lonely but talks to the birds and sometimes to herself
Her home is a park in the city
She lives near a busy street
She doesn't have a bed like you and I
She sleeps on park benches
occassionally in the winter she'll try to find a place near a heat vent to sleep
She is one of the many people who are homeless, she is reffered to as a baglady

—*Christina Wallace*

Baby

Sunshine and blue skies
The color of a baby's eyes
Promises of tomorrow
Pray there will be no sorrow
For our children will carry on. . .
Be strong little baby
Grow big and strong for me
Make the world see
How careless we've become
And save the earth before it's gone
Blue skies and sunshine.

—*Julie Ann Walter*

Rainbow

The colors of love,
The colors of hope,
Are in the rainbow
If you look.
If your eyes are
Nimble and weak,
Look up
By believing.
Look up and see
The stripes of colors
In the beautiful
Blue sky
And enjoy the nature
Of the earth
As you look up.

—*Klara Kastal*

Beaches

The beach is pleasing,
The cool breeze is easing,
I like to relax on the sandy shore.
But, more and more begins
To darken with pollution
And oil in the soil of the sea.
The beach should be forever,
But never will it last with
All the past trash, and never
Again will we see a wave crash.

—*Jennifer A. Howorth*

The Broccoli

The world was wickedly wimply
The country cuddled the cad
Friends fobbed flirty fatcats
So society sought to be sad.
It all began with the broccoli
Whose life was exuberant and wise
The broccoli was fickle and furtive
Which led to the world's demise.
The world embellished the broccoli
With bright brass bells and blue bows
The broccoli, in turn, gave the world a burn
As it exploited the world's friends as foes.
The broccoli lost all its friendships
As the world began to realize
The broccoli was really a sly guy
Who pulled the wool over our eyes.

—*Christi Kapp*

Untitled

The Kaleidoscope of hearts is a special place to be.
The crystals capture the light and spread its mood throughout the tunnel.
With each little turn you see something new, but the love is always there.
The chandelier makes it an exciting place, reflecting many lights.
Sometimes I like it there, but the bulbs are all burned out now.
The candlelight makes it a romantic place, everything so hazy and soft.
It's a nice place to be, but now I find no candles.
The blue light makes it a sad place, casting the mood in dark and violet tones.
That is where I am right now.
The sunlight makes it a real place, it masks nothing and shows all.
That is the best place to be, it seems, and I'll be back there soon.

—*Dawna Capps*

Dedicated to Jim and All My Friends Who Are Always There

The mist rises to allow me sight
The dawn emerges from the night
There's waves that crash against the rocks
And tremendous ships rest at the docks
Seagulls carol from up above
Their joyous songs I've grown to love
I lay upon the warm safe sand
And calmly sift it through my hand
The morning sky, so blue, so clear
Is a blanket of shelter to all life here
Up and up the sun floats higher
It seems to set the sky on fire
The brilliant rays pour into my eyes
I squint to peer up at the skies
I find this such a comforting place
The wind dries tears falling down my face
I never feel the need to run or hide
For in life there's always a peaceful side

—Debbie Kosinski

On Your Own

How does it feel to be loved
Yet feel unwanted too?
Everytime you're smacked around
You ask yourself why they do it to you.
You'd prefer to make the smallest mistake
Even spilling a glass of milk.
And heaven forbid you come home with a F.
You know they'll really be thrilled.
In school, you were always a loner,
Because you were so different from the others.
You grew up thinking your home was normal,
You even feared your friend's fathers and mothers.
Growing up was hard for you.
You had to do alot on your own.
But somehow you found the will to hang in there.
You're a fighter, you'll always be strong.

—Susan Obbagy

The Real Thing

I wish we were together
The days we are apart
Thoughts of you drift through my mind
There's no stopping once they start
I keep you in a memory
When we are away
Waiting for that one and only
Truly special day
I know that when you touch me
My body begins to shake
Quivering and shivering
With every move you make
We don't try to fool each other
Using some old line
Because when I say I love you
I know that you are mine

—Kerrilyn Kischer

The Lord's Gift of Light

As long as the Lord's light so shines upon me;
The devil's and dreariness shall never find me;
For the Lord gave us life, for that I do pray;
But the devil only gives painful deaths that the Lord helps us push away;
For the Lord wants to help us, to give us life eternal;
But the Devil wants us to die, to help him to kill;
The Lord gave us light to help to see;
But the Devil wants it night to hide his dark home;
For as long as the Lord's light so shines upon me;
The Devil's dark and dreariness shall never find me.
As I sit here, I sit here to pray;
I can't help to think that the Devil at one time could have had me slain;
I wish I could help some of those lost souls;
But I fear I'm too late to save them from him;
I still wonder how painful that could be;
But I've been helped, I'm no longer a lost soul;
I was saved that I may live to tell people this;
As long as the Lord is with me I will be safe forever.

—Corinne Schwartau

A Step in Time...

Waiting for the sun to shine
The dream of America.
Across the winding road
The look of life.
Backward ways of faded rainbows
The colors slip into the sky.
Nightfall behind the black curtains
The last temptation of society.
Tears well up in children's eyes
The silence is breaking.
Hearts are shattered into mirrored walls
The crashing sound of death,
But waiting
Waiting for the sun to shine
The lost thought to live again.

—Jennifer Cox

Dreams of Yesterday

Went away only to forget
The dreams of childhood
As if I could!
I came back to memories of how we met.
At the time not a care in the world.
It seems like days were hurled by.
Goodbye is not an easy thing to say for it is forever.
When you see me next I shan't be the same.
If our two paths don't ever cross, always remember my name.
Don't weep sorrowful tears for what used to be.
For time that seems like years is only days,
Soon enough thoughts of me shall be locked away.
They aren't forgotten for they're locked in your heart,
That is where I should stay.
Remember only our good times
Not have bitter fights
That used to keep me awake on a winter's night.

—Jessica James

Truth

I walk in the midst of an icy cold dream
While damp, chilling dew wets my skin.
I linger in shadows, in visions that seem
To motion my time to begin.
I move through the breeze like a whisper of song;
I shatter the silence with sighs.
I pass over bridges of evil and wrong,
Revealing my soul through my eyes.
I see in the distance a light from the past,
A brightness that breaks through my fear,
I reach for a moment of peace that will last;
As I stumble, I smile through a tear.
I touch my salvation with trembling hands;
I question which life I should lead.
I learn I must do what subconscious commands
So my heart, soul and mind may succeed.

—Melanie S. Andes

Cloudy Day in Phoenix

Quiet, somewhat heavy
The ever-present sunlight gone;
Different, this slightly brooding greyness.
The sky; not hot, stark, blue
But scudded up with fat, slow, clouds,
Patiently pensive and rain-wondering.
Stillness in the trees; leaves
Rest in windless meditation;
Present only to the not-yet-storm time.
Hushed, and with movements slowed,
Waiting, I turn my gaze within
To face my inner storm.
Ah! Feel the wind!

—Jeanne M. O'Craigham

Yesterday

I stand beside the window looking out at
  yesterday.
The faces and the feelings flowing
  through my mind.
Remembering the beauty, the tears, the
  hurts, the loves.
Stopping on each memory feeling each
  one out.
Unlocking all those tender feelings, held
  deep inside my heart.
Things that no one else can see, or hear,
  or feel or know.
Each memory brings back all those
  special feelings I once knew.
All those childhood dreams, all games
  that were so special long ago.
Making all those special plans that only
  friends can share.
So many warm, and tender moments only
  lovers know.
The years go by so quickly, and the
  memories pass so fast.
So hold onto every special thing you feel,
  before it slips away.
For tomorrow all to soon it seems becomes
  a yesterday.

—*Janet Lowry*

Somewhere Out There

There's got to be a place where dreams
  come true
Where everything is made of love and
  nothing blue.
Where you can be with the one you love.
And be in a cloud up above.
Where you can express your true feelings
With an affectionate hug
Or an intimate kiss
Maybe someday we will find that place
But before you do, you've got to believe in
  yourself
And your dreams will come true.

—*Melissa Miller*

The Perfect Pair

There is no point in hiding it,
The fact remains the same.
That there exists a special relationship,
Between us that cannot be explained.
We are always there for each other,
When sometimes things may go wrong.
Sharing the life together,
Our love is so strong.
There isn't a greater friendship,
Than the one that you and I share.
Continuing to trust each other,
We are a perfect pair.

—*Bernadette Torres*

Childhood Fear

Creeping slowly up steepened steps
The fear consumes the frame.
A hallway left before its time,
Tiny feet resist the motion.
Arrival at last, destination ahead
Heart pulsing the fear through shrinking
  veins.
A delicate arm stretches to claim the one
  hope of comfort left.
With one small "click" the light pursues
  the darkness.
A moment to peer, a second to breathe
Then darkness consumes the light.
Impulse rips, tiny feet scurry; one, two,
  three,
A flying leap of flinging child crashes to
  the bed.
No time to waste, a dive into sheets,
No noise, no motion, no beating or breath.
One more success, never an escape, from
  the monster beneath the bed.

—*Kerri Kristin Costley*

Happiness Is. . .

To me happiness is. . .
The feel of a soft rose petal
The rain on my face
And a cold crisp morning
Taking long walks in the country
Watching a sunset
And looking up at the stars
But most of all;
To me happiness is. . .
When I look in your eyes
The look on your face
And the way you make me feel

—*Angie Wilkie*

Scared

Scared,
The feeling of uneasiness
When that expected phone call
Does not come.
Seeing an open
Door or hearing
The creak of the house when
No one is home.
When the teacher
Hands back a test and you
Know you didn't
Study.
The feeling you get when you
Hear the clock ticking
Away and realize that the
Hours of life are
Slowly
Passing you by.

—*Christian Steele*

A Dream

We had a perfect romance
The feelings were so strong
I loved you, you loved me
Whatever could go wrong
You were everything I dreamed of
We almost were a team
How a man of your kind
Could bring this certain dream
It happened just one day
This day I dreaded so
The day you were to tell me
It was time for you to go
My heart broke into pieces
The tears they fell like rain
The feeling wasn't there
What had I to gain?
No other man is going to do
Though it does not seem
You have left me all alone
Was it just a dream?

—*Jill Lozon*

Remember

The moon, the stars, the gentle waves,
The fire burning, the empty cave.
We were there, we saw it all.
You and I, we'd never fall.
We'd love each other like we did then,
Forever and always, until the end.

—*Heather Higgins*

Candle in the Night

She held a candle in the night,
The flashing flame, the only light.
Shadowed images on the wall,
Exploding sparks with the wax crawl.
The fire grew greater, her face grew clear.
Upon her cheek was a salty tear.
A stream of pain beneath her eye,
A lonely weep, a helpless cry.
In a moment the room grew dark,
With one remain, a single spark.
Water and fire, a sizzling sound.
Her candle lit tear fell to the ground.

—*Hilary R. Ashworth*

Sunshine

When the rain stopped and the fog
    cleared,
The flowers will awaken and spread their
    cheer.
The sun will peer through the clouded sky,
And fill my soul of thoughts of you and I.
You've made me happy, and made my
    soul dance,
If it wasn't for you, we wouldn't have had
    that chance.
I hope you will keep me for quite
    sometime,
Because in my heart you'll always be
    mine.

—*Jennifer Collins*

Wondrous Power

Lord how infinite is thy power to create
    the beauty of a clear blue sky.
The fluffiness of the whitest cloud
To create the brightest of days and the
    mysteries of night.
The creator of all living things,
From the mysteries of the lightning bug
    whose light blinks off and on
To the creation of human life whose
    cycles we will never fully understand;
And in the midst of all your infinity sits I.
One of your created who can only sit in
    awe of all your wondrous and
    magnificent power.

—*Denise Washington*

24 Hours

The sun comes up,
The fog rolls in
The sun sets and the night grows dim.
The sky changes from blue, grey, to black.
The journeymen lay down their sacs.
The day has now been put to rest,
And it is time for all the blue birds to
    return to their
Nests.

— *Heather Patsis*

Nostalgia

Was it only yesterday that I watched
    them talk
The folks that seemed so old to me?
They spoke of days long since passed
No mention of the future or what could
    be.
I thought it odd that only things now gone
Could be the best there ever has been.
But now I can see as the years go by
How bright the past glows as the future
    grows dim.

—*John C. House*

The Life They Live

The rags they wear day after day,
The food they eat from can to can.
They're smart in so many ways,
Too bad they don't have a home like me.
I feel so bad to see a man or family
Not getting what they need.
If I had lots of money,
I would give so much away
To the people that starve day after day.

—*Jenny Smith*

I Know Two Seasons

Summertime is a brilliant miracle,
The gay companion of youth.
Now I have this wintry silence
Youth has to mellow
Lose the naive wisdom of playtime.
Now I know this wintry silence
The cardinal is more striking
The sunset is more inspiring.
Summertime is a brilliant memory
The gay miracle of youth.

—*Jane C. Storch*

Untitled

The way we met, I can't forget. . .
The gentle touch
I want so much
The sweeping smile
that warms all the while. . .
HAPPINESS-LOVE.
The way it end, we can't be friends. . .
Gone without a trace
like a mirage in a desert place.
So sudden, things begans to fade
Empty, lonely, I felt betrade. . .
ABANDONED-UNLOVE.
Through years, the hurt maintain to
    spread;
But how I try to mend it with needles and
    thread.
Look so sweet, but oh, so bitter, Love is
    never fair.
One gets hurt and the other one, does he
    care?

—*Adrienne-Diem Tran*

Untitled

Snowflakes fall all cold and white,
The green grass soon is covered.
Leaves are gone,
So are flowers.
All is at peace.
The car skids
Late at night
Since ice is on the road.
All that's left
Of that night
Is what's readable on the headstone.

—*Dayna Lawson*

Life

The misty rain fragranted
The ground with the
Smell of lilacs.
The air, refreshing and
Invigorating, encircled
Me with the knowledge
Of the world.
Yet I, alone and wanting,
Discarded my hopes
And dreams of the
Future, dwelling on the
Past.
Where could it all have gone,
The fun, the laughter,
The memories. It was
To be no more and
At last my anguish
Was over.

—*Angela Quinalty*

The Sands of Time

The sands of time are moving by don't let
    them go too quick
The hands of time are slowly starting,
    slowly starting to tick
The memories you had as a child. . .are
    slowly left behind
For the only memories that are left are
    the memories in your mind
The ones who knew you as a child, don't
    know you anymore
You are like a broken piece of
    time. . .washed upon the shore

—*Jody Fulton*

Until We Meet Again

Dusk befallen into night
The harvest moon actuating slowly
Upward in the east.
Clouds passing swiftly by, as not to
Distract the haunting moon's
 inquisitiveness.
An eerie feeling engrosses one's mind.
The night had finally elapsed but
The moon was still imminent in the west.
Now, greeting another adjunctive orb,
Facing each other
As earth's glory came to life.
Between them below was a
Welcoming guest spending
Morning pleasures with them. . .
Until each was to go
Their own separate way.

—*Krystyna M. Lowe*

Misery

As the days go by
The hatred grows
It's hard to understand why
No one knows.
Life is such hell
In this so called home
Where all should be well
Yet, misery still roams
The world seems to flash
As the tension grows worse
The two spirits must clash
Misery and creator converse.
The emotions are burning
The hurt dwells within
The table is turning
And misery now grins.

—*Cynthia Lee Manning*

The Night Song

The mockingbird flies to
The highest perch,
When the heat of the day
Is ore.
Lifting his head to his
God above,
He sings of old friends
Of yore.
He flits and flirts
Through the summer day
Tending to matters at hand.
But when the night
Breeze starts to cool,
He strikes up his
One bird band.

—*Alma J. Bridwell*

America, America

We love thee, we love thee
The home of the brave and the free
The home of all nationality
Where the big ball of gold comes up
Over the mountain in the early morn.
And the brids are singing good morning
A place to work, play, sing and cry
Under the same old sky
With the moon drifting by
America, we love thee, we love thee
Let freedom ring good and loud
Good and loud
For we are so proud of our flag
Red, white and blue
May it wave forever
In good U.S.A. so true

—*Emma B. Tousley*

The Game

Blindfolded with an azure scarf,
The hub of many outstretched arms,
He whirled, scarce pausing
At each proffered hand,
Until he came to hers
And caught and claimed it
As his own.
"Callouses", he softly said
In answer to our puzzled eyes,
And proudly drew her close
As all their wonderous brood
Descended in a shower
Of shining laughter.

—*Charlotte Tuttle Allen*

Everlasting Love

The pain,
The hurt,
The feeling and fears,
Leaves you alone at night in a bed of
 tears.
The crying,
The sorrow,
The heart filled with pain,
Those sunny days now turned into rain.
Those feelings of love that you once had,
Now up in smoke and flames to burn,
Those feelings now will never return.
You loved that one special person,
But now they're gone,
Taking away your heart ever-so-true,
Leaving you lonely, sad, and blue.
Those feelings that were there,
Those feelings that were shared,
Those feelings that once belonged in a
 fairy tale from above,
Now belong into the land of
 EVERLASTING LOVE.

—*Kim Anderson*

The Tower

Love locked in a tower
The key hid away
Picture a flower
On a warm summer's day
The tower heavy with gloom
The key found
And the flower ready to bloom
There is no sound.
The tower is awesome
The door is cracked
As the flower becomes a blossom
There is nothing to be lacked
The tower fades away
As the door opens wide
Picture a summers day
And love on the countryside.

—*Kenna Stout*

The Key to Your Heart

I have the key,
The key to your heart,
I'll cherish it, treasure it
So our love will never part.
I'll never let it go
I won't let it slip away,
If ever this should happen
A dear price I'd have to pay.
Your love is so important
I want it to last forever,
Please don't let it go
Please don't let it sever.
So we'll work together
To make it work out,
Just so our relationship
Will never be in doubt.

—*Jennifer Castro*

Forever Friends

Everyone needs one special friend,
The kind that will be there till the end.
Someone who is sad to see you cry,
The kind that will never tell you a lie.
Where do you find a friend like this,
Who wants to share your grief and all
 your bliss.
I want to be a forever friend to you,
And do everything a forever friend would
 do.

—*Crystal Punneo*

Down The Lonely Roads

I want to walk down the old lonesome
   brown dusty roads.
The lanes twist and turns around long
   rivers streams
A lonely road when you travel alone
   without you my love
Alone road for an old frailed spirit like
   me.
I walk along the twigs old woods vales
   trees tall and wide
I see today beauty you wished to see each
   day
You smile to view the wild grasses high
   green silks stalks
We laugh at birds loud trills sing choir
   song melodies
You walk with me along earths hilly red
   clays.
The beauty deep inside you is the beauty I
   see around me
Thy blue eyes sparkles in waters of low
   waves
Thy gentle voices rustless yellow big
   leaves to shade me
Your a geless love warms my aging hearts
   life.
You are companion as we walk on
   together down lonesome road
Two hearts as one as we stroll along
   Natures splenders
Once a lone road now a merry bright
   paths of sounds of success
I love you Ellen. We live together all my
   golden years of days.

—*Gertrude G. Jensen*

My Friend

The sun has gone down
The light is gone
The moon is now lightly
Shining the earth
But forever endlessly
Day or night
You're my friend
A friend who cares

—*Kelly Bierschbach*

Dinah

The little eyes that stare with wonder,
The little ears that stick up like tents
That sometimes have lights,
The little nose that is cold and wet,
The little tongue that cleanses the body,
The tiny head that tilts when it is curious,
Then finally when it is tired,
It will turn into a ball that is fast asleep,
And of course, I am speaking of my
   Dinah.

—*Carla L. Randall*

About Her

Her eyes are soft and gentle
The look they give is ever so warming
Her lips gracefully caress her beautiful
   smile
The moonlight dances with her long
   brown silky curls
Her tender skin radiates a soft warm glow
Her touch is so amazing
My body tingles from head to toe when
She runs her delicate fingers through my
   hair
Upon embrace, her passion flows to my
   heart
And takes control
When I feel her breath on my neck, my
   heart skips
Not one, but two beats
This power she has is one of a kind
I yield my body and soul for her to have
   and to hold
What I wouldn't give to have my heart
   skip two beats
Forever

—*Henry C. Kreske III*

Freedom's Voice

The highest point of your assumption,
The lowest of your degree,
Your life would be in easy consumption
Unless you are part of democracy.
Freedom sings as music for all
It brings nations to its utmost hark,
But sometimes it makes people fall
And be part of the endless dark.
Some would cherish the blessing
As a beggar his last dime.
Though being failible beings
We may abuse it as an alcoholic with his
   wine.
Therefore I speak in conclusion
That it is the individual's will,
To use his freedom in coordination;
With the wind that's considered still.

—*Joann Mainit*

A Rose Gift

The rose blossoms forth its rare beauty
The masque of inner delights
Hidden in the smoothly drawn petals of
   crimson
A history in ages of symbolic love.
A whisper of gentle fragrance
To caress the senses with heavenly wonder
Lending its mystical trail. . . . ...adorned
Gifted in this crimson rose of red.
A rose gift bespeaks forever
Of timeless beauty and care
The crimson red so deep in purest color be
The veil of sweet perfumed ages
Tenderly endowed for thee.

—*Joyce Lloyd*

An Angels View

The wind and rain had cast its spell
The mighty thunder lashed as well,
The rumble and the fury, the lightening
   and its glow,
Echoed from the valley in the distant hills
   below.
The sky so dark with agony and clouds so
   filled with pain
They sent their tears down to earth as
   drops of frozen rain.
The robin and the Meadowlark each had
   made a friend,
While perched together faithfully waiting
   for the end.
The churning clouds have passed away
   the rain began to slow,
The air so fresh the winds now calm the
   sun began to show
And over the valley, as you can see
Peace kindness, love and a rainbow from
   me.

—*Joseph Borda*

You and Me Forever

When I sit and think of life, I seem to
   dream about you.
The moments that we had were so very
   few.
I try to remember the good times we
   shared,
The thoughts and the feelings that we
   bared.
No matter where we were or what we
   were doing,
It seemed that you would be one person I
   wouldn't be losing.
Now I know better to close my eyes to
   reality
Or think that we'd feel the same way for
   eternity.
Our relationship has helped me in so
   many ways.
Falling in love helps you make more of
   each day.
Even though I don't have you for myself
   right now,
For you I would walk that extra mile.
Because I know that one day you again
   will be mine,
The love for me in your heart, you will
   find.
But until that day, whether it be on earth
   or above,
Always remember all of my care and my
   love.

—*Karena Mesich*

Once in a Lifetime

It only happens once not twice
The moments vanishing like mice
Scurrying past life much too fast
And only for the brave, the strong, the true
And when the moment comes for you
Don't let it pass you by
For in the twinkling of an eye
The love is gone, the moment dead
An empty ringing in your head
Your heart will know when fate has
Whispered in your ear
Oh, never fear beloved friend
For in the end
It's worth the price, the fee
The cost, when all is lost
But love has won
When true love comes
There is but one.

—Carla Jackson

The Stars of Night

The stars of Night glow so bright,
The Moon covered by a silver lining,
The breeze so gently blowing at the trees.
The Night so quiet and clear,
The birds lightly singing and the grasshoppers chirping,
And I just sit there gazing at the stars of night.

— Andrea Winslow

Starchild

I touch the stars; we are one.
The moon lies at my feet.
Miles below, lights glow;
They are great cities-insignificant.
A soft hum lulls me ever higher.
I search the heavens for my kin.
No one is above me-perhaps I have no equal.
There! Do I see light? But dark is the night,
And it's only a star, my fellow.
The cold clear air magnifies her smile.
I see the earth as round.
The tranquility of all my view belies evil.
Below, men strive, just to stay alive
And compassion swells in my breast.
Many who aspire to my station will fail their quest.

—James A. Wanless, Jr.

Her Candlelit Room

The wind swept through her candlelit room, rustling her lacy curtains.
The moon peeped into her candelit room, dancing on her walls.
The sweet scents of summer through her candlelit room aroused her from a dream.
The wind and the moon through her candlelit room lulled her back to sleep.

— Beth Susan Dombrowski

As I Wander

As I wander through the dark halls
The moonlight is dancing on the horizon.
The spirits flow freely.
In the moonlite cave they call me away.
Beckoning with me to come back.
They say that it's the cave of fears.
I no longer float freely but slowly sink.
My fears surround me and I lay
Lifelessly on the floor of the cave.

—Gerree Bollum

Life

The more faith I had, the more I believed,
The more goals I set, the less I achieved.
I picked a mountain too high to climb;
I dared to think big, it was a waste of time.
I came across mountains there was no detour around.
I climbed away too high and could not get down.
I came across water too rough to swim,
I did not think before diving in.
But with what little strength I had left inside,
I had finally given up and drifted with the tide.
I drifted to an island which wasn't too well known,
To find the road which I left off just to carry on.
I have found this road which has no end;
It just travels straight, it does not bend.
This highway of life is a one way track;
A straight journey forward with no turning back.
And it's just impossible to travel down this dusty road alone,
And I know right now, I'll never make it on my own.
It's not easy to talk with anyone today;
Because no one seems to understand why I feel this way.

—Cathy Bennett

Winding Down

Click, click, pop.
The old handle on the music box turns.
Pop, pop, click.
Old out of tune notes humm my favorite song.
Notes. Flat notes.
They wind down to a solemn two or three notes.
Winding down,
Just like me.
Winding down, a slow, solemn, and flat tune.
A flat life.
Life as dull as I've ever known it.
Beating slowly.
Slowly, solemnly, alone.
Oh God, please forgive my stubborn life,
My Godforsaken life.
Please, forgive me.

—Bobbi Humphries

Adapting

And so the wind blows. Slowly the ruffled leaves turn from green to brown,
The once painted house solely admired by all has deserted the town,
The tree outside that stood so proudly has now been torn down.
And as the hands of time tick away, again we reminisce of what was then. . .
Only to feel tears rise anew to our eyes
Only to hear our sobs and distant cries. . .
Yet, this moment itself shall be but another part of our past.
A small memory, a remembrance left of what was. . .
But as we gaze around the bended road,
Is that a tree with leaves of evergreens like a fairy tale foretold,
Is that not the place where the house once stood, now a new abode,
And do you remember the spot wherein we talked and sat
Where house of silence simply passed;
Do you not cherish these parts of our lives?
And as we tread life's different paths, do we not learn to adapt
To the changes it brings.
Do we not once again
Learn to sing. . .

—Karen Go

Always Love You

The one person.
The one boy.
You make me
Happy through sad times.
Yes, I can truly say
I love you for always.
You make blue skies bluer,
The sun shine brighter.
Yes, you are the one for me.
Our love will grow and grow
Forever and ever.
I will always love you.

—*Andrea Hochstetler*

Crossing Life's Rubicon

What is life like on the last track
The one sloping down to nil?
Will we still know, think, hope, fear, then,
As we slither down that last steep hill?
Will we wish we could clamber down
  slowly,
Grasping at straws as we go?
Will we wish for bare dirt or ice bumps
Instead of the smooth driven snow?
Will we roll ourselves up into snowballs
Rounded and ready to go?
Or bury our heads in a snowdrift
And scream, "No, no, no" as we go?
Will the landing be gentle and sweet
As we tumble into the vast chasm?
Will there be friends there to greet
As our lungs burst in one final spasm?

—*Dulcie Herr*

Him

I look over and see him.
The one who has always been there for
  me.
The one who could always comfort and
  cheer me.
He has made my life better and brighter,
  without knowing it.
He was the only person who cared enough
  to help me,
To listen to my troubles when no one else
  would.
Always willing to give me the comfort I
  needed.
Just laying there, looking up at the
  twinkling stars.
And even though it was a while ago,
  thinking back,
I know that I love him, and will always
  remember him,
And the things we did.
And I will always be there for him;
Like he was for me.

—*Jenny Hickman*

I Wonder If You're Out There?

I wonder if you're out there?
The one who'll catch my eye
The one who'll make a difference in my
  life
I sit and think—
I can picture you in my mind
I see us walking hand in hand on the
  beach
Watching the sun set together
Forever you and I
I wonder if you're out there?
The one I'd love to be with
Affection-strong, passionate
The ultimate romantic life
If dreams can come true
I dream of us and the day I'm standing
  right next to you.
I wonder if you're out there?

—*Amy Henderson*

In Love

I'll take hold of your hand,
the only way I know,
hold it close to my heart,
never letting it go.
Showing you how I feel
deep inside my soul.
I'll never hurt you
or even do you wrong;
for, the love I have for you
is too strong.
So give me a chance to come near,
and hold you tight without any fear.
That's the way I want to,
staring into your eyes,
and letting you know,
I love you.

—*Joel W. Smith*

Eternal Crush

You're the basis of my most wondrous
  thoughts,
The overwhelming passion I so often
  fought,
A score of gallant men couldn't halt my
  feelings,
Just the mere sight of you sends my heart
  reeling,
If you could realize my complete
  sincerity,
How may I tell you and spare my
  integrity?

—*Amy Catherine Bowman*

For One Moment

For one moment
the pain faded
the tears stopped
the flame of hate died out
For one moment
I died in his arms.

—*April Swartz*

Life

The pain grows deep inside of me.
The pain is all that I can see.
The feeling of emptiness shines through,
can't help wondering if life is true.
My eyes feel heavy and full of salt.
I'm the one who's blamed, it's all my
  fault.
Why does life go on if it's so cruel?
Who should I have to fallow that rule?
The hurt makes me want to cry.
Oh I wish that I'd just die.
No one can help me, no one cares.
This is about all that I can bare.
No one to talk to so I will just lie,
and think and sit and try to deny
life.

—*Audra Gibson*

Intentions

Self indulgence—
The philosophy
Of scholars
Free flying—
The belief
Of those with
Clear minds
When the sky
Is blue,
Take full
Advantage
Avoid the clouds
Do not compete
Come out immaculate
And feel the breeze
Of the birds. . .

—*Dana Tessel*

Requiem

Ominous black clouds.
The sky gray and black.
The wind beating at thy face.
A remembrance of death.
The loneliness,
The solitude,
I hear nothing,
Except the pounding of my weary feet.
The wind envelopes me,
In a blanket of fear.
Its whirling claws gripping me.
Its claws clenching my body.
The trees are moving in on me.
Their branches trying to grab me.
I feel the earth open up and I fall.
Into a hole of worries and fears.

—*Jennifer Wagner*

Tender Sunlight

Through the sunlight I could see
The snow melting so graciously.
Through all the days that I could
  remember,
I've never seen something so pretty and
  tender.
When I came out to see this,
There came to be a very thick mist.
But through the mist I heard a voice
Saying come to me, come to me, and let
  us rejoice.

—*Gretchen Dick*

Winter's Eve

Silence.
The sounds of night softened and shushed
  by
the cold winter snow.
Outside the world was disguised
in a wardrobe of winter white.
Occasionally a soft thud echoed through
  the night,
caused by the surrender of a branch,
  whose burden
of snow, became too much to bear.
Even the night itself had a sound,
the low wailing of the wind,
and the gentle murmur of night creatures
  hunting.
The shrill scream of a stalked animal
  dying
and when it fades silence settles.
Softening and shushing the sounds on a
cold winter's eve.

—*Jackie Barnhart*

A Time in a Dream

As I sit and dream about
The splendor I wish would soon come out
Of trees that sway, and birds that sing
And innocent children who love
  everything,
I dream of a time which perhaps never
  was
When the reason to live was simply to
  love,
A time with no war, a time with no hate.
When no one believed in locking their
  gate.
I guess that my dream is all it will be,
Our time is quite different, I now clearly
  see.

—*Amy Sims*

Untitled

Outside my window,
the stars shine bright.
I make a wish,
to hold you tight.
I close my eyes.
I say a prayer,
that we'll be together,
someday, somewhere.
I fall asleep.
I dream of you.
Special dream,
please come true.

—*Heather Rosewicz*

The Season's Surrender

The season is ending,
The Summer is gone,
The Spring flowers surrender,
For Fall is born,
For with colors adored,
Four o'clocks gone, now rest in their beds,
Where leaves and snow shall gather there
  instead,
Where bare is the earth of rainbow colors,
Where flowers once yearned...the sun,
  the rain
And leaves have fallen,
Yet colors adorned on trees linger,
For the flowers glow still remains,
In memory relived again.

—*Kathleen Ann Trainor*

Watching of a Rising Sun

I rose slowly that morning.
The sun had not yet come up, so I sat in
  utter darkness.
Quietly I walked toward my closet
And pulled out a pair of jeans and a
  flannel.
After reaching the kitchen, I pulled o
  piece of apple bread
And began to eat it. There wasn't a
  sound in the whole cabin.
Nothing stirred, it was as though
  world had stopped in dead sile
I walked out onto the porch. Th
  light around me,
Everything was dark. The wa
  crashed against the rocks,
In the cove that lay yards away
  where I stood. As I watched,
I wondered where the water that crashed
  before me had been before.
A ray of light shown from beneath the
  water. The sun slowly rose.
It was like a ball of fire shooting from the
  internal core.
I sighed, this is what I had come to see, as
  I did every morning.
I had come to watch the rising of the sun.

—*Fatimah Johnson*

Building Blocks

Motivation ebbs and wanes
Without the benefit of splashing tides
Slapping the inspirational strand
If only, but no, if only...if only, no
Wait then
For that exalted moment
When it all comes together
Wait. Hurry through, then resume
Your wait
It may never come
Guarantees are unicorns
And inspiration never "hits"
It creeps like a backache
Then consumes
Leap into the fire
Then wait
When the soul sizzles
It's time to write

—*Sharon Parker*

The Light

Pink and purple represent
The sunset of my earthly life
The dreams that I have followed
The work, the pain, the strife
Then comes night
A darkened space
Till a full silver moon
Gives light to his face.
Finally the sunrise
A burst of red and gold
Signaling the morning
As eternity folds.

—*Cash Young*

Mysterious Sunrise

A pink glow emanates from the light of
   the building buildings.
The swimming pool a sharp contrast of
   light blue.
Somewhere above there is a moon
but for now it's hidden in the heavy haze
   that is surrounding me.
I am high above every being looking
   down,
but I feel myself falling every moment as
   I look into the
deceivingly soft night.
Tomorrow all this world will be gone
and a blazing sun will hurt my eyes
while a cold wind scratches my skin.
For the moment, I will enjoy the alluring
   mystery
of a sunrise.

—*Kathryn M. McDonald*

Commandments

Let us return back to the basics,
The tablet etched with the
Simplest words of common sense,
Should be enough to reverse mankind's
   deadly course,
Back to the garden of Eden!
Man-made laws, rules, treaties,
   preambles,
Constitutions, so on and so forth,
Are mere interpretations,
Reverberating as signs of progress!
Let the eyes see, the tongue quiver,
The language of the mind, the politics of
   the heart,
Are sheer endeavors constantly probing,
The vulnerability of the commandments!
Find the love, beauty, and strength,
Of its simplicity,
Of its directness, so that
Adherence, deserves everlasting serenity,
Disobedience, facing the perils to oblivion!

—*Benjamin D. Jacobe*

Crippled Child Gone Away (dedicated to the memory of Mark Rigsby)

He came into this world as a crippled
   child
The tears he shed were tender and mild.
So young and determined he fought to
   live,
What gracious gift God could give.
Through the years he fought his way.
He learned to run, jump and play
Then the news came one awful day.
That determined young man had passed
   away
The accident he was in had brought his
   life to an end
Tears were shed from everyone's eyes.
They were shocked from this awful
   surprise.
He is gone and there is nothing I can do,
But I will always remember how he
   fought his way through.

—*Chasity Johnson*

Peer Leadership

I remember when you were upset.
The tears of mascara streamed down your
   face.
Those tears were your feelings
Pouring out into a world of reality.
Tears trickled down on my shoulder,
Where your head was lightly resting.
My shoulder was your security
To let out your emotions.
During that moment,
We both learned
How to open our hearts
And let someone else in.

—*Julie A. Colby*

Graduation

Now it's time to say goodbye.
The tears, they're falling,
I let out a sigh.
I realize you must go; I know why.
I'll miss you; I'll cry.
We've been through a lot together
You've always been there
To comfort me when things went wrong
I know you'll always care.
Remember all the talks we had,
All the things we've shared?
They'll carry on throughout our lives
Throughout those endless years.
I'll miss you.

—*Kelli Wilson*

To a Friend

So long my friend,
The time has come to say goodbye
But those are only words,
You cannot see what hides behind these
   eyes.
So many things to tell you,
Before you go away forever.
So many things I wished to say,
But did I have the courage? Never.
For when you go
I go, too.
A part of me
Will always stay with you,
And if I never see you again
Please always know I'm sorry
For anything that hurt you.
Cause time and distance cannot end,
The love I have for you, my friend.

—*Karen Ann Lewis*

Love

The days of love are endless,
The time of love is now,
The words of love are beautiful,
The trust of love, a vow,
The soul of love is divine,
To cross your path with mine,
The way of love is forever,
The hands of love are gentle,
The eyes of love are true,
The lips of love are tender,
The heart of love is truly you!

—*Cassie Meuth*

River

With it's slender trunk and bare branches,
The trees sway
With the breeze
While towering over the river.
So swift and fleet is the river.
Easily rushing over rough rocks and
   stones
With an occasional
Cool splash
Here and there.
So calm and quiet is the river.
Piled on the banks of the river
Are dry, crinkly leaves
With autumn colored
Bushes to accompany them.
The heart of a forest is the river.

—*Christine Ramos*

Mother's Love

Mother, the love you've taught me is
  buried so deep in the realms of my soul.
The true meanings, feelings, wants, and
  needs, all so real, so warm, so
  permanent.
From you I've learned to direct my life, to
  seek my wildest dreams, yet, remain
  intact and earthbound, realistic.
I now know I can channel this love, share
  it, radiating like beams from the sun, so
  precious like rare jewels and riches.
Through you I have found this unending
  wealth, a vein of gold, to spread
  through the universe, with each
  meeting of every being, this love is to be
  spread as a universal commodity.
As the years go on and our love grows, I
  see myself in you, and you in me, and I
  grow prouder, more secure, for I am in
  touch with my true reality.

—*Judith C. Middlebrooks*

A Year To Remember

A cool, breezy night on the beach,
The two of us walking hand in hand
Stopping often to watch a wave
Or to write our names in the sand.
Raking leaves in the backyard
You and I working side by side.
The colors beginning to pile up
Uncovering the last greens that they hide.
Playing in the large mounds of snow
In a world colored sweet, satin white.
Warming up by a blazing fire
And holding each other through the night.
Walking through the fields so green,
Stopping to gaze across the way.
Reminiscing about memories shared in
  the past
And talking about plans for some day.

—*Amy K. MacWilliams*

Life Lived And Remembered

As I sit under
The warmth of the sun,
I listen to
The joyful songs of the birds
While smelling the fresh blossoming air.
And as I sit and wonder
About the small little creatures,
I daydream about my childhood life
When I was a lot younger.
And when I come back
to the world that I left,
I think to myself,
What a wonderful life I have spent.

—*Jenny Grado*

What I Am

The soft breeze of twilight rippling
The waters of the deep shining lakes.
The sneaking deceptiveness of the
  shadows
That slip in with the falling darkness.
The chilling howl of a great wolf
Mourning for its mate.
The innocent beauty of maiden moon
Enfolding her wings of a shining glory
Around the earth.
If this is what I am,
Truly what I am,
Then I would not want to
Be anyone else.

—*Jo-Lynn Boule*

I'm Lost Without Him

I've loved before, but never like this.
The way he whispered into my ear,
And the way he gave me a kiss.
The way he touched me,
The way his body touched mine.
I can't stop thinking about him
And the way he made me shine.
I've never had such a pain in my heart.
I just hope when he's back,
That never will we be apart!

—*Jody Warren*

Lovers: Dusty and Brette

The softness of a touch
The whisper of a dream
The echo of a fantasy
Are found in you
The building of a hope
The answer to a prayer
The love of a lifetime
I've found in you
The touch of your hand
The smile in your eyes
The love on your face
All found in you

—*J. M. Broderson*

New York

Large buildings blocking out sunlight.
The whole world concrete.
Everyone hurries.
No time for laughter, only work.
The poor beg in the street.
The wind blows.
It is a cold wind.
The pace never slows.
People rush and hurry like there's no
  tomorrow.
Maybe they know something that we
  don't.

—*Donna Frederick*

Stop The Wild Hand

Endless pleas; ringing
The wild hand; fearing
The angry mouth; hurting
No where to run; no safe place
Stop the wild hand
Stop the wild hand.
A pull of hair; kicking
No matter what; there is no winning
A simple hello; violence
What can she do; be strong, be silent
Stop the wild hand
Stop the wild hand.
Nightmarish dream; terror goes on
Sure to return; someone come
Begging screams; one last time
Hoping; awaiting rescue
Stop the wild hand
Stop the wild hand.

—*Kathryn Leone*

Free Horses

Don't try to saddle
The wild ponies on the plains.
To tame the children of the wilderness
Is to distort the images of civilization.
For if the untamed became docile—
—What now are the docile?
Let them be free horses.

—*Christine Heying*

Telepathy

If it were but what a shadow feels
the wind across her lips
caress a leaf that falls onto his thigh. . .
a prayer is all but coming.
There is that which lives inside
Touch the painted elephant
free the sacred cow. . .
a reincarnate elevation upward fall.
The chasm closes forest and stream
as swallows sit to fly
then fly to sit. . .
and pollen shapes a myth around the glass
now drink.

—*Arline Bennett*

Life's Destiny

The snow was falling in the mountains
The wind began to blow
Then we knew it was time to go for our
    walk in the beautiful snow.
As we strolled along hand in hand
We began to get cold.
We knew we were lost in the snow.
We could no longer see where to go.
He took my hand in his and gently kissed
    it.
Then the world ended just as we knew it
    would.

—*Beatrice Lynn Seward*

The Desert Unicorn

As I look upon the mighty desert, I see a
    figure;
The wind blows in his grey mane.
He is the so called Unicorn of the Desert.
White in color, with a smoke grey mane
    and tail,
He looks so magical with the mountains at
    his back;
The foothills, grey like his mane,
The large desert cliffs, red like his dilated
    nostrils.
His eyes burn amber at the sound of
    jackals in the distance;
His large body quivers as he catches my
    scent.
His lion-like tail swishes in the breeze.
I blink. He is gone just as suddenly as he
    appeared.
He is the magical Unicorn of the Desert.

—*Amy L. Burrell*

Special Friends

The sky is there to scream on and to tell
    your secrets to.
The wind blows you along and leads you
    to something new.
The river flows beside you and guides you
    all the way.
The rocks are there to lean on and to help
    you on your way.
The grass is there to give you a soft and
    warm place to rest.
And the path is there for you to follow, no
    matter if you're at your worst or best.
So when you step into a world, that seems
    cold and hard to bear.
Just remember these special friends for
    they will always be there.

—*Kristina Colleen Bung*

Untitled

The trees whispered wistfully in the
    breeze;
The wind lifted her hair from her
    shoulders with ease.
They tried to comfort her but it did no
    good,
Though they tried as hard as they could.
She walked along the ocean shore
Caring for nothing she'd cared about
    before.
For life was precious to her no more.
Tears drifted slowly down her face
And in her heart nothing could ever
    replace
The love she had known or the hurt she
    had felt
And before the Lord that day she knelt
And prayed for God to take her soul
For Life was precious to her no more.

—*Chrissy Bubb*

Untitled

As I sit there among
the withering leaves,
I think of how things
might have been,
How they might have been
if time hadn't gone forth,
Gone forth toward the days
of my now changing world,
My now changing world
is starting to crumble,
Down around me it falls
like the mounds of an avalanche,
The avalanche won't stop
it just keeps falling,
It keeps falling around me
in an undying crash.
It is hard to try and cope.

—*Jessica D. Marchant*

Control

With a little self control, the mind can set
    you free.
The world is what you make it; you go
    where you want to be.
To a land of sunshine, that has no word
    for cold.
A land of silver fountains, where only for
    life is gold.
A solitary land of thought, where poets go
    to dream alone.
A land of fluffy cotton clouds, where can't
    be found a single stone.
You can change you life, control the way
    it seems.
Refine your perfective. Power by your
    dreams.

—*Helen Murray*

The Gift of Giving

How fascinating to look at
The world through the eyes
Of myself.
What joy can be found in
The simple pleasure of
Loving.
What real emotion lies in truth.
There for all to see
Tangible only to those who look.
I looked
I saw
I felt.
The beauty of real love
The joy of giving from the heart
The wonderful feeling of receiving.
In sight, I found myself.

—*Jennifer Dapsis*

I had A Dream

I had a dream last night.
The world was a beautiful place.
Everyone was kind to one another.
There were no longer any wars.
For all the weapons had been destroyed.
There were no longer any homeless
    people.
There was no longer any pollution.
The world was actually beautiful.
Everyone was treated the same.
And at night people didn't have to worry,
    about locking their doors.
Then I woke up.
I got out of bed,
and went over to the window.
Then I realized,
it had only been a dream.

—*Aimee Hudson*

Rocking, rocking, rocking —

He ponders his younger days.
The youth sees the sun as it rises;
He sees the sun as it fades.
Rocking, rocking, rocking —
He brushes a silvery lock from his brow.
The earth he plowed to make a living
Awaits his burial now.
Rocking, rocking, rocking —
Chances not taken crawl through his
    mind;
Regret becomes a burden to bear.
Although Death draws closer, as does the
    night,
His loved one awaits him there.
Rocking, rocking, rocking —
Darkness arrives, the stars shimmer
    above.
Death takes him higher and higher,
His soul twinkling brighter
Than the rest.

—*Colette Wells*

The World as I See it

As I look outside I see leaves falling. . .
Their colors a bright yellow, red and
　green.
But as I look past those bright pretty
　colors,
I see a dark gloomy world where people go
　hungry
And there is not enough shelter for the
　world to provide.
So as I look out the window I see not the
　pretty colors,
But the blanket that covers up the ugly
　gloomy world,
That with everyone's help we can make a
　better place!

　—*Julie Marie Rodriguez*

Tragic Comedy

Tragedy and comedy
Their synthesis is life
Our thoughts and movements are
Reflections when one confronts the other
Tragedy alone is darkness beyond the
Abyssmal spectrum of our soul
Comedy, unrestricted, defies the gravity
Of reality and hurdles into nothingness
The opposition of the two
Agitates the stillness of eternity
Creating ripples of contrast with
Which to guage one moment against the
　next.
To hope for the end of one
Is to hope for the beginning of none.

　—*Bryon K. Propst*

A Child's Love

First love at first sight
Then a smile of delight
A sweet kiss to remember me
That's how our love came to be
Your tender arms to hold me tight
To squeeze, to love, to make it right
If I should go don't shed a tear
Just feel in your heart that I'll be near.

　—*Angie Sorensen*

Nothing

A flash of light
Then darkness surrounds
A cry pierces the blackness
Followed by laughter
There's a feeling
Of love and a feeling
Of pain
Pictures
Accompany the sounds
They flicker by
Like a slide show
Soon an
Emptiness
So heavy
It goes to the very soul
And then
There is
Nothing.

　—*Jill Kleinsasser*

All for You

As he broke up with me, tears rolled down
　my colorless cheeks.
Then he spoke, ever so softly, "dry your
　crying eyes because I can't bear to see
　your big brown eyes cry."
I answered him, my voice as light as the
　wind, "it's not my eyes that cry these
　tears of pain, it's my heart."
"My heart cries for you. My body howls
　out in hunger for your touch."
"My ears weep as they strain to hear
　loving words come from your mouth."
"My lips shout orders to yours to touch
　them once again."
"So you see, as all of my body is
　mourning, it is not my eyes that shed
　these tears, it is my heart."
"And I have said before, I will die for you
　and your love."
"Now not only will my heart shed tears
　but also blood. So now I give to you my
　tears and my blood. All for you."
With that I plunged the arrow straight
　into my heart.
This arrow that I speak of is Cupid's
　arrow. The very same one that struck
　me three years before and introduced to
　me love and life with you in it.
But now it kills me for you no longer love
　me.
In my last minute of life, he bent down,
　took my hand in his, kissed me ever so
　gently and told me he loved me.
But it was too late.
Then he wept.

　—*Jennifer Lenna*

The Storm

The sun peeks through the clouds
Then hides once more
For it is a day for a storm.
The birds huddle in their nests
And the deer lay in the shelter for some
　rest.
As the sky turns gray and the storm grows
　power
The rain comes down on pretty, pastel
　flowers.
The plants say thank you and the trees
　say more
The rain comes harder into a pour.
Nearby a cabin's chimney blows out
　smoke in streams
As a forest ground turns to steam.
The mists of rain fall to the ground
And the rain is the only sound.
The rain turns to a quiet drizzle
The sun comes out and sizzles.
For all the animals come out and play
And there is only one thing to say. . .
There has been enough rain for the day.

　—*Amy Mix*

Dangerous Highways

It was the crack of dawn
When the bodies were found.
The tree was badly hurt.
Broken beer bottles on the ground.
The highway glistened
With transparent crimson.
It may be good that they died,
Or they would end up in prison.
The smoke had cleared
The bodies were young.
Now their blankets are grass,
And their pillows are stone.
Sister, it's been a year,
But it's still hard to see.
Through the tears in my eyes,
I can read: R.I.P.
My dear, sweet older sister
Was only seventeen.

　—*Rebekah Tiefenbach*

A Lonely Cry

I hear the cars and trucks go by
Then I look up into the sky.
I stop and listen a little more
And to my ears I hear the ocean roar.
Hear the baby cry,
No one actually knows why.
I'm all alone in this world,
I feel like I am in a whirl.
I cry, and cry, and cry some more,
Then I walked on the shore.
Waves coming, waves going,
Still no one knowing.
So when you hear a lonely cry,
Stop, think, wonder why.

　—*Amy Berdecia*

Dear Lord Why?

I awaken to see you at your place, sitting
 in front of a picture of her face.
Then I see you begin to cry, as you ask
 youself why did she have to die?
Then you sat down and started to pray,
 and this is what I heard you say;
Oh, dear Lord why did she go, I have so
 much love for her, much more than I
 must show.
Why did you have to take her away, why
 couldn't she be here, why couldn't she
 stay?
I can remember holding her so, hoping
 that I'd never have to let go.
Dear Lord, I wish I could have her to
 hold, and tell her things I've never told.
Lord, why did you take her away, why
 can't I see her and be with her today?
She has opened my eyes and my heart, so
 why did she leave, why did she part?
She has made my life much better, ever
 since we have been together.
Oh dear Lord, I beg of you, let this be a
 dream, don't let this be true.
I loved her and this is true, and now she's
 gone and there's nothing I can do.
But to remember all that we have done,
 all the good times, and all of the fun.
Dear Lord, I'll tell you this, I will never
 forget her warm, soft kiss.
I'll never forget the way she talked to me,
 the way she opened my eyes and helped
 me to see.
I guess there's only one thing to say,
 besides that I'll miss her in every way.
I'll never forget her pretty face, oh dear
 Lord, why didn't you take me in her
 place.

—Jennifer Ann Senft

War

First it was a game
then it was war
killing people
and knocking down doors
I feel sorry for the wives
and the kids with no fathers
getting killed with knives
as survivors go out farther.

—Amy McCoy

An Unknown Friend

If you only knew what you meant to me,
Then life would be different, you would
 see,
We would get along so fine,
I would be yours and you would be mine,
We could hang out around the school,
Boy, that would be so cool,
We could be good friends and it would
 seem,
Just how it had been in my dream,
And the world around us would be
 forever,
Laughing, talking, always together,
If you only knew what you meant to me,
Then life would be different, you would
 see. . .

—Cheryl Lehmann

Our Love

Love is something you feel together,
Then that's when you know it's forever,
The relationship might sometimes be
 unfair,
But together we must try hard to bear!
The relationship might be a little hard,
But together we must fight the battle to go
 so far,
And after we learned what to do
That's when I know it's the right time to
 say
"I Love You"!
Together we must be hand in hand
In order to keep our long time plan,
I know God will like that very much,
That He will bless us with His special
 touch!
I just hope this message goes through,
In order for you to know that "I Love
 You!"
So then when I think of you night & day,
I just hope our Love doesn't go away!

—Jesse Bocanegra

Is There a Tomorrow?

If there was no tomorrow
Then this day would never end.
If I had only one wish to be granted,
It would be for everyone to know me
Across the world and over the sea.
If there was only one message
I had to send,
It would be for everyone to
Know me as a friend.
If there was a tomorrow,
I would just want everyone
To know me as myself.

—Kim Ball

Stages of a Relationship

First we meet and are acquaintances.
Then we talk and are friends.
We share love and are very close.
There are broken promises; we're just
 friends again.
Lies and deceptions, we're enemies.
Then, nothing! Simply nothing!
Except for down deep in the heart,
There's an undying love which we both
 share
But are afraid to admit.

—Jennifer Joy Bennett

Snow Prints

The first snow has fell,
There are footprints everywhere,
A child has had fun.

—Amy Burnette

Peace

Everywhere you look,
There are peace signs
But it doesn't seem to be a belief,
Just a few fashionably drawn lines.
Is it all just talk
Without any real show of action?
Somehow that just doesn't seem
To bring much satisfaction.
Many people want to help,
They just don't know where to start
Just say what you feel and believe in,
And let it come straight from the heart.
It says in the Bible,
To live in peace with our brother
And continually in peace
We should live with one another.

—Carol A. Tedford

Love

True feelings of love.
There are so mamy ways love can be.
Love can be in poems that you won't be
 able to see.
Love can be pain,
You'd feel you won't have anything to
 gain.
Love can be hurting,
You'd feel you weren't getting what you
 were deserving.
Love can make you feel blue,
You'd be caught in a situation and won't
 know what to do.
But then again love can be love,
The kind of love that can be sent from
 above.
Love can be great,
If there is love, there's no place for hate.
Love can be sunshine,
With sunshine there is no place for rain
But my love for you has no certain
 amount,
I love you and that's all that counts.

—*Aretha Davis*

Lonesome Road

I was on a lonsesome road to nowhere
When you came along in my life to help
 me.
You gave me hope, faith, love and
 strength.
But what can I give you back.
A promise that I'll keep
Our friendship dear to me.
You stuck with me side by side
No matter what.
You were with me through the good times
And the bad times.
You're a good friend
To the end.
I hope it never ends.

—*Lara Fritz*

Perfection

Right, wrong
There are so many decisions to make.
Doors open, doors close
Does anyone reach perfection?
Is there anyone who really knows?
What is there to achieve or even do?
When all achievements are accomplished
Not by just anyone, but only by you.
So if you ask what is perfection
Take a glimpse inside,
Where the answer should ultimately
 reside.
You are the only person that it should
 matter
While all others are simply making idle
 chatter.
For when everything is over with,
Said and through,
The one that has to be satisfied with your
 decisions is
You.

—*Dean Powers*

Me, Myself and I

Me, myself and I
There are three in which I hide.
We can be happy and we can be sad.
One can be good and one can be bad.
We are all different but made of the same.
Playing around but all different games.
When I am not happy I become me.
When they are not happy
Myself I can be.
To all become one
Then we are we.
People like you
Find it hard to see
But there are differences
One who is me.
Also myself and I, I can be.

—*Krista Kuch*

Each Heart

There are burdens each heart must carry.
There are tricksters that make us wary.
There are troubles we each must bear.
There are people who just don't care.
There are thing we just can't change.
There is clutter we can't rearrange.
There are some things time can't erase.
There is humiliation one just can't face.
There is grief when loved ones die.
There is heartbreak that makes us cry.
Time robs us of our youth.
Deception often hides the truth.
Just when I feel that all is lost
And upon life's highest waves I'm tossed,
Something happens to change all that.
My teenage son stopes for a chat.
He brings to mind what I need to see—
The lesson of life: Each heart travels free.

—*Jean Osborn Downey*

Searching

How can I describe my love?
There exist no words eloquent enough.
Her beauty is indescribable.
No matter how poetic I write,
The words fall short and appear empty.
I am a beaten man,
Crossing a desert,
Scarching not for water, but words.
Words to quench the love I feel,
Love so indescribable,
Immune to all expression.
Desperately I grab at sentences,
But like the clouds,
They escape my clutches
And I fall to the earth.
My wretched heart beating a song
To which I am unable
To sing aloud.

—*Elliott Blackwell*

Be Patient

In every life of everyone
There falls a bit of light.
Someone who brings you joy and fun
And fills your heart with delight.
In every life of everyone,
No matter what others may say,
There will come a certain someone
That you look forward to seeing each day.
In every life of everyone
There are some insecurities.
But once you find that special one
Your insecurities become securities.

—*Blake Hildner*

In the Still of the Night

In the still of the night
There is
Silence
Suddenly a baby's cry
A light turned on
A mother walking
The low, soft, sweet sound of a lullaby
The light turns off
Silence
In the still of the night.

—*Jennifer L. Anderson*

Swirling Darkness

The torrent of swirling darkness
 surrounds me as I am a victim of the
 night
There is no escaping its growing density
The cold, windy jaws of the night air are
 enveloping my body.
Run, run faster. . .till I can run no more!
Hope, hope faster. . .that I can rid myself
 of this terrible nightmare!
Jingle the keys in my pocket, make sure I
 have not lost them. . .
Open the door.
Hurry, hurry faster. . .I must get in before
 the frostie night air swallows me whole!
The snow is piling at my frostbit feet, I
 am freezing to death, growing weary.
My eyelids are heavy, my eyelashes laced
 with snow.
Will this ever end?
My fingers are numb as I fumble the keys
 to unlock the door.
Turn the handle and step inside.
I shut the door behind me, locking out the
 evil storm that lurks outside.
Ah, a sigh of relief as I am safe in my
 living room—Merry Christmas!

—*Jennafer Kraus*

Nightmares

Golden tears of sorrow trickle down my face.
There is no one to turn to in this cold and lonely place.
Nightmares and terror will haunt me as they did so long ago.
They taunt me and attack me on awful waves they flow.
In the east the sun is rising, chasing the nightmares away.
The night time is frightening, but it is peaceful in the day.

—*Heather Strode*

Broken Hearts

My heart is broken
There is no way to mend it.
There are many things to say,
But I cannot find the words.
There are many people in this world,
My heart moans for only you.
Now you're gone.
I'm lost without you.
Why did you leave me?
Why did it have to be this way?
Why?

—*Julie Elsen*

Excuse Me, Sir

Pardon me, excuse me, sir
There is something I'd like to know
If I dare to ask
Will you tell me the answer?
If you will, please listen to me
Can I trust you to help?
Will you tell me if you know the answer?
Here's the question
Wait a second. . .
It's slipped my mind
I don't seem to remember
Thank you, sir, for your time
Next time we meet again
I'll remember the question
Will you know the answer?

—*Cynthia Rose Leusner*

The Broken Window

Beyond the broken window pane
There lays the glass of a shattered soul
Pieces of disappointment
Pieces of rescent
A breakable wall opened to vulnerability
Faced with problems of the past,
  re-opened into
today's sorrows
And through this shattered illusion a new
  escape is illuminated
To end the pain of a shattered soul.

— *Holly Damerville*

Heaven's Corpse

The sculpture stood strongly in my dream.
There. . .lit only by the moon and the sparkle in my eyes.
Surrounded by worn cobblestones
In a deserted city square, it stood magnific,
Larger than any known human could stand.
So delicately carved from white marble—
Flawless, its skin as smooth as porceline;
Draped in silk that seemed to ripple in the cool breeze,
Beyond earthly beauty it stood
With a face so fragile, eyes nearly crying—
Lips parted as if in speech. . .
Hands: graceful, elegant, rich, almost trembling. . .
Drenched with fear and sadness it stood
Gorgeous with its detail—a human perfection.
My breath escaped me as I stared—
Purity. Hard to believe your splendor is stone.
I imagine you moved when I opened my eyes.

—*Kate Nybakken*

The Beauty of Drugs

You loose you're pride and you're self respect too.
Your family can no longer mean love to you
A supplier is you're real love now
To say yes to drugs any coward knows how
To have control over you're mind and body as it should be
You're drugs instead will have control of you,
And will become you're worst enemy.
Making deals on the street or by phone
If you don't end up busted or dead,
You'll end up alone.

—*Linda L.Gage*

Fugitive Moments

As the waves hugged the shore
There she stood hugging the tree
Hearing the current roar
Feeling the gentle stroke of the autumn breeze.
Her naked feet caressed the sand
Her quixotic eyes traced the silhouettes of flying seagulls
While her fugitive thoughts
Dwelled beyond the foilage.
She heard the singing of mermaids
As music descended from above
And as the wind caressed her hair
She leaned her cheek on the tree.
She was a rare ensemble
Of an uncommon kind
Like a bedrock, unsoluble
Like a goddess, divine.

—*Carlos Moreno*

At a Very Young Age

At a very young age
There was a need, a crave
To hear the words
Those, never heard
A longing, if you will
That grew, and lives still
Those three symbols, laced in pearl
Songs are written about, curled
Around the artist' canvas
and a poet's pen, that traverses
Across the miles, to touch
The heart, give pleasure, such
Joy, those three words employ
Is it so difficult to say
I love you
At a very young age
There was a need, a crave
To hear the words
Those never heard?

—*Constance Jeanne Livernois*

Feelings and You

My world was full of confusion and pain
There was alot of guilt and shame
I was feeling hurt and alone
My depression was easily shown
You came along and turned my world Inside-out
Showed me what happiness is all about
You keep me smiling even though I Should frown
When I'm with you I could never be down
You brought out feelings I never knew I had
Spending the rest of my life with you Doesn't sound so bad
I'll wait for you until the time is right
But until that time you'll be in my Dreams each night

—*Jennifer Poole*

My Dream

You stole my heart one summer day.
There were so many things I had wanted to say.
The first time I saw you, my heart began to melt,
But I was so shy to tell you how I really felt
The way I feel can't be expressed,
It stays inside me never to be adressed.
Someday I hope we can be together,
Sharing our lives for ever and ever.

—*Alesha Chilton*

Treasure Within My Heart

As the sun rises over the ocean,
there's a feeling you get deep inside.
Your thoughts are mixed in with it's
  beauty,
and your heart drifts on out with the tide.
What beautiful miles of sand lay before
  you
as you walk in the bare of your feet
you notice that far beyond hope is a vision
that somewhere the end you will
For a teasure this has no limits,
and it's there to be given away.
How something so free could just win my
  heart over
is more than a few words can say.

—Crystal Sanger

A Day at a Time

Life for a parent in the NICU,
When you walk in, you're not sure what to
  do,
Babies are lying everywhere in sight,
You look at yours and wonder of its
  plight,
Nurses running around and monitors
  going off,
You get so nervous that you jump when
  someone coughs,
Days are endless and life seems to stand
  still,
The rest of the world keeps going, getting
  its fill,
You feel no one understands and you feel
  so alone,
You're learning words that before you'd
  never known,
Life becomes full of uncertainty for your
  baby and you,
But soon that becomes comfort in the
  NICU.

—Renee Thomas

Moose...You Above!

My dearest Moose...
there's just no excuse,
you're hardly obtuse.
When things slip-slide...
you're always by my side,
with love you provide.
You mean so much...
my heart touch,
and with no smutch.
You're not one to judge...
even when you nudge,
and I refuse to budge.
The things you do...
may seem very few,
but only to you.
Moose my love...
you're considered a dove.
people stand below,
you...above!

—Garilyn Kamalii

Star Lit Nights and Morning Sun

You have to believe me and know that it's
  true
There's never been another you
You've always been my only one
My star lit nights and morning sun
Your name has been embedded in my
  mind and on my lips
The very touch, the feel of you are prints
  upon my finger tips
The scent of you, your eyes, your hair
There is none other to compare
The memory of you has come between my
  every other plan or dream
But not once did I ever complain I needed
  to see your face in my rain
I needed to know a part of me would never
  ever be set free
I needed to cling to the little mood that
  rocked my very solitude
To cling to the thought that may be one
  day, I could turn to you and say
You've always been my only one
My star lit nights and morning sun
You have to believe me and know that it's
  true
There will never be another you

—Karen Kinses

Granddaughter

Watching the little blonde girl from
  across the street,
With braces on her tiny legs, yet acting so
  discreet.
Holding my breath with tears in my eyes,
  praying she wouldn't fall,
How pretty she is and oh, she has grown
  so tall.
Oh, to go to her and hug her and say, "I
  love you, dear,"
But to do that might frighten her and
  surely fill me with fear.
She doesn't know me, it's nothing I've
  done,
They prefer it this way, although her
  father is my son.

—Lois Nason

My Love, Real or Grim

My love for him is real
there's no denying how I feel.
Yet, to make him understand
seems totally out of hand.
I could lie,
I could die,
all for him
it sounds so grim.
Would that prove my love,
to the heavens above.
It may to them,
but not to him.

—Frieda Dawson

It Can Never Be

Although I know it can never be
There's nothing wrong with dreaming,
  dreams
Of just how wonderful it could be
From feelings that have grown with time.
Although I know it can never be
I want to make every moment special
To be moments we can always cherish
Not to regret, but remember
With love and tenderness forever.
Although I know it can never be
I'm happy we at least have had this time
  together.
A time to call our own
Moments to share ourselves.
Although I know it can never be
There's nothing wrong with dreaming,
  dreams
And through the windows of my heart
I see we will forever be, together.

—Cheryl Parker

My Big Scary School

In our big, scary school,
There's rule after rule.
No jackets, no hats,
No this, no that.
No radios, no gum,
No staying home, gotta come.
We're not allowed to have fun
And we're always on the run.
All teachers say is "sit down, shut up,"
"How many ounces in a cup?"
Well, I don't know, how can I tell,
Whew boy! Saved by the bell.
My locker is stuck,
But I can't make a fuss,
Oh great, I missed the bus!

—Becky A. Bishop

The Time we Spend Together

When we're together, day by day
There's so many things I'd like to say
But, nerves and shyness override
All the words I have inside
Although I may not say it much
My love for you, no one could touch
That's why the time we spend together
I wish would just go on forever
The time we're together is so precious to
  me
Your beauty is something I long to see
Without you my life would be so empty
Because you and I are meant to be
So, when we're apart and you're alone
And all we have might be time on the
  phone
Just remember the time that we spend
  together
And I'm sure that our love will go on
  forever.

—Cathi Jo Dinger

Untitled

the pain
there's so much pain
tears fill my eyes
my heart aches
I'm so alone
there's so much darkness
the darkness becomes light
the pain disappears
love fills my heart
as you put your arms around me
the coldness is shattered by
the warmth of your soul.

— *Cami Womack*

In Memory

When I talked to her on the phone
    Christmas Day
These are the words she heard me say
"I'll be there to visit with you during week
    after New Year's"
Now I write this through my tears
She could not wait for me to come
In a few shorts days—God called her
    home
I thought we'd greet each other with a
    hug and a smile
And like always—talk, eat and laugh
    awhile
I never planned to go to say
    good-bye—forever
Now the good times we shared—I can
    only treasure
The day I stood there with the family and
    wept
The promise I'd come—to think this was
    the way it was kept. . .

—*Harriet Shove Bedard*

Grandfathers

Grandfathers are very special people,
They are always with you, by your side.
They stand very bold,
With dignity and streams of pride.
Grandfathers will open their arms
And with a smile of glee,
Say, "come here, and sit on my knee."
Grandfathers will tell you stories
About horses and cowboys,
Along with Goldilocks eating her porrige.
Grandfathers are one of a kind,
They are very special people,
And keep this in mind,
When they are sad and feeling blue
Cheer them up
Because look at all they've done for you.

—*Jennifer Kennedy*

Outside

Bright green clovers marching across the
    land
They are laughing in the breeze
Tree branches are reaching out giving a
    helping hand
To the little lost daffodils trying to march
    in the band
The shy timid tree hides its faces in the
    leaves
While the gallant rabbits come out of
    their houses—
In rabbit language, beaves
The laughing brook babbles to the banks
Now the dirt is covered with a grassy
    blanket of leaves
While the moonlight casts a shadow in the
    eve.

—*Jenna M. Droluk*

Untitled

Stories come from the heart,
They are molded by love
And detailed by kindness.
The characters are thoughts,
The scene is the imagination.
The plot is life. . .
And what happens is fate.

—*Heather Pekoc*

Angels

Angels are like God o' Thee
They are so heavenly.
I think of them day and night,
By my side as a guiding light.
My father to heaven to which thee are
With me right now and forever more.

—*Amy Walter*

Church Bells

Church bells,
They are the Lord's way
Of telling us he loves us.
They play with the sweetest melodies,
As beautiful angels all dressed in white,
Singing and rejoicing, chime in
To make beautiful, everlasting music
Filled with love.
They tell the world there is hope,
There is peace.
God mounts his throne
To shouts of joy;
A blare of trumpets for the Lord.
As the Holy Bible says,
"Christ has died,"
"Christ has risen,"
"Christ will come again. . ."

—*Helena C. Tavares*

When You're in Love with Someone

When you're in love with someome,
They can do no wrong,
They're just loads of fun,
To have along.
As the days go by,
And you see their faults,
In your eyes,
The world may come to a halt.
However no one is perfect,
So don't you dare,
Try to reject,
The one for whom you care.

—*Janet Ockinga*

Blind People

Crazy people
They can't see
Who is taking over me
Are you blind?
Can't you see
I'm falling behind
I'm going crazy
Help me! Help me!
Someone help me before it's too late
He's waiting at the garden gate
For me to come outside and play
So he can come and take me away
Will you ever understand
Someone come and hold my hand
And help me through this awful time
Don't you know my soul is mine?

—*Candice Anderson*

People are Blind

People are so blind, they never seem to see
They can't see past sorrowful eyes that
    long to be noticed
They see only images, but not those of
    pain and burden
People are so blind, if only they could
    open their eyes,
They would make the darkness disappear
    and see that the light never dies

—*Alysia Knop*

Love and Hate

Love and hate
They go hand in hand
One can say they love
But seldom can they prove it
Often one says they hate
But really they despise it.
Why does one who knows better
Use words they know nothing of?

—*Deborah Marie DeVittorio*

Facing Something That's Gone Forever

They're gone away to a nice place,
They left us with a gloomy face,
But I know they'll live better up there.
Even though I still do care,
Now I know I'm facing something that's gone
But not lost.
My love for them
Can never be crossed.

—Katherine Gould

Lovers

Lovers are people and friends too,
They love and share like a couple of two
Who bring love and joy into the world.
We and God give and share
To those who need a friend that cares.

—Angela Crutchfield

Memorial

Those We love are like a dove.
They never stay, they always fly away.
And as they fly through heaven above,
May we always cherish their never dying love.
Their memories are left to linger on,
Even though their bodies are presently gone.
And in those memories are some good and bad,
Combined with others which are happy and sad.
For better or for worse, which every they may be,
All these memories linger on with me.
I'll never forget the day when may Mamaw passed on
It was almost as if My life had also gone.
She loved and raised me from the time I was born.
And when she passed away, I was left to mourn.
But why be unhappy, it was for the best.
She's no longer in pain, just a peaceful rest.
And as she watches over me from heaven above,
I'll never forget my Mamaw, flying away like a dove.

—Angela S. Dye

Walls

Walls really do have ears and mouths and eyes
They see and hear everything.
Sometimes when I think I'm all alone
I'll hear my wall give a heavy sign
And remember that my walls are always listening.
Walls like to talk amongst themselves.
I often hear them speaking to each other at night
When they think everyone is asleep.
Sometimes on happy occasions
The walls sing and shout
They may even dance, but I've never see it.
On Constitution Avenue in Washington, DC
There is a special wall that is entirely outside.
This wall hears a thousand cries in mourning every day.
It is totally silent yet it tells us a story.
It is totally silent yet somehow
It makes us remember.

—Amber Earley

The Shadowed Teardrop

A shadow, a face, a teardrop about to fall.
They see her but don't hear her words thought aloud.
A frightened scream only silently heard.
The shadows, they chase her. A faint noise is ignored.
By one, the silence is broken.
She hears the screams, calls for help.
No one comes. No one cares.
A stranger appears. A caring smile painted on her face.
Reaching hands for each other fade out of sight,
As her opening eyes bring her back to her life's reality.
Alone in her room.
A shadow, a face, a teardrop has fallen.
As she screams silently into the night.

—Krista Manganello

Flowers

Flowers are a beautiful sight
They shine in the warm sunlight
They sway when the wind blows
At night they sleep until the morning
Then they get their water and dry off in the sun
There are all kinds of flowers that bloom all day
Some are purple, and some are gray
My mom plants flowers all day long
And she loves to sing beautiful songs
I dream a wish I hope will come true
That someday I'll plant flowers too.

—Cathy Stevens

An Everlasting Love

So far apart just as we,
They shine so bright oh yes indeed.
As they hang high in the sky above,
They remind me of our forever love.
Just as they illuminate a sky of gray,
When I am blue you brighten my day.
On a cloudy night they disappear,
When the moment is right they are always near.
Just as you are nowhere in sight,
But when you are you hold me tight.
As they reach beyond eternity
Our love will remain everlasting.

—Angie Schmitt

The One's Left Behind

The one's left behind have it bad
They sit and think of who they had
They blame themselves for what went wrong
Especially when they hear a suicide song.
They feel as though they held the knife
That ended the young loved one's life.
They feel like it's them that caused the suicide
Then they asked why the young one died.
No one knows the answer to this awful fate
But the child's heart was filled with hate.
They're off in a strange and distant place
Where they don't even recognize a familiar face.
It's the wrong way to end an innocent youth
But this epidemic holds no truth.
The one's left behind only have doubt
But to the young one it's the only way out.

—Dawn Ellis

Shadows

Shadows lie silently,
They speak no harsh words,
Shadows are silent.
My heart is like a shadow,
It too speaks no harsh words.
Yet, it accepts the harsh
words that can break
The true meaning of love.
My heart is also silent,
Even though it wants to cry out.
I stay silent, I speak no harsh words.
I, myself, am a shadow.

—Kati Lai

Street Gangs

As I look outside the window, I see them
They stand out like the moon on a clear night
Concealing every type of weapon there is,
They feel confident
I see their faces and it frightens me
They look so young yet act so grown up
They fight to solve their problems
It's the only way they know
When you walk by them
It's like walking on eggshells
You have to be careful or something might snap
How can I worry about Russia
When I have a living breathing time bomb
Right here?

—*Gina Michelle Goon*

Christmas

The children are always excited about their toys.
They stay up late
So they can see Santa Claus full of joy,
Because they think he's so great.
Time to decorate the Christmas tree
And to be with the ones you love.
For this is time to be merry
And to think of the One above.
Putting up the Christmas lights,
Standing under mistletoe,
Waiting for the night,
To hear the sound, "Ho! ho! Ho!"
Christmas is the best holiday of the year
Because it is always full of laughter and cheer.

—*Gretchen Anne Wyble*

Friendships

Many travel near and far,
They take place everywhere,
But when it comes to friendships,
My fear is always there.
Losing friends and keeping them,
Are very important to me,
I hate to see them get mad,
Or try to hide from me.
Staying close is always fun,
Yet these times pass so fast.
Friendships are so very uncertain,
And sometimes never last.
I call them and write them,
To me that is the fun,
Of being friends with someone,
And I'm so glad you're one.

—*Dawn Prieskorn*

Untitled

Why is love a lie?
They tell you it's for real.
They say it's forever!
But everyone knows forever is;
Never forever.
Then you're left!
Left with nothing.
They say you'll get over it.
Maybe you will.
Only time will tell,
But time is always forever!

—*Kimberly Case*

The Beggar

As passers-by walk down the street,
They throw coins at his feet.
And he utters blessings in return,
To those who give and do not shun.
In the night he lies cold and weary,
Under the bridge so damp and dreary.
What protection have his rags to give?
From where gets he the strength to live?
In the harmattan when the cold is shocking,
From door to door he goes a-knocking.
"A loaf of bread and some tea to go with it,"
"Will warm up my body and put life in it."
But on the days when it's warm and bright,
He walks about and his steps grow light.
His flesh fills out, he can ecen smile,
As he hobbles along for many a mile.

—*Ifeoma Angela Chime*

Friends Are Forever

When friends are right
they will be bright
they will always be there
be able to bare
through the roughest
and the toughest
through right and wrong
to help you along
and they will always care
though friends are very rare.

—*Dawn Broomerkle*

Time's Efforts

Why when I try
Things make me cry?
How can I know
When to let things go?
Going through the present.
Thinking about the past.
Hoping for the future,
But will it all last?
Somethings are abstract
And then some are plain.
So how can we react
When we are in pain?
The moment is now.
Many moments have been.
We might not know how,
Yet someway we'll win.

—*Catherine B. Orzol*

The Crucifixion

Dear Jesus,
  I am so sorry
    It had to be
      Because of me.
        Your grateful sister,
          Kay

—*Kay L. Patton*

Smiles and Tears

If times are hard and you feel blue,
Think of the others, worrying too;
Just because your trails are many
Don't think the rest of us haven't any.
Life is made up of smiles and tears,
Joys and sorrows; mixed with fears.
And though it's us, it seems one sided,
Trouble is pretty well divided.
If we could look in every heart,
We'd find that each one has its part.
And those who travel fortune's road,
Sometimes carry the biggest load.

—*Kelly Lynn Dudley*

City
Noisy, Busy
Stealing, Frightening, Crowding
Crime, Skyscrapers, Freedom, Fields
Trusting, Exciting, Wide open spaces
Peaceful, Relaxation
Country

—*Dawn Smith*

A Far Away Land

Sitting here, pen in hand,
Thinking of a far away land.
A land full of sunshine and skies of blue,
A land where all your dreams come true.
A land full of love and joy,
Room for every girl and boy.
Take my hand and we will go,
To the land where our love will grow.

—*Diana Kuhaneck*

Thinking of You

Sitting beneath the sky of blue,
Thinking of love, me and you.
Wishing you were here with me,
But you broke it off how could it be.
We were not different, yet, not the same.
What is this you're playing this little game.
As I write my feelings down
I try my hardest not to frown.
If only you could understand,
If I could just once, just hold your hand,
I am in love that's how I feel,
You're something special, something real.
Everytime I lose a tear,
I'm getting rid of all my fear.
Let's try to talk, you think it over,
While I hold in my hand, this 4-leaf clover.

—Amy Bailey

The Pain of a Dream

Here I sit broken hearted,
Thinking of what I've always wanted.
Thinking of dreams that only I can see,
Knowing that they can never be.
Hoping for a love so true,
That we will be together as two.
Holding for you this place in my heart,
Just waiting for the pain to start.
Wondering if you will find,
A love for me you cannot hide.
I wish that I can hold you tight,
This feeling I have feels oh so right.
I only wish that you can see,
The pain that's building up inside of me.
My only wish is that it can be,
But I guess it's all just a fantasy.

—Becky Kosch

Goodbye My Darling

During the day, during the night
Thinking of you by candle light
Your're in my heart
Your're in my soul
Never wanting to let you go
Teardrops fall from my face
Glistening like silver in the sand
My heart it beats at such a pace
I invision us walking hand in hand
The moon is glowing in the sky
Our love so strong it makes me cry
We had to let it all go
Goodbye my darling
I love you so.

—Candi Billington

To Love Is Dear

Now here I sit upon this bench,
Thinking what was meant to be.
I lost a love a broken heart,
I must endure for thee.
When will I know when will I see,
What happened was really best for me.
Feeling the pain I can not see.
So many sobs so many tears,
A reason there must be,
To feel such love to feel such pain,
Which one do I really see;
To live the life to feel the love,
Is a goal I shall yet hope to see.
And it shall be or I shall die,
One of these two I will not lie.
And till that day I wll not cry.
But try to live forever.

—Ita Neymotin

This Land

Day after day it reappears,
This constant pain and hunger.
I watch people die day by day
But all I do is watch, never to walk away.
My main quest is to stay alive;
With my stomach empty and body weary,
I struggle to survive.
I see my mother slip into a deep sleep;
A sleep she will never awake from.
When will I be free of this enemy?
When will my cruel unkind world be gone?
When it is going to happen,
I shall never know;
I just pray to God all mighty
To please let it go.
Because far from this land of hunger
There is happiness; yes I shall be happy.

—Alain Gordon Bleau

Lost Love

As I sit in this quiet room
This day's about to end
I was thinking of who you are
And how you were my friend.
Remembering when I cared for you
When we couldn't go too far.
Remembering when I first reached out,
Then you took my hand.
How I longed to touch you again.
Remembering all those empty nights,
Filled with thoughts of you.
Wondering if you felt the same.
Wondering if you loved me too.
All those nights of wanting you
Will never fade away,
Because I still think of you,
Every night and every day. . .

—Angela Tagliaferri

Dreams

Dreams are hard to figure out
This I know without a doubt.
Some of them are very sad
And some of them are very bad.
Some of them I still remember,
Even dreams of last December.
In dreams you can go so high
That you could almost touch the sky
But if we just couldn't dream
How dreary would our world then seem?
Dreams make our lives so very full
Without them we'd be very dull.

—Angela Holmes

Our Dying Country

Our country tis' of thee?
This is a question asked often.
Nuclear bombs, pollution, the ozone layer,
All of these things are killing our country.
When are we to realize we live in a dying country,
Surrounded by enemies and war.
Why must we walk in fear.
We are the land of freedom, or so we think.
Nobody seems to realize that our freedom is dying.
Is there anything we can do to revive our country?
Our youth are maturing and all they see is war and death.
But they are blind and so is our country.
They may never know the joy of peace and harmony
As I and fellow friends have seen or felt.
So I pray that one day our country will live again in peace.
So please, all can save our dying country tis' of thee. . .
That is for us to decide.

—Jenny Esquivel

Now and Forever

I think of you now and all other times.
This is our game, without clowns or mimes.
I sit here now without you near
I say "I miss you" and wonder if you hear
I hope that you know how close you are to my heart
And really can't handle how long we've been apart
I know I'll love you for oh so long
It doesn't matter what others say
I love you forever and my feelings aren't wrong

—Jody Lynn Gallardo

Deep Down Inside

In your heart, deep down inside,
This is where true feelings hide.
All wrapped up in a package with pride,
And with a golden memory is tied.
This is where your feelings collide,
Should you be shy, or show your wild
    side?
And when in you others confide,
These private thoughts will stay inside.
In here your feelings cannot be spied,
And to yourself you cannot be lied.
Away from the world true emotions hide,
In your heart, deep down inside.

—*Heather Futscher*

Motherhood

We give life, feel that wonderful pain.
This new life is changing things.
From my bosom, precious baby was fed.
While I rubbed and shaped its sweet head.
I prayed for guidance each and every day.
Fro God to show me the proper way.
One Mother's Day I received a snake.
We released it into the woods for its own
    sake.
Then came flowers, some made me sneeze.
Had to grin and bear it, and look pleased.
We stumbled through the teenage years,
Without shedding too many tears.
All grown up and on their way.
I am very wellpleased, needless to say.
My mother informed me that a stork left
    me in her door step.
I say that God loaned them to me, and I
    cannot thank Him enough yet.
To be a caring and loving mother is such
    an easy thing to do.
Why on earth does it dawn on so very few.

—*Catherine J. Marshall*

Holding A Rose

To hold a rose should bring delight,
This sculptor of art within our sight,
Texture of velvet on each petal we touch,
Detecting the fragrant we love so much.
Lets just stop and think a moment,
How did this beauty come to light,
Who painted the petals a velvet sheen,
Then decided the stems to be green.
How did these stems become a prickly,
While their hue of colors shine brightly,
Seem as tiny bubs or in climbing form,
this magnificent array of charm.
As the rose is grasp unto our hearts,
Do give thanks for this work of art,
Which has been molded by an unseen
    hand,
A deep unsolved mystery to man.

—*Geneva M. Wyatt*

Essence

Petals slowly opening
This virginal white rose the ivory of a
    young maiden's skin
So pure and innocent
Like the silvery dew in the quiet twilight
    of spring
Reminding me of days long ago
When all was so simple
And life itself was a child's dream. . .
I am lost in the reverie of an ancient
    eternity
Of beauteous and ironic repose
Now the supreme song of the nightingale
Echoes through the empty garden
As I sit head between my knees
Mourning this loss more precious than
    anything

—*Erin Lindsey*

Terror And Tears

Last night was not a night to remember
though I did not cry I was terrified
I lay in bed with a pain in my heart
trying ever so hard to fall asleep
sleep did not want me
I just lay there frighteneed of what could
    happen
finally I met sleep and slept until morning
In the morning there was rain
God was crying for me

—*Heather Hughes*

Thy Heart of Wood

Speak not a word from lips that lie.
Though sweet their touch, for which I'd
    die.
Love to lust, for thy soul I cry.
Anger thy heart, no dreams to trust!
I search for Thee in dawn and dusk!
Heal of faith, for life I must.
Visions of death thy eyes do start.
So close the edge of steel to heart.
Stripped of dreams, thy faith departs.
Thy sheath was hope, but it has shed!
Battle thy darkness each night in bed.
Flight on lonely wings I dread!

—*James W. Hadley*

Untitled

Alone I walk,
Though you are there
I'm going someplace
But I know not where
You're leading me on,
Pretending you care,
When all along,
We're not really a pair.
All I know,
Is how very much I've tried
And thinking of you,
I only cried
I was yours
Into my life you pried
And now I've learned
That you only lied.

—*Donna McColligan*

Mind Stuck

You are verily as pretty as they get
Though your ways I've figured not yet
But boy oh boy am I not goin' to bet
That even now there's nothing but glitter
    to get.
The sparkle in your eyes escapes me not
For ever since I laid my eyes on you
All attempts to consider another are only
    naught
As my eyes behold all that's every good in
    you.
They say time does tricks to a man's mind
And I see how well it has done mine
'Cause ever since that first days work was
    done
I knew even then my wandering mind was
    stuck.

—*Joel E. Kalle*

Thoughts

Thoughts are wants,
Thoughts are needs,
Thoughts are anything
From desires to dreams.
Thoughts are conquests,
Although may be defeats.
Judge them carefully,
But without thoughts
There would be no dreams.

—*Doris Dorsett*

A Place Only I Understand

While the stars are sparkling,
Thoughts go through my mind.
The wind so soft in my face
While I see visions of dreams form
Images that only I understand.
Those dreams I pray will come true one
    day.
This place I speak about is beautiful to
    me.
It's a far away place in that only I see.
This place is secret, no one knows about it.
This place seems to understand me, not
    hurt me.
If I tell anyone about this place,
They will not understand what I am
    talking about.
They will just laugh and walk away.
This place seems to know my troubles
Even before I speak of them.

—Angela Keller

In the Rain. . .

When I stand and face the rain,
Thoughts of you come back again.
I remember that cold and rainy day
When my dreams were wiped away.
And those tears I cried
Had fallen from my eyes.
I knew what you wanted to say
When you called my name,
And as I slowly turned your way,
You looked at me in silence.
But before you could say goodbye,
I said these words to you:
"We could have made it together,"
"And it would have been forever."
You did not say a single word
But turned and walked away,
And you left me standing
In the rain. . .alone.

—Karen Ohmart

The Eagle

The eagle flying high,
Through a blanket of blue.
So wonderfully high in the sky,
And her young one flys with her too.
Her cry sounds loud and clear,
Across the mountain tops.
To one 'twould bring a tear,
Until her crying, stops.

—Amanda Bateman

Ghosts

They troop along, sad and weary,
Through ageless nights wet and dreary,
Keeping to darkness, black and cold,
Avoiding good cheer and life that is bold.
Slowly they drift, like mist on a breeze,
Making no sounds, not even a wheeze,
Speaking no thoughts, for none do they
    have,
As they suffer along, in need of a salve.
For pain is their lot, almost forever,
Never to laugh, be cheery or clever,
Only to wait in a dreamless state
Till all dues are paid and they no longer
    hate.
Then life will become them
And all will be well,
For though they don't know it,
There is an end to hell.

—Jeff Woodward

The Greatest Treasure

It glides softly, slowly
through the dark of the night.
Illuminating night objects
with its shimmering light.
It gently caresses each leaf,
each blade of grass
with stardust fingers.
It sweeps across, over rivers,
over lakes forming them into crystal pools
Reflecting the brilliant stars
of the night sky.
Forming the land into a
great treasure to the eye.
Serenity in the moonlit night.

—Brenna Schultz

Untitled

We thought we'd be best friends forever
    and always,
Through the saddest and the happiest
    days.
We were always together, never apart,
We understood each other from the start.
Until that day when our happiness turned
    to pain,
And we took every minute of our
    friendship in vain.
We forgot the good times and rememberd
    the bad,
It seemed like our friendship had just
    been a fad.
We threw away something special and
    unique,
Without us as friends, my life will never
    be complete.

—April Herr

The Light

The light shines
through the window
my eyes slowly open.
My mind
focuses
on th world
around me.
And then I
remember.
Today summer
is over.
The light seems
to fade
my eyes
shut quickly.

— Jennifer Schoenherz

Waiting

I keep peering out
Through the windows
Of my self
Because one day
Someone
Will be standing there
Watching me
From his heart
And I will know
In my depths
That here
Is the one who
Has been sharing
My dreams

—Ann Williams

Untitled

I see before me
Through the windswept rain
A single tree
It has few leaves
Hanging around waiting to drop
The bare branches
Curve upward
As if in a smile
And the tree shakes his head
As if to remind me
He is immortal
I am not

—Glynnis Vance

Everlasting

I raked my soul
through toils and snares
to search for what I was pondering.
I felt myself reach out
and touch your hand
because I knew you'd be there
through thick and thin
and forever more.
Yet I knew somehow
you needed someone
a soulmate or bosom buddy
but not just for that moment
for life is too short to forget
those that matter.
You needed a friend
and so did I
so we found in eachother
a friendship that would never die.

—Kim Bogden

Eyes of Mercy

A cry of mourning is heard
Throughout the air,
When they lay another body to be buried.
They wonder who will be the next one to go.
Their eyes of tears,
Their hearts of hope,
A life of many thoughts.
A hurting stomach from food not seen in days.
The eyes of mercy,
For a wish that someday
Their hopes will be known.

—Esther Sanzo

Peace

Peace is something I wish was
Throughout the world.
Peace is something I wish was in
All of our homes and hearts.
If there was peace everywhere,
The world would be pretty and quiet.
If there was peace, world wars
Would have never started.
If every family and couple had peace in their homes,
There would be no need for divorce.
If everyone had peace in their hearts and homes,
Everyone would be friends no matter what their color is or religion.
If everyone in the world tried to make peace with each other,
The world would be pretty and peaceful.

—Danita Brooks

Hover the Wings

Hover the wings of darkness
Thunder the winds of hate
Loom the darkness at noonday
Over humanities gate.
Crash the seas of tragedy
Tremble the minds of reason
Cry the dead of tomorrow
Beneath the knife of treason.

—Judy L. Drew

A Writer in the Mist

As I think with this pen and paper eagerly in my hand,
Thy mind begins to wonder.
Like having many stars sprinkling sparks.
Will such a poet, as I get the chance—
To use thy precious gifts which belay in my heart.
Will the opportunity of such open doors?
Where wiseness is so eagerly, willingly—
To share to a world, which has no knowledge,
Of one perhaps like me.
Will such a poet be in a lost land?
As I keep writing, wishing and waiting
For such possible thing to accure,
As God helps me to unfold myself,
As a writer in the mist—
Least to the world, but not to one,
Who has granted such gifts as his glory to thee.

—Janice R. Brown

Creative Process

He had never been much of a planter
Till his old friend erected the fence
And rambled a rose bush along it
To lend to his spite a pretense,
So he answered with roses in kind
A thorn in the side of his foe
With beauty as sort of an adjunct
On ground where once nothing would grow.
Still it wasn't the enemy's flowers
Or love that he'd lost on the side
That called for a growing rejoinder
But bareness he couldn't abide,
Not commerce that argument shattered
But structure that made beauty sense,
For it wasn't the roses that mattered
But just the response to a fence.

—David Curtis

Playground Affair

From the moment our eyes met
Till the second that they leave
We'll always be together
Together, you and me.
I guess it's like two children
With their playground affair
Push me on the swing
And I'll be forever there.
I hope you'll always love me
And show me that you care
And if you can, and if you will
The playground's always there.

—Dana Kofsky

Mirror Image

Looking in the mirror, I see a reflection of time;
Time flying quickly past me and into the future.
The mirror never lies.
I believe this as I watch all the opportunities.
I could have grasped slowly pass me by,
Not giving me a chance to reach out to them.
It's not a reflection of a person that didn't have a chance to care.
It's a reflection of a person that lives in the past.

—Beth A. Byrd

Money Talks

Money talks,
Time walks
And I,
Open to the nakedness
Of a world
Gone mad,
Sit quietly
In the park.

—Dennis L. Kellogg

My Angel, My Baby Boy

I can't even remember
Time when you didn't exist.
No blue eyes there to greet me,
Morning smile I can't resist.
I can't begin to imagine
How life would be without you.
Hugs and laughter you shower,
And know nothing else will do.
You are my angel, my baby boy,
You've stolen my heart away.
Oh for the chance to make time wait
While I hold you one more day.

—Kathy Dunign

The Gift

The birth and rebirth of such a delicate
    creature. . .
'Tis not a story of overcoming or power.
It's a relaxing, soothing, tinkling
    disturbance,
But one that's not always unpleasant.
Listen hard and try to hear,
For patience will be rewarded.
It can come in any form or appear in a
    raindrop.
And then late at night, through the cool,
    black air,
Passes the gift of the soundling.

—D. Suzanne Lewis

No Retreat

As a moth is drawn
To a burning flame.
I am to you
Just the same.
I'm the moth
And you're the fire.
When I get closer
You burn higher.
I fly away
And then return.
Only to find
You still burn.
I hover near
For your heat.
Only to find
No retreat.
You would have thought
I would have learned.
But instead
I got burned.

—Allison Osborn

Shangri-La

Come with me
To a place of dreams
Of unicorns, pegasis, and such things
Where good and evil abide and clash,
And overcome struggles to flourish and
    last.
Places of peril and places of peace,
Whereas love is rare but precious when
    found.
Accompany me to the lustrious world,
Come with me to the land of dreams,
The land of Shangri-La.

—Kendra Schweer

After Glow

I'd like the memory of me
to be a happy one,
I'd like to leave an after glow
of smiles when life is done.
I'd like to leave an echo
whispering softly down the ways,
Of happy times and laughing times
and bright and sunny days.
I'd like the tears of those who grieve,
to dry before the sun.
Of happy memories that I leave
when life is done.
"With Love,"

—Betty Ann Adcock

Too Much to Ask

That's all I wanted,
To be loved and accepted by the ones I
    love
And by my father looking down from
    above.
As for the kids on the playground, I know
    they don't matter,
But still when I'm around them, my teeth
    begin to chatter.
And I'm dizzy and I think I may fall.
And the sky turns dark;
And I'm all alone.
Sometimes I wonder.
Sometimes I groan.
Why me Lord? Why must I suffer? Don't
    you see?!
Wasn't it you that said,
"Suffer not the little children to come on
    to me?"

—Amber Helene Roeseke

One Final Look

I tried very hard
to be there for you
But it looks like I'v failed,
I'm finished, I'm through.
I just can't continue
to pretend anymore
Things just aren't the same
as they were once before.
We laughed, and we cried
and we knew we belonged
together forever
where did we go wrong?
And now as we watch
all our dreams slip away
I'll take one more look,
Then I'll be on my way.

—Cathy Bingham

Dark Night

"It's too dark a night"
"To be walking with your eyes closed,"
You told me once, long ago.
But the words that you spoke
Related more to yourself
Than you would ever know.
You were brought up on lies,
Deception and blind faith;
It was all in the game of child's play.
Must playing with lives
Always result in disaster,
The innocent unmercifully slay?
Betrayed by the Code,
The Order and Measure
You fought for your honor and life.
You turned to your heroes
Only to find
The dull edge of a menacing knife.

—Jenny Bigler

Belief

Belief is
To bet on God
Regardless of the world,
Regardless of your lot
And whether you
See love or not
To know it's there.

—Jenny Pair

Too Much Talent

You have too much talent, too many gifts
To blow away. . .you struggle against
    yourself
And mourn your imperfections. . .do you
    deny
You are feeling sorry for yourself?
You are your own worst enemy,
Others like you more than you do
    yourself. . .
You have had glimpses of eternity,
And are much too proud to ask for help.
You know you should do better. . .
Evolved in mind, you see the "truth",
It leaves you empty. . .you seek to ward
Against the base and superficial,
But have not learned what it means to
    love yourself.
Too much talent

—Jonathan Barry

The Dream

The glow of a candle,
To brighten a home,
On a dark and stormy night,
Portrays the gleam of a lover,
To loosen my heart,
When my soul is filled with fright.
And yet the breeze shall blow,
And the flame shall dance,
Till the wind has overcome,
And the sun shall shine,
And our hearts entwine,
Til the day he leaves me alone.
So again I shall sit,
In my dark, solemn corner,
And watch the shape of wax.
For my soul feels too bitter,
And my heart so alone,
To ignite my candle and brighten my home.

—*Anne Kacmarcik*

Gifts

Five precious gifts He did me make
To bring them up for His dear sake.
Babes dear, at first, they all did seem
Until they grew like in a dream
To men and women so mature,
Beholding them was like a lure.
And now as each one takes his place,
I thank Him for His special grace
In giving me five children dear
Who serve the Lord with godly fear.
May each continue in His peace
His gracious favour to bequeath,
That others too might see His face,
And live for Jesus by His grace.

—*Jean Dorothy Cox*

Life

It's the struggle of a baby
To come out into the world.
Wanting to expand
Instead of being curled.
As nine months go by,
Independence nears
Going through tough phases
With parents who are dear.
Why pressure, tension, and stress
Just to make it to this day?
It should be worthwhile
To at least arrive in May.
Because June is almost here
For this baby to be free,
Graduating with accomplishment
Is to be born successfully.

—*Celestine Asistido*

To Be

To achieve something you must discover it first;
To dance to the rhyme you must have a beat;
To think of an idea you must have a brian;
To cry over a feeling you must have a heart;
To have a friend, you must be one;
To laugh there doesn't have to be a joke.

—*Dayna Opferman*

Love Dreams

I have waited so long
To feel the way I do.
I never loved anyone,
The way I love you.
I may not always tell you
Exactly how I feel,
But what I feel for you
Could never be so real.
Even though we just begun,
You mean so much to me.
It seems you're much more
Than any other guy could be.
You're like a wishing well,
My dream come true,
'Cause I found love
When I found you.

—*Andrea Cullaro*

Pain

Yesterday, when you rushed,
to get to your home,
the sky cried.
And in a private moment,
I experience lonliness,
one more time.
But pain didn't hear me,
because sentiment answered me.
You weren't here to see how I grow old,
in a blank called life.
Because you taught me,
reading the verses of existence and possession.
The next days and nights,
When you wouldn't be here,
Just know somebody,
Is turning ove the memories.

—*Ellie Dehbozorgi*

Spring Has Awakened

After a long winter's rest It's time to rise
To greet the world with A colorful smile
Spring has awakened in its Beauty and splendor
To share with the world its Valuable treasure

—*Jennifer Neufeld*

Dreaming Real Life

Have you ever wished upon a golden star,
To have your perfect love?
But find yourself wondering where you are,
And realize it was just a dream.
But once again, you go back,
To think of that fine romance.
You imagine what the two of you could share,
That only your mind could enhance.
You know that you love him,
And think that he feels the same.
But as the two of you get closer,
Love turns into a broken-hearted game.
If you believe in your dreams,
They will always come true.
Just believe in yourself,
And do whatever you have to do.

—*Beth Schepanowski*

A Mother's Prayer

Dear Lord this prayer I say each night,
To help my boys in this great fight.
Keep each one, from great temptation,
While fighting for this great nation.
Watch over each one and everyone,
Until the day of peace has come.
Then send them safely home to me.
Dear Lord, my thanks, I give to thee.

—*Clara Cira*

Go Away

You were there to take away the pain,
To kiss away the hurt and tears,
Through a difficult time of my life.
You were there holding, cuddling me,
Making me feel needed and loved,
Through a difficult time of my life.
You were there making me laugh,
To see the sunshine and the smiles,
Through a difficult time of my life.
I have a lot to thank you for,
But not for the pain, loneliness,
And emptiness I am feeling now.
A difficult time of my life. . .
You're not taking this away,
But you are there.

—*Debbie Crawford*

Dream Away

I believe one day I'll find a way;
To leave this all behind,
To make a miracle arise,
To make my problems shrink in size,
A way that wouldn't take much time,
A way that wouldn't cost a dime,
But even if I found this way,
I'm sure I'd hesitate and stay,
Just so I could dream away.

—*Elizabeth Vanderpool*

That Special Guy

When you find that special guy
To love you during pain
To wait for you after class
And hug you in the rain.
To kiss and hug and cuddle
And take sometime out
To guide you through love
And what it's all about.
I'd found that special guy
But couldn't keep him long.
Although I tried to let go
My feelings were too strong.
He told me there was no one else
But secretly I knew.
There'll always be a place for him;
Juan Valdivia, I love you. . .

—*Elizabeth Taylor*

Untitled

For such a thing as great as death
to make one aware of
the necessity of friends
for such a thing as great as death
to make one appreciate
the need for family
for such a thing as great as death
to make one realize
the importance of every soul
for such a thing
I am ashamed.

—*Amy Bell*

Death Be Not Proud

Death be not known,
To mine heart whose pure,
Thy lie so still and silent,
Soft whisphers of prayer come from mine lips.
Death be not proud,
Ye steal a young life only to give missery.
Death came but fast,
To they beating heart,
Thy warm lips slowly turn cold.
Death be mine final wish,
Ye stole thy's heart and mine.
Thy has lost the warmth and life from thy body,
Mine is slowly going with thou.
Death stole not but one life.
Death be not proud.

—*Emily ViGotty*

The Snowdrop

It's such a delight after winter
To see the first snowdrop appear.
Her white delicate head is so graceful
As it hangs like a bell each year
On short slender stems & spear like leaves
She's such a glory to see.
After her struggle under ice cold soil
That's been bitten by frost & covered by snow,
How does she survive? It's a wonder to me
But so glad she does you know,
'Cause once this white maiden has bloomed each year
Others will follow her in a row,
To add splendor & color all over the world
In springtime, summer & fall
When once again we'll see the snowdrop
So great & yet so small.

—*Anne Brookover*

Mother

This is a poem for you Mother;
to show you how much I care;
To show you that I'm not mad,
and what you did was only fair.
Even though you were so young,
and I'm almost the age you were,
I hold nothing against you, Mother,
you did what you preferred.
I know you did the right thing
and I would have done the same.
But now it is so great to have
a big brother, and it was
well worth the wait.

—*Jodi Kidd*

A Moment of your Time

A moment of your time
To show you I care
That's all I need
To show you I'd be there
The touch of your lips
The feeling of your embrace
A moment of your time
That's all it takes
A place in your heart
To always be there forever
A moment of your time
Can pull us together.

—*Amy Walker*

Thank God?

Little girl
   —ripped dress
—lost
   —crying
Reaching out for only . . .
              a friend
Where are the sunshine and flowers?
She thanks God for his eternal love.

—*Lori Anne Brubaker*

Spring, a Time of Change

Time elapsed bringing anew breath of hope
To some lost souls.
The rank sweet smell of fields beneath the farmers
Plow, preparing the soil for some unknown harvest,
Reminds me of my childhood.
   Kaleidoscopic bloomage
Along the banks of creeks and oceans resonates the
Tides to Africa carrying with it my whole life. Legends
Of my slave ancestry still rise above the mountaintops
As the mourning sun awakens the dew-ridden canopy.
Lawnmowers stand fast awaiting the shred of grass
Only for some other blade of life to take its place.
Blades predating blade after blade. My dreams reach
Out with fully extended arms amongst those blades;
Seeking perhaps a more promising new refuge in time.
Turn the page signaling another postmortal chapter
In life. The road not yet traveled beckons me. Good luck
To me and all those whose new visions accept no boundaries.

—*J. H. Watson*

Something Special

Learning to love and becoming close,
To something special, you care for the most.
You live day by day with this presence so near,
And hold this special life to your heart, so dear.
You grow up and change and that friend is always there,
To help you through the rough times and show how much they care.
To help as you get older, and bring such happiness,
And what you did to deserve such love, you can only guess.
This someone watched over you, since you were a child,
And being in their presence, you just smiled and smiled.
You were so happy and content with your familiar companion,
That's probably why you now feel so abandoned.
As you got older, it didn't occur to you,
That your special buddy was aging too.
But you never noticed...as time flew by,
It was too late when you realized because you're special something died.

—*Joan Howard*

Perfect Words

I wish so badly for the perfect words
to sort of just happen along.
Or maybe I wish for the perfect phrase
Or the words to the perfect song.
I wish for the perfect moment
To tell you my secret thoughts,
But every time the moment comes
My throat is tied up in knots.
I wish for the perfect way
To tell you how much I care,
To tell you how much you mean to me,
and to tell you I'll always be there.
I wish I could convince myself
That it's not so hard to do.
But I have a lot of trouble
Saying the perfect words—
I LOVE YOU.

—*Kelly McGuire*

A Rainbow in Your Pocket

Each morning as you wake up
To start your busy day
Take an ounce of sunshine
And in your heart store it away
Hide it there with all the things
You save for a rainy day
Right next to love and laughter
Where all your memories stay
When there's a day that's stormy
And life threatens to make you blue
Remember above the darkest sky
There's a rainbow waiting for you
So just put it in your pocket
Then when problems get you down
Mix it with that ounce of sunshine
And spread it all around
You can paint your world with color
And tear the storm clouds all apart
With a rainbow in your pocket
And an ounce of sunshine in your heart

—*Connie L. Jacks*

Love

I'm writing this poem
To tell you how I feel
I never thought it would be like this
My love for you is real.
Right now, I'm very confused inside
But I guess that's the way love goes.
I want to tell you how I feel
Why I don't, who knows
I guess I'm afraid
Afraid of what you might say
I want you to smile
and say you love me the same way.
I wish that I could tell you
How I wish it could be
I'll probably always wonder
What your feelings are for me.

—*Betsy Walker*

Thank You

I want to take the time
To thank you for always being around
When I need someone special
To keep me from falling down.
You have helped me through hard times
And kept me on the road,
Pushed me toward the better,
But never let me go.
Remember that you are special
To me for evermore.
You always make me smile
When you walk through my door.

—*Bridget Sheets*

A Blessing

May your home be a haven
to the choicest people on earth
And your love be a leaven
that fills every life with mirth.
May the lives you make more full
and the hours you thus expend
Be the measure of your glory
and a joy that'll never end!

—*Justin Belitz*

Why Lord

Lord, I rode my horse upon this high ridge,
To try to find that heavenly bridge.
My heart is full, I need to talk,
With You my Lord, don't take a walk.
In this world where much is wrong,
You put so much beauty in a bird's song.
Here in this place so near the sky,
I humbly come Lord to ask you why.
Why is there sickness and pain in this world of ours,
Yet you put so much color in our flowers.
Why do we live with people mean and small,
Then we see Christians honest, broad and tall.
Why Lord, do some old reprobates live forever and a day,
While some young Christians you call away?
Please send me an answer my Lord,
So I won't be wondering so hard.

—*Joe N. Brown*

Wish I May, Wish I Might

I wonder what it would be like to be a star,
To twinkle in the sky and grant wishes.
I wonder what it would be like to be a horseshoe,
To bring luck and grant wishes.
I wonder what it would be like to be a rabbit's foot,
To feel soft and grant wishes.
I wonder what it would be like to be a four-leaf clover,
To be a one-in a million and grant wishes.
My wish has been granted though,
I can make my parent's wishes come true,
By twinkling, bringing luck to the family, and
By being their one-in-a-million, number one child.
That happened even before we all saw
The shooting star.

—*Amy Pignatella*

Younger Eyes

To see the world through younger eyes is
To witness all the rights
Instead of wrongs.
The world is but a speck
Of nothingness to them—
No worries,
No cares,
No tears.
How I wish
I could see the world
Through younger eyes.
For all I see is war,
No caring,
No love.
To see the world
Through younger eyes
Is to see the world
Through peace.

—*Jan Willis*

Yesterday and Tomorrow

Today is yesterday's tomorrow,
Today is tomorrow's yesterday,
Today is and was
Molding existence,
Giving birth to tomorrow.
Yesterdays, todays, and tomorrows
Framing what was
Producing what is
Creating what will be
Conceiving the truth that will free.
Tomorrow is spawned today
With shapes of memory and love
Of hopes and a dream
Embraced in my womb
Aching for sunrise tomorrow.

—*Carol Ann Lindsay*

Separate Ways

There we were, walking down the same
    road,
Together,
Hand in hand
Heart with heart
The moments we shared
Through good times and bad
The secrets we shared,
The thoughts that we had.
Now here we are, trudging down separate
    roads,
Apart,
Hand out of hand
Heart without heart
No moments to share
Of good times or bad
No secrets to share, or thoughts to be had.
Perhaps the roads will
    merge together. . .

—*Angela Soete*

My Love I'll Always Give

We'll walk together hand in hand
Together in the sand,
We'll hold each other very tight
Not wanting to end this happy night,
But then, you say good-bye
Not knowing that my heart may die,
Then we each go our own way
Because there's nothing we can say,
We just couldn't see
That this wasn't meant to be
But in my heart our love will forever live,
Because to you my love I'll always give.

—*Jennifer Prouse*

Together

Together we've laughed
Together we've cried
We believe in the truth
Telling no lies
Loving each other, more, as we go
    through life
Excepting me the way I am, me as your
    wife
We share the good times
Trying not to dwell on the bad
To comfort each other when we're feeling
    sad
The memories we've shared, making new
    ones too
The vows that we took will always hold
    true.

—*Chris Jesse*

Tomorrow

Tomorrow is the beginning of unborn
    dreams.
Tomorow unleashes unexpected things.
Tomorrow freedom rings.
Tomorrow heals the wounds of yesterday.
Tomorrow is a friend that way.
Although to tomorrow I am blind
Tomorrow is always kind.
Although yesterday's difficulties
Seem to entangle me
I know that tomorrow I will be set free.
Only tomorrow can find the dreams I
    pray.
Only tomorrow can take the blues away.
Only tomorrow can quench my thirsty
    soul.
Only tomorrow can make me whole.
Only tomorrow can be the brightest of
    dreams.
Tomorrow can be almost anything.
Tomorrow is anything our hearts deepest
    soul can tell.
And that I will settle for very well.

—*Cassandra Robinson*

Searching

Today we will search
Tomorrow we will search
We are always searching
for the best things in life
Hopes, dreams and wishes.
Some we will find
Others slowly fade away.
Keep on searching
Don't ever quit.
Because, if you quit,
You will have nothing,
Only memories of what was.
If you keep searching
You may find exactly what
You had always hoped for.

—*Heather Sakall*

The Race

The horses are in the paddock.
Trainers fussing, jockeys thinking.
"Riders up"! The loud speaker calls.
The bugle sounds.
Posttime.
The horses file to the gate.
The intensity is rising!
One by one, in the stalls they go.
One short minute. . .
The doors fly open!
"They're off"!
They thunder around the back turn!
The crowd is in awe.
The power, the beauty, the strength.
"And down the stretch they come"!
Their bodies surging for the wire.
The crowd is up and cheering!
The thunder fades.
The horses are resting.
The race is over.

—*Amy Lewis*

Paradox

Beyond the doors of reality,
Trapped withing the ridges of time,
A man walks there, alone,
Bearing news of an impending crime.
He marches to a lonely drum,
For his secrets are his alone.
Still He grasps to retain his sanity,
He believes it is completly gone.
The tailsman he bears takes its toll,
As he stubbornly marches on.
And he doesn't know it deep inside,
But his battle is nearly won.
And all the land beckons him onward,
Deeper weaving the dream,
And dreams are filled with realities
That are seldom what they seem.

—*C. Fox*

The Rose Petal

As the leaves or petals from a
Tree or soft rose fall,
And the way you form a family
Wall
Is kind of the same...
The children have come and came
And no one can love them as much as I
But as you grow you'll often wonder why,
And life isn't all bad...
Your family will always be there whether
　you're happy or sad,
And you remember the way your parents
　had kept you,
And you wish there was something more
　you could do,
It's easy to remember your family's
　beautiful touch,
And you want them to know that you
　appreciate them so much...
And as the leaves or petals from a
Tree or soft rose fall,
And the way you form a family
Wall
Is kind of the same...

—Jill Chavez

December Mist

The month when the winds arise
Whistling, whirling, through the skies,
Then this thing called snow arrives
Falling down in many sizes.
I look toward the sky as it tells me so
That this is the month of December you
　know.
Because the winds start to get colder than
　cold,
I feel it through my hands and freeze
And my ears that turn as red as leaves.
My feet are stiff, I can not walk,
I'll go inside for awhile to get warm, I
　thought.
But after awhile, I could not resist
To go back out in the December mist!

—Laquisha Hickman

Trees

Trees are big;
Trees are tall;
Trees are alive;
Winter through fall.
Trees have leaves;
Trees have bark;
Trees are seen
Even in the dark,
Their leaves are green;
Their leaves are red;
Their leaves fall into
People's flower beds.
When the bark comes off
It is sometimes said
The tree is old and
Will soon be dead.

—Christina Aquilano

Dream or Reality

I dream of you from heaven sent, an angel
　that has fallen from the sky.
Trying to catch you we meet eye to eye.
Love has sighted us again, as if we met in
　time again.
You grab my hand tight and we both ran
　into the night.
We stop for awhile and looked up, a star
　dying out.
And then we look at each other again, and
　by instinct we knew our love will never
　die.
Then I knew you had to say goodbye, so I
　hugged you and you were gone.
I wake up and there's reality at my side.
I wished this dream was true, because I'm
　still in love with the angel, but where
　are you?
I am not giving up, love has haunted me
　for you.
If I find you, I will be set free, and be
　brought to reality.

—Joy C. Morales

Untitled

I lay in the gray night looking to the stars.
Wondering only where you are.
Our love fades like a puddle in the sun is
　drying,
Our strength is easing as our love is slowly
　dying.
Why did our love go by so fast?
The sands ran so quickly out of the
　hourglass.
I guess the beatings of your heart
Squeezed away my little part.
Its not the arguing or breaking up that's
　making me go insane,
Its that throbbing in my heart "Oh" that
　powerful pain.
Our love was like a foolish game I don't
　think
I will ever feel the same.
I thought our love would last forever.
Like the Earth and the Moon.
But it ended so quickly as
The day broke at Noon.

—Michelle Kurth

Hope

Desperately gripping at nothing
Trying to make something
My hope pierces through darkness
Seeking the warm grasp of light
Defying finality
Purging dark reality
Like a broken winged heron
Struggling intensely to fly
Stunned by mortality
My hope conquers destiny
Confronting my heart
Crying within

—Elaine Wiggins

Lonesome

Lonesome as the wind at a midnight hour,
Trying to whisper a message, I feel its
　power.
Lonesome as the desert where no sound is
　heard,
There is only the flight of a lonely bird.
Lonesome as a single flower growing in
　the ground.
A single flower is me, waiting to be found.
Lonesome as a star alone in the night sky
I sit and watch this star, then I cry.
I know how it feels to be lonesome,
you're all alone and cold,
Always longing for someone to hold.
I'm always reaching out but nothing I
　grab.
In my heart there's a wound from a knife
　stab.
A stab of love.
A love I took advantage of.
I'm always wishing you were near.
Lonesome as my single tear.
　LONESOME.

—Candace Fountain

Lazy Things

These be
Two lazy things:
Honey dripping slowly...
And Papa taking a grand yawn
In bed.

—Kelly Blake

Paradox

Youth, wanting to,
Unable to,
Lacking knowledge.
Aged, wanting to,
Unable to,
Lacking youth.

—Kenneth H. Schwieder

Denial

Raindrops
uncertain as they
silently descend
against a backdrop
of cloudy innocence
molecules swim before my eyes
blurring the fine line
between reality and fantasy
my smile shrouds the inner turmoil
of desperation
demanding; how can I go on
knowing and hating the inevitable
separation
wrinkled hands;
so young yet so old
needing the touch of love to feed the
denied fire that will forever burn
in the shelter of unquestioned safety.

—*Courtney Beisner*

The Flower

Your love is like a flower, coming out of
　almost nowhere.
Yet, closed to all outsiders;
Left alone in your small world.
Then all of a sudden the flower opens,
Full of beauty and hope
Of a lifetime filled with happiness,
And a love as good as gold.
Then like a flower out of season, your love
　withers and dies.
So tired of being hurt,
And the cold, loveless lies.
Next season, when your flower opens
With new hope or revolations,
Lean your petals my way.
I'll meet your expectations.
Let me feed your flower;
Give it nourishment to grow.
Then let me have that flower,
The greatest gift, the gift of love.

—*Mary Ellen Versosky*

Life without the Silver Spoon

Cautiously, I reach into the fire
Uncertain of what is there
Hoping to find the amber of life
Expecting to get my share
You know. . .I'd vacate my very soul
To be sure to live complete
I'd harness the devil's passion
Or use up the gods I'd meet
But not all challenges can satisfy
My feelings appetite
For life lived inside my head
And dreams that flare at night
Are thoughts meant for times to come
And future's out of sight
So what I want and what I'll get
As different as night and day
May feed my very quest for life
Unknowingly. . .upon tarnished tray

—*James Crouch*

Springtime Air

Let us walk in the fields full of flowers; in
　a spring spritzy way,
Under misty white clouds like fog over a
　bay.
Fair rain that has come and gone
Has brought these flowers we walk
　upon—to brighten the day.
Let us enjoy the spring time air.
I shall gently walk. . .agile. . .in cotton
　blue,
And you, with grace, in white silk, like the
　color of morning dew.
Bluer than the sky floating above, and
　whiter than the wing of a free flying
　dove.
These are soft colors of springtime air.
Into the forest we shall solemly go,
To bid goodbye to the white shod snow,
And the colored air's blow, full of storms
　of the snow
That fell in the springtime air.
We shall step through spring air,
　wherever the spirit is. . .
It shall always be there.
It won't go away, for it won't ever dare
Leave us alone and unwanted;
We shall walk through spring everywhere.

—*Chloe Estrera*

Itemized Room

I live in a itemized room,
Where all my conditions of living
Are itemized with equal nerve,
To infuse themselves,
So I can't possibly miss them!
I fairly broker the memories,
Hoping to come by more memories,
To coral the day,
In the corners of my room,
Where I can better examine the
　memories!
I have to make a decision now,
It is for only a time being,
But I must part my room,
To go reconnirtoring for new memories,
To fill the spaces in my room.

—*Stantly Dubinsky*

Untitled

When you hold me in the moonlight,
Underneath a dark blue sky,
I feel a special love for you,
A love that will never die.
When we're walking hand in hand,
And we see a shooting star,
It makes me realize how rare,
The feelings we share really, truly are.
When we fight over jealousy,
It hurts the deepest parts of me,
I want so much for our love to be,
The kind of love we rarely see.
I pray for us to stay together,
Can you promise we will last forever?

—*Dawn Litak*

Untitled

Love is like a rose
Underneath a pale blue sky
Love to me is nothing more
Than simply you and I.
When I look into your face
I'm where I want to be
At all costs, no matter what
Only you and me.
As it seems it will be a while
Before we get together
As long as we have patience
Our love will last forever.
I only hope the day comes soon
When we can exchange "hello's"
But for now, I'll have to wait. . .
To never let you go.

—*Barbara S. Ivy*

Foolish Love

On a moonlit night,
Underneath the stars,
Just one kiss took away all my scars.
But when I woke up,
He was gone,
Leaving me lonely again just before dawn.
I should have known that what
we had couldn't last.
So why did I try to re-live
what we had in the past?
Even though he hurt me and
made me cry,
I just can't let him go and
I can't figure out why.

—*Jennifer Simon*

Untitled

I call to you
Understanding the illness that we share
You answer me with the silence
I have heard so many times before,
But its so different this time
Its the last time
Now I understand so much more.
If we had opened our hearts
We could have saved so much pain!
You won't so tell me—
How can I?

—*Gina Whaley*

Poetry Today

Thoughts, expressed by many.
Understood in misunderstandings.
Better left alone
Because the truth hurts.
In reality. . .
It is boring in its beauty.
The melodies
Are hard to comprehend.
Inspired by angels
Or demons passed on.
A language creation
Of times passed by,
Of times—gone by.
A shock for the future
In measuring cups.
To bring into order
Acts of today
To take and to share
A day at a time.

—Charlotte Martens

Soldier Of Addiction

Help me escape my private hell,
Undo the shackles at my feet,
Retrieve my soul that's up for sale,
Go forth and conquer when I retreat.
Kill the demon that locked these chains,
Imprison him, just send him away.
Take the needle from my vein,
Evict my deadly roomate today.
Stop his army before he wins the war,
Cease the mindless battles I must fight,
End his lies he's telling more,
Take the deadly powder that is virgin
    white.
End my daily torture and slow suicide,
Conquer what I cannot, cure my pain.
Pull him from my thoughts where he
    resides,
Evict my agonizing secret named
    Cocaine.

—Cassandra J. Meier

Love

Love, love is something we all need.
Unfortunately it is something we can't
    always have.
Sometimes it will come and just leave,
But it doesn't always turn out bad.
A lot of people become happy and forget
    about life.
Sometimes they can become mislead.
Some people are willing to try.
Others just want to take you to bed.
Love can trick and trick you well,
That's why you must understand,
Sometimes it is complete hell!
Other times you are in a fantasy land.

—Chaunda Anderson

Floating At the Botton

I tried to scream;
unheard my noise swept past a baffled
    society.
I tried to scream about the pain;
but my cries were drowned out by an
    ocean of tears.
So I thought of a love that brought sorrow
and cried,
I thought of the men who had spoken
and lied;
I've lived in a dream but now finally seen
the grave of great truths that have died.
So many good people have tried to explain
why we must live in a world so full of
    pain;
I can't understand why it must go on
but I know I'll be screaming
again
and
again.

— Joseph G. Shomo

Unending Love

In this moment in time we stand
Unmoving; forever unchanging
Our love that starts within two hearts.
Remaining the same; completing the
    game
That we play.
With you in my thoughts; drifting
Through my dreams.
I see your face and you smile at me.
My everything is you. You're everything
That's mine.
Our two hearts combine
As we're standing together
In a moment in time.

— Jaima Fawcett

The Dinosaur Age

The world was dark and the world was
    gray,
until the dinosaur came one day.
Some were as tall as the tallest trees,
but some were as tiny as bumble bees,
Some had eyes of gleaming green,
and some had eyes that looked so mean.
Some ate meats, and some ate greens
some were plumps and some were leans.
No one knows how they came or left,
it could have been some awful theft.
What ever it is, or whatever it was
the dinosaur is gone, just because.

—Carrie Heatherly

Careless Wish

Uninvolved by the constant demand
Untroubled by the race
That also ran
Worry free of the desires
That boggle the mind
Yet, yearning for a more
Fulfillment of idled time
While hoping for life
To hurry up and not finish
It's impulsiveness
For a careless wish
Having no interest
In the luxury of a wealthy treasure
Unconcerned by the
Lavishness of it's pleasure
With its selflessness
And mastery
Of a careless wish

—Dannie L. Carter

Autumn Wheatfields

The shadowed field of autumn wheat,
Where children have played since dawn;
Can rest her stalks beneath evening stars,
For now she's all alone.
The sun begins to slowly fade,
Over the field and all her peace;
As she kisses each grain upon her fingers,
With songs of autumn breeze.
She sighs to think of each laughing face,
That trampled in ever row;
Taking from her tender life,
That took so long to grow.
Once again the hazelies across,
Calling the children home;
Leaving tiny footprints in her soil,
For her to treasure while they were gone.
A day of pleasure has now ceased,
Her fingers can rest once more;
For the sun soon brings her little friends,
To continue as the day before.

—Regina Lynn Medders

The Windows Did Open

The windows have been opened
Up above this world that I live in
For this I do know the blessings
Of my Lord have fallen on and all around
    me
So many things have happened and
Are happening this I can tell
I was blind but now I see
Through all the darkness and the pain
My Lord and my God's
Grace was sufficient for me
Now that I have received my sight
I will praise and thank my Lord for
This one of many blessings that He
Has given unto me
For I was blind and now I see
All because the windows did open

—Juanita Hutson Kangas

Taken

With pain folding
Upon a gentle heart
A breeze sweeps by
From a cast
Of the blue sky.
Holding onto memories
They tear away the mind
Trapped by a force
Not inclined to see
But it's there
To take a hold of me.
By one or another
The desert wind blows
It takes the blood
Out of the cold.
From where it is I stand
A gentle heart
Was taken by a man,
Not yet known
And not yet seen
But he was there
I now believe.

—Kelly Gardner

Again
Your insincerity
Sweeps my brain
Again
Your lies pour down
Like acid rain
Again
I'm embarrassed
By your lack of shame
Again
Your words are sewage
And I'm the drain

—Rachel Douglass

Come Gentle Night

Come gentle night
Upon the shoulders of a summer breeze
Cover the world with your darkness
And hide its shame from all who have
   seen
Come gentle night
And spread your mystery upon the world
Let nothing show of what has gone before
Come gentle night
Wash and cleanse the sins of the day
Leaving only a hint of wonder
Of what is yet to come in the morning
   light
Come gentle night
Take the world into another dimension
Where there is no bewilderment and no
   shame
Come gentle night
Upon the winds wing and breathe new life
Set free the chains that had once confined
   the release
As now a new day is sure to follow
   starting fresh and anew

—Cheryl Frazier

Untitled

The hot blade slowly lands
Upon the surface of the flesh.
It was expected,
Bound to come,
But still it hurts inside.
It tears through like a burning iron —
Nothing is held in.
It goes deeper and deeper —
Seems endless and full of pain.
But the blade will pull back,
And the cut will heal —
In time —
Yet the scar will still remain.

—Barbara Tocko

Love

Love is a deep admiration
Usually acquired by two,
Love is having honor,
In everything you do
The sharing, caring and mutual respect
With a mate of your choice,
Love has a great understanding,
In him with whom you rejoice
Love is getting to know him
And taking time to see,
If all the things he want in love,
Is what I want for me
Love is a beautiful union
When it's felt within the heart,
When two people want to share a life,
That no other can tear apart.
So if you think you've found true love,
And things just don't seem right
Just read this poem and understand
Love don't happen overnight.

—Debra Cubbage

Rememberance

With glazed eyes I peer across the
Vast wakelessness of my ocean
Petrified wood does a dead man's float
As rippling waves incorporate a thousand
Dreams into my mind,
Past, present, future
Blend like a child's kaleidoscope
As the last embers of the sun's fire
Gloriously die and fall
Beneath the horizon into oblivion.

—Amy Bayne

In Memory of My Parents

The long journey in the stillness of the
   night
Vesper by the rooms of thunder storms
I recall memories of my childhood days
Mom and Pop differed by fate
Oh, those lingering graves as I face the
   dark desolate world
Is but like reveries of days gone by
Searching for the brighter promise of
   God—

—Concordia B. Brana

Falling Apart

All along the countryside,
Viewing contaminated seas.
Rolling is the white foam tide,
Drunk of medicine teas.
Moving down the sandy shore,
Sea gulls soar above.
Rememberance of peace and war,
Feels of hate and love.
Kicking needles, grains of sand,
What befalls my eyes.
Rambling over miles of land,
Guided by hazy skies.
Climbing over mountainous hills.
Way up over dunes.
Sighting unsanitary landfills,
Eclipsing suns and moons.
Finally reaching swayful docks,
Conclusion has been seeked.
Man destroyed our perfect world,
And nature slowly leaked.

—Alison Delaney

The Beauty Of Sleep

Make a joke and I will frown; you'll look
   up and I'll look down.
Visions fade from day to day; people ask if
   I'm o.k.
Hopes and plans seem so foggy; artificial
   life-drugs makes me groggy.
Reality strikes way too deep; Dreams are
   created-I go to sleep.
I now control the thoughts in my mind;
   my feelings were hatred;
now they are kind.
My dreams are as free as the birds in the
   sky; all problems gone and filled with a
   loving high.
I start to climax, I'm at the peak of my
   life.
I see myself married, with children and a
   wife.
Now filled with darkness; violence I reap;
The alarm clock goes off; I'm awakened
   from sleep.
Life is ugly because it keeps me alive.
Bored to death, I think I'll take five.

—Bruce Thornberry

Rejection

How could I be so stupid,
Vulnerable, and let my
Emotions control my destiny.
This must never happen,
I must be careful!
I made a promise long ago and
I'll see it to the end.
Until this place is a bad memory.
Hold your head up high and
Never let a tear show!

—*Gabriele Cartrell*

Is There a Tomorrow?

I see them sitting there,
Waiting for no one and
Watching life pass them by.
I see no tears in their eyes,
Only bitter determination not to
End up as their parents did,
Poor, tired and proud.
I see the hatred for the people
Who keep them there.
The prominent, the ignorant and
Their own depressive kind.
They want more than promises of
    tomorrow.
They want the security, the caring
And the love that no one can give.
They want what they feel cannot be—
Is there a tomorrow?

—*Kelly A. Kennedy*

The Drum Beats Steadily

I'm just an aging soldier in an endless war
    for freedom-
Waiting for reality to consume the
    beating drum's core.
My fellow man burdened with listless
    casualties-
Divided into countless numbers
Brothers still up in arms-
Fight an army of ambiguous Gods;
    finding the outcome contrast to belief
    beyond wealth;
Creating illusions of a nonexisting perfect
    world forced to fall prey to adolescence;
Their eyes dancing, like the colors of a
    child's imagination.
As twilight with all of its secrets dissolves
    around the flock-
Sleep never seems to befall their weary
    bodies
Dreams come, nightmares follow; the core
    within the drum beats steadily between
    breaths
Their space is lonely and empty; mine
    likewise, but we are staying on.

—*Eraka D. Head*

Suicide

I creep slowly down the road of life
Waiting for the end to near.
Suddenly I feel as though I cannot bear
To walk anymore.
I'm tired and I'm lonely.
I find I have no one to love and no one
    loves me,
So I end my road of life on my own.
Now as I sink down into the mighty
    depths of hell,
I feel my feelings are ten times worse.
There seems to be no way out.
I am imparticular to the method I used on
    earth.
I am trapped in the fiery depths of Hell.

—*Jennifer Wisling*

Pleasure and Pain

Pleasure and pain
Walk hand in hand, like lovers.
Creating hopes, then crushing dreams.
Bringing us joy then bringing us sorrow.
Pleasure and pain
Wait side by side, luring their victim with
    happiness.
While sadness lurks quietly around the
    bend,
Waiting to steal contentment and replace
    it with grief.
Pleasure and pain
Like glory and defeat,
Make us smile, make us frown,
Make us laugh, make us cry.
Pleasure and pain
Work like a see saw.
Lifting us up, bringing us down.
Until we take charge of our lives,
And bring our pleasure and our pain into
    balance.

—*Jacqueline P. Walker*

Here I Sit

Here I sit enmeshed in other people's
    rules
Walking round and round through other
    people's schools
Makes me wonder why I woke up today
Why I was molded from other people's
    clay
"What's the point", I ask, "Why don't
    they leave me alone?"
"Why am I always other people's when I
    want to be my own?"
Yet no one can tell me-they're all other
    people's too
So here I sit enmeshed, feeling rather
    blue.

—*Jonathan Laden*

Mary; Vietnam

Thou Lady of Bible ways
Walsingham, Paris, Sinai
Of New York in our hearts praise
Pray. . .pray our night and days
Thought in Christ, prevent Mylai. . .

—*George La Banca*

So Much to Offer

His eyes reflect years of srtuggle for
    acceptance
Wanting to trust, yet afraid to take a
    chance.
I love how they sparkle when he's pleased
    with me,
How they set my soul on fire and make
    my heart dance.
His smile fascinates me, it's always
    changing.
The way he grins when we first meet sets
    my heart aglow.
A laugh so genuine and boyish, it becomes
    contagious.
But when we must part, a smile so sad,
    my tears want to flow.
He has so much to offer, if only he knew.
But the years have taken their toll,
His confidence has steadily declined.
Second best is now what he settles for,
I could change all that, if only he were
    mine.

—*Bonnie Woolf*

The Wall

Tears, cries,
War; the unforgiven lie.
Families and friends wait
for their hearts to mend.
Now their loved ones
are gone, and tell me.
Were they wrong?
Lists of the dead
and missing bring
people forward with
their hopes and blessing.
Now the heroes are
carved in stone,
left alone, in
The Wall. . .

—*Andria Wekenman*

Israel

Land begin Love carries grief
War, Turmoil oncoming destruction
Stolen from a meager people by political thieves.
Robbed from their land leads great despair
Look to Hosea 2.23
Pray ye America you must care
Have we not been deceived
Our worst foe is discrimination
See the wolves disguised as sheep
Ironically, unbelievable these with our guns in hand
Be the last to desegregate the land.

—Cynthia Bean

Accident

So eager to be
Was I,
Embracing my chance
To experience life
Only to be shunned
By human's naivety.
Not a breath of mine
In the air.
Not a heartbeat had.
Not a chance to dream
All of the dreams
That I wanted to know.
Not a grain had fallen
In my hour glass of life.
Instead, here am I,
Left to wonder what could have been
If I had not been
ABORTED

—Jennifer Glatzer

Searching

What do we seek tomorrow, that could not be done today
Was time the element by which we let it pass our way?
Did all the whys and where-fores, somehow cancel out the plans
Is life ruled by a ticking clock, or the passing of the sands?
When Autumn turns to Winter, then Spring to Summer blends
Do we understand the process, or the message that it sends?
We know nothing of tomorrow, while today is so brand new
If we let it slip away from us, that "raincheck" just won't do.

—Claudia Knudsen

Love/Hate

Love
Warm, compassionate
Caring, helping, comforting
Kind, endless, deceitful, untruthful
Cheating, frightening, hardening
Cold, heartless
Hate

—Bobbie-Lee Howden

Joshua Encounter

The silent supplication of his eyes
Was met with ice blue "yes"
And he, in turn, felt in him rise
Firm strength and gentleness.
Across the darkness they reached out
Nor words were passed between
For words, they knew, enlarged on doubt
And trust was what they'd seen.
Hand touched hand and firmly closed
Vision magnified
In silence nothing interposed
As child to man replied.

—Benjamin Long

Untitled

The feeling of clean crystal waters
Wash away the sins that I soon forgave.
Even though my thoughts
Forgive those who hurt me,
Things start to wind into a strain
So full of powerful pain.
But those without care
Aren't as fair as the
Gracefulness of God himself.

—Ami Jenkins

Warnings of a Lonely Night

The trees whisper warnings in the wind.
Warnings that told people to leave
For something is coming.
A man, a man looking as old as time,
Slowly shuffling his feet on the cold asphalt.
A man for whom no one has any sympathy.
A man who has lived his life alone.
This man, arms laden with newspapers,
Newspapers serving as blankets.
Silently and thoughtlessly he looks
For a bench to be his bed.
This man is alone, utterly alone.
A man without a job, a family,
Without anything at all.
This man looks for a way out.
Now with a certain gleam in his eyes
This man sits listening to beautiful hymns.
No longer alone,
For he has found his peace with God.

—Dawn Marie Plover

The Day When He Sat Down and Cried

The day when he sat down and cried
Was the day he lost his mind
Furious at the world
Having nowhere to turn
After he had cried his tears
He felt more was on the verge
Reaching for a rainbow
Trying to pull his life from below
It was the day when he sat down and cried
He wondered for awhile
Longing to have power
And all his dreams were falling lower
On that day when he sat down and cried
He no longer wondered why
When he was trying to reach so high
It was too late, it was that day he died.

—Arlene Dunlop

Fireplaces

The eyes frightening, blazing like afire
Watching her go off, higher, higher
Your smile so devastating
The future you think, what will it bring
Tears flowing from those fireplaces
Remembering the love and its traces
Your skin so pure and so dreadfully innocent
Remembering on those days what you said and meant
Your fist pounds the table
Your love for her, it is no fable
Those rain drops still falling from those fireplaces
Only one thought recaptures your mind,
And this one thought is not many faces
But one thought overpowering them all
One face that will make you fall
Down on your knees forgetting all other painful cases
This one memory brings tears from Heaven
To those fireplaces.

—Ashley Foster

Pondering

Sitting in the cold
Watching minutes pass
Waiting for the hour
Wanting more from life
Shivering, rocking,
Needing a warmth
Waiting for the hour
Thinking of her
Golden hair,
Stormy smile,
Piercing eyes
Would she love me?

—*Jonathan Wood*

Untitled

i was sitting outside on a grey miserable day
Watching rain splatter on the ground
and clouds chase each other across the sky
When suddenly my immediate territory was obliterated by a shadow
And i looked up curiously
Only to see an image of perfection.
We touched fingertips
And walked away into the future.

—*Kathy Rickards*

The Circus

We stand in a great circle,
Watching with disdain,
The sight of prancing circus horses,
Colorful ornaments beautified upon their heads and manes.
Panic breaks out amongst them.
They jostle, rear, and kick one another in the back.
Their golden tails fly visciously,
Each creature for its own.
Bumping, clashing—hooves against hooves.
Contemptuous, we leave them alone.
The ring is desolate.
All the golden horses have gone.
In all the commotion,
The ornaments have fallen off
And lay strewn upon the ground.
Those that were once colorful hats and belts
Torn, broken, cruelly ripped apart,
Unrecognizable in any way, shape, or form.

—*Bridget Anfiteatro*

Alyssa Cali's Sea

The vastness of liquid motion, so this is the ocean.
Waves crashing on the shore.
Landing with a roar!
Lots and lots of open space, we could of sat anyplace.
The sky was not bright.
Seemed like the stars gave off the only light.
All those tiny pieces known as sand replaced the dirt
and pavement of the land.
Mom and dad held my hand.
Was this God's plan?
It's a little scary, the sea,
is what I think was observed by Alyssa Cali
On her first trip there with mom and me.

—*James Lore*

Love

A four letter word
We all strive to understand,
Of giving and sharing
The good and the bad.
L is for longing, to try once again to be wise,
O is for oval the shape of our eyes,
In seeing and believing in life.
V is for vanity we try to forget,
E is for eternity to last us forever.
Loving and giving, the ones that we care
Today and each day of the year.

—*Elisabet D. Engel*

Bridge to Glory

They are not yet known to us,
We are a bridge to their glory.
They live in God's heart as only a spark,
And each day, he chooses some of them and place them in His hand.
He smiles.
As with each one of us, they are given a purpose in life,
And He passes His hand over the earth; His will be done.
Those women whose time has come to conceive, are touched by the miracle of God.
He rejoices.
Many women fall to their knees and bless their Lord,
While some smile and accept their burden.
Lord have mercy on those who toss your gift of life away,
For not all of those chosen by God will cross over their bridge to glory.
He weeps.

—*Kim Delaney*

The Unknown

There is this guy,
We are friends.
He's tall, dark and handsome.
We are just friends though.
But I wonder if he knows,
How I really feel about him.
That secretly, I think to myself,
Will we ever be more than friends?
Could we be more than friends?
Would it work?
I might never know.
I wonder if he feels the same way I do,
If he is wondering how I feel about him.
We could keep our thoughts to ourselves forever,
Only to find out that we were meant to be together.
Or we could be friends and never give it a second thought.
A second thought about what secretly we are thinking of each other.

—*Jayme Gabay*

Show A Little. . .

Mother-daughter is a special thing
We are suppose to show our love and let our spirits sing.
As I can see this is something we do not do,
Do you love me and do I love you?
For hours and hours all we do is fight.
Mom, it's no different, every day and every night.
We need to talk and show we care.
Out loud—silently, the love we share.
The poem I wrote for you has come to an end,
And please don't just be my mother, be my best friend.

—*Crystal G. Craig*

The Game of Life

Placed on the Board of Life by Fate
We are the Players in the Game
Each turn of the card
Each roll of the dice
Moves us to another space
We choose a card and must decide
Which path we have to take
Once chosen we cannot look back
For the Game moves on ahead
Not so much who wins. . .who loses
But How you Play the Game

— *Debra Jane Rempel*

Untitled

Friends like you and me will last forever.
We can make it through thick and thin.
We, meaning you and me, can conquer
   anything.

—*Kristy Moore*

Friends

Looking back to the things we've done,
What me and my friends have overcome.
Even though we sometimes fight,
We figure out who's wrong and right.
There were times when I thought my
   world would come to an end,
But my friends were there to pick me up
   again.
Without my friends I don't know where
   I'd be,
They sure do mean a lot to me.
Remember I'm here for you and I'll
   always be,
No matter what, you're stuck with me.

—*Nikki Rondeau*

Something to Cling to

We must use lots of resistance
We can't just roll with the flow,
Or we would go cascading down the falls
To certain destruction below.
We have to find something to cling to,
It was a cleft in the rock for me.
A cleft in the rock of salvation
That kept me from drifting out to sea.

—*Deborah McIver*

Come Unto Me

Come unto me
Were the words he said to me
But I chose to ignore them and flee.
The day became oh so dark
And the sin grew heavy in my heart
My burdens bounded me down
And Jesus just frowned.
When all hope seemed to fail,
To sweet Jesus I hailed.
He took me beneath his wing
And now my heart sings,
For the father above
Gives me all his love.

—*Vickie Curry*

In Memory of You

We traveled down dark paths together,
We cried a river full of tears.
But our love proved to be a lantern
At each road's end, it would be near.
My mind was quickly put at ease,
Knowing you were there beside me.
Through Winter's chill and Summer's
   breeze,
We'd spread our love across the sea.
You know, it's really plain to see,
The only reason why I loved you
Was just because you chose to be
No one else you knew but you.

—*Kathy McDermott*

The House with the White Picket Fence

It was by chance that I saw my love's
   smiling face.
We had an extra special love, the kind you
   only read about.
Like seaweed entwined my love and I
   would sleep.
With a love as deep as the frond of the
   seaweed.
We told our secrets and we shared our
   dreams.
Her dreams became my dreams and mine
   hers.
We got married and found the house of
   our dreams.
The house with the white picket fence.
We were healthy and happy, we had it all.
But the times changed and so did we.
I journeyed far leaving the abode where
   my love dwells.
I suffered pangs of longing for my love.
Unable to sleep at dawn a sadness
   overtakes my soul.
While thinking of my love I doze to sleep.
My love's face before me I wish she were
   a bracelet I might wear.
I'd fastened her to my wrist.
For if I knew it was a dream, I'd never
   have awakened.
How many years passed until I wished to
   find a new love?
I grew that lonesome.

—*A. J. Sulz*

Father's Day Letter

As the years roll along they continually
   get faster.
We hasten to keep up with our day to day
   lives and sometimes it seems
We forget the most important things and
   people in our lives.
But we haven't they are forever etched in
   our hearts and*minds.
Sometimes I close my eyes and my
   childhood days roll into focus.
What a beautiful time of my life.
If everyone could hold such beautiful
   memories,
We'd have a more wonderful world today
   to live in.
Cause in my heart and mind I hold an
   essence of two of the most important
People in my life. Whom I'll forever
   cherish.
Thank you, Daddy, thank you Moma, for
   those beautiful memories I hold dear.
And from the two very special people in
   my life,
Who gave me a wonderful life to
   remember.
"I love you both, dearly."

—*Julie Winchell*

Three Little Words

There are three little words
We love to hear
Just three little words
That we hold so dear
There are three little words
That mean so very much
Just those three little words
And the thrill of your touch
Yet, those three little words
Can truly bring such pain
When those three little words
Are spoken, yet, spoken in vain
There are three little words
That we love to hear
Just three little words
That we hold so dear
Here are those three little words
Spoken honestly and true
Those three little words remembered
I Love You

—*KW Reaves*

Fantasy Land

Fantasy Land is a place you visit,
While you are asleep.
Anything can happen there,
No mountain is to steep.
You may be a prince or princess,
Dressed in fine rich clothes,
Or climb a giant beanstalk,
To where goodness knows.
In Fantasy Land,
You control your dreams.
Playing in brooks,
Or bright sun beams.
Anything can happen there,
At any time of day,
But then when you wake up,
Those Fantasy dreams slowly float away.

—*Wendy Fry*

The Portal

Through all our tears,
We never really learn
To hold on tight enough
To those we love.
Too soon they leave us
With the grief of untimely partings,
The dissatisfaction in ourselves
For being less than perfect.
And though I say
I will not again let time rob me
   unprepared,
I am old enough to realize
That life is a perpetual motion;
That moments crowd moments,
And all too soon
I will be caught up in the
Breathless anxiety of mere living;
Where I will allow memory to be dulled
Until death once again reminds me what
   is precious.

—*Kellie Jeane Scott*

Untitled

As we walk down life's long winding road,
We often wonder where it might go.
We never know what the curves might send,
Still we hope and pray it will turn out right,
Yet we always forget the struggle and fight.
As we continue to follow this long winding road,
Our body and mind slowly grow very old.
We have done several things, both good and bad,
We've traveled the map and chosen our path,
And we've done everything over a time and a half.
But of all the people we will ever meet,
We seem to forget the one's who accepted defeat.
The one special thing that these people brought
Was love and comfort when life was distraught;
But the one thing we definitely know,
Is how much they helped us grow.

—*Jennifer Boyd*

Salute to Single Parents

Although a mother we only have
We realize we need no dad.
To give us all the things we need
Our mother serves us cheerfully.
For food and shelter, clothing too
A single parent will always do.
Some say that it is not enough
Because they want the other stuff.
Well, our mom gives the greatest gift
She gives us love, a hug, a lift.
So, thanks to all the moms that try
That chose a life without a guy.
Let's lift our hearts and give a cheer
To single parents of the year.
We love you Mom!

—*Heather, Jennifer and David Piasta Jr.*

Young People

So full of energy and life.
We ride our bikes of dreams throughout the world
Like we're going to live forever.
Planning for tomorrow when the world
Could blow up or some tragic accident
Where we might not even be able to see the world change.
When you're a teenager, you feel that you're immortal.
And from the way we think,
Death's not really a part of our lives.
That's what makes being young so tragic.
You see, we haven't lived our life yet.
Not only do we have to deal with
The loaded gun of our family and peers
But that in the hands of the world as well.
Because it's not getting any warmer out there,
The world grows colder even as you read this.
And before long not just young people
But everyone will freeze.

—*Angela Hert*

A Question Of You

When I think of you,
What are my thoughts of?
Are they thoughts of sadness,
or are they thoughts of love?
When I hold you near me.
What questions do appear?
Am I happy with you or am I full of fear?
And when I'm thinking of you,
Can you feel it in your heart?
Can you feel my love for you,
and the need to never part?
And when you hold me near you,
Can't you feel me smile?
Can't you feel me loving you,
and my heart with no denile.

—*Tasha DiPietro*

Grandpa

I sit in his lap, his warm arms surround me
We rock back and forth
Slowly, I let my eyes drop, my body relaxes
I hear a faint voice in the distance
"Is she asleep?"
He answers, yes, hugs tighter
I open my eyes
Stare at his clean shaven face,
His blue eyes and Indian skin
I smile to myself
My heart sings
I recall fond memories
Sitting next to him
Waiting for the ice cream truck
Helping him in the garden
Wanting to be just like him
I look at his face
He sees me.

—*Amy Hethcoat*

Truth

In a time of change
We search for truth
For a piece to the puzzle
For the key to open
An unlocked dor.
In a dream
It seems a mystery
Each passageway
Leads to yet another
Impossible choice.
Must we wonder
Whether this journey
Will never end?
And whether these questions
Will be unanswered forever?
The truth
We may find
Is within.

—*Elizabeth Lake*

Can There be Peace?

Dear God,
What does the future hold?
Is it a world of death, disease and neverending pain?
Or is it a prosperous world full of hope and glory?
Dear Mother Nature,
What makes you work in your wondrous ways?
They say man is conquering nature,
But the way I see it,
It is you that conquers man.
Dear Leaders,
Why are you allowing our worlds to crumble?
Is it necessary to destroy one another?
If so, we are destroying ourselves.
Dear Father,
Why must you be so violent?
The creation of peace starts in the home.
Without amity,
How can the rest of the world be at peace?

—*Sara Therrien*

Revelation

With the coming of dawn
We see life renewed
And at dusk
We realize life is short
It is what we make of it
As we lie in pseudo-death
Dreaming of the next day
We see what we want
And hope to do
Only to realize
There aren't enough hours in a day
Or years in a life
To accomplish all we desire
With the coming of dawn
Try to grab all you can
And hold on
For at dusk
You may lose it all

—*Douglas S. Kneissl*

The Winter Season

Here it is winter again,
We sing the songs of now and then.
Hear the crackle of the fire long ago,
And watch the tiny trickles of the soft, wet snow.
Hear the children laugh and play,
And listen to them as they sled away.
They sound so pleasant if you've ever heard,
And listen in the tree that sweet little bird.
These things you hear during the winter time,
The church bells ringing and the sound of chimes.
It all is nice in the winter snow,
The children build snowmen and watch them fall.
They make some snowmen big and make others real small,
Some children don't make any snowmen at all.
Then we watch the snow all melt as the winter goes away,
But all children please don't fear,
For it will be here soon again next year.

—*Darlene Prince*

True Blue

True blue I love you.
Your eyes sparkle green,
Greener than the grass.
I love you, You love me.
You tell me I'm sweet
As the angels above.
I tell you you're cute as a dove.
I wonder why you're gone and why so long?
You don't phone.
I wish you come back cause I'm alone.
I wish you call.
Are you dead?
Who's your murderer?
Drugs, they're deadly.

—*Leslie Smith*

Spring and the Color Yellow

As we glance out of our back windows
We smile at this time of year.
The yard becomes filled with yellow reminders
That glorious Spring is here!
Yellow says "Yes! It's Spring!"
Yellow shows the forsythias are out.
It's like yellow bells begin to ring,
And dance in the breeze as the
Forsythia sprout.
They ring out a spring song only
They can hear,
But we see it and exclaim:
"At last, Spring is here!"
Their golden promise of Spring
Warms our hearts,
Just as their beauty brightens
Our views, as we start
Another lovely day.

—*Harriet Ahmels*

Best Friend

You are there for me,
We talk and share
Sometimes we laugh,
Others we cry
We may fight and disagree,
But we are still friends to the end
You and I have been since childhood,
And we are still of the best
We have gone through guys,
And other friends
Keeping the special times at heart,
You are my confidant and I yours
Listening and sharing is our secret,
Cause we care about each other.

—*Carri Shaw*

I Remember the Times

I remember the times when
We talked on the phone.
I remember the times when
You walked me home.
I remember the times when
We laughed and cried.
I remember the times when
You were by my side.
I remember the times when
We struggled with homework,
I remember the times when
We thought our friendship just wouldn't work.
I remember the times when
We cooked up a storm.
I remember the times when
Your smile was warm.
I remember all those
Endless hours of hatred and love.
I remember these special times when
I think of you my love.

—*Joan Thompson*

Special Moments

The day we met
We talked openly
With feeling
And emotion
Coming from inside
With a special touch
Of love.
The day we came together
We shared thoughts
With words
And expressions
Meaning more
Than touching itself.
The day we met
We showed the world
That we both could feel
And love for real
Like never before.

—*Brenda S. Austin*

We, The Children

Why is there hatred and war?
We, the children, don't need it anymore!
Why are the nations always at arms?
We, the children, want to be safe from harm!
Why do people argue and fight?
We, the children, want to set things right!
But, there is such a lack of trust,
That, our dream of peace is turning to dust!
Why do people give way to anger and hate?
It must be stopped before it's too late!
For each day our hopes fade more
And remember, we, the children, are the future!
We the children, want to laugh and sing
Think of the life and happiness it could bring
Listen, everyone, to our song!
Listen, now before all hope is gone. . .

—*Heather Edwards*

Darkness

As I walk in the darkness I wonder;
What ominous encounters await me.
The dark hazy mist surrounds my body,
Filling me with a gloomy emptiness.
Suddenly, a cold chill runs down my spine.
Am I all alone in the dark black night?
As I ponder all throught the frosty night,
I hear harsh echoing sounds scream with fright.
The darkness seems to be never ending,
Leaving me to walk an unknown pathway.
I now travel in the present darkness,
Having no past or future in my life.
My mind becomes captured within the night.
Visions run through my head, but are not clear.
As I scrape my way through the black darkness,
I realize I am lost forever.

—*Lisa Cowan*

The Moment

Touch me.
We touch.
In the spur of the moment.
Not another care in the world.
Just the moment,
All ours.
Just you and I
To share together,
Lost in time.
Knowing it's all going to end.
Knowing we must leave
Each other again.
All alone,
With the memories.
Memories of our times together.
Memories of things we've shared.

—*Annette Callahan*

Joys Quiet Moments

In silence much Beauty does flow.
We tune into hushed Wisdoms flow.
Inner pressures, outer stress,
Are relaxed in Silence, to bless
Problems forget when Answer's found;
In silence Light guides each rebound.
Quiet strings, yet, unheard choirs;
Blazeless blaze, purifying fire!
Faceless faces, such lovey beams;
Worldless figures, as in soft dreams.
Stand emblazoned in Lights Glory.
Now we unfold Lights Inner Story.
Lights diamonds color Medallion;
Emblem of Ture Loves Battalion.
Hear!—"Rise Oh! noble brave and
 stand,"
Protecting Good in all earths lands.
Limits break, limitlessness find;
Past, present future's HERE, combined.
Wisdom's mantled with sacredness.
Search loves answers that all LIFE Bless!

—*Eleanor M. Coleman*

Lost Love

You and I used to be so close.
We would spend every moment together.
You would hold me near
And kiss me gently.
I thought you loved me,
I thought I loved you,
But when you let me go
I felt so alone.
I wish you would come back
So we could be what we used
To be, but for now, I'm here,
Quietly waiting, with an
Empty space inside.

—*Christy Blom*

Cloudburst

Reminiscing musefully
Weather-beaten, toiler of soil
Waits prayerfully at dusk
For cool of night
To sweep torrid heat
Of humid, summery day
From land bleached as straw
Where velvety green grass,
Crops, flourished luxuriantly.
Suddenly, hopeful, echoic
Claps of thunder,
Flashes of lightning
Announce descent of heavenly relief
For nature, beast, man;
Thankful, Divine, cloudburst
Of salvable rain.

—*Clarice A. Merswolke*

Moonchild's Song

Cradled, warm, sheltered
Web of life woven thread over thread
Nourishment and comfort come
From soft whispers synchronized
With heartbeat and rhythm of breath
Then you, enduring flowing pain
Staining cold, sterile sheets
With the ruby wine of sustenance
Womb ravaged, yet fulfuilled:
Creator is your soul name
Now you instruct me in the way,
Showing me Selene's milk-white horses
Drawn across the sky since the beginning
 of time
You teach doctrines of cycles:
The crescent moon's secrets
The sea's tidal whispers
The season's steady, perpetual patterns
Helping me to begin to understand
What it is to be a woman

—*Katherine Hawkins*

Kepler and then

""'Klick click klock Clock" but it's He
 who says"" says Kepler
weeeEEooo...WeeeeEEoo
he could hear it—the harmony of the
 spheres
he couldn't hear
that it's a what
not a...
who..

—*Jim Davies*

Friends

Friends,
We'll always be,
Me and her,
Her and me.
Time may set us both apart,
But good friends
We'll stay at heart.
The good simple days
We'll always remember,
The crimson and gold
Of September.
We'll remember the forest trails,
And jotting down
Poems and tales.
Time may set us both apart,
A place for her,
Will stay in my heart.

—*Kerry V. Claypool*

My Special Feeling

Now that we have come to the end of our
 rainbow, we must leave.
We'll go our own ways of life to turn over
 a new leaf.
Now I will remember you how it once
 used to be.
It used to be of love and care, and now it's
 just my broken heart to spare.
But through the years to come I'll always
 carry a certain feeling of you that
 nobody could take away.
It'll be in my heart very deep carefully put
 away.
The one to find that special feeling of
 mine shall be the one to take over.
But until then I'll sit by the window
 crying.

—*Erica L. Cano*

Lessons

The greatest lessons I ever learned
were not in school
but at the bends of my grandpa's knees
looking up
into a face deep with knowledge,
an almanac of answers.
No question was too trivial;
no answer short of full.
He knew all about the seasons
and could read the skies.
He furnished me with reasons
and never lies.
He knew when to plant
and when to harvest
and when to simply sit
and watch things grow.
And, even now, if I looked up to ask
and he looked down below,
no matter what the task,
he would know.

—*Joe Wheeler Drennan*

Your Always Mine

It hasn't been easy
we've both been through so much.
Just put your arms around me
I'm forever in your touch.
With so much love to give you
and you treat me like a stranger,
Just tell me what I can do
to save our love from danger.
Together lets walk the miles in time
Please don't shut me out
Just tell me that your always mine
and rid my heart of doubt.

—*Karen Benson*

Fir Tree

Everything is here, exchange and
    interplay!
What a show, with music of it's own
    making.
There is no intermission, for the players
    are life cast,
As the wispy tip of evergreen reaches out
    to capture
A raindrop and another.
The wind plays a part, for it tosess the
    branches
Like a cloud duster, making victory all
The trickier for lacy fingers to hold the
    moisture.
Each struggling fiber plays it's part ot join
    the nectar
Into a nourshing silver strand.
A whiff of lightening and thunderous
    applause
Allow each player to be briefly seen in
    turn,
Only to resume a quieter role, without
    which
There would be no play, no life, no planet,
No pad, no pen, no me.

—Donna D. Valentine

The Clowns

There to make you laugh, they make you
    cry.
What are they really thinking?
Behind their masks of laughter,
Is always a forbidden, unseen tear.
Unseen to the real world.
Unseen to the crowds
Which wish to be kept away,
From the real tear.
Our comforting trauma—
The clowns.

—Jennifer L. Brady

Daydreaming

When you look out the window
What do you see?
The clear blue sky
Perhaps, even me.
When you look out the window
What do you see?
A child on a bike,
or flying a kite
Perhaps, even me.
When you look out the window
What do you see?
Raindrops falling
You think of calling
Perhaps, even me.
When you look out the window
What do you see?
A couple walking
Perhaps, you and me.

—Charlotte Procaccio

Where Has She Gone

A child, a woman, a mother,
What does it mean. . .
A child plays hard, filling their world with
    happiness
A woman loves with all her heart,
    wrapping her heart
around one man
He's gone, and now, she must go on,
A mother prays hard, works hard and the
    only hope she
has is that they will have more than she
Hold on tight as the world goes round;
Happiness and love growing into,
Emptiness, loneliness and hurt as time
    just rushes off
Where is the child?
Whats happened to the woman?
Leaving only the mother,
The child is gone forever,
The woman just left with a broken heart,
All that lives on is the memory of a child,
    the empty shell
of a woman, now only a mother.

—Eileen a. Souza

Reah Wings

I've had this dream inside of me every
    since I was to or three.
Whenever troubles come my way I close
    my eyes and fly away
far above the hurt and shame where
    no-one can cause me any pain
I fly so hight, so far away so free and
    peaceful is this day
Like a bird up in the sky, I get a feeling,
    shall never die.
but when it's time to open up my eyes,
I'll come crashing down and realize,
My imaginary wings are gone, I cannot fly
My real wings are wings of Love
That's all I need to rise above.

—Sandra N. Rhynes

Mystery

Sitting. . .often wondering
What I can do to change.
And wondering if I want to.
Hoping to find who I am
And what I want to be.
The mysteries of my world
Puzzling indeed
As I mentally try
To grasp hold
Of my deep inner self and
Feelings
Wanting to find someone
Who can understand me
Yet knowing, I have to
Undertand me first.
Do I really? I'm not sure.
Perhaps my biggest task is solving
The mystery of me.

—Aregeler Williams

Peace

Who seeks it?
What is meant?
Does it suggest calm,
or failure to do harm?
Individuals often pretend
in its name.
Nations often use it
as a game.
By promoting it some
gained fame.
Yet, to everyone its meaning
isn't the same.
Is it a feeling of being dead.
Or that restful feeling when in bed?
Is peace a mystical mystery
That exists in an auspicious degree?

—Juanita Terrell

Rubbish?

A philosophical question:
What is rubbish?
Is it an old bottle
Found drifting along the shore,
Or a far-out story
That no one really believes?
Is it a simple comment made
When an unfortunate mishap occurs,
Or an event in one's life
That one refuses to accept?
Rubbish is something unknown to man,
Rubbish is what one makes it.
To me rubbish is an incomprehensible
    thing
That needs to be explained.

—Felice Frederick

I Wonder. . .

As I lay at night wondering
what the next will be like. . .
. . .I wonder.
Will the sky be blue?
and the people too?
. . .I wonder.
Will my day go well?
And my grades be swell?
. . .I wonder.
Will my parents die?
And my brother cry?
. . .I wonder.
As I lay at night wondering
What the next day will be like. . .
. . .I wonder !!!

— Adrienne Renee Smith

Grim Wedding

Here I am in a gown of white.
What we did was wrong. Let's try to make it right.
Here you are in a suit of black.
So formal, so final, we can never go back.
We had nothing to lose, yet so much to gain.
How could so much pleasure bring forth so much pain?
There's nothing that binds us on Earth or above.
Why are we getting married? We're not even in love.
Yet here we are, two children, playing a grown up game.
We have to do the right thing or endure our families shame.
I have to let you go now. You were born to be free and wild.
Don't worry, I'll be all right, and I promise to love our child.
This will never make it right, it won't.
Do I take thee as my husband?
I'm sorry, no, I don't.

—*Chris L. Donovan*

My Gift

Long, long time ago
When I was just a lad
I would sit on a rock
And look over the sea
When I was feeling bad.
I would think of the things
That God has given me
Like the sun and the sand
And the birds and the trees
As I watched the children
Play by the sea.
I could see all that He had blessed
With His hand so gentle and true.
And I would look up into the sky
And no longer feel so blue.
God has given me a gift
That I must now share
And with this gift I give to you
My little prayer.
God, thank you for all that I can see
And for all that I can hear.
But most of all, I thank you God
For always being there.

—*Mary E. Rueda*

Sky High

We found each other through a friend,
What we have will never end.
My love for you is ever so strong,
And will last for oh, so long.
I have been waiting for someone like you,
But never found who.
I hate to be mad,
Because it makes you look so sad,
I guess what I am trying to say,
Is that I love my life this way.
You are the one guy,
That makes my love fly sky high.

—*Kristen Keech*

Will I?

When I'm 60, how will I feel?
What will I think of when I look back;
Replaying scenes, putting together pieces
Of a life confused and lost?
Will I sit there alone-as always?
Discontent with the outside world;
Hurting from things I could never change,
People I could never change-forever hoping.
Will I have any regrets of goals never reached,
Wasted moments, days so quickly gone by. . .
Or will I have reached an inner peace
Happy with my life, myself, and the beauty that surrounds me?
Will the little things please me still?
Sunshine warm my face, cool breezes calm my soul, quiet moments always.
Will I have been loved the way I've needed and dreamt of?
Will I have loved the way I've wanted and wished for?
An inner faith and spirit whispers to me. . .yes.

—*Ailsa Stewart*

One Little Lonesome Wish

If I had one little lonesome wish, what would I wish for?
What would anybody wish for? Such a simple question but
Does anyone know what they really want?
Would we wish to become rich and buy everything we see,
Or become a famous movie star and have people worship us?
Would we want to be rulers of countries and help govern them?
All those things are wonderful and anyone would want them,
But the question is do we really need those things?
What I think we really need to wish for is really such a simple thing,
Just peace and harmony throughout the world.
Won't you give one little lonesome wish for that?

—*Andrea Savala*

Sunset

Faded grey, medicinal eyes;
Wheelchairs aimless in their race
Accuse in weary, silent voice,
"When will you find the time?"
While others blank against the wall,
Dance their own tune, sing their own song.
We drop a smile along the way
And let it fall—wherever.
Rushing! Must escape condensed
Air overburdened with remains
Of death, antiseptic, and ham,
Too thick for youth to breathe.
And then within the doorway, Ethel,
Rocking in time to her Na-Na song.
For one sane moment, stopping to speak,
"Waiting. Na, Na, Na. . .waiting."
So on she rocks, too sad for sane
And Mother's Day Sunday, she waits.

—*Kathryn Jarka*

Untitled

Goodbye was all you could say when you left,
When al that time my arms longed to hold you,
Hold you so close and tenderly,
All you could do was resist.
Our feelings always seemed to collide,
But never bond within one another.
Now you are gone, and so am I,
Because me without you makes a life of nothing.
Nothing to hold except the memories of a love greater than life,
Life that is now gone.
I thought something so great would never die,
But I was wrong.
It now rest peacefully in a warm, darkened grave,
Below everything sadness, war, depression and heartbreak,
But it shall never rise again, for it lies silent everyday
And night for now because there is no forever.

—*Anitra Coomer*

Hosannah

The common sounds are bolder late
When all in the house are sleeping:
A vagrant breeze shakes the gate,
While a lonely faucet's weeping.
In the pale lamplight the teacups glow
And a jar of jelly is manna,
For through the window near there show
The stars that sing Hosannah.

—*Jay Davenport*

So Long Ago

Can you remember so long ago
when children knew no fear.
Of someone taking them away
from those who love them dear?
Can you remember so long ago
when gunfire, silence knew.
And people cared about the world,
the sky was purest blue?
There was a time, a time of peace
when love like flowers grew.
And words meant just the things they said
and everything was true.
Oh! For that life to come again
when happiness abounds.
And laughter fills the universe.
and peace flows all around.

—Donna Williams

A Grandfather's Wish

My grandfather loved the fall
When everything is so bright and
   beautiful
He loved when the trees turned colors
And when it started to turn chilly
But when my grandfather died
We knew he wanted us not to be sad
Because we knew in our heart
We would be seeing him sometime soon
   enough
In another lifetime far away
We wish we could see him very soon
But we knew it couldn't be arranged
We know we will see him soon enough
So we don't wish too hard
Because life's too short anyway
He's living a happy life in the sky.

—Dendy Shepherd

Someone Cares

There comes a time
When everything seems to go wrong
And you feel so alone
Be patient 'cuz someone cares.
Whenever you're down and out
And you feel like you can't go on
When you feel like giving up
Be strong 'cuz someone cares.
When everyone's against you
And you feel you can't do anything right
When they keep putting you down
Be brave 'cuz someone cares.
When you feel that no one cares
Please always remember
That someone cares for you a lot
And that someone is me.

—Jacqueline Lim Tanso

A Gift

I was sitting alone this morn' so blue. . .
When God said, "A gift I give to you."
I've often wondered, "What's my lot?"
For gifted, I thought I was not. . .
But now I see
God has a plan for me. . .
To put my words on paper,
So others will capture
Some things sent from above,
To prove his divine love.

—Gayle Wilson

Love at First Sight

That day in the park
When I first met you
It was getting a little dark
Our eyes locked
And I knew it was fate
Just for you and me to be together
My love for you will never stop
Til the day I die.
We were meant to be
In the eye of fate
We may argue and we may fight
But I know it'll turn out alright
Cause I know you love me
Just the same way I love you
Together, forever for always we'll be!

—Karolina Kowalczyk

Frances

All is beauty, all is grace
When I gaze upon your face
In spite of all the strife and tears
That occurred throughout the years
God has seen fit to provide
That you would still be at my side
You stuck to me through thick and thin
With God's help we'll surely win
A few more years of good health
Maybe even a trace of wealth
We give thanks to God above
It's so nice to be in love.

—Glenn B. Petitt

What Love Means to Me

Love is seeing your face every morning,
   Looking up and seeing you there.
When I need you, you're always there, To
   comfort me, to make me understand.
I am so alone when I'm not with you,
   When I am, my heart is filled with love
   and happiness.
When I want to cry, you make me laugh.
The most important words you say to me
   are, I love you.
This is what love means to me.

—Jennifer Skaggs

The Way it Was

I wish you still really knew how much I
   think of you.
When I see you, I can't stop thinking of
   how it used to be.
I know you haven't any more feelings for
   me.
I was always so happy when we were
   together.
Now I only wish of how it could have been
   better.
You and I made such a good pair.
Now it seems like you don't even care.
We were always laughing each and every
   day.
You now don't even seem to look my way.
We used to hold each other's hand,
As we walked across the sand.
We used to stare into each other's eyes,
Now it's all of these sad goodbyes.
I always feel that I'm falling apart,
You always seem to be breaking my
   heart.
I sit here alone feeling so empty because
I wish it could be the way it was.

—Janice Espinoza

Because I Love You

I am always near you
When I seem afar.
I am with you
When your days are long.
Think of me
When your burdens are too heavy to bear;
For I will be there
With a smile and a kiss to lift your cares.
When you feel
That you can't take one more step,
Think of me
And I am beside you to take your hand.
When you feel afraid
And doubt fills your mind,
This is the time in which to close your
   eyes
And think of me;
For it is then that I am near enough to
   touch you,
And for you to hold me.

—Corinna Murphy

I Love You

What is the true meaning of love.
When I think about it,
You're the one I think of.
Even though we see each other everyday,
My love for you grows in every way,
And nothing will ever tear us apart.
Every time I say I love you,
It's from my heart.
Forever and always it will be just us two,
All I really wanted to say is I love you.

—Jennifer Reed

At the End of My Rope

When I think of the failure I stand for,
When I think of the smile I last smiled,
When I think I have no more strength left,
When I think no one else cares or loves,
I think of quitting my life,
To lower my goals
For I have no faith in my task in life.
No more strength to seek
No shoulder to lean on,
I stop and think of what I thought
And I think, I should leave
Everything to God.

—Coleen Walker

Neverending Friendship

You make me smile
When I want to frown.
You bring me up,
When I'm feeling down.
When he breaks my heart,
Or yankes it around?
You make things all better,
When you come around.
You make me laugh,
When I want to cry.
You change my mind,
When I want to die.
I hope our friendship never ends,
You'll always be my special friend.

—Desiraie Storm

Depend on Me

When I was sad, you made me happy.
When I was hungry, you fed me.
When I cried, you comforted me.
Thanks for everything,
For without you,
I could not be.
I say this to you,
Because you are me.

—Kim Yedlosky

Catching Falling Stars

I tried to catch falling stars
When I was just a kid
But I could never catch them
No matter what I did.
I tried to find the pot of gold
On the rainbow's other side
But I could never find it
No matter how hard I tried.
I tried to jump up to the clouds
So I could float around
But, no matter how high I jumped,
I always fell back to the ground.
But I never stopped trying
No matter how hard the job would seem
For one day, I just might catch a falling star-
If only in my dreams.

—Jennifer Addis

Change

How I hate. . .
When it slips upon me unaware,
I try
To
Grasp my moment. . .unaffected by
The moody time of life's travail.
Someone save me, someone soothe me
Break my fall from my present
Happy niche.
Someone save me, someone bear me
Away from changes unsolicited,
Each painful switch
Unwarranted, unwanted always
Fetters my unfettered self
For worse or better I find
Each unwanted change brings sacrifice
Unwonted.

—Elizabeth Torres

My One and Only

My love was lost
When my boyfriend and dumped me
I paid the price it cost
Because he wanted to be free.
He heard a tale that wasn't true
From his friend, he thought.
And the next day I was blue
Then his friend got caught
In the middle of a lie.
So we both talked it out
And now I don't have a lost love
And no longer do I need to pout
Because we are doves on a clove.
Since we're together now
We are happier.
Happier than a cow
Could ever be.

—Christina Caddy

Friend to Friend

Crusing through life at a comfortable speed.
When reality sets in.
Things are not what they seem.
Friends are supposed to be faithful
Through the fire and the rain.
The fact they are not
Sets you up for considerable pain.
You have a choice in dealng with this pain.
Don't run away from it.
Go to your One true source of help,
The One whose blood has saved,
The One whose touch can make you whole,
And whose love will never let you go.
With Him you can face tomorrow.
Remember there are those
Who will stick through the stormy weather.
But most of all I want you to know,
You've got a Friend forever.

—Elizabeth Bergeron

Life

What's life worth,
When the birds don't chirp?
When the sun doesn't shine?
Or your puppy doesn't whine?
But if you look at the bright side of everything,
The sun will shine and the birds will sing,
And yes, oh yes, your puppy will whine.

—Kelly Jo Haycook

Love Arise

I arise with dreams of you,
When the winds are breathing low
And the stars are shining bright,
I arise.
Entwined within thine lovers arms
Beneath the blanket of night,
Warmed by the moon lover's delight,
I arise.
Breathe deep thy fragerance sweet
Touch thy lips through slumbers sleep,
Shadow lover of the night arise with thee
Upon dawn's first light, arise.

—Janis I. Crichton

Lay Me Down

When I've climbed all my mountains and
   traverse all my glens,
When there comes a time I seem not to
   have a friend,
Don't do a thing, just lay me down.
When I've wiped all the tears from each
   of my eyes,
When I've said goodbye to heartaches and
   fears,
Don't do a thing, just lay me down.
When I've read all the books and written
   my last line,
When energy and vitality says I've run
   out of time,
Don't do a thing, just lay me down.
When my steps have become but feeble
   and few,
When all of my days are lonely and blue,
Don't do a thing, just lay me down.
When I dream no more of the future, but
   reflect only on my past,
When no longer I can run and jump on
   my garden grass,
Don't do a thing, just lay me down.
When all my tools I've laid to rest and
   medical science has done its best,
And when I've descended life's ebbing
   crest and retire in my earthly crest,
Remember what I say, just lay me down.

—Ezekiel Stubbs

Springtime Friends

I used to watch them out my window,
When they began to play;
But now I cannot watch them,
Because they have gone away.
They would flit and float, as they soared
   up high,
Higher and higher into the sky.
Their brilliant hues with bold, bright
   sheen,
From far away could still be seen.
Beautiful monarch butterflies are they,
But now I cannot watch them,
Because they have gone away.

—Amanda Schloemer

Our Love

Our love was unknown
When we were alone.
But through our letters
We shared to each other that we cared.
Miles separate us,
But as I think of you today,
I say to myself "I love him oh so much,"
"More than words can say."

—Julie Nelson

My Secret Fear

My friends don't share this secret
When we're playing in the yard.
They don't know how I feel inside,
Or how my life's been scarred.
My friends have never been abused,
Or known this kind of sadness.
Their homes are always cheerful,
Never a hint of unhappiness.
My friends don't seem to question
Why today I cannot play.
Once more, I stay inside my room,
Badly bruised and in dismay.
My friends I think could help me,
If I'd only let them know.
I need someone who understands;
Someone to tell me so.

—Cathy Bryan

You and Me

You and me are two as one,
When we're together we always have fun.
You and me are known as double,
But when we're apart; we're nothing but
   trouble
You and me are not best friends,
But to me you are the best to the end—
You and me our hearts combine,
On Valentine's day I think of you as mine.
You and me can always have fun,
You and me are two as one.

—Amber Drake

School Time Goodbyes

At the end of the year
When we've all said goodbye,
Shed all our tears,
Let out all our sighs.
Promising we'll keep in touch,
Never realized school meant this much.
Here at the end
When things come to a close,
There's a feeling inside
That no one else knows.
We rely on each other,
And that's a big deal,
Cause friends are the ones,
Who know how we feel.

—Jaime Tyna

Summer

Summer is a time when you're out of
   school,
When you don't have teachers nagging at
   you.
You have swimming parties,
Stay up as late as you want,
You can have fun without worrying about
Homework or any sort of problems.
That's what summer
Is all about.

—Jami A. Dobretz

Time

Time is always too fast
When you have love that lasts
In family and friends
Who stick to the end.
But time will leave
Before you believe;
So cherish every day
Before time slips away.

—Kirsten Honaker

Friends

Friends are there through thick and thin,
When you lose and when you win.
Friends have a special bond,
To carry with them on and on.
They're there for you when you cry,
Or if you just lost a guy.
Even though friends sometimes fight,
They'll always be there day and night.

—Kristin Tyler

Untitled

Tis so hard,
When you miss someone so much;
To go on with your life,
Without their feelings and their touch!
You sometimes try to forget them;
But can't seem to succeed;
Because they are a part of you,
Something you will always need!
They seem so far away,
Farther than they really are;
And when people tell you this. . .
You think far is far!
You want to break away
Because you have become too close;
But for them to be back again,
Is what you want most!

—April L. Johnson

Alone

When you were crying, I gave you my
 shoulder.
When you needed to talk, I lent you my
 ear.
When you were happy, I celebrated with
 you.
When you were sad, I shared your sorrow.
When you were in trouble, I was there to
 bail you out.
When things fell apart, I helped put them
 back together.
Where were you when I cried out?
Where were you when I needed to talk?
Where were you when I was celebrating?
Where were you when sadness overtook
 my heart?
Where were you when my life fell apart?
You were gone, I was alone.
I left, to leave you alone,
Forever!

—Kate Stevenson

Your First Love

Did you ever get the feeling
When you really want to die?
All you do for days and days
Is bow your head and cry.
It feels like God is taking away
The best thing in your life
When he takes away your first true love.
It cuts you like a knife.
You'll never want to let him go,
Although you know you should.
You'd hold him for eternity.
He doesn't think you would.
Did he really love you?
Does he ever think about it?
Or were you on a one way street?
Sometimes I wouldn't doubt it.
You can't let go of your favorite
 posession.
I'll always love him. . .that's my one
 confession.

—Kerri Ethier

Majority Always Rules

What is crooked,
When you see a crooked picture
It seems crooked because everything is
 straight,
But if everything else is crooked
The picture would be crooked again,
And everything would actually be
 straight,
Would it not?

—Karla Lesh

The Cost of Living

The cost of living is so high.
When you think of it, it makes you almost
 cry.
All this inflation we have shatters your
 dreams;
When you are talking about getting
 wordly things.
They say you have to pinch and scrape.
That's why the world has robbers who
 have to take.
With the cost of living, you can hardly get
 by;
That's why some people on their taxes try
 to lie.
The cost of living will soon grow and
 grow.
You will have to get a job that pays more
 dough.

—Karen Everage

Forever

The sorrow that filled my heart,
When you were gone
Is unexplainable,
How I would of loved to have spent more
 time with you,
But you came and you left,
Just as everybody has to,
I did not know you as well as I should of,
But I know you are in heaven,
In good hands,
There you will live,
Forever,
So now it is time for me to say goodbye,
Forever.

—Destiny Ashworth

My Best Friend

When the cold wind is blowing, and no
 one's around
When you're alone in the darkness,
 without a sound.
When people around you are just being
 mean.
and everything seems so wierd and
 obscene.
When you're in need of help or feeling
 sick,
When you break a belonging, or a loved
 one has died,
and nobody else will stand by your side
These are all times when a friend comes
 along,
to make you feel happy, better, and
 strong.
Many friends can come and go,
but heres something more important to
 know,
Real true friends are precious but few,
Thats why I chose my best friend to be
 you!

—Cassia Ponusky

Endless Nights

Tonight, I wonder
Where did sweet youth go?
For it is as hopelessly lost to me now
As the tears that fell into a bottomless
 lake.
Night after endless night, it continues.
Seldom are there nights when I find relief.
I pray to God above for sweet slumber to
 come—
With it, a chance of dreaming of a world
Where dreams live, where they thrive.
Even then reality reigns, and I wake once
 more.
And yet the sunlight shines through the
 rain,
Its golden beams reaching me
Even in this dismal world.

—Katherine

Where Am I?

Where am I?
Where do I live?
I spend all my time in a place faraway
Deep in my heart
And my soul.
But what if I chance to meet reality?
What would I do?
What would I say?
It's been so long since we've met
My world revolves around fantasies and
 emotions
Reality revolves around fact and matter
If we chanced to meet someday
Would I push it far away?
Or hold tight to it?
So not to fall too deep within myself.

—Kathy Walsh

Where does all the Time go?

One day I stop to think,
Where does all the time go?
As I ponder I see the links
Of the chains of my existence,
Slowly intertwine.
I remember all the words unsaid.
And regret the things undone.
One of the things I've realized is,
From the future, you cannot run.
I know one day I must say goodbye
To the things I hold so dear,
Still everyday I try my best,
To keep the present here.

—Jessica Rumfelt

Destiny

There is a place
Where dreams come true
Where love is forever
And skies are always blue.
There is a place
Where water is crystal clear
Where there is no hatred, nor is there fear.
There is a place
Where love will always grow
Where is this place? Only you know.
How do I get there? you may ask.
To do so would be a simple task.
Where is this place?
There's only one clue
Look inside your heart
Your destination is you.

—*Heather Hopes*

Summer

Summer is a season
Where everything has reason.
The flowers, they bloom.
Because they know it's June.
The meadow becomes greener.
The pool becomes much cleaner.
The reason for this,
Is cause the pool was a mess.
The days become longer,
Your health becomes stronger.
That's why summer is great
And sure lots of fun.
So make sure to get out.
And get lots of sun.

—*Becky Kauffman*

Lost Love

I think to myself
Where has it gone.
The love I once
Knew that kept
Me so strong
Thinking, who
Will help me
Find it again.
Praying, wondering
Was it a sin
Someone, anyone
Will you help me.
Should I find this
Love or let it be?

—*Jamie Music*

A Christmas Night

Alone with you, up in the mountains,
Where it is snowing every minute of the day
As you're out cutting wood,
Me, cooking by the warm fire.
The snow is drifting lightly
As you and I lay by the fire
Cuddled together, thinking of only
Each other.
We have, for an old fashioned Christmas,
Strung popcorn upon a fully decorated
Pine tree with a few presents
From each other beneath it.
We lay cuddled together in each others arms
Thinking of all the things we've shared
Throughout the years,
Whispering in each other ears, "I love you",
Wishing this wonderful Christmas night
Would never end.

—*Amanda Blanton*

The Land of Cain

Have you ever heard of the Land of Cain,
Where lions cry as souls are drained?
The men are weak, it always rains,
The few untouched are barely sane.
For as you enter this bleak domain,
You become enveloped with their pain.
The fun you feel is only feigned,
Escape is tough, most times in vain.
Your health goes bad as good times wane,
You never sleep, your body's lame.
You're traveling down destruction lane,
But walking's slow—you catch a plane.
The days are nights, the night's the same,
You've lost all touch with nothing to gain.
But you try very hard, 'cause you want to obtain,
The one thing you still like,
Your last friend, cocaine.

—*Brian Goldberg*

My Friend

The heart is a sacred doorway,
Where love's the only key.
Someone's gotten in there,
And become a dear friend to me.
She's listened to me crying,
And soothed my anguished tears.
She's been kind and understanding,
She's calmed my savage fears.
A true friend till forever ends,
She helps me through each day.
Whatever happens, no matter what,
In my heart she'll always stay.

—*Debbie Barton*

Journey

I journey off into barriers of mind, into my past,
Where rain, storms, and cloudiness haunt me.
As rainbows, sunrise, and the sun please me.
I journey, deeper into my soul,
Where good is trying to overpower bad.
Off into my heart I go,
Wanting to love, but just can't trust.
Wanting to let go, but love is captured by frightened emotions.
I journey, into reactions.
Doing bad things to try to stop the pain.
I journey, until forever ends to find myself.
But I never accomplish this goal.

—*Cyndi Sawyer*

I Join My Brother

I join my brother today
Where there is no greatness
Or grandeur,
No fame or fortune.
I join my brother today
Where there is no
Night or day,
No yesterdays or tomorrows.
I join my brother today
Where our spirits meet
In God's realm
Of eternal love.

—*Kelle Carpenter*

Peace, Love, and Democracy

Living in a dangerous time
Where there isn't any security.
Criminals loose on the streets,
People carrying guns for protection.
Can't walk the streets after dark,
Don't know who to trust.
Everywhere you look, there's fear,
There's no longer any compassion.
Everyone is out for themselves.
Whatever happened to our heroes,
We only hear about our villians.
Prostitutes on the city streets,
Drug dealers there beside them.
Doors don't go unlocked anymore,
Windows are nailed and barred.
People watch over their shoulders.
Whatever happened to such things as
Peace, love, and democracy?

—*Delta Pierce*

Edification

My past is cold, entombed below
where waters flow beneath the ground.
Now, liquid time shall wear and score
as polished pebbles softly shine.
The drops of days construct a spire.
Stone altars bear dark, secret thoughts.
Without, the world must labor on.
Within, the crystal memories—mine.
Great caverns wait where once was life.
Yet precious moments still withstand
awaiting, now, the dousing rod
which, once extended, will divine.
Prove out my soul; reveal my core!
Stretch out the staff towards the cache.
Yes, time has done its patient work;
to shape, restructure, and refine.

—*Connie Crandall Crosby*

The Ocean and Sea. . .

The ocean and the sea.
Where waves move in and out
The peaceful sound of sea gulls.
The sun that sets at night.
The sand beneath your feet.
The animals that swim about.
The way they play in and out.

—*Kimberly Rylott*

Promise

Thomas promise you'll always stay near
Where we can live without fear
And share in all we see and hear
Thomas promise that when you take a wife
You will not go out of my life
That you will let me share in your sorrow and laughter
For a Mother's life is a lonely one once her son is grown
So—Thomas promise you will always stay near

—*Elaine C. Mandulak*

Untitled

Oh, de Study Hall
Where you can only study, study all;
Math book english book,
Reading book, science book;
It gets very boring after all.
You can't sleep or snore,
Even if it becomes a total bore.
If you talk, you'll have to walk
Right out the door with chalk
To write your sentences on why you talked.

—*Kjersti Thompson*

Common Entrapment

Religions are slaves of their own means,
Which are measured by their ability to enslave a degree of mankind.
Communities of market places, lions's dens,
That gives views to black holes of infinite buying of meaty flesh.
Woa, to the soul that lingers within these gates.
Grind the bodies to the institutions and let no follower free its soul,
For the way of God is through these doors of mankind's thinking
And nothing more, nothing more.
Individualism, a defeated thought, caused by the manipulation of groups
Who choose to control, leaving no room for self seekers.
Buy that soul and devour the senses for no one dares to defy
The path of glory.
Interpretations, confuse illusions, deadening the spirit to expand
Its growth, a losing battle for scrupulous ideas.
What tithing can be given to pay one's dues,
Not one penny for majority rules, majority rules.

—*Georgia A. Payne*

Untitled

Oh, bless the Lord and then bless the mountains
Which I love so much.
Do you kow where God is?
Do you know who we are?
Do you know everything that God has done for us?
I guess so many things, but I know some are wrong and
Some are right, that's all we can do is to guess
What life is all about.
But I know, deep down in my heart
That I love this world and you and I
Am going to make you understand
That I'm in love with you.
Don't you know by now that you're my only love.

—*Autumn D. Brahan*

Changes

I remember the times of my past
Which I thought one day, would never pass,
But I began to see that life
Was to change for me.
I asked God to show me the way
For I fear what was good,
Has now gone away, and I search for
The light to start a new day.
I remember the holidays and celebrations and all the jubilee,
The families and friends that would gather to create that unity;
And through love, these things were made to be,
God has put us on this earth for us to see.
The times are changing and it's hard to believe,
Yet I have faith that one day I will achieve,
The beauties of life and the will,
From God's shining light.

—*Joseph Geralis*

Love

When we first met, I was overwhelmed by your tender love and care,
Which in this day and age is not found everywhere.
Now as time is passing,
I realize that is was just a passing fancy,
We need not to cry till the end,
But I am happy to say I am still your friend!

—*Christine Mugavero*

Spools Of Love

Our love was like a spool of thread
Which thinned out everyday
Our love was never meant to be
We just left it to decay
We took for granted all the love we had
But didn't seem to care
And wasted our time for other things
When we had all that time to share
So I realize we should
End it all right then and there
Like spools of thread on a person's head
That turns bald and runs out of hair.

—*Annaliza Rodica*

Confusion

Dark black clouds torment the raging sky
While clashes of lightning race to ground;
Booming thunder pierces ear
As waters trample to get to below,
The wind billows through tree
With no sign of decreasing,
And I, with no heart, cry at the window
For what is outside is also within.

—Janet Spizzirri

Passion

Subliminal moods slowly surface,
while conscious thought takes a respite.
Desire undergoes a metamorphis,
becoming passion's insatiable delight.
Primeval urges seeking control,
combat lingering moral doubts.
Delirious illusions of the abnormal,
haunt each attempt of forestalling this lout.
Delayed satifaction increases desire,
while mental pictures imagine results.
Confusion reigns as diminished willpower,
holds hands with desire's sudden jolts.
The decision is made to no longer forestall,
as urgentcy overrules harm's way.
Need is seen as the motivator at fault,
when passion rules in its day.

—Donald L. Clegg

Untitled

Standing up for the view of the eagles swaying over the canyon,
While foxes crouch down on their ankles
And chickadees chirp in a race of tag,
The wheat whistling in the wind like a chime of beads
Pine trees bending and hovering over the ground,
The clouds swiftly spreading over the crystal blue sky,
Excitement and beauty at the state of the color green.

—Ashley Danenhoover

Ocean Beauty

Rolling in, drifting out.
While the fish jump about.
Winds blowing calmly and sometimes harsh
Tousling up the shore and marsh.
My eyes meet the waves and my fears drift aside
For this beauty you cannot hide.
White crests etched in blue meet the sand
And wash debris onto our land.
How can this heaven change so fast?
Why can't this beauty last. . .

—Debra Creech

Valdez Oil Spill

The people were making ready their fishing fleet
While the pipeline was furnishing us oil for heat
On the way south with its mighty black load
The Exxon Valdez was left in its auto mode
Now waters that were once blue and clear
Are now oily and covered with black smear
Fish use to swim and birds loved to fly
Now they await to be picked up right where they lie
The beaches were so quiet, the people so loving
They now are crowded with workers pushing and shoving
They come from afar, to help us clean and restore
To save and protect so destruction is no more

—Daphne Swearingen

The Popularity Race

Many people thrive on a high social standing
While they sit on a pedestal and are very demanding.
Looks must be perfect in every way.
In likeness with the styles of the present day.
Actions must be based on an attempt to gain
The respect of others, but it is all in vain.
For, in the end, who wins?
Do they ever catch up?
Are some left behind without the appropiate makeup?
And what is the prize for the most popular one?
To me it seems they're all overdone.

—Bristol Davis

Where is it?

I ran into my room looking for my earrings in a drawer that was an absolute mess.
While tossing everything out I found a used tissue that said "I was grounded from the pool." I began to laugh while looking at it.
I found old school papers, a locket my sister gave me, a Hershey kiss wrapper and an old cookie that was gross.
A few minutes later in a corner I found a box that said "To Jessica with love always Mom."
I opened the box and there they were plain silver earrings, but what made them special was "With love always Mom."

—Jessica Nowik

Years (from you)

They slip away from us
while we leisurely sit and let them go
neither caring enough to move in the other's direction
to halt this passage,
no need, it's only time
and we all have our quota to waste.
So let them go, for they will,
in spite of any attempts to hold them back.
Like people we have known through them
we have become a grand example of what their passing
can do, or undo.
So let them go, as we have our selves,
for life has not yet bestowed on us the magic handles to grasp,
and we have not yet learned the lesson of how to run in step.

—Monica A. Pearl

The Wretched Men—Which Ones?

Wretched are we
who abandon our integrity
who abandon our brothers.
Pathetic, isn't it
to be unaware of what we are becoming
to be unaware of who we are.
Like a woebegone man
lying in a pool of blood,
crippled, ostracized and now
ignored by man.
Dreary, isn't it
Are we not the ones who brought this
Upon ourselves?
What fools!
Why has man permitted himself
to have deteriorated to such a dismal state?

—Jose J. Cerecedo

Untitled

Like the distinguished hum of the fated
   life of the ingenious fly
Who found himself enclosed in a lifeless
   place,
With the saddening gesture of never
   traveling beyond that great wall of
   transparency,
Still existing in his own microcosm among
   the suffering and soon corpses,
He is still fully unaware that sameness he
   will become.
The lonely and somewhat savage fly
   desperately calls out from his
   entrapment,
In hopes a glimpse of understanding is
   caught.
Time is an important key, for the longer
   that is spent there,
The more easily it is to slip away from
   reality.
The farther reality seeps, the closer to
   death he finds.
Unable to comprehend, unaware he
   becomes.
Slower he moves, quieter is he, ridden to
   one place;
He is no longer able to see through the
   transparent wall.
His devotion is no longer there as he
   awaits his non-existence.
The sill turns into an endless corridor of
   white blandness.
The transparent wall has shrunk and now
   has bars across it;
A man begins to weep, for he just
   observed the fate of his entire life
From a tiny symbolic fly in the window of
   the asylum.

—*Kendra Cox*

Dreams of Insomnia

In search of the white crow
Who knows the sadness of witches
And the godspeed of despair,
Where paradise by the numbers
Fall by the wayside chapel,
And the magic of blue unicorns
Lie just beyond the mist
Of candles in the rain,
And the dusting powder of love
Retreats to the wine-dark sea
Where the amnesia of yesterday
Is memory enough. . .
And I breathe the silence
Of all she said,
And touch her perfect absence
When I wake to dream,
My dreams of insomnia

—*Eric Wallace*

Friends of Mine

Integral part of me are they
who steal my childlike heart away;
Their candid antics move me so,
in places where I, too, must go;
They live and play and have their fun
as children of the moon and sun;
Their only clock is night and day,
no rent for space do my friends pay;
They aren't encumbered with the need
to create gods, to heel and heed;
There is no reason for my friends
to live by laws which man depends;
They've claimed no right to judge or
   scorn,
no sins of which to weep or mourn;
They live a life that's free of blame
for ills caused by the money game;
They're synchronized within life's plan,
unlike the missing link called "Man."
. . .The animals.

—*Dale Patrick Hoffman*

Our Father

The Lord our God is my heavenly father
Who loves me with all my imperfections
Where would we be if He didn't bother?
We would be alone and without
   protection.
He is with us in both good times and bad,
He is with a child dying of cancer,
He is with a family who has lost their dad,
He is there to help us with the answer.
He has a never-ending love for us
That is like an endless burning candle,
Though we fall short of His glory we must
   not fuss,
For He is the foot and we are the sandal.
So, to bring this sonnet to an end,
Just remember that God is our friend.

—*Christy Wunderling*

Why Did You do It

Sitting quietly, I wondered why
Who were you, to decide to die
You were so young, and full of life
I feel you stabbed me with a knife
You were so selfish, I hope you know
It's God's decision when it's your time to
   go
We went to your funeral, the tears
   dropped like rain
You couldn't imagine the hurt, and the
   pain
Your family, and friends all gathered
   around
We watched them put you into the ground
I wish you had gone to someone for help
We had no idea, how bad you must have
   felt
When it came time to say goodbye
I couldn't believe you chose to die

—*Deborah A. Ferris*

Remembering

Remember the little boy
Who held the shabby toy,
With jelly on his face
And not a hair in place.
Remember his first deer
And the night he snuck a beer;
Girls, dates, the senior prom
Merrily his life would go on.
Graduation, then came Vietnam,
Letters home, how he missed Mom!
Then the telegram arrived at the door,
All that's left are memories evermore.
Remember the little boy
Who held the shabby toy,
Remember my son
Who lies in Arlington.

—*Amy Jo Newcomer*

The Old Oak

There once was many, but now there's one
Who stands alone, atop his throne.
He stands so brave, so strong and proud.
As though no force, could bring him
   down.
He's been through hell, so many times.
He's fought some battles, yet still he
   climbs.
He's all that's left, he's one and only.
Yet in this glory, he's so very lonely.
But he carries his burden, to live forever.
He's last to live, to die is never.
There once was many, but now there's one
Who stands alone, atop his throne.

—*Eric Tolman*

The Forgotten Generation

Who will help the children?
Who will rock them into sleep?
Who will help them now
that their troubles are too deep?
For the children, they are hungry;
the children, they are poor.
Yet no one picks them up as they
drop down to the floor.
Time is running out, you see,
the world is split in two.
Still no one picks them up,
if they don't, why don't you?
In their hands they hold the future,
so won't you hear their cries?
Can you give them back the hope
lost from their dying eyes?

—*Brooke Kelly*

La Professeur

There was a certain teacher, la professeur
　as they say in French,
Who'd grant you not a single point by a
　mile nor by an inch.
She sat behind her desk with books so
　neatly stacked,
And a host of half-checked papers tucked
　inside her sack.
Her diction was impeccable as she
　sounded every "t",
But her very best skill of mastery was
　termed philosophy.
The thin and fine-cut glasses sat sedately
　upon her nose
As she walked with perfect posture and,
　of course, on tippy-toes.
Her hair was fairly long, I assumed, for I
　never saw it loose,
And her face was straight and
　narrow-shaped—somewhat obtuse.
The cold and distant dark-grey eyes lay
　stiff within their shade
To show her heart-felt sympathy for every
　failing grade.
I supposed her smile was stolen, for it
　never did appear,
But that was fine because it matched her
　clothes which lost their cheer.
There must have been an unpleasant odor
　circulating beneath somewhere,
Because her nose was always turned up
　slightly in the air.
Indeed she was a character, quite an
　amusing sight to see;
Nevertheless, she was the one who held
　my passing key.

—Canangela Roquel Jackson Boyd

The Time Betwixt

Hence, lovely love
Whom Aphrodite and Hephaestos bore
On feathered cloud of formless form
'Midst dancing cherubs and celestial bliss
Come soothe my lonely heart
Where once lived mirth and her
　companion youth
Where brooding ravens now reside in
　dungeon dark.
Come fair Goddess and Eros too
Force an arrow through my chest
Let sparks of passion arise from ashes
And once again regain the throne
Thus I beseech thee gods above
Do not let love part first
And death come last.

—George Postupak

Missing You

There was a young man I once knew,
Whose eyes were brown and his life was
　blue.
When you were a child, I watched you
　grow.
You were funny, curious, and always on
　the go.
I have so many memories, some would
　curl your ears,
But when I think of them I end up in
　tears.
For no more memories will I make with
　you,
Because God decided he needed you too.
I can't say I understand why,
God never let me say goodbye.
So many questions, answers I have none,
Your life was a mystery, you were always
　on the run.
My mind would be at ease if only I knew,
Why your death was so violent,
And why it had to be you,
The Bible says we are not to question
　why,
I just wish I could have said goodbye.

—Frances G. McFalls

Little Girl

Little girl with the piggy tails
Why are you crying?
Are you sad?
Or have you not seen your dad?
Little girl with the freckled face,
Why are you laughing?
Or have you finally found you dad.

—Heather Nelson

Winter's Warmth

Big bright fire
Why are you there?
So people can snuggle together at night,
In front of your coals that burn so bright?
Or are you there to crackle and snap?
You sound like a hammer going tap, tap,
　tap!
You are so cozy, you feel so nice!
And you feel so good on a cold winter's
　night!

—Jodell Lang

Why Wear Clean Clothes

"Why wear clean clothes?" young Sibyl
　asked of me.
Why beat a weathered cloth against a
　rock
Or wash a weary gown or wring a sock?
To soil is wretched nature's dire decree.
From dust we came, to dust we must
　return,
And in the while sweep up on silver
　threads
Fortune's filth, as in the sordid bed.
We're buried long before the final bourne.
Yet nature's mortal law we must
　ammend,
And cleanse the imperfections of our lot,
Till death, the meanest error, we offend.
We soak the bloody stain and scrub the
　spot
To triumph over death's devouring pit,
Where dusty flood will drown our
　textured knit.

—John M. Clement

Bees

I loved you!
What do you want me to do?
I gave you my life.
I became your wife.
She is warm inside.
She never runs to hid.
She can't be your bride.
You'd run and hide.
No for me.
Yes for her.
What can I be?
er— er— er
Can't you see?
Nothing's for me.
There never was a me.
I can see a he.

—Rebecca Hendrix

Silent Flame

I love her—
Why can't I speak to her?
Why can't I tell her
Of my desire,
Of my longing,
Of the cherished, gleeful moments with
　her
Racing through my mind,
Only through my mind?
If I could bring our worlds together;
Hers fresh,
Jubilant,
Filled with living;
Mine quiet,
Lonely,
Flat with fear.
She is a stranger to me.
No, never to my eyes,
But always—
Always—
To my heart.

—George Foss

Come Back to Me

How could you cause all this hurting
Why did you have to keep on flirting.
Whatever happened to being together
And whatever happened to the forever
Why didn't you just stay
Why did you have to go away
I gave you all of my heart
Instead you just tore it apart.
Why can't I forget you
Why couldn't you have been true
I showed you all of my love and devotion
But you just turned around and showed no
  emotion
What do you want me to do
Just go on being blue
I want you for more than just a friend
Please just tell me it's not the end
Why can't you just see
I want you back with me.

—Heather Barnard

The Face of Death

The tears keep rolling down my face.
Why do I always come to this place?
I feel worse than I've ever felt before,
Or do I feel better? I can't tell you
  anymore.
I watch the stones, lying cold on the
  ground,
I too am frozen as I hear a sound. . .
I look up and see the Angel of Death;
He's so close to me I can feel his
  breath. . .
In his hand he holds a burnished blade
My life slowly begins to fade
I quickly reach out and take hold of the
  knife;
I point it toward me and take
My own life. . .

—Jennifer Turrell

Coffee Break

I sit and think of all I should have done
  today,
Why do I procrastinate my life away?
I'll wake up late again tomorrow and race
  to my work space,
Just to find the work I left set beside my
  place.
Another day to play Ms. Congeniality,
Fantasizing that I handled all to the best
  of my ability.
And don't you know I pulled it off with a
  smile of concern,
So more work is left undone, do you think
  I'll ever learn?
Traveling home I mentally organize my
  next days work,
Fooling myself once again that with my
  morning coffee
Suddenly I'll perk!

—Ellen R. Foodim

Sunshine

Sunshine, my sweet sunshine,
Why have you disappeared?
You've set into the earth,
And filled our hearts with fear.
Your eyes that once shined,
Your smile ever so bright.
Could lighten a dark room
On a cold December night.
So we must remember,
And I will never forget.
That, at one time,
Even the most beautiful sunshine must
  set!

—Karen Haas

Off Again On Again

Off again, on again,
Why is it, off again, on again.
Try as I may, I just can't say.
Off again, on again.
You just can't go, off and on again.
I hurts me deep, and I feel so beat.
When I think it's on, it's off again.
When I think it's off, it's on again.
Please take me out of my grief.
How can friendship stay a friend.
How can you and me change this trend.
Please jsut be there so you can help me
  share.
Thank you, no more neither or nor,
Yes or nor or maybe some more,
I think at last we understand the past.
Gee, golly and thanks. . .

—Edmond Bertrand

Frightened Children

Frightened children; Don't you wonder
Why they're afraid of mellow thinder?
Why when lightning strikes they flee;
Under the bed where they can't see.
Why on rainy days and nights
You see them crawl out of sight?
Frightened children, poor old souls
What comforts them; no one knows.
They jump about screaming; running
Without waiting to see what's coming.
Those little children break my heart
For happiness; they've always sought.
Frightened children hide when seeked,
Very seldom do they sleep.
Scurrying about and scurrying past
Like one that runs for the last
Up and above; below and beyond,
Don't look now the children are gone!

—Jackie Duylie

Some Friendly Advice

Sorrow, heartache, tears,
Why, why, does the earth have to be so
  cruel?
Why can't we live in harmony?
Is there no hope for tomorrow?
What will become of us?
Will we ever find life beyond the stars?
Or will we fight until we vanish all life
  from space?
As an angel I know I will never vanish.
Why not make the best of your life on
  earth.
Because you'll never know where your life
  there may take you.

—Amy Heidel

One Moment to Think

It was a sad time just to think,
We would shed that last tear in a few
  more winks.
We had to sit down and dry that tear,
When the twenty-seven people died,
All because of someone drinking beer.
My friends died all because of one bus
  ride.

—Luci Edmondson

Victims of Addiction

Twisted brain games used on blind
  victims
Wielded by masters of anarchy creation
The decay of intelligence obvious to no
  one
Because no one cares in a nuclear world
Sunken eyes and skeletal bodies are
  symbols
Mascots for the state of hopeless addicts
The government ignores them with cruel
  silence
Choosing not to see their desperate agony
  and pain
They live by a joint, taking every day as it
  comes
They don't look ahead and they don't look
  behind
Oh, to exist such a heinous and brutal
  truth
Where is their freedom? What is their
  peace?
Now we cry for those that have no
  paradise haven
Look inside our stony hearts and find
  compassion
This nation's indifference is an asinine
  shame
We are blind to the ones that are wasting
  within
Please, let us unite and fight to stop this
  needless suffering
Oh God, help us today with your superior
  strength.

—Carlita M. Barrios

In Love

All the times you made me smile,,
Will forever be remembered,
Every glance you ever gave me,
Will never be forgotten,
Any shiver ever sent throughout me,
By a touch of your loving hand,
Won't ever feel the same,
Given by another lover's hand.
A promise that was once said,
Will always be endeared,
The threat of breaking apart
Has been, quite forgiven,
But all of this has drawn me closer,
Than any of the greatest rides given by life to you,
Just because you've made me so happy,
By just being ourselves and being in love.

—Annie Cerasoli

Rose

Rose, rose, rose, rose
Will I ever see tomorrow
I will see tomorrow
Oh rose
Rose, rose, rose, rose
These memories are so sweet
They will be at my side
Oh rose

—Audrey Sorokach

The Giant Balloon

The world is like a giant balloon, floating in space.
Will the pace of its race, cause its disgrace?
Or will the world float on into space, never ending its race.

—Charles E. Washington

Untitled

More and more I find myself trusting him.
Willingly submitting to his every qualms.
Yes, I'll welcome him into my life, into my arms,
Yielding to his desires.
Wanting more of this-this love that makes you,
High spirited.
No quarrels will I make
No kisses will escape
His manly caresses of my eccentrically womanly possessions.

—Brenda Barnes

Haiku

still, sad pond
wilted water lilies. . .
even the frogs
are quiet

—Barbara Bell-Teneketzis

Baby Blue

It is so tender and soft,
With a gentle touch.
Cotton balls in shapes of moving objects
Maybe it's a tree, or could be a lion?
The sky is guided, and cradled with God's hand.
Some days we may float to dreams of an unknown land;
The vast baby blue reaches out to me,
In times of thought.
The sky is a pair of eyes watching our every move.
The baby blue is a palace of kingdoms.
Deep within us,
We are there: Wishing, Hoping, Praying.
The sky is a blanket
That warms us during trials,
And a bundle of cheer
During our triumphs!
The sky: My destiny.

—Amanda Johnson

When I Left This Place

I was living
With a heavy burden on my heart.
So, in that sense,
It was hard for me to see anything-
That was good in this world.
My heart ached with every false smile-
I lended.
I walked along the ocean shore and pondered my thoughts.
As I looked up from the sand,
I perceived the most beautiful sunset.
My sorry face, once without expression,
Had the most simplistic glow ever.
With this, I fell to the earth.
Able to hold on for one last breath,
I thanked God for letting me witness
One of his glorious masterpieces,
Before I went from this wretched place.

—Iris Raynor

Mathematical Love

I love you mathmetically
With a trigonomatrical love.
Because theoretically and practically
You are my decimal system.
I add you, subtract you, multiply you,
But I don't divide you.
When I came out with a dream without a factor,
You will be my loving cipher and
Maximum common divisor.

—Don Still

The Sea

She looks beautiful but carries harm,
She wants peace from all above.
We do things to her; that we regret,
And she harms us back the same.
The zone is burning so we must go.
While we sink in her sorrow.

—Stacy Paradis

A Sunday Afternoon

The sky looking a bright blue
With a wind rumbling through the trees
While a bird flies across the street,
Looking for its next meal.
Cars riding along on a backstreet,
Taking part of a leisurely afternoon
While laughter from a family picnic
Spreads throughout a neighborhood.
Smoke coming from backyards
With the aroma of barbecuing filling the air
While children run along,
Splashing through sprinklers.
Everyone in the area
Enjoying the warmth of the sun
While partaking in the activities
Of a Sunday afternoon.

—Kimberly A. Johannes

Perfect

We can't all be just perfect,
We can't all be just right.
We never do what's expected,
We always do what's not.
But if we were just perfect,
But if we were just right.
We would have no fun
Any day or night.

—Tanya L. Carter

Untitled

The sky is darkening
With faint traces of the blue of day;
And the wind carries
The smell of freshly fallen rain
As it blows cool and gentle
Across my face and through the trees,
Making each branch rustle softly.
A solitary cricket sings
A lullaby of peace to every child.

—Jenn Delci

No More Tears

My heart's completely parched,
With feelings that are dry.
It's not that I don't care,
It's just that I won't cry.
I picked you up when you were down,
And calmed all your fears.
I loved you for the longest time,
But now there are no more tears.
Why did I love your jealous heart?
It just broke mine in two.
You abandoned me a million times,
But I just kept loving you.
I always loved you best,
Away I never ran.
But now that you have run from me,
I'll never cry again.

—*Julie Stephens*

Little Hummingbird

Oh little hummingbird
With fluttering wings,
Up and down and sideways,
I watch you flit so fast,
Tasting of the nectar
From every flower.
You visit my feeder
and claim it as your own,
No brother or sister
Do you allow to drink,
E'en tho there are four spouts,
You think you own them all.
So small and so pretty,
You're fiesty as can be.
I've seen you chase squirrels,
Even attacking me,
Still to me you're special
My little hummingbird.

—*Greta Marie Brikowski*

In my Dreams

He was tall and bright
With his hair so soft and light.
With his eyes of royal blue
It's a wonder they don't talk to you.
They sparkle in the evening night
As though they were the only light.
So intelligent and smart
He stays up studying in good heart.
Guys like this are hard to find
Most are one of a kind.
As though it may seem
This is all just
In my dreams.

—*Christi Mueller*

Color

The serape
With its
Reds, blues, yellows, and greens
Purple, browns, oranges, and golds
A rainbow
Filling up the sky.

—*Jennifer Marek*

Tuscany

Tuscany is a land of awe,
with its hills that roll in harmony,
and embrace vintage farms, trim
    vineyards,
and ancient villas.
It is a peaceful place,
that's still but yet alive.
For the birds sing their melodies,
the wind whistles through the fields,
and from time to time the train lets its
steam out as it passes by,
its destination—a small villiage
hidden in the hills,
once protected by its wall of mighty stone
that tells a thousand words of glory and
    defeat.

—*Caroline Giffith*

Seashore

Show me the seashore
With its white, cool sand.
Where hearts intertwine
And we walk, hand in hand.
Where the birds call softly
And the breeze gently blows,
This is where my heart,
When troubled, goes.

—*Autumn D. Conley*

Come!

I'll take you far away, along a narrow
    path.
With lights, so bright to lead the way
Just step within my steps.
A grand reception is being prepared.
Such special honor waits you there.
Music, splendor, you shall hear
When sounds uncommon fill the air.
Now don't be fearful,
Trust me please.
I shall not harm you
Soon you'll see!
You ask—who am I?
The answer is clear!
For I'm death's messenger
Your time is here!

—*Christy Cay*

Untitled

Life is great and all too wild
With little games of every style.
The golden fleece that life does hold
Will proudly tell you that it is bold,
Because this love is far too free,
This love you find is much like gold
For there it stands above this world,
To love another that love you too.
Is only fortunate for those too few,
And when you find this love of yours
Treasure it beyond four scores,
And so I give to you a phrase,
"I love you each and every day".

—*Jeff Park*

Hard Times

I am a hard fist, crashing down on the
    table of nations.
With me come hatred and sorrow,
Death and rations.
Soon you will begin to believe in no
    tomorrow.
I make your calm life stressful,
You shall have no rest.
At the back of your mind horrible
    thoughts will pull,
And these thoughts will your mind infest.
Like the warning roll of thunder
    proclaiming a storm,
This is how the first blow will strike.
In all hearts will be coldness instead of
    warm,
I am something no one can like.
By now you must know me, of that I am
    sure,
This is my name:
I am war.

—*Bambi Gerrard*

To Let Go

I'm in my own little world,
With my lone, small self,
In a itsy bitsy cubbard,
On a teeny, tiny shelf.
No one knows who I am
As if I am concealed in a can.
They say my stare is far,
I am told, "Look into yourself;"
"Find out who you are."
I look into myself
And see the real me
I climb off the shelf
And go into the world to see. . .

—*Julie Meyer*

An Empty Heart

An empty heart is a broken heart,
With no feelings and no love.
I feel like my life,
Has come to an abrupt halt.
My feelings for you are strong,
Yet I can do nothing.
I want to hold you and love you,
Yet I have to wait.
She's stopping us, knowing,
And seeing, how we feel.
Yet, I wait patiently for you,
And your love.
An empty heart is a broken heart,
That's how I feel.
I can't cry or get angry,
I can't hate or love.
An empty heart is a lonely heart,
An empty heart is a broken heart,
And that's how I feel without you.

—*Billie A. Smith*

I Hear More Than The Ocean

Oh little shell where have you been
What stories lie there deep within
The ocean roar I'll no doubt hear
If held so close up to my ear
But speak to me and tell me more
I'd love to hear your ancient lore
Of ships above and sea below
Of men and times so long ago
Those ancient shores and distant lands
I seem to hold within my hands.
Oh little shell it must be known
I'd love to keep you for my own
But to the sea I give you back
Part of your history I'll remain intact
The waves shall take you far away
And you shall journey many a day
To be washed onto shore after shore
And share your secrets evermore.

—*Susan M. Franks*

What is it Like Being a Teenager

I'm all alone in one dark world
With no one to help me out,
I wish that someone could understand.
What my life's all about.
I want a friend to talk to,
I want her to understand,
Only if we could share our feelings,
And give each other a hand
I feel abandoned, hurt and alone inside,
When I feel this way,
I let my heart be my guide.
I know that being a teenager isn't easy,
I know it could be the best times of my life,
Only one person could change my way,
I'm the only one,
I only have one thing to say,
It's not easy being a teenager,
It's not easy at all.

—*Amy-Jo Akin*

Ancient Wars

Ancient wars were fought
With not knives
Or guns
Or nuclear weapons
But with love
And prayers of hope
Or sonnets
Of promising luck to be.
There were no wars
To prove superiority over others,
Or to gain power
And riches.
Ancient wars were against disease
And nature's unpredictable ways.
An ancient war victory
Is to live a rewarding life
And to have balance
Between peace and war.

—*Andrea Severson*

Who Am I?

When I look in the mirror I always seem
  to ask,
What does this over achieving world
  expect from me?
I want only the best from life
And I will do my best to fulfill my dreams.
I will learn to always be myself,
Let others know who I am and where I
  stand.
At this specific time in my life
I must welcome happiness and learn to
  deal with saddness.
I know that I am one of a kind,
Set in my ways, with my own personality
And no one will ever be exactly like me.
Everyone is different in their own ways.
So if you ever find yourself asking
Who am I, gladly I say,
I am me, and I am special.

—*Michelle Lynn Wilson*

Untitled

Sitting in a dark and dank room,
With nothing surrounding you but pails,
  buckets and brooms.
Knowing there is no way out,
Not even if you knock and shout.
Being kept captive like an animal,
How could he have been my best pal?
All that we went through together,
All was well until he received that letter.
That awful piece of paper,
And when he told me my eyes became a
  blur.
I just couldn't believe what he told me,
But he said that's what must be.
This is the evil price I must pay,
And I have nothing in the say.
It is not my fault,
That my life must come to this sudden
  halt.
So here I'll stay, wasting away.
In this dark and dank room!

—*Janna Ide*

An Evil Addiction

A spiral staircase
With silver railing
The oceans wild
But the boat is sailing
An evil addiction
Without any reasons
Your mind will change
Along with the seasons
A desperation inside
With a need to escape
Your spirit is dry
Like a desert landscape
An empty heart
With a lonely sensation
Your mind is blank
In complete isolation
A crystal pond with your reflection
You see yourself with no direction

—*Draga Millich*

A Fantasy

The petals of the Gardenia caress the
  earth
With soft, rich sweetness.
The wind circles the mountains.
The ground trembels and lightening
Splits the calm, indigo night sky.
The black stallion enters the canyon,
Looks about, moving slowly forward.
His gait becomes a gallop, then he breaks
  into a run.
There is a burst of sunrise, triumphant
  and golden,
Then there is peace.
Even the waves cease their pounding and
  the ocean is calm.
The sea gulls soar and dive contentedly.
The lilting sounds of a festival
Float up, circle the trees,
Fill the vally to overlowing,
And crown the mountain peaks.
At that instant the world is filled with
  goodness,
And there is no evil.

—*Joan Lowe*

Insight

I'll forever seek a blind man
with supernatural sight.
Who'll see deep inside a person
yet is denied his equal right,
Such a man is not so usual
for he is most superior,
He's a judge who is unpersuaded,
not mislead by false exterior.
Why grant him with your pity,
when he should grant you your share—
Alas, the inside is more than pretty,
the outside is only there.

—*Gina Petruzziello*

Fall's Mundane

Like a figment of my heart's own making
With the colors of fall's mundane,
I feel like a beggar and while taking
And with thankfulness, yet greed and
   shame.
In my heaven on earth and peace for
   awhile
Silence and glow stare back at me
To remember this touch, mental records
   I'll file,
Of the leaves and colors and rustle of
   trees.
Adulthood and its many blessings
Though Candor and winds display a mood
Love of touch and mellow speech, there's
   no guessing
My woods of people are now all nude.

—Faye Gibbs Hughes

The Country

The country is such a beautiful scene,
with towering trees and grass so green.
White, puffy clouds float in the blue sky,
while subtle flocks of birds silently fly.
Gusts of wind provide a gentle breeze,
and make the tall trees dance with the
   greatest of ease.
Thousands of little, yellow dandelions
   spread about the fields,
and for them, the trees provide a constant
   shield.
Two chestnut horses gallop and play,
and whinney at each other; a peaceful
   neigh.
The country is such a beautiful scene,
and now I know how much it can mean,
to see the green lands and the sky so blue,
and all the while, I'm sharing this with
   you!

—Beth A. Cheatham

The Unicorn

You came from far away,
With visions in your eyes.
A frame formed of the moonlight,
That dances in the skies.
The wisdom of your face,
Tells the number of your years,
For you're the arranger of disorder
With your magic and your tears.
How is it that they don't know you?
But listen with rising fear
As your cry pierces the night
And your thundering hooves draw near.
You move with the night's shadows,
And sleep within the day.
But you are an unsolved mystery,
It has always been that way.

—Allison Payton

The Airplane Field

A natural trail like "prairie days"
With wild flowers for a horse to graze
The smell of leather as I rode
Sweaty palms as I did hold
An empty wagon in the field
A wealth of history revealed.
Warm, summer air blew in my face
A snorting breath with Leah's pace
My riding partner would appear
A devilish smile—our race was near
A little nudge, a little show
With the words, "Get set and go"!
The wind screaming, the mud flying,
Oh, how both of us were trying
Hoofs pounding wet, brown earth
Thumping, rubbing against the girth
A finish line we soon would cross
None of us were at a loss

—Jeanie Rinker

Under the Silver Moonlight

I walk in the garden through the darkness
With wisps of hair blowing in my face
I think of the night so cold and rigid
And then I think of the moon so elegant
   and silver
And then I see you so handsome and
   thoughtful
For my days turn to dust without me
   catching a glimpse of your face
For so long I have wished that you would
   be caressing me
Under the moonlight. . .together forever
For my heart is aching for you to be
   standing next to me
Under the silver moonlight

—Hillary Ann Schornack

Waiting

I'm missing you and waiting for you to
   return;
With you gone, it seems my heart's on fire
   and if you don't hurry back, it'll burn.
What's been three days feels like forever;
I guess it just means our love is strong
   enough to stay together.
Each day you're gone, I seem to love you
   more;
And with each passing moment, it also
   grows stronger.
Don't ever leave me again; I may not
   survive;
Cause only when I'm with you do I feel so
   alive.
I've been counting the minutes till we can
   be together;
And when I hold you again, the moment
   will last forever.
I keep waiting for our next kiss;
And once I've received it, it will be deja
   vu to what I've missed!

—Kelly J. Slone

Memories

Life is a mystery
With young people budding
And older people cherishing fond
   memories.
Memories that will last an eternity.
Memories that will burn in our minds
Giving us nightmares or wonderful
   fantasies.
Our cherished memories will never leave
   us,
No matter who we are or how we act.
Dream and experience life's mysteries for
   as long as they last,
Go little one, go.

—Karen Oakjones

Raindance

Scattered gems
Within dark, wrinkled velvet
Gather light,
Or fall, and burn;
No wisp of smoke to bear a fragile dream.
"Dream vision? Nothing".
Doubt the dead star's empty socket.
Soft, dark shroud,
Purple velvet canvas running black,
Black dragon,
Cast a shadow,
Hear the dry air sigh.
Called down, cold wet fingers open eyes
At raindrop shatter touch;
Shatter rusted promise,
Shatter fragile bridge
That spans the burning day.

—Edward G. Stolte

Real Love

You can say a lot
Without saying a word.
You can scream and shout,
And never to be heard.
You may not be hurt
And still feel the pain.
You can be a winner
Yet never play the game.
But you can't be in love
And say that you don't feel.
Love is not a game,
Love is for real.

—Bree Bisnette

Love Lasts

Love lasts by caring, sharing,
Without tears are the time running down
   your face
And running away from people and love
   lasts by talking
About your feelings with each other,
   about your problems
And forgiving people's gifts for
   Christmas, Valentine gifts
To people show true love.
Love hasts even when you are dead and
   love lasts when you are even
Misbehaving. God loves you are the time
   and love lasts when you treat
People right and love lasts all the time.

—Christina Renee Bray

Release South Africa

South Africa is the country
Without true justice or liberty.
We shall not all be totally free.
We need to release our
Brothers across the sea.

—Chuck Ochelli

The Echo Of My Scream

A chillingly vacant room
Without windows or doors
A lonely place
Yet a haven of sorts.
The voices outside
Seem so very faraway
Low, hushed tones
Barely audible. . .
The place through the walls
Is not really my world
It is strange and distant,
Frighteningly absurd.
I beg you to hear me
Listen to the echo of my scream
There's madness out there
Nothing appears as it seems.

—Dianne E. Young

Lost Love

I lay in bed at night thinking thoughts of
   you,
Wondering where you are and what your
   going to do.
Wondering if you'll come back to me
and someday love me as I love you.
My heart aches inside.
My eyes fill with tears.
As I lie in utter darkness alone and in
   fear.
My friends tell me everythings
going to be o.k., but I know your
not coming back, not ever, not today.
Because your not there now when
I need you, I've often thought about
   killing myself.
But then what would that prove;
That I died for love and couldn't deal with
   the pain of losing you.
You ask yourself, "what could I do"?
The only words that came to your mind
I LOVE YOU!

—Gretchen Payson

Come Back

All I need is love.
What I need is you.
Can you come and be with me tonight.
Tonight and forever.
No one knows the pain I'm going through
I need you to understand me
Please come back, I need you
I want you.
I know I've treated you bad but forgive
   and forget
Can't you.
I need you to love, that's it
All I need is love, the warmth of your
   body near me as we
hold each other side by side.
My stomach gets excited everytime I
   think of you
Everytime I see you my heart beats a
   thousands more times.

—Nicole Larocque

Quiet

People yelling, radios blaring,
Workers with power tools, and people are
   staring
At a man who steps out of a building and
   yells,
"Quiet! Quiet please, my whole family
   can hear you"
"And they're in out of state hotels!"
The noise paused for a moment and then
   went on,
People yelling, radios blaring,
Workers with power tools, and people are
   staring
At the man, as he steps quietly back into
   the building.

—Erin Palmer

Ailing Mankind

That one man's error, greed, or strict
   belief
Would cause another's death, cannot be
   right;
How many of our fellows feel the grief
Of wartime's innocent's yet harmed in
   flight?
Of people who are crying as I write this,
Of children who are dying as I sigh,
Of creatures who do suffer long despite
   us,
Us thoughtless human beings shall hear,
   should cry.
Then, having cried, jump up and launch
   the questions:
What'll happen to the ozone now we've
   killed
A hefty mass of trees, what gives
   protection;
The friendly sun we love will have us
   grilled.
Some TV programs boast an earth of
   beauty,
But change the channel; smell that traffic
   jam,
Or see starved Asians suffer from law's
   duty;
South Africans, dealt death by bombs in
   trams.
But 'midst the worldwide strife intentions
   grow,
Computers, research, medicine, and art.
But how on earth will problems ever go
If peaceful visions rot locked in man's
   heart?

—Fiona Bayly

The Structure

Bare ground cracked by noon day sun
Wounded by big CAT's pummeling blows
Yields begrudgingly to ministrations of
   man
Foundation layer of cement and steel
Engineered to withstand earthquake's
   rumblings
Lofty pine and oak succumbed to interior
   needs
As the mighty structure reaches to azure
   horizon
Gabled roof with jaunty slant challenges
   sure foot workers
The warp and woof of architect's artifice
   takes shape
Soon it becomes clear to one and all
This is God's house-a temple of worship
Where faith, hope and love serve endlessly

—Dr. Stanley S. Reyburn

Nature

A purple lasso
wrapped around white mortars in your
  mouth
Soft brown hair
blowin' in the wind around your lips
that transcend in the dark
of our honeymoon room
tomorrow
Cat eyes and innocence
gullible minds need a wash and a rinse
Thank God
for the experience of a new birth
Yes, nature should exist on an earth like
  this one
Look in a mirror
reflection correct, no physical dissect
So short is this stanza
on a page made of paper
Mayby later they'll say
"Let's save the trees".

—*Jeremy Lane Combs*

Winter's Arrival

In the early rays of dawn, winter
  announces its arrival loudly,
Wreaking havoc, it displays its abilities
  proudly.
It moved quietly at first, sneaking in at
  dusk,
Attacking all in sight with a vengeful lust.
A dash of innocent rain soon changed to a
  constant sheet of ice,
Then a subtle shift to snow allowed peril
  to snuggle down and hide.
From far above, beautiful tiny puffs
  continued to float lazily down,
Adding inches upon inches of depth to the
  ground.
Tired of sneaking about, the wind began
  to howl,
Making the pristine white blanket a mess,
Like that of a late night sleeper unable to
  rest.
The abuse continued until it grew tired
  and weary,
And the winds began to die down,
The gentle shades of dawn breaking
  through as the skies started clearing.
In the early morning sun the last few
  flakes floated past,
Finding a peaceful place on earth, resting
  at last.
Mere humans awake to an awesome sight,
Their world, converted by nature's fury,
  to a sparkling white.

—*Dorinda Courter*

Bach

Bach you must understand was a clever
  little man but all the
years he sat and wrote he didn't write a
  single note but he
invented ten hundred robots at least and
  in evry robot he put
a flea. You must know that fleas know
  how to compose. They made
Bach famous and every year they shout
  and cheer and drink some
beer and yell hooray for the holiday. You
  see they worked every
day so Bach could get some pay. They did
  this so he wouldn't
spray, swat or hurt them. He would of
  course compromise if only
they were his size. But then on the fleas'
  holiday they would
work on a size machine and one day
  finished it they did and can
you guess what they'll do? They'll make
  themselves as big as
you! And that day Bach opened the door
  to the fleas' workroom
and then there was a big BOOM! All the
  fleas began to sneeze.
Then the fleas grabbed Bach and made
  him talk to all the land
and make them understand that they
  should get the dough because
Bach didn't even wiggle a toe and so the
  fleas are wealthy insects
who don't even have to move their index
  nor wandering inside a
robot trying to sing a long solo!

—*George Tourtellot*

Discovers

She listens and hears,
She walks and finds,
She loves and discovers.
Though she can't figure out
Why she's here,
What's her purpose,
What's her talent.
Does she understand,
Does she know that one day
She just may find out!

—*Rebecca Trout*

Beautiful Skies

Beautiful skies way above me,
Yellow, brown, auburn, I see.
Sunsets changing all the time,
Each more beautiful than the one behind.
Lakes below shimmering with light,
Reflecting the sign of day turning to
  night.
Trees towering high above,
Bearing the nest of a newborn dove.
Flowers blooming all around,
Sharing their sweet scents with all that
  surround.
Beautiful skies way above me,
How can such natural, vivid scenes be?

—*Emily May Leffler*

Untitled

They say love is blind
Yes, I do know
And it's all so true.
But honey if only I could be with you
I would no longer feel so blue.
You are the one I think of.
You are the love for me.
So once again I dare to ask
Is love no longer blind?
Or are you really the one for me?

—*Cindy Figueroa*

Love

Love is a far off country,
Yet a land I yearn to find
A home to joy and sorrow,
But seldom peace of mind.
I seek a bright warm country,
A place in my true loves eyes,
Where the sparkle of loves laughter
Bring stars to starless skies.
Yet in this country distant,
though the cold moon never chills
I am told the price of happiness
Is the thunder in the hills.

—*Julie Dircksen*

I Love You

You say "I'm sorry,"
Yet continue
As though nothing had happened,
And I'm tied to the fist—pounding
Road of frustration,
My love and hope have been rolled over,
Beneath you,
Flattened by newfound liberation.
I can see where your weakness will lead
  you
And cry out to save you the pain;
Yet I also see the strength you have,
The strength to say "I'm sorry,"
Yet refuse to turn over the reins.

—*Barbara Rysdorp*

Untitled

Long awaited days seem to bring me
  sorrow;
Yet I always find myself hoping for
  tomorrow.
And when I see a sky of grey, all my fears
  return;
For a flower am I, yet scared of the rain.

—*Heather Waldman*

A Poem of Love

I've tried so many times to erase your
    memory from my mind,
Yet it doesn't ever last for long,
I see your picture, then I hear your voice,
Our love must be stronger that before.
Here I stand defenseless as I look in your
    eyes,
There's nothing left to say or do,
You fill my head with promises, and all
    your pretty lies,
Would it be so wrong to want you by my
    side.
I'm captured by my senses, lost in your
    reverie,
Our love must be stronger than before.

—*Kimberly Baker*

Untitled

3 A.M. Through the blur of tears and
    darkness
She sees what she had closed her eyes to.
"Where do I turn? Who do I call?"
She dials the number with a blinding
    heart.
Her heart speaks without judgement to a
    comforting voice.
No longer alone in her world.
No more tears—only a true friend.

—*Tina Frost*

Day and Night

We travel through the day
Yet to our dismay
We travel once again in shadowy dreams
Or so it seems.
You see the unadorned side
That is always hidden away.
While I seal myself
Behind the mask of day.
I try to straighten out my illusion,
But it merely leads me to confusion.
And I still stand here with my plight
As the day once again dwindles into night.

—*Hana Velk*

Eagles

I am an eagle, free in spirit,
Seeking always vision's crest;
I soar on high—oh, to share it!
You'll know me by my eagle's chest.
In the fullness of my keen—eyed sight,
My eyes become majestic light.
You may come and fly with me,
And then together we will be free.

—*Ron Vail*

An Offering

Each passing tide
Yields gifts of toxicide
Homocide/suicide
We the murderers of the earth.

—*Jennifer O'Malley*

I Love You

I love you so much and I love to talk to
    you.
You always seem interested in everything
    I do.
You always make me feel very good.
If I ever asked anything of you, I know
    you would.
You always seem to have time for me.
No matter what my problem may be.
I think about you every day.
And every night for you I pray.
I love you deep in my heart.
And I really thank you for helping me get
    a brand new start.
You are always on my mind.
And that's because you are so good and
    kind.
You know that I will always love you.
And I will always be proud of you no
    matter what you do.
Take care and have a beautiful day.
And thanks for helping me along my way.

—*Angel Maria*

Together

Together forever,
You and me.
Together forever,
That is what we shall be.
Together forever,
For an eternity.

—*Angela Messmer*

Paradise

I look in your eyes and I can see paradise.
You and me together as one.
Together as two as long as I can be with
    you.
Together or apart,
You will always be in my heart.
So just go on your way,
I got no more to say
But I love you!

—*Charlotte Becker*

Together

You are always there,
You are always near.
I'm never alone,
I've no reason to fear.
You always stand right by my side,
I know now you always will.
Together. . .
I just reached my destiny,
You and me living in ecstasy.
Always together,
Never apart.
We've been linked together
Right at our hearts.
Together. . .
Here we are,
Side by side together.
Here we are,
Side by side forever.

—*Dawn Riess*

history of a meditation

alone
    allowing inimical thoughts to
    snowdrift the sides of my parka
    my furtive fingers (drumsticks
        of my mindself)
    become aching reminders of an
    arthritic tympany as intrinsic
    in me as tom-toms to homeless
    people of a lost civilization
along
    an aloneness trail always
                    i
                drift
            back
    and make connection with a time
    i knew before when aloneness was
    fiberfood for cleansing arteries
    of the second self

—*roger wilbur*

Sleep Good Sweetheart

I lie here it's midnight
You are asleep, I'm sure
Tightly tucked away for
A hard day you have endured.
I'm thinking of you
As tears fill my eyes
How I love you though
I'm sure you realize.
I can see you lying
Oh so quietly,
Many dreams I wish upon you.
Sleep good sweetheart
For tomorrow there will
Be more things to do and
People to see.
When you wake you will
Jump up, around so hurriedly
To do—to be—to see.
Don't hurry so much, take
Life slow not so fast and
Things will come more easily.
But for now sleep good sweetheart
And wake and think of me.

—*Donitta Young*

Mom

Moms are unique and you're no
  exception,
You are honest and true with no
  deception.
You are kind and sincere just what we
  needed,
Your advice we have sought and often
  heeded.
It is easy to take someone for granted,
That would be hard with roots solidly
  planted.
Values are something you worked hard to
  teach,
At times it is true we were hard to reach.
Love was given in generous portions,
We all left home to seek family fortunes.
Now families are grown and are quite
  secure,
As our ages increase you still lend an ear.
Mom you have been and remain
  wonderfully dear.

—Gwynn Sosa

Dream

Come along with me. I wan to share my
  dream.
See the beauty, see the picture, see the
  colors.
What's that over there! It's a water fall 50
  feet tall;
With flowers all sizes and a rainbow
  beautifully stretched
across the sky. Birds singing with all call.
Oh! over there, it's a rock shinning of gold
  as big
as the sun shines with a glow.
Feel the warmth in the air, dance to the
  rythem of the
water drops, oh! keep your eyes open this
  is for real
It's a dream with nature. It's fresh,
It's our Dream.

—Teresa Baker

The End

I sit here and now want to pout,
You are locked up and must long to shout
I cannot cry, but the tears are there,
They will not flow, but God knows how
  dearly I care
It must be hard, for you I believe,
And the thoughts keep running, but I still
  can't conceive
So much there is to do and so little time,
And me; I'm a help, writing this rhyme
You were my friend, a dear one it's true,
But now I feel we are finally through
We've been through it all together,
And I fear we must end it apart
I'll miss you now and forever,
And I'll always love you;
Like a brother,
With all my heart.

—B. A. Bramick

Time

When you fight with a friend, time seems
  to be standing still.
You are so dizzy with anger and
  frustration that you feel terribly ill.
Just thinking about that day makes time
  go in reverse.
Your hatred toward each other is getting
  steadily worse.
There's a terrible, aching pain in your
  broken heart.
The two friends that once loved each
  other grow further apart.
Time is only a torturous and merciless
  chain.
It lets you have nothing to loose and
  nothing to gain
Except a special and wonderful friend.
When time makes you loose a certain
  person, you want everything to end.
Deep down inside of you both is a
  friendship so strong.
You two finally realize that you were so
  very wrong.
The both of you forgive each other with a
  hug
And you realize time has trampled over
  you as if you were a rug.
"You never will hate each other—never."
Your special love and bond will live
  forever.

—Anne-Marie Moffa

Eternal Love

My love for you is like that to heaven.
You are the one to brighten my day,
And to comfort me at night.
You are always there when I need
  someone.
I feel as though I can tell you anything.
And know that you'll understand.
To be with you is my destiny.
Without you, my life wouldn't be the
  same.
Will you be with me eternally?

—Kimberly Sheets

Best Friends

You are the friend I confide in,
You are the one who could do me no
  wrong.
You are my love I go through life with,
You bring me joy and happiness.
You bring me up when I'm feeling blue,
You are my best friend and I love you!

—Juanita O'Neil

Yes

Thinking of the day gone by
You ask yourself "Why me?"
You say things just aren't fair, not right
Everything's against you, you don't
  understand
You think of giving up, ending it all
You say, "Is it worth it"
"Is it worth living for"
A strange feeling overcomes you, like
  something's there
You can't see it, but you feel it
You ask "Why keep living"
"Why"
A long silence comes, no sounds, just
  silence
You ask again
"Is life worth living"
Finally, a sound different from yours
"Yes"
Simply said, simply put
"Yes."

—Karen Perkey

Aging

You begin weak, you end weak
You begin being led, you end being led
You begin helpless, you end helpless
But between the beginning and the end
There is a line drawn. . .
You gain strength
You learn to prove yourself
You succeed, you fail
You love, you hate
You laugh, you cry
You gain, you lose
You remember, you forget
You grow weak
You grow old. . .
You begin with nothing, you end with a
  treasure.

—Christine Murphy

Ocean

In tranquility
Serenity all around
Nature is at ease
Silence interrupted by
Nature's soft whispering waves

—Sasha Mervyn

Sunshine

You're my sunshine when there is no light
You brighten me up on a cold rainy night.
You stay in my heart from night to day
And you'll always be there in a special
  way.

—Christy Key

Untitled

Though the day is just beginning
you can already feel the strain
the darkness closing in on you
the screaming, yelling, crying
Fighting for time
on the edge
the laughing, the tormenting
Then, boredom
a lull in life
you're going to explode
the darkness closing in on you
That torturing demon
thinking evil thoughts of you
true they not be
Close to tears
palms cut to blood
the darkness closing in on you.
The darkness, that horrid darkness.

—Elizabeth J. Meyer

Dreamland

The oceans breeze on a hot summers night
You can feel the beams of the everlasting light
No matter where you are you can hear the ocean by far
Even on the other side of the world where their is a war
The sparkling water shimmers by the moon
It is reflected so soon
The endless sea flows about from you to me
The waves crash when they hit the shore
But soon another will hit there more
That is what the feeling of the sea means to me.

—Chrissy Clark

Untitled

Trying to get close to you is like trying to tame a wild kitten.
You can sit for days with food in your hand and each day he comes closer.
In awhile, he's in your hand and you are stroking him and loving him and he is happy.
Until you scare him away by sneezing and you have to start all over again.

—Erin Hennessy

Sweet Child of Mine

Sweet child of mine you are so dear
You cannot speak but I know you can hear.
Remember I love you
Truly I do and would never do
Anything to hurt you
It's so hard for me to let you go
But it's all for the best and never the worst.
I will hold you in my heart forever
So that way we will always be together.

—Jamie Ann Lee

The Journey

Don't dwell in the past.
You can't change what you've already done.
Learn from any mistakes you've made.
Don't dream for the future.
You can never know what lies on the road before us.
Wait for your times to come.
Life is a great journey.
But always remember one thing as you travel this road.
Take it step by step.
Live for right now and today.
Now is the only time in your life you can make.
Hurry, before now slips away.

—Angie Herron

Raining Days

Rainy days always get everybody down,
You can't get out and around the town.
It's wet and muddy out of doors,
This means staying in doing my chores.
The morning has passed after noon has come,
It is still raining a little, kinda, well some.
Wishing the sun shine would please come out,
So that I could finally get out and about.
I guess I'll just listen to my radio,
Or maybe get hooked on a good t.v. show.
The afternoons past and evenings arrived,
It looks like I have survived.
The days almost over, wish the showers would pass,
Wonder how long the lighting will last.
I'll just go to bed, lay down my head.
Soon morning will come,
And so will the sun, I hope. . .

—Cassi Casto

Could have been

I've loved before, but not like you
You changed my world around
And tore my heart in two
As time passed, there were no
More tears to cry, my heart wasn't
So lonely and my love for you began to die.
Thinking of memories that we
Once shared
Remembering them showed how much
You really cared.
I'll always have a place for you
Deep in my heart,
But we can never be together
Since we've had to part
Don't stop and think how it
Could have been,
You let it go
And that was the end. . .

—Jennifer Enright

Come Back To Me

I wish you were here,
you could be with me.
Tell me your dreams,
tell me your deepest fantasies.
"The thing we could share"!!!
I wish I could show you,
Just how much I care.
We could make it through our problems,
and our bad days we could face,
you and I together,
would always leave a trace.

—Christy Sue Robinson

If Life Were Like a Storybook

If life were like a storybook,
You could savor every word,
Skip what you don't care to know;
Perhaps this sounds absurd.
Perhaps I'm just a dreamer
Living in a realistic world,
With a realistic government
Whose lies at us are hurled.
If life was like a storybook,
We could travel back in time;
You could be all that you want to be,
Life would be sublime.
We all must face reality
And all that it may seem,
Though I'd prefer imagination
To escape into a dream.

—Christy Handkins

Eternal Love

His love for her was truthful,
You could see it in his eyes,
For when he looked at her,
There was a feeling he could not hide.
He got nervous when he was around her,
Yet he didn't want her to go,
He wanted to confess his unending love,
Yet he didn't want her to know.
He wanted her to live forever,
So she could see all the bright, sunny days,
But things did not go as he had hoped,
And the Lord took her away.
His love would live forever,
It would strengthen through heartache and pain,
The only thing that he would regret,
Was not knowing she'd always felt the same.

—*Joni Mitchell*

Valley Green

A place of peace and happiness,
Where no darkness can be seen.
A land of only beauty,
In the place called valley green.
The sun is always shining there,
And a breeze so lightly blows.
It blows the clear, blue river,
As its water gently flows.
The flowers keep on blooming,
As the days go rolling by.
The clouds stay white and fluffy,
As they float across the sky.
The raindrops fall with rhythm,
While they sing a happy song.
And not too far behind them,
The rainbow rolls along.
Oh, in this place of wonder,
Where no darkness can be seen.
It's the land of only beauty,
It's the place called valley green.

—*Shannon Polachek*

Dreams

As the sunset came it was summer
You could see the clear moon an it wasn't a bummer.
Day by day I'd watch the sky
And as I did I'd wish I could fly.
If my dreams could come true
I'd be a kangaroo
Jumping up and down on the clouds.
It seems to me
That I could be
A bumble bee juicing my honey.
Or maybe a white haired bunny...
It really doesn't matter
I'd eat ice cream on a platter
Or maybe a bowl of fruit.
And I'd look cute
In a teeny weeny bikini
Still kind of dreaming
But maybe I'll wake up.

—*Corneilsha Malcom*

River Of Life

The river is deep, and the water is cold.
You got to get wet, before you get old.
Stay on the bridge, or your gonna fall in.
Deeper and deeper, tred water and swim.
Another man drowned, he got tired and died.
He swam for tree branch, with a cramp in his side.
Higher and higher, hold on to that breath.
The river is rising, your so scared to death.
Back above water, a bridge is in sight.
If your gonna make it, you better put up a fight.
The river is deep and the water is cold,
You got to get wet, before you get old.
Stay on the bridge, or you're gonna fall in.
Deeper and Deeper, tred water and swim.

—*David L. Smith*

Lightning

Lightning strikes on storm wet ground,
Shaking the earth with huge leaps and bounds.
As it jumps around from hill to field,
With thunder rumble for company,
It damages, sparkles, and flies a quiver.
It's piercing cry runs through the air.
The people full of fear have no time for despair
To mourn the loss of their once proud home.
The lightning takes care of it for them
To rebuild and start all over again.

— *Laura Wichmann*

Maybe

When I first met you, I never dreamed you would be there on my team.
You have a wonderful smile and maybe that's why I knew after awhile
That our being friends would never end.
Maybe I need you more than you need me,
Maybe you don't care but honey, tell me please,
Do you love me as much as I love you?
Now that you are out of school, I hope you will obey the rules,
Have a good, a very good life; I don't want to see you in strife.
Well I learned my lesson,
Never fall in love with a person who doesn't love you.
Now that I am grown up, I know life will be tough.
Will you call me when you're gone?
Cause friends like you can't be forgotten.
Maybe I need you more than you need me,
Maybe you don't care, but honey, tell me please,
Do you love me as much as I love you?

—*Julie Gardner*

Poems I Mean To Write

There are so many poems I mean to write.
You have filled my life with inspiration,
But somehow I always lack the time
To write it all down.
My hours of daydreaming are so few now.
But your love and inspiration are ever present,
And I am still filled with awe,
Thinking of what we have.
For all the poems I mean to write,
Know they were written once
In my heart.
Know that your love
Is the most important thing in my life.
Know that I love you truly,
Even when there's not time
To write it down.

—*Karen L. Stallworth*

Two Different Worlds

Somewhere along our path of togetherness
We grew apart, you walked ahead, I fell behind
Here I am alone without you, but not really alone
Some nights are worse than others
Remembering all of the times you were here
Reliving all of the nights you stayed with me
The pictures in my memory embedded for life
The confusion you left with me lies even deeper
Our future looked so bright, so promising
The ring on my finger, a symbol of our love
The love we shared ran deep, deep into my soul
I sometimes think of the fights we had, the words,
How they hurt, I read your letters over and over again
Wondering, I sit here now wishing it was me.
Me, who was holding you now

—*Wanda Hammond*

First Sign of Light

With the sun going down and the moon coming out
You hear the last cries of the children's loud shouts.
The light of the day and the dark of the night
You must wait again until the first sign of light.
As you sleep in bed, dreams form in your head
Dreams about what now lies ahead
Then, "pop", all of a sudden, you awaken from the night
But, alas! Guess what? It's the first sign of light!

—*Amy Bendell*

Reality

Gracious, old man, with gleaming white
  hair and deep piercing eyes of blue,
You just made my forever most dream
  come true.
Thank you so much for this Religious
  Symbol
I will hold it forever, here in my heart's
  dimple.
Proudly, I marched to school today,
So bursting with pride, my body swayed.
I placed my new gift on top of my desk,
To be seen by all, and honored at best.
Surprised me not, teacher rudely snatched
  it up,
Oh God, I prayed, she just drained my
  cup.
I ran to my dear old friend, grabbed hold
  of his hand,
And began to whimper,
I feel deep, deep down inside like a branch
  of fallen timber.
Don't cry my child, he said with a smile,
  you still own it pure and simple.
I see it so clearly, imprinted, right there,
  between your temples.

—*Janet E. Cook*

Open Your Eyes

Do you notice that when we are together,
  I am a different?
You know that I am a smartass around
  other people
But when we are alone, I am heart
  broken.
Open your eyes.
Do you remember the last time we
  hugged?
It was after we had that fight, after we
  had talked.
Did you notice that my hug lasted a little
  bit longer?
Wasn't it a little bit stronger, weren't you
  paying attention?
Open your eyes.
When I came over to your house and gave
  you that letter,
We sat on the bricks outside.
I watched your face as you read, you
  looked so perfect, so innocent.
I saw the tear fall from your blue eye.
  Why? Why were you crying?
As we talked, didn't you notice the hurt in
  my voice?
Can't you figure out that I love you?
Open your eyes.

—*Karen Bernards*

Lifes Course

You're born, you breathe,
You learn, you function.
It's like a ship at sea,
If you take the right course,
You reach your proper destination.

—*Alice Stengel*

As The Sun Sets

As the sun sets
You leave me all alone,
As the sun sets
I repeatedly wail and moan.
As the sun sets
My love for you dies,
As the sun sets
You hear my lonely cries.
As the sun sets
The woman in me appears,
As the sun sets
It's for you I shed these tears.
As the sun sets
You caress me in your arms,
As the sun sets
Your love, it is me it harms.
As the sun sets
You are mine no more.

—*Jacquelyn N. Coutre'*

Ryan

You left this life to forget all your
  troubles and strifes.
You left without a sound, disappeared,
I won't get to see you around.
I loved you from a view, now to see you, I
  have to sit in a pew.
I wish I could have read your pain, maybe
  I could have
Helped and we'd have something to gain.
I can't imagine why you took your life, my
  only guess is the strife.
To see you in a saddened state just isn't
  you; but you took the bait.
Depression wears down your soul, your
  life is how it took its toll.
I can't help but cry every time I hear you
  die.
I imagine you tried to make us see the
  pain that wouldn't
Let you be.
I guess we didn't think you had troubles
  too,
Now there's nothing we can do.
We're left asking why,
There's no note or words or a cry, to why
You had to die.

—*Crissi Ault*

Untitled

When you love
You love completely
Or you don't love at all
I love you, completely
But you don't love at all.
Love all the small things you do
Even love the things that hurt me too
Love you when you don't talk to me
Love you when it's not me you see
Love you when you ignore me
Kind of love you for not loving me.

—*Amy McDonald*

Lost Love

I loved you
You loved me
But now that you've left
We both are free
Free to run
Free to walk
Free to have fun
Free to talk
We had our love
But now it's gone
I lost the fight
That you have won

—*K. Whidden*

Breaking Up

Breaking up is hard to do,
You loved me and I loved you
But the time has come for us to part
I cannot handle the pain in my heart
Just turn and go so you don't see
The pain that you are bringing me

—*Danielle Enborg*

Perfectly You

You're so wonderful,
You make me smile,
Bring me joy,
But all the while,
I didn't know,
It was you,
That made me shine and made
  me glow.
Warm and gentle,
Funny and sweet,
Sentimental, and carefree,
Tender, loving,
My heart beats, faster,
When you're with me.
So comfortable to be around,
You make me feel at ease.
I'm so glad that I have found,
A guy so great to me.

—*Elena Olszewski*

Remembering

I lay in bed, the radio is playing a song
 which makes me think of you.
You moved away with your family almost
 a year ago. You said you would never
 forget me.
Now I'm wondering if you did. I knew I
 could never forget you.
I have a picture of you beside my bed. I
 have the tape which has our song on it .
 Every time I play it, I break down and
 cry.
All my friends go out to the mall
 Saturday. I'm staying home waiting for
 you to call.

—*Jenell Klinedinst*

Angel

Angel girl
You rule my world
You are my sunshine
You are my rain
You are my joy
And you are my pain
Angel girl
You are my true love
You have come from the heaven's above
Angel girl
Never leave me
For I will die
So do believe me

—*Christine Krupinski*

Untitled

You never mean to stray
You said so yourself
You never meant to hurt me
And put my love upon a shelf.
You never meant to leave
And go so far away
You called me and
How you wish you had stayed.
Will I never meant to fall in love
And give my heart to you
But once it had happened
There was nothing I could do.
What's done is done
And this I can trully say
I'll never take you back
And thats meant in every way.

—*Angel Giles*

Breaking Up

"It's for the better."
You say and I turn around
For I am weak and too ashamed
To cry in front of you
You whisper my name
So I take a last look
Only to see tears in your eyes too

—*Amber L. Kovach*

Impasse

Can you tell someone who dwells in a
 desert how healing the valley can be?
You see his shambling shack and tread his
 barren land.
You search for shade from searing sun;
 you seek a spring to quench the thirst,
but there is only sand.
His life was ever thus, vast void of
 nothingness? In your mind you find no
 answer for his choice,
no reason for his course.
But if he seeks no more than scorching
 sand and waste, can valley cool and
 brook and rainbows after rain
return him to his source?
You offer him your hand to cross the
 wilderness. He waits and hesitates.
 "This step might be too soon;"
"this step might be unwise."
He begs you stay with him, abandoning
 your goals. you know it is farewell. The
 healing of his soul
he'll never realize.

—*Charlotte Riepe*

Tear us apart

If death shall ever tear us apart,
You shall never be without my heart.
You shall never ever live a day,
That you don't feel the golden sun's rays.
That you don't feel the warmth of me,
Flying high, wandering and free.
Don't think of me all the time,
Keep on planning your next heart crime.
Let me be the one you'll love,
And let me be your angel dove.
If death shall ever tear us apart,
You shall never be without my heart.

—*Hannah Schauer*

Life

If you ever walk down a path through the
 trees,
You should pay attention to what you
 might see.
Notice the ground, passing you by,
Then take a peak up in the sky.
The clouds will follow as if they know,
Just exactly where you will go.
As soon as I know it, that's where I'll be,
I will be with my loved ones, just them
 and me.
The earth is where we live, it is where we
 are,
But soon enough we'll be there,
 somewhere afar.
So remember that God controls our
 destiny,
He will guide us and lead us until we are
 free.
So live your life and don't ever worry,
Just slow things down and try not to
 hurry.

—*Brian Wedlake*

Window

When rain streams like tears down my
 clear-eyed face,
you sit yearning outward on the edge of
 outdoors.
mist frosts my gaze in the winter hours,
and with your finger you trace
messages to the spiraling, swirling, snowy
 pyre
that will soon be transformed to dancing
 snowmen by fast-paced imps.
I am cloaked with fine tapestry trappings,
that hang like Buddha's robes to the floor
I let in only light, not dark, like the
 omniscient I am.
I see the whole of life:
mail boxes, white picket fences, roads that
 go on to forever
nowhere, postmen, and stray cats.
in the dark time that falls regularly
I reflect in again you as you pace between
 rooms
and light candles on a flowery table
you wave goodbye from the sanctity of my
 unblinking portal,
but sometimes I see you taper to the tip of
 the non-ending road,
and not once do you turn back to face my
 steady approval.

—*Kim Karr*

Teary Angel

You sit, like an angel,
You speak not a word,
Your face, a pale white,
Your mouth downward turned.
What is it that troubles you?
What makes you so blue?
Is it the change of the season?
Was your one love untrue?
Your hands folded neatly,
Upon your white dress.
Your hair hides your eyes,
It hides your duress.
Cast away your sadness,
You have nothing to fear.
Put sparkle in those angel eyes,
Wipe away your tears.

—Amy Varner

Love

Love is a feeling from deep inside,
You struggle and fight, but there's noting to hide,
You reach deep in your heart,
With your feelings so cold,
Then you finally realize you have something to hold,
Something that will not perish, till death do you part,
Something that will last, and never fall apart.

—Dawn M. Creekmore

Our Special Love

When I'm with you nothing else matters,
You take care of me when my world shatters.
As long as the stars shine,
I know that you'll always be mine.
My life is full now that your here,
And I have nothing to fear.
You stand by me when things are bad,
You hold me when I'm sad.
You wouldn't believe,
How much your love means to me.
Songs can't really express,
Our special closeness.
You and me will always be.

—Julie Canady

Let Go

You give me wings, but you won't let me fly.
You tell me to grow up, but you won't let me try.
You ask me to be responsible, but you won't give me any responsibilities.
You tell me to live my own life, but you want to hold my hand and lead me through it.
You want me to be my own person, but you want me to be just like you.
I want to do it on my own, but you're the one who has to let go.

—Jenn Anne Seigle

You and the Stranger

You—you're in and out of my life.
You think of me, you dream about me—
Until—she walks in and I become a
Small thought packed into you cluttered mind.
I'm in there whenever you may need me
I'll sit and wait for your walls of your world to crumble
So I can come out to rescue you.
I'm here for you
I'll listen to you
I'll talk with you
I'll even feel for you.
Maybe someday when you come back into my life.
When I become more than a "tucked away" friend
You'll realize—you mean the world to me!

—Amy Von Ville

Tomorrow Next

We walked.
You told me that my eyes were blue.
I told you that I knew.
Come with me.
I walk alone just every day—Please stay.
This heart—
Is so fragile, please just stand—
Please hold my hand.
I thought.
I hope this won't ever end—You were my friend.
We fought.
Until I had beguiled,
Until you smiled.
Look there.
We come now every day to see the sea, just you and me.
One day,
You told me, you said, "I love you".
I told you that I knew.

—Caroline McKoskey

A Love to Last Forever

A love to last forever is what you'll always be;
You took another pathway, which did not include me,
I loved you nice and tender until the very end.
My love you'll always be and my heart you cannot mend.
A love to last forever is what you'll always be;
Now that we've departed my life is empty.
Your smile made me tingle, something I just cannot explain.
I know you're lost forever, but it will never be the same.
A love to last forever is what you'll always be;
We were a unit like two songbirds sitting upon a small oak tree
It hurts so much to say goodbye and to let my feelings go.
My heart is broken and I am sad because I loved you so.
A love to last forever is what you'll always be;
You wanted more space between you and me.
You wanted more time so you could think things through totally.
Once a unit, my songbird has flown away and now I sit alone upon the desolate tree.

—Amy Propp

Love is

Love is when you care so much,
You tremble from a single touch.
Love is when you give your all,
Just because your loved one called.
Love is when the gift of a rose,
Makes you tingle right down to your toes.
Love is wanting to give all your heart,
To that true love who will never part!

—Evon Wood

Dream A Little Dream

Dream a little dream that won't come true
You want it to but you know it won't
Wishing it would, you find something new
What you have found is love
Love that will last forever
More greater than life is to spend your life with someone
special
Someone who loves you, as much as you love them
Someone you can turn to when you are blue,
Who will hold you tight and tell you it will be all right
Work things out and kiss you more passionately than life.

—Carrie Horton

Daddy's Girl

I was your little girl.
You were always so proud of me.
Every Sunday I sat by the window
And waited for your visit.
I always looked forward to Sunday,
But that Sunday, you didn't come.
Or the next one, or the next one.
I still sat by the window every Sunday,
But the joy I had always felt was gone.
That was so many years ago.
This Sunday when you come to visit
Your little girl won't be waiting
By the window.
Your little girl is all grown up now,
And you're not a part of her life anymore.

—Koren King

O' Dear Little Brother Of Mine

O' dear little brother of mine,
You were always so sweet
Like a glass of red wine.
O' Dear little friend of ours,
Your laughter would fill a room
For hours upon hours.
O' dear little child of love,
You always brought peace
Like a little white dove.
O' dear little son of all,
You knew no boundaries
You knew no wall.
O' dear little hero I miss,
You're a bundle of joy;
A bundle of bliss.
O' dear little brother of mine.

—Brooke Capps

Reflecting

I looked in the mirror today,
You were crying through my eyes,
I'm missing you again.
Memorable images reflected of you,
Exposing emotions of me,
Pulling at my heart,
Leading me into your immortality,
Through pain I did not feel,
Until now.
I looked in the mirror today,
I was crying through your eyes,
Remembering you again.

—Ken Konrad

Lonnie Ray

Gone? No never!
You will live in our hearts and minds forever.
As I gaze at your picture, I can trace
All of the kindness in your face.
Ah! Generous, kindly, loving soul
One who possessed a heart of gold.
Our thoughts will be of you as we gather summer's rose
And in the winter's night, as the north wind blows.
Gone? That can never be your generous personality
Is still afloat on life's great sea.
The lives you touched will always be
Better by far-far having known thee.
Entwined, entrenched in our memory
And in God's great mystery of earth and sky and sea.
Yes, you will always be.
Sleep on-dear one, beneath the sun
Your works are finished, all were well done.

—Agnes O. Thomas

Thinking About...

Follow your dreams,
You will soar high.
Lead your fears,
Sing a sad lullabye.
Capture the happiness,
Fill yourself with joy.
Shatter a bleeding heart,
Like a brand new toy.
People have minds,
A brilliant tool.
People forget,
Crying like a fool.
Time goes fast,
Prayers are often spoken.
The bear at the carnival,
Kept as a token.
Screams of love,
Almighty and strong.
Say goodbye to the nights,
That seem so lonely and long.

—Christine Kelley

Untitled

If you were to end it all right now,
You would leave behind all our vows.
We've been together for almost a year
And we both shed many a tear.
But then again we've had the best times of our lives
We were sad but then we revived.
We were destined to be together, you can't doubt that
If we can't be together, it would leave my heart flat.

—Amanda Pilcher

Eternity

No matter what I said to you,
You'd always turn away.
My smile was received by a frown,
My laughter received by a stare.
It didn't matter to you that I cared.
I had made some mistakes,
I had done the wrong thing,
But my happiness had been so strong,
All I had wanted to do was sing.
The lies had crumbled,
And the truth caught up with me.
Now I have to make up for it...
For an eternity.

—Becky Rahn

To Bee or Not to Be

Bees are good but sometimes bad.
You'd think so to if you'd been had.
Oh yeah! said the little bee.
What could I do, when he sat on me.
Made me mad enough to turn blue.
What would you do if it was you?
I was bright yellow, until I turned blue.
I was fat, but he changed that to.
I thought golly, something must be done.
So I popped my stinger into 42 ton.
I know one thing up he come.
I didn't live long enough to see who won.

—Joyce Willis

Longing For Desire To Be...

A bird, a feather, a beautiful
young girl, a tear. All longing for
desire...desire to be. Showing
feeling, growing up, shedding
feathers and tears. These are
silent renewals, happening to
everyone, and everything. Content,
that is when the bird sheds a
feather. Content, that is when the
young girl sheds a tear. She is
she, and also has fulfilled the
desire to be. Forevery everyone and
everything, will have and should
have the longing for desire to be.

—Heidi Eileen Green

Adolescence

Young men
Young women
All trying to grow up
School during the week
Many hours of homework
A few for fun
Dating on the weekends
Dreaming
Planning for the future
Applying for a job
Fighting with parents
Making up with friends
Happiness
Sadness
Teenagers

—Amy Blaskowski

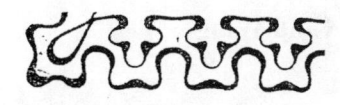

Reflections

I am a person whom you can share,
Your dreams, your thoughts, and you can
 declare
That I am yours and that you are mine,
Together is us, until the end of time.
For I am vindictive and I have much
 pride,
I'm desirous, invidious, and dignified.
If you shall detest my obstinate way,
Apologies to you, that's how I shall stay.

—Colleen Marie Judd

Seduction

When you touch me a shiver of a
 sensational jolt runs up my spine,
Your dulcet caress sends me into the
 heavens; I don't mind
Your wandering arms around my waist.
Your tender kiss indulged my lips. I knew
 then we
Had reached the decisive line.
I had to make the choice, would we go on
 to greater experiences
Or would this be our climax?
When I failed to do so, you proceeded
 with your concept of seducing
My mind. You wrapped your arms around
 my waist.
Your behavior became aggressive. Your
 talk all lies.
You wanted what I could give.
I felt I had to resist, but when I looked
 into your glassy eyes
I left my defenses unguarded. Your
 passion quickly enclosed me.
I was trapped, no way out, taking all you
 could give.
I struggled for a moment, I saw it was
 hopeless.
I was helpless in your arms. You didn't
 want to unleash me from your grasp.

—Alexis Winnell

Class of the 80's

Fast cars, fast music, and fast girls,
Seems the whole world is in a whirl.
Drugs, gangs, and people who don't care,
Are there any good people anywhere?
Everything is "money," "me," and
 "now,"
Words like "awesome," "rad," and
 "wow."
Slang that doesn't make any sense,
Too many people, uptight and tense.
Using bad language and lousy manners,
There is no courtship, love doesn't matter.
Obscene gestures and crude, rude talk,
Everything's giving me a real bad shock.
This generation is reckless and bad,
No wonder the parents are so mad.
Their poor children, what have they done,
In the end no one has won.

—Stacy Beversdorf

You

In the blinding darkness, I see your light.
Your eyes of fire, they shine so bright.
In the icy rain, I feel your warmth,
Like a thousand candles, a blazing hearth.
In the world's deepest despair,
I call your name and you are there.
Your warm, sweet words, they soothe my
 soul,
Melting all the memories that were once
 so cold.
Once my days were black and white,
But then your color came into my life.

—Elizabeth Warren

Passing Storm

My friend, why are you so down?
Your face is a gloomy winter day.
Your sorrow is shown by your frown.
What made the sunshine go away?
My friend, melancholy has taken you
 over.
The raindrops of misery streak your face.
The temperature of your emotions has
 gotten colder.
The joy you had in you left without a
 trace.
My friend, depression is a passing thing:
One day it's there, one day it's not.
Soon you will hear birds sing,
And your storm will be but a dot.
Until then, take care, my friend.
The storm your'e in will very soon end.

—Amy Larranaga

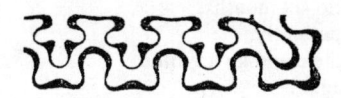

Unknown

What you don't know can not be seen,
Your only way to solve the unknown is,
to search deep within me,
If you dare to find what is hidden,
You will surely know it is forbidden,
For what is hidden within my heart,
will take a very commited part,
Until that day I will be searching,
for the person who will solve the unknown.

—Arayna Jayd Parks

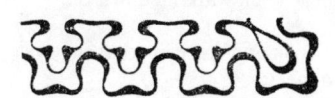

To My Father

You are alone in the world now
Your soul does not love
Your heart does not lust.
You are an iron pipe in the bitter
Winter rains—cold, dark, and full of rust.
But behind the moving sunset,
Behind its indigo and green
I have moved beyond you
Into a passion warm and mean,
I have taken your tokens,
I have played your game
And I have decided it is you and not I
Who has gone insane.

—Heather Laatz

Furtively

Try as you might
Your ways are severed
You'll never make your flight.
It's not fair to hold you back
But, be forewarned
Before you're thrown off track
You need your freedom as I do
Don't move too far
I'm jealous of you.
I suppose I was a friend. . .
No longer; my aversion is detestable
But, your faith in yourself will make
You stronger. . .understand.
Your goal is easy to attain
If you pay my falsity no mind
And no hatred remain.

—Christine A. Fore

Unfortunately

We are told six months,
We wait patiently,
Knowing he could go anytime,
Wondering. . .
If this is real,
Unfortunately it is.
We stand over the casket,
Staring into his eyes,
I see a tear roll down his face,
I wonder. . .
If it is real,
Unfortunately it isn't.

—Lori Rezendes

Why

What do you do when you're not the same,
You're different from the rest.
You're last in line for everything,
You settle for second best.
What makes everyone look at you so differently when walking down the street,
They stop, look and stare at what they've come to meet.
People don't care how you are inside,
How you act, or the feelings that you hide.
Throughout the world, they're all the same,
They hold that grudge, and feel no shame.
This feeling inside-it makes me want to cry,
Watching all the bigotry and really wondering why.
Why must others look down on those who are less fortunate,
Having nothing left, but a life to regret.
Why?
Because the sky is blue and the grass is green,
This, through my eyes I have always seen.
Those bigots are really out of whack,
Who discriminate against the black.

—Kathleen N.I. Bolles

Break the Chains

You can hear their singing but you can't see the birds
You're listening to the music but you're not hearing the words
Your destiny will take a course you must find
A twist of fate you can never unwind
You have the key to open the door don't be so blind
You can dream your dreams or you can live them
You can drown in the water or learn to swim
They're driving you away you better take the reigns
And when they're not looking break the chains
Do what you've always done and you'll get what you've always got
When you dance in the line of fire prepare to be shot
Never let them see you slip never let them see you slide
If your back isn't bent the devil can't ride
Envy is ignorance imitation is suicide
You can dream your dreams or you can live them
You can drown in the water or learn to swim
They're driving you away you better take the reigns
And when they're not looking break the chains

—Fred L. Taulbee Jr.

Introduction

Imagine
Yourself,
Traveling
Back into the 1800's
Where slavery was a big issue,
And everyone hated you,
No one had a heart
Or showed any mercy,
You had to try and to survive in order to fulfill your dream
Of becoming someone
You had to solve your problem, with pain and suffering around you.
So just take a few minutes out of your time and try to realize,
As you read this poem; what it was
To live or to die.

—Joy Apelquist

Our Friendship

You're in my thoughts so often, every night and every day.
You've come and touched my life in such a special way.
We understand each other and communicate so well,
A friendship with such understanding with others it would compel.
We have the best relationship because we're one of a kind.
Together we will search, and love is what we'll find.
The journey could be touch, along with aches and pains.
But if you're by my side I won't feel the strains.
I hope that we will be together, friends until we part.
I know your spirit will always be, enclosed within my heart.

—Kristen McClanaghan

A Daughter

A daughter is a very special person.
To her mother she's the memory
Of the challenges and trials
Experienced in the process of growing up.
To her father she brings to mind
All the beautiful and sweet
Young women encountered in his youth.
Together, parents, in their sometimes clumsy way,
Try to guide, teach and love her,
To protect her from their own imaginations.

—Sharron Lea Kanter

Honda, Gold Wing

Saturday
7 AM
Overcast
40 percent
— chance of rain.
8:25 AM
Sunshine
Don the Levi's
Cotton shirt and boots.
9 AM, to the shed
Steer the Honda out
Clean it up
Check it down.
9:25 AM
Cycle warmed up
Helmet on
Open road here I come.

—Sharron Sharp

It's What You Are Inside

As far as I'm concerned it matters not if a
    person may be a doctor,
A beggar or a king.
Because it's what a person is inside that
    really counts in life to me
Over some other superficial thing
First of all I simply look for honesty and
    the genuine goodness
Woven in that person's heart
Because they somehow seem to have that
    special something from others
Which sets them far apart
Many feel that their position at work
    gives them power, however, it
Alone doesn't make a man
Because it's the humility and many little
    things he does in life
That compose God's wonderous plan
It is also a fact that those here on earth
    who show understanding
Fill others lives with tenderness
However, the trouble unfortunately is,
    many people forget this quality
I now sadly do confess
Now there are only a couple of the many
    inward treasures that do
Fill this life with cheer
That is why I have found it is not who we
    are but what that
Counts most while we're here

—Nicole G. Williams

Heart Broken

My heart was being cut open.
A blade struck into soft flesh.
Blood pouring from my body.
Then frozen.
A tear of joy flows down my face.
I resolve that he will suffer.
Not me.

—Rebecca Miles

A Shattered Tear Fell From My Face

A shattered tear fell from my face
A broken heart was the case.
A love that once was true
By two hearts who shared the word love.
Two hearts ready to live
Two hearts ready to give,
A love that would last eternity
A love that would be forever more.
A shattered heart broken forever
Of two hearts longing to be together,
To share true love for a lifetime.
But then again how long do we have in a
    lifetime?

—Rebecca Jane Moss

Butternut Brook

Butternut Brook near a lake
A bubbly little stream that flows over
    rocks and stones
Water so pure and crystal clear dancing
    down the mountainside
Sometimes hurrying to the lake
    othertimes meandering dreamily
The trees around make music as the
    breeze sings its song
All nature is in harmony-no room for
    discord
I cup my hands and sip the cold water it is
    full of such vitality
May the life in me have the response as
    the water
And like the brook wherever my path goes
    may I
Bubble and dance and sing with joy.

—Norma B. Dixon

A Child in the Night

Noises in the night
A child cries
Why?
Abuse.
Why?
Reason? No reason.
Just because.
A hit or a slap at first
More drastic as they grow
A broken arm or leg
Maybe severe burns
Why?
Too young? Too much pressure?
Will the child die?
Last night I heard a child cry
Why?

—Tami Heilman

Beauty

Beauty is a flower blowing in the wind,
A child's face, so innocent and young.
Unicorns in the sky, so white and wild,
Rainbows reaching out to touch the land
With their brightness.
Beauty is a friend with no scorn,
And beauty is a rose with no thorn.
Time held in your hands as it sifts
Slowly through your fingers.
Sunset over a lake, colors melting into the
    water.
Beauty is in everything that is free
And beauty is part of the children, you
    and me.

—Marlene Miotke

Windblown Curls

i want
a cold bath
on a winter day
to use baby shampoo on my dog
eat butterscotch pudding at dawn
to be a
beach of white sand
sun—kissed
ocean drenched
to race cheetahs across Africa
softly sing us to sleep at night
we do not live
in a glass box
we can make love on rooftops
and not care who watches
and I can write you this poem
without even knowing your name

—M. Collier

A Writer's Sonnet

Before I sit down and begin to write,
A collection of thoughts is in my mind.
I pick out a feeling cordial and bright
To write sweet words that are gentle and
    kind.
Whenever I write my phrases rhyme,
All of my words come together and blend.
The feeling fits every moment in time
With a very special message to send.
Writing poetry fills the depth of my heart,
And it gives me so many great pleasures.
The words are tender and fresh from the
    start,
There's excitement within every measure.
Poetry is unique in every way,
It expresses all thoughts I wish to say.

—Stephanie Heim

About Chicken Noodle Soup

Like staring down into
A cup of steamy chicken soup
Yellowishly murky; dotted by
Tiny green pieces of broken parsley
    leaves,
And wedges of bright orange carrots,
Giant creamy noodles are
Swimming independently and
Big chunks of chicken that
Were expected in generous amounts are
Mysteriously unavailable.
You can see the gold dust floating
On a surface of oil, just meat and
    vegetables
And not trying to be
Anything as temperamental as spinach
    florentine with hollandaise sauce
But still just as good and, it's this you can
    gaze into
And nearly always find a poem.

—Mary Best

Halloween

Pumpkins glow, witches soar,
A curse a warlock mutters;
A scratching noise upon the door
And things beyond the shutters.
Apples in a water pail,
Tiny heads a-bobbing;
Sheets entangled in a gale
And little sister sobbing.
Candles drip, shadows creep,
Past paper skeletons flexing;
Goblin faces stare and leap
And on the porch are hexing.

—Robert Bartlett

Life...

We wake up every morning to find
  another one say
A day in which hate, war, and destruction
  rule
A time of killings and a time of science
We hope that each day is better than
  yesterday
We wish for gentle spring breezes,
Flowers and children with eyes that dance
But most of all we wish for love, hope and
  dreams
That will never die...because what is
  LIFE without LOVE.

—Loren Chavis

Lost

A day like the rest
A day of sorrow
The leaves falling from the trees
Rain sprinkling on the window
A day to think of the past
The love that has been lost
Over the years
The days of happiness are gone
Til you return to me
I will never forget you
Always you will be in my dreams
In my arms forever

—Laura Chester

No Greater Love

How fair the brightest star does shine
  within the darkest night
A dream, a magic wish, that cast it's own
  bright light.,
Held within the dreamers hand, to break
  an ancient spell.
Unfolding from a childhood heart to
  break the hold of hell.
As we stepped into the night the two of us
  were strong.
Armed in silver, truth and right we loudly
  sang our song.
One that proved our hearts were pure
  upon this fiery night
We stuck forth, in each our own with
  honor in our sight.
And each we conquered evil with our own
  bright sword.
With hearts as pure as fire we stood
  before our Lord.
As a light as gold as heaven rose into the
  sky.
We watched with awestruck wonder the
  night begin to die.
And we received our gift with open heart
  harkened from above.
Knowing from within we had no greater
  love.
From a childhood dream we had kept
  within our inner sight.
How fair the brightest star does shine
  within the darkest night.

—Valerie O. Donovan

A Cool Breeze

Stark and standing
A face that reads the truth
Beaming, glowing
Eyes that hide beyond the shadows of the
  moonlight
Too deep frustration, too little afterglow
  of happiness
And read between the words of wonder
To answer an inquisitive prayer
Follow the deepest emotions, live and
  breath a dream
Look, listen, learn
A face that reads the truth and lies
  forbidden
Eyes appear, stark and standing
One light that shines...One light holds
  the key
Whispering sweet words
Words that create the happiness, detour
  frustration
And the sound that shivers is lost
Lost within...Lost forever
And all that is felt
Is a cool, cool breeze.

—Tracee Becker

Untitled

I live is a fantasy.
A fantasy that has no end;
No line between reality.
My life goes on and on,
like a movie;
I watch from the outside
looking in on death and corruption
but not a part of it.
Just watching,
Waiting,
hoping to be remembered
but not to become involved.

—Ramsey Frazier

Mecca

Mecca, a place of worship, of pilgrimage.
A fulfillment of life's needs
A cleansing of the soul and a purging of
  sins.
Mecca, a poignant black wall, filled with
  names.
No race spared, mostly youth.
A generation's legacy.
Mecca, a journey of twenty years.
Of drugs, of guilt, of anguish, of loneliness
  and pain.
A difficult path filled with memories.
Mecca, it took so long to arrive, but now
  I've touched the stone.
I've seen my friends and said so long; not
  good-bye.
For they will never be gone while I live;
  just so long.
Mecca, a place where tears may be finally
  shed,
Where one's troubled mind may be put at
  ease.
A place where one may find peace again.

—Peter S. Gustin

Love "Conquers" All

To love is a gift, a gift from the heart.
A gift for the world of today,
Such a rare gift that is absent from
  mankind world today;
That man no longer cherish, nor care.
Love is "great, love is hate".
To love will make your heart pure
And your life will "shine" and "flourish"
All over the universe.
A problem will arise but love will erase.
Patient, I will be until the end.
"The word love is unique enough for me".
Love you can't buy.
Love you "cannot" destroy.
Love is for the world today.
Love "will conquer" all "problems".

—Mae Bell McKee

House vs. Home

A house is different than a home.
A house is a place that's considered a building.
A home is a comfy, cozy place to live.
A house is a shelter.
A home is a place to hang your hat.
People think house and home are the same.
But listen,
Do you say, "let's go house?"
No, you say, "let's go home."
A home is a nice place.
A house is a place that's not homey.
There is a major difference.
Do you say, "house sweet house?"
No, you say "home, sweet home."
A house is a house.
A home is a home.

—Michelle Bono

Alone

The dank dark despair of being a woman alone.
A husband, two cats,
And a beautiful home.
A job with benefits,
Graduate credits.
The dank dark despair of being a woman alone.
You exist.
He exists.
Bear a child.
Live awhile.
The dank dark despair of being a woman alone.
You talk.
He walks.
You cry.
He sighs.
The dank dark despair of being a woman alone.

—Leslie Nielsen

A Lifetime

A moment we arrest
A lifetime to capture
Love to unfold
Memories to create
Feelings untapped
Emotions released
Hands clasped
A kiss for guarantee
Moments we collect
A lifetime to share
Memories of love
Feelings of ecstasy
Emotions soar
Arms embrace
The moments a lifetime captures

—Lori O'Mel

Hidden Secrets

Violets blooming on the hill,
A little child wanders with a thrill.
The wind blows slightly caressing her skin,
She smiles gaily while dreaming within.
Her worries are few for her mind is strong.
She knows of right and never wrong.
To believe in something is all she can do,
For she knows her dreams will someday come true.

—Lisa Tupper

Love Story

My heart beats,
A little faster...
Adrenaline flows.
A slow blush,
Climbs.
A giggle sounds
Out of nowhere,
A brief smile,
A light touch,
Sets my heart racing.
A kind word,
A funny joke,
Your smile,
The one I see again and again,
The one I dream about,
Directed at me,
Makes me hope...
And wish...
And wonder...
Is it love?

—Robin A. Landals

How Loud My Sleeping Mind Rings

How loud my sleeping mind rings
A lonely call I hear.
Of desires yet unfilled,
In silence of my fears.
Tranquility has risen
Then faulters victory.
Blinded in open eyes,
Lives actuality.

—Lori Halla

A Night to Remember

A night to remember,
A memory to hide,
An everlasting love is
What we share inside.
Remember the night,
The night filled with love.
Remember the memory,
The memory that wanders above.

—Pia Christine Sisante

Life in the Moment

A moment in time that lasts forever.
A moment to live long and free.
Dancing in the wind like a flower wild and free.
To sing like a bird in the spring.
To love with your heart and soul.
To feel with yours, the feelings of love that is forever.
To dream and live the impossible dream.
To have life in the love that you have found.
To live life in the moment in time in which you live it.
A life to live for a moment in time.

—Michelle Grider

Mother

Mother, there is no one on earth, as sweet as you.
A mother so dear, and her love goes with her child.
The first look of her newborn, brings joy in her heart.
Mother, washes, cleans, cooks, keeps a clean house
Mother's warmth, and tender care goes a long way
As you grow, mother takes you by the hands,
To teach you your first step
You look at her and smile
When you grow to be a young child, mother is there.
When you need to talk, she takes time to listen
And give you good advice.
A real mother is more precious then pearls or diamonds
As you grow to be a teenager, mother is there, to guard
You into adulthood. To see her child live a christian,
Clean and decent life. A true mother doesn't want to see
Her child be with wrong people.
Sometimes, you think she is
Hard, but mother has been through the hurt that she is
Trying so hard to keep you from. I love you Mother.

—Tangerine Sokal

A Wonderful Mother

God made a wonderful mother,
A mother who never grows old;
He made her smile of the sunshine,
And he molded her heart of pure gold.
In her eyes he placed bright shining stars,
In her cheeks, fair roses you see.
God made a wonderful mother
And he gave that dear mother to me.

—Rhonda Martin

Under the Microscope

As you look to the ceiling, searching for
   one last breath,
A mysterious hand touches your soul
   leading you to a higher plane—
No worries, no pain; just
   serenity—Peace...one with the world.
A ring of keys is placed in front of
   you—the keys which everyone
Searches for.
The answers lie behind the bolted doors
   awaiting their brief moment of
   attention
All answers, thoughts become visible to
   the mind's eye.
Life and death become a cycle which
   repeats itself in time.
Nothing dies forever—not even a silly
   memory of the past.
Your identity is a ball of energy—no sex,
   just a simple figure of a
Physical—bodied veteran. You may feel,
   but you have no hands,
See, but without eyes;
Scream—but without sound. A figureless
   apparition waits the
Chance to be born again—a
   reincarnation—
Living, learning, dying again.
And again.
Forever.

—*Moone Gray*

Better Than You Know

You said I couldn't go through with it.
Well I proved you wrong,
Cause I went and did it,
Not the same old song.
A show of great independence,
Of course you're too dense to see,
I'm better than you know.
Now do you regret what you did?
You sure should.
I don't expect any apologies,
Only an ashamed face and an alibi,
Cause I'm better than you know.

—*Millie Turner*

The Path

Curiosity follows
A narrow path
It leads—
Through wooded areas
An opening, a light
The sun shines.
In the shadows—
I walk
Imagine...
The answers
Curiosity, questions
Strange dreams.
Impressions of nature
Colors—I seek
I wonder...
Content with my thoughts
At peace with my feelings
But curious nonetheless.

—*Tracy Nickloy*

True Love

Behind the fences of love
A new heart abides.
It's like a giant beanstock
That will grow higher than the stars.
There may be others who try to climb as
   high
But slip before their goal is reached.
For there is only one other heart
That will reach as high;
That is the heart of true love.

—*Michelle Miller*

Time

I feel the time drift away,
A painful tear rolls down my cheek.
The future's near, the past is gone,
And the sun I cannot see from the highest
   peak.
And as time sits still...
Love cries out for times helping hand.

—*Marella Benedetto*

A Subconscious World

Dreams are the goals of the subconscious,
A perfect reality.
Illusions of the mind, thoughts to set us
   free.
Wishes of utopias,
A view of life hidden inside thee.
People are what their dreams are
Their true selves hidden within an
   imperfect shape.
To really know someone you must look
   deep inside,
And pull out a dream.
Because the true inner person will never
   be on
The outside to see.

—*Summer Knight*

Sky

The sky is a most beautiful and
   wonderous thing.
A place that used to be clean.
The sky now is a place where even the
   birds don't want to be.
But if the people of tomorrow can fix the
   mess ups of the people of today;
We can fix this earth to be a place where
   it will be pleasant for everyone to live;
And a pleasant place for everyone to
   breathe.

—*Regina Keane*

Wildflower

There's a tree where the wildflower grows
A place where love abides
I want to take you there someday
underneath the autumn leaves
Where the wind blows gently
and the feeling is of peace.
Take my hand and come with me
to the place
where the wildflower grows.

—*Teresa Shupe*

To A Special Friend

To a special friend I think about alot
A poem that comes from deep down in my
   heart
It's a thank you to you from me
that I hope you will hold dear
Thanks for being there when I needed
   you.
Just plain thanks for being my friend.
Our friendship will hopefully never come
   to an end.
For what would I do without my dear,
   dear friend?

—*Lisa Kearns*

Continuous Glass Globe

There is no end nor beginning, you live in
   a continuous glass globe
A question may be asked, and an answer
   may be given.
But beyond that, another question awaits.
   There is no end.
The blue of the sky goes on for an
   eternity, like the cloud that creeps in
   which will never end,
Instead, will keep on blowing, existing in a
   mist or a flock.
Onwards, it goes, no sign of ending
Onwards, when did it begin?
Pain, sorrow, when did it ever flash so
   quickly before our eyes?
It never stops, there and then
The clock forever turns...
Seconds...minutes...hours...days...
If there comes the end, does it stop
   abruptly like a clock's second hand,
   suddenly, as a shock stops cold?
Will there be someone there to repair the
   clock?
Thoughts and thoughts tumble through
   mind, knowing, loving, hating, and
   losing.
Stop! It must end.

—*Lily Yung*

The Storm Of Thought

Echoes of thunder,
A ricochet of thought
The mind is a chest
Holding all life has taught.
A labyrinth of ideas, secrets, and dreams
Swimming in the realm of an open sea.
A storm awaits
in all, but some
The whirlwind rests
until the time has come.
Then all at once the waves start to prance.
Crashing together, dancing their dance.
Suddenly, it sleeps
And drops to a quiver
The raging waters still,
Like the surface of a mirror.

—Renella Mosqueda

Is There No End

A creaking door, a dim lit room,
A screeching roar, a dusty broom,
A cackling voice, a dreary night,
A weeping girl whose full of fright.
There's no escape, nowhere to go.
There's no hope for this poor soul.
If only she could find a friend,
All her fears and wounds he'd mend.
Her life would simply turn around,
The thought to her was so profound.
A friend could really change her world,
Add a sparkle to her eyes and a bounce to her curls.
A screeching door, that terrible face,
All hopes and dreams her mind erased.
Silently she weeps again,
Will this torture never end?
There's not escape, nowhere to go.
There's just no hope for this poor soul.

—Susan Watkins

Untitled

Growing deathless. . .
A seed that falls amongst the field,
I ammmmmm
Never more to fear nor dread
Life's travelling stream.
The current flows. . .onward
carrying me. . .weightless upon the hill.

—Virginia Iaizzo

Life

Life is like
A ship at sea on stormy nights,
Being cast about to and fro, up and down.
It's strong and powerful waves pounding away,
Trying to subdue, leading us astray.
To grasp from us
Our life's course, or sink us into the sea.
But only faith and courage guide our course,
Breaking walls of water, cutting our way through
To subdue the sea. . .

—Robert C. Prince

Wandering

I'd love to have
a ship good and strong
to leave the earth behind.
Just go sailing through the stars
to planets yet unnamed.
How wonderful it would be
to live an adventuress life
and never hear the 6 o'clock news.
My ship would be powered,
not with atoms,
but with shear will power,
imagination that knows no bounds.

—Randolph C. Reynoldson

Silent Love Song

My heart is singing,
A silent love song.
Sometimes I get so down,
That I sing along.
The song seems so familiar,
Though I don't know what it is.
It's in my head all night,
Still-I don't know what it is.
It always makes me cry,
Deep down inside.
I always ask myself why,
I guess it's something I have to hide.
It runs over and over,
Through my mind.
I don't understand,
I thought I was being kind.

—Stephanie Lykins

Selfish Rebel

Once, far from God, I dwelth apart,
A sinful, selfish, rebel;
But now, by grace, I sup with Christ
Upon faith's higher level.

—Shirley A. Owens

Untitled

A single flower by itself all alone,
A single ant on a journey to a place unknown,
A simple question, unanswered, denied.
The answer so easy yet nothing replied.

—Randi S. Hershman

First Kiss

The beach was waiting
A special cove prepared
The moon was bright
The stars were light and sparkling
The sand sat patiently
And the waves moved slowly
The night was silent
And the rocks sat still
Then from beyond came two silhouettes
Searching for a special place
They borrowed the sand, the rocks, and the sea
And asked for light from the moon
They held each other tight
And kissed for the first time.

—Sarah Glass

Shaking Bed

There's something I'd like to talk about,
A subject that goes unsaid
I sometimes have strange occurrences,
With an occasional shaking bed.
I often wonder if I'm possessed,
or has someone else experienced this too.
With all the people in this universe,
This can't be something new.
With frequent changes in my sleeping arrangement
The different places I'm fed.
Last night, again it happened,
The phenomenon of my shaking bed.

—Susan M. Smith

Untitled

To die is to live in another world,
A superior universe.
To participate in the transformation of mortals
Into a divine unity.

—Sarah K. Hughes

I Am You

I stand tall with pride and dignity
A symbol of truth, honor and liberty
I cry out to those who fought and died for me
Be it on land, in the air, or on an angry sea
My blue is for your loyalty
My white reflects for its purity
My red is for their courage, and the blood they shed
I was with you on the sands of Iwo; also Wake and Guam
On the bone chilling hills of Korea
And in the steaming jungles of Vietnam
You didn't let me falter, though torn and tattered at your side
A tribute to the many; a vision of your pride
So for those who shed their blood and tears
I proudly represent their courage and fears
America! Look up to me and as you do
Please remember always, that I am you

—*Thomas F. Whiteman*

Anti—Abortion

A tiny little hand
A tiny little foot
A tiny little face
Where a tiny smile is put
A faint but steady heartbeat
A flutter deep inside
A cry from God above
As another unborn died.

—*Shari L. Austin*

Confidence

Confidence is firm belief,
A trusted certainty,
That what we want to do, we can—
A winning quality.
For when a person needs to do
A thing requiring skill—
Confidence gives him the mind
To know he can, and will.
Perhaps it's hard to understand,
When times are rough on us,
That confidence gives us a hand,
And makes us extra tough.
So build your confidence up high,
And gain endurance thru,
Experience as days slip by—
Because they are but few.

—*Sherrie Van Dyke Harris*

Brand New Start

Brand new sneakers on his feet
A twinkling sparkle in his eye
Tell me there's hope now
He has a chance to try.
I remember when his grandpa
Had to go to the back door
I'm happy now to know
They don't do that anymore
The journey was a long one
I know it seemed an eternal night
But now if they choose to
They can walk the road of light.
Though my skin's a different color
Down deep within my heart
I'm glad to know the children
Can make a brand new start.

—*Marian Carpenter*

When I am with You

When I am with you, I feel so secure and happy-
A way I've never felt with another guy.
When I am next to you, I just want to reach out and touch you and stay close to you forever and never leave your side.
When I am not with you, I am scared and depressed.
All I can do is dream and hope that someday you will be mine and mine forever!
Don't ever forget that I will love you forever!

—*Michele Hinkley*

An Honorable Hero

Courage is his strength
A willing to want to accomplish something
A goal
A reason for mankind
Humanity
The concern for human welfare
But being somewhat modest
Plain or simple
Truthful and trusting
Is an Honorable Hero.

—*Randi Trainer*

My Life, Your Future

Looking at you I see the future,
A world that I cannot seem to penetrate.
How many times have I wished
Or at least imagined
What it would be like to enter this unit of life.
Looking at you I feel anger.
Everybody is envying you on your accomplishments,
Everybody is comparing me to you.
I try to understand why,
Life is so easy on everyone but me.
Looking at the future I see you,
And I am scared
Scared to be unable to join you there.
But maybe, one day, I'll catch up to you
In this world in which I see thee.

—*Marie-Eve Therien*

Where Did Grandma Go?

I asked mommy where grandma went
She didn't tell me.
I asked daddy where grandma went
He didn't tell me.
I asked brother where grandma went
He wouldn't tell me. But I don't think he knew.
I asked God where grandma went
But he never answered. Then I figured he was thinking.
He must have thought really hard.
Because it took him a while to answer
When he did answer, I didn't understand.
He said things like love, joy, peace and friendship.
But then he said one last thing that made little sense.
He said grandma was somewhere special.
A place she loved. And though we cannot see her
She's really in our hearts. Now that I know where grandma is
I don't have to cry. But one more question. Why did she have to die?

—*Taga Lin Dumerauf*

Untitled

Life is a passing of time—
A worthless stall.
Until the "final" day
As we live with never stopping time
We realize this is it and go about our business.
As if it were the most important object in the world.
Though it is just a passing gate of civilization.
The reason of existance is unknown.
So we mold to our superiors and imitate,
As if they're the ones who know?
We pretend to feel—
If there is such a word or emotion.

—*M. K. McGee*

Ten Hangers

In remembrance of my mother, a story
    must be told,
About a Christmas we once shared that
    close to me I hold.
My mother sat us all right down, all five
    of us you see,
Then she began to tell us of the Christmas
    she had no tree.
That year she said that all she wanted was
    something tall and green,
But since they could not buy a tree, she'd
    make one especially.
She found ten hangers all bent up and
    shaped them here and there,
Then hooked them to a stick of wood very
    slowly and with care.
To make some ornaments for this tree, she
    said would take some luck,
But she had found green paper and then
    began to cut.
When she had finished with this tree, she
    stared in disbelief,
But with her loving smile, she placed
    Father's picture right underneath.
Until this day I never knew if this story
    was really true,
And in time I had forgotten how it made
    me feel brand new.
But now that God has taken her, this story
    comes to mind,
And I am thankful for her love and what
    little time was mine.
Although I have the money and a tree I'll
    buy each year,
On her grave you'll find ten hangers and
    green paper to keep her near.

—*Randy L. Ford*

Untitled

Did you ever stop and think
About how much people change?
It's like their minds
Are rearranged.
People can go from friend to foe.
How? It doesn't seem possible.
I just don't know, I think it's odd
The way people change,
It's like their personalities rearranged.
Changing starts as a group of lies,
And one by one they break apart
Your friendship's ties.
Then they act like you're still friends,
And their ear to you they wish to lend.
If you tell the truth, or even if you lie
You'd better have an alibi.
They'll change your words as they've been
    changed
It's like their minds have been rearranged.

—*V. S. Holiday*

Friendship Lost

Whenever you mention his name, she
    begins to smile,
Acting like her love for him was worth the
    while.
She acts like what she's doing is not a
    bother to you,
But really child, it's breaking you in two.
She thinks she knows what love is, but
    hasn't experienced it before,
And talking about him around you is
    hurting you even more.
She acts like nothing changed, and acts
    all nicey—nice,
And doesn't bother to think about what
    she's doing twice.
It hurts to say, she really doesn't care,
Cause she's no longer a friend in whom
    you can confide and share.

—*Tammy Nelson*

An American Woman

Thinks like a man
Acts like a lady
Makes love like a tigress
Cooks like a chef
Honors her God
Nurtures her offspring
Defends her country
Follows her man
and
She does it all
With love

—*Noreen James*

Second Chance

Unpredictable was Our Feeling.
Advantageous was Our Meeting.
Opportunity was Knocking.
Us, A Possibility?
It was a Gamble.
But We had to Risk it.
It was not the Same as the Other.
Nor did it Resemble the Original.
Even though it Followed the First.
It was not an Alternate.
It was and Accidental Pleasure which
Became. . .
"A MOST WELCOME ADDITION TO
THE WHOLE".

—*Shirley A. Wynn Mashack*

Walls of Memories and You

I was wandering.
Afraid of being hurt by anyone or my
    memories.
Then trying to erase both, I withdrew.
Not just from the past, but from what was
    almost at my door, you.
When you arrived, the walls of hurt
    memories were fresh,
But you saw my need to be loved.
You sensed my need to be.
So with great gentleness, you began to
    seep through my walls.
You saw me with only love and
    understanding
Which made it easier for me to let you in.
I was afraid my hurt walls of memories
    would scare you off,
But you stayed, and not in vain.
For because of you, I, with new hope and
    love,
Removed my own walls.

—*Rebecca Sue Flowers*

A Chosen Choice

Two mirrors, I looked in one then the
    other.
After time I chose the second for it was
    the one I wanted.
In time, it shattered and I was left with a
    decision I had to make.
I could take the one I did not want or put
    the one I loved so much back together.
When it was completed, I realized I had
    done what I had set out to do.
I felt angry, hurt, lost, and without hope.
But yet, I felt I had the desire and
    strength to pull through
Anything life dealt me-good times or bad,
    I know I can do it.

—*Stephanie Lee Foster*

Mesmerized

The wind is cold
against my cheeks
The ground beneath me
shakes
Glass shatters
Screams are heard
In the distance
fog becomes thick
As I walk
a blinding light
slowly; takes over my sight
A voice is heard
A hand is gently opened
My heart is taken
from the sounds of love
I, myself, step into a different world.
Alone.

—*Nicole Howard*

Solace

We danced together in the temples of
 Egypt,
Ages ago, you and I;
Worlds apart, but drawn together by a
 bond that is timeless.
Not a word between us is necessary, for
I know your questions,
and you have my answers;
Your touch tells me everything,
and lets others know nothing
of the wholeness, the completeness of
 dancing with you.
So that in your arms, I am transformed by
 the beauty
of a love, born thousands of sunrises ago,
but fresh enough to feel like it is just
 happening to us now;
For to dance with you is to live each day
in a perfect heaven created for me—
to feel the comfort of your arms around
 me,
and to hold you forever in mine.

—*Lisa J. Braverman*

Pat O.

A young man the age of eleven or so
Seemed so grown—up in his actions,
Others could tell he was young at heart.
His hair would hang down in his face
 every so often.
His eyes a greenish color matched
 perfectly
With his beautiful, sparkling lips.
Wearing his jeans, a baggy shirt, and a
 smile
You can tell that he likes to be
 comfortable,
And have fun in any spare time,
Because skateboarding is hard, but fun
 work.

—*Tami Revers*

People

All the world and all its races,
All comes down to all its faces.
There are people who just can't say
 goodbye,
Or people who never dare to cry,
There are people who let life pass by,
Before their eyes.
The happy one or the deceiver,
The doubter or the believer,
The feeble or the strong,
The great ones without a song.
Those with hope and faith and joy,
Those who think your mind's a toy.
The ones who break hearts galore,
The ones who think life's a chore.
The stupid ones without a prayer,
The ones who don't know you're there.
The ones who walk without a friend,
The ones who have nothing in the end.

—*Susan L. Brumley*

The Old House

Laughter, sadness, love and hate
All dance down the old crumbled halls,
Trying to stand their ground; but slowly
 dying down.
No more; is it gone?
No balls or dances. No gowns. No
 beautiful rooms.
All have been swept away with a dusty
 broom.
The wind whistling along the pavements
 trying to scrounge up-
Knocking along the doors.
Peering into the window, longing for the
 memories-
The fanciful, yet the fantasy.
The breaking paint falling to the ground
The shutters hanging on the hinges, just
 dangling down.
While cobwebs, dust, dirt and other debris
 are being blown as hard as can be.
This old house isn't haunted.
It's just alone
Longing for a master to call its very own.

—*Tyra Boyd*

Sentimental Mood

There sits my ragdoll
All faded and worn.
Her hair is uncurled
Her dress is all torn.
She is missing one eye
And has shabby knees.
She was my favorite
As anyone can see.
Through the years we played
Now she is tired and old.
Raggedy Ann looks like trash
But she's better than gold.

—*Wendy Richardson*

The Dark, Deadly Pool

Gone
All his friends are leaving slowly.
They are losing the battle
with the deadly pool of darkness
created by man.
He waits patiently
swimming through the murky sea.
Looking up mournfully
at the clear blue heavens
for the last time
he spouts out a black fountain
from his humping back.
His time has come.
the huge body becomes still
And sinks to the depths of darkness.

—*Lucille Dauz*

Life of the Sea

As the sun rises over the deep blue sea.
All I can see lying next to me.
Is my lover and friend while the tide goes
 out another comes in,
Just lying here looking at and loving my
 friend.
I see someone I can trust and tell secrets
 to,
No one is better than someone like you.
As the sun goes down another day is gone,
At least I know my friend and I will keep
 going strong.
In love, life, faith and trust.
What would the sea do without friends
 like us?

—*Lysa Emmons*

The Day I Left You

Since the day that I left you,
All I do is feel so blue.
I still remember that very night
When in your arms you held me tight.
You whispered softly in my ear,
I wish that I still had you here.
Then when you kissed me oh so fine,
I knew that you were only mine.
And then you broke your lucky charm,
I thought to us there would come harm.
And when we said our long goodbyes,
I felt I was about to die.
But soon when I came back to you,
I heard you loved somebody new.
I left you for another guy,
But then found out he was a lie.
I wish that I could be with you.
To show you that my love is true.

—*Rachel Jimenez*

The Scars are Now on Me

I sat alone, and in that night
All my brave and strong—willed dreams
Were reduced to a pile of fright. The
 screams
Of sluggish sirens opened wide my eyes.
How long had they been closed to fright
 and fear!
The fierce and heaping flames, so near
And yet just far enough to scare and
 stare,
Loomed o'er me like ravenous sharks or
 missiles on their way.
"Save me!" I cried, and suddenly
The sun arose, the flames were gone, and I
 was not alone.
My memory grew dim. "Was it a
 dream?" I prayed of him,
And he replied, "No child. The price was
 paid,"
"But not by you. 'Twas me who laid"
"My life down for you. See?"
"The scars are now on me."

—*Mariana Brand*

Moments To Cherish

High school days—they were fun
All of us sharing laughters under the sun
Smiling here, talking all the way there
Staying together or walking by pair
It didn't matter how it was spent
All it matters were those good moments
As time has arrived, our days has end
And also a time, we lost a friend
To loose one friend as enough to break a
    heart
But I lost almost all of you in my part
Well I say to myself and wipe my tears
    away
Friends may not last long but memories
    will stay
Memories in Hanalie, enjoying and hiking
Memories in slep class, laughing and
    crying
Remember those days, my good friends?
You may have left me but memories never
    ends
I don't know what else to say so I just sigh
Nothing more, really, just an "I Love
    You"
goodbye.......

—Marlyn P. Tadye

Child's Lost Memories

I saw a child sitting in a corner
all slumped over, crying, with a
very frightened look on her face.
I looked into the child's eyes
and saw something so familiar.
The child was curious, wanting to
to know everything.
But afraid, so afraid, of what
knowledge might lead her to.
And afraid of the future for she
has listened to adults cry, laugh,
and curse the future.
I soon realized that child was
me in the back of my lost memories.

—Toni Antonicelli

Deep Ocean Blue...

Close your eyes and try to forget,
All the times of your regret.
Look onto the days with me,
Then together we'll be free.
I love you more everyday,
I think it's supposed to be that way.
My life I'd give to make you smile,
Even if it's for awhile.
It's scary to think of life without,
One to ever walk about.
Please remember I'm always there,
Taking sight of every care.

—Stephanie Danielle Anderson

Preparing For Winter

The leaves have now
All turned orange, red, and brown
The air is getting chilly
It is winter now in this little town
Chimneys puffing out smoke
Fathers gathering wood
You can smell logs burning
As you walk through the neighborhood.
Thanksgiving is soon coming
And Christmas not too far behind
There is lots of preparation
And we're running out of time.
As you walk down the streets
People and cars are buzzing by
Only having time
To say a quick "hi"
You see people all bundled up
With their gloves, coat, and hat
Hurrying here and there
Just to get this and that

—Sarah J. Chapman

To the Sand

My life is like the ocean's sand scattered
    upon the shore,
Allowing every tide to carry them through
    another wave once more.
Each lost grain of sand wandering around
    the beach
Is a moment in my life I will never be able
    to reach.
As each tide arrives then leaves again,
It's like each of my happy times that leave
    before they begin.
The waves crash upon you like each
    troublesome time in my life,
We share each other's burdens, loneliness,
    suffering, and strife.
So I say to you the sand, "What's the
    difference between you and I?"
We were both placed on the earth for a
    reason beneath the blue sky.
And for whatever purpose we both shall
    serve you will live and never die.
As I push that thought to the corners of
    my mind,
I look back across all the crashing waves
    to a memory and there I find
A vision I had not long ago that brought
    happiness not sorrow,
About a Lord that would one day return,
    maybe even tomorrow.
So to the sand I speak, "There is a hope
    we both can keep,"
"That above the beautiful, blue sky, we
    both shall live and never die."

—Melissa Ann Standley

The Path

I walk down the lonely road
—Alone
I feel your presence
—I turn
Only to find a shadow
—But no face
I want to cling onto your memory
—But it must be buried
For there comes a time
—Where
We must stand on our own
—And walk the lonely road
Alone.

—Rai-An Perrish

Calm before the Storm

Bare desolate landscape:
Alone and discreet.
Gentle waves kiss the horizon-
Sand beneath my feet.
Clouds collect in mock disguise
Sky meets the trees.
Rippling wind gathers strength to blow-
Water up to my knees.
A threatening feelings in the air
The land is cold and dead.
Rain now begins to fall-
Water over my head.
Storm erupts in sudden fury
Sand its trembling pawn.
Angry sea meets relentless sky-
Will you miss me when I'm gone?

—Lisa Hostman

Alone Is...

Alone is having a friend move away
Alone is having nothing to say.
Alone is being in your room at night
Alone is seeing nothing in sight.
Alone is having nothing to read
Alone is not satisfying a need.
Alone is being home all alone
Alone is not having a home.
Alone is not a friend to be seen
Alone is the trauma of being a teen.
Alone is having no friends around
Alone is not hearing a sound.
Alone is eating all by yourself
Alone is putting Mr. Teddy on the shelf.
Alone is my aching heart
Alone is when we are apart.

—Teri Hein

Bleeding Heart

I
Alone, she sits amidst a garden-bower
Gazing over grassy hills that unfold
Into layers of varying green hues,
And listening to the melancholy music
Of nature's harmonious instruments,
As the soft breeze whispers her sad secret;
A lone bird calls for its lover,
And the babbling brook slowly creeps
    along.
II
A shadow is sweeping across the sky,
Covering it with a heavy grey film;
And casting a spell over all the trees.
Suddenly, dead silence! There is a
    pause—
Annihilating language, time and space.
Only the loud beats of a heart are heard
While a hot crystal tear rolls down her
    cheek,
And shatters like mercury, on a lily;
For her love, lost, killed in bitter war!

—*Yvonne Sewall*

Different

That's the difference between
me and them who dream of
        foreign
        lands.
They write about the glass slipper
And the "Chateau de La Roue".
The criticism is so fancy and
Abstract that,
    When I speak my words of
            d
             i
              r
               t
                y
               r
              a
             g
            s
         And
                crying babies,
The classroom cringes from
me. Disgusted.

—*Tamara Conner*

The Beginning of the End

Alone in the dark
Alone with her thoughts
Her past and future
Written before her
The love and happiness
Slipping from her life
Slowly being replaced
By sadness and hatered
All her memories fading
Along with the sorrowful tears
What is to become of her
A blurry vision in the night
No one to turn to
No one to help her
She is left to dread
The beginning of the end.

—*Mindy Knicely*

Whatever Happened

Whatever happened to the long walks
Along the shore,
And your smiling face when you walked
Through the door.
Whatever happened to the thoughts
We shared,
And the laughter, I thought you
Really cared.
Whatever happened to the promises
You made,
I never thought your love would
Fade.
Whatever happened to you and me,
You always said we were meant to be.
Whatever happened to the fun times we
    had,
Their all gone now and my world has
Turned sad.
Whatever happened, I'll never know,
All I can say is,
"I will always love you so".

—*Rebecca Perito*

Alone

She sits, always alone.
Always looking for away to avoid, going
    home.
A smile comes across her face, once in
    awhile.
She's alone in a world of her own.
No one can help her,
No one but the one soul.
The one who only he, can take her
and give her, her dreams.
The one who can make her laugh and cry.
The one who can hold her, and assure
her, everything is alright.
The one who tells her he loves her,
and will never let her go.
For only the one soul, can take her away.
But until he comes, alone she must stay.

—*Ronal Palmere*

Life's Shadows

Through the shadows we
    follow—wondering what we will find,
Always searching for an answer when
    life's not always kind.
When will the time come—when
    everything will be clear?
Will it always be a mystery—or is it
    something we should fear?
Thought painful and difficult, we must
    learn to cope,
We must never give up, and never lose
    hope.
Life brings all kinds of changes—take it
    one day at the time,
Fill your heart full of desires, and
    everything will be fine.
For there will be hard times when
    everything looks cold,
But things always get better—that's what
    I've been told.
Give the best of yourself to new friends,
    loves, and dreams—
Look far beyond the shadows, and you'll
    find out what it means.
Even when things look sad, and nothing
    seems bright—
Force a smile to your face, and things will
    be alright.
Life is like a game, and winning we will
    do—
If we keep going on, our dreams are sure
    to come true!

—*Michelle S. Clune*

One Lonely Tear

All alone at night,
Always thinking it isn't right.
It isn't right that nobody's here,
And the only company I have is one lonely
    tear.
But I don't brush it away,
Because it symbolizes all my hurt in one
    small way.
That one small tear brings back hope,
And the feeling that I can really cope.
Cope with all that life has in store,
And every surprise through every open
    door.

—*Michelle Miller*

The Cat

There he sits on the windowsill,
Amazed by watching the gentle
Snow fall peacefully.
Mesmerized by this action,
He just stares at the unique
Snowflakes through his sharp eyes.
He thinks to himself, and wonders
Why this is happening, and who
Creates his beautiful scene.

—*Renee M. Dycio*

Lovely

In my moments of quietude, I reflect upon
  her loveliness,
Amid the glow of her radiance, I feel
  solace.
She moves among us touching our lives
  with her relentless love,
Thus we are richer in spirit for having met
  her.
For she is everything to everyone.
She is a tower of strength, which provides
  a refuse
From the raging storms of life.
She is like the warm sun on our face on a
  cold blizzard day.
She is as a beautiful star shining bright,
Suspended high in the heavens.
And though I have known her for only a
  season
And have pondered the depths of her
  loveliness,
Indeed, I have truly known her for a
  lifetime.
Knowing her is to comprehend the
  greatest gift of all to mankind,
Love.

—Paulette Torian

One February

A single tear
Among many
My reward
For the pain
I caused
My reminder
You are above all
Fragile
The thought
Of us no longer me
Your touch
Of love so close to my inside
Alone
I have not
Taken the care you deserve
I have instead
Run away
I have been
Afraid
That sigh
My heart suspended
That single tear
The last I can allow
No more
Living love on hold

—Marc Daniels

My Circle of Fear

Across the sandy shore
Among the horrid hills
Between there lies a hidden fear
Which brings to me a chill.
Memories of dancing figures
Under the moonlight,
Amid the pale floor.
Then doubtful thoughts and upsets
Come to life once more.
Tomorrow shall bring a tear or smile
Oh, this in life is true.
Loneliness does exist,
The fear is losing you.

—Marisa Munoz

Eden

Do you remember lying in fields of
  summer
Among violets and daisies and wild
  grasses,
Looking deep into the hollow blue of
  heaven,
Seeing so long and so far that it dizzied
  you?
Do you remember dreaming those days of
  angels
Singing eternal glories around that grand
  throne
Where God the Father sat looking down
  upon you
Probably happy you had nothing else to
  do?
Do you remember naming the
  cloud-shapes that passed
Through the azure field, like Adam in his
  garden
Calling one an alligator, one a giraffe,
One an elephant, and that last one a
  woman?

—Richard J. Daigle

The Beach

The beach was like a deserted battlefield
  littered with the remains of long, dead
  jellyfish that had struggled to get away
  from the enemy tide.
An empty bottle lay near the water's edge
  like a shell casing.
Birds preyed patiently, waiting for the
  wounded to die.
The water painted the areas of wet and
  dry sand like blood.
The tracks from children's feet
  crisscrossed in the sand where they had
  played unaware of the death behind
  them.
The sun slowly sank into its coffin earth,
  and the moon appeared freshly awake
  to shine its light over the land.

—Tammy Mize

A Different Song

Our love was like a song,
An endless melody sung everday.
Never changing words I sung every step
  of the way.
Words I listened to and thought I knew
  what meant.
But while I was still singing the love had
  come and went.
Now you're singing strong while I listen to
  the music fade.
You took away your love and made a
  small trade,
And you sang a different song as you hold
  her hand.
Now I have to learn these words that I'll
  never understand.

—Tori Strickland

Gabble Gourmet

You are a gourmet of self expression,
An epicure of the loquacious spread.
You're a quick-serve quip, a chatter chef,
Who will see that every ear is fed.
Your bready tales at our tables of talk,
Are sometimes cold, unbuttered rolls,
But the mixed-word-salads have laughter
  sauce,
And We can but swallow them whole.
The meat of this moment is roasted bull,
But its plenty makes pleasant the dine,
And you pour our glasses full to the brim
Of your deepest, experience-wine.
Desert is rich with your jokes of life,
A blabber mousse, sweetly spieled.
O, that the starving over the world,
For a day, could but be so filled.

—S. Diane Bogus

Cycles

A young man runs,
An old man stumbles,
The seas roll,
And the mountains crumble.
A child is born,
An old man dies,
Life goes on,
Under God's skies.
Fish swim,
birds glide,
If you have troubles
There's no place to hide.
Flowers blossom
The children grin,
When he world smiles
So does everyone within.

—Lindsay Romano

My Life

My life since the start has had its pick of
   ups and downs,
And a lot of put downs.
I try, try but no success.
When I succeed, and for people in my life,
I feel like I should be trying harder,
But if I wasn't around the people in my
   life,
There would be no joy.
My brother has a lot of advantages
In life such as books, grades, popularity.
But I have something much better,
I think and that is my love.

—Sarah Cecil

The Sound of Music

As my fingers fly over the keys
And air moves through the horn
People stop to listen
To the sound that is born.
I can feel the music coming from my soul
I can be anything achieving all my goals.
Happy, sad, and exciting,
All my music is very inviting.
People love the wonderful tone
Coming from my alto saxophone.

—Laura VonDeylen

The One Who Cared

Someone smiled as they walked by
And as the day went on I wondered why
Did I show a sign of love or kindness
Or did they want me to feel love more
   then less
Well I journied home and found nothing
   new
The trees still stood and the birds still flew
This time though I felt different, in a
   special kind of way
On my way home I felt love move in my
   heart to stay.
I felt a tear drop roll down my face
And I realized I needed your embrace
That somewhere deep, deep down inside
I let you in and threw away my pride.
I laughed a little with the whistling wind
And as I walked along, I knew, I'd come
   back again
I came back to loving, trusting and
   knowing how to care
I only wish I could tell you that you're the
   one who got me here.

—Patricia Olbeter

North Carolina

North Carolina has good times,
And bad ones too.
But the only things that count are me and
   you.
In all NC schools,
Grow brilliant minds.
Young Edisons, Washingtons and
   Einsteins,
Future doctors, lawyers and teachers too,
To make a better state for me and you.
Yes, we do have our bad times,
That are always in the back of our minds.
But at the cliff when there's no hope,
In our hearts there will always be a rope!

—Wendy L. Bigham

Love Beckoned Once More

'Twas Kismet that united two strangers'
   hearts as one,
And blossomed love eternal into their
   hearts and souls,
The dance of love, a lifetime dance, had
   swept them away,
To starry forevers filled with unspoken
   hopes and dreams.
Youth's passion quickly faded the dancers
   paused, confused,
Steps seemed empty, somewhat
   mismatched, the song unknown,
They stopped dancing, uunsure of the
   rhythm of their dance,
Then love's dance beckoned, and they
   danced on once more.
Their steps were slower as contentment
   filled their hearts,
Maturity defined the rhythm and they
   knew all their steps,
Starry forevers were sunlit moments
   shared together as one,
For their dreams became reality with
   each new step taken.
Too quickly the dance of love played as
   their lives passed,
Spring to summer and they were unaware
   when autumn arrived,
The music vibrant and loud through the
   years softly faded,
But their love's dance was incomplete,
   and they danced on.
They slowly danced from this world into
   the next together,
And earthly tunes metamorphosed into
   celestial arias,
Higher and higher on the tips of
   moonbeams they twirled,
To their love dance that beckoned them to
   beyond forever.

—Melody Ghandchi

Telephone Love

Touch me with your voice
And bring back memories of years past
Crashing down upon my head like
A summer shower
Torrential downpour with
Absolutely no fore—warning
That's what you do to me
When you touch me with your voice.

—Vikki S. Coale

Fetch Me Yet Another Star

Fetch me yet another star
And bring it over here.
I haven't got enough, you see,
And time is drawing near.
Then fetch me gold from yonder sun
And cotton from the clouds.
I make a cloak for honored guest.
Don't tarry. Do it now!
Emeralds from the grass and trees,
Rubies from the dawn,
Sapphires from the bluest sea,
And hurry, don't be long!
I hear it coming on the wind
Yes, Truth is on its way.
I thank you for your gracious help,
Your wages Truth will pay.

—Yvonne Behrens

Sunrise To Sunset

A silver shaft of light breaks through the
   black,
And casts a shade of grey across the sky.
Then periwinkle blue begins to crack
The darkness of the night that has gone
   by.
And as the day goes on, the hues grow
   bold-
From light to brighter blue, with wisps of
   white.
Dramatic is the sky, outlined in gold;
A luminescent picture shining bright.
Then darker, royal blue begins to merge
With burning flames of purple, orange
   and red.
The fire blazes in a brilliant surge,
Triumphant only when the day is dead.
Then, silently, the flames burn down and
   die,
As, once again, the blackness claims the
   sky.

—Melanie Robbins

Time

The minutes fly,
And days go by.
The seasons pass,
And years never last.
Centuries begin,
And then they end.
Time is never-ending,
Always descending.

—Shelly Elizabeth Bagley

Seashell

I went to the beach one day
And found a shiny shell; it was
Sitting in the shallow sheets
While the waves were shooting
Short showers over it, the
Shiny Shell was a shiny white
Inside it was a shiny pink.
The sand was cold beneath my
Bare feet, the golden light
Danced on the water and the
Seagulls screached overhead,
Slowly, I turned to go home.

—Serenity Ebert

Everything from Top to Bottom

Everything from top to bottom
And from bottom to top
Is what makes life.
Everything from top to bottom
Adds to a person's feelings
Of life around them.
Everything from top to bottom
Takes away from life
Only to give it.
Everything from top to bottom
Makes a person mad
At all the world.
Everything from top to bottom
Gives you a sense of goodness
Which helps an aching heart.
Everything from top to bottom
Makes life the way it is
And portrays it through its people.

—Shelby Diane Thiele

The Storm

I came upon a weary night.
And gave the kids a great big fright.
They were in their beds asleep,
I gave the house a midnight creep.
After I'd done my deadly deeds,
The storms of night had all been freed.
The kids awoke up out of their beds,
In fear that they all will soon be dead.
The cat pranced up onto the stairs,
While the kids sat patiently in their chairs.
The kids will soon go back to bed,
And the storms of night will then be dead.

—Nadia Garnett

Night Sounds

The vibrant moon comes out,
And glows upon the soft soil fields.
A wind howls,
Rustling the crisp leaves.
Along the hard, cool ground.
A light mist settles upon the cold ground.
In the distance there are the beautiful night sounds,
Traveling through the cold night air,
Echoing through the land,
As if playing music through the night.
There comes the radiant sun,
Upon the global earth,
And all is silent. . .

—Trisha Beadnell

The Candle That Glows

The candle that glows is the spirit of man
And God loves him in his hand,
God holds his hand and causes him to see:
That Jesus the saviour lives in him,
He holds his reign tightly, and causes him to know
That Jesus his saviour possesses his soul,
The candle that glows is the spirit of man:
And God bless him in his hand:
The spirit of man is the candle of God,
And God knows the path they all trod,
God blesses man for his own delight,
And we, believe him a great fight,
The spirit of man is God's delight,
And he is filled with a great insight,
The spirit of God possesses man, and they
Love him all they can.

—Rev. Drexil R. Evans D.D.

Destiny, the Heart

My feelings for you have passed love
And gone into a different dimension.
I don't know what this dimension is
But there are very few people here.
A couple are lovers who feel the same
For each other as I feel for you.
I don't know what the name
Of this dimension is
But I have my own name for it.
Cloud Nine.
Cloud nine is higher than the highest peak of love.
It breaks the boundaries of love.
It floats through the lowest tunnel of love.
It goes through the toughest skin
Only to reach its
Destiny, the heart.

—Tammy Hoover

My Mother's Hands

My mother's hands, that drew me to her breast,
And guided unsure steps along the years,
And cooled my fevered brow, and brought me rest,
And gently brushed away my childhood fears. . .
Those patient hands that taught me Heaven's way,
And toiled through the nighttime while I slept,
And wistfully touched my veil, my wedding day. . .
I long to hold them once again. Except,
Now mother's hands are cold and gray and still,
And 'neath the daised grass are laid to rest.
The pain of loss, I've learned, that love withstands.
So, I live on. . .her dreams yet to fulfill.
She lives in me. And now I know I'm blessed,
For in my own. . .I see my mother's hands.

—Nancy Crockett Gladson

Headed Home

Over my shoulder
And headed home
Round houses
Full fields
In singular waves
Distant voices
Cry, sun!
Weep, winds!
Bright evening
Sonatas
All composed
Inately pure and perfect.
Home
Can wait!

—Roman Eli Campion

Will You

Will you take my hand,
And help me find the light?
Will you hold me crying,
All through the night?
Will you always be there,
When I need a hand?
Will you always love me,
The best that you can?

—Michele Renee Sablotny

My Heart

Turn out the light
And hold me tight
Close your eyes
So you can't see my tears
They roll down my cheek
Onto the sheet
I watch as the wetness
Grows bigger and bigger
I look up to you and you're asleep
I feel as though I'm going to weep
I can't understand these problems we face
In this long, slow exhausting pace
We try so hard to make things right
But in the end we always fight
I close my eyes for the night
When I wake up you're not in sight
You have gone away to save my heart
But really you've torn it apart.

—Shawna Wilds

My First Love

He said he loved me and I him,
And I knew it was the truth when the lights were dim.
For that's when he gave me my very first kiss,
That special moment I'll always miss.
My friends all teased me,
And as you could see I was in the worst spot a person could be.
For they had never been kissed by a person they loved,
Or they had never felt like a flying dove.

—Shawna Gross

Here

Here I stand,
And I stand alone,
With or without you,
I'll get by on my own.
You made me feel happy,
You made me feel free,
But now you are gone on
Those waves out to sea.
I just look on the horizon
And there you stand,
To make me feel
Happy and free again.

—Patti Saurtelle

Ant Hills

I walk.
And I think.
About why people walk, when they can run.
Running avoids stepping on more ant hills.
People are selfish and inconsiderate.
That's why we walk.
Maybe if we had giants to step on our houses,
We wouldn't be so selfish.
I walk.
And I think,
About why I just stepped on another ant hill.

—Suzanne M. O'Connor

A Little Bit of Sunshine

I'm a little mouse
And I'm as sweet as I can be.
Whenever you need a boost
Just smile and look at me.
I'll always be your friend
In good times and in sad.
When you need a little lift
Just smile and don't feel bad.
Yes, I'm a little mouse
And I'm sweet as I can be.
I'll bring you lots of sunshine
When you SMILE and look at me.

—Michelle Smith

S & N

We were best friends
And it was said "to the very end"
But now we both see
That our dream will never be
I still love you so
And I never really wanted to let go
I guess it was time to let you know
Cause we both know my feelings never show.
I will always be there for you
So don't treat me like your old shoe
I will miss you, but I'll never kiss you
So on May 2nd, your special day,
Remember that I'll always go out of my way just to say
Happy B-day and I'll always love you in the very best friend way.

—Nikki Ross

Untitled

Pollution is something we all know about
And it's something we can all live without.
So if we all pitch in, it might not be too late
To save the world from this terrible fate!
We can all start by learning not to litter
So if you do, don't be a kidder
Because it won't be so funny
When the world's not sunny
And there's pollution up to our eyes
With all the smog hovering the skies.
So let's all give the world a hug,
And give that little extra tug
Let's not be a giant litterbug!

—Lorena Lowell

The Devil Speaks

I am the spirit that denies -
And justly so; things from the void
Given me, deserve to be destroyed.
Better you were not created
And all, which you call sin is rated,
Where evil, pain and death are spent,
Why, there's my proper element!
This modest speech I make to thee
If you, a blinded fool can see
Yourself as whole so frequently.
Part of me you were in primal night
Part of the dark which brought forth light,
Man's selfish light which now fights with my space
And claims my mother's night, her ancient place.
For yet the struggle goes, and light; it cries,
I hope, just as the bodies go, it dies!

—Roy Pace

Love

Do you ever love someone
And know they don't love you?
Did you ever feel like crying
But what would crying do?
Did you ever look into his eyes and say a
  little prayer?
Did you ever whisper "God I love him but
  he will never care."
Did you ever wonder where he's at or who
  he's with?
One day you'll feel so happy,
The next you'll feel so blue.
Still you're wondering why it's happening
  to you.
Please don't fall in love my friend, you'll
  find it doesn't pay.
Although it causes broken hearts it
  happens everyday.
You see my friend I ought to know.
I fell in love with you!

—*Tina Hubbard*

Thoughts Of Time

Oh age; thou crept upon me fast
And left my youth, back in my past
Before I gave much thought of time,
My life had long since, passed its prime.
Now the things that once excited me
They make me shake with fear, you see
And things once thought no use to be
Oh now I hold these, so dear to me.
My youth was spent in such a haste
That much of my time, was merely a
  waste
As a youth I gave no thought to time,
For I felt eternity, was surely mine.
Now I know; if only, I could stroll back to
That time when things were all brand
  new,
I know, if into the past, I could recede
My youth, I would not, so recklessly,
  deceive.

—*Pamela Y. Garrison*

Could I Share With you my Dreams?

Could I ever become a poet
And let all the world know it?
Could I write the words to rhyme
And still not have but a dime?
Could I share all my dreams
And not fall apart at the seams?
Could I? Could I? Share with you my
  dreams?
Could I hope for tomorrow
And not have to borrow?
Could I fall in love
And still see the heavens above?
Could I? Could I? Share with you my
  dreams. . .

—*Patricia J. Palmer*

Life is a Goal

Sunshine is life,
And life is sunshine.
But when you take a life,
You take a soul.
And if there is no sunshine,
There is no life,
And with no life,
There is no goal.

—*Maureen Ann Valler*

Crime

Stardust
And midnight's varied gems
Are precious things
That make the sky
A rendezvous
For thieves;
Stardust
On sparkling diadems,
Though crowning kings,
But tempt their eye.
Each hurries through
And leaves
Stardust
And shattered fragile stems,
And broken wings
That once could fly.
A crime, but who
Perceives?

—*Natalie Bergen di Paolo*

A Raining Evening

Cool, cold, and chilly,
And my friend had gone to sleep.
Looking up in the gloomy sky,
Where my friend usually smiles.
Tick! Tick! Tick!
The other friends visit me,
Dancing with the wind,
Jumping with the falling leaves,
Playing with the balcony.
Oh, my little friends, I wish I were you,
No color, no odor, no love, no hate.
No tremble, no idle, no depressed, no
  upset.
Tick! Tick! Tick!
Holding out the skinny hand
Wet, my hand was wet
By the rain or by my own tears
Tick! Tick! Tick! Tick!
The rain was still chasing me.

—*Thai Huynh*

Untitled

If I feel asleep one night
And never woke again,
Would the world keep on spinning
Or would it come to an end?
If I closed my eyes
For eternal sleep,
Would the tears of grieving angels fall
  from the sky
Or would the sun continue to shine?
If I passed on one night
Never to see you again,
Would you laugh and play
Or would you never live again.

—*Susan A. Kile*

The Child

A child that plays all day,
And never worries about the yesterday
Might grow up in a single day.
With his toys all put to stay,
The little child may run away.
The child ran away,
No place to go; no place to stay,
Always in danger, freedom is lost.
A good idea at the time,
But didn't know the cost.

—*Ray Newmans*

Mothers

Not always sugar and spice,
And not always something nice.
Not exactly a rose petal,
But yet deserves a medal.
A golden heart,
Often torn apart.
For the love they give,
Shall linger and live.

—*Ronda McMahon*

My Friend

When my world seems to fall apart
And nothing seems to matter,
You, my friend,
Are always there.
You are the best
That anyone would need.
So stick around my friend
You are the seed.
The seed to my life,
The seed to my heart.
I'm learning to live
So thanks for giving me my start.

—*Victoria Coleman*

Trapped

I scream and I fight while I hit the walls.
And now I regret why I hear no calls.
I'm trapped, and I can't get out.
I'm trapped in my life is that what I'm about?

—*Theresa Gordon*

Goodbye

The first time she saw you
She knew it was love at first sight,
And all that night,
She thought of nothing but you
Months had passed of secret love
When one day you descended like a dove
I, her best friend, had to break
The news of you leaving
She acted as if she didn't care
But you really left her heart bare
You even left without saying goodbye,
That's all she wanted
One goodbye.

—*Tonya Lynn Gutelius*

Beautiful Circle

Not a single day goes by but some lovely thing we see;
And oft we do not give a thought of how it came to be.
But when we pause to contemplate the beauty that is there,
We come to find a special time is given to things lovely and rare.
As rainbows are so beautiful after the grey and rain,
And a child's sweet smile when you've kissed away the pain.
Each of these are lovelier still as we realize whistfully
That something must die and go away to bring the next so beautifully.
So the precious plant we see must gracefully bloom and grow,
Then die and go to seed before it's new full beauty we know.
Such is life as we observe the cycle all around
Must be complete and start again before it's full grace and beauty are found.
And so our child, our lovely girl, waxed strong and tall and fair;
She walked the earth so gracefully but now she is not there.
Just like the flower to seed must go, and seed to grow again,
Our child has left this earthly life her heavenly one to begin.
Each year goes by so swiftly with joy and grief and pain,
And the circle is soon complete to when the beauty comes again.

—*Patti Kowalchuk*

To Life

I'm ninety—he said with a bit of a grin,
And, oh! You can't imagine the places I've been.
Traveled the world over — two times — maybe three,
Touched a few hearts. . .a few touched me.
Fought in a war in a far, distant land —
Left just a boy — came back as a man.
Settled on down to a quiet farming life;
Found a good woman; made her my wife.
She gave me a family — gave me her love.
Took me to heights I'd never dreamed of!
We'd rise each morning—see what we'd find;
Looked to the future, never glancing behind.
Yes, we had hard times — some pretty bad —
But, none — none can compare to the good times we've had.
Well, now here we are at life's farthest end —
You think that's sad but let me tell you my friend,
Life's been an adventure—and, oh, so much more!
And Death — well, death's just another world to explore!

—*Lesa Lunsford*

God First, Others Second and I'm Third

There are those who are undecided,
And others second sighted;
But we must find the reason why
We were created here on Earth,
Before we have the chance to seek
That important second birth.
You'll find so many people
Living in a herd,
But to find your goal, or Utopia,
List yourself as Third.

—*Matt Mullen*

Untitled

Soldiers of war, some go AWOL
And others stick it out
Others go on reliving things of the past
Trapped no way out
Lost souls of a raging war
Blind in the dark, fumbling for the exit door
Unable to find an answer
To a life long question
Unfortunately one hard quest to fulfill
For some relief is a cowards way out
Welcoming the darkness as escape
While others continue in life's many confusions
Seeing things through black illusions
Thoughts-feelings all together in one
Some fight to keep a war alive
And others to forget
Some will live on and some will die
This is the rough paths before lost hart lie.

—*Tricia Barone*

A True Friend

I have a friend,
She's there in times of sorrow,
She knows just what to say,
In all the right ways.
She's there to spend happy times,
Every birthday,
Year after year,
In case of any tears!
We have different backgrounds,
But somewhat the same!
She's there to lend support
And always gives you the report
Whether bad or good,
Laugh or cry, she's there!
We're friends forever!
Thank God!

— *Lori Koopmeiners*

Pets

Pets, everyone needs them
And pets need everyone.
It does not matter who you are,
Pets are for everybody.
When you are old and lonely,
Pets can take the place of a friend.
All you do is clean and feed them
And especially give a lot of love.
If you love and care for them,
Pets will always be there fore you.
Take time out and enjoy their company,
Then you will have an everlasting friendship.
You can talk to them, they will listen
And will not disagree.
When you are frightened and alone,
Pets can comfort in weary times.
So bring a little sunshine and happiness in life,
Find a special pet to love.

—*Shannon Gamble*

Living Arrow

It swiftly sails into the silent night,
And pierces darkness like a lonely flame.
Throughout the eagle's straight and
 narrow flight,
He searches for a target like a game.
His killing is consistent and yet,
I still am left in marvel, left in awe.
Each time his mark of gracefulness is met,
He seems to fly without a single flaw.
His destiny is to accomplish what he
 starts,
And will not cease until his death has
 come.
For as he strikes his prey through its
 heart,
The eagle and his target become one.
When he has taken what he flew to earn,
The living arrow leaves, but will return.

—*Nicole Tanner*

Mother's Conviction

Lord, I know my life has meaning
And purpose just to be.
I really didn't do much today
As human eyes would see.
I walked the beach with my little son
And kissed his injured knee.
We skipped stones and talked awhile
About our family.
Along the shore, we painted rocks
My little girl and me.
We built castles in the sand
For all Eternity!
Lord, I really didn't do much today
As human eyes would see.
I dried his tears and calmed her fears
And just made memories!

—*Patricia Comfort*

Dying Time

You can feel the hate,
and see the fate,
You can hear the guns,
father against son,
You can see the red,
where someone bled,
I hope one day our wars will end,
for soon enough,
There'll be no one to defend.

—*Theresa Cantwell*

Ceaseless Motion

My life is a ceaseless motion
And senseless does it seem
Lacking in direction,
Suffocating screams.
Bending brittle branches,
Whispering against the wind,
Twisting with the turmoil,
Wrenching from within.

—*Marge Bemis-Breznen*

Untitled

She loves him
And she fears to ask how he feels
For she knows his fateful answer
Undoubtingly it hurts her so
To see the two together
She needs to hear his irresistable voice
Calling to her sweetly
There's always the future, but maybe by
 then
He'll have forgotten her completely.
She feels alive when he is near
Though it is her friendship she betrays
And maybe for her love, or maybe
Her fear, it is, that he delays—
The story I impart, my friend,
Is far more than appears
True love 'til the bitter end,
When sight of death draws near.

—*Maggie O'Connor*

The Magic Key

The sun set high and bright,
And shot out a ray of light.
No more darkness will there be
Because I hold a magic key!
This key will open any door,
But its magic holds much more.
The magic will never fade away,
Even on the darkest day!
What can this magic be,
The one you can feel, but never see?
The one that makes you feel like you're in
 the clouds above,
It's the special magic called love!

—*Melissa Fasolo*

The Barn

The barn is dank and musty
And smells like hay.
It's like a church:
Silent,
Reverent,
Without ceiling; I see the sky,
Seeing sky and stars
And seeing stars, counting stars
Counting stars, dreaming dreams
And dreaming, wake.
Upon waking,
Drink a cold cup of decaf.
Go out to the barn
And do it all over again.

—*Paul Hanna*

The Rose

The rose lies there
Shattered and torn by hate and despite
Its petals red
Not with the color of love
But of blood, shed for anger
Its leaves hold no sign of life
Pounded into pieces
By brutal fists
Only one thing remains
Untouched, unharmed
Thorns
Odd, crude thorns
That hold no sign of beauty
But only remnants of war
All that is there of the rose
Is what is left
After love is gone

—*Wanchay Chanthadouangsy*

Holy War

Nations say they have faith in you
And some have even engraved on their
 money, "In God We Trust"!
But what trust have they put in You?
What trust have they shown?
Nations fight and kill and proclaim war in
 Your name, and that of Your Son.
Before going off to battle they pray and
 plead for Your help and protection.
They shout, "Hallelujah"!
As they claim victory over the destruction
 of cities
That held many innocent lives.
The religious leaders have mingled with
 the leaders of the world
And have sent their devoted followers
 with prayers and blessings
To go and destroy the human life that
 You have created.
They claim to know and do Your will, but
 does the will of God
Consist of blood-shed with brothers
 hating one another?
Is He not the Creator of all humankind?
So then, what war is holy?
And what is holy in war?

—*Rosie Vigil*

Growing Old

She sits in her chair and rocks
And sometimes just stares into space.
You can tell that she is weak
By the look on her face.
Her white hair still shines, though
But, her eyes grow older by the day.
Often she seems quite confused and scared
You can tell by the things she will say.
Her life is so different now
The day runs into the night.
She struggles just to walk or sit
And has difficulty with her sight.
Growing old is not an easy task
We must all face this, you see.
I look at her rocking in her chair
And wonder if that will be me.

—Sally A. Spirida Carlani

Goodbye

Watching from knee height
She sees many tears shed.
In the distance a statue, a religious statue,
Surrounded by flowers.
Do the flowers live forever?
Green grass as far as the eye can see,
Periodically interrupted by engraved gray slabs of cement.
The sun's glare on the glistening bronze box makes her eyes tear,
So she turns away.
Men in black suits and white gloves stand silently.
Faces, vaguely familiar, look upon her with pity.
The final amen is said and delicate rose petals are thrown on the box.
Not quite tall enough, the child is lifted off the ground
By hands unknown to her
To toss the petals and say goodbye to her father.

—Shannyn Lenihan

Small Town

In olden days the wall stood strong
And tall against the sky;
Its parapets looked out to warn
The least of passers-by
That none should dare to enter here
By force of might or sword.
The life of all within this town
Was guarded from discord.
Our town still has its outer edge
Secured from grasping hands;
The farmlands black are barriers
That stretch out like a band
To stop the march of progress from
Encroaching steel's cold spell.
A pastured peace enfolds the town
With rural sentinel.

—Sally McMillan

Love is Like a Butterfly

Love is something that can take you soaring to the sky,
And tastes of the many sweet nectars and pleasures life has to offer.
Its colors are many, varied and bright.
It is very delicate and carried on the lightest of wings.
It can be allusive and short lived, or as splendid as the early dew on the fragrant rose.
Love can endure in hopes and dreams, in pixie dust and in one's heart.
It may wane and fade, but as long as there is a wish for a breathe of life there can be love.
The butterfly flies to the rainbow for its colors and is free.
A heart in love is free and bound at the same time.
Love cannot exist without caring, touching, and someone to return it,
As the butterfly can't exist without the nectar, warmth from the sun, and freedom.
Love can hurt sometimes and is so lonely.
Is a butterfly ever lonely in it's flight, I don't know?
Please someday let me be like the butterfly free, lovely and not afraid to love.

—Mary E. Housh

Loneliness

I have tears of loneliness,
And tears of fear,
I have tears of sadness,
And tears of madness
Yet no one stops me from crying

—Michelle Anderson

Across the Nile

Finest violet does smear the air
And tempts the sun to fade to fair
And long the Nile does set for stare,
And long the Nile does set for stare.
For unannounced the moon will drift
Across the river, though course may shift
And Egyptian hearts will gloriously lift,
And Egyptian hearts will gloriously lift.
But eyes, those eyes, take to other heights,
To jewels and diamonds that soar with lights
And oh how fine when the sun is right,
And oh how fine when the sun is right.
So lost forever the former pride
Till found by beasts on river's side
Then the moon again will gently glide,
Then the moon forever will gently glide.

—Spencer Mansouri

Dear William

Conceived in much love
And tenderness...
Heaven has blessed us
With a baby...
I love you more
than you will
Ever know;
And I am proud to be
The mother of your child...
May all the angels watch over
This tiny life,
So precious...so special
And so very much wanted...
Congratulations dear
You are about to be
A father...

—Marge Kingcaid-Pizzute (Mek)

My Wish

If I could have one wish,
And that one wish would come true,
My one wish would be to be with you.
To be by your side through night and day,
Bad and good, to be the one you want to hold and love.

—Nicole Monia

Why? Friend

I thought you were my best friend
And that this relationship will never end
But now that I know of all the things
You done behind my back
I just wish you were full of lack.
Still I can't believe your doing such thing
But look at the reaction that
Unbelieveable truth being.

—Lourdes Sanchez

Love Gone Away

As the sun goes away
and the breezes blow in,
The feeling of your presence
warms the coming wind.
I think of how you came
of how you said goodbye,
I think of our past
while the night steals the sky.
You said I love you
in more ways than one,
And now its gone
gone away like the sun.

—Rosalyn Peace

The Rose Will Bloom

The rose will bloom and then it will die,
And the clouds above will cover the sky.
The sun will shine, and then it will rain,
And I'll look through a window and feel
 all the pain.
I'll hear a song that reminds me of you,
Then I'll see you with someone new.
My friends will tell me I'll be okay,
And I'll think of you often, day after day.
Then someday, the rose will bloom,
And all this I'm feeling will no longer be
 gloom.
The rose will bloom and again will die;
And clouds will begin to cover the sky
The sun won't shine, but it will not rain,
And I'll look through a window without
 feeling pain.

—Michelle Murray

Gone

Gone are the heroes of yesteryear,
And the gentlemen who hold doors open
 wide.
Gone are the duals over true love,
And gone are gunfire wars.
There is no longer joy,
Children no longer laugh.
Their futures consist of nuclear wars,
And crying silent cries of death.

—Susan Dulik

For One Pearl

Four winds blew on an Irish Mill
And the green Irish sea drew me still
In bluey haze I thought I spied
A boy or man smile and pearly cry
I strained my heart and eyes to see
Trees rocked like the silent sea
Then a small Natterjack toad ahead
 outgrew
Yet like a lion or dragon he regally stood
As we walked, he gently croaked:
"Some seas bear putrid pearly cloaks"
"Oily iridescence pours over sweet
 breath"
"O ominous oil slicks reek of death."
I gazed with wonder, attuned to hear
His yellow streak shone irradiantly clear
"Where is one pearl of a solitary sage"
"Who will seek one in this violent age?"
"Nature is the i in fertile and universe"
"Nature is not a fertile hearse"
"Where is one pearl of a solitary sage"
"Who will seek one in this violent age?"

—Lisa Clementson

Once

When the sun falls
And the moon rises
Like the lifting of a balloon
How beautiful the feeling
The feeling of—
Once loved
Once loved was I.
How two people could
Change the world
Nothing was more
Important than drifting
In each others arms,
Like a fairytale was the
Story, the story of
Once loved,
So once loved was
I. . .but only once.

—Patty Martinez

Real Love

We could talk forever and not even say a
 word.
We could listen to the songs and realize
 we never heard.
We could smile with laughter and cry
 with pain inside.
We could stand up for each other but
 really want to hide.
I know how to make you happy, I know
 just what to do,
But one thing I've never seen is the real
 you.
I know just how to kiss you, I know how to
 hold your hand,
But one thing I don't know how to do is to
 make you understand.
I know how to tell you what kind of day
 I've had,
I know just how to tell you the things that
 make me sad.
But I don't know who I'm loving and I
 can't tell you how I feel,
Why do we keep the love that never will
 be real?

—Steffi Rook

Untitled

When the days go by
And the nights drag on
I sit here dreaming,
dreaming of your love.
The way your arms hold me tight.
The whisper of your kiss.
The caress of your voice.
The way you make me feel at night.
As the night drags on
I sit here thinking,
thinking of your touch.
The eagerness of your lust.
You can say I'm a fool in love,
And probably that's what I am.
For when I'm away from you
I long for us to be together.
Forever.

—Olga Kosmadakis

Untitled

Cold, crisp, crackling air hits the hot,
 sparkling fire, bears and wolves are
 heard in the distance,
And the once green foliage up above has
 now turned black.
It is night time, bats are flying high, winds
 are dying down and the lake is calm.
Firecrackers are heard in a distance from
 the party going on at the opposite side
 of the lake.
Campfire songs are being sung, roasting
 tender marshmellows one by one.
Evening moon is hung big and gold,
 waiting for ghost stories to be told.
Children up way past bedtime running
 around. Sparklers in their hands,
 drawing pictures in the air.
The sparklers fall into the sand and
 they're washed away by the tide for
 next year.
It's time to go in now, and the children
 say goodnight, it's been a long day.
The mothers come back out and curl up
 on the green lawn chairs around the
 fire.
While husbands drink beer and talk of
 fishing.
In the cabin the children still awake, talk
 of tomorrow's events.
The candy store, bike riding, swimming in
 the lake, maybe a ride into town.
"Only five weeks left", one says with a
 frown.
Then she laughs and smiles, then says
 with a cheer,
"Ah, yes, but there's always next year."

—Michele Mojeski

The Lost Love

The moon filled with joy
and the sky filled with love
for the thoughts of a special
boy way up above.
The nights we were together
were the nights I hope to
Remember, for I am lonely and
all below tender.
When I lost you I cried with
sorrow realizing your love was only a
 borrow.
As the nights go by you run
through my head whistling and shouting
as I'm lying in bed.
Now that you're gone I can't go
on for I will always love, but
will continue on.

—Melissa Risley

Castles In The Sand

The ocean's breeze is flying through my
 hair,
And the stone gray clouds protect my eyes
From the sun's harsh glare. All around
Me seagulls troop with only the softest
 sound
Of fluttering wings to push them off the
 dampened ground.
It is only here I am released from limiting
 ties
And the relentless situation where the
 only words spoken
Are meaningless alibis. All around
Me the waves' soothing song is heard, my
 soul it does surround,
To stretch my heart's arms
 paradise-bound.
I leave only when I must and soon the
 spell is broken;
My hope never quite accepts the beauty is
 deceiving,
Missing the fresh air and choking. All
 around
I grasp for hidden dreams that cannot be
 found
On a desperate search like a determined
 bloodhound.
Perhaps the knowledge that I can escape
 should be relieving,
But it's always the same disappointing
 end—
Wishing your love was something I could
 believe in.

—*Traci Burch*

The Most Beautiful Thing of All

The world is a most beautiful thing,
We have summer, fall, winter, and spring.
We see the flowers bloom,
And the tragedy of doom.
There are the stars at night,
That are always shining bright,
And the sun at day,
That is beautiful in its very own way.
But I think the most beautiful things of all
Are the trees in fall,
Because the leaves are full of color
Right before they flutter to the ground.

—*Tamara L. Aumiller*

The Pattern of Life

If the pattern of life looks dark to us,
And the threads seem twisted here and
 there.
To the one who is planning the whole
 design,
It's perfectly plain and clear!
For it's all part of God's loving plan
When He weaves in the threads of grey
They will only make brighter the rose and
 gold. . .
Of another happier day!

—*Selma Foster*

The Rose

When the snow runs down the mountains
And the warm winds start to blow
And the spring rains on those winds
Come to make the roses grow
The hand of God gives life to all
From ocean depths to sky above
And the common thread thru all
The life that's given thru impartial love
When those who go in search of love
Feel their world is torn apart
Can see the love that grows the rose
Then will find it in their heart
And those who finally find this love
Find there's nothing that they need
For all they touch will be a rose
When love is given as the seed

—*Victor Leppky*

Another Land

The waves break at the shore,
And the white foam goes upon the sand.
The tide tells you what these waves are
 for,
And that they reach still another land.
But at the other land there are freedoms
 and rights,
And laws that protect you and I.
There is no fights,
And no one will ever die.

—*Sherrie Davis*

. . .And All My Dreams Came True

I dreamt of walking on the beach with you
And then it didn't seem we were really far
 apart
We chased the waves and ran down the
 sand
So Carefree and our problems seemed so
 far away
I dreamt of walking on the beach with you
And then I was reminded of how much I
 really do miss you
We walked and talked for hours
We laughed and cried as we reminisced
I dreamt of walking on the beach with you
And all my dreams came true
We were together again
And then I realized I love you so much. . .
Just because I dreamt of walking on the
 beach with you.

—*Mary Baker McWilliams*

Untitled

It is a jungle after all
And there are animals of prey
I have not yet named.
I have loved some
Whose arms and names I never knew
Streams and gulfs that separated us, and
 others lost at bay.
Seldom the blazing sun
Answers such questions
In which answers never come
Sometimes worrying for love once known
Then found guilty, a trial completely
 undone.
There ought to be something, something
 that's fair
For love that awaits the hungry in an
 electric chair
Love, at the very least
Ought to be pacified with relish
Camouflaged as a great feast.

—*Monica Williams*

The Gathering

I gathered the red and purple flowers
 today,
And they cried as I plucked them out of
 the soil.
Storm clouds appeared suddenly,
 protesting at my
Selfishness. They spit at me—large heavy
 pellets
Disguised as rainwater and I ran into the
 house afraid
And out of breath. The flowers laughed at
 my fears and
Vowed their revenge, and that night I
 dreamt that they had eaten
Me alive—and that I was trapped inside
 their stems unable to get
out.
The next morning I awakened early and
 gathered the flowers once
again
And walking out to the fields I tried to put
 them back into the soil,
But other flowers had grown in their place
 and so I was left
standing there,
Holding the flowers that I no longer
 wanted.

—*Marta Vega*

Pride of Baltimore

There were many great third basemen
And they were tough and fearless
But Brooks Robinson in comparison
Was monumental and peerless
He was the Dean of defense
Covering more ground than his hot corner
Many a good batter hitting toward him
Suddenly became a mourner
Sure clouts became sure outs
As Brooks' golden glove extended
To his left or to his right
It didn't make any difference where it ended
Paving his path to Cooperstown
He was also a prince at the plate
Leading his team to many pennants
His final tribute can never come late
And on his plaque should be added these words
A credit to baseball and the human race
Unlike any player before him
Brooks Robinson owned third base.

—*Louis Dominick*

I Will Love you Forever

Separate roads and separate ways,
We each have a different journey.
Our paths cross here and I must say,
A blessing it has been.
But on our way we each must go,
And never will we cross again.
But in my heart a song I'll sing,
Forever will I love you.
We sail our ships into the wind,
But never will we really end.
And now I say my last goodbye,
Forever will I love you.
One day we'll meet at last,
And reminisce of things gone past.
To say not much we missed together,
And in my heart I'll always know,
I will love you forever.

—*Lisa Shawn Byerley*

Thoughts Of My Love

Peering at the darkness, I lay awake at night
And think of his love; my eyes perceive a light.
A light burns pure and free, that twinkles like the stars,
That brightens a cold darkness, that darkness in my heart.
Still staring deep in darkness, I think of his touch,
So soft, so gentle, so loving, it proves his love so much.
My mind hears his voice, as he calls my name,
In it I hear his love—to others it's not the same.
Quietly, the minutes pass on. . .slowly my mind slips to shade.
I think of his arms wrapped 'round me. . .as my room begins to fade.

—*Laura A. Gascon*

Together

You were my one and only love,
And this I want you to know—
You meant much more to me than anything;
I didn't even want you to go.
Loving you gave me happiness,
The kind I needed everyday.
And if sometimes I didn't show it,
I loved you in each and every way.
If I sometimes got jealous,
It's only because I cared.
The love I felt for you was ever so rare.
If I could have one wish,
Do you know what it would be?
For us to be together for all eternity.

—*Lisa Williams*

Give Me Back My Child

Where is she? That inquistive little girl.
Where did she go? She was here not one minute ago,
Asking me to play house with her.
I told her I would, as soon as I finished my paper.
Where is she? I want to play.
Wait, is that her? No, that can't be her; that is a young woman.
Where could she have gone? Maybe the young lady would know.
Wait, was it really only a minute ago that she was here?
Why is my hair gray; my hands, why is my skin wrinkled?
The young lady, she is coming here, she is calling me daddy.
Could this really be my baby? Look at her, she looks like her mother.
"Daughter," I said, "would you like to have a tea party with me?"
"Oh, Daddy," she said to me, "I don't have time to play anymore."
How did I let time slip away?
Now, it is I who wants to play.

—*Lara M. Henson*

I Wrote a Poem

I wrote a poem,
And tried to find a meaning
In the words, but could not.
The flow of words
Became a silent music
That I heard within myself.
And yet, I hoped
That others who might read my words
Would hear the song,
And then would find
A meaning for themselves
From my meandering words.
For when I write
I hear the music that is mine alone,
As it must be,
But hope the words
Will speak to others silently
To bring quietude and hope.

—*Merle C. Hansen*

If You Could Just Love Me

If I could just hold you the whole night long
And wake up warm beside you to the birds and their song.
If you could just love me as I need to be,
Baby, like the sunshine your love could set me free.
Hold me close and love me as I know you can.
Your love leaves me peaceful, you're such a beautiful man.
I can melt in your caress for your touch is so tender.
I need you and I want you, and to you, I surrender.
Let me wake and meet your eyes, they make my smile bright.
And let me love you tenderly til the dawn emerges from the night.
I'd love, laugh, and grow with you and treat you like a king.
Because you are so sweet and kind and you make my heart sing.
How I wish this to you I could be, for I'd never leave you lonely.
I wish you'd come and take my heart, and be my one and only.

—*Michelle M. Montgomery*

The Beauty of the Land

I sigh at the sight of the deep blue ocean
And watch the fish and gulls in motion.
As I sit quietly by the sand,
I see the beauty of the land.

—*Tanya Schnarr*

Untitled

Let's take a walk along the beach
And watch the waves come in.
Listen to the peacefulness,
So quiet and serene.
The waves glisten with sunlight,
As they round to shore
The seagulls take to flight,
Watch them as they soar.
We are here together,
To picture all of this.
Hand in hand,
We stop to share a kiss.

—*Mary Ann Gonzales*

Quest

Now the challenge
And what a challenge indeed
To sail your own ship
And chart a course into tomorrow.
So I begin
Drifting in the sea with no course or
  reason
Not knowing where I'm going
Or where I've been
Looking for a place to call my own
A place to land
And stand tall where I can be
And find myself.
Again and agin I find what I believe
Is the land of my search
And slowly discover that the land is not
  the
Object of my happiness.
So long I sail through rough seas and
  calm
Discovering new lands only to find
That the place I seek is within my soul.

—*Randall W. Teets*

When I Think of You

There are times I still think of you.
And when I do, a tear comes to my eyes.
I sometimes ask myself why,
But I guess it's because
Deep down inside, I still have feelings for
  you.
I wish I could just get over you,
But I see now it's not going to be easy to
  do.
I guess it's because I still love you.

—*Michelle Lee*

Apology

I hurt you
And when you told me so
I was angry at myself, not you
Because I knew you were right
But I couldn't admit it, I wouldn't.
I had no excuse,
No reason for treating you the way I did
I'm sorry it was you.
You're the last person I'd ever want to
  hurt.
You treat me as though I were your own
When I'm good, and when I'm not good.
Thank you for showing me where I went
  wrong
Without trying to hurt me back
Although I probably deserved it.
I owe you an apology and I hope you'll
  accept
Because I love you
And to lose a friendship like yours,
Well, I'd really rather not.

—*Victoria L. Boldt*

I Love You

I wish this dance would last,
And will be my first not my last.
I feel more love and emotion,
Moving and growing faster than an ocean.
Why must you act this way?
I wish you felt for me, as I feel for you.
But what can I say?
We're not one we're two.
I love you more than words can say,
But love? you say it's not that way.
I wish we could go on forever,
But I know it's not that way.
You said I'm like a feather,
And my heart can just float away.
I feel it's love not lust,
Why do you insist you feel nothing?
You've broken my heart easily,
Can't you feel my heart breaking?

—*Sue-Ellen Dean*

My Last Wish of You

I gaze upon a wishing star,
And wish for love again,
For I've been dreaming endlessly,
Of a love that could have been.
I do remember hearts of gold,
And eyes of shimmering blue,
But what I don't remember,
Is why I fell in love with you.

—*Patti Yanochko*

Augur

Behold the brambled bush
And witness life at its worst and at its
  best.
A patch of twigs and thorns and vines,
Twisted, confused, going in all directions.
Seemingly dead, and yet very much alive,
Housing life, and protecting that life.
Do we ourselves in the bust?
What are we but sheep. . .part of the
  massive flock
Whose strength lies in the knowledge
That we are part of His flock
And that the shepard will not allow us to
  be lost.
That alone is an answered prayer.
That realization makes the trials easier,
The falls softer
And in the frustrations we will never
  settle for mediocrity.
So when asked, "What is it like
To be part of the brambled bush?"
The answer must be,
"Only perfect."

—*Thomas W. Allen*

Angel

Though man might dream of earthly
  things
And work hard to see them come true,
If I could hand-make a heavenly dream,
I'd make an angel like you.
The sound of your voice, that's all I need
To gladden my heart through and
  through.
The warmth of your smile, the touch of
  your hand,
The way you say, "I love you."
Though all of my dreams are not heavenly
  dreams,
God made an angel in you!

—*Lloyd McDavid*

There's Hope

One night I had a dream
And world peace was finally reached.
World hunger was no more,
Crime was down to its lowest score.
Our churches were full,
Our elderly happy,
And this country was rich with fellow
  humanity.
And when I awoke, I still kept the hope
That one day I would see,
This dream become reality.

—*Melissa L. Brody*

Why?

You told me you loved me
And would never cause me pain,
So why did you hit me again and again?
When I bruised on the outside,
My heart inside bruised too.
Why did you do it, Daddy-What did I do?
I look for a reason,
But one's so hard to find.
That night runs like a horror movie inside
  my mind.
A daughter should be held,
Cuddled and kissed,
Not beaten and bruised by her father's
  angry fists.
So each night I pray
To God up above,
That instead of your anger,
You'll show me your love.

—*Wendy Barkley*

The Life of a Flower

Flowering flowers shouldn't be mowed
  down
and wrapped in see—through noisy
  plastic paper
and tied together at the point of
  departure,
drowned in a brown Tupperware bucket,
  waiting
for someone to pick them up and
shove their deprive beauty in their nose,
pay a price to small and just
give them away to another accepting
  monster,
accepting flowers accepting conformity, to
  only
step up by being drowned in a nicer well
  and
forgotten about until they
drop their parts upon the linen tablecloth
  and
are thrown out by a heartless hand.
I know it sounds strange from someone
  my age but this
is the life of a flower and it's a sad sad
  thing.

—Tanya May

To Know Me

If you can see me through my laughter
And you can see me through my tears
Then you'll begin to know me.
If you have seen me in the rain,
And you've felt the pain that I've been
  through
Then you'll begin to know me.
But if you really want to know me,
Don't judge me with the public's eyes.
You'll see my best behavior.
You'll never know what's on my mind.
In every person, there's two people.
One's too shy to reach the top.
So what you see upon the surface,
You think is me, but it is not.
So, if you really want to know me
Then come and be my friend.
Love begins in friendship,
And knowing is for friends.

—Linda Macklin

Happiness is Like. . .

Happiness is like a bird that sings in the
  morning and flies away with gladness.
And you have that joyous feeling inside
  you, you just can't explain.
Happiness is like a warm, sunny spring
  day with laughter and good spirits all
  through the day.

—Tammy Hall

What You Are

True, you may not be Robert Redford,
And you may not be an Einstein.
You may not be perfect,
But neither am I.
You may not be rich,
But I don't mind.
I don't like what you aren't,
I just love what you are!

—Vicki Hulinsky

Cogitation For A New Beginning

The time will come
and you'll be gone,
I'll be alone
feeling forlorn,
But the love I felt
will linger on,
In my heart
that is now so blue.
Yet life must continue,
I have to move on,
Even without you
I must get through,
Sadness will pass
Fate will again be clear as a glass.
A new day will begin
For the sun will shine again,
A new beginning
will be the new happening.

—Mel Caranto

Lost Love

No one will ever know the love we shared
And you'll never know how I really cared.
Our love was one that can't be told
  through words
Its sole expression was through songs of
  birds.
I remember the times we'd spend
  laughing
And recall those times of doing nothing.
How I enjoyed the sweetness of your
  voice,
For all your whispers forced me to rejoice.
However, now you're gone, and I'm alone.
My voice has fallen to a joyless tone.
Never before have I felt so empty.
Together our happiness was plenty.
If only you'd one day return to me,
I'd belong to your for eternity.

—Linda S. Kurtz

Anger

Anger is something deep down inside,
Anger is something you don't want to
  hide.
Anger is something you want to let out,
Anger is something when all you do is
  shout.
Anger is something that makes you feel
  bad,
Anger is something that can make you
  feel sad.
Anger is something you feel against me,
Anger is something I don't like to see
Anger is something coming from you
Anger is something that makes me feel
  blue.

—Michelle Noftsinger

Untitled

A heart is broken,
Another one mends
After the tears
A smile again.
A loved one is born
Another may die,
A warm sense of joy,
For others there's cries.
The day starts so early,
The night comes too soon
The day with the sun
And the night with the moon.
The ocean is troubled
With reflections that glisten,
The ocean made of teardrops
But no one to listen.

—Maricruz Garza

Images

Images
Appear and disappear
Before my eyes
The rain overwhelms
Meshing pictures into one
And leaves
Fall encircling to the ground
Each covering another
Through the hourglass
Images are distorted
And confused
Everchanging as patterns
When the kaleidescope turns
The water moves, rippling and shining
And the silver weathered stones
Remain unmoved

—Michelle Superle

Cuts

Your words
Are a sword
To my heart.
Ripping to shreds
Kind love
Harboring there.
Sharp and swift
The blows
Cutting me to the quick.
I know their intent
Is innocent
Spoken in haste.
Understanding
In this case
Doesn't dull the pain.
Harsh words
Cause erosion
On the gem of love.

—Sue Lusk

Computers

Computers of the future
Are creations of yesterday
They're taking over jobs and such
Causing their creators much dismay
Although they are automatic
And are faster in so much
There still is nothing that can replace
The joy of human touch.

—Laura M. LaBell

Touch of Magic

People who can write a book or a novel
Are envied by those like me; if I tried I
  would grovel.
They pinpoint every event, each person,
  time and place.
Their concentration and ability makes
  them an admirable race.
They take us on fabulous journeys as they
  unleash their theme;
Leading us through reality or fantasy
  with a magical dream.
All I can do is paint little stories with
  words and rhyme;
Capturing a dash and a bit of what nature
  holds sublime,
From the ground to the clouds in the sky;
Small moments that appear to my eye.
But I love to take it, mold it, and do
  humbly share
What I've had the privilege to see, a
  moment so rare.
So, if I can bring to you a smile or a warm
  thought,
Then I've shared a touch of magic that,
  luckily, I caught.

—Patricia L. Heincy

Where are the Feminine Black Women?

Where are the feminine black women?
Are they as delicate blooms
To be picked off the face of the earth
As were Lady Day and Dandridge?
Or enigmas to redefine in dichotomies
Of strong and tough
vs.
Soft and delicate?
Perhaps they are mere bywords to be
  reasoned away
As luxuries beyond our purse.
Still
They remain
As desert flowers
Blooming midst adversity
In obscurity
Ever beautiful.

—Sandra J. Phillips

Dreams

Dreams. . .
Are what?
The thoughts of those who are asleep.
Can they be the wishes of one's mind?
The hopes of the future
Or memories from the past.
Pleasant,
Scary,
Humorous,
Mysterious,
Dreams are like plays.
As if you're the director
Setting the scenes and writing the moods.
Dreams are like illusions
Blurred, faded, or sometimes real as life.
Dreams may come to those awake, sitting,
  staring,
But not really seeing
These dreams are daydreams.

—Rhonda Nicole Sykes

The End of Another Day is Upon Us

Night sets in. . .
As
Day creeps out. . .
The moon beams in. . .
As
The sun fades out. . .
Dark clouds blankets over. . .
As
White cumulus disappears. . .
Stars pop out. . .
As
Sleepy heads go in. . .
As we bid farewell to the day
And watch darkness makes it way
Above our heads, where, on feathered
  pillows we lay.

—Tarita Wright

A World Of Peace

A child's cry is heard from the starlit
  night
As a man behind a gun commits another
  crime of violence
He shatters a mother's love, destroys a
  child's
innocence, hurts a world of people
Without doubt it will continue. . .Why?
Why do we destroy ourselves in a world
  that
destroys us?
So bitterly, so hurtfully
In a world full of promises
Why do we let time pass us by?
Crying alone in the darkness desolate and
  alone
I realize this is my world
But, do I want it?
Unpurposeful is the world we live in
It doesn't hurt to dream, to achieve
A world of freedom
A world of peace
Together as one, it can become a reality.

—Lori Anne Brodnicki

Rain

It begins
As a tiny spherical shape,
Descending from the sky.
But soon becomes a multitude of
  glistening diamonds
Reflecting the vast spaciousness of the
  universe
And malforming the everyday world of
  jagged edges,
Into a new world.
One of fluid, abstract images with no real
  shape or
Form that glide through life without
  retaining
The one thing necessary to live.
Gradually, it is absorbed into the world
Of routine precision, until it eventually
Becomes no more than a darkening pool,
Quickly vanishing, leaving no trace
It had ever existed.

—Leigh Reid

Homage to Georgia O'Keefe

There is a chill in the night
As blackness engulfs the artificial mesas,
'Round as morning begins to surround the sun,
In a voguish play with time against night,
Flat clouds steer a course opening the heavens
From dark stars to alight with their providential yoke
Harnessed to the sky and nearly blue; her art opens from
The direction of the sun and her flowers stretch over as long
As the eye can fetch. Far from the buttes and arroyos; distant
From the rain, inside, on canvas alive; a harmony swells and music
Becomes brushstrokes and flutters of light move the sands, yet.

—*Vincent Kamin*

Good-Bye

She remembers the beginning when their love was strong,
As he looks in her eyes and says it was wrong.
She wants to tell him that she knows he lied.
When he knew it was true, but only denied.
He wouldn't admit to cheating on her
'Cause he wanted things the way they were.
But she walked away with a tear in her eye.
He calls her name and he starts to cry.
He wants things to be like they were before,
But he's the one who asked for more.
Thinking of when she heard him lie,
She wiped her tears and said "Good-bye"

—*Sharon Russ*

Day Dreaming

One day
As I sat on the porch
Watching the clouds move away
I imagined a frame in the sky
The clouds have carved
A face I knew
As I look harder
My eyes began to water
The picture became distorted
The face in the frame
Seemed to call me by name
I felt mesmerized for the moment
As the clouds moved away
The face and the frame faded too.
See what day dreaming can do.

—*Russ Fitzgerald*

What You are to Me

You are as full as the moon,
As bright as a star,
Any kind of love there is,
Is what you are.
With the sun so big and with light,
Stay together forever?
With our love I'm sure we might.
You look at the sky
There's so much blue,
There's nothing as big
As my love for you.
The greenest grass,
The birds and the bees,
Anything so beautiful is..
What you are to me
I love you!

—*Scott Leclair*

Emilly

I cleanse myself with tears
As I awake to early morning's rise.
At a time gone by, she would
Stir me with soft gentle lips
And the charm of her lush green eyes.
Our harmonious love would have
Lasted forever, but alcohol took my Emilly away.
I still keep on waiting and
Hoping my sweet Emilly comes home to stay.
My weary eyes water and I start to cry.
The bottle that I drinketh has run dry.
Shame me O'Lord for I have failed thee.
I was strong once but cannot
Carry my love's burden any further.
Blessed be my Emilly.

—*Stacy Andrews*

The Bridge

I hear the night call
As I shiver and fall
I hear the water cry
As I look with a sigh.
This bridge where you fell
Is the secret I can't tell
I've come back to visit you
But where are you?
My anger that kills
Your body that fills
The dead air with sorrow
Haunts me with a claw.

—*Rowena Cadiz*

Vision Of Love

I look clearly
As far as I can see
But the visions of your love
Seem to be staring at me
I stare into the clearness
of the dark beautiful sky
I wish upon the stars
I see shining so high
I sit and wonder
Did my wish come true
But then I notice
There you are
You seem to have came
Out of the clear blue.

—*Rachael Ballard*

As Time Goes By

As I sit here, I think of you sometimes.
As I lay here, I see the look in your eyes.
As I sleep here, I hear your cries, telling me you love me.
As I look through the window, I see your face.
As I hear our song, the feeling will never be replaced.
As I lay in the dark I sometimes misplace your voice,
telling me your leaving.
As I see reality now in you.
As I remember the things you used to do.
As I relive my love for you
and you're gone.

—*Tina Thomas*

Another's Dream

Books can take me into another world
As I sit by the fire curled.
A place where lives myth and fantasy
For all those that wish it to see.
Another's dream printed on the pages,
Presented to last throughout the ages.
To share with all who believe
In the web that the author weaves.
Of things discovered, love's conceived,
Battles waged, and leaders deceived.
A goal to chase after,
A hall filled with laughter.
All is possible in these fairy lands,
Even purple seas washing upon red sands.

—*Patricia R. Gordon*

I'll Wait for You

Days may pass as does my fate,
As I stop my life to stand here and wait.
Other's lives may carry on,
But mine has stood still since you've been gone.
The tears of the future part from my eyes,
I try to hope, but all that's left are sighs.
All I have left is a devoted will,
My pride may be lost but I wait here still.
I miss you so much, I'm cried out from the pain,
I just can't help but wonder if I'll see you again.
My feelings for you I wish you knew,
But no matter what happens, I'll always wait for you.

—Tracie Lynn Mayer

Green

I remember diving into the lake, the warm water enveloping me
As I swam up to the surface for a breath of life.
The coolness, touching the tips of my toes, felt wonderful.
And as I dove again, under the water, I opened my eyes.
I watched as the rich shade of brown changed to a cool green.
The water was cold, and it kept me suspended in time,
For what seemed like years.
The icy paradise surrounded me,
Until I was pushed upward by an unknown force,
To be left gasping for air once more.
Reselence filled my mind.
When I thought of the green,
Tranquility filled the sky and the world around me.

—Lori S. Kirkpatrick

Splendor Of The Night

The sun sets upon the golden sand,
As I walk with you hand in hand.
Along the beach as we slowly stroll,
Upon the sand the waves do roll.
Through the dark flies a graceful gull,
While the rays of sun begin to dull.
As sparkling waves gently flow,
The water reflects the sun's last glow.
Over the top of the sandy dune,
I see the rays of the silvery moon.
The special beauty of its rays,
As they reflect on the foamy waves.
When I look up at the peaceful sky,
I see a shooting star go by.
I make a wish with all my might,
And enjoy the splendor of the night.

—Mandy Winters

Untitled

Serenity filled the summer breeze
As I walked along the lonely street.
Darkness filled the summer sky
While the soft, gray clouds began to cry.
The street was misty and very wet
Along the sidewalk I slowly crept.
Around me shadows gracefully danced
A kitten's shadow began to prance.
The full white moon lit the only lane
As if it were full of a giant, round flame.
The buildings stood tall and very brave
As if it were me they were trying to save.
And while the darkness crept to an end
I dreamed of when it would return again.

—Michele Izzo

As When I Believe

I will not be the same
As I was
when I believed.
I will not behold the magic
Of special wonder
without your Spirit.
I will not feel the eternity
Of sweet Eternity
the dreaming Child.
I will never
know my destiny
unless I suffer for it.

—Marcelle Jones

Midnight Dreams

The wind was blowing swift and light
As I watched the summer night.
The stars were big your eyes were bright
As you held me oh so tight.
Should I leave or should I stay?
Please don't make me go away!
I want you here from time to time,
My heart pounds faster out of line.
Seeing you there so innocent and fine
Knowing one day you'll soon be mine.
I want you now come with me,
Let's go watch the calming sea.
The waves are harsh yet crash as they may,
Now it's ending I see day.
Dawn breaks through as I awake a smile comes across my face.
It's nice to know I'll see you here.
Goodbye for now I have to go,
I'll see you after the midnight show.

—Sarah Berlint

Tranquility

I sit watching the blanket of twilight
As it outlines the background among the trees.
I hope that somewhere in the past I've left some measure of thought,
Or feeling of love as I passed along the way.
To love all as myself, and in loving receive love in return.
Share what measure of abundance I have,
And receive measure for measure.
Relish in the joy of children and be fulfilled.
Serve the sick and see the look of thankfulness
In their eyes to warm my soul.
While the flowers open to the first sunlight,
And the trees sway back and forth in the gentle breeze,
I am glad to awaken to see the dawn of a new day,
And the hope lingers on that I may live a little while longer,
For I may not pass this way again.

—Vivian M. Casey

Untitled

Time passes ever so quickly,
As love spreads throughout it.
You hold me tightly in your arms,
And I hope this passion will never quit.
I stare into your baby blue eyes,
Praying this flame will never die.
Counting the days as they pass,
Until the one when we say goodbye.

—Triniti Lisa Burton

Losing Him

The summer waves crash on the shore,
As my dreams are washed away...
My life was filled with happiness
But now our relationship is gone,
I cannot help but feel that your
Decendants was but my fault,
For maybe if I had muttered those
Three heartfilled words you would
Still be here.
As I watch the sand be washed away
My heart feels it's never too late
To say...
"My friend, I love you."

—Lori Vinch

Did your Heart Crush?

I felt your heart crush
As my prized ceramic trinket.
Toward the floor it fell
Slipping from my grip.
How was I to replace the prize
Left in a thousand pieces?
How was I to know
The effect of my careless grip?
How do I pick your heart from the floor
And glue it back together?

—Sarah Jane Walker

Dreams of Glory

Misty breezes blow
As seagulls call my name
They soar and swoop down low
But I have done the same
I have soared away up high
Gliding on dreams of glory
Sailing up way past the sky
Feeling the pride of victory
But I too have fallen down
As a gull swoops with the wind
It takes all strength to drown
The feeling of chagrin
I envy gulls and their flight
As I try to forget the past
I hope to accomplish without plight
A happiness that will last

—Stephanie Hoffman

An Eerie Silence

An eerie silence, absence of sound
As snowflakes gently swirl to the ground.
Beauty unsurpassed
As they billow and dance,
They eddy and twist, they flounce and curl
And slowly their way to the treetops unfurl.
The heavily laden branches bend and groan
As though they had a life of their own.
Precariously the snow perches on a fence
Lightly at first and then it becomes dense.
Shapes that were easy to identify
Become something different as time goes by.
Trees that are silhouetted against a darkening sky
Become hauntingly beautiful as night draws nigh.
In the warmth of the pearly pink sky of dawn
The snow glistens and shimmers virginally on our lawn.
An eerie silence, absence of sound, as snowflakes gently swirl to the ground.
What a multitude of sins are hidden there, only to be exposed when everything's bare!

—Rita Kornberger

Pieces of an Incomplete Child-Memory

Fuzzy evening clouds and black winter trees watch
as some man throws me down into sticky leaves
I whimper and a worm jumps from his pants, it tries to touch me
then Mommy fades with the sun
forever beyond some imaginary horizon
with all the good boys and girls following her
Left behind, I find a secret isolation
behind my thoughts, and try to understand
Why is it suddenly so cold here?
Then my paralyzed mind begins to notice
some sticky liquid leaking
I think it's my brain running down my legs
and I just hope I die
When left alone, I detach the dead leaves from my sweater
notice the trees have altered, the clouds are fragmenting now
Then I walk home,
forever infected with a phantom pain

—Marcie Matthews

I remember

I held tightly to your hand,
As tears rolled down my cheek.
I remember our walks in the sand,
We were standing looking off the peek
Now memories surround me at night,
As I lay silently in the dark.
I remember your shining light,
It haunts me like a spooky park.
When last I saw your face,
It was like a ghost in fright.
I remember my teddy bear in lace,
You bought me for that night.
You are now 6 feet deep,
In a world of loss.
I remember I was so cheap,
To let you try to be the boss.

—Mandy Mancuso

Your Eyes

They're as blue
As the bluest ocean,
As deep as the deepest sea,
And when I look into your eyes,
I feel you've just completed me.

—Trudi McGinnis

Sweet Dreams

It's late at night
As the breeze
Coming in through the window
Gently ruffles my hair.
Slowly, I toss and turn
As your voice
Filters in and out of my dreams
And I keep smelling
Traces of your cologne.
I see vague images of your face,
But never a whole picture.
It is as if a small part of you
Floats in with the breeze
Touches me
Deep in the night
And then is gone.

—Lisa R. Morrow

The Living Dead

One child and one drug,
As the child grows up
The drug grows in number.
And sooner or later, the drug seems larger.
Peer pressure,
The boy soon tries the life, that will bring his death.
High popularity, skipping school, stealing money,
A simple high on life becomes a desperate need.
The gun, the money maker,
Which now supports his habit.
Like: someone to get high with.
Marriage, money, drugs
Shooting up, popping, snorting:
No preference, no worries, no limit.
Pregnancy, money, drugs,
Celebration.
And now they are the proud parents
Of a child and a drug addict.

—Teri A. Durst

The Spirit Of Man

As timeless
as the earth,
and its solidarity;
As breathless
and exhilarating as a snowflake
melting into oblivion:
All the things in a lifetime
which are needed,
loved, and hoped for.
Your are
the will
to survive.

—Lawrence Anthony

Petals in the Wind

The wind blows softly through your hair
As the last petal falls from your hand
And blows gently in the wind.
As it travels in the wind,
You look for another and another.
But they all hold the same
I love you, you love me not.
Why must you listen to the petals
And not your heart?
All the petals will soon blow away,
But my love will not.
For you see I love you,
You love me not?

—Melissa Johnson

Holidays

For some, it's time of adventurous fun
As the old but pleasing sun,
Emerges behind the school-time tomb.
Galloping chill and refreshment come,
Luscious like a honeycomb.
While for others, it's time to contrast
The road that runs miles long.
Dilligently to criticize the past,
Praise the good and correct the wrong.
Heal the wounds and hurting heart,
To be a perfect rose and ever last.

—Rizwan Yusuf

The Storm

The storm is not scary but beautiful
As the rain outside my window pitter pats
Harshly onto the damp ground,
The thunder rocks the earth like a big
   rock
Falling to the ground.
Then the lightning brightly flashes
Across the violet sky.

—Nicole Flamer

Broken Heart

I walked along the shoreline
As the sea slapped silently
Against my feet.
I threw a rock into the
Waving waters
And picked up the small seashells.
With a stick I printed out
His name
And slowly drew a heart
Being
Broken.

—Natalie Nichols

Life

I see the lonely bird's flight
As the sky turns ashen gray,
He has a long, long way to go
Before he can once again play.
It's the turning of the seasons
When all things begin again,
I am starting on my journey
That leads away from all the pain.
Like the earth that changes its coat
Four times a year, without fail,
My happy heart has begun its singing
As I go to travel the new laid trail.
When I begin to ponder
All the things that might have been,
I'm proud to say with great conviction
It's good just to be alive again!

—Loretta M. Barrios

Lost Love

There I sit quietly in the sand
As the tears roll off my face and into my
   hands.
Remembering all of the times we shared
   together
And I thought that they would last
   forever.
If only I could have spent much more time
   with you
And show you I love you through and
   through.
For I never expected something like this
Now I wish I could see you again and give
   you one more kiss.
When I heard you were gone, I had never
   felt so much pain
I cried until I had no more strength to
   gain.
But now I'm living on,
But always remembering you before you
   were gone.
Just tell me one more thing,
Can you ever see me looking into the sky
With tears in my eyes,
Wondering, why did you have to die?

—Tracy Brewer

His Passing

She cried softly to herself
As they lowered the plain pine box
Deeper and deeper into the freshly dug
   hole
That was especially dug for that rainy
   day.
Tears brimmed on her lashes,
As the salt mixed with the droplets from
   the sky
Which seemed to echo her hidden
   feelings.
An image of a man, much older than she,
But looking much the same,
Passed quickly in her mind.
At last, she thought, he is at peace.
With that she picked up a handful of
   earth
And threw it upon the coffin
Of the man she loved but hardly knew.

—Laurie S. Yanow

Secrets

Cramped up in a bottle
As they sometimes are
Some are put away
In the back of a drawer.
Some are hidden
Some are sad
Some are heavy
Like a piece of lead.
Some are shared
And some points are carried out to
Some could be hearsay.
But some are true.
Some are short
Some are long
Some stay forever
Like in a wonderful song.

—Wendy Miller

Sonnet II

No pain rips, tears, destroys the very soul,
As this, alone, in darkness-the sun fell.
Liquid wine burns my eyes; no longer
   whole.
I am the prey, this life is mine to sell.
Beauty black, stars aligned by destruction
Graves fall to the dust, bodies cry out
   pain!
The mind whirls-impossible to function
This life to the living, nothing to gain-
Heavy hearts and blue-black thoughts
   take over;
Time moves slowly, then ceases to exist
Neverending as a former lover
Blood drips down like warm rain-hard to
   resist
Sorrows eat flesh-contentment no longer
Until tears have passed, the pain grows
   stronger.

—Ruth Anne Geyer

A Flower In The Junkyard

The human experience,
As we trod from the womb to the tomb,
Is often a garabage detail in a world of mud.
Where bigotry, intolerance, facism, fear
And anxiety permeate our society,
Making our struggle an uphill battle.
While around our shoulders, bureaucracy
And politics weigh us down.
When we meet a fellow traveler,
With feelings, sensitivity, and regard for other humans.
It is like a light in the darkness,
Or a flower in the junkyard.

—*Linda G. Wheeler*

Decay

Ice clear and cold
As your lips are
On red berries. The
Color of sweetness is
Foreign on your skin.
Kisses, smooth as
Creamed fingers,
Shiver up my hair,
Resounding like silk
On cool wet thighs.
Black eyes
Stripped of flowers,
Swept cold like death
Beneath the silver
Smooth slab of me.

—*Paige J. Swartley*

I Made All Things Right

You are just Lord, You are kind,
"Ask," you said, "and I shall find."
In whatever state I am be content,
I know in quietness and trust lies my strength,
But, soft murmurings in me rise and fall,
Then I seek to find, "Why do terrorists prosper at all?"
"Why in defeat—must my good endeavors end?"
You are my friend. I dream dreams which tend
To disburse nought, thus within the depths of contemplation
Something cries out. I think of You and your creation.
"You made it Lord" Sadly, He said, "In the genesis of life"
"I made all things-And They Were Right."

—*Lena E. Lewin*

The Wall

I have been coming to the wall,
at days and nights, in snow, rain and fog,
and it's something I have never lived before,
Touching the wall I talk to my men,
who never made it back home,
I have seen mothers, fathers, children,
widows, friends, comrades, to touch a name,
and all in silence wipe off a tear away,
Some remember, some to see, and some mourn to him,
and they all sing a farewell to him,
Walking tall I imagine faces behind names,
and holding our flag I please the sun,
to tell the moon and stars,
there is a peace at last,
and let's share the joy and sorrow of our lost love,
Because the wall reflects the great deed of nobody's war,
Now, I admit, that I have NO words to tell the world,
Why, we fought the lost war,
Why?

—*Ted Pagas*

Just You

The crowd
Seems so oblivious
To small, little
Me.
Performing on stage
Like a dolphin
For the sea.
Often
I ask myself
"Is it worth it?"
But then
I see your eyes in
The crowd.
For you
It's worth it all.

—*Pam Kolb*

Reluctant Prodigy

Who cares if Ashkenazy
at eight was playing Glinka?
I'd rather play hide and seek
than "Michael Row your Boat"
or a F major scale.
"B flat dear, try it again."
Did Shostakovitch's mom
pick on his minute faults?
Did the boys yell at Tchaikovsky
"Sissy, Mommy's little boy"
because he played piano
instead of playing ball?
I won't be sent to the gulag
for not practicing?
They hailed Rachmaninov,
and he was eighteen
before he wrote one opus.

—*Mike Hardin*

Untitled

Sometimes I feel afraid,
At night I even pray
Of the things that go on
In this great big world today.
Sometimes I feel secure,
Like I can face anything,
But then it all fades
Like a deaf person's ear.
The steam that builds up
Inside my frightened body
Is like all the people
Trying to outdo everybody.
The pressures that we face,
Alcohol, sex, and drugs,
Just lands on my head
With a great big thud.
I don't know if I can take it,
For it's all so much to face.
I'll just put my trust in the Lord,
And let Him take the grace.

—*Shannon Post*

Animals

A dying species to us all,
At night I often hear their call.
While man hunts them down, they search for a home,
It seems they always have to roam.
In the light of the moon I hear a wolf's cry,
With so much pain it brings tears to my eyes.
If the human race can learn to share their home,
Maybe the animals can be left alone.

—*Shawn McRae*

I See You

I see you bending in the wind.
At seeing you
I shout for joy.
Feathery stalks of wheat,
I think you are named "Fox Tail"
I have loved you since childhood,
Your yellow-green kernals in a straight row.
Your maroon fur
Soft and silky if stroked the right way,
The other, stopping and catching.
Lightly you tickle my face.
Straight, dry stalks held in my hand.
I feel guilty at killing you.
Just to enjoy your spiritless bodies.

—*Patricia May Hokanson*

Romeo and Juliet

First meeting between Juliet and
  Romeo. . .
At the dance. . .
Tenuous advances from an eager
  shy-brash youth.
In his reverie, joyfully careless with his
  tenderness. . .
Revelations to relations who ought not
  see.
$And Juliet loving the loving in her heart,
  walks in a dream. . .
Longing to proclaim such wondrousness
  and silencing herself with
propriety. . .
$Waiting until
Both can re-discover the strength in the
  solitude of their souls.

—*Victoria Magdalena S'anchez*

Cynical

Run and hide as fast as you can. . .
Away from the shame that comes from
  man. . .
This is a recording.
Who will listen? Who will hear?
Who is willing to lend me their ear?
At the tone, please leave a message.
Oh pain, pain go away. . .
Find another place to lay!
The number you have reached has been
  disconnected.

—*Veronnica Rupp*

Among the Clouds

Here I stand,
Awed. . .
Amazed. . .
The world below me,
The heavens above me.
I reach up and touch an angel's wing,
I bend down and gently brush the leaves.
Before my eyes, the Earth stretches to her
  full lengths,
The sun sinks slowly behind tree covered
  mountains.
My heart soars with pride,
My eyes fill with tears.
Here among the clouds, peace on the
  wings of wind, doth ride.

—*Rebecca Hardin*

To the Scientist in All of Us; for Ellen

here we go again
back to the lab
all those brown bottles and finely tuned
  instruments
delicate is a first cousin to fragile
we weigh out our thoughts, our worth, our
  feelings
to precise calibrations
it's such a tricky business this measuring
we jab our fingers with pointy razors
and under the microscope we see the
  stain,
and strain
who will be as careful with us as we are
  with ourselves
perhaps time released is really easier on
  the system
sensitive is a sister to pain
so much data. . .
how to trust
who to entrust

—*Sabley Sabin*

Love Is Like A Rose

The love I have seen is like a rose,
Barely visible as it grows.
As a young bud it blends in well,
Hidden beneath a protective shell.
Forever in dark it may stay
From those who search everyday.
Love, like a rose, is built upon time;
Quiet and gentle, much like a mime.
Without a warning, it could disappear,
Making us grasp for whatever is near.
The memories made won't fade away,
Forever in the heart, they will stay.
As time goes by, a new bud will grow,
Leaving a chance yet to be known.

—*Meredith Dawn Smith*

Gentle Rain

Mother Nature
Bathed herself,
On this autumn day;
In delicate little drops,
Gentle was her rain.
David, I know
If you were here,
You'd be out there too!
Caressing all the raindrops
She to fall on you!
Written October 16, 1974

—*Lisa Michelle Brunell*

Battered Abuse

I would kill anyone I found,
Beating or knocking kids to the ground.
They are hurting them for the rest of their
  lives,
And the abusers don't care and should
  think twice.
They must think they are cool,
By hitting kids like an eight-ball in pool,
But actually they're as cruel as the devil,
And should be locked up to the highest
  level.
If we could take the law into our own
  hands,
I'd search the town in military vans.
I'd break and rip them apart,
Like they did to that kid's heart.
I hope that anyone in trouble will speak
  now to the town,
And I would be there for a shoulder to cry
  on.

—*Teri Lyn Beilke*

Heart of Gold

A heart of gold
Beautiful and bold.
Healing touch so sweet
Like a special treat.
Faithful friend
Always a hand to lend.
Cheery smile, sparkling eyes
Mirroring the skies.
Laughter that fills the room
Blows away all gloom.
If only to have, to hold
That beautiful
Heart of gold.

—*Michelle Neubecker*

Flowers

Flowers sway in the wind
Beauty clinging to every petal
Grace to every stem
The gentle breeze increases
As rain begins to fall
And the flowers hide their faces
Hiding the beauty in all.

—*Mindy Shepherd*

No Turning Back

He went away
Because he had to.
They never knew
When they were going to see him again.
But it was the vicious system
Under which they all lived,
That was the cause of his
Necessary, but unnecessary departure.
He could never go back
And they didn't know
If they could ever leave.
The pain was indescribable.
As he stepped onto that plane
In search of a new life.
He could never turn back.
But that's the pain.
That goes with a life
Under Apartheid.

—*Samantha Liddell*

Love is Like a Rose

Love is like a rose's roots,
Because it grows deep into my heart.
Love is like a rose's thorns,
Because it pierces deep into the soul.
Love is like a rose's bud.
Because it begins to grow more,
Lovely each and everyday.
Love is like a rose's blossom.
Because it finally blossoms out!

—*Tandy Marie Arthur*

My Dream

I wish so much that my dream could come true,
Because the only one I want to be with, is you.
The minute I close my eyes you appear next to me,
You tell me there is no where else you would rather be.
I wish you could really exist (that would make me so happy),
But you're only a guy in my dreams and that makes me feel so lonely.
When we are together in my dream, we walk up our favorite hill.
It is so beautiful, with extraordinary views,
I wish that all of this could be real!
This morning I realized what you said to me last night.
You said that you love me, and I was all you want in life.
You said, "Don't worry one day our dream will come true,"
"And finally I will be with you, but for now you have to wake up,"
"Let me give you one last kiss, I will be waiting til you sleep again,"
"Just remember..."
"One day I will exist"!

—*Roxana Partida*

Honey

Honey,
Bees make honey,
And it's not eaten by bunnies.
It's eaten by bears,
Not by mares.
It's eaten by children,
Not by a chicken,
It's good to eat,
So it can't be beat.

—*Nathan Williams*

A Bride's Prayer

Oh, bride to be
Before he slips the ring on thee,
Pray that he will never forget
The time you and he have spent.
Pray to be strong
To resist temptation
That is oh so wrong.
Pray that his love for you will grow
And will always show.
And pray that he
Prays a similiar prayer as thee.

—*Tracy Lovell*

Intoxication

The grass is greening always
Before the red of the human eye.
Her bloodshot eyes do see the grass.
Her bloodshot eyes do.
When she is drunk,
The bells on her ears jingle like mad
And it won't stop,
I promise you it won't stop.
A twinkle for the ear,
That is what the sun
And diamonds must,
Must sound like.
Her bloodshot ears in the visionless dark
Do hear the sun,
Until it comes up the next morning.
The street concrete is blacking always
Before the Visine of the human eye.

—*Meghan Wynne*

Wishful Eye

Half giraffe is she
Behind the veil, blinks and blinks,
Eye of morning.
The lonely sky betrayed
Eye of night, dark sky
You hear the sounds of day
Creeping from below.
Day has arisen.

—*Marcie L. Sturdivant*

Number One

You have never wanted anything from me but love.
Being number one, you deserve that and more.
You always told me you would be here,
When all the others had waved goodbye.
I counted on that!
You are number one alright.
You always gave me enought rope,
To hang myself.
Like a fool, I did
Maybe I did because I knew old number one
Would be there to cut me loose
And set me free.
You deserve my love and more.
You are number one.
I only hope you are still around
When I'm tired of being someone
Else's number two.

—*Wyolene Solomon*

Friends

What does friendship mean?
Being there when you're needed,
listening and understanding.
Giving advice when asked and
keeping quiet when not.
Remaining a constant source of
strength and love.
Knowing what to say and when to
say it.
Sharing, giving, and protecting.
And, most of all, being true to
yourself and your friend.
A friend is forever.

—*Sarah Pruitt*

Always

Above the clap of thunder
Below the sprouting grass
There lies your very image
Upon a crystal glass

—*Shannon Hedglin*

What is Love?

A fragile rose crushed
Beneath the careless
Foot of a running child.

—*Terry Propst*

Intimacy

Tonight your eyes sparkle from afar
Beneath the eloquent flicker of
  candlelights
The reflection of wine from dainty
  crystals,
Arrogantly protrudes an intimate whisper
While the quenching thirst from my moist
  lips,
Has been induced by the reality of your
  true beauty
My will begins to weaken and desires
  intensify,
As music persuades me to romance
I ten pause, as we both savour this
  evening's
Elegantly prepared meal
Then we look, smile, and realize we're in
  love

—Omar Lopez

On-On Just On an On.

Hand and hand they walk
Beside the stream of strife.
Empty shells of silence
Tortured cries engulf them.
Old hurts awaken unanswered sighs of
  hope.
Already gone but not apart.
Hearts broken long ago,
Just seem to go on alone.
Their feet lead them on.
Are they drifting home or beyond.
Hand and hand they walk.
Beside the stream of life.
On and on.
Just on and on.

—Roberta Stevens

Love

Love is something shared
between two people
Love is like a heart in
love for the very first time
Love is like a flower just
blooming in the spring breeze
Love is special like you and me
Love is everything

—Lisa Kralik

Storms

On a torrid afternoon,
Beyond the sun;
Clouds are waiting,
For night to come.
When dusk is here,
And mortals are sleep;
Out of the clouds,
Rain will peep.
Soft drizzle, silent showers,
Then pouring rain;
The delicate newborns,
Of paths in pain.
The animals go home,
To seek cover;
One, two thunderstorms
After another.

—Reliina Faronii

Time

Morning roses,
Birthday kisses,
They all fall in line,
As moments of time.
Like pebbles in the dirt,
Or fish in the sea,
Just segments,
Seconds away.
As an hour glass fades,
We forget who gave us time.
But we should never,
Forget who gave us time,
Because time is so fragile,
And is only here for a second.

—Lori Robbins

My Love for Him

Oh kind and gracious Father,
Bless my feelings I have for him,
Bless the kisses that I wish were his,
Bless those thoughts I hold inside,
God only knows exactly why.
I watch the stars every night,
Hoping for his gentle touch in the
  sunlight.
He fills my days with no sorrow,
And my nights with hope for tomorrow.
Bless the prayer I have for him,
I say every night beside my bed.
Bless this love I have for you,
But sometimes I wonder. . .is it true?

—Robin Boswell

Lord's Prayer

Heavenly Father up above,
Bless the guy I really love.
He's the guy I can't forget,
I loved him since the day we met.
Make him know I'll always care,
For my love to him I'll always share.
Bless the moments when we walked,
Forget the moments when we fought.
His heart is like a ton of gold,
Hard to get and hard to hold.
Don't let our love come to an end,
For broken hearts are hard to mend.
Heavenly Father up above,
Bless the guy I really love.

—Lena Miles

To You—With Love

To the only person who I can talk to about
  my problems,
Secrets, and dreams knowing that he will
  listen,
To the only person who I would give my
  life for,
To the only person who I can trust my life
  with.
To the only person who I love to hug and
  laugh and have a good time with—
And to this person I give my life, my
  heart, my world and hope that this
  person will love me for forever.
And never quit loving me no matter how
  bad I mess up—
And I also hope that this person will trust
  me with his life and all of his dreams!
The only person I give this all is to
  you—Dear God—With all my heart
  and love!

— Valerie Stephens

My Stage

The lights shine down to my eyes,
Blind me with their colorless glare,
The shameless stare of many faceless
  people,
My heart pounds, my eyes water,
  suddenly. . .
Every face becomes the image of interest,
My features fade away, She appears. . .
Now I am a queen, a star, a mother, a
  widow, a wife.
My life is laid out for others to see,
The roars, the cheers, then the lights fade
  into darkness,
I am now myself and no one else,
I now have a past, a present, a future,
Unlike Her, who only lives three hours of
  her life,
For others to see.
I turn to find myself alone on fate's stage,
As I turn to face my audience,
I find that to them, I am Her, not me,
So I speak my final and closing line,
  "Who am I"?

—Tamara R. Parks

Hello

"Nomaste," "guten tag," "buenas dias,"
 "hello!"
Bloody good to see you my dear fellow.
"Howdy," "aloha," "gut morgon," "good
 day,"
You can say hello almost any way.
So many languages under the sun,
There's English, Chinese, and Hungarian.
Latin and Russian, Mexican too,
So many ways I can say "hello" to you.
"Ello—hay" in Pig Latin,
"Bonjour" in French.
In Chinese it's "zao,"
Suh-bye-dee is Lao
In Danish "go morn,"
Italian "pronto."
Indionesian it's "salam,"
In Russian "arro."
But out of 2,803,
"Kalimera" really is Greek to me!

—Michelle L. Sleater

Society

A flower
Blooms and grows,
Shows life and hope.
A new bud sprouts,
More life.
To pick a flower shows love of life
While still showing hate toward it.
To stop a flower from growing, we kill.
Kill to place a flower in our hair.
Society is very selfish sometimes
Toward things which we do not
 understand.
We do not kill to harm others
But for personal gain.
So what do we accomplish
Besides nice hair?

—Sandy Phillips

Love

Love is like a breeze
Blowing in the trees
Love is a flower
Growing prettier every hour
It's still as a pond
Calming as the beach
When two are in love
No flower is prettier
No breeze is cooler
Bo beach is calmer
No pond can be still
Only that special moment
When lips meet lips
And the bride and groom
Say. . ."I do".

—Mandy L. Marziaz

The Life Cube

Small box; red on top
blue on the sides
four blank walls stare
Down at me
On each wall a huge door
does exist
each door of brilliant green
Doors that can't be opened
With knobs out of reach
trapped inside with no way out
the walls get closer
Slowly shutting in
And folding up
until there is no more
small box; red on top

—Mary T. Harte

Rabbit

Frightened little rabbit
Bolts into the bushes,
Afraid of what he might find
Or what may find him.
He darts and dashes, trying to escape
From the predators that follow; those
Who will catch him. He hasn't got much
Time, to determine his strategy,
All he can hope for is luck.
Maybe there will be a ray of sunlight
As he crashes through the brush,
To help him find his way.
But then, it takes a turn for the worse,
As the heat of hungry breath is upon his
Heels. And the poor little rabbit is
 exhausted,
And cannot run anymore.

—Lana Schneider

Alone Again

I sit alone on the couch
Breathing strong feelings that make me
 yell ouch.
No one is ever at home to be with me,
I wish they would come instead of letting
 me be.
I do so many things around the house,
They act as if I did so little,
They probably think of me as a small
 mouse.
They always say they don't have time, or
 sometimes say not now.
I hope someday they will change their
 way,
"Would someone please tell me how?"
So there you have it, the family just isn't
 mine,
But I still don't understand why they
 haven't time.

—Tara Tomalinas

A Little Girl Lives Next Door

A little girl with golden hair, eyes of blue
 lives next door to you
Bright eyes went to the garden to see
 diamonds-morning dew!
She played jump rope, hopscotch, hide
 an'seek, farmer in the dell,
She skipped merrily with buckets of water
 from Grandpa's well
Wishing to be a boy; to climb trees, to see
 the bird's nest
She made peach pies, apple delight; her
 desserts—the best!
She picked Arbutos an big Violets, she
 saw birds on the wing!
'Neath her bedroom window she heard
 the little wren sing!
She found wild strawberries, blueberries;
 gathered nuts 'neath trees
Cooked, sewed, cleaned; thought she knew
 'bout "birds and bees"!
Visited Uncle's farm;—herded cows thru
 meadows dotted with flowers
Thru fern woods, past cool spring where
 butter kept for hours.
Glad she was a girl—she met an engineer
 knew all 'bout birds-bees.
They visited "Minnie ha ha"! The Great
 Lakes-enjoyed the breeze!
Starry eyed she wore a diamond; climbed
 mountains-hiked through trees;
Happily married; they lived carefree;
 kneedeep in clover; daisies
If you meet a white-haired Lady with a
 cane-eyes of blue,
Remember she could be that little
 girl-lives next door to you!

—Mary Lou Darnielle

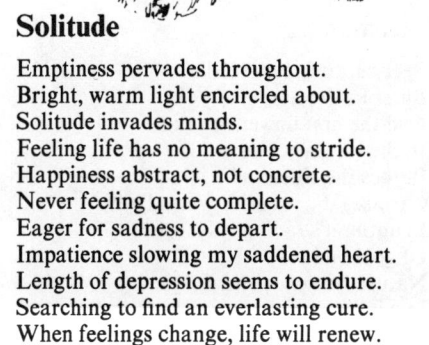

Solitude

Emptiness pervades throughout.
Bright, warm light encircled about.
Solitude invades minds.
Feeling life has no meaning to stride.
Happiness abstract, not concrete.
Never feeling quite complete.
Eager for sadness to depart.
Impatience slowing my saddened heart.
Length of depression seems to endure.
Searching to find an everlasting cure.
When feelings change, life will renew.
Til then my heart will strive to continue.

—Marilen Samson

The Nostalgia Of The Waxed Eye...

My sculpted,
broken soul,
given the color of life,
the power of his hands tell of my
  story...and
i touch the infinite with the grandeur of
  his idea.
not thinking of my original sentence to
  solitude,
and never begging;
i have a singular season, a perpetual
  embrace with
time
no past and no future...

—Vasile Preda

Untitled

Candle
Burning bright
Dripping molten war
On the fingertips of a believer.
A gust of wind blows out the flame,
The wax is cold
And hardened
Again.

—Vivian Krotzer

Seasons

In the spring, tiny seeds
Burst forth anew
And the first flowers awake.
In the summer, the sun
Bathes the trees and
Caresses the sea with warm light.
In autumn's fading colors
Of gold and red,
Nature stretches and sleeps.
In winter's harsh embrace,
Thin icicles silently
Weep single tears.

—Pamela J. Castles

Good Morning

It's snowing,
But,
Then,
it's has been
for three days...
Snow,
soft...
Have you even caught
a snowflake in your mouth?
It's a beautiful here.
Clean, open,
almost untouched...
I miss you!
I Love you
Fond memories
are ever present...

—Noel

The Tree

The tranquil silhouettes of dreary,
  melancholy trees
Seems to be so mysterious and full of
  wonder.
As the fog casts a dreary haze which
  surrounds the vast forest,
The single tree set aside from all of the
  others
Seems so sad and fragile.
Each tall figure having a story to tell
And a song to be sung.
Yet, who really stops to listen?

—Leah R. Weiss II

Constant Lover

Dear Constant Lover bear with me now
  I'm not that good at words
But as you well know no one's perfect so a
  "chance" from you I deserve.
I've tried to show you, in more ways than
  one, how I really feel
About the dream concerning you & I, if
  only it was real.
But when I try to express myself, my
  words get all screwed up
Which reminds me of a game I played
  and "Out 3" I always struck.
Although you never can read my mind,
  my eyes tell it all
But you Constant Lover are never
  straight-up for with me you always
  stall.
I even tell my friends how much of a
  husband you would mean to me
And hoping with all things possible "Your
  Wife" I'll someday be.
So, now that I've taken this chance with
  you, to open up my mind
I think you should do likewise to me and
  stop wasting precious time.
For I believe either sooner or later we two
  can work something out
And help each other overcome the agony
  of being in total doubt.

—Teresa R. Glenn

The Way of Justice

Some people deserve what they get
But do they get what they deserve?
Some people die when they are born
But do they deserve to die so young?
Some people have a perfect life
But do they deserve to have it so nice?
Some suffer when it's not their fault
But don't they deserve a better life?
Some people commit crimes and get away
But do they deserve to escape?
Some people...in life, try their
Hardest and fail
But don't they deserve success?
Some people try their hardest
To love
And don't get loved back
But don't they deserve to receive
What they give?

—Lisa Zeman

Wedding Vows

Drawn to each other by a force beyond
  control,
We close the space between us,
A charge across two poles,
Our touching, a universal truth.
The combination of elements
Separated by circumstance
Without purpose or meaning.
But the fusion cannot be denied
Balance is restored, the chasm closed
The lark sings; pines sigh in relief.
For always have we been together
And always will it be
Not our doing but our destiny.
To cling, to close, to be complete,
We need no vows or promises.
For us there is no other way.

—Marvin Rosen

Learning to Care

They tell her she's so marvelous, so
  wonderful, so great.
But do they really understand or even
  appreciate?
She knows they do not want to know she
  knows they do not care.
But the flame in her keeps on pushing her
  to do the things others would not dare.
She does not know what to say. She does
  not know what to do.
So I guess she'll go through life just
  saying, "Thank you."
She feels so lonely, so useless, but she
  knows God is there.
But to her He does not tell her things she
  would really like to hear,
Like, "Dear, I think you are so beautiful,
  I love you, I care."
Although she fears she cannot feel she
  does deep down inside.

—Marie Jorns

Visions from the Other Side

I call to you
But don't know if you even hear me.
I feel you with me
Sometimes,
But I wonder. . .
Is it my imagination?
Wishful thinking, maybe?
I don't understand.
Why must I love you from so far away?
This distance cannot be measured
Really, logically
It does not exist,
Yet fathomless darkness is between us.
I call to you
From across the bridge.
You are on the other side. . .
Never to return
But soon I will join you.

—*Lois Patterson*

Death

I know that they will always be there,
But I am wrong.
Ignorance is bliss,
Taking away worry and pain.
Then reality comes,
Making us insane.
They'll always be there
Through heart and mind,
But to touch and talk to,
Is love of a different kind.
Who knows there is heaven?
Who proves there is hell?
Ignorance is bliss,
And I guess it's just as well.

—*Namiko Kunimoto*

To Love The Unlovable

I see you
But I can't feel you.
I need you, but I can't have you.
I want you, but I can't touch you. I love
   you.
But I can't love you. I want to hold you
But you're already being held.
I want to kiss you, but you're being kissed.
I want to spend time with you
But you have no time to offer,
I want to walk with you
But you have someone to walk with.
Wanting to hold, kiss, and love you
Is the way I really feel.
To love the unlovable is to
Love what's not mine.
To love the unlovable is the
Type of love I'd like to find!

—*Sonia J. Nina-Gomez*

Love

I thought I was in love once,
But I guess that I really wasn't,
I'd stare at the image of him
That jumped in my eye,
But I could never see the image of me,
Neither did he,
I tried to catch him,
But he kept running,
I tried to fall into his arms,
But he would never extend
His arms to catch me,
That's when I realized
There can never be love
Unless there are two in it.

—*Mary Harrison*

Dreams of Wandering

There are many things
I have never felt,
Like the force of the winds
In the typhoon belt;

Or the heavy rains
Whose torrential flow
Can isolate places
Like Baguio.

I'd like to travel
to that far off place
Where the platypus swims
And the kangaroos race.

And I'd like to see
The flowering hordes
Of Haleakala's
Famed silver swords.

—*Frances E. Sines*

Thinking Back

I always thought I would see you again,
But I guess that I was wrong.
The time we spent together,
Seemed to last so long.
If I were to meet you again,
I wonder what we would say.
Right now, I only wish that you
Were here with me today.
I'll write these lines of feelings,
To try and win your heart.
There's really no distance,
That can keep us apart.
When reading these lines,
Think of me with a smile.
Even though we may not,
See each other for awhile.

—*Pietro A. Costa*

For Keeps

They try to tell me I'm too young for you
   and that we'll never last,
But I have a feeling fate thought different
   when the dice were cast.
I think we were meant to be together to
   share our love through the years,
To share the laughter and happiness along
   with pain and tears.
My heart is full of love for you and I can't
   ask for anything more,
You make me feel peace and happiness
   like I've never felt before.
I can't stand it whenever we're apart, I
   need you by my side.
You're always going to be in my heart,
   about that, I would not lie.
You'll always be mine, mine forever, no
   one can take you away.
And, that you'll always love me, too, is
   something I always pray.
When we met, I never thought that it
   could be like this,
It all started with a word and a smile, and
   then a little kiss.
I'm never going to let you go now that I'm
   in this deep.
Now that we've come this far, I know that
   what we have is for keeps.

—*Samantha Faye Stubblefield*

Him

A simple little "hi" from him,
Sends me whirling into space.
And for endless days afterwards,
I can't forget his face,
I often come so close,
But always blow my chance.
Yet when it's least expected,
I steal a worthless glance
Someday I'll be able
To tell him how I feel.
I hope he doesn't doubt me,
For my feelings are quite real.

—*Nancy Reiman*

Goodbye

You liked me so much,
But I never dared,
'Cause I liked you too,
Yet I was still scared.
The fun time we had
Put hope in my heart,
A kiss on the cheek-
Thought it was a start.
I opened my heart
And began to flirt,
Blindly led on,
I just got hurt.
Time will heal my pain.
Like you thought I never knew—
Your sudden change of attitude,
Meant there was someone new.
I think back to our memories with a sad
   tear in my eye,
That long-lasting kiss, was meant to say
   goodbye.

—*Xenia Woloszczuk*

Going Back

I was once a Christian in church,
But I resorted to the devil to stay.
I left church because I lost my trust in
   God
When He took my best friend away.
Now I am losing more friends,
And my beloved family is breaking.
So I want to go back to church
To stop my restless nerves from shaking.
I don't know if God will let me back in
After devil worship has been in my life.
But I think I will give it a try, just to show
That God had cut my heart out with
   Death's knife.
If it works and I get to go to Heaven,
I will be happier than I am now.
I have faith that He will forgive me,
But I have to escape the devil somehow.

—*Pamela Painter*

My Meadow

I sit and think
But I'm really on the brink,
Of sadness or is it madness,
For I cannot say.
It is such a rotten day,
In the house.
I left the house,
As quiet as a mouse,
For if I stay
I will be in such dismay.
I must escape,
I know the perfect place,
My meadow.
I love to play
THe day away,
And talk with a certain flower,
For I have the power.
To stay here forever in my meadow.

—*Rhiannon L. Evans*

Our Future

The world of tomorrow is growing today
But it isn't with dolls, just guns that we
   play.
Our forefathers spoiled this once good
   land
And all they left us is the destruction they
   planned.
We are doomed to deletion,
Hanging in a time that doesn't seem to
   exist,
Completely inferior, waiting for our name
To be called from the list.
How will we build our future? With guns
   and poisoned minds?
What is our alternative? We didn't choose
   to draw the blinds.
I pledge allegiance to what is left of the
   United States of America,
And to a world that once had meaning,
One nation, pure hatred, for which we
   stand,
Inferior, no liberty or justice for all.

—*Suzanne Blanchard*

Giving Up

I know that you don't understand my
   feelings,
But I see that you're smiling and
I know everything is okay,
Didn't you know all I wanted to do was
   make you happy,
Now that you are smiling I can only pray
That you'll be smiling at me someday,
I was always told never to give up, but it's
   okay,
Giving up is something that I'm getting
   used to,
Didn't you know I only wanted the best
And that was you!

—*Tami Workman*

Those Words

I want to say those words to you,
but I'm so afraid —
I don't think I should ruin
the new trust we have made
I need to feel those words toward you —
they make my life worthwhile.
And if you feel those words for me
I'll go that extra mile
Those words were used so loosely,
like any other ones.
Those words stressed our bonding —
our time, our lives, our fun.
You wonder what those words are —
They're shining through and through.
This way I can explain it:
Those words are "I love you".

—*MaryAnn Paterno*

Best Friends

Friends mean alot
But it's best friends who count
for you are mine
And I am yours
forever we'll be.
You were there for me
I was there for you
And always will be.
Though we're miles apart
Our love is with each other
I can only say, I miss you
And hope you can find the
worth of such simple
Words that sound so small
But are the biggest words
On earth.

—*Phyllis St. Thomas*

Love Me Not

Here I am lonely inside,
but I won't call because of my pride.
I don't know why we can't be together,
but I do know that I'll love you forever.
It seems as though my face is always in
   the dirt.
You may still love me in ways,
Only if I would have known who
your love belonged to,
I wouldn't be here alone realizing how
   much
I love and miss you.
The secrets I have learned have hurt a lot.
Only to learn that you love me not.

—*Lori Dehart*

Life

Life is unfair,
But it can be fun,
When we choose
To be wise,
And don't think
Otherwise.
Striving for success
Is that golden key,
To become what
You were meant to be.
So never give up on life,
And continue to strive!

—*Matilda Naputi*

There are Times

There are times to care and there are
   times to cry,
But just because I'm gone doesn't give you
   a time to cry,
But yet a time to care.
Show your friends you love them,
Don't forget they ever stood,
Show them you can still have a good time.
Please don't cry but please care.
I am gone and crying isn't going to bring
   me back,
So go have a good time.
Love and laugh,
Just remember,
There's a time to cry and
There's a time to care.

—*Tabitha Jean Porfido*

Laure Ellen

An angel came in early fall
but knew she could not stay;
Her time on earth was four short years
and ended one spring day.
Her name was Laure Ellen,
hair of blonde, eyes of blue;
A dimpled chin, her daddy's grin
and strength compared to few.
She loved a sparkling rainbow,
sun drenched flowers, clear blue skies,
Dogs, ducks, fish, birds
and graceful butterflies.
Fly free sweet angel, Laure Ellen,
sing songs 'round every bend;
And find the peace that waits for you
beyond the rainbow's end.

—*Linda Czumak*

Tender Moments

Your touch that says hello
But never goodbye.
The smile that breaks the silence
With a twinkle in your eye.
An embrace in your arms
That is very warm.
Tender moments are as sweet
As a new spring day.
As pleasant as a late summer
Breeze from across a bay.
As beautiful as a rainbow's glow
And soft as a new fallen snow.
Tender moments are ours to share
In times when we want to care.
Love is ours to hold so deep
In our hearts forever to keep.

—*Lawrence Paradis*

Love is Blind

Love is blind, or so they say
But some believe that that's okay.
They get what they can, and then they leave.
While their partner sits alone, alone to grieve.
Some people choose darkness over light
Maybe to believe that their love is right
But don't be blind to anything
Only unhappiness it will bring.
If in love, make it sure
Love can bring hurt, jagged and pure.
Only time can heal a broken heart
It won't be needed if stopped at the start.
You're unique, but there is someone for you
A feeling in your heart will tell you it's true.
Don't look for that feeling, let it arrive,
Only with it will your love survive.

—*Todd Giese*

Untitled

You were once my friend, and, you were once my lover.
But something in our hearts, clouded our feelings over.
You didn't believe in me, when I really needed you to,
And I didn't believe in the love to follow you through.
I thought what we shared would bind us together, but instead,
It seems to have torn us apart forever.
I will always remember me and you, you and me.
We shared a passion, no one else could ever feel,
Understand or see, it was only me and you.
You and me. . .

—*Lorrie Smith*

Imprint a Tone

The green marker offers life
   to those who want not to live.
The red screeches
  as it runs across the page
    while bearing a frightening
     flushed-fever shade.
The orange gleams with vivacity
  it senses hilarity
    in all.
The blue cries out
  with a deep and hollow voice
    to the multitudes
      who merely pass by . . .
Each impression
  a marker makes
   is a basis
    of
   our
  dying world.

—*Amy White*

Friendship of Life

The friendship of life is rare and true
But sometimes confusing to me and you.
Worth more than diamonds, precious and rare-
And as good as a heartfelt prayer.
It's a gift through difficulty and strife
And helps you face the hardships of life.
It gives you comfort in time of grief
And a friendly shoulder to cry on when you want to weep.
It's a bond to share in the goals you've won
And gives us courage to get up and run
For what you believe in and not for what other's do. . .
And makes life worth living for me and you.
Friendship's something that lasts forever.
In which you should endeavor
And something there, not for wealth
So friendship's greatly heartfelt.

—*Nirmala Bahall*

Family

It's time for grocery shopping,
But the sun is shining bright.
Let's walk a while together,
Enjoying warmth and light.
Home needs some attention.
There's dreary rain outside.
Let's splash a couple puddles
And share our sense of pride.
There's a business obligation
While the grass is turning green.
Let's touch the land together
And enjoy a future dream.
A parent has a schedule.
A child has a need.
With massive understanding
They can sow a sharing seed.
These precious little moments
Are the bonds of family life,
Proud stories for the future
Sharing love and warmth and light.

—*Linda Jessie-Jones*

The Night That Shouldn't Have Happened

The night was young so were we.
Your feelings were more than they could ever be.
I wasn't yours, you weren't mine.
I couldn't wait in another line.
We knew it was wrong from the start
But you were the one with a broken heart.
You were taken, that I knew.
The feeling was intense because it was you.
There was a time you felt mistreated,
The time was when you knew you were cheated.
I tried to make you forget that one night
But all the moments weren't quite right.
By making me smile it took away your anger
No longer to you (was I) a stranger.
This horrible night couldn't go on any longer,
It would both make us weak and not any stronger.
For right now this is the end
Since your the boyfriend of my best friend.

—*Sheree Barbee*

The Mist

In the mist I hear no sound
But the wind blowing the trees
Small dark clouds cover the ground
One should take pride in what he sees
The mist covers only a small part of land
It sits silently over the sea
I try to grasp it with my hand
But it only goes through me
How could anyone overlook it
Such beauty in a calm way
This sight I won't forget
Wait for mist night and day

—*Melissa Hawes*

A Patient's Perspective

Sitting in your waiting room, there's not
  too much I'm saying.
But the worst please don't assume; it's
  just-I'm busy praying!
When I'm underneath the gas, euphoria's
  my fate.
Really, it's too much to ask that I
  articulate!
Later, if I'm all ahush, you must think me
  nearly dumb;
But my words resemble mush when my
  mouth is still so numb!
My dentist, ever calm is he; such peace of
  mind he brings
Whistling, oh so cheerily, initialing my
  fillings.
How can he be so mellow? How can I be
  so crass?
To think this charming fellow might be
  nipping at the gas!
The oral surgeon has such flair, an expert
  on tough cases.
So far back he tilts my chair while my
  poor heart just races!
Now I know all things must pass-(if what
  they say be truth),
But, Lordy, do turn up the gas-here comes
  my wisdom tooth!
Insurance hassles now begin; with my
  agent I've a bet:
Will "any" teeth be left within when my
  deductible's been met?
But, if pressed to tell the truth, which pain
  is really worse?
The one that's in my tooth or the one
  that's in my purse?

—Paula Yohman

All In One

Nothing in my world rhymed anymore
But then you came along and brought
  poetry...
You brought inspiration and motivation
Into my pointless and colorless life...
You are a poem; everything about you
Makes sense and fits perfectly together...
All the beginnings and endings are
  smooth;
They connect to form the beautiful
  melody of you...
No other poem or song could be so perfect
No other inspiration so pure and grand...
When God thought of creating you,
He must have been in an artistic
  mood—for you are art...
You are music; every note so perfectly in
  tune
The harmony that forms when we are
  together is breathtaking...
You alone are breathtaking, you alone are
  a sigh...
You brought color back into my life—you
  are color...
You are everything beautiful all in one...

—Sandra Teresa Montes

Unheard Cry

I may be unable to speak
but there's something you should know,
I have lots of time to think
and my ideas I wish to be shown.
At one time I was thought as fun
then suddenly it turned to hate.
You didn't think too much of me
and continued to frequently date.
But soon people saw you differently
as though they were disgusted.
So you shut off all the world
and decided no one was to be trusted.
Now you sit in silence
and I can hear you breathe.
No matter how bad things should get,
Mommy, please don't abort me!

—Malinda Hernandez

City Limits

The city has many limits;
But they cannot stop me.
No matter what they do,
I am going to be what I want to be.
Life may put many obstacles in my path;
And I will just keep pushing them aside;
  to go about my way
Even though the city has many limits;
My dreams are still growing,
And my spirit alive.
Someday I will make my dreams come
  true.
Although I'll have to strive;
I will do whatever it takes,
Because in the end;
I'll have proved to myself and to my peers,
That I could make it on my own.
After it all;
I know I will be able to stand up
To stand up, tall and proud.

—Sonya Miller

Pretty Blue Eyes

I'm in love once again,
But this time it's not pretend.
I love him, he loves me.
Hopefully for all eternity.
We have our ups and downs,
When I'm around him I never frown,
He tries his hardest to understand me,
But there's a part of me no one can see,
He has the prettiest blue eyes,
Which hold no lies.
We love and live as it comes,
Never have to run.
We learn from each other,
Never bothering one another,
We will make it through thick and thin
In the end we will "Win"

—Traci Schuster

The Poor

Poor people have rights.
But those who have things, can't see the
  light.
They need food, clothes and even a home.
But people don't care and they won't
  share.
It wouldn't be fair if we all were out there.
Give to the poor, show them that you
  won't leave them in despair.
They are humans just like us,
So we can't treat them like rust.
Show that you care.

—Robin Elzie

My Broken Heart

My foolish heart has suddenly shattered;
But to you, I guess it doesn't really
  matter.
You've crushed it into many painful
  pieces,
And you're not going to even try and fix
  the creases.
I even thought that you might care,
But you've obviously shown your love
  wasn't to share.
I thought of you as more than a friend,
And now my broken heart will never
  mend.

—Shannon Mooney

Better Days are Coming

Better days are coming everyone
  proclaims.
But when you stop and look at your life, it
  just seems the same.
On a merry—go—round that you can't
  get off,
Going in circles around and around,
Feeling like a puppet on a string being
  pulled up and down.
It's not fair your heart and mind proclaim
  within.
Life has turned the lights off and your
  whole world is dim.
What have I done? Is it bad karma or just
  fate?
Why won't this life give me a break?
I need a vacation, a time of respite,
I want to experience laugter and get a
  taste of the good life.
But I'll be patient and wait till it's my
  turn,
I'll show a smile and share your joy while
  inside I yearn.
I know weeping may endure for a night
  and joy will come in the morning,
So I'll stop my crying and wearisome
  mourning
For I know that I know that better days
  are coming.

—Nicole Lovell

English Roses

I've never touched your beauty
but while those around you fall
one can find you standing proud
way up tall
and the English roses
have dignity and grace
the English roses
like fine silk and knitted lace
so bend but never break
always keep your pride
when others try to make you look small
if you can't stand alone, cling to me
while ladies where their hair up
fancy dresses
with a matching shawl
you stand proud as great Moses
never die, English roses

—Tammy Sue

Untitled

You always say you love me
but you can't seem to understand
I don't want to be your lover
I just want to be your friend
if we could do it all again
this time I'd do it right
where we could spend the days alone
and learn to talk all night
now you're just a stranger
I can't talk and I can't trust
the love that we had built of stone
is turning now to dust
tonight let's take the clocks
and turn them back to yesterday
and teach ourselves to love again
and friendship how to stay.

—Tamra D. Brinkmeier

Forbidden Love

To fall in love with your best friend
By nature's law is forbidden.
And if you do you have committed
A sin that's unforgiven.
For all your life you must be shown,
Forbidden love is best unknown.
And the punishment that you must pay
When your best friend turns away,
Is lasting and will never end
Because your love lost your best friend.

—Tonya Holmes

One Crisp and Shining Star

One crisp and shining star
can purify the heat
that cracks the melon-colored dusk,
that mutes the starling's accented sigh
into a fatiqued retreat.
Feathered clouds seek to close the
     companionship
behind the palm silhouette of a Norway
     pine,
a giant fan the earth idly waves
to cure the kiln-hardened sky.
One crisp and shining star
that cleanses all regrets,
a pinhole to the lighter side of the universe
that pierces the wispy clouds
which neither shield nor weep.
One crisp and shining star
on a canvas by O'Keeffe to heal
like a laser this cacaphonous ruin
and precede the coming of the thief.

—Neal K. Bachman

Life May Be Our Destiny

Life may be our destiny
But with death walks hand—in—hand.
Some bright day young children will see
This God-forsaken land.
Life may be our destiny
But war ruins the dream,
Never again will we have to see
Our country as a team.
Fighting, bleeding, and slowly dying
To win their homes' respect,
The only result of their trying
Is a cause with no effect.
So when our dreams begin to shatter
Into tears upon the ground,
Remember the destiny of climbing the
     ladder
To keep us freedom—bound!

—Michelle Kemper

Brutal Beating

You hear a scream in the middle of the
     night,
But you're hoping it is only a dream.
You get up to find flashing lights
     terrorizing the sky.
Then the tears roll out of your eyes.
That night, a husband spent his time
     beating on his wife.
No matter what happens, the violence
     never ceases and
Tears seem to be performing everywhere.
The night dies and so does someone else,
But you can't help to wonder if that could
     have been you.
You aimlessly wonder and finally fall
     asleep only to
Be awakened by a child's deadly,
     brutalizing scream.

—Yenere Spack

To Robert

I have held many loves
but you are my every one
And if you should go
There'd not be another
For where could I find
Another atuned to my soul
As you
And where would there be
One able to accept the gift of me
As willingly
Only you have taken
The gifts I have offered
And managed somehow
To give them back
More beautiful
Than given

—Lois M. Baker

The Thief

It's breath of life was stolen,
By carelessness and greed,
No sooner was it planted,
Than gone, this loving seed.
The thief had wanted it so desperately,
That he was blinded by it's light,
He saw it's kindness and beauty,
Like an eagle in mid-flight.
Captivity doesn't create love,
It brings resentment, pain and fear,
Not a hug, a kiss, a smile,
But the drying of ones tear.

—Lizzie Henderson

Kids on the Run

Who, what, where, when and why?
Can they not see the sky?
Can I help them in any way-
Some food; maybe a place to stay
I wonder why,
Sometimes they cry.
What makes them leave?
Who can they believe?
Is it cause someone they
Love and trusted passed away
Someday they may find a home.
But for now they will find a street to
     roam.

—Wendy Weaver

Untitled

Flakes of water drops upon each other
Cannot really hold the pen,
write the letters I want across the page
A wide sheet like dancers—
it is not me I know or don't, writing.
There is a bousculade of words in torrents
Cascade of light and words—
So very close, exquisitely tired
wondering impatient.
Memories came yesterday and today—
I was reminded of large paintings
wanted to spread colors,
place my hand, head down on a cushion
of love
and be joyous and free.
Thoughts are like perfumed,
Waves
giving life unhindered
giving love unrestrained
to share and receive
absorbed.

—Monique Adam

The Rose

A singe rose blooming wild and free,
captures my eye as I sit beneath a tree.
Its petals are so delicately spread apart.
And it brings the true meaning of love, to
  my heart.
As I sit beneath this tree of green.
It reminds me of many a roses I've seen.
But this rose doesn't seem the same,
for this one is special, so it is this rose that
I will claim.

—Tanya Wasser

Crowds

Wild rain falling,
Careless wind blowing,
Air pressure tightens
As tension heightens.
Leaves flutter by,
Clouds cover the sky,
Birds fly low,
As winds still blow.
Wild flies my hair,
The dark clouds tear,
Down falls the rain
As people rush in vain.
Bright flashes the lightening
People find frightening,
Loud claps the thunder
As people shudder under.
Quick leaves the storm,
With very little warn,
Sudden leave the clouds
As out come the crowds.

—Sue Butzlaff

A Day Before Always

Silently the dawn
Caressed the face of creation
Speaking its peace with time.
The dew of the morning
Rested upon the bosom of mother
Gently touching.
Romantically, magic
Waved her wand
And all seen went quietly away.
Instant forever,
Cast the light of love,
A day before always.

—Robsol G. Pinkett, Jr.

Sunshine's Mistake

Sunshine's dead
'Cause someone said,
Amy was gonna beat in her head
With a giant piece of lead.
Sunshine called Amy a name,
That was really lame.
So Amy got mad and her the same,
But Sunshine got most of the blame.
Then Sunshine opened her mouth which
  now is badly cut,
But Sunshine knew she should have kept
  her mouth shut.
And then after she got her mouth all cut
up,
She went and kicked herself in the butt.

—Trisha Intintoli

Life

We live in a destructive world
Caused by profit-greedy people.
Those who care more about money
Than the planet they live on.
They've poisoned the water, air, land,
And now our precious minds.
Our lives are being threatened
Each day by one another.
Some of us begin to wonder,
"Will I be here tomorrow?"
While others do not care,
Throwing their lives away.
How long can this go on?
Until there is nothing left?
The future is very uncertain
If something is not done.
Imagine the world years later,
What will be there for the children?

—Tina Zengerle

Summer Sanctuary

The heat rises slowly,
Causing blurry waves
To drift about.
The only sound is that of a
Nearby creek.
The sunlight is
Blocked by a
Curtain of tree branches,
Reaching up to grasp
The bright indigo sky.
The earth is carpeted
By a layer of
Last year's leaves.
In the ravine,
There are no problems,
No concerns-
In my summer sanctuary.

—Lanelle Pronych

shivers in the night

a silent scream sounds through
choked tears rooted in the growing
barrenness that gnaws at the
fibers of my being,
a shell that mirrors
some poor coke addict whose life
is almost spent,
hollow eyes that pierce the darkness
for a glimmer of hope

—Paula A. Buckner

The Hill to Equality

The road to understanding is all up hill,
Climbing,
Climbing,
But will we ever reach true equality?
Or will we forever be forced to live as
  black and white?
Never to live together as one race,
The human race.
Are we really all that different?
Does the color of our skin really matter
  over the content of our hearts,
Our souls,
Our selves?
Do we have to climb this hill forever?
Or will we all, someday, be able to live
  together in peace?

—Sandra Dube'

Spring Path

Our grassy playground
Clutters
With golden dandelion dreams,
Miniature suns
Scattered in a green sky.
Carefully we pluck a path
To the sidewalk—
Turn and eye
Our perfect trail
Then eyes avert
To our sticky hands,
Filled with
Yellow bursts
Of light.

—Robertta—Jeannette Ludwig

The Guilt Of Sin

In the darkness of the night
Comes a still, silent fright
From the wood not creaking in the wind,
And the windows not rattling. It's a sin.
As a footstep appears before you,
No body follows behind.
And later, you hear it coming
Sound travels slower.
Gone away from the house are you?
Moving faster and faster.
In your car, you speed away,
But guilt is close behind.

—Tammy Deemer

Is it Love

The mist in your eyes tells me you're
    confused,
Confused about the feelings you feel for
    me.
You hold me tight, but at the same time
Our hearts aren't touching as they should.
In a helpless voice, you whisper "I Love
    You" over and over,
But I have doubts those words mean
    anything
You lie next to me silent, and in my mind,
I can hear you telling me it's over,
Is it over, or are you're helpless actions
    love?

—Norma Jean Raczkowski

Pale Shadows

Fingers interlocked
Colors embrace
Darkness enfolds
Shadows on a pale face
The difference
An attraction
The sameness
A satisfaction
Why can't others see
The beauty
Revealed to me
The sweetness
Of ebony
Intertwined with ivory...

—Stacey Schlosser

Just the Two of Us

A friend like mine
Comes just one of a kind.
She is honest and fair,
She understands and she cares
About the times that I lied
And came back sheepishly and cried.
Together we laugh,
Together we smile.
Together we walked
Hand in hand for awhile.
We are two friends of one kind.
Yet we both keep in mind
That it takes time to be friends.
That time never ends.
We are friends.

—Stacey Van Wazer

The Pain Inside

Her eyes full of secrets, just staring in a
    gaze
Confusion burning up inside, her mind is
    like a maze.
There is nothing there to figure out, you
    cannot see her through
She blocks you from her mind completely,
    there's nothing you can do.
She lacks the love needed to live a life of
    joyous times,
She doesn't express her true feelings, they
    are just mimes.
She needed someone to give her time, but
    no one ever did,
Now she is lost in her mind, those secrets
    she has hid.

—Sandra Savin

Minority Majority

My color marks me, my skin molds me.
Comedians ape me, but their humor
    escapes me.
Prejudice greets me, and illiteracy cheats
    me.
Your votes could free me, but politicians
    don't see me.
Equality eludes me, oppression includes
    me.
Surely heaven awaits me, since this old
    world hates me.
Poverty haunts me, no employer wants
    me.
Welfare feeds me, where hunger leads
    me.
Who can help me? Look in the mirror and
    see thee.

—Sharon Bailey

A Glimpse Of Hope

Afraid.
Confused.
Misunderstood.
Feeling lost or unloved.
True feelings not expressed.
Just of lonely heart.
A tearful eye.
And a desperate hope for the future.
A desire to be loved.
A passions to be needed;
burning deep within my soul.
It can be revived our, love.
My love for you will never die.
All I need, is a promise.
Just a glimpse of hope;
That I am in your future.
And in the end; for each other,
We will be together.

—Tamera Murray

False Love

An umblemished mind
Conquered by lust
Struck by the hand
Once held with trust.
Worn upon the face
Diminishing pride
Crawling for shelter
It's so hard to hide.
Believing in dreams
Shattered within time
Relentlessly wanting
To curl up and die.
From the book of love
Was ripped a young heart
Silently screaming
Ending at the start.

—Teresa Smigielski

Reflections

Dark midnight sky
contrasting snow,
crystal white.
Tinsel shimmering, sparkling,
shining bright.
Reflections of merging
Pulsating Christmas light.
Music floating, lightly, gently.
Caress the night.
Dazzling snow tinted gold.
Day replaces night.
Christmas love, soft glowing light.
Icicles glistening, gleaming,
clear or frost white.
Christmas past. Memories,
Reflections shining bright.

—*Mary Burnette*

Some Doubt

Some doubt there is a God!
Could I? No!
Whenever I travel, the beauty of what I
　see
Is so evident, it leaves no doubt with me.
"We will place all manner of terrain on
　the face"
"Of the earth to give beauty and variety
　to man."
Stand in awe of mountains as imposing as
　the Alps.
Float in sapphire lakes of cool, clear
　water.
Explore canyons deeper than the Grand.
Play in dunes of rippling, clean sand.
Gaze upon the desert, painted soft and
　calming tones.
Majestic, statued formations, made of
　stone.
Look down upon stalagmite pinnacles of
　salmon colored hues.
And waterfalls each named so well.
Why? No need to tell.
Oh, you who doubt! Just open to the Holy
　Writ,
Then somber be, and ponder.
Behold the expertise that only those
　supreme
Could make this hallowed land with such
　beauty and variety for man.

—*Wilda Haskett*

Courage

Courage is finding solutions to problems
　there are no answers for.
Courage is rising above your disability to
　soar.
Courage is knowing when you make a
　mistake and admitting that wrong.
Courage is forgiving the one you love and
　knowing in his arms is where you
　belong.
Courage is holding onto your dreams with
　all your might,
Yet being able to sacrifice to reach new
　heights.
Courage is believing in yourself enough to
　take a stand,
Yet knowing whatever difficulties one
　goes through,
There are those who need a helping hand.
Courage is the terminal patient who fights
　for their life
On a day to day basis,
With a smile for their loved one, no
　matter what he or she faces.
Courage is the homeless who hunger and
　shiver in the alley ways,
Yet having enough faith to bow their
　heads to pray.
Courage is the teenage mom who gives up
　the child she bears,
For she knew the life the child needed, she
　was not prepared.
Courage is within all of us, look deep
　within your heart,
Then you can begin each day with a brand
　new start.

—*Lucille A. Rinaudo*

Nature and Me

My hair is like long brown grass
Covering the sandy land blowing in the
　wind.
My forehead is like a patch of sand
Lying lonely without an object on it, only
　around it.
My eyebrows are like dead pine needles
　resting on the ground.
My eyes that sink down in the valley are
　like patches of fresh green grass
Which the animals graze on.
The nose on my face is like a cliff that
　drops down
And on each side of it are hills sand with
　freckles
That resemble shrubs waiting peacefully
　to be a meal for a hungry animal.
The lips on my face are like a bed of roses
Lying peacefully under the shade from
　the cliff standing in the sun.
Dunes glazing in the sun, reminds me of
　the chin that sits below my bed of roses.

—*Maggie Callaway*

The Crashing Waves

Out of the darkness of night they come.
Crashing on the sandy beaches.
They crash as if angry,
But at what could it be?
Calmer and calmer they become
As the glistening sun taps on
The shoulder of darkness.

—*Michele Anthony*

Waves

I often think of the sea, its endles waves
Crashing upon the sand. . .and look to it
　for
The answers I seek to find. Each wave is
Like a day of my life, all different,
Yet they are still waves. . .

—*Ralph H. Frazier*

Possessor of Love

Possessor of love,
Crept; through me.
Our God! Our God! Our God and me,
Throughout eternity!

—*Sharon P. Wyatt*

Suicide

Blood trickled down fingertips
crimson drops on dirty white tile
Insects crawling in cracks
faded in his eyes
Rats decayed in the molded tub
winds howled shutters banded
He was isolated in a fetal position
rocking slightly in the dust webbed corner
Soon the boearded up windows
on the half charcoaled house
would not be seen with his tired eyes
With his heavy head at rest
against the chapped sink
he cried for help
chapped lips split
ice-filled motionless veins. . .slowly
He gasped for one more breath
a tear fell
all was lost
the gift of life. . .was gone

—*Tracy Zakhar*

Children of Reality

Tortured children
Crying eyes
Bloody faces
Leave the children, let them grow
Look, their eyes
They're filled with fear
Their eyes mirror your actions
You see your real self in the eyes of the innocent
You see what you have become
And you punish them for your faults
You torture the children, to rid yourself of your pain
The pain of reality
Leave the children, they have done nothing
None of them asked to be born
But you brought them into this world and look what you've done
You've killed them, out of the hatred you have for the children
Hatred because of their innocence
Tortured children, that never wanted to be born

—S. Kulas

Moonlight Mist

A light transcends from heaven to earth.
Crystal shards enter my room
Giving off an incandescent glow.
I awaken from a quiet slumber
And gaze out the window.
The moon is in full bloom.
Ethereal beams cascade silently downward.
The lake reflects the moonlight mist
Into my soul.
Peaceful sleep comes quickly
Promising eternal rest.

—NancyAnn Anderson

Dagger In My Heart

Harsh words are like a dagger,
cutting through my heart.
As you try to explain,
The hatred you felt.
I would never understand
Why you hated me
Because I did nothing
But love you.
And listen to those harsh words
Being thrown in my face
and being drowned by my tears.
You left me in pain with a
Dagger in my heart.

—Rachel Rosamond

Dancer

He lightly floated across the floor,
Dancing in a melody of silence;
Leaping into nothingness with outstretched arms,
Like a swan. . .
Gliding over a lush meadow, and
Crystal streams on gossimer wings.
Pausing only a moment,
He went forth to twirl;
Like a dust devil in a summer breeze,
Displaying wondrous gyrations;
Whirling about.
The drifting sand dunes.
Those graceful movements,
Made time so precious;
Yet he continued to flow forever,
As an everlasting fulfillment;
Adrift. . .
In a tide of dreams.

—Michelle R. Hessell

Puppet Love

Like a puppet on a string
Dancing through a faded dream,
I have lived my life.
Overlooking other's pain and strife,
Retreating to my inner side,
Now I think I will let my fortunes ride
On the flight of a dove,
Or on love.
Even if not sent from above,
And as foul as the marrow of a bone,
It would be better than being alone.

—Robert Neal

Leaf Dancer

One solitary leaf,
Dancing to the silent
Music of the wind.
Like a ballerina
Floating through the air.

—Sharon Waltman

Reminiscence of Autumn (For Trisha)

Leaves of red, yellow, and orange
Dangle from a faltering tree
As Autumn displays its brilliant colors
For all the world to see.
A gentle breeze sweeps through the limbs,
And leaves flutter to the ground.
Softly and relentlessly
They dance without a sound.
The backdrop for this setting
Is a pure sky of crystal blue.
Nothing compares to a cool Autumn day except. . .
A brisk Autumn night before a fire with you.

—T.J. Danchess

Untitled

Black as death,
Dark as night,
Overtakes the firelight.
Creatures whisper,
The moon's a sliver,
It's not the cold that makes me shiver.
Shadows breathing,
Darkness creeping,
Comes for me as I lay sleeping.

—Suzanne Grundtner

Darkness

As my mind wanders I imagine
darkness in the distance light behind me.
I'm heading for the darkness
for that is where I belong.
In the darkness,
I cannot be harmed.
I'll fade into the darkness.
Not living just there, in the darkness. . .

—Marie Bartoni

Life

Life brings to people joy and pleasure.
Day by day brings moments to treasure.
In the morning God opens our eyes.
God makes it possible for people to see
Different colors, shapes, and sizes.
God made so many things in this world to adore.
Like the white sand on the ocean shore.
Life is like a child with a new toy.
It shall bring the child happiness to enjoy.
God created the ocean, lake, and the sea.
Just think if it wasn't for him, where would man be.
We wake to see everything in motion at one man's command.
This man is God and the whole world is in His hand.

—Renita Simmons

Silently

Silently I sit thinking of my future,
Day Dreaming, pondering of what it may bring.
Silently I lay thinking of my past,
Remembering and feeling, each hidden memory.
Silently I ponder my present life,
And realize that time, will always care for itself.

—Melanie Owlett

Happy Easter

As this Easter morning dawns
Dear Friends, I wish for you,
The richest of all blessings
On a day that brings anew.
The knowledge that we live today
Because of one who cried,
Because he gave his life for us
Because for us he died.
And as he rose to heavens high
Free from death and pain,
He set us free and cleansed our souls
That we might live again,
He took our sins, absorbed them all
There upon that cross,
He gave his life that we might live
In freedom through his loss,
So now rejoice, Dear Friends of mine
Sing praises to our king,
Christ has risen from the dead
Let Hallelujahs Ring.

—Lucille West

Death

What is death?
Death is not good nor bad,
Right nor wrong.
To me, death is the leaving of one world,
And the entering of another.
To me, this world is a joyous one,
A world of love and peace,
To me, this world. . .is heaven!

—M. Gendall

Dreams

Dreams of having you
Deep in my heart,
Dreams of us never
Wishing to part.
Do you realize the dreams?
The meaning "forever"?
Do you realize I dream
Of us being together?
Together I mean -
For always, forever.
Being with you,
Stop loving you never.
Our dreams have been shattered
A couple times—maybe more,
But my dreams of us now
Are just like before.
Hold onto your dreams,
Don't let them slip away.
If you believe in your dreams
They'll come true for you someday.

—Mikki Embry

Untitled

Mark of Cain?
What causes him to stand out?
Why is she so special?
Different?
Like the beautiful delicate snowflakes,
We are all distinct.
No two are alike.
Yet, still we search to clone.
Conform.
All must dress the same, act the same,
Think the same?
A heat wave stuck!
All have melted together.
True it is cold and icy by yourself,
But you can soar and float with freedom.
Nothing can trap those points of life.
Never allow yourself to melt,
For then all you can ever be is a tiny drop of water.

—Sarah Chase

The Silver Ghost

The silver ghost
Demands nothing but perfection
Quality is your right
He says, and
All those happy endings
In Hollywood
Made there
The American Way
Enjoy that chaotic peace of mind. . .
What a completely different
Cry for help we hear
From beneath that wild, wild, river
Every man's most
Lovable enemy
Drowns perfectly
Sucked in by the dollar's deadly vivaciousness
Shine me, you silvery devil
Shine me

—Rachel Douglas

The Death of Someone Special

With Death. . .
Departure, loneliness, emptiness, great sadness.
Suffering, grief.
Realization of the brevity of life.
A definite need
To immortalize the departed.
With Death. . .
A sudden urge
To accomplish the extraordinary,
To make up for lost time.
With Death. . .
Finally a trace of optimism.
An understanding
That he enjoyed life,
That he would will us to.
A need to live up
To his expectations.

—Susan Waltman Sanchez

My Playhouse

Blossoming apple trees all around,
Dew on my feet from a brand new day,
The damp and musty smell after a fresh rain,
All this disturbed by honks and horns from a nearby road.
As I sit with my dolls having tea,
A gentle breeze flows in through the window,
The same breeze which rustles the leaves,
The smell of apple blossoms lingers in the air.
A rolling golf course greets me when I look out the window,
I feel grown—up with all my pretend kids,
Suddenly, mom's voice drifts from the kitchen,
To tell of a feast that is awaiting.

—Sara Murray

Enchanted Song

Wishing wells and shooting stars,
diamond rings and flashy cars;
The world's a play, we all have parts,
lovestruck fools with broken hearts.
We often dwell on times gone by,
of private words beneath the sky;
From making friends and making love,
to endless songs from heaven above.
Oh how I wish that I could see
all that there could ever be;
But for now I sit and write so long,
a lovestruck fool's enchanted song.

—Mark Harrison

A Little Too Far

Did you ever move away from home and wish that you had not?
Did you meet so many strange people that you really missed home a lot?
Did you ever cry alone at night when you thought no one could hear?
Did you ever think of fond old friends and wish that one were near?
Did you ever remember a friend when you heard ones favorite song?
Did you ever look at their picture and here their laughter ring out strong?
Never move away from home for you'll find it's very bad.
You'll dream of once happy memories that now all make you sad.
You'll wonder where loved ones are and if they feel alright.
At one point you'll think you've adjusted, then you'll feel uptight.
So here is my conclusion, never wander too far when you roam
For if you do you might find yourself just a little too far from home.

—Sherri Plowman

Mirror, Mirror

Mirror, mirror on the wall
What lies behind your cool reflection?
Could it be another world
A distant place
Of years past?
Through the years you've seen many things
And captured them all in your reflective way.
Untold stories
Of days of glory.
All captured and locked in your gaze.
Locked away safely
Are memories of many.
Who might you capture
From their reflection next?

—Tammy Short

The Iconoclast Dream

Hey there, little girl, with the cold, dark hair
Did you see the show? Think I saw you there
With your maniac ways and melancholy eyes
You were strung out on acid and full of your lies
Did you see your family there, did you see the parade?
Wondering why you killed yourself with a tubular blade
With your blood-striken attitude, occupied scream
They all say you lived the iconoclast dream

—Steven Bloomfield

Antiqued

Youth leaves each day.
Diminished physique.
Tears, just at the thought
Of bygone moments of tenderness and passion.
Flecks of gray, facial decay, bodied disfigurement.
Wiser yet weaker.
It's sad, It's madness
Forever gone, forever lost
This is life's truth,
Life's rule.
Best to use the day given
For finding what's taken for granted.
Seek what the heart yearns for
That the body, mind, and soul be satisfied.

—Lori L. Wilson

Whispers of Supernova KRD-TDA '89-B

Words dilate, distend, and depart;
Displacing forces they once secured,
Expanding in bands of unyielding yellows,
Orphaning oranges. The adverb actions
Of rumaging reds replying steal censored crimsons
Across the wandering view midnight confidences
Sold of beauty, and the gravity is lured
Away from feeling. At the heart of the core
Growing heavy, dense as iron, neutrinos echo
The pulse of atoms compressing
Beneath the weight of no remorse. Exploding
Through the surface, despair, in whispers
Of drying blood stain, with no remorse
The black, drop, of space. Whispering
To five billion surviving stars, no remorse,
Across a wondering, deaf, universe.

—Thomas D'Antonio

From an Army Bus Window

I saw a score of birds,
diving against dusk. . .
or so the size seemed.
And as their wings winked to me
Rapidly,
They flew away with life
Oh!
unlike us. . . .

—Tina Thurmond

First Date

My first date I musn't be late.
Do my hair, find shoes to wear.
Try on a dress, Oh what a mess!
Find stockings to wear, but now they tear.
Put on earrings, then the doorbell rings,
When I run downstairs he's not even there.
Half past nine, oh this is just fine.
Our date was eight and he is late.
The doorbell rings he has on blue jeans.
Our reservations were at eight but now we're late.
The man at the counter says now you must wait.
Then he bugged me by saying
"Do you see how long it takes?"
So I tell you never go on your first date
Especially if they're at eight!

—Tatanisha Johnson

Dreams

Can anyone define the meaning of a dream?
Do people really know what they mean?
Everyone has dreams because its a part of life,
But if some dreams don't come true,
life may be ended with a knife,
In society today, people need dreams to survive!
Dreams can help people thrive, or cause them to conive,
I don't really care just as long as they're alive,
Being alive is what a dream means to me,
I thank God that I'm able to speak, hear, and see,
I wish people would consider being alive as one of
their ultimate goals,
May it be eternal in our everlasting souls.

—Patricia Peden

Do You Know Why?

Do you know why the whales are dying?
Do you know why the eagles are crying?
The last of the rhinos sits in his bed,
While the deers await their fate with dread.
The innocent panda, bamboo he holds,
And the elephant's tusks are being sold.
The bottlenosed dolphin swims with hope in the sea,
The white tiger knows that he will soon never be.
So I ask you, why won't they be there when you call?
For you who do nothing has no answer at all.

—Nina Raba

Autumn's Eve

In the light of the moon he cried out his
    ever-lasting love.
"Do you love me?," The voice echoed in
    the cool of the night.
"Fair maiden, in all your beauty I cry out,
    do you love me?"
"Do you not know I live for your touch."
    The moon lit up the
Sky in hopes to see the porcelain features
    of the maiden fair.
"Now my beauty before me, I implore
    you, do you not love me?"
And the night air lingered to hear the
    reply.
And before her he cries, "From you no
    love can I deny."
You are my true love, and in the night you
    do glow.
I refuse you nothing, for the love of you is
    all I know.
I give to you all the love I can endure in
    my heart.
If for me there is no love, this world I shall
    depart.
And in the calm of this cool autumn's eve,
You deny your love, then I shall leave.
With the dignity that I did search to find,
The love of a fair maiden who is one of a
    kind.
And in the search for the only life I knew,
I give my mortality to this sword before
    you. . .

—*Robin Jensen*

Friendship

Friendship
Doesn't care about
Popularity or looks.
It's like a book
That never
Runs out of
Pages.

—*Mara Burginger*

The Suicide

Your love drowns me in its sweetness
Don't dare rescue me
But let me drown
For even if I die today
I'll die securely
Knowing that no torture in Hell
Can ever compare with the pain
Of losing you
And that the very fruits of Heaven
Have no comparison
To our first delicious kiss

—*Susan Brook*

Hope

Hope for the future,
Don't dwell in the past.
Live in the present
And make today last!
Pray for tomorrow
Cause yesterday's gone.
Just hope for the future
Because your life must go on!

—*Nancy Brazeal*

Don't Look Back at Me

Don't look back at me if you're leaving.
Don't look back at me if you go.
Don't say you love me if you don't.
Don't say you're leaving if you're not.
Don't look back at me if you're leaving.
Don't look back at me if you go,
'Cause I won't be watching you leave.

—*Lisa Weaver*

Autumn Blessings

Like bright laughter in the sun,
Down the leaves come one by one;
From the maple tree they fall;
The frosty wind kissed them all.
Elms in yellows, oaks in brown,
See the leaves come tumbling down;
Flaming sumace, goldenrod,
Make the heart feel close to God.
Oh, world of crimson, golden hue,
Nothing can compare to you.
Most lovely time of the year
Autumn comes to bless us here.
This blessed gift he taught 'em,
I'm sure the sent them, Autumn.
Tomorrow will be winter,
And God will still be center.

—*Melinda Y. Wallace*

Lonesome for You

Drifting, drifting, out on the lonely sea,
Drifting, drifting, wishing you were with
    me.
Floating, floating, farther away from
    shore,
Floating, floating, wanting you more and
    more.
Drowning, drowning, such an awful
    thought,
Drowning, drowning, hoping I will not.
For I want to live so that I can be,
Back at home with your arms around me.

—*Melanie Rinne*

Election Money

It's just no fun
During any election
Especially those Presidencies
Cause having a lot of money
Is like having a lot of honey
For the candidates are around me like
    bees.
But for only this occasion
And a little personal persuastion,
Will I rid the candidates of their fears.
Oh, I'll just give them a little dough
And they'll put on a little show,
Then I'll sigh, "Just four more years."

—*Nighthawk*

What Was Vietnam

Vietnam was young and old men
Dying and fighting, for what?
Our country.
Our country spit on the soldiers
And veterans after the war was over.
America was their home.
America sent them to Vietnam.
And what did they do?
The soldiers gave us freedom,
Others died to protect us.
What did we do?
Spit on them and look down on them.
What was Vietnam really?
Tell me.

—*Shana Bockelman*

Dedicated to Larry

I love the way you tell me you love me,
Each and every day
And you know I would not want it
Any other way
I love your shining eyes
And your sweet adorable smile,
I love the way you hold me
And you know I love your style.
I hope you never think my love
Is anything but true,
And I hope you never doubt me
When I say that I love you.

—*Laurie Laube*

My Guy (Dedicated to Larry)

I love the way you tell me you love me
Each and everyday,
And you know I would not want it
Any other way.
I love your shining eyes
And your sweet adorable smile,
I love the way you hold me
And you know I love your style.
I hope you'll never think
My love is anything but true,
And I hope you never doubt me
When I say that I love you.

—Laurie Laube

My Best Friend

You are constantly remembered
Each minute of the day.
You make me laugh
When I want to cry.
You are honest with me,
You never lie.
You make my problems
Seem so dear.
You make my fears disappear.
You understand me and you care.
I hope our friendship will never end
Because you, Stephanie Grant, will
 always be my
Best friend!

—Veronica Rocha

Interlocking

The world is made of many facets
Each person part of a city
Each city part of a state
Each state part of a country
Each country part of a global expanse
So too am I, a puzzle within myself
Strengths, weaknesses, ups and downs,
Trusting, trustless, sensitive, loving and
 kind,
Awareness, confusion, body, soul and
 mind,
Individual and global
Pieces interlocking in time

—Rachel R. Dubois

Elegy For My Gramp

Pockets full of candy.
Eager Grandkids faces.
Stories of the past.
Gramp full of energy doing little jigs.
"Give Gramp a hug".
Eager Grandkids faces.
Bouncing us on his knee.
Grandkids running to meet Gramp down
 the road.
Heaven has him now.
Pockets full of candy.
He's doing his little jig.
Waiting on his Grandkids to bounce on
 his knee.

—Stephanie Cook

Early October Morn

Cool breeze blows in the open door
Early October morning
As the kittens run in and out
Chasing each other
Life for them seems to be simple
As this complicated world turns
A lesson for humanity
Doubtful too many see it
Seems fewer even care
Cool breeze blows gently across my face
As I sit in the open door
Taking a look at early morning nature
Wishing others would too
And not let the world around them
Complicate natural feelings
But money matters more
It's a shame it's that way
Cool breeze blows in the open door
Early October morning
When thoughts turn to a cruel world
Then they are ignored

—Pat Willis

True Friendship

Come to my house and rest awhile,
Eat at my table, let me know how you are.
Sleep in my bed for as long as you want,
Don't give me your money,
Your friendship is enough.
Give me your love, give me your care,
Share your dreams, your goals,
Don't think for one minute
That I am not here for you.
Take my blankets, take my food,
Take all my prayers,
Take it all with you.
Make yourself at home,
All of mine, it is also yours,
Stay for as long as you want,
I don't care, as long as you are
At peace and comfortable.

—Marcie Warner

The Box

There is complete
emptiness,
hollowness,
and loneliness.
in the box that I sleep
in and when I wake
up I never know
where I am.

—Shannon Haidsiak

The Lone Rose of Spring

It is the place I make for myself
Where the rose never ceases to unfold
And the wind never ceases to blow the
 petals.
I am at home in this garden...with its
 extraordinary brightness.
Its many whispers saying, "turn up your
 face to dew kissed morn"
"Make yourself a rainbow." For your
 span on earth is short.
The future has not happened and the past
 folds away.
The sun throws down its gold and the
 green of spring bursts forth.
Diminutive unparalleled on earth as I am;
 I have no wings to fly.
Only thorns upon my stem, I cannot hide
 myself from visitors of night.
Cold of winter comes and the sweep of
 snow upon my fading throngs,
And the agony of fading into forever...
For non remembers my beauty, save
 Heaven herself.
And maybe perchance to dream and
 bloom again another morn another
Spring.

—Lee Fissori Wright

Untitled

Take from me my frown
Enchant me with your smile
Enter my shades of darkness
Color me with brightness
Stop my shivering with cold
Share with me your warmth
Eluding my world of sadness
You've brought me always gladness
Within my dreams of illusions
Come, be my reality.
Hallow, with the feeling of emptiness
Fulfillment from you I receive
Taken from me my shyness
Beside you I'm no longer withdrawn
Tears falling from crying
Instead with you, there's laughter
Weary and feeling down
By the touch of strength you lift me
When obstacles are there to distract
To clear my path, you're there
So with many emotions admidst each day
Together with reason
You guide my way.

—Liz Baker

Reaching for Your Dreams

I have dreams that I long to see become
   reality in my lifetime and have
   long-term effect beyond my passing.
Encouraging others through my successes,
   yes, but also through my failures, for
   success finally comes through our
   failures and their lessons.
I want to touch the soul, the very core of
   their being.
The dreams within my spirit, although not
   revealed in their completion, are alive
   and strong.
Pressure builds a yearning to do more, see
   more, to live my life as I choose.
In my quest for my identity, I hope to
   share myself with my fellow man and
   learn from them.
I hope that the dreams I have are not too
   lofty for others to hear with open hearts
   and minds.
I hope that the angry and hurtful words
   can be laid to rest and relationships can
   return to the way they once were, the
   way they were meant to be.
If my hopes are not shared, then the
   future is dimmed but not darkened.

—*Tim Touchton*

Untitled

Slowly the tears fall from my eyes,
Erasing all the deceitful lies.
Always thinking "I can believe!"
I never thought that you'd deceive.
You brought such joy to my life,
After all that struggle and strife.
I loved you and thought you loved me too,
But a liar's words are never true.

—*Veronica Lee Mitchell*

The Story of Jim

Jim loved all little girls
Especially ones with lots of curls.
Jim was such a sweet little boy
But thought a girl was just a toy.
There was a girl with bright red hair
Who thought that just wasn't fair.
So she thought up a plan
And told girls across the land.
When Jim you meet
You must walk on his feet.
So when your boyfriend starts to think big
Remind him politely of Jim, the 20 inch
   footed
chauvanist pig.

—*Tiffanie Nieukirk*

Rose

Aromatic fragrance unsurpassed
Especially teamed with fresh mown grass
A bee's delight to say the least
On birthdays, anniversaries, grads
Just a little token of esteem from Dad.
By the dozen or singly, it's always a treat
To give or get a rose.
Throw all cost to the wind
When you receive the whim to send a
   rose.
So many varieties from which to choose
It does one' heart good to muse
All in selecting just the right rose
Petal soft and infant pure
A dew drop just adds more enjoyment
Of a rose.

—*Mattie Dobey*

Why?

Why does love always seem to hurt,
especially when your treated like dirt.
When you do everything you can,
just to try to please your man.
Why does everything turn out the wrong
   way,
and leaves you with nothing that you can
   say.
All you have left me with is pain and
   sorrow,
but still I'll love you even more tomorrow.
Why are my feelings so strong for you,
when I know you don't feel the way I do.
Why can't you see how much pain you've
   caused,
it seems when you left me my whole world
   had paused.
Why does it seem my lifes at a stand still,
Oh I know the answer, I loved you then
   and always will.

—*Nina Velez*

Migratory Soul

I saw a flight of geese
Etched against a drear November sky.
Their wild raucous cries
Caught ear and eye and heart.
I'm flying, too,
High and hard,
Beating against the wind,
Seeking the warmth.
Do you hear the wild cries of my heart?

—*Norma Lemley*

Windblown Heart

Before the scent of the romantic rose
Even hits my nose,
I feel blue
Because I'm searching for you.
It's the waiting that's the hardest part.
Why couldn't our love have lasted
Like the blue in your eyes that never lie?
They were so quiet, so shy.
No one guessed the fire they had.
But they will always burn in my memory
   and my heart.
But as the wind blows through the open
   window,
I think of you, and all we've ever done
   comes
Crashing upon my memory.
I wish you hadn't gone.

—*Marti Green*

Impression

To me your mem'ry will ne'er grow old,
Even if I live many long years more.
And, too, my love for you will ne'er grow
   cold,
But I will live again those mem'ries o'er.
For even if I know your faults so well
That I can enumerate them to you,
Nevertheless you are my true ideal,
And one I never will change for a new.
Doubtless you no longer remember me,
Because you are not meant for just one
   love,
Forever asking only to be free;
Dwelling in dream castles which are
   above
The heights attained by ordinary man,
Ever soaring just as high as you can.

—*Reva M. Scott*

Love Never Dies

The love we shared will never die.
Even though things will just be memories
   for me.
For now they've put him in a long black
   limosine.
He told me he loved me and would never
   leave.
But they took him away in that long black
   limosine.

—*Vicky Lynn Rose*

Wrong Kind of Love

My love for you cannot be told: for it is wrong.
Even though you have confessed your love to me, I cannot tell mine.
Your eyes mesmerize me.
Your warm hands, softly touch me.
You do not know of my love; as of now, no one knows.
Is it love?
Is it love that makes my skin burn underneath your touch?
Or is it the wrong kind of love?
I wish upon the stars but they cannot help.
I talk to the moon asking for advice, but it doesn't hear.
Every night I lie awake, thinking of you.
Every song I hear reminds me of you.
Am I to confess my love?
Will your love last forever?
Or is it the wrong kind of love?

—*Tessie Falconer*

Our Journey

We are moving forward along a special path
Even when we stumble or laugh in the bath
Each second brings us closer to our true selves
Even for those in their elevens or twelves
A life full of poor eating habits
Propels us forward like eager rabbits
To change and grow and be more pure
To look within and about for a natural cure
Everything we do both right and wrong
Is just as special as a beautiful song
From lifetime to lifetime our souls do pass
Even for those who won't mow the grass
The bee is more than a thing that stings
And a plane is more than a couple of wings
It is all very special we all should know
How God helps us learn and grow.

—*Ralph Weinstein*

Days Of Reality

I sigh with the knowledge of changes
Ever occuring in a world of uncertainties
Reflecting times of past and future dreams.
I cry for the loss of all hope
Buried beneath the fear of reality
Destroying life as it should become.
I cringe from a bitter and cold heart
Frozen by ignorance to learn and love
Feeling the loneliness of one.
I sink into a deep and restless sleep
Praying that righteousness will rein
Awakening soon to the light of a new day.

—*Michele Lee Adelman*

Tomorrows Memories

Have you ever tried to capture
every moment in your mind?
Only to face the reality;
some things must be left behind.
The little things that mean alot
are easily forgotten, lost in all the rest
Life's only highlight is our memories
of a few shining moments, at best.
But as you walk the road of life
Don't walk in gloom and sorrow
because the life you live today
is but a memory tommorow.

—*Melissa Simmerly*

Time

Every second that ticks by,
Every moment that has passed,
Will no longer be with you,
Will no longer last.
But you can remember all the goodness and the kind,
That is very deep inside you in your heart and in your mind.

—*Tara McBride*

Star-Crossed Love

Looking out my window,
Every starry night,
I watched a bright star
Hang outside in the darkness.
While it twinkled and glimmered,
It would sing me a sweet lullaby
Filling my heart and night
With silver-woven dreams.
One night, I reached for
That star, and reaching back,
It gently kissed me on my forehead.
It's fairy dust beam covered my face,
Creating magic.
I felt its brilliance cradle me
With its loving touch caressing and
Warming my soul.

—*La Tonya Henry*

Mourning Tide

I see the waves of life lashing against the beach of time.
Every time a wave hits, someone or something dies on this earth.
In the Spring I see the salmon swimming upstream only to reproduce and meet their death.
Antelope die to feed hungry lions. Fish, birds, and other animals die to meet human's needs.
Everything dies so another can live. But why humans? Nothing uses us for food.
Do we die so another can live, or do we die so another can mourn?

—*Sarah B. Finn*

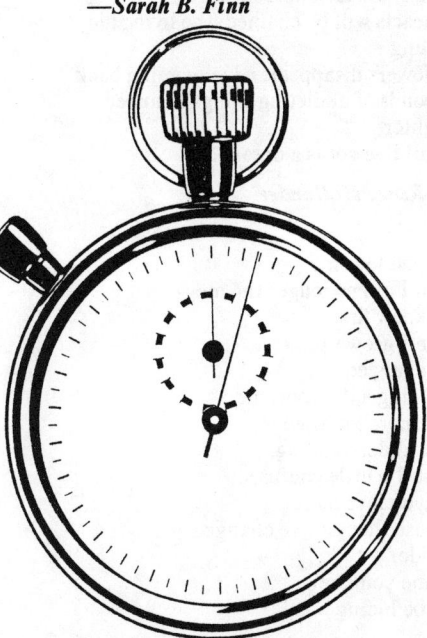

Unproclaimed Killer

They kill, they hurt many, and get off easy,
Every type of race all are part of the crime,
Under a haze of pretenses it starts,
The first scent fermented or demented,
The haze deepens, the scent is stronger and the mind is clouded.
They kill, they hurt and get off easy,
Mindless fools stumbling in their worlds of drunkeness.
They falter but still reach the weapon,
In the hands of the killer now it is more dangerous than a gun,
It moves, the killer unknowing is a stalker looking for a victim.
They kill, they hurt many and get off easy,
Seconds, minutes, hours all can pass but in a blink,
The victim is found, hot metal, cold of life,
The unproclaimed killer has struck and now waits,
Waits for the call to the soft lap of Mother Justice and a slap on the wrist!

—*Nancy Peterson*

My Dream

If one day somehow,
everyone in their own way could change
    that person
what would the world be,
and how would it manage now?
Could we set all the hearts free?
the dead live a full life
the flowers come back in the spring
the bonds of tangible things broken
and all I've got is a dream.
Yesterday I wanted to help
but whose gonna help me,
If I'm helping you?
And this, the card we have been dealt?
One day we look up and see
the hearts will be chained, the living die
    young
the flowers disappear, never coming back
the bonds of addicting things wrapped
    tighter
and all I've got is a dream?

—Renee Hollander

Me

Will you love me
When I am no longer the me
You knew first.
When I grow up,
And change,
Becoming a different me
With more knowledge,
More understanding,
But still a little confused,
Will you love me.
Because though I've changed
Outside,
The me you knew
Will be hiding
Inside.

—Lisa Bailey

For a Friend

Through thick and through thin, good
    times and bad
Experiences everyone I'm sure we've all
    had
And through it all, could we survive
Without a good friend to stand by our
    side.
We've helped each other through our ups
    and downs
Because our friendship knows no bounds
We talk and we talk of our lives to come
We keep it between us because we are
    one.
We've loved and we've lost, that's
    something we shared
Because of true friendship, nothing is
    spared
And as we grow old we'll take different
    paths
But in the end, we'll share all the laughs.
The sun set slowly and we've come to an
    end
I just want to thank you for being my
    friend.

—Louie Flores

Teardrops

A teardrop is an emotion
Expressed in many ways,
Either happy or sad
Many words it can say.
It can say I miss you
When you're not here,
This can't be said easier
Than in a tear.
It can also say you're happy
When someone is around,
It may be hard to hear
Tears don't make a sound.
But the tears that mean the most
Are the ones that say,
"I love you and I need you,"
"Forever and today."

—Nadine Enright

Leaving Me

A few weeks is all we have left,
We'll try to make them the best,
A few loving moments is all we share,
We both know we'll always be there,
Caring too much to let go,
We love each other that's all we know,
In a few weeks you will leave,
The pain in my heart I cannot believe,
I promised I'd be here waiting for you,
I meant that, it's true,
I will be waiting here forever,
For worse or even better,
Even though we'll be apart,
You will always remain in my heart,
Even though you're leaving me,
My love for you shall remain true as can
    be.

—Susan Angermeyer

I Tried

When life gets tough, they told me
"Face it with a grin, just be happy!"
So I tried and I tried and I tried and I
    tried
I smiled when I'd rather have cried
And this, my friend, is what happened you
    see.
A car came by, the driver stopped and
    looked at me
I waved, said "hello", and gave a big grin
All he did was sigh, shake his head, and
    look again
Then he yelled, "Hey you! Come here!
    Get in!"
"We're taking you to the loony bin!"
So this is where I am today
Moral of the story? I don't think there's a
    way
To make it through life without a tear
For if you're always happy, and you make
    it appear
As if you have no problems, all is good
    cheer -
Then watch it fellow, you'll end up in
    here!

—Lisa K. Huddleston

My Protector

Alone in a crowd
Faces that seem unfamiliar rush at me
I am being called
I turn away
The sound is coming from every direction
It's growing louder and louder
I start to run
Behind me I hear footsteps
Now they are in front of me
My heart is pounding
I cry out
Someone embraces me
A tear drips down my cheek
I am crying
I peer through dampened eyelashes
To identify my comforter
Mom

—Rachel Reimer

World War III

I stand alone
Facing what is left of world
I have seen devestation and destruction
And the rebirth of nothingness,
No longer can I take this silence,
This utter isolation.
Humanity has been destroyed
By the force of its own hate,
And as the last survivor
Of a forgotten world
Raises the gun to her head,
I whisper and unanswered prayer
And pull the trigger.

—Pandy A. Jansen

Wings of a Dove

On a cold, fall day when the bright
    camoflauged leaves
Fall like snow and the wind is stinging
    your face
Like a hornet after honey.
Yet in this lonely cold place you feel
    comfortable
Thinking about the good times when it's
    been warm
And you've felt like a dove gliding
    carefree through the air
When you feel so happy no one could
    bother you,
Yet it just comes upon you as if you have
    no wings.
You just seem to fall to the ground and
    think bad things
Of how you can go do evil, and feel better
But yet the wise discover the only way you
    can feel
Like a carefree bird in the wind is to pay
    no mind to the one
Who tempts and tries to take your wings
    away!
Just do good against evil and good shall
    win.

—Lisa Layfield

Autumn

Ageless leaves breaking away—
Falling motionless.
I stumble through them—
Not noticing their cries or
Feeling their pain.
The sky overhead is brisk—
Unfriendly.
I hurry home to escape the chill—
While glorious colors are silent
In the street.
Not alive anymore,
Just blowing.

—*Sarah Jehle*

Deceased Desire

Blood and venom set me free, no angel of
    mercy could rescue me.
Far beyond the walls of glee, for death I
    summon as my only plea.
Haunting my escapes through desperate
    dream,
As exquisitely angelic it may ironically
    seem,
Truly it is a vicious gleam
For no one can hear my silent scream.
Toiled forever now, lost in a trance,
    darkness and gloom my partners in
    dance.
My freedom deastroyed, offering no last
    chance as my Prince of Dusk fires a
    glance.
He tells me He loves me as He locks me
    tight
Caressing me, embracing me to His
    delight.
Not a lover is He, just an angel of fright
I try to break free with all my might.
Do not ever fall in love, it deviously kills
In peace I shall lie, forever still.
Listen to my words, a boding shrill
As armourous as you are, avoid love's chill.
Farewell forever, my Lord is my only love.

—*Rosmarie Bilicic*

My Best Friend

She has moved,
Far, far away,
And I won't see her,
Everyday.
I'd like her to know,
That even though,
She's moved away,
I'll be thinking of her,
Everyday.
I think of her,
As my best friend,
And our friendship,
Will never end.

—*Nicole Mata*

The Unicorn

White as the cloud's with a colored head
Fast as the wind but gentle as a lamb
He walks through the forest looking for
    a quiet friend to talk to.
I spot him drinking from a sparkling blue
    pool
And I sit down to wait for him on the cool
    green grass.
He looks up and runs to me
He whispers softly as I pet his smooth
    white mane.
Then a light shines from above,
And he is gone.
He does not return as the years go by
But I never will forget him.
For the last time that I walked in the
    forest
I found his golden horn.
I knew it was from him
For on it was a picture of him and me
Sitting by the sparkling blue pool.

—*Michelle Northrup*

Come Back, I Doubt It

The last couple of years with you
Were the best years of my life.
Anything I'd do as your friend
I'd do it and try.
To be there you were there
And still is today.
But the heart of me the part of me
Misses you in everyway.
I thought I saw you standing
You were an image of white
I came close to touch you
You disappeared cause I was right.
I'm still waiting for you to return
But that day will come not ever
I'll remember you and won't forget you
Will you come back to me?
No, no, never

—*Yolanda Fullard*

Sacrifice

One night I knelt in solemn prayer
Father what have you done for me
Follow me He said go to the stair
At the top only three doors did I see.
I have blessed all because I'm the Creator
But of these blessings three are the key
Life Death & Sacrifice-choose one door
And see My child what I've done for thee.
Without hesitation I chose door number
    three
Afterall to man life and death seem no
    mystery
Wise choice my child for you soon shall
    see
Why life was given especially to thee.
On a cross hung the Son ready to die
As His scarlet blood streamed down His
    cheek
With His last breath He looked in mine
    eye
My child what have you done for Me.

—*Sonja M. Drake*

Lonely Calls

Desolate cries in the cold, dark night
Fear of life and death
In Flander's Fields, beneath rusted bombs
100,000 Canadians lay silenced forever.
A game of chance, despair and tears
Nowhere to hide or run
And yet far away, in a poppy bed
An innocent scarlet bloom.
The setting of sun, the moon so bright
The twinkling stars; they shine at night
The village so peaceful and friendly
Is now a scene of devastation and
    destruction.
Speak now, or forever hold your peace
Before war begins again, to take its toll
Their gift of freedom is set aside forever
As lives resemble a tattered rag doll.
Yet a time much later, memories return
To haunt us of the courageous peoples
We can now worship without fear, and set
    aside
A moment of silence as we commemorate
    you all this day.

—*Petra Ohnoutka*

A Summer Day

Listen the the whispering wind
Feel it against your skin
Hear the voices of the birds
Singing, full of cheer,
With the sky so clear
Children laughing so gay
On this summer day!

—*Mary Wilson*

Walking at the Beach

I see the shells, here are the waters
Feel the breeze blowing through my hair
The sand at my feet going through my
    toes
While walking at the beach
I see little children building sand castles
The birds above flying in the air
I wonder why they dare to fly in the air

—*Tiffany Johnson*

Hands

See the pleading eyes
Feel the reaching hands
Hear the lonely cries
Reaching across the lands.
They are very real
Just like you and me
Pain we feel they also feel
How long before we see?
Reaching across the lands
To answer pleading eyes
Taking hold of reaching hands
And comforting lonely cries.
Only then we understand
The fullness of Jesus' love
As we grasp reaching hands
Pointing to God above.

—Sarah Bridle

You're My Guy

No ther guy could make me
Feel the, way I do, with you.
When we're together, you never
Make me feel blue.
The times I spend with you,
Are my dreams come true.
If miracles do happen,
Then you would always be mine.
I have feeling inside,
They're so strong I can't hide.
You're tender face is like
Paradise to my eyes.
My feelings for you are all
Truth, no lies
I LOVE YOU!

—Libby Valentine Ortega

Untitled

There is nothing worse than being sad,
Feeling all alone with no hand to hold.
It's hard to be happy instead of mad,
When your deepest secrets have all been
    told.
When you feel you've fallen from cloud
    nine
And the strength to climb you cannot find.
Then you can't find someone to drop some
    line.
It is impossible to be ever so kind.
You can't find anyone who really cares for
    you.
All you want to do is have a good cry.
It's hard to say why you are so blue,
Your troubles are hard to identify.
When your sadness eventually departs,
Don't forget we love you deep in our
    hearts.

—Marla J. Boomershine

Peace

The young man came home, so troubled
    by war,
Fighting in Vietnam had left a permanent
    scar,
He couldn't recover, death haunted his
    nights and days,
He couldn't readjust to peace and quiet
    peaceful ways.
The nights were the worst, filled with
    awful dreams,
He could still hear the noise and the
    woundeds' screams,
Drinking dulled the pain, it helped him to
    sleep,
But the memories stayed alive, these he
    would keep.
He couldn't fit in, not in this peaceful
    world,
He even tried marriage to a wonderful
    girl,
She tried to understand, she loved him so
    much,
But he started to reject, even her tender
    touch.
She left one day and took away their tiny
    child,
That was the last straw, he went crazy
    wild,
He loaded a gun and shot himself in the
    head,
Vietnam was finally over, the young man
    was dead.

—Mary A. Mullens

Dreams

Oh secret depart but do not leave me void
Fill me with yearning for what is truth.
Cause the tide to cycle on the land
The vibration that my hearing knows.
Oh sad the tale comes from love and
    memory
Show us all the light and color for each
    day,
And yet the glimmer keeps the edge of
    night away.
While we slip our bands and fly in dream
Do not come to us or take us to true light.
We cannot see for it is but a glass
And we the image bear 'til in the
    morning,
Shatters, breaks at dawn and real will be
    replaced.

—Ruby Anne Lewis

Anticipation

The warm sun hits me,
Fills my body through and through
With the anticipation of summer
Looking forward to what could be the best
    one yet.
The waves gently caress the sandy shore
Pure heat covers my body
I brush my hand across the burning sand
Nothing else could possibly make me feel
    this way
I am totally relaxed
I have only one care in the world
The sun will soon be setting.
But I know,
No matter what happens
I can count on the sun
To rise again,
And lure me to the beach once more.

—Stacey Hallbeck

dusty sunlight
filters full from
the window
landing brightly
on wooden floors
simple serenity
a cat on the
wooden window sill
lying lazily in the
dusty sunlight

—Patrick Clare

Yellow Canary

Little canary of love
Find my heart and bring it back to me
Rid me of the deep dark that rules my
    soul
Rid my mind of the cold and unwanted
Open my heart up
Warm its walls with your bright yellow
    feathers
Mend my conscience
It is torn and dark
It has been abused
Rub your magic yellow dust against my
    mind
Brighten it up with love
Make a warm nest in the rough and
    stormy corners
Coo. . .my surging thoughts
Sing a summery tune
Lead me to the Light of Life
To the Light of Love
Guide me
Little canary of love.

—Pamela Roberts Aue

Follies Bergere

An ocean of gams
flailing on stage.
Moving in waves,
swells of outrage.
Bare breasts gaze
from frontless attire.
Tempting, enticing,
promoting desire.
Confident, upbeat,
the music continues.
No doubt headlines
of raving reviews.
Intermission, the
pause that refreshes.
A welcome respite from
the bounce of pink fleshes.

—Linda R. Steyding

Fall

Raging mountains of brilliant colors are
    towering infernos.
Flakes of a golden brown, float to the
    ground like the flakes at
    Christmastime.
Small children, zipped up to noses, giggle
    and crunch into piles of leaves.
Bubbling brooks, with them bring colder
    weather for the days ahead.
Slowly, the season's changing, soon will be
    upon us an icy cold winter.

—Stefanie Nelson

At a Drop

And the rain, she did fall
Flat and wide and clean
And every drop
Every scintillating spark
In the dark
Splashed a memory
Broke it open, and flowed
From the guitar of the old
To the hands of the new
And the magic walks, and stone forts
My words, and his voice
In the dark once again.
The smooth, blue water
And the changing leaves
My tears roll
He hears. . .he listens. . .makes me laugh.
The rain, she brought this;
This memory, and this feeling.

—Posie Danby

Tears

A tear is like a waterfall
Flowing down your face
Into a little pool
Then to a flood of tears
That's when I drown
Into my own flood of tears
Then I cry more
Until everybody else drowns with me
Even the one I am crying about

—Stephanie Harris

Untitled

Tears fall from the lonliest of eyes,
Flowing freely, as the river does
Through the mountains.
Tears fall from the eyes that have felt
    pain,
The pain felt
From falling deeply in love.
Tears fall from the eyes that are hurt
By one who plays
Silly love games.
Tears fall from the eyes that belong to
Hearts trampled over
And thrown away as a lost idea.
Tears, foreshadowing pain.
Fall from the eyes of mine.

—Michelle Craig

The Net

Her heart is a butterfly
flying its crooked course
over the multi colored field flowers.
I am the boy hiding among
the yellow, purple and pink flowers,
who desires the butterfly, net and hand—
however, the butterfly eludes his net.
Perhaps the butterfly
is better off free,
not mounted in a display case,
a pretty, dead trophy.

—S. N. Isaak

English

Acknowledge the language you have
    adopted
For all of the wealth in all the world
Hath not its excellence
Acknowledge the power of homely,
    simplistic words
For all of the mundane babble
Does not draw a parallel amidst
With my pen, scribbling down silent
    feelings
On the threshold of a dream
Significant poetry and literature
Brings my weary mind to an infinite halt
in the midst of an answer to my
    questionability
Leading me on to face yet another
    judgement
Made on a higher ground
Witnessing all others fading away
Like the haziness time inevitably reveals
A marked devotedness molded
My heart stands still for a boundless
    degree of time
For a distinctive language.

—Tara D. Walter

Tears of Grief

Here I rest upon your grave
Wiping those tears of memory away
I've shed a tear for when our eyes first met
And for when I fell in love with you!
I've cried many for just sitting here
    without you
And for not sharing our thoughts and
    sweetheart
I've feared many nights for remembering
    just you,
How you made me smile, and for the
    twinkle in your eyes.
For there's just one tear I've shed
That's for not telling you that "I Love
    You."

—Laurie Diane Bullard

Life

Life is a joy
For all to explore
The answers to our questions
are full of poise.
Life is not complete even
In our hurried ways
For a choice of exploration
our new ways.
For a complete life
Turn to God
He will explain
His glories ways
For he gave us life
To enjoy each day
He created us as gentle human beings
For he stood there wishing up a very
beautiful thing. LIFE.

—Rebekah Simmons

Untitled

Thank you for every sacrifice
For being my closest friend
For all the laughter and smiles
Lifting my spirits again and again.
You've always been there to listen
Not once did you turn away
There to lend support and guidance
Knowing just the right thing to say.
I know I could never repay you
For all you've given so willingly
Your unconditional love
The way you took such good care of me.
If I could, I'd take a rainbow
And place it right outside your door
I'd give you everlasting happiness
The stars, the moon, and even more. . .
Just to thank you for being my mother.

—*Lydia Marie Kislig*

A Winic In Time

I really must thank the man
for coming as fast as he can
My papers are piled high to the ceiling
and I'm getting a sinking feeling
I won't make my one o'clock deadline
if I can't get the computer on line
I feel my face getting very red
and wish that I could have stayed home in bed
The technician stops by and gives me a wink
and then he shows me the plug and tells me to think

—*Pamela F. Berglund*

Grandma Irene

One day I was lonely and sad,
For grandma Irene had died,
God mad me so mad,
That I wanted to hide.
Now that she's gone and not here,
The world feels so dead,
For God gave me fear,
But, now she's in her own bed.
I thought that God didn't care,
So, I wanted to die,
And to me it wasn't fair,
So, I cried.
Life can be tough,
To the ones we love,
But to us it can be rough,
When they get sent above.

—*Theresa J. Worden*

Love In Absence

Within me, I feel him;
For he is always there
I've captured him in mind and spirit,
Of his soul, I am aware
Anxiety overwhelms me,
In times of needful sleep
It really matters not now;
For the night is obsolete
Of his origin, I have no idea,
Yet, I love him, there is no fear
Between the confusion, I am sane;
I have no energy left for pain.

—*LaShonda Powell*

Proud To Be Alive

I am proud to be alive,
for I am here to see the
beautiful sunsets,
smell the beautiful fragranced flowers,
and feel the breeze as it gently blows
againist my face.
I am proud to be alive,
for I am a special human being
free of diseases and viruses and
also caring for the old and ill.
Everyone is special and is
proud of something they've done.
for it's beauty and reality.

—*Tania Andersch*

Bonds of Freshness

A breath of freshness seems to be, your overwhelming view
For I have witnessed beautiful, reflections cast of you
While in these visions I have felt, my heart begins to grow
With tantalizing feelings of, a love that I should know
My dream is one of passion, as I drift with wanton lust
Engulfed within your memory, of tender loving trust
And as I reminisce about the freshness of your ways
I wish inside, that you were mine, I'd worship you with praise
Your personality is so, intensified by fate
For you have come into my life, and truly made it great
I love you very much sweetheart, as you can plainly see
I cherish your emotions, that's become a part of me
The bonds within our love are now, the bonds within our life
That binds us with affections as we live, as "man and wife"
Appealing bonds of freshness are, as intimate in view
Alluring sweet, with memories, when I envision you. . .

—*Noble T. Clinton*

A Love Story

He turned to me and said goodbye,
For my love has gone away.
I turned to him and said "Oh, God,"
"Please make him stay."
He kissed my lips
And held me tight.
I stayed up thinking of this
For half the night.
He whispered "I love you"
Into my ear.
He whispered so softly
I could hardly hear.
A tear drop fell from
My eye,
I turned around and
Cried "goodbye."
I never saw him from that moment on,
He wasn't lying, he was really gone.

—*Stacy Steward*

Broken Love

We were lovers,
We were friends,
We were there for each other
Until the final end.
I could never say what happened,
I thought we both cared.
But there was something,
Something we had to spare.
I told you I loved you
But you didn't seem to care.
When I needed you
You held your head in spare.
I hope now you're happy
Because now we have nothing
To share.

—*Stacey Woodford*

Inner Beauty

What is a body without a soul?
For one could look upon me and think they know me,
when all they see is an outer surface,
not the Godly being covered by an exterior.
To them my thoughts mean nothing.
Maybe I am not a flower, but in my dreams I can fly.
Behind this mask is a spirit waiting to be free.
Why do people always judge only by what they see?
Remember when He died for us, nailed to a cross that day,
blood pouring from the hands that once healed our pain.
Now we are held by the strength of God's love.
For we know we are forgiven,
if we lift our hearts and pray.
Flesh means nothing,
when life starts inside.
Peaceful is what the world should be.
Someday in Heaven we will all be. . .free.

—*Nicole L. Morby*

The Mighty Eagle

Soar gracefully, Eagle, through the great sky,
For you never know when it is your turn to die.
As you begin your flight way up high,
Soar gracefully.
Fly high, Eagle, as high as your wings can,
Above the mighty ocean blue and golden sand,
Up over the mountainous land,
Fly high.
Eat heartily, Eagle, while you have the chance.
Then, you may fly into the wind and dance your special dance.
While on the ground do not waste your time to prance,
Eat heartily.
Strut proudly, Eagle, for you stand alone,
You sit upon a mightly throne in a world that's all your own.
We will remember what you have shown,
Strut proudly.

—*Michelle Yale*

Forever

Forever I want to hold you, but how can that be?
Forever is such a long time, will you want to stay with me?
My feelings for you will never die, they run too deep to ignore.
I could make it to Forever, and many Forevers more.
Your love is the world to me, I live and I'd die for you.
Forever with you is my wish and I know it will come true.
Many things have tried our love and times I thought we'd sever.
But all along our hearts knew we'd stay together Forever.
I'm not worried about the future as long as I'm with you.
You keep me happy, you keep me sane, but that's not all you do.
So forever is what I'll strive for, Forever I'll stand by you.
As long as I'm with you Forever, all of my dreams will come true.

—*Stacey Wright*

A Gilded Horse Speaks

I am but a painted horse on a merry-go-round,
Forever running in circles without my own purpose
and always propelled into motion without my own efforts.
I am merely a wooden dream maker that feeds the ticket taker.
Hordes have been touched in my presence
excited by my simple function and fascinated with my intricate ornamentation.
Once crafted into a beautiful creation now worn
and ravaged by age and wear though still a form of awe to the onlooker.
Created to give pleasure to the young & old alike
to all whom wish to take part in my fantasy.
Spellbound, the youngest clutch my reins with might
too overwhelmed to know if they are frightened
by my reeling spirals or amused by them.
Even when the ride is over they still wonder. A curiosity to be satisfied
during their next spin on the carousel.
Outside of the world beneath my canopy
stand the friends and folks of my lighthearted rides.
I warm myself in the glow of their faces and listen as they whisper tales of their own past encounters with my kin.
They look on as their loved ones whizz by shrieking with delight and throwing kisses to the air.
I feed on those smiles that grace my boundries.
I am but a tool, a catalyst for laughter in the carnival atmosphere.
I am separate from, but then again I am part of the crowd.
For the crowds existence is my own.

—*Tammy L. Ryan-Lucky*

My Heart

My heart you hold within your hands,
Forever yours to keep.
Hold tight to it and life's demands
Won't make it break and weep.
Conceal it from all emotions
That may make a single tear.
Don't let those many angry frustrations
Cause it to start to wear.
Because my heart I give to you,
I trust you'll keep it strong.
The thoughtfulness in all you do
Shows where my heart belongs.

—*Nichole Phillips*

Children of God

Children of God get down on your knees.
Forget about the stimulated visions that you see.
In your mind runs wild secrets locked inside.
Draw your hidden powers; take them on a ride.
Children of God raise your hand to the spirit.
Children of God learn to obey and fear it.
Draw your sword, aimlessly swing;
Always careful, forever missing.
Children of God don't be mislead by the light.
It's the devil's dark deception you must fight.
So call to the God who guards you so well.
To the devil your soul you may sell.
When the gates of heaven call your name.
Children of God pray for your soul; eternity is what you claim.

—*Roses Channel*

My Heart

My heart melts
When I feel the touch of your hand
Or the caress of your lips against me.
The feeling of you-near me
Brings my stomach to a flutter
And the world stops
For one precious moment to be shared.
Yet, when you are not here
My heart aches for your return-
No longer can I sleep
Or even recall anything but you.
But as the tear slowly trickles
Down my face,
You are there to wipe it away
And bring a smile back into my heart.

—*Rebecca Riemer*

Honor thy Celebration

"Rejoice, rejoice" the prophet had said,
"Forgive the living but don't excuse the dead."
"For we celebrate life in the face of death"
"Until the day of that very last breath."
"Revolt, revolt" the soldier would warn,
"Cherish the right for which you were born."
"Those who retreat to a desolate cave"
"Are soon destined to an early grave."
"Remit, remit" the bishop had preached,
"Stop grasping for what cannot be reached."
"Pray to the Lord and continue to give"
"Because without him you would not live."
"Revise, revise" the scholar would suggest,
"Let us struggle to pass that final test."
"For it is in failure where we must succeed"
"To become something being our greatest need."

—*Steven Patrick*

Mystic Lover

I'm in awe! Your beauty is like a
    desert—flower,
Forlorn and idyllic;
Your lips are like a shining star,
    scintillating
And distant;
Your walk is like a cat on a moonlit night,
Cautious and mysterious.
And—aha! When I look into your eyes, I
    see
The eternal light of the universe, and
Its cosmic children at play.
Ah, it is for this reason that I've called
    you
My mystic lover; mystic lover don't ever
    stop loving me,
For your love has catapulted me into a
    new day.

—Ravi Arupa

Made by You

This was made by you,
Formed by all the pain you've caused me,
All the lies you've told me,
All the times you've used me,
All the hell you've put me through.
This was made by you,
This tear I cry, was made by you.

—Robin Long

Take me Away

Take me away
Free me from his hold
Let your words
Be true
And my heart I will
Give to
You
Please let your love
Not be in vain
For my heart can't take
Any more pain
Bring me in. Take me
From the cold
Take me away
Free me from his hold

—Laura Lewis

Friends

Friends are forever so they say
Friends are always there to make your
    day
When a friend is in need a friend you
    should be
But my friends are not always there for
    me
I lend, they borrow
I plead, they leave
Who needs friends like these
A true friend is one who will overlook
    your faults
And one who shares in your joys and
    sorrows.
When I'm with a good friend I'm so
    happy I could burst,
The next thing you know things couldn't
    be worse
So if you think you have a true friend
Look again around that bend
Is that friend there to lend, or to borrow
Or are they there to mend your sorrow
Never the less I say to you
Be a good friend and your friends might
    come thru!

—Robin DuPont

Friends

Friends are people who believe in you,
Friends are people who won't make fun of
    you.
True friends don't say things behind your
    back,
True friends don't write notes about you.
I had this one friend who claimed to be
    my friend,
But every time I turned around, she would
    stab me in the back again.
She was really two-faced and I didn't like
    it,
And because of it, she isn't a friend!

—Melinda Tyler

Friendship is. . .

Friendship is like a sweet lullaby that
    sings you to sleep.
Friendship is like a shoulder when you
    feel you must weep.
Friendship is comforting, fun, loving and
    true,
And the best part about friendship is
    friends like you!

—Rachael Wamsley

The Sun

Soon the sun will rise
Frightening the night away
Then the world wakes up.
Again the sun changes,
Now it is high, very high in the sky
People laughing and talking,
Children playing.
Soon again the sun changes,
People slide into bed,
And soon they're fast asleep
Just as the last light of the sun
Creeps over the mountain peak.

—Mandy Ewing

Three Words To Say

I have three words to say,
From deep inside my heart.
Today and every day,
But I don't know where to start.
I is the first word,
In this small phrase.
Please say your heard me,
And will remember it for days.
Love is the one,
Spoken from the inside.
But only for some,
It is the word that is hard to confide.
Now just say to me,
Since the last word is you.
That you will confide in me,
And I love you too.

—Melissa Frederick

Rainbow's Promise

Rainbows promise "love"
From God above.
Believes in happy ending
Through life's tribulation.
Giving "hope" to those who are sad.
Bringing smiles of happiness.
Rainbows promise "friends"
To whom dare risk love.
Special friendships encouragements
Genuine care upliftments.
"Faith" for the future.
Sweet memories of a special gentleness.
Rainbows promise "creativity"
A gentle sensitivity.
Telepathic in nature
Loyal love reassure
It says "Give of your best"
Talents telepathy will bless!

—Vicki Ann Wong

Where did the World Go

Where did the world go?
From Greek Gods at Olympus
To Caesar's reign as king,
From marches in the South
To Martin Luther King.
Where did the world go?
From cancer to AIDs in just one year,
To starvation in Africa with a baby's first tear.
Where did the world go?
And where are we headed?
To a life full of pain
And no one left to tell it.

—Nanette Parker

Metamorphosis

Have you ever seen a year flutter by like a butterfly,
From spring's flower to fall's leafless tree?
Or have you seen the remnants of its reproduction multiply,
Like unseen minutes crawling toward its destiny?
As if time had one hundred legs to march through crisis,
Eventually being covered by the shield of chrysalis.
No longer to be a caterpillar beneath the weeping willow,
It shed its past for wings of victory,
And the beauty of its soul flutters through history.

—William Samuel Sullins

From My Heart to Your Heart

From my heart to your heart, I love you so.
From the dawn of light to the darkness of night, I love you so.
From my heart to your heart I have waited for you my love, but
Forlorn and dreary I sought my life,
Till my heart becomes your heart.
From the long wait, the dawn is bright,
The darkness is light, I have found your heart
To my heart my love.

—R. J. Biesiadecki

Our Promise

Life begins as we all know,
Full of enchanting dreams untold.
Envision the sky and clouds above,
Two soaring spirits falling in love,
Bound together in pure deight,
Their souls combine, their hearts take flight.
To the winds they promise each other,
To love, cherish and honor
To keep alive forever the love shared together.
But soaring spirits begin to fall,
Dreams lose clarity and seem quite small.
While ups and downs may try love thin,
A strength will implant deep within.
Remember the vows made not long ago
Together can love only grow.
May God embrace your loving unity
Warmest thoughts and wishes for you,
To my son, and now my daughter too.

—Penny L. Knight

Life

Life is a rose,
Full of sweet surprises.
Life is a robber,
Great with disguises.
Life is a thistle
That scratches your skin.
Life is a whistle
Which calls you within.

—Lanita Quastad

Valiant Eagle

When the clouds are drifting and the soft wind rustles the leaves, I'll see you
Galloping with your lovely arched neck gleaming in the sun, running to me, I'll see you
All those many years of loving and caring-how you made my dreams come true, I'll see you
Your black mane flowing in the wind, your neigh so real, so enduring-I'll see you
And when the moon shines over the misty meadows, fading the green to silver, I'll see you
You lay there now, buried forever, but I will always see you
Running to me, tossing your lovely head, oh yes, I'll see you

—Melva McLean

February Thoughts

The wipers scribe their measured arcs across the glass,
Gathering, mashing, raindrops with each pass.
Asphalt, black and wet with rain, unwinds before my speeding wheels,
As twists and turns the highway through the hills.
Trees with bare and leafless arms upreach,
To shred and rend each passing Nimbus cloud.
Whose ragged skirts caress each moss hung branch,
Leaving moist, life giving, sustenance.
The winter still sits hard upon this land,
And not a bud has burst with promises of spring.
The leafless forest blooms and glows,
A pale and golden growth upon each branch.
And moss is king again.

—Wesley A. Johnston

Colors

The sinking sun
gathers the colors of the evening
and covers them all with a blanket
of darkness.
My sinking heart
gathers the colors of my soul
and covers them all with a blanket
of despair.
I can't see
past the blackness
the dark is so thick—
but I am not afraid.
The colors are still there
and they will emerge
more brilliantly hued than before,
Washed with the strength of pain defied.
Darkness does not fade colors,
just too much sunshine.

—Miken Bayles

Paranoid

Soft clicking of the blinds
Gently rapping against the window frame
Sounded like. . .Footsteps.
Wind whistling through the trees outside
Sounded like. . .Voices
A cat's moaning meow somewhere in the night
Sounded like. . .a scream.
Fear. . .but not real fear.
Only manifested into reality
By my own mind.
Paranoid.

—Melanie Meadows

Untitled

They say life is a bowl of cherries
Getting bruised by our carelessness,
Eating up what life gives us and spitting out the pit.
We take life for granted
Dumping our waste on it.
Now as the little ones grow up
They are the ones to clean the mistakes we made.
But as they try
Life gets even by making it harder on them,
Harder to survive.
Making that bowl of cherries easier to crush.

—Lisa Simhiser

Untitled

Perk up and smile
Give happiness a fairer trial
Your frown goes on for a mile
dont take an hour
just smell a flower
they'll be a delight
and make the world seem all right.

—Susan Hall

The Meaning of True Love

It is sharing and caring,
Giving and forgiving,
Walking hand in hand,
Talking heart to heart,
Seeing through each other's eyes,
Weeping together,
Praying together,
Laughing together,
And always trusting,
And believing,
For each other,
For love that is shared,
Is a beautiful thing.
It enriches the soul
And makes the heart sing.

—Tracy Reeder

Untitled

Can you soar with the wind?
Gliding high above, using clouds as your landmarks?
Navigating the deep valleys,
Flowing up the mountainsides
With wind-ruffled feathers?
I can.
Can you swim in the sea?
Flitting deep below, hiding in the coral reefs?
Playing in the shore's shallows,
Exploring the watery graves
Of sailors who lived long ago?
I do.
Can you live in your dreams?
Experiencing your imaginings, surviving your nightmares?
Diving deep into fantasy,
Daydreaming of victories
Yet to be accomplished
I am.

—Malia Du Mont

Chasing a Dream

I am chasing a dream
With plenty of schemes,
I require a team.
My friends I am scanning
Doing lots of planning
For money we are panning,
Cruel rivals we are banning.
I want to be on top
I know that I may drop,
For an image I shop.
Controlling my fears,
Can't show any tears.
Rejection I bear,
Scoffing at their jeers.
I want to ride on a victorious steed,
Hoping I'll be proved by many a deed.
Desperately striving to succeed,
A friend in need is a friend indeed!

—Verena D. James

Pain

"Shut up," "Don't bother me"
"Go away"
Is what they say
When I dare
To speak up
"Of course we care"
Is what they say
I don't understand
How can they lie?
Don't they see-when I cry?
And my screams echo
Inside my empty heart
How I wish for just one hand, to reach out;
And caress my trembling soul.
How I need just one touch, to assure me-
That I am here,
That I am real.

—Megan Navahright

Untitled

Sometimes it's nice to
Go away with your thoughts
Not really thinking
About much
Just bits and pieces
Of little things
Not anything really
Important
Just thoughts. . .
Bits and pieces of insignificant
Things
Things you never thought
Of before
Or things you think
About everyday
Just thoughts. . .
Thoughts that come when
The wind blows
And then. . .they're gone.

—Vanessa Olevia Davis

Deep Within Me

I can feel a struggle,
Going on in my soul,
Deep within me.
It feels as if
World War III
Is occurring,
Deep within me.
Fighting to destroy
Every remnant
Of my very self.
Days, weeks,
Even months pass by.
The war is now
Coming to an end.
Who will win?
Deep within me,
Who?

—Michelle Vega

Love

Love means many things,
Golden bracelets and diamond rings.
Those special moments
Filled with warm smiles,
Soon to be married people
Walking down the aisle.
Going steady,
Promising to be true.
But most of all,
Love is the way I feel
When I'm with you.

—Suzanne Conduff

Gone, Gone, Gone

Gone is the sun, gone is the light,
Gone is the day, gone is the night.
Gone is a flower, gone is a tree,
Gone is the grass, Gone is the breeze.
Come the bleakness, come the black,
Come the nuclear war attack.

—*Meredith Smith*

Letting Go

I came home about a quarter to four,
grabbed the pictures of us
and threw them on the floor.
Mad at myself,
for the things I have done;
I really thought you were the one.
I love you so much that I think I'll set you free.
You know where your life is going
and you deserve someone better than me.
Sometimes my emotions are things that I can't hide.
I have to face this reality, so I'll
set your love aside.
Please don't think my feelings have changed,
they're all just mixed around inside,
and my heart can't break this stride.
I hope you can forgive me for the things I do,
on the outside I may look happy,
but on the inside, I'm missing you.

—*Sharlee Teel*

Grandfather

Grandfather sings, I dance.
Grandfather speaks, I listen.
Now I sing, who will dance?
I speak, who will listen?
Grandfather hunts, I learn.
Grandfather fishes, I clean.
Now I hunt, who will learn?
I fish, who will clean?
When my grandfather dies, I will weep.
When my grandfather is buried, I will be left alone.
When I'm dead, who will weep?
When I'm buried, who will be alone?

—*Tammi Beers*

Reflections

Bonnets and pinafores, high top shoes;
Grandma and Pap, my rag dolls too.
Sweet honeysuckle, tempting the bees.
Conner and George in the ole' peach trees.
There! I see a reflection of me. . .
The train track, the creek;
Our house on Monroe Street.
Mama and Daddy and Bobby made three;
Then I see, a reflection of me. . .
Cracked sidewalk, the chinaberry trees,
Wash day and lye soap and many skinned knees.
See! There's another reflection of me. . .
Sometimes I'm sad those times have passed.
But remembering can make it last.
If I close my eyes I still can see;
Reflections of those days, and me. . .

—*Shirley Steponaitis*

Untitled

The fearless fish, struggling,
Grasps for air as the world floats by.
Strenuous efforts for survival fail
As it drowns in the familiar sea which it calls
Home.

—*Robin N. Winship*

The Bag Lady

Alone on the bench amidst the scattered debris of Central Park
Gray and wrinkled, she shakily opens the tattered bag
Handling each object longingly, with wistful eyes
The golden necklace, her 16th birthday party
The key to a long lost jewel box, was it wooden?
The watch proudly worn on her first day of high school
The candle and corsage, memories of her first prom, what was that shy, young boy's name?
The calendar booklet, her first real job, how businesslike, how organized she had wanted to appear
The stereo jack, her son's boisterous, rollicking music fills the air of her dreams
Slowly, lovingly she places each treasured item into its place in the worn bag, a sad smile spreads across her creased face
Lifting her cumbersome, rag covered body from the bench she ambles slowly through the garbage and disappears into the homeless community.

—*Laurie Swinwood*

Of Whipporwills and Crows

Azure has turned deep blue.
Green hills have ever
So subtly turned purple.
Diamonds on the lake
No longer dance on
Its now gray surface.
And I—I sit silently sinking
Under the weight of the dusky
Blue, purple and gray.
And as the day ends in one
Deep sigh, no one speaks
Save the whippoorwills and crow.

—*Theresa J. Orwig*

Why?

So young; so innocent-yet full of life.
Growing among darkness,
This miracle lies.
Waiting; just waiting-to explore what's beyond
The small sac it call its home.
Small fingers; small toes-even a nose
A human child,
Just look how it grows!
A boy; a girl-a product of love
Normal and healthy,
Blessed by God above.
Then why, oh why, does man do such a thing?
By hanger or syringe
It's all the same.
Abortion is murder.
Life is no more
The actions of Satan
A young child pays for.

—*Rhonda M. Watts*

War

Bombs may fall
Guns can fire
Gases are spread
War Continues
Peace is forgotten
Friendship lost
Hatred grows
Fighting hovers over
Night brings death
Day carries more
I pray for my life
For soldiers lay still
Under shells
That killed so many.

—*Michelle Grebin*

What Is Lost

They ran through the meadow,
Hand in hand;
They walked on the beach,
Upon the sand;
They watched the sun,
Rise and fall;
And now he does it alone.
You see, his love was taken,
Called by God while in her prime.
Now he does what they once did
Just to pass away the time.
Time has passed.
The pain has eased.
But sometimes late at night
He looks out his window at the stars above
And all he can think of is his lost love.

—Lisa Diane Martin

Untitled

Sad children
Haunting children
Their faces gaunt and pleading
Needing love
Having none
Can you give them some?
Watch them crying pitifully,
Watch them dying painfully.
Having you ever seen such a terrible sight
As the children weeping?
Pain holds them
Sorrow grips them.
It's terrible to see
What they can be
But then it all crashes down upon them.
Have you ever seen such a horrible sight
As the children sobbing?

—Tanya Olson

Composition of Grey

I was just
having a brush
with the white
of my canvas
when
a black
sear of pain
from
the cold nights
of your soul
crept in between.
Grey flashes
touched my canvas
in a fission of colour
and a casual encounter
of brush and canvas
became poetry.

—Rooma Mehra

Friendship

Friendship is like a state of mind
Hard to keep and hard to find
Sometimes friendship can be mislead
By what other people have done and said
Friends get mad and want to fight
And lose their friendship out of spite
So just be thankful for the friends you got
Cause they're the ones you cherish alot.

—Mandy Schrepp and Cathy Fleming

The Ocean

On that day, the ocean
Has lost it's usual motion
It was still and quiet
As though it had never been loud, like a riot
The waves curled gently into a sleep
Without a single peep.
What a queer day
The ocean had let me have my way
By not being loud like a riot
But rather being very still and quiet.

—Michele Elms

Love and Hate

Hate is a pain,
Hate is a number,
Love is a gain,
Love is a hunger.
The hunger of love is lovingly high,
So hate is the biggest black lie.
The number of hate is hopefully low,
But love has and is an everlasting glow.

—Mica Shy

Leaving

I know you
have to leave,
it's just something
I don't want to believe.
To see you leaving
hurts me so.
I really wish
you didn't have to go.
I know you're leaving
is not for good.
I know you would stay
if only you could.
Soon we won't be
so far apart,
but until then we'll be together
right within my heart.

—Melissa DeMoss

Together Forever

Have you ever loved someone who didn't
    love you back?
Have you ever felt the pain of knowing
    you can't hold on forever?
I love you but you don't love me, you love
    someone else.
You don't seem to notice the love I have
    for you,
You don't care that without you my life
    means nothing.
I would lay down and die if you would
    promise me
Someday our souls would unite in heaven
And we could be joined as one forever.

—Lori Knowlton

Horses Are My Best Friends

As I saddled him up, and leaped on his
    back;
He bolted away, his mane and tail
    flowing.
My hair was streaming out;
Oh, what a joy how we were going!
Over the pastures, over the fences, we
    flew.
I steadied him up, and turned him 'round.
But he snorted and didn't listen;
He leaped over the brook with ease.
I took my stick out of my boot.
Tapped him lightly on the rump.
And he poured on instant speed; oh, how
    we soared!
I turned him around and headed for
    home.
And my mother asked me, "Where have
    you been"?
But I smiled at him; he whinned to me.
For it was our secret; just Ruder and me.

—Tammi S. Garvey

Jesus

Jesus is the one that filled my heart,
He filled it with an everlasting spark.
He helps us whenever things are going
    bad,
He makes me never ever feel sad.
Jesus is so special in my life,
He lets me go through no strife.
He's always there for me and you,
He helps us and shows us what to do.
I will love Jesus with all my might,
He will be by my side the rest of my life.

—Lynn Hotalski

The Creator

He built the stars and made them shine,
He gave the moon its glow.
He sent to me the life that's mine,
Though his intentions I may never know.
He made the sea with its waves of blue,
And the forests with their trees so green.
He has for us a love so true,
Just think what his gestures must mean.
He made the mountains so lovely and
    high,
The whole earth he shaped in a sphere.
He created the birds so they could fly,
And in our eyes he placed gentle tears.
In a single day he created the sun,
And on the seventh day his work was
    done.

—Tonya Beavert

You Were There

Through the days I was feeling blue
He gave up on me, I needed you
Each hour of every day we shared
I needed a friend, you were there.
I've been waiting for so long
Now I finally found someone.
I always hope we'd stay together,
In my life now and forever.
When you asked me to be yours only
I knew no more would I be lonely.
This was a decision I had to make
And a promise I couldn't break.
The love you showed I began to feel
As my heart began to heel.
I never knew you had cared,
I needed a friend, you were there.

—Stacey Carr

First Love

My first love was very special,
He had such great potential.
He was so big and strong,
He made my love go on.
He was so sweet and kind was this a
    crime.
People said, "It's only puppy love".
But I feel that it was true
His love for me I could hold.
He made my heart pound,
When he held my hand.
And when he held me I would just melt.
I could love him forever.
But they said the true love wasn't there.
They were right.
Even though we're apart,
He still holds that special place in my
    heart.

—Malia Loudermilk

No Love

Missy loves Blain, but it can never be
He left without saying
So much as even caring about me.
So as I write this, I'm thinking of him
Always and forever
I will be at a loss
For my true love, I will never find
One that I loved as much as him
He doesn't care
But it's okay
Because it never really mattered anyway
As I see two doves cuddling in a tree
I see true love, unbroken love
THe kind of love I know I'll never find
Because no one will give me the kind of
    love I need
So I search on, trying my best
It never does any good
So I'm putting love to rest

—Missy Luther

Good Friends

I watched him play basketball
He played well
I said "Hi!"
He winked
He talked to me for about an hour
He likes me, alot
He jokes around
Making fun
I like him too!
More than you can imagine
I told him who I like
He wouldn't tell
Brothers are like that

—Shannon Polly

Untitled

God is the sun,
He provides us with light,
But blankets us in darkness
Throughout the night.
Demons lurk in darkness,
Never in light.
Child sees a monster
Late at night.
He protects us from evil,
That divine God of ours.
He knows day and night;
Sun, moon, and stars.
He does what he can
To keep good in our lives.
A deed is done;
A soul survives.

—Mary Hill

Junior High Romance

It started when I saw him in the hall,
He pushed my best friend into the wall,
I asked if she would be all right,
Then I saw him, love at first sight.
His eyes were so blue,
It was then that I knew,
I'd never be the same,
'Til I found out his name.
I couldn't say a thing,
I just played with my ring.
I felt really stupid,
But I'd been shot by cupid.
I looked in his eyes,
I got quite a surprise,
He gave me a kiss,
Oh, nurse check my wrist.

—Michelle Oman and Kacie Powell

I Know a Boy

I know a boy named Kyle
He really has got the style.
His eyes are blue
As the sky,
His voice is deep
As the ocean.
He uses sunscreen lotion
On his beautiful skin.

—Nancy Carter

Mystery Man

As the dark settles,
He rides in
On his black steed.
His eyes are the color
Of gray, stormy clouds.
His hair the color of black coal.
He wears his black clothing
As to blend in with
The mystifying night,
For he is the
Mystery man of the night that
I know sometime
Soon I'll have to meet.

—Mandie Robinson

Adoption

We looked and saw the little boy
He seemed like a discarded toy
No love from a mom and dad
It must be why he looked so sad.
Hurt and anger made him cry
His childhood is passing him by
We'll give our love to him to share
He'll know we'll always care.
Happiness will light his eyes
Love and childhood won't pass him by
Come and be our little boy
Our hearts will fill with joy.

—Tricia Stevens

The Neighbor

There once was a man whose name was Wayne;
He tended his flowers in sun and in rain;
Whatever he planted just flourished and grew;
Each year to his flower-bed he added one new;
The walkway was made of stone and bricks;
All was neat, you nver saw sticks;
His patio was quite cozy;
The fence was a clinging vine filled with roses;
Robins and Wrens flew down for a bite;
The birds were beautiful, Oh what a sight;
He never tired of working in his yard;
To him it was play, nothing was hard;
All those around enjoyed his labor;
He was just that kind of a neighbor.

—*Sheila McDonald*

A Single Rose

A single rose lay in her hand
He tried not to cry
He tried to take it like a man.
He took the rose and held it tight.
He tried not to look at her
For she was a painful sight.
Her face so pale,
Her hand is cold,
Although he didn't want to
He had to go.
As he walked away,
He turned for a final look
A single tear fell from his eye
And his heart let out a painful cry.
At that moment, no one made a sound,
As they placed her casket
Beneath the ground.

—*Tonya Sons*

A Young Man

There was a man I knew,
He was strong and full of happiness.
He did everything he could do,
He was full of love and life;
Until the other night
It all ended,
I tried to believe everything would be alright,
But I looked at his skin
Sunken into his cheekbones,
His lifeless body,
Gasping for one last breath.
I tried not to cry.
I asked for reasons why.
I stared at his body
Thinking of the past
And as he lie, with nothing said,
I realized he's gone forever
And my father's dead.

—*Susie Marino*

The Bigot before God

The bigot stood before his God, his king.
He was such a pitiful human being.
His sins he did dread.
When he saw God's skin was red.
The man looked to the ground.
When he saw God's skin turned from black to brown.
When he saw God turn brown, he also saw God frown.
The man looked back to the ground.
All around was so quiet—no one made a sound.
When God told him how he had treated his next door fellow.
God's skin turned yellow.
When God started to turn to a bright light.
The man shook with such fright.
The bigot stood when he heard his greatest sin—
When he judged man for the color of his skin.

—*Sheryl Plyer*

The Joy

The joy abounds
    around the door
        that leads
            to me
                inside.
But when I think
    I've got the key
        my mind
            I find
                has lied.
I put the key
    into the lock
        and hear
            the hollow
                click.
Instead of joy
    to fill
        my heart,
            I find
                a wall
                    of brick.

—*Mickey Baker*

OM.

Like a seed I want to grow this very moment,
hearing the cracking of the mountains...
become the sea!
Let me have all the dreams of human being
feeling their joy within the stars.
Like the wind blow and in the thunder, flash
into the scream of a newborn...
Then I will know, that you are my
FATHER
for I have plough, and the whole
great extension of your heart.
Father. My Father, please embrace me;
let me weep, for all the sorrow in the Earth.

—*Laura Morgenroth*

Yearning

One fine day,
Heaven came my way,
Her beauty shown as up above,
For this fine woman is my love,
She captured my heart,
Only she has done.
This lonely heart.
Only her could have won.
Her glowing smile surrounded me burning,
To kiss her lips was my yearning,
All the features of an angel she possess at hand,
For she is wonderful,
The best in all the land,
When our love as now is strong,
We know it will last long.

—*Raymond Dougherty*

Bruised Reed

"Lord, it's me again".
"Help your bruised reed to mend".
"This world is so cruel"
"Makes me think I'm the fool"!
"But to your open arms I run".
"You know the world's no fun".
"And if I feel this way",
"How did you bear your stay"?
"You, more sensitive than I",
"How they must have made you cry"!
"Oh, man of sorrows"
"Help me face tomorrow".
"And thank you for being there":
"Close as my nearest prayer".

—*Mary Ellen Reynolds Amato*

Her breathing soft and low,
As in her breast the wave of life
Kept heaving to and fro.
So silently we seemed to speak,
So slowly moved about.
As we had lent her half our powers
To eke her living out.
Our very hopes belied our fears,
Our fears, our hopes belied;
We thought her dying when she slept,
And sleeping when she died.
For when the morning came,
Dim and sad and chill with early showers,
Her quiet eyelids closed,
She had another morn than ours.

—*Shannon Polley*

Father and Daughter

He remembers the castles she built on the
　beach,
Her chubby face shining with pride.
Now the dreams he built seem so out of
　reach,
As if they'd washed away with the tide
As he puts a seashell to his ear,
He remembers the nights he was too tired
　to play,
The little voice he didn't hear,
The smile that never went away
Kicking the sand that blankets his feet,
He wonders where all the time went.
He remembers the puppy she wanted to
　keep,
The hours on the phone that she spent.
Dressed in white, face aglow.
As he realizes he must let go.

　　—Traci York

Untitled

She shyly opens the door and plods in.
Her eyes scan the bar as she disappears
　into another self.
Her head is up and she saunters through.
An exchange of smiles, a touch of the
　hand, a slow dance.
She retreats with him into her own world
　which, unknown to her,
Is witnessed by all. Their worlds become
　dark as their eyes close
In a passionate kiss. Others are disgusted
　but she doesn't notice.
A tormenting emptiness is being
　temporarily filled.
A false fulfillment her only feeling.
There's no meaning but she doesn't care.
The slight glow of alcohol warms her.
Closer and closer, more physical.
Heads turn away in embarrassment.
But they are alone in their world.
They leave together.
The next morning, the loneliness is still
　there.

　　—Linda S. Looney

Bath Time

Because my cat is so fastidious,
Her grooming can be rather tedious!
The principal reason being that,
Her tongue must cover a lot of cat!
It's a fascinating thing to see her wash
　that ear so thoroughly!
The whole procedure is very slow;
I have watched it, I ought to know.
It's lick the paw and wash the ear;
A dandy job she's doing here.
Lick and rub and rub some more,
She's done it fifteen times before,
And when the left ear's finally done,
She's forgot about the other one!

　　—T. A. Hodges

To Ashley

A gift from heaven in my arms
Her sky—blue orbs did sunder dawn.
Hearts could but smile behind eyes' rain
At life renewed within this fawn.
Fresh, fragile flower from God's home;
A newborn rose in earth's bouquet.
With earnest hope each day I pray
That she 'til my life's eve will stay.
Where do you go, what do you see,
My angel daughter, as you play?
What joys has life reserved for you?
Who will you grow to be someday?
Together we'll unfold life's scheme
And not demand too much from you.
We'll seek the beauty of life's dream
To guide you tenderly and true.

　　—Steven A. Seager

The Unicorn

Swiftly she runs
Her white mane
Blowing in the wind
Her eyes shimmering
In the light.
And if you were to look into them
You would see not your reflection
But the reflection of the forest.
Her elegant prance
Is what prides her most.
Her coat and hooves
Always shiny
Her horn the color of gold
Reminds you of the sun
On a clear morning.

　　—Maria Jensen

Runaway

I feel so frightened,
Here on the streets alone.
I have no real friends,
I call a cardboard box home.
At first it was a way out,
A place away from rules and stuff.
But now I'm just scared,
I've already had enough.
I haven't seen mommy,
In what seems like years.
I want my daddy,
To come and dry my tears.
I finally got up the nerve,
And called home today.
They said. . .they still love me. . .
And want me home to stay.

　　—Laura Morgan

The Coming

Over the clouds, I see Him coming,
He's coming for me, I can feel it, I know.
I'll know it for sure when I hear trumpets
　blowing,
And hear people singing His praises and
　songs.
He'll be calling our names, softly and
　tenderly,
Leading us all to His mansions above.
I can't wait to see His face, so loving and
　kind.
To think he'll be my king, forever, He's
　mine.

　　—Miklyn Erin Green

Skitso

He's neither insane nor dangerous
he's merely passing.
he's very vulgar, but delightful.
he has an insecure mind
brimming with growing suspicion.
he lacks arm control
his eyesight is somewhat impaired.
he dresses in gloomy plaid pastels
sort of a boring spectacle
with a dashing style.
he always has this big grand design
stored away in his pockets.
he's roaming in delicate movement
in a higher plane
without structure!

　　—Ruben Gerard Martinez

Worlds Apart

We cast ourselves a world apart,
Hiding behind the words that scar,
And all that remains is two broken hearts,
And friends ashamed of who they are.
A simple "I'm sorry" was all we did
　require,
And so we said in the end,
It all adds up to inspire,
The understanding of a friend.

　　—Staci Perfetto

A Memory

I saw a man walking in the heat.
His clothes were torn and tattered, his
　back bent.
Baskets piled above his head,
Brought him but a few pesos a week.
Today was market day.
People came from near and wide,
But seeing that poor old man
Touched a part of me deep down inside.

　　—LeAnn Neal

Untitled

He was as romantic as can be.
His hair was blonde, only to be covered by
   the warm sun.
Hers was the color of a tigers black
   stripes.
He loved to see her hair blow in the wind.
Their's was a truly romantic love affair.
Until another man entered her life.
He fell in love the minute he saw her.
She knew that it would mean that her true
   love would have to
forget about her.
But he wouldn't he was so heart broken;
   no one could ever
take the place of his love.
She went to say goodbye to her lost love,
   but when she got
there he was gone.
As she lie on his bed she took a knife and
   drew her last
breath as the sun arose over the
   mountains.

—Lisa Lattimer

As the Horse Paints his Masterpiece

The horse gallops to the music's beat;
His sheen fur sweats from the heat.
He pushes off with his strong feat.
As he hurdles the humongous wall,
The music stops and he starts to fall,
The jockey atop him isn't having a ball.
And if by chance the music starts,
His galloping will be like beautiful art,
As the horse paints his masterpiece.

—Taryn M. Oatley

Untitled

My broken heart bleeds my burning tears,
His words confirming my silent fears.
He said our love would never die,
Now I know it was just a lie.
What we had was perfect, it was meant to
   be.
There was something special between you
   and me.
Was it something I said, what did I do,
What stopped you from saying "I love
   you, too?"
What happened to those nights we would
   sit and talk,
Or go to the beach for midnight walks.
How can you say it's over and done,
We've really only just begun.
How can you leave me crying alone,
If before this had started I had only
   known.

—Marjonie Gabriel

Hold

Hold me close
Hold me tight
Kiss me too
And I'll be alright
It's love I'm in
Please whisper to me
"I love you" I hear your
Heart beat and I know
This is love I forever feel!

—Sandra Kruse

Mirage

From a distance
Hollow mountains
Seem to stride across the land.
Artificial
Skins of concrete
Genuflecting in the wind.
Called skyscrapers
Multistoried
Buildings, reach to touch a cloud.
Monumental
Castle towers
Man—made structures tall, strong,
   proud.

—Paul M. Lamb

Ben's Song

Darkness will be set afire when love,
hope,
and honesty
breath dandelions into the shadows.
Fade to ivory bonewhite gravestones.
Blackness is only ignorance,
Evil is only a dream of
sadness,
despair,
unreality.
Life, love, and shards of fire
seep, flood, wash like rain clouds
into Evil's shuteyes,
and they
open
to
the
Sun.

—S. Moore

Darkness

As I walk. . .
Hopelessly to find
What the night
Has hidden behind.
Then I turn on the light
Wide—eyes and aware
I see what the night
Has hidden me there.

—Rochelle Ann Clark

With Her Face to the Sun

She greeted the world with a smiling face,
Hoping that she could bring new hope to
   those around her.
For three decades and seven years, she
   walked with her face to the sun,
Hand in hand with those who love her.
Life was great for her until the Orphan
   messenger came with grieving news
"You have a disease from which you may
   never recover," says the messenger
"I can't! I won't! I shall not!" But she did.
It hurt and still hurts, but she fights with
   a wild vigor.
"I'm not the only one. I'll find others to
   help me and in turn, I'll help them"
Thus, her fight for life carries on, and one
   day soon she hopes to walk again
With her face to the sun, hand in hand
   with all those who love her.

—Robert L. Roberts

Summer Breezes

The summer has come,
hot in the Florida sky,
Time slowly passes,
and the wind carries a gentle breeze.
The breeze smells of the Atlantic,
soft and cool on my warm skin,
The same breeze carries me off,
to different places, different worlds,
and different times.
The summer has come,
hot in the Florida sky,
Time slowly passes,
and the wind carries a gentle breeze.

—Tiffani Page

Baby

I watch you grow up,
How come you grow so fast?
I watch you play by day and night,
I have grown fond of you.
When I hear your laughter,
You make me happy.
You are a joy to be around,
You showed me how to love you, so much.
How can I not love you?
I know one day you will grow up to be a
   young lady.
May you grow with kindness,
Willing to help others, respect,
Dignity and pride in yourself.

—Yvonne M. Sims

Self

How high is the mountain?
How deep is the sea?
How much is my life worth,
If only to me?
To sit on a shelf
And not get involved,
Is selfish and ignorant,
And you won't be absolved
Till you get out and take action,
And see issues resolved!
To know that others lives
Have around you revolved.

—Patricia Nelson

Home

I walked the empty rooms alone.
How I ached to jump in bed and hide
  beneath the covers.
But all our familiar belongings were all
  packed and gone.
My stomach twisted and turned as I
  glanced over the bare walls
That once held our precious families by
  picture frames.
Every nail hole now seemed only a scar to
  my memory
As I ran my hand down the wall.
Oh! How I'll miss this place.
It seemed only months ago it was a
  hopeless case.
It's hard to imagine anyone taking our
  place.
Hanging their pictures in the same empty
  space.
This place has become a dear friend to
  me.
How could I possibly hand over the key?

—P. L. Button

For Michael

Have you any idea
How much I care for you?
Your shy little grin
And your deep, sparkling eyes.
A smile comes to my face
When I think of you.
Today you're sixteen
So much time has passed.
No matter how old we get
Always remember this;
You can always depend on me
My dear little brother.

—Stacey Uffelman

The Unknown Solider

The unknown solider,
How quietly he lay,
Under the ground,
Day by day.
Knowing that he,
With his heart so true,
Knowing he died,
For me and you.

—Molly Cage

Seasons

These tracks have come together
However long or brief they meet
Despite the chilly weather
Time spent is warm and sweet
Alone and isolated
They are hidden but not lost
Surely it was not calculated
To feel so safe among the frost
Winter melts and spring reveals
The yearning life beneath the snow
The silver blanket once concealed
The hearts that froze so long ago
Ice dissolving into rivers
Sunshine's rays, they warm the soul
In the spring we will not shiver
Seasons change, that much I know

—Susann Ehringer

Through My Eyes

Through my eyes, I see hunger.
Hunger so terrible it cannot be explained.
I see wars. Wars that scare me
Until I must close my eyes.
But what worries me,
Is if anyone else sees this.
Am I a child whose eyes are too negative
To see anything else?
Maybe I'm just paranoid.
Mom tells me not to worry,
That I'm too young.
But this world is ours,
And I, for one, shall try to help it,
No matter how old I am.

—Vivian Lee

Deception Of Terrorism

Brutalizing, torturing, killing
Hypocrites all across this damn world
Stealing lives of others to perfect your
  hateful world
With your warped minds and your bloody
  hands
But you program your minds that you're
  one of God's creatures
It's time you stop pleading forgiveness
and live up to your self-image.
Stare hard in that mirror, and into those
  cold eyes
and see the reflection of all those helpless
  souls
that you've forcefully snatched from this
  earth
And bluntly wonder if this same bastard
  is cruelly
slaying YOUR family
With satisfaction written all over his face
And let it be like icy water splashing you
Then, maybe you'll realize what a
  monster you've become.

—Natalie Anne Bowen

The Final Countdown

There she was, atop a cliff.
She looked so cold, and her eyes were stiff.
She thought she didn't want her life
  anymore,
She hated this world, and all its war.
She decided to jump and end this terror.
She thought that afterlife would be more
  fair,
She decided to count to ten and jump.
While doing so, came to her throat a
  lump.
She saw her life pass before her eyes.
And then remembered death brings many
  cries.
She decided to give life one or two more
  tries,
She decided to be a little more wise.
And in her frantic joy of realizing this,
She slipped and accidently fell off the
  cliff.

—Rebecca Goessl

Untitled

I can hear what "I Love You" says
I accept the goodness of what you are
  made of
In which, I havee selected to learn
For that is what is all I want to be
This is my goal. . .this is my challenge
To replace the energy of experiences
To maintain a postive state of mind
Oh! howw I can hear. . .I love you
Can be so tranquil to the ear
Can you hear it too?

—Sharon Long

The Essence of My Life

Each day when I go home alone, I miss you.
I also realize just how much I love you.
You haunt my dreams and my reality.
You are a mixture of love and desire.
You signify my meaning and symbolize my very existence.
You are the substance of my soul, the essence of my life;
You are what I am made of.
Within each drop of my blood a memory of you remains;
Each memory a sincere motive for loving you more.
You are what nurtures me and gives me hope.
With you, time has no end and no beginning.
Throughout time, the essence of my love in my heart,
Body and soul will always be spelled. . .C-A-R-L-O-S.

—*Viviana Garcia*

The Girl in the Glass

She is vivid.
Her sharp eyes await
   sullen tears.
Her breath is weak.
She whispers,
   again . . .
      it's cloudy on the fragile wall between us.
The tips of her hand
   touch,
     tap . . .
      tap . . .
Her glare is
   focused on luminous beads
   drizzling past her fingertips.
She doesn't know she isn't alone,
I am.
For she is me.

—*Ladena Martineau*

A Tear Broke Upon My Window Sill

A tear broke upon my window sill as I watched the day go by,
I always think of him and never wonder why a friend of mine,
He's come so close to being so much more, but as that time
Came around we had to close the door! Even though I wanted more.
Life is long, and lots of time to find out what to do
But no matter how hard I try I come out number #2

—*Sue Humphreys*

i am myself

i am a neglected child in a dark corner, hopeless and destroyed, an abandoned hope.
i am a shattered dream now unwanted, passed over by the brilliant light of the world.
i am the bitter tears that fall from hollow eyes, soothing the pain that is kept inside.
i am the whip of hostile anger, ready to lash out at those who wander by.
i am a mass of wounded flesh, huddled in a corner trying to hide.
i am the soul that's torn and battered, seeing the world through frightened eyes.
i am the one who stares ahead blankly, waiting for heaven's glory to come.
i am the lonely, the hungry, the homeless, i am the one you left alone.
i am the one who knows of the future, of the two roads that ahead lie.
i am the symbol of peace and justice, the road that we may never ride.
i am the path of war and pain, the one you've always deliberately chosen.
i am destruction, death and shame, i am your heart that has been frozen.
i am the neglected child in the corner, the one the world has destroyed.
i am your shattered hopes and dreams, the ones you've decided to avoid.
i am forever huddled and frightened, scared of this cruel and bitter life.
i am the candle that has been conqured, never again to shine my light.

—*Lara Ras*

Running

entering my head, you reiterate
the pull, the pull
   drags me
across green sheets of water.
     d
      r
       o
        w
         n
          i
           n
            g
sucking for breath
only to suffocate on your taste.

you god-like devil, holding me
to the sun
warm flames lick over
my ice body.

their beauty caresses
and burns hotter
i am combustible and
endlessly burn.

scars of your sickness run
the length of what is left
of my soul.

—*Kristine N. Chambers*

Untitled

In a dream, a colorless dove glides on a gentle breeze, unobstructed on his journey.
I am there too, walking far below the dove.
I come to a fork in the road-which path I take does not matter, for neither points toward my freedom.
Each time the beautiful bird offers me a ride upon his outstretched wing, I refuse; I am afraid.
He does not beg but simply accepts my answer and continues on his way.
I stop.
And just as I am about to give up, as I always have before, I realize that my eyes are closed and my ears shut.
When I open my eyes I can see the hope and the promise that my life offers.
"It is meant to come in the form of my courage."
We fly as if we own the bright blue skies.
I can feel the freedom pulsate through my soul as it satisfies the hungry cries inside of me.
When I look downward and gaze upon the many wrong roads I had traveled in the past I see them slowly disappear.
I am now able to see off into the distance-where my future lies.
It is bright, for it waits for me on the horizon.
And the dove, on which I soar, has many colors, as does a shimmering rainbow.

—*Tracey K. Wertz*

The Moon By Night

All our yesterdays
Were photographs of dreams
I looked into your eyes
And thought that they were real
But now we're standing face to face
And I am a sad lonely artist
My paintings have faded away
The moonlight caresses your tears
And softens those sad words of goodbye
The shadows hide your smile
It used to be meant just for me
I thought your words of love were forever
But those words have faded like the sun
Now you've left like the moon by night
And I'm the lonely one. . .

—*Laura Jean Beck*

I Believe

I believe in you and me
I believe in my heart you hold the key.
I believe wherever we are on earth we're together.
I believe that we're forever.
I believe whatever we become that we had more than some.
I believe that I'm the sun and you're the sea.
I believe in you and me.

—*Tanya Sparks*

Friendship

Friendship is like a crystal.
I can break into a thousand pieces and
 never be put back the way it was before.
Friendship is like a star.
You can shine in all your glory, or feel as
 though your whole life is a worry.
Friendship is like a yo-yo.
You can go up and down in times of
 hardship, or in times of happiness.
Friendship evolves around your whole life.
Without friends your life would be lonely
 and unreal.
Friendship is like a banana peel.
It can go up and go down,
But friendship takes time and not a simple
 line.
Friendship is like going fishing.
You can catch a friend or lose one, but
 whatever you chose,
Will stay with you your whole life, and
 without friendship your life won't be
 real,
But it will be like an envelope with a seal,
That will never open, once you have
 closed it.

—*Wendy Frances Bennett*

Perception

One Man-
with a tender touch,
eyes as serene as a star
Love in his voice
as the words he speaks
of a life which lives afar. . .
One Child—
with an innocent smile
a glow of happiness and pride
Peace fills her heart
as she knows she returns
as faithful as the tide. . .
Together they share—
a special bond,
love as warm as the sun
Dreams of the night
live through each day,
the promise of laughter and fun. . .

—*Terrie Gajewski*

Janie

On that sunny day,
I can hear the cars beeping,
I can see the kids playing,
And there lies Janie sleeping.
On that sunny day,
I can hear the bees buzzing sighs,
I can see the planes flying above,
And there strains Janie's cries.
On that sunny day,
I can hear fire sirens screeching for miles,
I can see flowers blooming,
And there shines Janie's smiles.

—*Marissa Vescuso*

Moments like These

As I gaze across the sky tonight
I can see many stars shining bright
The full moon is looking down from above
Should be a time for romance, a time for
 love
Sweet memories of you make me feel so
 high
As I watch a shooting star fall from the
 sky
I close my eyes, make a wish for you and
 me
I pray that in time, God will let it be
I walk alone in the sand, as the tide moves
 in
Wondering when we'll be together again
The reflections on the waves, are a
 beautiful sight
But would never match your beauty, if
 you were here tonight
As I return to shore and sit on the sand
I still long for the time we'll sit hand in
 hand
Together we'll gaze at the moon up above
And share moments like these, as we
 share our love

—*Noel Grover Nelson*

You're My Pal

When I need you. You are there
I can't live without your friendship.
I'm glad I have a pal like you.
When I'm gone I think of you.
I'm sorry I had to go but I'll always
Remember you because your my pal.
I'm not happy right now. Your fun and
exciting to be with. You cheer me up
 when
I'm down. I wish you were my sister but
 your
just a very close friend. As you can see I
take you for more then that. I hope you
 think so too.
I know you are sweet and kind to me.
When I'm really mad you understand
 why.
I wish I'll be there for you.
But I have to go. But I just know
You'll always be my Pal.

—*Patricia Quaider*

Try as I Might

Try as I might
I can't get rid of the leaves
in my heart.
The more I rake my emotions
The more they fall
If the wind decides to pick up
I'm done for.
Why do I feel eyes upon me?
I don't expect you to help me
because I never claimed you
were my friend.
It is night now
and I'll sell my rest
to the highest bidder
stay up to reflect and ponder
what was lost and won
many times
over the course of my emotional lifetime.

—*Matundu Makalani*

Guiding Light

I am the light at the end of the tunnel,
Yes I am the shining one.
I can turn nights of darkness,
Into days of warmth in the sun.
I can bring you happiness,
Put a final end to the night.
I'll bathe the world in my glory,
And shine my sparkling light.
I'll guide you every step of the way,
I will never let you fall.
But if you should ever need my help,
You'll know just who to call.
For I am the guardian of the day,
And enemy of the night.
But if the night should ever attack,
I'll chase away the fright.

—*Regina Tuozzo*

Devotion to Starlite (For Tonya)

As I looked into her eyes tonight,
I caught a glimpse of ascending Starlite.
As I heard her voice a benevolent sound,
I thought a part of me long missing had
 been found.
I only know her in appearance,
But her smile reveals, emotions, the
 dearest,
I thought true love was what I felt,
But with my true passion I had not dealt.
I had to come to terms with reality,
Look in the mirror of my morality,
I had thought of her only, these past two
 years,
Looking through eyes of wanting tears.
I have not felt the warmth of her embrace,
Nor experienced the soft touch of her lips
 on my face,
I know not what defines devotion,
Trust, honor, or respective emotions,
I only confess what is inside,
My eternal love, a burning flame that will
 never die.

—*Matt Mulkey*

Mixed Emotions

I love the one,
I cherish the other,
A friend of his we love each other.
The other on I wait upon,
To be with hime and spend so long.
My mixed emotions about one or the other,
Get caught up inside me to wonder forever.
Shall I ever know whether to forget or prolong?
My love for one or the other
Grows stronger and more painful
As the days go on so long.
Stronger is friendship.
Painful is love.
The one or the other depends on his love.

—Megan Barnett

My Mind's Closet

Pictures of memories hang in my mind's closet—
I choose each as if it were a garment carefully examining it in
Remembrance of when I had last worn it.
Often I remember no feelings—
Just pictures on a canvas—
And those that I feel have touched me I keep in the front—
Others that have not, are kept in the back—
I may shuffle them from time to time—
But all stay in my mind.

—Maria L. Cruz-Morales

A Letter From Mary

Nothing unusual happened today.
I cooked and cleaned,
And after work,
Met with some friends to play.
My husband lies peacefully sleeping,
While I record the days events.
His work calls him out at all hours,
So he rests while he has the chance.
At the post office was a letter from a friend,
We haven't written for quite some time.
Her grandfather had passed on,
And a note of sympathy I had sent.
She said she is doing fine,
And for Grandpa now there is no more pain.
Although she would miss him in his pick up
Driving up the tree lined lane.
Snowflakes fall outside the window.
And the clock shows the lateness of the hour.
I'm off to bed then up early in the morn,
To prepare a little something for a friends baby shower.

—Sandy Bilyeu

The Voice Inside

My life was filled with dread and sorrow,
I could not think about tomorrow.
I only thought about the past,
But help arrived in time at last.
A voice so quiet and gently,
Reached down and said inside of me,
You do not have to worry or fret,
For what you think has not come yet,
But is approaching and quite near,
To what I say please lend an ear.
Make ready today, don't live in sorrow,
For what you think may come tomorrow.

—Rachel Rogers

Soldier Boy

I watched you pack your suitcase
I could only think "No! Please don't go!"
I can't let you out into that awful place.
Where will you hide when the chances are low?
I already miss you so very much.
I can't believe you've been taken to war.
I can still feel your gentle touch.
Why did I let you walk through the door?
In school you were always so clever.
So don't play around like your life is a toy.
Because death is forever.
My little soldier boy.

—Nicole Wittmeier

Now I'm Alone

When I saw him in the twilight
I couldn't believe my eyes,
Was he the one I've been
looking for all of my life?
Or was he like the other ones,
Who would pass me by in time?
I guess I'll have to take a chance,
And try to make him mine.

—Samantha Eversoll

You and Me

We've known each other for some time,
I couldn't sell you for a dime.
I could never forget the way we talked.
We tried to lose weight when we walked.
I can't remember when this started,
But I would cry if we parted.

—Susan Pickrell

Untitled

Every night before I fall asleep
I count each tear drop fall down
My cheek as my tears dripped one by one
I thought you were the only one.
Those who thought they were my honeybun did
Nothing but burn me with the sun.
As it comes to the bottom of this, you'll
Soon have to face your thought of
In each teardrop that's been falling down my face.

—Sara Bock

I Cried Last Night

I cried last night for God called you away.
I cried this morning for all the things I never got to say.
But now my crying is done, for you're locked away in my heart.
You're in a place where you've been from the start
And from this place I know you'll never leave.
I know I will see you again if I only believe.
I'll turn my crying into laughing whenever I think of you
Because I know this is what you would want me to do.
You may be gone from this life, but you'll always be a part of me.
I'll always have my memories, they can never take that away you see.
So rest in peace my love,
I promise someday I'll see you up above.

—Sandy Grunder

When I Think of You

I think of you night and day, wishing my tears would go away.
I cry for you, I live for you.
I die for you, and hoping I never have to say goodbye to you.
I love you more than you will ever know.
I have this feeling in my heart that my love for you may never grow apart.
I look in the mirror with a tear in my eye wishing you were standing by my side.

—Renee Smith

The Web

The sound of the television is at a dull
  roar—Along with this is the honking of
  a car and the noisey yelps of the
  children playing in the street below.
I don't hear this. The only sounds to me
  are the endless ticking of the
  grandfather clock and the creak from
  my grandmama's chair as she rocks
  back and forth.
As I watch my grandmama, as I watch
  her fingers, I am amazed at what I see.
Magically appearing from old, bony
  knotted fingers is a delicate precious
  web.
The clumsy fingers move on and on, as the
  web of lace grows even more beautiful
Minutes pass as seconds while the day
  melts into night—
Suddenly I realize that the television is
  off, and all children have gone for
  supper.
The clock begins to sing the
  time—one...two...three...four...five...
  six...seven...eight. It goes back to its
  unending, uninterrupted tick.
Now, the only thing left to listen to is the
  creaking of my grandmama's
  chair—then that stops.
Questioningly, I look into my
  grandmama's face and I receive a heart
  warming smile.
I'm aware of the gift I've been given—the
  smile and being able to watch the
  process of the old making honest
  beauty. I know no gift could be better.
Sitting in my room, staring at the sky, I
  hear someone enter my room.
Stepping from the shadows, grandmama
  gives me a final smile and in my hands
  places a dream...

—Sarah Vinatier

Daddy, Don't Hit Me

Daddy, don't hit me anymore.
I don't know what you hit me for.
I am just your little boy,
And I should be your pride and joy.
I don't know the mood you're in,
Or when your fist will hit again.
Daddy, just what can I say
To make all the hurt go away?
Daddy, you love me, it's true.
But there is something wrong with you.
You are hurting, I can see,
But please, don't take it out on me.
Please smile at your little son.
Can't you see the harm you have done?
I love you, dad. Please don't cry.
Things will be better if you try.

—Rachel G. Wilson

Baby, I Love You

When I say I love you, I mean I love you.
I don't want you for what you have.
I don't want you for who you are on the
  outside.
I don't want you for the materialistic
  things you have,
I don't love you because you can buy me
  anything my heart desires.
I love you for your sunny smile.
I love you because you're understanding,
  honest and fun to be with.
I love you for you and for what you are on
  the inside.
I love you because you're easy to get along
  with and you brighten my everyday.
I love you because you're there each and
  every moment that I'm in need of you.
I love you because you're always there for
  me to run to and when I need a
  shoulder to cry on.
There is one thing in this world that
  money cannot buy and that's true love.
Which is being giving to you freely and
  from the heart.
Love comes naturally and purely from the
  heart and without second thoughts.
I want your love freely without doubt and
  mistrust.
Love means giving and receiving but I
  would rather give to you than receive
  from you.
I love you baby now and forever.
Love me baby forever true.

—Rosemarie A. Whitelocke

Dreams

Everynite when I am asleep
I dream of what we could have had.
And it makes me feel oh, so sad
I wish I could have wished a thousand
  dreams
With all your brilliant schemes
But right not you left my heart
Leaving me all torn apart
I told you once and only once that I
So dearly loved you
But it just never seemed to be so true
I think of you all the time
And wish you still could be mine.

—Theresa Ott

The Park

Relaxing in the beautiful park
I enjoy all of nature's spark.
Pretty scenery beyond compare
Is waiting to greet me there
Until the gates close at dark.
You perform a silent escapade
Walking under the tree shade.
You have a lot of clean fun
Protected from the hot sun.
Flowers give a quiet parade.
You may play some silly pranks
On trails along the riverbanks.
Remember God's love is so free
For He created all this majesty.
Let us stop to give God thanks.

—Roy Doskoch

Undying Love

Just when I thought things were going
  great
I even thought you might of been the one.
I did my share of loving, then I turned my
  back
And you were gone.
I didn't even have a say in it, you just
  went and did it,
It's done.
You didn't give me a chance, just picked
  up and left
I wonder if you really did love me like you
  said
But now it's gone, and the love we shared
  is dead.
It wasn't supposed to happen like this,
It ended so fast.
Now all I have to remember you by is
  memories,
Memories of the past.
I loved you so much, I just wish you
  would've opened your eyes,
Because that love I had for you, was the
  kind that never dies.

—Staci Miller

I Feel Nothing

I sit in listless life
I feel no anger,
no pain.
I await my demise
I feel no sorrow,
no gain.
I want nothing from life
I feel no love,
no hate.
Isn't it better this way?
I feel nothing,
not even the rain.

—Rebecca Kilbreath

No Name

What am I doing here
I feel only fear
Tomorrow will be the same
Another day—more shame
Nobody cares—nobody hears
Wasted lives—wasted times
Cold, uncaring cities
Faceless, nameless bodies
Out in the cold, out of a home
Together—we're alone
Dirty streets—aching feet
Only to eat—to sleep
And not die—in the street.

—Rayford Woodall Sr.

Another Day

I don't know,
I feel so out of place,
I only know people by their face.
No one here can understand,
No one to take me by the hand.
I feel so strange, like I could cry,
But slowly the times passes by.
Before it's over, the worst is past,
It all went by so very fast.
Soon I knew it was to be,
Another day in my history.

—Shannon Gibson

Spring Morning

As I awake this sunny morning,
I feel the sun on my face.
I hear the birds chirping,
And I sense it getting warmer.
I lie still, unmoving.
Awaiting the shrill sound of my alarm.
I slowly open my eyes,
A breeze blows,
Oh, how nice that feels,
It's getting darker now.
A storm is coming
As the rain begins to drop, drop, drop,
I slowly close my eyes again
And sleep.

—Sandra M. Edling

The Ghetto

My heart beat wildly as I walked down
  the street,
I felt like they were the lions and I was
  the meat.
A feeling of constantly being watched
  made me want to stop,
People sat on their front steps, others on
  the rooftops,
But, I continued on walking, trying to
  appear brave,
Some people started to whistle, others
  began to rave.
My pace began to quicken, I really
  yearned to run,
I kept my cool, still going on, wishing I
  posessed a gun.
Glancing through an alley I saw a man
  nestled in a ball,
Four boys were picking his pockets, then
  left him there by the wall.
At this point I was terrified, but what was
  I to do?
My head was screaming, my palms were
  hot,
My feet throbbed from inside my shoes.
The more they kept on staring, the more I
  seemed out of place,
A gang paraded through an old building,
  then up a staircase.
My heart beat wildly as I walked down
  the street,
I felt like they were the lions and I was
  the meat.

—Melanie Russo

To My Love

When I first saw you,
I felt my love so true.
I thought I'll never love anyone,
As much as I'm loving you.
When I am around you,
I usually stay mute.
That should explain to you,
You are to me, very cute.
Whenever I'm being felt,
By you, oh sweet you,
I begin to get weak,
I begin to melt.
When I first saw you in my class,
I felt my heart jump.
I just stood and stared,
And a desk was what I first bumped.
And now that you have moved away,
I have been so blue.
And now to you, I want to say,
Something caring like "I love you".

—Viengkeo Luangkhoth

Through You

Your voice is my guide
I follow your song
Through the path of my life
Stretching far and so long
Your eyes are my windows
And through them I see
A world full of wonder
And all that is free
Your lips are the passage
To the depths of your soul
A kiss, and once two
We now become whole

—Olga de Sousa

Rainbow Of Emotion

I get the blues, when I think about you.
I get red, when I think of what you said.
When I think of white, I feel delight
When I think of pink, I sigh,
When I think of black, I cry.
When I think of something mean, I think
  of green,
When I think of yellow, I feel mellow.
When I dream of orange, I think of the
  sun.
Purple and brown bring melancholy, no
  fun.
A rainbow of colors that have emotion,
To show the colors and their love and
  devotion.

—Samantha Sanchez

Tear Me Down (With Your Love)

I woke up this morning feeling blue
I get this feeling everytime you're with
  me.
I can't resist, this feeling's coming all over
  me.
Don't you call the police; they just can't
  help me.
It's only you, girl, who can help me
I have been through many moods like this,
So you've got to tear me down,
Tear me down with your love.
There's a fire; it's in my heart.
Don't you try any trick; it won't help me
This fire, it's burning in my heart.
Don't you stand and stare till I burn
  down.
It's only you, girl, who can help me
I have been trough many moods like this,
So you've got to tear me down,
Tear me down with your love.

—Prince Dave Kprake

Now and Then

Look at me, I'm down again,
I get this way, now and then
It's not that I have a reason to cry,
I'm just not happy; I don't know why!
Seems I can't look forward to anything
  new!
Seems life feels old and much too used!
These problems I've known throughout
  my past!
And happy moods don't seem to last.
I guess it's time to change this scene,
Throw out the old and start clean!
Pick up my life, start over again
I get this way, now and then!

—*Lee A. Savidan*

When Love Is Gone

As I walk into the night,
I glance up at the sky.
The tears begin to roll down my face,
  without a fight,
And I start to wonder why.
I can still see pictures of you,
And of all the times we spent together.
I never wanted to leave you,
But maybe it was for the better.
You said it would last forever,
That you would never say bye,
We would always be together,
But it was all a lie.
You're always on my mind,
And I start to cry,
When I think of the time,
That we said good-bye.

—*Renee Ryan*

Dreams of the Future, of a Little Girl

When I was a little girl,
I had great dreams for the future.
When I was twelve, I lost my dream.
When I was sixteen, I began to dream
  again.
When I was seventeen, I lost my dream
  again.
Fifteen years later, I had my hopes and
  dreams again,
To see my son grow into a young man.
Twenty years later, I began to dream
  again
To see my granddaughter grow into a
  young lady.
I have almost fulfilled my dreams of the
  future.

—*Nannie J. Wethington*

Today is Just Another Dull Boring Day

Today is just another dull boring day.
I hate getting up early, but I do it
  anyway.
It's not because I hate school,
It's the kids that'll make fun of you if
  you're not, I quote, "Cool".
They'll make fun of the clothes you wear,
But I don't really care.
'Cause if they want to be my friends,
They'll pay attention to me, not my trend.

—*Tiffany Cerra*

Deaf

             Plunging
rocks drill the desert floor
                        No
eardrum rattle
Amplified silence
    —*Yvette Aarons*

Untitled

I love you but
I hate you.
I want you but
I can't stand you.
I trusted you but
You lied to me.
I need you but
You don't need me.
Why? Why?

—*Nancy Auvil*

That Very Special Place

In the brightest corner of my heart,
I have a secret place.
A place where all my special thoughts,
Are crammed into one space.
The place I put my memories,
Of love and you and me.
The place I like to visit,
So very frequently.
The thoughts that make you seem so
  close,
When you are far away.
The thoughts that help to cheer me up,
Every single day.
The brightest corner of my heart,
Has just one thing to do.
To store up all my special thoughts,
Of times I've shared with you.

—*Shannon Lape*

The Testimony of a Dreamer

I have outrun the cold winds of loneliness
  when darkness was on every side.
I have overcome the bumpy road of
  disappointment
When trouble seemed here to stay.
I have broken the unstable grip of the
  hand of desire
And outwitted the trap of my own lust.
I have survived the all consuming fire of
  jealousy that
Has sort to burn like an uncontrollable
  fire in my soul.
I have worked through the destructive
  web of impatience
And made peace with dreams yet
  unfulfilled.
I have outstretched the limited world of
  self—pity and
Found strength to rise above the scars of
  failure.
I have broken the hold of a poor
  self—image and have
Accepted myself as an imperfect but
  growing child of God.
I have kept hope in the chilly presence of
  sorrow and despair
And crossed the low roads of uncertainty
  on the shoulder of imagination.
I have experienced life and I shall be alive
  forevermore!
I have looked beyond what is in order to
  find hope in what could be.
I am a dreamer!

—*Reggie T. Cleveland*

Timing

I'll catch you
in an unguarded moment
when you are daydreaming about
your prince charming
and a faint smile
is playing across your lips
and then—
I'll kiss you.

—*Joseph Krkljus*

Life

I see the pain and happiness on peoples
  faces.
I hear the cries of glee and the cries of
  distress.
I touch the wet dew of the morning, the
  rough bark of the trees.
I feel the happiness collide with the
  sorrow in my own heart.
I see a new baby cry, an older person die.
I taste the salty air of the oceans, the
  fresh water of the mountain streams.
I hear wind rustling the leaves of new
  spring trees.
I experience life as only life can be
  experienced, with pain and with joy.

—*Melisa S. Hile*

A Soldier's Last Thoughts

As I lay in the dirt, my face towards the sky,
I hear the great roar as bullets fly by.
I look towards the sun knowing my time is near;
My heart full of glory, my mind full of fear.
I fought for my country, with my soul and heart,
This is not just the end, it's a beginning a start.
My eyes are just closing, my mind is at ease;
As I lay in the dirt below the oak trees.

—Sean E. Sullivan

Peaceful Moments

As I sit here gazing at the pastel colored sky,
I hear the sound of crickets,
And see the light of a fire fly.
The air smells of flowers so fresh and new,
I walk into the dusk,
And my bare feet touch the dew.
All my problems drift away,
In the still evening night.
Its growing darker now,
And the stars are in my sight.
Its so safe and peaceful,
The night is growing late.
I know that I must leave now,
Though its parting that I hate.

—Sherry Bond

Distant Friends

Though you may be far away,
I hear your laughter every day.
Your laughs are captured in my heart
And I feel like we are never apart.
When I'm blue I read your letters.
I immediately feel so much better.
It seems as though your voices are near
And I pretend that all of you are hear.
When you call I jump for joy,
I have so much to say, but I get coy.
We only hang up when our jaws start to ache
And I wonder if moving is one big mistake.
I miss you all, my dearest friends,
But no matter where we are, good friendship shouldn't end.

—Lata Murti

In My Soul, In My Heart

Every night I go to bed
I hope I'll wake
But if I don't, I want you to know
That forever so
You're in my heart, in my soul
No matter what will happen next
We'll always be together forever
But if we should part
You're in my soul, in my heart.

—Michelle Howland

A Rainbow of a Dream

Things are a little cloudy now.
I hope that one day soon
I'll be able to see through
The clouds and see the
Beautiful colors of the rainbow.
The majestic unicorn will prance
Over those seven stripes and
Take me away to paradise.
Paradise will be full of
Green grass, beautiful flowers,
And blue skies that will last forever.
It is a world built for just
The unicorn and myself.

—Tammy Jeschke

Something To Tell You

I have something to tell you.
I hope you feel the same.
I feel it in the way it sounds,
when I say your name.
I feel it everywhere I go,
whether we're together or apart.
I realize that specialness,
of what I've newly got.
The thing I had to tell you,
is that I love you true.
I can only hope and pray,
that you love me too!

—Wendy Pelleman

Can You Live With It?

You blow my mind, with the things you do.
I just don't understand.
Where others would have stayed and fought,
You turned around and ran.
You leave me no alternative, but to give up on love.
We teetered on the edge a while, but you gave the final shove.
Now live with what you've done.
Get your loving on the run,
Never know now if it could have been.
Keep on running, you'll never win.
You're happy now, you've got your way,
Or so that's what you've said.
It doesn't matter to you at all,
That now, our love is dead.
Things gone by, can never be
The way they were before.
It took a while, but now I see,
I can't love you any more.

—William Michael Holbert

Goodbyes

Please hold me tight,
I just need to cry.
Just help me through the night,
Then I'll just say goodbye.
I feel so lost and all alone,
I need someone to love.
My heart feels just like a stone,
And as small as a dove's.
It's time for me to go,
You seem to say.
I scream, "no",
Please don't leave today.
Goodbye.

—Stacy Phillips

My Crystal Tear Drop

When I have troubles or a problem,
I know exactly how to solve 'em.
I look down, without a frown,
At the crystal hanging from my neck.
I pick it up,
Into my hand;
It glows just like a grain of sand.
And when the tears are boiling inside,
My crystal tear drop is my guide.
It tells me always, without a doubt,
Just to simply let it out.

—Leila S. Gonzalez

You and Me

You and me, me and you, together what
  could we be. . .
I know I've only seen you once or twice,
  three times the most, but the
  attachment is there eternally,
I continually think about you from dusk
  to dawn, a feeling that may never
  descend,
In the distance I can see us embraced with
  each other, a distance too far to attain,
I look in your eyes, and I see affection and
  questioning,
I feel love and comfort, and I hear nothing
  around us,
I perish each time our eyes meet, but the
  division is too soon to come,
Songs of devotion remind me of what we
  could be,
But my tears remind me of the situation,
  you and me,
Only together once every few weeks,
Which to me seems like an eternity
  longer, I long for you to see the
  confusion I have,
Wondering if you know me, if you'd like
  me, or if we could ever have a
  relationship,
Now I drift into deep thoughts about what
  could happen between us,
But I'm always returned to the real world,
  I know your a year older,
But doesn't it matter about fondnes
  instead of age?
You remind me of an enchanting rose just
  beginning to open, and people
  wondering of the outcome,
You and me, me and you, together what
  could we be. . .

—*Tammie Huschka*

Little Brother

Remember the days we went to the park?
We'd sit on a bench and talk until dark.
I'd verbally dissect the teachers and
  school.
I'd teach you to talk and act and dress
  "cool".
We dreamed and set goals and gossiped
  alot.
Taught you how to rebel and never get
  caught.
There were many things I never could
  share.
Of my anger and pain, you were not
  aware.
I moved far away and now we don't speak.
I've wanted to phone you each day this
  week.
Though most of the memories now bring
  tears,
I want you to know of my love all these
  years.

—*Linda St. Michel*

A House and Mind Neglected

My mind, cracked like a dry sponge,
  refuses to comprehend the loneliness;
I lay in bed, dirty month-old covers pulled
  up and around my neck-
The footboard cluttered with stale
  clothing and last semester's books.
My hands clutch around a pillow, chipped
  fingernail polish resting like drops of
  blood on a microscope slide;
I rise out of my secure womb to pace, my
  bare feet step on popcorn kernals and
  hairy dustballs-
Mounds of cigarette butts and ash
  overflow from ashtrays scattered
  around the boundaries of the small
  space.
My gaze falls to long dead daisies and
  carnations, decaying leaves dropping
  into a pool on the coffee table;
I return to my cradle, pulling the stained
  flannel sheets over my head-
Surrounded by the darkness, I close my
  eyes, desperate solitude twisting into
  my sockets.

—*Robin Mitchell*

Colors

Black is a color
White is one too
But color doesn't matter
It depends on you.
For white may be pure
And black may be beauty
But beauty fades
And white gets dirty.
For your true beauty
Is what lies within
Regardless your looks
Or the coat of your skin.
Cause color doesn't matter
It doesn't at all
So remember to be proud
And stand real tall.

—*Natalie Gibson*

Long Time, Long Distance Friends

We were friends since we were two,
I learned through the years that I could
  confide in you.
We shared our triumphs, our failures too.
We continued marching on two by two.
We laughed a lot until my moving day,
Then together we choked the tears away.
I moved hundreds of miles away,
But that didn't affect our friendship to
  this day.
Through endless letters,
Long distance phone calls too,
We keep our friendship going through and
  through.
Even though we're far apart,
We keep in touch heart to heart.

—*Lisa Moncur*

Thank God for this Day

Do you remember the day we both ran
  away?
I let the police chase me and you made a
Safe get away, I met a stranger on the bus
When I was a frightened child running
  away
This lady understood why I was a
  runaway.
I felt like a motherless child who came
  from
A long hard way, met with foul play
Thank God for this day, I am a
  professional
Person today, I made it from a long way.
Sisters and brothers who've never been
  seen
They felt like they had been treated mean.
As bad as it might have seemed, all ten
Have said we are just human beings.
Tears rolling, hurt feelings, disappointed
Lost all of your best friends,
Sitting alone thinking who is a true
Friend, God is a true friend.

—*Linda Redding*

As I Wish Upon A Star

As I wish upon a star,
I look above the heavens afar.
The stars twinkling and smiling remind
  me of you
And how much I realize what should be
  true.
As I sit and watch in the loneliness of
  night,
I miss you so much, it fills me with fright.
When we were together, nothing went
  wrong.
I was caught up in my own love song.
How could I have let my own heart fall
Just as a wishing star does for all.
You know my wish, my wish is for you,
So please give me a chance and make it
  come true.
Fulfill it for me and I'll love you once
  more.
For you, my heart will never be sore.
My feelings for you will always be shown,
Just tell me you have me and let it be
  known,
And if the wind carries a silent plea,
It will always be whispering, "Please
  come back to me."

—*Tracy Haycook*

Patience

I look back to the past.
I look ahead to the future
Awaiting and vast.
If I attain my future,
And take a glimpse behind,
I look at everything
All soon to remind.
It reminds me of patience.
Patience is the question of when.
How long it takes to obtain
What I wanted then.
How long it took my dream to tend.
All the hopes and prayers you must send.
The hopes which made life today
A dream come true.
The faith which is patience. . .
To have what is now in view.

—Michelle R. VanScoyk

Silence

A silent darkness falls upon my empty
  soul
I look for a god
But even he has let me down
When there is no one left to turn to,
I cry out in sadness
Waiting for something good to come
I ask myself if there's any kindness left in
  this evil world we live.
But all hope is lost
And I, forgotten
Standing alone, surrounded in a world of
  loneliness where no one listens.
Silently, I hear whispers of sorrow
Beckoning to me in my desperation.
I only grasp onto what is left in my
  deserted life,
And try angrily to piece them back to
  reality.
Now all is left for me to give
Is this rose placed silently
On the ground which you lay beneath.

—Susan Chaggaris

Morals

You look for trouble.
I look for peace.
You look to have a good time
Tonight.
I look to be happy the rest of my life.
You live life fast.
I live life at a pleasant pace.
You learned how to fight.
I learned how to forgive.
You learned how to steal what you want.
I learned how to work for it.
You see, our personalities are
separated by one thing.
MORALS

—Toni Lee Dragoo

Who Do I Love?

I know now that of my feelings
I love neither he nor she,
I love but only one person
And that is thee.

—Tami Jo Hall

Untitled

To my guy I'll know one day.
I love you.
I need you.
There's so much to say
To you that I need so much
To kiss
To cuddle
To even touch.
I need you now, but I can wait.
For many years
That special date
That tells me I am what you need
To love
To live
To even sleep
Together in our favorite room
To make a dream for me come true.

—Scott Barnard

Prison of Love

"Elvis, we love you," the crowd cried. "I
  know," said he,
"I love you, too, but I'm just a country
  boy at heart."
"You are crowding me into a prsion of
  your own making."
"I need to roam alone at times without"
"The constant screaming faces and hands
  reaching out for me."
"I cannot move without hands tugging,
  tearing at me."
"Boddies hurdling toward me, pushing,
  shoving, crushing"
"Out the air, the life in me. I want at
  times to roam"
"Freely, quietly, but I cannot.
  Everywhere I go"
"I must give, give, give of myself until
  there's"
"Nothing left for me — or anyone else."
"But, Elvis, we love you," they cry. "I
  know," he answers,
"I love you, too. I have given my all to you
  — my song, my body,"
"My soul. Everything until there is
  nothing left to give."
"I cannot stand this 'glass prison'"
"You have made for me. I must be free,"
  he cried
As he said, "Goodbye."

—May Thompson

Could've Been

Do you ever think about what could've
  been?
I mean you and I until the end.
We could've built something special
something strong
But no matter how hard we tried,
We couldn't hold on
I've tried to forget you, I really have tried.
But it's no use you're always on my mind.
In my dreams you're there by my side
on a beach or down a long country road
it's just you and I
But I know we'll never be together again
But I'll always remember you and I and
what could've been.

—Sabina Janel Bowman

I Still Care

I tell you I still love you,
I miss you very much. . .
How often I long to hold you,
And feel your kiss, your touch. . .
I told you I wasn't happy,
During the time we spent apart. . .
I want to be together again,
And make a fresh new start. . .
My head is telling me not to,
You'll hurt me once again. . .
My heart is saying I need you,
Just name the time and when. . .
I know that I'll come back to you,
I need to have you near. . .
I'm placing my heart into your hands,
Please handle me with care. . .

—Marianne Stahlnecker

I Must Drop My Crutches

I must drop my crutches
I must let them go
Now is the time and here is the place
I will probably stumble and often crawl
But I must stand alone
Just once
So that I know
I am able to depend on myself
I must drop my crutches
They have given me support
They have helped me survive through the
  hard days
And that is why
I have to leave them behind
To prove to myself
I am worthy of me
I must drop my crutches.

—Megan McGonagle

Aborting

All the time that I remained inside,
I never thought I would have died.
Everything went by so fast,
I'll probably just end up a memory of the past.
I know my parents weren't ready to have me,
And freedom was probably all they could see.
I'm sorry if I caused you so much pain,
But I'll never come back, I swear in vain.
I don't think you'll ever really know,
But I will forgive you for not letting me grow.

—Michele Grondin

Catching Fire

Take my hand for together we can fly.
  Open your heart and we can aim higher.
When I look at you, I realize, my heart has long ago caught fire.
My heart long ago set pain free, as you helped me to take chances.
Love on the rocks, love as bright as the stars. Together we see what romance is.
Your tender words to reasure me, when my eyes have thought of rain.
Your sympathy which through all endures. A kiss to ease the pain.
Take my hand, gaze into my eyes, abolish my every fear.
Help me cure this rare disease, show me things aren't as they appear.
Look at me, tell me you can feel the love.
  Promise you'll always stay.
Love me, stand by me forever, never wander or stray.
For if you were to leave me, those words would cut me to the bone.
A part of me would die, and I'd never make it on my own.
Dream with me, for the heavens have our answers fulfilling my every desire.
When I look at you, I realize you've let your heart catch fire.

—Mindy Goldstein

A Last Goodbye

I think of you day and night.
I only wonder if I was right.
I remember so many things.
Now they seem like childish dreams.
I held you once, next to me.
We were in love, so wild and free.
Now we are too far apart.
A continuous break grows in my heart.
I once saved you from all retorts.
But over time our faith grew short.
Now I seem to cause only pain.
I lost the heart I tried to gain.
So now I must say goodbye,
Spread your wings, learn to fly.
Soar strong against the wind,
Remember me when you need a friend.

—Theresia Stone

D.W.I.

My fingers run through the sticky mud.
I open my eyes and see it is blood.
Hearing the screams of the wretched one inside,
I cannot move and there's no place to hide.
The mangled corpse of the shiny red car
Reminds me of the descent which my sanity will marr.
It is futile to hope that I will ever stand.
I cannot unclench the beer can locked in my hand.
The whirling scenery that flows before my eyes
Is filling me with malice and hatred at the lies.
The cataclysmic pounding and scratching in my head
Are contradicting parasites, and soon I will be dead.
I'm drowning in something which I've tasted before.
I'm closing in on death now; I can see the door.
This pain is burning through me; nothing can assist.
As I watch myself from somewhere else, I cease to exist.

—Wendy M. Frechette

Give me Back my Innocence

In my childhood, in my innocence
I perceived the world with wonder
Everything was beautiful
Everyone was kinder
My eyes were closed to the evils of the world
My heart had never felt pain
Time was mine to squander away
Oh, how I want to live that life again
Give me back my innocence
Take me back in time
Back to my carefree years
When I never saw crime
I want to close my eyes again
I cannot face reality
Take me to a different place
This world is not for me

—P. Ilagan

The Star

I look outside my window and see all the stars,
I pick the brightest, prettiest one and I make it ours.
I see that star shining bright
Deep within the wicked night.
I can't help but notice our star is slowing dying.
At that moment, I notice I start crying.
Crying out your name within the sheet of black.
Something is missing, there's something it lacks.
I try to think of what it is, what's causing all this pain,
My heart still icy, still much cold it fills up with vein.
That's it I know the reason for that dying star above
That star has room, it has the sky, but it has no love.
I close my eyes and release all the love I behold,
My heart slowly released all of the cold.
The star grows brighter, more alive with all that love,
I then look at that star and see you above.

—Penny Oliver

I Know A Place

I know a place
Where there is no pain,
No sorrow, no danger.
I know a place
Where dreams come true
And there is love.
I know a place
Where black and white
People live in harmony.
I know a place
Where there is no violence,
War but peace.
I know of such a place
But only exists in my heart.

—Roland Perez

Just You and I

To you my secret love is who I write this for.
I pray that you will one day come knocking at my door.
We then will fall in love and never split apart;
That's my wildest dream I hold closest to my heart.
The deepest feelings ever felt are my feelings felt for you.
Because I think of you always I know this love is true.
Whether you feel the same, I will never know.
If you do, please tell me; just let your feelings show.
I love you so much, for you I would die,
I hope for eternity it will be, just you and I.

—Rhonda L. Cogburn

The Secret

I know this secret
I promised not to tell
It's not a secret to keep
Not if I know well
My friend wants to go out and drink
I read it in a letter
She's too young to drink
She's knows much better
If I let her go, I may loose a best friend
If I make her stay our friendship may end
If the drivers drinking, they wont get that far
She won't visit or call if I make her stay
She'll find a way to make me pay
Well I kept my mouth shut
And tried to be a good friend
Now I have to wake up early
I have a funeral to attend
"To Stay Alive—Don't Drink And Drive"

—*Simah Lopes*

Word

I stretch my mind, like a tree reaching for itself in the wind.
I quest, with my thoughts spanned across my field of vision.
I endeavor to attain what fits, like the hand in the perfect glove.
I hunt through limited knowledge, in pursuit of what will only betray me.
And as I am just about to grasp,
During the split second between have—not and have,
The uncaring, impeccable word loosens and slips through my fingers,
Like granules of sandy thoughts, now dispersed by the wind of my soul.

—*Lisa Bassett*

The Boy Next Door

I see your face every single day
I read your words, understanding what you say
You move with ease across the floor
You give it your all, I see much more
I can only see a star in my sight
But it doesn't seem quite right
I don't understand you are just like them
I just see you shining like a sparkling gem
I don't understand I know only you
You will always be number one no matter what you do
Just how much I care, you don't realize
But I can really see it when I look in your eyes

—*Tonya Shelhamer*

Questions

I stop my busy schedule and think;
I really let my mind wander into the future.
You know what! I really find myself asking a lot of
"Suppose's" and "what if's."
I feel so young and so vulnerable and so darn afraid.
I don't know what my future will bring;
Whether it will be full of happiness or sorrow.
I don't like to be pessimistic, but I feel so uncertain.
I think about death now in a way that I've never thought about before.
I feel young and, in a way, very grown up.
I realize now through life's experiences
That things are not always so rosy.
Problems do occur and we do not always have answers for them.
Slowly you realize that life will always be giving us tests
And no matter what you do or how hard you try,
You will never figure everything out.
There will always be questions in our minds,
But the answers won't always be there.

—*Lisa Roberts*

Your Beautiful Eyes

As I stare up at the blue, blue skies,
I remember something about your eyes.
The laughter in them that made them shine,
The person I wished was all mine.
A smile that took my breath away,
A look that left me with nothing to say.
I sit here and think about those days
When my love was as strong as a summer sun's rays.
I dreamt of ways of telling you—
That this love in my heart was forever true.
Though time has gone by and years have passed;
I know that my love for you will always last.
From the first time I met you, till the time of my death,
I'll love you all the more with each taken breath.
I'll always remember you-and your beautiful eyes-
Every time I look up and see blue skies.

—*Lena Scunziano*

Our First Kiss

I remember the day,
I remember the place,
I remember the thrill
As we stood face-to-face.
I remember your lips as moist as dew,
But I can't remember me without you.

—*Shelley Reagan*

My Feelings for You

Even though we are worlds apart
I remember you in my heart.
Losing you was hard to do,
Why it was you there is no clue.
To keep my hopes up high
I remember thing we used to do.
I remember the walks in the park,
I remember the times in the dark.
Even thought these memories are full of pain,
I need to remember there is something to gain.
We'll be together another time,
But for not you'll be in my heart and mind.

—*Shawna Boyca*

I Understand

I didn't realize until yesterday so many days had gone by,
I remember your eyes staring into mine and I cry,
You say no longer love me, I understand
The warm air embraces me, the moon kisses my face,
The stars light up my eyes, I can almost feel your arms around me,
"We belong together" that's what everyone says,
Yet you say you no longer love me, I understand
...Because I know you once loved me and only me,
You caressed my face, dried my tears
I could have sworn we'd be together for years,
The times you told me you loved me,
And the times we spent together can never be taken away,
So when you say you no longer love me, I understand.

—*Nicole Suares*

Travelling Through Monument On The John Day River

Trust, they call it trust; that trust called
   boy
I ride and rein a metal insect
Pulling a jagged broken leg
Turning lines of dirt; deep lines
In Oregon highland's summer heat
Chasing trails of sweat
Down the sweet brown boy chest
Pulling and clutching
The noise and dust settled by a quiet Thin
   boy watching his
insect father
With orders on a slanting field
Two miles far across
Across an Eden watered canyon
Full of shade and grassy fields of
Troutdeerporcipinesrattlesnake
A big man swarmed with frustration
Two miles of clear clear air away
I stand for many years alone with that fire
That burnt my inside black.

—*Sean Kelly*

Infinity

Infinity a description
When we talk of loving you
A love we know can only grow
Through memories we now hold
The things you did to make our day
Hurts that might get in the way
One thing in your life you knew
Love for you was always true
A fete you earned from everyone
Who had contact with you
Until every life touched by you,
Enters Heaven's gate.
A part of you will live on through
Souls that God creates.
All these lives will better be,
Because of touching you.

—*Shirley Winner*

Alone Now

When the phone rings,
I run to answer it;
Almost yelling my "Hello!"
But to my dissapointment. . .it's not you.
I hear the car door slam,
I rush to the window;
Pressing my face to the clear pane,
Only to find a strange face. . .staring at
   my empty eyes.
But wait, I hear someone knocking at my
   door,
I jump up to greet you;
But it's only my dad's friend. . .returning
   my unsmiling smile.
The tears flow down my pain-etched face,
I'm no longer able to hold back;
I hug my knees to my body. . .rocking
   back and forth in anguish.
I dry my tears and face the world again,
Holding back the pain,
And pretending I don't care
That I lost you. . .my life and my love.

—*Lisa Karosas*

A Decision

I'll take that chance, I really don't care
I said I'd do it, it's another big dare.
I know it's wrong and I know I shouldn't,
But if I don't they'll say I couldn't.
And I know I could whether I want to or
   not
I want to be one of them, one of the lot.
The decision is now left to me
And I'll show them, I'll make them see,
That I can do it, and do it right
Without even causing a fight.
But now it's final, who cares about them,
I'll show them who I really am,
I won't do it, I'll let them see
That I'm not anyone, but me!

—*Margaret Lymburner*

In the Eyes of a Child

What is the matter little one?
Why are the tears welling in your eyes?
Are you lost in the hustle and bustle of
   this strange adult world?
Has no one heard you cries for help?
You are but a child and already you are
   cast into a world
Where humanity is lost and only hatred
   survives.
Man is at war with man and your future
   is the price to be paid.
You watch, silently contemplating your
   destiny
As man slaughters man in a struggle to
   satisfy his greed
And lust for power.
You go unnoticed. . .a miniscule observer
   of this harsh,
Unfeeling world.
This is the world you are predestined to
   inherit.
Inevitably, you will soon be encompassing
   in the cruelty
And blinded to the children as your youth
   is stolen from you.
It hardly seems fair. . .this world offers
   you only age
And you have no choice but to accept.

—*Tina Renee Pratt*

You

When I looked into your eyes,
I saw a reflection of myself.
I thought I didn't understand,
the true meaning of love.
But then, when I found you,
I knew love was all around me.
I cannot yet describe,
my feelings of you,
I have built up inside.
But I know
those feelings are good,
because
when I'm with you
things are perfect
just the way they should be.

—*Renee Stearns*

Past, Present, Future

Do you see what I see. . .
I see a bright and clearly figured out
   future
Inside of a dream that's neverending,
Always trying to do better than what you
   are or have now.
Then you think you have awakened from
   your dream
To realize you're in a fantasy world.
Did you see what I saw. . .
I saw an awful and dreadful past with
   little to be proud of
And a lot to be ashamed of.
It's time to face reality, there's nothing
   you can or cannot do,
All you need is the inspiration.
Do you feel what I feel. . .
I feel like a useless piece of paper that is
   thrown away
Because it isn't needed, then found and
   put to good use
For something really important. Then the
   whole thing is over and
You find yourself sitting in a corner
   holding on tight to a
Teddy bear wondering about your past,
   present, and future.
Then you have your future in your hands
   and what you do is up to you.

—*Tami Jordan*

To Dreams

The porcelain elephant sits on my desk,
Wearily supporting discarded butts.
Dressed in regal splendor and ready for
   the hunt,
His unfailing eyes scan the savannah for
   tiger.
His trunk upraised, poised for a bellicose
   roar,
A false charge.
His tusks short, sharp, stand as armed
   sentinels
Against danger.
Upon his tinted base, he awaits the
   direction
Of a maharajah.
Weary not, proud elephant.
You were conceived in cruel jest,
But I will join you on the hunt.
And we will slay tigers, you and me,
By the thousands.

—*Saverio De Ruggiero*

Silent Cry

As I look in the mirror
I see a young girl
With a candle burning bright.
She speaks but no one listens.
She sins and everyone suddenly cares.
She is locked in her own private world
With walls as strange as steel.
There is no way out,
For she will die here.

—*Tiffany Hobson*

The Future in my Eyes

I'm in the future, I see what I see.
I see all my friends, and they're talkin'
  about me.
I died seven years ago in a sabotaged
  plane,
On my tombstone it's written, "He rode
  the fast lane."
The markets are closed, and so is Times
  Square,
And everyone's wearing a gas mask for
  air.
The subway is under the gravel, I think,
For the dust rises up, and it makes my
  eyes blink.
The air's very toxic and so is the ground,
There aren't many people for miles
  around.
I'm in the future, I see what I see,
I see all my friends, they've stopped
  talkin' 'bout me.

—Michael S. Leffler

China Doll

As I sit here and look at my china doll
I see how fragile she is.
I see how careful one should hold her,
And how much she longs to be kissed.
My china doll is like a heart, if you
Hold her too tight she'll break.
But yet don't treat her like a lady,
She needs love and warmth
Like a doll, but remember too much fame,
Will only make her fall.
But do not forget that she is there,
  because
Then she will only think you do not care.
What I'm trying to say to you about the
  china doll,
The one that needs to be loved so that
She is not the only one that needs love,
As you may see the other that needs
To be treated like a china doll is me.

—Mindy S. Hoppal

Tonight the Sky is Mine

Through the mystic fog
I see silver studded skies.
The sparkling of the stars
That shines in my eyes.
A falling star fell onto my open hand,
Seeming to know just where to land.
The magic moon in the silvery skies,
The laughter in his smile, the twinkle in
  his eyes.
As I look up into space
The heavenly lights shine upon my face.
As I reach to touch the light,
I'd love to touch the sky tonight.

—TaggyLee Mermis

Just One Look

As my eyes open as wide as they can and
  my heart pounds 5 times a second,
I see the one I want to love forever.
Just one look is all it takes to make me
  tense.
it only takes one look to make me feel
  warm all over.
When I go home and sit down I look out
  the window
And only then do I think of him.
"How wonderful it would be to love him",
  passes through my mind.
Every love song I hear reminds me of him.
Nothing on this earth can make me hate
  him.
As I lay myself down on my bed beautiful
  thoughts lullaby me to sleep.
As I recite my love prayer I wish him by
  my side.
Only then I will know and live the true
  beauty of love.

—Ramona E. Meza

Hidden Land

As the sun shines upon a lake,
I see what is called daybreak.
As the ducks and swans swim up and
  down,
The animals come from all around.
As the deer stop to stare,
The wild horses could give a care.
Oh, what a beautiful site to see,
But the only one there was me.

—Michelle McAllister

Untitled

Just when I thought I loved you no more,
I sent you away and you came to my door.
Just when I thought you were out of my
  mind,
I searched for new love but there was
  nothing to find.
Just when I met someone else to embrace,
I opened my eyes and saw only your face.
Just when I knew you had gone far away,
I cried and cried and wished you had
  stayed.
Just when I realized it was the end,
I sent you away and lost a friend.
Just when I thought
Just when I knew
Just when I realized
I loved you too.

—Lisa P. Caccamo

The Twelve Vows

I shall not be a slave
I shall not buy a slave
I shall not starve
I shall not go naked
I shall not be without shelter
I shall not be without work
I shall not walk or live in fear
I shall not commit crime or murder
I shall not discriminate one human
  against another
I shall not deliberately harm any living
  creature in the world
I shall not knowingly defile or destroy the
  earth's environment
Live and let live shall be the principle and
  philosophy of my life

—Shanti La

Deserve

I am waiting for life,
I sit and wait for all that I deserve.
It is a long wait for life.
But I wait patiently for my reward.
I suffer today's life.
So that I might enjoy tomorrow's.
I am still waiting for life.
The crowd passes me by.
I have waited too long for life.
It has left me behind.
I must jump for life.
And grab on to all the remains.
I might fall and die.
But I might not and live.
I am no longer waiting for life.
I am laughing and singing with him.

—Seth Sachson

A Rose

I finally grow up and fully open.
I sit soaking up the sun, enjoying life.
I'm just thinking about the reason people
  kill us.
Wondering why after all that growing,
Do they just kill us slowly,
When we are only beautiful for a couple
  of days.
Why can't they understand we have
  feelings too?
Why can't they enjoy us as we're
  growing?

—Tammy Trombley

Untraceable Soul

My heart grows cold as I sit here and
 stare.
I speak not a word, and say not a prayer,
I see nothing now nor hear a sound;
Confused by emotions that keep going
 round;
Caught in the emptiness of the time and
 the place,
My body sits still, my mind races through
 space.
My love, she has gone, and she's not
 coming back.
With her far away, joy, I do lack.
Our love was beautiful and strong, yet we
 knew not the cost;
With her departure, two lives were lost;
One body was buried, the other
 misplaced,
One soul went to heaven, one soul can't be
 traced.
The one who was buried, is much luckier
 than I;
My love, who I married, had but one time
 to die.

—*Robert M. Bay*

Reason

It makes me spin
When you say
You care for me
It makes you smile
When I say
I adore you
But somebody says
All we do is just
Pretending, pretending!
But honey, for God's sake
Keep it up, keep it going
Keep it shine, keep it coming
Least we have
A reason to
Get together
Least we have
A hope to
Go further.

—*Syed Razzak Ali Shah*

I Wear a Mask

I wear a mask and I'm all alone.
I stand alone, I eat alone,
I cry alone; I will also die alone.
Over the mask is happiness and laughter.
Nothing wrong but under the mask is
 crying,
Sadness, pain, and depression.
I call it a mask of death and pain
Or in others words, life.
Everyone has one, but I wish to wear it
 out.
I wear my mask-
So everyone can't see the pain and misery
 on my face;
So they won't put me through anymore.

—*Thomasenia Elexsi*

You In My Eyes

Everytime I think of you
I start to wonder if you really love me
Or is it just a game you play?
I love you will all of my heart
But do you really love me?
I think of you in my dreams and in my
 thoughts
But do you think of me?
I wonder if you really love me or am I
 some
Kind of toy
You call me when you need a shoulder
Or when you're lonely
But when I call you you're always too
 busy
So when you make up your mind
Look into my eyes and tell me you love me
Until then I love you.

—*Stacy Cox*

                I
              sit
            in our
             old
            home and
          wonder what it
        would be like to live
      in those glorious days of
   floor-length gowns and big silk bows.
                I
              then
           see through
         the window and
        look at the old slave
        house—two hundred
          years old—and still
           standing—Dignified.
and i think maybe i would not like to
have lived back then . . . . at all.

—*Kelly Kenny-Edwards*

Lost Love

As I watched the clouds pass by,
I suddenly see a patch of blue sky.
I hoped to see some sunshine too,
But that idea is no can do!
In those clouds I also see,
A vivid vision of you and me.
Us together, full of cheer,
Now that vision isn't so clear.
I wonder why I could not see,
Since it was so clear to me.
But now I understand so well,
The love we had, slipped and fell.
I had to make it rise again,
To make it the way it had always been.
I needed you to help me through,
But I guess my love just wasn't for you.

—*Linda Barton*

Dear Love

Dear Love, I ask you, "how do you think
 of me"?
I tell you I need love and whatever else
 you can give.
Will you say, "I need you too; please stay
 with me forever"
Or will you say, "go away, you mean
 nothing to me".
I wonder if I asked you, "what would you
 say to God"?
Would you answer, "how do dear soul".
Or would you say, "please don't bring
 Him up"!
I'm leaving you before you leave me; I
 need you no more.
I asked you, "do you love me"?; you
 asked,
"why do you need to know"?; I answered
 with, "good-bye"
This is my world as much as yours; I'll
 govern my own fate.
Goodbye, Dear Love, I'll see you again
 some cold and dreary day.

—*Nikko Adkins*

Time

I know where age begins
Where wisdom thrives,
Where thunder cloudstrust
And wind revives.
I own the power of unspokeness
And the power of words.
I learned how to dance with the stars
And sing with the birds.
I am time itself
And I do what I please,
I talk with the rain
And learn from the trees.
Yet amid all this power and freedom and
 joy,
I am wistful because
What I touch grows old instantly
And what I am-already was.

—*M. J. Waugh*

Changes

It's time to say goodbye,
I think love was on our side.
We were always there for each other-
Always loving one another.
True love is hard to lose,
But losing you is like losing part of me.
All our hopes, dreams, and fears-
Shared under starry nights, wishing upon
 moonlight.
Our love was once so sweet,
But now our lives are changing.
Challenging us anew.
Oh, all the times we've shared
Now just seem to make me blue.
Now I'm leaving you this day,
With a good word of advice too.
Take all your hopes and dreams
And share them with good friends,
Because there will never be someone as
 special as you!

—*Melanie Abram*

Reality Hurts. . .

When I look back to our past,
I think of how my future is surrounded
   with memories of
Yesterday,
For living until tomorrow only brings
   pain,
The dreams we had together were so
   special.
But without love it wasn't real,
My life is now reality,
My heart was only free to fantasize when
   I was with you,
The warmth and security my soul once
   felt is gone forever,
My hopes were lost with yesterday,
But every tomorrow brings thoughts of
   your return,
The tears I cry are ones of sorrow and
   grief,
And I wonder if you ever loved me,
For when I look back to our past,
I think of how my life is surrounded with
   memories of
Yesterday,
A yesterday so dearly treasured,
A yesterday I will never forget, for my
   soul won't ever be the same,
But at least I now live in reality. . .

—Leigh Rychener

Life

I think of dying, I think of lying,
I think of living, I think of giving.
So many things run through my head,
To the point I wish I were dead!
I think of sorrow, I think of pain
I think of happiness, it's all a game.
I'm so confused, and I feel so used!
I just wander when this life will end.

—Leslie Raye Molbert

Forbidden Memories

I think of you,
I think of me,
I think of things,
That cannot be.
I had you once,
In the past,
As I looked in your eyes,
My heart beat fast.
I kissed your lips,
Once or twice,
If I only knew,
I was to pay the price.
When you held me tight,
I believed in you,
Then it happened,
We were through.

—Michelle Baker

Untitled

I've been sittin' here feeling blue,
I think of the days and nights of loving
   you.
Deep down I knew we would depart.
Wondering what it would really be like to
   be apart.
I wish I knew just how you felt,
To me it feels like my heart is being hit by
   a belt.
You hurt me so bad,
But you didn't care if it made me sad.
I know our love was meant to be,
But it's not just up to me;
I still love you!
But it's all up to you.
Whether you love me too.
So if you ever want me back,
Just give me a call because
Our love was meant to be!
I love you!

—Sheri Reeder

Betrayed

As I sit here,
I think of the night we met.
I think of all the lies you told me,
How you said you really cared.
Now you say you want to be friends.
Do you really think it works that way?
No, not after you've been betrayed.
You treated me like a piece of dirt,
How many other girls did you use for fun?
For I know I'm not the only one.
Do you really think I want to be friends?
I don't know if I really could.
After all,
You haven't said you're sorry.
I guess I must have been mistaken,
For I thought,
That's what friends should say after
They've betrayed you.

—Miranda Saastad

Flowery Red

While walking in a field of flowers,
I though of my love so far away.
As I picked a fresh daisy for his flowery
   bed,
A tear fell silently from my cheek.
I think he can see me from where he lies,
And I know he cares for me still.
He left me abruptly without a good-bye,
But I know that soon enough I'll be at his
   side.

—Sarita Araiza

A Prayer

God, at first I thought I was alone.
I thought I had no friends to talk to,
But now I know I'll always have you.
I know you will hold my hand,
And walk with me through life.
No matter how I treat you
I know you will always be there for me.
You're someone I can tell all my secrets
   to,
And I don't have to worry about everyone
   knowing them.
I know you will never leave my side.
I'll always need you,
No matter where I am.
I'll always love you,
And I know you will forever love me.

—Tonya Shelton

My Son the Soldier Boy

Watching my young son at my feet
   playing with his toy,
I thought, I won't raise you to be a Soldier
   Boy.
He was in and out my old kitchen door,
From early mor'n to half past four.
He teased and taunted, with his beguiling
   ways,
Putting frogs and things in my purse on
   many days.
The day his head hit my dashboard and
   cut his eye,
It was Mother who had to cry.
Armed with Beebe Gun, the Salamanders
   for game
He marched to War, but it wasn't the
   same
Because, one day, it was a game no more,
The battle was real—the game was War!
The Beebe's are Bullets, and I knew the
   stance
Now, my heart is still as he takes his
   chance.
My little boy, how you've grown so wise,
But The starlets still glisten in your big
   blue eyes.
I know a Soldier job is never done,
Just remember I love you, and please
   come home safe, MY SON.

—Sherry Rorick

A Puddle Of Tears

I have loved you for so long.
I thought it was right but now it is wrong.
You have put me through so much pain.
For the love I wish from you will never
   gain.
Why can't you see that I love you so.
Do you see and won't let it show.
The love I have for you will still gain.
The memories of you will always remain.

—Tammy R. Whitt

Regretfully Yours

I didn't know that our love was a thing of
   the past.
I thought it was strong and was going to
   last.
Now I've seen the truth and my heart is
   bruised but not broken.
In time you'll be replaced and remain only
   a small token.
Of the youth I'll leave behind—
Only a small memory of my mind.
I don't want you to think that you mean
   more than you do.
Or that I'll never recover from my love for
   you.
My love is strong, but it is fading fast.
And I know now that it would never have
   last.
The only thing I hope and pray for. . .
Is that one future day, we'll meet again.
And you'll regret how you treated me
   then.
So—Goodbye, My Love.
I wish you no harm, or unhappiness.
I just wish you to regret how you treated
   this.
Of this relationship—we're closing the
   doors.
And I sadly sign this letter. . .Regretfully
   yours.

—*Tamera Miller*

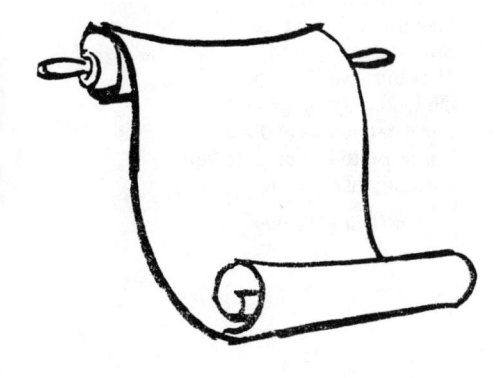

Untitled

i took your hand and gave you my trust
i took your hand and brought down your
   lust
you took my hand and showed your desire
you took my hand and stood with a liar
we held each others hand and stared into
   opposing eyes
whispers of love and echoes of lies
you said you'd stop
i said i've been trying
two lovers. . .stood lying
now it's our last chance
and i will try
for if our love fails
a great part of me dies

—*Min-aha Beeck*

A Never-There Kind of Love
(Dedicated to Zerzell A. Smith)

There's something I need to tell you, I
   think that you should know.
I tried to be so perfect, in the feelings I
   tried to show.
To me you were the one, almost perfect in
   every way.
There's nothing I wouldn't do, or nothing
   I wouldn't say.
I know the times between us weren't the
   best that they could be.
But the ones set between us, we'll have to
   wait and see!
I'm sorry it wasn't me, the one to be for
   you.
But of course when we're together, we
   equal the perfect two.
I'm sure that we'll be friends throughout
   the years to come.
Even through the hard times and the
   mean things said and done.
I'll close my eyes and pray for happiness
   in what you see.
And pray five times harder that you wish
   the same for me.

—*Shelley Lynn Bailey*

Liaisons

Mirrored
Self—images,
Dank and stoic,
Writhe in a mute orgasm.
Pacified
In twilight,
The good old days;
Incarnate,
The sphinx
Of childhood.
Decency,
A small town,
Blunts emotions'
Half—life
At parting.

—*Robert Kappel*

ME

I feel it's really hard,
I try to be like everyone,
Maybe too hard,
But I feel such a fool,
I feel the need to be accepted,
Not used as a tool,
I'm just afraid of being rejected,
I don't even know myself,
Who am I really?
Everyday a different side,
What is it I have to hide?
Sometimes it scares me to be confronted,
I've alway said what they wanted,
I'm so afraid to let myself show,
Sometimes I wonder if I even have an
   inner glow,
Maybe someday. . .
I'll know.

—*Shawn West*

No Gain, Only Pain

I fill the empty space with my thoughts
   and my anguish
I try to leave a message for certain people
   to keep
I often cry with every verse that I write
Hoping, that I can give the people I love
   the gift of sight
There are many times when the message
   has been overlooked
These are not only words written in black
   and white
My poetry describes the emptiness of a
   broken heart
Also a young poet that knows what it is
   like to fall apart
They will read my poetry, but they cannot
   feel my pain
They do not have to struggle to survive
   every single day
Their lives will continue and I will
   continue to suffer in silence
I abhor the idea that I am gradually
   wasting away
Their intentions are not to let me hurt any
   day of my life
I can certainly see that they do care
I am not ready to reach out and hold onto
   their hands
So I will continue to stand alone and
   watch the moments that they will share

—*Linda A. Wilkens*

Civilization's Pen

All by myself the visions of what is to pass
   we can comprehend.
I try to wait out the efficient killing spree
   in hopes that it will cease—
Don't you believe in means of life to an
   end?
Oh, but for if I acquire the state of
   controlled chaos mankind is
Smothered in, there will be no drying to
   infinity of our bloodstained
Tears my friend and it will contaminate
   future generations of you,
Me and him. Until then though, once
   again, in never ending delusions
I'll live with images of myself in
   civilization's pen.

—*Richard Bruno*

The Day

It is the morning,
I walk to school,
My step is quick and light.
It is the evening,
I walk back home,
My step is slow and weary.

—*Michelle Miller*

Untitled

As the van stopped under the tree,
I walked without hesitation to your door.
You came and opened it, like a dream in a fantasy.
I strongly admire your gentle and kindness at my first sight of you.
I traveled thousands of miles through mountains and rivers,
But never did I expect to be in a love valley.
Time flew like quicksand that cannot be stopped.
Until the day came I was to be shipped home.
For I still remember that night we went riding on your bike,
Singing happy melodies throughout the night.
As the morning came, we watched the sun rise.
Then we left, riding back on your bike with silent lips.
I hoped you could have come with me, but facing with reality,
I moved my lips and said goodbye.
Now, as I sit in my classrooms, loneliness overcomes me with each class.
But the happy memories of us brings me back into the world of fantasy
With the sweet days we had.

—*Yun Ngan Wong*

The Clay—Horned Unicorn

I once had a unicorn,
which had no horn,
so I got me some clay,
and I made him one,
he was so proud,
he never took it off,
'til the day he died,
I sat and sat,
I cried and cried,
I loved him so much,
'til that day,
he died,
so let us never forget,
that one time unicorn,
which had no horn. . .

—*Tamara Fleming*

The Events

You scare me with your familiar race.
I wander alone in an empty place.
Feeling as stale as air,
My act performed.
Gliding to where times is reformed.
Free while he slept upon a watery distance.
Buried a dead soul without any resistance.
Agony in the eyes showing a dark silver.
Power in an arm that will always prefer.
Turning gold stars with questions in an answer.
Design a forseen dream on a strange dancer.

—*Louise Annis*

I'm Sorry

So here we are our first fight, did we move to fast?
I want so much for this to last
I didn't want it to seem like I spied on you
I care so much I don't know what to do
Inside I'm hurting bad
Outside I'm feeling sad
The time we are staying away
I hope it will give us time to think of what to say
I hope our problem will mend
I don't want us to end
Please forgive me
Just think about it, wait and see.

—*Marla Kelly*

Love so Real

I wish I could let you know just how I feel.
I want to tell you that my love is so real.
We've been through so much good and the bad.
Memories of us remind me of what we once had.
What did I do to push you far away?
You ended our love without a word to say.
I don't care what other people say or feel.
Because my love is so strong, my love is so real.
Maybe someday we'll be together once again.
I don't know how and I don't know when. . .

—*Natalie Berman*

Hidden Feelings

My love for you, I could no longer hide
I wanted you to know how I was feeling inside
I kept it within me for such a long time
But now I realize how much you should be mine.
I never loved anyone as much as I love you
But I need to know if you feel the same way too.
You weren't the first I ever loved but you'll be my last
All the ones before you are lost deep within the past.
Can't you see how much you mean to me?
Wrapped around your arms is where I want to be.
Your love to me is the drug that keeps me high
Love me always, love me forever, love me till the day I die.
If I sleep and never wake
Addicted to your love was only my mistake?

—*Raechel R. Guerra*

Drifting Apart

I've known you since we were young
I was happy to be with you
You were the best friend
Anyone could have
Now we're drifting apart.
We shared all our secrets
I told you my fears and joys
You told me yours
We cried through the bad times
And laughed through the good
Now we're drifting apart.
I thought we'd be friends till the end
But now you're going your way
I guess I'll go mine
Maybe we'll meet again
And talk about the old times we had
Whoever thought we'd be drifting apart.

—*Tracy Bartus*

God's America

In 1988
I was near the Pearly Gate,
The doctor shook his head
And this is what he said:
"1 chance in 5,000"
"Is all that I can give."
But God above said,
"Let him live."
Oh God, I am so grateful
For what you have done.
I promise to live close to you
Until my life is done.

—*William Tucker*

Judy's Blue Eyes

My pretty Judy, with eyes so blue
I was so concerned
What the future had in store for you.
From the moment I held you by the arm
I said I will keep you from all harm.
Though you could not hear anything I say
I knew you would be able
To understand me someday.
I caught german measles before you were born.
I would pray every night and every morn.
I prayed God would be merciful to you and me
And please don't be born blind.
There are so many beautiful things
For you to see.
I know grandmother Hyatt
Looks down from above
And somehow she still shares her love!

—*Ruby Hyatt*

Untitled

It was a nothing afternoon
I watched as he slowly, with a razor
Drew white lines with this forlorn crystal.
This, the same razor that tomorrow would
    end another line.
Placing the rolled bill in his nostril,
The enticing powder disappeared.
Not knowing why I repeated his actions,
Then leaned back in the safety of his
    arms.
The curtains blew softly in the breeze,
Calling. . .calling. . .calling to me.
They reached out and brushed my cheek,
Carrying my body and soul out the
    window.
I was floating. . . floating. . . floating on
    the back of an angel.
The breeze turned to a fierce wind,
Ripping at my skin until-
Thud!
Now I will only be floating among the
    angels. . .the angels. . .angels. . .

—Lori Mullen

Eyes of Brown

What is he thinking,
When he looks at me,
With those eyes of brown?
Our eyes, unblinking,
Locked eternally,
Never to look down.
His eyes of the earth,
Mine of stormy skies,
Share secrets hidden.
Today is the birth,
No need to disguise,
Of our love forbidden.
Our eyes, all too soon,
Slip away, but install
Promises for hereon.
Reality. . .noon,
Standing in the hall.
The moment gone.

—Melanie Thompson

No Matter What

I will not judge you
I will not bring up the past
For fear of wiping out the present.
I will not possess you
Even though I want to own your every
    breath
I will not plan our every moment
Surprises are more fun.
I will not lie to you
Even when the truth will hurt you more
I will not try to change you
I accept you as is
I will not take away your pain
You need it to grow on too.
I will not have expections of you
The ones you have of yourself are great
    enough
I will not stop loving you. . .
No matter what!

—Patti Kelly

Masterpiece in Time of Undying Memories

I will take to eternity the taste of my
    mother's homemade vegetable soup.
I will remember how she made each
    dumpling with a labor of love rolling
The dough flat and letting it dry on the
    old formica gray table top.
And the day I stood at my parents back
    door watching the sun glisten
Through my father's white hair which
    had once been raven black surrounding
The high cheeks of his indian smile.
A tear fell from the corner of my eye, it
    ran down my cheek.
I started to cry. For where there had been
    a stowic smile, a wrinkle
Did now reside.
A card from my brother which simply
    said, "How much more I appreciate"
"You now than when we were kids."
    You're not only my sister, but
Also my friend.
A handicapped son whom I watched grow
    from a small helpless child
Into a fine strong man.
A daughter who grew up to be my best
    friend, a more lovely child
God could never send. The childhood
    memories of my sister and I.
The games we played, the love we shared.

—Lee Cooper Meade

Hurt

in darkness,
    i hear laughter.
    —the voice is yours—
        I can tell
    only few have dared
        dream of love
'though thought i to be a chosen
            one
        wrong was the
            assumption
        and futile
            the
                dream.

—Sheryl H. Sesack

I Wish

I wish all day I wish all night,
I wish I could make this darkness bright.
I wish all day I wish all week,
I wish I could make this world be meek.
I wish all day I wish all month,
I wish this world would be peaceful for
    once.
I wish all day I wish all year,
I wish all the hungry children could eat
    dinner here.
I wish all day I wish all of my life,
I wish we could all live a long, long life.
I wish all day I wish all night,
I wish I could make this darkness bright.

—Misha McNabb

Just to See Him

When he first touched the earth,
I wish I were there.
On the day of his birth,
I wish I were there.
When he united the heavens and earth,
I wish I were there.
When he first made man, a new birth,
I wish I were there.
When he looked down on the world
For all that it's worth,
I wishI were there.
And when he returns to claim his earth,
I hope I'm still here.

—Natasha A. Williams

Lost Love

I wish there could be no more crying, but
    the tears never seem to end.
I wish the pain was over, but I hurt more
    every day.
I hear his words in other people's voices.
I see his face in all the darkness,
    sometimes I think I cannot go on.
I trust the memories to move me along,
    but they only hurt me more.
I want others to understand, but no one
    feels the way I do.
At times my anger feels so strong, but I
    have no one to blame,
I know God must have had a reason.
I thought the crying was over, but other
    tears did fall.
I thought the pain was gone, but the
    nights hurt me so.
I wish I could explain how special he was,
    but now no one seems to care.
I want my thoughts to bring a smile, but
    only tears can come.
I will think of him until the day we share
    life again.

—Stacey Staggs

A Secret Love

I see you in the distance,
I wish you were here.
Your eyes hold secrets,
As well as dreams.
May you realize the feelings,
I feel.
I think about you day and night.
You're the star in my dreams,
As well as my life.

—Shelly Yamaguchi

I Am

I am a country girl at heart
I wonder how it is to be a city girl
I hear hooves in the near, yet distant night
I see a radiant stallion poised at a stream
I want a horse of my own, someday
I am a country girl at heart.
I pretent to ride upon a glorious Quarter
　Horse
I feel myself in the saddle
I touch the silky horse's hide
I worry I will wake from my wonderful
　dream
I cry that my dream will fade
I am a country girl at heart
I understand my dream is that, a dream
I say that horses and myself go together in
　harmony
I dream of a grand stallion and a sandy
　sea shore
I try to imagine myself caring for such a
　glamorous creature
I hope my dreams will come true, one day
I am a country girl at heart.

—*Shera Wilhoite*

Boys

I sit here staring at the wall
I wonder if he'll ever call
Slowly I begin to sing
I wish the phone would start to ring
He said he'd call to say "Hi"
Maybe that was just another lie
The phone finally rang, it was his call
Maybe he's not so bad after all.

—*Tara Stevens*

Yesterday's Love

As I look upon my broken wounds,
I wonder if they will ever heal
And it's all because of him
He came along and destroyed all
My hopes and dreams
And now it seems I live in yesterday
But what will become of my life today
Sometimes I cry, others I just want to die
Why, you say, there are other fish in the
　sea
But no one is right for me
I'll never see tomorrow's sun
Til the one I love is back with me
On the outside, I seem as fine as can be
But inside, my heart is broken in more
　than three
So I say goodbye to tomorrow and today
And remember only yesterday

—*Vicki MacKenzie*

The First Rainbow

Blue, green, yellow, and red,
I wonder what Noah must have said.
First he prayed and God had heard,
Then God sent that special bird.
So 'till this day we see a streak
Of many colors our hearts may keep.

—*PFC Sharyn M. Mitchell*

The Shark Around my Neck

There you hang, though only a tooth.
I wonder what you did,
When your powerful body was full of life.
Were you a nasty creature?
No one will ever know, I suppose.
Since you've been attached
To the cheap chain,
I feel, even when I'm alone,
You'll be my friend.
There's nothing you can't do.
Yet you're only a simple shark tooth.
The dreams you give me!
We float through the grey waters,
We fought deadly harpooners.
Together, we can do anything.
Hope, that is the gift you give me.
Hope that maybe someday, I'll be great
　too.

—*Sarah Suzanne Westcott*

What I Am

I am a shy and different girl
I wonder where dead things go.
I hear the noise of a jungle far away.
I see people in far away places.
I want to become a doctor.
I am a shy and different girl.
I pretend that I am going to other planets.
I feel the troubles of life.
I touch the stars in my dreams.
I worry about my future.
I cry when I think of war and other sad
　things.
I am a shy and different girl.
I understand the emotions of hurt, love,
　and pain.
I say that everyone should have a chance.
I try to do my best.
I hope there will be world peace.
I am a shy and different girl.

—*Shanita Foreman*

Hiding Inside

As each day passes by
I wonder why I still love you.
I feel like a stranger that
Has wandered into your life.
I know only what you say
And nothing what you feel.
Often I wonder why you hide so;
Must be from your childhood.
Is it hard for you to accept
That one loves you so deeply,
That you cannot let me in
To share your joy and your pain.
Instead you hide behind words
That I have slowly learned were lies.
If time has not already let me
Then we must part, for I need
Emotions that are true
And feelings that are love.

—*Sherri L. Rivera*

Untitled

As I sit by the window and think of time
　gone by,
I wonder why I wasted it on a dream that
　could never come true.
The silence I have grown to know is
　deafening,
And the painful feeling of my heart is
　killing me,
Because the only one I ever loved, never
　really loved me.
I did not lose just a friend, I lost my best
　friend.
I may be able to forget about us in time,
But no amount of time will help me to
　forget you.
I will always love you with all my heart
　and soul.
We gave all we had to give, I guess it
　wasn't enough.
My life is the same as before I met you,
But somehow, someway, it seems
　different, emptier,
And I feel more lost and alone than ever
　before.
I remember a time when we held each
　other tight,
And did not want to let each other go,
But all that has changed and now I am
　left feeling sad and blue.

—*Melissa Pallotti*

Time in Space

Time in space
i won't forget
We ripped apart each other,
We ripped apart the state,
The country
We ripped apart our world,
Our universe
We laughed at many lifes now
And cried about an infinity later
We had ripped apart ourselves
We had looked at the pieces
There alone on the floor
We wondered what in this
World we had done
Because we realized finally that
Those pieces were nothing alone
That somehow they have to get all
 together.

—Marie L. Mapes

I Wish I Were but a Butterfly

I wish I were a butterfly,
I would fly the sky so high,
The earth where people sigh,
And many more, they cry,
For others lie,
And yet more die,
If only I were a butterfly.
I wish I were but a butterfly,
As free as I can be,
I would fly away by nigh,
And hurt, I'll never have to see,
Ah, to be but a butterfly,
As free, as free can be.
I wish I were a butterfly,
For butterflies, they never never cry,
If only a butterfly were I,
Surely happiness is forever my.

—Melody Yeoh

Love's Tough

In my bedroom, on my bed,
I wrote a letter to my boyfriend that read,
"In the back seat of her car,"
"I saw you two together."
"In my mind, in my heart,"
"I truly never thought we'd be apart."
"You can't deny or try to hide it,"
"Let's not even attempt to fight it."
"The pain is so rough. . ."
"One conclusion: Love's tough."
"Now we put our love to the test,"
"We always thought love came with the
 best."
"But now you have another girl,"
"I'm your least care in the world."
"Broken hearts, the pain so rough,"
"We always wanted more than enough."
"Together, we faced the fact. . .love's
 tough."

—Tanya Guillory

I'd be a Tree

If I could choose one thing in nature to be,
I'd be a tree.
It stands so calm and poised from day to
 day,
I could be that way.
It does not resist life's storms, but with
 them bends,
So must we, my friend.
There are many lessons of life the tree can
 teach,
It does not need to preach.
It is beautiful example of the kind of life,
We can have without strife.
If we but learn a lesson from the tree,
We too can be free.

—Rita Jean Smith

If only

My life is a book of open pages being
 turned by the wind.
If only I could turn them back again.
I remember days of happiness and sitting
 here with you,
If only I could turn the pages back.
A single tear is the sign that those happy
 days are gone.
The roses you sent me are wilted and
 dead.
My eyelash of dreams is lifted to the
 wind.
The flowers seem to struggle to stay alive.
Maybe just to be a single reminder of
 days past and gone. . .

—Tara Mantsch

Apart

We haven't talked since we've been apart.
If only you knew how much I miss you.
I feel as though I need you so.
For what can I do since I'm crushed by
 you.
Now that we've been apart
I feel so helpless in my heart.
What I would give to be in your arms
Just maybe that would help my lonely
 heart.
I love you so but I guess there is no hope.
I'll now let you go
With one thing you should know.
How I love you so.

—Michelle Whitney

Family, Friends, and Changes

If you don't take the time to love they
 might be gone.
If you don't take the time to care they
 might just move on.
Like everyday as if your last because
 changes come around real fast
So while you have the time
Love them
Care for them
And live as if today is your last
And the changes won't seem to come so
 fast.

—Sarah Smith

Distant Love

I love it when I hear your voice.
If you only knew, you're my choice.
I saw you for a short time,
And right then I wanted you as mine.
I left you for a little while,
Then the love I felt grew within every
 mile.
This feeling I have for you
Is starting to make me blue.
It's the distance between that hurts me.
But its hurt no one can see.
I want to touch and to hold,
To lie next to you and hide the cold.
If you don't feel the same way,
Please tell me now and I will sadly go
 away.

—Monique Cabrera

Life

Life is what you make of it,
If you think of it as challenges
Instead of obstacles you'll be more
Likely to succeed.
Look at mistakes as a learning
Experience and remember people
Have a great impact on life itself.
One single person can brighten
The world like a rose growing
Among poison ivy.
All it takes is a kindred spirit,
Caring heart, and beautiful soul.
One person who stands out among
The crowd and shines
Brilliantly with benevolence is you.

—Tammy L. Briceland

Time

Time is something like a rhyme
If you're late you pay a fine
Time goes by fast
And won't always last
Time has gone on and on
And hopefully will until we are gone
Time is something everyone has
Sometimes it gives you pazazz,
It has a never ending cycle
Like the wheel of a motorcycle
Sometimes time goes by slow
Almost like wind always blows
God created time
And it doesn't rewind
So be kind
And share yourself with mankind

—Leigh Freeman

It's Hard to Say Goodbye

When you leave I'll miss you so.
I'll hunger for the inner beauty that you
    display,
The companionship you always flourish
    me with,
The friendship that rises above the
    surface with your smile,
And the love you've given me by keeping
    me warm when I am cold.
You are a ray of sunshine, you brighten
    the darkest of days.
Every time we embrace, I know we were
    meant to be,
A twist of fate, he wanted us to be
    together.
Every time I look into your eyes,
I realize you're the one I could never be
    without.
Since you will be leaving in a short while,
I want this message to be as special as can
    be.
You filled the emptiness in my heart, it
    meant so much.
Still together hand in hand, separated we
    will never be.
I'll miss you much but remember, I love
    you much,
So hold my hand, hold me tight,
    remember me as yours.
Upon returning from your long journey,
    open arms are what you'll see,
Because babe, it's forever you and me.

—Lisa Timmins

A Child's Words From Heaven

I was once here but now I'm gone
I'll leave these words to carry on.
My soul is with you I'll be in heart
With my family I'll never part.
I love my daddy and he loves me
But he'll never see me climb my first tree.
I'm in heaven with God I'll stay
All I ask is that you will pray.
For all those children who loved me
Let them know I am now free.
Help those children to get well
Make them hear you but do not yell.
Don't cry now the pain is gone
That's why God let me hear His song.
Please remember, I love you
I'll be here each day to help you through.
I must go now to my new home
Where I will never be alone.

—Lori Smith

M.I.A.

Memories
forcIng the
  unShed tears to fall
    Saluting him, whom
    I
    Never knew.
  A Grave for
    hIm
  staNds at
    Arlington
    Cemetary; a
    sTone for the stranger
    I
    lOve
My uNcle John.

—Amy L. Yunek

Grandmother's Trunk

Today I am going through Grandmother's
    trunk.
I'll probably find a lot of junk.
Well what do you know, a picture of me
    from long ago.
A lock of hair so black, just like
    Granddad's long
time back.
A photograph of a girl and boy.
Their faces full of joy.
Old-timey clothes and faded rose.
Tears came to my eyes, I had to stop and
    blow
my nose.
Through tear dimmed eyes.
I saw a flag, scrapbook, a memo of a
    dance
All this belonged to a son killed in France.
I looked it over through and through.
I had, had a glimpse of Grandmother's
    life, by
looking in her trunk.

—Patsy Bockman

I Care

I hope that you know that I care about
    you,
I'll try to show you so that you know it's
    true.
I care about what happens each day of
    your life,
I want you to tell me of each struggle and
    strife.
I want to tell you I will always be here,
It doesn't change anything whether I'm
    far or near.
I want to share your smiles and tears,
I want you to tell me your hopes, dreams,
    and fears.
I've told you before and I'll tell you again,
Now and forever you'll always be my
    friend.

—Michele Pritchard

The Pearl

Stunning is the moon,
illuminating the darkness that surrounds
    it,
dancing along the stars,
with gracious beauty,
leaving a glimmer of hope among
those captivated by its song,
Yet, if it were to reveal its many moods
harmoniously together,
at one glorious moment,
beyond the mountains,
and deep within the sea,
It would take the breath right
from the soul,
for it is a glamorous pearl that was
stolen long ago by the lonely night...

—Lisa Rayfield

Night Flight

Watching out into the night,
I'm flying high, just like a kite.
Carried through the sky so high,
I never knew that I could fly!
I feel the wind upon my face,
Still soaring higher, into space.
"Now what?" I thought, "Can I get
    down,"
"Back in the direction of homeward
    bound?"
Terrified over my bad luck,
Suddenly, I wake up.

—Melissa Gugni

Whenever

Whenever you need to talk things out;
I'm listening.
Whenever you need a shoulder to cry on;
I'll be there.
Whenever you need a smile;
I have extras.
Whenever you need the sound of my
 voice;
I'm by the phone.
Whenever you need advice;
I'm right by your side.
Whenever you need a friend;
I'm yours forever.
Whenever you just need to be with me;
I'm in your heart.

—Terri Barker

My Little One

My little one,   I feel you
  Beside me always near,
    My Heart is yours
      forever — you took
        a large part when
  you went away.

My little one — your eager hands
  were always reaching
    out for new worlds
      to explore — and new
        meadows to run in
  forever in God's fields.

My little one — you greeted me
  each morning with a
    smile, and tender
      baby kiss —
        may you grace
          the Angels with
            you presence —
and share forever your sweet smile
  with me, in memory.

—Michael J. Guida

Missing You

I lie here awake thinking of you, the rain
  falls softly upon my window pane.
I'm missing you now and wanting you too,
  when will I see you again?
I remember the night, the night you were
  here. You held me close to your heart.
The night was so short, daybreak had
  come, and my love, we were now soon
  to part.
You held me once more and said that you
  cared, my feelings were so very strong.
I wanted you then but I was so scared,
  this feeling had lasted so long.
We parted my love, early one day, the
  pain was so real to me.
Fate had its chance, time took its toll, but
  I love you babe, still don't you see.
We're miles apart and futures away; it
  keeps us from holding on tight.
But I lie back and dream sweet mem'ries
  of you and be thankful for one special
  night!

—Shannon Thornton

The Wonder of Children

I sit on a bus going anywhere, lost in my
  thoughts.
I'm not in a bad mood really, just heavily
  in thought.
You wouldn't say I was in a good mood
  either.
I don't have a smile on my face.
But no matter how I feel, there's one
  thing,
One thing that can always bring a smile to
  my face. . .
The face of a child.
The innocence of their smile, their
  questions,
The look on their face when they see,
Discover or hear something new.
Oh, that can always make me smile.
It can always cheer me up.
I stare at the child pointing out the
  window
She has no idea, no inclination
As to how she makes me feel
The wonder of children. I can always
  count on them,
To put a smile on my face, and laughter in
  my eyes.

—Stephanie C. Pacelli

It's Love

Sky of blue. Colors of the rainbow are
  one.
I'm so in love with you!
A summer breeze passes by.
A beautiful day has begun.
Birds dance about up above to music all
  their own.
Our hearts sing. It's love.
A feeling all our own.
Our smiles are the sunshine.
Our secrets are the key. It's love.
Forever I'm yours.

—Rita M. Sutherby

Morning Time

I watch the waves erase my
imprints in the sand.
My mind lurks from reality
to the thoughts of my subconiousness.
I try to see past the clouds
but I can't
Is it someone with their hand
held out?
I run to greet this person; but
only to be disappointed.
For when I got there,
The only thing I found was a
picture of me
I close me eyes, returning to
reality.
Only to find part of me gone.

—Sharon Reynolds

Sight

Did you ever stop to smell a flower
In a meadow filled with dreams,
And wonder if this world of ours
Is ripping at the seams?
Did you ever stop to hear the rain
Beating on the earth,
And doubt about your feelings, hopes
That plainly have no worth?
Did you ever feel the power
Of a love to never end,
Or anticipate a letter,
Which you pray that he did send?
Yes, life without these miracles,
How queer it has to be.
If yours is truly sight,
I choose to never see.

—Lara Pitaro

Subconscious Awaken

The rain fell soft
In a misty haze
As the clouds twisted
To form an infinite maze
With my alter image
I blindly proceed
Toward the depth
Of hatred and greed
Coming upon an eternal light
I trudged wearily on
Melting away my coldness and fright
All my insecurities now gone

—Rachelle Prisco-Braido

Grandpa

Trapped, not unlike an animal
In a ringside cage
A victimized prisoner
Of the silent war
A body has waged.
Captive, within the lucid limbo
Of some unjust reward
Grasping at a distant thought
An ineffective mind
Is stumbling toward.
Isolated, like an earthly alien
Separate from the crowd
Craving a familiar word to communicate
The answer out loud.
Shackled, by the heavy iron chains
Of an antique jail
Seated, patiently waiting for the end of
  pain
And a heart to fail.

—Laurie Chalko

My Spirit Explains

My earthly presence does not cause me to
   be
In a world any finer than I could.
If it were that I could rise
Above all that was
It would be a finer being I would be.
There without the moon and sun
It is my light that would follow me.
Never once was I able to say to you
That this was my love come back to you.
But here in my heart the sea shall turn
Though calm it would be along the shore.
Never could I say this to you
For it is your ear would hear it differently.
But morning comes and in a dream
I partly step to hear the scream
And carry you in flight gone by
Across the world that I call I.

—Mary Adamowski

Don't

Don't sit too close
You'll ruin your eyes
If you eat that cake
It goes right to your thighs
Brush your teeth
Before they turn yellow
If you're that hungry
Have some sugar-free jello
Get your beauty rest
You need it.
If you really want a dog,
You'll have to feed it
Harmless advice
From a parent to a child?
Or the voice from within
That drives you wild!

—Linda Tamuccio

Feelings Of Love

Love and despair, Love and hate,
In everyday there's more to take.
You climb the love ladder, and then fall
   down.
You try to climb back up,
But it's a hopeless battle,
Your mind is confused,
It won't stop the rattle.
You wonder if there's any way out,
If the hurt will ever end, voices begin to
   shout,
And, you're looking for a friend.
You're crying and upset, because the love
   you had is lost,
You're trying to forget, and now you pay
   the cost.
To think you know someone, whose love is
   true,
Then they turn their back,
And really hurt you.
So whatever you do, and whatever you
   say,
Remember what I told you, when your
   love runs away.

—Laura Whitlow

The Outside World

The sadness of hope
in fear of thou lonely world
a world where no one can turn.
All shut out of this happyland.
Without even a breath in this silent light.
With fear of darkness.
Shutting out nothing,
Yet life itself.
This is more than blank
Darkness flashing in the light it is a place
With no one to care.
What is this world?
But what we fear makes no difference
This different world is nothing more than
   life,
life itself.

—Nadia Drew

That Girl

That girl I know is out to get me,
In her sardonic mind, she's thinking up
   schemes to hurt me.
Her peevish ways destroy my soul.
Those rumors she starts destroy my heart,
Yet, she gets her way like a devil would,
I wish her to die more than anyone could.
But I have to live with that unruly girl.
But as I look in the mirror,
That girl looks a lot like me.

—Melinda Lutes

The Witches in the Woods

The girls have been standing in the
   darkness
In the black woods with no stars above
With slow paces, the girls were dreaming
   of nothing
With the straight long blond hair
In the hands, the girls were having the
   wild flowers
And they were dancing on the dark green
   fields
Being put off the white clothes
With no echoes, it was silent
In no smiles, the faces were so white,
Calm and cheak with less voices
If the girls found any aims to move
They gathered and walked so slowly
By the rivers, the girls were just sleeping
Listening to the river's moving

—Yoshimi Iwano

My Dream of Him

As I was walking along
In the cold,
Still night dark
There he was still so alone
That he was still in my heart
Tears fell, when I looked at him
From my eyes that were weeping
I thought of him
Until he adores me indeed
With dreamful eyes
He, his spirit lies
When my dream will never die
He will glow and shine
In front of my eyes.

—Leslie Hambrick

Royal Palms Overhead

Up ahead a shimmering light
In the distance a beauty pure sight
I mustn't pass this moment to stop
For only it takes palms to cast my thought
As the sun's extended rays do glow
For when my hair breezes, winds do blow
Unaware of the coldness that lays
My body stands and softly sways
Easily captivated in this trance
My horizon beholds the sea in one glance
My smoke beholds the scent of relief
To escape who I lusted for,
Is yet fading
As does the sun only time waiting
A time of sure pleasure
To come forever to treasure
This place a sun set, is said
Royal Palms overhead.

—Monika Nunez

Wars for Fools so Peace Rules

Soliders who fight by day and night,
In the eyes of kids, have no right,
God, why don't we let everyone live?
Let hostages go along with captive,
Peace is good. War is evil.
Ask me what's to rule
And I'll simply say
Peace should!

—Vickey Whelan

Untitled

The world today is pretty messed up;
In the minds of christians, it's simply
   corrupt.
There are drug addicts, pill poppers, and
   thieves,
Murderers, liars, and blasphemers, I
   believe.
Today the decision is yours, my friend,
To help save the world from the soon
   coming end.
The end of the world is hell, torture, and
   sin
While for christians, our lives are about to
   begin.
The end is near so there's no time to
   waste,
We must act now and act with much
   haste.
There are hurting people searching for life
But are filled with hatred, resentment,
   and strife.
The life that they want has been given to
   you
To plant in their hearts and tell them it's
   true.
So start planting now; don't ever stop,
And soon you will reap a great big crop.
Never give up and soon you can say,
Dear Jesus, my sheaves, please show them
   the way!

—*Terri Weber*

Secret Garden

I know a place where no one ever goes,
Where roses bloom, and weeping willows
   sway in the breeze.
A place where the grass grows green and
   sweet.
Sometimes I go there and lie in the grass,
   or sit in a tree,
And just listen to the duet the birds and
   crickets sing.
Other times I take a walk or smell the
   roses.
But most of all, I love to let my
   imagination run wild and be a princess
   with a beautiful crown,
Or just a girl lost in her dreams.
This place I talk of is my secret garden,
   and will be forever.

—*Rebecca Morris*

Yesterday

She sits in her porch rocker
In the moonlight
Remembering what it was like
To be in love
Back in the days of petticoats
And Model T's
When gentlemen came to call
With flowers
Or to ask a father's permission
For a stroll.

—*Michele McMullen*

Observations

I see your strength, O God
In the swelling of the sea
In the grandeur of the mountains
I see your majesty.
A tiny shell now empty
Displays your gentle hand
Lying on the shore
With countless grains of sand.
I hear your joy in laughter
Around me everyday
Sounds of little children
Happy, lost in play.
Never changing sky
Floods me with your peace
Heights and depths unknown
Timeless creativity.

—*Wanda Dyer*

White Fence

Story of tears fenced in white,
Inside a story as black as night.
Carved in stone for all to see,
It's the future of you, the future of me.
It's a story of pain fenced in white,
The fence can be seen day and night.
Children of four who all went close,
The loss of a child hurts the most.
To lose all four, little time between,
Tears and pain it can be seen.
This story I tell is not my own,
This story I found cut in stone.
Many years pass till the story's complete,
The parent's now rest at the children's
   feet.
This story is true, this is known.
Their story is cut deep in the cold, grey
   stone.

—*Michael R. Hanley*

Growing Old

I'm growing old and my beauty has faded.
Inside myself I still feel young,
But the youth I feel within does not show
In my wrinkled and toothless face
Nor in my slumpy, dumpy body.
I don't appeal to anyone's eye.
I'm alone within myself,
Hiding away from society and
Wishing that I would have never grown
   old.
Maybe there is something called
   reincarnation
And when I die, I could come back
Young and pretty once again
And enjoy life one more time.

—*Teri Payne*

Somewhere It's Written

No better than the idea or worse than
   another's thought,
interpretation is left to the reader whose
   mind cannot be bought.
Alive isn't dead and that is close I'm sure,
to knowing the profundity of reason which
   I abhor.
If we don't know what dead is, then why
   purport the lie,
of knowing purposes and reasons when we
   can never die?
Take time and hold fast to the mercy of
   fate,
nonexistence is all there is, so we cannot
   be late.
Patient, calm reasoning of yourself, the
   soul,
let it take you to the places that fill the
   ancient hole.
Stop pulling the lead to where it's
   supposed to go,
supposing and surmising are better left to
   the gods above
than to the mortal question mark below.

—*Susan A. Sager*

Little Neo Hippy

I'm just a little neo hippy,
Into peace and flowers.
I could sit and play guitar,
And sing folk songs for hours.
I want to change the world,
Into a better place.
Showing love to friends and neighbors,
With the smile on my face.
I walk around bare-foot,
With a twinkle in my eye.
I'm comfy in my torn up jeans,
And T-shirts of rainbow tie-dye.
It doesn't get me up-tight.
When people frown at what they see.
Because I've never been so happy,
As I am just being me.
A little neo hippy!

—*Rachel Wisda*

Sunsets

Sunsets are stunning colors
Intricately woven in the heavens.
They are delicate flowers
Dancing across the evening sky
Casting their wonderous shadows
Upon the abandoned earth.
They are scarlet, pink,
Rose, and blush rainbows
Jumbled and stretched
Throughout millions and
Millions and millions of miles.

—*Shannon Jones*

In Friendship

This hand I offer
is
hardened with toil,
scarred
with time. . .
yet,
this hand of mine
is
tender and loyal. . .
longing
to touch you.
Won't you accept
this hand?

—Lee Anderson-Pike

The Window

All between me and the outside world
Is a thin piece of glass.
Material so fragile,
Yet so tough.
This is all that keeps me from a world
I once knew.
A transparent wall,
Letting me see what I can't have.
Tempting me,
As though I were a babe
And it were candy,
And me wanting of it's sweetness.
Oh so tempting,
Yet I don't want the bitter,
And there's still the glass,
That transparent wall that takes my world
  away.

—Venis Weaver

Memories, Hopes and Dreams

When you feel the world
Is against you
And there is nowhere
To turn,
Think about old
Memories
Think about our hopes,
Our dreams
And what we can achieve
In the future.
The present is a time
In our lives
That will soon be lost
In our history.
So make the best of this
Present time
So we can have more
Old memories
And more
Hopes and dreams.

—Rachel Schueller

Awakening

The pungent aroma of spring
Is all around;
The taste of blossoms and
Fecund earth is on the tongue.
The dew-*renched grass
Gently caresses the feet
Of those who walk
Upon it.
The morning sky lifts out
Over the horizon,
Searching, seeking to renew
Those who would understand.

—Sharon Clark Smith

Desert Sea

A vast, vast sea
Is all I see.
Where does it end?
Cactus, tumbleweed. . .
Not much more
Until
The spring
Where everything is flowery
And green again.

—Melanie Velez

Love

If your love for me
is as strong as mine for you,
We shall live together
in harmony.
Who knows what will happen
if our hearts are purely true,
Filled with love and caring
for just us two.
I know my heart beats true
but what if your heart or mine
should happen to skip a beat?
A second of love we shall never see,
A second of love that will never
come to our hearts,
And all the rest may just be
a memory

—Rayanne Shattuck

True Feelings

Fresh as the morning dew,
Is how true my love is for you.
I just wich you new,
How strong my feeling are for you.
Words can't say what my heart feels
  inside.
My actions show the sensitive side.
If I only new what you felt,
That would make my heart melt.
The thought of you saying no,
Makes me want to crumble.
When I see you my face starts to light up,
And when your not around I practically
  fall to
The ground.

—Lukendra Hurt

Circle of Life

My circle of life
Is intertwined with many others.
We do not form a chain,
Nor a mere second circle,
But rather a network
Of interlocking strength.
Each is touching the other
And equally contributes
"Each in his own way"
To the massive structure.
We are the frame of life,
The scaffolding of truth,
The cover of justice,
And the armor of peace
Containing the courage of love
And the happiness of friendship.

—Terry L. Dollar

Wishing

What is wishing?
Is it a place where destiny is your goal
Or a flower growing tall in your soul?
If it is somewhere, or if it exists
Maybe I'll find it while lost in a kiss.
A single breath can say yes or no
Or even if I will go
To this place where wishing is true.
Wishing is magical
A never-ending road where I can go and
  see
Or two people holding hands underneath
  a tree.
Maybe one day as I'm skipping down a
  hill
The stars will sing to me and tell me what
  I've fulfilled.
But until that day I'll have the strength
To go on in life, not in pain.

—Lisa Sizemore

Love

Do you know what love can be?
Is it being here. . .
With my love for you unknown?
Can I know what love is?
Do you embody what I want to love?
Is your name love's alter-ego?
Forever I hold love.
Forever as long as I have you.
For although you remain a friend,
I love you for an eternity.

—Tracy Fox

Is It All Really Worth It

Is it all really worth it
is it really worth it all
the hardships with the goodtimes
the defeat with the triumph
should you have to fall down just to get up
should you have to lose just to win
over and over
again and again.
Is life just something
that is short but not long
is it the difference between what is right
    but not wrong
is it the balance between no music and a
    song
the world would be too different
the world would be too strange
the world would be too unfamiliar
the world just wouldn't be the same.

—Stacie Cheryl Darr

The Mirror and the Glass

I often wonder who's behind the Mirror?
Is it realy me or a Man of Horror?
Or just a reflection of my inner Soul.
Nay, a Vestige in an outer shawl.
Am enclosed in a capsule of dream?
Is it reality, a reflection of your gleam? or
    just a puppet on my hand,
Who does as I wish and obeys my
    command.
I know who's behind the glass,
A living Soul solid as the brass.
He maybe anyone who moves and sway.
To see them. . .in a clear sunny day.
To touch who's behind the glass is like a
    mirage,
How to fulfill without a barrage,
No mortals thought dares to comprehend.
But my source I'll always spend.

—Ulysses S. Alumbro

Untitled

Waiting for that day
Is like a million years away.
Standing by the window,
Staring at the stars,
It's a pretty lonely place.
I'm all alone
Waiting for that moment.
I'll stand here forever
And when you come
We'll meet
You're in my thoughts
Day and night.
I could hear your voice
Calling me
And that brings all the memories
We had together.

—Shelly Kim

Dreams

The waves that crash upon the sand
is like the feeling when you hold my hand
the glorious winds that blow through the
    trees
will you come with me. . .please!
To a place where apples bloom
and waterfalls rumble
where the moons of Venus shine a glorious
    blue
I can't believe this is true
that I am alone. . .here. . .with you!
Where rainbows never end
where shamrocks always bloom of four
where white, blue, or even purple horses
    fly
amongst the stars, against the moons.
Do you understand this crazy afternoon?
My love, my life forever we shall be
but these are just dreams. . .
well. . .maybe.

—Telfair Mason

Too Tired to Run

Is love real
Is love fantasy
My fate is sealed
It's my destiny
To find what's real
Fantasy loves, life's common mistake
Falling in love with the ideal of it all
Rushing in, another common mistake
I get so tired of taking the fall
Yet I rush in with my heart at stake
Have I met the one
Is she on my list
Or is she yet to come
I scream and clench my fist
I'm too tired to run!

—Lonny David Ricker

Dreamland

The hole in life
Is my domain.
The power of thought
Is my escape.
Dreamland
The island of isolation.
Surrounded by the sea of grief.
Abandoned by life.
My subconscious kingdom.
Dreamland
Free life
Free thought
Free soul
Free.
Dreamland

—Roland Hofstede

The Harvest Time Of Love

The harvest time of love
Is not to wait for another day—
Wisdom dictates if it would be now, is
    now;
"Gather ye rosebuds while ye may".
Heaven, a tantalizing prospect, I must
    confess
Is not what I feel under my dress;
Utopia differs in more than degree
From the hard-fought proving of your
    masculinity.
Love's not love that unnecessary delay
    makes;
Let's not quarrel for our own sakes.
If my flesh, my hair, my cherry lips thee
    offend,
Of this affair let's quickly make an end.
To wait and wait till our soul's escape
Would be living, loving, lifeing much too
    late.

—Mary McGreevy

Untitled

Who is that?
Is she looking at me?
What does she want?
What does she see?
Why does she cry?
Is that a frown?
Is her world turning upside down?
What does she fear?
She's so far yet so near.
As I turn away,
I don't want to believe
That girl in the mirror—
That girl is me.

—Rosalind Kemp

Companion

Is someone you can trust.
Is someone who can keep your secrets.
Is someone who is there for you.
Is someone who loves you.
Because you are you, your own person.

—Wendy Jeya Haigh

My Mom

My mom,
Is someone who's a friend.
My mom,
Is someone who knows who you are.
My mom,
Is someone who will take you
Shopping when you're feeling down.
My mom,
Is someone who knows that when
I am angry that I love you.
But most of all,
Mom, you are my best friend.

—Michelle Bastiani

Nuclear Age

The breeze you feel that you cannot see
Is telling you the time is now for you and me.
We must ask for his hand and gather our strength,
For we are moving into an uncertain future across time and space.
We have much to do if we are to insure the survival of our race,
For you and I are the ones who have been chosen by fate.
Nuclear age you blew in like the breeze,
And you are hereby informed forever and a day
That you shall not and will not ever blow us away.

—Steven M. Cameron

Your Secret Place

Line after line after line
Is that what you do?
To be with you, I would have never guessed
That you are promised to a certain death
It won't happen to me, is what you thought?
But guess what, it did
You don't feel the pain and betrayal that I feel
Only others know of it and dislike it
All you care about is getting high
And your friends are the ones who are always feeling low
I keep my thoughts on paper so you don't see
The feelings I have for thee
You keep yours in the air
Because you are always hiding there

—Stephanie Christian

Confidence

Having confidence in yourself
Is the most important thing you can own;
In everything you do,
It just sets the tone.
Do the best you can
In everything you try to do,
And you'll see that others
Really look up to you.
You must believe in yourself
And like yourself, too,
Then confidence will come very easily
In everything you do.

—Linda Nelms

Prevail

What is the beginning and where is the end
Is there a heaven—is there sin
They say no man an island is
But if he has it, it is his
They say no man a rock can be
He can't stand alone eternally
But if what they say is true
Then ask yourself are you really you
They'll tell you what it takes to be men
They say swords hold less might than a pen
They'll say don't take the easy way out
And still you don't know what it's all about
So you make things hard for yourself
And marvel at the success of someone else
They say that charity begins at home
That's one thing thay say that may not be wrong
Remember that what they say won't bring you wealth
If you want to be successful. . .try being yourself

—Richard Chapman

Everything

It to be that can it be
Is to find all that we can be,
And never fear to find which is true.
Is to find all that we can be
That which is everything?
Or is everything nothing?
Or is nothing everything,
That of which we truly are?

—Michel Demyen

World Today: Year 1989

The world in my point of view
Is very busy, has many things to do.
Not caring much about important things,
Such as home, family, and friends.
A world of love and hatred
And of peace and war.
Everywhere people are dead
But we want to see more.
The world is so unfeeling,
It keeps our minds reeling.
Bush, Gorbachev, and nuclear arms,
Don't you say we should turn on some charms.

—Wendy Weinkauf

My Charlie

Is Freud right?
Is what I feel
Merely an overflow of my libido
And now the pain results
From its return to my ego?
But intellectualizing
Diminishes the pain
None whatsoever.
I only know
I'll never again
Hold my Charlie.
Did the man in the car
When he struck
That black ball of fur
Know he crushed
Part of my heart?

—Shirley E. Curtis

To Be A Kid Again

To be a kid again
is what I wish to do
To be young and free
And start anew.
To run and play about
is what I wish to do
To climb old oak trees
For the sky to be blue.
To watch flowers bloom
is what I wish to do
To run through the meadows
My dreams to come true.

—Vanessa Ward

Winter Love

Just when the flowers begin to die.
Is when my love soars high.
As leaves whither and plunge to their grave
It is through you my world is saved.
And as the outside air begins to chill
Beside you I am warm still.
The snow from the sky
Is as pure as my heart
I love you as much now
As I have from the start.
As long as there's a chill in the air
I now beside me, you'll be there
But when the warmth has come to stay
Will you find a new life and go away?
For when it's warm outside.
My own coldness I shall have to hide.

—*Michelle Pinto*

Wind, It's a Breeze

The wind is like an ocean of air in the sky.
It blows my hair in my face and cools me on hot summer days.
When I go to the beach, it blows the salty water on my face.
I can feel drops on my cheeks.
I love the wind when it blows my way.

—*Samantha M. Franks*

Pain

Screaming like the rising sun,
It breaks over the horizon,
Swelling into the sky,
Bursting into a torrent of piercing hues.
It festers as a boil,
Burning with the flames of the sun.
Slowly, silently its poisons escape from its crusty armor.
Hysterical diffusion engulfs the skies,
Resounding with echoing cries.
It is alive with ardor,
Scattering in a suffocating web.
Pain is born,
Alive with grief
That smothers the living.

—*Tracy A. R. Krug*

Love Can Be Found

Love is like a lost puppy,
It can be found.
Days worrying, crying, and thinking,
Love takes time.
So when you find it,
Put it in your heart
And throw away the key.

—*Michelle Gleason*

The Thing

It is the thing everyone sublimely fears,
It could happen at any time,
Or in many years.
It's like a volcano on the brink of eruption,
But this could cause total destruction.
It takes one large shake to make the volcano blow,
But one small finger can make it all go.
It's the bomb
The nuclear bomb

—*Vanessa L. Wyrick*

The Distance

The wave. . .
it crashes, it dashes, it splashes
Enticing a reckless delight.
You wave. . .
unhurried, unflurried, unworried
I sense your eyes wild and bright.
Your footsteps. . .
so feline, the sea brine's drunk with wine
Your hand must I reach out to take
The distance. . .
first crying, the whying, now dying
A murmur that's left in your wake.

—*Stacey Leong*

My One And Only

With your love, I'll never feel alone,
It feels so good, our love has grown.
In my heart, you have a place,
Because you definitely got, what it takes.
You make me feel so secure in many ways,
that's why I'm so glad, it's you
I'll be spending the rest of my days.
I have alway's looked for someone
To love to the total extreme, and
It was you all along, you have fulfilled my dream.
My feelings for you are so deep,
You my dear, I think I'll keep.
Life with you, I know will be great,
You are my best friend, my lover, forever my
Soul mate.

—*Rose Jordan*

Water

Water. . .
it fills the sea
makes dusty ground muddy
cools you off on a hot summer day
some may wonder why oh why
can such a thing come
from one little thing
Water

—*Lynn Schmitz*

The Angel Of Light

The silk pony had wings of a heraldic bird.
It flew fiercely against the strongest and angriest wind.
Wisps of clouds suddenly burst into orange flames
The stars fell on dry earth like shattered pieces of glass.
I walked slowly until my feet bled! but I felt no pain nor fear.
My eyes were in ecstatic focus to the immaculate vision of an ange.
Our hands met and I fell into a sudden embrace.
The smile I could not forget—it was oh I so gentle, so holy—
my heart wept with joy!
It was the ANGEL OF LIGHT.

—*Marth Baldemore*

Forgotten Past

The story was forgotten
It had the lives of many
On its cover
Written forever in stone
For all to see
But not understand
The young are curious
The old are stuborn
Holding onto old beliefs
Closing the mind
Afraid of the past
Ignoring the future.
Caught in a void
Only breakable by remembrance and wisdom
Will it happen again?
We will relive Vietnam?

—*Tiffany Ann Bruner*

One

One is a very lonely number,
It has no friendship, love, or success.
It's best friend is it's own shadow,
Doing nothing, loving nothing, saying nothing.
It's life is one dark whole of unheard cries,
Cries calling for someone else,
But no one listens to lonely one.
It shall stay that way until that one's life is deceased.
No one will notice.
No one will care.

—*Libuse M. Zburll*

A Cry Through Darkness

You're in a darkness though it seems
    you're alone
It is a sickness that you must realize on
    your own
I am here for you, if you could only see
Through the darkness, it's true, I am here
    for thee
How can you fade away? Leave people
    that really care?
Why won't you stay? Nothing in life is
    fair
Once you're gone, you're gone, there is no
    turning back
You'll find out before long that suicide is
    a fact
It's a fact of life, it's a fact of pride
It's a fact by a knife, it's a fact by a free
    ride
A free ride into dying, a free ride into hell
Don't keep in your crying, find someone to
    tell
Remember the good times, but don't
    forget the bad
Life and death are all rhymes once you're
    gone, it'll be so sad
Because you're playing with death and
    you don't realize
That you do have friends that hear your
    cries
Living is life, by all means don't play
And dying is death, for that there's hell to
    pay.

—*Stephanie Davis*

Love

Love is like a rose,
It is beautiful and special.
Love is like a waterfall,
It flows forever.
Love is a special feeling,
Reserved for special people.
When I'm in love,
I feel on top of the world.
And the one I'm in love with
Stands there with me.

—*Marnie Flesher*

Christian Poem

A new day, a new year,
It is only I
On an ordinary Monday
Requesting the honor of your presence
At my kitchen table
For coffee and conversation.
Comfort comes in knowing
You require only an invitation.

—*Thomas Creel Lanham*

Memory

When the rose is tightly closed,
It is only the beginning.
As the rose opens,
Its petals show off its beauty.
Even though those petals fall,
The beauty is still there.
Memory. . .

—*Stephanie A. Neil*

Mist Of The Mind

In my minds eye I see what is yet to come
It is so clear and yet so far away
But before its meaning can be read
A mist of despair tears my soul apart
Death rides in the wind
It surrounds and consumes me
And nothing that I do can stop it
For how can you cure the pain
That others leave behind
And as my heart turns to stone
I say my last, goodbye.

—*Tamara Renee Carlson*

So Free

Walk along and meet. . .
It is so nice to greet. . .
The grass and fields of wheat. . .
Around us. . .
Feeling the breeze. . .
It is good to be free. . .

—*M. Padilla*

Lost Love

The pain of a lost love is too great to bear,
It leaves on your heart a little tear.
Which is known as a scar throughout the
    years,
So you'll always remember those bitter
    tears.
But one day you are sure to find,
A man who's as loving as he is kind.
So until then don't be too blue,
A Mr. Right's out there for you.

—*Robin McRee*

Listen to the Rain

I listen to the rain because it makes a
    beautiful sound.
It makes a sound like little mice running
    to their home.
When it gets hard it sounds like cats and
    dogs fighting.
The cats are running away from the dogs.
When it gets soft it makes a beautiful
    rainbow.

—*Sarah K. Warnecke*

Silence

The silence captures me.
It makes me sit and think, for I am not
    perfect.
I sort out people's problems as I walk
    through time.
I come back to Earth.
I'm back to a different world,
For I have learned so much, it would take
    man infinity to absorb it.

—*Lorraine Bratis*

The Very Essence of Life

Life is like a sparkling star that enlightens
    us with its presence.
It makes us feel the way we do.
The glowing light of nature is our guide in
    the continuing saga of life.
Nature sews a beautiful quilt for the
    creatures who live in the universe.
We are sustained by the music of the sun.
The universe will flicker as long as nature
    moves on the trail.
Every creature of nature keeps up the
    plentiful goods of life.
We must let nature shine its face on us.

—*Syndee Jundt*

The Child

I grew up so long ago,
It seems I was never a child.
I quite forgot what it was like
To frolic free and wild.
But now my child I need you.
Please come out and stay. . .
Let me see you dance about
And teach me how to play.
Laugh and cry and sing,
Show me how you feel.
I want to know this part of me
So elusive, yet so real.
What a glorious ending
At the ebb of life to say,
"When I grew up I became a child"
"And a child I'll stay".

—*Tracie LR Ojakangas*

Forever

When it's night and you're near me
It seems like it is day time forever
Your pale white skin
Your curly black hair
Your dark eyes
Your kissess
Your touch
Your looks
Your strong arms
When I close my eyes
I picture myself on a beach alone
Wearing a white sheer dress
Laying on the wet sand
Letting the cold water pass through me
Chilling my body
Slowling going down between my legs
When I open my eyes
You're Loving me Forever

—Mayra Ramirez

The Wind Rolls Across the Sea

The wind rolls across the sea.
It seems so beautiful to me.
As the waves jump and the wind roars.
The sea is the same to me.

—Sarah Heng

Untitled

The wind warned of the coming storm
It smelled of rain waiting to break and
    pour down on the earth.
The sky was fogged over with blackened
    clouds,
Drifting, drifting in melancholy
    formations.
Blanketing the earth with dark shadows,
Swallowing up the color and bringing
    blackness.

—Marie Tripp

Peace

Peace is white
It sounds like people singing.
It tastes like cream pie.
It smells like a flower garden.
It looks like silk.
It makes me feel comfortable.

—Michelle Bochner

From a Single Note

From two hearts,
It starts,
This magic that is you,
As a single violin,
It begins,
A symphony for two.
Note by precious note,
We wrote,
Two sonnets of our love.
Now in harmony
The four of us, will sing,
Life's changing melodies.

—Martin Mathers

True Friendship

How lovely is true friendship?
It warms like morning sun.
It gives each day new
Meaning makes things we do more fun.
It gives us strength and courage for
    problems we must face,
Helps us keep our bearings throughout
    this hurried pace.

—Stephanie Doan

Love is a Fish

You tossed the fish up onto the beach—
It was just a shiner
"Worthless," you said.
It flopped around, frantic
To find water.
Later, the seagulls came.
They picked out the vital parts—
And eyes. . .
I may be blinded
But I still see—
Oh, I still see.

—Pamela Berreth Lyons

Finally Love

I've finally found love,
It wasn't hidden far.
It was in a place so tender and so close,
So close that anyone could find it.
But to find love,
I had to experience the kindness and
    caring,
Needed to feel my emotions.
And after the search I was surprised to
    find,
That love was so close to me,
That I could have had it the entire time.
For love was just two breaths away,
It was in my heart.

—Wendi Brown

Listening

I heard a cloud that stopped to cry,
It whispered on the breeze.
It told of travels near and far
And things that it had seen.
It thundered black and roared with pride
And racked the earth with rain.
Then, lightning stilled and thunder quiet,
It softly slipped away.

—Laurel Reinholz

Love as it Happens

When it grabs control of your heart
It will tear you apart.
When it invades your mind
Your thoughts become blind.
When it captures your sole
It will leave you alone.
Enjoying it can be a treasure
When coupled with physical pleasure.
All senses race
With nerve ending pace.
The past is a blur
The future holds no cure.
Without knowing or direction
A body starves without affection.
This yearning has to be attended
By only that person to whom you
    surrender.

—Lisa Pontarelli

If I could Fly

If I could fly,
It would be lonely without you.
You make my dreams come true,
When you're with me.
If I could soar,
Up into the blue,
It wouldn't be right if you weren't there,
To share it with me.
If I should get lonely,
I wouldn't know where to go,
If you weren't there.
If I should get sad,
If you weren't there,
I wouldn't know where to turn.
If I could fly,
It would be lonely without you.
You make my dreams come true,
When you're with me.

—Tonya Lance

My Room

I'm sitting here all alone in this room I call my own,
It's a place where I think and do what I want to do,
When I'm happy or sad, or even mad, it's the place I think things through.
My room is my world; it's mine to keep.
I have all my things in here and this is where I sleep.
My posters are hung on the walls,
And next to my bed is my telephone where I make all my calls.
My jewelry is laying everywhere,
But I promise I layed it there with much care.
My room is here and it always will be,
Why don't you come over and visit me?

—*Stacey Howard*

My Love for You

My love for you is hard to explain.
It's a type of love that only you can claim.
My love for you is within the depth of my soul.
Full of understanding, and yet out of control.
My love for you is like an open book.
You baited your line, and I swallowed the hook.
My love for you will never be shared.
For God knows it's only yours to bear.

—*Sharon Washington*

A Broken Heart Without a Place to Go

A broken heart without a place to go.
It's all alone without knowing how to grow.
It's broken because of another heart that was so untrue.
It never could find the time to tell the broken heart why it was blue.
But the broken heart is floating on,
Just like the words of a beautiful love song.
And the heart that was so untrue,
Well it's just there without knowing the broken heart is blue.
As time goes on, and the beautiful love song floats along.
The broken heart is finally mending.
While the untrue heart is steadily pretending.
Pretending that it's not it's fault,
And it wasn't the one that always got caught.
But as the untrue heart listens to the beautiful love song float away.
Well it's friend the broken heart, it has another place to stay.

—*Sylvia Renee McClain*

Changes

My world is often being compared to a light bulb.
It's always being turned on, switched off, burnt out,
Or just too bright.
I often can't seem to see through the changes to make the right decision.
It's being used for much more than supplying life
Or in the bulbs case, light.
Although it appears so quiet, it is screaming out with pain,
Fear, and torture from above.
How can a world that is created by your inner self
Be destroyed by a single heart.
You have to obtain the courage and strength to pull yourself
Together and start over with a better and stronger soul,
While the bulb needs changing and you decide to put in a bigger
Bulb to produce more light.
What you put in yourself is the real you.
You make your world. Don't be switched off by a foolish
Misunderstanding or wrong doing.
Your world is your life. A bulb can be changed
Like your decisions, but the new will never be like the one before it.
Each different in its own way, as you are different in your own way,
But a bulb can be replaced, your life cannot.

—*Sylvia L. Joyal*

The Promise

SOMEDAY,
   When the mind's rankling clears,
SOMETIME,
   When the misty cobbled web thoughts assume original order.
   (Allowing my spirit
   to grasp the talons
   of the muses,
    and hang on for
     ONE
     LONG
     FANCIFUL
     FLIGHT!)
THAT TIME,
   (That one time only)
   I will ride the wave's crest,
   and speak profoundly of the sublime.

—*Andria Parry Witman*

Your Presence

As I sit here, I can feel your presence in this room.
It's as beautiful as a red rose, in the midst of its bloom.
It's such a feeling of security, found within my heart.
It is warm and gentle, and never to depart.
There's really no words that can absolutely describe,
It's just a smooth gracious melody, that gives me the vibe.
I feel your presence while chills run up and down my spine,
And I bet those people felt it when you turned water into wine.
It's like a river flowing down a mountain stream.
If I didn't know any better, I'd think I was in a dream.
It seems funny, I can't visibly see you with my human eye,
But I can feel your presence now, and I'll see you when I die.
I'm thankful for your presence, it's really like a gift,
Especially when I'm feeling low and needing an uplift.
The very day, I accepted you, my life started to enhance.
I'm just thankful of your presence, that has given me a chance.

—*Mark A. Milam*

Life

Life is like a flower
It's beauty often dies,
Living in a world
That's nothing but lies.
The problem of a sixteen year old
Seems so little
But when things get rough
The problems become riddles.
What has life turned into
To put us teenagers through so much hell
It makes life seem
Like a bad fairytale.
When life gets rough
Suicide comes into mind
While parents wonder and cry
As a life slowly dies.

—*Tonya McIntyre*

Sunrise

The new dawn unfolds
Its beauty to the world.
The earth is calm and quiet;
Not a sound is heard.
It's still early in the morning,
But, already, darkness is backing away.
Just a subtle hint from the Lord
To start a fresh, new day.
I hop out of bed, but cannot resist
One more glance at the sunrise.
Suddenly, I change inside, and then I see
The world with brand-new eyes.

—*Susan B. Muaddi*

Fear

A shadow in the dark, lurks among the present
It's cold and unsteady, and rumbles with action
Its point of view is within all living things
Its power is beyond uncontrollable
Its rage is invincible
The strength of this emotion can only be stopped by one thing
The mind

—*Miranda Marie Lundeen*

Untitled

Shhh.
It's coming close
But do not fear,
For it's just a squirrel
Collecting roast
For another year.

—*Tricia DiMeo*

Lost Heart

My heart weeps in the shadows of the night,
It's crushed into a thousand pieces,
It was once full and healthy,
Now it's nothing but stone.
How can I feel anymore?
Where do I go from here?
What does everyone want from me?
I can't go on living like this.
Suicide is not an answer,
Death will not solve these problems,
They'll stalk me forever.
What should I do?
Where shall I go?
I have no answers.
Only time can heal these wounds.

—*Lori J. Dukeshire*

Apart. . .

It's something that makes this love so special; being apart.
It's difficult; we both know, but it will work out in the end.
We've gone so far now so we can't hold back what we feel for each other.
This world was meant for people who love each other to be. . .apart!
But not for long, because it's you and me that make this
Relationship happen, even tho' we're. . .apart for now.

—*Nickole L. Marcincak*

Youthful Heart

Deep within lies a young, growing heart
Yearning to be free
Hoping
Begging
Longing for life to be worthwhile

Filled with thoughts of unending joy
Hoping to succeed without being destroyed
Striving to please family and friend
Yet hurting one in the end

Pressure will succomb this treasured heart
Who's defence was not yet known within
Destined to learn a lesson of pain
In a world where youth find it hard to restrain

A youthful heart needs love and attention
Direction in morals and constant affection
The struggle is difficult but can be won
With wisdom, courage and determination

—*Karen Bather "Jade"*

The World, Why Can't it Change?

The world means everything to me.
It's large yet it's small in its own way.
The world is full of different people.
It has its good and its bad people.
The world is full of grief and sorrow,
Yet is full of joy too.
But we each are enclosed in our own small world.
Whether we live in depression, togetherness, loneliness, or happiness
Which are our own moods in our own small world.
But because we are so wrapped up in our world,
We forget about the larger world which surrounds us.
We forget about the homeless, the runaways, the poor, and the needy.
We become ignorant and self centered.
Why can't this all change?
Why can't we all live in the same world and the same ranking?
Why?

—*Lisa Khoury*

Goodbye, At Last

As I wake from the past,
It's like looking into an hour glass.
I used to see your smiling face,
And remember your warm embrace,
But now no longer do I see
The dreams of you and me.
I no longer imagine your gentle sighs,
Or our sweet, loving goodbyes.
No longer do I dream of you,
How I wanted them all to come true.
I'm finally letting go of you,
And all the memories I've held on to.
It hurts a little don't you see,
Because you were once a part of me.
My world revolved around you,
And all we used to do.
But no longer are you what you were in the past,
This is goodbye forever, goodbye, at last.

—*Reann McGlothlin*

The Beach

When the sun shines on the sandy beach,
It's like shining diamonds.
The waves rolling in, like soft curls of hair.
The seagulls flying high in a light blue ocean of freedom.
The boys and girls in a place, that feels like freedom.
When they go to this sacred place,
They leave all worries behind.

—*Tracy L. Wood*

To Frank

To Frank-
It's not easy being me,
is it easy being you?
Perhaps, that's why
I cannot be true.
Wearing a mask
to cover my personality,
I live everyday with
what they call a reality.
There's peace on my face
but such war inside,
Pretending, I'll smile for them
but from you I can't hide.
It's not easy being me,
and I wish I was you
So sensitive, yet so strong
but mostly-so true.

—*Yana Wolfson*

Untitled

Pressure, pressure all around.
It's pushing me into the ground.
My troubles hound me every day.
Screaming, kicking, and making me fray.
My mind is intruded by thoughts so deep.
My heart must guard the watch they keep.
So lonely and vacant is my heart.
I am sometimes afraid to live and take part.
This life I live must mean something to me.
'Cause otherwise my heart, would have given up on me.
So, the sights of my thoughts,the blades and the knives.
My heart will now conquer, so I can take part in life.

—*Tammy L. Long*

I Wish I Could Fly

I wish I could fly, way up in the sky
Where the birds are, and the clouds so high
I'd soar like an eagle, then flap my wings high
If I could only just fly.
I wouldn't ever be at blame.
No one could ever say I'm stupid,
They wouldn't know me if only I could do it.
I would never have to answer to anyone, what I did I would only know.
It would be my home, way up in that sky.
I'd fly all day and fly all night.
If I knew just where to go, I'd buy some wing and away I'd go.

—*Sally Goatley*

Decision

I'm lying in my own world of blackness.
It's starting to close in on me.
I think of the things that happened today.
The kids at school are always happy.
I feel as though I am the only one who sees the real world.
The dark, bleak one.
I'm in a shadow of darkness, and that keeps me from their circle of light.
I think of the things that happened today.
My parents fighting, my sister crying.
The look on my father's face as he drove away for the last time.
The way my mother hasn't left her room since the fight.
I think of the things that happened today.
The way I wish I could be like others and escape reality.
The full bottle of pain killers I hold in my hand.
The packed suitcase under my bed.
I think of the things that happened today,
And I wonder which escape route I'll choose.

—*Melanie Clark*

Old White House

There's an old, white house just down the road,
It's thought of as a treasure, it's worth more than gold.
Inside a heart, it holds such a place,
For love and devotion, it left quite a trace.
That one small heart, it belongs to me,
It's touched my life, like no one can see.
I go there for peace, when I'm sad or down,
It brings me such joy, like that of a clown.
In a beautiful day, after morning's fresh dew,
It appears so sweet, so clear and new.
Some day, I know the roof will give in,
I hate to admit it, but time shall soon win.

—*Tara Luther*

Uncovering a Dream

Wipe away the dust and dirt that covers your dream.
It's time to make it come true!
Every thought and idea that comes to you,
Try, try, and make it come true!
Life is too short to waste,
Dreams are the main things upon which life is based!
So, the next time a dream comes to your head,
Don't drop it like a piece of lead.
Try, try and make it come true!

—*Suzanne Capito*

Best Friend

When I think my "best friend"
It's you on whom I depend.
To bring me up when I'm down;
You make me smile instea of frown.
When he and I have a fight;
You help me see when I'm wrong or right.
Together we've seen some real tough times;
Happy times too, the memories ring like chimes.
The hurt and happiness that we've shared,
Can never ever be compared.
I know you know just what I mean;
Feels sometimes like an awful dream.
When I say to you we need to talk;
Then, we take again that friendship walk.
I can never repay what you've done for me,
But a friend to you I can also be.
All I've written here, I know is true.
My "best friend" is you.

—*Tessi Hollis*

Your Kiss

Your kiss says everything
I've always wanted to hear.
It's like never before
And to me is very dear.
Your kiss is special,
And can never be beat.
It's kept with my heart,
Until again our lips meet.
I'm always thinking
About you,
And how the love we share,
Is so very true.
Our kiss, our love,
It all means so much.
So I'll be loving you forever,
And will always remember your sweet touch!

—*Nicole Vogt*

All Your Love

I don't know what to do anymore,
I've cried all the tears I can cry
Over all the dreams I've ever dreamed,
Just to watch them shatter,
Over all the falling stars I've wished on,
Just to watch them die.
When all the things I do
Won't bring me any closer to you.
I've tried to make it die,
This love I feel for you.
I can't though, no matter how hard I try,
So I've decided to just let go
Of everything that reminds me of you.
But it's still there
Back in the lonliest corner
Of my heart, all of your love.

—*Shelley Letzig*

Alone

Here I am, alone again
I've loved too many
I want no pity
All the love was given
All the love was taken
Alone again
Never enough love to make it last
No more tears will fall
No one to call
I won't think of the past
Alone again
Never totally alone
Just alone again

—*Lois Sitchenkov*

Too Fast

Since you've been away,
I've thought of the past;
I think my feelings
Moved too fast.
I've had feeling for
Other guys, too,
But not like the feelings
I have for you.
Life moves on. . .
It won't wait for me;
I wish it would because
I want you to see.
I think that I love you;
I wish you loved me.
But dreams don't come true
At least not for me.

—*Lagena Dowding*

An Unknown Soldier

I've been here for years
I've tried hard to control my tears
And to hide my deep fears.
I wait here everyday for someone
To finally say I can go home.
I have to watch for the enemy
My orders are, "shoot to kill."
How can I kill someone who has a family
Just like mine?
I decided not to shoot and here I lay alone
    and cold.
Surrounded by people I don't know
The fighting stopped a year ago but I'm
    still here.
An unknown soldier.

—*Vanessa Gallihugh*

Waiting for the Vampire Bats to Come

In that days push through the
Jungle there had been only
Exhaustion, and concern over becoming
Lost. Now each lay underneath his
Mosquito netting which hung down
    between
Us like fisticuffs between friends,
Partitioning off the darkness. I
Was left to be alone with my sweat, the
    roar
Of the bush at night, and a
Sense of silently flapping wings.

—*Tim N. Hartzell*

Love, What is it?

Love, what is it?
Just an emotion?
No, it's a feeling in the heart.
A feeling that makes you feel wanted.
Love is not love without someone to share
    it with you.
Love is not whole unless there's
    something.
Someone to give and return this special
    feeling.
I'm confused,
I need help to understand this awesome
    feeling!
If I don't get help soon,
I'll never be able to understand this
    feeling.
I know what it is, but I don't know quite
    how to use it.
It's new and unknown to this heart!
Will you help me?
Someone help me, please!

—*Tina Province*

Untitled

Times unwind. . .
Just as the wind passes
Through the leaves of life,
Chilling those cold and
Forgotten memories,
Cooling off the new and
More memorable.
And the still of a summer
Breeze. . .
Caresses my soul
And uplifts the love that
Fills my heart,
Only to remind me of life;
Chilling and frightening one
Minute,
Still and simple the next.

—*Stacy J. Rice*

Untitled

A shadow is an area of darkness,
Just like my heart,
Lonely and scared,
Almost falling apart,
I try to choose everything that's right,
But my heart will ache, and my throat
    feels tight,
I try my best in everything that I do,
Trying to tell someone, simple like you,
Trying to tell you, you the only one,
That I am in a closed world,
Caught like a wild bird,
Wanting to fly to be free,
Or waiting to die, in misery.

—*Tatiana Tuttosi*

The Last Moments

I love you, he whispers
Just then all is silent.
My heart going out to him,
A tear trickles slowly down my pale face,
I am still
I love him so yet he deceives
My mind tells me no
Inside I ache
I push his hand away
Outside I feel fragile
Goodbye I whisper
It is over.

—*Nicole Brand*

You Came to Me When

You came out of the blue,
Just when I needed you,
You give me comfort and love,
And you give me happiness beyond
The stars above.
Your devilish smile gives me a thrill,
And my love for you no one can kill.

—*Nicole Roy*

A Young Mind

I'm lying in bed not thinking of much,
Just wondering about my future and such.
When my mom banged on the bedroom
    door,
What she said was something I tried to
    ignore.
"You're too young to be daydreaming of
    things so far ahead,"
"Stop being lazy, get up from there and
    make your bed".
I don't know why moms just don't
    understand,
But as soon as she left, I was back
    dreaming again of a far away land.
A land far away from all pain, just
    happiness there,
Surrounded by love and people who care.
Away from all stress, the heartaches and
    riot,
I could think of nothing else so peaceful
    and quiet.
There's no doubt in my mind I'll be there
    someday,
I'll be in that land that's so far away.
For now, I'll keep my little secrets locked
    inside of my head,
And I'll mind my mother get up from here
    and make my bed.
It was filled with content that land far
    away,
As I dreamed in my bed-still as I lay.

—*Stephanie Hurst*

Love is Like Dying

They loved each other secretly, nothing that can hide
Kept it only to themselves, kept it only inside
She risked her life to save his, now she lies asleep
Unawake, unconscious, unwilling in deep sleep
Remembering things and days of old
Treasures for both of them to hold
Now he whispers "I love you and I wish you were at home."
His face flushes as a tear escapes from his eye
She flinches slightly as if to say "I love you"
And raises her arm to touch his and sighs
Another tear filled with love leaks from his eye
She lifts her head and opens her eyes
And brings it down again and cries
Sorrow overwhelms him
For he knows she will not survive
And still she clings to her hand,
As she closes her eyes and dies.

—Shelley D. Ely

School

School is here and we're not ready,
Kids are shaking and very unsteady,
Homework is coming, but so is death,
So count to ten and take a deep breath.
But it's not so bad, it's kind of fun,
Because once you start you've just begun,
A new beginning to a good education,
If you get real good, you could rule the nation.

—Shelcey Harding

Easy Living

I wake up in the mornings, refresh myself.
Kids off to school.
Off to work and well done job
And refresh, retired with supper, to bed.
Socialized on my spare time and fun.
Learning more about high society worlds.
We cope with life everydays
Facing problems, strive for higher career jobs.
To make living more enjoying and easy living,
In today's worlds.

—Mary O'neal

People/World

Infants are sleeping eating and crying,
Kids want everything except they're not buying.
Teenagers are just trying to have fun,
You know partying and bathing in the sun.
Adults acting worried and furious,
Or just overworked and a little serious.
Elderly people some sick or even dying,
Can we help these people stop their crying.
The world is not the perfect place,
Who knows maybe either is space.

—Tracy Panza

And Gentle is His Name

Oh, son of the sun, child of the moon,
Kindred spirit of the night.
Such a warm glow he radiates,
Upon his handsome face—
When beaming his enchanting smile,
Of tender charm and grace.
Beauty surrounds him like the mist,
Of a soft sleepy dream—
His haunting features embraced,
By the mystery of a moonbeam.
His laughing eyes sparkle,
With unfathomable light—
They have stars twinkle,
Devilshly merry and bright.
Oh, son of the sun, child of the moon,
Restless soul: At last acclaimed!
Understanding at heart; his caring the same—
For tender is his touch and gentle is his name.

—Sandra Justus Atkins

No Tomorrow

Tears flowing down my face,
Leaving behind a definite trace,
I have soon a decision to make,
And maybe even my life to take.
At nights I cry
And only try
To forget the things
Bad luck could only ever bring. . .
Right now I need
Someone to take heed
To show me they care
And not leaving my flesh to tear
I need to hear
That someone would shed a tear
If my life
Were ended with the knife!

—Shannon Clausen

The Inside Meaning

The sun shall pass through the horizon.
Leaving darkness
So shall pain and sorrow
Even joy and pleasure
But not thy confusion.
that was laid on us til day.
It was just swept away,
with but one touch
that seeks and absorbs our body.
It enchants our soul,
our eyes for what it sees
Brings a smile form upon lips
It is noticed by a free spirit.
or of a simple clear mind.
For this one day,
the sun shall rise above a thin line,
offering the real trueness of beauty.

—Melanie Payawal

Moving On

Finally the years have past,
leaving joyous memories behind,
for us to share with,
newly found friends.
This has meant parting,
seperating,
from the ones we love.
They filled a place in our hearts,
that is now empty,
Bare.
Crying softly, we pull back,
and look into the faces,
that are engraved forever,
within us.
And through it all,
we must face a single fact.
We will move on,
as the days go past.

—Yvonne Gastelum

Sun Goddess

The sun goddess moves among the earth,
Leaving us briefly, but always returning.
She is more precious than any jewel is worth,
More luminous than any fire burning.
Warming our faces, brightening our days
Casting her radiance for the world to see,
With her beautiful rays.

—Theresa Nelson

Share With Me

Where there is little
Left to cherish,
Stay with me.
Let's cherish each other.
When there is no need
To look back,
Delve into your mind.
I want to know what
You think.
As the sun shines
Outside your window,
Walk outside
And feel what you see.
I want to know
What it makes you feel inside.
At your lowest point,
Forget who you are,
Tell me
Who you want to be.

—Vanessa Janulis

Tiannamen Square

My China bleeds and ever has
she stomped and trumped to leader's find
to only go along that road
again to shed her blood anew
and raise again that banner o'er
same field of evil as before.
But now she cries in People's Square
and braves the flames of dragon mad;
it's tail has swept the students off
their place of freedom tried anew
where courage stands acute and tall
to never more let freedom stall.
Though thousands die the millions live,
it is by shed of rivered blood
the conscience breaks Pagoda Morn
where spirits fly just overhead
to sun the soul in People's Square
in memory love's lotus shared.

—Yon E. Fearshaker

Colorless

To thine own humanity
let all attempt to be fair and true
For all to be colorless
the hopes depend on you
If all should die
before they awake
A residue of Blackness
their corpse shall surely make
Oh what a sheer delight
if one day it would be
Gazing into the mirror
you'd be as black as me
If by chance some day we realize
twas so rediculous to be labeled
by color of skin or eyes
Me not a pedestial and not professing to
    be
For in thine own image he created you
    and me.

—Ralph Hogges

Your Past, Our Future

I want to know everything in your years
    gone by
Let's go sit on the beach and chat while
    watching the seagulls fly.
Did you get your first trike when you were
    three or four?
Was learning to read a pleasant
    experience or did it seem an awful
    chore?
Did you like girls at the age of seven?
Probably not — I bet you were eleven.
Did you ever sneak the car out before you
    were of age?
What did it take to make your father
    furious and your mother fly into a rage?
It's hard to imagine you ever being small
Did you ever think you'd grow so tall?
You know, it's really insignificant now to
    recall all the years gone by
For it's our future now that I want to
    discuss eye to eye.
Oh, please stand up and hold me tight
Don't let go, this feels so right.
Look at me and tell me what you feel
Are we living in a dream world or is this
    dream real?
Take my hand, let's go for a walk
I want to feel the sand on my feet while
    we talk.

—Teri Epperson

Forgiveness

In order to forgive, you have to forget
Letting go of your fears so the caring can
    set—
I don't know if I, can truly forget
But I can try to work through the
    hardships I've met.
I'll turn my eyes up to a higher force
And let the good Lord, help set my new
    course
I can no longer do this all on my own
My heart's been broken, the hole can't be
    sewn.
Please teach me your ways
Show me the fork in the road—
I will rise up to meet you
And you'll carry my load.

—Paula D. Roberts

Beginning Life

You and I, lying in the sun
Life is a pleasure, everything is fun.
How could anything be better than this,
This life so happy, so full of bliss.
Then the day came to our everlasting
    shame
That a mistake was made, with only us to
    blame.
What should have been good in its own
    time
Was now ruined, the act now a crime.
In a world like this on a day like today,
We look upon the price of lust we pay.
This small life so full of love and wonder,
Brought into this world in one nights
    blunder.

—Shannon Harrison

Kaleidoscope

My
Life is like
A kaleidoscope
Oft times with soft hues
Harmonizing
In a lovely design;
Other times with
Brilliant colored symmetry
As a stained glass window
Through which
The sun may shine;
But sometimes
As pieces of jagged glass
Crumbled in a pile,
Until a loving hand
Begins to turn it
Into his pattern
Divine.

—Pat Gladden

A Life of an Ill Child

Young and frail
Life won't go beyond
White brick walls
Eyes only know
The yellow gowns
And the pink small blanket
Little hands won't know
The touch of a rumpled leaf
Not even your mother's own skin
Ears have heard
Voices that surround you
But also of the
Small dull beep
As you breathe each breath

—Lesley Ann Roberts

Dear Lord,

Now that I have reached my prime,
Life's own fortune soon confronts me.
May I always keep my rhyme,
This, in prayer, I now request thee.
Life may come and life may go,
But one thing my soul will savor,
Love's own gift that I may show
To You, forever.

—Sara O. Newberg

The Wedding

Dark emptiness
Light spoken into being
Blue skies open up with but a word.
Grassy fields, flowers spring forth.
The sun, the moon, the stars,
Brought to life.
Again he speaks. . .
Seas they are filled,
Fields come alive.
Nature's corucopia
The stage has been set.
You and I now placed on the scene
In their likeness made.
Stewards together
To all that is given.
Taking our first step in
The Kingdom of Heaven.

—Michael and Tina Johnson

The Penetrating Moment of Dawn

He took my heart,
like a bandit
in the night,
For to him all I was
was another face,
In the penetrating moment of Dawn,
His voice,
like thunder,
Striking me in ways
I hadn't thought amaginable,
The feeling of temptation
races
curiously through my mind,
but then—
alas—
he was gone.

—Stephanie Woods

Let Me Be

My love ran through
Like a burning flame
But the heat of his body
Was my only gain.
Let me be
Like a bird with wounded wings,
Maybe then we'll see
Just what happiness his love brings.

—Sarah Ann Moise

The Wind

Sweeping along the sky
like a butterfly in the air
Is the wind that flies so high
Like it had not a care,
Through the trees
And through the grass
With a look
As clear as glass
Brushing petals
Off of flowers
Fluttering high
As the highest towers
Flying low
And through my hair
Is the wind
Without a care

—Shannon M. Taylor

I Got Stoned

Later. . .
Like a cool
Springtime night
Driving
With you arm
Out the window
As always,
The false wind
Moving the hairs
Around,
Then you hit
A cold pocket
In the air
As if you
Just passed death,
Swampy and thin,
Only long enough
To send shivers
Down you spine.

—Lisa Rissmiller

Passages

Time flies down the lonely hallway,
Like a dove soaring aimlessly toward the sun.
I find myself sitting, and I wonder,
Staring into the darkness, between
What seems like endless rows of secret dreams.
I can see you in the memories of my mind.
With the shadows on the wall, you sit by the window,
A moonbeam captures your silhouette in the glass.
My memories have become a blanket, shielding you from the flourescent glow,
Like our dreams once did together. I reminise about the times we shared,
Helplessly hoping you would return. As I reach for the light a song comes
To my ears, a song that has been in my mind for what seems like an endless
past, and following behind this forever future.
I remember the first time I ever saw you, the feelings race back.
I long to feel that closeness again, I know I must forget.
With the feeling of total frustration, I fumble to turn the switch,
I feel the numbing silence erase all the pain and memories of you,
But not to long I can never forget, not the way I feel everyday,
Not anything not you, I know I can't but do I even want to?

—Stephanie Cooke

The Night

The night is long and mellow
Like a good turkish cigarette
I take a puff and inhale deeply
I lie back and contemplate the ceiling
The swirls of the plaster take my mind on trips
The morn comes so swiftly
I have scarcely left on a journey to dreamland before
The alarm awakens me
Jarring, demanding that I respond.
Did you ever notice how much better things are in the
Morning before consciousness of things past return
Past thoughts have a shattering effect on how you face today
And then there are the good days when everything goes right
When you wonder what happened and
How can I get a repeat performance?

—Patsy Edwards

Remember

The summer days flew by so quickly
like a shadow darting hesitantly over a
    distant tree.
I stood here once. . . . with you
But now I stand alone.
The breeze makes a wisp of hair
Fly into my eyes
And I can see you standing here beside
    me.
Shimmering, not solid, not real
Here in spirit
To remember with me,
The tears of happiness and the laugh of
    pain
You are hiding in the past as a memory
And as I turn and walk away
That summer dream
Explodes in reality's air
To become exactly what I want it to be
Nothing at all.

—Rebecca Sargent

Vase of Life

A vase opened
like a shell wanting release
from the boundary of
his hatred sea life.
A vase held
the flowers
cut,
like grass shedding
the life of torment
that bounded the earth.
Visions (were revealed. . .)
that showed life
in a new perspective. . .

—Michael William Morales Donnelly

Burning Blood

I see my swarthy hero
like a vision in front of me,
and passionately pray, day after day
that he'll not be long at sea.
For he promised to take me with him
when next he did return,
and the thought of sailing with my love
makes the blood within me burn.

—Nancy D'Annolfo

Like Father, Like Small Sons?

God is our father, when people look at
    you, can they say
like Father, like sons?
God is so good, so honest, so truthful,
God grants forgiveness, does not hold
    grudges,
God does not shout and scream, He
    speaks in a still small voice,
God does not condemn, has no evil
    thoughts,
God sees need and supplies, without
    talking about it to everyone,
God does not make wounds, he heals
    them,
God is no respecter of person, treats
    everyone on an equal basis,
God does not put down or bad mouth
    others to make himself look better,
God is willing to give everyone a chance,
    again and again,
God's love never fails, He is faithful,
God said, "love your neighbor as
    yourself,"
God said, "love your wife as Christ loves
    the church-husbands,"
God said, "honor, respect, and love your
    husbands-wives,"
Like father, like sons?
John 1:12- "But as many as received Him,
    to them gave He power to become the
    sons of God, even to them that believe
    on His name."

—Rose Marie Pickard Cashwell

Times

Expressions of the time, gathered
Like flowers from a field, picked
With care-as a rose from a bush.
We give ourselves free to one another,
Our love blossoms with time.
As a rose is precious to the woman,
So the woman to this man;
Showers of adornment pass your way
With expressions of the times.
These times with you speak for
    themselves,
Filled with laughter
Filled with love-
Expressions of the times,
Our times.

—Michael Weston Roger

Idiosyncrasy

Some peoples' mouths are
Like flowing streams running on
Until they're dammed.

—Mary Jean Carnevale

Anger

The two faces of hatred stand in
    confrontation,
Like good and evil, but undecided which
    is which,
And travel up and down the river of
    denial
Because there still is no answer to the
    unasked
Question of where to draw the thin red
    line on
This ridiculous facade, and melodramatic
    punch
Line filled meeting of the minds.
Too impossible to hear the echo in the
    middle
Of the mess, and also too impossible, or
    unheard
Of, to care.

—The Caterpillar

His Daugther's Eyes

As green as jade, or April's blade,
Like her mother's but more innocent, less
    wise.
Precious jewels, sparkling pools
That dance with reflections of childish
    joys.
Purity protected, memories collected
Of love that strengthens as mind's
    pictures fade.
Life's reality, childhood's brevity
Effect bittersweet emotions that hearten,
    and hurt.
Her father's eyes (more quiet than wise)
Survey events that will change, disrupt
    and distort.
Unwilling to chasten, reluctant to hasten
A tearful look from the eyes of wounded
    heart.
Countenance sweet, even in sleep
The unquestioning love illumines her eyes.
As his own tear shows, a father knows
The power of his weakness, and the
    weakness in his strength.

—William Reed

Soul Surviver

A reflection
Like no other only to be seen as a
    memory,
of an effortless perfection.
In a world of dreams
Emptiness as an emotion
Peace and Hate is all it seems.
Is there no love
Within a dream,
Looking for help, above.
A hope survives
To all the World to see,
Finally no one willing to deny.

—Robin Hyatt

Disapperence

You slipped through my fingers
Like rain in my hand.
Where are you hiding
Lover of my dreams?
Night after night in every tavern
With hungry eyes I search for you
In the face of every man I see,
Then come away alone and empty.
Were you an illusionary shadow
Without real substance,
Someone I conjured up in my brain,
Someone I needed I pleaded for?
I thought as I persued the dream
I was a step closer to your heart
But like a magical illusion,
You disappeared from my view again.

—*Marianne Lazur*

My Apology

We were once best friends. . .
Why did it have to end?
Because.
A simple answer to a complicated question.
We got too emotional..too physical.
Lust made us blind to what lay ahead.
Now look at us!
We don't even speak. . .
Glances are made often.
Why do I feel it was my fault?
Did I push our friendship too far?
Am I to blame for the end of a blooming relationship?
I apologize with all I have to give. . .
If I could, I'd promise you the world.
I dream of holding you in my arms again. . .
If that is possible.

—*Tina Gerber*

You

Your eyes are of blue,
Like the color of the clear blue sky.
It tears me up inside. . .
To see a raindrop tear fall from your eyes.
Your smile. . .so warm.
It lights up an entire room. . .
With happineess and love.
Like the white dove that soars in the sky. . .
My hand fits inside your glove.
Your arms so secure,
I'm content when they embrace me.
Like a mother who embraces her baby,
. . .I embrace you.
The way you speak to me,
With the words from the bottom of your heart. . .
They are so sof and gentle. . .
Like a rose's petals falling apart.
Our love will last forever,
Like a river flowing free.
Our dreams will be built together. . .
Our relationship, an unselfish memory.

—*Martha Webb*

Precious

How many times have I confessed my love for you? Told you you are precious-
Like the prospector's find-the rare jewel, obscured beneath the matrix.
Passionate fires leaping from my soul-naked crest.
Inner voices muffled by the drone of intimate longings.
Even against the slat of darkness
You shimmer.
Your hair, your eyes, fingertips
Skinny-dipping in undulating waves of invisible light.
And you, your blushing sweetness and tragic shyness-you flutter away,
Like a leaf in the wind.
Denying me your soft, lovable qualities, not even affronting reality.
You're plain, you say, simple,
Not even beautiful.
Never was, never could be.
But you are beautiful, precious.
And you don't even know it.

—*Reginald Sinclair Lewis*

Peaceful Awakening

The cloud spits forth the first light drops of rain,
Like the spray that flies from a freshly-cut, ripe watermelon.
A great gust of wind blows through the grass,
And decapitates the bright blossoms of the most delicate flowers.
Sand blows across the yard, stinging my arms, my face.
A bright burst of light illuminates the northern sky,
Outshining Polaris.
The rain falls harder, and I know I should go inside,
But the branches of the trees are beckoning me.
The wind whispers my name, and then rises to a howl.
Branches swirl at my feet—
Scratching random lines in the soil
Like Chinese wrtiting. It makes no sense.
What are they trying to tell me?
I open my eyes wide, and brush the sleep from them.
The sun is shining—
On my now red face.
Slowly, as if in a daze, I move to the shade of a friendly maple.

—*Michele Anstine*

Untitled

The words ripple over the page
Like waves kissing the shore.
A dreamer.
A wizard of rhymes,
I reach out to pluck the perfect
Phrase from the branches of my mind.
A watcher.
A student of nature
I write of her glory.
A painter.
An artist modeling empty words
Into life, I write.

—*Sarah Rohret*

Dear Daddy

Back when I was little there were lots I didn't know,
Like why I asked my mommy did daddy have to go.
Mama said when I was bigger I would understand,
But years have went by and where is that man.
As I lay here with stars shining bright,
I wish on one daddy please come home tonight.
I know I'm very small but I still have hopes and dreams,
That your love will outshine all the years in between.
Will it be tomorrow or maybe the next day,
So please come home daddy, please don't stay away.

—*Patty Turner*

Alchololism

It pulled us apart,
Limb by limb,
The evil darkness,
Which lurks within.
In every bottle,
It will hide,
Never trying,
To subside.
It's a losing battle,
Can't you see,
Trapped by tears,
We can't be free.
The slowest death,
Full of pain,
Everything to lose,
Nothing to gain.

—*Tanya Cervinka*

Revive Me

The splintered and wind-twisted
Limbs of my soul are now heavy
Laden with my own loneliness.
They desperately grasp for the last chance
Of life restoring contentment known,
At least until my real life can be given
    back to me.
The only care of this weather-chilled
    heart
Is to be rejuvenated to its earlier life
Before this hard hitting season came
And sapped it of what was most dear.
But, alas, nothing can be done to bring
    this
Refreshing air of spring any sooner,
So I must wait with my brittle,
Chilled bows until I will at last be revived.
Please hurry.

—Naomi Wells

This Moment

Inside my windows
listening to
a many year old
who can't see
that leaves
are a part
of the trees
in my backyard
where the wind
makes everything
uncomfortable,
i wait.

—Rawn Slo

A Child's Silent Cry

Little children laugh and play,
Little children sing and say:
How innocent are we,
Subjected to crime and violence.
Never known is peace,
But always known is silence.
The silence of laughter,
The silence of tears,
The silence of peace,
In the children's hearts and fearful tears.
Little children sing and say:
Please bring us a better day.
We give our love and shed some tears,
And now, today, we share our fears.
Give us your heart and lend us your ear,
For this is love we seek year to year.

—Tiffany Davis

Untitled

God made all
living creatures,
the plants,
the trees
even you and me.
He knew when
he made us,
we were without sin,
But Adam and Eve
just had
to give in.
Even though they
had sinned,
And sorry they were
A blessing in
disguise was
sent upon this earth.

—Teresa Stanley

My Mother

The memories will always be there
Locked deep inside my heart.
Of the happy times that we had shared
Right from the beginning, right from the
    start.
That smile that was on her face
And the twinkle in her eyes.
She was always warm, loving, and honest
She always told no lies.
And now she is no longer suffering
May she rest in peace.
And the stillness of her sweet breath
Has now come to a cease.
I will never forget the times we shared
You were my mother, my sister, and my
    best friend.
I love you mom, and always will.
My love for you will never end.

—Lee Shriberg

The Pain of Youth

Tears and fears,
Loneliness and emptiness,
Children trapped,
In a world that has no peace.
The need to grow is in the air
Broken hearts and shattered dreams,
Open hand and empty hand,
Hope that never grows,
And hands that need a hand to hold,
Reach out but seldom grab,
So I whisper a silent prayer,
Hoping they find that hand to grab
And I pray they don't let go.

—Trish A. Hilgendorf

Dark

Here I sit in my dark world,
Lonely, cold, and sad.
My heart aches from friends I've lost,
My eyes hurt from tears I've shed.

—Tracy Feathers

Life is but a Dream

Enchanted with the heavens, I peer into a
    cloud,
Longing to be up there, enveloped by its
    shroud.
Soaring with the angels, upon a golden
    beam,
Everything so beautiful, I wish it weren't
    a dream.
Passing over the golden gate, gleaming
    with its glory,
Wanting everything in sight, nothing here
    is boring.
Approaching now our destination, never
    looking back.
My life lies past the desolation, to sorrow
    I give no slack.
Landing now I realize, though many
    things were missed,
All the simple pleasures in life, as being
    gently kissed.
Turning now to walk away, and knowing
    more it seems,
I remember my trip through heaven,
    saying life is but a dream.

—Lynda G. Marsh

Amorelle

Amorelle, my long lost love,
Look down to me from clouds above.
Your whisper in the wind I hear,
You sing your song so soft, yet clear.
Oh, Amorelle, you were my own,
You left to sing around the throne.
So high above, I cannot see,
Your whisper pleads, "remember me."
Your sapphire eyes and golden hair,
You came and went without a care.
Remembering your gentle touch,
Your loving words is not enough.
I long to be with you again,
One day I will, someday I can.
The Lord knows why He's taken you,
Someday in heaven you'll see me too.
Oh Amorelle, in heaven above,
You're the only girl I'll ever love.

—Nikki Klassen

The Essence of You

We spend a lifetime looking for our real self.
Looking for what we think is lost or hidden.
We look for what others define as the purpose God gave us in this life.
We serach high and low for the illusion of a happy material life.
When death comes knocking at our door, we are ready to go on another journey;
If we have fulfiled the illusion of a happy material life.
We pass on into another life without ever knowing the true essence of who we really are.
What are we made of?
Why are we here?
So many questions are to be answered in order to get to the truth.
That truth about the real self that comes from within.

—*Nora Belle Bynum*

Little Pup

Peering little eyes
Looking through the grass
Hearing little ears
Listening through the wind
Smelling little noses
Sniffing for a scent
Dainty little paws
Pouncing in the dirt
Wondering little heads
Searching for an answer
Pondering little questions
Thinking of the meanings.

—*S. E. Messina*

Untitled

She stands on the bridge,
Looking up at the sky,
There is no place for her to go,
Except down into the water.
She holds inside her a silent pain,
For if she doesn't jump, it will always remain.
As she walks closer to the edge,
She talks a silent prayer in her head.
As she falls,
Getting closer to death,
She yells out,
One last shout is all we'll hear,
From the girl on the bridge,
With all those tears.

—*Sue Eger*

Jesus the Savior

Jesus the Savior
Lord of all land
We are the people
Who obey your command
You were nailed on a cross
Dying for our pride
Jesus the Savior
We are strong and we stride
You died for us
Making us understand
That you didn't want war
Just man to love man
Jesus the Savior
The one we look to
For guidance and promise
Jesus, we love you.

—*Michelle Majers*

America. . .

Would you now return to me? declares the Lord.
"Lord up to the barren heights and see".
Is there any place where you have not been ravished?
You have defiled the land, "You burn your own flag in flames"!
Therefore the showers have been witheld, and no spring rains
have fallen. You refuse to blush with shame.
Have you not just called to me: My Father, will you always be
angry? Will your wrath continue forever?
This is how you talk, but still you kill your babies.
Drugs fill your veins and minds where once you let me live!
Alcohol and greed have become the idols of your game,
Weeping from your inner streets echo thru the night,
Tis the call of all the hungry as they continue in their blight!
Trees are down and fish are dead,
One day soon. . .there shall be not a crust of bread.
The shame is mounting in once such a great land. . .
America. . .would you now return to me?
declares the Lord.

—*Linda Hinds Peterson*

Fly in the Cobweb

There is a fly of heartbreak and sorrow,
Lost in a crowd
Being awaited by a black widow
And her web; of her work,
She is proud.
Tell this fly to disappear, disappear,
Then all we can see is a tear,
Of a fly in a cobweb.

—*Tara Ann Gillis*

Final Aria

An old man wanders aimlessly down the endless road.
Lost in the darkened recesses of his mind,
Searching musty attics of forgotten time.
His shoulders distorted, twisted from heavy loads,
Contorted features, damnation foretold.
Pain emitting punishment for some horrendous crime,
Committed somewhere in his perverted prime.
Shivers rack his tortured body with forebode.
Tears eroding flesh, silently, with forsaken cries.
Escaping breath, no other sound is heard.
Finality etches his ravaged, deformed face,
Captured pawn in death's race.
Vanishing embers of a sordid life slowly dies,
Freed spirit soars on the songs of a bird.

—*Patricia A. Kelly*

Because of It, I Lost

Because of it, I lost.
Lost my hopes and dreams,
Lost my last inch of freedom.
Because of that unfortunate day,
I will never again be the same.
So, erase my love and my saying,
Throw away my "stuff", and sell my room.
Keep only your memories of me.
Keep your dignity because
Mine was denied to me.
I have nothing left.
But, as you're going through
My belongings
Promise me you won't blame
Me for the accident.
I swear, I only had a "few beers. . ."

—*Summer Lepak*

Love Can Be

Love can be heartache
Love can be pain
It can be like an
Endless rain
Love can be happy
Love can be fun
It's best if you take
Your steps one by one

—*Virginia S. Lee*

Gifts of Life

Oh, beauty on earth. Oh, glory of the skies
Love for us over and around us lies
Hill and vale, sun and stars of brilliant light
Joy of ear and eyes, for heart and mind delight
Thy justice of mountains high soaring above
Clouds which are foundations of goodness and love
Hear birds sing sweetly in the trees
Listen to the brook and feel the gentle breeze
If down in the valley or upon the mountain steep
Close to my savior would my soul ever keep
We blossom and flourish as leaves on the tree
And wither and perish but naught changes thee
Gifts of earths beauty inspire my heart to praise
How gracious are thy mercies, sunshine hallow my days
You're the chart and compass over life's surging sea
From harm and danger keep thy children free

—*Mildred Capps Jerome*

Love is. . .

Love is so good yet unreal;
Love is a feeling that two people feel.
It's like a rainbow in the sky.
Without love I think the earth would die.
It would be such a great depression
And that's why love is such an obsession.
If our relationship ever died,
I think my heart would forever cry.
I'd feel the hurt and the pain,
Without you I think I'd go insane.
I don't think you know what you mean to me,
But it's hard to put it in words you see.
I hope that you will always be true,
Cause I could never love another the way I love you.

—*Latasha Williams*

Love

Full of joy and pain
Love is not a game
Not a toy to fool around with
Nor a thing to put down or forget.
You must keep love
And share love
With all your heart
And most of all be very careful with your love.

—*Stefania Czernow*

Love

Love is like a breath of fresh air sweeping you away.
Love is what somebody feels for a man, woman, or child.
Love you feel for your families and friends
It's really very silly,
But. . .I feel it's like a blossoming lily.
So delicate and gentle.
Love.

—*Nadine Ruland*

Are We Really So Different

The sun rises, the sun sets,
Love lost, love found,
All balanced, all equal
As life is to death.
The sun, the moon,
The sea, the land,
All balanced, all equal
As night is to day.
The man, the woman,
The white, the black,
All balanced, all equal
As love is to hate.
The sun rises, the sun sets
People die, people live,
All balanced, all equal
As I am to you.

—*Rayanne Crampton*

Friends and Lovers

Friends are one thing,
Lovers are another.
You have learned
To love each other.
You've been through good,
You've been through bad.
You've been happy,
And you've been sad.
He loves you a lot,
And you love him too.
"I love you" comes from
The both of you.
The both of you hope
This never ends.
Because you're more,
Than just good friends.

—*Michelle Atkins*

Once More

Touch my heart just one more time,
Loving each other is not a crime.
Hold my hand as we walk side by side,
Then I can forget the times I cried.
Touch my lips with one more kiss,
Although it's something I know I'll miss.
Say the words I long to hear,
I love you so much, I love you dear.
What comes in the future,
Will soon be the past.
I want these moments,
TO forever last.

—*Leslie Hinzman*

The Beach
Lying on nature's warm, white blanket
Under a daring blue—green sky.
The soft, white clouds of cotton gently soothe my eye.
Lingering in the tranquility of God,
I feel the sun's striking rays
Painting me shades of gold.
It's heartfelt warmth, peace, and brilliance
Is a memory, forever to behold.
I am dreaming, yet I'm awake.
I hear the waves roaring, crashing boldly on the shore.
While the wind whispers secrets of patience, tolerance and understanding.
Why does the ocean act so fierce for a moment. . .then no more?
How quickly the tide changes!
Not unlike the hearts of men.
Soft, subtle scents surround me,
Aroma's found only in my perfect land.
The wings of time fly and fade, for dawn is already at hand.
I leave my earthly utopia, knowing I may never return.

—*Susan M. LoGiudice*

Dragon of Glass

Dragon of Glass, sits so proudly
majestic, yet sallow; strong, yet weak;
different, mild, yet so special to me,
reminding me of something I once had,
 but lost,
of beasts, and wild animals, and things of
 long ago,
as I sit and dream of magic.
Dragon of Glass, watching me
silently staring, wishing; longingly,
silent, unmoving, still,
making me wonder what really happened,
 long, long ago,
of jesters and emperors, palaces and
 kingdoms,
as I sit and dream of magic.
Dragon of Glass, frozen in fright,
mouth open, eyes bulging, feet stomping,
frightening, scary, monsterous; yet small,
making me scared, small, and wondering,
of dragons and beasts, elves and dwarves,
as I sit and dream of magic.

—*Libby Ferguson*

The Eyes of Love

The eyes of love turn me inside and out
While showing me what life is all about!
Love shines like a beautiful vase
Floating in the heavenly sky with grace,
Springs at the right place
And moves around at a tender pace!
The eyes of love are so brand new,
It will dwell in the heart
And just might never depart.
It's a dream come true in the night sky
 blue,
Which will always touch the heart.
Hold on to dreams, for if dreams die,
Life would be like a broken wing
That cannot fly high in the night blue sky!
The eyes of love bides people together and
Turns the world around and around
 without
Making a single sound!

—*Steve Nee*

Unspoken Words

That special day,
Makes all your dreams awake,
And prepares you for the world again,
As you walk the road of hope,
The memories will but never fade,
The unspoken words I will say,
When crossroads meet,
That is not the end,
But will God send,
From the heaven above,
The love that wonders without end,
To guide you past the crossroads freely,
And to help you through the nights,
The love from above will but make
 everything,
So bright.

—*Sarah Cornelison*

Looking Back

Looking back on times that passed,
Makes me wonder how it went by so fast.
The good times with the bad times too,
Just go to show, time really flew.
The times I thought would never move-
Time again was up to prove.
The memories I've always had,
Seem to be all the sad.
The fun and action I've gone through.
I've never known one could do.
In school I have studied hard
To make a career and take charge.
I ask myself, "will we ever find the
 answers within our range-"
If we do, will the questions change?"
Looking back to see
Memories that will forever be.
Now, I've woken, and taken in the slack,
I see myself now, looking back. . .

—*Renee Gilbert*

War and Roses

War and roses, roses and war,
Makes no difference anymore.
Because of war people die,
After a while roses go by.
There's no more time for another lie,
No one can tell us why.
Greedy people who want more power,
The blooming of the flower.
All beautiful while they last,
Then all is in the past.
Everything just gets worse,
With ease or with force. . .

—*Sharon Bose*

Being With You

Being with you in this splendid way
Makes up for the words we cannot say.
Always remember while we are apart,
You will always and forever be in my
 heart.
Just hold me real tight, and I'll be strong.
Because I know our love is not wrong.

—*Linda Landry*

Anger

Her fury spreads like wildfire
Making her heart and mind begin to
 flame,
And setting her soul ablaze.
She understands that she has to release,
This consuming evil that has invaded her.
Before it entraps her,
And possesses her spirit.
She is confused, with a cloudy mind
And shudders as she thinks rash thoughts,
That can't be halted.
Then she shrieks aloud from the turmoil.
Suddenly she feels composed
And knows that the sinister poison
Is gone from her blood.
Until the next time,
When it begins all over again.

—*Ruth Pappa*

Love in the Wind

The wind running over me,
rushing through my hair,
maneuvering my body and soul.
It gives me the speed and momentum
that I dearly need,
in order to be me.
Suddenly I stop.
The wind leaves with a whoosh,
to one more deserving than I.
Who manipulates this wind?
Only those who lend me their love,
and in return, abuse my love for them.

—*Pam Graben*

Fighters

There is one kind of fighter, that goes
 through the world with a bow,
Making himself look forward since
 nothing could come out worst.
He wants for others, what he feels is right,
Knowing that is not easy getting what he
 wants without a fight.
He'll never let himself be pushed down by
 those hungry cowards with rich smiles
That prefer to have a helping hand, than
 to win a poor coward's fight.
Walking down the other side comes a true
 armor knight.
That fighter that walks through life with a
 smile, without a fight;
Letting others have what they want, not
 caring if he lives or if he dies.
The one who never cries, never bites.
The one who smiles when you should cry.
The one who works when you should rest.
The one who walks when you should
 crawl. He is the one.
The one who doesn't fight men nor
 problems.
He fights shattered dreams, broken
 illusions.
He fights himself, urging to go on living,
 without going down
The shadowy streets of suicide.
He is the one. He is the fighter.

—*Sophia Mitiavila*

The Confused One

The baby who made it in the world of living,
Making promises for life and giving.
Promising to make everything perfect,
Making it's goal to a certain limit
Promising it will follow its elders steps
Hoping to step in the right direction.
But little did it know, it wasn't going to have real parents
After finding this bit of knowledge out,
After looking out of its disappointment and grief.
It finally forgives his real parents because they let it live
And gave it a chance of the real world and a nice family.
And environment to live with.
Thanking them silently it goes on living happily with life its self.

—Sarah Baird

Decisions

I am walking through a hallway of life.
Many doors are open,
Yet some are closed.
As I slowly continue through this hallway,
I stop to stare every now and then.
I see many hardships and pleasures as I pass by.
I'll have to choose one day in life,
And choose my whole life through.
Friends and family will pressure me,
To choose the right thing to do.
Folks say the hardest decisions come
When you are all grown up.
But even though my choices are simple,
They still are very hard.
So even though my whole life through,
Decisions I still must choose.
I'll wait until I'm a little older
To choose the right thing to do.

—Samantha Hasting

A Child is Born

A child is born.
Many everyday.
It's a bundle of love
Given to a couple this way.
A child is born.
Many every minute.
We give it our love to its fullest limit.
It is a miracle
That's hard to explain.
But it brings us joy
That's worth all the pain.
A child is born.
This one today.
We love this child in a very special way.
It's sweet and innocent, like a dove.
But really this child is a bundle of love.

—Stacey Fenn

Where Do I Come From

Where do I really come from?
Many might think that question is dumb.
But, if you stop to think what the answer may be,
You may find your whole life is a fantasy.
Yes, I know the color of my eyes and hair,
And I know what style of clothes I wear.
But those are things only you can see,
None of them express the real me.
You see, deep in my heart is my beginning and my end,
Because that's where I carry my most precious friend.
If you want to discover where you came from, too,
Just reach into your heart and God will take care of you.

—Marla Summerhill

Secrets of the Sea

The sea I gaze upon beholds,
Many secrets not yet told.
The breeze whispers softly in my ear,
Things the seagulls can only hear.
Crash go the waves,
With a mocking roar.
Then they race away laughing,
Form the shore.
The birds call and smile at me,
For I cannot know what the secrets mean.
I think to myself, "What can they be,"
"The secrets that the sea hold from me."

—Shannon Hartung

Roasie

Many's the time, we gathered roses,
Many's the time, we shared life's trails;
Many's the time, we looked around us,
Found out friendship, never fails.
You're resting here in my memory—
Your grandma's house, a sentinel stands;
My steady steed a childhood treasure,
Journeyed hours throughout the land.
Childhood treasures, sweet sweet memories,
They made life, how secret it is;
Friend oh friend, you I do treasure,
Childhood sunlight, pleasures bliss.
Forget not, lest we perish,
Forget not, remember youth;
They the best times, oh precious tender,
Glorious moments of our youth.

—Vonnie Hayseed

Inspiration To Love

May you be inspired with love
May God be with you always
May you be guided by his love
May you find happiness and peace
May you look on new horizons tomorrow
May you never ever suffer any sorrow
May the sun always shine brightly
May the rays of sunlight be your pot of gold.
May the dew that falls nightly be your diamonds.
May it be added to your crown of jewels.
May the moon and stars be your compasses.
May the clouds be your pillar of wisdom.
May each season bring a horn with blessing plentiful.
May the birds who sing, bring a soft smile to your lips.
May the frogs and crickets who chir-rups sommers nightly,
be your symphony.
May the May flowers with their beauty, bring you hope and cheer.
May the faith you have in God, give you strength and be of
comfort through the years.

—Marie C. Weber

My Love

My love is like a river,
Rolling on and on and on;
And after all these teardrops
My river still rolls on.
My love is like a flower,
Blooming in its bed;
But if the sun should lose its shine
My flower will be dead.
My love is like a soldier
So brave and proud and true
Maybe this is all because
My love's for only you!

—Stacy Miller

Untitled

May the sun always shine on my face God
May the sunshine always shine on my face God
To help hide the tears when I am sad
And help light it up again
So I may shine for you
May the wind always blow on my back God
May the wind always blow on my back God
To help me get back up again when I fall
Or take the wrong turn somewhere along the way
God help the wind blow my way to give me the strength
To get back up again so I can get back on the right track
Again so I may do good for others and you too God

—Rhonda Montgomery

Below the Low

It's going to be a different day
Maybe, even a good one.
Listening to the radio,
"This is the day your life will surely change."
I feel so torn, ever since I was born.
Life is easy when you set your death point by your own theory.
I'm wondering, how many layers are there in depression?
As I look to the window, hearing Christine sing to Eric,
Daydreaming of going away in a three mast ship.
In a blink of an eye I could cross the threshold.
My intriguing scene shakes me.
Below the low, here it comes;
Sinking, oh no, not again, God help me in my need to feel complete.
Playing with diamond cards
But the joker always knows whats on your mind.
Violins are playing in my darkest hour
And the sweetest melody I hear is from the musical figurine
That plays on...

—*Michelle Joan Barulich*

I Hate To Be Alone

I find it hard to travel down the road of love alone.
I wish that you could join me in this dark and lonely place.
Love is supposed to be of beauty, not so shy and vaguely dull. It's supposed to be of kindness and of caring too.
I'll be on my way again going very slow, praying you'll catch up to me because I hate to be alone.

—*Tori Anne Penrod*

Today's Love

I seek and grope a true lover to love.
Merely not I, everyone, even a philander.
Who reads his shortcoming but smart to read to others.
I was a lover, I am, and would do.
On the following day for new taste.
I knew not. I know nothing, would
Say same on my following day.
That's called the way of modern life.
Reflection and refraction is like a daily meal.
Where is the true love?
In the market or in town or in villages?
All are fed with same ideology.
But my granny is right.
Life in her days, at least with my grandfather.
The true love died off.
As my granny died.
At last, we have ideology of true love.
For we are their descendant.

—*Prakash Gurung*

A Hypocrite?

Yesterday with pen in hand
Mighty words were spoken
Of inspiration courage and good token;
Ah! I knew it all.
Today, mind in travail
This writing seems of no avail;
Do I write of what I know not?
Wondering am I a hypocrite or not,
Or merely passing through
The everchanging renewal
Of the opening of mind
In the passage of time.

—*Paddy Stewart*

Long Love For We...

Long love for we have fought;
Mine heart to keep this thought.
Two faces coming together
Sealing a kiss to last forever.
Loving and leaving to adore
Is something that I never explored.
Telling you the feeling that I have
For you to know where I stand.
You are the only one I need;
Show me that you do believe,
I have learned so many things;
Loving everything that you did bring.
Both of us together in love
Was a wish that came down from above.
Now, I sit here dreaming of you
Hoping all this will always be true.
Precious dreams is what it brought...
LONG LOVE FOR WE HAVE FOUGHT!

—*Tanya Dacri*

Death in thy Passing

From The waters swirling, white,
Mist rose in the dark of night,
Share-borne, barren limbs adorn,
Enshrouded trees, that sombre mourn,
Thy passing.
In the gimlet eye of dawn
Rising from its cloudy down.
Gem encrustled, bright halo,
Light thy passage as thee go,
In thy passing.
But when tide and time have run
And my skein of life is spun,
Having given up the race,
I'll meet thee, bravely, face to face,
Death, in thy passing.

—*Steven Muransky*

May the Lord Brighten your Night

As the remote environment paves the way,
Mobility has so much to say.
Each private drive along the expressway
A perfect lifeline and tranquil day.
Safe precautions blares out from the roadside.
Have a happy and safe vacation this time.
May the order of St. Michael's archangel
Bless and promote your grand knight command
May you walk with caution, during each errand.
The remote environment paves the way
Have a safe and tranquil day.
May the Lord brighten your night
And enhance the spirit of the risen Christ.
There's all kind of delight to see you through.
Safe precautions will protect you.

—*Lady Louisa Reeves Sebaskin*

Lost Innocence

The call came early that morning.
Mom knew even before she answered.
"Let's go," she whispered, "we have to see if Nana's okay."
The drive over was the longest of our lives.
"Stay in the lobby. I'll go see if Nana needs help."
What seemed like forever passed and then two old men walked by.
"Another one's gone. I can't believe it."
The lobby was stuffy and the minute hand on the clock crawled with a maddening slowness,
And as we saw Mom emerge from the elevator, the look on her face told us everything.
Nana was gone.
Mom's crying had stopped as not to upset her young children.
She tried to look strong as her world was crashing, but there were tears in her eyes and a weakness in her knees as she came toward us.
For the first time, we could see that she wasn't invincible.
She could hurt just like we could. Our world was forever changed.

—*Melissa Fox*

Happy Father's Day

Oh, Father, what shall I do?
Mom's on the run and the cat's in the stew.
One day I ran in and then ran out,
So I'm coming home and you don't have to shout.

—*Tammy Nash*

Heart of Deep Blue

Wider than a sea of blue
More peaceful than the great ocean waves
Faster than the crystal blue current
Deeper than the ocean depths
Yes, a heart of deep blue.

—*Nancy Roth*

Rainbows

Rainbows are one of the
Most beautiful things
God created.
Rainbows make people feel refreshed
After a long day
Of pouring down rain.
Did you ever hear the old saying,
At the end of every rainbow
There is a pot full of gold.
I'm not too sure of that
But there is one thing I know for sure,
At the end of every rainbow,
There is love,
God's greatest gift.
Rainbows are the most peaceful things,
As they hang in the blue sky
So everyone can see them.

—*Shelly Hebert*

The Closing Door of Summer

The closing door of summer,
Mother nature has a key.
September's sun grows weaker,
Leaving August a memory.
The lazy walks of summer,
The brisk steps of fall.
The fading call of robins,
The Loons aren't heard at all.
My summer friends are leaving,
An emptiness of heart.
The frost is on the flowers,
Long shadows are sure to start.
Beaches are deserted, the roads
South are full. Nine months
Left till summer, and I will
Be here still.
The door will slowly open,
And Loons will soon be heard.
My friends and all that traffic,
And don't forget the birds.

—*Robert J. Eastman*

Mother's

Mother's are the ones who care
Mother's are the ones you don't want to
   ever share
When I get hurt, you put a bandaid on my
   cut
Whenever I asked you something, you
   never said what
Words can't even tell you how much
   people love
Love is like the color of a dove
The wings of a dove sore through the skys
Like the day you hugged me and looked in
   my eyes
You glisten me up every time I am sad
You punish me when I am extremely bad
I know I will grow up and marry
But I will still treasure the love that we
   carry
The way you talk to me and make me
   gleam
You and me, we make a wonderful team
Though words get in the way
And sometimes I will forget to say
Mother, I Love You

—*Tracy Berry*

Death

The people
Mourn
In desperate agony,
Their cries are
Too much to stand.
The people wail
Over a
Loved one
They have lost.
They should not
Mourn
For they will see their
Loved one
Tomorrow.

—*Miriam Kavanagh*

Tears of Eternity

Softly the rain falls to the ground,
Much like the tears I shed for you.
No, I am not at all sad,
But instead overwhelmed with joy.
I am feeling emotions never before felt,
And dreaming of things so sweet.
A shine in my eyes, a bright smile,
I owe it all to you.
You've softened my days,
And caressed my nights.
Filled my heart with a warm glow,
And gave me love, I'll never forget.

—*Lisa Focken*

A Grandmother's Memories

I became a grandmother at forty-two
Much to my joy and delight
Needless to say, in just two years
I now am looking a fright
But, I love my grandson
The terrible twos is an age to beware
I find that only too true
A few more months and he'll turn three
Then I won't have to scream till I'm blue
Still, I love my grandson
I noticed I started to shake alot
Also my hair is turning gray
Whenever someone close to me says,
"Little Jason is coming to stay"
I think, I love my grandson
Everything now is quiet and neat,
Since putting Jason to bed
I think, what a blessing after all,
As I lean over to kiss his head.
I know I love my Grandson.

—*Sandra Musselman*

Confusion

          is
     a tiny ballerina
         inside
     a music box
         who spins
           around
         to music
     whenever you peek.

     She sees the world
          always
     in rapid motion
       with everything
         whirling by
     the images blurred.

         She tries
     to put them back
         together
       like a puzzle
           but
         one piece
           is
         always lost
       beyond the music.

—*Jennifer Taylor*

Eloise

How many days upon this earth
Must I walk untrod ground,
Times my lips of dewy rich pearls,
Calls at dusk and longs for serenity.
Beyond the patch of fresh turned earth,
A snarly apple limb points a finger right
   at me.
I turn away toward the path,
My back to those I will nevermore see,
The loved one's face I'm destine not to
   meet.
I hear a voice and turn to flee,
I cannot bear to hear,
His whisper calling me,
Oh Eloise, oh Eloise,
How can thee leave me so.

—*Sandra Stalford Austin*

Last Letter Home

From the sea we came, to the rock
 cragged shores,
My comrades and me, where we'd not
 been before.
To battle and conquer, this paradise
 lost—
The unknown enemy, whatever the cost.
An errie dawn's mist, made ghosts of us
 all,
And on the beach, I saw men began to
 fall.
Amid the turmoil of battle, fear mirrored
 in eyes,
Took hill number five, where a lone plane
 flies—
A rugged terrain, of worn-down
 mountains,
By late afternoon, blood spurted like
 fountains.
This is my sunset, flashing in the sky;
No stars this night, no familiar winds that
 sigh.
There is no breath, of lasting scented air,
Nor a wife's kiss, just a Chaplain's prayer.
Wounded and spent, no doubt can there
 be,
Desperate and alone, they fight without
 me.
With sympathies I enfold, my memories
 abate;
For God tells me, I won't be late. . .

—*Linda L. Lung*

Homeless

Stranded in life
My day to day cry.
A hunt for food,
I can't tell you why.
I hide in my vicies
The evil and the lie.
Eyes on me with shame even death,
I can't tell you why.
A thousand dreams
Burning bright in the night;
These are my points of light.
My clothes draped on me
Are my castle, my home;
Away I just roam.

—*Lowell Baker*

Don't Go

My love for you will never end,
My dear, great, loving friend.
I asked, "Why do you have to go?"
You said, "I guess God found someone He
 wants to know."
My heart is filled with love to share,
And love I might never know.
But, my heart will surely break my friend,
When your time has come to go.

—*Lisa Fernandez*

Pue No More

As luck would have it
My dream came true
I won a goldfish
And named it Pue.
His water was clean—he was always fed,
And Pue became my special friend.
There isn't much left to be said,
But I didn't expect his life to end.
Pue and I were soon to part
By a ruthless boy with a stone cold heart.
Pue was swallowed in the wink of an eye
On the dare of another who stood close
 by.
I now know and always will
That goldfish are so easy to kill.
In the future I will never leave
Any goldfish near a boy named Steve.

—*Tracie Lynch*

My Love for You

When the sun rises
My eyes awake,
By looking into your eyes
I see a deep, but shallow
Love for you.

—*Linda Sanchez*

The Lost Lover

As I look out the window into the snowy,
 gray day,
My eyes fill with tears and my mouth
 opens in pain.
I see so much, yet sometimes I am blind.
I try to tell myself that soon the sun will
 come out,
But I can't say the words for right now I
 can only cry,
Because I got too attached and now I am
 a lost lover.
I walk outside and the beautiful snow
 burns a hole in my arm.
Then I look down to see a solitary rose
And a piece of paper with the words, "I
 love you".
My eyes fill with tears as my face breaks
 out into a smile.
Then the long journey starts over again.
The rose withers and dies,
My heart slows down,
One last breath of life,
A scream rings out into the night,
Then the silence once again rolls in as my
 mind goes blank
And I slowly fall to the ground,
A dead rose clutched in my hand.

—*Lydia Brownlee*

Wishing for You

Seeing you always makes me smile.
My feelings for you are a never ending
 mile.
When we spend time together it makes
 me wish
That you'll be mine forever.
Though your eyes are telling me that you
 are confused,
Knowing whether or not you are being
 used.
I wish there was something I could do or
 say
To make this feeling go away.
Maybe one day you will let me know.
I don't think I could stand to see you go.
In your heart I know you want me.
It just takes time.
Why don't you try me?

—*Laura Payan*

He Loves me

The flower picked my loveless fate
My fingers picked the petals;
Of war and peace and love and hate
And all that Jesus settles.
I chanted those enchanted words
While soft the flower crumbled,
The noiseless thoughts that could be
 heard;
Afraid of being humbled.
Alas the last were in my line,
I found he loved me not.
Another vacant valentine. . .
Another hopeless thought.

—*Leah Eddens*

Farmer

I write these words in blood
My friends,
To remind you of the pain
I have had.
My weathred, cracked hands,
They bleed, my friends,
From the work and labor
They have done.
Oh Lord I wish that
I may quit
So that I may heal
And rest,
For I have worked
All these years,
And Lord, I'm
Still in debt.

—*Stacia Weaver*

You Are...

The world is cold.
My heart has froze, much like those of the
    past.
The sky has darkened, black as coal,
    empty as the eyes of a hungry child.
I can't find my way through the crowd.
Like my heart, my cane has broken in
    two.
I need you more now than ever.
For you are my eyes.
For you are my light.
Through you I see all.
The avenue of life is rugged and long.
They say time heals all wounds, but my
    scars are more visible than the sweet
    smile of a newborn baby, than the
    bruises on a battered child.
The sweat from my brow burns the deep
    cuts from within.
I can't find my way.
I keep walking in circles.
I need you more now than ever.
For you are my eyes.
For you are my light.
Through you I see all
For you are my eyes.

—*Lynn Lohner*

Music

Rhythms of the Universe
Not the tone of the instruments
We know so well —
But the wind through the trees —
The rustle of leaves in the fall
And, he by my side!

Or the earth in sweet complacency —
reaming beneath her robe
of snowy white —
Flowers in the spring — delicate yet
Bold in coloring
Whispering to the bees!

Then sweetest, dearest sound of all —
A cry in the night
A tiny voice beneath the coverlet —
His child and mine.
MUSIC, music to my years . . . .

—*Adele Hunn Pritam*

Across the Miles

Across the miles-
My heart has traveled so far.
Distance doesn't change a thing,
I still follow the same connecting star.
When I wake up in the morning,
I picture the smile on your face.
But the deeper I get,
The smile changes to only a trace.
Why can't I touch your face?
Why can't I be by your side?
Why can't I see what you are doing
To see if ours is a true bond?
Even though this is for a short time,
Each day I miss you more and more.
The wind has changed its direction
And the sun shines no more.

—*Marla Stickel*

Hearts Are...

My heart is soft
My heart is true
My heart is a gift
from me to you.
So if you care as much
as you say
you won't throw all this
love away
Hearts are precious
and often break
but I guess thats a
chance we'll have to take.
For now I love you more
than ever.
and honey, I hope
We're forever together!

—*Tina Hager*

For the Brave

Rush quickly to me, my sarcastic wit,
My heart's battlements are yet under
    seige
For the world torments me as it sees fit,
Unrelenting to thee, my faithful leige.
Bring the sharpest of words that I may
    war
That the loss of so piteous a life
May be reflected in its final score
To say bravery housed within was rife.
Oh muses' armor, truest pen to hand
The stage is set and curtain call is nigh
'Ere blood is spilled upon this dying land,
My words on wings must climb into the
    sky.
Before my words become a faded thought
I'll shed the tear for which I've bravely
    fought.

—*Robert M. Durney*

Hopeless Love

I feel as if my world has ended.
My hopes and dreams vanished
    completely
Because the love of my life is no longer
There to give me support and make my
    dreams reality.
For in this part of my life,
The sun no longer shines.
It's just a dark, cold, and scary pit,
In which I often think of the love
I knew could never be.
All of my grief and sorrows dwell in this
    pit,
In which the sun used to shine
But no longer does.

—*Latasha McCants*

Darkness

The metal is cold; the hand is warm.
My left index finger is securely wrapped
    around the trigger.
The gun rests against my flushed left
    cheek.
I am lying on my right side in a fetal
    position.
The tile is cold; the puddle of tears, warm.
The thundering bang still echoes in my
    ears.
I cannot find the strength to blink my
    eyes,
they are becoming dry little balls.
If only I could close these lids this would
    all be over.
The light is so bright, it seems alive.
I realize I am drooling, but it is out of my
    control.
I hear anxious pounding, pounding.
The door burst open.
Call an ambulance, someone's shrieking.
The voice is faintly familiar.
My lids are finally down. They came
    down like shades,
darkness.

—*Sareesa Boyd*

Hope is of the Sun

Haloed mist with pink and golden
Rising past stars lonely, bare.
Turning slow from black to purple
Night sky fading, day is near.
For a moment stars suspended
In a pinking mauve of dawn
Brightness giving way to brighter
Dwindling stars engulfed, forlorn
Gentle colours cleared the way now
Orange blazes threatening dark
Swirls of quickly lightening blackness
Disappear the sky is stark
Only for a passing moment
All is still before the day
Scarlet sun so warm with promise
Shadows linger, cannot stay

—*Wendy Ormerod*

My Life With You

You are the light my life shines through,
My life could never be greater than when
    I'm with you.
You are the sun when my day is filled
    with rain,
Without you my life would never be the
    same.
You are the sun in my blue skied day,
All the things you have done for me, I
    could never repay.
You are the rainbow after a storm of
    great might,
You brighten up my days and lighten up
    my nights.
You are the light, the sun, the moon, and
    the rainbows,
Nothing could ever explain why I love you
    so!

—*Michael D. Rhoten*

Shoprite Batteries

My life is like my reflection, plain, simple and dull.
My life is like a country, a long road to haul.
My life is like a love-filled heart, it skips many beats.
My life is like warm, green grass lulling at my feet.
My life is like eternity, which never comes to an end.
My life is like total darkness, which never really begins.
My life is like a railroad track, a repeating pattern that goes on and on.
My life is like a tornado, it comes, but soon it's gone.
My life is like a circle, never knowing where to start.
My life is like a dagger, forcing pain within my heart.
My life is like a wrist watch, ticking away the hours.
My life is like a haunted house, filled with many cowards.
My life is like a question mark, always asking why.
My life is like Shoprite batteries, always wanting to die.

—Shana Waldo

Sea

White asteroids shine.
Sea drops wet the edges
of my dress.
Slowly a warm humor
rises from a deep
crevice.
Brittle tears blended
with a humid saliva
conceal foaming an
opulent body.
A psalm, far away,
is pursuing an beating
one divine melody!

—Santa A. Lalli Marazzani

The Leaves that Fell

When leaves were falling from the trees
My life was beginning to fall apart
Then there came that silent breeze
That came and left and broke my heart.
It came so fast I didn't really think
That love itself could hurt so much
Our bond of love was our link-
But now I must forget that touch.
Now all the leaves that fell are gone
So I must say goodbye to the breeze
So now my life still must go on
Even forget about the fallen leaves.
If that breeze is to come back
I don't believe the leaves will fall
I really don't know how I'll react
If it was to come back to me at all.

—Perla Belteton

My Little Sister

You would have been seven this year.
My little sister, I always wanted to say that I had a little sister.
You would have been the best, we could have done so much.
We would go to the park for a walk, we could have went shopping at the mall.
I missed that. I would have dropped anything to be with you.
We would have had so much fun together.
I would always be there for you. We could have made it through anything.
I kissed this dream goodbye. I know you're out there helping me. I can hear you.
I know someday I will meet you somewhere, my little sister.
I always wanted to tell someone, "Yes sir, she is my little sister."
Now is the time I need you the most.
But for now, I know she will help me.
I know someday I will meet her somewhere.
I miss my little sister.

—Stephanie Day

The Rose

As the days go by with the night to day,
My love for you grows in a certain way.
I count the days until we meet,
With the rain coming down and so is the sleet.
When the rain falls off the petals of a rose,
My heart aches and my love for you shows.
It shows like the sun that dries up the rain,
But the sun when it dries,
It never does gain.
My heart will love again and again,
It will still love you just as it's been.

—Pam Jolly

Untitled

Since I first met you,
My love for you has grown more and more.
I consider you more than a friend,
You're someone I adore.
I don't know why I feel this way,
Yet, you seem to be perfect in every way.
Everytime I see you,
You seem to smile just right,
And say the sweetest things,
When you call me every night.
Sure I've loved before,
But never anything like this.
Nothing will ever be more special,
Than our first kiss.

—Stacey Winnan

Empty Arms

Empty arms are what I had the day I fell in love with you.
My love grew stronger everyday, like a little baby's grip.
At first I was content with seeing your green eyes and seeing your beautiful smile.
Every night I dreamt of holding you tenderly in my arms until the dusk turned to dawn.
The day I found you didn't love me was the longest day of my life.
That night I fell asleep with empty arms.

—Virginia Figueroa

Circle

The sun sets in the west
My love rises in the morning
Now love is like a circle
Always turning, turning, turning.
Life is like a marriage
It has its up and downs
But you'll see it like a circle
Always going round and round.
Friends they come and go
But the good ones always stay
The circles turning faster
Every single day
The circle stands for life
And so it spins forever
It's hanging on a thread
But the thread will never sever.

—Mark Wolkon and Jeremy Hoch

Broken Hearts

The back of my mind is filled with broken hearts and lost dreams
My nightmares are endless with washed away grays
I have no pictures, just sad memories.
Disappointed in the way our friendship had to end
Your heart had been broken so many times,
I wondered how you could go on
I cared about you the most, only to have it all end like this.
My days seems endless with the heartache I feel
If you looked inside my heart, you would see a large piece missing
It's been stolen by you, only to have it crushed by your bare hands
So here I sit in never ending time,
Trying mend my broken heart
And find my lost dreams.

—Sharie Larson

Tears of Love...

Tears of love, fall from my eyes, are like
 raindrops falling from the skies.
My only love told me lies and said our
 love I thought was there just died.
I wonder why but the tears of love will
 always stay because my only love left
 me and went faraway...
I wait and pray everyday that some day
 he will come back to me and stay.

—Loungthyva Tia Chantharack

True Reality

As I work on my english paper in jail
My paper becomes soggy from salty, grey
 drops
My sweat combines,
All day
All night
No happiness
No peace
I develop a very shy bordom
It approaches me heavier, then heaver
I will soon die and laughter will arise
My ghostly spirit will look below—I will
 not laugh
Although those very familar salty, grey
 drops
My sweat combines—will linger
The laughter will haunt me until the end
 of the earth and sky
But it will never die
I never knew that ghosts can not die
I am very sorry and wish to awake.

—Lisa Ann Levy

Journey

Mother of Life and prossessor of my sons
my reach to the stars has just begun
Oh, how I wonder what discoveries await
on the far distant worlds beyond this gate
Where mortals are trapped and securely
 bound
in thoughts of kingdoms yet unfound.
My ship heads outwards to the rim of
 space
in search of the wisdom that will bring us
 grace
And deliver our spirits unto the suns
that fill the voids
where life began.

—William R. Bowman, Sr.

There just can't be

"I pray the Lord"
"My soul to keep"
She prays to God
And my soul weeps
She does not know
What I believe
There is no Lord
There just can't be
With all this crap
Drowning eternity

—Shannan L. Rogers

Seclusion

My emptiness engulfs
My strength and power to love.
All alone with nothing, nobody to tell me
 they love me.
So I sit in my room desperately wanting to
 know of love,
To feel its touch, to kiss its sweet,
 sensuous lips.
Instead, I am commiserated by the
 animals of no life.
Frozen smiles plastered on their faces of
 unending happiness.
What joy, to be put in their place,
To never know the pain and anguish of
 flesh.
But I, the unlucky, still sit in my room.
No attempts for the door.
I just sit in a place where I know I can't
 be found, to be hurt.

—R. D. Adamec

To Ana My Beloved Friend

The days have went much to quickly;
My time to say good-bye has begun to
 draw very near.
As I think of all that has happened,
I feel the warmth and running of a
 trickling tear.
Saying good-bye is such a hard thing to
 do,
Especially if you love someone as much as
 I love you.
You entered my life as a stranger, from a
 very different land.
Together we have walked the way, always
 hand in hand.
Sometimes the road was difficult, and it
 all seemes so up hill.
But together we survived all that, with
 heart and soul and will.
We gave what it took to be the close
 friends that we are.
Now being in my mind and heart, the
 distance won't seem so far.
Good-bye is such a hard thing to say,
But as you leave me along the way;
Remember me with a smile, not a tear,
And remember as sisters, you are always
 very near.

—Lorna Kay Winter

The Ocean

Down in the deep, dark depths
Mystery lies where no one steps
All the animals large and small
There are too many to name them all
Sunken ship, many treasures
All the beauty many pleasures
Down in the deep, dark, depths
You shall find where no one steps.

—Nicole Marsh

Yarning

Weaving stories like baskets of straw
Mythical beasts and crows that go caw
Legends of love and pain and desire
Fables for children, tales by the fire
Knights in shined armor save damsels
 distressed
With legions of stories by God we are
 blessed
Aesop and Twain, Shakespeare and more
Steal from the rich and give to the poor
Fiction or fact, folk tale or truth
Flight of fancy of a daydreaming youth
Just an old wives tale or cute anecdote
Adventure and drama, the rhymes of a
 poet
Reminiscinces, romance, biographies,
 plays
Diaries, letters, and the good old days
Yes, we're all yarners with tales to debate
Just accounts of our lives we love to
 narrate.

—Wayne Van Coughnett

Untitled

Nell M.
Nell was hell
Because she always heard bells
But she never smelled
So she was loved as you can tell.
Cynthia R.
Never smoked because she didn't like tar
And she was always drinking from a jar
At least she didn't have a scar
So you see we loved our star
Cynthia R.

—Mike Stewart

The Blue Green Calling

Like countless precious gems sparkling in
    the morning light,
Neptunes abundance of treasure a teasing
    yet desireable sight,
Offering a cool inviting haven in escape
    from the burning sun
The depth of the blue green calling
    promising pleasure and fun.
The herons with their long legs running
    jauntily across the sand
Join forces with the seagulls searching for
    a repast on sea or land.
The tinkling of children's laughter as they
    run to catch the waves,
The pride in the colorful seashells they've
    collected throughout the day.
So quickly the time has passed as dusk
    makes its rightful claim,
And the sun sinks below the water to wait
    its turn again.

—Lucy C. Pruett

Man

Drifting along life's ardous road,
Never listening to a thing he's been told.
He has his hat, his coat, his shoes,
Figures he doesn't have a thing to lose.
So why at night when it's cold and gray
Does he look up into the sky and pray?
I'm searching for the truth you can hear
    him say—
I am not blind, but I can't find the way.
Alone and afraid he weeps in the night,
Hoping that the darkness will cover his
    plight.
Never before has he felt so distraught,
Counting the years he's battled and
    fought,
He remembers the scars, the pain, the
    cries.
But he can't remember the reasons or
    why.
Terrible screams below from his soul as
    his anguish grows and grows,
He empties his gut of his rage,
Releasing the prisoner of its cage.

—Suzin M. Innaimo

Hugs

The hurt that I am feeling,
Never seems to go away.
I need one of your special hugs,
Each and every day.
When you put your arms around me,
I feel so safe and secure.
I only hope you feel the same,
But I don't know for sure.
I hope someday you might love me,
The same way that I love you.
But for now your hugs are just enough,
To get me through this life.

—Meg Coffey

Friends

Friends are forever
Never shall be apart
They're stuck together
Heart to heart
Side by side
They walk together
In the glorious light
No hatred just love
That there only can be and
That's why friends are forever
Just like you and me.

—Melissa Leggett

For Daddy

Always there for me,
Never would you leave me,
Take time to spend with me,
Taught right and wrong to me,
Gave me all I needed, and more!
Dried my tears,
Made me laugh,
Stuck up for me,
Never let me down;
Made me into what I am.
Knowing I could always count on you
I write these words for you
As a "thankyou" for everything.
Daddy, I love you!

—Rachel Cline

What can Life be?

Life can be a light
Nice and bright
Or like a black wall
Dull and dark
Life can be like an amusement park
Filled with adventures
Or like a flower
Filled with fresh air
What can life be?

—Monica Hastings

Hugo Grotius

Read today?
No
In New Amsterdam colony?
Yes, now.
Impact?
World wide.
The UNA, the United States, salutes
Grotius, the genius prodigy on his
Four hundredth birthday anniversary
April 10, 1983, as our
Father of international law and law of the
    sea
Writer of theology, poetry, prose, drama,
Philosophy, history and philology.
Rediscovered by America through
Ruth Steinkraus Cohen.
Now Grotius is recognized throughout the
    world,
At the UN and in your birthplace, Dutch
    land.

—Rose Marie Pace Barone

Halloween Spring

No robins, no daffodils,
No hymns filtering through the
    stained—glass windows.
The churchyard stands deserted.
I sit in the cafe on Madison,
Drinking espresso,
Watching the wind scatter the chill of
    grey skies
Around the steeple across the street,
Around the sound images of Mussorgsky
    playing in my head.
Rain beats on the timpani.
Witches fly on broomsticks of discarded
    straws.
A cat's eyes shine from the fire escape
And street lights flicker with wild grins.
As late night customers float out the door,
The waitress picks up half—filled coffee
    cups,
Used napkins, and wearily hangs the
    "closed" sign on the window.
I walk into the "Night on Bald
    Mountain."

—Melanie Hunnicutt

All's Quiet

All's quiet on the western front,
No indians shouting wild.
No cowboys riding through the town
Endangering mom and child.
Cowboys and indians call a truce
No changing lead for lead.
All's quiet on the western front,
My children are in bed.

—Virginia Sewell

Untitled

No matter what,
No matter where,
Just think of me
And I'll be there.
Remember all the fun.
Together we have had.
Treasure all the memories
Of the good times and the bad.
Never forget
The little things we shared,
Because I know I could not forget
How much I've always cared.

—Michelle McHone

Eden

Spring breezes flow throughout,
No more weeping, suffering, nor pout.
There shall be light,
No more fight.
This fair place. . .
EDEN.
Beyond the England hills,
The hunted eagles will,
They'll hunt for her. . .
EDEN.
In this expected generation,
There will be no celebration,
People will only hear,
The shedding of a tear,
For this thing. . .
EDEN.
When hundreds goest even,
It will be time for EDEN.

—Olivia Smith

Desperate

I want to be desperately in love.
No, not love.
Painful.
I want to be desperately in like.
No, not like.
Fleeting.
I want to be desperately in lust.
Yes lust, but there is something wrong.
Desperate.
No.
I never want to be desperate.

—Linda M. Cangialosi

Why Bother for Fathers

Why bother for fathers
No one really cares
What the heck, let's change
From that bad unusual flair
Now what should I get him
A hat or a new reclining chair
Or stop giving him that look
As he sends me to my room
In a great, great blair
Sometimes I sit and stare
And wonder what he'd do if
He knew what really happened
To his old reclining chair
So I've narrowed it down
To a reclining chair
Or maybe I should get him
That new toupee of hair.

—Nicole Due

My First Auto

I purchased my first auto,
No other could compare.
It cost me all my savings.
The price was more than fair.
I oiled it and tuned its horn,
I checked its wheels all four.
One thing I forgot to do,
Was lock its protective door.
I planned on showing it to friends.
I had paid it special care.
But when I went to take it out,
I found it was not there.

—Mae Futter

Suicide Wonders

Over the bridge I go
No second thoughts
I just had to see,
What the world would be,
Without me. Will I see?
Maybe I'll only see what will be.
In my mind as I dwell
Of a life only in hell.
I had a glimpse of the past
Although it was sincerely vast.
I only have come to see
My life I once lived to see.
Oh, I get those vibes so
Creepy and evil.
Oh well, at least my life was
Not all that feeble.

—Lynn Gush

Time

You think of the world as it goes by.
Nobody knows that time does fly.
All the nature, all the trees.
Nobody cares, nobody sees.
Times of wonder, times I've had.
Times of value, times I've been sad.
Time is special, yet no one knows.
When time goes by everything glows.
Time is love, time is hate.
Time is fun when you're on a date.
Time is fast, time is slow.
Time is white like a beautiful snow.
Time goes by without a trace.
It goes through us and into space.
But nobody knows if there was no time.
Clocks wouldn't tick tock and chimes
 wouldn't chime.

—Rodney Black

Beloved Mate

There are no words to ease the pain
Nor any you'd want to hear
When you're so lonely, tired and scared
And you've lost the one most dear
You try to seek comfort with the Lord
Hold on to His guiding hand
And though you try with all your might
You still don't understand
Why he has to be taken from you
He has always been your life
It's been that way since you were married
He is your husband; you are his wife
You will get through this darkest time
You'll never walk alone
The Lord will carry you in His arms
And give loving comfort to His own

—Wanda Mowatt

God's Love

I cannot weigh out God's love in dollars or
 dimes
Nor can I measure in th palm of one's
 hand,
How far God's love reaches down to the
 fallen man
God's love spans the globe
All over the world in every land,
God's love cannot be stopped
It keeps flowing from the Sea of Time,
You and I cannot fathom God's love
Nor understand the height, the depth, the
 width,
God's love is not measured in dollars or
 dimes.

—Mary E. Coleman Pinion

A Cry for Help

A cry for help, and no one listens,
Nor pauses to see who said it.
A cry for help, and they chat away,
Forgetting it, and forever holding their peace.
A cry for help, and everyone thinks it will get better,
Never thinking about the consequences.
The cry for help was from the world,
So now it will die, because no one listened.

—Matthew Damico

Homeless in the Land of the Free

It's hard to imagine
Not having enought to eat
Cardboard in your shoes
And no place to sleep
There have always been poor people
Since life began on Earth
At one time you'd find a steeple
And the warmth of a church
Now traveling through the city
I was sadly shocked
I think it's such a pity
The church doors are all locked
It's really quite a problem
And a price that must be paid
I think we should help our homeless
Instead of foreign aid.

—William F. Bowers

Ode To Poetry

About this subject,
Not many have written
Which is created in
Joy, sadness or when someone's smitten
Used as an adjective
To describe a ballerina's motions
It soothes the sores of many
Like a doctor's potion
It's found everywhere
in sports, drama, and even T.V.
Yes, it all makes sense
in the world of poetry.

—Michael E. Dunlap, Jr.

Long Lonesome Journey

There I am on the long desolate road, walking all by myself.
Not one single care in the world, and nobody to talk to
Except listening to the crickets talk amongst themselves.
Every now and then a car may pass by.
Their headlights flood me with their light, and my enthusiasm grows stronger,
As if I'm going to make friends from these people.
They probably say amongst themselves, "Hey there lonely girl, what are you doing your here by yourself?"
But then my enthusiasm is shot down in sorrow when the car passes by.
Then I walk up by the still waters of the pond, where I see leaves drop in
One by one like they are trying to catch a ride with a beautiful swan.
I take a quick glance at myself in the water. Am I laughing or crying?
No, as I take a longer and more careful look, I see a very still and serious me.
And if the water could talk, it would be saying, "Never fear, I will be your good friend for life."
So now I walk home in a joyous state of mind, and my long lonesome journey is over.

—Sandra Mattison

Strangers

Sometimes,
When I look in the mirror,
I don't recognize
The face
That I see.
I wonder
Who I am,
And
Why I'm here.
I look in the mirror,
And I see a
Stranger.
One that's
Not real.
But one
Who looks like
Me.

—Rachel E. Forehand

Loving

Nothing can be solved in a day.
Nothing can be solved in a lifetime.
It takes you and me,
Loving each other,
Day by day,
Year by year.
Life goes on,
The seasons change,
But my love for you never will.
I will protect you,
With my last breath,
My last bullet,
My last hand.

—Rose Stephenson

The Game

We're all bound by the same chains,
Nothing ventured, nothing gained.
I knew I shouldn't go along with the ride,
I guess the grass just grew a little greener on the other side.
Now it seems every day is the same,
That's because everybody's playin' the game.
Sleeping with danger, kissing the lips of death,
Tell me, is there really anything left?
Sometimes you have to close your eyes to see the light,
You'll find, it gets harder to resist temptation,
All because I once was filled with fascination.
"Trust me" is a phrase you should never believe,
People who use it are only out to deceive.
No longer do I live on hunger of desire,
Or thirst for the flames of the fire.
Power made its move, but I won the game.

—Patti Leigh Croft

They're Just Words

Quiet. Frightened. Black and blue.
She sits battered and alone,
Afraid to speak or move.
No one knows why yet, no one wants to.
The truth?
Well, it shocks most so they turn away.
She knows only anger and hatred,
Words that reject,
Blows that strike her soul.
She doesn't have any friends,
Besides, no one cares!
The reason?
She is trash, no good.
She doesn't deserve anyone or anything.
Or so he says.
Are they just words?

—Troy Altman

Song of the Sea

Once the sea was filled with happiness and music
Now it is filled with a weeping silence
We won't see them dancing
We won't hear their song
Look what we have done
To their magical song
Sadness and sorrow has replaced their gay playfulness
They long for the freedom to swim in the sea
They are trapped in their own kingdom
Of magic and grace
Their land was invanded
By people with wrong hearts
Their sea was intruded
With a wrong kind
Please help us
Right our wrong
Before the whales have gone away

—Melissa Goodlad

The First Step

I think about you—
Now that you're gone.
Wishing you'd come back to me.
I know, now, that I was wrong
and you were right.
I think about the way things used to be
and may never be again.
Everything has changed,
nothing stayed the same.
Sitting here thinking,
I wish you were here.
But I know we must start over-
from the very beginning.
And I know I must
make the first step.
And that is by saying,
"I'm sorry".

—*Pam Barnett*

Best Friend

It is really amazing that we are so close.
Of all the friends I've ever had,
I depend on you the most.
I know we've had our ups and down,
We've had good times and bad.
And how we've gotten through them,
I don't know, but I am truly glad.
I hope you keep in touch
When you move away.
I hope we can stay as close
As we are today.
You are so special to me,
I consider you my best friend.
I hope that I can call you that
Until the very end.

—*Trent Fontenot*

Crater Lake

Infinity is blue, a sapphire glow
Of depths unsounded, color deep and rare.
An ancient place, it's only lately known
To those of us who were not always there.
The ones who knew this place so long ago
Tell tales of warring gods and skies of fire.
We wonder, look and think perhaps it's
   so-
And leave in silence, or perhaps, inspired.
It matters little how the lake was made;
Whose artist's eye devised this brilliant
   hue.
For whether God or gods prepared the
   shade,
Here in this place, infinity is blue.

—*Linda M. Koeniguer*

Drowning

Drop to fall beneath the water
Occult's kin but sunlight's daughter
Quick and silent, smother life,
But slay isolation, vanish strife;
Now able, in this precious sleep
To feel the good and breathe the deep
Lurid things are all let go
And gentle drops caress and flow
Come and sing a song with me,
Under gentle, giveing sea
No memory of passing days
Which now slip by in opaque haze
The light is strong, the light is blind
I have no eyes but touch is kind
Come to me and take my hand
You never need return to land

—*Lise-Ann Davis*

Untitled

Listen to the sea
Of all the sounds
That hold the key
To the secrets found.
Sailing through the waves,
Settling my restless mind,
Finding the hopes I crave,
Leaving my past behind.

—*Sheila Cohn*

Appearing in Absentia

Wrapped in a mantle
Of dramatic black,
The pale ghost of Echo leans
Forward to catch the winged words
Soaring from the lips
Of the sibylline priestess
Who guards the temple,
Set in the lyrical grove.
Their touch, in the shimmering light,
Dual auras of aqueous gold.

—*W. John G. Martin*

Untitled

Staring down the barrel
of a loaded gun
trigger-happy world
itchy fingered
Absolute loneliness abounds
Restless bullet
Cold steel chamber
Total blankness
in velvet night
Reaching out in vain
midnight whistle blows
blinding lightening bolt
earth-shaking thunder roll
Pouring bloody rain.

—*Marc Gendron*

Lies and Deception

Lies and deception
Of an endless war, are the results of the
   hearts
That have nothing to fight for.
Though blinded by the tears
And a heart that only bleeds
Love for you is the one thing I do see.
Alone in my heart, where the memories
Come to haunt, I'm still in pain
I have a feeling this is just the start.
Though the love was sweet
And I thought the love was true
It turned bitter and so did you.
My ears were deceiving
So were the words you spoke.
You were gone, the moment I realized
   and awoke.
If I had only one wish
I know what it would be, I also know, too
Wishes are only a dream.

—*Shelley Stromquist*

My Only Wish

My only wish is to leave this place
Of evil and misery.
I see an eagle fly across the lonely sky,
As a tear falls quietly down my cheek.
My only wish is to be left alone for life
To be witthat eagle away from the world.
So I, me, the one who hates this awful
   place,
Could go where I want.
To go where I wish.
Live how I please.
That is my only wish.
No more pains.
No more heartache.
Tears I cry aren't tears of misery,
But of hate, red of life.
My hope are broken everyday.
Why can't I fly clear Lord?
That is my only true wish.

—*Tonya Henson*

America's Final Invitation

We invite you to a world
Of freedom and equality
Where everyone can control
Their own destiny, is our policy
Here you have total access
To peace and liberty
And the right to pursue
Your own happiness completely
However there are conditions
As there is to everyting
Hatred and hostility
You may not bring
Prejudice is ignorance
And you must leave this behind
For here cultural diversity,
Which leads to richness you'll find
We only ask that you
Love your country
With committment and dedication
And this my friend
Is America's final invitation

—Rachel A. Rouse

Imprisonment

Looking out the window
Of my wildly confused mind,
Thinking of the presence
That I'm soon to leave behind.
A world of pure uncertainty,
Afraid and all alone,
Soon these frightening memories
And feelings will be gone.
Happiness will overcome
Terrors fast construction,
And I will spread my wings once more
To flee from further destruction.
Now I have to face my fears
For I know where terror can be,
And dream of the day of happiness
When my mind will be set free.

—Sharla Stephens

Your Past, Too

You have given pause in the pursuit
Of presumed fact
For a chance to clarify
Those missed intentions.
You don't look the part of your poetry.
More that of an overseer whose stares
    permeate
The shades of confusion
Which you painted with twisted hands.
You'll write your way out of this
You always do find a way to set the scene
Bribe the situation and
And discreetly direct your own
    disappearance.
You and love fugitive companions
Reside in honor alongside a fable
Recited in silence so you won't have
To hear the fall of your name from grace.

—Rod Stearns

Desert Sands

My love for you is compared to the
    endless grains
Of sand in a vast desert plain.
So immense that it is impossible to be
    counted.
It burns,
It glows,
It is alive and hot like the mere presence
    of the sun.
But as the sun fades and leaves,
The sands remain.
Growing sad,
Losing its warmth and vitality,
Its sparkle.
It's alone in an empty darkness.
You are like the passing of the sun
From day to night.
And I am like the desert
That always remains.

—Patricia Holliday

Night Beat

Slumbering men pull a comfort
Of soothing dreams over their care.
Some dutiful watchdog, or cat on the stair
May test the stealth in the midnight air.
Night snuggles into the crevices,
Cold creeps out to the street,
While doubt and dismay
By a solid blue shadow and steady step
Are moved to retreat
When a cold, watchful cop on his
Late night beat,
With a hand to his stick
And an eye to the stars
Makes familiar overtures to the cement
With his size-twelve shoes
Down his own street.

—Margaret Shires

Desperation

As the silence overtook the pressures
of the day.
She began to reflect the images of a
life gone astray.
Death and loneliness had locked her in a
asylum of her own.
The search for a way out had become a
long and futile journey.
Alas, one day a shimmer of light was
    showing
her the door of life.
As she reached to unlock her soul, she
finally realized hell has no doors.

—Robert W. Roach

Special Touch

My eyes reflect the memories,
Of the love we once shared.
From them roll the tears,
To tell me I still care.
In my heart there is a space,
That is always sad and blue.
It is a broken heart,
And it was cracked because of you.
In my mind, there is your smile,
And the sparkle of your eyes.
I often daydream of you and me,
And it usually makes me cry.
But mostly, there is all of me,
And without you, that isn't much.
I want to hold you,
And feel your special touch.

—Paige M. Hagen

Smylnos

The faces of screams interconnect,
Why reality?
For one to embark upon the distant quest,
The search for realness.
For I have seen the myth,
And I have witnessed the unreal
    coexistence,
The gate for the rendezvous has been
    open,
I have seen the reality—
But never touched it.
If I could but congregate innocent
    derelictions,
To my advantage,
Reality would be more tangible.
Must I see what branded eyes only see?
Must I hear what sweet tongues on the
    snakes?
Yes I must, for I lead myself to it.
Reality could not be found,
For patience will be continued,
Until reality is met—head on.

—Talley Griffith

Self Portrait

Salt crystals glisten white on the wrinkled
    face
of the pier; forming a new image
with every stroke of the winds brush.
The low sun ignites the sky.
Red and orange explode
across the pale blue canvas
and fill his head with the flames
that burn on the horizon
and melt like wax drippings
into the green water.
Time drifts softly like the hanging fog.
It is a kaleidoscope vision;
Slowly the bits of colored glass disband
and disappear. Only one glowing white
crescent is left against the blackness.
The colors have melted dark
into the deep water, on which the moon
now performs its dazzling light.

—Margaret Dawson

Flight of the Nez Perce

The Nez Perce, they fled from the evil hand
Of their captors' uncaring, harsh demands.
Disease and sickness haunted that last flight.
Why were they hounded for doing but right?
The greed of the white man had caused this shame
That rousted a nation by misplaced blame.
An honest and good life now turned to a plight.
Why were they hounded for doing but right?
Chief Joseph gathered his people around.
The Nez Perce ways would no longer abound.
A losing battle it would be to fight.
Why were they hounded for doing but right?
This is the story of the Nez Perce flight.
Why were they hounded for doing but right?

—R. Owen

Remembering

Listen
Your friend is dead
From his picture you shall cry
From his laugh you shall laugh
From his smile you shall smile
From his likes and dislikes you shall remember.
From his other friends you will hear
All good and no bad about him
In school you will hear stories,
You will hear untrue stories, lies about him,
But you will know the truth.
Though good men like him die,
Life must go on.
And the dead won't be forgotten.
Life must go on.
In Loving Memory of Jeff Powers LeFebvre

—Michelle L. Cavallo

My Thoughts

Remember all the memories
Of times in the past
When we were together
Too bad they didn't last.
You used to say you loved me
Too bad it wasn't true
Cause I want you to know
I still love you.
I wish you hadn't left me
But you thought it was right
Cause we're both alone now
On this cold and lonely night.

—Nikki Lawrence

I Soulfully Remember You

Sultry seductress sea...I watch the groping sea fingers
Of your seaweed waters, fold and roll invitingly, over the
Soft, warm uneven neckline of these southern sands.
Tell me a sweet love novel, with untold chapters, I will listen.
Your rhythm gives solance to my dusty, wandering soul.
Within me, I recall sweet friend, your radiant love spirit,
How our tender hopes and ambitions were a sacred vigil,
My moods, doubts, hesitations were always tropical storms.
"How do I come to your bare virgin soul?" I would wonder.
Me, the vibrant suncatcher, who danced to an unseen fifer
Deep within the treasure cove, of my sweet, endearing memories?
Once more...in memory, I walk and soulfully remember you.
As we counted yellow cacti flowers on the dunes,
You would greet me..."You look so Florida, honey?"
How do I fully understand the mystic powers...
Of the sunkist touch, my friend, of your hand in mine
The times we slipped between the pages of a Florida afternoon?

—Nancy D. Chamberlain

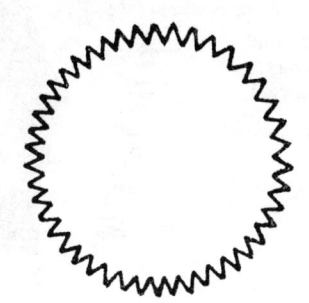

Dreams of Forever

I dream of a wonderful love,
Oh, his eyes do glisten
Though he may not speak
I do always listen.
As he pulls me closer,
I hear him whisper
Dreams of summer evenings
And of "us" forever
As we grow older.
Forever lasts
As I dream
Not of the past
But of the future we hold.
Though our souls may die
Our love will never grow cold.
No, our love will never die.

—Rose Hobbs

Fifteen Years

You're the wind in my sails, you're my tranquil sea,
Oh, my darling, how I love thee.
You're my Rock of Gibralter: you're my feather bed,
For fifteen years, we've been happily wed.
You have lifted me up when I was way down,
I'm always happy when you're around.
When life had me beaten, you made me see,
That no one could get the best of me.
You're my warm winter hearthside,
You're my cool summer breeze
You have comforted my sorrows on life's stormy seas.
You've fought all my battles and brought peace to my heart.
I could not bear it if we should part.
Yet, if we were parted by death's final blow,
Our years together would shine with a glow.
Of all the plans God had for me,
Finding you was surely meant to be.

—Rebecca W. Costner

Dawn Dance

Woman
Sea seen
distance
On sunrise sand.
Long-striding lithe
Song raised
dance
Pirouette
Flecked waves
Sea green
sketch
Tilted-cap greetings.
Dawn dance
Sea lyrics
swirl
Morning dreams
Woman

—M.D. LeDoux

Gone, Yet Always Here

He sat here, in this very chair,
Oh, so often;
Reading and reading.
Then he'd close the book,
Hold his finger in his place
And shut his eyes and think.
Sometimes a furrowed brow
And other times a dear smile.
He must have thought often
Of his many students.
Our love was such a quiet thing;
So deep, so secure, so unending.
Now, only the body is gone
While much of his great soul
Is a part of me —
And I, the richer for it.

—Margaret Dahl Aamoth

A Love Story

As I sit and think of the good times we had
Old feelings arise and make me sad
How could I have just let you go
You were my very first beau
I gave my heart for you to hold
And you made it worth its weight in gold
We made love under the stars every night
Each time reaching a brand new height
Then you left and I was all alone
Waiting every moment near the phone
I hated the war for taking you from me
Each night I'd wonder where you could be
A knock came suddenly at my front door
And as I answered my heart fell through the floor
My worst fear had finally come true
You were dead and I didn't know what to do
I told our daughter of our love story
And that you died with honor and glory

—*Tereasa Booher*

Jealousy

To say I have feelings for you
would be untrue.
To say I have fantasized
would not be a lie.
Vicious thoughts of jealousy emerge
When you talk to another
How I wish I could fill her shoes
And speak and dress like her.
Just so that it would be
Me that you notice,
Me that you talk to,
Me that you long for.
Please,
back to reality.
It is not me that he cares for.
Who needs conversation
When you can have more than her mind.

—*Marian Krueger*

Memory of Life

I can remember carved oak boxes
On dark and dreary mornings, on sad days;
Faces masked in black with tears that are
Streaming down faces, trying to think positively
Seeing desperation while seeking comfort,
Wanting to help-
Realizing what is out of control, like a blazing
Fire that moans and groans as it destroys
The things you hold most precious.
Looking at the haunted faces of the moon,
As it looks on in undying sympathy.
Some may slip into the void of endless thought;
Only to realize what is not there.
There is something behind the costume of death,
And the finale will be greater than life-
Won't it?

—*Stephanie Bova*

Love And Devotion

We decided to take a ride,
on one warm summer day.
I never wanted that day to end,
holding on to you, I wanted to stay.
We rode all over town,
greeting people as we passed by.
I felt so close to you,
like there was no-one near by.
Since that day, some things have changed,
like having no motorcycle to ride on.
But one thing has remained the same,
and this we can count on.
Our Love and Devotion,
that keeps our relationship strong.
This is what makes us grow together,
and keeps things from going wrong.

—*Laura-Lee Robinson*

Good-Bye

Standing
On the shore at sunset,
Alone.
Holding in my hand
A red rose wet with tears
From my eyes.
Slowly
I let go of the rose—
Forever.
It plunges
Into the deep blue
And drifts away.
I will never forget.

—*Lisa McDowell*

Moon Cat

The crystal moon is shining down
On the snow in the backyard.
The snow looks like a sea of blue
With tiny sparkling diamonds suspended in it.
Here and there are islands of lilac bushes and spruce.
A snake freighter made of rotting wood
Separates our sea from our neighbors.
From far away one can see the "lighthouse"
Which illuminates a path on the water.
My cat is beached by one of the lonely islands.
He is the only living thing out there tonight.

—*Michelle Havens*

Our Dreams Come True

As we stand here paused
On the threshold of our dreams,
Prepared to commit our lives
And love to one another
The excitement and joy of the moment
Has now taken hold it seems,
And we ask you to share in it
Both as sisters and as brothers
Our love for each other is boundless,
The future as bright as we choose it to be
This special love so long in coming,
Beside me now and all our days through.
The comfort of being oneself
While nurturing our special unity,
Our dreams have come true dear
Your love for me and my love for you

—*Theodore Radford III*

Blindness of the Night

Depression and loneliness, that's all that exists
On this cold and dreary night of December.
I can hear the wind howling like hungry wolves,
Now, as I sit in my chamber I think about this useless life.
It seems as if there is no daylight, ever.
I am always in a hole, it's always dark and lonely.
The blindness of darkness I cannot bear
The loneliness involved I did not dare to reveal.
All I am thankful for is the presence of the night
It feels as if I am in my own world, confused and weak.
My life is like an alarm clock, it always keeps me up,
Each day I am waiting for someone to pull the plug.
I disagree on my life, but dwell on my death.
Now that I have nothing, I shall take nothing with me,
Nothing but this hand that prepared me for my death, by writing.
I look out that big window beside my bed and I see my grave waiting for me.
Well, it shall wait no more for my time has come,
There shall be no sorrow for who would sympathize.

—*Michelle L. Houck*

The Walk

Take a walk up this road past ponds of quiet reflection.
On this road you need not think of lifes's pressing moments.
Leave the world behind to follow the quiet serenity of the silent wood.
Walk past trees of changing colors preparing for winters sleep.
Breathe deep the cold crisp air for it warms the soul.
For there is no cold when you are the moment of self discovery.
Grant yourself the moment to notice the heavy gray sky of snows to come.
The carpet of fallen leaves laid beneath your fee to support a light walk,
In the bare branch is the silent summer song of birds preparing for a winter lodging.
Walk along this road before the quilt of snow snuggles the nested animals in time honored carring sleep.
Help yourself to the fragrance of wet damp smells of mossy covered bark of smoke from farm cottages across the fields.
The wind beckons with bare branch to follow the road to explore uncommon things in life.
Hope begins to dawn on a harried life as you walk down the road.

— *Stephen P. Croston*

One Red Rose

Upon the note lay
One beautiful, red rose
Perfect in every way.
Just as she thought
Their love had been.
Why did he leave?
Had she sensed a change?
Not a coldness in his eyes,
Not an edge to his words,
But a longing.
A restlessness in his heart.
Love blinds you from the danger
Of pain to endure.
The cut that will
Forever remain a scar.
Her tears touched the rose
Perfect in all ways but one.
Its only fault that it would die.

—*Michelle Gallant*

Forever

Dreams pass me by
One by one
Into the night
Until the darkness
Fills the chasms.
Of my empty
Lonely state
A corpse devoid
Of any hope
I dream no more
Of living life
But merely drift
Forever caught
In crescent waves.

—*Trinh Ngo*

This Day

Each day brings upon us a new and fresh beginning.
One can take that day and live it
Like they have the last one or two or forty
But you
Must look at that beginning
And enjoy every breathtaking minute of it.
The ocean air, sunny gardens, snow filled fields, and whispering winds
Can fill your days with a very special magic.
I awoke this morning and saw the vast blue sky
And the sun winking at me.
On my way out I saw birds laughing and playing
While little children sang and danced
Under a red maple tree.
I was filled with a brilliant love for life
And promised myself to make each day
As beautiful and special as this.

—*Susan A. Lynch*

A Lonesome Me

Oh, how I'd like to be a different fellow than me.
One like a swift honey bee
And could sing like a little Towhee (a little bird).
A fellow like me just can't be as lonesome as me.
I wonder what could be the matter with me.
I should have built a house under a tree
And had pretty flowers planted by me,
And a pretty wife a waiting for me.
And then maybe I'd feel like loving
And wouldn't be as lonesome as me.

—*Paul E. Fouse*

Wishing for Love Upon A Star

There's one star in the sky tonight
One star trying to last through the night
A star so beautiful it show's me to hold on tight
To what love I have and what love that might.
I know that my day will come
that love should have already begun
I hope and I dream for a love that lasts forever
but I have this feeling it's next to never.
Sometimes I wonder if love should be
cause love never seems to happen to me
For once I would like a love that lasts
cause love seems to leave me so fast
Sometimes I think if I hold on tight
the love that is will last through the night.

—*Lynne Fontano*

Seek as to Find

Seek as to find one love
One very special love
Care as to take sometime
To hide away the fear of falling deeply in love.
Baby, if you'd care
Then baby you'd bare
Your heart to me
Please hold me dearly in your arms
Care a little
Care a lot
Baby, give it all you've got
Don't tell me you love me not
Seek as to find one special moment
Seek as to find some lovin'
But not just any kind of love
But the special kind you find inside!

—*Maritza De La Guardia*

Tears on my Pillow

The tears on my pillow mean nothing to anyone but me.
Only one person can understand, only I can see.
But that does me no good.
Because from where you have stood.
You have not seen me fall apart.
You have not seen my lonely heart.
I've called for help, but no one can hear.
It seems to get worse with each shedded tear.
But I'll sit in my room of four cold walls,
Until someone answers my calls.

—*Lynne E. Rice*

A Love Affair

For once there are no tears nor sadness,
    no loneliness nor solitude,
Only the burning fire of an intense love
    affair.
Tease a part of nature lurking within
    passion;
The embodiment of private obsession
    mascaraded by purity.
Discretly aspirations soar, quiet moments
    esculated by ectasy,
Frozen in our thoughts are illusions of you
    and me.
Fragile as "China doll" the priceless jewel
    of love;
Charades given birth from past events,
    highlights of a love affair.
Dawn, another time arriving soon, the
    cornerstone of pleasure's haven;
Light absorbs the darkness created by the
    blind.
Paradise made of fantasies, dreams of two
    people alone;
Flowers growing outside my window,
    come lay down with me.
Sunshine seeps in through open creases,
    the night was spent together.
Touch me, let me know it's real, the true
    meaning of a love affair.

—Wayne A. Williams

Tales

When I was young, my friend and I.,
Would sit upon Grandpa's knee
Listening to him tell tales
Of kings and queens, princes and
    princesses
Of faraway countries, of distant lands.
Then we would imagine
What it would be like
To live as those people once did.
We would be draped from head to toe
In velvets and silks and satin;
We would be the ones sitting in splendor
While those we knew, and we ourselves
Fought dragons and villains
And went on daring adventures.
But for now
All we do is dream,
And listen to Grandpa
Tell his tales.

—Nina K. York

Love

Lovely is love,
Open minded and free,
Rushing throughout your body
Eternity being yours.
Never will it die,
Amazing what love can do.

—Lorena Chacon

Love Unbound

I always seem to conjure this dream about
    us
Opening this door to a world we could
    trust
A certain voice that was rich and gentle
    spoke
Which we held each other close as the
    silence was broke
The shadowy voice began to ask, "You
    two lovers are chosen"
"To stand firm on thy feet from your
    generation"
"To tell the whole universe your true
    happiness."
The silhouette figure, as were all objects
    in the distance,
Continued the discourse, "You, my
    friends, do you believe"
"The love you bear in the morning to be
    the same as in the eve?"
"Yes, I do believe that it is." I vividly
    replied.
"In truth, we have each other as our most
    beloved."
Than you, my lady love answered, "I do
    say for the better"
"And that we could hold it forever
    together."
The shadowy voice again asked, "You
    trust this love guides you?"
In one beautiful rhythm we sang, "Yes,
    we do!"
The rich, gentle figure smiled as the other
    shades happily weep
As we returned to the earth knowing it
    was ours to keep.

—V. W. Oliveira

Today's Youth

Troubled and confused,
oppressed left out in the rain
Oh where shall they find shelter
From all that is vain.
All that is forward,
All that is dark,
Is filling the emptiness
that was made in their heart.
For May shall seek,
but few shall find,
That untreaded pathway,
So many has left behind.
Trangressors and opressors,
shall take the souls of many,
The pathway is dark and,
The numbers are plenty.

—Scotty Burns

Inner Peace

Why should I smile
Oppression
World hunger
Tyranny
War
Failing economies
Terrorism
Why should I smile
Well for starters
It's a beautiful day
My cousin just had a baby
And they named it after me

—T. L. Hart

My Reality

The moon is not crusted cheese
Or a smiling man,
And there is more to fear
Than simply fear.
Also, I have seen love
And felt love,
And each instance
It was disguised in hate.
And even worse,
I have seen hate
Disguised in love.
I have rejected both
As worthless,
And in so doing,
I have hidden reality
And sealed my fate.

—Todd B. Dean

What Should I Write About

Should I write about a tower, leaning in
    the sky?
Or about a flower that blossoms in July?
Should I write about a sunset, seen on the
    shore?
Should I write about a murder, or a very
    bloody war?
Shall I write about devastation, famine or
    one's without homes?
Shall I talk about God's creation, or
    elders all alone?
I have no clue of what to write, in this
    present age
So tomorrow flip over, and read the next
    page.

—Lisa Sisler

My Magical World of Dreams

I can soar higher than a rocket
or dive deeper than a submarine
I can touch a star
or kiss the ground
In my magical world of dreams.
There are no nuclear weapons here
and no animal experimentation
There is no hunger or poverty
and there is no sickness
In my magical world of dreams.
I knew only happiness in my magical world
because I never allowed my sadness in
Then one day I woke up
and locked the door
To my magical world of dreams.

—*Lady Phillips*

Why

Why did you do this?
Why is there blame?
All the time we were together, and yet there is another flame.
Does she love you?
Does she care?
This burden you have put on me
I can feel only despair.
You felt the love I deeply held.
The burning in my heart.
Just to tell you that I love you would only be start.
But then if you are happy,
then she is the one for you.
And then if you find that you are not,
I'll still always be here for you.
As I have loved you
I always will.

—*Mary Stimburys*

Can't You See

Can't you see it, see the little girl picking daisies
Or her mother smelling a rose,
Can't you see out yonder,
This I need to ponder.
Welcome them abound for they won't stay,
There, can't you see the kids out to play.
Not kids, just stumps growing up in the baseball diamond
Like grim reminders of a torn today.
Can't you see, out yonder,
Me neither, so I start to wander.
There, can't you see, the farmer among his cows
And his wife tending to baby chicks.
No, just bewildered deer, dead trees and baby vultures
Reaping the last bearable fruit, my mind plays tricks
Can't you see, out yonder.
No, I see, there is nothing left to squander.

—*Rodney Cogbill*

My Dearest Love,

I will always love you forever, because every time I think of
Or look at you I think of what could have been if we had gotten together.
But now I can only think and dream of that and the only reason I do is because
My heart refuses to let you go. When I look into your eyes
I see all of the dreams I've had about us being together and staying together forever.
I want you to keep this poem as a token of my love and to show you how much love I have to give you.
My heart seems to think that you might one day give this same love in return,
But my mind still stays confused on why I still hold onto these dreams.

—*Monica Jones*

The Wall

Was Pink in sink?
Or was he really mad?
Look at love today
And I think you might say
It really can get that bad.
Did Pink know a way
To live day by day?
When illusions blur right to wrong?
But Pink understands
Rejected love to a man
Can only be expressed
In mother's song.
Yes, love is a trip
From sanity I slip
To the place of the infamous wall
And let it be known
I've counted its stones
And by so I've answered it's call.

—*Michael Gowling*

Image

The sun peaks over the mountain.
Orange.
Yellow, fills the sky.
Black glittery stars.
Gone.
The moon fades.
High noon. Clouds roll in.
Birds pass above.
Soaring.
Singing.
Dusk. The sun sets.
The day cools.
Purple.
Orange.
The moon rises.
Twinklers fill the sky.

—*Robin Morgan*

Poverty

Some walk by day
Others by night
Some never have a say
It's a never ending fight.
Does anyone hear their cry
The cringing shriek
Most, constantly try
Some are children so mild and meek.
The sidewalk seems endless,
All the boxes full
Completely defenseless
Like a kitten against a bull.
These are the children of the circle
The poverty chain
Dreaming of a miracle
Something to end their pain.

— *Sarah Eno*

Being Old

People call me dumb and naive
Others just can't understand and turn to leave.
Why do they treat me as though I don't know
Why they are leaving or why they must go?
A wrinkled old shell is what they all see,
But deep down within anything I can be.
As I sit near the window and feel the sun's rays,
I look out and wonder if anyone will come today.
I remember the days when I was so young
And the possibilities were yet to come.
But now I am lonely, tired, and old
All I want is some love and someone to hold.

—*Laura Riss*

Through the Broken Window

Peering through the broken window I sit with a sad heart.
Our biggest fear of growing apart was just beginning to start.
Endless days turned into endless nights
While thinking of our petty fights.
Blinding tears grew very clear
As reality was almost near.
Our love should've been forever
Just as the window should've stayed together.

—*Stefanie Myers*

The Day Our Country Grew Up

He rode by as our president,
Our hero,
Our protector.
We looked at him with respect,
With adoration,
With love.
Then he was shot,
He was killed,
He was assassinated.
Down with him went our country,
Our security,
Our innocence.
Our eyes were filled with tears,
With horror,
With grief.
We became a nation of violence,
Of sadness,
Of pain.

—*Sarah Raye Marshall*

Reflections

"Reflections": LOVE, for too long we
　have sold ourselves. Lived
our lives like statues on shelves. It has
　been too bad, for too
long. I'm tired of singing the same old
　song. I am a black butter-
fly, I am free. FREE to be what I damn
　well please to be. To live,
to love, to soar the skies above. As
　beautiful to me, as a pretty
white dove. Now I have done all I can od.
　I won't do anymore, I re-
fuse too. No more wishing, alot more
　seeing. Seeing the world and
actually living. I'm tired, I've had enough.
　If you can't understand
that's too bad, that's tough. You'd better
　try to understand, you
better see the point. There is no more love
　in which to annoint.
For Once, let me live, let me love, let me
　go. I'm leaving anyway
just letting you know. I've done all I can
　for you. Although I can
not say the same of you. I've took all I'm
　going to take. I'm leav-
ing for my won sake. I've had enough of
　you using me. I've opened
my eyes and now I can see. All my life
　I've lived for love. Wishing
on the stars above. Now it's time to live
　for me. Become the person
I want to be. I've died, Yet survived, I
　have been revived. . .

—*Stephanie L. Brown*

Our Love

You are the one who is meant to be,
Our love is so strong but free,
Free as a bird gliding with the wind,
Circling each rainbow and chirping
　within,
A love so strong no one could win,
For by the Grace of god we're not a sin,
So as love and peace flows through our
　souls within,
We'll not be lead through Hell but
　Heaven,
We'll never lose, we'll always win,
Cause our love is so pure I can feel it
　within,
So we'll do as the bird and glide with the
　wind,
We'll take it day by day and never give in,
We'll stay hand to hand and heart to
　heart,
We'll never ever be broken apart.

—*Pamela Marie Saut*

Song of the Leaves

Swinging, swaying, to and fro,
With the wind that's where we go.
Delicate, slender, crisp, and free.
Look at us falling, we have motions key.
When autumn comes and the breeze gets
　so cold,
We say farewell to the trees as winter
　unfolds.
Our bountiful colours light up the sky,
We daren't say so long, but bid you all
　"goodbye."
The snow is coming: "Adieu to thee."
You'll see me in the springtime, sprouting
　joyously.
When happy cries can be heard from all
　around,
From the children wading in the puddles
　on the ground.
My life is short, yes a mere two and
　one-half seasons,
Time won't permit me to relate the
　reasons.
I am but a leaf amongst all the leaves,
We are calling to you when we rustle in
　the trees.
May the leaves bring pleasure to your
　eyes,
For we are a small wonder in disguise

—*Wanda Head*

Me and You

Our love is something right,
Our love is something true.
But when it comes right down to our love,
It's just me and you!
Me and you.
You and me.
That's how it's meant to be!
Being ourselves is what keeps us strong,
In our hears is where it belongs!
And I know some day it's true,
It will all come down to me and you!

—*Tami Murphy*

Cry for Yesterday

Deep inside the mist of the night my spirit
　cries out for you.
Our love was born upon the wind many
　years ago.
My sky is filled with reflections of our love
And they speak to me of a time when we
　were young
And tomorrow was so far away.
Today your my angel and through the
　years your love taught me to believe
So cry for yesterday, it's where our love
　was born
Cry for yesterday, it's where I long to be
Too many days slip by and so many
　dreams seem to die.
How can I find tomorrow when you're so
　far away?
Just put your hand in mine and we can
　dream of how it was
In the beginning because it lives on
　forevermore.
Yesterday is lost in a dream but I'll still
　carry on
Because there's a tear in my heart and a
　dream that was lost
Cry for yesterday, it still holds our dreams
Cry for yesterday, because the dream still
　remains

—*Tracy Damron*

Our troubles seem to build like mountains
　to the sky.
Our problems seem to echo in the
　mountains when we cry.
When alone we hear the sound, amidst the
　sadness of our sorrow.
Let alone no words we hear and not a
　word we seem to borrow.
It seems we are alone when we are
　despaired.
Then we wittle and we hone over someone
　whom we cared.
To know that all things cease; to know
　that even the wind
Is truly not a peace until the very end.
To know that every rose never really dies,
Its beauty is always there and it lives
　among the skies.
To know that every bird has wings, that it
　will always fly.
To know that it will drop to the ground, to
　know that it will die.
To know that every living thing on earth
　can be half serene.
To know that God can see your very soul's
　light beam.

—*Mary Hahn*

We're All Alike

We're all alike
Our skin color maybe different
Our religion may vary
But no matter what
We're all the same
We're all alike
In our own special way
Some may have green eyes,
Some may have blonde hair
But no matter what
We'll always be loved
We're all alike
No matter where we live
No matter what our family background is
We'll always be together

—Stephanie Adams

Love is Deeper than Philosophy

Your love is stronger than the universe,
Wider than the sky,
Deeper than philosophy, in
Unconditional supply,
You make me feel vitality.
You make me see the best.
You give my heart contentment;
My soul, eternal rest.
I want to feel the strength you have.
The power from inside.
I want to be forever free
From pain this life provides.
Your love is stronger than the universe,
Wider than the sky,
Deeper than philosophy
Always in supply.

—Paulina Hrcan

Someday

Someday, when we die, we'll fly beyond the sky.
Our tears will be wiped away in that great resurrection day.
Our sorrows will come to an end and our joys will just begin.
Someday, we will no longer give up the right for the wrong,
And we'll meet our loved ones who're already gone.
Someday, all men will live as brothers
And there will be no more hate toward one another.
No one will be hated for the color of their skin,
And this world will be free from all sin.
Someday, we'll live in perfect peace and never worry about grief.
Love and joy will be ours
And we'll blossom like beautiful flowers.
Someday, we'll never grow old, and we'll never die again.
There will be eternal rest for our weary souls.
Someday, we will sit around the welcome table and every man
Will be at peace with his neighbor.

—Marandia Ross-Porter

Hidden

Hidden away
Out in the beautiful ocean,
There lies the truth about love.
As the waves come and go,
They take away a part of the ground,
And hide it down deep in the sea.
And so when love comes and leaves,
It takes a part of your heart,
A part that never comes back.
The feeling of love never leaves your soul
For you and I know how fast it comes,
And how slow it flows and goes.
That love goes into a place
That people call nowhere
Hidden
Yes it's that love that longs to become free.
Hidden away
Down deep inside of me.

—Stella Luna

Untitled

The moon and the stars
Out of this world love affair.
Guitars!
Whisper hysterical screams in my sleep
Make my pathetic dreams die of thirst.
You're stepping on my soft spot-ouch!
Say you will be sorry.
Say you love me.
Nylon or still—Your choice.
Are you as innocent as I look?
Or are you as soft as I want to be?
Make up your mind!
Give me all that you've got
We can make something of it, I'm sure.
Black velvet on white skin feels so good at midnight.
Yummy! Microwave bubble gum!
Confused? Talk to Mr. Nehi—He knows!

—Lauren Spiridigliozzi

The Birth

I am all alone in a dark abyss.
Outside is a world,
Full of hate, and bitterness.
For many months
This has been my bed.
I don't want to go,
Where many a tear are shed.
I begin to see a bright light
No longer will I live
In a world of night.
I will live where people
Kill and fight.
Something, something strikes me
My head begins to spin.
From the hollow of my throat
I emit a sharp cry.
I now belong to the outside world
I live now, only to begin to die.

—Shawna Zee

Together

Laughter echos
Over and over
the happiness within us
Comes out when we're together.
The smiles begin
When we share a funny thought
Always one sees the bright side
When the other one is down.
We can't stay sad for long
When we're together.
You're always there for me
I'll always be there for you.
No other friendship could be the same
As this one we have together.

—Megan Thomas

Untitled

Pictures and phrases conjure up in the mind,
Over I think, "What word can I find?"
Everything wants to come out at one time,
Though I still restrain them, letting loose line by line.
Reveals my pen my emotions so mixed,
Yet my mind is at rest when on paper they're fixed.

—Linda K. Goswiller

Spirit Ridge

Souls of ancient Indian warriors set adrift
Over sacred burial mounds and lofty cliffs.
Their ghostly presence all around, guarding
Artifacts of arrowheads and fire rings, evidence
Of ancestral hunting and camping grounds.
A swirl of haunting sound and color lift the
Spirits into ceremonial dance, painted faces,
Feathered headdresses, limbs leaping all around;
Souls of ancient Indian warriors set adrift.
Eyes like piercing pointed arrows shift,
Their sharpness like spears with poisoned tips.
To the rhythm of beating tom-toms they listen,
A war cry, spilled blood, horses hoofs pounding. . .
The Souls of ancient Indian warriors set adrift.

—Patricia J. England

The Grass

Soft, sharp warlike
Over the years becoming angry
Under everything in its
Little green suit;
Fighting, struggling, growing,
Nature promising victory:
Adaptable swift Chameleon!

—*Teresa A. Winters*

On the Threshold of a Dream

Will you tell me why I have not heard
 from your family?
What did I do, she asked, pain burring
 her voice.
You burned your bridges with Dad, he
 said, grey eyes luminous
In a face gone crimson. How, she asked.
 When you told me
He said to be patient with me—that I
 would come around,
He spoke softly, the light glinting off his
 glasses
With the mild tremor of his head. But he
 did not say that.
The Bishop said that. Your father told me
 to be patient with you.
That was all. It was the Bishop who. . .she
 said. . .her steady
Voice denying the blood cyclotroning
 through her head.
That moment of de je vue, that was when
 she finally knew.
That in his need to win, he had lied to his
 father.
It was also the beginning of something
 new. . .heavy weights of pain
Attributed to the long silence from the
 family of 22 years began
To peel away as the redness of his face
 increased, the pounding of
Her veins calmed. Now, she was freed
 from the spell of tightly
Woven lies that caged her loving, celestial
 spirit with his
Alcohol and earth stained soul.

—*Mary Sewell Causey*

Peace

As my soul fills me within
Overwhelming sensations of peace appear
Strands of love, which are long and thin
Intertwine in my heart
Calling out in song for the world to hear
I am sure to fast to the balance inside
And my message becomes clear,
For there is nothing to hide
Let joy fill the air
As it fills me
People join hand in hand
Bonding the different and the same
All are one; one are all
A circle of love is formed
And finally,
Peace cries out its name!

—*Nicole Harris*

A Painting of the Mind

I think I'll paint a picture of winter
 wonderland,
Paint the lovely scenery while by my
 window I stand.
I painted the birds as they flew high in the
 trees.
And watched the mother bird cover her
 young from the cold and the breeze.
I painted the leaves as they turned from
 green to brown, and gold,
Twas a beautiful sight like a portrait of
 old.
The snow began falling, at first very slow,
The flakes became larger and the cold
 wind began to blow.
I watched the mother bird push her young
 from the nest,
"Tweet, tweet," as if she was saying,
 hurry we have to go.
I watched as they took off and flew out of
 sight,
"Treet, treet," we'll be back in the spring,
When everything's green and the sun is
 shining bright.
I painted the children, riding their sleds
 down the hill by the road,
I painted the elves as they danced quietly
 through the snow.
Now I'm not an artist, I have no paint or
 brush,
To smooth the rough edges, or give it the
 finishing touch.
And even though it's a picture I can't
 hang on the wall,
To me it's a master-piece, whatever it is
 called.

—*Margaret Halcomb*

War

Children are crying
Parents are fighting
There's a war going on
Everyone's shouting.
Families are being departed
Love is being discarded
How did this war get started?
After all this has ended,
We have to straighten up
Everything that has been bended.

—*Nancy Del Toro*

Sunrise and Sunset

What do you think of when you see the
 sun
Peek over the horizon?
Do you let your mind wonder into another
 world,
Your world, where only you can go?
And what do you think about?
Do you think of beautiful waterfalls
And wide open fields?
Do you picture your dreams coming true?
Because that's what it is
When you see a sunrise or sunset,
And like your dreams,
It's something you can't forget.

—*Pamela A. Turner*

Saddness

I don't have a life worth living
People listen
For wrong words to be said
My boyfriend is gone
Yet I still love him
His firey-red hair
And ocean-blue eyes
Suicide is the only answer
I had a knife
I could feel it pierce my stomach
The feeling went through my body
My soul began to leave
I could see my lifeless body
Floating up and up
The clouds all around me
The gate opens to the heavens above
He is there, waiting
Waiting for the warmth of my love

—*Stacey Zbytowski*

I See; But I can't Explain

Many things in this world,
People see only through the human eye.
See the beautiful girl of fourteen,
Beaten and left in a closet to die.
What pains my heart so very much,
Is that we just ignore,
The things we see that are so bad in life,
Like dirty trash by our shores.
I cannot explain why we make these rules,
That people aren't supposed to break,
When people rob and steal,
And take things they aren't supposed to
 take.
See the old man with his hat and cane,
Out on the street, alone, with not a penny
 to his name.
Please help me find an answer
To these questions that I ask.
Please help me find an answer,
That my friend, is my task.

—*Tiffany Byrdic*

What is Life?

Why must we get old?
People we are so close to,
They enjoy their youth.
They have fond memories,
That remain vivid throughout life.
The joy and pain that we endure.
The joy of falling in love.
The pain of losing someone,
In a war that has no purpose.
The older and wiser must look back,
The mistakes they made,
And they watch the young make the same.
Although I haven't experienced this.
In my eyes I see them afraid,
Afraid of not awaking,
And reaching the end as we know it.

—Mark Nelson

To Mother, with Love

I defied you with purpose
Perhaps in search of reaction
I walked in defiance
In search of praise
I wanted to carry your burden
Thus, I created my own
I wanted to be bigger than life
Thus, I grew faster than my years
The knowledge we both share
Secrets held within
The sealed lips that want to say too much
But, the language is unknown, foreign
I'm sorry, I do understand
I would drink your tears to cleanse my soul
The greatest sin,
My love for you, left unspoken

—Shadow (S. Lucken)

Our Lives, The Way I See It

There's a place in life called happiness
Perhaps you've seen its doors.
An illusive place of images, fixed and free.
Sometimes, on clear days, it appears
With flowers on its floor.
With windows opened wide through which to see.
Ten thousandfold the trails will be
That lead us to these doors
And each is clouded by a haze of life's uncertainty.
To venture down an unmapped path
We lone conquistadors,
May reach the door to happiness
But might not find the key.
Our lives the way I see it
Are a reason to explore
The tangled web of trails that lead to happiness' door.

—Mark Einstein

The World is a Wonderful Place

The world is a wonderful place
Petals on roses remind me of a baby's face
The bluebirds sing tweet, tweet
The sound is so charming and sweet
I love to hear the crickets at night
But I seem to never find them in sight
Somehow their sound helps me to go to sleep
It's a sound I will always treasure and keep
Sometimes I just look up at the sky, sigh
And say, "The world is a wonderful place."

—Michele Marcucci

King of the Skies

Your majestic wings spread out to such lengths.
You may seem new,
But your idea is old.
You are the dream of many men.
You are the passengers' delight.
Travel is ever possible now that you are here.
Places never dreamed of are being reached from afar
Thanks to your fantastic speed.
Only surpassed are you by the bird,
But is there a bird so strong
As to carry hundreds of people?
You do mean so much to me.
If not for you, would going beyond be at all possible?
To end this now, I shall thank you
From your giant wings to your tiny struts:
May you forever fly.

—Leesa Magoch

Hopeless Memory

She walks in deafening silence
Phantom feet a-tremble on the path.
Thin fingers twisting tousled ringlets
Of blood, roses or brandywine.
Her eyes wander, searching the twisted route she follows.
Looking, looking for what?
But stay — a faltered step, eyes wavering
Brimmed with tears.
A breathless sigh as she drops to her knees,
Then hesitates.
Longing for the ruins
Of the past to return
Trying to deny, yet knowing
That it can never be.
At last, the ghostly fingers softly brush the cracked remains
Of stone dandelions.

—Natasha Hook

Untitled

If only you could feel the pain of what you've done to me,
Place your hand upon my breast and feel my broken heart.
Put your cheek to mine and feel the tears coursing down my face,
Listen to me, the timidness in my voice
Where has my self confidence gone?
You have broken my spirit.
I would have preferred you to have broken my arms and legs.
They will mend.
But a broken heart, oh, a broken heart
Takes more than a splint to knit.
A broken spirit takes more than a bandage to heal.
I suppose I shouldn't complain. You broke my heart and spirit,
But you also cracked my shell.
You made me unafraid to be me. You helped me realize that people
Will love me for who I am, not who I pretend to be.
Through your openess and consideration, you taught me how to love.
Not only myself, but others, and for that I love you.
Thank you.

—LaShonda Smith

Charleston, The Southern Lifestyle

The southern flowers blooming,
Plantation's southern beauty booming.
The sun is high in the afternoon sky,
A little Charleston smile in the southern lifestyle.
The oak trees shade, the magnolias cascade
In weak and brittle branches.
I long to be with,
No, it's not a myth; the southern lifestyle.
Dainty belles and gallant beaus,
In the shadow, the loyal slave.
This was known,
To have grown in the southern lifestyle.
Oh Charleston, the city; southern should be fitting.
The people, the faces, plantations, the places.
They all thrive,
They all survive in the southern lifestyle.

—Stacey Beakes

Youth

Let's run barefoot through dew-bathed
    violets
Play hide-and-seek all the day through
Let's play dress-up in a silk with lace
    eyelets
Under a cloudless sky, baby blue
Let us take warmth from the sun's smiling
    rays
Quench our thirsts by a sweet, babbling
    stream
Living and loving in summer's bright days
Loving is living, and life's but a dream.

—*Sharron D. Walker*

Friendship

Through the years and through the miles,
Remember me with lots of smiles.
For friends can stand the test of time,
Through life's long and treacherous
    climb.

—*Mandy Sternbergh*

The Eyes of Sand

The eyes of sand will watch me
Please never turn your thoughts
When the night wind blows,
The eyes of sand will fade
But not far
Only far enough to dream
And escape to the world that he loves
The eyes of sand will watch me
Never turn your thoughts

—*Quinta J. Bartleson*

The Land of the Free

What is happening around here?
Please take note
Of who our leaders are leading
Or taking care of
So much help has gone out
To the other teams
Playing wounded lamb
It is we
Who are wounded now
A developing infection
Thirsting
For the action of another land
Taking in trade
What was already ours
From the beginning of time
Soon we won't belong to ourselves.

—*Lorrin Barnes*

Daisy

Pluck, he loves you.
Pluck, he loves you not.
Pluck, pluck, pluck.
Now, there are no other
petals to pluck.
He loves you not.
The Beauty and Fingers of it's life
have been taken away.
It can no longer feel the wind.
Now you are left with—Nothing
Except!
a green stem
with a yellow center,
Ugly.
Don't pluck nature
to wich someone
loves you.

—*Mariah Manners*

Poetry in a Glass

Poetry can be the hand of a small child
    reaching out
Poetry's destiny of knowing what life is all
    about
Poetry's so fragile and delicate not ever
    crass
So as the child needs to be protected
I've learned to keep my poetry in a glass!
Not so wise, you say!
What if the glass should shatter?
Not to worry-no matter
For as my poetry was made to last in that
    glass
Said glass, was made of brass!

—*Terri Amarante*

Friends

Friends are like diamonds,
Precious and valuable.
Friends are people you can trust,
Like a member of the family.
Friends are special in their own way,
Like everyone else is.
Friends are faithful and there when you
    need them,
Somewhat like a dog is to its owner.
You are indeed a friend, you are all I have
    mentioned,
And much, much more.
I could never find another friend quite like
    you,
No matter how hard I might try.
I'm so glad to have you as my friend,
And I hope I'm a good friend to you too.

—*Sarah Shoate*

The Serpent and Me

Cleverly wrapped lies
Pretty colored capsule lies
To soothe the raging sea
Inside my head
Friendly sea serpent
Feeding on debris
Inside that raging ocean
Somehow co-existing
Serpent and sea
Lies and me
Until the tidal wave
Destroys us both

—*Sharon L. Gibson*

The Line

Though a pristine source, exquisite its
    display:
Primal ancestry refines an awesome skill.
Beguiling and omnific, taciturn yet strong.
Etching the rugged scape by rote and
    conception,
Tools of wisdom and time.
Each essence defined:
The intangible embodied into images,
Irrefutable orchestrations of kinds.
Dimension and space: relations of being.
Description: a consequence of man.
Such unchallenged majesty, this patriarch
    of arts:
To reveal the unperceived,
To conceive the unimagined,
To set a time unsearched by human
    minds.
Without it how could life be?

—*Rick Matos*

Aids the Silent Reaper

Growing, gnawing, searching
Probing through my body
Darkness getting darker
Pain, depression, desolation
My mind is functioning
Who are all these people
Scuttling, whispering, sympathetic faces
Starched, white uniforms
Cold to the touch
Cold to the heart
I'm so infantile
I want to cry
I cannot let them see me
How frightened-please hold me
My mind hears echoes
My body is falling apart
Yet my brain functions clearly
Please, please release me

—*Rena Brady*

The Promises Beyond

How does the night so long and deep
protect me in a peaceful sleep?
So vainly puffed much like a cloud
it settles around me like a shroud.
I hear ny heart beat steadily
and breathing grow so peacefully.
Don't disturb me in my sleep;
I've countless missions yet to keep.

— *Martha Hayter Peterson*

What Could This Be?

A soft, warm blanket,
Protecting me from all.
A wise old man,
Knowing what is in my heart.
A sunscreen,
Warning me when life is too bright.
A pat on the back,
Helping me search for tomorrow.
All of this,
What could it be?
The special type of friendship
You give to me.

—*Trista Strauch*

White

White is the kitten,
Purring gently in my hand.
White is the sunlight,
That surrounds me in bands.
White are the clouds,
So cottony and new.
Dotting winter skies,
On days too few.
White are the stars,
That light up the skies.
Their twinkle and sparkle,
Bounce in my eyes.
White is the blanket,
Of snow in my yard.
While I am asleep,
It silently stands guard.
Tomorrow I'll awaken,
To a day new and bright.
Filled with things that I love,
Many will be white.

—*Theresa Miner*

Patriotism 1970

Take a man, then put him alone;
Put him ten thousand miles away from
    home.
Empty his heart of all but blood,
Make him live in sweat and mud.
This is the life I have to live
And why my soul to the devil I give.
I heard them say, this one's dead.
It's a large price he had to pay
Not to live to see another day.
He had the guts to fight and die
He paid that price and what did he buy
He bought your life by losing his
But who gives a damn what a soldier
    gives,
His family, his friends, or maybe his son
But they are about the only ones.

—*Larry J. Allen*

The Closed Door

It's time to move on, time to forget
Put it all aside and close the door
Life's too short to hold on to the
    memories.
Think of the times you shared,
Was love really there?
Something to open,
Something to face,
Things that time cannot replace.
If he really loved you,
If he really cared
He'd forget your song
And let you be free, he would honestly see
    reality
But. . .you keep sitting back waiting
Hoping he would change,
So many times you let it slide by,
Its time to open a new door
Before the old one gets too old
And the man behind it dies.

—*Maria T. Tighe*

Why

Why was I,
put on this earth
to live or,
to die.
To make peace
or war,
why, can't I understand
this world,
It's odd,
Why, do you have
so many different
kind of people,
some good,
some bad and
some you can't tell,
so I ask myself,
why was I, put on this earth.

—*Mandeline Lucas*

Personification of Myself

The Pacifist—
Quiet;
Accepting with a smile.
The Anarchist—
Angry;
Practicing defiance and rebellion.
The Radical—
Impatient;
Knowing what's wanted and wanting it
    now.
The Conservative—
Wondering;
Why can't things be like they were
    before?
Myself—
I am many people,
Combined into one.
Others—
Disregarding all,
But the person they want to see.

—*Stephanie Janci*

The Old Adam

Was God slightly wounded
when Adam expressed a bone
saying creation was not beautiful
living with God alone.
For the old Adam,
desired his Eve's personification
not content to have her whisper
as a muse of inspiration.
But many view this discontent
as his fatal flaw
there are these who do not
view imagination as a bore.
Many still prefer to keep their eves
    concealed
beneath their bones
so in the paradise of
their psycles, God lives
within their homes.

—*Thomas F. Smith*

Footsteps

Footsteps in the darkness
quiet and unrecognized
Slowly growing faster
Across the bare floor
Outside the howling winds grow louder
Crying in the night
The footsteps stop outside the door
All is silent
Quietly the footsteps enter the room
Nearing their destination
Suddenly stopping at the crash of thunder
Then continuing on
Nearer and nearer they come
Stopping at the foot of the bed
Seeing the child safe and warm
A satisfied grin, and a scamper back
    across
The bare floor.

—*T. Robinson*

The Masterful Sea and Sky

Though the sea and the sky are miles
    apart, there really
quite close.
Flowing forever, yet not destined for a
    time nor a place,
they seem to at times express emotions of
    pain, anger,
happiness, and joy.
The Masterful Sea and Sky
Shining blue on the good days, a turbulent
    gray on the bad.
A nature that is fasinating to humans
    keeps growing endlessly
within.
The Masterful Sea and Sky
Man seems to be conquering and
    destroying this beautiful
part of our landscape.
The destroyers are innumerable and raze
    the beauty of its
significance,
making the once masterful sea and sky
    now vulnerable.

—*Michelle Naumann*

What Does Friend Stand For

F—is for the Faith a person has in you.
R—is for Reliability that person can give.
I—is for the Impression ones life leaves on
    another.
E—is for Enjoying the times that you
    share together.
N—Notices you for who you are and not
    for who they want you to be.
D—is for helping ones Dreams come true.

— *Melinda Meisel*

Almighty Power of God

The grace of Almighty power of God.
Radiance of the moon and the stars above.
Upon the Universe shine for the childrens'
    light;
Leading them to hail and worship God.
From time to time straightway You lead.
And to walk with You day and night.
Now and then You guide and protect us;
Pardon our sins and not forsake us.
For wars and calamities to come;
Your hands protect and guide us away;
Strenghten faith and develop more to
    convey:
Because Your unfaded Love and grace do
    not betray.
Enfold us love, honor and respect;
Our life with the people every day and
    night.
Fill our hearts the joy and sincere love;
Satisfaction obtained from grace of the
    commandments of God.

—*Pete G. Galozo*

Arrow of Time

Artificial, clever smiles
Rain on my spirit.
Raked over by a cruel fidgeter,
On occasion I disintegrate like a dead
    leaf.
When unfaithful promises are recalled, I
Occupy my piercing bitterness, renting
    hatred by the hour.
Fingers of pain fingerpaint with my tears.
Time wounds with shattering suddenness.
I forget my resolve to forget.
My mind tricks me into trouble.
Every sling of thought hurls me into the
    black hole of the past.

—*Rebecca Wilson*

Fear

Fear is like cold blasts of ice
Ripping through your veins
Fear takes over your mind
Terrorizing you, commanding you
Controlling your every move
Sending repeated chills
To unknown nerves
Fear makes you alert
More than you have ever been
Every sound is heard
Every move noticed
You are careful, so careful
Not to make a sound
And then you are caught

—*Laura Bratt*

The Mending Wall

I saw a pasture yesterday, filled with
    sweet lavender. The sun's
rays layered a shimmering glow across
    waves of tiny purple heads gently
nodding. Some of them bumped into an
    ancient decaying wall built long
ago by careful hands, whose purpose was
    surely to protect the field, giving
room for living things to be born. . .and
    grow.
My heart filled with tears as I watched a
    farmer run his hands over
the wall, soothingly patting a stone or two.
    He then looked out over the
field and smiled. Reaching down and
    picking up a fallen piece, he
prudently positioned it into the wall,
    turning it over and over to make
it fit — purhaps not the way it did long
    ago, but a different way. . .and
a good one.
Now butterflies can flourish protected
    from the wind, and the seeds
the birds scatter will not wash away in
    tomorrow's rain. I can return
tomorrow and bring my children to smell
    the lavender and feel the sun's
warmth on their skins.
I just wanted you to know, that yesterday,
    I saw you at the mending
wall and I was healed.

—*Nancy S. McDonald*

Beautiful as could Be

Beautiful as could be, looking so alive
Reaching for the air filled sky
Just like a tree planted by the waters
Beautiful as could be, branches high
Swinging tossing to and from
Just like a tree planted by the waters
Beautiful as could be, producing seeds
Restin on the sun soaking up the rain
Just like a tree planted by the waters
Beautiful as could be, aging changing
Embracing the seasons purging to earth
Just like a tree planted by the waters
Beautiful as could be, looking so alive
Returning to dust you and me
Just like a tree planted by the waters.

—*Mildred Hodge*

Friendship

Sharing laughs and clothes and tears,
Ridding me of foolish fears.
Special moments, special times,
Forgiving me for little crimes.
Helping when you think you can't,
Knowing when to rave and rant.
Being honest when you should,
Knowing you did all you could.
Staying when you'd rather run,
All the times we've fought and won.
Not believing all you heard,
Friendship, what a special word!

—*Sheila E. Wilson*

Reagan

Reagan, Reagan, he's so great, he was
    bound to keep the country straight.
Reagan came from Hollywood, where
    heros they do make.
The public saw another man and sent him
    to Washington (D.C.) land, for he had
    to take a stand.
No job for me, no free ride, Reagan made
    no place to hide.
No welfare you'll get, you'll have to work,
    so look for that job don't act like a jerk.
Old Glory now waves with strength on
    high; stand proud America, one must
    cry!
Stop the bombs, cut down now, no defense
    would that create.
Keep peace, let's not fight was said, but
    that would make for all to be dead.
Stand up America! Comes the cry, peace
    with strength not to deny.
Granada yelled help us please, freedom
    we want, and not with ease.
The Cubans ran and ran they did, for
    Castro learned he could not win, for
    had paid for that great sin. . .
Stand tall our "hero" of the day, for you
    have shown us all the way.
Rise up America and join this race, for
    then our streets won't reap of mace.
Reagan, Reagan, he's so great, he was
    bound to keep our country straight!

—*Sharrie Lynne*
(Sharon L. Venkatesan)

Mine Armor

Mine armor hath brought the sheen vault to mine eyen
With chances of Life able to stroy fermentations.
The welkin is a fell dudgeon on my actions;
And the safeties of mine armor has the speed
Of wondrous opportunities to extend to the qualities
Of the most winsome wines of Life: the anomaly of character.
An mine armor persists for the essence of nature,
Wherefore hath the road been traveled an the gravel
Hath been journeyed erenow?
But, nay, the sword that doth slay the swine
Eke doth the sword slay the boar eftsoon.
While that time approaches, mine armor shall last
Home forever, though the valley of writhen faculties
Design the signs of anguish and grief
Ere mine own eyen.
But, gramercy, mine armor hath stood ere the minions
Of everyone's nightmares—
Or so it shall.

—Russell Vallotton

The Dawn of Destiny

Luminescent waves of the moon reflect apon the silken river,
While a bitter breeze causes a blossom of velvet of shiver.
A gentle dew drop of silver settles apon a delicate frond,
As a swan awakens from a near-by lilly pond.
Its slender neck glistens with a sparkling white,
Meanwhile, the dawn disturbs the peace of the night.
The sun smils upon the newly awakened lands,
Trees worship the sky with outstretched hands.
The call of the lark echoes in the assortment of breezes,
While a brooke babbles about whatever it pleases.
The swan calls to its love with a romantic song,
The other calls back, its answer just as strong.
The sun bids farewell its labor is now done,
The land responds "good bye" to its friend the sun.
Letting out a heavy sigh, the sun floats beneath the sea,
Once again to sleep in the arms of its destiny.

—Terri Farrow

Grandpa

He was tall and thin like a stalk,
Red hair and sharp blue eyes as the sky,
His mustache matched that of the straw,
Broad shoulders, long legs and hands like a tree.
He pulled the plow with the mules in lead,
Raised and fed a familky of nine and me,
Hard days of dust and storms on his land,
His laughter was not many, a smile never.
God led him away before I was born,
He left this hard earth to join the happy,
But he left his strength with us all
We are all proud because he was
Grandpa.

—L Youngblood

Harlequin Doll

I am a mind without an owner
And a body without a purpose
I am owned by anyone who pulls my strings
My mind is cluttered
Yet my body is empty
Empty
without love
Empty
without feelings
Yet my mind is filled with
Desperation, stoicism, and envy
When you pull my strings take special care
For I am a harlequin doll;
Not at all
like the people who love you dearly

—Alicia Bobo

Memories

An autographed book of your school years.
Remembering laughs,
Remembering tears.
Times together,
Times apart,
Words that came straight from the heart.
Special moments with each other,
Time spent with a sister or brother.
Love and hate,
Friendship and war.
Good times and bad times,
And much, much more.
Remembering laughs,
Remembering tears,
Memories of good and bad things
Throughout the years.

—Megan Michelle Hills

Fly High Til The End

If I could fly
Rise real high,
You wouldn't see me
For a long time.
Visiting rainbows,
Go 'til the end
Never come back
I would stay there.
I've got to go
God is waiting,
I am waiting,
For the sun to rise
And then shine real bright.
Butterflies on the sky
Reflecting on clouds,
Different colors, different shapes
And they all wonder. . .
Where is the end?

—Morella Contreras

Our Sun

The Sun is shining bright and warm today.
We see no clouds, the sky is clear and blue.
No blackened clouds will ever block the way.
The Sun will shine forever, always true.
But wait! We see a storm's approaching clouds.
The storm will cruely snatch our streams of light.
Impending storm! The clouds become a shroud—
It wraps the Sun and holds the beams, once bright.
The rain began to fall. I stood alone.
The pain I feel inside is very deep.
I wish the Sun would shine. I shouldv'e known.
I stand alone and cry and weep.
A ray of light now proves the storm has gone.
It shines so bright upon both you and me.
We both must wait until tomorrow's dawn.
Our Sun will shine again, just wait and see.
My friend, the storm is over. Persevere,
Our Sun will rise again; our dawn is near.

—Valerie Schwader

Todays, Tomorrows, Yesterdays

Moments,	drifting,	timeless...	I have escaped.
Feelings,	unknown,	real...	I am free.
People,	caring,	life...	I am alive.
Leaving,	questions,	goodbyes...	I am dead.
Todays,	tomorrows,	yesterdays...	I have been.

—*Tami Rosenberg*

The Promise

SOMEDAY,
   When the mind's rankling clears,
SOMETIME,
   When the misty cobbled web thoughts
   assume original order.
   (Allowing my spirit
   to grasp the talons
   of the muses,
    and hang on for
      ONE
      LONG
      FANCIFUL
      FLIGHT!)
THAT TIME,
   (That one time only)
   I will ride the wave's crest,
   and speak profoundly of the sublime.

—*Andria Parry Witman*

Pondering Over Patrick

Wandering aimlessly through my cabin at midnite
like a mournful soul, lost in purgatory
I warm my buns on the earthstove
touch cool windowpanes with my forehead and
gaze up through the trees to a zillion brilliant stars.

   I see your face
   I smell your scent
   I remember your touch
   And I miss you so much . . .
   it's just ridiculous,
      I need to
     sit on your lap
        rest my head on your shoulder
               and feel
        the warmth
        the security
        the goodness
that you exude through every fiber
of your being.
And I want you.
        I wonder if you want me, too?

—*Theresa Urie*

The Scheme

In the scheme of life (people say)
We are nothing (an atom of helium in a large balloon)
Floating nowhere (at all)
But up (and perhaps down)
Yes, we are nothing (in the scheme).

So no use doubting (though we do it well)
About the sun running out of fuel
Like a bucket of water (mere H_2O — nothing in the scheme)
Being poured on a fire (which promptly goes out)
Like life itself would (and may?).

So where do we go? (now that we know)
In the scheme it really doesn't matter.

—*Sarah Middleton*

Three Thoughts Intertwined

Seeds

It was in the garden of joy that I planted my seeds of love
And it was with God's help everlasting happiness sprang up
Wisdom, patience taught, and a fond request dreams fulfilled
And resignation to the Lord's will
Some seeds flew around recklessly and had no special plan
And some had a special place but all of them grew tall
With the help of God's grace.

Virtue

I longingly searched for the truth
As seen in God's light
I wondered thoughtfully day and night
And then after looking how he ran his world
Each day and the way he guarded those who pray
I decided that courage was the name of the game
Wisdom and kindness were both the same
And the truth and virtue ran alongside of each other
And it was through them that we learn and discover

God's Offering

A rose bloomed to its fullest; an example of the bountiful,
Robust love of a tree in the season of blossom
A band of baby opossums, still another beautiful offering of God
A ripe orange bursting with perspiration
Let us praise with exaltation the beautiful offerings of God

—*Coco Lemar*

Hiding Yourself

He rushed through the fields,
Over the fence of flowers,
Down the hall of bricks from the unknown,
Into a secret place of towers.
He shook in the corner until it went away.
The sun rose and the clouds covered him like a blanket.
A silver blanket.
There he lay sleeping until his enemy returned.
Finally, the lonely rose said, "Leave me alone, leave me alone."
The wind said, "You — I'm not your enemy.
  No matter how many times you've been scorned."
The rose said, " You must be. You have to be. I'm so misunderstood."
"I'm not like the others, " the wind said, "I'm an individual mood."
"So am I," the rose said, "But no one seems to accept me.
  I am all I have
  I'm strong so I hold on.
  I have to hold onto me."
The wind said, "Well, don't hide in here,
  "In a place where
  You can't be seen!
Otherwise, you're creating a fiend."

—*Pearl L. Thomas*

Two Hearts

Two hearts, taking different paths
  along the same journey
By chance? — They meet, and share
  the journey . . .For a day, for a night, for a
Thousand days and nights — Who can say?

Two hearts; needing to heal, wanting to feel
Two hearts guarding themselves so carefully
Wrapping their insecurities in a blanket of protection
Two hearts; afraid of unknown emotions, uncharted waters
  Waiting to be explored

Two hearts that long to give
  the best they have to offer
Two hearts that feel at home . . . with each other
  Just two hearts, hoping to be loved
  Who knows?

Two hearts, weary from their travels
Silently aching from the bumps and bruises of life
Two hearts, looking for someplace, somewhere,
  someone to provide relief . . . and release
  They meet; By chance?

—*Bruce Brint*

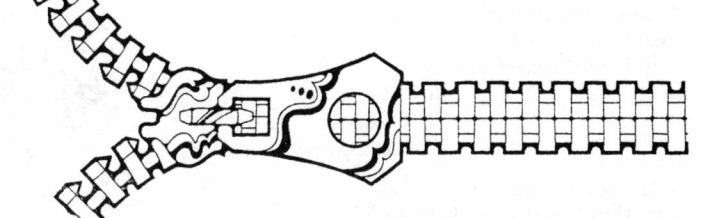

Untitled

As if in a dream, she floats onto stage.
  Graceful yet precise,
She dances each move with practiced
  care. Beautifully draped,
She attracts and captures the attention of
  one and all.
Soundlessly she glides in a world all her
  own. She drifts up and down
The stage as if inviting us to enter her
  private domain.
Another and another and yet another join
  her. I picture myself
With them, but I know I will never be one
  of them again, for I am
Unable to walk. Watching the activities
  going on about me backstage,
I remember when I was part of the flurry
  of getting ready for a show.
I miss dancing, but as I sit in my
  wheelchair, it hits me that dancing
Is now only a dream I once fulfilled. I cry
  sorrowfully and almost
Bitterly at the thoughts whirling through
  my head like little dancers.
I was once the star, the prize of the
  company. Why did it happen to me?
Why not one of the other dancers? Does
  God think me vain and conceited?
Why am I not dead instead of paralyzed
  for life? What do I have to live for,
With my dreams shattered? Did I only
  live to pay for my actions when
Fighting my way to the top? Everything I
  ever knew is gone!

—*Natasha Densmore*

When you Leave Will You Stop Loving Me?

Will my smile fade away?
Will you erase me from your memory or
  will I remain in your heart?
Could you forget me and find someone
  new and still be able to say, "I love
  you?"
Will you write and call or just let me sit
  here wondering where you are?
I gave you my heart and soul.
All I wanted in return was something that
  is true.
You gave me something, something
  special, but will our love survive?
Will I be able to stop your fears?
Will you be able to stop my tears?
Will I be able to limit your pain?
Will you be able to limit the rain inside
  my heart, even though we're so far
  apart?
I'm willing to take a chance, will you take
  it with me?
It takes two people to make love, and one
  to make a fantasy.
I will never forget you, even if I could.
We can make this work, we should at
  least try.
For every tear I cry, I cry for you.
I won't give up on you because I got you
  to see what I see,
I'll always love you and you'll always love
  me.

—*Sheree D. Fletcher*

Island of Hawaii

The sun has risen on a clear blue sky,
With gentle winds from snow covered
  mountains.
The sea has sand as white as snow, endless
  and calm as can be.
Flowers of all varieties spill their
  fragerance with beauty,
So come to my island surrounded by sea.
Islanders and visitors share smiles and
  friendliness
So visit our beaches to share the Aloha
  Spirit.
Here everyone relaxes, and time lingers
  on,
So come, come to my island surrounded
  by sea.
Blacks, browns, blues and greens of our
  island coast,
And the gentleness of the sea, will all help
  you to relax
On our island surrounded by sea.
The warmth of the sun, the gentle sway of
  the trees, the beauty and
Fragrance of the flowers, will make you
  want to stay.
Roses, Hibiscus, Anthuriums, Plumerias,
  Orchids and Bougenvillas,
Give beauty, fragerance and enjoyment to
  all who are present.
The abundance is here, reds, yellows,
  oranges and purples,
So come, come to my island surrounded
  by the sea.

—*Paulette Oliveira*

Don't Miss A Minute

Minute by minute, hour by hour, day by day,
The clock ticks, the time slips away.
The birds soar into infinity,
Singing their cheerful melodies.
A blossom is born,
A bee comes,
To pollinate,
Rejuvenate.
The seasons revolve, it's a cycle, you see,
The leaves on the trees
Change color,
Blow in the breeze.
A blade of grass evergreen,
There's so much to be seen!
Don't miss a minute, an hour, or a day,
The simplicity of our world is beautiful
In every way.

—Kathleen Kneifel Varga

Lost Sisterhood

      Sister . .
I love you,
 though reluctantly,
 secrets divulged.
 winds of difference,
     blow you away.
      Sister . .
       Sister . . . . .
Rose vines,
 beat against our skin,
 thrashing, word winds blow,
     Distance is suffered.
      Sister . . .
      Sister . . .
       Sister . . .
I can forgive.
 But why?
 Never forget.
 You do not ask.
   winds blow chills,
     no response.
      Sister . . .
      Sister . . .
       Sister . . .
I see you more,
 lies rise in score.
 perception lessened, dim.
   winds blow . . . .
     sweeping empty echoes.
      Sister . . .
      Sister . . .
       Sister . . .
The route is blurred,
 direction indistinct.
 Don't step in darkness.
   winds blow . . . .
     winds blow . . . .
      Sister . . .
      Sister . . .
       Sister . . .
I am waiting.
 Are you aware?
  Are you lost?
   Where is common ground?
    Will our sisterhood be found?
      Sister . . .
      Sister . . .
       Sister . . .

—Annette Dixon

Yesterday

Scenes of yesterday,
Reflected in your eyes. . .
Scenes of time
When there were no lies.
A time
When what you said was true. . .
A time
When I believed in you.
But now all that is through—
You destroyed my trust in you.

—Stephanie Christian

Life is Hard

When walking down that depression road
While trying to bare that heavy load
Talk to the Lord, He answers prayer
Believe me I know cause I've been there
It may take awhile but it's a while worth
 wait
So don't do something stupid before that
 date.
Life is too precious to give up hope
Even if it's hard to cope
If you keep on striving you'll get your
 reward
Just keep on living by the Lord.
It may be hard, I understand
But I want to enter the Promised Land
It's up to you to make the choice
So one day you might rejoice.

—Robin Oakley

There You Are

Where was it we met?
What time, what place?
How does it happen that I start a sentence
 and you finish it?
It could not have been in this
 lifetime—you were halfway round the
 world til now.
What led you to this place?
Did we somehow ordain this reward for
 ourselves when we had finished out
 life's work?
I watch you as you listen to the stereo,
 your eyes closed.
Would you flinch to know that I think
 "The Lonely Shepherd" is
A reflection of your soul? Serene and
 stately. (Yes, you, the one on your
 knees this afternoon
Planting that jungle in the backyard,
 trying to force the bougainvillea to
 grow.)
Maybe one day we will recall the words to
 that English tune
We can both almost remember. Is that
 where we met,
In some other lifetime, dancing at a
 country faire?
We will probaby never solve this mystery.
Yet one thing is certain—
I have always known you.

—Treva Myatt

Poem to a Friend

I watch you
    once again
        sail to your distant land
Your ship has left the harbor we have shared
You are destined for unexpected storms.

If you must leave for so long
Let me be the crew of your ship
    and watch and listen and learn . . . and understand
        what you, the captain, must do.

When the waters have calmed
I will beckon to you to return
    to the safety we know.
Here we can dock our boats
    and leave the unpredictable waters behind
And walk the stable earth.

—*Alysson Zatarga*

View from an Airplane's Window

Blinding white, tinged with grey.
Glimpses of Blue
d
 o
  w
   n
past the silver wing
Checkerboard patches
Brown and Green and Tan
Clouds vying for space
with the sun.

—*Christa Chamberlin*

Untitled

Walking on into the light
Reminds me of that glorious night.
The night you held me in your arms
And smothered me with all your charms.
You held me close so lovingly,
So that I knew I could never flee.
You were always close enough to touch
But never so close that it was too much.
My love is so great, I crumble inside
When our eyes passionately collide.

—*Traci Mizlo*

At Anchor, Curlew Bay

So still,
the silence broken
only by a loon
proclaiming peace.

Reflections,
mirrorlike
until, just now,
a leaping salmon,
shattering the glass,
left liquid rings behind.

It's dusk,
and at the inlet's end
between the tall-treed shoulders of the hills
a strip of amber sky below the cloud
holds in suspense a crescent, setting moon
of purest gold.
Here we are safe,
serene.
So let us sleep.

—*Hereward Allix*

Something To Remember

Edna would talk of the days of old
we would rather play
She would worn us with important advice
we would rather be adventurous
She would cook to keep us healthy
we were never hungry
She would ask us to go to church
we could never make time.
Edna became ill. . .
We cared for her every need
The finest doctors
But no cure
Loosing her sight but not her great mind.
Edna struggled
Sick for three year, this woman, so frail
Asked for one last thing. . .
A painless death
Another favor we could not provide.

—*Tracy Phillips*

Never Gone The Spirit Of Tiananmen

Stared at our dead comrades, we cried
In tearless grief, the merciless Heaven denied the voice of the people.
The belief in our government, as a dream, was wakened by the gun,
And looking at butchers' smile, we waited for the answer.
How could the Communist Party rejoice over a victory
To kill the innocent people, the patriotic youths?
Still remember our oaths? Our comrades?
    No one wants to die,
    But when we could irrigate the ground with our blood,
    And plant countless flowers of freedom and democracy,
    Without regret we go, for our country . . .
    Blood is ours, while floweres left for posterity.
The memory written on the date of June 4 in 1989, you've gone
Mourn over your death, we swear we'll be back;
Even tanks smashed thousands of bodies with flesh and blood,
For the democracy, the freedom, and the movement, the spirit of Tiana
Be alive forever, in Peking, in the history.

—*Pang-Jen Kung*

Cave

Metallic drip drops
reverberate off
jagged rocks
Cave
Taking refuge
in spider-filled nitched
Murmuring to mites
that hide in the crevices
between my legs
Wanderer
strayly approaches
squinting and peering
into the rut
Go away

—*Laura Axelrod*

Dreaming

What is it to be a dreamer without a
 dream to dream?
What is it to be a dancer without a dance
 to dance?
Why do we have to have a dream to be a
 dreamer?
Isn't our life full of enough love to be a
 dream?
Why do we have to have a dance to dance
 to be a dancer?
Aren't all the people running around us
 enough to be a dance!
All the people within the world fill it with
 enough love to be a dream.
All the love floating around us in the air is
 enough to be a dance!
Don't you wish that all of this could be
 true!

—*Shelly Collins*

Can We?

I miss your loving arms around me, that
 secure feeling,
Saying everything will work out.
Your eyes used to look into mine and
 they'd shine,
Now they look away as if they are in pain.
Your hand clinging to mine,
As if we would never touch again.
Loving words once escaped your lips,
Now they're cruel, hard.
Our minds used to think alike,
Now I'm not evern sure what to say to
 you.
We didn't have to speak, just look at one
 another.
Now we don't even look.
Have we lost that special thing only
 between us?
Will we have to fight to get it back.
Will we ever, can we ever be the same?
Can we?

—*Robin Hunt*

You

I gave so much to you
You expected so much more
Than I could give
But that, that I gave
You expected.
And gave so very little in return.
Why?
You only wanted to use
That, that I had to offer
To supply your need, for
That time, and only that time
But my feelgns were involved.
SO, you saw no way out.
Only to take my heart,
My mind, my soul,
And drain my body of
All the love and emotions that
I might give to someone
Who really needed me
For always.

—*Marion Brown*

Words

Words of truth,
Words of wonder,
Words of curiousity,
Are your words,
Words of truth?
Your words stick in my mind
Were they meant to hurt
Or meant for happiness?
Words,
Always alive.
Wonder, promise, curiousity,
But are they for real?
Will our words meet?
Will we love one day?
Tell me,
Tell me,
With words of truth
And with words of love.

—*Pam Barry*

I'd Rather

Ah, wits nor brawn don't mean a thing,
 They help me not one mere whit,
 With things I should do.
 But I want not.
My head does not hold what it should,
 Not precise in smart thinking,
 Dreams keep floating by,
 Enticing me.
Ethereal things do sooth my mind,
 While beauty not so true,
 Does blast my senses,
 And I am lost.
A jogging start brings me to life,
 What I didn't do is there,
 I lay aside my dreams,
 I still want not.

—*Monette Courtney*

Letters III

You stole my song
Sang it
You whispered in my song
Gave it back softer, lighter
You stole my song
Added a new wind
Sang a new line
You kissed my eyelids
Opened my hand
Blew tenderness and honey on my arms,
Sang to my recessed and hollow dreams
You sang and
Held my song
You stole my fears
Sang them away.
You stole my song
Sang it
Sang to my dreams and whispers

—*Melvin E. Lewis*

The Break

His eyes were as cold as rain,
while mine stung with hurt.
I felt no gain.
He was just being curt.
As tears trickled down I tried to hold
 them in.
It seemed to be a battle I could never win.
I looked into his eyes,
the feeling was all gone.
There we were breaking the ties,
there was nothing that could be done.
I wanted to yell and tell him how I felt,
but the time wasn't right.
Now I realize I've lost him,
without putting up a fight.
Sometimes I sit and wonder if he really
 did care,
or if life is supposed to be unfair.

—*Tiffany Carroll*

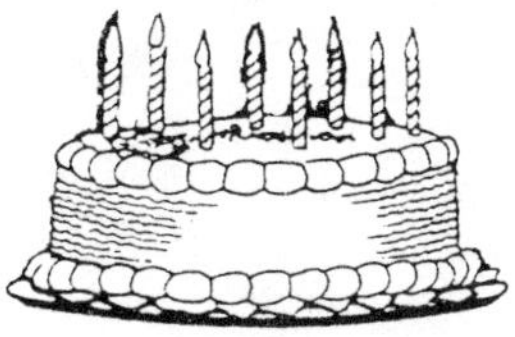

Birthday

7 years old!
What a surprise
I can't believe how time flies.
7 years ago today
you were new in my life
in every way.
So cute, so cuddly
and so full of love.
I am so glad you were
sent from above.
It would have been boring if
you hadn't been here.
You give us happiness year after year.
So don't ever forget how much
I love you.
You know you're my only little sis
through and through.

—*Laura Markel*

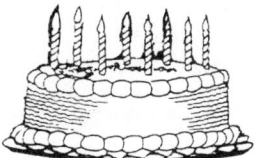

Isn't It Confusing

Isn't it confusing
when you are liked today
and hated tomorrow
or a hobby of today
is only a hobby of yesterday, tomorrow
or a person treats you like an adult today
but tomorrow your way to small
or when someone's upset
but don't know why
or the way a person acts
around everyone so different
Isn't it confusing
but it seems like thats the way it goes!

—*Tammy Lynn Glidden*

Memories

Memories shall always
Remind you of
Times forgotten
And though you may try
For the longest time
In the worst ways
You can't touch them
They're just memories
Of a wonderful past
Remember them
And treasure them
But don't stop dreaming
For your dreams
Will become the
Memories of the
Future.

—*Todd Wright*

Sounds of Chariots

Waves from the sea
Rush upon the beach
Before the storm. . .
Uneasiness touches the air
As smokey clouds
Shroud the heavens.
In the horizon
Stormy winds lifts aquamarine waters.
Waves mount to heaven,
And shoreward,
With foaming rage
In a roaring chariot race.
Ten thousand chariots collide
In a thunder clap and lie scattered
On a sandy beach.
When the storm calms with gentle waves
The breath of peace
Impregnates the air.

—*Lorraine Hicks*

Biographies of Poets

ADCOCK, BETTY ANN
Pen Name: Betty Ann Adcock; *Born:* October 31, 1960, Tacoma WA; *Parents:* Burnett and Betty Adcock; *Spouse:* Robert Brian Smith, July 10, 1982; *Occupation:* Supervisor; *Honors:* Honor Roll Student; *Other writings:* Keeps a diary; *Personal note:* Departed her life 27 February 1989 and will be sadly missed, her goal in life was to go as far as possible; *Address:* Petersburg, VA.

ADELSPERGER, JOCELYN L.
Born: March 19, 1975, Parkersburg, WV; *Parents:* Carol and David Adelsperger; *Education:* Little Hocking Grade School; *Occupation:* Antique Dealer; *Memberships:* 4-H Club, National Antique and Doll Club; *Other writings:* "A Special Place"; "Argument"; "The Stranger"; *Personal note:* My poems are inspired by things I see everyday, they seem to take a dim view of life, although I am a very happy person, maybe it's because Edgar Allen Poe is my favorite writer; *Address:* P.O. Box 398, Little Hocking, OH.

AHMEL, HARRIET
Born: February 27, 1915, Ridgewood, NY; *Parents:* John & Hedwig Hansen; *Spouse:* Carl-Heinz, December 14, 1935; *Education:* Bushwick High School; Drakes Business School; New York University; *Occupation:* Assistant Legal and Licensing Asst/Sec'y; *Memberships:* Presbyterian Woman's Guild; Christian Education; Pen League, National Sec'y Assn; *Honors:* Medal for first Poem; Phi Beta Kappa; Queen of Empire State; *Other writings:* Published in local papers; *Personal note:* I write as I see things and feel, sometimes I see what others can't see or feel; *Address:* 18B Park Drive, Lakewood, NJ.

ALLIX, HEREWARD
Born: 1922; England; *Spouse:* Louise, 1954; *Occupation:* Freelance Writer; *Other writings:* Written one novel, short stories, articles, numerous poems, essays and two plays; *Personal note:* What is written is forever, so write it well!; *Address:* Bristish Columbia, Canada.

ALONZO, ERLINE MARY
Born: July 10, 1972; Honolulu, Hawaii; *Parents:* Tranquilino T. Alonzo, Erlinda Molina Alonzo; *Education:* Radford High School Senior; *Occupation:* Student; *Memberships:* Amnesty International; *Honors:* Principal's Honor Roll; Excellence in Spanish, Social Studies, and Math; Appreciation from Special Olympics Program, Sterling Scholar Nominee; Scottish Rites Bodies, Certificate of Appreciation; *Other writings:* Several unpublished poems, feature articles in the *The Ram Page*; *Personal note:* Beauty is within and without, to perceive with the eyes is without; to acknowledge with the soul is within...I love you, emerald eyes! *Address:* P.O. Box 163, Kaaawa, HI.

ALTMAN, TROY E.
Pen Name: Troy Elaine Altman; *Born:* February 16, 1974, VAFB, CA; *Parents:* James H. Altman, Kelly J. Altman; *Education:* La Purisima Catholic Elementary School; Central High School; *Occupation:* Student; *Memberships:* FHA, Student Council, Sophmore Representative; *Honors:* Daughters of American Revolution, Essay Contest, Knights of Columbus Essay Contest; *Other writings:* Several Notebooks full of poems, three essay contest prizes and writing journal entries as a hobby; *Personal note:* I write so that people may see my light, as a beginning poet, I hope to convey messages that are important to today's society; my light may some day encourage another's light; *Address:* 1759-B Iowa Street, 6FAFB, ND.

ANDERSON, CHRISTA
Born: March 30, 1977, Kansas City, KS; *Parents:* Barbara Anderson, Michael Anderson; *Education:* Mark Middle School; *Memberships:* Spotlights Dance Troop; *Honors:* Backflip Trophy; *Address:* Kansas City, MO.

ANNESSE, MARY JOYCE
Born: February 29, 1956, Providence, RI; *Parents:* Antonetta Annese, Pasquale Annese; *Education:* North Providence High School, Rhode Island College, BA, 1978; MAT, 1983; *Occupation:* Teacher, Grade 5; Marieville Elementary School, North Providence, RI; *Honors:* Dean's List, Honor Award, Best of New Poets, 1988; American Poetry Assn; *Other writings:* "Remember with the Heart"; "I'd Like to", American Poetry Assn, 1988 *Personal note:* My poetry is a reflection of the goodness and kindness I see in those I deeply care about, those I love have strongly influenced my writings; *Address:* 23 White Court, No. Providence, RI.

ANTHONY, LAWRENCE
Born: January 21, 1955, Baltimore, MD; *Parents:* Christine and Albert Anthony; *Education:* Federal City College, Fashion Institute of Technology, Washington Technical Institute, New York School of the Bible; *Occupation:* Minister, Menswear Designer; *Memberships:* FIT Alumni Assn; American Society of Composers, Authors and Publisher, and Maranatha Gospel Hall; *Honors:* Tribute to Black Designers; Madamoiselle Magazine, Honorable Mention; Student Design Competition, 3rd Place; Boy's Design Competition, 3rd Place, Studio 54 Art Exhibit; Featured in New York Times Articles; *Other writings:* Published in Bethelite Journal and Word Magazine; *Personal note:* A Godlike consciousness, as to women as well as men, is essential to achieving a sense of purpose, one must liken himself to the Lord in order to obtain this consciousness, writing is a reflection of our conscious abilities; *Address:* Alexandria, VA.

ANTONICELLI, TONI
Pen Name: TRA; *Born:* October 5, 1972, Long Island, NY; *Parents:* Heidi Ann Antonicelli; *Education:* Law Magnet High School; *Honors:* National Honor Society; Outstanding High School Students; Honorable Mention and the Golden Poet Award for 1989, The World of Poetry; *Other writings:* I have written a short story, "Always and Forever", that I entered into Seventeen Magazine fictional short story contest; *Personal note:* I believe there are many different ways of viewing life and poetry is definitely one of them; *Address:* Dallas, TX.

ARMAS, JENNIFER C.
Born: February 8, 1978, New York, NY; *Parents:* Genaro Armas, Teresita C. Armas; *Education:* Blessed Sacrament School; *Honors:* 3 Sports Trophies, Violin Scholarship, Honor Roll; *Personal note:* In a way, my poems says that a call for help, love, or anything else is not always answered positively, or in some cases, the call is not answered at all;

ASISTIDO, CELESTINE B.
Born: October 2, 1971, San Francisco, CA; *Parents:* Rosalia and Crispin Asistido; *Education:* Notre Dame High School; California Polytechnic University; *Memberships:* Sacred Heart Community Volunteer; Pilipino Cultural Exchange; *Honors:* Music Teachers Assn of California Presidential Fitness Award, National Honor Society, Religion Awards, Community Service Award; *Other writings:* Poems published in school newspapers; *Personal note:* "Live life to its fullest because you're only given one chance, strive to be all that you can be"; *Address:* San Jose, CA.

ATKINS, MICHELLE
Born: August 6, 1974, Columbia, SC; *Parents:* Ronnie Atkins, Glenda Atkins; *Education:* Gilbert High School; *Occupation:* Student; *Memberships:* Vocational Industrial Clubs of America; Anchor Club; Pep Club; *Other writings:* I have written others, but this one is the first to be published; *Address:* Lexington, SC.

AUNAN, TOMMY
Born: April 11, 1959, Svarstad, Norway; *Parents:* Anton Aunan, Edel Aunan; *Education:* University of Oregon, School of Business; *Occupation:* Student; *Memberships:* Associate member of American Symphosium of Authors, Composers and Publishers; *Honors:* UN-Medal In-Service of Peace; Outstanding Student; *Other writings:* Songs: "Dreams of Peace", "Nevada Trucking", "New World", "Magic Tears"; *Personal note:* It is working to reach life's goals which is meaningful, not necessarily reaching them; *Address:* 1255 Mill Street, Suite 4, Eugene, OR.

AUSTIN, SHARI
Pen Name: Shari Austin; *Born:* March 6, 1957, Austin, MN; *Parents:* James C. and Lois L. Poole; *Spouse:* Garry A. Austin; *Children:* Samara; *Education:* Henderson High School; *Occupation:* Switchboard Operator, Receptionist; *Honors:* Placed in top 25 of Nashville Music City Song Festival with Poem/Lyric "It Could Have Been Me"; *Other writings:* Many Unpublished Poems and Lyrics, Presently Working on a Novel; *Address:* Alden, MN.

AUTEN, AMY K.
Born: June 26, 1974, Indiana; *Parents:* Douglas and Tanya Auten; *Personal note:* I believe love should never be forbidden because of race, religion, or nationality; *Address:* 352 King Den Dr, NW, Cleveland, TN.

BACHUS, KERRI
Born: February 8, 1975, Tulsa, OK; *Parents:* Nona, James Bachus; *Education:* St. John's Episcopal; Mann Jr. High School; Cooper High School; *Memberships:* The National Society Daughters of the American Revolution; *Honors:* Educational Fitness Award from the President; Student Writing Award, Achievement Award, Merit Award; *Other writings:* Many poems and short stories unpublished; *Personal note:* Writing thoughts down on paper has always been a great way to learn about yourself as a person; *Address:* 3774 Wilshire, Abilene, TX.

BAGLA, AMISHI
Born: March 29, 1969, Calcutta; *Parents:* Sushil Bagla, Pushpa Bagla; *Education:* Modern High School; Loreto College; *Occupation:* Student; *Memberships:* Loreto Debating and Dramatic Society, Calcutta Racket Club; *Honors:* Trinity College of Music Performers Certificate in Effective Speaking, First Prize, All India Youth Art Competition; *Other writings:* Various Articles Published in *The Telegraph, Calcutta Skyline* and *Amrita Bazaar Patricia*; *Personal note:* Though it takes a great deal of courage on my part, I continue to hold faith in human nature, I do believe poetry to be the spontaneous overflow of powerful emotion; *Address:* Culcutta, India.

BAILEY, SHARON
Born: March 25, 1954, Dalton, GA; *Parents:* Calvin Postell, Marie Postell; *Spouse:* Jack L. Bailey, June 2, 1972; *Children:* Scott, Timothy, Marcus, Sarah; *Personal note:* A few words well written, can say more than many words spoken aloud; *Address:* Dalton, GA.

BAILEY, SHELLEY LYNN
Pen Name: Jessica Lee; *Born:* April 23, 1973, Colombus, OH; *Parents:* Ronald E. and Peggy J. Bailey; *Education:* Hugh High School; *Occupation:* Student; *Memberships:* Pep Club, Literary Magazine, SADD; *Honors:* Editor's Choice Award; Golden Poet's Award; *Other writings:* Many poems published in other anthologies; *Personal note:* I believe you have to believe in yourself, and no matter what people say; stand up for what you believe in; *Address:* Reno, NE.

BAKER, JOHNNIE
Born: April 26, 1946, Cleburne, TX; *Parents:* Skeets Baker, Mr. and Mrs. R.D. Bowers; *Children:* Lee Roy, Tammy, Rodney, Michael; *Occupation:* Accounting; *Memberships:* American Legion Auxiliary; *Other writings:* "Old Sol, Rising"; "Unrequited Love"; *Personal note:* Everyday I wake up is going to be a good day and only I can make it happen; *Address:* Cleburne, TX.

BAKER, LOWELL NEILL
Born: November 30, 1959, Norfolk, VA; *Address:* 3922 Roebling Lane, Virginia Beach, VA.

BAKER, MICHELLE
Born: May 15, 1972, Durango, CO; *Parents:* Jim Baker, Diana Baker; *Education:* Battle Mountain High School, International Correspondence Schools; *Occupation:* Housekeeper; *Other writings:* Written other poems that were entered in several poetry contests; *Personal note:* Poems are inner feelings expressed through the pen and printed on paper; *Address:* P.O Box 165, Red Cliff, CO.

BALL KIMBERLY N.
Pen Name: Kim Ball; *Born:* October 1, 1974, Marion, VA; *Parents:* Kay Breedlove, J. T. Breedlove; *Education:* Marion Senior High School; *Occupation:* Student; *Memberships:* Marion Senior High Concert Choir; *Honors:* 3 Certificates for A+B Honor Roll; *Other writings:* I have wrote several other poems and songs; *Personal note:* I strive to reflect the way I feel in my writing, I have been influenced by circumstances of life; *Address:* Rt 6 Box 657, Marion, VA.

BARNETT, PAM
Born: September 1, 1973; Coldwater, MI; *Parents:* Willard Barnett, Patty Barnett; *Education:* New Hope Christian School; *Address:* Rt #2, Box 74, Union City, MI.

BARONE, TRICIA
Born: March 28, 1972; *Parents:* Salvator Barone, Sandy Barone; *Education:* Yorktown High School; *Occupation:* Student; *Address:* 1572 Amazon Road, Mohegan Lake, NY.

BARR, SARAH

Pen Name: Sarah Barr; *Born:* August 21, 1975; Omaha, NE; *Parents:*Jeanne Barr, Dale Barr; *Education:* Millard North High School; *Occupation:* Student; *Honors:* Honor Roll; *Other writings:* I have only written poems for school and friends; *Personal note:* I think people should take a good look every once in a while and look at the beauty that surrounds them; *Address:* Omaha, NE.

BARRANCO, KATHYLYNN

Born: May 17, 1962, Washington, DC; *Parents:*Salvatore Dominic Barranco; Patricia Mockey Barranco; *Children:* Stephen Salvatore; *Education:* University of North Carolina, Charlotte; George Mason University; *Occupation:* Subsidiary Rights Manager, National Academy Press; *Memberships:* Society for Scholarly Publishing, International Publishers Assn; *Personal note:* Life is a mystery to be questioned and cherished; *Address:* Alexandria, VA.

BARRIOS, LORETTA MAXINE

Born: October 7, 1933, Merkel, TX; *Parents:*Roy Harold Buchannan, Mattie Lee Price Buchanan; *Children:* Binky Ann, Cindy Gail, Mandy Ellen, Rene Ramiro, Juan Alberto; *Education:* Merkel High School; *Occupation:* Restaurant Owner, Worker 25 Years in Administration; *Memberships:* Notary Public for 4 Years in Florida, Member of Various Women's Club; *Honors:* Won Several Bronze, Silver and Gold Zero Defects Awards while Working at McClellan AFB; *Other writings:* Three Short Stories and Two Novels that are Being Prepared for Shipment to Prospective Publisher; *Personal note:* I get inspiration from my daily surrounding mostly, my friends, animals and memories; to me most things are beautiful to someone and I try to express it, and share my thoughts and feelings; *Address:* Abilene, TX.

BARRY, JONATHAN

Born: March 21, 1946, Bronx, NY; *Education:* Temple University, MA, 1975; *Occupation:* Psychologist; *Honors:* Graduated Summa Cum Laude, Golden Poet Award; *Other writings:* Composed over 7000 Poems; *Personal note:* Major Source of Inspiration: Eastern Philosophy Existestialism, Humanistic Psychology, Romantic Writers, Major Themes: Search for Self, the Human Condition, Love; *Address:* 526 Stanbridge Street, Norristown, PA.

BARTON, LINDA L.

Born: February 10, 1973; Grand Haven, MI; *Parents:*-Roger Barton, Virginia Barton; *Education:* Rockford High School; *Other writings:* Written numerous poems and stores; *Personal note:* In my spare time I love to write of fantasy and wishes, I also love to read poems to find the true meanings; *Address:* 3060 Roger River Road, Belmont, MI.

BEAM, PHILIP H.

Pen Name: P.H. Beam; *Born:* Dodge City, KS; *Children:* Rosemary; *Education:* Oakland Junior College, Oakland CA; University of CA, Berkeley CA; Emporia State University, Emporia, KS; *Occupation:* Race Car Driver, Designer; *Memberships:* VFW, AARP, California Alumni Foresters; *Honors:* Korean Service Medal, United Nations Service Medal, National Defense Service Medal; *Other writings:* "Remembrances", Now is the Archives of the Normandy Battlefield Museum; *Personal note:* I believe man's ultimate desire is for the freedom of creation; to express without suppression, to pursue interest without intervention; *Address:* Scandia, KS.

BECK, DANA

Pen Name: Dana Beck; *Born:* April 16, 1974, New Bern, NC; *Occupation:* Student; *Memberships:* Cheerleading; *Honors:* National Honor Society; Achievement Academy, 1988; National Award and Physical Science Award; *Other writings:* "Best Friends Green"; "Guys to Trust", "A Friend"; "Friendship"; "CAT"; "Here's To You"; "Through the Years"; *Personal note:* Find your strong hold in the strongest; *Address:* New Bern, NC.

BEILKE, TERI LYNN

Born: March 31, 1976, Grand Island, Nebraska; *Parents:*Timothy and Karen Beilke; *Occupation:* Student; *Memberships:* YMCA, YWCA, WJH Band, Grand Island Full City Orchestra, St. Stephen's Episcopal Church; *Honors:* Straight A Student, Superior Ratings at both Band Festivals and Orchestra Festivals, Fitness Badges; *Personal note:* I strive to write poems showing the good things and bad things of nature, that is how I get my point emphasized to the readers of them; *Address:* Grand Island, NE.

BELITZ, JUSTIN

Born: April 3, 1935, Omaha, NE; *Parents:*John T. Belitz, Helen Belitz; *Education:* BA in Philosophy; STB in Theology; Doctoral Certificate in Psychorientology; MA in Music Education; *Occupation:* Roman Catholic Priest Educator; *Memberships:* Academy of Religion and Psychical Research; Institute of Noetic Sciences; Accelerative Learning Society of Australia; *Honors:* President's Cup from SMCI for Outstanding Lecturer in the United States; Honorary Doctorate from American Institute of Psychical Research; *Other writings:* "Achieving Your Career Goals", *Chemical Engineering*; "Musical Perceptions", A General Music Textbook; Regular Publication of Poems in the *The Journey*; *Personal note:* I am dedicated to the cause of world peace by helping others to take charge of their lives and generate love; *Address:* The Hermitage, 3650 E. 46th Street, Indianapolis, IN.

BELLEMARE, KIMBERLY

Born: August 27, 1958, Scottsdale, AZ; *Children:* Luke Benjamin, Blake Joaquin; *Education:* Healdsburg High School; Santa Rosa Junior College; Empire College; *Occupation:* Legal Assistant, Office Manager; *Memberships:* Santa Rosa Evening Active; 20/30 Club; Legal Secretaries Assn; RLC Choir; *Honors:* Gospel Music Award; *Other writings:* Poem Published in "Paths Less Traveled" Several, Newsletters and National 20/30 Newsletter; *Personal note:* I write my heart; the wonder, the beauty, the humor, the sorrow, the pain of life; I always strive for a message that may touch someone else; *Address:* 14040 Chack Hill Road, Healdsburg, CA.

BELLINGER, JESSICA

Born: September 5, 1973, Grand Rapids, MI; *Parents:*-Mark Bellinger, Terri Bellinger; *Education:* Forest Hills Northern High School; *Other writings:* "Rings of Color", "And the Earth Became A Hell", "Blinded by Your Own Darkness"; *Address:* 5967 Knapp, Ada, MI.

BELTETON, PERLA REBECCA

Pen Name: Gidget; *Born:* August 27, 1972, Los Angeles, CA; *Parents:*Olga G. Belteton; *Education:* Immaculate Heart of Mary Elementary, John Marshall High School; *Honors:* 1988 U.S. Achievement Academy Award; *Personal note:* My writing reflects what my heart feels;

BENNETT, CATHY

Pen Name: Kitty Wilbur; *Born:* May 3, 1972, Albany, NY; *Parents:*Joanne Bennett and Robert Arseneau; *Spouse:* Roger Wilber, May 1, 1991; *Education:* Albany High School; *Occupation:* Part time Cashier at Price Chopper and PVT in the USAR; *Memberships:* Vice President of Personnel of a Junior Achievement Sales Company; Albany High Swim Team; *Honors:* Recipient of Numerous Poetry Awards; *Other writings:* "My Only Love"; "A Question of Love"; "Work"; "Don't Give Up"; "Best Friends"; "Winter"; "All Alone"; *Personal note:* Don't Give Up; *Address:* 30 Morris Street, Albany, NY.

BENNETT, WENDY FRANCES

Born: November 20, 1972, Oakville, Ontario; *Parents:*-Peter Bennett, Frances Bennett; *Occupation:* Student; *Other writings:* I have written dozens of poems kept in a notebook which all of my friends love and feel that I have a talent, especially my mom; *Personal note:* I love writing poems which reflect how I am feeling at the time I am writing them, while some are about racism, aging and other world issues; *Address:* 52 Douglas Drive, Toronto, Canada.

BERGERON, ELIZABETH

Born: September 2, 1972, Hartford, CT; *Parents:*D.H. Bergeron Jr., Alice H. Bergeron; *Education:* Agawam High School; *Occupation:* Student; *Memberships:* Agawam Assembly of God, American Field Service, Students Against Drunk Driving, Christ's Ambassador's Church, Youth Group; *Honors:* MVP Softball, Softball Soccer Champions, Youth Evangelism Explosion Award, Biology and History Award, 7 Year on Honor Roll; *Other writings:* 1st place in town Memorial Day essay contest; 1st place in school poetry contest, several essays published in school magazine; *Personal note:* Love never fails, it's power source is God, so it will last forever, let us not love with words or tongue, but in actions and in truth; *Address:* Feeding Hills, MA.

BERNARD, JAMES MICHAEL

Pen Name: Michael Aquarius; *Born:* March 18, 1947, Portsmouth, VA; *Children:* James Michael Bernard, Jr; *Education:* Manatee Junior College; *Occupation:* Teacher; *Memberships:* Cataclysmic Humanity; *Honors:* Editor's Choice Award, 1989; Coach of Bronze Medal Basketball Team; Championship Coach of Hardee County; *Other writings:* "Limited Living"; "Unlimited Living"; Two Short Stories, "Nobody Died", "The Immersible Invitee"; *Personal note:* For those of no talent and faith with a third reich mentality, who offered a final solution because they thought my poetry was suicidal or life threatening to emotionally average persons, I drink to your ideological death with the golden chalice of the muses; *Address:* Brooksville, FL.

BERRY, TRACY

Pen Name: Tracy Berry; *Born:* September 15, 1974, Bartow, FL; *Parents:*Bill and Pat Berry; *Education:* Bryan High School; *Memberships:* Student Council; *Honors:* Ribbon for a book of poems, selected for student council, academic achievement award; *Other writings:* Poems published in school newpaper, have gotten awards on poems published through my school years; *Personal note:* I want my writings to influence people to love and live a better life, people need to tell their personal feelings and I do it by writing poems; *Address:* 4100 Green Valley Drive, Bryan, TX.

BETTER, KERRIE ANN

Born: September 23, 1976, Worcester, MA; *Parents:*-Robert J. Better, Roxanne Better; *Education:* Quabbin Regional Junior and Senior High Schools; *Personal note:* I hope to write many more interesting poems in my future life; *Address:* Gilbertville, MA.

BEWLEY, JENNIFER

Born: October 17, 1972, Syracuse, NY; *Parents:*Karen Bewley; *Occupation:* Student; *Memberships:* Band; *Other writings:* Written numerous poems and short stories; *Personal note:* Through my writings I try to reflect both the joys and downfalls of life and improve upon them, writing is a way for me to truly express my feelings both real and fantasy; *Address:* Houston, TX.

BHANGOO, KAMIL

Born: March 29, 1977, Richmond, IN; *Parents:*Dr. Dulwant S. Bhangoo, Gurder K. Bhangoo; *Education:* Nichols; *Other writings:* I have written several other poems which I keep to myself inside of a locked diary; *Personal note:* No need to complain of lack of sleep, for when you die you shall sleep eternally; *Address:* 4 Valley View Drive, Orchard Park, NY.

BHUSHAN, ARYA

Born: July 11, 1918, Meerut India; *Parents:*Vishwa Mitra, Gyanwati Devi; *Spouse:* Swarn Lata Bhushan, October 12, 1942; *Education:* Manjula Waldron, Abhay Kumar, Rajiv; *Occupation:* Ewing Christian College; Allahabad University; Thomason College of Civil Engineering; *Memberships:* Retired Chief Commissioner of Railway Safety; *Other writings:* Short stories, poems and articles published in journals, newspapers and magazines in India and the United States; *Personal note:* I am interested in spirituality, reincarnation and parapsychology, I believe in one world brotherhood and the existence of a universal cosmic consciousness in all beings leading to ultimate sublimation; *Address:* 3838 Mumford Place, Palo Alto. CA.

BIGLER, JENNY

Pen Name: Lauran Castyll; *Born:* January 22, 1972; Iowa City, Iowa; *Parents:*Sharon Hyde and Sterling Bigler; *Education:* Westwood Traditional School; Central High School; *Occupation:* Student; *Address:* 2232 W. Weldon Avenue, Phoenix, AZ.

BILICIC, ROSMARIE

Pen Name: Rosmarie Bilicic; *Born:* July 31, 1972, Hamilton, Ontario; *Parents:*Steve Bilicic, Carol Bilicic; *Education:* Cardinal Newman High School; *Occupation:* Model (Fashion Shows) Robinson's Sales Associate; *Memberships:* Croatian Folklore Group, Holy Cross Parish; *Honors:* School Honor Roll, Vice President of Student Council; Royal Canadian Legion Literary Contest; *Other writings:* "Nevermore"; "And Now, the Sun Shines"; Sealed Within a Frame"; "Desolate Enchantment"; "Vague Intrigue"; *Personal note:* Fear not of weeping and releasing your emotions, for it is our tears that water and replenish our growing souls; *Address:* Stoney Creek, Ontario.

BIRCH, JESSICA

Born: February 2, 1976, Bannod County Pacatello; *Parents:*Bruce and Ginger Birch; *Occupation:* Student; *Other writings:* Some small poems and stories not published; *Personal note:* Writing is a way of expressing your innermost thoughts, I write from my heart not my mind; *Address:* 1840 2nd Avenue N, Payatte, ID.

BIRKS, CHERIE

Born: March 24, 1969, Mt. Holly, NJ; *Parents:*Thomas D. Birks, Molly A. Birks; *Education:* Burlington County College; *Occupation:* Student; Waitress; *Personal note:* Life is nothing without the people who love you close by; *Address:* Vincentown, NJ.

BISHOP, DENISE

Pen Name: D.T. Bishop; *Born:* April 7, 1970, Orange, CA; *Parents:*Robert Taylor, Jean Taylor; *Spouse:* Paul C. Bishop, May 20, 1989; *Children:* Nichole; *Education:* Orange High School; *Occupation:* Housewife, Secretary; *Other writings:* One Poem Published by National Library of Poetry, 1989; *Personal note:* If it wasn't for my family and friend's encouragement I wouldn't write the things that I do; *Address:* Garden Grove, CA.

BISHOPS, BECKY ANN

Born: August 10, 1976, Lansing, MI; *Parents:*Elizabeth and Bernie Bishop; *Education:* Kingston High School; *Occupation:* Student; *Memberships:* Kingston United Methodist Church, Sue's School of Dance; *Honors:* Three Years of Perfect Attendance, Piano and Band Award; *Personal note:* I like dancing, playing the piano and cheerleading; *Address:* Mayville, MI.

BLACK, RODNEY

Pen Name: Hot Rod, Alfy; *Born:* July 12, 1975, Altanta GA; *Parents:*Anita Cross and Wayne Black; *Education:* Sulphur Springs High Schools; *Occupation:* Manager; *Memberships:* Olympic Sales Club; Public Library of Sulphur Springs; *Honors:* Athletic Awards, Honor Roll Awards; *Other writings:* I'm trying to write a bibliography of my life that includes my poetry and it explains the poems meanings; *Personal note:* I live on a dairy and work on a dairy is very hard, most of my spare time is used in writing poetry; I devote these poems to my country and maybe they'll understand them; *Address:* Rt 5 Box 817, Sulphur Springs, TX.

BLASKOWSKI, AMY

Pen Name: Amy Blaskowski; *Born:* April 17, 1975, West Allis, WI; *Parents:*Gregory, Celeste; *Education:* Pius XI High School; *Occupation:* Student; *Memberships:* Pius Girl's Swim Team; *Other writings:* "Posters" in *Against the Grain*; *Personal note:* My writing reflects my feelings; *Address:* 2140 South 62 Street, West Allis, WI.

BLOM, CHRISTY

Born: March 24, 1976, Waterloo, IA; *Parents:*Fred and Carol Blom; *Occupation:* Student; *Memberships:* FHA, Girl Scout of America; *Honors:* Girl Scout Leadership Award, Girl Scout Silver Award; *Personal note:* I like to express my feelings by writing poems and short stories; *Address:* Sherburn, MN.

BOCKELMAN, SHANA

Pen Name: Banana; *Born:* December 10, 1974, Wichita, KS; *Parents:*Judy Ewertz, Ron Bockelman; *Memberships:* 4-H Kansas High School; Rodeo Assn; *Personal note:* I was inspired to write this poem because my father is a Vietnam Veteran; *Address:* 3966 Calvert, Wichita, KS.

BOGGAN, BRIDGITT F.

Pen Name: Bridgitt F. Dunn; *Born:* March 23, 1960, Memphis, TN; *Parents:*John E. Boggan, Kay R. Boggan; *Education:* Spelman College, Atlanta GA, BA; *Memberships:* World Citizen, Spelman College National Alumni Association, NSA, Soka Gakkai International; *Honors:* The Golden Poet Award, 1987-88, The World of Poetry; Honorable Mention, World of Poetry; Poet of Merit Award, American Poetry Assn; *Other writings:* "The Sign", *Hearts on Fire*, Vol. IV, The American Poetry Assn; "Electric", *Echo*, American Poetry Anthology; "The Flame Factor", *Hearts on Fire III*, The American Poetry Assn; *Personal note:* I write poetry as my gift to the world; *Address:* 173 North Avenue #2A, Plainfield, NJ.

BOLLES, KATHLEEN NOREEN ISABELLE

Pen Name: Kathleen N. I. Bolles; *Born:* July 29, 1974, Manchester, CT; *Parents:*Gene and Loretta Bolles; *Education:* Rockville High School; *Occupation:* Clerk; *Personal note:* Live laughing, loving, shopping, party hardy and you'll die with a smile, my writing reflects my views on what I see, I find I express my feelings better on paper than in speaking; *Address:* Vernon, CT.

BOLLUM, GEORGE

Pen Name: Nic; *Born:* March 13, 1974, San Diego, CA; *Parents:*Raymond and Linda Bollum; *Education:* Brownwood High School; *Other writings:* Several Unpublished poems; *Personal note:* When I write, I may write from experiences, dreams, or just from a feeling, most of my poems are personal and always of releasing my problems; *Address:* Brownwood, TX.

BORTRAND, DANA SUE

Pen Name: Yvonne; *Born:* December 9, 1973, Lafayette, LA; *Parents:*Don and Sue Bortrand; *Education:* Guaydan High School; *Memberships:* Girl Scouts, Guoydan High Band; SADD Club, Evangelism Fellowship of LA; *Honors:* District Honor Band, 1987; Most Valuable Player in Band, 1987; District Honor Band, 1988; 2-Blue Ribbons for Local Writer's Contest; 2-Band Solo Metals; *Other Writings:* Writing for the Guoydan Journal on local reading program; *Personal note:* I dedicate my talent to my mentor, Kris Potier, and I thank my teacher and friend, Mrs. Linda Hair and Mrs. Wilda Marceaux; *Address:* Rt 1 Box 339-B, Guoydan, LA.

BOVA, STEPHANIE A.

Born: April 21, 1974, Syracuse, NY; *Parents:*Samuel V. Bova, Jean M. Bova; *Education:* Genesee Senior High School; *Memberships:* Student Government, Wind Ensemble, Symphony, Yearbook Committee *Honors:* Creative Writing Award, Summer Music Scholarship to Syracuse University, Presidential Academic Fitness Award; *Other writings:* Several Unpublished Short Stories and Poems; *Personal note:* I'd like to say thank you to my parents and sister, Amanda, for being so supportive. I also owe a great deal of thanks to my english teacher, Mrs. Lorraine Bedy, who encouraged me to make dreams reality; *Address:* 109 St. George Drive, Comillus, NY.

BOWEN, NATALIE ANNE

Born: February 20, 1976, St. Matthews, KY; *Parents:*-Marnie and Joe Bowen; *Education:* Carrithers Middle School; *Memberships:* 8th Grade Chorus, Diane Moore Dance Academy; *Honors:* Selected for the Duke University Talent Search; *Other writings:* A lot of unpublished poems and short stories; *Personal note:* Most of my poetry is about the world and its problems, I think it is important to realize our mistakes and never repeat them; *Address:* 10810 Cherry Grove Court, Louisville, KY.

BOYD, CANANGELA ROQUEL BOYD

Born: October 3, 1972, Holly Springs, MS; *Parents:*Huldia Jane Jackson Boyd; *Education:* Holly Springs High School; *Memberships:* Physics Club, Stupid Council, Academic Team; *Honors:* National Honor Society; Second Runner Up in Mississippi' Miss Teenager Pageant; Miss Calendar Girl for Wal-Mart Discount Store; Choral Award; *Other writings:* Writings Nominated for the National Council Teachers of English and the English Journal; *Personal note:* I strive to enhance the true beauty and power of ideas and emotions through my writing, the outflow of freedom that I feel when I write is magical an ecstasy beyond explanation; *Address:* P.O. Box 351, Holly Springs, MS.

BOYD, TYRA

Born: May 15, 1975, Brooklyn, NY; *Parents:*Daisy and Ulysses Boyd; *Education:* Francis Lewis High School; *Occupation:* Student; *Honors:* The Principal's Honor Society; Certificate of Merit, Student of the Month; *Personal note:* Dream always and your imagination will come. Learn to live together with other people as one; *Address:* 134-39 224th Street, Laurelton, NY.

BRADLEY, DONNA MAY

Pen Name: Dawn Lopes; *Born:* New Bedford, MA; *Parents:*Lillian L. Lopes, Rene Breault *Spouse:* Russell B. Bradley, May 25, 1985; *Occupation:* Machinist, Carpenter, Nurses Aide; *Memberships:* American heart Assn, Cancer Society, Mentally Retarded Assn; Equal Rights Assn; *Honors:* Plaques and Certificates of Achievements for Poetry, Volunteering Myself to the Needy, Homeless, The Poor, as well as the Handicapps and Elderly; *Other writings:* "Long Ago"; "How Do I Tell the Story"; "I'm Your Dream"; "Not Your Dreamer"; *Personal note:* I was taught to strive and reflect onto others my teaching in the works of my writing, I've been influenced by my mom and famous poetry writers, and hope that someday my work can reach all people, so we can all live in unity, let your teaching be taught at home with pride; *Address:* Glen Burnie, MD.

BRADLEY, EDITH INEZ

Pen Name: Edie Bradley; *Born:* March 10, 1970, New York, NY; *Parents:*Joseph Walter Bradley, Geneva H. Bradley; *Education:* Hunter College; *Occupation:* Student; *Memberships:* Carribbean Club; American Museum of National History; *Honors:* Who's Who Among American High School Students, 1987-88; Who's Who Among American High School Student, 1988-89; Who's Who Among American College Students; The National Dean's List; *Personal note:* Above all worship God the good Lord, just under that, honor the mother until thy days cease, and even beyond; *Address:* 95 Lenox Avenue, Apt. 10-A, New York, NY.

BRAGA, DENISE

Born: October 8, 1969, Paterson, NJ; *Parents:*Arlene Braga, Edward A. Braga; *Education:* Parsippany High School; *Occupation:* Clerical Worker; *Honors:* Talent Show, Singing Award, Finalist in State Championship Spelling Bee; *Other writings:* Presently working on my own personal book of poetry; *Personal note:* I have been strongly influenced by my boyfriend, Chris, he inspires me to write and allows me to explore every angle and possibility of love and life, with which I express in my poems; *Address:* 10736 Hearthstone Drive, Jacksonville, FL.

BRAHAN, AUTUMN DAWN

Pen Name: Autumn Brahan; *Born:* October 19, 1975, Bennington, VT; *Parents:*Teresa E. Markiewicz, Ronald C. Brahan; *Education:* Hoosick Falls Central School; *Honors:* Art Awards, Student of the Month; *Other writings:* Short Stories, poems and songs; *Address:* Hoosick, NY.

BRAND, MARIANA

Pen Name: Mari; *Born:* September 23, 1973, LaGrange, GA; *Parents:*Douglas C. and Deena R. Brand; *Education:* Oakside Christian High School; *Occupation:* Volunteer DJ at WOAK Christian Radio, Lagrange, GA; *Other writings:* A few works published in WOAK Newsletter; *Personal note:* I want to give my heavenly Father glory through my songs, poetry and singing, God is my inspiration; *Address:* 1002 Vernon Street, LaGrange, GA.

BRANSON, BETH

Pen Name: Ashley Lauren; *Born:* August 14, 1973, Huntsville, TX; *Parents:*Walter Branson, Margaret Melinder; *Occupation:* Student, Clerk at Photo Finish Lab; *Memberships:* Junior Achievement, HOSA; SADD; *Honors:* Honor Roll, Reginal Choir, Best Poem Award; *Other writings:* "Hidden Lies"; "Times"; "Another Place"; "Forgetting"; "Lost Love"; "Forevers End"; "Thinking Back"; "Inside Dreams"; "Her Inspirations"; "Dreamer and Drowning"; *Personal note:* Keep your words nice and sweet, someday you may have to eat them; *Address:* 219 Calaclium, Lake Jackson, TX.

BRAZIS, STEVEN J.

Pen Name: Steven J. Brazis; *Born:* November 28, 1946; E. St. Louis, IL; *Parents:*John C. Brazis, June C. Brazis; *Spouse:* Rose C. Brazis, August 19, 1989; *Children:* Curtis, Milena, Mick, Jerome, Elise; *Education:* San Jose State College; University of Heidelberg; University of the Pacific School of Dentistry; *Occupation:* Dentist; *Honors:* Moo Duk Kwan, Society of Tae Kwon Do; *Other writings:* Written Book Entitled, "Withdrawal"; *Personal note:* I write to try to express the internal experience of living to reflect how personal choice shapes our inner environment and growth; *Address:* 2436 Elvyra Way, Sacramento, CA.

BREWER, TRACY

Born: September 18, 1974, Muscatine, Iowa; *Parents:*Arlin Brewer, Jean Brewer; *Education:* Palatka High School; *Memberships:* Drama Club, NAHS, FCA/FCS, SADD, Beta, SAGA; *Honors:* Eighth Grade Certificate of Achievement; *Personal note:* Anything can be achieved as long as you put God to your mind and your mind to your goals! Never give up, and you"ll never go down! *Address:* Rt 5 Box 2008, Palatka, FL.

BREZNEN-BEMIS, MARGE

Born: April 27, 1956, Claremont, NH; *Parents:* Hugh and Janet Bemis; *Spouse:* William J. Bemis Breznen, May 15, 1983; *Education:* Stevens High School, University of NH; *Occupation:* Secretary, Teacher; *Honors:* Salutatorian, High School, 1974; Rennsselaer Award, Math and Science; Outstanding Employee, 1987; *Personal note:* I appreciate all forms of art as a wonderful gift, a means by which man has the opportunity to express beauty and strive for perfection in a world where beauty and perfection are not always within our power to create; *Address:* Redmond, WA.

BRIDLE, SARAH

Born: April 21, 1973, Burlington Ontario, Canada; *Parents:*Don and Trudy Bridge; *Education:* Oakville Christian School, Lord Elgin High School; *Occupation:* Student; *Memberships:* Lord Elgin Swin Team; *Other* *writings:* Several other unpublished poems and several short stories; *Personal note:* In my poem I try to bring the reader to a place or a time and then give them something to think about; *Address:* 960 Long Dr. Burlington, Ontario Canada.

BRIGGS, LATOYA
Born: May 24, 1971, Washington, DC; *Parents:*Leroy Briggs, Jr., Nancy M. Clark Briggs; *Education:* T. Roosevelt High School; *Occupation:* Student; *Memberships:* Softball, Basketball, Teddy Ready's; Young Black Writers; *Other writings:* "I'm Young and Black", *Poetic Voices of America*; "Jazzeville City" Young Black Writers; *Personal note:* Life is like a cherry, short and sweet; *Address:* Capitol, Heights, MD.

BRINKMEIER, TAMRA D.
Pen Name: Tamra D. Brinkmeier; *Born:* July 26, 1971, Puerto Rico; *Parents:*David and Shirley Kruse; *Spouse:* Charley Brinkmeier, September 23, 1989; *Education:* Polo High School; *Other writings:* Published in Local Newspaper; *Address:* 1110 Wild Street, Sycamore, IL.

BROOKE, YANKTON
Born: October 2, 1976, Devils Lake ND; *Parents:*James Yankton Jr., Mary Lou Jetty; *Education:* Carrington Junior High School; *Occupation:* Student; *Honors:* A-Honor Roll; Participant in Language Arts Festival; *Other writings:* Poem Published in Junior High Midwest Writer; *Personal note:* I like to write about the beauty of nature and almost everything can bring me to write a poem; *Address:* Carrington, ND.

BROOKS, DANITA
Born: September 17, 1976; Pittsburg, PA; *Parents:*-Teddy and Maryann J. Brooks; *Education:* Shull School Elementary, Lone Hill Intermediate; *Honors:* Running Awards; School Awards; *Other writings:* Well, I wrote a few other poems but they were just for fun; *Personal note:* I write poems because I'm really good at it; *Address:* 713 North Amelia Avenue, San Dimas, CA.

BROOKS, MELISSA
Born: November 12, 1975; Scottsbluff, NE; *Parents:*-Sam Brooks, Jo Brooks; *Education:* Ft Laramie/Lingle Jr High School; *Occupation:* Student; *Honors:* 4.0 Honor Roll; Student of the Month, 3rd in District Mathematics Contest; *Other writings:* Written poems and short stories; *Personal note:* My writing give me a way to escape from the real world and relax for awhile; *Address:* Torrington, WY.

BROWN, TANYA Q.
Born: December 17, 1973, Jamaica, WI; *Parents:*Joyce and Delroy Brown; *Education:* Cardinal Spellman High School; *Occupation:* Student; *Honors:* National Junior Honor Society; *Address:* Bronx, NY.

BROWNLEE, LYDIA
Born: March 9, 1975, Winston-Salem, NC; *Parents:*-Jerry and Judy Brownlee; *Memberships:* Volunteer at Baptist Hospital; *Honors:* Several piano awards, elected to student council in high school; *Personal note:* I write for myself and others, never can you have too little, for someone will always have less; *Address:* 3650 Lakeview Drive, Pfafftown, NC.

BRUMLEY, SUSAN LYNN
Born: May 28, 1974, Amsterdam, NY; *Parents:*Robert L. Brumley, Jackolyn Freer Brumley; *Occupation:* Student; *Memberships:* Drama Clubs, Track, Community Leadership Programs, Anti Drug Activist; *Honors:* Various Public Speaking Awards, High Honor Roll; *Personal note:* I am 15 years old and wrote this particular poems at the age of 11; *Address:* Amsterdam, NY.

BUCKLEY, PATRICIA E.
Pen Name: Patty Buckley; *Born:* September 3, 1972, Delaware; *Parents:*Paul and Paula Buckley; *Education:* Smyrna High School; *Personal note:* I write straight from the heart; *Address:* RD 2 Box 581, Smyrna, DE.

BUCKMAN, MALINDA
Born: April 9, 1976; *Parents:*Beverly and Billy Joe Buckman; *Education:* St. Agnes School; Union County Middle School; *Occupation:* Student; *Personal note:* At my age, I am still growing and changing; I am striving to create my own personality and style; *Address:* Rt #1, Box 142-A, Uniontown, KY.

BULVER, JULIE
Pen Name: Jules; *Born:* February 21, 1971; Waterloo, IA; *Parents:*Janine Smith, Ronald Bulver; *Education:* Columbus High School; Kirkwood Community College; *Occupation:* Student; *Memberships:* Swim Team; *Other writings:* Numerous poems and short stories; *Personal note:* Once dreams become real they escape the power of the dreamer and become their own deadly things capable of independent action; *Address:* 729 Downing, Waterloo, IA.

BUSH, JENNIFER M.
Born: July 3, 1973, Syracuse NY; *Parents:*Elizabeth Roberts and Fred Wagner; *Spouse:* Scott S. Bush, July 15, 1989; *Children:* Toni Michelle Bush; *Education:* Mexico High School; *Honors:* French Honor Award; Honor Roll; *Other writings:* Several poems reflecting my personal experiences and the feelings that I have felt toward others; *Personal note:* Unless you know every aspect of one's life, don't pass judgment on them; *Address:* Oswego, NY.

BUZIKIEVICH, JENNIFER
Born: Octobner 12, 1974, Prince George, BC; *Parents:*-Ron Buzikievich, Marchien Buzikievich; *Education:* Anne Stevenson Junior Secondary School; *Occupation:* Student; *Personal note:* I hope to make the world a better place for the children of tomorrow; *Address:* 1065 Slater Street, Williams Lake, BC.

BYERLEY, LISA SHAWN
Born: April 1, 1966, Melbbourne, FL; *Parents:*Jim and Alicia Byerley; *Education:* Tigard Senior High School; Portland Community College; *Occupation:* Library Clerk; *Memberships:* Willamette Writers; *Other writings:* Several Poems Published in Various National Anthologies; *Personal note:* I strive to reflect my inner self in my writing. I believe that I have been greatly influenced by the courage and goodness of mankind; *Address:* 20756 SW 84th Avenue, Tvclatin, OR.

CADIZ, ROWENA
Born: December 29, 1971, Philippines; *Parents:*Jaime Cadiz, Norma Cadiz; *Education:* Hubbard High School; *Memberships:* Science Club; Math Club; *Honors:* United States National Art Awards, National Leadership and Service Awards, All-American Scholar; *Address:* Chicago, IL.

CALDWELL, ALISA KATHERINE
Pen Name: Alicia Maria Marclano; *Born:* November 3, 1974, Orlando, FL; *Parents:*Brenda Caldwell; *Occupation:* Student; *Memberships:* Drama Club, Campus Ministry; *Honors:* Talent Show Award; Science Fair Ribbon; *Other writings:* Written for school literary magazine; *Personal note:* Dreams can become reality through prayer and hard work; *Address:* 1611 Barkwood Drive, Florissant, MO.

CALL, KRISTEN M.
Pen Name: Kristy, Shelly; *Born:* February 10, 1972, Los Angeles, CA; *Parents:*Jeffery Call, Collene S. Call; *Children:* Charity Jeannette, Lynn DeSanto; *Memberships:* Loch Haven Baptist Church; *Other writings:* Written Numerous Poems; *Personal note:* I hope one day to inspired others as Poe and Shakespeare inspired me, I love poetry and I express it in my poems; *Address:* 5625 S. 37th Court, Green Acres, FL.

CAMERON, STEVEN M.
Pen Name: SMC; *Born:* January 5, 1958, Cincinnati, OH; *Children:* Hillary Rose Cameron; *Occupation:* Central Plant Engineer, Body Builder, Writer, Model; *Other writings:* Written Several Poems; Currently Compiling Material for Book; *Personal note:* I live for the day when I can devote all my time to the improvement of mankind; *Address:* P.O. Box 296, Amelia, OH.

CARANTO, MEL
Pen Name: Pamela; *Born:* July 23, 1960; Philippines; *Children:* Melanie, Carl Patrick; *Education:* St. Mary's College; San Sebastian College; *Occupation:* Bookkeeper; *Honors:* Gold Medalist, Dean's List, Scholarship on Computer Programming; *Other writings:* This is my first attempt to write poetry, this is also my first published poem; *Personal note:* My dreams are the outset of my reality; *Address:* Guam.

CARDONNEAU, ANDRE
Pen Name: Cachet; *Born:* September 24, 1957, Ange Gardien, Quebec; *Parents:*Evariste; Jeanne D'Arc; *Spouse:* Marianne Elley; July 24, 1982; *Children:* Christine, Sarah, Philippe; *Education:* BS; *Occupation:* Teacher; *Other writings:* Poems published in local Teacher's Association Newspaper, Information; *Personal note:* Des centaines et des centaines, des milliers et des milliers, des nullions et des millions, et toujours un seul poems; *Address:* Otterburne, Manitoba, Canada.

CARLSON, PATRICIA BROUN
Born: February 16, 1924, Wilmington, NC; *Parents:*Kathryn Broun, Horace Broun; *Spouse:* Dr. Alden L. Carlson, November 26, 1958; *Children:* David Alden Carlson; *Education:* State University, MS, Cortland NY, 1957; *Occupation:* State Uni *Memberships:* Presbyterian Church; *Honors:* Theta Phi; First place in North Carolina for High School Patroitic Essay Contest; Won Golden Poet Award from World of Poetry; *Other writings:* Several poems published; Poems published in a Syracuse paper and several articles in local newspapers; *Personal note:* I like music, poetry, travel, civic work and children literature; to me poetry is a beautiful art form; I would like to see a renewed and restored interest in poetry; *Address:* 14 Stewart Place, Cortland, NY.

CARROLL, HEATHER LEIGH
Born: March 31, 1973, Portsmouth, VA; *Parents:*Michael and Nancy Carroll; *Education:* McHenry High School; *Occupation:* Teaches Tennis and Full Time Student; *Memberships:* USTA, Inv. American Ambassador Soviet/American Youth/Student Exchange Program; *Honors:* Honor Roll; Major Letter for Cheerleading, Varsity Tennis Award; *Other writings:* Sports and feature story writer for the Star News; *Personal note:* If you find something you want be persistant follow thru and your dream will come true, thank you TCG for the inspiration; *Address:* McHenry, IL.

CARSON, MARCELLA
Pen Name: Marcella Jones; *Born:* August 5, 1960; *Children:* Alexander Noel; *Education:* Kennedy High School; F.J. Brennan High School; University of Windsor, St. Clair College; *Occupation:* Writer; *Honors:* Silver Poet Award; *Other writings:* Several poems being published in other anthologies, including the American Poetry Annual and the Amherst Society; *Personal note:* In my poetry, the loss of faith and the regaining of that faith are main themes; love is both a blessing and a responsibility; *Address:* 1607 Commonwealth Avenue, Apt #5, Brighton, MA.

CARTER, AMBER DENISE
Born: January 17, 1971, Joplin, MO; *Parents:*Mary Ann Ketcheside, James P. Carter; *Occupation:* Music Education Student; *Memberships:* Quill & Scroll; Music Educator's National Conferences; *Other writings:* Writer for high school yearbook staff and newspaper and literary magazine staffs, feature in local newspaper; *Personal Note:* Whether I write in a style that is humorous, factual, or sentimental, my writing is a reflection of the person I am; *Address:* Rt 1, Box 661, London, AR.

CASTLES, PAMELA J.
Born: May 13, 1959, York, SC; *Spouse:* Lamar B. Castles, November 13, 1982; *Children:* Amanda Nicole, Andrew Lamar, Emily Lauren; *Education:* Crest Senior High School; Gardner-Webb College; *Occupation:* Homemaker, Freelance Writer; *Honors:* Martha Mason Award for Creative Writing, 1977; English and Dramatic Awards, 1976, 1977; *Other writings:* Editor of a literary magazine entitled, *The Pegasus*, 1976-1977; first prize awards for poetry in country fair, 1977; *Personal note:* Poetry gives me an ease of expression unlike any other form of writing, often, I find my soul bared and my wings free; *Address:* 3321 Circles End, Charlotte, NC.

CASWELL, CAROL A.
Pen Name: Blondie; *Born:* April 1, 1974, Lynn, MA; *Parents:*Harold R. Caswell, Jr., Stella N, Caswell; *Education:* Keansburg High School; *Occupation:* Student, Model, Junior Policeman; *Memberships:* 4-H Club Square Dancer, Keansburg High School Band; Keansburg Police Explorer; *Honors:* Square dancing competition, volunteer cub scout, beach cleaning, blue and gold banquet award; *Other writings:* Personal and school writing; *Personal note:* I love to write poems, an expression of yourself, others, or fictional; It's a good way to release tension and I plan to continue possibly with the thought that someone somewhere may be helped by my poetry; *Address:* 61 Twilight Avenue, Keansburg, NJ.

CECIL, SARAH ELIZABETH
Pen Name: Sarah Cecil; *Born:* August 25, 1971, Honolulu, Hawaii; *Parents:*Richard Lee Cecil, Dorcas Ann Cecil; *Education:* O'Fallon Township High School; *Memberships:* St. Nicholas Catholic Church; *Personal*

note: My writing is a personal achievement to me, writing let's the real me show; *Address:* 15 Brandonwood Drive, O'Fallon, IL.

CHAPPELL, HEATHER
Born: March 23, 1975, Rochester, NY; *Parents:* William L. Chappell, Kathy Chappell; *Education:* Williamson High School; *Occupation:* Student; *Address:* Williamson, NY.

CHARBONO, MAIRI
Born: April 13, 1971, Enfield, NH; *Parents:* Lawrence Charbono, Sandra Charbono; *Education:* University of Maine; *Occupation:* Substance Abuse Counselor; *Honors:* Numerous Cheerleading and Band Awards; *Personal note:* Poetry to me, is my way of revealing my inner thoughts to others, I'm a shy person and poetry helps me to express myself, I am the words in my poems; *Address:* Enfield, NH.

CHAVEZ, JILL
Born: March 29, 1974, Paso Robles, CA; *Parents:* Greg and Janelle Griffin; *Education:* Paso Robles High School; *Occupation:* Student; *Memberships:* "Jazz n Company" Dancer; *Honors:* Golden Poet Award; *Other writings:* Editor of Junior High School Newspaper; *Personal note:* I dedicate this poem to my mother, she taught me this; be your own person, hold on to your dream, Jill, be a dancer, a singer, an actress, a writer, believe in yourself; *Address:* P.O. Box 2346, Paso Robles, CA.

CHESROW, CATHLEEN GWEN
Born: January 16, 1947, Chicago IL; *Parents:* Mar Q. Gras, Vernon Gras; *Spouse:* Eugene Joseph Chesrow, October 1965; *Children:* Albert John Chesrow, Alexis Marie Chesrow; *Education:* Art Institute, BFA; University of Chicago; *Memberships:* Chicago Council of Foreign Relations, Indiana Shariffs Association, Amnesty International, Disabled American Veterans, The Cousteau Society, The Planetary Society; *Honors:* Numerous inclusions in biographical reference books, World Jewish Congress Diplomat, certification to teach horsemanship; *Other Writings:* Has published numerous newspapers and newsletters, has had many poems published in national anthologies; *Personal note:* A country has to fight at times, the effort to find with Allah the right way to fight is the true effort; not to be deterred from by dishonoring women and children within their own homes on their jobs in their communities; *Address:* South Bend, IN.

CHIME, IFEOMA ANGELA
Pen Name: Ifeoma Angela Chime; *Born:* March 8, 1972, Nsukka, Nigeria; *Parents:* Charles Chika Chime, Augusta Chinwe Chime; *Education:* University of Nigeria Primary School; Nsukka; Federal Government Girls' College, Onitsha; *Memberships:* Young Readers Club, Nigeria; FGGS, Onitsha Press Club and Dramatic Society; *Honors:* 1st and 3rd Prizes for Poetry, Inter-Collegiate Competition, 1984; and National Award for Junior Prose, 1986; *Other writings:* Poem about "My Guardian Angel, "Success and My Sister, a prose about fear that won a national award; *Personal note:* It's quite easily forgotten, when you're given a little warning, but a lesson learned the hard way, goes along way; *Address:* 177-10 Croydon Road, Jamaica, NY.

CLARK, CONNIE L.
Born: March 27, 1949, Cleveland, OH; *Parents:* Edward Tyhulski, Lucille Tyhulski; *Spouse:* Richard M. Clark, November 30, 1979; *Children:* Jenny R. Hendricks, *Education:* Garfield Heights High School; Cuyahoga Community College; *Occupation:* Accounting; *Honors:* Dean's List; *Personal note:* Writing is like a mirror which reflects our experiences, our loves and our views; *Address:* North Ridgeville, OH.

CLAY-MOON, JULIETTE
Pen Name: Julie Juice; *Born:* Chicago Illinois, February 20, 1956; *Parents:* Claude and Beatrice Moon; *Spouse:* Anthony Clay, August 5, 1989; *Education:* Chicago State University, BSED, MSED; *Occupation:* Teacher for the Profound Mentally Handicapped; *Memberships:* Junior Achievement and Girl's Service Club, 4-H Member; *Honors:* Wendell Phillips High School Honor Society, Journal Art Award, 4-H Awards, Choir Awards; *Other writings:* I have a collection of profound and heart warming poetry ready to be recognized; *Personal note:* Writing is my source of energy it is therapeutic to me, whenever I need a friend, I'll pick up paper a pencil or a pen; *Address:* Atlanta, GA.

CLEGG, DONALD L.
Born: March 28, 1940, Harrisburg, PA; *Parents:* Dorothy R. Clegg, Elmer B. Clegg; *Children:* Brenda Lee, Tammy Lou, Donald Lee, Mark Brooks, Tina Louise, Michael, Margaret; *Education:* Newport Joint High School, Newport, PA; *Occupation:* Electrician; *Honors:* Quill and Scroll Honor Society; Honorary Staff Writer for Majestic Records and Countrywine Publishing; Best Poets of the 1988 and 1989 American Poetry Assn; *Other writings:* Song lyrics, newspaper articles and various poetry anthologies; *Personal note:* The known poet glories in his/her sense of immortality, like prayers to the statue of the unknown God, the unknown poet's labors are for nought; *Address:* 221 East 10th Avenue, Homestead, PA.

CLEMENT, JOHN M.
Pen Name: John M. Clement; *Born:* May 10, 1964, Dallas, TX; *Parents:* Jerry L. Clement, Jane M. Clement; *Spouse:* Lisa W. Clement, January 20, 1990; *Education:* Southern Methodist University, Universidad de Toledo, Oxford University, University of North Texas; *Occupation:* Self Employed; *Memberships:* Kappa Sigma Fraternity, Highland Park United Methodist Church; *Honors:* Outstanding Young Man in America; *Personal note:* To read these works, which are the result of thought, is common enough, but to sit in pleasant company and join in the act of thinking is a rare pleasure in deed; *Address:* 9648 Crestedge, Dallas, TX.

CLEVELAND, REGINALD T.
Born: March 7, 1956, Richmond, VA; *Parents:* Leroy Franklin, Irene Tilton; *Spouse:* Yolanda Cleveland; May 25, 1988; *Children:* Tyrone Leroy Cleveland; *Education:* Morehouse College, Atlanta GA, BA; Virginia Union School of Technology, Master of Divinity; *Occupation:* Chaplain, United States Air Force; *Memberships:* Moore Street Baptist Church; *Honors:* Company Grade Office of the Quarter; *Personal note:* I believe spiritual people should solve problems in spiritual ways, the job of every spiritual man or woman is to bring awareness; *Address:* 1300 S. Farm View Drive, A-34, Dover, DE.

CLINE, RACHEL
Born: January 29, 1973, Hammond, IN; *Parents:* Rose Cline, Roy Cline; *Education:* Volunteer High School; *Memberships:* Greenvale Baptist Church; *Other writings:* Written many other poems but none published; *Personal note:* I show my feelings in my poetry, but it is extremely difficult for me to write unless I have a strong feeling toward something, most of my inspiration comes from my mother, she has taught me that I can do anything I want, if I try; *Address:* Rt #1, Box 317-2, Church Hill, TN.

CLINTON, NOBLE T.
Born: 6 December 1954, Detroit, MI; *Parents:* Richard & Ida Morris; *Children:* Oleen, Richard, Michelle, Terilyn; *Occupation:* Military Veteran; *Memberships:* NAACP, National Coalition; *Other writings:* I have personally put together a private collection of over two hundred and fifty poems and songs I've written over the years, until one day they can finally be published, and be available to the world; *Personal note:* Writing for me surpasses my intimate zeal in revealing to the world, just what's inside this man, it also gives me a sense of personal satisfaction, comparable to the thrilling sincerity of an experience, with your first true lover, and inseparable friend; *Address:* Cherry Point, NC.

COGHILL, RODNEY
Born: October 9, 1968, Richmond, VA; *Parents:* Phillip Coghill, Lois Coghill; *Education:* Clover Hill High School; John Tyler Community College, Kee Business College; *Occupation:* Trust Research Specialist, Sovran Financial Corp, Richmond VA; *Honors:* 1st Place Prose, Sherwood Literary Magazine; *Other writings:* Over 150 Poems, 200 Songs and Several Short Stories; *Personal note:* Writing is a form of art, but also a form of expression, I wish to express my innermost feelings, but my concern for mankind and mother earth take center stage; *Address:* 8400 Bethia Road, Chesterfield, VA.

COLBY, JULIE A.
Born: August 16, 1972, Olean, NY; *Parents:* Donald Colby and Ann Colby; *Education:* Allexis I Dupont High School; Randolph High School; *Occupation:* Student; Parttime Student Aide; *Memberships:* Culture Club and Key Club; *Honors:* Honor Roll; *Other writings:* A couple of my other poems have been published in my school's literary magazine and newspaper; *Personal note:* I wish to thank my eleventh grade english teacher for introducing me to poetry; *Address:* 24 Leight Court, Randolph, NJ.

COLLINS, EUGENIA ANNE
Born: April 24, 1972, Albany GA; *Parents:* Jimmy Collins, Penny Collins; *Education:* Monroe Comprehensive School; *Occupation:* High School Senior; *Memberships:* Future Business Leaders of America; Annual Staff, Academic Decathlon, Debate Team, DECA; *Honors:* Who's Who Among American High School Student 1988-89; Senior Superlative, 1990; *Other writings:* Poems published in local newspaper, The Albany Herald; *Personal note:* I love poetry and writing, after graduation I plan to attend Middle Georgia College and the University of Georgia School of Journalism to major in journalism; *Address:* Albany, GA.

COLLINS, JESSICA A.
Born: April 13, 1975, Raceland, LA; *Parents:* Paul A. Collins Sr., and Laura Collins; *Education:* Golden Meadow Jr. High; *Occupation:* Student; *Memberships:* FHA, HERO Member, Golden Meadow Jr. High Quiz Bowl; *Honors:* Principal's List, 1988, English Fair Award; *Personal note:* To my fellow Americans I say: try your best in everything you do and never doubt yourself or your abilities, to my family and friends I say: thank you for always being there for me; *Address:* P.O. Box 892, Galliano, LA.

COMFORT, PATRICIA
Born: December 14, 1953, Clearfield, PA; *Parents:* James Wright, Mary Virginia Wright; *Children:* Melissa Comfort; Benjamin Comfort; *Education:* Jersey Shore High, Pennsylvania College of Technology; *Occupation:* Library Assistant, Williamsport PA; *Other writings:* Poems and Personal Writing; *Personal note:* This poem is dedicated to the community of Williamsport for helping me to grow as an individual, I can be myself when I am closest to nature and try to reflect that in my writing; *Address:* Williamsport, PA.

COMPTON, SHEILA DIANNE
Born: March 18, 1948; Buxton, ME; *Parents:* Frank & Jean Colson; *Spouse:* Douglas Compton; February 21, 1987; *Children:* Sean, Heather, David, Mikie; *Education:* Bruhs Randolph, Vermont; Laney Junior College, Oakland, CA; *Occupation:* Artist, Writer, Butterfly Publishing; *Other writings:* "Memories", "Who Gives a Hoot"; Poem published in *Wide Open Magazine*; *Address:* 4050 Wonder Stemp Road, Crescent City, CA.

CONTI, MICHELLE L.
Born: December 27, 1971, Fort Wayne, IN; *Parents:* James Conti, Nancy Kramer Conti; *Honors:* Tri Kappa Award; Rotary Youth Leadership Award, Graduated Salutatorian; *Other writings:* "A Lost Rapture", "An Influential Sky", "You Left Me More", "Lost at Sea", "The Courage to Love", "Love at First Sight"; *Personal note:* One can always find the rainbow after the rain, if through the storm, he keeps sight of the light; *Address:* 2701 Poinsette Drive, Ft Wayne, IN.

COOK, JENNIFER
Pen Name: Jennifer Cook; *Born:* APril 29, 1976, Rome, GA; *Parents:* Jimmy and Judy Cook; *Education:* Cedar Hill Middle School; *Memberships:* Cedar Hill Middle School Band; *Honors:* The Honors Club; *Personal note:* Believe in yourself and live out your dreams; don't let what others think get in your way, this poem was written for Kim Cooper and Mr. Montgomery; *Address:* 606 Collard Valley Road, Cedartown, GA.

COOK, KIMBERLY CARLENE
Born: September 17, 1969, Beckley, WV; *Parents:* Roland Cook, Shelby Cook; *Education:* West Virginia University; *Occupation:* Student; *Memberships:* Accounting Club; *Honors:* Alphi Phi Omega, Golden Key National Honor Society, Honor Program; Presidential Award for Outstanding Academic Achievement; Outstanding Pledge Award for Fall 1989 Pledge Class; *Personal note:* Poetry helps me express what I feel and sort of acts like a catharsis for me; *Address:* P.O. Box 914, Mullens, WV.

COOK, LESLIE KAREN
Born: December 4, 1969, Wellston, OH; *Parents:* Lawrence W. Cook, Phyllis M. Cook; *Education:* Green Run High School; *Occupation:* Air Force, Fuels Specialist; *Other writings:* Personal poems, none other published; *Personal note:* I love to write and if my poems bring happiness to others, then I've accomplished what I wanted to do; *Address:* Virginia Beach, VA.

COOMER, ANITRA LYNN

Pen Name: Anitra Coomer; *Born:* February 7, 1975, Colombus OH; *Parents:*Donald Coomer, Kathy Coomer; *Education:* Athens High School School; *Occupation:* Student; *Memberships:* LASCU School of Ballet, Chicago City Ballet; *Honors:* Honor Roll, Sports Medals and Awards; *Personal note:* Your dreams can come true but only if you dare to dream; *Address:* 1025 Woodside Trail, Troy, MI.

COPPLE, JENNIFER ANNE

Born: June 27, 1976, Erie, PA; *Parents:*John and Mary M. Copple; *Occupation:* Student; *Personal note:* Writing is a good way for me to sort through my own emotions and feelings and by sharing them with others it may help them to understand their own, no matter what their ages are;

COSTLEY, KRISTIN

Pen Name: Kerri Kristin Costley; *Born:* August 27, 1970; Atlanta, GA; *Parents:*Wayne and Carole Costley; *Education:* Pebblebrook High School; Kennesaw State College; *Occupation:* Secretary, Receptionist for General Contracting Firm; *Memberships:* Orange Hill Baptist Church, Single's Council; *Honors:* Dean's List; *Other writings:* Poem published in *Poetic Voices of America*; *Personal note:* My writings are a very special part of me and my dream has always been to write a piece of work that will touch someone's world as it has never been touched before, that through the grace and beauty of my words, I might carry someone to a place completely unknown, it is then that I will be fulfilled as a writer; *Address:* Powder Springs, GA.

COSTNER, REBECCA W.

Born: December 26, 1940, Larens, SC; *Parents:*Reba R. Wood, John H. Wood; *Spouse:* Harley L. Costner, June 9, 1973; *Children:* John Riddle, Mark Costner; *Education:* Newberry High School; Columbia Commercial College; *Occupation:* Branch Manager; *Other writings:* Unpublished Short Stories and Poems; *Personal note:* Generally Circumstance Make Decisions Inevitable; *Address:* 4409 Bonnie Forest Blvd, Columbia, SC.

COUGHNETT, WAYNE VAN

Born: August 15, 1959, Mahopac, NY; *Parents:*Robert and Gladys Coughnett; *Education:* New Milford High School; *Occupation:* Residential Building Contractor; *Other writings:* Hope to have collection of 50 poems published soon; *Personal note:* The lock and key; My Secret Heart; The Soul of Me; My Humble Art; *Address:* 4-C Kent Road, Gaylordsville, CT.

COURTER, DORINDA

Born: August 30, 1957, Omaha, NE; *Parents:*Don and Lorraine Dean; *Spouse:* Terry Courter, August 1, 1981; *Children:* Michael, Crystal, Donny, Angel; *Education:* South High School; *Occupation:* Homemaker; *Honors:* Golden Poet Awards; *Other writings:* Several Honorable Mentions in World of Poetry, and on The Threshold of a Dream; *Personal note:* Write poems is my way to express myself best; *Address:* 1520 Fifth Corso, Nebraska City, NE.

COUTURIER, ELAINE

Born: July 3, 1933, Riverton, NH; *Parents:*William Luther, Virginia Roberts; *Spouse:* Leo Couturier, April 2, 1967; *Children:* Leland Joseph, Robert Paul, Ronald James, Betty Bernice, Virginia, Evelyn, Brenda; *Occupation:* Seamstress; *Other writings:* Have written a lot of poems which I have never done anthing with; *Personal note:* In my poetry I can open my heart and say the things my mouth will not. There is a beauty in words and I'd like to help others find that beauty; *Address:* Whitefield, NY.

COVERT, POLLYANNA

Born: November 4, 1971; *Parents:*Naaman Coveat, Jean Covert; *Education:* West Union High School; *Occupation:* Student; *Honors:* National Honor Society; Top Honors Award in Art and English; Recipient of Numerous Art Show Award; *Personal note:* Being from the midwest and Living on a farm gives me the opportunity to view many facets of life; poetry is just one outlet for me express my thoughts; *Address:* 999 Delong Road, Otway, OH.

COX, REBECCA ANN

Pen Name: Becky; *Born:* August 29, 1974, Little Rock, AR; *Parents:*Earl Joseph Cox and Betty Sue Bailey Cox; *Education:* Lonoke High School; *Occupation:* Student; *Memberships:* Marching Band; SADD, Math Club; *Honors:* Honorable Mention in the Science Fair; Several first and second divisions at our solo and ensemble band contest; *Other writings:* Several other poems, but none have been published; *Personal note:* Hard work and determination means a job well done; *Address:* 815 England Street, Lonoke, AR.

CRANE, BETSY SUZANNE

Born: March 26, 1973, Gainesville, GA; *Parents:*Shirley Crane, Kenneth Crane; *Education:* White County High School; Tallulah Falls Boarding School; *Memberships:* Church Choir, Ensemble; *Other writings:* Poems: "Hugs", "Looking Beyond the Barriers", "Managing to Survive"; "Two Hearts", "Christy and Rodney"; *Personal note:* As I write my poems I think of the problems of life, I write to feel better and to show emotions on paper; *Address:* P.O. Box 374, Cleveland, GA.

CRAWFORD, ROBERT F.

Born: May 3, Norfolk, VA; *Parents:*Robert L. Crawford, Lucy Petit Dumville; *Children:* Joyce Hanlon, Lindsay Crawford; *Education:* Cornell University, Owego, NY; *Personal note:* I strive to be in harmony with the universe around me, without hate, malice or hypocracy; *Address:* P.O. Box 15323, Sarasota, FL.

CROASMUN, GEORGE W.

Born: September 11, 1950, Erie, PA; *Parents:*George & Dorothy Croasmun; *Spouse:* Roberta A. Croasmun, March 20, 1984; *Children:* Angela, John, Nathaniel; *Education:* East High School; *Occupation:* Electronics Technician; *Memberships:* Poets of Now; *Honors:* 1989 Golden Poet Award from World of Poetry; Honorable Mention from Nashville for "Is This the Way It Should Have Been?"; *Other writings:* Written Numerous Poems; *Personal note:* The poet possesses such a wonderful gift, the saddened spirits of others to life, we cannot claim 'tis of our own accord, for it's God who gives the poet his word; *Address:* Orlando, FL.

CROWELL, ELIZABETH

Born: February 19, 1971, Englewood, NJ; *Parents:* Merrill Crowell, John Crowell; *Education:* Montclair Kimberley Academy; Smith College, Northampton, MA; *Occupation:* Student; *Honors:* Graduated Cum Laude; *Personal note:* Expression is a responsibility for humanity;

CUBBAGE, DEBRA

Pen Name: Debbie; *Born:* November 11, 1950, Luray, Virginia; *Parents:*Elna P. Johnson, Melvin Washington; *Spouse:* James L. Cubbage, July 14, 1968; *Children:* Angela Marie, Lora Christine, Lisa Michele, Carol Ann, Crystel Lynne; *Education:* West Luray School; *Occupation:* Floor Supervisor; *Memberships:* Bibleway Church of God; *Other writings:* Write for family and friends and others as a hobby; *Personal note:* I would love to make something come of my writings; I love to write and I write for my own experiences or heartfelt feeling; *Address:* Shenandoah, VA.

CULLARO, ANDREA

Pen Name: Taylor Sands; *Born:* August 7, 1974, Trenton, NJ; *Parents:*Daniel Cullaro, Dolores Cullaro; *Education:* Nottingham High School; *Occupation:* Student; *Memberships:* Hamilton Aquatics Club; *Other writings:* Written Several Poems in the School Caelestis; *Personal note:* My style is unique and entirely contemporary, my work strikes at the sensitivity of my readers stirring lost emotions that continue after the poem ends; *Address:* Mercerville, NJ.

CUMELLA, BALDASSARE BANY

Pen Name: Ben B. Cumella; *Born:* January 1, 1920, Ogrigento, Italy; *Parents:*Salvatore, Rose; *Spouse:* Mary, September 10, 1950; *Education:* Academy Don Bosco, Royal Lyceum Umberto I, University of Palermo; *Occupation:* Physician; *Memberships:* KCMS, NYSMS, FICA, Regina Pacis Residence, Pres; Legion of Merit; *Honors:* Dean's List, Knighted by the Italian Government, Men of the Year, Golden Award in Poetry; *Other writings:* "The Eagle", "The Vietnam Heros", *Marisa, The Miracle*; *Personal note:* I strive to reflect love and peace in all my writings; I have been influenced by classic studies; *Address:* Brooklyn, NY.

CUNNINGHAM, DARLENE D.

Parents: Leon Cunningham Sr., Mattie B. Cunningham; *Occupation:* Registered Nurse; *Memberships:* United States Tennis Assn; *Honors:* National Honor Society; *Other writings:* Written numerous poems and short stories; *Personal note:* Flowing thoughts in the form of poetry is one of the greater releases; *Address:* P.O Box 1123, Maryland Heights, MO.

CURRY, PAGE

Born: July 8, 1976, Knoxville, TN; *Parents:*David and Ernie Page; *Education:* Gap Creek Elementary School; Doyla Middle School Student; *Occupation:* Student; *Honors:* School Honor Roll; Language Arts Award, Science Award, Drawers Award; *Other writings:* Articles in School Newspaper; *Personal note:* Writing a good poem is hard work, but once you try and have the right inspiration you can write a wonderful poem; *Address:* 7921 Hodges Ferry road, Knoxville, TN.

CUSTODIO, ULDARIO P.

Pen Name: Dayono Dario; *Born:* October 14, 1904, Lezo Aklare, Philippines; *Parents:*Santiago Custodio, Ursula Prado; *Spouse:* Anisia T. Custodio; August 25, 1934; *Children:* Edgar, Edsel Edwin, Sherwin, Winston, Evelyn; *Education:* Normal College; *Occupation:* Retired Public School Teacher and Principal; *Memberships:* Aklon Public School Teachers Assn; Philippines Public School Teachers Assn, President and Advisor of Local Community Organization, Boy Scout Leader, President of the APSTA; *Honors:* First Prize Award for Poetry Contest in Local Dialect Competition during Rizal Inauguaration of the Monument on Dec. 30, 1951; *Other writings:* Several Poems Unpublished in English and Dialect; Have Written Almost More than a Hundred Poems in English; *Personal note:* Writing poems and essays as inspired during my reading of poetry and stories of lives of famous authors, my dreams and desires to put my feelings in writings so it could influence the lives of others to do noble deeds; *Address:* 29 Grant, Irvine, CA.

CZUMAK, LINDA

Born: January 11, 1948, Long Island, NY; *Parents:*Charlotte Doerrbecker, DeWitt Doerrbecker; *Spouse:* Michael Czumak, September 10, 1977; *Children:* Michael III, Christopher James; *Education:* Carle Place High, Nassau Community College, Long Island University; *Memberships:* Order of the Eastern Star; *Honors:* Graduated Magna Cum Laude; *Personal note:* I enjoy writing about people, places and things that I love; *Address:* 246 Soundview Road, Huntington, NY.

D'ANGELO, LAUREN

Born: August 5, 1976, Waterbury CT; *Parents:*Cynthia D'Angelo, Fred D'Angelo; *Education:* Swift Junior High School; *Occupation:* Student; *Other writings:* I enjoy writing poems and books and hope to accomplish other publications in the future; *Personal note:* I dedicate this poem to anyone who has lost the certain someone they loved and cared deeply for; *Address:* Oakville, CT.

DAUZ, LUCILLE

Born: May 30, 1973, Belleville, NJ; *Parents:*Dr. Urbano A. Dauz, Dr. Virginia B.C. Dauz; *Education:* Junior High School; *Occupation:* Student; *Memberships:* OHSA, Scholastic Bowl; *Honors:* Honor Student, Band and Chorus Awards, Illinois Music Assn Awards; *Personal note:* Pollution is man's worst enemy, everyone should pitch in and clean up; *Address:* Shelbyville, IL.

DAVENPORT, JOHN W.

Pen Name: Jay Davenport; *Born:* June 9, 1927, Greenville County, SC; *Parents:*John B. Davenport, Edna Crews Davenport; *Spouse:* Catherine Browning Davenport, December 26, 1943; *Children:* Carole, Roy, Elizabeth, Curtis, Pamela Gregory; *Education:* Mauldin High School; Spartanburg Methodist College; Wofford College, BA; Candler School of Theology; Duke Divinity School; *Occupation:* Ordained Minister, The United Methodist Church; *Memberships:* Chaplain, Newberry Civitan Club, Lions International, President of Rock Hill Ministerial Assn; Clover International Poetry Assn; *Honors:* Scholarship from Wofford College; Four Years on Dean's List; Salutatorian for 1950 class at Spartanburg Methodist College; Third Place Winner in National Writing Contest; *Other writings:* Articles and Poems in the S.C. Methodist Advocate, Articles in The Upper Room (devotional booklet published by the United Methodist Church), wrote column "Table Talk" for the Edgefield County News, Ghost wrote Editorials for the Same Paper, Poem "Albert Sweitzer" Published in the Clover Collection of Verse; *Address:* 21 Seyle Street, Greenville, SC.

DAVIS, ATHENA M.

Born: December 4, 1974, Miami, FL; *Parents:*Sharon C. Davis; *Other writings:* Poems Published in Local Newspapers; *Personal note:* Writing is the key to the world, with words all doors can be opened; *Address:* 10611 Turkey Scratch Lane, Jacksonville, FL.

DAVIS, BETTIE MARTIN
Born: August 8, 1948, Bowman, GA; *Parents:* Jessie T. Martin; *Children:* Roosevelt Davis Jr., Jessica Marie, Connie, Melissa; *Occupation:* Housewife, Writer, Photograph; *Memberships:* CRS Records, Top Record, Hollywood Artist Records, World of Poetry, American Poetry, Quill Hooks, Five Star Music; *Honors:* Certificate for Song, Merit Award for Poems, Golden Poet Award; *Other writings:* Several poems published in other books; *Personal note:* Writing is a hobby for me I am a association member of six record companies, I am also an associate member of four poetry societies; I am a songwriter as well, my poems are about love, life and dreams; it makes me happy, writing always brings out my inner feelings when I can't talk to people; *Address:* P.O. Box 92, Bowman, GA.

DAVIS, CORI LYNN
Born: November 3, 1972, Bethpack, NY; *Parents:* Sandi, Glenn Davis; *Occupation:* Student; Sales Consultant; *Other writings:* Several poems not yet published; *Personal note:* I dedicate this poem to my boyfriend, David, who has taught me the real meaning of love; *Address:* 20 Bobcat Lane, East Setauket, NY.

DAVIS, DONALD L.
Pen Name: D. Lee Davis; *Born:* February 18, 1937, Niagara, WI; *Spouse:* Shirley A., December 26, 1964; *Children:* Cynthia, John Darrell, Jeffery; *Education:* Niagara High School; Northern Michigan University, BA; MA; *Occupation:* English Teacher; Diary Farmer; *Memberships:* WEA, National and Wisconsin Holstein Assn; *Other writings:* Two Novels in Progress; *Address:* Florence, WI.

DAVIS, STEPHANIE K.
Born: June 2, 1973, Los Angeles, CA; *Parents:* Jim and Debbie David; *Occupation:* Student; *Memberships:* Parent, Teachers, Student Assn; National Cheerleading Assn; *Honors:* Nomination in Who's Who Among American High School Student; Nominated for awarded of excellence at NCA Cheer Camp 1989; *Other writings:* Writing poetry for 4-5 years for family, friends and myself; *Personal note:* Someone cares; *Address:* 9772 Medina Drive, Santee, CA.

DAVIS, TIFFANY FRANCES
Born: October 23, 1972, West Covina, CA; *Parents:* Janet Lee Davis; *Education:* Nogales High School; *Occupation:* Elementary Teacher; *Memberships:* Dehaven Community Center; *Honors:* Bronze Congressional Award for my dedication to my community as a volunteer; *Personal note:* A smile in your heart gives you a world of happiness; *Address:* West Covina, CA.

DAY, STEPHANIE
Born: March 6, 1972, Meriden, CT; *Parents:* Jan and Bill Day; *Honors:* A Sketch book Award; Award from Barbizon; *Personal note:* My poems mean a lot to me, all of this comes from the heart, to all my friend, I am nearly famous, miss you all; *Address:* Wayne, PA.

DEAN, TODD BISHOP
Pen Name: Bishop Dean; *Born:* July 11, 1966, Baton Rouge, LA; *Parents:* Gerald and Pat Dean; *Education:* Louisiana Tech University, Ruston, LA; *Occupation:* Parttime employee at Wal-Mart; *Memberships:* Officer in SAE Fraternity; *Other writings:* Several poems, none of which have been published; *Personal note:* I hope to write movies, plays and comedy for stand up comics, my first love is poetry; *Address:* 1728 Bellfort Drive, Baton Rouge, LA.

DEHBOZORGI, ELLIE
Born: May 12, 1966, Tehran, Iran; *Parents:* G. Husien Dehbozorgi, Z. Setayesh; *Education:* Montclair State College; *Honors:* Outstanding Speaker at the North Arkansas Community College; *Personal note:* We never know when we will die, so the best gifts that we can give each other are love, peace and trust; *Address:* 53 Morse Avenue, Bloomfield, NJ.

DELANEY, ALISON
Pen Name: Allison Delaney; *Born:* February 18, 1975, Philadelphia, PA; *Parents:* Carol and Jack Delaney; *Education:* Lower Moreland High School; *Occupation:* Student; *Memberships:* SADD; *Honors:* Honor Roll, Distinguished Honor Roll; *Other writings:* Short Stories, Epics, Poems for School; *Personal note:* Although this is my first success in writing, I am confident that many more await me, I also want toencourage other kids my age, to keep reaching for the stars!; *Address:* Huntingdon Valley, PA.

DEMOE, KATHLEEN A.
Born: March 16, 1939, Bronx, NY; *Parents:* Teresa and Edward Roche; *Spouse:* Donald DeMeo, June 24, 1961; *Children:* Teresa, Donald, Edward; *Education:* Staten Island Community College; Notre Dame College; Richmond College, MS; *Occupation:* High School English Teacher; *Memberships:* UFT, Blessed Sacrament Church; *Honors:* Dean's List, College English Teacher of the Year, 1987; *Other writings:* "DeJa Vu", a poem published by Amherst Society; poem published by National Library of Poetry; *Personal note:* I greatly appreciate the support of my colleague in the New York City Teacher Consortium and the Creative Writing Instructor at the college of Staten Island;

DEVOE, JANA
Pen Name: Nae-Nae; *Born:* November 23, 1978; Savannah, GA; *Parents:* Frances DeVoe Reynold; *Spouse:* Charles Reynolds; December 24, 1985; *Children:* Marcus; *Personal note:* I like to be by myself to write; I have beenwritingpoems for two years; Shakespeare, other poets and story writers have influenced me; *Address:* Savannah, GA.

DIBBLEY, MEGAN
Born: July 7, 1976, Lake Charles, LA; *Parents:* Pamela Dibbley, David Dibbley; *Education:* Gillis Elementary, Moss Bluff Middle School; *Occupation:* Student; *Memberships:* Beta Club, 4-H, Our Savior Lutheran Church; *Honors:* Art Award from the American Press; Science Award for Outstanding Achievement; *Other writings:* Nature, Alex the Great, Bayou Monster, Our Constitution; *Personal note:* I believe in peace for the world, I hope we can all learn to love each other; *Address:* Rt 15 Box 2685, Lake Charles, LA.

DICK, GRETCHEN
Pen Name: Ginger; *Born:* May 24, 1977, Lake Forest, IL; *Parents:* Jeff and Deanna Dick; *Occupation:* Student; *Memberships:* 4-H Madame Alexander, Doll CLub; *Honors:* High honor roll student, ribbons from horse and dog shows, award for best penmanship; *Other writings:* School writing of poems and won an award for writing the best scary story out of grade; *Personal note:* I believe that each person holds their own destiny, and has a responsibility toward mankind and toward the earth; *Address:* 30913 Manor Hill, Grayslake, IL.

DINIS, ANA C.
Pen Name: Tina; *Born:* March 20, 1965, Portugal; *Parents:* Roger and Luisa Silveira; *Education:* Elizabeth High School; Roberts-Walsh Business School; *Occupation:* A/R CLerk; *Honors:* Dean's List; *Personal note:* I want to capture the beauty of love in my writing; *Address:* 982 Floyd Terrace, Union, NJ.

DINKEL, CRISTA LYNN
Pen Name: Crista Dinkel; *Born:* January 23, 1974, Long Prairie, MN; *Parents:* John, Cheryl; *Education:* Long Prairie High School; *Occupation:* Announcer; *Memberships:* Volleyball Team, Golf Team, SADD, AFS; *Other writings:* Written Numerous Poems; *Personal note:* I enjoy putting my personal experiences in my work, I also enjoy reading and writing all types of poetry; *Address:* Long Prairie, MN.

DIRCHSEN, JULIE
Born: October 31, 1974, North Platte, NE; *Parents:* Stephen, Roberta; *Occupation:* Student; *Address:* Stanfield, OR.

DIXON, MAUDEAN ANNETTE
Pen Name: Maudean Robinson; *Born:* September 20, 1960, Covington, KY; *Parents:* Don Robinson, Sypsy Mae Robinson; *Spouse:* Edward Brehm; *Children:* Konean Nikole Dixon; *Education:* Yuma High School; Cerritos College; *Occupation:* Staff Writer, Long Beach News; *Memberships:* Jobs Daugher, Thespian; *Honors:* Alpha Gamma Sigma, Dean's List; *Other writings:* News articles for the Long Beach Press; *Personal note:* Meaning is an essential component of life, strive for that rarely equaled richness and don't forget your atlas, help each other find the way; *Address:* 15918 Orizaba Avenue, Parmount, CA.

DOLIN, HARRIET
Born: Worcester, MA; *Parents:* David and Rosa Goldstein; *Education:* Montclair State College, AB: Clark University; *Occupation:* Sales Representative, Linco Products, Inc; *Memberships:* Senior Citizens Club, Writer's Club of Charlotte; *Honors:* Plaque, Cedar Grove Senior Citizen's Housing Assn; Council of the American Institute of Chemists; Dean's List; Many letters and news releases in newspaper; *Other writings:* 7 Monographs on food additives; Resume Writing; Four Books in Process; *Personal note:* My writing stems from experiences of myself and my friends; *Address:* Charlotte, NC.

DOMINICK-SCALZETTO, LOUIS
Pen Name: Louis Dominick; *Born:* July 10, 1931, Albany, NY; *Parents:* Gelardo Scalzetto, Angeline Scalzetto; *Occupation:* New York State Civil Servant; *Memberships:* NY State and Federal Civil Service Assn of Employees; *Honors:* Citation from the baseball hall of fame board of directors for a poem, 1974; *Other writings:* "Contemporary Poetic Experience of 1975"; *Personal note:* I was inspired as a youngster by the works of John Steinbeck and especially biographies of all art. I have been lucky to be blessed by excellent teachers; *Address:* Albany, NY.

DONEY, JOHN T.
Born: January 13, 1933, Punxsutawney, PA; *Parents:* Daniel, Dorothy; *Children:* John, Martha, Stephen, James, Joseph, Mary; *Education:* Dale High, Cambria-Rowe Business College, AA: Waynesburg College, BA; *Occupation:* Transportation Sales; *Honors:* Chevalier Degree, Order of DeMolay; *Other writings:* Numerous Poems for special occasions; *Personal note:* Humility is wanting God's perfect will in your life, life is fulfilled in that same humility; *Address:* P.O. Box 3019, Independence, MO.

DOTY, TAMARA LYNN
Pen Name: Tami Doty; *Born:* March 13, 1976, Ukiah, CA; *Parents:* Dan Doty, Phyllis Doty; *Education:* Pomolita Junior High School; *Occupation:* Student; *Memberships:* Pomolita Marching Concert Band; Hopland 4-H Club; *Honors:* Citizenship Award; *Other writings:* Written various poems; *Personal note:* I hope in the near future, we will all be living in an honest and drug free world; *Address:* Hopland, CA.

DOUGHERTY, RAYMOND
Born: April 21, 1943, Hammonton, NJ; *Parents:* Raymond Dougherty Sr., Mary Dougherty; *Spouse:* Joseph Dougherty, April 4, 1970; *Children:* Ray Anthony Dougherty; *Education:* St. Joseph's High School; *Memberships:* American Legion; *Honors:* Honorable Mention in World of Poetry, 1982; World of Poetry, Golden Poet's Award, 1989; *Other writings:* "Diaster", World of Poetry; *Personal note:* I find that their is much beauty in the poets of the past and yet poetry to me is like the soul of manking; *Address:* P.O. Box 382, Hammonton, NJ.

DOUGLAS, EMILY
Pen Name: Emy Sue; *Born:* April 1, 1977, Orriville, OH; *Parents:* Nancy Douglas, Robert Douglas; *Honors:* Merit in Scholarship; *Address:* 48-21 Street N.W., Massillon, OH.

DOWDING, LAGENA
Pen Name: Lagena Dowding; *Born:* March 23, 1975, Lincoln, NE; *Parents:* Lyle, Diana Dowding; *Education:* Palmyra High; *Occupation:* Student; *Memberships:* Happy-Go-Lucky; 4-H Club, Our Saviors Lutheran Church; Volley Ball; Basketball, Track, Band, Omnibus; *Honors:* Honor Band, Honor Roll; *Other writings:* Won Young Author; *Personal note:* I reflect my poetry on personal and general problems, suicide and outlook on life inspires me the most; I'd like to pursue a career in art and also illustrate some of my poetry with my art; *Address:* Bennet, NE.

DRAKE, ALI MARIE
Pen Name: "Drake, the Snake"; *Born:* March 2, 1971, Indianapolis, Indiana; *Parents:* Samuel I. Drake and Jessie M. Drake; *Education:* Graduated from Arlington High School; *Occupation:* Soldier in the United States Army; *Memberships:* Honor Roll, National Honor Society, French Club, Who's Who Among High School Students; *Honors:* National Merit, Varsity Volleyball 3-year Award, Honor Roll; *Other writings:* I received recognition for an Essay on Martin Luther King, Jr. I have had poems published in school literature; *Personal note:* I hope to one day become a veterinarian and graduate with honors from Purdue University; *Address:* 9534 Tower Lane, Indianapolis, IN.

DRAKE, ELEANOR LYNN
Born: May 31, 1967, Syracuse, NY; *Children:* Virginia Commonwealth University; *Education:* Student; *Occupation:* American Quarter Horse Assn; *Other writings:* Written many poems and short stories; *Personal note:* I own two horses that I trained myself, they have taught me that patience and kindness may not be the fastest road, but the best path to success; *Address:* Mechanicsville, VA.

DRENNAN, JOE WHEELER
Born: February 19, 1924, Seneca, SC; *Parents:*Joseph Wheeler, Rosa Lee Jordan; *Education:* Indian University, BS, MS; West Georgia College; *Occupation:* Counselor and Instructor; *Memberships:* NEA; Pi Kappa Phi, Omega Chi; *Honors:* Teacher of the Year, Star Teacher,2nd Prize Albany, GA; Writer's Guild Competition; *Other writings:* "Suck Egg Mule", "The Deer and Daschund", "The Naked Ear"; *Personal note:* Interested in Helping the Disadvantaged Youth; *Address:* Moultrie, GA.

DREW, JUDY L.
Born: September 10, 1946, Atlanta GA; *Parents:*John and Adelia Matthews; *Education:* BSN; *Occupation:* Nurse, Freelance Writer, Poet, Author; *Memberships:* Writers in Touch, Charter Member South Georgia College Literary Society; *Address:* 3661 Anneewakee Road, Douglasville, GA.

DUKESHIRE, LORI J.
Born: December 8, 1969, Silver Spring, MD; *Parents:*Patricia J. Dukeshire, Stephenson Robert I. Dukeshire; *Education:* Linganore High School; Frostburg State University; *Occupation:* Elementary Education Student; *Honors:* Alpha Sigma Tau, Dean's List; *Other writings:* Written numerous poems; *Personal note:* The poems that I write reflect my personal feelings, tragedies and triumphs; Writing poetry gives me the chance to understand the events in my life; *Address:* 3019 Sunflower Drive, Ijamsville, MD.

DUMERAUF, TAGA LIN
Pen Name: Taga Lin; *Born:* May 3, 1975, Davenport, IA; *Parents:*Terry Lee Dumerauf, Cynthia Straight Dumerauf; *Education:* North Scott Community Schools; *Honors:* Honor Roll Student;

DUNBAR, JENNIFER
Born: Febuary 13, 1975, Brantford, Canada; *Parents:*Arlene Dunbar, Keith Dunbar; *Education:* Grand Woodlands; Mohawk College; *Honors:* Honorble Mentions; *Other writings:* "A Dream", "Imagination", "Confusion"; *Personal note:* I won't forget the ones who inspired me the most in memory of Andy Mackenzie, George Janos and Jason Eisler; *Address:* 17 Allwood Street, Brantford, Canada.

DUPONT, ROBIN
Pen Name: The Bird; *Born:* September 7, 1966, Cambridge, MA; *Parents:*Joseph Dupont, Frances Dupont; *Education:* Stoughton High School; *Occupation:* Information Systems Personel; *Honors:* 2 years 1st place company softball team, also won MIP award for softball; *Other writings:* Written several other poems, I'm working on a manuscript in the hopes of being published; *Personal note:* I try to show people reality thru my words, I believe in telling what's in your heart, we need to believe in each other and love one another! *Address:* Stoughton, MA.

DUTCHY, DAWNA
Born: September 23, 1974; *Parents:*Dale and Terry Dutchy; *Education:* Glenpool High School; *Honors:* 1st place in singing contest; *Other writings:* National Essays; *Personal note:* I express my deep feelings for people I admire in my writings, I'm inspired greatly by romantic poem and poets; *Address:* Glenpool, OK.

EBLACAS, TERRIE
Born: September 3, 1975, Honolulu, HI; *Parents:*Teresita Eblacas, Raymond Eblacas, Sr.; *Education:* Waianae High School; *Occupations:* Student; *Memberships:* Waianae High School Band; Waianae Sacred Hearts Church Music and Youth Ministry; *Honors:* Principal's List; National Band Award Nominee; *Address:* 87-137 Pelanaki Street, Waianae, HI.

EDMONDSON, SONYA V.
Born: December 18, 1949, Trion, GA; *Parents:*Hillard and Frances Marbutt; *Spouse:* Neal Edmondson, May 5, 1972; *Children:* Darlene, Johnny, Stanley, Samanth, Pamela; *Education:* Chattooga High School; *Other writings:* Gospel Songs; *Address:* Rt 2, Box 357, Henagar, AL.

EDWARDS, JANICE A.
Born: 1954, Decatur, GA; *Parents:*Emma J. Anderson, Bennie L. Anderson; *Spouse:* Lawrence H. Edwards, 1979; *Children:* Lawrence II, Janelle; *Education:* AA; BS; MS; *Occupation:* Senior Disability Adjudicator, Teacher; *Honors:* Dean's List; Semi Finalist on a Number of Poems, Interviewing Skills Award, Outstanding Young Women of America; Who's Who of American Women; *Other writings:* Several poems published in other anthologies; *Personal note:* Writing poetry about the Lord comes easy for me because He is my light; *Address:* Decatur, GA.

EKLUND, COLLEEN
Born: November 11, 1974, Emporia, KS; *Parents:*Becky and Rocky Eklund; *Education:* Emporia High School; *Honors:* Academic Awards; *Address:* 3720 SW 29th Street, Topeka, KS.

ELLEDGE, ELLIS HUGH
Pen Name: E. Hugh Elledge; *Born:* August 6, 1950, Nashville, TN; *Parents:*Dorothy Jean Elledge, Ellis H. Elledge Sr; *Spouse:* Julia; January 27, 1979; *Education:* Middle Tennessee State University; *Occupation:* Furniture Maker, Carver; *Memberships:* Sierra Club, National Geographical Society, Audubon Society, Greenpeace, Wildernesss Society; *Other writings:* Various Political Essays, Satirical Short Stories, Numerous Poems and Songs; *Personal note:* We live in a time when success and aggression over shadows ethics andmorality, the poet remains the mirror for society to see itself as it really is; *Address:* 685 Kittrell Road, Franklin, TN.

ELMS, MICHELE
Born: February 2, 1975, Boston, MA; *Parents:*Cynthgia Elms, Frank Elms; *Education:* Holliston High School; *Occupation:* Student; *Memberships:* Trevor's Campaign for the Homeless, Girl Scouts, Town Soccer Association; *Other writings:* Many poems such as: "Dieing", "Thanks", "Friend", "Thank You", "Mom"; *Personal note:* I write about things that are effecting me at that specific time, writing poems helps me sort out my feelings; *Address:* 167 Jerrold Street, Holliston, MA.

ELSEN, JULIE LYNN
Pen Name: Julie Lynn Elsen; *Born:* April 17, 1978, Fort Pierce, FL; *Parents:*Robert Dean Elsen, Cynthia Camp Elsen; *Education:* Garden City Elementary School; *Occupation:* Student; *Memberships:* Garden Club, Safety Patrol, Newspaper Committee at Garden City Elementary; *Honors:* Principals Honor Roll, Outstanding Student Coordinator Student Coordinator for United Way, 1st Runner Up in Miss St. Lucie County Pageant; *Other writings:* Articles for Garden City Nightly News; *Personal note:* My poetry comes from deep feelings within me; *Address:* 2721 South 35th Street, Ft. Pierce, FL.

ENBOR, DANIELLE
Born: March 14, 1975, San Bernadino, CA; *Parents:*Doug, Cindy; *Education:* Rim of the World High School; *Occupation:* Student; *Other writings:* Love is a rose so tender and true but nobody knows of my love for you, I hold it inside so one day you will see all the love I had deep inside of me; *Personal note:* If you were a tear in my eye, I would never cry for fear of losing you; *Address:* 286 Hwy 138, Crestline, CA.

ENERSON, HEIDI R.
Pen Name: Deidre A. Siemons; *Born:* April 24, 1974, Rockford, IL; *Parents:*Barbara Enerson, Gordon Enerson Sr; *Education:* Middleton High School; *Occupation:* Student; *Memberships:* Yearbook Staff, Literary Magazine; *Honors:* Certification of Merit, Yahara River Writing Contest; *Other writings:* Writes column in two local newspapers, several articles for social services, another poem published in a different book; *Personal note:* Even in grade school I knew what I wanted to be; I'm working toward my goal to be a successful writer; *Address:* Cross Plains, WI.

ENRIGHT, JENNIFER M.
Pen Name: Jenny; *Born:* January 3, 1972, Duarte, CA; *Parents:*Marian L. Enright, Lee Osbourne Enright; *Occupation:* Student; *Honors:* First Miss Princess, 1989; *Other writings:* I have many various types of poetry in which a few were published in school newspaper; *Personal note:* Influenced by everyday life allows me to express feelings and thought in poetry; *Address:* 1020 Bradbourne #7, Duarte, CA.

ESCOFFIER, AIMEE
Pen Name: Yvo; *Born:* November 19, 1974, Glen Cove, NY; *Parents:*Deindle Escoffier, Edward Escoffier; *Education:* Our Lady of Mercy Academy; *Honors:* Winner of Numerous Drawing and Writing Contests; *Other writings:* "URU", "Friendship", "Nightmares", "Death", "Ending Relations", "Love", Confusion",. "Sucide"; *Personal note:* In order to overcome it, you must grow from it first; *Address:* Locust Valley, NY.

ESTES, JEANNA
Born: February 3, 1975; *Parents:*John T. Estes, Carol O. Estes; *Education:* Athens Drive High School; *Occupation:* Student; *Memberships:* First Baptist Church; *Other writings:* "Forbidden Love", "A Nature Call", "My Everything", "True Love"; *Personal note:* Love makes the world go around, each person should search and find a little love to share; *Address:* 5220 Leiden Lane, Raleigh, NC.

EVANS, DREXIL R.
Pen Name: Drex; *Born:* January 26, 1928, Hackleburg, AL; *Parents:*J.M. Evans and Della Evans; *Other writings:* Wrote the Holy Bible Song Lyrics, Manuscripts, Testimonials; *Personal note:* I am greatly influenced ny the inspirational words of God; *Address:* Fairdealing, MO.

EVANS, JENNIFER LEA
Born: November 23, 1974, Fairfax, VA; *Parents:*Jesse and Carol Evans; *Occupation:* Student; *Honors:* Presidential Academic Fitness Award; *Address:* Sterling, VA.

EVANS, SARAH
Pen Name: Rosanne St. Patrick; *Born:* December 28, 1974, George Air Force, CA; *Parents:*Dennis and Brenda Evans; *Other writings:* Unpublished Fiction Novel;

EVERINGTON, KAREN L.
Pen Name: Alexandria Jewel; *Born:* November 5, 1974, New Bern, NC; *Parents:*Janice P. Everington, Alfred L. Everington, Sr; *Occupation:* Student; *Honors:* Southeast Regional Education Center, Student Council Representative; *Other writings:* Several others poems, some published in school newspaper; *Personal note:* My goal is to write from the heart and soul of what I really believe in, I was greatly influenced by Edgar Allen Poe, and also my eight grade teacher, Cole Jones; *Address:* Beaufort, NC.

EVERSOLL, SAMANTHA
Pen Name: Sam Eversoll; *Born:* October 18, 1976, Little Rock, AR; *Parents:*Mr and Mrs Troy Eversoll; *Education:* Highland Schools; *Occupation:* Student; *Memberships:* Highland Junior Band; *Honors:* Most Outstanding Woodwind Player 1988, 1989; Metals for Achieving the Highest Honors at Solo and Ensemble; *Other writings:* "Christmas", "Dreamin" published in the local newspaper; *Personal note:* I try to make people happy with my writing; *Address:* RT 1, Box 290, Ash Flat, AR.

FARONII, RELIINA
Pen Name: Rae; *Born:* August 27, 1978; *Education:* Helion Hall School; *Memberships:* 4-H Club, Liberty Gymnastics; *Other writings:* I have been creating poetry since the age of three;This is my first time published; *Personal note:* Poetry is an inspirational from the heart put on paper to be shared with others; *Address:* Monticello, NY.

FERGUSON, DESIREEN U.
Pen Name: Dez Ferguson; *Parents:* Mary and Cie Ferguson; *Honors:* Recipient of numerous awards; *Address:* P.O Box 2101, Oxnard, CA.

FERRIER, GAIL
Born: December 3, 1961, Lowell, MA; *Parents:*Arthur and Elizabeth Ferrier; *Spouse:* Michael Hamrick; *Education:* Lowell High; Actors Workshop; Santa Rosa Junior College, S.R. CA; *Occupation:* Administrative Assistant; Proofreader; *Memberships:* Mendocino Area Park Assn; *Other writings:* Poetry published in National Anthology other than this one; *Personal note:* I write to express the emotions struggling inside of me, and hope that others can relate to those emotions and derive some good from my expression of them; *Address:* Petaluma, CA.

FEWKES, CLARA E.
Born: January 6, 1901; *Parents:*James H. Enden, Anna J. Hagen; *Spouse:* William Fewkes, 1974; *Children:* Nada LaVoie, Donal Brock; *Occupation:* Homemaker; *Memberships:* HEO Club, TVIA Montana Board of History, OES, Eureka Quilters; *Honors:* 3 Community Service Awards; *Other writings:* Co-author of the book *The Story of the Tobacco Plains County*; and Several Magazine Articles; *Personal note:* Let Nothing You Dismay!; *Address:* Rexford, MT.

FISHER, JENNIFER NICOLE
Born: September 18, 1974; *Parents:* Donna M. Fisher, John A. Fisher; *Occupation:* Student; *Other writings:* Poem published in school newspaper; *Personal note:* My parents, family and surroundings inspire me, I have a very loving family, I have written many poems that reflect how I feel; *Address:* Springfield, IL.

FITTRY, CHARITY
Born: December 23, 1973; *Parents:* Sherry Fittry, James Fittry Sr; *Occupation:* Student; *Memberships:* HOSA, WIBC; *Honors:* Honor Role; Student of the Quarter; *Other writings:* "Darkness", "Defeat"; Wondering Love"; "Wondering Body"; "Love is Rain"; *Personal note:* All my poems have some sort of meaning to them, for instance darkness and defeat is about my trying to kill myself; *Address:* 29 South High Street, Apt #1, Newville, PA.

FITZPATRICK, WINNIE E.
Born: October 26, 1926, Atlantic City, NJ; *Parents:* John and Catherine Nolen; *Spouse:* James P. Fitzpatrick, September 23, 1950; *Education:* Josephine, James, Martin; *Occupation:* Retired Santa Rosa City Employee; *Memberships:* National League of American Pen Women, California State Poetry Society, California Federation of Chapparral Poets, California Redwood Writers; *Honors:* Has received 322 Awards for Poetry; One Award for Photography; *Personal note:* If people can forget their own troubles while reading my work then I will have been successful writer; *Address:* Kenwood, CA.

FLAMER, NICOLE
Born: Maqy 17, 1977, West Chester, PA; *Parents:* Russell Flamer, Linda Flamer; *Occupation:* Student; *Personal note:* Keep your dreams because dreams do come true; *Address:* Coatesville, PA.

FLEMING, MARY ELLEN
Pen Name: April Showers; *Born:* April 3, 1956, Cleveland, OH; *Parents:* Charles and Janet Fleming; *Spouse:* Michael; April 28, 1978; *Children:* Bryan Michael; *Education:* Cuyahoga Community College, Associate of Arts Degree; University of Nevada, Reno NE; *Occupation:* Nurse; *Memberships:* Southwest Bible Church; Diabetes Assn of Greater Cleveland; *Honors:* Won a 1989 Editor's Choice Award for a poem published in *Days of Future's Past*; Also won the spelling contest; *Other writings:* Currently writing two books; *Personal note:* I attribute my writing talents to all of the nuns that taught me in grade school and encourage me to do well in english class; I also thank all of the people in my life that I met for all of my life's experiences; *Address:* 3788 W. 22nd Place Down, Cleveland, OH.

FLORES, LILLIAN
Pen Name: Lilly; *Born:* June 27, 1972, Brooklyn, NY; *Parents:* Iris Colon; *Education:* Senior at Eastern District High School; *Occupation:* Parttime Office Worker; *Memberships:* Tennis Team, Frisbee Club, Job Training Program; *Honors:* Who's who Among American High School Students, Arista Honors, French Achievement; *Other writings:* Several Poems published in school literary magazine and short stories; *Personal note:* My writing reflect what I feel at the moment, I can't ever predict what my poems will be about; therefore, writing is interesting; *Address:* Brooklyn, NY.

FOLEY, EILEEN KATHERINE
Born: November 15, 1974, Manhattan, NY; *Parents:* Eileen Jenks, Tom Foley, Gregory Jenks, Jill Foley; *Honors:* First Runner Up in New York Hemisphere Beauty Pageant; *Other writings:* "In Your Heart", *Garden of Shadow*; *Personal note:* I consider myself very lucky to be so young and still have the ability to write and I encourage other people my age to follow their dreams; *Address:* Danbury, CT.

FOLEY, HEATHER
Born: May 20, 1973; Westminster, CO; *Parents:* Laura Jackson, Sgeve Foley; *Education:* Westy High School; *Memberships:* National Forensic League; *Honors:* I have received superior and excellent awards in forensic; *Other writings:* I have written other poems and short stories, all unpublished; *Personal note:* Poetry is a reflection of the heat; *Address:* 7830 Yates, Westminster, CO.

FONTANO, LYNNE
Born: October 30, 1974; Bayshore, NY; *Parents:* Robert Fontano, Nadene Fontano; *Education:* East Islip High School; *Occupation:* Student; *Address:* Islip Terrace, NY.

FORD, PETER A.
Born: April 16, 1966, Dermott, AR. *Parents:* Johnnie F. Blackman, Peter A. Ford, Jr; *Education:* McGehee High School; *Occupation:* Avionics Technician; *Memberships:* NCOA; *Honors:* One Army Commendation; Five Army Achievements; One Good Conduct; and AIr Assault Wings; *Other writings:* Currently writing TV scripts for Ocranic Cable HI to be aired in the near future, working on writing script for movies and soundtrack, looking for production company; *Personal note:* Before a man correct the faults of another first he should correct the faults of himself; *Address:* Schofield Barricks, HI.

FOSSUM, DARLA
Born: September 13, 1974, Sparta, WI; *Parents:* Richard Fossum, Violet Fossum; *Education:* Independence High School; *Occupation:* Student; *Memberships:* FFA, Swing Choir; *Honors:* National Honor Society; Dairyland Honors Choirs, FFA Chapter Degree, Awana Church Club Award; *Other writings:* Poems for Nursing Home Activities, Poem in School Newsletter; *Personal note:* I enjoy writing about the closeness of my family and friends, who have greatly influenced my life and poems; *Address:* Independence, WI.

FOSTER, LEE, STEPHANIE
Pen Name: Stephanie Lee Foster; *Born:* October 23, 1974, Ironton, OH; *Parents:* John and Welhelmena Foster; *Occupation:* Student; *Address:* Ironton, OH.

FRANK, SARAH E.
Pen Name: Sarah E. Frank; *Born:* September 2, 1973, Portage WI; *Parents:* JoAnn, Marlin, Groskreutz, Ronald Frank; *Education:* Westfield High School; *Occupation:* Student; *Memberships:* Active in Jazz Choir and Students Against Driving Drunk; *Other writings:* Has written many poems, none other published at this point; *Personal note:* Love helping others, wants to go into the field of counseling after high school; *Address:* Westfield, WI.

FRANKLIN, PIERCE KIE
Pen Name: Franklin Kie Pierce; *Born:* May 23, 1938, Peoria, IL; *Parents:* Jane and George Pierce; *Children:* Jane, Ericks, Sarah; *Education:* High School; *Occupation:* Police Officer; *Memberships:* Police Benevolent Assn; Professional Law Enforcement Assn; *Other writings:* Has written numerous poems; *Personal note:* Our country is based on individual freedoms of man; we must not forget the price we have paid for these freedoms, God bless America; *Address:* 12420 SW 11 Court, Davie, FL.

FREDERICK, DONNA
Pen Name: Donna Sue; *Born:* May 20, 1971, Muncie, IN; *Parents:* William A Frederick, Sandra L. Frederick; *Education:* Muncie Southside High School; Ball State University; *Occupation:* Lifeguard; *Other writings:* High school yearbook articles, several unpublished poems; *Personal note:* Dreams can only be reached through diligence, patience, understanding, hard work, and trust in God; *Address:* Muncie, IN.

FRENCH, PRUE
Born: March 29, 1938, Seattle, WA; *Children:* Deborah, Jennifer, Todd, Candace, Jon; *Education:* Lewis and Clark High School; University of Idaho, BS; *Occupation:* Teacher, *Memberships:* NCTE, BPW, OES; *Honors:* Delta Delta Delta; Paprys Creative Writers Award; *Other writings:* Many poems and short stories; *Personal note:* Some people write with words, I write with my heart, for without heart behind the words, the words have a shallow meaning and are of little worth; *Address:* P.O. Box 376, Potlatch, ID.

FREW, CAROLE J.
Occupation: Editor/Publisher of Feelings Poetry Magazine; *Other writings:* Creator and Writer of the annual Easton Christmas book and has written two chapter books, *Letters to a Lost Love*, 1976 and *Letters*, 1984; Freelance articles have appeared in various magazines such as *Single Parent Magazine*, *Singles Alive!* and *Editor's Digest*; Poetry has appeared in numerous journals, magazines and anthologies; Currently working on a third chap book and a handbook for singles titled *Being Single, Being Happy: Not a Contradiction in Terms*; *Personal note:* The philosophy of *Feelings* is to provide a publishing experience for the first-time and amateur poet. Any poetry when written from the heart is of itself artistry; *Address:* P.O. Box 390, Whitehall, PA.

FRISK, CARRIE
Pen Name: Haily Mertz; *Born:* March 14, 1976; Gravenburst Ontario Canada; *Parents:* Alec and Barb Frisk; *Education:* Joseph Gould School; *Occupation:* Student; *Memberships:* Uxbridge Swim Club, Uxbridge Swim Team; *Personal note:* Discrimination: I hope that someday people will learn that everyone and everything is equal and should no longer be segregated by an invisible barrier; *Address:* General Deliver, Sandford Ontario, Canada.

FULLARD, YOLANDA
Born: April 3, 1972, Wilmington, NC; *Parents:* Vivian Fullard; *Occupation:* Student; *Memberships:* Mount Calvary Baptist Church; *Honors:* Miss WIlliston; *Other writings:* Other poems submitted in the literary club and literary magazine of New Hanover High; *Personal note:* My writing reflect my personal thoughts and feelings towards my personal life; *Address:* Wilmington, NC.

FULTON, JODY
Born: October 31, 1973; Sewickley, PA; *Parents:* Judy and Dave Fulton; *Education:* Humble High School; *Occupation:* Student; *Memberships:* St. Mary's Catholic Church; *Personal note:* Go forward looking for the good in people, not the bad, love one another and make a positive difference in our world! *Address:* 19515 Hurst Wood, Dr. Humble, TX.

FURNE, ALANNA DENISE
Pen Name: Al, Alf, Plu, A-lane; *Born:* March 5, 1974, Atlantic, Iowa; *Parents:* Dennis Furne, Elaine Furne; *Education:* Atlantic High School; *Occupation:* Student; *Memberships:* Maurice's Fashion Board; *Honors:* Honor Roll for four quarters; *Personal note:* I try to relate to people in fantasy and reality, I like to feel that all people can understand and appreciate my writings;

FUTSCHER, HEATHER
Pen Name: Jasmine Jericho; *Born:* March 21, 1975, Redding, California; *Education:* Freshman at Lake Brantley High School; *Memberships:* Drama Club, Spanish Club at LBHS; *Honors:* National Junior Honor Society, honor roll, honors classes, trophy in English; *Other writings:* Various poems and short stories, none published; currently working on a book; *Personal note:* I would like to thank my parents and relatives for their encouragement, my friends for standing by me, and my Romeo for the inspiration; *Address:* Altamonte Springs, FL.

GALOZO, PETE G.
Pen Name: Pete; *Born:* August 30, 1917, Candon, Illocos Sur, Philippines; *Parents:* Florentino Galozo, Pia Garunta Galozo; *Spouse:* Petronila Pagaduan Galozo, January 25, 1947; *Education:* Carmencita, Rudy, Rogelio, Danilo, Angelito, Evelyn, Jocelyn; *Occupation:* Central Mindanao College; *Memberships:* American Legion, AARP, Songwriters Club of America, Sarsota, Florida; Five Star Music Master; *Honors:* 2nd Lt Presidential Award in Recognition of Military Services during the World War II; *Other writings:* Several writings published; *Personal note:* I always strive to be honest and truthful to work for quality and perfection to beginning to finish to see the result of the performance; *Address:* Jersey City, NJ.

GAMM, MARILYN
Born: July 27, 1961, Louisiana, Missouri; *Parents:*-Wayne, Georgia Gamm; *Education:* Bowling Green High School; William Woods College; *Occupation:* Radio News/Operations Director; *Memberships:* Providence-Concord Presbyterian Church, Raintree Theatre Guild, Raintree Arts Council, Pike County Sheltered Workshop Board; *Honors:* Bowling Green Business and Professional Women Club's Young Careerist, Alpha Psi Omega, Dean's List; *Other writings:* Several Poems Published in Anthologies and Two Church Christmas Pageants; *Personal note:* Poetry, like other writing forms is a way not only to express myself but also to comment on the world in which we live, thereby effecting change; *Address:* Bowling Green, MO.

GARDNER, BONNIE L.
Born: March 22, 1977, Jackson, MI; *Parents:* Gene L. Gardner, Sallianne Gardner; *Education:* Williams Elementary School; Jonesville Jr. High School; *Occupation:* Student; *Memberships:* Girl Scouts of America, School Volley Ball Team; *Honors:* State Board of Education Certificate of Recognition; Susan Vaughn School of Dance Certificate, Award for Tap and Jazz, Williams Elementary School Good Citizen Award; *Other writings:* Poems published in local newspaper; *Personal note:* I would like to be a famous poet or write for Hallmark, American Greeting Company or Gibson Card Company; I like to write about people and feelings with the world around me; *Address:* 5200 Mosherville Road, Jonesville, MI.

GARDNER, KELLY

Pen Name: The Kid; *Born:* August 27, 1971; *Education:* Covina High School; Mount San Antonio College; *Occupation:* Telemarketing, Eric Edwards Photography Studios; *Memberships:* United Cerebral Palsy, Alcyonians Service Club; *Honors:* Most Valuable Player for Junior Varsity Badminton and Tennis, Dean's Honor Roll; *Other writings:* Poems published in Quill Books; *Personal note:* Poetry is important in my life because it allows me to show an expression of myself that otherwise, no one would ever see; *Address:* West Covina, CA.

GARVEY, TAMMI S.

Pen Name: Tammi G; *Born:* July 6, 1979, Albany, GA; *Parents:*Michael Garvey; *Memberships:* World Wildlife Fund; *Honors:* Montgomery Counts Superintendent Award; *Personal note:* I'd like to become both a jockey and an author; *Address:* 9629 Shadow Oak Drive, Gaithersburg, MD.

GERALIS, JOSEPH CHARLES

Pen Name: Joe; *Born:* May 8, 1950, Atlantic City, NJ; *Parents:*Mr. and Mrs. James Geralis; *Education:* Associate Degree in Fire Technology; Certificate for Medical Technician, CPR Instructor; *Occupation:* Security Officer at Harrah's Casino; *Memberships:* American Red Cross; *Other writings:* Newspaper articles in the Atlantic City Press, other poems in American Poetry Assn; The Poetry Center from California, New York Poetry Anthology; *Personal note:* Poetry is an expression of one's most inner thoughts and secrets of their life, and the character of their destiny; *Address:* 1 Queen Street, McKee City, NJ.

GEYER, RUTH ANN

Born: September 14, 1973, Bridgeport, CT; *Parents:*-Laura and Edward Geyer; *Education:* Moorestown Friends School; *Occupation:* Student; *Memberships:* Student Council, Religious Life Committee, American Fields Society, Spanish Club; *Personal note:* Dedicated to Steve T. and Janey K. for his memory and her support, and of course, Mom, Dad and Blaine; *Address:* 205 Independence Blvd, Lawnside, NY.

GHOSTON, ERMA

Born: Coahoma, MS; *Parents:*Willis Ghoston, Willie Ghoston; *Education:* Booker T. Washington High School; *Occupation:* Retired Secretary; *Memberships:* Liberty Baptist Church Women's Guild; Oak Grove Baptist Church Training and Development Organization; Memphis Tennessee Poetry Society, AARP, NAACP; *Honors:* Award of Merit for Poem Entitled "Ship Wrecked On a Lonely Island"; Golden Award, 1989; Golden Award Trophy, 1989; *Other writings:* Have had numerous poems published; *Personal note:* Writing is rewarding and relaxing, it is a hobby I have pursued since the age of 12, I write whenever God gives me something to write about no matter where I am or what I'm doing. I strive to paint pictures in words so that others may understand and enjoy what I write about; *Address:* 1803 Bismark Street, Memphis, TN.

GIBSON, CAROLYN PATRICIA

Born: February 18, 1942, Washington, DC; *Parents:*-Nannie Payne, Robert Payne; *Spouse:* Sylvester Gibson, November 26, 1970; *Children:* Nathan, Robert, Gregory; *Education:* Eastern High School; Howard University; *Occupation:* Staff Assistant, U.S. House of Representatives; *Memberships:* Member of the Fifth District Police Department Advisory Council and Kingman Park Civic Assn; *Other writings:* Several Letters to the Editor of the Washington Post Regarding Community Issues; Poems Published in Community Newsletters; *Personal note:* I'm a community activist whose prespective focuses on influencing modern critical thought and opinion; *Address:* Washington, DC.

GILBERT, JACK ALFRED

Pen Name: Jack Alfred Gilbert; *Born:* July 28, 1954, Hollywood,CA; *Parents:*Robert Gilbert, Bea Gilbert; *Education:* Fairfax High School; University of Southern California; *Occupation:* Customer Service; *Memberships:* European Health Club; Bowling League, Active in Political Campaign; *Other writings:* Submitted a true story to Filways, now Orion in 1983; *Personal note:* I write poetry from my heart with feelings, I copy nobody and at all times speak forwardly, whether liked or not, if you have a goal be persistent in life and you will obtain your goal; *Address:* 385 East 2nd Street Apt #312, Reno, NV.

GILBERT, RENEE

Born: February 24, 1974; *Parents:*Carol Gilbert, Walter Gilbert; *Education:* North Star High School; *Memberships:* Band, Chorus, Constellations, All County Band, All County Chorus; *Personal note:* If you get a chance to do something honorable do it, for you might not ever get that chance again; *Address:* 959 Boswell Heights, Boswell, PA.

GINN, LEROY

Pen Name: Ginn; *Born:* May 23, 1972, Baltimore, MD; *Parents:*Louise Ginn, Roy Ginn; *Occupation:* Student; *Memberships:* AP English Club; *Honors:* Golden Poetry Award; *Other writings:* "If Time Would Stop", "The Old Man", "Time With Christ", "Love", "Selfish", "So Called Friends"; *Personal note:* If it were not for the Lord Jesus Christ, I would not be able to do what I have done; *Address:* 314 Sherwood Street, Kingstree, SC.

GIZZO, DEBBIE

Born: January 2, 1967; *Parents:*Mary Gizzo, Frank Gizzo; *Education:* Berner High School; *Occupation:* Receptionist; *Address:* New York, NY.

GLADSON, NANCY CROCKETT

Born: March 27, 1948, Pittsburg, KS; *Parents:*James Nelson Crockett, Mabel Magee Crockett; *Spouse:* Robert J. Gladson, October 3, 1970; *Children:* Elizabeth Anne, Dina Gayle; *Education:* Liberal High School; PSU, Pittsburg KS; *Honors:* Golden Poet Award; *Other writings: ation:* Student; *Memberships:* First Christian Church; Published in the *World Treasury of Great Poems*; *Personal note:* Create golden memories for these are the true treasures of life; *Address:* 610 Village Drive, Girard, KS.

GLESMANN, AMANDA

Born: March 3, 1978, Walnut Creek, CA; *Parents:*Linda Butler, Dan Glesmann; *Education:* Federal Terrace Elementary School; *Other writings:* An Indian Legend Published in the Vallejo Times Herald, Five Poems Published in the American Poetry Association Anthology; *Personal note:* I am eleven years old and in the sixth grade, my hobbies are writing short stories and poems, someday I hope to become a professional writer; *Address:* Vallejo, CA.

GODDARD, HAZEL FIRTH

Born: Jordan Ferry, Nova Scotia; *Parents:*Laura and Gustavus Firth; *Spouse:* Roland Bernard Goddard; *Occupation:* Retired School Teacher and Federal Government Public Service; *Memberships:* Canadian Authors Assn; N.S. Poetry Society, Kentucky State Poetry Society; *Honors:* 3rd Place Poetry Writer's Digest in 1988, 7th in 1987, 65th in 1989; *Other writings:* Published a non-fiction book *My Loyalist Years* in 1988; sold out except a dozen copies, *Personal note:* One's talent has been bestowed as a sacred trust, scatter its seed and be rewarded with its spiritually rich harvest; *Address:* #404-40 Rose Street, Dartmouth, Nova Scotia, Canada.

GODFREY, MICHELLE MARIE

Born: August 30, 1971; Winchester, VA; *Parents:*Stephanie Rene Godfrey; *Education:* James Wood High School; *Occupation:* Student; *Memberships:* Basketball, Ski Club, Varsity Club, Swimming Team, Youth groups; *Honors:* Basketball, Swimming and Cross Country; *Other writings:* Only poems for school papers; *Personal note:* Always believe in what you're doing and never give up then, you may survive; *Address:* Winchester, VA.

GOODWIN, MATTHEW D.

Born: June 16, 1972, Cincinnati, OH; *Parents:*Lynn and Penney Goodwin; *Education:* Ohio State University; *Occupation:* Student;

GOON, GINA MICHELLE

Born: November 20, 1974, New York, NY; *Parents:*Jeffrey and Jane Goon; *Education:* Public School 124; Yung Wing, Robert Wagner Jr High School; Stuyvesant High School; *Occupation:* Student; *Honors:* 1988 Take Pride In New York Photo Contest, 2nd Place, 1987 Honorable Mention in the Scholastic Writing Awards Contest; *Other writings:* Numerous poems published in other anthologies, yearbook poet and writer; *Personal note:* Never let anyone tell you that you can't pursue your dreams because of your age, we are the future who will prove to past generations that we are competent;

GRAINGER, GAYLE DUNCAN

Pen Name: Gayle Grainger; *Born:* February 17, 1951, Loris, SC; *Parents:*Annie Jane, Lee Duncan; *Spouse:* Donovon Grainger, Richard Donovon Grainer; *Children:* Richard; *Education:* Tabor City High School; Finklea Career Center; *Occupation:* Service Advisor, Bell Pontiac; *Memberships:* President of Parent Assn, JROTC at Green Sea Floyds High School; *Other writings:* Poems published in local newspaper and church newsletter I have written over 70 poems in two years; *Personal note:* My poems reflect my inner feelings, I hope when they are read, they can help someone find a peace of mind like I do when I write them; *Address:* Rt 1 Box 275, Loris, SC.

GRAY, LEAH

Pen Name: LETC Gray; *Born:* April 17, 1931, Flushing, NY; *Parents:*John B. Leah, Helen V. Cole; *Spouse:* W. Gray; 1952; *Children:* June R. Evans; *Occupation:* Registered Cardiology Technologist; *Memberships:* Deliverance Tabernacle Nurses Aide, National Society for Cardiovascular/ Pulmonary Technology Inc., American Red Cross; *Honors:* Valedictorian; 2nd Place in National Pepsi Cola Spelling Contest; *Other writings:* Compiling books of poems for copyright; *Personal note:* Every child should read King James version of proverbs, to direction, careful not to cut rungs on the upward ladder of life, top can be shakey, rungs may be needed on the way back down, be yourself, act your age; *Address:* Newark, NJ.

GREEN, MARTI

Born: September 13, 1971, Eureka, California; *Parents:*-George Green and Marjorie Peterson; *Education:* Public high school until 1987, 1987-89 Christian Boarding School in Oregon, currently attend college; *Occupation:* Full-time student, part-time worker with disabled; *Memberships:* Grace Chapel Church in Fortuna, California; *Honors:* Award for Caligraphy work in 1986; *Other writings:* Small peoms; *Personal note:* In my poems I hope to show the love of God and the light He has reflected into my life; *Address:* 162 Page Way, Fortuna, CA.

GREENING, JENNIFER

Born: October 16, 1973, Hartford, CT; *Parents:*Bruce H. Greening, Mary N. Greening; *Education:* Duffy Elementary School; William H. Hall High School; *Occupation:* Student; *Honors:* Editor's Choice Award; *Other writings:* Love to write poetry and short stories; *Personal note:* When writing, look around you and there will be many things to inspire you; *Address:* West Harford, CT.

GRENIER, TERRY L.

Born: March 30, 1972, Westerly, RI; *Parents:*Keith L. Grenier, Debra E. Grenier; *Education:* Charino High School; *Other writings:* Many other unpublished poems that I hope someday will be published; *Personal note:* My poetry is my biggest hobby. I find it an exhilarating way of opening my mind to an inspiring world; *Address:* 15 Prospect Square, Wyoming, RI.

GRIDER, MICHELLE

Pen Name: Michelle Grider; *Born:* February 22, 1974, Springfield, MO; *Parents:*William Gene Grider, Judy A. Grider; *Education:* Marian C. Early School; *Occupation:* Student; *Memberships:* Speech Club, Music Club, FBLA, FHA; *Honors:* Won Numerous Poetry Awards; *Other writings:* Poems published in local newspaper; *Personal note:* I always make my writing come from the heart and mind and no one can take it away from you; *Address:* P.O. Box 512, Bolivar, MO.

GRIFFITH, TALLEY

Born: October 13, 1972, Stuart, Virginia; *Parents:*Bruce and Cindy Griffith; *Education:* Patrick County High School; *Occupation:* Student; *Memberships:* Spanish Club, 4-H, Student Government Association, Boy Scouts, Stuart United Methodist Church; *Honors:* District Forensics Winner, 4-H All Star, Virginia Boy's State, Presidential Classroom, 4-H State Award; *Other writings:* High school literary magazine; *Personal note:* "Man cannot see what he feels, but man can always see why he feels"; *Address:* Stuart, VA.

GROSS, DENISE D.

Born: July 27, 1975; *Parents:*Dennis H. Gross, Robin L. Gross; *Education:* Jackson Center High School; *Occupation:* Waitress; *Personal note:* I would like for peace to win at war; *Address:* Jackson Center, OH.

GUMM, ERICA

Born: November 6, 1971, Colfax, Wa; *Parents:*Lon & Deniese Ottosen; *Education:* Tekoa High School; *Memberships:* Explorer's Program; *Honors:* 1st Place in the state for 4th grade through 8th grade in a national VFW essay; *Personal note:* I write my poems from my heart mostly on what I am feeling at that moment; my boyfriend, Mike, is the inspiration for all of my poetry; *Address:* 18517 Dunn Road, Fairfield, WA.

HAGEN, PAIGE MOANA

Born: March 18, 1971, Chippewa Falls, WI; *Parents:*-Ronald Hagen, Christine Hagen; *Spouse:* Herbert

Swope; *Children:*Hapaki Ronald Swope; *Education:* Mason City High School; *Occupation:* Secretary, Management Technical Services; *Honors:* Track and Field Awards, Softball Trophies; *Other writings:* Several poems written, but never went public until now; *Personal note:* Poems express my deepest emotions when words just aren't enough; *Address:* Honolulu, HI.

HALL, CRYS

Born: August 15, 1974, Manchester, MO; *Parents:*-Linda Harris, Jeff Hall; *Education:* Pacific High School; *Memberships:* Queen's Own, Drama Club, French Club; *Personal note:* I try to capture a feeling when I write and to create a visualization of that feeling, I just hope it comes through to others; *Address:* 8 Pacific Summit East, Villa Ridge, MO.

HALL, TAMMY

Pen Name: Eden Matthews; *Born:* March 20, 1975, Collins, MS; *Parents:*Allmon and Ruth Hall; *Education:* Mt Olive School; *Occupation:* Student; *Address:* P.O. Box 59, Mt. Olive, MS.

HALVERSON, JENNIFER

Born: June 17, 1975, Wichita KS; *Parents:*Leonard and Vicki Halverson; *Education:* Andover High School; *Memberships:* Fellowship of Christian Athletes; National Pigeon Association; *Honors:* Principal's Honor Roll; *Other writings:* Other Unpublished Poems and Short Stories; *Personal note:* Through my poetry I try to reflect my christian values, I believe that a man is only as good as the word he speaks; *Address:* Wichita, KS.

HAMILTON, BELVA DOBYNS

Born: February 24, 1930, Tulsa, OK; *Parents:*David Edger Doyyns, Grace Simpson Dobyns Jones; *Spouse:* Jack A. Hamilton; May 6, 1950; *Children:* Deborah, Paula, James; *Education:* Tubman High School, Hurst Business College; *Occupation:* Secretary, Freelance Writer; *Memberships:* Romance Writers of America, Georgia Romance Writers, Warren Baptist Church; *Other writings:* Poems currently accepted for publication: "Ride a Magic Pony", "Life Without Changes", "Gifts and the Giver", "Inside Out",
"Disguises"; in addition to several unpublished books; *Personal note:* A writer voluntarily reveals his innermost perceptions in print; and is awarded a silent glimpse of the person within himself; *Address:* 3211 Winding Wood Ct., Augusta, GA.

HANNEBAUM, SHEILA

Pen Name: Sheila; *Born:* September 24, 1974, Lawrenceburg, IN; *Parents:*Phil and Donna Hannebaum; *Education:* Bates High School; *Occupation:* Student; *Memberships:* New Kinds on the Block Fan Club, FHA, Drama Club; *Other writings:* Wrote several poems; *Personal note:* I write about my life or someone else's life or experiences, most of my poems are about my best friend, Wendy Howard; *Address:* Batesville, IN.

HANSEL, VICTORIA J.

Personal note: Jonquils and vervains...; *Address:* 355 North Street #A, Pullman, WA.

HARDIN, ANGEL LYNN

Born: September 7, 1971, Greenville, MI; *Parents:*Debra Welch, Fred Welch; Bob Hardin, Marilyn Hardin; *Education:* Belding High School; *Other writings:* One poem published; *Personal note:* Thank you to my friends and family for their love and support; *Address:* 603 Alderman, Belding, MI.

HARRIS, DANA L.

Born: February 18, 1972, Downey, ID; *Parents:*Wayne and Carolyn Harris; *Education:* Marsh Valley High School; *Occupation:* Student; *Memberships:* Performing Arts Club; Pep Band; *Address:* P.O. Box 298, McCammon, ID.

HARRIS, JENNIFER

Born: September 7, 1974, Cambridge, MD; *Parents:*-Donald & Barbara Harris; *Education:* Wicomico Senior High School; *Occupation:* Clerk at flower Shop; *Memberships:* Former Girl Scout; *Honors:* Honor Roll, Reading Awards, Softball Awards, Volunteer Awards; *Personal note:* I try to write poems about feelings and ideas that other people can relate to; *Address:* 424 Largo Terrace, Salisbury, MD.

HARRIS, JULIE

Born: April 18, 1976, Stoughton, MA; *Parents:*Kenneth Harris, Maryanne Harris; *Education:* Middleboro Memorial Junior High School; *Other writings:* I have written many other poems, but they have never been published; *Personal note:* In all my poems I write about past experiences, I think it's a great way to express yourself; *Address:* Middleboro, MA.

HARRIS, SHERRIE L.

Pen Name: Sherrie Van Dyke Harris; *Born:* December 21, 1938, Pekin, IL; *Parents:*Henry J. Van Dyke; Veda Thomas Van Dyke Cook; *Spouse:* Howard D. harris, May 24, 1958; *Children:* Thad Howard; Gail Elizabeth Christopher, Lynne Anne Hangartner; *Education:* Pekin Community High School; *Occupation:* Freelance Writer; *Honors:* Several Ribbons and a First Place Trophy for Area Oil Painting; *Other writings:* Presently engaged in finishing a book based on a true area murder; compiling a book of poetry, music composition; *Personal note:* During my oil painting years, I never thought I could enjoy anything more until I began writing, during my newspaper writing years, I never imagined becoming a poet, but creating poetry soon became a best friend of sorts, a personal therapy I had no intention of sharing with the world; *Address:* Pekin, IL.

HARRIS, STACY ANICE

Born: July 30, 1975, Columbus, GA; *Parents:*Wayne, Glenda Harris; *Education:* Tate High School; *Occupation:* Breeds and Shows Registered Quarter Horse; *Memberships:* Tate High School Equistrian Clubs; Diamond N 4-H Club; Ensley Baptist Church; *Honors:* Honor Society; Presidential Scholastic Achievement Award; *Other writings:* "The Last Ride" published in Western Horseman Magazine; *Personal note:* Many of my poems strive to express the great injustices man has committed against nature and the severity of the results of the acts for our future; *Address:* P.O. Box 387, Molino, FL.

HARRISON, EDGAR M.

Born: November 24, 1912, Avalon, Catalina Island, CA; *Parents:*Edgar M. Harrison, Florence Bates Harrison; *Spouse:* Donna Lee Harrison, November 1, 1947; *Children:* Kathleen, Gregory, Christopher; *Education:* Avalon High School; Long Beach Junior College, San Jose State College; *Occupation:* Shipmaster; *Memberships:* The Retired Officers Assn; *Honors:* World of Poetry Prizes; James T. Phelan Award; *Other writings:* *Tidepools*; *Personal note:* Hiker, biker, snorkeler, wilderness traveler; and doting grandpa of one boy and three girls; *Address:* P.O. Box 1332, Avalon, Catalina Island, CA.

HAUPT, CECILIA G.

Born: January 5, 1919, Los Angeles, CA. *Parents:*Josephine Jedofsky, Reinhard F. Guedemann, Jr; *Spouse:* William Dean Haupt, Jr., December 27, 1942; *Children:* Cecilia, William III, Maria Christine, Kevin, Teresa, Monica, Bridget; *Education:* Ramona Convent; Occidental College, Los Angeles CA; Laval University, Quebec Canada; *Occupation:* Retired Psychological Interviewer; *Memberships:* Catholic Press Council, Medial Communion Mass and Breakfast; Pacific Pioneer Broadcasters; Pasadena Crime Prevention, Women's Parish Council; SCRC; *Honors:* World of Poetry, Silver, Gold and Merit Awards; The National Library of Poetry, Merit Awards; *Other writings:* Written for Kathleen Lee Mendel Publications; Southern Poetry Assn; Sparrowgrass Poetry Forum; The Poetry Center; *Personal note:* Iattempttoincorporate into my writings the fantasies as well as sorrows of love,spiritualandhuman;myworkhasbeengreatly influencedbytoday'sliberal catholic things, also I have drawn heavily on life's experiences and travel; *Address:* 3300 Florecita Drive, Altadena, CA.

HAWKINS, DAVID M.

Pen Name: Cloudland Jim; *Born:* December 14, 1939, Trion GA; *Parents:*Virgil D. Hawkins; *Spouse:* Brenda S. Hawkins, August 4, 1959; *Children:* Janice, Stephen; *Education:* Summerville Elementary Grade School; Mt. Berry School for Boys; Tennessee Temple Bible School; *Occupation:* Auto Worker; *Memberships:* DAV, Commanders Club, PALS, Poem & Letter Society; *Honors:* World of Poetry Award of Merit and Golden Poet Award; *Other writings:* "Four Facts You Must Face", A Gospel Track; *Personal note:* If we could live life, as most poets portray: there would be no need for drugs today; *Address:* 1 Soutee, St. Peters, MO.

HEIDEL, AMY LORINE

Born: November 14, 1975; *Parents:*Donna and Danny Heidel; *Education:* Sonora High School; *Occupation:* Babysitting, Student; *Memberships:* Richardson's Family Fitness, Girl Scouts; *Honors:* Honor Roll, 1st Place, 1989; Patroitism Contest, 2-2nd Place Awards in 1988 Speech Festival; *Other writings:* Currently writing for school newspaper "The Wildcat"; *Personal note:* I try to make everything I write make someone stop and think; *Address:* P.O. Box 271, Groveland, CA.

HENDRIX, JENNIFER S.

Pen Name: Jeni Hendrix; *Born:* Orange, CA; *Parents:*-Roger Hendrix, Ginger Hendrix; *Education:* Ramona High School; *Other writings:* Written Several Other Poems; *Personal note:* My poem is about suicide; it was a very depressing time in my life, to all readers, suicide is not the answer; *Address:* Riverside, CA.

HENRY, BONNIE AILEEN

Born: 4 November 1936, Jackson's Hole, Wyoming; *Parents:*Edith Pearl Hodges, Joe Herman Spalding; *Spouse:* Dale Robert Henry, 5 November 1955; *Children:* Dale Lawton, Danny Lee; *Education:* Gunnison County High School; North Idaho College, Coeurd' Alene ID; *Occupation:* Student; *Memberships:* Coordinator of Shoshone County Idaha Oral History; Creative Writing Club; *Honors:* 1985 Honorable Mention in Poetry Contest; *Other writings:* Various Articles on Different Subjects for Local Newspapers; *Personal note:* To be truly free we must love and respect all living things, I try to reflect this in my writings; My writings are part of my growing process, a gift from God; *Address:* 121 Kellogg Avenue, Kellogg, ID.

HENSLEY, JACK

Pen Name: The Unknown Poet; *Born:* December 13, 1948; *Children:* Angela; *Other writings:* "Natural Beauty", *World of Poetry*; "Our Dad is Gone", *The Newport Plain Talk*; *Personal note:* I write to inspire all children to get a good education, so the world will be at peace forever; *Address:* Rt 14, Box 542F, Greenville, TN.

HICKMAN, LAQUISHA

Born: December 30, 1976, Chicago IL; *Parents:*Corliss Hickman; *Honors:* Upper Academic Olympic, Speech Arts Winner, 1st Place, Black History Winner; *Personal note:* Poetry provides an outlet for me to express my feelings; *Address:* Chicago, IL.

HICKS, JENNIFER

Born: October 10, 1975, Fairfax, VA; *Parents:*Tom Hicks, Caroline Hicks; *Education:* Rocky Run Intermediate School; *Memberships:* Drama Club, Rocky Run Choir; *Honors:* Science Fair, Merit Awards, Music & Drama Editor, Presidential Physical Fitness Award; *Personal note:* Someday I would like to be an actress, model or writer; *Address:* Centerville, VA.

HICKS, MELISSA M.

Pen Name: Melfin, Boekey; *Born:* June 18, 1973, Ft Belvior, VA; *Parents:*SusanC.T. Hicks; *Education:* Potomac High School; *Occupation:* Lifeguard; *Other writings:* Many othe poems and a few short stories; *Personal note:* Poetry is my expression of all thoughts and emoitions, I love to try to keep a journal to explain my feelings toward things in my life, but I find poetry much more personal, poetry is memories recreated, unable to be express by emotions; *Address:* 8110 Goergetown Pike, McLean, VA.

HIGGINS, HEATHER

Born: June 14, 1974, Evergreen Park; *Parents:*Michael and Kathy Higgins; *Education:* Marian Catholic High School; *Personal note:* The best poetry comes from the heart, the best of everything comes from the heart; *Address:* Peontone, IL.

HILGENDORF, TRISH A.

Born: January 21, 1975, Wausau, WI; *Parents:* Stan, Diane Hilgendorf; *Education:* First Lutheran Elementary School; *Memberships:* Volleyball teams at Badger High School; *Honors:* MVP Award; *Personal note:* I understand that sometimes asking for help is the hardest thing to do, I just want people who are sad and feel alone that they don't have to feel this way, God is always there and he's eager to listen, he can always help and he loves you no matter what you do, he's my life, my hope and my way to a better life; *Address:* 1199 Rolling Lane, Lake Geneva, WI.

HILLER, DANIELLE

Born: June 9, 1973, Diluth, MN; *Parents:*John Hiller, Jarvis Baldwin; *Occupation:* Education; *Memberships:* 4-H Horse Club; *Personal note:* I would just like to let people know what I'm feeling; *Address:* Star Rt 1, Box 176,Iron Mt, MI.

HILLS, MEGAN M.

Born: October 14, 1976, Kansas City, MO; *Parents:*Robert Hills and Vicki Hills; *Education:* Blue Ridge Elementary, Raytown South Middle School; *Memberships:* Camp Fire; Girls Civic Softball; *Honors:* Recipient of Young Authors Award for Short Story, American Royal

Contest for Art Work and Missouri Reflections Program for Art Work, Founder of Scribblers Writing Club at Raytown South Middle South; *Personal note:* I enjoy writing as it helps me to express my feelings, I hope to have a book of my poetry published; *Address:* Raytown, MO.

HINKLEY, MICHELE R.
Born: September 9, 1976, Effingham IL; *Parents:*William H. Hinkley, Shelia R. Roberts; *Occupation:* Student; *Address:* 701 S. 5th Street, P.O. Box 367, Effingham, IL.

HINSON, BARBARA CLARK
Born: September 28, 1944; Edison, GA; *Parents:*Mary L. & Talmadge A. Clark; *Education:* Smith's State High School; *Occupation:* Executive Assistant, Education Coordinator; *Memberships:* NAFE; *Honors:* National Outstanding Young Woman of America; *Other writings:* Published poetry in the Poetry Center's *Heartland*; The Poetry Press *Yesterday's Memories*; *Personal note:* My writing reflects memories of the rural southwest area of my youth and the music, lyrics, and love that always filled the air; *Address:* 3333 Eastside Ste, 139, Houston, TX.

HOLLANDER, RENEE
Pen Name: rh; *Born:* February 9, 1971, Beaumont, TX; *Parents:*Benjamin, Euvah Hollander; *Education:* Clyde High School, Cisco Junior College, McMurry College; *Occupation:* Student; *Other writings:* Poems published in high school yearbook; *Personal note:* There is no life without living; *Address:* Clyde, TX.

HOLLIS, THERESA T.
Pen Name: Tessi Hollis; *Born:* March 14, 1952, Jacksonville, NC; *Parents:*Edward L, Maureen Turnage; *Spouse:* William A. Hollis, II, December 29, 1973; *Children:* Floyd William Hollis, II; *Education:* Columbis High School; Coastal Carolina Community College; Beaufort County Community College; *Occupation:* Cosmetologist; *Memberships:* Wesley Memorial United Methodist Church; Tyrrellinean Club; *Honors:* Outstanding Student of the Year; Who's Who in American beauty; President List, Beaufort Community College; *Other writings:* Just things for my family and friend; *Personal note:* Writing seems to release your heart and soul, but at the same time feed your mind; *Address:* Rt 2, Box 317, Columbia, NC.

HOOPER, ARAMENTA L.
Pen Name: Menty; *Born:* December 31, 1975, Cleveland, OH; *Parents:*Malinda L. Hooper, Derrick M. Hooper; *Education:* Maryland City Elementary, MacArthur Middle School; *Occupation:* Student; *Memberships:* Girl Scout, Cadette Senior; *Honors:* Maryland Science Center, Nutrition Essay Contest, Fire Prevention Awards 1st, 2nd, 1st, 3rd; Illustration Contest 1st Place, AACO Art Show 1st Place; *Personal note:* My thoughts lie in the hearts of kindness; *Address:* Laurel, MD.

HOPE, ROBERT B.
Pen Name: Robert B. Hope; *Born:* December 30, 1903, New York, NY; *Parents:*Hugo K., Queenie Margaret Hope; *Spouse:* Marian DeWitt Hope, June 24, 1930; *Children:* Stephanie; *Education:* McKinley High School; University of Hawaii, Honolulu HI, BA; University of Oregon Medical School, MD, 1928; *Occupation:* Doctor of Medicine, Freelance Writer; *Memberships:* American College of Cardiology; American College of Gastroenterology; Writers Club Leisure World; AMA, CMA, American College of Physicians; *Honors:* Thea Alpha Phi, Alpha Omega Alpha; *Other writings:* History of Peritoneoscopy Forum on Medicine, August 1978; *Pioneering in the Delivery of Healthcare*; Forum on Medicine, March 1979; "The Fishing Barge", *The lookout*; "Westward Ho", *American History Illustrated*, January, 1987; *Personal note:* Have written poetry since age 15, did not try to publish until 1985 when I started creative writing classes, poems and stories about the sea, ships and world war II; prefer rhymed verse but write both types; *Address:* Laguna Hills, CA.

HORNE, REGINA
Pen Name: Peggy; *Born:* September 3, 1973, Hot Springs, AR; *Parents:*Gene and Sharon Horne; *Education:* Lake Hamilton High School; *Occupation:* Student; *Address:* Hot Springs, AR.

HOUSE, JEN
Born: October 23, 1976; Phoenix, Arizona; *Parents:*Diana Hauser; Diana Elczyshyn; *Occupation:* Student; *Other writings:* Various poems that are not yet discovered; *Personal note:* This poem is one of many I have written for my ex-boyfriend, RH, I hope for the best for everyone I know in Half Moon Bay, especially BB and RC; *Address:* 5 Anchor Way, Half Moon Bay, CA.

HOUSE, JOHN C.
Born: August 4, 1941, Winder, GA; *Parents:*Henry and Geraldine House; *Spouse:* Page Hutcherson House, August 17, 1963; *Children:* Shannon, Paul, David, Mary Beth, Mahlon; *Education:* Winder-Barrow High School; North GA College, Medical College of GA; *Occupation:* Family Physician; *Memberships:* Medical Assn of GA; Southern Medical Assn, American Academy of Family Practice; *Honors:* Distinguished Alumnus at North Georgia College; *Other writings:* Poems published in Mag Journal; *Address:* 705 N. 5th Avenue, Winder, GA.

HOWARD, DEBORAH ELLEN
Born: January 25, 1953; Glendale, CA; *Parents:*Marcus and Stuart Howard; *Children:* Howard Matthew, Cameron; *Education:* Occidental College; Glendale College; Harvard University; *Occupation:* Author, Nurse; *Memberships:* Glendale Teacher Assn; American Heart Assn; *Honors:* California Scholarship Federation; Tick Tockers Scholarship; Scholarship from American Heart Assn; Runner-up to Miss Glendale, Miss Crown City Optimist; *Other writings:* "Rosebud", Annual Anthology of College Poetry; *Personal note:* Poetry is an expression of art in its most beautiful form, because it is from the heart; *Address:* Glendale, CA.

HUBBARD, TINA
Pen Name: Tina Hubbard; *Born:* June 11, 1976, Lawrenceburg, IN; *Parents:*Paul and Diane Hubbard; *Education:* Dixon Israel Middle School; *Occupation:* Student; *Other writings:* Like to write poems in my spare time; *Personal note:* I love animals and nature, I also love to play the guitar and sing, that is my inspiration for writing poems; *Address:* 4291 Lakeland Terrace, College Corner, OH.

HUDDLESTON, LISA K.
Born: February 25, 1971, Norman, OK; *Parents:*Daniel and Dorothy Huddleston; *Education:* Dayspring Christian Academy, Rose State College; *Honors:* Editor's Choice Award; *Other writings:* Several poems and short stories read over the broadcasting company in Zambia, Africa; *Personal note:* Poetry is a great relaxer and I strive to write it with a purpose whether it's just to make a statement, cheer a person up, or express the way I feel; *Address:* Midwest City, OK.

HUFFAKER, STACEY REY
Born: August 1, 1974, Caldwell, Idaho; *Parents:*Stan Huffaker, Dana Huffaker, Vicky Davis; *Education:* Middleton High School; *Occupation:* Full-time student; *Memberships:* Poetic Society, Saga Journalists, RLDS Member, Greenpeace, Student Recycle Inc.; *Honors:* Honor Roll, 3rd Place in District Write-Off, Scholarships; *Other writings:* Poems entered in many contests, prizes won. I also write for the Middleton Saga; *Personal note:* Writing was a gift given to me from God. I can only hope that my talent can be used and reused; *Address:* P. O. Box 66, Middleton, ID.

HUGHES, FAYE GIBBS
Pen Name: Sherry Lynn; *Born:* July 4, Indiana; *Parents:*Fred and Georgia Gibbs; *Children:*Mark, Sean; *Occupation:* Magnetic Healer, Artist, Musician; *Memberships:* National Health Federation; *Honors:* Earned the honor to belong to World Healing Assn through Psychic Association of Great Britian; *Personal note:* Happiness is first and above all, good health; what we think and what we eat, this we become; if we please God, we will please others and then ourselves; *Address:* Tarpon Springs, FL.

HUGHES, LEO
Born: October 14,Cushing OK; *Parents:*Elzie, Martha Hughes; *Education:* BS; MA; PHD; *Occupation:* Teacher; *Memberships:* Chaparral Poets; *Honors:* Three Scholarships to Kansas State University; President County Assn for Retarded Persons of KS; *Other writings:* The Barracks; Poems published in 6 national anthologies; *Personal note:* I am a romantic at heart searching for a similiar person to work with, prefer adventurous young man who loves new experiences and traveling; *Address:* Ponca City, OK.

HURST, STEPHANIE ANN
Pen Name: Steph; *Born:* March 20, 1971, Boron, CA; *Parents:*Warren Hurst, Wanda Hurst; *Education:* Boron High School; *Occupation:* Professional Model; *Memberships:* First Southern Baptist Church, N. Edward, CA; *Honors:* Senior Class President, Miss Boron Representative; *Other writings:* Compilation of Several Poems, Read at Public Functions on Varying Subjects; *Personal note:* I am a creature of moods, most of my poems are the results of spontaneous reaction to happenings in my own life, the intrinsic events of living, provide me with ample thoughts; *Address:* Boron, CA.

HUTCHISON, GEORGE L.
Born: 17, 1915, Catawissa PA; *Parents:*Jenny and Ross Hutchison; *Spouse:* Mildred; October 15, 1983; *Occupation:* Security Guard; *Memberships:* Westwood Baptist Church; *Other writings:* "Enchanted Gardens", "Perseus of Sassaman's Hollow", "The Legendary Masters of the Sheebeen House"; *Personal note:* It is my prayer to have my novels published and to continue being an author and poet in the world in which we live; *Address:* 8103 Martin Way, Olympia, WA.

HUTCHISON, MEGAN ELIZABETH
Born: July 30, 1976, Pasadena, TX; *Parents:*Jack and Dianna Hutchison; *Occupation:* Student; *Honors:* National Honor Society; *Address:* Deer Park, TX.

IRRGANG, MARILYN J.
Pen Name: Mary Jean; *Occupation:* Psychiatric Technician; *Honors:* A Letter from the President of France concerning the "Status of liberty" poem; *Other writings:* "Freedom", "Our Flag", "4th of July", "America"; *Personal note:* Kindness is strength, cruelty is weakness, the righteous will prevail and the wrong will fail! *Address:* Indianapolis, IN.

JACKS, CONNIE LISSA
Born: September 22, 1959; Jasper, AL; *Parents:*Jerry Humphries, Sylvia Humphries; *Spouse:* Dwight Keith Jacks, August 18, 1978; *Children:* Brian Keith Jacks; *Education:* Walker High School; *Occupation:* Housewife; *Memberships:* Northside Baptist Church, Lupton Jr. High Parent Teacher Organization; *Personal note:* My writing is not only a gift but a reflection of my heart. Just simple thoughts and feelings that surface from somewhere deep within, and from time to time find their way into my mind...and into the hearts of those special people that I hold dear; *Address:* Rt 2, Box 447, Nauvoo, AL.

JACKSON, CARLA
Born: August 7, 1974, Columbus, OH; *Parents:*Byron & Sandy Jackson; *Education:* Circleville High School; *Occupation:* Student; *Memberships:* Key Club, Good Shepherd United Methodist Church; *Honors:* Little Miss Pumpkin School Attendent; *Other writings:* I am 15 Year old and this is the first thing I have ever had published; *Personal note:* Someday I would like to see world peace, no wars, no hatred, nothing but peace and love! *Address:* 362 Cedar Heights Road, Circleville, OH.

JACKSON, CHARIS
Born: June 3, 1974, Lancaster, PA; *Parents:*Shirley N. Jackson; *Education:* Manheim Township High School; *Occupation:* Cashier, Cook; *Memberships:* Key Club, Performing Arts, Gymnastics Team, Track; *Honors:* Honor Roll, Spelling Bee Champion, Letter for Track, Semi Finalist in Pennsylvania State Essay Contest; *Other writings:* Articles for Hi Lite Magazine, Semi Finalist for Essay Contest for Penn State; *Personal note:* Personal experiences and creativity add to the writing of poetry because they are *Address:* 520 Somerset Road, Lancaster, PA.

JACOBE, BENJAMIN DACALANO
Spouse: Carolina Cortez Jacobe; *Education:* USNTC, San Diego, CA; *Memberships:* Fleet Reserve Assn; American Legion, Santa Cruzans of Hawaii, Inc; *Honors:* Honor Certificate from the US Navy's Boot Camp; Two Golden Poet Awards; *Other writings:* "I Love You" "Be My Valentine" are the awarding winning poems for 1988 and 1989; *Personal note:* Dedication to my adopted country is unquestionable, I consider loyalty not a cheap commodity that can be bought or sold at will, but an individual's prerogative; *Address:* 99-108 Kalaloa Street, Aiea, HI.

JAMES, NOREEN
Born: August 13, 1947, Clarkston, WA; *Parents:*Asa C. David, Esther Davis; *Children:* Dustin; *Personal note:* One of the Greatest things in this world is to be an American; *Address:* APO New York, NY.

JEFFRIES, JODI L.
Born: June 30, 1970, Lancaster, PA; *Parents:*Richard W. Jeffries, Linda L. Krieder; *Education:* Solanco High School; *Occupation:* Medical Secretary; *Memberships:* PETA, Greenpeace; *Honors:* Modern Miss Finalist,

Honor Roll; *Other writings:* Several Poems have been published in anthology publications; *Personal note:* Patience is your greatest strength and I am very thankful to J.D. for lending me some of hers; *Address:* 308 Smithville Road, New Providence, PA.

JENKINS, AMI
Born: March 9, 1974, Beverly, MA; *Parents:*Roxanne Sutherland, Tom Jenkins; *Education:* Lake Region High School; *Honors:* Won 2nd Place in a Science Pair, 4th and 2nd Place in Horse Shows; *Other writings:* I keep my other writings, safely in a pile; I'm trying to write a whole book of my poetry; *Personal note:* I've always looked at things in life differently when I write it helps me explain how I feel; *Address:* P.O. Box 162, Bridgeton, ME.

JETTE, DEBRA
Born: April 25, 1976, New Haven, CT; *Parents:*Stephen Jette, Patricia Jette; *Education:* Saints Peter and Paul Grammar School; *Occupation:* Student; *Memberships:* American Heart Assn; National Wildlife Federation, SSPP Cheerleader; *Honors:* Honorable Mention in City Fire Prevention Poster Contest, First Place in City Poetry Contest; *Personal note:* I have a great interest in creative writing and drama and hope to pursue these interests as I further my education; *Address:* 165 Woodbine Street, Waterbury, CT.

JOHANNES, KIMBERLY A.
Born: January 5, California; *Occupation:* Student; *Other writings:* Several unpublished poems about life's trials and tribulations; *Personal note:* My writing is inspired by the surroundings and feelings I encounter through people I meet and know, places I go and like, and things I do and that are being done; *Address:* Milford, CT.

JOHNSON, CHRITINE MICHELLE
Born: November 26, 1977, Granite City, IL; *Parents:*-Robert & Teresa Johnson; *Education:* St. Elizabeth's School; *Occupation:* Student; *Memberships:* Paddlers' Swim and Dive Teams; *Other writings:* Written essays and short stories; *Address:* 1 Frontenac, Granite City, IL.

JOHNSON, FATIMAH
Pen Name: Fatimah Johnson; *Born:* April 7, 1976, New York, NY; *Parents:*Gregory Johnson, Claire, Bardes Johnson; *Education:* Brooklyn Friends School; Nyack Junior High School; *Occupation:* Student; *Honors:* Honor Roll; *Other writings:* Several Poems to be Published in the Spring in the *American Poetry Anthology*; *Personal note:* I try to base my writing on inner feelings and emotions, along with experiences which I have had; I have been inspired by Robert Frost, Carl Sandburg, and my teacher, William Robert Caramella; *Address:* Grandview, NY.

JOHNSON, MICHAEL ALAN
Born: July 7, 1960, Albuquerque, New Mexico; *Parents:*-Joseph and Leona Huber; *Spouse:* Tina Louise Johnson, September 12, 1987; *Children:* Kristy Louise and Maurice William; *Occupation:* Electronics Technician; *Memberships:* Christian Motorcyclists Assn; *Honors:* Numerous Military Awards; *Other writings:* Several Poems Written But Unpublished; *Personal note:* I strive to glorify God in my writings, inspired by the experiences of my life; *Address:* Lewiston, ME.

JOHNSON, TIFFANY
Born: March 4, 1977, Knoxville, TN; *Parents:*Wilford & Frances Johnson; *Education:* Jacksboro Middle School; *Occupation:* Student; *Memberships:* JMS Cheerleader, 4-H Club, JMS Student Council, Band, Member of the Fine Arts Dance Academy and the Fine Arts Concert Dance Company; *Honors:* School Honor Roll; *Other writings:* None at this time but plan to continue writing; *Personal note:* I have always loved poetry from a very young child, I plan to write more poetry and hope that someone reading my poetry will be influenced as I was, I strive to portray the happiness and love that life can bring through my writings; *Address:* Caryville, TN.

JOHNSTON, PATRICK J.
Born: December 27, 1970, Greenville, SC; *Parents:*-Barry R., Nancy A. Johnston; *Education:* Allen D. Nease High School, Florida State University; *Occupation:* Phebotomist; *Other writings:* Published in *Trouvere's Laureate II, Poetry Forum*; *Windows on the World*; *FSU's Flambeau, American Poetry Anthology*; *Personal note:* The heavens declare the glory of God and the firmament sheweth his handywork, day unto day uttereth speech, and night unto night sheweth knowledge, there is no speech nor language where their voice is heard, Psalms 19:1-3; Every rainbow, every breath of oxygen, every breeze, every full moon, every songbird, every cup of cold water, every flower is God's way of telling us he's there and he loves us, I don't want to take that for granted, so I write about it; *Address:* FSU Box 60173, Tallahassee, FL.

JONES, CURTIS RAE
Pen Name: C.J. Stomper; *Born:* May 6, 1953, Michigan City, IN; *Parents:*Norman K. Jones, Alice Greene; *Spouse:* Paula A. Jones, July 17, 1983; *Occupation:* Chef; *Other writings:* Written several books of poetry; *Personal note:* Life's nest, is but only a test, conspired everyday; For what is life's best, but only a test, conspired everyday; *Address:* 114 Stimpson Court, Michigan City, IN.

JONES, JEANNE B.
Born: July 28, 1927, Chicago, IL; *Parents:*Alvin DeHeight, Elsie DeHeight; *Spouse:* Thomas W. Jones, March 25, 1948; *Children:* Gayle Barbara, Geri Jeanne; *Education:* Oak Park River Forest Township High School; Brevard Community College; *Occupation:* Retired; prior Administrative Assistant, Mental Health Field/Judiciary; *Memberships:* National Assn Legal Secretary; National Registry of Medical Secretaries; *Honors:* Certificate for dedicated service to the David Lawrence Center; *Other writings:* Poem in American Anthology; local newspaper articles and commentary; Novel unpublished to date; *Personal note:* I strive for reflections of better family living in all of my writings, morale values become very important in our world where youth seem so indecisive; *Address:* Sugar Land, TX.

JONES, LONA MARIA
Born: February 23, 1975, Morristown, TN; *Parents:*-Dana C. Jones, Sr., Margaret Joan Crizer; *Occupation:* Student; *Honors:* Cheerleading and 4-H Club; *Other writings:* Have other poems and song but have no titles; *Address:* Rt 2 Box 931-A, Whitepine, TN.

JORDAN, TAMI
Born: June 16, 1972, New Orleans, LA; *Parents:*Bennie Jordan, Rita Jordan; *Education:* East Jefferson High School; *Other writings:* Several unpublished poems: "In Between", "Alone"; *Personal note:* I try to do my best at everything I do and I hope to accomplish my dreams, as you should accomplish yours; *Address:* Metairie, LA.

JOYAL, SYLVIA L.
Born: November 6, 1973, Springfield, MA; *Parents:*Joseph Joyal Sr., Sylvia D. Joyal; *Education:* Central High School; Barbizon School of Modeling; *Occupation:* Student; Certified Babysitter; *Memberships:* Girl Scouts, Dancing Gymnastics, Foreign Language Club; *Honors:* Honor Roll; *Other writings:* "Wanted for Living a Dream"; "Just A Whisper Once Heard", "Life"; *Personal note:* Look toward the future and never forget the past; *Address:* Springfield, MA.

KANGAS, JUANITA HUTSON
Pen Name: JK *Born:* April 23, 1933, Urbana, IL; *Parents:*Eva Collins Hutson, William Hutson; *Spouse:* Marvin Raymond Kangas, December 3, 1987; *Children:* Brenda Ann Lott, Robert Wayne Richardson; *Education:* Grant Pass High School; *Occupation:* Writer, Housewife; *Memberships:* Ilnco Community Church; *Honors:* The Publishers Choice Award; 4th Place with The National Library of Poetry *Other writings:* Written Poems that were Published in the Hometown Newspaper; *Personal note:* Always loved writing, working on another book, my writings are all dedicated to my children and grandchildren; *Address:* Ocean Park, WA.

KASTAL, KLARA
Born: August 29, 1973, Gyergyoszentmiklos, Romania; *Parents:*Elizabeth and Laszlo Kastal; *Education:* High School Student; *Memberships:* Ligonier Valley Senior High Band, PTSA, AMC Club; *Honors:* Trophies for basketball, and plaques for basketball and several certificates for school such as science fairs; *Other writings:* I wrote other poems, but they were not sent in for publication, I usually write when I get inspired by something or someone; *Address:* 218 Kalassay Drive, Ligonier, PA.

KATSIFIS, GLORIA
Born: February 24, 1970, Bronx, NY; *Education:* Christopher Columbus High School; Westchester Community College; *Occupation:* Student; *Other writings:* Write song lyrics, poems and potential story plots for novels; *Personal note:* If you can't tell your dreams to someone, the pen and paper are always around, never under estimate your goals and always reach for them, no matter what stands in your way; *Address:* 44 East 208th Street, Bronx, NY.

KAUFMANN, JENNIFER
Born: November 28, 1971; Abilene, TX; *Parents:*John and Peggy Kaufmann; *Occupation:* High School Student; *Memberships:* FHA, Annual Staff, Student Council, Church Youth Groups; *Honors:* Who's Who Among American High School Students, Honor Roll, Second Place in State Wide Drawing Contest; *Other writings:* Published in school newspaper; *Personal note:* I have been greatly influenced by the romantic poets; *Address:* P.O. Box 175, Chillicothe, TX.

KELLER, ANGELA
Born: August 15, 1974, Freeport, IL; *Parents:*Dennis and Rita Keller; *Occupation:* Student; *Honor and Awards:* Recipient of Award from World of Poetry; *Other Writings:* "A friend"; *Personal Note:* I feel free when expressing my feelings in my poems, I never thought I had a talent until the 8th grade, the talent has stuck with me and I now love to write poems; *Address:* 5605 Squires Drive, The Colony, TX.

KELLOGG, DENNIS L.
Born: June 23, 1947, Des Moines, IA; *Spouse:* Deborah A. Kellogg, May 20, 1978; *Education:* Southeast Missouri State University, MA; *Occupation:* Paralegal; *Memberships:* Iowa Natural Heritage, Audubon Society; *Honors:* Golden Poet Award, Graduate of Academic Distinction; *Other writings:* "No Need Now"; "A Single Yellow Leaf"; "Brother, Brother"; "River"; "The Behrle Cabin, "Post War Hysteria"; "Young Men Once Old"; "Pain"; "I'll Sing Your Song"; *Personal note:* We're told not to get everything we want but we get everything we need, don't cling to life, experience it! *Address:* Des Moines, IA.

KENDALL, JEANNIE MATTOX
Born: Bourbon County, Kentucky; *Parents:*Silas and Norma Clark Mattox; *Spouse:* Wayne Kendall, October 1, 1977; *Children:* Brady Jameson, Jeana Waine, Neil Patrick, Nicholas Christian; *Occupation:* Tutor in Adult Education; *Other writings:* Written several poems published in local newspaper; *Personal note:* My poetry feels inspired and I write it very quickly with few changes, I write best about people and emotions; *Address:* Route 4 Box 480, Cynthiana, KY.

KENNEY, JOHN
Pen Name: John Kenney; *Born:* March 17, 1959, Philadelphia PA; *Parents:*Joseph & Stella Kenney; *Education:* Deptford High School; *Occupation:* Stationary Engineer; *Other writings:* Numerous other poems, several short stories; *Personal note:* I never thought much of publishing my writing, I really have just written as a release, away to release tension; *Address:* 429 Baylor Road, Wenonah, NJ.

KIDD, JODI D'ANN
Born: May 13, 1974, Groom, TX; *Parents:*Larry and Paulette Kidd; *Education:* Clarendon High School; *Memberships:* Student Council, FFA, Varsity Basketball, Track Tennis Gold, Explorer Scouts; *Honors:* Junior Varsity Cheerleader, Sophomore Class Favorite, Freshman Class President; *Address:* Clarendon, TX.

KINSES, KAREN
Born: Dayton, OH; *Parents:*Kenneth and Marian Kinses; *Children:* John Christopher; *Education:* Magnolia High School; Fullerton College; *Occupation:* Sales Administrator; *Honors:* Golden Poet Award, 2 Awards; Silver Poet Award, 3 Awards; *Other writings:* Written over 7000 poems, several published; *Personal note:* Somewhere in my youth or childhood I must have done something good to see the love in my child's eye and know he is my best audience; *Address:* Buena Park, CA.

KIRKMAN, ANGELA S.
Born: March 18th, 1975, Winston Salem, NC; *Parents:* Charles and Sue Kirkman; *Education:* West Forsyth High School; *Occupation:* Student; *Memberships:* Students Against Driving Drunk; Latin Club; *Other writings:* Written Several Poems; *Address:* 6209 Parkfield Lane, Clemmons, NC.

KITZAN, JENNIFER
Pen Name: Jennifer Ketzan; *Born:* April 13, 1973, Mitchell, SD; *Parents:*Ronald Kitzan, Maria Kitzan; *Education:* Carl Hayden High School; *Occupation:* Student;

Other writings: Several poems published in school's writer's guild; *Personal note:* My poetry is a window to my thoughts; *Address:* 3742 W. Portland, Phoenix, AZ.

KLASSEN, DENICE NICOLE
Pen Name: Nikke Klassen; *Born:* September 8, 1975, Morden, Manitoba Canada; *Parents:* Peter and Eileen Klassen; *Education:* Winkler Elementary School; Garden Valley Collegiate; *Honors:* Honorable Mention for a Short Story Contest in a Local Newspaper; *Other writings:* A short story published in a local newspaper, a poem in the school yearbook; *Personal note:* I think it's time for people to open their eyes and see the mess we're making in the world, and try to do something about it before it's too late; *Address:* 337 Pembina Avenue, Winkler, Manitoba Canada.

KNICELY, MINDY
Born: July 24, 1975, Phoenix, Arizona; *Parents:* Robert Knicely, Anne Knicely; *Education:* Cactus High School; *Occupation:* Student; *Memberships:* Musical Horizons Club; Peoria's Pride; Heritage Presbyterian Church; *Honors:* Silver and Golden Honor Rolls; *Personal note:* Poetry is one way I express my feelings, knowing it won't betray me; *Address:* Glendale, AZ.

KNOWLES, ALBERT STANLEY
Born: January 6, 1915; *Education:* Rutgers University College, New Brunswick, NJ; *Occupation:* Retired Major of the US Marine Corps Reserve; *Personal note:* I am interested in collecting fine books in literature, history, art, horticulture and religion; *Address:* Brick, NJ.

KOEMPEL, KRISTINE
Born: June 13, 1969, Pittsburgh, PA; *Parents:* John and Gerry Koempel; *Education:* Baldwin High School; University of Pittsburgh; *Honors:* National Honor Society; *Personal note:* The exchange between observation and the inner self leads to creative expression; *Address:* Pittsburgh, PA.

KORUSIEWICZ, MARIA
Born: February 3, 1956, Katouice, Poland; *Parents:* Bronislaw Machnik, Miroslawa Machnik; *Spouse:* Lech Korusiewicz, April 2, 1977; *Children:* Leszek, Anna; *Education:* Academy of Art, English Philosophy; *Occupation:* Graphic Artist; *Memberships:* Polist Art Assn; *Honors:* National Literature Foundation; Scholarship from Ministry of Culture; *Other writings:* "Women's Hard at Dawn"; Translations of American Poetry; *Personal note:* Living for so many years in a grey east european country behind the old iron curtain, far from the noisy colorful streets of San Francisco a writer has two possibilities: he can engage himself fully in a political struggle or he can explore his own personality; as a poet, I have chosen the second way, looking at the world through the kitchen window, I try to describe my own self: a woman; *Address:* 1120 Jackson Street #16, San Francisco, CA.

KOSINSKI, DEBORAH
Born: May 23, 1973; *Education:* Mother McAuley High School; *Occupation:* Student; *Address:* 3912 101 Street, Chicago, IL.

KRICK, KIRI
Born: January 24, 1973, Illinois; *Parents:* John and Mary Krick; *Education:* St. Joseph's School; Highland High School; *Occupation:* Student; *Honors:* Various Drama, Vocal and Athletic Awards and Honors; *Other writings:* Short Stories and Speeches; *Personal note:* I focus on my deepest emotions and apply them to physical things around me; *Address:* 9430 Hampton Drive, highland, IN.

KRUEGER, PHYLLIS A.
Born: July 27, 1922, Apple River District, WI; *Parents:* Leroy and Norma Powell, *Spouse:* Elmer Leroy Krueger, August 27, 1938; *Children:* Roland A., Rosalyn Bell, Delmar, Delena Gibson; *Education:* School of Cosmetology; *Occupation:* Retired; *Memberships:* United Foursquare Women; *Other writings:* Published one poem in American Anthology; *Personal note:* I enjoy pointing out the goodness of my Lord and Savior; *Address:* 244 6th Street, St. maries, ID.

KRUG, JACQUELYN
Pen Name: Tracy A.R. Krug; *Born:* September 18, 1961, Austin, MN; *Children:* Michael Krug, August 1, 1987; *Education:* Winona State University, BA; *Occupation:* Doctoral Student; *Memberships:* MASGW, MCGC, MMHCA, ISSMPD; *Honors:* Phi Theta Kappa, AFS Scholarship, Summa Cum Laude, Dean's List, MN State Scholarship; *Other writings:* Clinical writings in the areas of cancer, color usage in children drawings, the single parent child, group therapy design and "What's Wrong with Mommy"; *Personal note:* I write because, I am; *Address:* Marshall, MI.

KRUPINSKI, CHRISTINE
Pen Name: Cee-Cee Luv; *Born:* April 7, 1975, Suffern; *Parents:* Audry and Kenneth Krupinski; *Education:* Kakiat Junior High School; *Occupation:* Full time Student; *Memberships:* Yearbook Committee Kakiat Jr High School; *Honors:* APA Poets Award; *Other writings:* "True Love"; "Broken Hearts", "Revenge of a Broken Heart", "Mystery Man", "Limbo"; "The Night Dreams Edge"; *Double Lives; Personal note:* I write mainly for adults, even though I am very young, people don't understand that not only adults should be writers, it does not mean that all people my age will be good writers but there are some out there; *Address:* 11A Fletcher Road, Monsey, NY.

KRUSE, SANDRA LYNN
Born: March 1, 1976, Brookings, SD; *Parents:* Leroy and Belinda Kruse; *Occupation:* Student; *Personal note:* Active in basketball, track and declam; *Address:* Volga, SD.

KUNTZMAN, KIM
Born: November 28, 1974, Springfield, IL; *Parents:* David Kuntzman, Linda Kuntzman; *Education:* South Fork High School; *Memberships:* Student Council, Spanish Club; *Honors:* Member of World Champion Cheerleading Squad, High Honors; Honors Club; *Personal note:* I am honored to have my writing selected by the National Library of Poetry, I hope to continue to express my personal beliefs through more literary work; *Address:* P.O. Box 498, Kincaid, IL.

LAGARDE, KIMBERLY
Born: March 10, 1971, Providence Rhode Island; *Parents:* John and Lorraine LaGarde; *Education:* University of CT; *Personal note:* In the spirit of Jim Morrison and Arthur Kimbaud, I attempt to reveal that which lies beyond reality, I wish to both portray and inspire spiritual love, harmony of the soul and knowledge of what exists after death;

LANDRY, LINDA
Pen Name: Lin; *Born:* February 28, 1969, Nashua, NH; *Parents:* Donald Landry; Noella Landry; *Education:* Nashua High School; *Occupation:* I work for Xerox Corporation; *Other writings:* I write lots of poems but this is the first publication of my poem; *Personal note:* I love to write poems and wish to publish more; *Address:* Nashua, NH.

LANHAM, THOMAS CREEL
Born: July 24, 1971, Illinois; *Parents:* David and Jean Lanham;

LASALLE, MICHELE
Born: January 29, 1975, Bronx NY; *Parents:* Louisa LaSalle, George LaSalle; *Education:* Elijah D. Clark Junior High School; *Occupation:* Student; *Memberships:* United Command Corps Cadets; *Honors:* Math Team; *Personal note:* Life should always be lived to the fullest for you could always die tomorrow, I encourage young writers to write now; *Address:* 681 Courtlandt Avenue #9E, Bronx, NY.

LAUDE, LAURIE
Born: August 13, 1975, Viking, Alberta; *Parents:* Reuben Laube, Sonja Laube; *Education:* Holden School; *Occupation:* Student; *Memberships:* Holden School Badminton Team; *Honors:* 2nd Honorable Mention, Holden Literary Contest, 1989; Gold and Silver Award in Fort Saskatchewan Gymnastics Meet, Safety Essay Award; *Other writings:* Several other poems, essays and songs; *Personal note:* I like to write poems based on real life and I prefer to use a definite rhyme scheme; *Address:* Holden, Alberta, Canada.

LAUFENBERG, CHRISTINE M.
Born: December 26, 1967, Madison, WI; *Parents:* Ken and Rose Marie Laufenberg; *Education:* Mount Horeb High School, Madison Area Technical College; *Occupation:* Production Artist, Widen Colourgraphics, Madison WI; *Memberships:* Quill and Scroll, Thespians; *Honors:* Special Merit Award for Portfolio, High Honor Roll; *Other writings:* "Revenge of the Rose", "The Iris", "The Star", "The One Constant", "The Rainbow", "Regret", These other poems will be published in *The American Poetry Anthology; Personal note:* I often use nature in my poetry to symbolize stages of my life and people that I have placed on pedestals in my mind, ususally, these people would rather not be placed on my pedestals; *Address:* 4831 Country TK Hwy J, Mt. Horeb, WI.

LAUNDRY, MONICA A.
Pen Name: Monica Anne; *Born:* September 20, 1972, Burien, Washington; *Parents:* Rosalie Landry, Jesse Landry; *Education:* Mt Rainier High School; *Occupation:* Writer; *Personal note:* The difference between dreams and reality is you; *Address:* 22782 13tth Avenue, Des Moines, WA.

LAVENDER, BRENDA
Born: August 30, 1971, Oregon; *Parents:* Norman and Sylvia Lavender; *Occupation:* Student; *Other writings:* Other poems; *Personal note:* My poems reveal my deepest feelings, ones that are unable to be expressed in conversation; *Address:* Springfield, OR.

LAVENWORTH, COLLEEN
Pen Name: Kathrine Loring; *Born:* August 30, 1972, Anaheim, CA; *Parents:* David Leavenworth, Gerri Doster; *Occupation:* Student; *Address:* Santa Ana, CA.

LEIBY, TRACEY A.
Pen Name: The Same, Why Hide? *Born:* July 11, 1969, Williamsport, PA; *Parents:* Douglas Leiby, Marlent Leiby; *Education:* Troy High School; Lock Haven University, Coastal Carolina Community College; *Occupation:* Student; *Honors:* Presidential Academic Fitness Award, Good Samaritan Award, Honor Society, Class Salutarian; *Other writings:* Myriads of poems as of yet not published; *Personal note:* The only dreams that can ever come true, are ones shaped from your own reality; *Address:* 115 Pelletier MHP, Jacksonville, NC.

LEWIS, RUBY ANNE
Born: April 18, 1941, Santa Barbara, CA; *Parents:* Cecil A. Talmadge, Elna E. Talmadge; *Spouse:* Robert Flint Lewis, Jr., December 17, 1960; *Children:* Pamela Gwynn Row, Sandra Pauline; *Education:* Carpinteria High School; Santa Barbara City College; *Occupation:* Administrative Assistant for Health Care Center; *Memberships:* Presbyterian Church, Choir; *Other writings:* Several poems in area newspapers; *Personal note:* I like to write about feelings and nature and God; *Address:* 265-A Fifth Street, Solvang, CA.

LIDDELL, GAY FONTAINA WILLIS
Pen Name: Gay Widdell; *Born:* May 30, 1954, Tulsa OK; *Parents:* Augusta Willis; *Spouse:* Cornelious Liddell Jr., February 28, 1983; *Children:* Kiya, Shamale, Micah, William; *Education:* Booker T. Washington High School; Tulsa Draughon School of Business; Rose State College; *Occupation:* Teacher for Head Start, Community Action Agency; *Memberships:* Missionary Board; *Honors:* Child Development Associate, President's Honor Roll, Outstanding Volunteer Awards; *Personal note:* I write from my heart, hoping to touch others, God is my inspiration; *Address:* P.O. Box 392, Spencer, OK.

LINCOLN, ESTHER G.
Born: March 19, 1911, Guys Mills, PA; *Parents:* Barney Pennell, Mary Pennell; *Spouse:* John L. Lincoln, June 2, 1949; *Children:* Gordon L. Lincoln; *Occupation:* Nurse Aide; *Memberships:* United Brethren in Christ; 700 Club; Inner Circle; *Other writings:* Written Non Fiction Poetry; *Personal note:* I am a christian, love people, I believe in standing up for what's right; *Address:* Meadville, PA.

LIPICKY, JOSH
Pen Name: Snow Dog; *Born:* December 16, 1970, Cincinnati, OH; *Parents:* Raymond J. Lipicky, Janet Lee Lipicky; *Education:* Kings High School; Ohio State University; *Other writings:* "Knights of Conaway, Wyward", "My Liquid State of Euphoria"; *Personal note:* "A Dying Flame" was inspired by Amy Rosenbach earlier in my life, I still await your return someday, until then, there once was a man from Nantucket...; *Address:* Loveland, OH.

LOFTIN, PATTI
Born: July 13, 1976, Greenville, NC; *Parents:* Glenn Loftin, Wilene S. Loftin; *Education:* Chocid Elementary School; *Occupation:* Student; *Honors:* Honor Roll, Principals List, County Spelling Bee; *Other writings:* Short Story for chidlren's section of local

paper; *Personal note:* My writings are always afterthoughts or reflections of perosnal experiences; *Address:* RT 2 Box 363-D, Ayden, NC.

LOGUIDICE, JOANNE

Born: January 18, 1974, San Jose, CA; *Parents:*Vito A. LoGuidice and Sarah M. LoGuidice; *Education:* Sacred Heart School; *Occupation:* Student; *Memberships:* California Scholarship Federation; Scholarship to Notre Dame High School; *Honors:* Knights of Columbus Award, The George J. Mifsud Memorial Award for Literary Achievement; *Other writings:* Written Various Poems; *Personal note:* Every poem I have ever written has been for someone important in my life, this particular poem was written for Brent Edwards; *Address:* 200 George's Drive, Hollister, CA.

LOGUIDICE, SUSAN M.

Born: December 7, 1973, Flushing, NY; *Parents:* Emanuel LoGuidice, Josephine C. LoGuidice; *Education:* St. Robert Bellarmine Elementary; St. Francis Preparatory High School; *Occupation:* Student; *Honors:* National Honor Society; Optimate List; *Address:* 56-25 226th Street, Bayside, NY.

LOUDERMILK, MALIA

Pen Name: Lia; *Born:* December 15, 1973, Oakland, CA; *Parents:*Gary, Lani; *Education:* Oakland Technical High School; *Occupation:* Salesclerk; *Honors:* Honor Roll; *Other writings:* Writings in Literature Classes; *Personal note:* Don't just be a friend be a listener; *Address:* Oakland, CA.

LOWE, KRYSTYNA MARY

Born: October 18, 1952, Victoria, Australia; *Parents:* Michael Smyk, Maria Smyk; *Spouse:* Gerald W. Lowe, September 19, 1978; *Children:*Geraldine Maria, Natalie Michelle; *Education:* Sion College; *Occupation:* Homemaker; *Memberships:* Americans Women's Assn; Petroleum Club; Elk's Lodge; *Honors:* Phi Sigma Alpha; *Personal note:* God's beauty has many man's expressions and impressions to find, to follow, to share, and to leave! *Address:* Rt 5 Box 910B, Abilene, TX.

LOZADA, FRANCES

Born: May 24, 1972, New York, NY; *Parents:*Carlos and Frances Lozada; *Education:* Forest Hills High School; *Occupation:* Student; *Memberships:* St. Gerard Majella Parish, Law and Humanities Internship; *Honors:* Award Received from Poem Contests, Dean's List; *Other writings:* Written Numerous Poems; *Personal note:* I express love in my poems, I feel love differs from person to person; *Address:* 90-61 198th Street, Hollis, NY.

LUCKY-RYAN, TAMMY L.

Born: May 17, 1962, Portland, OR; *Parents:*Ralph Ryan, Cathy Ryan-Wilson; *Children:* Joshua and Jessie Lucky; *Education:* Centennial High, Mt. Hood Community College; *Occupation:* Communications Dispatcher Portland International Airport; *Memberships:* Portland Music Assn, Oregon Jazz Society, Coalition of Labor Union Women, PTA, AFSCME #1847, Cascade Blues Assn, APCO; *Address:* P.O. Box 30533, Portland, OR.

LUNSFORD, KATHRYN

Born: January 28, 1978, Milton, FL; *Parents:*Mr and Mrs Larry G. Lunsford; *Education:* Chumukla Elementary School; *Occupation:* Student; *Memberships:* Mary Lous Models, Rascals Unlimited, Troll Student Book Club; *Honors:* 6 Trophies, the include: beauty pageants, best television commercial, best comedy talent; 6 ribbons for art, spelling and math tournament; *Personal note:* I feel that everyone should follow their own conscience to make their dreams come true; *Address:* Rt 6 Box 245, Tracy Road, Milton, FL.

LUTES, MELINDA

Born: October 3, 1974, Portsmouth, VA; *Parents:*Lois Lutes, Clarence Lutes; *Education:* Hillcrest High School; *Occupation:* Hospital Volunteer; *Honors:* Language Arts Fair Winner, Honor Roll; *Other writings:* Written Several Poems; *Personal note:* I write the reality of being a teenager, the good and evil side; *Address:* 1441 E. Snider, Springfield, MO.

LYNCH, TRICIA LORENE

Born: June 20, 1973, Stuttgart, Arkansas; *Parents:*Tom and Pat Lynch; *Education:* Clarendon High School; *Memberships:* FHA, (President), Beta Club, Student Council; *Honors:* 1st and 3rd Place Science Fair Awards, Home Economic Award, Star Events Award; *Other writings:* I write poems all the time, I have written several for special occasions and school events; *Personal note:* Writing to me, is a special way of expressing my inner feelings; *Address:* Clarendon, AR.

MACKENZIE, VICKI

Born: January 9, 1974, Brooklyn, NY; *Parents:*Connie MacKenzie, Michael MacKenzie; *Education:* Our Lady of Perpetual Help High School; *Personal note:* My poetry reflects the emotional turmoil and heartaches experienced by teenagers; *Address:* Bay Ridge, Brooklyn, NY.

MACWILLIAMS, AMY KATHLEEN

Born: March 15, 1970, Washington, DC; *Parents:* James and Judith MacWilliams; *Education:* Northern High School; Salisbury State University; *Memberships:* Concerned Women of America, Republican Women's Club of Wicomico County; MD Federation of Republican Women; *Other writings:* Several Poems Published; *Personal note:* I have been writing poems since I was eight years old, my main sources of enlightenment are my romantic dreams; *Address:* Owings, MD.

MALDONADO, YVETTE

Born: February 23, 1973; *Parents:*Felicita Aviles and William Maldonado; *Education:* Seward Park High School; *Occupation:* Student; *Honors:* Reading Awards; *Personal note:* Poems, Dreams, hope and life are priceless; *Address:* New York, NY.

MANDULAK, ELAINE C.

Born: July 31, 1948, Hartford, CT; *Parents:*Thomas Constandilo, Diana K. Constandilo; *Spouse:* Robert James Mandulak, January 9, 1972; *Children:* Elaine Diane, Thomas John; *Education:* Central High School; Housatonic College; Sacred Heart University, University of Bridgeport; *Memberships:* Assumption Greek Orthodox Church; *Honors:* Won Golden Poet Award of 1989; *Other writings:* Several poems published through poetry contests; *Address:* Sandy Hook, CT.

MARCHANT, JESSICA

Born: February 17, 1976, Nashua, NH; *Education:* Juilliard School; *Occupation:* Student; *Memberships:* United States Gymnastics Federation; *Honors:* Junior Olympic State Class IV Gymnastics Championships; *Other writings:* This is my first published piece of writing; *Personal note:* Live life to the fullest extent and appreciate what you have, don't dwell on what you've lost; *Address:* Hollis, NH.

MARSH, ANKE LIZABETH

Born: November 17, 1969, Honolulu, HI; *Parents:* James and Elke Marsh; *Education:* Iolani School; Syracuse University; *Occupation:* Student; *Memberships:* Japan Society, Lead Singer in a Local Band; *Honors:* Dean's List; *Other writings:* "Sometimes" published in another poetry collection, I also write lyrics for the band; *Address:* 143 Avondale Pl. #14, Syracuse, NY.

MARSH, DOROTHY R.

Born: February 24, 1920; Gallup, New Mexico; *Parents:*Arthur Childers, Ruth Neubert Childers; *Children:* Richard Marsh; *Education:* Sacred Heart High, San Diego Jr Business College; *Occupation:* Artist, Writer; *Memberships:* National Extension Homemakers Council, Inc.; *Other writings:* "Das Madchen aus dem Wilden Western" in collaboration with Maria Klingler of Kirchdorf, Austria; *Address:* 1109 Calle Del Valle, Belen, NM.

MARSHALL, ERIKA

Born: July 24, 1970, Honolulu, HI; *Parents:*James R. Marshall, Connie S. Marshall; *Education:* Iolani High School, Seattle Pacific University; *Occupation:* Student; *Other writings:* "Haiku" Published in the Honolulu Advertiser; *Personal note:* I hope to bring deep feelings to the surface of every person who reads my poetry, a smile to their lips or a tear to their eyes; *Address:* 15130 NW Oak Hills Drive, Beaverton, OR.

MARTIN, ALFRED NAPOLEON

Born: August 5, 1926, Birmingham, AL; *Parents:* Bennie L., James Napoloen Martin; *Education:* A.H. Parker High School; UCLA; Booker T. Washington; *Occupation:* Retired; *Memberships:* California State Poetry Society, National Federation of Poetry Societies, Christian Writer's Association of America; *Honors:* 3-times winner of the Golden Poet Award, Certificate of Merit in 1987 & 1988 from Music City Song Festival, APA Award from American Poetry Assn, Editors Choice Award from the National Library of Poetry; *Other writings:* Published in an International Poetry Anthology, Inclusions in the World's Best Poet's of 1986 & 1987 by American Poetry Assn; *Personal note:* The thoughts that come to mind is from the works of my favorite, Ralph Waldo Emerson;He said, "there are two classes of poets, the poet by education and practice and the poet by nature—these we love"; *Address:* 1061 East 4th Street, #3R, Ontario, CA.

MARTINEZ, RUBEN GERARD

Pen Name: Boo Boo; *Born:* November 18, 1960, Phoenix, AZ; *Parents:*Herlinda Martinez; *Education:* Ima Community College; *Memberships:* LULAC, MECHA; *Other writings:* My poems have appeared in Santa Fe Review; *Personal note:* I've been encouraged by some of the most famous poets of today; Richard Sheldon, Willin Man just to name a few, and the support of my family; *Address:* 1411 E. Monte Vista, Phoenix, AZ.

MASHACK, SHIRLEY A. WYNN

Born: December 27, 1955, Portsmouth, Virginia; *Children:* Five; *Education:* Graduate of Cardozo High School; Currently attending school for Computer Programming; *Occupation:* Word Processing Assistant; *Personal note:* My oldest child Rina encouraged me to enter one of my writings in this contest. Making life better is a daily task. We must use our senses to view life wherever we may be. Let's not ignore those who are seen as outcasts of society. Though the majority of us are far from being rich, we do have something valuable to give -one's self. As you view on's life, someone views your life, for the windows on the world are you and I. So take a second to say hello, give a warm smile and also give some time to listen and share ideas. These acts of kindness could help turn just one life around for the better. Open you windows on the world.

MASILOTTI, DOROTHY

Born: October 26, 1952, Salem, NJ; *Parents:*Robert F. and Dorothy V. Ayars; *Spouse:* James Masilotti; September 30, 1985; *Children:* April Anne, Raymond Robert; *Education:* Salem High School; Salem Community College, Cumberland County College; *Occupation:* Moldmaker; *Memberships:* AFGWU Local 7, Recording Secretary for the Union; *Other writings:* Local news articles printed monthly for Flint Magazine; *Personal note:* This enrichment of ones own inner self is by far the largest fortune one can achieve; *Address:* 92 Seventh Street, Salem, NJ.

MASTRACCHIO, JULES

Born: July 26, 1972, Edinbrugh, Scotland; *Parents:* Robert Mastracchio, Beatrice Mastracchio; *Education:* Randolph High School; *Occupation:* Student; *Honors:* 1st team all county; 1st team all conference in soccer; *Personal note:* My poetry is an expression of my innerself, my writings express the fantasies that many people dream of; *Address:* 28 black birch drive, Randolph, NJ.

MATTESON, STEPHANIE ANN

Born: April 8, 1973, Knoxville, TN; *Parents:*Harland and Mary Matteson; *Occupation:* Student, Courtesy Clerk; *Honors:* National Honor Society; Mu Alpha Theta; Perfect Attendance, Second Honors Awards; Silver Card at West High School for Honors; *Personal note:* I try to tackle things with a positive attitude and always wear a smile; *Address:* 2804 Chillicothe Street, Knoxville, TN.

MAY, CHRISTINA

Born: July 15, 1974; Toms River, NJ; *Parents:*Ernest and Beatrice May; *Education:* Toms River High School East; *Memberships:* Peer Leadership, East Side Theatre Company; *Other writings:* I have written a childrens book call *Bug and Bubble*; *Personal note:* Take one day at a time, don't feel sorry about the past and don't worry about the future, for the past is gone and the future hasn't come yet. Live in the present and make it beautiful; *Address:* Toms River, NJ.

MAYER, TRACIE LYNN

Born: May 29, 1970, Chicago, IL; *Parents:*Peter and Marlene; *Education:* Maine East High School; Oakton Community College; *Occupation:* Student, Works as Clerk at Medi-Check International Foundation; *Honors:* Ice Skating Trophies, Cheerleading Certificate, and Pom Pom Certificate and Plaque; *Personal note:* There is a reason for everything; *Address:* Des Plaines, IL.

MCCABE, SHARON
Born: July 2, 1976, Providence, RI; *Parents:* Bruce McCabe, Marcia McCabe; *Education:* Scituate Junior High School; *Memberships:* United States Figure Skating Assn; *Address:* 7 Overhill Road, North Scituate, RI.

MCCOY, AMY E.
Born: March 14, 1972, Shreveport, LA; *Parents:* Carole McCoy and Richard Garner; *Personal note:* I write about things that make me happy or sad, also, about things that happen in the world or to me; *Address:* Garwood, TX.

MCCOY, HELEN T.P.
Born: October 26, 1936, Bronx, NY; *Parents:* Anna and Anthony Piano; *Children:* Anthony J. McCoy; *Education:* Jane Addams Vocational High School; *Occupation:* School Aide and Receptionist; *Honors:* Several Poems Published in Yearbooks; *Personal note:* I write what I feel; *Address:* NY.

MCDONALD, AMY
Born: December 20, 1973, Houston, TX; *Parents:* Cynthia McDonald; *Other writings:* Has Written Short Stories and Poems; *Address:* Oldfields School, Glencoe, MD.

MCDONALD, KATHRYN MICHELLE
Born: February 9, 1975, Fort Walton Beach, FL; *Parents:* Ethel Quinn McDonald, Victor J. McDonald; *Occupation:* Student; *Address:* Oak Ridge, TN.

MCFALLS, FRANCES G.
Pen Name: Frannie; *Born:* August 7, 1959, Lancaster, PA; *Parents:* Ronald and Phyllis Kurtz; *Spouse:* William H. McFalls; *Children:* Billy, Christine, Andrew, Matthew; *Education:* Lancaster Catholic High Willow Street Vo-Tech; *Occupation:* Cashier; *Memberships:* Saint Ann Catholic Church; *Personal note:* I started writing poetry as the only way to put my thoughts down on paper. My only hope is to stir the emotions; *Address:* 74 South Grant Street, Manheim, PA.

MCGREEVY, MARY
Born: November 10, 1935, Kansas City, KS; *Parents:* Donald Hamilton McGreevy; Emmy Lou Neubert; *Spouse:* Phillip D. Rosenbaum, January 21, 1960; *Children:* David Steve, Mariya, Chay, Allyn, Dora, Jacob; *Education:* Vassar College, BA; Columbia University, University of California, PHD; *Occupation:* Scholar, Poet; *Memberships:* AAUW, AWP, Nelson Atkins Museum of Art, Los Alos Museum of Art; *Honors:* Distinguished Full Professor of Psychology; *Other writings:* Written Articles on Drug Addiction; *Personal note:* I feel Aristoles expresses my philosophy when he says: "Amicus Plato, Se'd Magis Amica Ver'tase", Plato is dear to me, but dearer still is truth; *Address:* St. Laud, FL.

MCKEE, ELLYN
Born: July 3, 1972, Painsville, OH; *Parents:* Jim and Jane McKee; *Education:* Fairfax Elementary Memorial Junior High; Mentor High School; *Occupation:* Student; *Memberships:* National Order of the Rainbow for Girls; Mentor, Plains United Methodist Church; *Honors:* President of Students Against Driving Drunk, 1989; Young Musician of the Year; Scholarship Award; *Other writings:* Several poems published in high school poetry magazine *Reflections*; *Personal note:* I write poems that best explain the mood I'm in or poems that describe world situations; *Address:* 8285 Eldon CT, Mentor, OH.

MCRAE, SHAWN DENISE
Born: May 19, 1977, Irving, TX; *Parents:* William and Dorothy McRae; *Education:* Truman Middle School; *Address:* Grand Prairie, TX.

MEDINA-BERDECIA AMY
Pen Name: Eve; *Born:* September 18, 1977, Ponce, PR; *Parents:* Rosa M. Berdecia, Joseph Berdecia; *Education:* Immaculate Conception School; *Occupation:* Student; *Memberships:* Drama Club, Beta Club; *Honors:* Honor Society; *Other writings:* Some poems published in school newspaper; *Personal note:* I feel I must take every munute as it was my last, I have been inspired by my family and my 5th grade teacher, Mrs. Stewart; *Address:* 1300 Warren Hites Drive, A-102, Augusta, GA.

MEHRA, ROOMA
Born: January 24, 1957, New Delhi, India; *Parents:* Harbans Lal Mehra, Sushil Mehra; *Education:* Lady Irwin School; *Occupation:* Painter, Sculptress, Freelance Writer; *Memberships:* The Poetry Society; *Honors:* Certificate of Honor from the Skylark Poetry Academy; *Other writings:* Three volumes of poetry called "Sunshadow"; "Reaching Out", and "For You" have been published in India; *Address:* New Dehli, India.

MENKE, JENNIFER LYNN
Born: October 30, 1974, Michigan City, IN; *Parents:* Ronald and Penny Menke; *Education:* Springfield Elementary, Krueger Junior High School; Rogers High School; *Honors:* Junior Honor Society; *Address:* LaPorte, IN.

MERCY, SHELLEY
Born: September 25, 1969, Rapid City, SD; *Parents:* Sandy Mercy, Charles Mercy, Jr; *Education:* Sturgis Brown High School; *Occupation:* Store Clerk; *Honors:* Honor Society; *Other writings:* Poems and short stories, I would like to write children's books and articles on controversial subjects that would make a difference; *Personal note:* There is so much more to life than what people see, I like to write about what comes from within, what makes people feel, God is my inspiration!; *Address:* P.O. Box 32, Whitewood, SD.

MERKER, ALICE DAVIS
Born: January 17, 1926, Harrison County, IN; *Parents:* Hubert A. David, Minnie A. Davis; *Spouse:* Robert A Merker, February 1, 1946; *Children:* Rand, Dinah, Louise, Robert, Mark, Katrina, Cynthia; *Education:* Corydon High School; *Occupation:* Marketing; *Memberships:* American Gold Star Mothers Inc., Elmwood United Methoidst Church, Faith Bible Class Camilla United Methodist Church; *Other Writings:* Includes 3 books of poetry, a children's book,co-authored a book, a few short stories, the reading of which is shared with family and friends; *Personal Note:* Any talent I may possess is a gift from God and I can take no credit for it, however, as a gift from God, it is wasted, unless it is shared with others; *Address:* Rt 1 Box 783, Baconton, GA.

MERZ, KRISTIN
Pen Name: Kristin Merz; *Born:* McKeesport, PA; November 17, 1973; *Parents:* Terry and Sharon Merz; *Education:* Norwin Senior High School; *Occupation:* Student; *Memberships:* Student Council, Treasurer of Youth Fellowship, Newspaper at School; *Honors:* Honor Roll, All Star Softball Team; *Other writings:* Written Articles for the Knight Krier; *Personal note:* Being myself and writing poems that reflect the way I feel are the only ways for me to write true poems; *Address:* North Huntingdon, PA.

MICHALSKI, BONNIE
Born: July 14, 1974, Bad Axe, MI; *Parents:* Joseph Michalski, Jean Michalski; *Education:* Harbor Beach Community High School; *Honors:* Young Authors Award; *Personal note:* I would like to thank my family and friends for standing by me thorough these last few years; *Address:* 2840 N. Lakeshore Road, Port Hope, MI.

MIGLIACCIO, ERICA ADELE
Born: March 17, 1978, Hudson, NY; *Parents:* Lola Migliaccio, Edward Migliaccio; *Education:* Cairo Elementary School; *Occupation:* Student; *Memberships:* Treasurer of Student Council, Merritt Dance Studios; *Honors:* Highest Academic Achievement Grades K-6, High Honor Roll, Many other School Related Awards, Aysma Music Achievement; *Other writings:* A story about my hamster published in the Mountain News through 4-H; *Personal note:* I enjoy amusing people with my writings and have been greatly inspired by Shel Silverstein; *Address:* Rt 32, Box 324, Freehold, NY.

MILAEGER, CORRIE LYNN
Born: May 28, 1976, Rockford, Illinois; *Parents:* Richard and Robin Milaeger; *Education:* St. Paul's Elementary School; *Occupation:* Student; *Personal note:* I have been influenced by my faith and love in God and my need to spread His word; *Address:* 6261 Brookhill, Oconomowoc, WI.

MILAN, MARK A.
Born: July 21, 1965, Carthage, TX; *Parents:* Paul and Bennie Fay Samford; *Occupation:* Advertising Representative; *Memberships:* Crestview Missionary Baptist; *Other writings:* "My Dear Friend" published in the Poetry Centers, *Many Voices, Many Lands*; "God is Everywhere" published in the Poetry Centers, *Heartland*; "He" published in the Amherst Society; *Personal note:* God has been so good to me throughout the years and I want to do all I can with my poetry and life to reflect that to whomever with the understanding that's what he has done for me; He will also do unto you, He is the best friend anyone could ever have. My prayer is that my poetry will inspire everyone to accept him as their personal savior and began a life of everlasting happiness and peace, God bless you! *Address:* Grand Prairie, TX.

MILES, REBECCA
Pen Name: Becki; *Born:* June 18, 1974; *Parents:* Sandra Hart, Paul Miles; *Education:* Saratoga Springs Senior High School; *Occupation:* Secretary at Camp Saradac during Summer Vacation; *Personal note:* I like to help people through rough times and I like for people to ask for help or advice from me, It makes me feel good because I could be making someone else's life just a little bit better; *Address:* 9 Garside Road, Saratoga Springs, NY.

MILES, SELENA
Pen Name: Lena Miles; *Born:* March 27, 1975; *Education:* Mt Carmel High School; *Occupation:* Student; *Personal note:* The limit is what's given to you, to strive is to go beyond; *Address:* San Diego, CA.

MILLER, ALISON
Born: February 13, 1976, Americus, GA; *Parents:* Eugene T. Miller, Camille C Miller; *Education:* Lee County Middle School; *Memberships:* Millie Lewis Modeling Agency; *Honors:* Jr. Beta Club Award and Medal for Citizenship; *Address:* 132 Delham Drive, Lessburg, GA.

MILLER, AMY
Born: December 15, 1976, Waterloo, NY; *Parents:* Elizabeth Miller, Thomas Miller; *Education:* Romulus Central High School; *Occupation:* Student; *Memberships:* Romulus Central School Band and Chorus; Romulus Presbyterian Church; Youth Group and Junior Choir; Phyllis Griffith School of Dance; Girl Scouts; *Honors:* Honor Roll; *Personal note:* I hope that one day, we can accomplish a peaceful and drug-free nation; *Address:* P.O. Boc 134, Romulus, NY.

MILLER, BRANDI
Born: January 29, 1978, Wheeling, WV; *Parents:* Daniel and Brenda Miller; *Education:* Sardis Elementary, Sardi, OH; *Memberships:* 4-H, Tap, Ballet, Jazz, Gymnastics; *Honors:* Principal's List; 4.0 Student; Young Authors; *Other writings:* "The Blind Miracle"; "Always and Forever", "The Finer Things in Life"; "Why Live", "Alone in the Sky", "Take Me Now"; *Personal note:* Don't be afraid to march a parade, to be in the lead, to do anything, if you believe it you can achieve it, if you dream it you can become it; *Address:* 37432 th Avenue, Sardis, OH.

MILLER, ERICA T.
Born: July 24, 1972, North Tarrytown, NY; *Parents:* Ronald Miller, Thelma Miller; *Education:* Woodlands High School; *Memberships:* Union Baptist Church, Africa Study Group, Church Choir, Church User Board; *Honors:* Commended Black Scholar; *Personal note:* I write from my heart, and about things that are heavy on my mind; *Address:* 15 Midway Road, White Plains, NY.

MILLER, JAMES
Born: February 7, Charleston, SC; *Parents:* Elijah Miller, Geneva L. Miller; *Spouse:* Janette L. Miller; *Children:* Angelia A., James, O'Neal, Matthew; *Education:* Laing High School; Mt. Pleasant, SC; *Occupation:* Supply Clerk; *Memberships:* The American Legion, NAACP, AARP, AFGE Local 2082; *Honors:* Two Golden Poet Awards, 1988-89 World of Poetry and a Poet of Merit Award from American Poetry Assn; *Other writings:* "Smile", *American Anthology of Contemporary Poetry*; "Lemon", "Bullfrog", "Dr. Martin Luther King Jr.", *American Poetry Anthology*; "Love Begin", *Treasured Poems of American Winter*; *Address:* Marina, CA.

MILLER, MICHELLE
Pen Name: Michelle Miller; *Born:* February 2, 1974, Watertown, SD; *Parents:* Michael G; Marilyn Ries; *Education:* Watertown Senior High School; *Occupation:* Student; *Memberships:* USTA, Holy Name Catholic Church; *Honors:* Honor Rolls; *Address:* 157 14th Street N.E., Watertown, SD.

MILLER, SONYA

Pen Name: Tina, Pumkin, Shorty; *Born:* February 8, 1974, Boston, MA; *Parents:*Linda E. Yancey, Allen B. Miller; *Education:* Boston Technical High School; *Memberships:* Mattapan Youth Outreach Program; *Honors:* Student of the Month; *Other writings:* Poems for a personal collection; *Personal note:* I want to inspire all young people to be the best they can be; *Address:* Boston, MA.

MILNER, ERVIN

Born: May 25, 1927, Gibsland, LA; *Parents:*Buster Milner, Ida Clark Milner; *Children:* Ervin J., Rochelle D., Keith E; *Occupation:* Custodian; *Memberships:* The American Legion, American Cancer Society; *Honors:* Korea Veteran, Honorable Discharge, Good Conduct Medal, Army of Occupation Medal, National Defense Service Medal; *Personal note:* Poetry is expressing your feeling of a person or subject;

MINOR, REBEKAH LYNN

Pen Name: Ashton Lace; *Born:* September 1, 1974; Little Rock, AR; *Parents:*Rose Ann, Jerry Minor; *Education:* Harmony Grove High School; *Occupation:* Student; *Memberships:* Fitness Unlimited; Beta Club, Science Club, FBLA, FHA, Student Council; *Honors:* Most School Spirit of Homecoming, 1989; Beta Club Award, Piano Awards, Civics and Geography Awards, 7-10 Grade Honor Roll Awards; *Other writings:* Several Poems published in local newspapers; *Personal note:* I like to reach the hearts of others in my poems as well as in the way I live. A smile is the cure for anything; *Address:* 805 Turtle Creek, Benton, AR.

MITCHELL, VERONICA LEE

Born: October 21, 1972, Lynwood, CA; *Parents:*Robert H., Terri E. Mitchell; *Education:* Marysville Junior High School; *Occupation:* Student; *Memberships:* Rocky Horror Picture Show Fan Club; *Other writings:* Several poems entered in school district competitions; *Personal note:* What diabolical plan has seized my crazed imagination? *Address:* 4706 122nd Place NE, Marysville, WA.

MOBLEY, PAUL R.

Born: January 15, 1931, Paintlick, KY; *Parents:*L. Herbert Mobley, Lola Mobley; *Spouse:* Shirley A. Mobley, July 17, 1954; *Children:* Michael R., Paul R. Jr., H. Allen, Danita Colleen; *Education:* University of Cinti; *Honors:* Patent Awards; *Other writings:* Engineering type technical writing, newspaper column, miscellaneous publications; *Personal note:* I strive to contribute growth information and pleasure in my writing, to be a contributor to humanity; *Address:* Cynthiana, KY.

MOFFA, ANNE MARIE

Pen Name: Angel Spencer; *Born:* March 2, 1977, Pursan, South Korea; *Education:* Roslyn Elementary School; *Occupation:* Student; *Memberships:* Just Say No to Drugs Club; *Honors:* Honor Roll; *Other writings:* "Oh Delicate Rose", "My First Kiss"; *Address:* 2443 Avondale Avenue, Roslyn, PA.

MOJESKI, MICHELE

Pen Name: Raven Barbee; *Born:* February 29, 1972, Niagara Falls, NY; *Education:* Fairport High School; *Occupation:* Student; *Memberships:* Amnesty International; *Honors:* Human Rights Club Award; *Personal note:* Appreciate the art within your soul; *Address:* 1 Crossbrook Trail, Fairport, NY.

MONIQUE, JEWEL

Born: New York, NY; *Parents:*Maurice Brown, Patricia Brown; *Education:* Joan of Ark High School; Louis D. Brandis High School; *Occupation:* Home Health Aid; *Honors:* Won Golden Poet Award for 1989; *Other writings:* Several poems have been published in the World of Poetry Press Brooks, and another poem which I had won an award for in 1989 has been published; *Personal note:* I like to be able to share my writing's of peace, love, and with hopeful meanings with other people in the world, and it's a great joy to be able to do this in my life; *Address:* 875 Amsterdam Avenue, #5-B, New York, NY.

MOORE, CHAD

Pen Name: Chad Brady; *Born:* October 3, 1969, Plainview, TX; *Parents:*Ronnie Moore, Judy Moore; *Spouse:* Tammy Moore, December 1989; *Children:* Jade Brady Moore; *Education:* Canyon High School; *Occupation:* Refrigeration Technician; *Memberships:* LIXX Array Club; *Honors:* Best Male Model; *Other writings:* Written song lyrics for certain rock-n-roll bands; also, in the process of writing a book entitled, *Midnight High*; *Personal note:* Never let anyone tell you, that you're limited to one type of writing, always express your self opinions; *Address:* 7816 Acton Rd, Indianapolis, IN.

MOORE, DEBORAH

Born: January 23, 1971, Dallas, TX; *Parents:*Allie Mae Moore, Carl Potts; *Spouse:* Willis Brown; *Children:* Nakita Moore; *Occupation:* Typist; *Memberships:* Business Professional of America, Bayside COGIC, Adult Choir; *Honors:* Voluntary Income Tax Assistance Award, High Honors Graduate; *Personal note:* Reach for the unreachable expect the unexpected never be disappointed; *Address:* Dallas, TX.

MOORE, STACY ERIN

Pen Name: S.E. Moore; *Born:* March 7, 1971, Onionta, NY; *Parents:*David Moore, Gina Moore; *Education:* Lafayette High; Virginia Commonwealth University; *Occupation:* Student; *Memberships:* Quill and Scroll; Advertising Club; *Honors:* Governor's Seal on High School Diploma; Art Scholarship; *Other writings:* Poems and short stories in school newspapers, edited and wrote copy for high school yearbook; *Personal note:* A piece of writing must dig to the depths of it reader's souls and unearth memories and secrets. It must throb of life otherwise it is as dry and lifeless as a dead leaf; *Address:* 112 Sharps Road, Williamsburg, VA.

MORGAN, CYNTHIA A.

Born: April 2, 1974, Princeton, NJ; *Parents:*Granvil, Estelle Morgan; *Education:* Ridgeway High School; *Memberships:* Senior High Art Club; Speech and Drama; *Honors:* School Wide Poetry Contest, 1st Place; *Other writings:* Currently working on first book of poems; *Personal note:* I feel that writing poetry defines any emotion tossed my way, however, Emily Dickenson has made a tremendous impression on my thoughts; *Address:* Memphis, TN.

MORGENROTH, LAURA LORA

Pen Name: Laura Lora; *Born:* January 22, 1940, Mexico; *Parents:*Jorge Morgenroth Romero; Enriqueta Lora Cruz; *Spouse:* Tomas Meraz Marin; *Children:* Tomas Meraz; Veronica Meraz; *Education:* Kindergarten Teacher and Bilingual Secretary; *Occupation:* Housekeeping; *Honors:* Latin American Poetry, Golden Poet Award for 1989; *Other writings:* About to finish two or tree books in Spanish and a dictionary for students in english; *Personal note:* I believe in love's energy and God's will. Mainly I enjoy the classics, also I like Shakespeare and Federico Garcia Lorca, Leon Felipe, Amado Nervo, Juan Rulfo and Pearl Buck; *Address:* San Jeronimo Lidice, Mexico.

MORROW, LISA

Born: January 13, 1968; Little Rock, AR; *Parents:* Randy, Linda Morrow; *Education:* Fort Zumwalt High School; University of Missouri; *Occupation:* Employed by Wal-Mart; *Memberships:* Amnesty International, University Players; *Other writings:* Working on short stories in a workshop at UMC; *Personal note:* I like personal writing that other people can relate to, I try not to be obscure, my greatest influence is John Lennon as a writer, musician and human being; *Address:* Columbia, MO.

MOSQUEDA, RENELLA FRANCO

Born: November 6, 1973, San Pedro, CA; *Parents:* Ricardo Mosqueda, Nelmida Mosqueda; *Education:* Mount Vernon High School; *Occupation:* Student; *Memberships:* SADD, National Honor Society; American Studies Club; Senior Math Team, International Social Club; *Honors:* Honor Roll, French Proficiency Award, First Place Lyric Poetry; *Other writings:* Written several unpublished poems and short stories; *Personal note:* I am fascinated by fantasy, the unusual, the mysterious, and the magical, my inspiration comes from all that is beautiful to me; *Address:* Fort Belvior, VA.

MUGAVERO, CHRISTINE

Born: February 24, 1974, Port Jervis, NY; *Parents:* Madeline Mugavero, Christopher Mugavero; *Occupation:* Cashier; *Address:* Beohmler Road, Sparrowbush, NY.

MUHAMMAD, AMIR

Born: October 17, 1954, Bridgeport, CT; *Parents:*Mr. and Mrs Herbert West; *Children:* Rasheed, Charles, Atiya, Aisha; *Occupation:* Accounting; *Memberships:* LIFE, Living Ideas for Family; *Honors:* Minority Business Award, Community Service Award; *Other writings:* Written Book Entitled, *From the Heart of A Man*; *Personal note:* To reflect the unity of man and the oneness in human nature;

MULKEY, MATT

Born: October 5, 1971, Carrollton, GA; *Parents:* Charles Mulkey, June Mulkey; *Education:* Mt Zion High School; *Occupation:* Student; *Memberships:* HEART; Senior Play Committee; *Honors:* Nominee for Who's Who Among American High School; Honorable Mention Cultural Arts Poetry Contest; *Other writings:* Poetry Published in School Newspaper, Written and Performed Several Songs Locally; *Personal note:* Having had childhood cancer I can say, "as long as their is a spark of hope in your heart your goodwill will be the flame that shows it"; *Address:* 200 State Park Road, Carrollton, GA.

MULLIGAN, RENEE

Born: August 4, 1976, Hackensack, NJ; *Parents:*Regina Salice, Thomas Mulligan; *Occupation:* Student; *Address:* Wyckoff, NJ.

MURAWSKI, DOLORES ELLEN

Born: October 17, 1972, Philadelphia, PA; *Parents:* Joseph Ann Delores Murawski; *Education:* Lower Cape May Regional High School; *Occupation:* Student; *Other writings:* Several Non Published Poems, Short Stories and A Novel; *Personal note:* Dreams bring on the creation of new worlds; *Address:* 201 States Avenue, VIllas, NJ.

MURTI, LATA

Born: March 28, 1976, Oakland, California; *Parents:* Saty Satya-Murti, Viji Satya-Murti; *Education:* Currently in 8th grade; *Memberships:* National Federation of Music Clubs; *Honors:* Music Festival Awards, a 3rd Place Plaque for the County Spelling Bee; *Other writings:* Several poems published in newspapers, have won a music essay contest; *Personal note:* I enjoy writing poetry for it is an outlet through which I can express my feelings; *Address:* Box 262, Route 4, Parsons, KS.

MYERS, JENNIFER M.

Born: November 24, 1974, Tampa FL; *Parents:*Kim Myers, George H. Myers; *Education:* Boca Ceiga High School; *Address:* St. Petersburg, FL.

MYERS, LESLIE ALLENE

Born: December 2, 1970, Savannah, GA; *Parents:*John R. Myers Jr., Carol C. Myers; *Education:* Manning High School; *Occupation:* Student; *Memberships:* Manning High School Marching Band, Hero Chapter; *Honors:* Band Hall of Fame, Honor Society; *Other writings:* Many other poems and stories; *Personal note:* This poem was written in memory of Kevin Scott Fenters who was a friend and a member of the 3A state championship football team in South Carolina; He was taken away from us in a automobile accident in March of 1989; *Address:* PO Box 535, Godwin Drive, Summerton, SC.

NAPUTI, MATILD MARIA

Pen Name: Deedee; *Born:* December 2, 1973, San Diego, CA; *Parents:*Joaquin Nangauta Naputi; Julia Santos Naputi; *Education:* Pacific Basin Education Center, Computer Pacific Institute; *Occupation:* Student; *Memberships:* SPIRIT Committee, Athletic Committee SADD Committee of Notre Dame; *Honors:* National Junior Honor Choir and Safety Award, National Bible Essay Contest Award, St. Francis School Reading Trophy, Notre Dame Scholarship Award; *Other writings:* "Today's World"; "Achievement"; "Improve Your Health, Relationships and Happiness"; *Personal note:* I usually create poems about reality, self improvement, and the qualities a particular subject should have, however, if I was asked to make a poem that does not acquire my usual themes, I would be able to carry out such request; *Address:* Merizo, Guam.

NASH, SHARON LEE

Pen Name: Sharon Crooks Nash; *Born:* March 10, 1940, Hamilton, MT; *Parents:*Sammy Crooks, Evelyn Crooks Daniels; *Spouse:* Harold Lee Roy Nash, September 1974; *Children:* Gerald, Gene, Gordon; *Education:* Stevensville High School; Pharmacy Tech Training College; *Occupation:* Pharmacy A-Tech, Artist, Photographer; *Memberships:* Washington State Art Society; Cougar Club, Washington State Pharmacy Assn, St. Patrick's Parrish; *Honors:* Editor's Choice Awards on both Poetry and Lyric Competition; *Other writings:* Poetry Short Stories, "Tales of Jacob

McNaughton", "Joshua McTavish Finds a Home", "Welcome Home"; *Personal note:* I hope my poem "Rose in the Snow", can help ease some of the pain of SIDS, my purpose is to touch on everyday life and bring joy to someone who lives it; *Address:* 217 E. Kiernan Avenue, Spokane, WA.

NASH, TAMMY LYN
Born: February 28, 1976, Bangor Maine; *Parents:*Allen L. and Carolee M. Nash; *Education:* Hayfield Secondary School; *Occupation:*Student; *Memberships:* Hayfield Secondary School Band; *Other writings:* This is my first published writing; *Personal note:* I took pen and wrote something on paper, then showed it to my teacher and she said "what beautiful poetry, Tammy." *Address:* Ft Belvior, VA.

NATIONS, JACINDA
Pen Name: Jacinda Nations; *Born:* October 31, 1975, Grapevine, TX; *Parents:*Perry and Charlene Nations; *Occupation:* Student; *Other writings:* Written several unpublished poems; *Personal note:* Poetry is my life and my goal is to become a published poet; *Address:* 805 Jarvis Lane, Azle, TX.

NEISIUS, DAWN RENEE
Born: October 10, 1973; Wauwatosa; *Parents:*Richard and Bonnie Neisius; *Education:* San Marin High School; *Occupation:* Student; *Personal note:* World Peace Starts with Inner Peace; *Address:* 3 Rosemary Ct, Novato, CA.

NELMS, LINDA
Born: May 6, 1953, Brady, TX; *Parents:*Roy Hilliard, Wanda Hilliard; *Spouse:* Toby L. Nelms, November 27, 1970; *Children:* Tammy Lynn, Joshua Lee, Roy Mack; *Education:* Burnet High School; *Occupation:* Homemaker, Volunteer Teachers'Aide; *Other writings:* Poem published in local newspaper with article; *Personal note:* Only through experience, do we learn, through my new learned experience, I hope to help many others deal with their new life changes; *Address:* 5350 Garner Road, Weaatherford, TX.

NELSON, JENNY
Born: June 24, 1975, Milwaukee, WI; *Parents:*Alan and Betty Nelson; *Education:* Peshigo High School; *Memberships:* 4-H, Yearbook Staff, Peshtigo High School Concert, Marching Band, Senior High Chorus; *Honors:* 1st Place in Marinette County Writers Contest; *Address:* W3070 Hale School Road, Peshtigo, WI.

NELSON, MARK A.
Born: January 10, 1974, Ottawa, Ontario; *Parents:* Barbara and John Bissett; *Education:* Carleton Secondary School; *Memberships:* International Arabian Horse Assn, Canadian Pony Club, 4-H Club; *Personal note:* I have been greatly influenced by my grandfather; *Address:* RR #4, Almonte, Ontario.

NELSON, NOEL GROVER
Born: January 15, 1942, Mena, Arkansas; *Parents:*Nel W. Nelson, Greta K. Nelson; *Children:* Kay, Kenny, Kevin; *Education:* Ball High School, Galveston, TX, 1959; Art Institute of Houston, AA, 1985; *Occupation:* Security Officer, Graphic Designer; *Honors:* Golden Poet Award, World of Poetry, 1988, 1989; *Other writings:* "Faces are Pictures"; "Salute to Veterans"; "Loves Touch"; "God Knows All"; *Address:* 5109 Sealy #1, Galveston, TX.

NEWCOMER, AMY JOAN MARIE
Born: April 15, 1972, Uniontown, PA; *Parents:*Donald Raymond and Martha Karchnak Newcomer; *Education:* Tri Valley Sr High School; *Occupation:* Newspaper Carrier, Student; *Memberships:* Tri Valley Art Club; Students Against Drunk Driving; Junior and Senior High National Honor Society; *Address:* Uniontown, PA.

NEWTON, DENISE
Born: October 28, 1957, North Miami, FL; *Parents:* Grant Johnson, Karin Rubin; *Spouse:* William Newton, June 2, 1979; *Children:* Jesse Michael, Thomas William, Chad Andrew; *Education:* North Miami Beach High School; Central Florida Community College; *Occupation:* Housewife and Mother; *Memberships:* Right to Life Assn; Concerned Women for America; *Other writings:* Several other poems and cards; *Personal note:* Much of my work was inspired by family and loved ones, I only hope they all know how important they are to me; *Address:* Rt. 2 Box 896, Williston, FL.

NILES, ANGELA
Pen Name: Angie Niles; *Born:* July 5, 1977, Carson City, Nevada; *Parents:*Arlene Niles Huls, Richard Niles; *Occupation:* Student; *Memberships:* 4-H; *Honors:* Presidential Academic Fitness Award; *Personal note:* One can get the greatest pleasures out of the simple things in life; *Address:* Box 151, Silver Springs, NE.

NORMAND, JEANINE A.
Born: December 2, 1949, New Orleans, LA; *Parents:* Jack Normand, Gene Normand; *Education:* MA, Cum Laude in French; MA, Cum Laude in English Linguistics; PHD, Scholar in French; *Occupation:* Technical Writer, Technical Communication Specialist and Concert Pianist and Orchestra Leader; *Memberships:* Society for Technical Communicators, National Lesbian Agenda, Atlanta Lesbian, Feminist Alliance; *Honors:* Honorary PHD, International Language School, NDEA Fellowship in French, President's List, Woman Writes Coordinator, 1986-1990; *Other writings:* Fiction and Poems Published in Maize Magazine, Articles in Evergreen, Literary Criticism in Scholarly Journals, Fiction and Poems in Women Writes Anthology, 1985, 86, 87, 89; *Personal note:* The Great Women Poets, Especially Adrienne *Address:* Decatar, GA.

OAKLEY, ROBIN A.
Born: February 28, 1973, Greensboro, NC; *Parents:* Charlene Floyd and John Oakley; *Education:* Harry P. Harding High School; *Memberships:* Honor Society, Beta Clun; *Other writings:* When in six grade poem was published in Mecklenburg County Childrens Book of Poetry; *Personal note:* I write to get things off my mind and about everyday happenings; *Address:* Rt 3 Box 52C, Huffstetler Street, Gastonia, NC.

OBBAGY, SUSAN NOEL
Born: March 21, 1968, Parma, OH; *Parents:*William and Patricia Obbagy; *Education:* Lakewood High School; *Occupation:* Works as Housekeeper; *Other writings:* I have written many poems since high school but I haven't been successful in getting any published until now; *Personal note:* I believe we should all accept everyone for who they are, we are all equal but different in our own way, no one is better than you until you believe you're better than they are; *Address:* Cleveland, OH.

ODEN, SHAWN M.
Born: February 16, 1973, Shreveport, LA; *Parents:* Carol Cowan Gullette, Paul Edward Oden; *Occupation:* Student; *Honors:* Quill and Scroll, 1st place in city's poetry contest; *Other writings:* "Obsession", "Way it Should be"; "Turn Around"; "Missing You"; "Chain of Friendship"; "In Your Arms"; *Personal note:* Contemplations are much more than words; *Address:* Rt 9 Box 142A, Little Rock, AR.

ODOM, KAREN KAY
Pen Name: Kay Kay; *Born:* June 6, 1970; Houston, TX; *Parents:*Sheila Holder, Ricky Kumpt; *Spouse:* Earl Aldridge; *Children:*Erica, Raymond; *Occupation:* Housewife; *Honors:* Track Awards in School; *Other writings:* Several other poems; *Address:* Magnolia, TX.

OKORO, ANEZI N.
Pen Name: Anok; *Born:* May 17, 1929, Arondizuogu, Nigeria; *Parents:*Okoro Okereke, Onuaku Okereke; *Spouse:* Eseohe Aneziokoro, August 3, 1971; *Children:* Chinyere, Onuake, Chukwuma, Anezi, Ogbonnaya; *Education:* Methodist College, Uzuakoli, DMGS, Onitsha; University College, Ibadann; University of Bristol, England; *Occupation:* Medical Practitioner, Professor of Medicine; *Memberships:* Nigerian Medical Assn; British Assn of Dermatologist, American Academy of Dermatology; *Honors:* Ahiajoku Lecture, 1988; *Other writings:* "The Village School"; "The Village Headmaster", "One Week One Trouble"; "Febechi in Cave Adventure"; "Febechi Down the Niger"; "Education is Great"; *Address:* University of Nigeria Teaching Hospital, Enugu, Nigeria.

OLBETER, PATRICIA LOUISE
Pen Name: Pattie, Smurf, Angel; *Born:* March 19, 1973, New Kensington; *Parents:*Shirley Louise Black, Richard James Olbeter; *Education:* Lower Burrell Westlyn Academy; Cheswick Christian Academy; *Honors:* Academic Trophies; *Other writings:* I have not gotten anything else published as of yet but I have hundreds of poems that I hope to get published someday; *Personal note:* I would just like to thank my family for encouraging me to write and I would like to dedicate all my writings to my parents especially to my dad, may he smile on me writing in heaven; *Address:* Brackenridge, PA.

OLIVEIRA, VICTOR WILLIAM
Born: March 23, 1966, Woodstock Ontario; *Parents:* Eduino, Oliveira, Inez; *Education:* College Avenue Secondary School; *Occupation:* Woodworking, Apprentice, Parcel Boy, Laborer, Custodian; *Honors:* Received 25 Free Albums for Having a Song in the Nascho Record Company; *Other writings:* A country song called "Lovewaves, Lovewaves" on the Nascho album entitled "Lovewaves; A poem in the American Poetry Anthology; *Personal note:* I have been influenced greatly by the classical greek and roman poets from Homer to Dante Algheiri; I've also been inspired by the Holy Scriptures which I can say, may the sacred heart of Jesus be adored, glorified, loves and preserved in the world now and forever; *Address:* Woodstock, Ontario.

O'MALLEY, JENNIFER
Born: July 11, 1973, Straford, NJ; *Parents:*Peter O'Malley, Diane Ewell; *Education:* Gulf High School; *Occupation:* Bus Girl and aspiring Poet; *Memberships:* Artwise; *Personal note:* In those solitary hours the fear that overpowers shatters glass unseen; *Address:* New Port Richey, FL.

ORMEROD, WENDY ANN
Born: November 12, 1972, Chinhoyi, Zimbabwe, Africa; *Parents:*Beverly and George Ormerod; *Education:* Rydings Junior, Lomagunoi College, Chisipite Senior; *Occupation:* Student; *Memberships:* Wildlife Society of Zimbabwe; *Honors:* Milton Arts Award; *Other writings:* Poems in magazines and in *Of Diamonds and Rust*; *Address:* 11 Ettington Road, Greystone Park, Harare, Zimbabwe, Africa.

OWLETT, MELANIE SUE
Pen Name: M.S. Owlett; *Born:* May 1, 1976, Hornell, NY; *Parents:*David Owlett, Elva Owlett; *Education:* Student; *Occupation:* Writer, Actor, Dancer, Singer; *Memberships:* Girl Scouts of America, 4H, Alfred Ballet Academy; *Honors:* NYSMA Medal; *Other writings:* Written numerous poems and short story entitled, "Upon a Daydream"; *Personal note:* To write is to use your pen as a paintbrush and your imagination as a subject; *Address:* 37 Twin Valley Terrace, Almond, NY.

PALMERE, ANN
Pen Name: Ronald Palmere; *Born:* May 9, 1971, Melrose IL; *Parents:*Ann M. Holt, Joe D. Palmere; *Education:* York High School; *Occupation:* Villa Park Veterinary Hospital; *Honors:* Illinois High School Assn III Division for Solo Voice; *Other writings:* I have written many other poems and songs, but none have been published outside of school; *Personal note:* Always reach for your dreams because one day they will come true; *Address:* 505 Willow Road, Elmhurst, IL.

PARADIS, STACY
Born: August 14, 1975, Rochester, NH; *Parents:* Richard and Linda Paradis; *Education:* Kingswood Junior High School; *Personal note:* I send a reminder and hope to stop the world of pollution. Follow your dreams for hope that this reminder will come true; *Address:* 38 Ridge Road, New Durham, NH.

PARIS, AMY
Born: March 1, 1974; *Parents:*Sandra L. Paris, Richard C. Paris; *Education:* Assumption High School; *Address:* Louisville, KY.

PARKER, SARAH JENNIFER
Pen Name: Sarah Parker; *Born:* June 11, 1975, San Francisco, CA; *Parents:*Marcy Parker; *Occupation:* Student; *Other writings:* Written several poems; *Personal note:* My family is very important to me and my love of family is reflected in my poetry, the loss of my grandparents affected me deeply, I dedicate this poem to my grandfather who I love and miss very much; *Address:* 14315 Riverside Drive, #207, Sherman Oaks, CA.

PARKS, CLARENCE H.
Pen Name: Apid Abdullah Rasheed; *Born:* July 18, 1949, Miami; *Parents:*Clarence H., Anna A. Parks; *Children:* Tommy, Gregory, Stacey Mikkita, Clarence II, Ontika, Cody; *Education:* Miami Carol City High,

University of Maryland, Columbia College and Metro State College; *Occupation:* Retired Air Froce; *Memberships:* F&AM Masonic Order Consistory, Shrine & Holy Royal Arch Masons, PHA, USA; *Honors:* Dean's List; *Other writings:* Several Poems published in other anthologies and newspapers; *Personal note:* Poetry is but precious stones that fall from the unmined caves of of our very souls...we must learn to leave the stones untouched until they have been cultivated by time and emotion..then; *Address:* 1273 Lima Street, Aurora, CO.

PARSON-COALE, VIKKI

Pen Name: Vikki S. Coale; *Born:* May 12, 1961; *Spouse:* John C. Parson; *Education:* Florida State University; Canal Zone College; *Memberships:* MENSA, National Forensic League; *Honors:* Phi Theta Kappa, Dean's List; *Other writings:* The life I live true love magazine; *Personal note:* I am an adventurer and explorer, currently living in Alaska; Future plans include living off the land in southeast Alaska; Someday, I plan on visiting Australia; *Address:* Juneau, AK.

PARSONS, JENNY LYNN

Born: May 8, 1972, Dallas Texas; *Parents:*Herbert L. Parsons Jr., Linda M. Parsons; *Education:* Spotwood High School; *Occupation:* Student, Works Parttime in Convenience Food Store; *Honors:* First Place in Water Color Painting Contest; Won 6th Place in Horse Show; *Other writings:* "Only A Fantasy", The American Poetry Anthology; *Personal note:* This poem is dedicated to my grandfather, John W. Bracken, and all who loved him. I wrote this for everyone who will miss him because of his death, we love you, Grandpa, always! *Address:* Grottoes, VA.

PARTIDA, ROXANA

Born: March 29, 1972, Brownsville, TX; *Parents:* Ramon and Amparo Partida; *Education:* Canales Elementary and Gladys Porter High School; *Other writings:* I have written numerous poems, but this is the first that has been published; *Personal note:* Writing has been my hobby since I was 13 years old, I write about the facts of life and personal feelings of human beings, I have been influenced by Shakespeare's writings; *Address:* Brownsville, TX.

PATRICK, KEVIN

Born: January 19, 1971, Hummelstown, PA; *Parents:* Dennis and Linda Patrick; *Education:* Warwick High School; Millersville University; *Honors:* Who's Who Among American High School Students; *Personal note:* I love to write poetry, I love to write in many different styles and a variety of themes; Most often my writings are stirred by strong feelings on a subject; *Address:* Lititz, PA.

PATTON, KAY L.

Born: December 7, 1922, Dallas, TX; *Parents:*Charles and Willie Patton; *Education:* Abilene Christian University, Abilene, BA; *Occupation:* Counselor, ACU; *Memberships:* Church of Christ, *Honors:* Alpha Tau Lambda Literary Society; Who's Who in American Colleges and Universitiws, Alpha Chi, Alumni Citation Award from ACU; *Other writings:* Various Published Poems and Articles in the United States and Germany; Thesis on Unwed Mothers' Problem in Libraries of Abilene Christian University; *Personal note:* My purpose in life is to honor and praise God, My Faith, and Jesus, His Son and my Brother, by living as best I can by Their direction in Their Holy Bible and sharing Their Message with Others; *Address:* 851 E. N. 16th Street, Abilene, TX.

PAYNE, GEORGIA A.

Born: June 2, 1945, Springfield, OH; *Parents:*Ralph and Wilda Hanson; *Spouse:* Elmer R. Payne; March 7, 1964; *Children:* Penny Lee, Rick Allen; *Education:* Edison State Community College; *Occupation:* Vista Volunteer; Project Coordinator for Literacy Program; *Memberships:* St Marys of the Wood; Literary Council; *Honors:* Dean's List; *Other writings:* "Circle of Life", Independent Review; "Silent Friends", Pegaus Press; *Personal note:* As a beginner in the field of writing I find persistence and positive attitude eventually gives gratification to the heart; *Address:* Quincy, OH.

PELKOFER, ELIZABETH JUNE

Pen Name: Elizabeth J. Pelkoper; *Born:* June 16, 1974; Pittsburg, PA; *Parents:*Frank and Melanie Pelkofer; *Education:* Moniteau High School; *Occupation:* Student; *Memberships:* Spanish Dance Troup; Saxaphone Ensemble; Jazz Band; *Honors:* National Honor Society; YSU Honors; *Other writings:* Published poems in the Moniteau Literary Magazine; *Personal note:* Climb hard, fast and high until you have touched your sky, and then find another just as blue; *Address:* RD 1 Karns City, PA.

PELTIER, SHERRY

Born: October 14, 1973, New Westminster, BC; *Parents:*Richard Peltier, Wilma Peltier; *Education:* Robert L. Clemitson Elementary School; Valley View Junior High School; *Occupation:* Waitress; *Honors:* Most Valuable Player Award in Softball; *Address:* 1000 Todd road, Kamloops, BC.

PENNER, KIMBERLY S.

Born: August 15, 1974, Gettysburg, PA; *Parents:* Steven and Linda Renner; *Education:* Littlestown Senior High School; *Honors:* National Peace Essay; Contest winner for 2nd Place in the state of PA; *Personal note:* Writing poetry is not a difficult thing, you must first capture an emotion and then the words flow from within; *Address:* P.O. Box 261, Littlestown, PA.

PERRISH, RAI AN

Born: May 28, 1971, Cheektowago; *Parents:*Marilyn Perrish, Paymond Perrish; *Education:* Cardinal O'Hara High School; University of Buffalo; *Occupation:* Student; *Memberships:* Greenpeace; *Other writings:* Published in School Newspaper; *Personal note:* Through poetry I am able to bring out my innermost feelings that otherwise may not be expressed; *Address:* Buffalo, NY.

PETERS, KASIE

Born: November 14, 1974, Orange County FL; *Parents:* Dana and Vicki Peters; *Occupation:* Student; *Memberships:* Georgia Cattleman's Assn; *Honors:* 1984 Elementary All Star Chess Champion; Dean Rusk Middle School Music Accomplishments Award; *Other writings:* Written Several Poems not Yet Released to the Public; *Personal note:* I believe the extreme usually gets the most response and if I can influence someone to take a chance or risk in life to succeed then I am truly an artist; *Address:* Canton, GA.

PETERSON, NANCY

Born: April 25, 1975, Spearfish, SD; *Parents:*Donald and Suzanne Peterson; *Education:* Sundance High School; *Occupation:* Student; *Memberships:* Sundance High School German, Speech, and Drama Clubs; St. Paul's Catholic Church; *Honors:* Sundance High School Honor Roll; *Personal note:* Hanging on to depressing yesterdays, dims the hopes for tomorrow; *Address:* Star Route 1, Box 41, Sundance, WY.

PHILLIPS, DIANE TRAPMAN

Pen Name: D.T. Phillips; *Born:* February 11, 1952, E.S. PA; *Education:* St Joseph's University, BA; University of London; *Honors:* Dean List; Named one of the final top 25 poetry chapbooks in the 1988 Annual T.S. Eliot Memorial Competition by the Florida State Poet's Assn; *Other writings:* Author of two full-length plays: "The Crossing" and "The Perfect Blend"; *Personal note:* The production of poetry (music and art alike) is an irrepressible pull on man toward bridging the realities of the physical and the metaphysical, without which true understanding is most unlikely; *Address:* Narberth, PA.

PHILLIPS, JULIE

Pen Name: J.P.; *Born:* February 2, 1953, MO; *Parents:* Robert and Margaret Brown; *Education:* Central Missouri State University, BSE; *Occupation:* Account Representative, Metropolitan Life Insurance Co; *Honors:* Phi Sigma Pi, Kappa Delta Phi Honor Society, 1977 and 78; Who's Who in American Women, 1990; *Other writings:* I am also a professional artist and write poems on the subject of paintings; *Personal note:* My philosopy is to describe life in the simplest form for all to understand; *Address:* S-5A Lake Lotawana, Lees Summit, MO.

PHILLIPS, TERESA DIANE

Pen Name: Ameralis Aldrich; *Born:* March 29, 1964, Spartanburg, SC; *Parents:*Phillip R. Phillips, Irene Phillips; *Education:* Woodruff High School; *Occupation:* Home Worker; *Memberships:* American Red Cross; *Other writings:* Several Poems in 7 Different Anthologies; *Personal note:* I am affected by simple things, all of my poetry is emotion based, and comes from the heart; *Address:* 112 Harbor Town Court, Montgomery, TX.

PIERCE, FRANKLIN KIE

Pen Name: Jann Ross *Born:* January 25, 1975, Spokane, Washington; *Parents:*Jerry and Jackie Ross *Education:* Wilbur High School; *Occupation:* Student; *Memberships:* Future Business Leaders of America; *Honors:* Student of the Month, September 1989; 2nd Place Impromtu Speaker; *Other writings:* Written poems entitled, "Tear Drops", "Promises Made", "Promises Broken; *Personal note:* I strive to let my emotions come out in my writing, so everyone that reads them will experience the feelings I had when I wrote them; *Address:* P.O. Box 28, Wilbur, WA.

PIERCE, JENNIFER LEE

Born: October 13, 1972, Peterborough NH; *Parents:* Timothy R. Pierce Sr., Susan E. Pierce; *Education:* Hillsboro Deering High School; *Occupation:* Student; *Memberships:* Lifetime member of Hillsborough Historical Society; Basketball Junior Varsity Team, Drama, Chorus Youth Group, Big Sisters; *Other writings:* Many poems, short stories, Working on a book for teens about depression; *Personal note:* I express myself through writing, if I can make one person happy with my writing, it's all worth it; *Address:* Hillsboro, NH.

PILCHER, STEPHANIE LEIGH

Born: September 29, 1974, Ripley, TN; *Parents:*Steve and Charlene Pilcher; *Education:* Ripley High School; *Occupation:* Student; *Memberships:* Spanish Club, Goal Card Club, Faith United Methodist Church; *Honors:* Lauderdale County Junior Auxiliary Award for Achievement; Savings Bond for English and Literature; Savings Bond for Achievement, Honor Roll; *Other writings:* Poetry, Short Stories, Essays; *Personal note:* I have been greatly influenced by nature and my surroundings, I greatly enjoy expressing my feelings by writing; *Address:* Rt 6 Box 231A, Ripley, TN.

PINDER, CHRISTINE LYN

Pen Name: Christine Pinder; *Born:* May 21, 1972, Danbury; *Parents:*Diana Pinder Fortunato, James Pinder; *Education:* New Milford High School; *Occupation:* Student; *Personal note:* I write well when my emotions are at a peak; *Address:* Deer Run Shores, Sherman, CT.

PLAUMER, JODI LEA

Pen Name: Jodi Lea; *Born:* July 8, 1970, Connersville, IN; *Parents:*Jerry and Sharon Pflaumer; *Education:* Madison Consolidated High School; Carson-Newman College; *Honors:* Dean's List, National Honor Society; *Other writings:* My poems have been published in the Orange and Blue College Newspaper and in the Difference Baptist Student Union's Newsletter; *Personal note:* My poetry is my way to express my thoughts and dreams, I hope it may touch one reader and then it is all worthwhile; *Address:* 2127 Flint Street, Madison, IN.

POFF, PATSY

Pen Name: Patsy Poff; *Born:* Freeport, TX; *Parents:* Curtis Pate, Lottie Pate; *Spouse:* Malcolm Poff; *Children:* Kirk, Kristie, Kelley, Shelley, Miranda Monae; *Education:* Galveston College of Nursing, Brazos College, AAS; *Occupation:* Registered Nurse; *Memberships:* First Baptist Church, YMCA, Several Nurses Assn; *Honors:* Golden Poet Award; *Other writings:* Several poems published in school and hospital papers; *Personal note:* I try to write down personal feelings that I feel about life around me and things that happen to me and people I love; *Address:* P.O. Box 802, Palestine, TX.

POLACHEK, SHANNON

Pen Name: Jordon Eleigha; *Born:* July 19, 1974, Lakenheath, England; *Parents:*Bernard C. Polachek, Jane Polachek; *Education:* Rome Free Academy; *Occupation:* Student; *Memberships:* American Red Cross, Griffiss Air Force Base Cheerleading Squad; *Honors:* Placed 2nd in State Writing Essay Contest; State of Montana American Red Cross Volunteer Award of the month; *Other writings:* "Devil's Beast", "Autumn Leaves"; "This Earth Has Room for Everyone"; *Personal note:* My poetry represents peace and harmony and equalibrium between man and nature, I've been greatly influenced by two of my english teachers, Judy Jones and Devon Coon, I've also been inspired by Robert Frost; *Address:* Rome, NY.

PONTO, SUSAN

Born: July 1, 1973, Seoul, Korea; *Parents:*Betty A. Ponto; *Education:* Ladywood High School; *Occupation:* High School Student; Professional Dancer; *Memberships:* SADD, Taylor Ballet Americana; *Honors:* CCS

Full Scholarship; *Other writings:* None of my other works have never been published; *Personal note:* Words said will sometimes be forgotten, but words written will always be in the eyes of the beholder; *Address:* Dearborn, MI.

POPE, SANDRA

Pen Name: Sandra Pauline Pope; *Born:* Washington DC; March 12, 1955; *Parents:*Mr. and Mrs. James Ashe; *Spouse:* Henderson J. Pope, March 19, 1975; *Education:* Lincolnton High School, Athen Area Technical Institute; *Occupation:* Esthetician Skin Care; *Memberships:* NAACP; *Other writings:* "Broken Dreams"; "Me"; *Personal note:* Through life there is one thing that I have, the gift of writing; *Address:* P.O. Box 1042, Washington, GA.

PORTIER, R. ELAINE

Pen Name: Lane Cannon; *Born:* November 12, 1952, West Palm Beach, FL; *Parents:*Mymie & Elisha Shuler; *Education:* University of Delaware; *Occupation:* Copywriter, Appraiser; *Memberships:* Mid Atlantic Notary Assn; National Writers Club, National Board of Realtors; *Honors:* Outstanding Young Women of American, Elected Town Council-Colmar Manor; *Other writings:* "How to Campaign on a Shoestring"; Various Poems published in Community Newsletter; *Personal note:* Life deals everyone the same card: Birth; Some keep dealing and taste success, others just spectate and never know what they've missed! *Address:* Adelphi, MD.

POWELL, LASHONDA DEE

Born: October 26, 1972, Sampson County, NC; *Parents:*Eddie N. Powell, Teresa F. Powell; *Education:* Lakewood High School; *Memberships:* NAACP; *Honors:* National Achievement Academy; Who's Who Among American High School Students; National Future Leader of America; Biology Award; *Other writings:* A variety dealing with love, depression, etc, also numerous depicting the mind; *Personal note:* Through poetry, I can express my inner-most thoughts, but most of all it's a way I can escape the real world and live in my own world, it's an experience like no other; *Address:* P.O. Box "N", Roseboro, NC.

PRAZNIK, MONNICA

Pen Name: V.S. Holiday; *Born:* January 16, Medina, OH; *Occupation:* Student; *Memberships:* Greenpeace, Bonita Orchestra; *Personal note:* Save the planet, shop the mall, rock-n-roll; *Address:* LaaVerne, CA.

PRICE, MICHELLE KATHLEEN

Born: April 7, 1972, Ridgewood, NJ; *Parents:*Daniel J. Price, Helma J. Price; *Spouse:* Thomas Licursi; *Education:* West Milford Township High School; *Occupation:* Student; *Memberships:* Humane Society of the United States Special Olympics Volunteer, World Wildlife Fund, SADD, St. Joseph's Church; *Honors:* National Honor Society, Garden State Scholar; *Personal note:* In writing, it is exceedingly imperative to be veracious, thus, I elect to portray life through both pleasant and unfavorable personal experience; *Address:* 52 Yorkshire Avenue, West Milford, NJ.

PRUITT, DEBORAH

Born: July 21, 1975, Lower Merion, PA; *Parents:*John Pruitt, Elizabeth Pruitt; *Education:* Ocean City High School; *Occupation:* Student; *Memberships:* St. John's Lutheran Church Youth Group, Ocean City High School Choir, OCHS Band, SADD; *Honors:* National Junior Honor Society; Distinguished Honors; 2nd Place for Water Conservation Essay; *Personal note:* I tend to write from a teenager's point of view, I write this way, because I feel that they look upon the world as a wonderful place, whereas adults don't have the time; *Address:* #1 Evio-John Court, Marmora, NJ.

QUASTAD, LANITA

Born: July 5, 1978, Fairmont, MN; *Parents:*Mr and Mrs. Marlyn Quastad; *Education:* Ringsted Middle School; *Occupation:* Student; *Memberships:* Armstrong-Ringsted Student Council; Chorus, Christian Youth Club, Christian Life in Progress; *Honors:* Writing Awards for Winning Writing Contests at School; *Other writings:* "Seventh Heaven", "Tonjan Yika", "Life is a Rose", "The Split Up Family"; *Personal note:* I try to show through my writing the reality of life and I hope to give to those who gave me strength a piece back of what they gave me in knowledge; *Address:* Armstrong, IA.

QUINALTY, ANGELA

Born: October 25, 1969, Columbia, MO; *Parents:*Larry and Linda Quinalty; *Education:* Cassville High School; University of Missouri; *Occupation:* College Student; Business Secretary; *Other writings:* Various poems and short stories; *Personal note:* I really like writing poetry because it expresses feelings and emotions that you can't express in everyday life; *Address:* Cassville, MO.

RAU, ELKE ZOSKE

Pen Name: Elke Zoske; *Born:* August 5, 1957, Giessen, West Germany; *Parents:*Kurt and Mathilde Zoske; *Spouse:* Glenn L. Rau, August 31, 1988; *Children:* Nina Ortega, Vincent Ortega; *Education:* Mt. San Jacinto College; *Occupation:* Pre-school Teacher; *Honors:* Golden Poet Award, 1989; Honorable Mention; *Other writings:* "Love and Pain", "Silence", "Sealed with a Kiss", "Without You", "Precious Moments"; *Personal note:* I enjoy writing especially poetry, most of my writings reflect moments of my personal Llife; *Address:* P.O. Box 632, Banning, CA.

RAYNARD, JENNIFER

Born: March 9, 1975, New Glasgow, Nova Scotia; *Parents:*Ron Raynard, Jean Raynard; *Education:* New Glasgow Jr. High School; *Honors:* Examination Honors; *Other writings:* Written Numerous Poems and Articles; *Personal note:* I hope we start taking care of our world so it can take care of us again!; *Address:* 100 Cardinal Court, New Glasgow, NS.

RAYNOR, IRIS LYNN

Born: May 5, 1972, Muncie, IN; *Parents:*Joseph and Juanita Raynor; *Education:* Jeffersontown High School; *Honors:* Honor Roll; Received Several Young Author's Awards; *Other writings:* I write for the school newspaper, I have articles and many poems published in it, I keep a journal of all my poems ever written; *Personal note:* A peom should be written to first satisfy the writer, then, it should be shared with the world, in hopes that the world may find in it, it's own personal meaning; *Address:* Louisville, KY.

REED, CRISTAL

Born: April 18, 1973, Bronx, NY; *Parents:*Thomas Reed, Leslie Reed; *Education:* Monsignor Scanlan High School; *Memberships:* Msgr Scanlan Drama Club; Bronx YMCA Barracude Swim Team, BCL Futuremakers; *Honors:* BCL 1988 Cotillion Scholastic Award, Typing, Attendance, Spanish Award, Bridgefield Civiv League; *Other writings:* Several other poems written, one published in school yearbook; "Looking Back"; *Personal note:* I didn't always shoot for the stars, now I am and the feeling is undefinable, don't neglect yourself or your talents, you'll miss a world of joy; *Address:* 1162 East 223 Street, Bronx, NY.

REED, JENNIFER REAGAN

Pen Name: Jenny; *Born:* August 5, 1973, Alexandria, VA; *Parents:*Scheenren F. Reed, Sandra K. Reed; *Education:* Robert E. Lee High School; *Occupation:* Student; *Address:* Springfield, VA.

REEVES, CARLA

Born: August 22, 1972, Cleveland, OH; *Parents:*Ronald and Linda Reeves; *Education:* Vienna High School; Bucyrus High School; *Occupation:* Student; *Other writings:* "Obsession", "I Remember", "Dreams", "Generations",
"Memories"; *Personal note:* My poems range from emotions and love to vivid dreams, sometimes poetry is the only way I know how to express myself; *Address:* 625 Plymouth Street, Bucyrus, OH.

REISINGER, CHARLES W.

Pen Name: C. Willis Reis; *Born:* November 26, 1931, Beaver, OH; *Parents:*Cecil and Beatrice Reisinger; *Spouse:* Dorothy M. Reisinger, July 25, 1953; *Children:* Gina, Tonya, Charles; *Occupation:* Pastor; *Memberships:* Fairfield Family Association; Kiwanis, AARP; *Other writings:* Numerous Poems; *Personal note:* I desire to communicate the Lord and His way of living for the good of all mankind; *Address:* 321 E. Allen Street, Lancaster, OH.

RENNER, KIMBERLY S.

Born: August 15, 1974, Gettysburg, Pennsylvania; *Parents:*Steven and Linda Renner; *Education:* Littlestown Senior High School, presently a Sophomore; *Honors:* National Peace Essay Contest Winner for 2nd Place in the State of Pennsylvania (1989); *Personal note:* Writing poetry is not a difficult thing. You must first capture an emotion, and then the words flow from within; *Address:* P. O. Box 261, Littlestown, PA.

REYNOLDSON, RANDOLPH C.

Born: 21 September 1952, Sacramento CA; *Parents:* Buzz E. Reynoldson, Lila J. Reynoldson; *Spouse:* Emily M. Reynoldson, 1 September 1973; *Occupation:* United States Air Force; *Personal note:* I write in the hope of reaching others that feel as I do; *Address:* 2012 Weeden Drive, Clovis, NM.

RHYNES, SANDRA N.

Pen Name: Rosie; *Born:* October 23, 1952, Centralia, Illinois; *Parents:*Laura and Walter Sexton; *Children:* Cora, Jason; *Education:* Centralia High School; *Occupation:* Food Service Worker; *Honors:* 5 Honorable Mentions in World of Poetry; *Other writings:* Fantasy called "Dream Heart"; Written Short Stories and Several poems in local paper; *Personal note:* No mountain is too high, if you spread your wings of faith and fly; *Address:* P.O. Box 1658, Davenport, FL.

RICHARDSON, HEATHER

Born: April 17, 1974, Houston, TX; *Parents:*Tom Richardson and Lisa Miller; *Occupation:* Student; *Memberships:* Parkaire Olympic Ice Skating Team; ISIA; *Honors:* ISIA Metals Awarded for Two Gold, One Silver and One Bronze; *Other writings:* Published in Cherokee High School Review; *Personal note:* Established your dreams and make them happen! *Address:* L.A. Station 1088, Waleska, GA.

RICHARDSON, ROBERT G.

Born: May 7, 1946, Cookeville, TN; *Parents:*James G. Richardson, Mildred E. Richardson; *Children:* Shannon Kelly Richardson; *Education:* Algood High School; Livingston Area Vo-Tech School; Columbia State Community College; *Occupation:* Correctional Officer; *Memberships:* Tennessee State Employees Assn; NRA; *Personal note:* Most of my poems are based upon my childhood memories and my memories of Vietnam, I would like to write a book of children's poems using local legends and stories; *Address:* P.O. Box4754, Nashville, TN.

RIFE, KIMBERLY S.

Born: October 12, 1973, Fremont, OH; *Parents:* Kenneth Rife, Diane Rife; *Education:* Oak Harbor Schools; *Occupation:* Student; *Personal note:* I've always felt that poetry comes from inspiration, not education. It isn't the size of the words I use, it's the feelings behind them; *Address:* 1140 S. State Rte 19, Oak Harbor, OH.

RINAUDO, LUCILLE ANN

Born: September 13, 1955, Rochester, NY; *Spouse:* Vincenzo Rinaudo; June 19, 1976; *Children:* Jennifer, Patrick, Vincenzo; *Education:* High School Graduate; *Memberships:* New York State Head Injury Assn; 700 Club; *Honors:* Four Honorable Mentions from World of Poetry, Golden Poet for 1987 and 1988, Silver Poet for 1989 from Word of Poetry; *Other writings:* "The Unloved Child", "Being a Mother", "Was I Ever Young",
"The Miracle of Birth", "A Disabled Women's Prayer"; *Personal note:* I have learned with the love of Jesus and family there is no obstacle that can't be overcome, this is what I write in my poetry so others can see there's hope; *Address:* 3 Reddick Lane, Rochester, NY.

RISLEY, MELISSA

Born: November 25, 1973, Fort Benning, GA; *Parents:* Jose Hernandez, Sandra Hernandez; *Occupation:* Student; *Memberships:* American Karate Academy; *Honors:* Honor Roll; Perfect Attendance; Cheerleading; *Other writings:* Written Numerous Stories; *Personal note:* I feel all people have the right to express their real thoughts; *Address:* 2323 Vicky Avenue, Columbus GA.

RIVERA, SHERRI L.

Born: April 6, 1962, Trenton, NJ; *Parents:*Phyllis and Ismael Bolivora; *Education:* Mercer County Community College; *Occupation:* Cosmetologist; *Personal note:* I have been inspired by family and friends;

RIZZO, STEVEN M.

Born: October 3, 1958, Boston, MA; *Parents:*Joseph J. Rizzo, Florence C. Rizzo; *Spouse:* Deborah M. Rizzo; September 18, 1988; *Education:* North Reading High School; New Style Barber School; *Occupation:* Barber, Hair Stylist; *Memberships:* Church of the Open Bible; *Other writings:* Several unpublished poems, Have also written many songs; *Personal note:* Better or worse? Striving to be what you truly want may sometimes alter who you truly are; *Address:* Medford, MA.

ROACH, ROBERT W.
Born: July 17, 1956, Memphis TN; *Parents:* William Roach, Betty Roach; *Children:* Cortney Michelle, Whitney Danielle; *Education:* Bartlett High School; *Occupation:* Salesman; *Personal note:* As we all pass through this world together, may honesty, truth and trust prevail; *Address:* Memphis, TN.

ROBERTS, LISA ELAINE
Born: July 28, 1966, Nassau, Bahamas; *Parents:* Nehemiah and Elaine Malone; *Spouse:* Chet Roberts, March 26, 1988; *Education:* High School at St. Augustine's College; *Occupation:* Teacher; *Other writings:* Several other poems; *Personal note:* I write exactly what I am feeling at the time I write a poem. Most of my poems were written when something was going on in my life. *Address:* Great Guana Cay, Abaco, Bahamas.

ROBERTS, ROBERT L.
Pen Name: R.L. Roberts; *Born:* August 5, 1958, Logan, UT; *Parents:* Karen Ann Roberts, Robert Roberts, Jr.; *Spouse:* Julie W. Roberts, March 17, 1988; *Children:* Christina Martie Roberts; *Education:* Corrigan Camden High School, Kilgore College, Tyler Jr College; *Occupation:* Correctional Officer; *Memberships:* Boy Scout Committee; *Honors:* Regional Finalist, 1977; UIL Speech Contest, East Texas Area; Church Speech Contest Winner; *Other writings:* "Seeking Guidance"; *Personal note:* Do not hide your God givens talents under a bushel, express yourself and you may be blessed for it! *Address:* 508 East Lamar, Palestine, TX.

ROBICZEK, HOPE
Born: September 17, 1916; Quincy, MA; *Spouse:* Fred F. Robiczek, June 21, 1942; *Children:* Nadine Melody Robiczek, Bonita Jewel Robiczek Meadow; *Education:* Brooklyn College, BA; *Occupation:* Retired Teacher; Computer Executive; *Honors:* American Poetry Assn, Poet of Merit; *Other writings:* Class News editor, Brooklyn College Magazine; *Personal note:* Love to write poems for special occasions and/or special people, like to pun; *Address:* 3718 Avenue T, Brooklyn, NY.

ROBINSON, BRANDI
Pen Name: Nicole; *Born:* February 24, 1975, Giles County; *Parents:* Jerry and Mary Robinson; *Education:* Ardmore High School; *Address:* Rt 3, Box 311-1, Elkmont, AL.

ROBINSON, CASSANDRA
Pen Name: Sandra Lee *Born:* October 27, 1970, Raleigh, NC; *Parents:* Charlie Robinson, Carolyn Robinson; *Education:* Student; *Occupation:* Poet; *Memberships:* Martin Street Baptist Church, YWCA, BTU; *Honors:* Editor's Choice Award; *Other writings:* "One Shining Day"; "The Adventures of Katherine McCoy"; *Personal note:* I press toward the mark of excellence in my poetry and I deeply encourage others to do so; *Address:* 111 Star Street, Raleigh, NC.

ROBINSON, CHRISTY
Born: December 1, 1972, Wamego, Kansas; *Parents:* Verbie and Esther Robinson; *Education:* Wamego High School; *Occupation:* Valley Vista; *Memberships:* SADD, Kayettes, Weight Lifting, FBLA, Chorus; *Honors:* Volleyball, Chorus, GPA, and Track; *Personal note:* This poem is dedicated to Kristian Robert Sylvester; *Address:* Louisville, KS.

ROBINSON, LAURA LEE
Born: August 27, 1970, New Haven, CT. *Parents:* Barbara J. Robinson, James F. Robinson; *Education:* Branford High School; *Occupation:* Accoutns Receivable/Administration; *Honors:* High Honors; *Other writings:* Several other poems and short stories; *Personal note:* If the Lord hadn't wanted us to reach for the stars, he wouldn't have blessed us with the power to dream; *Address:* 39 Pompano Avenue, Branford, CT.

ROCKETT, HOLLIE V.
Pen Name: Hollie V. Rockett; *Born:* January 12, 1973, Florida; *Parents:* SR Cockrell, Lynda Cockrell; *Occupation:* Student; *Other writings:* Written Several Poems; *Address:* P.O. Box 1618, Prentiss, MS.

ROSS, JANNOTT J.
Pen Name: Jann Ross *Born:* January 25, 1975, Spokane, Washington; *Parents:* Jerry and Jackie Ross *Education:* Wilbur High School; *Occupation:* Student; *Memberships:* Future Business Leaders of America; *Honors:* Student of the Month, September 1989; 2nd Place Impromtu Speaker; *Other writings:* Written poems entitled, "Tear Drops", "Promises Made", "Promises Broken; *Personal note:* I strive to let my emotions come out in my writing, so everyone that reads them will experience the feelings I had when I wrote them; *Address:* P.O. Box 28, Wilbur, WA.

ROSSA, ANGELA RENE
Pen Name: Angela Rossa; *Born:* April 10, 1973, Millington, TN; *Parents:* Peter Rossa, Kathleen Rossa; *Education:* Spaulding High School; *Memberships:* Health Occupation Students of America; AFJROTC; *Honors:* National Honor Society; *Personal note:* I would like to dedicate this poem in remembrance of Marcia Bailey who died a few days prior to her graduation due to a car accident; *Address:* Rochester, NH.

ROY, NICOLE
Pen Name: Nicole Roy; *Born:* March 9, 1974, Maple Ridge BC; *Parents:* Joseph and Maaike Roy; *Occupation:* Student; *Memberships:* BC Cross County Ski Club, Swim Club; *Honors:* Girl Aggregate Citizenship Award; *Other writings:* Lots of poetry and some short stories in grade school; *Personal note:* Everybody should be able to live as they want to, not as they should; *Address:* Lacha Hache, BC.

RULAND, NADINE
Born: June 5, 1977, Danbury, CT; *Parents:* Robert and Patricia Ruland; *Personal note:* My favorite pastime is poetry and writing; *Address:* Wilton, CT.

RUSSELL, EMILY KATHERINE
Born: July 18, 1974, Ridgewood, NJ; *Parents:* James Russell, Deborah Steed Russell; *Education:* West Milford Township High School; *Memberships:* Environmental Club; *Other writings:* Personal Collections; *Personal note:* Most of my poems focus on peoples' emotions and feelings towards one another; *Address:* 10 Oakwood Avenue, West Milford, NJ.

RUSSELL, TERRY A.
Born: May 18, 1963, Barnwell, SC; *Parents:* Eddie P and Chappell Howard; *Spouse:* Charles R. Russell; *Children:* Jewel; *Education:* Williston Elko High and Orangeburg Calhoun Technical College; *Occupation:* Highway Worker; *Other writings:* Several poems published in school newspaper; *Personal note:* I try to write as realistically as possible because things won't always have a happy ending; I have always love Poe; *Address:* Rt 1 Box 367, St. Matthews, SC.

RUTTENBERG, DANYA
Born: February 6, 1975, Evanston, IL; *Parents:* Roger and Janice Ruttenberg; *Education:* New Trier High School; *Memberships:* Amnesty International USA, People for the Ethical Treament of Animals; *Other writings:* Several poems published in local newspaper and school literary magazine; *Address:* Glencoe, IL.

SABRERA, MONIQUE RENEE
Born: August 14, 1973, Downey, CA; *Parents:* Gloria Jean Soto; *Education:* Carmino High School; *Other writings:* Other poems in the process of being published in the American Poetry Anthology; *Personal note:* My poems are inspired by feelings I have had throughout my teenage life; *Address:* Whittier, CA.

SAENZ, GILBERT
Pen Name: Gil Saenz; *Born:* October 17, 1941, Detroit, MI; *Parents:* Valentine Saenz, Lena Mireles Saenz; *Education:* Wayne State University, Detroit MI, BA, 1968; *Occupation:* Computer Programmer, Analyst; *Memberships:* Latino Poets Assn; *Honors:* 3 Honorable Mentions, 2 Editor's Choices, 2 Golden Poet's Award; *Other writings:* Published a small collection of 19 poems on my own; Booklet is entitled *Where Love Is* and consists of some of my previously published poems; *Personal note:* Poetry is a very good way of expressing thoughts and feelings which are not easily expressed in some other way. Also, poetry is a challenge to try and capture moods and thoughts and put them into an artistic form; *Address:* 17250 Raupp Road, Apt. 17A, Melvindale, MI.

SALOMONE, ERIN LYNN
Born: May 17, 1972; *Parents:* Philip Salomone, Linda Salomone; *Education:* Newman Smith High School; *Occupation:* Student; *Memberships:* I am a christian member of this world; *Honors:* First place medals in tuba solos; 2nd place in a PTA poetry contest; President of national german honor society; *Other writings:* Several poems published in local literary magazines; Written unpublished short stories and a novel; *Personal note:* I hope to affect people in anyway with my writing, if I can make one person stop and think and reflect than I have accomplished something, I believe that everyone can overcome anything they need to, by recognizing the strength and love they have already used throughout their lives; *Address:* 2206 Glascow, Carrollton, TX.

SAMUELS, LEESA FALASHADEH
Pen Name: Leesa Falashadeh Samuels; *Born:* August 4, 1976, Jamaica; *Parents:* Violet Elizabeth Hart Samuels, Lynval Samuels; *Honors:* Valedictorian, Winner of Storytelling Contest, Principal's Honor Roll; *Other writings:* Poems published in elementary school paper for 3 years; *Personal note:* We must view the depth of a man's soul, and there we will discover the characteristics that make him human; *Address:* Laurelton, Queens, NY.

SANCHEZ, MONA
Born: January 22, 1975, Big Spring, TX; *Parents:* Ruben, Cyndi; *Spouse:* Nicky; *Education:* Stanton High School; *Occupation:* Presently in a hospital volunteer program; *Memberships:* Student Council, FCA, FHA; *Honors:* 1st Place U.S. Constitutional Bicentennial Essay Contest; 1st Place, Knights of Columbus, Achievement Academic Awards; *Other writings:* "The Hardest Thing for Me to do"; "The Goodness of Him";
"Jesus Lives" and many other short poems; *Personal note:* I try to live each individual day to its fullest and I lift up every event to Jesus Christ, my Savior; *Address:* P.O. Box 1191, Stanton, TX.

SANCHEZ, SOPHIA MITJAVILA
Pen Name: Sam Brown; *Born:* January 26, 1972, Costa Rica, CA; *Parents:* Isabel Sanchez Oller, Alvaro Mitjavila Lemus; *Education:* Lincoln High School, University of Costa Rica; *Occupation:* Law Student; *Memberships:* Rotary Club; *Honors:* IIE Scholarship; *Other writings:* Unpublished writings; *Personal note:* Writing is not only words in a page, it is feelings locked up on ones mind and ones heart. my dream is to make people understand that there is much more behind writing than just simple words; *Address:* San Jose, Costa Rica, C.A.

SANCHEZ, VICTORIA
Pen Name: Victoria Magdalena Sanchez; *Born:* November 13, 1956; *Parents:* Pete S. Sanchez; *Education:* BA in Fine Arts; Nursing Degree; *Occupation:* Registered Nurse; *Honors:* Home Health Professional of the Year; *Other writings:* Several poems published in anthologies; *Personal note:* Much of my poetry is created through exploration of a character for a stage production, writing is a creative catharsis and a complementary intertwining of the drama of emotion in theatre, literature and medicine; *Address:* Scottsdale, AZ.

SANDOVAL, BERNABE G.
Pen Name: Trey Sandoval; *Born:* November 4, 1973, Farmington, New Mexico; *Parents:* Bernabe C. Sandoval, Lynne Miller, Howard Miller; *Occupation:* Neosho High School; *Memberships:* Key Club, Future Christian Athletes; *Honors:* Presidential Academic Fitness Award; *Personal note:* I use poetry as a way of expressing my feelings for every situation always signing it with just another thought never to be remembered again; *Address:* Neosho, MO.

SARGENT, AMY E.
Born: August 11, 1976, Mt. Lebanon, PA; *Parents:* Edward J. Sargent, II, Mary E. Sargent; *Education:* Thomas Jefferson Elementary School; Herbert Clark Hoover Elementary School, Mt. Lebanon Junior High School; *Occupation:* Student; *Other writings:* One poem published in school magazine; *Address:* Mt. Lebanon, PA.

SARTINI, EMILY
Born: March 26, 1977, Lexington, KY; *Parents:* John Sartini, Kathy Sartini; *Education:* Sayre Middle School; *Memberships:* Young Musicians Club; Sayre School Chorus; *Honors:* Honor Roll; *Other writings:* Poem published in the local newspaper; *Personal note:* I enjoy writing about abstract feelings, I enjoy poets such as Emily Dickinson and Elizabeth Barret Browning; *Address:* 1022 Richmond Road, Lexington, KY.

SARVER, DEANNA
Born: May 17, 1969; Meyersdale, PA; *Parents:* Donna L. Weyant Trent, Harvey B. Trent; *Education:*

Meyersdale Area High School, Somerset Area Vocational Technical School; *Occupation:* Cashier; *Personal note:* I write about every important event that happens in my life, I was very greatly inspired by Karlten Ashley Benzies! Thanks so much! *Address:* Somerset, PA.

SAVORY, JOHNNIE LEE

Pen Name: J.L. Savory; *Born:* July 25, 1962; Peoria, IL; *Parents:*Y.T. Savory and Claudine Savory; *Education:* Danville Community College; *Occupation:* Poet; *Memberships:* Concerned Citizens for Criminal Justice; *Other writings:* Articles published in the Traveler Weekly; *Personal note:* I was inspired to write poetry and articles about my life and the world around me by a very warm, understanding, and loving person, my God Mother; *Address:* 2124 W. Kettelle Street, Peoria, IL.

SCHMIDT, JACQUELINE

Born: July 18, 1973, Appleton, WI; *Parents:*John L, Elaine Schmidt; *Memberships:* Mt Olive Lutheran Church; *Honors:* Outstanding High School Students of America, Endless Inkpen Awards; *Other writings:* Various poems in national magazines; *Personal note:* I admire the rather insane approach used by Edgar Allan Poe, I try to be a touch off centered in my poems, forming them after my emotions, you have to feel something in order to write, there is nothing more stale than unemotional writing; *Address:* Appleton, WI.

SCHMIDT, JODI

Born: December 16, 1970, New Hampton, IA; *Parents:* Larry and Doris Schmidt; *Education:* New Hampton High School; Kirkwood Community College; *Occupation:* Student; *Other writings:* Poems published in local newspaper and in the book entitled *Quiet Moments*; *Personal note:* I never look to the past only work harder to make my future brighter, my friends inspire me most and my world revolves around them; *Address:* 253 East Logan, New Hampton, IA.

SCHORNACK, HILLARY

Born: January 5, 1978, Genoa NE; *Parents:*Julie and Philip Schornack; *Education:* St. Isidore's School; *Address:* Columbus, NE.

SCHORR, KRISTIN

Born: March 5, 1975, Alexandria, VA; *Parents:*Barry Schorr, Marilynn Schorr; *Education:* Osbourn Park High School; *Occupation:* Student; *Memberships:* Osbourn Park Forensics Team; *Honors:* Special Youth in Film Award for Writing a Polaroid Commercial, Three Time Recipient of Prince William County Best All Around Young Author's Award; *Personal note:* Carpe diem! *Address:* 13764 Coronack Ct, Manassas, VA.

SCHUTTEN, MICHELE LEE

Born: February 17, 1973, Joliet, IL; *Parents:*Rosemary, Richard; *Education:* Wilmington High School; *Occupation:* Cashier; *Memberships:* Chorus, Bowling, Student Council, Church, School Newspaper, SADD; *Honors:* Honor Roll; *Personal note:* My poems reflect feelings and problems I've faced in my life, I hope to influence others with my poems; *Address:* 600 S. Water Street, Wilmington, IL.

SCHWADER, VALERIE

Pen Name: Symphoni; *Born:* September 19, 1972, Bethlehem, PA; *Parents:*Nydia and Fransis Schwader; *Education:* Saucon Valley High School; *Occupation:* Full time student; *Memberships:* Jehovah's Witness; Arthritis Foundation; *Honors:* Various Certificates of Achievement and lettered in Academics; *Other writings:* Various Unpublished Material Including Poems, Short Stories and Novels; *Personal note:* In writing, I escape to a world that allows me to experience things I'll never experience in real life, meanwhile, I hope to discover a way for my reader to vicariously experience those things too; *Address:* Box 133A RD1, Hellertown, PA.

SCOTT, ANNE

Born: June 14, 1974, Wiesbaden Germany; *Parents:* Jean Scott, James Patrick Scott; *Education:* York High School; *Occupation:* Work during summer vacations; *Memberships:* Amnesty International, Art Club; *Personal note:* My writing is based on what I see and feel; *Address:* P.O. Box 614, York Harbor, ME.

SCOTT, KELLIE JEANE

Born: January 5, 1971, Baltimore, MD; *Parents:*R. Lawrence Scott, Kathleen L. Scott; *Education:* North Stafford High School; George Mason University; *Address:* 47 Greenridge Drive, Stafford, VA.

SCOTT, REVA M.

Born: September 19, 1918, Winterset, IA; *Parents:*Allen Dotson, Ethel Este; *Children:* Kathleen Ethel Scott; *Occupation:* Accountant-Systems-Analyst (Retired); *Personal note:* Life is like a painting; we learn to enjoy the lights in a picture because of the darks and in life we come to treasure the happy times because of the sorrows we bear; *Address:* Winterset, IA.

SEALE, ANDREA SUE

Pen Name: Andrea Sue Howard; *Born:* June 25, 1944, Leeds, AL; *Parents:*Andrew Howard, Nell Alexander Howard; *Children:* Kenneth, Sharon, Angela, Brian; *Education:* Jefferson State Junior College; *Occupation:* Office Worker; *Honors:* Dean's List, 3 Honorable Mentions, Two Golden Poet Awards; *Other writings:* Poems published by World of Poetry, the National Library of Poetry and Star Publishing; *Personal note:* At the age of 44 a hidden talent came forth to express the pain of having been a victim of child abuse, I have been greatly influenced and encouraged by my therapist, Arlene C. Caplan; *Address:* 2428 Briarcliff Drive, Leeds, AL.

SEALS, DANA

Born: March 1, 1969, Salinas, CA; *Parents:*Bobby Seals, Rella Seals; *Education:* Living Word Christian High School; *Occupation:* College Student; *Memberships:* NAACP; *Personal note:* My life with and without Leon inspires my poetry; *Address:* 516 Dallas Avenue, Salinas, CA.

SENIUK, JODEAN

Pen Name: Joey; *Born:* August 10, 1974, Winnipeg, Manitoba; *Parents:*Diana and Emil Seniuk; *Occupation:* Student, Waitress; *Honors:* TADD, Gimli Youth Task Force, Teen Centre Planning Committee; *Personal note:* Never give up hope in achieving a goal; *Address:* Gimili, Manitoba.

SEOL, EDWARD SCOTT

Born: June 25, 1970, Landcaster, CA; *Parents:*Phyllis N. Cowdery; *Education:* Hermiston High School; *Memberships:* Church of the Nazarene; *Honors:* Academic Awards; Selected to attend the Oregon State writing festival at University of Oregon; *Other writings:* One poem published in school literary magazine; write poems all the time, still hoping to be discovered; *Personal note:* I try to inspire one's heart, let people relate a little on the subject I have written, goals are stepping stones on my walk of life as well as God; *Address:* 990 N. Juniper Street, Hermiston, OR.

SEWALL, YVONNE R.

Born: October 12, 1945, Norwalk, CT; *Spouse:* Mickey Ruckin; *Children:* Jessica, Christina, Michael; *Education:* University of Connecticut, BA; New York University, MED; *Occupation:* Manager; *Other writings:* Written novel entitled "Max's Kansas City"; Written articles published in Fame and Metro Magazine; *Address:* 474 Greenwich Street, New York, NY.

SEWELL, VIRGINIA

Born: May 18, 1917; Redkey, IN; *Parents:*James, Agnes Main; *Spouse:* Kelley Sewell, January 23, 1943; *Children:* Beverly, Reginald, Ronald, Loren, Thomas; *Occupation:* Occupation; *Memberships:* Baptist Church, Church Senior Citizens; *Honors:* Honorable Mention from World of Poetry; *Other writings:* Published two poems; other poems and some short stories not published; *Personal note:* I want to reflect the love of God and family in my writing; *Address:* Rt 2 Box 916, Selma, TN.

SHAH, SYED RAZZAK ALI

Pen Name: Gogloo, Ibn-E-Nasir; *Born:* October 3, 1958, Karachi, Pakistan; *Parents:*Syed Nasiruddin Kamal Shah (deceased), Syeda Fatima Bibi; *Education:* BSC, Diploma in Advanced English, many other sertificates; *Occupation:* Income Tax Inspector; *Memberships:* The American Center Klarachi, YMCA, Goethe Institute, Income Tax Library, Liaquat Memorial Library Karachi; *Other writings: Visions of Agony* and *Burning Ice*, both under composition; *Personal note:* I write for myself and for all crazy people who believe in universal poetry! *Address:* 250, C. P. Berar Society, Block 7/8 Karachi-5, Pakistan.

SHAHINIAN, ERICA

Born: August 2, 1971, Lynchburg, VA; *Parents:*Mr and Mrs. A.H. Shahinian; *Education:* Mary Washington College; *Other writings:* "Keeping Up"; *Address:* 5217 Boonsboro Road, Lynchburg, VA.

SHARROCK, KANIKA

Born: November 14, 1975; Tarrytown; *Parents:*Starkie and Eulah Sharrock; *Personal note:* I try to base my poems and stories on everyday life situations, I hope one day every child will have a home; *Address:* 927 Albert Road, Peekskill, NY.

SHERWOOD, HOLLY ANNE

Born: July 17, 1975, Glendale, CA; *Parents:*Maris A. Sherwood, Roy H. Sherwood; *Education:* Temple City High School; *Other writings:* I have written many other poems and short stories but have never submitted any for publication, I began writing when I was 9 years old; *Address:* San Gabriel, CA.

SIMIC, MICHELLE

Born: April 10, 1972, Enid OK; *Parents:*Donna Simic; *Education:* Garber High School; *Occupation:* Student; *Memberships:* Future Business Leaders of America; *Honors:* Student of the Quarter; Principals Honor Roll; *Other writings:* Several Unpublished Poems and Stories; *Personal note:* I like to write people's inner most passions and desires; *Address:* R R Box 155, Garber, OK.

SIMMONS, SHEILA DARLENE

Born: March 20, 1959, Kingston Ontaria, Canada; *Parents:*Dorlan Gerald Sudds, Geraldine LaVecque; *Spouse:* Ronald Cecil Richard Simmons, December 2, 1983; *Children:* Shantel Lee Ann, Jeremy Cecil, Ronald Richard; *Education:* Napanee Secondary High and Quinte Secondary High School; *Occupation:* Housewife; *Other writings:* Written Numerous Poems; *Personal note:* I write to release inner emotions and express to others the joy or sorrows I feel; *Address:* Ontario, Canada.

SIMS, AMY

Born: April 16, 1975, Amarillo, TX; *Parents:*Stevan Sims, Anita Sims; *Education:* Alamo Catholic High School; *Occupation:* Student; *Honors:* National Junior Honor Society; *Other writings:* Written Many Other Poems; *Personal note:* The only way you can become a good poet is by letting your true feelings and emotions show; *Address:* 4008 Beaver, Amarillo, TX.

SINCLAIR, BIL ANTHONY

Born: New York, NY; *Parents:*Oneater Sinclair, William B. Sinclair; *Spouse:* Inga Watkins Sinclair; *Education:* Long Island University, BS; George Washington University, JD; *Occupation:* Film/TV Writer, Producer, Director and Attorney; *Memberships:* Fairfax Cable Assn, Arlington Community TV; Pennsylvania Bar Assn; *Honors:* Merit Award, Best Use of Art and Graphics in a Cable Video Production, Service Award, Dean's List; Graduate Cum Laude; *Other writings:* "Listen Up"; "Mourning" and "Sometimes"; *Personal note:* My creative inclination is to reveal the subtle yet potent dimensions of the human condition and the human spirit; *Address:* Alexandria, VA.

SISLER, LISA

Pen Name: Lisa Sisler; *Born:* April 10, 1976, Morristown, NJ; *Parents:*Helen Sisler and Bruce Sisler; *Education:* Villa Walsh Academy; *Occupation:* Student; *Personal note:* Make the most out of life, it only comes once, so live for the day; *Address:* Morris Plains, NJ.

SKILLMAN, FRANKLIN JOHN

Pen Name: Franklin John Skillman; *Born:* November 3, 1933, Brooklyn NY; *Parents:*William E. Skillman, II; Dorothy Skillman; *Education:* Hofstra University, University of Arizona, Florida State University, Virginia Commonwealth University; *Occupation:* Medical Record Technician; *Memberships:* Presbyterian Church; *Honors:* USAF Outstanding Unit Award, State Service Award, Phi Alpha Theta; *Other writings:* Several Poems published in newspapers and bulletins; *Personal note:* I strive to show sensitivity in my writing since I am influenced by the romantic poets; *Address:* Crestview, FL.

SKRDLANT, VIRGINIA

Born: June 17, 1930, Batavia, IL; *Parents:*John Joseph Skrdlant; *Occupation:* Teacher of Emotionally Disturbed; *Honors:* Poet of Merit Trophy, American Poetry Assn; *Other writings:* "Mother", Published by Sparrograss; "Rose Garden"; "Lonely Roads", JMW Publishing; "On the Mountain", Amherst Society; "Termination", American Poetry Assn; *Address:* 700 Old Lancaster Road, Bryn Mawr, PA.

SMITH, BRENDA W.
Pen Name: Brenda Whitehead Smith; *Born:* October 26, 1946, Kewvir, KY; *Parents:*W.E. Whitehead, Marie H. Whitehead; *Spouse:* James Charles Smith, June 4, 1966; *Children:* Brent Edmond; *Education:* Broughton High; Hardbarger's Private Business College; Fonville Morisey Real Estate School; Institute of Real Estate Management, Meredith College; *Occupation:* Certified Property Manager, Real Estate Broker, Insurance Broker, Notary Public; *Memberships:* National Assn of Realtors; Raleigh Board of Realtors, Irem Chapter #56; Irem International; *Honors:* Beta Sigma Phi, Editor's Choice Award; *Other writings:* Poetry selection in "Creative Dreamwork"; various newsletters in sorority and professional publications; *Personal note:* "To lay haphazardly upon one's own self, looking pristine, yet have no know value is a feeling of utter loneliness, yet existing"; *Address:* 912 Hemingday Drive, Raleigh, NC.

SMITH, CYRIL E. JR.
Born: December 10, 1954, Trinidad, West Indies; *Parents:*Cyril and Ermyntrude Smith; *Children:* Jason, Jacqueline, Jillian and Jamie; *Memberships:* Horizons of Fellowship, (C'da), The National Author's Registry, U.S.; *Honors:* Award of Merit from the American Poetry Association, Edotor's Choice Award from the National Library of Poetry. *Other writings:* Several poems published throughout the United States. Have written 4 country gospel songs recorded in the U.S. by N.C.A. Recording Company, Nashville, TN; *Personal note:* I wish to continue my creative writing in the form of poetry. However, there is a way out of all our sorrow; *Address:* Toronto, Ontario, Canada.

SMITH, DAWN M.
Born: April 24, 1973, Corry, PA; *Parents:*Clifford Smith, Patricia Smith; *Education:* Lawton High School; *Honors:* Honor Roll Student; *Personal note:* I enjoy my writings of poetry, songs, and stories, although this is my first publication, my inspiration comes from my family, friends, and teachers, I hope to continue my writing; I would like to dedicate my poem to Mrs. Donahue and Mrs. Pendley; two of my teacher at TJHS; *Address:* Spartanburg, PA.

SMITH, DOREEN M.
Pen Name: Dorrie Smith; *Born:* September 8, 1968, Brockport NY; *Parents:*Edward and Laila Smith; *Education:* Spencerport Central High School; State University of New York College; *Occupation:* Teacher; *Memberships:* Odyssey of the Mind; *Honors:* Paul Douglas Scholarship; Phi Eta Sigma, Kappa Delta Pi; *Other writings:* A Publication in *Our Hidden Selves*; *Personal note:* Intense emotional situations filled with anything from love to despair are most inspirational for me; *Address:* 445 Trimmer Road, Spencerport, NY.

OSSMITH, HEATHER ANN
Pen Name: Gizmo; *Born:* April 3, 1975, Stroudsburg, PA; *Parents:*Ronald Smith, Margie Rossar, Doris Smith, Bob Fields; *Education:* Pocono Mountain High School; *Occupation:* Student; *Honors:* High School Distinguished Honors; *Other writings:* Several other poems and short stories; *Personal note:* I strive to reflect my true feelings about Bob, other loved ones and just life in general, I wish to be the best I can be in my life for whatever I may do; *Address:* HCR 72, Box 72, Pocono Pines, PA.

SMITH, LENNOT C.
Pen Name: Len; *Born:* Trinidad; *Parents:*Cieriani Smith, Maria Smith; *Spouse:* Jeannette Lee Smith; August 4, 1979; *Children:* Reuel, Laura Lee, Maria; *Education:* Carribbean Wesleyan College; *Occupation:* Safety and Security Assistant; *Memberships:* Writer's Digest Book Club; *Honors:* Recipient of Several Awards for Poetry, honored at Montgomery County Public Schools for Writing; *Other writings:* Poems published in New Voices; *Personal note:* Worthwhile goals can only be achieved by sacrifice and hard work; *Address:* 7714 Scotland Drive, Potomac, MD.

SMITH, ROBIN ROCHELLE
Pen Name: Robin Ipolani Smith; *Born:* July 14, 1973, San Diego, CA; *Parents:*Florentina Smith, Roy Chris Smith; *Education:* Lanai High School; *Occupation:* Student; *Memberships:* Girls' Volleyball, Hoby Alumni; *Honors:* Hughs' Brian Youth Ambassador; *Personal note:* If you ever need a friend, God's there, don't turn to drugs because it's not the answer, don't kill yourself because you feel unloved, God put you on this earth for a reason and that's because he loves you; *Address:* Canai City, HI.

SMITH, SUSAN M.
Born: September 16, 1950, Mississippi; *Parents:*Eddie and Ethel Smith; *Children:* Tanja, Purnell, Catina; *Education:* UWM, Sawyer Business College; *Occupation:* Bus Driver; *Other writings:* Published in National Anthology of Poetry; *Personal note:* To capture beauty in every person or object on earth in my writing; *Address:* 4218 W. Auer Avenue, Milwaukee, WI.

SMITH, VICKIE L.
Born: March 5, 1946, Scottsbluff, NE; *Parents:*Floyd Davis, Mildred Davis; *Spouse:* Dwight E. Smith, June 1, 1968; *Children:* Todd Edward Smith, Laureen Marie Smith; *Education:* Torrington High School; Hastings College, Hastings NE, BA; *Occupation:* Office Manager; Medical Records Medical Clinic; *Memberships:* Beta Sigma Phi, BPW, Methodist Church; *Other writings:* Several poems published in other collections, writing speeches for friends, etc, to this point nothing outstanding; *Personal note:* My writings are always a reflection of deep, inner emotions be it happy or sad, I feel my writings help reflect emotions of others who have trouble expressing themselves; *Address:* Box 147 1301 5th, Chappell, NC.

SNISKY, MICHELE RENE
Born: September 16, 1973; Freeport, Grand Bahama; *Parents:*Mary Anne, Edward Snisky; *Education:* St. Paul's College; *Occupation:* Student; *Memberships:* Hawksbill Explorers Club, YMCA; *Other writings:* Several other poems for my person all satisfaction; *Personal note:* This contest was my first attempt at sharing my writings outside my family, I hope you enjoy it, my poems was written to my boyfriend, Rodney Burrows;

SOKAL, TANGERINE
Born: June 16, Washington, DC; *Parents:*Thomas D. Sokal, Ozella Sokal; *Children:* Rachel Ozella Charity Unsire; *Education:* Bible College; CTI University, PHD; *Occupation:* Freelance Writer; *Memberships:* Pentacostal Faith, Self Confrontation of Counseling; *Honors:* The Standard Leadership Curriculum; Certificate of Award Bible Catechism; *Other writings:* Several Poems Published; Written Greeting Cards and Articles for Various Magazines; Unpublished Recipes and Songs, Currently working on Three Novels; *Personal note:* I love spending time with my mother and daughter; I enjoy writing, traveling and gardening, I am a good cook and decorator; I pray that what I write will inspire others; *Address:* Germantown, MD.

SOLOMON, WYOLENE B.
Pen Name: W. B. Lene Solomon; *Born:* May 20, 1947, Columbus GA; *Parents:*Mr and Mrs Walter Louis Boddie; *Spouse:* Tobe Solomon Jr., December 28, 1966; *Children:* Merrick Tobe, Lewis Tobe; *Education:* Carver High School; Columbus VoTech; *Occupation:* Register Lab Tech; *Memberships:* International Society for Clinical Laboratory Technology, PTA; *Honors:* Certificate of Appreciation, Employee of the Month, Medical Center Hosptial; *Other writings:* Four books that are being considered for publication; *Personal note:* I felt the need to capture your spirit; I felt I must touch your soul, I felt the need to embrace your body, I felt the need to look into your mine; I felt the need to get to know your spirit, soul, body and mind; *Address:* Columbus, GA.

SPERRY, CARISSA
Born: April 3, 1975, Moscow, ID; *Parents:*David, Monta; *Occupation:* Student; *Author; Memberships:* Humane Society; *Honors:* 1st Place School Poetry Contest, Twice Received Presidential Academic Physical Award, Honor Roll; *Other writings:* Poems and Short Stories, Published in School Magazine and Local Newspaper; *Personal note:* It is not over until you've gained your dreams, don't quit until there are no more goals to strive for; *Address:* 111 Franklin Street, Brevard, NC.

ST. DAWN, GRACE GALASSO
Education: Central High School, Paterson, NJ; The World Academy of Arts and Culture; Universal Orthodox College; National Academy of Management, PHD; *Memberships:* Life Fellow of the American Biographical Research Institute; Life Fellow of the International Platform Association and The Knight of Malta; The World Academy of Arts and Culture and the United Poets Laureate International; *Honors:* World Decoration of Excellence; Gold Commemorative Medal of Honor; Historical Preservations of American Biographee of the Year, 1986; Golden Poet Award, Silver Award; *Other writings:* "The Gift of Peace", "God Gave Me His Peace", "Trust God"; *Address:* 340 Elliot Place, Paramus, NJ.

STAM, MELISSA
Born: August 21, 1970, Dubuque, Iowa; *Parents:*Diane Stam, Charles Stam, Jr; *Education:* Worthington High School; *Occupation:* Student; *Memberships:* HITS; *Honors:* Honor Roll; *Personal note:* Most of my poems have a meaning behind them, a loss of a loved one inspired me to express my feelings in my writing; *Address:* 1315 East Division Street, Faribault, MN.

STEPHENS, JULIE
Born: January 21, 1975, Owensboro, KY; *Parents:* Joanne and George Stephens; *Education:* Precious Blood Grammer School; Owensboro Catholic High School; *Occupation:* Student; *Personal note:* I am greatly influenced by music from hard rock groups, DeFleppard, Poison, Great White and many others, and hope to write ballards like theirs in the future; *Address:* 820 Worthington Road, Owensboro, KY.

STEWARD, JODI L.
Born: December 3, 1976, Flagstaff, AZ; *Parents:*Mike Steward, Linda Steward; *Education:* Oak Creek Junior High School; *Occupation:* Junior High Student; *Other writings:* Submitted several poems in local poetry contests; *Personal note:* Writing to me is away of expressing my feelings and letting other people know how I feel about them; *Address:* Cornville, AZ.

STEWART, AMBER CAROLINE
Pen Name: Amber Caroline Stewart; *Born:* December 3, 1974, Pensacola, FL; *Parents:*Janice C. Stewart, James R. Stewart; *Education:* Baker High School; *Occupation:* Student; *Memberships:* Future Business Leaders of America, Future Teachers of America, Spanish Club, Drama Club; *Honors:* 11 Years Perfect Attendance; Good Citizenship Award; *Personal note:* I write poems about life and good things that happen; *Address:* Holt, FL.

STILL, DONALD E.
Pen Name: Don; *Born:* February 26, 1946, Brownsville, TN; *Parents:*O.F. Still, Sr., Maudie Lee Still; *Children:* Stephanie Dawn Still; *Education:* H.V. Cooper High School; Hinds Junior College; *Occupation:* Rural Mail Carrier; *Memberships:* National Rural Letter Carrier Association; *Honors:* American Poetry Assn, Poet of Merit, 1989; *Other writings:* Poems published in the National Rural Letter Carrier Assn Magazine, The Miss Rural Carrier Magazine, and Clark County Newspaper; *Personal note:* I strive to reflect on all subjects that affect a person's life, I have been greatly influenced by my mother and friends; *Address:* 102 Bailey Avenue, Ovitman, MS.

STIMBURYS, MARY ANN
Born: July 19, 1973, Cleveland, OH; *Parents:*Diane M. and Allen J. Stimburys; *Education:* Euclid High School; Brush High School; *Occupation:* Student, Writer, Musician; *Memberships:* Institute of Children's Literature; *Honors:* Musical Awards and Writing Awards; *Other writings:* Several poems published in magazines; *Personal note:* No matter how old you are, you must always believe that your dreams can come true, you're the only one who can make them a reality; *Address:* South Euclid, OH.

STOLDER, MELISSA C.
Born: July 2, 1976, Mentor, OH; *Parents:*Chuck Stolder, Della Stolder; *Education:* Rock Creek Elementary; Jefferson Junior High School; *Occupation:* Student; *Address:* ROck Creek, OH.

STONE, ANDRA LYNN
Born: April 16, 1950, Aruba, Netherlands Antilles; *Parents:* Joseph J. Stone, Clara A. Stone; *Education:* Idaho State University, BA; University of Houston, MA; *Occupation:* Academic Advisor, Saudi Cultural Mission; *Memberships:* American Assn University Women, National Academic Advising Assn; *Other writings:* "I am Like a Willow", American Poetry Anthology, VII, 5, American Poetry Assn; *Personal note:* I strive to reflect upon my personal life experiences, the work of Samuel Taylor Coleridge has been a great influence and incentive to the creativeness of my work; *Address:* Houston, TX.

STONE, RUTH
Pen Name: Maggie Ruth Stone; *Born:* November 22, 1917, Crewe VA; *Parents:* Roy and Lucy Long; *Spouse:* Harlan A. Stone, October 12, 1940; *Children:* Leslie Ruth, John Robert, Paul Harlan; *Education:* University of Illinois; Champaign Business College; Blackstone-Sprague Writer's Institute; *Occupation:* Executive Secretary; Director of School Transportation; *Memberships:* Phi Beta Dramatic; *Honors:* Interviewed on Christian Radio; Appeared on the Learning Circle, WDCN Public Television; *Other writings:* Writes a weekly column for two community newspapers; Have had articles published in two baptist magazines, have written nineteen christian romances; *Personal note:* The Lord brought me through a serious cancer operation 21 years ago and if I can help people deal with their problems in a positive way, I want to do that; *Address:* 76 Tusculum Road, Antioch, TN.

STORCH, JANE C.
Born: May 7, 1943, Northampton, PA; *Parents:* Fred and Jane Storch; *Education:* Allen High School; Edinboro State College; *Occupation:* Writing, volunteer work at school or retarded children; *Honors:* Achievement Award for overcoming personal disability, April 16, 1980, Golden Poet Award, 1988; *Other writings:* Poetry published in Gospel Carrier, December 16, 1973; Joyful Noise, September 1985, American Poetry Anthology, 1989; *Personal note:* I enjoy writing poems for special occasions; *Address:* 4230 Dorney Park Road, Apt 112, Allentown, PA.

STORM, DESIRAIE
Born: August 10, 1975;

STOVER, APRIL *Born:* February 25, 1973, Delaware, OH; *Parents:* Mollie and Harold Stover; *Education:* Oakridge High School; *Honors:* Young Authors, Principal's List; *Other writings:* Short stories not yet published and children's short books published by my elementary school; *Personal note:* I don't give up and I always finish what I start; *Address:* 3922 Auburndale Avenue, Orlando, FL.

STOWELL, CURTIS
Pen Name: The Honest Con, Technical Criminal; *Born:* January 21, 1962, Tacoma, WA; *Parents:* Alfred and Donna Doiron; *Personal note:* I am a Criminal that uses the knowledge and experience which I've learned through the years with the criminals, in and out of prison, to help the juvenile, as well as the prison system to reduce the climbing crime wave; I hope to show and convince that crime in all shapes and forms, isn't the better life style; *Address:* P.O. Box 900 IMV, F-104, Shelton, WA.

STRODE, HEATHER
Born: November 17, 1974, Pesotom, IL; *Parents:* Charles and Diana Strode; *Education:* Unity High School; *Memberships:* Student Council, Track, Cross County, Future Business Leaders of America; *Other writings:* I have 42 other poems that I have written for a hobby but have not yet been published; *Address:* 203 E. Maple Street, Pesotum, IL.

STUBBS, EZEKIEL
Pen Name: Zeke; *Born:* Cat Island, Bahamas; *Parents:* Reverend and Mrs Aaron A. Stubbs; *Spouse:* Joycelyn Elizabeth Stubbs, December 20, 1980; *Children:* Jamal, Chrislyn, Zekiah; *Education:* Teacher's College, Teachers Certificate, BA; University of Miami, MA; Century University, PHD; *Occupation:* Research Statistician; *Memberships:* Bahamas Satistician Organization; South Beach, Baptist Church Evangelistic Ministry; Government Public Schools Laison Officer; *Honors:* Bahamas Representative at OAS Seminar, 1987, 1988, 1989; *Other writings:* "Carribbean Soul"; "Aspects of Bahamian Culture"; "We Live on Cat Island"; "Art for First Graders"; *Personal note:* Dream big, hold on to your dreams and let nothing turn you back; *Address:* P.O. Box N 7029, Nassau, Bahamas.

SUDNIK, KATHY
Born: September 6, 1975, Dawson Creek, BC; *Parents:* John and Vicky Sudnik; *Education:* Central Middle School; *Honors:* Academic Awards and Honor Roll; *Other writings:* Written a children's book for a school library; *Address:* P.O. Box 966, Dawson Creek, BC.

SULZ, ANN JEAN
Pen Name: A.J. Sulz; *Born:* April 28, 1962, Troy, NY; *Parents:* Eugene Sulz, Jean Sulz; *Education:* Troy High School; Communication Center Operator School for the Marine Corp; *Occupation:* Lab Technician for Lens Crafter; *Honors:* Outstanding Young Women of America Award, 1987; 2 Letter of Appreciation; 2nd Award for firing expert with the M-16 Rifle while enlisted in the USMC; *Other writings:* 2 poems published in local magazine; *Address:* 1215 S. Ditmar Street, Apt A, Oceanside, CA.

TANIS, JOEL
Born: February 16, 1966, Kansas City, MO; *Parents:* Jesse and Alta Tanis; *Other writings:* "Reflection", American Poetry Anthology, 1985; "Dawning Eyes", Words of Praise Vol. II; "Musing of the Subconscious"; "Dreams and Delusion; *Personal note:* I strive to write poetry that catches the mind's eyes, captures a concept, and communicates the abstract with the concrete; something with depth reproduces my emotions and insights on the readers' wave length of discernment intertwining our points of view, if only for an infinitesmal instance; *Address:* 1080 Western Avenue, Williams Lake, BC.

TEDFORD, CAROL ANN
Pen Name: Carol A. Tedford; *Born:* August 13, 1973, Clarkesville, AR; *Parents:* Phillip, Kim; William, Barbara; *Occupation:* Student; *Memberships:* FHA, Future Busienss Leaders of America; Abundant Life Fellowship Church; *Honors:* I have written one other poem for a church Christmas play; *Address:* Ozark, AR.

TEEPLE, B.J.
Pen Name: B.J. Teeple; *Born:* May 25, 1918, Livingston, TN; *Parents:* Nora Ethel and Millard Teeple; *Children:* Billy, Nelenne; *Education:* DDS; *Occupation:* Dentist; *Other writings:* Written over 400 poems and songs; *Personal note:* Let there be songs to sing and poetry to read, to each his own; *Address:* P.O. Box 1017, South Hill, VA.

TESSELL, DANA
Pen Name: Dana Tessel; *Born:* January 30, 1972, New Jersey; *Parents:* Carol Tessell, Jack Tessel; *Occupation:* Student; *Memberships:* Greenpeace; *Personal note:* I try to find the peace of mind that will allow me to deal with the unkind; *Address:* 53 Frost Avenue, West, Edison, NJ.

THACKERAY, BETTY FERN
Children: Daniel, Debra; *Education:* Williamson High School; *Occupation:* Semi-retired Administrative Secretary/Medical-Legal; *Memberships:* Idaho Writer's League, Community Theater, Women's AGLOW, St Mark's Lutheran Church; *Honors:* Academic Scholarship, Miss Lucas County; Golden Poet Award, Certificate of Appreciation; *Other writings:* Poems published from time to time, been writin 'em since I was 9, use skits 'n stuff in church programs etc. I'm presently writing a novel entitled Undaunted Soul featuring my deceased husband; *Personal note:* I know that I am not so great of my own self, but I also know that I was created in the image of God; and He is great, so when I strive as hard as I can to follow His plan for me, no one can successfully undermine me, but, alas, I lack! *Address:* 1902 Thomas Lane, Coeur d'Alene, ID.

THOMAS, BETH
Born: May 5, 1976, Sylvania OH; *Parents:* Larry and Diane Thomas; *Education:* Arbor Hills Junior High School; *Occupation:* Student; *Honors:* Honor Roll Student, Has Won Numerous Academic Awards; *Personal note:* I have played the piano for 6 years, I have taken ballet lessons and jazz dance lessons for 7 years; *Address:* Toledo, OH.

THOMPSON, JOAN
Born: February 2, 1973, Fort Worth, TX; *Parents:* Robert B. Thompson; *Education:* Richland High School; *Honors:* Girl Scouts of the USA; Outstanding High School Student of America; *Other writings:* Girl Scout Silver Award, Richland Junior High Business Award; *Personal note:* I dedicated "I Remember the Times" to my good friend, Michael Hoover, may our friendship last a lifetime; *Address:* Ft Worth, TX.

THOMPSON, KJERSTI LEIGH
Born: June 20, 1976, Rochester, MN; *Parents:* Bruce and Dianna Thompson; *Education:* Stewartville High School; *Memberships:* Zion Lutheran Church; Youth Group; *Personal note:* I strive for peace and love on earth for eternity; *Address:* RR1 Box 376, Stewartville, MN.

THOMPSON, MELANIE LYNN
Born: February 5, 1975; *Parents:* Alan Thompson, Lynna Thompson; *Occupation:* Student; *Memberships:* Key Club, Jr. Beta Club; *Honors:* Rotary Club 4-Way Test Essay Contest; Regional and District Winner; *Personal note:* My main inspiration has been from the new found emotions of my early teen years; *Address:* 5931 Trinity Road, Raleigh, NC.

THURMOND, TINA TARESSA TANYA
Pen Name: Patrick McGuiness; *Born:* March 13, 1966, Lima, OH; *Parents:* Ada Lee Thurmond, Sandy Thurmond; *Occupation:* US. Army, Military Intelligence; *Honors:* Honor Student, French Fleur de Lis, Hi Ho Scholarship, Hauss-Helms Scholarship, Good Conduct Medal, Army Achievement Medal; *Personal note:* I am a patron of the arts to me, any type of art must spontaneously flow from the burst of an emotion, such art is above any technical analysis; *Address:* 1105 S. Metcalf, Lima, OH.

TIERNO, CATRINA
Pen Name: Tina Marie; *Born:* November 27, 1970, Boston, MA; *Parents:* Donna Jean Sikes Tierno, Joseph Tierno; *Education:* Boston High School; *Honors:* HonorRoll; Perfect Attendance, English Award, Certificate of Recognition; *Personal note:* This is dedicated to my mother, my best firend, life and love; *Address:* 134 Everett Street, E. Boston, MA.

TIGHE, MARIA
Pen Name: Maria T. Tighe; *Born:* April 26, 1972, Huntington, NY; *Parents:* Theresa Tighe, Thomas Tighe; *Education:* Commack High School, Junior College of Albany; *Occupation:* Student; *Memberships:* Christ the King Church; *Honors:* 1989 Silver Poet, Award by World of Poetry; Captain of Cheerleading; *Other writings:* Several poems published in magazines; *Personal note:* Take the time to express a feeling and look back years later and remember the memories forever...I've only just begun; *Address:* Commack, NY.

TOPPERT, NANCY DEA
Born: September 13, 1947, Davenport, IA; *Parents:* Hazel and George Toppert Sr.; *Education:* Annawan High School; Blackhawk College East; *Occupation:* Night Receptionist; *Personal note:* I am very excited that my poem will be included in Windows on the World; I hope that in someway my poem "My Son" will touch the heart of all those who read it, and give comfort to those who have lost a child; *Address:* R.R. 3, Kewanee, IL.

TORIAN, PAULETTE
Born: June 15, 1947; *Parents:* Eddie and Alice Torian; *Children:* Tamela A. Harvey, Shoovie Ihezue; *Memberships:* National Wildlife Federation, American Society of Notaries; Top Records Songwriting Assn; *Other writings:* Has Written Many Poems, Songs and a Short Story, Currently Working on a Book of Poetry on Various Subjects, Four Poems are Pending Publication in Anthologies; *Personal note:* "Lovely" is dedicated in loving memory of my mother, Martha Davis and to mothers everywhere, the ability to reach within myself and extract words to form a poem is a blessing; *Address:* P.O. Box 12065, Baltimore, MD.

TORO, NANCY DEL
Born: July 10, 1973, Chicago, IL; *Parents:* Angel L. and Francesca Del Toro; *Education:* Schaumburg High School; *Occupation:* Retail, Salem Place Office Supply; *Honors:* Honors in Art; *Other writings:* Poems in school paper; *Personal note:* Love cannot be written on paper, but feelings can be; *Address:* 756 Bode Circle, Hoffman Estates, IL.

TORRES, BERNADETTE
Pen Name: Maridette Christina Torres; *Born:* February 6, 1974; Guagua, Pampanga, Philippines; *Parents:* Brigido Torres, Helen M. Torres; *Education:* Stephen M. White Junior High School; King Drew Medical

Magnet High School; *Occupation:* Student, Parttime Secretary; *Memberships:* Easter Seal, Students Against Drunk Driving, Mothers Against Drunk Driving, Share-A-Ride; *Honors:* California Scholarship Federation; *Address:* 1433 East 220th Street, Carson, CA.

TORRES, ELIZABETH
Born: November 14, 1950, Brooklyn NY; *Children:* John Glenn High School, BA, 1988; CW Post University; *Occupation:* NY Army National Guard; *Membership:* NY Road Runners Club, LI Road Runner Club; *Honors:* Dean's List; *Other writings:* Play Entitled "Sir Rock"; Several Poems and Short Stories; *Personal note:* Everyone is obligated to strive for perfection and achievement in all their goals, falling short of your goal is better than not trying at all; *Address:* Huntington, NY.

TOUCHSTONE, TIM
Born: October 5, 1951, Wichita Fall; *Parents:* Mr and Mrs. A. Touchstone; *Education:* Winton Church; *Memberships:* Chose Hand; *Other writings:* Written Essay; *Personal note:* I am trying to write things that will make people think, give hope and be proud of themselves, that's all; *Address:* Tim Touchstone, 4107 Lennox #4, San Antonio, TX.

TOWSLEY, EMMA BERSAW
Pen Name: EM; *Born:* March 9, 1907, West Rutland, Vermont; *Parents:* Valier and Josephine Bersaw; *Spouse:* Nathan Ransom Towsley, September 10, 1927; *Children:* Ransom Webster, Barbara Jean, Bryce Barton, Errol Ross, Sandra Lee; *Occupation:* Own and Operate Laundramat; *Honors:* Recipes published in cookbook; Rotary Club; Letter of Thanks from President Bush; *Other writings:* I have written 12 to 14 songs, some of which have been recorded; *Personal note:* I think the good Lord above He has given this life, I'm just trying to express a small amount of thanks; *Address:* 26 North Main Street, Wallingford, VT.

TRENZ, HEATHER
Pen Name: Tokia; *Born:* May 24, 1972; *Parents:* Raymond Trenz, Darlene Trenza; *Education:* Carlson High School; *Personal note:* I write to express and explain my feelings better, my favorite deals with love and how I would like to express it to someone; *Address:* 23451 W. Ditner, Rockwood, MI.

TROUT, REBECCA
Born: October 11, 1974, Silver Spring, MD; *Parents:* Richard Trout, Ruth Harrell; *Education:* Smithsburg High School; *Personal note:* The world only has what each person feels they have, and you only get what you deserve. Then that determines how much the world has; *Address:* Rt 2 Box 21 Schaller Lane, Smithsburg, MD.

TUTTOSI, TATIANA
Pen Name: Tat, Kitten; *Born:* September 7, 1975; Winnipeg, Manitoba; *Parents:* Debra J. Tutosi; *Education:* MacGregor College; *Occupation:* Student; Waitress; *Honors:* Mary Stewart Scholarship; J. Mendenhall Scholarship, Honor Roll Scholarships; *Personal note:* Poetry makes up a big part of my life, it takes a lot of time and effort to succeed in writing a poem but it's a wonderful experience; *Address:* Manitoba, Canada.

TYLER, GRETCHEN
Born: November 6, 1974, Oronomo, WI; *Parents:* Sherry Clark Tryler, William Isreal Rank; *Address:* 432 Coronado Hills Drive, San Marcos, CA.

URANTA, EUGENE TONYE
Pen Name: Gene James; *Born:* June 26, 1964, Okrika, Nigeria; *Parents:* Rawson James Uranta, Comfort Uranta; *Education:* University of Lagos, St. John's University; *Occupation:* Public Relations Practitioner; *Memberships:* National Council for Arts and Culture, Assn of West African Young Writers, Nigerian Youth Organization; *Honors:* 1989 National Library, Editor's Choice Award; Award for Exceptionally Creativity and Artistry; *Other writings:* Several Poems published in local newspapers; written magazine articles for *Something Else* Magazine; *Personal note:* If you can dream it you can achieve it; *Address:* P. O. Box 8744, Ikeja, Lagos, Nigeria.

VANESSA WYRICK
Born: March 20, 1974, Redwood City, CA; *Parents:* Gerald and Lynn Wyrick; *Education:* Burroughs High School; *Personal note:* This is my first published poem; when I write, it explains how I feel at that time; *Address:* 224 Richard Ct., Ridgecrest, CA.

VANPATTEN, JENNIFER
Born: January 28, 1972; *Parents:* Jerry VanPatten, Geraldine VanPatten; *Education:* Gibson Southern High School; *Occupation:* Student; *Address:* Fort Branch, IL.

VASSOS, IRENE
Born: July 17, 1967, Stuttgart West Germany; *Parents:* Aurora I. Vassos; Basil H. Vassos; *Education:* Grinnell College, BA; University of Michigan, PHD (Antic.); *Occupation:* Student; *Memberships:* Alpha Phi Omega; *Honors:* NSF; *Personal note:* I believe everyone has beauty and goodness in them, I believe in true love and in the power of an individual to make a difference; *Address:* 403 Village Green Blvd, Apt 203, Ann Arbor, MI.

VICKERY, HEATHER LYNNE
Born: December 9, 1974, Indianapolis, IN; *Parents:* Neda Ward, Jerry Vickery; *Education:* North Central School; *Occupation:* Writer; *Honors:* 3rd Runner Up in Miss American Pre-Teen, 5th Place in International Modeling and Talent Assocation; *Other writings:* Many poems published in several books; *Personal note:* I have the hope that someone will read my writing and it helps them see the rainbow through the cloud; *Address:* 3317 Baypoint Drive, Indianapolis, IN.

VIOLETTE, KRISTEN
Born: December 2, 1974, Milford MA; *Parents:* Leslie Violette, Carl Violette; *Education:* Northridge High School; *Other writings:* I have written other poems that are on their way to being published; *Address:* 55 Sherry Street, Whitinsville, MA.

VISGER, JENNY
Born: February 29, 1976, Hancock, MI; *Parents:* Michael Visger, Deborah Visger; *Education:* Swift Creek Middle School; *Occupation:* Student; *Honors:* Youhg Authors, Write Now Contest; *Other writings:* War Poems, Miscellaneous Poems; *Personal note:* I live by this statement: but at my back I always hear, time's winged chariot hurrying near; *Address:* Richmond, VA.

WADE, SHERINE
Pen Name: Beth; *Born:* December 23, 1969, Brooklyn, NY; *Parents:* Myrtle Wade; *Education:* Boys and Girls High School; *Occupation:* Baby Sitter; *Honors:* Honor Roll List, Best Word Processor; *Personal note:* Photographs make great illusions but writing creates a innovative idea; *Address:* 94 Chauncey Street #6E, Brooklyn, NY.

WALDMAN, HEATHER
Pen Name: Maggie St. Clair; *Born:* October 19, 1974, St. Louis, MO; *Parents:* Darlene Waldman, Lee Waldman; *Education:* Parkway West High School; *Occupation:* Student; *Memberships:* Parkway West Pom Squad, Space Club; *Honors:* Citizenship, Vocal Presentations, United States Space Academy Diploma; *Other writings:* Wrote "Dreams" and other untitled poems such as "Smile Sadly", "Up and Down", "Changes"; *Personal note:* Don't be scared to be yourself; *Address:* Chesterfield, MO.

WALKER, JACQUELINE P.
Born: October 29, 1961, Jamaica, West Indies; *Parents:* Josephine G. Walker; *Education:* Woodrow Wilson High School; Hofstra University, BA, 1984; University of Maryland, MA; *Occupation:* Research Analyst; *Memberships:* Alpha Kappa Alpha; Assn of Female Executives; *Personal note:* People are our greatest resources. The successes or failures of society is directly related to the personal successes or failures of each person, therefore, it is our responsibility to help each other strive to be the best that we can be; *Address:* Hyattsville, MD.

WALLACE, MELINDA
Born: October 30, 1972; *Personal note:* We hold the cards to our future; *Address:* San Bernardino, CA.

WALSH, KATHLEEN
Born: March 18, 1975, Northridge, CA; *Parents:* Myrna and Marty Walsh; *Education:* Notre Dame High School; *Occupation:* Student; *Memberships:* Dance, Tall Flags, Scouts and Powder Puff Football; *Other writings:* I have my own personal collection of poems and short stories; *Personal note:* A dreamer creates poetry as a composer creates music, with emotion and often passion; *Address:* Sherman Oaks, CA.

WALTER, TARA DENISE
Pen Name: Tara D. Walter; *Born:* Fort Leavenworth, KS; December 2, 1969; *Parents:* Mr. and Mrs. J. Douglas Walter; *Education:* Habersham Central High School, Piedmont College; *Honors:* Who's Who Among American High School Students; *Personal note:* My hope and prayer for my writing is that I reflect upon my own personal experiences in life with a greatful heart and mind, I wish to gain a stronger appreciation for the art of writing; C.S. Lewis remains an inspiration to me always; *Address:* 359 B. Ridgewood Estate, Cornelia, GA.

WALTMAN, SHARON
Pen Name: Beth Summers; *Born:* September 19, 1973; Johnstown, PA *Parents:* Duane Waltman, Nora Waltman; *Education:* Patapsco High School; *Occupation:* Student; *Memberships:* West Inverness Dance Program; *Honors:* 5 and 10 year trophy in dance; *Other writings:* Other poems published in school newspaper; *Personal note:* To understand life's true meaning, I allow God's energy to shine through my darkest days and make them whole again; *Address:* Baltimore, MD.

WARD, ONEITA M.
Born: April 16, 1939, Mississippi; *Parents:* Modean Embry, Hubert Jackson; *Spouse:* Elmer W. Ward, July 8, 1960; *Children:* Allen W. Ward, Susan R. Ward; *Occupation:* Song Writer; *Other writings:* Written song that is being released from Coltrain Records New Country Sound and NCA Recording; *Personal note:* We must remember it is never to late to follow your dream and work to make it true; *Address:* 1386 Avon Road, Plainfield, IN.

WARRNE, GENE
Born: August 12, 1916, Denver, CO; *Parents:* Leonore and Francis Joseph; *Spouse:* Eleanor Gale, August 19, 1946; *Children:* Gene Jr., Ronald, Michael; *Memberships:* Academy of Motion Picture Arts and Science; Academy of Television Arts and Sciences, American Youth Symphony Society, Producers Guild of America; *Honors:* Academy of Motion Picture Arts & Sciences Special Effects Award; *Other writings:* Teleplays, Scripts for Animated Shorts and Children Programs; *Personal note:* I take my credo from John Donne, "No Man is an Island" and "Any Man's Death Dimishes Me..."; *Address:* 701 Island Avenue #4A, San Diego, CA.

WASHINGTON, SHARON
Born: March 4, 1951, Clifton Forge, VA; *Parents:* Otis and Mable Washington; *Children:* Monique Marcelle, Alyce Farquay; *Education:* Clifton Forge High School; *Occupation:* Mother; *Address:* Alexandria, VA.

WATSON, JOHN H.
Born: April 1, 1954, Dawson, GA; *Parents:* Christine Watson, Major L. Watson; *Education:* Terrell County High School; *Occupation:* Employed at Philadelphia Naval Shipyard; *Address:* Philadelphia, PA.

WEBER, BEVERLY JOY
Pen Name: B.J. Weber; *Born:* November 30, 1932, Swickley, PA; *Parents:* Mr and Mrs A.E. McCormick, *Spouse:* J.P. Weber, September 1, 1966; *Education:* Roy Miller High School; C.C. Business College; *Occupation:* Professional Artist; *Memberships:* Byliners Writing Club; Art Center of Corpus Christi, Elizabeth Simpson's Traditional Art Assn; *Honors:* Listed in Notable Women of Texas, 1st Edition Awards and Certificates in Art, Honorable Mentions in Poetry; *Other writings:* Poems in American Poetry Anthology, Best New Poets of 1986, New American Poetry, New York Poetry, Honorable Mentions in Poets Review, Poetic Page, Quill Books, Poets at Work; *Personal note:* I love to write, I love to paint, it can bring great pleasure and hopefully for the enjoyments of others; *Address:* 402 Longview East, Corpus Christi, TX.

WEBER, MARIE
Pen Name: McWeber; *Born:* October 18, Taylor Springs, IL; *Parents:* John and Blanche Eveland; *Spouse:* James R. Weber, March 6, 1949; *Children:* Pam, Nancy, Alice, Patricia; *Occupation:* Licensed Practical Nurse; *Memberships:* LPNAI; *Other writings:* Written Numerous Poems; *Personal note:* May the

world be a better place tomorrow, may the spoken word bring a smile to the face of a stranger in passing; *Address:* Decatur, IL.

WEBSTER, DONALD
Pen Name: Sir Donald; *Born:* July 21, 1973; Montgomery, AL; *Parents:* Archie, Donna Webster; *Education:* Carver High School; *Occupation:* Student; *Honors:* Won Speech Contest in School; *Other writings:* "Peace", "Remembrance of You", "A Drop"; *Personal note:* I bring forth some of my deepest thoughts in my writings and like for everyone to enjoy my poems, the world needs to find the meaning of life, and live in peace; *Address:* 2669 Drake Street.

WEEKS, BERNADETTE
Pen Name: Angel; *Born:* July 3, 1968, Long Island, NY; *Parents:* Bobette Weeks, Raymon Weeks; *Education:* Lindenhurst High School; *Occupation:* Electronics; *Personal note:* I strive to be honest it means a lot to me and to believe in Gods; *Address:* Lindenhurst, NY.

WENTZLOFF, KARI
Born: December 26, 1972, Gaylord, MN. *Parents:* Gary and Sandra Wentzloff; *Education:* Gaylord Public High School; *Memberships:* St. Michaels Youth Group, Gaylord Declamatory Team; *Honors:* Student of the Month; *Other writings:* Poems in High School Paper; *Personal note:* I write about my real feelings and I strive to write about current affairs; *Address:* Gaylord, MN.

WESTERFIELD, BRIAN
Born: September 5, 1962; *Parents:* Charles and Gertrude Westerfield; *Occupation:* Foreman; *Other writings:* Won Several Awards for other Poetry; Won the Annual Golden Poet Award from the World of Poetry; *Address:* 7503 Challis Road, Brighton, MI.

WHITE, DARRELL ANTHONY
Pen Name: The Original; Awesome Dreamer; *Born:* AUgust 5, 1967, Chicago, IL; *Parents:* Mary Louise White, Ulysses Merideth Woodard; *Education:* N. Chicago High School; College of Lake County, Northeastern Illinois University, Chicago, IL; *Occupation:* Data Entry Operator; *Memberships:* Church of Christ; National Authors Registry; *Honors:* National Achievement Academy, Government, 1985; Mr. Midwest, 1987; Golden Poet, 1989; *Other writings:* "The Man in the Mirror"; "No Justice, It's Just Us"; "Take a Closer Look"; "Peace Be still"; *Personal note:* Day by day in every way through the grade of God, I am getting better and better and better; *Address:* 4847 N. Kimball Avenue #2F, Chicago, IL.

WHITELOCK, ROSEMARIE A.
Born: August 5, 1969, Jamaica; *Parents:* Muina Perry, Ronald Whitelocke; *Education:* Business Major; *Occupation:* Administrative Secretary; *Honors:* Presidential Award; *Other writings:* Book entitled, "Deadly Shadows" not published as yet but almost finish; *Address:* Alexandria, VA.

WHITEMAN, THOMAS F.
Born: February 16, 1939; Collingswood, NJ; *Parents:* Walter F. Whiteman, Helen C. Whiteman; *Spouse:* Dolores L. Whiteman; June 19, 1976; *Children:* Thomas Michael, Richard Lee, Daniel Paul; *Education:* Lew Wallace High School; *Occupation:* Warehouseman/ Fork Life Operator; *Memberships:* Teamsters Union Local #142; U.S. Navy Veteran; *Honors:* Silver and Golden Poetry Awards; *Other writings:* Written spiritual poem, "Confidence" published in Marine Corps Leatherneck Magazine; *Personal note:* In my writing my pen, in hand, is guided by what I feel and want to express from my heart, I find poetry an ideal form of expressing one's thoughts; *Address:* Portage, IN.

WIGNEY, AYSHDOV YOSEF
Pen Name: Joseph Wigney; *Born:* March 23, 1943, San Jose, CA; *Parents:* Helen and Merle Oxley; *Spouse:* Barbara Ann Wigney, September 16, 1989; *Children:* Jayson Daniel Wigney, Anthony Harrison Wigney; *Education:* DeAnza College; *Occupation:* Information Specialist; *Other writings:* A musical comedy childrens play entitled, "I Can't Believe I Ate the Whole Thing!" *Personal note:* My writings reflect extremes of two areas: either they over simplify complex issues or they mask or disguise a simple meaning to challenge the reader; *Address:* 1220 Tasman Drive, Sunnyvale, CA.

WILBUR, ROGER
Born: July 17, 1936, Wood River, IL; *Spouse:* Edie L. Wilbur; *Education:* Illinois Wesleyan University, Illinois, BFA; Bowling Green State University, Ohio, MA; *Occupation:* Associate Professor; *Memberships:* Georgia Freelance Writers; Speech Communication Assn; *Honors:* Teacher of the Year, 1986; *Other writings:* "Mind Rambling"; "Reflections on Becoming", "Odysseus Seachild"; Has written three academic books, *Being Yourself; Communicating with People: A Natural Approach*; *Personal note:* I am part of the human potential movement, believing in creative energizing of people; *Address:* Ellenwood, GA.

WILKENS, LINDA A.
Born: April 23, 1963, Bayonne, NJ; *Parents:* Edward Dominguez, Gwen Dominguez; *Personal note:* This is for my parents and my dear friend, Susanne Parente, I thank them for their patience and understanding through some very difficult times; *Address:* Port Reading, NJ.

WILLIAMS, GRETCHEN
Born: April 27, 1972, Spartanburg, SC; *Parents:* Michael, Jan; *Education:* Woodruff High School; *Occupation:* Student; *Memberships:* Future Business Leaders of America, National Honor Society; *Honors:* I dare you leadership award; *Personal note:* Appreciate loved ones in the present and look for the good in all; *Address:* 133 Racetrack Road, Woodruff, SC.

WILLIAMS, KELLY J.
Pen Name: Kelly J. Williams; *Born:* October 19, 1970; Ashland, KY; *Parents:* Miles and Margaret Lawhorn; *Spouse:* Keith A. Williams, December 27, 1986; *Children:* Michael C.D, Williams; *Occupation:* Assistant Manager; *Honors:* Dean's List, Extemporary Honor Roll; *Other writings:* Written Over 30 Poems; *Personal note:* Poetry comes from the heart and reflects off the mind; *Address:* HHC 2/15 Infantry, Box 907, APO, NY.

WILLIAMS, NATASHA ANISE
Pen Name: Tasha W.; *Born:* January 8, 1973, Chicago, IL; *Parents:* Julienne B. Williams; *Education:* Cathedral High School; *Occupation:* Student; *Memberships:* Greater Institutional A.M.E. Church Junior Usher Board; *Honors:* Greater Institutional A.M.E. Church Black History Contest; *Other writings:* Creating Writing Book; *Personal note:* I like imagination mixed with a little realism; I believe that with a little imagination you can go anywhere; *Address:* 2921 S. Michigan #201, Chicago, IL.

WILLIS, CONNIE
Born: August 9, 1970, Stratford, NJ; *Parents:* JoAnne William; *Education:* Highland Regional High School; *Occupation:* Student, Babysitter; *Personal note:* Keith, this poem was written to you, I really found love when I found you, I love you and I mean it with all my heart; *Address:* Sicklerville, NJ.

WILSON, ANNIE L.
Pen Name: Andrea Lynn Welsh; *Born:* July 10, 1937, Vaughans, NC; *Parents:* Sallie Lillian Strong, Roland Wilson; *Children:* Yvette, Monique, Andre; *Education:* Holabird Elementary School; Paul Lawrence Dunbar Junior and Senior High School; *Occupation:* Creative Design and Fabric Art Work, Monogramming and Crafts; *Other writings:* Published twice in the World of Poetry; Several unpublished books of poetry, also unpublished writings on heath and beauty; *Personal note:* Influence by Dunbar, favorite poets who inspired me, their style touches me, Edgar A. Guest and Rudyard Kipling; *Address:* P.O. Box 4254, Van Nuys, CA.

WILSON, GWENDOLYN S.
Pen Name: Wendy Wilson; *Born:* June 20, 1975, Jefferson, LA; *Parents:* Richard Z. Wilson, Catherine R. Wilson; *Education:* Arch Bishop Chapelle High School; *Occupation:* Student; *Honors:* High School Academic Scholarship; *Address:* Metaire, LA.

WINESTOCK, JILL K.
Born: December 20, 1957, Arlington Heights, IL; *Parents:* Mr and Mrs. J. Freeman; *Children:* Jennifer, Robert, Tahra; *Occupation:* Full Charge Bookkeeper; *Memberships:* Friends Church; *Personal note:* I have found poetry to be my way of expressing myself, as well as a release of my emotions; *Address:* Phoenix, AZ.

WINESTOCK, JILL K.
Born: December 20, 1957, Arlington Heights, IL; *Parents:* Mr & Mrs. James Freeman; *Children:* Jennifer, Robert, Tahra; *Occupation:* Full Time, Full Charge Bookkeeper Parttime Warehouse Account Representative; *Memberships:* Coach, Soccer; *Honors:* Several poems published in American Poetry Anthology; *Other writings:* Several Poems Published in American Poetry Anthology; *Personal note:* I write as a way of releasing my emotions and write from my heart; *Address:* 6711 N. 35th Avenue #57, Phoenix, AZ.

WINNAN, STACEY
Pen Name: Stac; *Born:* December 3, 1973, Elk Grove, IL; *Parents:* Susan Kraus, Richard Winnan; *Education:* Eastern High School; *Occupation:* Student; *Other writings:* "Mr. True Love"; "Cover for a Broken Heart"; "Never Forever"; "Living in the Past"; *Personal note:* If you strive hard enough you can reach any goal; *Address:* Louisville, KY.

WINNER, SHIRLEY ANN
Born: October 15, 1937, Casey County, KY; *Parents:* Ray Lay, Bessie Lay; *Spouse:* Glenn A. Winner, December 31, 1975; *Children:* Philip L. Miller, Sandra Ann Griffin, Peggy Denny; *Memberships:* Lady of Lords Parish, Columbia, MO; *Honors:* Award of Merit Certificate, World of Poetry; *Other writings:* "Memories", "Last Light" published by Sparrow Grass Poetry; "Image", "Last Journey", American Poetry Assn; "Miracle", World of Poetry; *Personal note:* My poetry is written in honor or my son, Philip Lennie Miller, Born July 4, 1962, died October 30, 1988, dedicated to his son, J.P. Miller, June 16, 1985; *Address:* 2701 E. Nifong Blvd #170, Columbia, MO.

WOEBKENBERG, SARA
Pen Name: Sara Woebkenberg; *Born:* November 30, 1974, Jasper, IN; *Parents:* Mary Ann Woebkenberg, Tony Woebkenberg; *Education:* Spring High School; *Occupation:* Student; *Address:* 23310 Upper Falls Court, Spring, TX.

WOLFE, MARY ANGELA
Born: February 9, 1972; *Address:* P.O. Box 295, Roy, WA.

WOLFGANG, DIONNE
Born: May 6, 1971, Wichita Falls, Texas; *Parents:* Clair and Shirley Wolfgang; *Education:* North Schuylkill High School; *Address:* #1 Preston Street, Lavelle, PA.

WOOD, TRACI
Pen Name: Dawn Crain, Kyla Henderson; *Born:* March 24, 1975; Okeene, OK; *Parents:* Skip Wood, De Wood; *Other writings:* Published work in recent National Library of Poetry Anthology; *Personal note:* I set goals toward christian life and living with God, I highly believe in the wisdon and sincerity of the sixth sense, common sense; *Address:* P.O. Box 112, Ames, OK.

WORDEN, THERESA JANE
Pen Name: Tonya Lisa Ellis; *Born:* February 23, 1971, Liberty; *Parents:* John Worden Sr, Vivian Worden; *Occupation:* Student; *Memberships:* Lisa Whelchel Fan Club, Honeycomb Hideout Club; *Honors:* Fair Housing Contest, Won Awards for Art Contest and Attendances; *Other writings:* A short story published in the Times Herald Record; written book entitled, *Tenth Grade Rumors*; *Personal note:* I practice writing a lot and I hope someday to be famous a writer, I want to be another Laura Ingalls Wilder, I love Laura Ingalls Wilder's stories; *Address:* P.O. Box 628, Neversink, NY.

WRIGHT, GAYLE ADAMS
Born: November 16, 1952, Illinois; *Parents:* Thomas Adams, Eileen Gregory Adams; *Spouse:* Carl Wright, October 3, 1987; *Children:* Rhonda, Ronnie, Kerry, Cristy, Charlie, Tommy, Tammy; *Honors:* Awards of Recognition from the World of Poetry; *Other writings:* "A Little Girl's Prayer"; "To Be a Twin", "Happy Number Nine", "Happy Anniversary"; *Address:* 303 E. Jefferson, Sullivan, IL.

WRIGHT, TARITA
Born: January 12, 1970, Manchester, Jamaica; *Parents:* Laura and Dolman Wright; *Education:* Manchester High School; York University; *Occupation:* Student; *Honors:* Eva Smith Award, Funcia Award, Rotary Club Scholarship, Honor Roll; *Other writings:* Written

short stories and poems published in school magazine; *Personal note:* The only limitations are "Man-Made" and through my writings I hope to encourage other black students that the sky is the limit!; *Address:* Rexdale, Ontario;

YAGER, CHRISTIANA A.
Born: September 11, 1974, Norwich, NY; *Parents:* Darrel Yager Joan Yager; *Education:* Sidney Senior High School; *Occupation:* Student; *Personal note:* My work expresses my intermost thoughts of love, life and eternity. I hope that my poems will enlighten the life of whomever reads them; *Address:* RD 3, Box 216A, Bainbridge, NY.

YENTER, NIKKI
Born: September 21, 1972, Milwaukee, WI; *Parents:* Brenda Cannestra, Robert A. Yenter; *Education:* Homestead High School; *Other writings:* A few poems and stories in school newspaper; *Address:* Thiensville, WI.

YOUNG, TRACY
Born: December 28, 1973, Niskayuna, NY; *Parents:* Gerald Young, Carol Young; *Education:* North Spring High School; *Occupation:* Student; *Memberships:* Young Life, Interact, PSTA; *Honors:* Dance Scholarship, Music Performance Award, Outstanding Student, S.A. Finalist, Science Award; *Other writings:* Poem published in school magazine, several unpublished poems; *Personal note:* The vision that you glorify in your mind, the ideal that you enthrone in you heart, this you will build your life by, this you will become; *Address:* Atlanta, GA.

YOUSE, LINDA M.
Born: December 20, 1949, Philadelphia, PA; *Parents:-* Gaetano and Marie D'Orazio; *Spouse:* William Youse, June 16, 1968; *Children:* Cherie, Stacie; *Education:* Pennsauken High School; South Jersey Business School; *Occupation:* Housekeeper, Parttime Secretary; *Memberships:* World Vision and Save the Children Projects, Whale Adoption Project, MADD; *Honors:* Honorable Mention Award for a poem entitled, "Paradise" from the World of Poetry Contest; *Other writings:* Wrote a book containing a complete collect of my poetry entitled, *Sincerely Yours*; *Personal note:* I enjoy expressing my views, ideas and opinions, while emphasizing my love and respect for people, nature and life in general; *Address:* Mt. Laurel, NJ.

ZACHARIAS, TRACEY
Pen Name: Tracey Zacharias; *Born:* June 25, 1963, Sacramento CA; *Parents:* Gus and Connie Reich; *Spouse:* Casey Zacharias, July 29, 1985; *Children:* Elisabeth Claire Zacharias, Michelle Marie Zacharias; *Occupation:* Casino Employee; *Other writings:* Assortment of short stories and poems; *Personal note:* Doing the Best I can with What I Have; *Address:* P.O. Box 937, South Lake, Tahoe CA.

ZBYTOWSKI, STACEY
Pen Name: Space-Ace; *Born:* February 24, 1975, Alpena, MI; *Parents:* John A. Zbytowski; Cheryl A. Zbytowski; *Education:* Thunder Bay Junior High School; Alpena High School; *Memberships:* Huron Shore League; Girls Softball; *Other writings:* Articles in the Alpena News under Town Talk; *Personal note:* My goal is to become a great author of many books, I love to write and I hope my dream will be fulfilled someday, although this is just the beginning; *Address:* 2794 County Park Road, Alpena, MI.

ZEE, SHAWNA
Born: October 27, 1972, Edmondton, Alberta; *Parents:-* Cor and Joan Zee; *Education:* Edmonton Christian High School; *Honors:* Art Award; *Address:* Edmonton, Alberta.

ZEMAN, LISA ANN VERONIKA
Born: May 26, 1975, Lincoln, NE; *Parents:* Leonard Zeman, Ann Zeman; *Other writings:* "Always Remember"; *Personal note:* You can never succeed if you don't try; *Address:* 230 Monroe, Bennet, NE.

ZIPTKO, ALICIA
Born: July 17, 1973, Passaic, NJ; *Parents:* Fred and Carolyn Ziptko; *Education:* Wallington High School; *Occupation:* Student; *Memberships:* Treasuer Class of 1990; Chorus, Dancing; *Honors:* Honor Roll; *Personal note:* Writing permits me to express myself in the way in which I really feel; *Address:* 13 Fradkin Street, Wallington, NJ.

Index

Aamoth, Margaret Dahl 393
Abbate, Christine 148
Abbot, Kathryn 190
Abbott, Dawn 13
Abney Amy 48
Abram, Melanie 351
Accardi, Alisa Marie 144
Adam, Monique 310
Adamec, R. D. 387
Adamowski, Mary 360
Adams, Connie 133
Adams, John 27
Adams, Kari 14
Adams, Stephanie 399
Adcock, Betty Ann 227
Addis, Jennifer 246
Adelman, Michele Lee 319
Adelsperger, Jocelyn L. 123
Aden, Jacquelyn 155
Adkins, Nikko 351
Adlhock, Krista 71
Adur-Rassaq, Barria Muntaz 61
Ahmels, Harriet 241
Ahn, Jessica 132
Akin, Amy-Jo 257
Alburas, Evie 194
Ales, Beverly 79
Alexander, Alisha Nicole 115
Alforque, Audrey 129
Ali Shah, Syed Razzak 351
Allen, Adelle 96
Allen, Charlotte Tuttle 206
Allen, Larry J. 403
Allen, Thomas W. 292
Alley, Cynthia 25
Allie, Christine 64
Allison, Aimee 75
Allix, Hereward 409
Alma, Anita 26
Alonzo, Erline 120
Altman, Troy 390
Altmann, Jennifer 64
Alumbro, Ulysses S. 363
Alvarez, Rosemarie 64
Amador, Claudia 14
Aman, Jill 43
Amarante, Terri 402
Amato, Mary Ellen Reynolds 334
Amywensel, D. 35
Anctil, Kerry 123
Andersch, Tania 324
Andersen, Kristen 126
Anderson, Alameta Yvette 191

Anderson, Beth 112
Anderson, Candice 220
Anderson, Chaunda 234
Anderson, Christa 83
Anderson, Emlyn 199
Anderson, Endia 31
Anderson, Jenna 46
Anderson, Jennifer L. 217
Anderson, Karen 105
Anderson, Kim 206
Anderson, Michelle 288
Anderson, NancyAnn 313
Anderson, Pauline 326
Anderson, Stephanie Danielle 279
Anderson-Pike, Lee 362
Andes, Melanie S. 203
Andrews, Billy F. Sr. 28
Andrews, Stacy 295
Andriekus, Christine 94
Anfietatro, Bridget 238
Angermeyer, Susan 320
Annis, Louise 354
Anstine, Michele 376
Anthony, Lawrence 297
Anthony, Michele 312
Antonicelli, Toni 279
Apelquist, Joy 270
Aporta, Amy 53
Aquilano, Christina 232
Araiza, Sarita 352
Archer, Katie 135
Arent, Chris 154
Armas, Jennifer C. 40
Armendariz, Anna 96
Arney, Jerry 18
Arnold, Barbara 26
Arnold, Dawn 193
Arrington, Christina 40
Arsenault, John 138
Arthur, Tandy Marie 301
Arupa, Ravi 328
Ashbrook, Carmen 155
Ashcraft, Brenda 115
Ashcraft, Joy 190
Ashley, A. 56
Ashworth, Destiny 248
Ashworth, Hilary R. 204
Asistido, Celestine 228
Atkins, Michelle 379
Atkins, Sandra Justus 372
Aue, Pamela Roberts 322
Auliff, Alice 10
Ault, Crissi 265

Aumiller, Tamara L. 290
Austin, Brenda S. 241
Austin, Sandra Stalford 383
Austin, Shari L. 276
Auten, Amy 39
Auvil, Nancy 343
Avampato, Christa 60
Avery, Danielle Terese 114
Avery, Kira 179
Axelrod, Laura 410
Ayetigbo, Ayodele 159
Babcock, Carol 57
Bachman, Neal K. 309
Bachus, Kerri 36
Backo, Heather 182
Bagla, Amishi 21
Bagley, Jenna 129
Bagley, Shelly Elizabeth 283
Bahall, Nirmala 307
Bailey, Amanda 22
Bailey, Amy 223
Bailey, Henria S. 176
Bailey, Lisa 320
Bailey, Sharon 311
Bailey, Shelley Lynn 353
Baird, Sarah 381
Bairow, Ginger 95
Baisden, Charity 137
Baisley, Freedom 191
Bajor, Beth 172
Baker, Ginger 54
Baker, Johnnie 178
Baker, Kimberly 261
Baker, Kristal 51
Baker, Liz 317
Baker, Lois M. 309
Baker, Lowell 384
Baker, Michelle 352
Baker, Mickey 334
Baker, Teresa 262
Balckburn, Amy 103
Baldemore, Marth 365
Baldwin, Melissa 83
Ball, Kim 216
Ballard, Rachael 295
Ballesteros, Gloria I. 102
Bangerter, Adrian 112
Banick, Erika 107
Banks, Bob 154
Bannis, Clarissa 11
Banzet. Christy 144
Barbee, Sheree 307
Barber, Amanda 65

Barce, Kymberdo 100
Bard, Catherine 189
Barker, Carla 113
Barker, Terri 359
Barkley, Wendy 292
Barnard, Heather 254
Barnard, Scott 346
Barnes, Brenda 255
Barnes, Candice 18
Barnes, Gail 61
Barnes, Lorrin 402
Barnett, Jennifer 125
Barnett, Megan 340
Barnett, Pam 391
Barnhart, Jackie 211
Barnhart, Jessie Ruth 196
Barns, Tracy 354
Barone, Rose Marie Pace 388
Barone, Tricia 286
Barr, Lois 108
Barranco, Kathylynn 71
Barrett, Joseph E. 54
Barrios, Carlita M. 254
Barrios, Loretta M. 298
Barry, Jonathan 227
Barry, Pam 410
Bartels, Cindy 33
Bartleson, Quinta J. 402
Bartlett, Julie 31
Bartlett, Robert 272
Barton, Debbie 249
Barton, Dena 178
Barton, Linda 351
Bartoni, Marie 313
Barulich, Michelle Joan 382
Bassett, Lisa 348
Bastiani, Michelle 364
Bateman, Amanda 225
Bateman, Tricia 7
Bather, Karen ``Jade'' 369
Bator, Ellen 180
Baumgardt, Kimmi L. 12
Bay, Annette 199
Bay, Robert M. 351
Bayles, Miken 329
Bayly, Fiona 259
Bayne, Amy 235
Beadles, Terry W. 165
Beadnell, Trisha 283
Beakes, Stacey 401
Bean, Cynthia 237
Bean, Elizabeth Dawn 182
Beardsley, Dana 85
Beausoleil, Cherrin 58
Beaver, Tonya 333
Beck, Dana 170
Beck, Jessica 38

Beck, Laura Jean 338
Beck, Paula 197
Becker, Charlotte 261
Becker, Tracee 272
Bedard, Harriet Shove 220
Beebe, Debbie 143
Beeck, Min-Aha 353
Beers, Tammi 331
Behrendt, Kim 102
Behrens, Yvonne 282
Beilke, Teri Lyn 300
Beisner, Courtney 233
Beisner, Kara 37
Belitz, Justin 230
Bell, Amy 229
Bell, James 7
Bell-Teneketzis, Barbara 255
Bellamy, Cindy 32
Bellemare, Kim 148
Belles, Donna L. 151
Bellinger, Jessica 143
Belteton, Perla 386
Bemis-Breznen, Marge 287
Bendell, Amy 264
Benedetto, Marella 274
Benedict, Brooke 143
Bennett, Arline 213
Bennett, Cathy 208
Bennett, Jennifer Joy 216
Bennett, Wendy Frances 339
Benson, Karen 242
Benton, Jena 103
Berdecia, Amy 215
Berg, Holly 112
Bergeron, Elizabeth 246
Berglund, Pamela F. 324
Berlin, Dana 103
Berlint, Sarah 296
Berman, Natalie 354
Bernard, James Michael 163
Bernards, Karen 265
Bernet, Jolene 138
Berrry, Debi 198
Berry, April Renee 65
Berry, Kimberly 56
Berry, Tracy 383
Bertrand, Dana 124
Bertrand, Edmond 254
Best, Mary 271
Better, Kerrie-Ann 170
Betz, Diona 116
Beversdorf, Stacy 269
Bewley, Jennifer 88
Bhangoo, Kami 107
Bhushan, Arya 198
Bicherl, Robin Marie 29
Bieber, Katrina 174

Bierschbach, Kelly 207
Biesiadecki, R. J. 329
Biggins, Angela 140
Bigham, Wendy L. 282
Bigler, Jenny 227
Bilicic, Rosmarie 321
Billington, Candi 223
Bilyeu, Sandy 340
Bingham, Cathy 227
Bingham, Kelly 175
Birge, Katharine Ann 150
Birkowski, Greta Marie 256
Birks, Cherie 198
Bishop, Becky A. 219
Bishop, D.T. 126
Bisnette, Bree 258
Bissas, Despina 113
Black, Elizabeth 52
Black, Kimberly 114
Black, Rodney 389
Blackwell, Elliott 217
Blair, Kellie 73
Blair, Kristi 178
Blake, Kelly 232
Blanchard, Carol ReNee' 150
Blanchard, Suzanne 306
Blankenship, Julia 5
Blanton, Amanda 249
Blaskowski, Amy 269
Blazak, Kelly 84
Bleau, Alain Gordon 223
Blecha, Judy Atwell 4
Blom, Christy 242
Bloom, Allie 81
Bloom, Edgar S. 182
Bloomfield, Steven 315
Bober, Jennifer 152
Bobo, Alicia 405
Bocanegra, Jesse 216
Bochner, Michelle 367
Bock, Sara 340
Bockelman, Shana 316
Bockman, Patsy 358
Boestche, Kim 82
Bogden, Kim 226
Boggan, Bridgitt F. 176
Bogus, S. Diane 281
Bojorquez, Holly 100
Boldt, Victoria L. 292
Boling, Celeste A. 52
Bolles, Kathleen N. I. 270
Bollum, Gerre 208
Bolton, Heather M. 126
Bolton, Joy 37
Bond, Kristine 76
Bond, Sherry 344
Bonish, Amy Marie 130

Bonnell, Helen J. 15
Bono, Michelle 273
Booher, Tereasa 394
Boomershine, Marla J. 322
Borba, Jennifer 27
Borda, Joseph 207
Bose, Sharon 380
Bossarte, Eileen 71
Bosse, Anne 74
Bosse, Kristi 105
Bosshard, Jessica 190
Boswell, Robin 302
Boucher, Karen 154
Boule, Jo-Lynn 213
Boulton, Anastasia 175
Bova, Stephanie 394
Bowen, Natalie Anne 337
Bowers, Elizabeth 94
Bowers, William F. 390
Bowles, Jennifer A. 39
Bowman, Amy Catherine 209
Bowman, Sabina Janel 346
Bowman, William R. Sr. 387
Boyca, Shawna 348
Boyd, Canangela R. Jackson 253
Boyd, Jennifer 240
Boyd, Sareesa 385
Boyd, Tyra 278
Bradley, Connie S. 42
Bradley, Donna May
Bradley, Edith Inez 15
Brady, Jennifer L. 243
Brady, Rena 402
Braeutigan, Aimee 195
Braga, Denise 133
Brahan, Autumn D. 250
Bramick, B. A. 262
Brana, Concorida B. 235
Brand, Mariana 278
Brand, Nicole 371
Branson, Beth 56
Brant, Kristen 132
Brashares, Crtystal 8
Bratis, Lorraine 366
Bratt, Laura 404
Braun, Audrey 90
Braun, Cathryn 69
Braverman, Lisa J. 278
Bray, Christina Renee 259
Brazeal, Nancy 316
Brazis, Steven J. 325
Brennan, Julie 23
Brewer, Tracy 298
Brice, Brenda K. 20
Briceland, Tammy L. 357
Bridges, Amy M. 112
Bridle, Sarah 322

Bridwell, Alma J. 206
Brigitta, 91
Briner, June 185
Brinkmeier, Tamra D. 309
Brint, Bruce 407
Britt, Erica 36
Broadwater, Hazel 26
Broderson, J. M. 213
Brodnicki, Lori Anne 294
Brody, Melissa L. 292
Brook, Susan 316
Brookover, Anne 229
Brooks, Danita 226
Broomerkle, Dawn 222
Brouillard, Frances 55
Brown, Angel 137
Brown, Bob 29
Brown, Bobbie Ann 18
Brown, Candi A. 48
Brown, Charla 105
Brown, Debbie 29
Brown, December 175
Brown, E. Talley 83
Brown, Erika 123
Brown, Hilda 160
Brown, Janice R. 226
Brown, Joe N. 230
Brown, Marion 410
Brown, Stephanie L. 398
Brown, Wendi 367
Browning, Chris Biasini 46
Browning, Dawn 162
Brownlee, Lydia 384
Brubaker, Lori Anne 229
Brumley, Susan L. 278
Brunell, Lisa Michelle 300
Bruner, Tiffany Ann 365
Bruno, Richard 353
Bryan, Cathy 247
Bryan, Cathy 36
Bryant, Amanda 188
Bubb, Chrissy 214
Buch, Jennifer 166
Buchanan, Catrell 183
Buckless, Amy 62
Buckley, Lydia 152
Buckner, Paula A. 310
Budai, Christine A. 15
Buell, Carol 16
Bullard, Arlan P. 69
Bullard, Laurie Diane 323
Bulver, Julie 37
Bunch, Frenchie 173
Bung, Kristina Colleen 214
Burch, Traci 290
Burginger, Mara 316
Burnette, Amy 216

Burnette, Mary 312
Burns, Scotty 396
Burr, Brian J. 35
Burrell, Amy L. 214
Burton, Deana 80
Burton, Triniti Lisa 296
Bussey, Alex W. 4
Butler, Andrea 194
Butler, Carolyn D. 47
Button, P. L. 337
Butzlaff, Sue 310
Buzikievich, Jennifer 186
Byerley, Amy D. 58
Byerley, Lisa Shawn 291
Bynum, Nora Belle 378
Byrd, Beth A. 226
Byrd, Cindy 164
Byrdic, Tiffany 400
Cabal, Jesus Alberto 141
Cabrera, Monique 357
Caccamo, Lisa P. 350
Caddy, Christina 246
Cadena, Elizabeth 89
Cadena, Leticia 163
Cadiz, Rowena 295
Cage, Molly 337
Caldwell, Alisa 85
Call, Kristen M. 25
Callahan, Annette 241
Callaway, Maggie 312
Cameli, Christy 10
Cameron, Aileen 81
Cameron, Becky 186
Cameron, Joyce 87
Cameron, Steven M. 364
Camilletti, Jeanne 77
Campbell, Alicia 172
Campbell, Cheryl Ellen 47
Campbell, Christy J. 32
Campion, Roman Eli 283
Canady, Julie 267
Canavan, Jack E. 71
Cangelose, Donnajean 196
Cangialosi, Linda M. 389
Cano, Erica L. 242
Cantwell, Theresa 287
Capil, April 14
Capito, Suzanne 370
Capps, Brooke 268
Capps, Dawna 202
Caranto, Mel 293
Carbonneau, Andre' 184
Carlani, Sally A. Spirida 288
Carle, Amanda 145
Carlson, Tamara Renee 366
Carnevale, Mary Jean 375
Carney, Diane 193

Carney, Jeannette Johnson 179
Carpenter, Jennifer 133
Carpenter, Kelle 249
Carpenter, Marian 276
Carr, Stacey 333
Carrfagna, Angelo 6
Carroll, Kathleen 194
Carroll, Tiffany 410
Carstens, Dawn 50
Cartee, Anthony 85
Carter, Amber 50
Carter, Ashley 70
Carter, Dannie L. 234
Carter, Nancy 333
Carter, Tanya L. 255
Cartrell, Gabriele 236
Carver, Judy 142
Casanta, Isabelle 159
Casavant, Karen 45
Case, Kimberly 222
Casella, Amy 114
Casey, Elaine 147
Casey, Kristen F. 158
Casey, Vivian M. 296
Cashwell, Rose Marie Pickard 375
Castles, Pamela J. 304
Casto, Cassi 263
Castro, Amber 23
Castro, Jennifer 206
Caswell, Carol A. 140
Caterpillar, The 375
Causey, Mary Sewell 400
Cavagnudo, Judy 84
Cavallo, Michelle L. 393
Cavanaugh, Angie 198
Cay, Christy 256
Cecil, Sarah 282
Centeuo, Jesse 180
Cerasoli, Annie 255
Cerecedo, Jose J. 251
Cerra, Tiffany 343
Cervinka, Tanya 376
Chacon, Lorena 396
Chaggaris, Susan 346
Chalko, Laurie 359
Chamberlain, Nancy D. 393
Chamberlin, Christa 409
Chambers, Kristine N. 338
Chandchi, Melody 282
Channel, Roses 327
Chanthadouangsy, Wanchay 287
Chantharack, Loungthyva Tia 387
Chapman, Richard 364
Chapman, Sarah J. 279
Chappell, Heather 167
Charette, Anne 65
Chase, Sarah 314

Chavez, Jill 232
Chavis, Loren 272
Cheatham, Beth A. 258
Chechik, Catherine 9
Chesrow, Cathleen 17
Chesrow, Cathleen 75
Chester, Carol A. 59
Chester, Laura 272
Childs, Eugene E. 189
Chilton, Alesha 218
Chime, Ifeoma Angela 222
Chisolm, Jamie 155
Cho, Jane 62
Chorvat, Janice L. 87
Chossek, Harold 30
Chow, Karen M. 156
Christian, Stephanie 364
Christian, Stephanie 408
Cincotta, Deana 201
Cira, Clara 228
Clapp, Janet & Clark, Rich 4
Clare, Patrick 322
Clark, Chrissy 263
Clark, Christopher A. 45
Clark, Connie L. 153
Clark, Melanie 370
Clark, Rochelle Ann 336
Clary, Emily Garrett 83
Clausen, Shannon 372
Claypool, Kerry V. 242
Clayton, Annette 98
Clegg, Donald L. 251
Clement, John M. 253
Clemente, Kim 120
Clementson, Lisa 289
Cleveland, Reggie T. 343
Cline, Rachel 388
Clinton, Noble T. 324
Clune, Michelle S. 280
Coale, Vikki S. 282
Cob, Janelle Luelen 133
Coffey, Meg 388
Cogbill, Rodney 397
Cogburn, Rhonda L. 347
Cohn, Sheila 391
Colby, Julie A. 212
Cole, Dana R. 127
Cole, Elizabeth 94
Cole, Jack E. 146
Coleman, Eleanor M. 242
Coleman, Hilary 176
Coleman, Victoria 285
Collier, M. 271
Collins, Elizabeth 28
Collins, Eugenia 123
Collins, Jennifer 205
Collins, Jessica 78

Collins, Kelly 132
Collins, Shelly 410
Comberiate, Josephine Bertolini 66
Combs, Craig Thomas 58
Combs, Jeremy Lane 260
Comfort, Patricia 287
Commisso, Angel 131
Compton, Sheila 153
Conduff, Suzanne 330
Conklin, Carli 24
Conley, Autumn D. 256
Conner, Bethann 156
Conner, Tamara 280
Connor, Tracy 142
Consola, Amy 119
Conti, Michelle 79
Contreras, Morella 405
Contristano, Audrey 188
Cook, Janet E. 265
Cook, Jennifer 51
Cook, Jennifer 63
Cook, Kimberly C. 197
Cook, Stephanie 317
Cooke, Stephanie 374
Cooks, Tina L. 179
Cool, Rita M. 25
Coomer, Anitra 244
Copeland, Angela 111
Copple, Jennifer A. 3
Coppler, Holly 91
Cornelison, Sarah 380
Corrente, Cindy 122
Cortese, Jocelyn 189
Costa, Pietro A. 305
Costes, Heather Ann 125
Costly, Kerri Kristin 204
Costner, Rebecca W. 393
Cotton, Heather 63
Cottrell, Cathy 72
Courter, Dorinda 260
Courtney, Monette 410
Coutre', Jacquelyn N. 265
Couturier, Elaine 73
Covington, Amanda 147
Cowan, Lisa 241
Cox, Becky 75
Cox, Carolyn 145
Cox, Jean Dorothy 228
Cox, Jennifer 203
Cox, Kendra 252
Cox, Marci 77
Cox, Stacy 351
Coyle, Bill 31
Coyne, Gwendolyn 140
Cracolici, Cindy 60
Craddock, Haze 114
Craig, Connie 98

Craig, Crystal G. 238
Craig, Jennifer 153
Craig, Michelle 323
Cramer, Heather 68
Crampton, Rayanne 379
Crane, Betsy 16
Cranford, Donald G. Sr. 71
Crawford, Debbie 228
Crawford, F. Robert 24
Crawford, Gloria Parks 52
Crawford, Jonathon Jr. 89
Creager, Brandee 47
Creech, Debra 251
Creekmore, Dawn M. 267
Crichton, Janis I. 246
Croasmun, George W. 104
Crobaugh, Emma 184
Croci, Eva 173
Croft, Patti Leigh 390
Crosby, Connie Crandall 250
Crosby, Joanne 199
Croston, Stephen P. 395
Crouch, Glenn 170
Crouch, James 233
Crowell, Elizabeth 80
Crowne, Kerri 202
Crutchfield, Angela 221
Cruz-Morales, Maria L. 340
Cubbage, Debra 235
Cufton, Gretchen 184
Cullaro, Andrea 228
Cumella, Ben B. 21
Cummins, Harriet 193
Cunningham, Darlene Denice 76
Cunningham, Joanne M. 46
Cunningham, Kelli 137
Curry, Vickie 239
Curtis, David 226
Curtis, Eleanor R. 31
Curtis, Shirley E. 364
Cutler, Crystal 24
Czernow, Stefania 379
Czumak, Linda 307
D'Amora, Ashley 135
D'Annolfo, Nancy 375
D'Antonio, Thomas 315
D'Asto, Cymber 150
D'Lutz, Daniel 132
Dacri, Tanya 382
Dady, Rose 136
Daigle, Richard J. 281
Dallas, Kristi 143
Dalton, Carla 130
Damerville, Holly 218
Damico, Matthew 390
Damm, George E. 121
Damron, Tracy 398

Danby, Posie 323
Danchess, T. J. 313
Danenhoover, Ashley 251
Daniels, Marc 281
Danioth, Jennifer 97
Dapsis, Jennifer 214
Darnell, Joanna 186
Darnielle, Mary Lou 303
Darr, Stacie Cheryl 363
Dascole, Kristin 120
Daugherty, Elizabeth 196
Daughtry, Anita Pierce 196
Dauz, Lucille 278
Davenport, Jay 244
Davey, Boyd T. 186
Davidson, Anna 149
Davies, Jim 242
Davis, Amy 97
Davis, Aretha 217
Davis, Athena 121
Davis, Bettie Martin 88
Davis, Bristol 251
Davis, Cori Lynn 197
Davis, D. Lee 116
Davis, Elizabeth 44
Davis, Elizabeth 6
Davis, Holly M. 93
Davis, Jeni 82
Davis, Kimberly 111
Davis, Lise-Ann 391
Davis, Sherrie 290
Davis, Stephanie 366
Davis, Tiffany 377
Davis, Vanessa Olevia 330
Davison, Jennfifer Anne Francis 141
Dawson, Frieda 219
Dawson, Margaret 392
Day, Charles 154
Day, Stephanie 386
Day, Joan L. 122
De La Guardia, Maritza 395
De Ruggiero, Saverio 349
DeBiase, Danielle 144
DeCarteret, Amy 210
DeLancey, Connie M. 111
DeLand, Allison 67
DeMeo, Kathleen 89
DeMoss, Melissa 332
DePriest, Patricia 326
DeSantis, Karin 165
DeSurra, Desiree 64
DeVittorio, Deborah Marie 220
DeWaard, Jayna 3
Dean, Anne Louise 168
Dean, Brandy 155
Dean, Diana 117
Dean, Sue-Ellen 292

Dean, Todd B. 396
Deemer, Tammy 311
Dehart, Lori 306
Dehbozorgi, Ellie 228
Del Rio, Judity 67
Del Toro, Nancy 400
Delaney, Alison 235
Delaney, Kim 238
Delap, Missy 117
Delci, Jenn 255
Dell'Accio, Elizabeth 167
Dematteis, Christina M. 53
Demyen, Michel 364
Denney, Jennifer 116
Densmore, Natasha 407
Denton, Diane 168
Denty, Christi 160
Derrick, Jillian 187
Desrosiers, Diana 78
Detro, Jill 127
Devoe, Jana Lashun 37
Di Pasqua, Kendra 97
DiFrancisco, Gabrielle 136
DiGrazia, Gina 88
DiMeo, Tricia 369
DiPietro, Tasha 240
Dias, Lena 22
Diaz, Idania 78
Dick, Gretchen 211
Dickinson, Katie 35
Dickman, Kelly Marie 97
Dill, Christine 113
Dillender, Kelly 144
Dinger, Cathi Jo 219
Dinis, Ana C. 95
Dinkel, Crista 101
Dircksen, Julie 260
Dispigno, Joe 156
Dixon, Annette 408
Dixon, Norma B. 271
Dlouhy, Dee 121
Doan, Stephanie 367
Dobey, Mattie 318
Dobretz, Jami A. 247
Dollar, Terry L. 362
Dombrowski, Beth Susan 208
Dominick, Belton 10
Dominick, Louis 291
Donesa, Therese B. 64
Doney, John 21
Doniger, Eden 136
Donnelly, Michael William M. 375
Donovan, Abigail 151
Donovan, Chris L. 244
Donovan, Kathy 164
Donovan, Valerie O. 272

Dornburg, Beverly 192
Dorsett, Doris 224
Dorsey, Albert W. 86
Doskoch, Roy 341
Dotoli, Elaine Anne 7
Doty, Tami 77
Dougherty, Raymond 334
Douglas, Emily 28
Douglas, Rachel 314
Douglass, Rachel 235
Dow, Deborah 39
Dowding, Lagena 371
Downey, Jean Osborn 217
Doyle, Clarie 54
Dragoo, Toni Lee 346
Drake, Ali Marie 8
Drake, Amber 247
Drake, Eleanor Lynn 168
Drake, Sonja M. 321
Drennan, Joe Wheeler 242
Drew, Judy L. 226
Drew, Nadia 360
Droesch, Jenniefer 119
Droluk, Jenna M. 220
Du Mont, Malia 330
DuPont, Robin 328
Dube', Sandra 310
Dubinsky, Stantly 233
Dubitsky, Joanna 135
Dubois, Rachel R. 317
Ducharme, G. & Schukar, H. 166
Dudley, Kelly Lynn 222
Due, Nicole 389
Duffy, Erin 195
Dukeshire, Lori J. 369
Dulik, Susan 289
Dulin, H. Cajo 177
Dull, Amy 94
Dumerauf, Taga Lin 276
Dunalp, Michael E. Jr. 390
Dunbar, Jennifer 80
Dunham, Heather 166
Dunign, Kathy 226
Dunlop, Arlene 237
Dunn, Jennifer 52
Dunn, Kim M. 171
Duong, Diana ThiHuyen 97
Dupree, Adora L. 40
Durney, Robert M. 385
Durst, Teri A 297
Dutchy, Dawna 96
Duylie, Jackie 254
Dycio, Renee M. 280
Dye, Angela S. 221
Dyer, Wanda 361
Dyke, Aviance 42
Dzikowski, Deanne 97

Eader, Angela 192
Earley, Amber 221
Eastep, Christine 35
Eastlund, Brandy 69
Eastman, Kelly 105
Eastman, Robert J. 383
Eaton, B.J. 34
Ebert, Serenity 283
Eckman, Detra 57
Eddens, Leah 384
Edling, Sandra M. 342
Edmondson, Luci 254
Edsall, Amber 201
Edwards, Amanda 140
Edwards, Dana 187
Edwards, Heather 241
Edwards, Janice Anderson 30
Edwards, Krista 158
Edwards, Patsy 374
Eels, Ann C. 56
Eger, Sue 378
Ehrig, Judi L. 72
Ehringer, Susann 337
Einstein, Mark 401
Eklund, Colleen 129
Elexsi, Thomasenia 351
Eliot, Jennie 155
Elisofon, Barry 180
Elizabeth, Jane 95
Elledge, E. Hugh 111
Ellis, Courtney J. 74
Ellis, Dawn 221
Elms, Michele 332
Elsen, Julie 218
Ely, Shelley D. 372
Elzie, Robin 308
Emans, Cassie 169
Embry, 314
Emerson, Bernadette Hillery 108
Emery, Linda S. 61
Emig, Cindy 61
Emmons, Lysa 278
Enborg, Danielle 265
Enerson, Heidi R. 5
Engel, Elisabet D. 238
England, Amy 78
England, Patricia J. 399
Eno, Sarah 397
Enright, Jennifer 263
Enright, Nadine 320
Epperson, Teri 373
Eppinette, Christy 55
Escoffier, Aimee 105
Espinoza, Janice 245
Esquivel, Jenny 223
Estes, Anne L. 169
Estes, Joanna 109

Estis, Alicia 32
Estrera, Chloe 233
Ethier, Kerri 248
Evans, Caryn 119
Evans, Drexil R. 283
Evans, Harry 162
Evans, Jennifer 166
Evans, Julie A. 34
Evans, Krista Marie 10
Evans, Rhiannon L. 306
Evans, Sarah 170
Everage, Karen 248
Everington, Karen L. 155
Eversoll, Samantha 340
Ewing, Mandy 328
Fabiszak, Toni 59
Fahrner, Cheryl Lynn 183
Falconer, Tessie 319
Famolare, Christy 186
Fankhauser, Kari 181
Fantl, Andrea 58
Farmer, Gary 176
Faronii, Reliina 302
Farrar, Heidi 161
Farrow, Terri 405
Fasolo, Melissa 287
Fawcett, Jaima 234
Fay, Christa 156
Fearshaker, Yon E. 373
Feathers, Tracy 377
Fegley, Jeannette C. 82
Felan, Jacquie Danette 147
Fellows, Elizabeth 189
Fenn, Stacey 381
Ferguson, Deci 154
Ferguson, Dorothy M. 198
Ferguson, Libby 380
Fernandez, Lisa 384
Ferrer, Arlene P. 73
Ferreria, Immx 3
Ferrier, Gail 90
Ferris, Deborah A. 252
Fettweis, Heather 93
Fewkes, Clara E. 48
Ficarro, Kate 161
Figueroa, Cindy 260
Figueroa, Katie 56
Figueroa, Virgina 386
Findlay, Anne 84
Finkle, Amanda 105
Finn, Sarah B. 319
Finnicum, Barbara 13
Firmingham, Kelly A. 130
Fisher, Britney 30
Fisher, Floy 111
Fisher, Jennfifer Nicole 59
Fitzgerald, Russ 295

Fitzpatrick, Jordan 190
Fitzpatrick, Josie 41
Fitzpatrick, Joy 116
Fitzsimmons, Charles 169
Flamer, Nicole 298
Fleischhauer, Renee 193
Fleming, Tamara 354
Fleniken, Brandi 172
Flesher, Marnie 366
Fletcher, Jesse 176
Fletcher, Sheree D. 407
Fliss, Catherine 173
Flores, Louie 320
Flowers, Amy P. 78
Flowers, Rebecca Sue 277
Floyd, Jeanne 162
Floyd, Jennifer 38
Fluharty, Karen 47
Focken, Lisa 383
Fogler, Elizabeth 155
Foley, Eileen Katherine 191
Foley, Heather 146
Foner, Jill 74
Fontano, Lynne 395
Fontenot, Desiree J. 76
Fontenot, Trent 391
Foodin, Ellen R. 254
Foot, Laura 108
Ford, Damantha 16
Ford, James Wesley 142
Ford, Randy L. 277
Fore, Christine A. 270
Foree, Jennifer ` 184
Forehand, Rachel E. 390
Foreman, Shanita 356
Form, Hazel Morvant Master, 84
Forster, Cindy 148
Foss, George 253
Fossum, Darla 197
Foster, April 199
Foster, Ashley 237
Foster, Fina 117
Foster, Kanda Rae 92
Foster, Selma 290
Foster, Stephanie Lee 277
Fountain, Candace 232
Fouse, Paul E. 395
Fowler, Jessica 184
Fowler, Joyce 22
Fox, C. 231
Fox, Melissa 382
Fox, Tracy 363
Foye, Angela Kathleen 124
Frahme, Erin 52
Fraley, Jaime 181
Frank, Sarah 136
Frankel, Courtney 179

Franks, Samantha M. 365
Franks, Susan M. 257
Frantz, Tamara
Frazier, Cheryl 235
Frazier, Ralph H. 312
Frazier, Ramsey 272
Frechette, Wendy M. 347
Frederick, Donna 213
Frederick, Felice 243
Frederick, Melissa 328
Freeman, Danica 157
Freeman, Leigh 358
Frew, Carole J. 75
Frisk, Carrie 101
Fritz, Lara 217
Frost, Tina 261
Fry, Wendy 239
Fulks, Gina 91
Fullard, Yolanda 321
Fulton, Jody 205
Furne, Alanna 111
Futscher, Heather 224
Futter, Mae 389
Gabay, Jayme 238
Gabriel, Brian 137
Gabriel, Marjonie 336
Gage, Linda L. 218
Gajewski, Terrie 339
Galazin, Kathleen 151
Gallagher, Lisa 111
Gallant, Michelle 395
Gallardo, Jody Lynn 223
Gallihugh, Vanessa 371
Galozo, Pete G. 404
Gamble, Jeremiah 132
Gamble, Shannon 286
Gambone, Brian 109
Garafolo, Andrea 101
Garcia, Viviana 338
Gardiner, Jocelynne 20
Gardner, Bonnie L. 41
Gardner, Julie 264
Gardner, Kelly 235
Gareau, Dawn 149
Garlisch, Kathleen L. 9
Garner, Kim E. 33
Garnett, Nadia 283
Garrison, Pamela Y. 285
Garvey, Tammi S. 332
Garza, Jaime D. 95
Garza, Maricruz 293
Gascon, Laura A. 291
Gaskin, Donna 75
Gaskins, Karen 93
Gastelum, Yvonne 372
Gaston, Ann 161
Gauden, Kim 52

Gaudiano, Frances 58
Gaulin, Diana 188
Gavitt, Sherry 6
Gaydos, Beth A. 173
Geary, Danielle Leigh 74
Geddes, Jennifer 36
Geebaman, Charity 94
Gelineau, Jan 3
Gemmell, Amber 180
Gendall, M. 314
Gendron, Marc 391
Geralis, Jospeh 250
Gerber, Tina 376
Gerling, Denise 48
Gerrard, Bambi 256
Gerry, Amber Marie 146
Geyer, Ruth Anne 298
Ghoston, Erma 33
Gibert, Anna 26
Gibson, Audra 209
Gibson, Carolyn P. 194
Gibson, Natalie 345
Gibson, Shannon 342
Gibson, Sharon L. 402
Giebultowski, Krystyna 156
Gielow, H. R. 7
Gierich, Anna 152
Giese, Todd 307
Gietzen, Shawna 86
Giffith, Caroline 256
Gilbert, Jack 19
Gilbert, Kim 137
Gilbert, Renee 380
Giles, Angel 266
Gill, Dorothy 185
Gillett, Jennifer 81
Gillis, Tara Ann 378
Gittler, Danielle 156
Gizzo, Debbie 142
Gladden, Pat 373
Gladston, Nancy Crockett 283
Glass, Judith 19
Glass, Sarah 275
Glaza, E. J. 139
Glazer, Jennifer 237
Gleason, Jennifer 159
Gleason, Michelle 365
Glenn, Teresa R. 304
Glesmann, Amanda J. 171
Glidden, Tammy Lynn 411
Go, Karen 208
Goatley, Sally 370
Goddard, Hazel Firth 45
Godfrey, Michelle M. 110
Goessl, Rebecca 337
Gofis, Georgia 16
Goldberg, Brian 249

Goldstein, Mindy 347
Goldstone, Blake L. 146
Goncalves, Elaine 47
Gonzales, Anita 109
Gonzales, Mary Ann 291
Gonzalez, Jacqueline 112
Gonzalez, Leila S. 344
Good, Christine 90
Good, Jennifer 153
Goodlad, Melissa 390
Goodlett, Heather 9
Goodrich, amy Marie 9
Goon, Gina Michelle 222
Gooze, Heather 57
Gordon, Elizabeth 70
Gordon, Partricia R. 295
Gordon, Theresa 286
Goren, Emily 191
Gorman, Ellen 174
Goswiller, Linda K. 399
Gottesman, Edward 35
Gould, Katherine 221
Gould, Lara 7
Gowling, Michael 397
Graben, Pam 380
Grado, Jenny 213
Grady, Bridget 143
Grainger, Gayle 177
Grau, Amy 74
Gravely, Katherine 109
Gray, Dwight A. 137
Gray, L. E. T. C. 85
Gray, Moone 274
Grayson, Stacey 19
Grazulis, Debra Pepis 143
Grebin, Michelle 331
Green, Debbie 98
Green, Heidi Eileen 269
Green, Lisa 30
Green, Marti 318
Green, Miklyn Erin 335
Greenamyer, Ginger 157
Greenfield, James G. 73
Greening, Jennifer 79
Greet, Kim 165
Grenz, Holly 144
Gresham, Rebecca 26
Grider, Michelle 273
Griff, Heather C. 189
Griffin, Heather 8
Griffis, Gena 44
Griffith, Talley 392
Grimm, Aimee E. 123
Grometer, Karen 189
Grondin, Michele 347
Gronke, Raquel 9
Gross, Denise 58

Gross, Shawna 284
Grossmith, Edward J. 60
Grot, Bonnie L. 144
Grubb, Brandi 27
Grumbling, Brandee 168
Grunder, Sandy 340
Grundtner, Suzanne 313
Guenther, Aimee 99
Guerra, Lisa 165
Guerra, Raechel R. 354
Guggenheim, Debra E. 29
Gugni, Melissa 358
Guida, Michael J. 359
Guilford, April 127
Guillory, Tanya 357
Gumm, Erica 182
Gunby, Carol L. 70
Gurung, Prakash 382
Gush, Lynn 389
Gustin, Peter S. 272
Gutelius, Tonya Lynn 286
Haas, Karen 254
Hackney, Gladys M. 142
Hadary, Judith 4
Hadley, James W. 224
Hagan, P. 347
Hagen, Paige M. 392
Hager, Tina 385
Hahn, Mary 398
Haidsiak, Shannon 317
Haigh, Wendy Jeya 364
Halbeck, Stacey 322
Halbrook, Charlie 193
Halcomb, Margaret 400
Hall, Adrienne 163
Hall, Barbara J. 169
Hall, Denise 69
Hall, Susan 330
Hall, Tami Jo 346
Hall, Tammy 293
Halla, Lori 273
Hallock, Shaunna 325
Halmas, Joanne 115
Halonen, Briita, 196
Halverson, Jennifer 19
Hambrick, Leslie 360
Hamill, Wendy L. 10
Hamilton, Belva Dobyns 81
Hamm, Dee Dee 157
Hammond, Wanda 264
Handkins, Christy 263
Handy, James 49
Hanley, Michael R. 361
Hanna, Paul 287
Hannah, Janice 165
Hansen, Merle C. 291
Hardin, Angel L. 143

Hardin, Mike 299
Hardin, Rebecca 300
Harding, Shelcey 372
Hargrove, Jynnifer 171
Harkness, Christa 46
Harler, Beverly L. 25
Harness, Betty B. 128
Harnot, Joseph J. Jr. 118
Harper, Dawn 170
Harper, Jennifer 87
Harrington, Heather 15
Harris, Dana 188
Harris, Jennifer 130
Harris, Julie 86
Harris, Nicole 400
Harris, Sherrie Van Dyke 276
Harris, Stephanie 323
Harrison, Edgar M. 210
Harrison, Jancie L. 195
Harrison, Mark 314
Harrison, Mary 305
Harrison, Shannon 373
Harrison, Wendy 84
Hart, T. L. 396
Harte, Mary T. 303
Harth, Jennifer 62
Hartung, Shannon 381
Hartwell, Heidi 98
Hartzell, Tim N. 371
Hartzfeld, Joseph Leroy 46
Harvey, Jean 131
Haskettt, Wilda 312
Hasting, Samantha 381
Hastings, Monica 388
Hatfield, Angela 127
Hauff, Heather 75
Haupt, Cecilia G. 46
Haupt, Erin 66
Havens, Michelle 394
Hawes, Melissa 307
Hawkins, David M. 85
Hawkins, Jeri 116
Hawkins, Katherine 242
Hawthrone, Jennifer 167
Haycock, Tracy 345
Haycook, Kelly Jo 246
Hayden, Amanda 200
Hayden, Jennifer 199
Haydon, Annette 43
Hayseed, Vonnie 381
Hazelton, Jamie Lynette 179
Head, Eraka D. 236
Head, Wanda 398
Heaps, Barbara Wolfe 77
Heard, Diana V. 70
Heatherly, Carrie 234
Hebert, Shelly 383

Heckmman, Carrie 196
Hedglin, Shannon 301
Heffelmeier, Jennifer 156
Hefter, Gillian 106
Heidel, Amy 254
Heilman, Kristie 76
Heilman, Tami 271
Heim, Stephanie 271
Heiman, Dora L. 11
Hein, Kristal 96
Hein, Teri 279
Heincy, Patricia L. 294
Heirbout, Heather 99
Henderson, Amy 209
Henderson, George E. 155
Henderson, Jospehine 77
Henderson, Kelly Renee 128
Henderson, Lizzie 309
Hendrickson, Heather 95
Hendrickson, Jill 85
Hendrix, Jeni 88
Hendrix, Rebecca 253
Heng, Sarah 367
Hennessy, Erin 263
Hennigan, Eddie III 117
Henry, Bonnie 72
Henry, La Tonya 319
Hensley, Ellouise 181
Hensley, Jack 119
Henson, Lara M. 291
Henson, Tonya 391
Hernandez, Andrea 56
Hernandez, Malinda 308
Herr, April 225
Herr, Dulcie 209
Herrin, Heidi J. 120
Herrington, Jennifer 48
Herron, Angie 263
Hershman, Randi S. 275
Hert, Angela 240
Hessell, Michelle R. 313
Hethcoat, Amy 240
Heying, Christine 213
Heyman, Jill 126
Hickman, Jenny 209
Hickman, Laquisha 232
Hicks, Jennifer 141
Hicks, Lorraine 411
Hicks, Melissa 174
Higginbotham, Kitten-Kathie 173
Higgins, Heather 204
Hildebrandt, Christina 38
Hildner, Blake 217
Hile, Melisa S. 343
Hilgendorf, Trish A. 377
Hill, Cheryl 36
Hill, Joan 160

Hill, Mary 333
Hiller, Danielle 119
Hills, Megan Michelle 405
Hilsinger, K. 75
Hinkley, Michele 276
Hinson, Barbara Clark 102
Hinzman, Leslie 379
Hitchcock, Inez 79
Hite, Amy 146
Hladky, John A. 57
Hoart, Carole B. 135
Hobbs, Rose 393
Hobson, Tiffany 349
Hochstetler, Andrea 209
Hodge, Mildred 404
Hodges, T. A. 335
Hoffman, Alice M. 190
Hoffman, Dale Patrick 252
Hoffman, Heather 63
Hoffman, Stephanie 297
Hoffmann, Joanne E. 180
Hofstede, Roland 363
Hogan, Kelley Marie 210
Hogges, Ralph 373
Hokanson, Patricia May 299
Holbert, William Michael 344
Holby, Esther Hughes 80
Holcomb, Dreama 92
Holden, Eric 160
Holiday, V. S. 277
Holland, Lisa 99
Hollander, Renee 320
Holliday, Patricia 392
Hollis, Joanna Pauline 114
Hollis, Tessi 370
Holloway, Heather 59
Hollub, Jennifer 168
Holmberg, Anne 195
Holmes, Angela 223
Holmes, Kristen 139
Holmes, Tonya 309
Honaker, Kirsten 247
Hoogland, Staci 48
Hoogstad, Jenne Barbasiewicz 130
Hook, Natasha 401
Hooper, Aramenta L. 33
Hoover, Tammy 283
Hopes, Heather 249
Hopkins, JoAnn K. 148
Hopkins, Veronica Dianne 25
Hoppal, Mindy S. 350
Horne, Regina 325
Horton, Carrie 268
Horworitz, Katie 91
Hostman, Lisa 279
Hotalski, Lynn 332
Hotte, Jessie 51

Houchens, Kristy 169
Houck, Michelle L. 394
House, John C. 205
Houser, Jenny 116
Housh, Mary E. 288
Hovis, Jennifer A. 11
Howard, Andrea Sue 102
Howard, Deborah Ellen 7
Howard, Joan 230
Howard, Nicole 277
Howard, Stacey 368
Howden, Bobbie-Lee 237
Howell, Allison 49
Howell, Keith R. 148
Howland, Michelle 344
Howorth, Jennifer A. 202
Howton, Christina 66
Hoyle, Janine 73
Hrcan, Paulina 399
Hubbard, Carmen D. 21
Hubbard, Tina 285
Hubbs, Alyce L. 182
Hubner, Angela Noel 54
Huddle, H. 145
Huddleston, Lisa K. 320
Hudson, Aimee 214
Hudson, J. Blaine 36
Hueppehen, Gary S. 135
Hughbanks, Rachel 79
Hughes, Faye Gibbs 258
Hughes, Heather 224
Hughes, Sandy 101
Hughes, Sarah K. 275
Hulinsky, Vivki 293
Hull, Crys 103
Humphreys, Sue 338
Humphries, Bobbi 208
Hunnicutt, Melanie 388
Hunt, James 65
Hunt, Robin 410
Hunter, Carol 183
Hupy, Desiree M. 174
Hurst, Stepahnie 371
Hurt, Erin 171
Hurt, Lukendra 362
Huschka, Tammie 345
Hutchings, Crystal 6
Hutchison, George L. 118
Huynh, Thai 285
Hyatt, Robin 375
Hyatt, Ruby 354
Hyio, Geraldine 49
Hyunn, Andrea 194
Iacobucci, Dana 28
Iaizzo, Virginia 275
Ide, Janna 257
Imperial, Joseph John 103

Innaimo, Suzin M. 388
Intintoli, Trisha 310
Isaak, S. N. 323
Islas, Sara Angelica 104
Issendorf, Jennifer 202
Ivy, Barbara S. 233
Iwano, Yoshimi 360
Izzo, Michele 296
Jacks, Connie L. 230
Jackson, Angela D. 157
Jackson, Carla 208
Jackson, Charis 183
Jackson, Clance 200
Jackson, Jeanette L. 38
Jacobe, Benjamin D. 212
James, Gene 68
James, Jessica 203
James, Noreen 277
James, Verena D. 330
Janci, Stephanie 403
Jansen, Pandy A. 320
Janulis, Vanessa 373
Jarka, Kathryn 244
Jarzynka, Julie 128
Jehle, Sarah 321
Jendrzejewski, Ingrid Anne 139
Jenkins, Ami 237
Jenkins, Angie 108
Jenkins, Denise 104
Jenkins, Hollie 129
Jennings, Jenni 69
Jensen, Amy 91
Jensen, Gertrude G. 207
Jensen, Jennifer 47
Jensen, Margaret 92
Jensen, Maria 335
Jensen, Robin 316
Jepson-Gilbert, Anita 160
Jerome, Mildred Capps 379
Jesca, 35
Jeschke, Tammy 344
Jesse, Chris 231
Jessie-Jones, Linda 307
Jette, Debra 74
Jewett, Gail A. 88
Jimenez, Rachel 278
Joblon, Edna 122
Johannes, Kimberly A. 255
Johnson, Alycia W. 95
Johnson, Amanda 255
Johnson, Anthony 210
Johnson, April L. 247
Johnson, Ardith 54
Johnson, Chasity 212
Johnson, Christina 24
Johnson, Christine 44
Johnson, Connie 192

Johnson, Dixie 133
Johnson, Fatimah 211
Johnson, Jaylynn 14
Johnson, Mark A. 82
Johnson, Melissa 298
Johnson, Michael & Tina 374
Johnson, Tatanisha 315
Johnson, Tiffany 321
Johnston, J. Patrick 30
Johnston, Wesley A. 329
Jolly, Pam 386
Jones, Amy C. 108
Jones, Beth 120
Jones, Brandie 107
Jones, Jeanne B. 26
Jones, Jennifer 194
Jones, Jennifer 67
Jones, Jenny 4
Jones, Karen 146
Jones, Kaye 70
Jones, Kristine 31
Jones, Marcelle 296
Jones, Monica 397
Jones, Shannon 361
Jordan, Dana 6
Jordan, Rose 365
Jordan, Tami 349
Jordann, Dawn 44
Jorns, Marie 304
Jortner, Helen J. 44
Joyal, Sylvia L. 368
Joynes, Ashley 137
Juarez, Jessica 199
Judd, Colleen Marie 269
Jundt, Syndee 366
Junior, Jeanette 133
Kacmarcik, Anne 228
Kaiser, Anne 135
Kalies, Joanne 58
Kalle, Joel E. 224
Kalmey, Christine 164
Kamalii, Garilyn 219
Kamin, Vincent 295
Kangas, Juanita Hutson 234
Kanter, Sharron Lea 270
Kapp, Christi 202
Kappel, Robert 353
Karosas, Lisa 349
Karr, Kim 266
Kastal, Klara 202
Katherine, 248
Katsifis, Gloria 17
Katz, Hazel Hoff 18
Kauffman, Becky 249
Kauffman, Christine 51
Kaufmann, Jenny 128
Kavanagh, Miriam 383

Kay, Jennifer 187
Keane, Regina 274
Kearns, Lisa 274
Keech, Kristen 244
Keefer, Dusty 100
Keith, Anne 60
Keith, K 110
Keith, Kathy M. 49
Keller, Angela 225
Kelley, Christine 268
Kellogg, Dennis L. 226
Kelly, Brooke 252
Kelly, D. H. 197
Kelly, Deidre' A. 138
Kelly, Erin 77
Kelly, Joan Auer 17
Kelly, Marla 354
Kelly, Patricia A. 378
Kelly, Patti 355
Kelly, Sean 349
Kemp, Rosalind 363
Kemper, Michelle 309
Kendall, Jeannie Mattox 12
Kendra, Heather 60
Kennedy, Cheryl 138
Kennedy, Jennifer 220
Kennedy, Kelly A. 236
Kennedy, Kim J. 135
Kenney, John 147
Kennison, Eudora Tree 173
Kenny-Edwards, Kelly 351
Kent, Sandra Lee 147
Keran, Durae 181
Kernodle, Karen 121
Kerr, Renee 159
Kerzner, Jackie 75
Key, Christy 262
Key, Erica 169
Keys, Karen 17
Khoury, Lisa 369
Kidd, Billy D. 131
Kidd, Jodi 229
Kieber, Amy 128
Kilbarger, Karen 89
Kilbreath, Rebecca 341
Kile, Susan A. 285
Kim, Caroline L. 134
Kim, Shelly 363
Kincaid, Kerry C. 157
King, Beckie 52
King, Brietta 181
King, Koren 268
Kingcaid-Pizzute, Marge 288
Kinnamon, Angie 66
Kinse, Karen 219
Kinsey, Parisha 83
Kirchhevel, Deborah 65

Kirchhoff, Jennifer 39
Kirck, Kiri 79
Kirk, Andrea 23
Kirk, Andrea R. 63
Kirkman, Angela S. 26
Kirkman, Diane 49
Kirkpatrick, Deborah E. 41
Kirkpatrick, Lori S. 296
Kischer, Kerrilyn 203
Kislig, Lydia Marie 324
Kitchen, Candi 122
Kitzan, Jennifer 175
Klassen, Nikki 377
Klavikorn, June 185
Kleinsasser, Jill 215
Kleppinger, Ethel H. 119
Klinedinst, Jenell 266
Klinger, Kim 125
Knapp, Gray Senior 149
Kneissl, Douglas S. 240
Knicely, Mindy 280
Knight, Bett 90
Knight, Penny L. 329
Knight, Summer 274
Knop, Alysia 220
Knopp, Angela 53
Knowles, Albert Stanley 198
Knowlton, Lori 332
Knudsen, Claudia 237
Koempel, Kristine 20
Koenig, Angie 192
Koeniguer, Linda M. 391
Kofsky, Dana 226
Koger, Denise 139
Kohler, Heather 4
Kolb, Pam 299
Konrad, Ken 268
Konrad, Krissy 99
Koon, Elizabeth 192
Koopmeiners, Lori 286
Kopetz, Susan 325
Koren, Annette 62
Kornberger, Rita 297
Korpos, Kristin 128
Korsbeck, Judy 42
Kosch, Becky 223
Kosinski, Debbie 203
Kosmadaklis, Olga 289
Koun, Elizabeth A. 175
Kovach, Amber L. 266
Kowalchuk, Patti 286
Kowalczyk, Karolina 245
Kprake, Prince Dave 342
Kralik, Lisa 302
Kraus, Andria 6
Kraus, Jennafer 217
Kravcisin, Kim 99

Kreske, Henry C. III 207
Krivda, Edward R.J. 171
Krkljus, Jospeh 343
Kronmiller, Christine 195
Krotzer, Vivian 304
Krueger, Jo Ann Chiari 32
Krueger, Marian 394
Krug, Tracy A. R. 365
Krupinski, Christine 266
Kruse, Sandra 336
Krysz, Christine 33
Kubinski, Kerrie Ann 199
Kuch, Krista 217
Kuhaneck, Diana 222
Kuipers, Kristie 150
Kulas, S. 313
Kunesh, Barb 47
Kung, Pang-Jen 409
Kunimoto, Namiko 305
Kuntzman, Kim 12
Kurth, Michelle 107
Kurth, Michelle 232
Kurtz, Linda S. 293
Kyler, Eloise 180
La Banca, George 236
La, Shanti 350
LaBell. Laura M. 294
LaBianco, Dolores 67
LaGarde, Kimberly 154
LaPlante, Cherie 4
LaSalle, Michele 87
Laatz, Heather 269
Lacky, amy 170
Laden, Jonathan 236
Ladislaw, William 23
Lahr, Christal 87
Lai, Kati 221
Lake, Elizabeth 240
Lamb, Paul M. 336
Lambert, Julie Anne 79
Lance, Tonya 367
Land, Kieth O'Brien 44
Landals, Robin A. 273
Landry, Linda 380
Lane, Barbie 53
Lane, Dani 116
Lang, Jodell 253
Lanham, Thomas Creel 366
Lanier, Hallie 120
Lape, Shannon 343
Larocque, Nicole 259
Larranaga, Amy 269
Larson, Sharie 386
Latchaw, Ruth 200
Latchinian, Sally 326
Latourette, Doreen Michelle 23
Lattimer, Lisa 336

Laube, Laurie 316
Laufenberg, Christine 19
Laurie, A. G. 152
Lavender, Brenda 190
Lawhorn , Amy 76
Lawrence, Nikki 393
Lawson, Charly 177
Lawson, Dayna 205
Lawson, Jana M. 124
Layfield, Lisa 320
Lazarus, Chady 65
Lazur, Marianne 376
LeBlanc, Claudette 92
LeBlanc, Kelly Christine 115
LeDoux, Delphine 174
LeDoux, M. D. 393
Lea, Jodi 81
Leathers, Kristy 57
Leavenworth, Colleen 10
Leavitt, Donna M. 18
Leavy, Colleen A. 57
Leclair, Scott 295
Lee, Connie 192
Lee, Emily Ann 201
Lee, Jamie Ann 263
Lee, Michelle 292
Lee, Virginia S. 378
Lee, Vivian 337
Leffler, Emily Mae 260
Leffler, Michael S. 350
Leflar, Jean 14
Legg, Alice L. 27
Leggett, Melissa 388
Lehmann, Cheryl 216
Lehmann, Joyce 66
Lemar, Coco 406
Lemley, Norma 318
Lenihan, Shannyn 288
Lenna, Jennifer 215
Lenz, Kelly 166
Leonard, Dorothy 39
Leone, Kathryn 213
Leong, Stacey 365
Lepak, Summer 378
Leppky, Victor 290
Lesh, Karla 248
Leslie, Kellie M. 120
Lester, Jessica 8
Letzig, Shelley 370
Leusner, Cynthia Rose 218
Levy, Lisa Ann 387
Lewallen, Melissa 57
Lewin, Lena E. 299
Lewis, Amy 231
Lewis, D. Suzanne 227
Lewis, Donna 151
Lewis, Edwin 50

Lewis, Joseph 159
Lewis, Karen Ann 212
Lewis, Laura 328
Lewis, Melvin E. 410
Lewis, Reginald Sinclair 376
Lewis, Ruby Anne 322
Lewis, Sara 326
Li, Diane 58
Liddell, Gay F. 42
Liddell, Samantha 301
Lieber, Dian 15
Lien, Daniel R. 181
Liesch, Krissy 125
Limberger, Stacy 6
Limprecht, Eleanor 153
Lincoln, Esther G. 158
Lindsay, Carol Ann 231
Lindsey, Erin 224
Lingenfelter, Dawn Lynne 196
Link, Carol B. 131
Linn, Becky 186
Lipicky, Josh 57
Lira, Silvia Lopez 118
Litak, Dawn 233
Litzenberg, Kim 195
Livernois, Constance Jeanne 218
Lizewski, Beverly 74
Lloyd, Joyce 207
LoGiudice, Susan M. 379
LoGuidice, JoAnne 163
Lobera, Alex 78
Lock, Jocelyn 97
Lockhart, Juli 37
Loecher, Becky 87
Lohmuller, Jennifer 69
Lohner, Lynn 385
Lomax, Angie 86
Lombardi, Julie 15
Lombardo, April 177
Lombillo, Patricia M. 80
Lominac, Keith 14
Long, Benjamin 237
Long, Carri 25
Long, Cecilia 24
Long, Denise 119
Long, Denise 145
Long, Elizaeth 193
Long, Jennifer 50
Long, Robin 328
Long, Sharon 337
Long, Tammy L. 370
Looney, Linda S. 335
Lopes, Simah 348
Lopez, Barbara I. 168
Lopez, Heddy 187
Lopez, Omar 302
Lore, James 238

Lotman, Elizabeth 16
Loudermilk, Malia 333
Lovell, Nicole 308
Lovell, Tracy 301
Lowe, Joan 257
Lowe, Krystyna M. 206
Lowell, Lorena 284
Lowry, Janet 204
Lozada, Frances 145
Lozon, Jill 204
Lu, Nhien-Phuong 30
Luangkhoth, Viengkeo 342
Lucas, Mandeline 403
Ludwig, J. L. 37
Ludwig, Robertta-Jeannette 311
Lueking, Angela 125
Lujan, Joleen 135
Luna, Stella 399
Lundeen, Miranda Marie 369
Lundy, Krista 101
Lung, Linda L. 384
Lunsford, Kathryn 197
Lunsford, Lesa 286
Lusk, Sue 294
Lutes, Melinda 360
Luther, Missy 333
Luther, Tara 370
Luttrell, Shannon M. 104
Lyczkoswki, Karrie 167
Lykins, Stephanie 275
Lymburner, Margaret 349
Lynch, Susan A. 395
Lynch, Tracie 384
Lyons, Pamela Berreth 367
M, Addy 141
Mabry, Karen 148
MacKenzie, Vicki 356
MacPherson, Kathy 166
MacWilliams, Amy K. 213
Macaluso, Giovanna 93
Machicek, Donna 51
Mack, Diane Bowman 7
Mackett, Kelly 70
Mackey, Carol 56
Mackin, Abby 96
Macklin, Linda 293
Madaffari, Cindi 81
Madden, Carrie Ann 119
Magee, Joseph 187
Magoch, Leesa 401
Mahafaj, Kiran Antoinette 98
Mahoney, Jackie 12
Mailer, Jewellee 195
Mainit, Joann 207
Majers, Michelle 378
Makalani, Matundu 339
Malcolm, Jonor I. 163

Malcom, Corneilsha 264
Maldonado, Yvette 118
Malinowski, Laura 183
Malott, Krista 160
Mancuso, Mandy 297
Mandulak, Elaine C. 250
Manganello, Krista 221
Mani, Bakirathi 210
Manker, Crystal 13
Manners, Mariah 402
Manning, Cynthia Lee 206
Mansouri, Spencer 288
Mantsch, Tara 357
Manzo, Danielle 142
Mapes, Cricket 200
Mapes, Marie L. 357
Marazzani, Santa A. Lalli 386
Marchant, Jessica D. 214
Marcincak, Nickole L. 369
Marcucci, Michele 401
Marcum, Christie 62
Marcus, Jody 160
Marek, Jennifer 256
Maresh, Rachel 72
Maria, Angel 261
Marietta, Annette 21
Marino, Susie 334
Markel, Laura 411
Marley, K. D. 66
Marquais, Chris 183
Marsh, Anke 22
Marsh, Dorothy R. 78
Marsh, Lynda G. 377
Marsh, Nicole 387
Marshall, Catherine J. 224
Marshall, Edie 90
Marshall, Erika 164
Marshall, Jaime Lynn 128
Marshall, Sarah Raye 398
Martel, Jenny 63
Martens, Charlotte 234
Martin, Alfred Napoleon 27
Martin, Alison 194
Martin, Angela 38
Martin, Dawn-Mari N.E. 23
Martin, Heather 173
Martin, Jessica A. 133
Martin, Karen 172
Martin, Lisa Diane 332
Martin, Rhonda 273
Martin, W. John 391
Martineau, Ladena 338
Martinez, Patty 289
Martinez, Ruben Gerard 335
Martinson, Connie 175
Martorana, Rosann 134
Mary, David 74

Marziaz, Mandy L. 303
Mashack, Shirley A. Wynn 277
Masilotti, Dorothy 174
Mason, Heather 16
Mason, Telfair 363
Mastracchio, Jules 45
Mata, Nicole 321
Mathai, Beena 171
Mathers, Martin 367
Matos, Rick 402
Matson, Alexandra 59
Matteson, S. 90
Matthews, Katie 19
Matthews, Marcie 297
Mattison, April E. 123
Mattison, Sandra 390
Maurone, Dori 115
Max, David M. Jr. 179
May, Christina 173
May, Heather 58
May, Janice L. 53
May, Jennifer F. 161
May, Tanya 293
Mayer, Tracie Lynn 296
Mayhew, Angela C. 111
Mazeika, Kristine 121
McAbee, Jennifer 162
McAdams, Coleen 18
McAllister, Michelle 350
McBee, Amy 28
McBride, Tara 319
McBurnett, Cecil Edwin 165
McBurnett, Cecilia Edwina 70
McCants, Latasha 385
McClain, Sylvia Renee 368
McClanaghan, Kristen 270
McColligan, Donna 224
McCoy, Amy 216
McCoy, Helen 201
McCraine, Brandi 91
McCrary, Kristin 25
McCreary, Jen 162
McCrory, Alexandra 43
McCurdy, Kenzie 155
McDavid, Lloyd 292
McDermott, Betsy K. 38
McDermott, Kathy 239
McDonald, Amy 265
McDonald, Kathryn M. 212
McDonald, Kristin 46
McDonald, Nancy S. 404
McDonald, Sheila 334
McDowell, Billy Ray 136
McDowell, Lisa 394
McEntee, Barbara 186
McFalls, Frances G. 253
McFerran, Christina 103

McGee, M. K. 276
McGinnis, David Jr. 175
McGinnis, Trudi 297
McGlothin, Reann 369
McGonagle, Megan 346
McGreevy, Mary 363
McGuire, Ellen 188
McGuire, Kelly 230
McHaney, Angela 17
McHone, Michelle 389
McIntyre, Tonya 368
McIver, Deborah 239
McKee, Ellyn 68
McKee, Mae Bell 272
McKeehan, Denise 54
McKissick, Amy 115
McKnight, Ida Lewellen 34
McKoskey, Caroline 267
McKoy, Dawn C. 43
McLain, Alta 106
McLean, Melva 329
McMahon, Ronda 285
McManus, Brandi 158
McMillan, Sally 288
McMinn, Collena 131
McMullen, Michele 361
McMullin, Danielle 191
McNab, Helen 85
McNabb, Misha 355
McNally, Ginnie Jean 100
McNeely, Kimberly 144
McRae, Shawn 299
McRee, Robin 366
McReynolds, Jennifer 60
McStravick, Kirstin 185
McWilliams, Mary Baker 290
Meade, Lee Cooper 355
Meadows, Melanie 329
Meckley, Joellen 93
Medders, Regina Lynn 234
Meek, Anissa 144
Mehra, Rooma 332
Meier, Cassandra J. 234
Meisel, Melinda 404
Melbott, Ginger 41
Mellett, Brenda 41
Mendoza, Cynthia 164
Menke, Jennifer Lynn 21
Menz, Michelle 80
Mercer, Marlo 92
Merker, Alice Davis 22
Mermis, TaggyLee 350
Mernone, Dawn Marie 61
Merriman, Diana 13
Merswolke, Clarice A. 242
Mervyn, Sasha 262
Merz, Kristin 88

Meseraull, Gary D. 192
Mesich, Karena 207
Messina, S.E. 378
Messmer, Angela 261
Metz, Charity 84
Meuth, Cassie 212
Meyer, Cheryl 94
Meyer, Christy 96
Meyer, Elizabeth J. 263
Meyer, Julie 256
Meyres, Edith 39
Meza, Ramona E. 350
Michalski, Bonnie 103
Michaud, Josee 117
Micheal, C. P. 89
Middlebrooks, Judith C.
Middleton, Sarah 406
Migliaccio, Erica 14
Milaeger, Corrie 77
Milam, Mark A. 368
Miles, Crista 16
Miles, Lena 302
Miles, Rebecca 271
Millender, Laura Ellen 57
Miller, Alison 37
Miller, Amy 196
Miller, Amy Leigh 34
Miller, Andree 122
Miller, April 155
Miller, Barb 92
Miller, Becky 170
Miller, Brandi 106
Miller, Byron G. 77
Miller, Byron Glenn 132
Miller, Corrine L. 15
Miller, Dara 108
Miller, Dawn 53
Miller, Erica T. 62
Miller, James Sr. 131
Miller, Jerry Edward Jr. 186
Miller, Jonancy 55
Miller, Kelly 166
Miller, Melissa 204
Miller, Michelle 274
Miller, Michelle 280
Miller, Michelle 353
Miller, Sonya 308
Miller, Staci 341
Miller, Stacy 381
Miller, Tamera 353
Miller, Tanya 27
Miller, Wendy 298
Millett, Melissa 102
Millich, Draga 257
Milner, Erwin 126
Miner, Theresa 403
Minor, Rebekah Lynn 140

Miotke, Marlene 271
Miranda, M. 182
Mitchell, Joni 264
Mitchell, Kristie 63
Mitchell, Robin 345
Mitchell, Sharyn M. 356
Mitchell, Veronica Lee 318
Mitchell-Rizzo, Deborah A. 104
Mitiavila, Sophia 380
Mix, Amy 215
Mize, Tammy 281
Mizlo, Traci 409
Moder, Stacy 14
Moffa, Anne-Marie 262
Moise, Sarah Ann 374
Mojeski, Michele 289
Molert, Leslie Raye 352
Molina, Cheyenne 167
Monacci, Corrine 36
Moncur, Lisa 345
Monia, Nicole 288
Monique, Jewel 139
Montes, Sandra Teresa 308
Montgomery, Michelle M. 291
Montgomery, Rhonda 381
Moody, Ashley 172
Moody, Kelly 36
Moon-Clay, Juliette 117
Mooney, Shannon 308
Moore, Deborah 72
Moore, Grin 27
Moore, Jacquelyn 26
Moore, Jacquelyn J. 130
Moore, Kristy 239
Moore, S. 336
Morales, Joy C. 232
Morazzani, Barbara J. 179
Morby, Nicole L. 324
Moreno, Carlos 218
Morgan, Cynthia A. 165
Morgan, Debbie 67
Morgan, Jackie 12
Morgan, Laura 335
Morgan, Robin 397
Morgenroth, Laura 334
Morris, Cyndi 99
Morris, Rebecca 361
Morrisette, Deborah A. 97
Morrow, Lisa R. 297
Morse, Amanda L. 134
Morse, Gloria 109
Morton, Cheryllynn A. 128
Moskal, Kimberly 100
Mosqueda, Renella 275
Moss, Rebecca Jane 271
Motaze, Emilienne 114
Mowatt, Wanda 389

Muaddi, Susan B. 369
Mueller, Christi 256
Mugavero, Christine 250
Muhammad, Amir 98
Mulford, Clare 123
Mulkey, Matt 339
Mullen, Jennifer L. 35
Mullen, Lori 355
Mullen, Matt 286
Mullens, Mary A. 322
Munoz, Marisa 281
Muransky, Steven 382
Murawski, Dolores 22
Murawski, Karen J. 8
Murphy, Christine 262
Murphy, Corinna 245
Murphy, Kerry Lynn 185
Murphy, Tami 398
Murray, Helen 214
Murray, Michelle 289
Murray, Sara 314
Murray, Tamera 311
Murti, Lata 344
Music, Jamie 249
Musselman, Sandra 383
Myatt, Treva 408
Myers, Jennifer 197
Myers, Jennifer L. 102
Myers, Stefanie 397
Naputi, Matilda 306
Nash, Tammy 382
Nason, Lois 219
Nation, Kristen 5
Nations, Jacinda 170
Naudus, Deborah 16
Naumann, Michelle 404
Navahright, Megan 330
Navicki, Bonnie Lou 40
Neal, Amy S. 178
Neal, LeAnn 335
Neal, Robert 313
Nedomatsky, Cornelia Bruck S. 169
Nee, Steve 380
Neece, Barbara 91
Needles, Kara 76
Neil, Stephanie A. 366
Neisius, Dawn Renee 20
Nelms, Linda 364
Nelson, Christina 49
Nelson, Heather 253
Nelson, Jenny 49
Nelson, Julie 247
Nelson, Mark 401
Nelson, Noel Grover 339
Nelson, Patricia 337
Nelson, Stefanie 323
Nelson, Tammy 277

Nelson, Theresa 372
Neubecker, Michelle 300
Neufeld, Jennifer 228
Neuschafer, Kerri Dawn 136
Newberg, Sara O. 374
Newcomer, Amy Jo 252
Newman, Karla Janel 190
Newmans, Ray 285
Newsome, Gina 6
Newton, Ann 90
Newton, Denise 22
Neymotin, Ita 223
Ngo, Trinh 395
Niazi, Halide, 127
Nichols, Anna 37
Nichols, Barbara 137
Nichols, Natalie 298
Nickloy, Tracy 274
Nidever, Jack 20
Nielsen, Kristine 189
Nielsen, Leslie 273
Nielsen, Ruth Naomi 94
Nieukirk, Tiffanie 318
Nighthawk, 316
Niles, Angela 66
Nina-Gomez, Sonia J. 305
Nissen, Janna 32
Noel, 304
Nofsinger, Michelle 293
Noiman, Julie 69
Norman, Georgette M. 71
Normand, Jeanine 45
Northcutt, Jessica 75
Northrup, Michelle 321
Notes, Abbey 134
Nouwels, Chandra 151
Novara, Marisa 56
Nowik, Jessica 251
Nunez, Angela Michelle 117
Nunez, Guisselle 38
Nunez, Monika 360
Nybakken, Kate 218
O'Connor, Maggie 287
O'Connor, Suzanne M. 284
O'Craigham, Jeanne M. 203
O'Dowd, Colleen 114
O'Field, Joanne 110
O'Gorman, Amy 167
O'Malley, Jennifer 261
O'Mel, Lori 273
O'Neal, Mary 372
O'Neil, Juanita 262
O'Rouke, Daniel 187
Oakjones, Karen 258
Oakley, Robin 408
Oatley, Taryn M, 336
Obbagy, Susan 203

Ochelli, Chuck 259
Ockinga, Janet 220
Odom, Karen 87
Ogden, Christie 118
Ogrodnik, Carri 51
Oh, Janet 189
Ohlerking, Anjanette 124
Ohmart, Karen 225
Ohnoutka, Petra 321
Ojakangas, Tracie L. R. 366
Okoro, Anezi 7
Olbeter, Patricia 282
Oldfield, Alicia 210
Oliveira, V.W. 396
Oliver, Penny 347
Olivera, Kathy 71
Oliveria, Paulette 407
Oliverio, Elena 169
Olsen, Cara 129
Olsen, Kate 66
Olsen, Kristin 199
Olson, Heather 159
Olson, Tanya 332
Olszewski, Elena 265
Oman, Michelle & Powell, Kacie 333
Onabe, Estuko Ogi 76
One, Graceful 17
Opferman, Dayna 228
Orlowske, John G. 131
Ormerod, Wendy 385
Ormsby, Deana 165
Orr, Erica 167
Ortega, Cirila 177
Ortega, Libby Valentine 322
Ortiz, Cynthia 16
Orwig, Theresa J. 331
Orzol, Catherine B. 222
Osborn, Allison 227
Osborne, Jessica 42
Osburn, Crystal 144
Ostermeier, Cora 11
Ott, Theresa 341
Otts, Andrea Nicole 29
Owen, R. 393
Owens, E. B. 45
Owens, Elizabeth 100
Owens, Shirley A. 275
Owlett, Melanie 314
Pace, Roy 284
Pacelli, Stephanie C. 359
Padilla, M. 366
Pagas, Ted 299
Page, Curry 134
Page, Jennifer & Erin 159
Page, Tiffani 336
Pagliocca, Annamaria 152
Painter, Pamela 306

Pair, Jenny 227
Palazzolo, Grace 40
Pallotti, Melissa 356
Palma, Dilma 113
Palmer, Erin 259
Palmer, Patricia J. 285
Palmere, Ronal 280
Panagiotou, Alexia, 164
Panza, Tracy 372
Papier, Cheri 190
Pappa, Ruth 380
Paradis, Lawrence 307
Paradis, Stacy 255
Paris, Amy 127
Paris, Cheryl 55
Park, Jeff 256
Parke, Amy 118
Parker, Carlyn 5
Parker, Cheryl 219
Parker, G. C. 80
Parker, Nanette 329
Parker, Robert T. Sr. 326
Parker, Sharon 211
Parks, Arayna Jayd 269
Parks, Tamara R. 302
Parr, Kendra 139
Parrotte, Kelli 64
Parsons, Jenny L. 98
Partida, Roxanne 301
Passanisi, Katie 17
Paterno, MaryAnn 306
Patin, Cheryl Anne 8
Patrick, Billie Ann 132
Patrick, Kevin 198
Patrick, Steven 327
Patsis, Heather 205
Patterson, Cassie 151
Patterson, Lois 305
Pauly, Christina 33
Payawal, Melanie 372
Payne, Charlotte 30
Payne, Emily 32
Payne, Georgia A. 250
Payne, Teri 361
Payson, Gretchen 259
Payson, Laura 384
Payton, Allison 258
Peace, Rosalyn 288
Peake, Kiana 109
Pearce, Brandi 50
Pearl, April 140
Pearl, Monica A. 251
Pearson, Karea 158
Peden, Patricia 315
Pederson, Patrice 68
Pedroza, Minerva 63
Peek, Becky Lynne 89

Peel, Janet 45
Pekoc, Heather 220
Pelkofer, Elizabeth J. 193
Pelleman, Wendy 344
Peltier, Sherry 136
Pendell, Judy 153
Penrod, Tori Anne 382
Perbeck, Amy 31
Pereira, Jennifer 157
Perez, Diane 181
Perez, Ismael R. Jr. 172
Perez, Jeanine 97
Perez, Roland 347
Perfetto, Staci 335
Perito, Rebecca 280
Perkey, Karen 262
Perpignano, Kristin 73
Perrish, Rai-An 279
Perry, Allyson 19
Peters, Kasie 176
Peterson, Linda Hinds 378
Peterson, Martha Hayter 403
Peterson, Nancy 319
Petitt, Glenn B. 245
Petro, Joseph D. 158
Petruzziello, Gina 257
Philips, Jean 109
Phillips, Carolyn 100
Phillips, Chisty 101
Phillips, D. T. 147
Phillips, Diane 121
Phillips, Julie 112
Phillips, Kristen 156
Phillips, Lady 397
Phillips, Nichole 327
Phillips, Sandra J. 294
Phillips, Sandy 303
Phillips, Stacy 344
Phillips, Tracy 409
Phinney, Alison 6
Piasta, H., J., & D., Jr. 240
Pickrell, Fred III 104
Pickrell, Susan 340
Pierce, Adam Franklin 125
Pierce, Delta 249
Pierce, Franklin K. 201
Pignataro, Beth M. 95
Pignatella, Amy 230
Pilcher, Amanda 268
Pilkington, Barbara 185
Pinder, Christine 184
Pinion, Mary E. Coleman 389
Pinkett, Robsol G. Jr. 310
Pinna, Angelica 29
Pinto, Jennifer 166
Pinto, Michelle 365
Pipkin, Jennifer 42

Piscke, Bobbi 85
Pitaro, Lara 359
Pitchford, Judy Darlene 190
Planchard, Amanda 139
Ploss, James 124
Plover, Dawn Marie 237
Plowman, Sherri 315
Plyer, Sheryl 334
Pochatila, Joy 179
Polachek, Shannon 264
Polk, Amy 196
Polley, Shannon 334
Polly, Shannon 333
Pontarelli, Lisa 367
Ponto, Susan 325
Ponusky, Cassia 248
Poole, Jennifer 218
Poremba, Holly 121
Porfido, Tabitha Jean 306
Portier, R. Elaine 41
Post, Shannon 299
Postupak, George 253
Poulsen, Marie 22
Pound, Bobby Jo 110
Powell, Denisha D. 184
Powell, Katie 168
Powell, LaShonda 324
Powers, Dean 217
Pratt, Tina Renee 349
Preble, D. J. 129
Preda, Vasile 304
Prenderfast, A. Hull 65
Preston, Anne 154
Prieskorn, Dawn 222
Prince, Darlene 241
Prince, Robert C. 275
Prisco-Braido, Rachelle 359
Pritam, Adele Hunn 385
Pritchard, Michele 358
Pritchett, Donna M. 59
Privette, Christel 67
Procaccio, Charlotte 243
Pronych, Lanelle 310
Propp, Amy 267
Propst, Bryon K. 215
Propst, Terry 301
Prothero, Libby 210
Prouse, Jennifer 231
Province, Tina 371
Pruett, Lucy C. 388
Pruitt, Debbie 62
Pruitt, Heather 93
Pruitt, Sarah 301
Ptak, Casey 38
Punneo, Crystal 206
Quaider, Patricia 339
Qualset, Anna 108

Quastad, Lanita 329
Quinalty, Angela 205
Quinones, Dinorah 147
Raba, Nina 315
Rachoner, Becky M. 200
Raczkowski, Norma Jean 311
Radford, Theodore III 394
Radice, Chrissy 89
Raffaghello, Dawn 101
Rafique, Joyce 46
Raftery, Dawn 50
Rafuse, Ruby 109
Ragan, Amy 181
Rahn, Becky 268
Ralston, Ellen 108
Ramirez, Joseph L. 33
Ramirez, Mayra 367
Ramnanan, Lakshmi 170
Ramos, Christine 212
Ramos, Deborah 13
Ramos, Rebecca 158
Randall, Carla L. 207
Randels, Lori 95
Rarick, Jody L. 51
Ras, Lara 338
Rasheed, Adib Abdullah 145
Rattenborg, Chris 180
Rattenni, Anthony 138
Rause, Sheila 33
Raveill, Frankie 159
Ray, Christopher 10
Ray, Junaita 53
Rayfield, Lisa 358
Raymond, Faycial 104
Raynard, Jennifer 18
Raynor, Iris 255
Reader, G. T. 9
Reagan, Shelley 348
Reaves, K. W. 239
Redding, Linda 345
Reed, Bernice Anita 142
Reed, Danylle 150
Reed, Jennifer 245
Reed, William 375
Reeder, Sheri 352
Reeder, Tracy 330
Reeves, Carla 192
Reid, Leigh 294
Reiman, Nancy 305
Reimer, Rachel 320
Reinhart, Joe 8
Reinholz, Laurel 367
Reisdorph, Daphne 188
Reiser, Evelyn J. 147
Reisinger, Chuck 31
Reitzler, Michelle 19
Rempel, Debra Jane 238

Renner, Kimberly S. 182
Repine, Becky Denise 164
Revers, Tami 278
Reyburn, Stanley S. 259
Reynolds, Alaina Nicole 185
Reynolds, Brandi 182
Reynolds, Ernest F. 210
Reynolds, Kim 54
Reynolds, Sharon 359
Reynoldson, Randolph C. 275
Rezendes, Lori 270
Rhoten, Michael D. 385
Rhynes, Sandra N. 243
Rice, Lynne E. 395
Rice, Stacy J. 371
Rich, Carol 163
Rich, Jenny 15
Richardson, Amber 110
Richardson, Bill 105
Richardson, Heather 13
Richardson, Robert G. 94
Richardson, Wendy 278
Rickards, Kathy 238
Ricker, Amy 105
Ricker, Lonny David 363
Ridenour, Joann 200
Riedel, Charidy 23
Riemer, Rebecca 327
Riepe, Charlotte 266
Riess, Dawn 261
Rife, Kimberly S. 77
Riffle, Kimberly 112
Rinard, Jenny 201
Rinaudo, Lucille A. 312
Rinker, Jeanie 258
Rinne, Melanie 316
Rioux, Catherine Noelle 163
Risley, Melissa 289
Riss, Laura 397
Rissmiller, Lisa 374
Ritch, Angela 129
Rivers, Sherri L. 356
Rizzo, Steven M. 326
Roach, Robert W. 392
Robb, Christine 175
Robbins, Lori 302
Robbins, Melanie 282
Roberts, David Thurston 142
Roberts, Jennifer 11
Roberts, Lesley Ann 373
Roberts, Lisa 348
Roberts, Paula D. 373
Roberts, Robert L. 336
Robertson, Amber 91
Robiczek, Hope 100
Robinette, Jennifer 12
Robinson, Alice 82

Robinson, Brandi 51
Robinson, Cassandra 231
Robinson, Christy 185
Robinson, Christy Sue 263
Robinson, Jennifer 149
Robinson, Laura-Lee 394
Robinson, Mandie 333
Robinson, T. 403
Rocha, Veronica 317
Rockett, Hollie 105
Rodenberry, Erik 151
Rodica, Annaliza 250
Rodio, A. Mario 138
Rodriguez, Julie Marie 215
Roeseke, Amber Helene 227
Roger, Michael Weston 375
Rogers, Jan 177
Rogers, Rachel 340
Rogers, Shannan L. 387
Rohert, Sarah 376
Roma, Joanne 195
Romano, Lindsay 281
Rondeau, Nikki 239
Roney, Jodi C. 158
Rook, Steffi 289
Roots, Julie 28
Rorick, Sherry 352
Rosamond, Rachel 313
Rose, Vicky Lynn 318
Roselle, Amy 34
Rosen, Marvin 304
Rosenberg, Tami 406
Rosenfelt, Heidi 34
Rosewicz, Heather 211
Roshini, A.K. Ayesha 153
Ross, H. 139
Ross, Jann 73
Ross, Nikki 284
Ross-Porter, Marandia 399
Rossa, Angela 141
Roth, Nancy 383
Rotter, Dustin 28
Rouse, Janice E. 160
Rouse, Jodie 113
Rouse, Rachel A. 392
Roy, Nicole 371
Royce, Berni Anne 36
Rubin, Diana Kwiatkowski 84
Rueda, Mary E. 244
Rueger, Shawna 325
Ruland, Nadine 379
Rumfelt, Jessica 248
Ruminski, Angie 37
Rupe, Kelli Janae 78
Rupp, Veronnica 300
Russ, Sharon 295
Russell, Charlotte 112

Russell, Emily 116
Russell, Jacqueline R. 193
Russo, Melanie 342
Rustad, Dawn 22
Ruttenberg, Danya 32
Ryan, Laura 178
Ryan, Marilyn 4
Ryan, Renee 343
Ryan-Lucky, Tammyy L. 327
Rychenerr, Leigh 352
Rylander, Amalia L. 45
Rylott, Kimberly 250
Rysdorp, Barbara 260
Saastad, Miranda 352
Sabin, Sabley 300
Sablotny, Michele Renee 284
Sachson, Seth 350
Saenz, Gil 120
Sager, Susan A. 361
Sakall, Heather 231
Salahi, Kim 68
Salazar, Grace 188
Salkins, Erica 175
Salomone, Erin 153
Salzman, Elyse 94
Sambas, Jennifer 109
Sams, Carrie 100
Sams, Melissa 12
Samson, Marilen 303
Samuels, Leesa Falashadeh 39
Sanchez, Linda 384
Sanchez, Lourdes, 288
Sanchez, Samantha 342
Sanchez, Susan Waltman 314
Sanchez, Victoria Magdalena 300
Sander, Jennifer 61
Sanders, John 134
Sandiford, Jeanine 24
Sandoval, Trey 138
Sandt, Betsyann 75
Sanger, Crystal 219
Santi, Joanne Delli 54
Sanzo, Esther 226
Sargeant, Erin 39
Sargent, Brooke 5
Sargent, Rebecca 375
Sartini, Emily 168
Sarver, Deanna 93
Saucier, Georges J. B. 43
Saurage, Gabrelle 137
Saurtelle, Patti 284
Saut, Pamela Marie 398
Savala, Andrea 244
Savidan, Lee A. 343
Savin, Sandra 311
Savory, J. L. II 53
Sawyer, Anne B. 31

Sawyer, Cyndi 249
Sayers, Alicia Monique 97
Scarlett, Eileen M. 55
Schapira, Gabrielle 124
Schauer, Hannah 266
Scheller, Judith Ann 45
Schepanowski, Beth 228
Schimetz, Kimberly 71
Schlegel, Julie 28
Schloemer, Amanda 247
Schlosser, Stacey 311
Schmeck, Kathleen 184
Schmidt, Corina 153
Schmidt, Jacqueline 125
Schmidt, Jodi 115
Schmitt, Angie 221
Schmitz, Lynn 365
Schnarr, Tanya 291
Schneider, Lana 303
Schoenherz, Jennifer 225
Scholz, Kimberly 150
Schoppa, Chelby 55
Schornack, Hillary Ann 258
Schorr, Kristin 134
Schrepp, M. & Fleming, C. 332
Schueller, Rachel 362
Schulte, Cathy 40
Schultz, Brenna 225
Schumaker, Bob 124
Schumaker, Elayne 60
Schuster, Traci 308
Schwader, Valerie 405
Schwartan, Corinne 203
Schwarz, Dawn 117
Schweer, Kendra 227
Schwieder, Kenneth H. 232
Scott, Anne 9
Scott, Annette 40
Scott, Clarissa 127
Scott, Eva O. 195
Scott, Heather 168
Scott, Kellie Jeane 239
Scott, Reva M. 318
Scott, Shaun-Marie 84
Scunziano, Lena 348
Seager, Steven A. 335
Seals, Dana R. 191
Seamon, Betsy 171
Sebaskin, Lady Louisa Reeves 382
Seelos, Kristin Ann 197
Seginak, Donna 10
Seigle, Jen Anne 267
Senft, Jennifer Ann 216
Seniuk, Jodean 191
Senninger, Karen 29
Serrano, Cheryl 55
Sesack, Sheryl H. 355

Severson, Andrea 257
Sewall, Yvonne 280
Seward, Beatrice Lynn 214
Seward, Jennifer Lynn 67
Sewell, Virginia 388
Sgambati, Judy 110
Shadow, (S. Lucken) 401
Shahinian, Erica 11
Shapton, Joyce 70
Sharp, Jennifer 90
Sharp, Sharron 270
Sharrock, Kanika 21
Shattuck, Rayanne 362
Shaver, Kimberly A. 120
Shaw, Brenda 81
Shaw, Carri 241
Sheehan, Timothy 113
Sheely, Jamie 163
Sheets, Bridget 230
Sheets, Kimberly 262
Shelhamer, Tonya 348
Shelton, Christopher 136
Shelton, Tonya 352
Shepherd, Dendy 245
Shepherd, Mindy 300
Sherrill-Krasinski, Lori Ingrid 154
Sherwood, Holly Anne 167
Shiban, Kristi 4
Shields, kelcie D. 91
Shires, Margaret 392
Shoaf, Angie 68
Shoate, Sarah 402
Shobe, Aniece 99
Shomo, Joseph G. 234
Shores, Gloris J. 194
Short, Tammy 315
Showers, Kelly 123
Shriberg, Lee 377
Shultz, Annette 27
Shumard, Alicia 67
Shupe, Teresa 274
Shy, Mica 332
Silva, Kathleen 32
Silver, ChrisAnn 68
Simhiser, Lisa 330
Simmerly, Melissa 319
Simmons, Kim 130
Simmons, Rebekah 323
Simmons, Renita 313
Simmons, Sheila 154
Simms, Jennelli 11
Simon, Jennifer 233
Sims, Amy 177
Sims, Amy 211
Sims, Yvonne M. 336
Sinclair, Bil Anthony 9
Sines, Frances E. 305

Sinnreich, Helen 119
Sipes, Christina Marie 188
Sirch, Julie Anna 43
Sisante, Pia Christine 273
Sisler, Lisa 396
Sitchenkow, Lois 370
Sizemore, Lisa 362
Skaggs, Jennifer 245
Skala, Kim 127
Skiba, Deborah 58
Skillman, Franklin J. 83
Slater, Edward D. 121
Sleater, Michelle L. 303
Slo, Rawn 377
Sloan, Katherine 202
Slobodian, Lori 146
Slobotski, Kendra L. 5
Slone, Kelly J. 258
Smigielski, Teresa 311
Smith Jonnia Walker 47
Smith, Adrienne Renee 243
Smith, Alberta L. 46
Smith, Barbara J. 168
Smith, Billie A. 257
Smith, Brenda Whitehead 171
Smith, Cenita 106
Smith, Danielle K. 86
Smith, David L. 264
Smith, Dawn 222
Smith, Dawn 225
Smith, Dorrie 152
Smith, George Harmon 162
Smith, Heather 118
Smith, Jamie 24
Smith, Jennifer 113
Smith, Jenny 205
Smith, Joel W. 209
Smith, Karri 194
Smith, Kelly Luicelle 88
Smith, Kim 69
Smith, LaShonda 401
Smith, Lennx C. 325
Smith, Leslie 241
Smith, Lori 358
Smith, Lorrie 307
Smith, Meredith 331
Smith, Meredith Dawn 300
Smith, Michelle 284
Smith, Olivia 389
Smith, Renee 340
Smith, Richard 110
Smith, Rita Jean 357
Smith, Ruth Lokele 11
Smith, Sarah 13
Smith, Sarah 357
Smith, Sharon Clark 362
Smith, Susan M. 275

Smith, Thomas F. 403
Smith, kathryne Kinnison 10
Snider, Eloise 8
Snisky, Michele 69
Snow, Bonnie 7
Snow, Elizabeth G. 131
Soete, Angela 231
Sokal, Tangerine 273
Sokalski, Andrea 104
Solomon, Wyolene 301
Solt, Kristina M. 87
Somach, Sindy 98
Sondrini, Kathryn 180
Sons, Tonya 334
Sorensen, Angie 205
Sorensen, Keirsten 92
Sorenson, Brandine 179
Sorokach, Audrey 255
Sosa, Gwynn 262
Soto, Grace 84
Souza, Eileen A. 243
Sowards, Amanda 5
Spack, Yenere 309
Spahr, Denise 191
Spalding, Wendy Jean 134
Sparks, Tanya 338
Spaulding, Beckie 181
Speicher, Kevin R. 163
Spencer, April 125
Spencer, J. Warren 165
Sperry, Carissa 198
Spiridiglozzi, Lauren 399
Spitsen, Christina 50
Spivey, Herbert C. 149
Spizzirri, Janet 251
Spotts, S. L. 123
St. Thomas, Phyllis 306
St. Dawn, Grace Galasso 115
St. Michel, Linda 345
St. Pierre, Danielle 177
Staggs, Stacey 355
Staheli, Nicole 68
Stahlnecker, Marianne 346
Stallins, Chasity D. 106
Stallworth, Karen L. 264
Standley, Melissa Ann 279
Staniec, Karen Lee 13
Stanley, Teresa 377
Star, Alein 64
Starling, Melissa 177
Steager, James J. 132
Stearns, Renee 349
Stearns, Rod 392
Steding, Jane 70
Steele, Christian 204
Steimle, Jennifer 21
Stein, Cara 169

Stein, Collen 62
Steiner, Kim 134
Stengel, Alice 265
Stepankow, Denise 160
Stephens, Edgar wyatt 20
Stephens, Julie 256
Stephens, Kristie 104
Stephens, Sharla 392
Stephens, Valerie 302
Stephenson, Karen 10
Stephenson, Rose 390
Steponaitis, Shirley 331
Sterling, Marilyn 146
Sternbergh, Mandy 402
Steven, Kay 171
Stevens, Cathy 221
Stevens, Julie 150
Stevens, Roberta 302
Stevens, Tara 356
Stevens, Tricia 333
Stevenson, Kate 248
Steward, Jodi L. 139
Steward, Stacy 324
Stewart, Ailsa 244
Stewart, Amber Caroline 144
Stewart, Carol L. 65
Stewart, Heather 112
Stewart, Jennifer 189
Stewart, Mike 387
Stewart, Paddy 382
Steyding, Linda R. 323
Stich, Jessica 185
Stickel, Marla 385
Still, Don 255
Stimburys, Mary 397
Stockinger, Eric 178
Stodghill, Jody 160
Stokely, Jeannie 69
Stolder, Melissa C. 129
Stolte, Edward G. 258
Stomper, C. J. 166
Stone, Andra Lynn 128
Stone, Joan 64
Stone, Theresia 347
Storch, Jane C. 205
Storm, Desiraie 246
Stout, Brenda M. 61
Stout, Kenna 206
Stover, April 102
Strauch, Trista 403
Strickland, Tori 281
Striegel, Janet 88
Stripe, Gina A. 72
Strobel, Bonnie 79
Strode, Heather 218
Stromquist, Shelley 391
Stubbert, Eric 150

Stubblefield, Samantha Faye 305
Stubbs, Ezekiel 247
Stupansky, Erica 186
Sturdivant, Marcie L. 301
Sturm, Kelly J. 199
Suares, Nicole 348
Sudnik, Kathy 156
Sue, Tammy 309
Sulak, Catie 325
Sullins, William Samuel 329
Sullivan, Kelly R. 174
Sullivan, Sean E. 344
Sulz, A. J. 239
Summerhill, Marla 381
Sumpter, Jennifer 191
Sunderland, Janine Leigh 162
Superle, Michelle 293
Sussman, Jennifer 201
Sustaita, Annessa 187
Suszek, Jaime 100
Sutherby, Rita M. 359
Svieta, 142
Swails, Gloria 172
Swartley, Paige J. 299
Swartz, April 209
Swartzfager, Brian 57
Swartzfager, Jill 28
Swearingen, Daphne 251
Swier, Dana 172
Swinwood, Laurie 331
Sybil, Erma J. 126
Sykes, Rhonda Nicole 294
Symonds, Cathy 41
Tabak, Kimber 149
Tadye, Marlyn P. 279
Tagliaferri, Angela 223
Tait, Bobbie 187
Tait, Christine Annette 122
Talbert, Cynthia Jo 188
Talifer, Jean 114
Talltree, Cinamyn 197
Tamburin, Tanya 4
Tamsin, Ken 59
Tamuccio, Linda 360
Tang, Diane 110
Tanis, Joel 151
Tanner, Jenni 76
Tanner, Nicole 287
Tanso, Jacqueline Lim 245
Tapley, Katherine 82
Tappen, Christine 107
Tatianna, Deanna 107
Taulbee, Fred L. Jr. 270
Tauriello, Ericka 92
Tavares, Helena C. 220
Taylor, Darniele 125
Taylor, Elizabeth 229

Taylor, Hana 8
Taylor, Jennifer 383
Taylor, Robert A 21
Taylor, Sara 98
Taylor, Shannon M. 374
Teal, Kathy 99
Tedford, Carol A. 216
Teel, Sharlee 331
Teeple, Amy Catherine 71
Teeple, B. J. 3
Teets, Randall W. 292
Teller, Bonnie 44
Tennis, Heidi 48
Tepe, Kimberly 82
Terrell, Juanita 243
Terry, Heather 113
Tessel, Dana 209
Thackeray, Betty Fern 200
Tharp, Yuli 141
Therien, Marie-Eve 276
Therrien, Sara 240
Thibeault, Kelly A. 116
Thiele, Shelby Diane 283
Thisse, Angi 26
Thomas, Agnes O. 268
Thomas, Beth 114
Thomas, Bobbi 128
Thomas, Megan 399
Thomas, Pearl L. 407
Thomas, Renee 219
Thomas, Tina 295
Thompson, Joan 241
Thompson, Kjersti 250
Thompson, L. 161
Thompson, May 346
Thompson, Melanie 355
Thompson, Nicol Marie 326
Thorell, Alana J, 86
Thornberry, Bruce 235
Thornton, Shannon 359
Thurmond, Tina 315
Tiefenbach, Rebekah 215
Tighe, Maria T. 403
Timmins, Lisa 358
Timpany, Kimberly 96
Tiritilli, Belinda 110
Tisdel, Kelly 163
Titkemeier, Angie 106
Tocko, Barbara 235
Todd, Carrie 48
Tolle, Kristin 34
Tolman, Eric 252
Tomalinas, Tara 303
Tompkins, Heidi 29
Tonkin, Joelyn A. 140
Tonra, Jennifer 147
Torian, Paulette 281

Torres, Bernadette 204
Torres, Elizabeth 246
Touchton, Tim 318
Tourtellot, George 260
Tousley, Emma B. 206
Tozier, Ethel 106
Trainer, Randi 276
Trainor, Kathleen Ann 211
Tran, Adrienne-Diem 205
Trent, Julia Diana 85
Trent, Robbyn Dianne 178
Trexler, Jeff 44
Tripp, Marie 367
Trombley, Tammy 350
Trousil, Heather 154
Trout, George E. 148
Trout, Rebecca 260
Truax, Tammie 117
Trussell, Lori 180
Tucker, Christine 68
Tucker, William 354
Tullgren, Jospeh W. 149
Tuozzo, Regina 339
Tupper, Lisa 273
Turner, Kara 93
Turner, Mille 274
Turner, Pamela A. 400
Turner, Patty 376
Turrell, Jennifer 254
Tuttosi, Tatiana 371
Tyler, Gretchen 41
Tyler, Kristin 247
Tyler, Melinda 328
Tyna, Jaime 247
Udell, Chrissy 201
Uffelman, Stacey 337
Uhlig, Bethany 140
Uhrinek, Jennifer 106
Underwood, Barbara L. 74
Underwood, Kendra L. 41
Unger, Ammie L. 151
Upright, Ginger 189
Uranta, Eugene Tonye 64
Urbach, Elizabeth Ann 133
Urie, Theresa 406
Utley, Antoinette F. 145
Vail, Ron 261
Valenzuela, Fred A. 83
Valkentine, Donna D. 243
Vallandingham, Cathy 92
Valler, Maureen Ann 285
Vallotton, Russell 405
Van Coughnett, Wayne 387
Van Hollen, Angela 73
Van Houten, Diane 78
Van Velzer, Diannah 74
Van Wazer, Stacey 311

VanDeburgh, Desiree 99
VanScoyk, Michelle R. 346
Vance, Glynnis 225
Vanderpool, Elizabeth 229
Vandervelde, Bonnie 93
Vanpatten, Jennifer 42
Varga, Kathleen Kenifel 408
Varner, Amy 267
Vass, Jenny 122
Vassos, Irene 11
Vecere, Andrew James 35
Vega, Marta 290
Vega, Michelle 330
Velazquez, Amy L. 3
Velez, Melanie 362
Velez, Nina 318
Velk, Hana 261
Venberg, Amy 61
Venkatesan, Sharon L. 404
Vermette, Kelly 105
Versosky, Mary Ellen 233
Vescuso, Marissa 339
Vetter, Amy 158
ViGotty, Emily 229
Vickery, Heather 180
Vigil, Karen 148
Vigil, Rosie 287
Vigliotti, Gina 55
Villa, Carol 33
Vinatier, Sarah 341
Vinch, Lori 296
Violette, Kristen 175
Vitale, Elaine 101
Voeltz, Howard L. 85
Vogt, Nicole 370
Von Ville, Amy 267
VonDeylen, Laura 282
Votuno, Brenda J. 49
Wadlington, Elaine 35
Wager, Elaine 38
Wagner, Jenni 52
Wagner, Jennifer 211
Wald, Danielle 87
Walden, Brenda D. 12
Waldman, Heather 260
Waldo, Shana 386
Waldron, Florence M. 145
Walgenback, James 187
Walker, Amy 229
Walker, Betsy 230
Walker, Coleen 246
Walker, Jacqueline P. 236
Walker, Janice 108
Walker, Sarah Jane 297
Walker, Sharron D. 402
Wallace, Christina 202
Wallace, Eric 252

Wallace, Jenny 145
Wallace, Melinda Y. 316
Wallace, Yvonne 161
Wallwe, Eva 72
Walsh, Kathy 248
Walter, Amy 220
Walter, Julie Ann 202
Walter, Tara D. 323
Waltman, Sharon 313
Walton, Jennifer 29
Wamsley, Rachael 328
Wanless, James A. Jr. 208
Ward, Vanessa 364
Warnecke, Sarah K. 366
Warner, Marcie 317
Warnock, Jayme 201
Warren, Elizabeth 269
Warren, Gene 146
Warren, Jody 213
Warshaw, Dalit 126
Washington, Charles E. 255
Washington, Denise 205
Washington, Sharon 368
Wasser, Tanya 310
Watkins, Susan 275
Watson, J. H. 229
Watson, Kristine 42
Watters, Dana 30
Watts, Rhonda M. 331
Waugh, M. J. 351
Weatherford, Brenda 72
Weaver, Christopher 183
Weaver, Lisa 316
Weaver, Stacia 384
Weaver, Venis 362
Weaver, Wendy 309
Webb, Carmen 124
Webb, Deeana 88
Webb, Erin 143
Webb, Gail 88
Webb, Martha 376
Weber, B, J. 5
Weber, Marie C. 381
Weber, Terri 361
Webr, Brandi 53
Webster, Donald 15
Wedlake, Aimee 95
Wedlake, Brian 266
Weeks, Bernadette 182
Wegert, Chrissy 157
Weikel, Kimberly 152
Weinkauf, Wendy 364
Weinstein, Ralph 319
Weiss, Diane 126
Weiss, Leah R. II 304
Weitzer, Brenda 89
Wekenman, Andria 236

Welch, John 138
Wells, Colette 214
Wells, Naomi 377
Wensel, Brenda 107
Wentzloff, Kari 106
Werner, Donna 103
Wertz, Tracey K. 338
West, Angela R. 183
West, Lucille 314
West, Shawn 353
Westcott, Christine 96
Westcott, Sarah Suzanne 356
Westerfield, Brian 47
Wethington, Nannie J. 343
Wethington, Priscilla 31
Wetter, Jennifer L. 129
Whaley, Gina 233
Wheaton, Ida D. 178
Wheeler, Amanda 199
Wheeler, Arville 80
Wheeler, Joy 115
Wheeler, Linda G. 299
Whelan, Vickey 360
Wherry, Amanda 200
Whibbs, G. 161
Whidden, K. 265
White, Alicia 122
White, Amy 307
White, April S. 136
White, Darrel Anthony 3
White, Donna M. 86
White, Jennifer 82
Whitelocke, Rosemarie A. 341
Whiteman, Thomas F. 276
Whitlow, Laura 360
Whitney, Michelle 357
Whitt, Shannon 141
Whitt, Tammy R. 352
Wichmann, Laura 264
Wieczorek, Anna 184
Wiggins, Elaine 232
Wightman, Dawn 192
Wigney, Joseph 80
Wilbur, Charlene 126
Wilbur, Roger 261
Wilds, Shawna 284
Wilhoite, Shera 356
Wilkens, Linda A. 353
Wilkie, Angie 204
Wilkie, Carrie Colleen 25
Wilkie, Jaime 13
Wilkinson-Anderson, Elizabeth 129
Williams, Angela 83
Williams, Ann 225
Williams, Aregeler 243
Williams, Bridgette 72
Williams, Carolyn R. 63

Williams, Denise 72
Williams, Dennis A. 51
Williams, Diane 133
Williams, Donna 245
Williams, Gena 34
Williams, Gretchen 48
Williams, Guinelle 172
Williams, James M. 27
Williams, Jenny A. 164
Williams, Kelly 54
Williams, Kelly J. 162
Williams, Latasha 379
Williams, Lisa 291
Williams, Monica 290
Williams, Natasha A. 355
Williams, Nathan 301
Williams, Nicole G. 271
Williams, Wayne A. 396
Willis, Connie 143
Willis, Jan 231
Willis, Joyce 268
Willis, Joyce 91
Willis, Pat 317
Wills, Amanda 60
Wills, George Roland 125
Wilson, Annie L. 86
Wilson, Bethany B. 32
Wilson, Corey 12
Wilson, Gayle 245
Wilson, Jessica 193
Wilson, Kelli 212
Wilson, Lori L. 315
Wilson, Mary 321
Wilson, Michelle Lynn 257
Wilson, Rachel G. 341
Wilson, Rebecca 404
Wilson, Sheila E. 404
Wilt, Christine A. 121
Winchell, Julie 239
Winestock, Jill 118
Winnan, Stacey 386
Winnell, Alexis 269
Winner, Shirley 349
Winship, Robin N, 331
Winslow, Andrea 208
Winson, Angela 43
Winter, Lorna Kay 387
Winters, Mandy 296
Winters, Teresa A. 400
Wisda, Rachel 361
Wisling, Jennifer 236
Withrow, Bonny 44
Witman, Andria Parry 368
Witman, Andria Parry 406
Witsil, Angela R. 157
Wittmeier, Nicole 340
Witusik, Karen 24

Woebkenberg, Sara 140
Woerpel, Denise 60
Wolfe, Jennifer 167
Wolfe, M. 65
Wolff, Jennifer L. 148
Wolfson, Yana 369
Wolkon, Mark & Hoch, Jeremy 386
Woloszczuk, Xenia 305
Womack, Cami 220
Wonderling, Cindy 40
Wong, Hein Jee 59
Wong, Vicki Ann 328
Wong, Yun Ngan 354
Wood, Amy 192
Wood, Evon 267
Wood, Heather 200
Wood, Jennifer F. 107
Wood, Jonathan 238
Wood, Tracy L. 369
Wood-Tisdale, Gwendolyn 83
Woodall, Rayford Sr. 342
Woodford, Stacey 324
Woods, Stephanie 374
Woodward, Jeff 225
Woolf, Bonnie 236
Worden, Theresa J. 324
Workman, Tami 306
Worley, F. George 81
Wright, Andrea 62
Wright, Gayle 90
Wright, Lee Fissori 317
Wright, Stacey 327
Wright, Tarita 294
Wright, Todd 411
Wunderling, Christy 252
Wyatt, Geneva M. 224
Wyatt, Sharon 312
Wyble, Gretchen Anne 222
Wyninger, Amy 13
Wynne, Meghan 301
Wyrick, Vanessa L. 365
Yager, Christiana A. 173
Yale, Michelle 327
Yamaguchi, Shelly 355
Yamorsky, Julie 43
Yang, Eme 102
Yankton, Brooke 133
Yanochko, Patti 292
Yanow, Laurie S. 298
Yedlosky, Kim 246
Yeoh, Melody 357
Yetter, Deanna 143
Yoder, J. J. 71
Yohman, Paula 308
Yoo, Kristie 52
York, Nina K. 396
York, Traci 335

Young, Cash 211
Young, Dianne E. 259
Young, Donitta 261
Young, Jenny 120
Young, Neila 326
Young, Rebecca 176
Youngblood, L. 405
Yucas, Jessyca Pearson 178
Yunek, Amy L. 358
Yung, Lily 274
Yunker, Martha 4
Yusuf, Rizwan 298
Zacharias, Tracey 66
Zaidi, Farhana 107
Zakhar, Tracy 312
Zambino, Deb Chadwick 43
Zatarga, Alysson 409
Zboril, Libuse M. 365
Zbytowski, Stacey 400
Zee, Shawna 399
Zelinsky, A. 152
Zellermayer, Jessica 40
Zeman, Lisa 304
Zengerle, Tina 310
Zidek, Julie Marie 111
Zimmer, Jenn 174
Zimmerhanzel, Heidi 190
Ziptho, Alicia 141
Zoller, Candice 162
Zoller, E. 67
Zook, Daniel Forie 18
Zoske, Elke 24
Zumbrun, Heidi M. 194
de Leon, Jesselyn 103
de Sousa, Olga 342
di Paolo, Natalie Bergen 285